Quinlan's
Film Directors

Quinlan's Film Directors

DAVID QUINLAN

B.T. Batsford Ltd, London

Contents

© David Quinlan 1999
First published in 1983
Reprinted 1983
Published in paperback 1991
Reprinted 1991
New edition 1999

Typeset by Bernard Cavender Design & Greenwood Graphics Publishing

Printed in Hong Kong

for the publishers
BT Batsford
583 Fulham Road
London
SW6 5BY

ISBN 0 7134 7753 9

A catalogue record for this book is available from the British Library

Introduction

When I first became a three-times a week visitor to the cinema some 30 years ago, directors of films were of hardly any significance to the great paying public who made the box-office tills tick over. The question was always 'Who's in it?' or 'Have you seen the new William Holden film at the Plaza?' 'or' What kind of a film is that?' or even 'Did you see the trailer of that last week?'. Directors who became a name or, rarer still, managed what Frank Capra called 'the name above the title' were rare birds, to be counted on the fingers of two hands: perhaps Lubitsch, Hitchcock, Welles, Capra himself and, for a brief, heady while, Preston Sturges, but very few more. Even of this select group, probably only Hitchcock meant anything to audiences outside the big city centres. The director remained a vague, shadowy figure in the background, the last name on the credits, frequently missed while saying something to one's companion, or accepting a pre-film chocolate. I gradually came to realize that the director was responsible for the pacing, style and approach of a film, and a great deal more; but for most, I think, the director remained one of the least important cogs in the wheel until the films themselves began to assume a greater importance than the stars who played in them.

In the last 20 years, things have completely changed. In a high percentage of cases, the director's name now precedes the film. Although most filmgoers in the early eighties could tell you that Alan Parker directed *Fame* or that John Carpenter made *The Thing*, they would almost certainly be pressed to name even one of the starring players. More and more seasons are devoted to directors, especially on television. An inevitable consequence of this for the director of repute is that *he* and not his players is now likely to bear the brunt of a major failure. No longer for him the protection of a studio contract should he lay the egg of a turkey. It is his reputation that will suffer and not those of the players he employs. One major failure could blight his career for life, especially as he now has to set up his own projects and consequently makes far fewer films than the studio director of 40 years ago.

Not that the pressures were absent in other decades: some men, as you will read, were driven to suicide. Others, fired by the excitement of creativity and driven by talent or ambition, triumphed over limited budgets to produce high-quality screen entertainment.

I hope that I have made the lives and achievements of those 750-or-so directors who appear in this book as illuminating and entertaining as possible – as the idea of the book is to bring the world of the film director out from behind the camera and into the lives of ordinary once-a-week cinemagoers, as well as buffs, fanatics and students.

Even given the opportunity by my publishers to include this many film-makers, selection, eliminations and additions were still very difficult. Although I am sure there will be some omissions that will provoke howls of outrage, I decided in the end to include as many British and American directors as possible, as well as some major directors from elsewhere in the world who have made a reputation for themselves outside their own countries, and whose names at least are likely to be familiar to the middle-of-the-road filmgoer.

As to 'borderline' choices, I admit to having been drawn to those directors with long, interesting or varied careers, and, at the other end of the scale, to those whose flourishing careers were cut short in their prime.

I have adhered largely to the journeyman working director of mainline feature films, whether he be auteur, genius or artisan. Thus you will find no cartoon directors (save those who did other work), few documentarists (although one or two personal favourites have been included), and no 'underground' directors.

The filmographies that follow the career studies are as complete as human endeavour can make them, and should include shorts, documentaries and TV movies in almost all cases, as well as *bona-fide* feature films.

Alphabetical order has been strictly adhered to: thus DeMille and De Palma come after Dean but before Deray, and Mac and Mc are not treated as one.

Dates of films: the one given is, hopefully, the copyright date on the credit titles of the film.

Awards: Academy Awards should be noted in the text on the director concerned.

Titles: the original title of the film appears first in almost every case, save for a few odd instances where foreign-language films are better known internationally by their English titles – thus American spellings for Hollywood films, British spellings for British films and so on.

A single asterisk in the text * indicates that the film it precedes is a short. Similarly, the letter (D), thus, indicates a documentary and a dagger † a co-directed credit. Any additions and exceptions to these signs will be explained beneath the filmography in question.

Now that the achievements of directors have been granted full recognition, a detailed guide to their work is an essential companion to filmgoing. I wish everyone happy browsing in the pages that follow.

Acknowledgements

My thanks are due to Lionel Perry, for diligent research on years of birth for those shrinking violets who seemed reluctant to give them, and to Gary Parfitt, for his contribution to the pictorial content of this edition. Additional thanks are, as usual, due to Richard Reynolds and the staff at B T Batsford, for their help and for their continuing [in]tolerance of my disregard of deadlines.

Almost all of the pictures in this book (the remainder are from my own collection) were originally issued to publicise or promote films or TV material made or distributed by the following companies, to whom I gratefully offer acknowledgement: Allied Artists, American-International, Artificial Eye, Associated British-Pathé, ATP, ATV, Avco-Embassy, BFI, BIP, Brent-Walker, British Screen, British and Dominions, British United Artists, Cannon Classic, Carolco, Channel 4 Films, Cinerama, Columbia, Walt Disney/Buena Vista, Eagle-Lion, Ealing Studios, EMI, Enterprise, Entertainment, Filmakers Associates, First Artists, First National, Gainsborough, Gala, Gaumont/Gaumont-British, Goldwyn, Granada TV, Grand National, Guild, Hammer, HandMade, Hemdale, Hollywood Pictures, Lippert, London Films, London Weekend TV, Lorimar, Mayfair, Medusa, Metro-Goldwyn-Mayer, Miracle, Monogram, New Line, New World, Orion, Palace, Paramount, PolyGram, PRC, The Rank Organisation, Rediffusion, Republic, RKO/RKO-Radio, Hal Roach, Starlight, Selznick, Touchstone, Tri-Star, 20th Century Fox, UIP, United Artists, Universal, Vestron, Virgin, Warner Brothers and Yorkshire TV.

ABRAHAMS, Jim 1944-

American writer and satirist whose most successful work has, along with long-time collaborators David Zucker and Jerry Zucker (qv) lain in spoofs of already established film or TV genres. Their successes as writer-directors have been less consistent outside this range. All three men hail from Milwaukee in Wisconsin, all three (at different times) attending the University of Wisconsin. Abrahams was working as a private investigator there in 1970 when he re-encountered the Zuckers and threw in his lot with them after they rented the rear of a bookstore and created their own comedy troupe, Kentucky Fried Theater, there. This was a multi-media show that often featured the trio in live improvisations interspersed with video-taped and filmed sketches. Following local acclaim, the trio moved to Los Angeles, where they opened up a new Kentucky Fried Theater in an abandoned warehouse. Over a four-year period they played to more than 150,000 customers and became the most successful small theatre in Los Angeles history. A ten-minute film reel of their funniest material led to a feature-length film: *The Kentucky Fried Movie* (directed by John Landis, qv). Their next venture, *Airplane!* written and directed by all three of them, remains commercially their most successful with the exception of Jerry Zucker's *Ghost*. Abrahams himself has continued to make mildly successful spoofs, comedies and light drama, staying longer in the wacky comedy genre than either of his collaborators. A move to TV movies in 1996 seemed to signal an acceptance of lower-profile work.(See also Zucker, David, and Zucker, Jerry).

As co-director: *1980: Airplane! 1984: Top Secret! 1986: Ruthless People.*
As director: *1988: Big Business. 1990: Welcome Home, Roxy Carmichael. 1991: Hot Shots! 1993: Hot Shots! Part Deux. 1996: First Do No Harm (TV). 1998: Jane Austen's Mafia!*

ADAMSON, Al 1929-1995

This American director of exploitation movies would probably not win a place in this book were it not for a death more grisly and macabre than anything in his own blood-soaked thriller and horror films. After being missing for five weeks in the late summer of 1995 Adamson was found entombed beneath the whirlpool bath at his home, which had been filled in with cement and tiled over. It took 18 hours of digging before the body was discovered. Police later charged a local contractor with Adamson's murder. The son of another director, Denver Dixon (Victor Adamson; 1890-1972), who made low-budget westerns in the 1930s, Al Adamson developed an enthusiasm for films while helping his father on what would prove to be his last picture, *Halfway to Hell*, in 1963. He made his own debut as director a year after, and entered his most prolific period some three years later, after founding Independent International Pictures with his long-time partner Sam Sherman. Using veteran stars, buckets of blood and a crude but effective approach, Adamson made a series of lurid shockers that did quite well for a while on independent circuits. At one time he was known as 'the king of the drive-in movie'. Later efforts though, were even shoddier and less successful and Adamson's last film directing credit came in 1982. In the 1990s, he became involved in producing children's and science-fiction films, before violent death intervened.

1964: Two Tickets to Terror. 1967: Blood of Dracula's Castle. 1969: The Female Bunch. Gun Riders/Five Bloody Graves. The Fakers/Hell's Bloody Devils/Smashing the Crime Syndicate (released 1973). 1970: Satan's Sadists. Horror of the Blood Monsters. Blood of Frankenstein (US: Dracula Versus Frankenstein). 1971: Last of the Comancheros. 1972: Blood of Ghastly Horror. Doomsday Voyage. The Brain of Blood. 1973: Angels' Wild Women. 1974: The Dynamite Brothers. I Spit on Your Corpse/Girls for Rent. 1975: Stud Brown. Blazing Stewardesses/Texas Layover/Naughty Stewardesses. 1976: Black Heat. Jessie's Girls. 1977: Black Samurai. 1978: Uncle Tom's Cabin revised version of 1965 film with added footage). Nurse Sherri/Hospital of Terror/Beyond the Living. Cinderella 2000. 1981: Carnival Magic. 1982: Lost.

ADLON, Percy 1935-

Innovative German director whose stylish treatment of offbeat subjects created some beguiling entertainments from unlikely sources, and made him an arthouse favourite through the 1980s. In the following decade Adlon's magic touch seemed to desert him. His work rate also slowed disappointingly, almost to a stop. Maybe his successes were woven inextricably into those of plump Marianne Sägebrecht, whose triumphs in his films put her briefly on the international map. Separately, neither Adlon nor Sägebrecht has prospered. Adlon has worked in radio and TV for the greater part of his working life, and he was 43 before a full-length documentary feature for TV led him into the world of films. Adlon's first success on the commercial scene came with *Celeste*, a handsome if typically offbeat account of the memoirs of Marcel Proust's housekeeper, caring for him in his dying days. The breakthrough to international recognition came four years later with *Zuckerbaby*. Marianne Sägebrecht, who had appeared in Adlon's previous films *Die Schaukel*, came into her own in this black romantic comedy as an overweight mortician who sets her cap at a handsome subway worker. She and Adlon moved to America for the next two, *Bagdad Café* and *Rosalie Goes Shopping*. The first film is quirkily endearing, as a Bavarian hausfrau is stranded in a tiny community in the middle of the Mojave desert There were signs of the partnership wearing thin in *Rosalie Goes Shopping* with Sägebrecht this time at large in Arkansas, where she has developed smart lines in shoplifting and major credit card fraud to keep her American family in the style to which she has accustomed them. Even Adlon's deftly black touches, though, couldn't sustain the anecdote to a feature. Since then, Adlon has languished in the sidelines between mainstream cinema and arthouse acceptance. There were some good reviews for *Younger and Younger*, described by one critic as 'a mad, wild soufflé', but very few people saw the film, and it has been too quiet on the Adlon front since then.

1978: Der Vormund und sein Dichter (TV). 1981: Celeste. 1982: Letzte Fünf Tage/The Last Five Days. 1983: Die Schaukel (GB and US: The Swing). 1985: Zuckerbaby (US: Sugarbaby). 1987: Bagdad Cafe. 1989: Rosalie Goes Shopping. 1991: Salmonberries. 1993: Younger and Younger.

AKERMAN, Chantal 1950-

Belgian-born director who makes long, often tedious, but sometimes hypnotically watchable arthouse films in which the camera's concentration on scenes for a long period of time can turn the viewer's pleasure into discomfort, interest into boredom or disinterest into perception. A unique film-maker, she continues to alternately baffle and fascinate her audiences.

Ill-at-ease on the range. Director Robert **Aldrich** (right and inset) gives Gene Wilder a few pointers on how to look frightened on a horse in *The Frisco Kid*.

Couch in New York. 1997: Chantal Akerman par Chantal Akerman (D).

ALDRICH, Robert 1918-1983

The violence and toughness in *Kiss Me Deadly* and *The Big Knife* that first helped attract critical attention to this American director's films ran through all his subsequent work, right up to (and especially in) *The Choirboys* in the late 1970s. Even the glamorous lady wrestlers in his last movie *All the Marbles* are no shrinking violets once they climb inside a ring. Indeed, most Aldrich films were set in arenas of one kind or another, metaphorically speaking, within which the combatants claw and scratch each other to pieces, ripping away each other's protective layers. The Aldrich camera crams in as much shock impact as possible, whatever the genre. More often than not, his heroes are cynical loners, even in the lighter films. Aldrich entered the film business in 1941 with RKO, working as an assistant director from 1944, several times under Lewis Milestone and Joseph Losey (both *qv*). Despite these distinguished tutors, the films that influenced his own style more than any others were probably two John Garfield vehicles, *Body and Soul* and *Force of Evil*: he was assistant director on both. The brooding power of these films is reflected most purely in Aldrich's mid-1950s work: one can almost see the bared fangs of the protagonists in *The Big Knife* and *Attack!*, both prize-winning films, although if a player is inclined to overact, it must be said that Aldrich's style will only encourage him. The most successful of his films, in both critical and box-office terms, were made in the 1960s. *What Ever Happened to Baby Jane?*, *Hush ... Hush, Sweet Charlotte* and, to a lesser extent, *The Killing of Sister George*, owe as much to the dominant personalities of their female stars as to their director. But *The Flight of the Phoenix* and *The Dirty Dozen* are ensemble successes, kept afloat by the skills of their all-star casts, but driven along by powerful direction that compels and sustains interest by careful concentration on the performances themselves. The talent for vigorous western comedy that Aldrich showed in *Vera Cruz* was never as evident again, and, of the 1970s films, only *The Longest Yard*, with its happy mixture of modern violence and pleasant, old-fashioned dialogue, is of real note. He died from kidney failure.

1953: Big Leaguer. 1954: World for Ransom. Vera Cruz. Apache. 1955: Kiss Me Deadly. The Big Knife. 1956: Autumn Leaves. Attack! 1957: The Gar-

Born to Polish-Jewish concentration camp survivors, Akerman was inspired by watching Godard's *Pierrot Le Fou* in 1965 to make films. Her precocious talent enabled her to make her first short film while still at film school in Brussels. Later, she went to America, still determined to make her own kind of films from whatever financial source she could scrape up. She took a job as cashier at a New York porno cinema, admitting to 'borrowing' $4,000 from the takings there to make two more short films. Since the controversy over her film *Jeanne Dielman* in 1975 – 'angry men shouted abuse or walked out while angry women yelled at the men to shut up' - she has worked mainly on the continent, making films with bold, sexual themes, whose slow, detailed

approach is an acquired taste, and makes Jacques Rivette look like John Woo in terms of editing and pacing.

*1968: *Saute Ma Ville/Blow Up My City. 1971: *L'enfant aimé. 1972: *Hotel Monterey. *La chambre. 1973: *Le 15/18 (co-directed). Hanging Out in Yonkers. 1974: Je...tu...il...elle. 1975: Jeanne Dielman. 1976: News from Home. 1978: Les rendezvous d'Anna. 1980: *Dis-moi. 1982: Toute une nuit. 1983: Les années 80. 1984: *L'homme à la valise. *J'ai faim, j'ai froid. 1986: Golden Eighties. Letters Home. 1987: Seven Women, Seven Sins (co-directed). 1988: Les ministères de l'art. Un jour Pina m'a demandé. 1989: Histoires d'Amérique/American Stories. 1993: D'est/From the East. 1996: A*

ment Jungle (uncredited). 1959: The Angry Hills. Ten Seconds to Hell. 1961: The Last Sunset. 1962: The Last Days of Sodom and Gomorrah/Sodom and Gomorrah. What Ever Happened to Baby Jane? 1963: Four For Texas. 1964: Hush. . . Hush, Sweet Charlotte. 1965: The Flight of the Phoenix. 1967: The Dirty Dozen. 1968: The Legend of Lylah Clare. The Killing of Sister George. 1969: Too Late the Hero. The Greatest Mother of Them All. 1971: The Grissom Gang. 1972: Ulzana's Raid. 1973: Emperor of the North Pole (GB: Emperor of the North). 1974: The Longest Yard (GB: The Mean Machine). 1975: Hustle. 1977: Twilight's Last Gleaming. The Choirboys. 1979: The Frisco Kid. 1981: All the Marbles (GB: The California Dolls).

ALEA, Tomás Gutiérrez 1928-1996

A leading intellectual and something of a father figure to the Cuban cinema, the strikingly-handsome, Havana-born Alea studied law in Italy but soon became a leading light of the Nuestro Tempo society on his return to Cuba, organising film clubs and screenings. Alea, or Titón, as he was affectionately known, also became involved with ICAIC, the Cuban Film Institute, and served as advisor on several of its most influential projects. Under the circumstances, it is perhaps surprising that he found time to make films as well. The best of his early work is *Memories of Underdevelopment*. A delicate and absorbing study, the underdevelopment to which it refers could perhaps be that of the central character, an intellectual unable to integrate himself into the revolutionary fervour of the new Cuba. Alea himself had no such problems with Fidel Castro's regime. But, as a committed writer (the author of a book on film theory) and vigorous speaker, his films were fewer than his compatriots would have liked. After a five-year gap in film-making, he co-directed the controversial *Strawberry and Chocolate*, which broke through the Cuban cinema's taboos on the subject of homosexuality, and earned an Oscar nomination in the Best Foreign Film category. This, like other of Alea's films, such as *Death of a Bureaucrat*, which lampooned red tape, and *Up to a Point*, which mocked sexism, underlined flaws in a Cuban society and regime which, to their credit, continued to allow Alea to make such films. Married to the actress Mirta Ibarra, Alea died from lung cancer at 67.

*1955: *El mégano. 1959: Esta tierra nuestra. 1960: Asamblea general. 1961:*

*Historias de la revolución. †*Muerte al invasor. 1962: Las doce illas/The Twelve Chairs. 1964: Cumbite. 1966: La muerte de un burocrata/Death of a Bureaucrat. 1968: Memorias del subdesarrollo/Memories of Underdevelopment. 1971: Una pelea Cubana contra los demonios. 1974: El arte del tobaco. 1976: La Ultima cena/The Last Supper. 1979: Los sobrevivientes/The Survivors. 1983: Hasta uncierto punto/Up to a Certain Point. 1988: Cartas del parque/Letters from the Parks. 1993: †Fresa y chocolate/Strawberries and Chocolate. 1995: †Guantanamera.*

ALLEGRET, Yves
See Allégret, Marc

ALLEGRET, Marc 1900-1973

Benign, bespectacled, Swiss-born Allégret was, like his pupil Roger Vadim (*qv*), a celebrant of lovely women. He it was who first noticed the special qualities in Simone Simon and Michèle Morgan, and he also worked with Brigitte Bardot, Danielle Darrieux, Hedy Lamarr, Mylène Demongeot, Jeanne Moreau, Corinne Calvet and other Continental love goddesses. Britain's Valerie Hobson and Joan Rice were *femmes* never quite as *fatales* as under Allégret's eagle eye. After a brief period of documentary film-making and assistant direction (most notably to Robert Florey, *qv*), Allégret began a long series of films dealing with women whose emotions ruled their lives. He worked mainly in the French cinema, and his classic films are all from the 1930s – *Fanny, Lac-aux-Dames, Zouzou, Orage* and *Gribouille*. His decline was predictable, as French tastes changed from Darrieux to Bardot, but it also made one realize that he had probably been more reliant than his contemporaries on superior screenplays and skilful actors. But his films continued to be smoothly, often elegantly made until his retirement in 1970. His younger brother Yves Allégret (1907-1987) also directed a number of films, most notably *Dedée d'Anvers/Dedée* (1947), *Une si jolie petite plage* (1948) and *Oasis (1995)*. Yves was married to the actress Simone Signoret from 1944 to 1949.

1926: Voyage au Cotigo (D). 1930: Papoul. Le blanc et le noir. J'ai quelque chose à vous dire. La meilleure bobonne. 1931: Les amants de minuit. Mam'zelle Nitouche. La petite chocolatière. Attaque nocturne. 1932: Fanny. 1934: Sans famille. Lac-aux-Dames. Zouzou. L'hôtel du libre échange. 1935: Les beaux jours. 1936: Aventure à Paris. Les amants terri-

*bles. Sous les yeux d'Occident. 1937: Orage. La dame de Melacca. Gribouille (US: Heart of Paris). 1938: Entrée des artistes (US: The Curtain Rises). 1939: §Le corsaire. 1940: *§Jeunes filles de France. 1941: Parade en sept nuits. 1942: L'Arlésienne. La belle aventure (US: Twilight). Félicie Nanteuil. 1943: Les petites du Quai aux Fleurs. 1945: Lunegarde. 1946: Pétrus. 1947: Blanche Fury. 1949: Maria Chapdelaine (GB & US: The Naked Heart). 1950: Blackmailed. 1951: La demoiselle et son revenant. 1952: Avec André Gide. 1953: Le film de Jean. Julietta. Jean Coton. 1954: Eterna femmina/L'amante de Paride/The Loves of Three Women (GB: The Face That Launched a Thousand Ships. US: The Loves of Three Queens). 1955: Lady Chatterley's Lover. Futures vedettes (GB: Sweet Sixteen). 1956: En effeuillant la marguerite (GB: Mam'zelle Striptease. US: Please, Mr Balzac). 1957: Ma femme, ma gosse et moi. 1958: Sois belle et tais-toi (GB: Blonde for Danger). 1959: Un drôle de dimanche. Les affreux. 1961: §Les démons de minuit. Les Parisiennes. 1963: L'abominable homme des douanes. 1967: *Exposition 1900. *Lumière. 1968: Debut de siècle. *Jeunesse de France. *La Grande-Bretagne et les Etats-Unis de 1896 à 1900. 1969: *Europe continentale avant 1900. *Europe méridionale au temps des rois. Le bal du Comte d'Orgel.*

§ unfinished

ALLEN, Irwin 1916-1991

Latterly known an a master of disaster Allen's career developed along clearly understandable lines as his ambitions grew. Basically a showman, New York-born Allen was a magazine editor, Hollywood columnist, radio director and literary agent before venturing into film production from 1951. After two Groucho Marx vehicles, Allen turned to the world of documentary. Nature features were being popularised by the Disney 'True Life Adventure' series, as well as by naturalists Armand and Michaela Denis and Hans and Lotte Haas. Allen's *The Sea Around Us*, based on Rachel Carson's popular history of the ocean and its flora and fauna, was both engaging and exhilarating, and as good as anything around in its field. It won him an Academy Award. Allen's next venture as director, which he sold with the line 'Two billion years in the making', was *The Animal World*, a winningly-made account of the evolution of animals from prehistoric times. If its model work in the dinosaur scenes was variable in quality, the film was a hit with the public, and showed as an 'A' feature in cinemas. Although the historical charade *The Story of Mankind* was mainly ludicrous, Allen was clearly developing his interests into big-scale adventures, sometimes with science-fiction elements. *The Lost World* and *Voyage to the Bottom of the Sea* were clever audience-pleasers, but *Five Weeks in a Balloon* pleased rather fewer people, and Allen drifted into television for a very successful decade in which he was responsible as producer for the sci-fi series *Lost in Space*, *Voyage to the Bottom of the Sea* and *Land of the Giants*. All were successful enough to run for several seasons. Allen returned to films and directed some of the action scenes in two hugely successful disaster films, *The Poseidon Adventure* and *The Towering Inferno*, both of which he produced. They were, however, his last major successes, and his last three films, including *When Time Ran Out*, which he produced but did not direct, were disasters in the worst possible sense.

1953: The Sea Around Us. 1956: The Animal World. 1957: The Story of Mankind. 1959: †The Big Circus. 1960: The Lost World. 1961: Voyage to the Bottom of the Sea. 1962: Five Weeks in a Balloon. 1972: †The Poseidon Adventure. 1974: †The Towering Inferno. 1978: The Swarm. 1979: Beyond the Poseidon Adventure.

† Directed some action sequences only

ALLEN, Lewis 1905-1986

Born in the heart of the English countryside, Allen was an actor in British films of the thirties, but had moved behind the camera (following experience of stage management in the theatre) by the time he went to Hollywood in 1941 to study directorial techniques with Paramount. Fifteen years later, he was one of the first emigrés to television. Few seem to have mourned the transition, and yet Allen began his career as a film director with two winning slices of Americana, *Our Hearts Were Young and Gay* and *Those Endearing Young Charms*, and two splendid ghost stories, *The Uninvited* and *The Unseen*, both of which engender fear rather than horror, shivers rather than revulsion. 'Proceed at your own risk if you are at all afraid of the dark' said the *New York Times* about the former. Allen returned to England to make *So Evil My Love*, an exquisitely detailed portrait of a murderess, with Ann Todd perfectly icy-hearted – appearing so much more suited to total evil than to the equivocal maybe-murderess of David Lean's *Madeleine* – as Olivia, sending her friend to the gallows

for the crime she herself committed. This is the performance one remembers from Ann Todd's career. One could say the same of Gail Russell in *The Uninvited*, and in fact almost all of Allen's films are the better for his having worked on them. *Valentino* is admittedly a low point – the only kind of film that Allen seemed unable to handle. And it heralded a break from the cinema for him after eight years of working for Paramount and RKO. In the 1950s he returned to form and, with Edward G. Robinson, turned two inferior projects with low production values into commercially viable properties that carry fascinating undercurrents of menace. If there's a Lewis Allen Appreciation Society anywhere around, count me in.

1943: The Uninvited. 1944: Our Hearts Were Young and Gay. 1945: The Unseen. Those Endearing Young Charms. 1946: The Perfect Marriage. The Imperfect Lady (GB: Mr. Loring's Secret). 1947: Desert Fury. 1948: Sealed Verdict. So Evil My Love. 1949: Appointment with Danger. Chicago Deadline. 1951: At Sword's Point (GB: Sons of the Musketeers. Completed 1949). Valentino. 1954: Suddenly. 1955: A Bullet for Joey. Illegal. Cavalcade (TV). Christopher Bean (TV. GB: cinemas). Man on the Ledge (TV. GB: cinemas). 1956: Gun in His Hand (TV. GB: cinemas). 1958: Another Time, Another Place. 1959: Whirlpool. 1963: Decision at Midnight.

ALLEN, Woody (Allen Konigsberg) 1935-

Someone says to Woody Allen in the semi-autobiographical *Stardust Memories*: 'I prefer you in your earlier, funny films.' The character is seen an a mosquito, getting under the skin of someone who has moved on to higher, better things. It seemed at that time that Allen himself would have preferred to forget the hit-and-miss romps of the 1969-1973 period. Yet the brightest and best of their ideas have a freshness, ingenuity and invention unparalleled in Hollywood since the 1930s. Gleams of their gaiety have resurfaced in Allen's work in the 1990s. Some of the visual gags in these early ragbags of comedy are dazzlingly original, immaculately timed and tear-streamingly funny, establishing Allen's on-screen character as a small, bespectacled, self-doubting Jewish-American defeated by both the machinery and machinations of life. 'If you need me,' he tells Diane Keaton in *Play It Again, Sam* (which he wrote but did not direct) 'I shall be at home on the floor having an anxiety attack.' Alas, angst replaced anxiety after the late 1970s. Encouraged perhaps by highbrow critical applause, Allen

more and more paraded his private neuroses in public under the flag of entertainment. *Annie Hall* was a watershed constructed for him by the Establishment, who awarded him the Best Director Oscar – although he declined to turn up and claim it. Here, and for the next 15 years, the comedy content was reduced to satirical shafts, often aimed at his own detractors. *Stardust Memories* proved too self-indulgent even for some of the faithful. *Interiors*, in which he did not appear, but which underlined his affection for Ingmar Bergman (later more amusingly treated in *Shadows and Fog*) was simply gloomy.

Honourable exceptions from this unproductive period are two films all of a piece. *Zelig* is a charming original about a mysterious character from the past who turns up at all sorts of historical events (predating *Forrest Gump* by 12 years) and whose longing for friendship and companionship gives him the power to turn himself into likenesses of those he's with. More clever than funny, but with a few typically goofy Allen asides, the film is marvellously hypnotic to watch. *Radio Days* is perhaps his most complete film to date. It has warmth, many shafts of humour, a setting perfect in look and feel and a title that is no cover of convenience, the theme of radio running richly through an immensely enjoyable story about a childhood in a central American town around the years 1939 to 1944. Mia Farrow has never been better than in this film. Yet it was her off-screen relationship with Allen which reduced his never huge box-office power still further with their acrimonious break-up after ten years, over his affair with her adopted daughter from her marriage to musician-conductor André Previn. Since her departure, Allen's most recent films have taken on a cleaner, mellower look, while retaining a talent for one-line belly laughs. Despite his Oscar nomination for his direction of *Bullets Over Broadway*, the best of these 1990s films is probably *Manhattan Murder Mystery*. A reunion with Diane Keaton, the star of his triumphant *Annie Hall*, it's a comedy-thriller vaguely in the tradition of an older era that balances the comedy and thrills in precisely the right proportion.

1969: Take the Money and Run. 1971: Bananas. 1972: Everything You Always Wanted to Know About Sex *But Were Afraid to Ask. 1973: Sleeper. 1975: Love and Death. 1977: Annie Hall. 1978: Interiors. Manhattan. 1980: Stardust Memories. 1982: A Midsummer Night's Sex Comedy. 1983: Zelig. 1984: Broadway Danny Rose. 1985: The Purple Rose of*

"This is how I remember it..." Woody **Allen** (right) and cinematographer Carlo Di Palma (second right) re-create the past in *Radio Days*.

Cairo. 1986: Hannah and Her Sisters. 1987: September. Radio Days. 1988: Another Woman. 1989: † New York Stories. Crimes and Misdemeanors. 1990: Alice. 1991: Shadows and Fog. 1992: Husbands and Wives. 1993: Manhattan Murder Mystery. 1994: Bullets Over Broadway. 1995: Mighty Aphrodite. 1996: Everyone Says I Love You. 1997: Deconstructing Harry. 1998: Celebrity.

† co-directed

ALMODOVAR, Pedro 1947-

Plump-faced Spanish director whose cult comedies customarily have a daring and provocative sexual content. Their resemblance to 18-certificate cartoons probably reflects that part of the director's own younger days when he worked as a strip-cartoon writer for *avant-garde* publications. Although the films are largely a mixture of tedium and irreverence, the showiest of them have built a considerable reputation both inside and outside their native country, making their creator

Spain's most successful director on the international scene since Luis Buñuel. And the viewer is guaranteed a few nuggets of gold even in Almodóvar's least successful work. Almodóvar began his working life as a clerk with a telephone company in Madrid, but soon became involved with Madrid's equivalent of off-Broadway theatres, combining writing with acting and even at one time running his own rock 'n' roll band. His first attempts at film-making came with Los Goliardos, an independent theatre company with which he was involved as actor and writer. These were in Super-8mm, running from 1974 to 1977. It would be 1978 before he attempted a 16mm feature. His second such film, *Pepi, Luci, Bom y otras chicas del montón*, was blown up to 35mm for general distribution, and made his name. From here on, Almodóvar rapidly became an expert at what might be called the shocking farce, combining moments of inventive hilarity with graphically improbable sexual shenanigans, involving much coming and going among bright, shallow characters who could be heterosexual

homosexual, bisexual or even transsexual. These situations are strung together most successfully in the director's international hits of the late 1980s and early 1990s – *Women on the Verge of a Nervous Breakdown!* (which won an Oscar nomination as best foreign film), *Tie Me Up! Tie Me Down* and *High Heels,* in which prison block inmates go into a song-and-dance number while the heroine, a convicted murderess, awaits her fate. Many of Spain's most popular stars of this period, including Victoria Abril, Antonio Banderas and Carmen Maura, made their breakthroughs in Almodóvar films, although only Banderas has consolidated his stardom on a worldwide stage. In recent times, the director's critical profile has been lower, and it will be interesting to see the direction in which the films of his middle age take him.

*1974: *Dos putas, la historia de amor que termina en boda. *La caída de sodoma. 1975: *Homenaje. *El sueño. 1976: *El estrella. 1977: *Complentos. Sexo va: sexo viene. 1978: *Salomé. Folle, folle fol-léme, Tim. 1980: Pepi, Luci, Bom y otras chicas del montón. 1982: Laberinto de pasiones (US: Labyrinth of Passion).*

*1983: Entre tinieblas. 1984: Qué he hecho yo para merecer esto? (GB and US: What Have I Done to Deserve This?). 1985: *Trayler para amantes de la prohibido. 1986: Matador. 1987: La ley del deseo. 1988: Mujeres al borde de un ataque de nervios (GB and US: Women on the Verge of a Nervous Breakdown). 1990: Atame! (GB and US: Tie Me Up! Tie Me Down!). 1991: Tacones lejanos (GB and US: High Heels). 1993: Kika. 1995: La flor de mi secreto (GB and US: The Flower of My Secret). 1997: Live Flesh/Carne tremula. 1999: Todo sobre mi Madre.*

ALTMAN, Robert 1922-

Hollywood's most determined maverick has remained throughout his career one of the most difficult of contemporary American directors to pigeonhole. Even with directors who tackle a wide variety of genres, common ground in their films can usually be detected. But there is little such consistency in Altman's work, unless it be a charnel-house humour, first evident in his breakthrough film, *M*A*S*H*, that could almost have escaped from the banned or censored writings of scriptwriters for the Marx Brothers. He is depreciative of his own tal-

ent, and amusing on the subject of his early, very chequered career. 'I've had a lot of experience of live theatre but, before films, I failed at everything I tried. I tried selling insurance, I tried tattooing dogs ... I tell you, I tried everything. Now I make movies which is like jumping off the high [diving] board with every new picture. Believe me, the very fact that the guy got up there and jumped in the water is something. Admire me for that, not for how I succeed, and not for how "good" the films might be, but for the fact that I kept going back and jumping off the high board.' Altman first 'jumped off the high board' with shorts, documentaries and TV work. But (belatedly) he made his name with irreverence and items guaranteed to shock the sensitive, and has since followed just those paths down which his fancy has taken him. His best films are generally considered to be *M*A*S*H*, *Thieves Like Us* (a remake of Nicholas Ray's *They Live By Night*), *Three Women*, *A Wedding*, *The Player* and *Short Cuts*. Although parts of *M*A*S*H* are superbly choreographed, most of these films are perhaps tedious and ponderous at least in part. My favourite Altmans are the less considered *Images* and *Quintet*, cleaner, tighter, more fascinating films, with a steely chill at the marrow – in keeping with a director who never set out to please all the people all of the time. He certainly failed to please many of the critics with *Popeye*, his musical adaptation of the cartoon characters made famous in the 1930s by Max Fleischer. The film, however, was aimed at young children, for whom it provided cleverly and carefully contrived enjoyment, and not at hidebound scribes judging it as an adult film from an adult entertainer. Altman himself seems to retain his child-like delight in the medium. He remains his own man and, despite Oscar nominations for his work on *The Player* and *Short Cuts*, determinedly outside the mainstream.

*1954: The Builders. 1955: Delinquents. 1957: The James Dean Story. 1964: Once Upon a Savage Night (TV. Later: Nightmare in Chicago). *The Party. 1965: *The Kathryn Reed Story. 1966: *Pot au feu. 1967: Countdown. 1969: That Cold Day in the Park. M*A*S*H. 1970: Brewster McCloud. 1971: McCabe and Mrs Miller. 1972: Images. 1973: The Long Goodbye. 1974: Thieves Like Us. California Split. 1975: Nashville. 1976: Buffalo Bill and the Indians, or Sitting Bull's History Lesson. 1977: Three Women. 1978: A Wedding. Quintet. 1979: A Perfect Couple. Health (released 1982). 1980: Popeye. 1982: Come Back to the 5 and Dime, Jimmy Dean, Jimmy Dean. 1983: Streamers. 1984: Secret Honor. OC and Stiggs. 1985: Fool For Love. 1987: †Aria. Beyond*

Pedro **Almodovar** strikes a worldly pose with the cast of his big hit, *Women on the Verge of a Nervous Breakdown*. That's an almost unrecognisable Antonio Banderas at top right.

Robert **Altman** gets the whole picture during the making of Sam Shepard's *Fool for Love*.

Therapy. 1988: Tanner 88: The Dark Horse (TV). The Caine Mutiny Court Martial (TV). 1990: Vincent and Theo. 1992: The Player. 1993: Short Cuts. 1994: Prêt à Porter (US: Ready to Wear). 1996: Kansas City. 1997: The Gingerbread Man. 1999: Cookie's Fortune.

† co-directed

AMIEL, Jon 1948-

'I've always had an interest in that intriguing place, almost between sleeping and waking, where the reality of the mind and the reality of the outside world meet. In my films, fantasy, myths and dreams all have, in a sense, equal weight to physical reality.' Jon Amiel was talking about his film *Aunt Julia and the Scriptwriter,* a winning mixture of romance, lunacy and bitter-sweet humour set against the world of radio in 1951. But the comment might easily refer to his later film *Copycat* or especially to the TV series that made his name, *The Singing Detective,* in which the division between fantasy and reality is indeed memorably blurred. Amiel began his career writing music for the theatre, but soon began directing productions for a North London theatre club. Progressing to the Royal Shakespeare Company, Amiel then joined the BBC as a story editor, beginning to direct films for them in the early 1980s. His first work for the cinema, *Queen of Hearts,* drew praise for its depiction of the feuds and fortunes of an Italian family in England, as seen through the eyes of its ten-year-old son. Since then Amiel has made overtly commercial films without quite repeating the combination of critical and popular success that he found in 1986 with *The Singing Detective.*

1984: Romance, Romance (TV). 1985: Silent Twins (US: TV). 1989: Queen of Hearts. 1990: Aunt Julia and the Scriptwriter/Tune In Tomorrow. 1993: Sommersby. 1995: Copycat. 1997: The Man Who Knew Too Little. 1999: Entrapment.

ANDERS, Allison 1954-

Although Allison Anders continues to hover on the fringe of American mainstream cinema, her portraits of strong, independent, down-and-dirty women are beginning to carve out a special niche and a cult following. Anders grew up without a father and became a single mother at a young age. Made while raising two teenage daughters on her own, the stories of some of her films, especially *Gas, Food – Lodging,* cut deeply into the experiences of her own past and present. Growing up in rural Kentucky, Anders was the victim of a gang rape at 12. She spent her teens running away from home and hitchhiking across the country, resulting in a series of adventures that often ended in jails and foster homes – a tough girlhood which she credits with giving her inspiration for her cinematic portraits of rural Americans. On an even darker note she was committed to a psychiatric hospital in her late teens after 'hearing voices'. She was eventually released but dropped out of high school and moved to England where she had her first daughter, Tiffany. Returning to Los Angeles, Anders, after spells as philosophy student, poet, waitress and childbirth teacher, enrolled in the UCLA Film School. She became a great fan of the German director Wim Wenders, met him when he made a trip to LA, and subsequently got her first film work as an assistant on his 1984 film *Paris, Texas.* After winning several screenwriting awards, including one for *Lost Highway*, subsequently made into a film by David Lynch, Anders made her first film, a low-budgeter called *Border Radio*, which she co-directed with UCLA colleagues. But it was *Gas, Food – Lodging,* made three years later, that put her on the map. Shot on location with a real sense of camera movement, this is the story of a single mother living in a caravan in New Mexico while battling to raise two teenage daughters, one of whom loses herself in the world of the local cinemas while her older sister has sex with any boy who'll have her. The New York critics gave her their Best New Director award for the film. Since then, like most modern directors, she's filmed infuriatingly sporadically. *Mi Vida Loca*, an abrasive tale of poor Chicana 'homegirls' in LA, was not successful, partly because it telescoped three stories clumsily into one. After the folly of the multi-director *Four Rooms*, however, Anders came up with *Grace of My Heart,* a down-the-line winner for most of the way (until it descends into soap opera towards the end) about a girl songwriter, who finds success in showbusiness but not with men: more echoes from Anders' own life, although she did adopt a son to add to her two daughters. Most

of the film is beautifully constructed, in a way that suggests a still romantic, but more mature Anders is now with us. 'I still feel marginal,' she says of her status in today's Hollywood, 'but I guess I'm really not any more.'

1988: †Border Radio. 1991: Gas, Food – Lodging. 1993: Mi Vida Loca/My Crazy Life. 1995: †Four Rooms. 1996: Grace of My Heart.

† Co-directed

ANDERSON, Lindsay 1923-1994

With long gaps between his feature films, and ever mightier running times, Lindsay Anderson became the David Lean (*qv*) of the British cinema's anti-establishment, rising to critical favour as Lean fell from it. Born in India, Anderson moved back and forth from film criticism (co-founding the magazine *Sequence*) to documentary film-making in his twenties and thirties, winning an Oscar for the brilliant documentary short *Thursday's Children*, which he made in 1953. These regional documentaries, full of flavour and strongly influenced by the work of Humphrey Jennings (*qv*), represent the backbone of

Anderson's cinema education. He stayed in the same vein for his first dramatic feature, the harsh, low-key study of rugby league and the industrial north of England, *This Sporting Life*. The film came along at the height of the critical vogue for working-class drama, and established Anderson as a leading director in Britain. His next big feature film remained among his best. This was *If ...* , a scathing, quirky, entertaining and powerful black satire, an indictment of the public school system which owed much in spirit to *Zéro de conduite*, directed by the Frenchman Jean Vigo (*qv*) 35 years earlier. After that, alas, *O Lucky Man!* was a sad contrast, a series of sideshows looking for strength; and all Anderson's best work in the 1970s was done for the stage. He disappointed again in 1982, after a long pause with *Britannia Hospital*, a bitter, black and bloody satire (although the satirical content in actually fairly crude) on hospitals, unions, snobbery, spare-part surgery and society itself: indeed anything within its reach. The whole unstable brew explodes in a final reel that lapses into bathos and pretentiousness, haranguing its audience with an unnecessary diatribe then leaving them in mid-air. Anderson was still a director of talent. But his dedication to

Lindsay **Anderson** on location for his last film (and one of his best), *The Whales of August.*

his films had become so total that one worried about his ability to look at their overall structure with an objective eye, in view of their vast lengths. A return to simpler values (echoing the days when he turned out episodes of TV's *Robin Hood* by the handful) seemed justified and indeed duly arrived in the form of *The Whales of August*, a little gem about two elderly sisters (Lillian Gish and Bette Davis) living on an island off the coast of New England. Tightly woven and full of poignant moments, the film has an ending that is certain to leave you on the verge of tears. Anderson regained more lost ground with *Glory, Glory*, a joyous satire of TV evangelists made for American cable TV. But, just as one looked forward to a more incisive autumn of his years, Anderson died in France from a heart attack.

1948: *Meet the Planners* (D. and narrator). 1949: **Idlers That Work*, (D. and narrator). 1952: *Wakefield Express* (D). **Three Installations* (D. and narrator) *Dreamland* (D) †* *Thursday's Children* (D). 1954: *Trunk Conveyor*. 1955: **Green and Pleasant Land* (D). *Foot and Mouth* (D. and narrator). **The Children Upstairs* (D). **A Hundred Thousand Children* (D). **£20 a Ton* (D). **Henry* (D). **Energy First* (D). 1957: *Every Day Except Christmas* (D). 1959: **March to Aldermaston* (D). 1962: *This Sporting Life*. 1966: *The White Bus*. 1967: **Raz, Dwa, Trzy/The Singing Lesson*. 1968: *If. . . .* 1973: *O Lucky Man!* 1974: *In Celebration*. 1979: *The Old Crowd*. 1982: *Britannia Hospital*. 1987: *The Whales of August*. 1989: *Glory! Glory!* (cable TV). 1994: *Is That All There Is?*

ANDERSON, Michael 1920-

Like many British directors of his time, Michael Anderson did most of his best work in the thriving British cinema of the 1950s. A gripping, well-made second feature, *The House of the Arrow* (based on an A.E.W. Mason novel) attracted attention, and quickly Anderson was a man with a reputation for making a variety of entertaining, commercial films. His films from 1953 to 1958 were all quite well received: this cycle ended with the best of them, the identity-crisis suspense thriller *Chase a Crooked Shadow*, which Anderson steered skilfully through its several twists. After this, however, Anderson worked in America, on splashy colour films with big stars and, apart from a return to form in the mid-1960s with *Operation Crossbow* and *The Quiller Memorandum*, his later output has been disappointing. His minor successes, *Operation Crossbow*, *Quiller*, *The Naked Edge*

Michael **Anderson** ponders the art of scaring the daylights.

and *Conduct Unbecoming*, have all been in that mystery-suspense vein in which he proved himself earlier. One still remembers with pleasure the ingenuous fun of *Will Any Gentleman . . . ?* and the simple emotional appeal and professionalism of the war films, but it seems unlikely now that Anderson will ever climb back to those relaxed entertainment peaks. His son is the actor Michael Anderson junior (1943-). Latterly resident in Canada, he has continued to direct, mainly in lower-profile projects and TV movie adventures.

1949: † *Private Angelo*. 1950: *Waterfront* (US: *Waterfront Women*). 1951: *Hell is Sold Out. Night Was Our Friend*. 1952: **Dial 17*. 1953: *Will Any Gentleman . . .? The House of the Arrow*. 1954: *The Dam Busters*. 1955: *1984*. 1956: *Around the World in 80 Days*. 1957: *Yangtse Incident* (US: *Battle Hell*). 1958: *Chase a Crooked Shadow*. 1959: *Shake Hands with the Devil. The Wreck of the Mary Deare*. 1960: *All the Fine Young Cannibals*. 1961: *The Naked Edge*. 1963: *Wild and Wonderful*. 1964: *Flight from Ashiya*.

1965: *Operation Crossbow* (US: *The Great Spy Mission*). 1966: *The Quiller Memorandum*. † *Eye of the Devil* (uncredited). 1968: *The Shoes of the Fisherman*. 1972: *Pope Joan*. 1975. *Doc Savage – the Man of Bronze. Conduct Unbecoming*. 1976: *Logan's Run*. 1977: *Orca – Killer Whale*. 1978: *Dominique*. 1979: *The Martian Chronicles* (TV). 1981: *Bells* (later *Murder By Phone*). 1983: *Mafia Kingpin. The Devil Imposter*. 1984: *Second Time Lucky*. 1985: *Separate Vacations*. 1986: *Sword of Gideon* (TV). 1987: *La boutique de l'orfèvre/The Goldsmith's Shops*. 1988: *Millennium*. 1991: *Young Catherine* (TV). 1993: *Rugged Gold* (TV). *The Sea Wolf* (TV). 1995: *Captains Courageous* (TV). 1998: *Summer of the Monkeys*.

ANNAKIN, Ken 1914-

A craftsman who has made few bad films, but few memorable ones – *Battle of the Bulge* is probably best of his bigger movies – this British director's films run in sequences: rural shorts, all the Huggett

On the road again. Ken **Annakin** on location on an Italian mountain road for his late Sixties' comedy *Monte Carlo or Bust.*

The Seekers (US: Land of Fury). You Know What Sailors Are. 1955: Value for Money. 1956: Loser Takes All. Three Men in a Boat. 1957. Across the Bridge. 1958: Nor the Moon by Night (US: Elephant Gun). 1959: Third Man on the Mountain. 1960: Swiss Family Robinson. 1961: Very Important Person (US: A Coming Out Party). The Hellions. 1962: Crooks Anonymous. The Fast Lady. †The Longest Day. 1963: The Informers. 1965: Those Magnificent Men in Their Flying Machines. Battle of the Bulge. 1966: The Long Duel. 1967: The Biggest Bundle of Them All. 1969: Monte Carlo Or Bust! (US: Those Daring Young Men in their Jaunty Jalopies). 1972: Call of The Wild. 1974: White Fang. Paper Tiger. 1977: The Fifth Musketeer (GB: TV). 1978: Murder at the Mardi Gras (TV). The Pirate (TV). 1979: Institute for Revenge (TV). 1980: Cheaper to Keep Her. 1982: The Pirate Movie. 1986: The New Adventures of Pippi Longstocking.

ANTONIONI, Michelangelo 1912-

A former film critic and editor, this Italian director first worked in films as a scriptwriter for Roberto Rossellini (*qv*), and has continued to write his own films, in whole or part, since turning director himself. Although he did not make his first feature film until he was nearly 40, Antonioni found himself an immediate hit with the intelligentsia of numerous countries with his pain-wracked portraits of people losing touch with the world. These doubtless reflect in some measure the director's own early struggles to find a place in the film industry, after years spent slaving in a bank and working for a provincial newspaper. In 1939, he went to Rome, but was hard put to make ends meet (he frequently tells the story of the day he stole a steak from a butcher's shop), although selling some articles of criticism to the magazine *Cinema*. But in 1942, he was finally hired as a writer by Rossellini, and began directing his own first film, a documentary about fishermen, the following year. Because of the war, however, he was unable to complete it until 1947. After several more two-reel documentaries, he made his first feature film in 1950. His best films are still perhaps this earliest batch of work, from *Cronaca di un amore* to *Il grido*, although it was his association with the actress Monica Vitti in four films – *L'avventura, La notte, L'eclisse* and *The Red Desert* – that brought his work to the attention of a wider international audience, with bleak, fragmentary pictures of characters drifting away from each other, and even from reality. His unique control of camer-

films, intrinsically British comedies and dramas of the 1950s, several films for Walt Disney, the first three James Robertson Justice-Leslie Phillips-Stanley Baxter comedies, the 'long-distance rally' marathon comedies, the Jack London adventures and, latterly, a string of TV movies. Many of his pictures portray groups of people banded together in a common cause, and battles against the odds. He began life as an assistant cameraman (he was also assistant director on Carol Reed's *The Way Ahead*) and his most successful films are generally the comedies, especially the first in their respective series, which are fresh and funny.

1942: **Cooks (D). 1943: *A Ride with Uncle Joe (D). 1944: *Black Diamonds (D). *The New Crop (D). *Combined Cadets (D). 1945: *A Farm in the Fens (D). Make Fruitful the Land (D). *Pacific Thrust (D). *Three Cadets (D). 1946: *The West Riding (D). It Began on the Clyde (D). *English Criminal Justice (D). 1947: *Turn It Out (D). Holiday Camp. Broken Journey. 1948: Here Come the Huggetts. Miranda. †Quartet. 1949: Vote for Huggett. Landfall. The Huggetts Abroad. 1950: †Trio. Double Confession. 1951: Hotel Sahara. 1952: The Planter's Wife (US: Outpost in Malaya). The Story of Robin Hood and his Merrie Men. 1953: The Sword and the Rose. 1954:*

awork, often moving in long, slow, sometimes circular pans, stamped his work with a highly individual quality of emotional tension His control of colour in *The Red Desert* is masterly but the move away from black-and-white seems generally to mark a slackening-off in his work, and, although *The Passenger* was highly regarded in most critical quarters (to me, its impact is dulled by its laborious pace), the international films he has made since the mid-1960s have on the whole been less satisfactory than his earlier pictures. Antonioni suffered a heart attack in 1985, and the film on which he was working, *Sotto il vestito niente*, had to be abandoned. Ten years later, he co-directed *Beyond the Clouds* with Wim Wenders (*qv*), but it was a sad occasion, almost like an old man's sexploitation film, only redeemed by the occasional felicitous touch. One fears it might be the last shot in the locker.

1947: **Gente del Po (D. Begun in 1943).* 1948: **N. U. (D). *Oltre l'oblio (D). *Roma Montevideo (D).* 1949: **Romarzo (D). L'amorosa menzogna (D). *Superstizione (D). Ragazze in bianco (D).* 1950: *La villa dei mostri (D). *La funivia del Faloria (D). *Sette canne e un vestito (D). Cronaca di un amore.* 1952: *I vinti/I nostri figli (US: The Vanquished).* 1953: *†Amore in città (GB & US: Love in the City). La signora senza camelie (GB: The Lady without Camellias. US: Camille without Camellias).* 1955: *Le amiche (US: The Girl Friends).* 1957: *Il grido (GB & US: The Cry).* 1958: *†Nel segno di Roma. †Tempest/La tempesta (uncredited).* 1960: *L'avventura.* 1961: *La notte (GB & US: The Night).* 1962: *L'eclisse (GB & US: Eclipse).* 1964: *Il deserto rosso (GB & US: The Red Desert).* 1965: *†I tre volti.* 1966: *Blow-up.* 1969: *Zabriskie Point. La cina/Chung Kuo/China (D).* 1975: *Professione: reporter (GB & US: The Passenger).* 1980: *Il mistero di Oberwald.* 1982: *Identificazione di una donna.* 1995: *†Beyond the Clouds.*

APTED, Michael 1941-

British director who, after a long apprenticeship in television, took to films and proved that his strength lay in dramas with a rural or regional background of some kind. His initial ventures were not successful outside Britain, although praised by critics of his own country. Some unhappy experiences followed, notably on *Agatha* and *Trick or Treat*, before Apted made a spectacular breakthrough on the international scene with the success of *Coal Miner's Daughter*. Again, there was a rural backcloth, although this time American, in the shape of the poverty-ridden mining territory of Kentucky. Apted told the story of the poor-born girl, married at 14, who eventually becomes a nationally popular country-and-western star, with the right mixture of reality, insight and what the public would probably want to see, aided by a performance by Sissy Spacek that won the year's Academy Award for best actress. He followed up with *Continental Divide*, an unusual story of love between a plump newspaperman and the eagle conservation lady he has been sent to interview in the Rockies. The stars, John Belushi especially, and gentle persuasiveness of the direction actually make you believe it could have happened. It all made a refreshing change from the general rush of X-rated movies of the 1980s – a civilized film with wit and sophistication, the sort of stuff Tracy and Hepburn would once have done, and a distant relative of *A New Leaf*. With this film and others, Apted proved that strength in character development is one of his greatest assets, and most of his best films concentrate heavily on one character or two characters only. This is shown by the two biggest hits of his most recent years, *Gorillas in the Mist* and *Class Action*. In this period, he has also returned to his documentary roots, among his work in this field being the latest two films in the 'Up' series surveying lives at seven-year intervals, a series with which he has been associated, in one capacity or another, since 1963.

1973: *The Triple Echo.* 1974: *Stardust.* 1976: *Trick or Treat (uncompleted).* 1977: *The Squeeze. Stronger Than the Sun (TV).* 1978: *Agatha.* 1980: *Coal Miner's Daughter.* 1981: *Continental Divide.* 1982: *P'Tang Yang Kipperbang (TV).* 1983: *Gorky Park.* 1984: *Firstborn.* 1985: *28 Up (D. TV. US: cinemas). *Bring On the Night (D).* 1986: *Critical Condition.* 1988: *Gorillas in the Mist.* 1989: *The Long Way Home (D).* 1990: *Class Action.* 1991: *35 Up (TV). Thunderheart.* 1992: *Incident at Oglala (D).* 1994: *Blink. Nell.* 1996: *Extreme Measures.* 1997: *Inspirations (D).* 1998: *Fortune's Fool. Always Outnumbered (TV).*

ARCHAINBAUD, George
(Georges Archainbaud) 1890-1959
You might be hard-pressed to cite even one of Archainbaud's many films without a prompt. In his last ten or so years, though, you could hardly have missed his name on television, as he made literally hundreds of episodes of *Hopalong Cassidy, The Range Rider, The Gene Autry Show, Champion the Wonder Horse, Annie Oakley* and, from 1954 until his death from a heart attack, *Lassie*. These TV years must have been pleasant ones for Archainbaud, who throughout his career had revealed himself most at home making outdoors adventures with simple, straightforward values. He was born in Paris of French parentage and became interested in stage management soon after leaving university. In 1915, he went to America, started to direct films two years later and quickly struck up a working relationship with the young David O. Selznick, for whom he was often to work through the years. Although Archainbaud worked consistently through the silent era, his best films date from the 1930s, especially some of those made at RKO between 1930 and 1934, which include the 'Hildegarde Withers' murder mysteries, and at Paramount between 1937 and 1940. His finest film is probably 1932's *The Lost Squadron*, a touching, exciting, bitter-sweet story about World War I flyers working as film stuntmen. He was impressively in charge of hurricanes, volcanic eruptions and all the usual periphera of Dorothy Lamour films in *Her Jungle Love*. His 1940s films are almost all 'B' movies, and he had run all the way down to Gene Autry westerns by the 1950s, although these did lead to his steady work for TV and are much more polished and professional than many of their contemporaries.

1917: *The Maid of Belgium. The Awakening. Diamonds and Pearls. As Man Made Her. Yankee Pluck. The Brand of Satan. The Iron Ring.* 1918: *Divine Sacrifice. Cross Bearer. The Trap. The Love Cheat.* 1919: *A Damsel in Distress.* 1920: *In Walked Mary. The Shadow of Rosalie Byrnes. What Women Want. The Wonderful Chance. Marooned Hearts. The Pleasure Seekers.* 1921: *The Miracle of Manhattan. The Girl from Nowhere. Handcuffs and Kisses.* 1922: *Evidence. Clay Dollars. Under Oath. One Week of Love.* 1923: *The Common Law. Cordelia the Magnificent. The Midnight Guest. The Power of a Lie.* 1924: *The Flaming Forties. Christine of the Hungry Heart. For Sale. The Plunderer. The Mirage. Single Wives. The Shadow of the East. The Storm Daughter.* 1925: *Enticement. The Necessary Evil. The Scarlet Saint. What Fools Men.* 1926: *Puppets. Men Of Steel. The Silent Lover.* 1927: *Easy Pickings. Night Life.* 1928: *The Tragedy of Youth. Woman Against the World. Ladies of the Night Club. Bachelor's Paradise. The Grain of Dust. George Washington Cohen.* 1929: *The Broadway Hoofer (GB: Dancing Feet). The College Coquette. Broadway Scandals. Man in Hobbles. Two Men and a Maid. The*

Voice Within. 1930: Shooting Straight. Framed. Alias French Gertie (GB: Love Finds a Way). The Silver Horde. 1931: The Lady Refuses. Three Who Loved. 1932: State's Attorney (GB: Cardigan's Last Case). Men of Chance. The Lost Squadron. Thirteen Women. Penguin Pool Murder (GB: The Penguin Pool Mystery). 1933: The Big Brain (GB: Enemies of Society). After Tonight. 1934: Keep 'Em Rolling. Murder on the Blackboard. 1935: Thunder in the Night. My Marriage. 1936: The Return of Sophie Lang. 1937: Clarence. Hideaway Girl. Blonde Trouble. Thrill of a Lifetime. Hotel Haywire. 1938: Her Jungle Love. Campus Confessions (GB: Fast Play). Thanks for the Memory. Boy Trouble. 1939: Some Like It Hot. Night Work. 1940: Untamed. Comin' Round the Mountain. 1941: Opened by Mistake. 1942: Flying with Music. 1943: Hoppy Serves a Writ. False Colors. The Woman of the Town. The Kansan/Wagon Wheels. 1944: Texas Masquerade. Mystery Man. Alaska. 1945: The Big Bonanza. Girls of the Big House. 1946: The Devil's Playground. Fool's Gold. The Unexpected Guest. 1947: King of the Wild Horses. The Marauders. Dangerous Venture. Hoppy's Holiday. The Millerson Case. 1948: Silent Conflict. The Dead Don't Dream. False Paradise. Strange Gamble. 1950: Border Treasure. Hunt the Man Down. 1952: The Old West. Night Stage to Galveston. Apache Country. The Rough, Tough West. Barbed Wire (GB: False News). Wagon Team. Blue Canadian Rockies. 1953: Winning of the West. On Top of Old Smoky. Pack Train. Goldtown Ghost Riders. Saginaw Trail. Last of the Pony Riders.

ARGENTO, Dario 1943-

One of those Italian film-makers of the 1960s and 1970s – other examples are Mario Bava and Riccardo Freda – who set out simply to scare us to death. Their films are all noteworthy for distinctive use of colour, clever editing and effective use of shock tactics. Argento, the youngest of this group, started as a writer (his father is producer Salvatore Argento) and has since proved something of a one-man band, writing or co-writing almost all the films he has directed, and lately contributing their clangorous, menacing background scores as well. The mechanics of fear, nothing else, are what concerns Argento, and the stories, which seem to make less and less sense as the films become more recent, are strictly of secondary concern in his frighteningly successful efforts to grind an audience into its seat. In *Suspiria*, his best film to date,

overlapping dialogue and stereophonic whispers combine with a fortissimo blend of music and moans to help him achieve his ambition; while editor Franco Fraticelli's work tightens the suspense like a steel cord at the director's bidding. Although the pillars of these terror-thrillers are a series of set-pieces which often seem to have little connection with the central story, they are staged with eye-opening flair and often contain (almost wilfully obscure) clues to the denouement of the plot. In these key scenes, the central figures are often threatened by a terror unseen but underscored by a screeching soundtrack that sounds like a thousand cymbals crashing at the devil's bidding. Argento has proved so good at this modern extension of the Val Lewton philosophy that one regrets the excess of bloodshed in his later films. As critical approval receded his profile has become lower in more recent times, and his output more sparse. His daughter, Asia Argento, is a promising young actress in continental films.

1968: †Probabilitá zero. 1969: L'uccello dalle piume di cristallo (GB: The Gallery Murders. US: The Bird with the Crystal Plumage). 1971: Il gatto a nove code (GB & US: Cat o' Nine Tails). Quattro mosche di velluto grigio (GB & US: Four Flies on Grey/Gray Velvet). 1973: Le cinque giornate. 1976: Profundo rosso/Deep Red. Suspiria. 1979: Inferno. 1982: Tenebrae. 1984: Phenomena/Creepers. 1985: Demoni/Demons. 1987: Opera (US: Terror at the Opera). 1990: †Two Evil Eyes. 1996: The Stendhal Syndrome. 1998: The Phantom of the Opera.

ARDOLINO, Emile 1943-1993

Born into the wrong era as far as films were concerned, Ardolino's speciality was dance and, if not another Vincente Minnelli, he could certainly have become another Charles Walters had musicals still been in style. As it was, a semi-musical, *Dirty Dancing*, made his name in the cinema after years of TV specials, and almost all the best moments in his few subsequent films were musical ones, After taking film courses at two universities, Ardolino had begun his career as a grip on *The Wedding Party* (1966), an early Robert De Niro film, but had soon progressed to film editor. Seven years later, he began directing for TV, mainly on dance-oriented specials, including 29 programmes in the award-winning *Dance in America* series. After winning an Oscar for his exhilarating documentary *He Makes Me Feel Like Dancin'* (about Jacques D'Amboise – once one of the

seven brothers who pursued seven brides – and 1,000 of his dance students), Ardolino made a belated move into films. Although romantic and dramatic scenes in his work hit few heights, his films take wing when music is involved – thus the 'rap' number in *3 Men and a Little Lady* is the scene most people associate with the film. This and *Sister Act* were the biggest hits of his movie career, although he also completed a new version of *Gypsy* for cable TV with Bette Midler just before his death from AIDS.

1982: Alice at the Palace (TV). 1983: He Makes Me Feel Like Dancin' (D). 1986: The Rise and Rise of Daniel Rocket (TV). 1987: Dirty Dancing. 1989: Chances Are. 1990: 3 Men and a Little Lady. 1992: Sister Act. 1993: The Nutcracker/George Balanchine's The Nutcracker. Gypsy (cable TV. GB: cinemas).

ARLISS, Leslie 1901-1988

Stern-looking (though more handsome than his father, the noted actor George Arliss) Leslie Arliss was a journalist and critic who became involved with writing for the British film industry from the early 1930s. A decade later, Arliss became the director responsible for some of the most flamboyant and successful films of World War Two. In post-war years, he left his home studio, Gainsborough, and was unable to find fresh inspiration elsewhere. Throughout the 1930s, Arliss was busy as screenplay writer, mostly in collaboration with others, on high-profile subjects in both comedy and drama. His first steps into direction, from 1941, came with Associated British, but a move to Gainsborough along with the star of his last film, James Mason, catapulted him into the public eye. Mason insisted in his biography that he and Arliss couldn't get along, so it's surprising they made three films together, two of them sensationally successful. Their first Gainsborough collaboration was *The Man in Grey*, whose period histrionics – audiences cheered as evil Mason thrashes equally wicked Margaret Lockwood to death at the end – proved just the ticket at the wartime box-office. So did Arliss's next film, the lachrymose *Love Story*, again with Lockwood. And he had Lockwood and Mason together for the most successful of all, *The Wicked Lady*, which gained valuable publicity with its low-cut costumes, and turned out to be Britain's top money-making film of 1946. Arliss's style in all these films is a brisk, no-nonsense one, encouraging his actors to emote positively, personably and at times even fiercely. With the end of World War Two, the Gainsborough talent fragmented. Arliss chose the inviting arms of Alexander Korda's London Films/British Lion organisation, but he was never the same force there. There were rows between Arliss and Korda and, although Arliss made three fairly unmemorable movies there, he was dropped from at least one, *Bonnie Prince Charlie*, a costume drama his touch might have enlivened. The Korda connection ended, there was a three-year gap to Arliss's next film, *The Woman's Angle*, which found him making films to a formula that no longer worked. But it was his last of any stature. There followed two poor comedies, some amusing Peter Sellers shorts, and a great deal of TV work, mainly on 30-minute telefilms produced under the banner of Douglas Fairbanks Jr.

1941: *The Team. †The Farmer's Wife. 1942: The Night Has Eyes (US: Terror House). 1943: The Man in Grey. 1944: Love Story (US: A Lady Surrenders). 1945: The Wicked Lady. 1947: A Man About the House. 1948: The Idol of Paris. 1949: Saints and Sinners. 1952: The Woman's Angle. 1955: See How They Run. Miss Tulip Stays the Night. 1957: *Insomnia is Good for You. *Dearth of a Salesman. *Danger List. 1958: *Man With a Dog.*

ARMSTRONG, Gillian 1950-
Women battling to escape the traditional roles forced upon them by society are, perhaps unsurprisingly, a recurring theme in the work of this feminist (but not in your face) Australian director who has filmed steadily in Hollywood in recent times without quite matching the accolades received for her first great Australian success, *My Brilliant Career*. Adept at portraying characters that grow with the film, Armstrong has perhaps done even more distinguished work in the documentary field. From the study of costume design in her native Melbourne, Armstrong leapt into the direction of her first short film before she was 21. A scholarship to the Australian Film and TV School followed. After graduation from film school, Armstrong plunged herself into a busy schedule. *Smokes and Lollies*, the first of three documentaries about young Australian women that would span almost 15 years, was followed by her first 'story' film, *The Singer and the Dancer*, which won the 1976 Australian Oscar as best short film (although it was in fact almost an hour in length). In light of the haul of seven Australian Oscars that followed her next Australian venture, *My Brilliant Career*, which made Judy Davis's name as the girl fighting to hold true to

her literary ambitions in turn-of-the-century Australia, the subsequent invitation to Hollywood was not unexpected. Her work there since 1984 has met with mixed fortunes, her most successful movie in box-office terms being the third screen version of *Little Women*. This shares both the virtues and vices of her other films in America, with a strong female protagonist fighting her corners but a rather gloomy atmosphere overall. Being a woman in a man's world, one might infer from Armstrong's films, is a rather cheerless thing. She was at this theme again with a new ally in the luminous Australian actress Cate Blanchett, in a role once intended for Judy Davis, in the stunningly shot romantic period epic *Oscar & Lucinda*.

1970: *Old Man and Dog. 1971: *Roof Needs Mowing. 1973: *Gretel. *Satdee Night. *One Hundred a Day. 1975: Smokes and Lollies (doc). 1976: The Singer and the Dancer. 1978: My Brilliant Career. 1980: *Touch Wood (doc). Fourteen's Good, Eighteen's Better (doc). *A Busy Kind of Bloke. 1982: Starstruck. 1983: *Having a Go (doc). Not Just a Pretty Face. 1984: Mrs Soffel. 1986: Hard to Handle – Bob Dylan in Concert. 1987: High Tide. 1988: Bingo, Bridesmaids and Braces (doc). 1991: Fires Within. 1993: The Last Days of Chez Nous. 1995: Little Women. 1996: Not Fourteen Again (doc). 1997: Oscar & Lucinda.*

ARNOLD, Jack 1916-1992
American director, a former actor (in British films from 1937 to 1939) and documentarist who, despite some memorable science-fiction films for Universal-International from 1953, and much reverence in cult critical circles, did not weather wholly successfully the general film recession from the late 1950s on. Critical applause for his work on *It Came From Outer Space, Creature from the Black Lagoon, Tarantula* and (especially) *The Incredible Shrinking Man*, films in which he showed great skill at conjuring up genuine excitement from unlikely situations, did not manage to keep him in top assignments after 1960. He seemed to have a flair for zany comedy with the emergence of *The Mouse That Roared*, but his Bob Hope vehicles offered only faint echoes of the great comedian's former wisecracking glory. After that Arnold raised only the odd spark of excitement and originality from a series of limp comedies and lumbering black-power thrillers for the cinema, although working extensively on TV. He never returned to the science-fiction genre, leaving the bulk of his important work to remain in those productive early

years. He died from arteriosclerosis.

1950: With These Hands (D). 1951: The Challenge (D). World Affairs Are Your Affairs (D).1953: The Glass Web. Girls in the Night (GB: Life After Dark). It Came from Outer Space. 1954: Creature from the Black Lagoon. 1955: Revenge of the Creature. †This Island Earth (uncredited). Tarantula. The Man from Bitter Ridge. 1956: Outside the Law. Red Sundown. 1957: The Incredible Shrinking Man. The Tattered Dress. Man in the Shadow (GB: Pay the Devil). 1958: Monster on the Campus. The Space Children. The Lady Takes a Flyer. High School Confidential! 1959: No Name on the Bullet. The Mouse That Roared. 1961: Bachelor in Paradise. 1964: A Global Affair. The Lively Set. 1967: The Pill Caper (TV). 1968: Hello Down There. 1973: Black Eye. 1974: Boss Nigger (GB: The Black Bounty Killer). Games Girls Play (GB: Sex Play). 1975: The Swiss Conspiracy. 1977: Sex and the Married Woman (TV). 1981: †Marilyn: the Untold Story (TV GB: cinemas). When the Snow Bled.*

ARZNER, Dorothy 1900-1979
Although there had been women directors in silent times – Lois Weber, Cleo Madison and Mabel Normand among them – Dorothy Arzner was for some years in the 1930s and 1940s Hollywood's only woman director. Arzner was a university graduate who nonetheless had to work her way slowly up the ladder after starting in the script department of Famous Players as a typist. Her determination got her promoted in turn to script clerk, film cutter and finally film editor. In the 1920s, her career benefited from her close working relationship with the prolific and sometimes innovative director James Cruze, (qv), who encouraged her ambitions to direct. In 1927, Paramount gave her a chance at direction with *Fashions for Women*, and the majority of her films with this studio (from 1927 to 1932, her best period) are social comedies with women as the central figures – 'women's pictures' perhaps, but with a bite and astute observation not always evident in similar vehicles directed by men. She was the victim of a degree of male prejudice after she left Paramount, and she worked irregularly, although some of her 1930s movies, most notably *Merrily We Go to Hell, Craig's Wife* and *The Bride Wore Red*, are strongly if rather heavily presented. There was a cutting edge to the in-fighting among the showgirls of *Dance, Girl, Dance* that suggested Arzner had regained some of her old touch and most attractive traits. But then she was off

directing training films for the WACs of World War II. After the dismal *First Comes Courage*, there were regrettably no further opportunities.

1927: *Fashions for Women. Get Your Man. Ten Modern Commandments.* 1928: *Manhattan Cocktail.* 1929: *The Wild Party.* 1930: *Paramount on Parade. Sarah and Son. †Behind the Makeup. †Charming Sinners (GB: The Constant Wife). Anybody's Woman.* 1931: *Honor Among Lovers. Working Girls.* 1932: *Merrily We Go to Hell (GB: Merrily We Go To –).* 1933: *Christopher Strong.* 1934: *Nana.* 1936: *Craig's Wife.* 1937: *The Bride Wore Red. †The Last of Mrs Cheyney (uncredited).* 1940: *Dance, Girl, Dance.* 1943: *First Comes Courage.*

ASHBY, Hal 1929-1988

This American director had such a wondrous way with actors that it can't be churlish to wish that he had actually made better movies. Look almost anywhere in an Ashby film and you'll find a performance, sometimes two or three, worthy of an Oscar nomination. Ashby had the happy knack of helping actors to get right inside their characters so that emotions as contrasting as anger and self-pity could pour out of them with complete naturalness. One wonders what the man might have done if he had ever been able to work on a wholly excellent script. Certainly the performances of Jack Nicholson in *The Last Detail* and Jon Voight in *Coming Home* remain highpoints in their careers (even given the limitations of the material) while Lee Grant won one Academy Award and was nominated for a second under Ashby's direction. He began in the business as a humble clerk with Republic Studios in their dying days, before graduating to assistant editor and then striking up a profitable relationship (as editor) with director Norman Jewison (*qv*) in the mid-1960s. Jewison also produced Ashby's initial film effort, *The Landlord*, although Ashby's directorial career needed re-establishing after the comparative failure of *Harold and Maude*, too offbeat a film to attempt so early on. After *Being There* (which contained another Oscar nomination, this time for Peter Sellers), Ashby's films of the 1980s were considerably less successful. Before he had time to recoup, he was struck down with liver cancer at 59. He was four times married and divorced.

1970: *The Landlord.* 1971: *Harold and Maude.* 1973: *The Last Detail.* 1975: *Shampoo.* 1976: *Bound for Glory.* 1978: *Coming Home. The Hamster of Happiness (released 1980 as Second Hand Hearts).* 1979: *Being There.* 1981: *Lookin' to Get Out.* 1982: *Time is On Our Side (D).* 1983: *Let's Spend the Night Together (D).* 1985: *The Slugger's Wife.* 1986: *8 Million Ways to Die.*

ASQUITH, Anthony 1902-1968

Although the recent critical trend has been to downgrade Asquith's work, reviewings of his most interesting pictures confirm that his war films were tight, tense and well observed, and that no-one fared better at conveying the sense of fun in Bernard Shaw's work from stage to screen. His association with the playwright Terence Rattigan was also a highly profitable one in its early years and produced some engrossing film entertainments. Asquith's films are intensely patriotic and romantic and, at least until 1955, of a consistently high quality and very affecting in their direct audience appeal. Born in London, the son of a man destined to be British Prime Minister from 1908 to 1916, Asquith studied film-making in Hollywood before returning to England in 1926: a year later, he co-directed his first film. With the coming of sound, he soon proved to have a sensitive rapport with actors that propelled him to the forefront of young British directors. Unaccountably, after his success with *A Cottage on Dartmoor*, bleakly melodramatic triangle tragedy, and *Tell England*, a moving story of the Gallipoli campaign, the 1930s were years of struggle for Asquith, who only re-established his reputation after Gabriel Pascal gave him the opportunity to co-direct his version of Shaw's *Pygmalion* in 1938. *French Without Tears* (which began the Rattigan connection and for which Ray Milland came back to Britain from Hollywood) and *Quiet Wedding* furthered his reputation, and his patriotic instincts stirred him to make two fine war films with intense concentration on wartime *camaraderie* between men from different walks of life: *We Dive at Dawn*, dealing with the submarine service, and *The Way to the Stars*, with its famous opening tracking shot through a now-deserted airfield. The postwar years, marred as they were by a (finally victorious) battle against alcoholism, were less happy for Asquith, although the partnership with Rattigan continued to flourish In *While the Sun Shines* and, especially, *The Winslow Boy*. Under Asquith's tight and attentive direction, the famous story of a naval cadet whose life seems ruined when he is accused of theft gripped the attention throughout. Asquith continued his moving, emotional studies of people under stress with *The Browning Version*, which contains one of Michael Redgrave's finest performances, as an embittered schoolmaster. Redgrave was also in the delightful *The Importance of Being Earnest*, in which Asquith rightly gave the treasurable Edith Evans her head as the trenchant Lady Bracknell. Asquith's subsequent films are more varied in impact, although *The Young Lovers* and *Carrington VC* are both underrated pictures. But the misfires did grow more frequent after 1950, and *The Millionairess* (again from Shaw) is the last highpoint of a career that ended disappointingly. He was known to his friends as 'Puffin'.

1927: *†Shooting Stars.* 1928: *Underground (and German version).* 1929: *The Runaway Princess.* 1930: *A Cottage on Dartmoor (US: Escaped from Dartmoor).* 1931: *Tell England (US: Battle of Gallipoli).* 1932: *Dance Pretty Lady.* 1933: *The Lucky Number.* 1934: *†Unfinished Symphony (US: Lover Divine).* 1935: *Moscow Nights (US: I Stand Condemned). †Brown on Resolution/For Ever England (US: Born For Glory.* 1938: *†Pygmalion.* 1939: *French Without Tears. *Guide Dogs For the Blind.* 1940: *Freedom Radio (US: Voice in the Night). *Channel Incident. Quiet Wedding.* 1941: *Cottage to Let (US: Bombsight Stolen). *Rush Hour.* 1942: *Uncensored.* 1943: *The Demi-Paradise (US: Adventure For Two). We Dive at Dawn. †Welcome to Britain.* 1944: *Fanny by Gaslight (US: Man of Evil). *Two Fathers.* 1945: *The Way to the Stars (US: Johnny in the Clouds).* 1946: *While the Sun Shines.* 1948: *The Winslow Boy.* 1950: *The Woman in Question (US: Five Angles on Murder).* 1951: *The Browning Version.* 1952: *The Importance of Being Earnest.* 1953: *The Net (US: Project M7). The Final Test.* 1954: *The Young Lovers (US: Chance Meeting). Carrington VC (US: Court-Martial).* 1955: *On Such a Night.* 1958: *Orders to Kill.* 1959: *Libel! The Doctor's Dilemma.* 1960: *The Millionairess. *Zero.* 1961: *Two Living, One Dead.* 1962: *Guns of Darkness.* 1963: *The V.I.P.s. †An Evening with the Royal Ballet.* 1964: *The Yellow Rolls-Royce.*

ATTENBOROUGH, Sir Richard 1923-

After the many war films in which he appeared as an actor, it was perhaps not unexpected that this British film-maker should turn to epic subjects when he began a belated directorial career at the age of 46. He has proved a workmanlike and capable director of these massive undertakings and, although the results may have been somewhat over-praised, he is undoubtedly capable, through careful pacing and camera placement, of achieving inspiring moments. In 1982, he achieved his long-cherished ambition of completing a film of the life of the great Mahatma Gandhi. It won him the Best Director Oscar. Attenborough entered films as an actor in 1942, and made an immediate impact with his faint-hearted seaman from *In Which We Serve*. This typecast him as weak and blustering youths for the next ten years, but he gradually escaped the mould to become a well-respected star character actor from the late 1950s on. He turned to direction in 1969 with an impressively mounted film version of Joan Littlewood's stage success, *Oh! What a Lovely War*, a satire on the mismanagement and waste of life seen in World War I. The sea of crosses at the end of the film remains Attenborough's crowning achievement in one scene. He continued to act, no doubt building funds for the next movie epic. The next two on his schedule were both war films of sorts – *Young Winston* dealt in proficient but faintly uninspired fashion with the adventurous early career of the future British prime minister Winston Churchill and *A Bridge Too Far* was a multi-star action spectacular about the disastrous British attempt to parachute into Arnhem in World War II. Although these films are made with great technical expertise, one feels a certain lack of blood and guts, reflected also in the later *Chaplin*; audience sympathy with their characters is not encouraged beyond a certain point. But the large-scale film of this kind was clearly Attenborough's forte; his next film, *Magic*, on the theme of a ventriloquist taken over by his dummy, suggested that he was less at home with more intimate drama. The film fails on all directorial levels save the good performances that Attenborough gets from Anthony Hopkins and Ann-Margret. One could have made the same comment 15 years later about Hopkins and Debra Winger in *Shadowlands*. *Gandhi* sounded a challenge too far, but Attenborough met it triumphantly, proving himself capable of touching the heart. Stars continued to be attracted to his movies in droves, but his films by and large have not had the same emotive effect as *Gandhi*.

1969: Oh! What a Lovely War. 1971: Young Winston. 1977: A Bridge Too Far. 1978: Magic. 1982: Gandhi. 1985: A Chorus Line. 1987: Cry Freedom. 1992: Chaplin. 1993: Shadowlands. 1996: In Love and War. 1999: Grey Owl.

AUER, John H. 1906-1975

Although Auer had the right background for success in Hollywood in the early days of sound – born in Hungary, educated in Vienna – there was little in his films to suggest he could be another Lubitsch, or Wilder, or even Curtiz, and he remained entrenched in (sometimes stylish) 'B' features for much of his career. Failing to find work in America's film capital in the late 1920s, Auer moved south to Mexico, where he did manage to get a start in direction by 1933. Two years later, he had retraced his steps to Hollywood, and made his first film for Republic, the studio where he was to spend most of his working life. Auer loved working in black and white, and never made a film in colour, not even the Trucolor beloved of Republic Studios. He returned there after a sojourn at RKO, and was put in charge of several of the studio's 'semi-A' monochrome features, some of which, notably *The Flame, I, Jane Doe, Hell's Half Acre* and *City That Never Sleeps*, are roughhewn and edgy but also fast-moving, exciting and strongly atmospheric. *The Eternal Sea*, a 'big' film by Auer's standards, is also of interest and shows his gentler side. In the mid-1950s, he finally left Republic and the majority of his last working years were spent in television.

1933: Una Vida per Otra. 1934: The Pervert. Rest in Peace. Su ultima canción. 1935: The Crime of Dr Crespi. Frankie and Johnnie. 1937: A Man Betrayed. Circus Girl. Rhythm in the Clouds. 1938: Outside of Paradise. A Desperate Adventure. I Stand Accused. Invisible Enemy. Orphans of the Street. 1939: SOS Tidal Wave (GB: Tidal Wave). Forged Passport. Smuggled Cargo. Calling All Marines. 1940: Women in War. Thou Shall Not Kill. Hit Parade of 1941. 1941: A Man Betrayed (later Wheel of Fortune. GB: Citadel of Crime). The Devil Pays Off. 1942: Pardon My Stripes. Moonlight Masquerade. Johnny Doughboy. 1943: Tahiti Honey. Gangway for Tomorrow. 1944: Seven Days Ashore. Music in Manhattan. 1945: Pan-Americana. 1946: Beat the Band. 1947: The Flame. 1948: I, Jane Doe (GB: Diary of a Bride). Angel on the Amazon (GB: Drums Along the Amazon). 1950: The Avengers. Hit Parade of 1951. 1952: Thunderbirds. 1953: City That Never Sleeps. 1954: Hell's Half Acre. 1955: The Eternal Sea. 1957: Johnny Trouble.

AUGUST, Bille 1948-

Danish director at his considerable best with close examinations of the problems of the proletariat. Trained as a photographer he soon graduated from advertising

to films following studies at the Danish Film School. After several films as cinematographer he began directing for TV in the 1970s, segments from his successful series *Buster's World* being edited into a feature film. That followed August's debut as a film director with *My Life*. The really big breakthrough, however, came in 1985 with *Twist and Shout*, a perceptive portrait of two teenagers growing up in the era of The Beatles. This proved Denmark's most popular film to that date, and two years later August took the Best Foreign-Language Film Oscar with *Pelle the Conqueror*, the study of a Swedish widower who takes his son to Denmark in search of a better life in the late 19th century, but finds only hardship serving landowners on a bleak farm. And there were more awards for *The Best Intentions*, an internationally popular portrait of an unconventional marriage, written by fellow director Ingmar Bergman, who based the story on the lives of his own parents. August had now come to the forefront of those directors adept at crystallising the (sometimes extraordinary) lives of ordinary people. So it was not surprising that, despite an ardent pursuit of author Isabel Allende to film her novel *The House of the Spirits* (which deals with people far from ordinary), August proved hardly the ideal director for her story, and recorded his first major flop. Since then he has regained some ground with *Jerusalem* and *Smilla's Sense of Snow*, the former again set in turn-of-the-century Scandinavia, the latter a partially successful first attempt at a thriller.

1978: Honning maane/In My Life. 1981: Buster's World. 1983: Zappa. 1985: Twist and Shout. 1987: Pelle the Conqueror. 1992: The Best Intentions. 1994: The House of the Spirits. 1996: Jerusalem. 1997: Smilla's Sense of Snow/Smilla's Feeling for Snow. 1998: Les Misérables.

AUTANT-LARA, Claude 1903-

Autant-Lara led a chequered career through his near 60 years in the cinema. It took him 20 of those years to achieve recognition in his native France, but there followed a golden decade of success. He continued to work, though, long after the critical applause had died. He began as a set decorator and costume designer before beginning to direct experimental shorts, in one of which, *Construire un feu*, he devised a fairly revolutionary wide-screen system. It was to try to sell this system that he went to America in 1930. He couldn't find a studio to buy it, but did stay on for a year or two directing French-

Funny business. Dan Aykroyd (left) and director John G **Avildsen** discuss ways of making their audience laugh on the set of *Neighbors*.

language versions of Hollywood films, including two with Buster Keaton. But it was not until the late years of World War II that Autant-Lara hit his stride, first with *Sylvie et le fantôme*, a delicate fantasy-comedy made in 1944 but not shown until after the Liberation, then with *Le diable au corps*, a strongly charged and beautifully acted (by Micheline Prèsle and Gerard Philipe) story of a doomed love affair between a boy and a much older woman. Almost all of Autant-Lara's subsequent films up to 1956 are of note in one way or another. The *diable* theme was repeated in *Le blé en herbe*, but there are also comedies, especially *L'auberge rouge*, one of Fernandel's strongest films, and *La traversée de Paris*, a film with excitement, atmosphere, charm and fun in equal proportions, as Bourvil and Jean Gabin attempt to transport a black-market pig from one side of a wartime, blacked-out Paris to the other. After this, Autant-Lara's light touch and elegant ways seemed gradually to desert him, not as suddenly as, say Preston Sturges' talent had declined, but just as irrefutably. Overtaken by *nouvelle vague*, he sank into the routine and never re-emerged.

1923: *Faits divers. 1926: *Vittel (D).

*Construire un feu. 1931: Buster se marie (French version of Parlor, Bedroom and Bath. GB: Romeo in Pyjamas). Le plombier amoureux (French version of The Passionate Plumber). Le fils du Rajah (French version of Son of India). Pur sang. La pente. 1932: Le gendarme est sans pitié. L'athlète incomplet. Monsieur le Duc. Un client sérieux. La peur des coups. Invite Monsieur à diner. 1933: Ciboulette. 1936: The Mysterious Mr Davis (US: My Partner, Mr Davis). 1937: †L'affaire du courier de Lyon (US: Courier of Lyons. Uncredited). 1938: †Le ruisseau (uncredited). 1939: †Fric-Frac (uncredited). 1941: Le mariage de Chiffon. 1942: Lettres d'amour. 1943: Douce (US: Love Story). 1944 (released 1946): Sylvie et le fantôme (GB: Sylvia and the Ghost. US: Sylvia and the Phantom). 1947. Le diable au corps (GB & US: Devil in the Flesh). 1949: Occupe-toi d'Amélie (GB: Keep an Eye on Amelia. US: Oh Amelia!). 1951: L'auberge rouge (GB & US: The Red Inn). †Les sept péchés capitaux (GB & US: The Seven Deadly Sins). 1953: Le bon Dieu sans confession. Le blé en herbe (GB: Ripening Seed. US: The Game of Love). 1954: Le rouge et le noir (GB: Scarlet and Black.

US: Rouge et Noir). 1956: Marguerite de la nuit. La traversée de Paris (GB: Pig Across Paris. US: Four Bags Full). 1958: En cas de malheur (GB & US: Love is My Profession). Le joueur. 1959: La jument verte (GB: The Green Mare's Nest. US: The Green Mare). Les régates de San Francisco. 1960: Le bois des amants. 1961: Tu ne tueras pas/Non uccidere (GB & US: Thou Shall Not Kill - released 1963). Le comte de Monte-Cristo/The Count of Monte-Cristo. 1962: Vive Henri IV, vive l'amour. 1963: Le meurtrier/Der Mörder (GB & US: Enough Rope). Le magot de Joséfa. 1964: †Humour noir. 1965: Le journal d'une femme en blanc (US: A Woman in White). 1966: Le nouveau journal d'une femme en blanc/Return of a Woman in White. 1967: †Le plus vieux métier du monde (GB & US: The Oldest Profession). 1968: Le Franciscain de Bourges. 1969: Les patates. 1971: Le rouge et le blanc. 1977: Gloria.

AVILDSEN, John G. 1936-
Although he has been associated with two Oscar-winning films (winning an Academy Award himself for *Rocky*), Avildsen's

career has not shown the consistency that might have established him as one of the foremost American directors of his time. After working as director of photography, production manager and assistant director on various films, major and minor, through the 1960s, he made several semi-sexploitation films before leaping into the limelight with *Joe*. Like many of his more successful films, this has an eye-catching central-performance (in this case by Peter Boyle as a loud and foul mouthed, all-American bigot) and it was followed by others, from Jack Lemmon in *Save the Tiger*, winning him an Oscar), Burt Reynolds in *WW and the Dixie Dancekings* and Sylvester Stallone in *Rocky*. Thanks to the success of this last film, it seemed that Avildsen could write his own ticket in Hollywood, but it was followed by the impossibly maudlin and sticky *Slow Dancing in the Big City* and by *The Formula*, which wasted the talents of Marlon Brando and George C Scott on a strictly routine power-in-high-places thriller. It was 1984 before he had another hit, and then it was with *The Karate Kid*, a sort of junior version of *Rocky*. Since then, Avildsen has mixed (too many) more Karate Kid and Rocky films with such feelgood message movies as *Lean On Me* (which contains another strong leading performance, from Morgan Freeman) and *The Power of One*. Avildsen married the actress Tracy Brooks Swope.

1964: **Smiles.* 1967: **Light, Sound, Diffuse. Turn On to Love.* 1968: *Sweet Dreams/OK Bill.* 1969: *Guess What We Learned in School Today?* 1970: *Joe.* 1971: *Cry Uncle* (GB: *Super Dick*). 1972: *The Stoolie/Roger the Stoolie.* 1973: *Save the Tiger.* 1974: *†Foreplay.* 1975: *WW and the Dixie Dancekings.* 1976: *Rocky.* 1978: *Slow Dancing in the Big City.* 1980: *The Formula.* 1981: *Neighbors.* 1983: *Heaven.* 1984: *The Karate Kid.* 1985: *Happy New Year* (released 1987). 1986: *Karate Kid II.* 1987: *For Keeps?* (GB: *Maybe Baby*). 1988: *Lean On Me.* 1989: *The Karate Kid Part III.* 1990: *Rocky V.* 1992: *The Power of One.* 1994: *8 Seconds.* 1999: *Inferno. Fashion Wars.*

AVNET, Jon 1949-

Although Brooklyn-born Avnet won, early in his career, a directing fellowship from the American Film Institute, he has until recently directed remarkably few films. After years as a producer and sometime writer, he does now seem to have settled in to the director's chair, mainly on the strength of his deserved success with the nostalgic 1991 film *Fried Green Tomatoes*

at the Whistle Stop Cafe. Avnet was a film producer as early as 1979 (firstly for nine years) in partnership with award-winning writer Steve Tisch and then (from 1986) with Jordan Kerner, a partnership that produced trailblazing telefilms as well as successful movies. Avnet's success with *Fried Green Tomatoes*, however, encouraged him to make the switch. His storytelling here proved strong enough to grip the attention almost all through what is quite a long film about the friendship between two Southern States girls in times past. He has not yet repeated the critical success of that film, the highest profile of his subsequent films being that of *Up Close & Personal*, a glossy romantic wallow through the world of TV reporting with occasional striking sequences.

1975: **Confusion's Circle.* 1985: *Between Two Women* (TV). 1991: *Fried Green Tomatoes at the Whistle Stop Café/Fried Green Tomatoes.* 1994: *The War.* 1996: *Up Close & Personal.* 1997: *Red Corner.*

BABENCO, Hector 1946-

'A man at the bottom of the world is still a man.' Argentinian-born film-maker Hector Babenco was talking about the character played by Jack Nicholson in his film *Ironweed*, but the quote is as apposite to aspects of almost all Babenco's films, as he confronts the lowest and most oppressed forms of life. There may be beauty even in the gutter if you search as diligently as Babenco, but you may feel you need a quick bath after watching one of his films. In these gruelling sagas, those living on life's edges frequently find themselves holding centre stage. The son of Russian-Polish immigrants to South America, Babenco rebelled against parental restrictions and left home at 17 to travel, via Puerto Rico, through Europe and North Africa. Settling in Brazil, he directed his first film, *King of the Night*, after toiling four years to scrape together the $250,000 needed to make it. It set the pattern for the rest of his work in its portrayal of a middle-class man's descent into degradation after passing up the chance of life with the prostitute who loves him. His second, *Lucio Flavio*, was a fact-based story of a professional thief who splits his

proceeds with the police and is murdered by them when he threatens to spill the beans. But it was with his next film, *Pixote*, that Babenco really leapt to international attention. This study of juvenile vagrants in Rio de Janeiro is an unflinching look at the underbelly of a city where children of ten or 12 become prostitutes and thieves and sometimes even killers. *Kiss of the Spider Woman*, uncompromising but never unsavoury in its portrait of two cell mates, a homosexual and a political prisoner who become drawn into the former's fantasy world of (bad) old movies to preserve their sanity, won Babenco an Oscar nomination but his work since then has been disappointing with the exception of the underrated *Ironweed*, a study of vagrants in America and one in particular (Nicholson) making faint attempts to re-enter the society that had rejected him.

1975: *King of the Night.* 1978: *Lucio Flavio.* 1981: *Pixote.* 1985: *Kiss of the Spider Woman.* 1987: *Ironweed.* 1991: *At Play in the Fields of the Lord.* 1994: *†Erotic Tales.* 1997: *Foolish Heart.*

BACON, Lloyd 1890-1955

An expert at conveying fun and joie-de-vivre, this American director hasn't received half the credit he deserves. If the spark of genius in such musicals as *42nd Street* undoubtedly belonged to Busby Berkeley (*qv*), a lot of craftsmanship still came from Bacon, the officially accredited director. He came to Hollywood as an actor, initially a comic foil for Charlie Chaplin from 1915, in *The Champion, The Bank, The Tramp* and others. He took his first faltering steps as director with three shorts made during 1923 and 1924, although not making his first feature until 1926. Al Jolson's *The Singing Fool*, Hollywood's first all-dialogue film, was his most important assignment, and it gave him a reputation as a maker of musicals (which he never entirely lost: he was still turning them out in the early 1950s) and a career with the brothers Warner that was to last 17 years. At the studio, Bacon tackled a wide variety of genres without quite contributing any of Warners' outstanding work. But, besides the musicals, the fast-moving *The Picture Snatcher* (the first of several films in which Bacon combined with James Cagney), *Marked Woman, San Quentin, The Oklahoma Kid, Invisible Stripes, Brother Orchid, Action in the North Atlantic* and *A Slight Case of Murder* are all enjoyable professional movies with touches that put them above the average. His Fox films in the 1940s are grindingly routine, but there were still a few goodies left in the locker. At Columbia in 1949 and 1950, Bacon made a quartet of farces (two of them with Lucille Ball) which, for sheer slickness, paciness and simple, direct belly-laughs, are four of the funniest co-feature comedies ever made: *The Fuller Brush Girl*, *The Good Humor Man*, *Miss Grant Takes Richmond* and *Kill the Umpire!* And *Golden Girl* is one last great musical. The tunes are full of life, the period feel impeccable. Mitzi Gaynor was never livelier or more appealing, and the ending draws the tears in vintage four-handkerchief fashion. He died from a cerebral haemorrhage.

1923: *The Host. 1924: *Don't Fail. *The Wild Goose Chaser. 1925: *The Raspberry Romance. *Merrymakers. *Breaking the Ice. *He Who Gets Smacked. *Take Your Time. *Good Morning Madam. *The Window Dummy. 1926: *Wide Open Faces. *Two Lips in Holland. *Meet My Girl. Broken Hearts of Hollywood. Private Izzy Murphy. *Kitty from Killarney. Finger Prints. *Circus Today. *The Prodigal Bridegroom. 1927: The Heart of Maryland. White Flannels. *Smith's Customer. *Smith's Surprise. *Smith's New Home. A Sailor's Sweetheart. Brass Knuckles. 1928: Pay As You Enter. The Lion and the Mouse. Women They Talk About. The Singing Fool. *The Question of Today. 1929: Stark Mad. Honky Tonk. No

Defense. Say It with Songs. So Long Letty. 1930: Moby Dick. The Other Tomorrow. She Couldn't Say No. A Notorious Affair. The Office Wife. 1931: Fifty Million Frenchmen. Sit Tight. Gold Dust Gertie. Kept Husbands. Honor of the Family. 1932: Fireman Save My Child. †Alias the Doctor (uncredited). The Famous Ferguson Case. Miss Pinkerton. Manhattan Parade. You Said a Mouthful. Crooner. 1933: The Picture Snatcher. Son of a Sailor. 42nd Street. Mary Stevens MD. Footlight Parade. 1934: Six Day Bike Rider. He Was Her Man. Wonder Bar. A Very Honorable Guy (GB: A Very Honourable Man). Here Comes the Navy. 1935: In Caliente. Devil Dogs of the Air. Frisco Kid. Broadway Gondolier. The Irish in Us. 1936: Sons o' Guns. Cain and Mabel. Gold Diggers of 1937. 1937: Ever Since Eve. Marked Woman. San Quentin. Submarine D-1. 1938: Cowboy from Brooklyn (GB: Romance and Rhythm). Boy Meets Girl. Racket Busters. A Slight Case of Murder. 1939: The Oklahoma Kid. Indianapolis Speedway (GB: Devil on Wheels). Wings of the Navy. Espionage Agent. Invisible Stripes. 1940: Three Cheers for the Irish. A Child is Born. Brother Orchid. Knute Rockne – All American (GB: A Modern Hero). 1941: Honeymoon for Three. Affectionately Yours. Footsteps in the Dark. Navy Blues. 1942: Larceny Inc. Wings for the Eagle. Silver Queen. 1943: Action in the North Atlantic. 1944: The Sullivans. Sunday Dinner for a Soldier. 1945: Captain Eddie. 1946: Home, Sweet Homicide. Wake Up and Dream. 1947: I Wonder Who's Kissing Her Now. 1948: You Were Meant for Me. Give My Regards to Broadway. Don't Trust Your Husband/An Innocent Affair. 1949: Mother is a Freshman (GB: Mother Knows Best). It Happens Every Spring. Miss Grant Takes Richmond (GB: Innocence is Bliss). 1950: The Fuller Brush Girl (GB: The Affairs of Sally). Kill the Umpire! The Good Humor Man. 1951: Call Me Mister. The Frogmen. Golden Girl. 1953: The 'I Don't Care' Girl. The Great Sioux Uprising. Walking My Baby Back Home. She Couldn't Say No (GB: Beautiful But Dangerous). 1954: The French Line.

BADGER, Clarence 1880-1964

Almost all of this American director's work lies in comedy. He was 35 when he made the big decision to quit journalism and go into films, where it so happened that his mentor was Mack Sennett. When Badger joined Sennett at Triangle-Keystone, it was initially, naturally, as a writer, but, inside a year, he was directing two-reel comedies at the studio. While Badger must have been deeply immersed in Sen-

nett slapstick, a gentler, drier, more elegant style of his own soon emerged. Such actresses as Gloria Swanson, Bebe Daniels and Clara Bow quickly realised that Badger could help them make the most of their talents for comedy, and he also made almost all of Will Rogers's silent films. In his talent he somewhat resembled Leo McCarey, Lloyd Bacon and all too few others, in that he mastered the art of making a whole string of hilarious visual situations form themselves into a coherent and enjoyable film: *Paths to Paradise* and *Hands Up!* are only two of the many examples of Badger's fast, funny, but affectionate and warm-hearted farces. With the coming of sound, Badger's eyes turned increasingly to Australia, where he had always fancied living. In 1934, he finally gave Hollywood the heave-ho and emigrated. Badger made a couple of undistinguished films in his new country but, by the time World War II had ended and the Australian film industry started up again, he had settled into retirement. Sometimes credited as Clarence G. Badger.

1915: *A Duel at Dawn. 1916: †A Modern Enoch Arden. †*Gypsy Joe. †*His Wild Oats. A Family Affair. *A Social Cub. *The Danger Girl (GB: Love on Skates). *Haystacks and Steeples. 1917: *Teddy at the Throttle. *The Nick-of-Time Baby. *Whose Baby? *The Sultan's Wife. *The Pullman Bride. 1918: The Floor Below. The Venus Model. The Kingdom of Youth. Friend Husband. A Perfect Lady. Day Dreams. 1919: Sis Hopkins. Daughter of Mine. Leave It to Susan. Through the Wrong Door. Almost a Husband. Strictly Confidential. Water, Water, Everywhere. Jubilo. 1920: Jes' Call Me Jim. Cupid, the Cowpuncher. Honest Hutch. The Strange Boarder. 1921: Guile of Women. Boys Will Be Boys. An Unwilling Hero. Doubling for Romeo. A Poor Relation. 1922: *The Ropin' Fool. Quincy Adams Sawyer. Don't Get Personal. The Dangerous Little Demon. 1923: Potash and Perlmutter (GB: Dr Sunshine). Your Friend and Mine. Red Lights. 1924: The Shooting of Dan McGrew. Painted People. One Night in Rome. 1925: Eve's Secret. New Lives for Old. Paths to Paradise. The Golden Princess. 1926: Miss Brewster's Millions. The Campus Flirt (GB: The College Flirt). Hands Up! The Rainmaker. 1927: Man Power. Senorita. It. Swim, Girl, Swim. She's a Sheik. A Kiss in a Taxi. 1928: The Fifty-Fifty Girl. Hot News. Red Hair. Three Week-Ends. 1929: Paris. 1930: No, No, Nanette. Murder Will Out. The Bad Man. Woman Hungry (GB: The Challenge). Sweethearts and Wives. 1931: The Hot Heiress. Party Husband. 1933: When

Experienced maker of action comedies John **Badham** sizes up the situation on *Another Stakeout*.

Roy Ward **Baker** took something of a break form the horror films that dominated the latter stages of his career when he made *Moon Zero Two*.

Strangers Marry. 1936: Rangle River. 1941: That Certain Something.

BADHAM, John 1939-

British-born Hollywood director, mainly of star-driven entertainment subjects that often hit the target in terms of popular appeal. A sharp visual stylist, Badham makes flashy, eye-catching films, although only in his early 1980s subjects does he consistently match his flair for visual effects with a sense of how to pace a film. *Dracula, Bingo Long* and *Saturday Night Fever,* however pleasing in patches (and there are bits of each that stick in the memory) are all over-inflated and at times positively creep along, a fault that sometimes reappears in Badham's work in the 1990s. Finding his Master's degree from Yale Drama School did not open doors for him in the film world, Badham resolved to learn the trade from the ground up, beginning in the Universal Studios mail room. By 1969, he had graduated to assistant director (on the Steven Spielberg-directed segment of the triple-decker TV movie

Night Gallery) and worked patiently in television before being given his first solo assignment in 1971. His TV movies are a variable crowd (*The Law* and *Isn't It Shocking* are well worth watching for different reasons, while *The Keegans* and *Reflections of Murder* are pretty awful), but *Saturday Night Fever,* a worldwide success, put television behind him. It was *Blue Thunder,* a first-rate helicopter action film, with no messing about, that heralded a winning streak for Badham that also included *WarGames,* an early example of kids hacking into the world's computer systems, *Short Circuit* – a robot takes on a life of its own - and the joky detective thriller *StakeOut.* Since 1990, Badham's films have been less successful, although there were felicitous moments in *The Hard Way,* about a film star joining the police force as practice for his next film. Badham's sister is the 1960s child player Mary Badham.

1971: The Impatient Heart (TV). 1973: Isn't It Shocking? (TV). 1974: The Law (TV). The Gun (TV). Reflections of Mur-

der (TV). The Godchild (TV). 1976: The Bingo Long All Stars and Traveling Motor Kings. 1977: Saturday Night Fever. 1979: Dracula. 1981: Whose Life Is It Any Way? 1982: Blue Thunder. 1983: WarGames. 1985: American Flyers. 1986: Short Circuit. 1987: StakeOut. 1990: Bird on a Wire. 1991: The Hard Way. 1993: Point of No Return (GB: The Assassin). Another Stakeout. 1994: Drop Zone. 1995: Nick of Time. 1997: Incognito. 1999 The Jack Bull.

BAKER, Roy (Ward) 1916-

This British director served a 13-year apprenticeship, first with Gainsborough Films, then making wartime films for service personnel; he emerged in post-war years as one of Britain's most solid stylists, very aware of shape and shadow and ahead of his time in editing techniques. There was an interesting Hollywood period, too; although it ended unfortunately, with Baker resigning from *White Witch Doctor* (something he was well rid of), it does contain the splendid *Inferno* which, like some of Baker's British films, shows admirable control of mounting tension. People living on the edges of themselves and their resourcefulness, like the character (Robert Ryan) abandoned in the desert in *Inferno*, have formed something of a recurring theme in Baker's work, right from his initial film as director, *The October Man* (his first of several with John Mills). His movies also include some of the most enjoyable popular successes of the British cinema in the post-war years, including *Morning Departure*, *A Night to Remember* and *The One That Got Away*. From 1960, however, he was hard at work on television, in such series as *Danger Man*, *The Saint* and *The Avengers*. On his return to the cinema in 1967, billed as Roy Ward Baker, he no longer seemed the same director, and indeed directed entirely different kinds of subjects, mainly horror films. Of these, only *Asylum* and *Dr Jekyll and Sister Hyde* carry a genuine charge of fear. In 1981, he returned to television to direct his first entire series – *The Flame Trees of Thika*.

1947: *The October Man*. 1948: *The Weaker Sex*. 1949: *Paper Orchid*. *Morning Departure* (US: *Operation Disaster*). 1950: *Highly Dangerous*. 1951: *The House in the Square* (US: *I'll Never Forget You*). 1952: *Night Without Sleep*. *Don't Bother to Knock*. 1953: *Inferno*. 1955: *Passage Home*. 1956: *Jacqueline*. *Tiger in the Smoke*. 1957: *The One That Got Away*. 1958: *A Night to Remember*. 1960: *The Singer Not the Song*. 1961: *Flame in the Streets*. *The Valiant*. 1963: *Two Left Feet*. 1967: *Quatermass and the Pit* (US: *Five Million Miles to Earth*). *The Anniversary*. 1969: *Moon Zero Two*. *The Spy Killer* (TV). 1970: *The Vampire Lovers*. *Foreign Exchange* (TV). *The Scars of Dracula*. 1971: *Dr Jekyll and Sister Hyde*. 1972: *Asylum*. 1973: *And Now the Screaming Starts!* *Vault of Horror*. 1974: *The Legend of the Seven Golden Vampires*. 1980: *The Monster Club*.

BANKS, Monty
See Kimmins, Anthony

BARDEM, Juan Antonio
(J.A. Bardem-Muñoz) 1922-
Although he almost single-handedly brought the Spanish cinema into the international limelight in post-war years, Bardem has lost much of his early critical reputation in the last 30 years and, if his international co-productions – a strange bunch, indeed – are anything to judge by, not undeservedly. The early successes, if still far superior to his later work, can now be seen to be lingering some way behind (and in the shadow of) their Italian counterparts of the neo-realist wave

from a few years before. From a theatrical family, Bardem was a writer and critic who, with his collaborator and friend Luis-Garcia Berlanga, put together several unproduced screenplays before succeeding with *Welcome, Mr Marshall*, a charming village comedy which Berlanga directed. Bardem's best films subsequently are also set against, or involve small-town life, with its charm, its restrictions, and its prejudices. *Death of a Cyclist* is a strong psychological drama about the repercussions of a road accident, and his next film *Calle Mayor*, benefiting greatly from a poignant performance by the American actress Betsy Blair, a penetrating portrait of loneliness and a scathing condemnation of those who seek their fun by preying on those more vulnerable than themselves. Bardem had much trouble with the Spanish censor under the Franco regime (he was briefly imprisoned for 'political reasons' in 1956) and by the late 1960s he had descended to very routine thrillers and adventures that could have been made by any run-of-the-mill French or Italian director. He usually scripted his own films.

1948: †**Paseo sobre una guerra antigua*. 1950: **Barajas, aeropuerto international*. 1951: †*Esa pareja feliz*. 1953: †*Novio a la vista*. *Cómicos*. 1954: *Felices pasquas*. 1955: *Muerte de un ciclista* (GB: *Death of a Cyclist*. US: *Age of Infidelity*). 1956: *Calle Mayor* (US: *The Lovemaker*). 1957: *La Muerte de Pio Baroja* (unreleased). 1958: *La venganza*. 1959: *Sonatas*. 1960: *A las cinco de la tarde*. 1962: *Los inocentes*. 1963: *Nunca pasa nada*. 1965: *Los pianos mécanicos* (US: *The Uninhibited*). 1969: *El ultimo dia de la guerra* (GB & US: *The Last Day of the War*). 1971: *Variétés*. 1972: *La corrupción de Chris Miller*. 1973: †*The Mysterious Island of Captain Nemo*. 1974: *Behind the Shutters*. 1975: *El poder del deseo*. 1976: *Foul Play*. 1977: *The Dog*. 1978: *El puente*. 1979: *7 dias en enero*. 1982: *The Warning*. 1987: *Lorca, la muerte de un poeta*.

BARTLETT, Hall 1922-1993
An independent American producer and director who aroused some interest with hard-hitting black-and-white dramas in the 1950s. In later times, however, several of his films received only limited distribution. His subjects always leaned towards being exploitative, or to having rather odd angles that would catch the public eye, but tended to be soft-centred and silly from the 1960s onwards. He was married to actress Rhonda Fleming from 1966 to 1971.

1952: *Navajo* (produced only). 1955: *Unchained*. 1957: †*Drango*. *Zero Hour!* 1960: *All the Young Men*. 1963: *The Caretakers* (GB: *Borderlines*). 1969: *Changes*. 1971: *The Wild Pack* (later *The Sandpit Generals*). 1973: *Jonathan Livingston Seagull*. 1978: *The Children of Sanchez*. 1982: *Comeback*. 1983: *Love is Forever* (TV). 1984: *The Defiant*. 1986: *Leaving Home*.

BARTEL, Paul 1938-
Although it seems he has now been finally defeated by the constant battle to get his films financed, this American director's anarchic work was consistently more entertaining than nearly all of his 'underground' contemporaries. Unfortunately, a secondary career as a bald, lugubrious, bearded character actor now seems to have swamped his directorial ambitions. He began as a director of animated shorts, following studies at the University of California, supplemented by summer work at the New York studios of UPA Cartoons. Like Frank Tashlin, who also started in animation, the surreal style of the cartoon suffused all of Bartel's subsequent work, outrageous in its subject matter and blackly zany in its treatment. The early car crash films *Cannonball* and *Death Race 2000* owe much to Tom & Jerry and to Wile E Coyote's fruitless pursuit of The Road Runner, but Bartel's reputation rests most securely with *Eating Raoul*, a film which took him ages to finance and almost as long to distribute until its success at film festivals. A wild black comedy about a penurious couple (Bartel himself and Mary Woronov) who raise the money to buy a restaurant by murdering perverts they lure into the house via the sex-ad columns, the film's uneven but has some wonderful darkly comic moments. Bartel also co-wrote the script, giving Woronov such lines as : 'Do you think we could buy another frying pan? I'm getting a little squeamish about using the one we use to kill people.' It was still tough to see Bartel joining the mainstream but, of his remaining films, *Lust in the Dust*, a spoof western, is too wild-eyed and knowing by half, while *Scenes from the Class Struggle in Beverly Hills*, his last to date, is light, lusty and luxuriously lewd, but only occasionally funny. Bartel once said of one of his films 'If this doesn't offend anybody, it isn't working.' He was right, of course, but making them laugh loud and long at the same time would have helped.

1962: *Progetti. 1967: **The Secret Cinema*. 1968: *Naughty Nurse. 1972: *Private Parts*. 1975: *Death Race 2000*. 1976:

Cannonball (GB: Carquake). 1982: Eating Raoul. 1984: Not for Publication. 1985: Lust in the Dust. 1989: Scenes from the Class Struggle in Beverly Hills.

BARTON, Charles T. 1902-1981

Barton was an American, and he made intrinsically American pictures – films that couldn't have been made, or set, anywhere else. His affection for the country and the values it wished to project in entertainment films, especially in the 1940s, reflected itself in all his work. From the westerns through the homely series films about Five Little Peppers, the wartime musicals, the Abbott and Costello films and outright Americana. Many of his films bore American place names that caused their titles to be changed abruptly in other lands, and even Abbott and Costello in Africa or Mexico were never far away from the Hollywood Canteen. Barton knew about comedy and he knew about movement and few of his films are low on entertainment value. In the latter stages of his film career, before stepping wholeheartedly over to TV to make comedy series there, he visited the Disney studio to make *The Shaggy Dog* and *Toby Tyler*, affectionately remembered pieces that burrow deep into the America of Americans' fondest imagination. Barton was a wiry little man, a knockabout vaudevillian who appeared as a boy in westerns with Broncho Billy Anderson from 1915. He also appeared on stage, but in the late 1920s, he returned to movies as a prop man, then, in the early 1930s, an assistant director under his friend William Wellman (*qv*) and on several Marx Brothers films – *Monkey Business, Horse Feathers* and *Duck Soup.* Although he did not possess Wellman's breadth of vision, Barton soon became a hard-working and reliable director of popular 'B' features, at first with Paramount, then Columbia and finally and most memorably at Universal, where he proved himself one of the few people able to handle the equally diminutive Lou Costello. And he gave as much enjoyment in the cinema as many better-known, critically more esteemed names.

1934: Wagon Wheels. 1935: Car 99. Rocky Mountain Mystery. †The Last Outpost. 1936: Timothy's Quest. Nevada. And Sudden Death. Murder with Pictures. Rose Bowl (GB: O'Brien's Luck). 1937: The Crime Nobody Saw. Forlorn River. Thunder Trail. 1938: Born to the West. Titans of the Deep. 1939: Behind Prison Gates. My Son is Guilty (GB: Crime's End). Five Little Peppers and How They Grew. 1940: Babies for Sale. Five Little

Peppers at Home. Island of Doomed Men. Five Little Peppers in Trouble. Nobody's Children. Out West with the Peppers. 1941: Honolulu Lu. Phantom Submarine. The Big Boss. Richest Man in Town. Two Latins from Manhattan. Sing for Your Supper. Harmon of Michigan. 1942: Tramp, Tramp, Tramp. Shut My Big Mouth. Hello Annapolis (GB: Personal Honour). Sweetheart of the Fleet. Parachute Nurse. A Man's World. Lucky Legs. The Spirit of Stanford (GB: Fighting Spirit). Laugh Your Blues Away. 1943: What's Buzzin' Cousin? Reveille With Beverly. Let's Have Fun. She Has What It Takes. Is Everybody Happy? 1944: Jam Session. Louisiana Hayride. Beautiful But Broke. Hey, Rookie. 1945: The Beautiful Cheat (GB: What a Woman!). Men in Her Diary. 1946: Smooth As Silk. White Tie and Tails. The Time of Their Lives. 1947: Buck Privates Come Home (GB: Rookies Come Home). The Wistful Widow of Wagon Gap (GB: The Wistful Widow). 1948: The Noose Hangs High. Abbott and Costello Meet Frankenstein (GB: Abbott and Costello Meet the Ghosts). Mexican Hayride. 1949: Africa Screams. Abbott and Costello Meet the Killer Boris Karloff. 1950: The Milkman. Double Crossbones. 1952: Ma and Pa Kettle at the Fair. 1956: Dance with Me Henry. 1959: The Shaggy Dog. 1960: Toby Tyler. 1962: Swingin' Along (originally filmed in 1960 as Double Trouble).

BAVA, Mario 1914-1980

Despite his 40 years' work in the cinema, the memory of Bava remains in its own microcosm somewhere in the early and middle 1960s. The world of this Italian director, peopled by vampires, witches and murderers, strikingly shot for the most part in lurid pastel shades, spun in parallel (but not twin) orbit to that of Roger Corman on the other side of the Atlantic Ocean. Indeed, several of Bava's films were released outside Italy by American-International, Corman's studio, and he actually worked for them on the unfortunate *Dr Goldfoot and the Girl Bombs*. Not surprisingly, in view of the startling visual content of his shockers, Bava began as a cameraman, working for Rossellini and other prominent Italian directors from 1939. His first great success (and first feature film as director) *La maschera del demonio/Mask of the Demon*, was in (very atmospheric) black and white, depicting an enclosed world of witchcraft, within which arise some memorably horrific set-pieces that hark back to the best American and German chillers of the late 1920s and 1930s. Since then, his chills and thrills have come in colour,

sometimes with quite extraordinary results. In the 1963-65 horror films especially, it seems that every shaft of light is shot with translucently pale turquoises, magentas or shades of ochre, with deep orange-red reflecting the blood of the victims. Outside of their style and Bava's bravura approach, these films have rather less to commend them than the earlier black-and-whites, of which *Evil Eye* is another notable example. *Operazione paura* is the last genuine highlight in Bava's career, in which his camera stalks in sinister style through a story which for once matches his visual skills, about a ghostly golden-haired little girl exacting revenge for past injustice; and the director's effects complement and enrich the genuinely creepy tale instead of bolstering some creaky murder plot.

*1946: *L'orecchio. 1947: *Santa notte. *Anfiteatro Flavio. *Legenda sinfonica. 1949: *Variazioni sinfoniche. 1950: *L'amore dell'arte. 1959: †La battaglia di Maratona (GB & US: The Giant of Marathon. Uncredited except as director of photography). 1960: La maschera del demonio (GB: Revenge of the Vampire; later Black Sunday. US: Black Sunday). 1961: Gli invasori (GB: Fury of the Vikings. US: Erik the Conqueror). Ercole al centro della terra (GB: Hercules in the Centre of the Earth. US: Hercules in the Haunted World). 1962: La ragazza che sapeva troppo (GB & US: Evil Eye). 1963: I tre volti della paura (GB & US: Black Sabbath). La frusta e il corpo (GB: Night is the Phantom. US: What!). 1964: La strada per Fort Alamo/Arizona Bill. Sei donne per l'assassino (GB & US: Blood and Black Lace). 1965: Terrore nello spazio (GB: Planet of the Vampires. US: Planet of Blood). Raffica di coltelli (US: Knives of the Avenger). 1966: Operazione paura (GB: Curse of the Dead. US: Kill Baby Kill). Dr Goldfoot and the Girl Bombs (GB: Dr G. and the Love Bomb). 1967: Diabolik (GB & US: Danger: Diabolik). 1969: Il rosso segito della follia (GB: Blood Brides. US: Hatchet for a Honeymoon). 1970: Cinque bambole per la luna di agosto (GB: Five Dolls for an August Moon). Roy Colt and Winchester Black. 1971: L'antefatto – Ecologia del delitto (GB: Blood Bath). 1972: Gli orrori del castello di Norimberga (GB & US: Baron Blood). Quante volte. . . quella notte (US: Four Times That Night). 1973: Il diavolo e il morto/Death and the Devil. 1976: Shock. 1979: La venere dell'ille.*

BAXTER, John 1896-1972

Just as Charles Barton (*qv*) was quintessentially American, so John Baxter was

English through and through. All his films, whether comic or serious, have a common rough edge: his productions (and he often did produce the films he directed) were home-grown and uncompromisingly so. His regional comedies were treated with critical disdain (and, like most of his work, wear badly) but they cleaned up at the country box-offices nearest their heart. Baxter's more caring films, such as *Doss House, Song of the Plough, A Real Bloke, Song of the Road, Love on the Dole, Let the People Sing* or *The Shipbuilders*, pursue the backstreets, by-ways and fields of England's working classes as determinedly as they wear their heart on their sleeve. One can almost see the dirt under their characters' fingernails. Although overtaken by the glossier studio productions of post-war years, Baxter had, in his own unpolished way, opened the door to the tougher, bleaker kitchen-sink realism of the late 1950s and early 1960s. Though his comedies are best left in limbo, a retrospective of the other side of Baxter's nature is now overdue.

1933: *Doss House. Song of the Plough. Taking Ways.* 1934: *Lest We Forget. Say It with Flowers. Music Hall. Floodtide. Kentucky Minstrels.* 1935: *A Real Bloke. Jimmy Boy. The Small Man. Birds of a Feather.* 1936: *Men of Yesterday. Hearts of Humanity.* 1937: *The Academy Decides. Talking Feet. Song of the Road.* 1938: *Stepping Toes.* 1939: *What Would You Do, Chums? Secret Journey (US: Among Human Wolves).* 1940: *Old Mother Riley in Society. Laugh It Off. Crook's Tour. Old Mother Riley in Business.* 1941: *Love on the Dole. The Common Touch.* 1942: *Let the People Sing. We'll Smile Again.* 1943: *Theatre Royal. The Shipbuilders.* 1944: *Dreaming.* 1945: *Here Comes the Sun.* 1946: *The Grand Escapade.* 1947: *Fortune Lane. When You Come Home.* 1948: *Nothing Venture. The Last Load. Three Bags Full (serial).* 1950: *The Dragon of Pendragon Castle. The Second Mate.* 1951: *Judgment Deferred.* 1956: *Ramsbottom Rides Again.*

BAY, Michael 1965-

An award-winning American director of commercials and music videos, Bay broke into the film big-time with his first film and looks ready to become one of the major action-film directors of the 21st century. Leaving film school at 24, Bay made rapid strides, turning out videos for singing stars and then moving into commercials with such major clients as Coca Cola, Reebok, Budweiser and Nike. The Directors Guild of America named him Commercial Director of the Year in 1995,

the same year that he brought out his first feature film *Bad Boys*, a big crowd-pleaser for its explosive action scenes; audiences ignored inconsistencies in the plot and made the film a box-office blast and a big boost to the career of star Will Smith. Bay had established stars, though, for his next *The Rock*, a heavy-duty action film about a slice of America held hostage by mercenaries on Alcatraz wielding rockets armed with a deadly gas. Nicely weighted performances from Nicolas Cage and Sean Connery attested to Bay's quickly growing authority with actors. And the action, though as powerful as in *Bad Boys*, is better varied. Critics declared his next, the disaster epic *Armageddon*, to be a turkey. But the public made it a massive hit.

1995: *Bad Boys*. 1996: *The Rock*. 1998: *Armageddon*.

BEAUDINE, William 1892-1970

Say that William Beaudine directed Mary Pickford, W. C. Fields, Will Hay and The Bowery Boys, and you'll see what a difficult man this prolific American director is to pin down. The plethora of brash 'B' features that smothered the latter half of his career has tended to obscure the gems of the 1920s and 1930s. He had entered the industry at 17, as a prop boy for D.W. Griffith, with whom he stayed for three years. He began directing in 1915, but it was not until 1922, after scores of comedy two-reelers, that he was put in charge of his first feature. Comedy, children and Americana were his fortes at this juncture, but his reputation received a boost following his polished and delicate handling of two Mary Pickford vehicles, *Little Annie Rooney* and *Sparrows*. For the next ten years, Beaudine enjoyed life in the upper echelon of Hollywood directors, culminating in his direction of W.C. Fields' *The Old Fashioned Way*, for my money the funniest and best knit-together of all Fields' vehicles, showing off both the scurrilous and the vulnerable sides of his screen nature. The visit to England that followed seems in retrospect to have been a watershed in Beaudine's career. Although his 13 British films included four with Will Hay, all well received critically and publicly, Beaudine found himself unable to regain his former footing on his return to Hollywood. There is little to say about these post-1937 years, save that the Torchy Blane films are fun (although that's as much to Glenda Farrell's credit as anyone else's), some of The Bowery Boys films, which he directed from 1943 to 1958, are better than others and the pieces of Cinecolor

Americana – *County Fair, Pride of the Blue Grass, Rodeo, The Rose Bowl Story* and *Blue Grass of Kentucky* – often more pleasant entertainment than his poverty row studio, Monogram, had any right to expect. The moustachioed, pipe-smoking, drily witty Beaudine made only one recorded comment on the dire nature of most of his programme fillers. When asked to rush the completion of some long-forgotten Monogram action film, he is reputed to have replied: 'You mean, Someone out there is actually waiting to *see* this?' Besides the films listed below, he also directed several 'Ham and Bud' comedies for Kalem, sometimes uncredited, in 1915 and, according to his own records, more than 50 one- and two-reelers for the Christie company between 1918 and 1921: titles remain untraceable.

1915: **Almost a King.* 1916: **The Inspector's Double. *Musical Madness. *Beans and Bullets. A Shadowed Shadow. *Their First Arrest. Scrappily Married. *Their Dark Secret. *Love in Suspense. *When Damon Fell for Pythias. *A Crooked Mix-Up. *In Love With a Fireman. *A Janitor's Vendetta. *The Tramp Chef. *Jags and Jealousy. *The Tale of a Turk. *Mines and Matrimony.* 1917: **Love Me, Love My Biscuits. *Barred from a Bar. *His Coming-Out Party. *Mule Mates. *Wanta Make a Dollar? *Whose Baby? *A Boob for Luck. *The Leak. *The Man With a Package. *The Boss of the Family. *One Damp Day. *The Cross-Eyed Submarine. *20,000 Legs under the Sea. *The Battling Bellboy. *Out Again, In Again. *Why They Left Home. *Hawaiian Nuts. *Who Done It. *A Bad Little Good Man. *Out For the Dough. *Passing the Grip. *Art Aches.*What the - - - ? *The Careless Cop. *Left in the Soup. *The Onion Hero. *Uneasy Money. *His Fatal Beauty. *He Had 'Em Buffaloed. *Canning the Cannibal King. *O-My, the Tent Mover. *Behind the Map. *Officer, Call a Cop. *The Fountain of Trouble. *What'll We Do With Uncle? *Secret Servants.* 1918: **Eddie, Get the Mop.* 1919: **Mixed Wives.* 1922: **Punch the Clock. *Strictly Modern. Watch Your Step. Heroes of the Street. Catch My Smoke.* 1923: *Penrod and Sam. Her Fatal Millions. The Printer's Devil. Boy of Mine. Lovers' Lane (uncredited). The Country Kid.* 1924: *Daughters of Pleasure. Daring Youth. Wandering Husbands. A Self-Made Failure. Cornered. The Narrow Street.* 1925. *A Broadway Butterfly. Little Annie Rooney. How Baxter Butted In.* 1926: *Sparrows (GB: Human Sparrows). That's My Baby. The Social Highwayman. Hold That Lion. The Canadian.* 1927: *The Irresistible Lover.*

Frisco Sally Levy. The Life of Riley. 1928: Home James. Heart to Heart. Do Your Duty. Give and Take. The Cohens and the Kellys in Paris. 1929: Two Weeks Off. Fugitives. Hard to Get. The Girl from Woolworth's. Wedding Rings. 1930: *A Hollywood Theme Song. Road to Paradise. Those who Dance. 1931: *One Yard to Go. *The College Vamp. Penrod and Sam (remake). Father's Son. Misbehaving Ladies. The Lady Who Dared. The Mad Parade. Men in Her Life (and Mexican version). Three Wise Girls. *The Great Junction Hotel. 1932: Make Me a Star. 1933: The Crime of the Century. Her Bodyguard. 1934: *Dream Stuff. *Trick Golf. *See You Tonight. The Old-Fashioned Way). Dandy Dick. 1935: Mr Cohen Takes a Walk. Boys Will Be Boys. So You Won't Talk. Get Off My Foot. Two Hearts in Harmony. 1936: Educated Evans. Where There's a Will. It's in the Bag. Windbag the Sailor. 1937: Feather Your Nest. Said O'Reilly to McNab (US: Sez O'Reilly to McNab). Transatlantic Trouble (later Take It from Me). 1938: Torchy Gets Her Man. 1939: Torchy. Blane in Chinatown. 1940: Mr Washington Goes to Town (uncredited). Misbehaving Husbands. Up Jumped the Devil. She Done Him Right. Lady Luck. 1941: Emergency Landing. Blonde Comet. Mr Celebrity. The Warden's Daughter. Desperate Cargo. Federal Fugitives. The Miracle Kid. 1942: Broadway Big Shot. Gallant Lady. The Panther's Claw. Foreign Agent. Duke of the Navy. The Living Ghost (GB: Lend Me Your Ear). Men of San Quentin. One Thrilling Night. Phantom Killer. Professor Creeps. 1943: The Ape Man (GB: Lock Your Doors). Ghosts on the Loose (GB: Ghosts in the Night). Follow the Leader. Clancy Street Boys. Here Comes Kelly. The Mystery of the 13th Guest. Spotlight Scandals. Mr Muggs Steps Out. What a Man! 1944: The Arizona Story. Mom and Dad (GB: A Family Story). Crazy Knights. Hot Rhythm. Oh, What a Night. Detective Kitty O'Day. Voodoo Man. Bowery Champs. Leave It to the Irish. Shadow of Suspicion. 1945: Black Market Babies. Fashion Model. The Adventures of Kitty O'Day. Blonde Ransom. Come Out Fighting. Swingin' on a Rainbow. 1946: Mr Hex (GB: Pride of the Bowery). The Face of Marble. Below the Deadline. Don't Gamble with Strangers. Girl on the Spot. One Exciting Week. Spook Busters. 1947: Gas House Kids Go West. Bowery Buckaroos. News Hounds (GB: News Hound). Too Many Winners. Hard-Boiled Mahoney. The Chinese Ring/The Red Hornet. Killer at Large. Philo Vance Returns. 1948: Angels' Alley. †Jiggs and Maggie in Court. Jinx Money. Kidnapped. The Golden Eye. The Shang-

hai Chest. Smugglers' Cove. Incident. 1949: Jackpot Jitters (GB: Jiggs and Maggie in Jackpot Jitters). The Feathered Serpent. Forgotten Women. Trail of the Yukon. †The Prince of Peace. Tough Assignment. Tuna Clipper. 1950: Blue Grass of Kentucky. Blonde Dynamite. Blues Busters. Jiggs and Maggie Out West. Second Chance. County Fair. Lucky Losers. Again – Pioneers! 1951: Ghost Chasers. Bowery Battalion. Havana Rose. Cuban Fireball. A Wonderful Life. The Congregation. Let's Go Navy. Crazy Over Horses. 1952: Here Come the Marines. Rodeo. Bela Lugosi Meets a Brooklyn Gorilla (GB: Monster Meets the Gorilla). Hold That Line. Feudin' Fools. Jet Job. No Holds Barred. The Rose Bowl Story. 1953: Jalopy. Murder without Tears. Roar of the Crowd. Born to the Saddle. For Every Child. The Hidden Heart. 1954: City Story. Paris Playboys. Yukon Vengeance. More for Peace. Pride of the Blue Grass (GB: Prince of the Blue Grass). 1955: High Society (Bowery Boys). Each According to His Faith. Jail Busters. 1956: Westward Ho! The Wagons. 1957: Up in Smoke. 1958: In the Money. 1960: Ten Who Dared. 1963: Lassie's Great Adventure (originally TV. GB: Lassie's Greatest Adventure). 1966: Billy the Kid vs Dracula. Jesse James meets Frankenstein's Daughter.

BEAUMONT, Harry 1888-1966

This American director had a sure and elegant touch when it came to stories of flappers and gold-diggers. He knew just what the public wanted from 1923 to 1933: he gave them frills, furbelows and surface brightness and did as much as any other man to make Joan Crawford a star. As Clara Bow's light dimmed, so Crawford's brightened and, in four Harry Beaumont films, *Our Dancing Daughters, Our Blushing Brides, Dance Fools Dance* and *Laughing Sinners*, she became the personification of the Jazz Age. When this frenetic time faded, so did Harry Beaumont. He made few films after 1933, and those he did turn out do not have the spark of his earlier work. During his time as an actor with the Edison company (1912-1916), Beaumont began collaborating on scenarios, and made himself familiar with lighting, editing and production. He began with the direction of broad comedies (in one of which Jackie Coogan made his infant debut) but it was 1923 that brought him his first great success, when he made *Main Street* and *The Gold Diggers*. He worked steadily on prestige pictures of the 1920s, before *Our Dancing Daughters* won him the plum assignment of MGM's first sound musical, *The Broadway Melody*, with scenes in

two-colour Technicolor, including the big production number *Wedding of the Painted Doll*, a quintessential product of its era. The film won the 1928-1929 Academy Award as best production, although Beaumont lost the best director award to Frank Lloyd (for *The Divine Lady*). It was to be Beaumont's (only chance. In the years of his decline, M-G-M generously kept him employed on co-features until his early retirement at 60.

1915: The Call of the City. 1916: The Truant Soul. 1917: *Skinner's Baby. *Skinner's Dress Suit. *Skinner's Bubble. *Burning the Candle. Filling His Own Shoes. 1918: Brown of Harvard. Thirty a Week. 1919: Wild Goose Chase. Little Rowdy. A Man and His Money. One of the Finest. Heartsease. Toby's Bow. Go West, Young Man. City of Comrades. Lord and Lady Algy. The Gay Lord Quex. 1920: Stop Thief! The Great Accident. Going Some. Officer 666. Dollars and Sense. 1921: Glass Houses. The Fourteenth Lover. 1922: Very Truly Yours. The Ragged Heiress. June Madness. They Like' Em Rough. Seeing's Believing. The Five Dollar Baby. Lights of the Desert. Love in the Dark. 1923: Crinoline and Romance. A Noise in Newboro. The Gold Diggers. Main Street. 1924: Babbitt. Beau Brummell. The Lover of Camille. Don't Doubt Your Husband. A Lost Lady. 1925: Recompense. His Majesty Bunker Bean. Rose of the World. 1926: Sandy. Womanpower. 1927: One Increasing Purpose. Our Dancing Daughters. 1929: A Single Man. Speedway. The Broadway Melody. 1930: †Lord Byron of Broadway (GB: What Price Melody?). The Florodora Girl (GB: The Gay Nineties). Children of Pleasure. Our Blushing Brides. Those Three French Girls. 1931: Dance Fools Dance. The Great Lover. Laughing Sinners. West of Broadway. 1932: Faithless. Unashamed. Are You Listening? 1933: When Ladies Meet. Made on Broadway (GB: The Girl I Made). Should Ladies Behave? 1934: Murder in the Private Car (GB: Murder on the Runaway Train). 1935: Enchanted April. 1936: The Girl on the Front Page. 1937: When's Your Birthday? 1944: Maisie Goes to Reno (GB: You Can't Do That to Me). 1945: Twice Blessed. Up Goes Maisie (GB: Up She Goes). 1946: The Show-Off. 1947: Undercover Maisie (GB: Undercover Girl). 1948: Alias a Gentleman.

BECKER, Harold 1938-
New York-born director mainly of gritty thrillers charged with dark atmosphere. Like many modern film-makers, Becker's

output has been shamefully sparse – just ten feature films over a 27-year period. Trained as a painter and illustrator, Becker began his career as an in-demand stills photographer and soon had his own studio. From here he branched out into directing TV commercials, to which field he returned after an inauspicious film directing debut in England with *The Ragman's Daughter*, a rich-girl-has-an-affair-with-poor-boy drama flying in on the fag-end of the once-popular kitchen sink wave. Back in America, it was 1979 before Becker hit his stride with *The Onion Field*, a black, bitter and violent true-life case study, involving the shooting of a young policeman and the gradual mental disintegration of his partner. In a key role it featured the menacing James Woods, who would star in two further Becker features, *The Black Marble* and *The Boost*. Those were unexpected failures, but Becker (and his star, Al Pacino) made a triumphant comeback in 1989 with *Sea of Love*, a strong, adult who-dunit which sees Becker keeping a tight grip throughout on a story about a killer who places romantic rhyming ads in lonely hearts columns, and getting smouldering star portrayals from Pacino and Ellen Barkin. *Malice*, the next in Becker's all-too-spasmodic output, was one of those foolish but fun (but typically dark) puzzle pictures, before Becker and Pacino reunited to somewhat lesser effect than before, in *Town Hall*.

1964: *Interview with Bruce Gordon. 1972: The Ragman's Daughter. 1979: The Onion Field. 1980: The Black Marble. 1981: Taps. 1985: Vision Quest. 1988: The Boost. 1989: Sea of Love. 1993: Malice. 1995: City Hall. 1998: Mercury Rising/Simple Simon.*

BECKER, Jacques 1906-1960

One suspects that, if this most civilized of French film directors had not died at the early age of 54, he might have been struggling in the 1970s to bring his unique attention to detail, and talent for the warmth of ordinary human relationships, to a handful of routine dramas and thrillers. In other words, it is difficult to imagine Becker being able to produce his best work outside the climate of the French cinema of the immediate post-war years. He learned his art at the feet of Jean Renoir, who considered him shallow when they first met – Becker was apparently something of an upper-class gad-about in the Paris of his youth – but soon recognized the latent talent. Renoir used Becker as actor and assistant director on some of the most memorable French films

of the 1930s – *Boudu sauvé des eaux, La nuit de carrefour, Toni, Les bas-fonds, La grande illusion, La bête humaine* and *La règle du jeu* among them. Becker struck out under his own flag in the war years, but it was the ten years from 1945 to 1954 which brought him his greatest acclaim. During that time, he made affectionate social studies (*Falbalas* and *Rendez-vous de juillet*) and romantic comedies of manners (*Antoine et Antoinette* and *Edouard et Caroline*), all of which celebrate love, life and laughter, and made Becker's films sure-fire prospects at the box office. Later came the low-life thrillers with a human touch, *Touchez-pas au grisbi* and *Le trou*, but before these Becker made his greatest film, *Casque d'or*. Probably all the elements in Becker's films come closest to meeting in this story of love against a turn-of-the-century criminal background, with Simone Signoret at her youthful, glowing best for perhaps the last time, and the lovers' backcloth of warmth, sunshine and perfect naturalness contrasting starkly with the cheap, dark, violent criminal world which will ultimately part them in tragedy. At the time of his death, Becker was married to the actress Françoise Fabian (Michele y Fabianera. 1935-) and is the father of Jean Becker (1933-) also a director, whose best known film is probably the 1966 *Tendre voyou*.

*1934: †Le commissaire est bon enfant. 1935: Tête de turc. 1936: †La vie est à nous. 1938: *Communist Party Congress à Arles (D). 1939: †L'or du Cristobal (uncredited). 1942: Dernier atout. 1943: Goupi Mains-Rouges (US: It Happened at the Inn). 1945: Falbalas (US: Paris Frills). 1946: Antoine et Antoinette. 1948: Rendez-vous de juillet. 1951: Edouard et Caroline. 1952: Casque d'or (GB & US: Golden Marie). 1953: Rue de l'Estrapade (GB & US: Françoise Steps Out). 1954: Touchez-pas au grisbi (GB: Honour Among Thieves. US: Grisbi). Ali-Baba et les 40 voleurs (GB & US: Ali-Baba). 1956: Les aventures de Arsène Lupin. 1957: Montparnasse 19 (GB: The Lovers of Montparnasse. US: Modigliani of Montparnasse). 1959: Le trou (GB: The Hole. US: The Night Watch).*

BEEBE, Ford 1888-**

Another American serial specialist, but not one to set alongside William Witney, John English or Spencer Gordon Bennet. Some writers have found merit in Beebe's work, arguing that he often produced highly effective results despite the poverty of the material at his disposal. I find his direction very rudimentary, even some-

times in the best of his serials, *Flash Gordon Goes to Mars* and *Buck Rogers*. Although some of these lesser scenes may be the work of co-directors (almost all serials were handled by two men), his solo feature films have very little to offer in the way of originality or style, and are almost all minor pot-boilers. Originally a freelance writer, Beebe first came to Hollywood in 1916, although it seems to have been 1919 before he began getting regular work on scenarios for two-, three- and four-reel westerns and other action adventures. On one of these, Beebe received his first taste of directing when the man who was making it, Leo Maloney, fell ill. It was not until 1932 that he settled into the groove that was to run through his career for the next 25 years, as a director of serials and small-time action pictures for various Poverty Row studios, including Columbia, Screen Guild, Mascot, Monogram, Republic and Lippert. At one time in the 1940s, it looked as if he would become a regular contributor to the cycle of cut-price horror films – one, *Night Monster*, is perhaps his best movie – but he spent the last years of his film career making Bomba the Jungle Boy films. At least he probably outlived all his contemporaries, even the extraordinary Allan Dwan (*qv*). His son, Ford Beebe Jnr, has also worked as a director, principally for the Disney studio.

1920: †The Honor of the Range (serial). 1932: The Pride of the Legion/The Big Pay Off. †The Last of the Mohicans (serial). The Shadow of the Eagle (serial). 1933: Laughing at Life. 1935: †The Adventures of Rex and Rinty (serial). Law Beyond the Range. The Man from Guntown. 1936: Stampede. †Ace Drummond (serial). 1937: †Jungle Jim (serial). †Radio Patrol (serial). †Secret Agent X-9 (serial). Tim Tyler's Luck (serial). †Wild West Days (serial). Westbound Limited. 1938: †Flash Gordon's Trip to Mars (serial). †Red Barry (serial). Trouble at Midnight. 1939: †The Phantom Creeps (serial). The Oregon Trail (serial). †Buck Rogers (serial). Oklahoma Frontier. 1940: †The Green Hornet (serial). †Flash Gordon Conquers the Universe (serial). †Junior G-Men (serial). †The Green Hornet Strikes Again (serial). †Winners of the West (serial). Son of Roaring Dan. 1941: †Sea Raiders (serial). †Sky Raiders (serial). †Riders of Death Valley (serial). 1942: †Don Winslow of the Navy (serial). †Overland Mail (serial). Night Monster (GB: House of Mystery). 1943: Frontier Badmen. 1944: The Invisible Man's Revenge. Enter Arsène Lupin. 1945: Easy to Look At. 1946: My Dog Shep. 1947: Six Gun Serenade. 1948: Shep Comes

Home. Courtin' Trouble. †Return of the Mohicans (feature version of 1932 serial). 1949: Bomba the Jungle Boy. The Dalton Gang. Red Desert. Satan's Cradle. Bomba on Panther Island. 1950: The Lost Volcano. Bomba and the Hidden City. 1951: The Lion Hunters (GB: Bomba and the Lion Hunters). Elephant Stampede (GB: Bomba and the Elephant Stampede). 1952: African Treasure (GB: Bomba and the African Treasure). Bomba and the Jungle Girl. Wagons West. 1953: Safari Drums (GB: Bomba and the Safari Drums). 1954: Killer Leopard. The Golden Idol. 1955: Lord of the Jungle. 1972: †Challenge To Be Free.

**Believed deceased

BENEDEK, Laslo (Laszlo Benedek) 1907-1992

One of the marginals who hardly merits a place in this book, save for his brief period in the late 1940s and early 1950s when he looked like being one of those Hungarian imports who might really settle down and make an impact on the Hollywood scene, in this case with some powerful black-and-white dramas. After the infamous Marlon Brando motor-cycle drama *The Wild One*, which itself now seems fussy and staged, Benedek's films proved an extraordinary mixture: few of them downright bad, but all pretty flabby in parts. From 1927, after studying psychiatry at the University of Vienna, he became cameraman and editor on a number of German and Hungarian films of the 1920s and 1930s, before following his mentor Joe Pasternak to Hollywood. Here (from 1938), he became regarded as something of an expert on montage sequences, inserted into other director's films, before getting his first solo directorial credit in 1948. After he descended into colourful melodramas and adventures, Benedek turned to TV, directing hundreds of episodes for *Mannix*, *Rawhide*, *Perry Mason*, *The Untouchables* and others. He seemed to have given up all pretence of seriousness when he suddenly came up with the sombre, brooding and definitely out-of the-ordinary *The Night Visitor* in 1971. Made in Sweden, this tenebrous, cold and compelling story of a man's revenge after being locked away in an asylum for a crime he did not commit was not widely shown at the time. But several television airings have revealed it to a mass audience and shown that the strange, unsettled talent of Laslo Benedek was probably there, submerged under a ton of candy floss, all the time. In the 1980s he taught film at American and German universities.

1948: The Kissing Bandit. 1949: Port of New York. 1951: Death of a Salesman.

1952: †Storm over Tibet (uncredited). 1953: The Wild One. 1954: Kinder, Mütter und ein General. Bengal Brigade (GB: Bengal Rifles). 1957: Affair in Havana. 1960: Moment of Danger (US: Malaga). Recours en grâce. 1966: Namu the Killer Whale. 1967: Daring Game. 1971: The Night Visitor. 1974: Assault on Agathon.

BENNET, Spencer Gordon 1893-1987

If George B. Seitz (qv) was the father of the American serial, Spencer Bennet was both its first child and its longest-serving disciple. Born to Anglo-French parents, Bennet was playing truant from school in his teens to act with stock companies. But it was as a stuntman that he broke into films at the Edison studio in the winter of 1911-12. He worked as a stuntman-actor in Seitz's serial *The Perils of Pauline* in 1914, and was second unit director on Seitz's follow-up serial *The Exploits of Elaine*. When Seitz turned to feature-film making in 1925, Bennet struck out on his own in the serial world. Although he was to continue making serials until 1956 (the last year of serial production by an American company), Bennet rarely surpassed the work he did in the 1920s. Such 'chapter plays' as *The Green Archer* and *Hawk of the Wilderness* still look sharper and more exciting than their counterparts 20 years on. Bennet's reputation for achieving 'terrified' reactions from his players at the appropriate time was partly explained by his habit of creeping up behind his actor – usually the leading lady – and firing blanks in the air to create the desired wide-eyed horror. But he was also genuinely skilful in the cutting room and, from pressure exerted by low budgets, became an expert at camera techniques that made silk purses out of sows' ears. His westerns with Buck Jones, Tim McCoy, 'Wild Bill' Elliott and Ken Maynard are all imaginative, if no-nonsense affairs that move along at a rattling clip. In later years, Bennett co-directed such notable Saturday-morning serials as *Superman*, *Captain Video*, *Batman and Robin*, *Zorro's Black Whip* and *Brick Bradford*. Right at the end of his career, and working for almost the first time in colour, Bennet made two 90-minute feature films that reunited many of the famous action stars with whom he had worked through the years. The films were, needless to say, hectically edited and crammed with action and adventure.

1921: †Behold the Man. 1923: †Plunder (serial, uncredited). 1925: Play Ball (serial). The Green Archer (serial). 1926: The Fighting Marine (serial). The House without a Key (serial). Snowed In (serial).

1927: Melting Millions (serial). Hawk of the Hills (serial). 1928: The Man Without a Face (serial). The Yellow Cameo (serial). The Terrible People (serial). Marked Money (serial). The Tiger's Shadow (serial). 1929: †The Black Book (serial). The Fire Detective (serial). Queen of the Northwoods (serial). Hawk of the Hills (feature version). 1930: Rogue of the Rio Grande. *Nick Harris (series). 1931: *Nick Harris (series, continued). *Mystery of Compartment C. 1932: The Last Frontier (serial). 1933: The Midnight Warning. Justice Takes a Holiday. 1934: The Ferocious Pal (GB: His Ferocious Pal). Badge of Honor. The Fighting Rookie (GB: Dangerous Enemy). The Oil Raider. Night Alarm. Young Eagles (serial). 1935: Calling All Cars. Rescue Squad. Get That Man. Heir to Trouble. Western Courage. Lawless Riders. 1936: The Cattle Thief. Heroes of the Range. Avenging Waters. The Fugitive Sheriff (GB: Law and Order). The Unknown Ranger. Rio Grande Ranger. Ranger Courage. 1937: The Law of the Ranger. Reckless Ranger. The Rangers Step In. The Mysterious Pilot (serial). 1938: Rio Grande. 1939: Across the Plains. Riders of the Frontier. 1940: Westbound Stage. The Cowboy from Sundown. 1941: Arizona Bound. Ridin' the Cherokee Trail. Gunman from Bodie. 1942: They Raid by Night. Valley of Vanishing Men (serial). The Secret Code (serial). 1943: Calling Wild Bill Elliott. Canyon City. The Masked Marvel (serial). Secret Service in Darkest Africa (serial). 1944: Mojave Firebrand. Beneath Western Skies. California Joe. Tucson Raiders. Code of the Prairie. †Zorro's Black Whip (serial). †Haunted Harbor (serial). †The Tiger Woman (serial). 1945: Lone Texas Ranger. †Manhunt of Mystery Island (serial). †Federal Operator 99 (serial). †The Purple Monster Strikes (serial). 1946: †The Phantom Rider (serial). †Daughter of Don Q (serial). †King of the Forest Rangers (serial). 1947: †Son of Zorro (serial). Brick Bradford (serial). †The Black Widow (serial). 1948: †Superman (serial). †Congo Bill (serial). 1949: Adventures of Sir Galahad (serial). †Bruce Gentry – Daredevil of the Skies (serial). Batman and Robin (serial). 1950: Cody of the Pony Express (serial). Atom Man vs Superman (serial). †Pirates of the High Seas (serial). 1951: †Captain Video (serial). †Roar of the Iron Horse (serial). Mysterious Island (serial). 1952: Brave Warrior. Voodoo Tiger. Blackhawk (serial). Son of Geronimo (serial). †King of the Congo (serial). 1953: Savage Mutiny. Killer Ape. The Lost Planet (serial). 1954: Riding With Buffalo Bill (serial). Gunfighters of the Northwest (serial). 1955: Adventures of Captain Africa (serial).

Devil Goddess. 1956: Perils of the Wilderness (serial). Blazing the Overland Trail (serial). 1958: Submarine Seahawk. 1959: Atomic Submarine. 1965: The Bounty Killer. Requiem for a Gunfighter.

BENNETT, Compton

(Robert Compton-Bennett) 1900–1974

Soberness was in the very backcloths of this British director's films. If it weren't for the mood of *It Started in Paradise*, one would suspect a lack of humour, for there is very little evidence of it even in his lighter subjects. But his earlier films were cleverly crafted towards what the public wanted and his first feature, *The Seventh Veil*, with Ann Todd as the pianist much beset by James Mason in another of his 'evil cad' roles, was an immense success at the box office. He was invited to go to Hollywood in 1947, but he could not make his characters spring to life within the American studio environment and his films were as disappointing as his 1946 British work has led one to fear they might be. Even in the successful 1950 version of *King Solomon's Mines*, he directed only the static dialogue scenes. After the inevitable return to Britain, Bennett briefly returned to form: all four of the 1952–53 films are good examples of their genres (weepie, war film, melodrama, thriller). He was out of

All wrapped up and somewhere to go. Robert **Benton** directing *Nobody's Fool,* which won Paul Newman an Oscar nomination.

films from 1954, busy in theatre and TV, before a final burst of quality product in 1957, including the skilful, atmospheric and under-valued life story of Vesta Tilley, *After the Ball* (although it was made totally at the wrong time), and a taut and polished little thriller, *The Flying Scot*. After this, there was nothing of note, and much, on big and small screens, that was not. Bennett was in turn bandleader and commercial artist at the outset of his career before making some amateur films, one of which got him a job with Alexander Korda's London Films in 1932. He became a film editor there and later made instructional and propaganda films for the British armed forces during the early part of World War II.

*1941: *Freedom Must Have Wings (D). 1942: Find, Fix and Strike (D). 1944: *Men of Rochdale (D). 1945: *Julius Caesar. The Seventh Veil. 1946: The Years Between. Daybreak. 1948: My Own True Love. 1949: That Forsyte Woman (GB: The Forsyte Saga). 1950: †King Solomon's Mines. 1952: So Little Time. Gift Horse (US: Glory at Sea). It Started in Paradise. 1953: Desperate Moment. 1957: That Woman Opposite (US: City After Midnight). After the Ball. The Flying Scot (US: Mailbag Robbery). 1960: Beyond the Curtain. 1961: *First Left Past Aden. 1965: How to Undress in Public without Undue Embarrassment.*

BENTLEY, Thomas 1880-1953

London-born Bentley was a Charles Dickens fanatic who made his mission in life the bringing of Dickens' novels to the screen. Although his films lack polish, they are full of charm and character, qualities which he also brought, in some measure, to his later regional comedies. Although trained as an engineer, Bentley was weaned on Dickens' works, and was determined to bring them to the public. As early as 1901, he was to be found on the London stage, offering a series of impersonations of Dickens' best-known characters, including Fagin, Uriah Heep, Mr Pickwick and Mr Quilp. In 1912, he began directing silent film versions of such books as *Oliver Twist* and *David Copperfield*. By 1934, when he made his last Dickens film (his third version of *The Old Curiosity Shop*), he was firmly established as a middle-range director, making mainly films which appealed to the working classes of the years between the two world wars. With the coming of World War II, Bentley soon retired from active film making and was appointed Technical Adviser to the British Film Council in 1945.

*1912: *Leaves from the Books of Charles Dickens. Oliver Twist. 1913: The Miracle. David Copperfield. Hamlet. 1914: The Old Curiosity Shop. The Chimes. 1915: Hard Times. The Woman Who Dared. Barnaby Rudge. 1916: Milestones. Beau Brocade. 1917: Daddy. The Labour Leader. Les cloches de Corneville. 1918: Once Upon a Time. The Greatest Wish in the World. The Divine Gift. 1919: The Lackey and the Lady. 1920: General Post. Beyond the Dreams of Avarice. 1921: The Adventures of Mr Pickwick. The Old Curiosity Shop. 1922: A Master of Craft. 1923: Through Fire and Water. *The Shadow of Death. *The Velvet Woman. *The Battle of Love. *The Courage of Despair. *The Last Stake. *The Secret Mission. 1924: Love and Hate. Wanted – a Boy. *After Dark. *The Cavern Spider. Old Bill Through the Ages. Chappy That's All. 1925: A Romance of Mayfair. Money Isn't Everything. 1926: White Heat. *Man of Mystery. 1927: *The Antidote. The Silver Lining. 1928: Not Quite a Lady. 1929: The American Prisoner. *Accidental Treatment. Young Woodley. 1930: Harmony Heaven. Young Woodley (remake for sound). Compromising Daphne. 1931: Keepers of Youth. Hobson's Choice. 1932: After Office Hours. The Last Coupon. Sleepless Nights. 1933: Hawleys of High Street. The Love Nest. The Scotland Yard Mystery. 1934: Those Were the Days. The Old Curiosity Shop. The Great Defender. 1935: †Royal Cavalcade (US: Regal Cavalcade). †Music Hath Charms. 1936: She Knew What She Wanted. 1937: The Last Chance. Silver Blaze. The Angelus. 1938: A Night Alone. Marigold. 1939: Me and My Pal. Dead Man's Shoes. Lucky to Me. 1940: The Middle Patch. Three Silent Men. Cavalcade of Variety. 1941: Old Mother Riley's Circus.*

BENTON, Robert 1932-

For a man of 66, this Texas-born director has made remarkably few films, even accounting for those in whose script he had a hand – *Bonnie and Clyde, There Was a Crooked Man, What's Up Doc?* and *Superman*. These films, and most of the few he has directed, reflect the vigour and the violence running through the mind of a man who was once art director of the magazine *Esquire*, set decorator on several films and has written a number of imaginative books for children. This violence has a comic-strip element that often belies the more down-to-earth touches of the directors assigned to Benton's projects. But *Kramer Vs Kramer*, a tug-of-love story that pushed Meryl Streep's career forward and was a big success at the box office, finally revealed Benton's softer side and won him Academy Awards for writing and direction. His films have promised much: their ideas are delightful, but often the elements in them have not quite gelled. This was somewhat true of Benton's next weepie, *Places in the Heart*, even though its script won the director his third Academy Award. The underrated *Nadine* was warm-hearted comic-strip comedy, and, after the failure of *Billy Bathgate*, Benton returned to basic human values with *Nobody's Fool* which won star Paul Newman an Oscar nomination, Newman was impressed enough to work with Benton again four years later on *Twilight*. Benton's films continue to be thinly spread, although those quality scripts no doubt take time to perfect.

1964: *A Texas Romance – 1909. 1972: Bad Company. 1977: The Late Show. 1979: Kramer Vs Kramer. 1982: Still of the Night/Stab. 1984: Places in the Heart. 1987: Nadine. 1991: Billy Bathgate. 1994: Nobody's Fool. 1998: Twilight.*

BERESFORD, Bruce 1940-

Beresford's comparatively sudden transformation from an ugly duckling of the Australian cinema into its shimmering swan is not very easy to explain. Certainly there is much interesting work in his early career, suggesting a man of greatly varied interests and talents, but it did seem by 1976 that crassness had irretrievably claimed him. Then came *The Getting of Wisdom, Money Movers* and *'Breaker' Morant*, which delighted critics and the discerning public, and probably totally baffled most lovers of *Barry McKenzie* and his chundering, clod-hopping comedy capers. However, if their success gave Beresford the backing to make his highly praised later films, one can only stand back and applaud the strategy. After making his first short film while still at Sydney University, Beresford travelled the world in search of experience: his own getting of wisdom in fact. From 1964, he worked for two years as a film editor and occasional director in Nigeria, before moving to Britain, where he was Films Officer for the British Film Institute's Production Board from 1965 to 1971, directing a number of short subjects and producing a great many more. Back in Australia from 1972, Beresford started his career as a feature-film director in earnest. His first film, the outrageously coarse comedy *The Adventures of Barry McKenzie*, about the outsider's typical Australian, forever in digger hat with corks hanging down, and swigging endless cans of Foster's lager,

established his box-office 'clout' and was followed by an equally successful (and slightly better) sequel. *Side by Side*, however, was worse, and *Don's Party* was merely boorish and travelled badly outside its native country. It was at this point that Beresford sloughed off his stubby brown feathers and, in a flurry of eiderdown, became a film-maker of international repute with *The Getting of Wisdom*, a beautifully-made and astutely observed story of the stultifying existence undergone by teenage girl students of an exclusive ladies' college in late 19th-century Melbourne. *Money Movers* was an exciting and very efficiently made robbery thriller. Skilfully edited, it moves at a tremendous clip throughout. More successful than both of these on an international scale, however, was *'Breaker' Morant*. The whiff of authentic courtroom drama hangs over this enthralling reconstitution of a 1901 court-martial in South Africa, in which one British and two Australian officers were set up as 'scapegoats for the empire'. The film gains its grip from the fact that, although it was almost inevitable that these men would be condemned to death, they were brilliantly defended by a small-town Australian lawyer who, in the great tradition of courtroom underdogs, made mincemeat of a court that refused to let him win. Beresford misses none of the opportunities proffered by a skilful script. Since 1982, he has worked mainly in Hollywood with rather spotty overall results. Although a number of acting Oscars have been won in his films there have been too many misfires for comfort, although he has stuck to a schedule of roughly a film a year. His *Driving Miss Daisy* won an Academy Award as best picture, but his own direction was overlooked. Since then, the best of his work has been shot in far away places and deals with varying degrees of primitivism: *Mister Johnson, Black Robe* and *Paradise Road*.

1960: *The Hunters. 1962: The Devil To Pay. 1963: *Clement Meadmore (D). *It Droppeth as the Gentle Rain. 1965: *Film for Guitar. *Eastern Nigerian Newsreel No. 30. 1966: *King Size Woman (D). 1967: *Picasso's Sculpture (D). 1968: *The End. *Extravaganza. *Lichtenstein in London (D). *Barbara Hepworth at the Tate (D). 1969: *Martin Agrippa (D). 1970: *The Cinema of Raymond Fark. *Arts of Village India (D). 1971: *View from the Satellite (D. Originally for TV). 1972: The Adventures of Barry McKenzie. 1973: Poor Fella Me (TV). 1974: The Wreck of the Batavia (TV). Barry McKenzie Holds His Own. 1975: Side by Side. 1976: Don's Party.*

1977: *The Getting of Wisdom. 1978: Money Movers. 1980: 'Breaker' Morant. The Club. 1981: Puberty Blues. 1982: Tender Mercies. 1984: The Fringe Dwellers. 1985: King David. Batavia (D). 1986: Crimes of the Heart. 1987: †Aria. 1989: Her Alibi. Driving Miss Daisy. 1990: Mister Johnson. 1991: Black Robe. 1992: Rich in Love. Bessie (D). 1993: A Good Man in Africa. 1994: Silent Fall. 1996: Last Dance. 1997: Paradise Road. 1999: Double Jeopardy.*

BERGMAN, Andrew 1945-

Something seems to have gone wrong for this New York-born writer-director since his directing career finally took wing at the beginning of the 1990s. He has continued to direct movies, but they have gradually declined in quality, and the delightfully wacky screenwriting with which he made his name is now all but forgotten. A publicist and author of film books for the first eight years of his career, Bergman's association with comedians through his father (a radio and TV columnist) led him to suggest the story and co-write the script for Mel Brooks' *Blazing Saddles*. Bergman's own directorial debut came with the self-scripted *So Fine*. Undervalued in its time, this is a splendidly silly farce, frantically paced by Bergman, about the invention of see-through jeans. Its failure kept him away from the director's chair for several years. in 1984, he was replaced as director of *Big Trouble* by John Cassavetes, a director with no reputation for comedy. Not surprisingly Bergman took his name off the credits (the script is credited to 'Warren Bogle') and the resultant turkey stayed on the shelves for two years, by which time Bergman had written the splendid comedy-thriller *Fletch*. Five years later, the delightfully dry humour of *The Freshman* gave Bergman a fresh start as writer-director in an O Henry-style yarn of the relationship between a student (Matthew Broderick) and an influential underworld figure played by Marlon Brando. Full of delightfully offbeat ideas,, the film has unfortunately proved a false dawn. *Honeymoon in Vegas* was a hit, if uneasily caste but the changing of Bergman's next from *Cop Gives Waitress $2,000,000 Tip* to the anodyne *It Could Happen to You* somehow conveys a notion of where the resultant candyfloss romantic comedy lost its way. Bergman hit a career low with Demi Moore's *Striptease*, before attempting to bounce back with *Intolerable Cruelty*. He feels that there is a common thread running through all his work in that 'the plot is always about someone trapped in circumstances they can't seem to get out of'. This is true, but it's a theme of which Bergman has all too rarely taken full advantage and one feels he needs to return to his comic roots to do so.

1981: So Fine. 1990: The Freshman. 1992: Honeymoon in Vegas. 1994: It Could Happen to You. 1996: Striptease. 1998: Intolerable Cruelty. 1999: Isn't She Great?

BERGMAN, Ingmar 1918-

The odds are that Bergman would be in almost everyone's top five living directors. Despite the disappointment I have felt with his work since the mid-1970s (coincidental with his own nervous breakdown that saw his films spiral into psychological and psychosexual blind alleyways), his eminence is richly deserved. Few, if any, directors can match his record of consistency, his probing into the human soul and his remarkable evocation, through an obsession with death, of dark worlds of allegory and fantasy. Torment, angst, inner turmoil, despair, madness and self-reproach are themes he cannot escape, many of them stemming perhaps from a repressed childhood in which a stern father would keep him locked away in the darkness of a cupboard for hours on end for some infringement of family discipline. Who knows what flights of demonic fancy wing their way across the mind of a child at such a time? Whatever they might have been, they were welded to Bergman's early passion for the theatre and he became a trainee director at a Stockholm theatre in 1938, entering the film industry in 1941. He first came to attention as screenplay writer and assistant director of Alf Sjöberg's Frenzy (the film that made Mai Zetterling an international name) and directed his own first film, Crisis, the following year (1945). Although his sexually-free portraits of emotional crises, penetrating deeply into the innermost feelings of his female protagonists, made him an international name in the early 1950s, the period from 1957 to 1968 is breathtakingly golden, one bleakly memorable masterpiece tumbling over the heels of the last. This period begins within The Seventh Seal and ends with Hour of the Wolf, each full of haunting images, the first concerned with a knight's 14th-century Sweden, the last verging on the world of horror as the leading character is driven into madness by the assault of his personal demons. These films are agonizingly well acted by a group of players never as effective outside Bergman's influence: Liv Ullmann, Bibi Andersson, Gunnel Lindblom, Max Von Sydow, Harriet Andersson and Gun-

"It's only a film, Ingrid..." Ingmar **Bergman** directed one of his favourite actresses, Ingrid Thulin, in Cries and Whispers.

nar Bjornstrand. And their powerful images, brilliantly organized, are all the stronger for being photographed in black and white. His film The Virgin Spring won the Oscar as best Foreign-Language picture in 1960. His screenplay for the 1992 film The Best Intentions was based on the lives of his own parents. That too won several awards.

1945: Kris (GB & US: Crisis). 1946: Det Regnar pa var Kärlek (GB & US: It Rains on Our Love). 1947: Skepp till India Land (GB: A Ship to India. US: Frustration). 1948: Musik i Mörker (GB & US: Night is My Future. Hamnstad (GB & US: Port of Call). 1949: Till Glädje (GB & US: To Joy). Fängelse (GB: Prison. US: The Devil's Wanton). Törst (GB: Thirst. US: Three Strange Loves). 1950: Sånt Händer inte Här (GB: This Can't Happen Here. US: High Tension). 1951: Sommarlek (GB: Summer Interlude. US: Illicit Interlude). 1952: Kvinnors Väntan (GB: Waiting Women. US: Secrets of Women). 1953: Sommaren med Monika (GB: Summer with Monika. US: Monika). Gycklarnas Afton (GB: Sawdust and Tinsel. US: The Naked Night). 1954: En Lektion i Kärlek (GB & US: A Lesson in Love). 1955: Kvinnodröm (GB: Journey Into Autumn. US: Dreams). Sommarnattens Leende (GB & US: Smiles of a Summer Night). 1957: Det Sjunde Inseglet (GB & US: The Seventh Seal). Smultronstället (GB & US: Wild Strawberries). 1958: Nära Livet (GB: So Close to Life. US: Brink of Life). Ansiktet (GB: The Face.

US: The Magician). 1959: Jungfrukällan (GB & US: The Virgin Spring). 1960: Djävulens Oga (GB & US: The Devil's Eye). 1961: Sosom i en Spegel (GB & US: Through a Glass Darkly). 1963: Nattvardsgästerna (GB: Winter Light. US: The Communicants). Tystnaden (GB & US: The Silence). 1964: För Att Inte Tala om Alla Desse Kvinnor (GB: Now About These Women. US: All These Women). 1966: Persona. 1967: †Stimulantia. 1968: Skammen (GB: The Shame. US: Shame). Vargtimmen (GB & US: Hour of the Wolf). 1969: Riten (GB: The Rite. US: The Ritual. Originally for TV). Faro-Dokument/The Faro Document (originally for TV). En passion (GB: A Passion. US: The Passion of Antia). 1970: Ber iörigen (GB & US: The Touch). 1972: Viskningar och Rop (GB & US: Cries and Whispers). 1973: Scener ur ett Aktenskap (TV. GB & US cinemas, as Scenes from a Marriage – also GB TV title). 1974: The Magic Flute. 1975: Ansikte mot Ansikte (GB & US: Face to Face; originally for TV). 1977: Das Schangenei (GB & US: The Serpent's Egg). 1978: Autumn Sonata. 1980: Aus dem Leben der Marionetten (GB & US: From the Life of the Marionettes). 1982: Fanny and Alexander. 1984: After the Rehearsal (TV). De tva saliga/ The Blessed Ones (TV). 1997: Siska skriket (US: The Last Gasp). 1998: In the Presence of a Clown.

BERKELEY, Busby
(William Berkeley Enos) 1895-1976

Berkeley is remembered not so much as one of the foremost dance directors of the cinema – although he was that, too – but as an innovative arranger of dozens of chorus girls arranged in kaleidoscopic but almost always symmetrical patterns. These breathtaking effects were often shown at least once from above, as Berkeley perched on some dizzyingly high camera – having, on more than one occasion, bored a hole in the Warner Studio roof in order to improve the effect still further. He came to Hollywood from Broadway, of course – the 'Busby' was an extension of 'Buzz', a childhood nickname that clung for life – and was soon at work inventing new routines for the Goldwyn Girls, especially in such Eddie Cantor extravaganzas as *Palmy Days, Flying High, The Kid from Spain* and, most notably, *Roman Scandals*. Enjoyable though these inventive interludes were, they were little more than dry runs for Berkeley's immense work at Warners through the 1930s. The films included *42nd Street, Footlight Parade, Wonder Bar, Dames, Go into Your Dance* and the Gold Diggers series, the stars were more often than not Joan Blondell, Dick Powell and Ruby Keeler. and, when Berkeley was choreographer only, as opposed to choreographer-director, the films were directed in complementary mood by such men as Lloyd Bacon (who collaborated six times with Berkeley between 1933 and 1951), William Keighley and Ray Enright (all qv). But the highspots were always the Berkeley routines. The eroticism and surrealism that formed part of their unique appeal has been somewhat overstressed in recent retrospectives. What Berkeley was after more than anything was to impress an audience with an eye-catching effect that would dazzle the senses and make people gasp with disbelief. Who can forget the little men under the swaying pianos in *Gold Diggers of 1935*, the giant portrait of Ruby Keeler on the backs of the girls in *Dames*, the waterlilies of *Footlight Parade*, the Depression marchers of *Gold Diggers of 1933*, or the cuttingly sharp choreography of the 100 dancers in Berkeley's masterpiece, the 'Lullaby of Broadway' sequence from *Gold Diggers of 1935*? Showman, organizer and inventor, Berkeley was all three. He went to M-G-M in the 1940s and made Garland/Rooney teen-swing musicals but, from the mid-1950s, apart from such flashes of the old 'Buzz' as the musical instruments coming out of walls and floors in *Small Town Girl*, his talents were allowed to stagnate in semi-retirement. He married six times.

1930: *Whoopee!* (c). 1931: *Kiki* (c). *Palmy Days* (c). *Flying High* (c: uncredited. GB: Happy Landing). 1932: *Night*

Those beautiful dames... Director Busby **Berkeley** puts himself among the girls on the set of the 1934 film *Wonder Bar*.

World (c: uncredited). *Bird of Paradise* (c: uncredited). *The Kid from Spain* (c). 1937: †*She Had to Say Yes. Roman Scandals* (c). *42nd Street* (c). *Gold Diggers of 1933* (c). *Footlight Parade* (c). *Fashions* (c. GB: Fashion Follies of 1934). 1934: *Wonder Bar* (c). *Twenty Million Sweethearts* (c: uncredited). *Dames* (c). 1935: *In Caliente* (c). *Stars over Broadway* (co-c). *Go Into Your Dance* (c: uncredited. GB: Casino de Paree). *Gold Diggers of 1935. Bright Lights* (GB: Funny Face). *I Live for Love* (GB: I Live for You). 1936: *Gold Diggers of 1937* (c). *Stage Struck.* 1937: *The Singing Marine* (c). *Varsity Show* (c). *The Go Getter. Hollywood Hotel.* 1938: *Gold Diggers in Paris* (c. GB: The Gay Imposters). *Comet over Broadway. Men Are Such Fools. Garden*

of the Moon. 1939: *Broadway Serenade* (c. GB: Serenade). *Babes in Arms. Fast and Furious. They Made Me a Criminal.* 1940: *Strike Up the Band. Forty Little Mothers.* 1941: *Babes on Broadway. Ziegfeld Girl* (c). *Lady Be Good* (c). *Born to Sing* (co-c). *Blonde Inspiration.* 1942: **Calling All Girls* (c). *For Me and My Gal* (GB: For Me and My Girl). 1943: **Three Cheers for the Girls* (c). *The Gang's All Here* (GB: The Girls He Left Behind). *Girl Crazy* (co-c). 1945: **†All-Star Musical Revue.* 1946: *Cinderella. Jones.* 1948: *Romance on the High Seas* (c: uncredited. GB: It's Magic). 1949: *Take Me Out to the Ball Game* (GB: Everybody's Cheering). 1950: *Two Weeks with Love* (c). 1951: *Call Me Mister* (c). *Two Tickets to Broadway* (c). 1952: *Mil-*

lion Dollar Mermaid (c. GB: The One-Piece Bathing Suit). 1953: Small Town Girl (c). Easy to Love (c). 1954: Rose Marie (c). 1962: Jumbo/Billy Rose's. Jumbo (c).

(c) As choreographer/dance director only

(co-c) As co-choreographer only

BERNHARDT, Curtis

(Kurt Bernhardt) 1899-1981

As this German director's first film was a version of Jane Eyre, it isn't perhaps surprising that after many adventures, including a narrow escape from the Nazis, he ended up in Hollywood directing Devotion, Warners' biography of the Brontë sisters. It was in the swirling mists of high melodrama throughout the 1940s that Bernhardt was at his best. When he moved into colour and gloss, his films became dull. Although I'm one of the few champions of Beau Brummell, I concede there is not much to be said for Gaby or Miss Sadie Thompson, nor for any of the later Continental films. In the Germany of the 1920s, Bernhardt soon became a prominent director, a man who worked with big stars, such as Marlene Dietrich and Conrad Veidt. But after a brush with the Gestapo, he took to his heels, making a few films in France and Britain on the way to Hollywood. Here Warners signed him in 1940, but gave him unsuitable projects until Devotion (1943, released 1946) struck the mould (and mood) for his best American work. These 1943-1951 films are mainly psychological thrillers or melodramas about people with problems, weaknesses or destructive tendencies. The stories bulge with atmosphere, whether shot on location (Possessed) or in the studio (Conflict and others) and feature the studio's top stars, Barbara Stanwyck, Humphrey Bogart, Joan Crawford and Bette Davis, in somewhat off centre and out-of-character roles that allow them to go slightly, if enjoyably, over the top.

1926: Der Waise von Lowood. Qualen der Nacht. 1927: Kinderseelen Klagen euch an. Schinderhannes (GB & US: The Prince of Rogues). Das Mädchen mit den fünf Nullen. 1928: Das letzte Fort. 1929: Die Frau, nach der man sich sehnt (GB & US: Three Loves). 1930: Der letzte Kompagnie (and French version). US: 13 Men and a Girl). 1931: Der Mann der den Mord beging (and French version). 1932: †Der Rebell (and French version). Der grosse Ratisch. 1933: Der Tunnel (and French version). 1934: L'or dans la rue. 1936: The Beloved Vagabond. 1938: Carrefour (GB & US: Crossroads). 1939: Nuit de décembre. 1940: Lady with Red

Hair. My Love Came Back. 1941: Million Dollar Baby. 1942: Juke Girl. 1943: Happy Go Lucky. Devotion (released 1946). 1945: Conflict. 1946: A Stolen Life. My Reputation. 1947: Possessed. The High Wall. 1949: The Doctor and the Girl. 1951: The Blue Veil. Sirocco. Payment on Demand. 1952: The Merry Widow. 1953: Miss Sadie Thompson. 1954: Beau Brummell. 1955: Interrupted Melody. 1956: Gaby. 1960: Stefanie in Rio (US: Stephanie in Rio). 1961: †The Tyrant of Syracuse (US: Damon and Pythias. Credited as Supervising Director). 1964: Kisses for My President.

BERRI, Claude (C. Langmann) 1934-

Despite some early promise, Berri seemed securely placed in the second rank of French film directors. Until the mid 1980s. Not for nothing had Berri spent six years pursuing, then two and a half years setting up two epic films based on Marcel Pagnol's stories in L'eau des collines. The two films that resulted, Jean de Florette and Manon des Sources, secured Berri's place in French film history. The expressive little. Paris-born filmmaker has enjoyed a unique career as actor, producer and director, sometimes combining all three. He had begun, like his father, as a furrier, but was already acting at 17. He began directing films in 1962, much of his early work having autobiographical elements, especially Le vieil homme et l'enfant/The Two of Us, which won its veteran star Michael Simon best actor awards at film festivals, as the anti-Semitic old man trying to cope with the eight-year-old Jewish boy sent to stay with him in the final days of World War II. After four films in which he starred himself, culminating in the opportunist but shallow Sex Shop, Berri's reputation began to decline. He turned increasingly to producing, until regaining lost ground as a director in 1983 with Tchao Pantin, a noirish study of a lonely alcoholic played by the music-hall comic Coluche (to be killed in a road accident in 1986) in a radical departure from type. And so to Jean de Florette and Manon des Sources, a stunning double-act of films made for a French record of the equivalent of $17 million. Spun around life in a Provençal village in the 1920s, the carefully structured story evolves into the deceit and skulduggery involved in the fight for a fertile piece of land and the efforts of two farmers to ruin their neighbour. Years after the latter dies, his daughter takes a well-calculated revenge. The acting and direction cannot be faulted, and the photography, especially in the first film, is rich with the warmth of the French countryside in

summer. The star of Jean de Florette, Gérard Depardieu, has since appeared again for Berri in the impressive Germinal and the disappointing Uranus. Berri won an Oscar in 1965 for his short film, Le poulet, made two years earlier.

1962: *†Jeanine/Janine. 1963: *Le poulet. †Les baisers. 1964:†La chance et L'amour. 1966: Le vieil homme et l'enfant/The Two of Us. 1968: Mazel tov ou le mariage/Marry Me! Marry Me! 1969: Le pistonné/The Man with Connections. 1970: Le cinéma de Papa. 1972: Sex Shop. 1974: Le male du siècle. 1976: La première fois. 1978: Un moment d'égarement/One Wild Moment. 1980: Je vous aime. 1981: Le maître d'école. 1983: Tchao Pantin. 1985: Jean de Florette. 1986: Manon des Sources. 1991: Uranus. 1993: Germinal. 1997: Lucie Aubrac. 1999: Mookie.

BERRY, John 1917-

Would this American director have become one of Hollywood's top men without being blacklisted by the Un-American Activities Committee? His early career was spent with Orson Welles' Mercury Theatre (he was an assistant director on Welles' 'lost' 1938 feature Too Much Johnson) and he was snapped up by Paramount after staging an outstanding production of Cry Havoc (later filmed with Margaret Sullavan) on Broadway. The best of his films – From This Day Forward, Tension, He Ran All the Way – are about people fighting to escape circumstances that threaten to crush them, but there is little to the European work except a certain bravura flourish, and some hard edges to portraits of the Paris underworld. He went to India to make the beautifully photographed, if rather languid jungle adventure Maya, before returning, via stage work in London, to making (not very good) films in America in the early 1970s. He continued to chase offbeat subjects in atmospheric locations until 1990.

1944: Miss Susie Slagle's (released 1946). 1946: From This Day Forward. Cross My Heart. 1948: Casbah. 1949: Tension. 1950: *Dix de Hollywood/The Hollywood Ten. 1951: He Ran All the Way. 1952: C'est arrivé à Paris (uncredited). 1954: ça va Barder! (US: There Goes Barder). 1955: Je suis un sentimental (GB: Headlines of Destruction). 1956: El Amór de Don Juan (GB: Don Juan. US: Pantaloons). 1957: Tamango. 1958: Oh! Qué Mambo! 1966: Maya. 1967: A tout casser (US: Breaking It Up). 1974: Claudine. 1977: Thieves. 1978: The Bad News Bears go to Japan. 1980: Angel on My

The Italian straw hat...as sported by Bernardo **Bertolucci** while filming the 1976 epic *1900* in baking summer weather.

Shoulder (TV). 1982: Sister, Sister (TV). Honeyboy (TV). 1985: Voyage à Paimpol. 1987: Maldonné/Il y a maldonné. 1990: A Captive in the Land.

BERTOLUCCI, Bernardo 1940·

One of the cinema's greatest masters of visual beauty, especially when assisted by cinematographer Vittorio Storaro, Bertolucci's films are also dramatically naive and pretentious far too often, even addled at times, resulting in risible scenes even when respected actors are used. But at least the nine Oscars won by *The Last Emperor*, one of his three near-masterpieces, have assured that Bertolucci will not simply go down in history as the man who made *Last Tango in Paris*. Although that film has its remarkable aspects, it is in many respects the director's least typical and reflects least his use of cinema as a visual art, composing scenes like great paintings and dazzling the eye with richness of colour, be it in a costume or a landscape. All the finer qualities in Bertolucci's work came together in *The Last Emperor*, which won him the best director Oscar. Bertolucci's other triumphs, both commercial and critical successes, are *The Spider's Stratagem* and *The Conformist*, both made in 1970. These are elegant, intricate,

absorbing films. On the other hand, any middle-of-the-road cinemagoer watching some of the director,s more recent works particularly *La luna*, *Little Buddha* and *The Sheltering Sky*, is entitled to ask what the fuss is all about. He began, after making his own amateur films as a teenager, as an assistant to Pier Paolo Pasolini (*qv*). He branched out on his own in 1962 (the year in which he also published a volume of poetry) and gained his first critical success two years later with *Prima della rivoluzione*. This is a very accessible and moving film about a liberalised young man ten years after the Liberation who discovers that his upper-crust inheritance runs far deeper than his newly acquired radicalism. There are remarkable scenes in all of Bertolucci's films and especially *1900*). But too often the material in between is overstretched into tedium. This is particularly true of the over-praised *Stealing Beauty*. Its actors pose modishly about the Tuscan countryside in summer and there is much fornication which, under Bertolucci's cultured hand, almost passes for art. He is married to the English-born director Clare Peploe.

1962: La commare secca (GB: The Grim Reaper). 1964: Prima della rivoluzione (GB & US: Before the Revolution). 1966:

*Il canale (D). 1967: La via del petrolio (D. TV). 1968: Partner. 1969: †Amore e rabbia (GB: Love and Anger). 1970: La strategia del ragno (GB & US: The Spider's Stratagem). Il conformista (GB & US: The Conformist). 1971: *La salute è malata o i poveri muoiono prima (D). 1972: Last Tango in Paris. 1976: 1900. 1979: La Luna (US: Luna). 1981: Tragedia di un uomo ridicolo. 1984: **Red Harvest. 1987: The Last Emperor. 1990: The Sheltering Sky. 1993: Little Buddha. 1996: Stealing Beauty.

** Uncompleted

BESSON, Luc 1959·

Although not strong on logic or plot development, this enthusiastic French director's films are all razzle-dazzle and adrenalin-surging excitement. Each new film by him has been an event, although crowd-pleasers rather than critical masterpieces. Eye-catching and innovative, Besson's too-few films are frequently triumphs of style over content. Born in Paris, his earliest interest – deep-sea diving and underwater photography – led him to begin working in films as a third assistant director at the age of 19. His first feature film, *Le dernier combat*, is shot through with the same audacious imagery (here in black and white) and technical mastery that was to characterise all his films, although the budgets grew

Luc **Besson** (left) and cameraman Carlo Varini line up a shot for Besson's 1988 film *The Big Blue*.

progressively larger. Besson made a breakthrough to international recognition with *Subway*, with Christopher Lambert (not the last Besson hero to sport weird-coloured hair) as a safecracker who flees to the tunnels below the Paris *Métro*, where he's protected by a bizarre collection of subterranean denizens. Criminal underbellies of society were further explored by Besson in *Léon* and *La femme Nikita*, notable for unconventional themes and spiky performances but less successful in their dramatic content and quieter moments. Science-fiction, though, has always looked Besson's natural home, and *The Fifth Element*, helped by the presence of a Hollywood star in Bruce Willis, proved his biggest international success. Stunning in its visual detail, it's a rip-roaring futuristic adventure (first envisioned by Besson when he was 16) about a battle to save the earth in the 23rd century. Besson's mind-blowing funfair rides look set to entertain us for some years yet.

*1981: *L'avant dernier. 1982: Le dernier combat. 1985: Subway. 1988: The Big Blue. 1990: Atlantis (D). 1991: La femme Nikita/Nikita. 1994: Léon/The Professional. 1996: The Fifth Element. 1999: Joan of Arc.*

BIGELOW, Kathryn 1952-

At the rate she makes films, this American director's career list is unlikely to be counted on more than the fingers of two hands. What films she has made have usually proved noisy, nasty and watchable: there are few smiles in a Bigelow movie. Bigelow switched from painting to filmmaking in her mid twenties, but she was

30 before she got her first feature film, *The Loveless*, off the ground. The next, *Near Dark*, didn't follow for five years, but it established a cult following. A dark and unpleasant vampire black horror comic, it has its vampires expiring in painfully protracted ways, as well as offering some genuine chills. Most of Bigelow's subsequent films have looked promising, but drawn disappointing responses from public and critics alike. The most innovative and ambitious of them has been *Strange Days*, a violent but very watchable hybrid of science-fantasy and whodunnit, set in Los Angeles at the turn of the millennium. Though its brutality is sometimes hard to bear, the film works well enough both as an action-thriller and as a chilling portrait of a movie nightmare near future. With the marketable Ralph Fiennes in the lead, the movie should have achieved better results than it did. Bigelow married blockbuster movie-maker James Cameron in 1989, but they were later divorced.

*1978: *Set-Up. 1982: The Loveless. 1987: Near Dark. 1989: Blue Steel. 1991: Point Break. 1995: Strange Days.*

BIRD, Antonia 1959-

British director who makes confrontational films that turn over stones to reveal things that some people would rather not know about society today. The only child of 'an unsuccessful actor', she admits to being influenced by the work of Martin Scorsese in her decision to start making movies of her own. After cutting her teeth on a rather unconventional TV detective thriller, she made *Safe*, which focused on the lives of homeless young people. This

was followed by her most controversial work, *Priest*, which looked at the struggles of a young cleric to repress his homosexuality. A trip to Hollywood to make *Mad Love* proved largely unrewarding, and Bird was soon back on Britain's mean streets, working with the country's newest superstar, Robert Carlyle, on a very violent gangster thriller called *Face*. Her style is hard-hitting, down-and-dirty, relying on close-up performances and skilful cross-cutting for its impact. She should thrive in the present British cinema climate.

1991: A Masculine Ending (TV). 1993: Safe. 1994: Priest. 1995: Mad Love. 1997: Face. 1999: Ravenous. Days Like These.

BIRT, Daniel 1907-1955

A skilful editor who worked steadily in the British cinema throughout the 1930s, Birt seems to have drifted into direction almost by accident, after moving from editing to producing in the war years, during which time he also made two interesting documentaries; the Welsh slant of the first of them, *Dai Jones*, was carried into the first of his features, *The Three Weird Sisters*. This was a very strange and sinister film – which scared a lot of audiences in its time (although no-one seems now to have seen it for years) – about three elderly Welsh spinsters who, to carry out a promise to restore local cottages, ruined by a cave-in at their father's mine, make various attempts to murder their rich half-brother for his money. This vein of unpleasantness also ran through Birt's subsequent features, but the 1950s began a decline which included several 'B' features, one of which, the truly dire *Circumstantial Evidence*, hit a new low even for British second-features of the early 1950s. The only bright spot in this last period of Birt's career *is Background,* a pleasant and affecting family drama which suggested that Birt might have shared some of Philip Leacock's talent in extracting moving performances from child actors. But in 1955, he died at 47, of a heart attack following a bout of pneumonia.

*1931: *Silt (D). 1941: Dai Jones (D). 1943: Butterfly Bomb (D). 1948: The Three Weird Sisters. No Room at the Inn. 1949: The Interrupted Journey. 1950: She Shall Have Murder. 1952: The Night Won't Talk. Circumstantial Evidence. 1953: Three Steps in the Dark. Background (US: Edge of Divorce). 1954: Meet Mr Malcolm. Burnt Evidence. 1955: Third Party Risk. 1956: Laughing in the Sunshine.*

BLACK, Noel 1937-

Seldom can the reputation of a director have rested so squarely on one film. Alas, poor Black is one of the very few American directors to have arrived on the cinema scene in the late 1960s or early 1970s with a low budget success, who has not subsequently made the big time. The film was *Pretty Poison* and madness lurking in the mind beneath a beautiful and tranquil exterior (admittedly with a magnificent assist from Tuesday Weld) has seldom been more chillingly or strongly captured. This theme of things being much darker than they seem on the surface runs through several of Black's films, even in the early short *Skaterdater*, which also caught both the public eye and critical approval. But bathos and pathos alike fatally flaw what there is of his sparse later work. Still, *A Man, a Woman and a Bank*, though lightweight entertainment, had some good things in it, and we can only hang in there and hope for another *Pretty Poison* or two. From 1980 on, however, Black has ostensibly turned out only poor films and mediocre TV movies, although he has also done some fine work in the field of short one-off TV dramas.

*1964: *Skaterdater. 1967: *The River Boy. 1968: Pretty Poison. 1970: Cover Me Babe. 1971: Jennifer on My Mind. 1977: Mulligan's Stew (TV). 1978: Mirrors. 1979: A Man, a Woman and a Bank/A Very Big Withdrawal. 1981: The Other Victim (TV). 1982: Prime Suspect (TV). 1983: Private School. Quarterback Princess (TV). Happy Endings (TV). 1985: A Time to Triumph (TV). Promises to Keep (TV). 1986: My Two Loves (TV). 1987: Conspiracy of Love (TV). 1988: The Town Bully (TV).*

BLAIR, Les 1941-

British director who has been making improvised drama for 30 years, sometimes to great effect, although inevitably with this genre he has had occasional failures. Born in Salford, Blair studied film in London and Prague before embarking on a TV career in the late 1960s. Since attracting attention with *Honest, Decent and True*, a satire on the advertising industry, Blair has also essayed two or three feature films. Easily the most accessible of these is *Bad Behaviour*, a gently amusing domestic comedy about an Irish couple living in North London who find themselves at the mercy of cowboy workmen, a wheeler-dealer shark forever on his mobile phone, and friends and relations with all the troubles in the world. It's a tribute to Blair's relaxed and unfussy direction here that all the performances

have a nice natural feel. A more tightly structured UK/South Africa venture, *Jump the Gun*, however, proved the director's first outright flop.

1984: Number One. 1986: Honest, Decent and True (TV). 1987: Leave to Remain. 1989: The Accountant (TV). 1990: News Hounds (TV). 1991: Filipina Dreamgirls (TV). 1992: Bad Behaviour. 1997: Jump the Gun/Babel.

BOETTICHER, Budd (Oscar Boetticher jnr) 1916-

An all round sportsman at Ohio State University, where he excelled at basketball, football and boxing, Boetticher became fascinated by bullfighting and turned professional matador at 19. Today, the bullfighting films he was to make – *Blood and Sand* (his entry to Hollywood in 1941 as technical adviser), *The Bullfighter and the Lady*, *The Magnificent Matador* and *Arruza* – are less well remembered than the series of virile westerns that he made with Randolph Scott as star between 1956 and 1960. Boetticher had already built up a reputation as a fast-working maker of vivid action films with a theme of male comradeship. Girls never seem to come across very strongly in his world, even when – as with Julie (then Julia) Adams in *Wings of the Hawk* – they have a prominent

part to play in the action. They are little more than prizes to be fought over in the Scott westerns, in which Scott is almost like a matador taking on cruel enemies who charge at him headlong. This is especially so in the final duel with Lee Marvin in the best ,of these films, *Seven Men from Now*, in which Marvin's guns (horns) uselessly plough through the air as he receives the *coup de grâce* from the lightning thrust of Scott's bullet. Boetticher received his own *coup de grâce*, career-wise, when he left Hollywood for Mexico in 1961 to make a feature-length documentary about Carlos Arruza, a famous matador and personal friend. The next six years brought Boetticher nothing but disaster. He nearly died of a lung ailment, he and his wife were divorced, and Arruza and three of Boetticher's crew were killed in a car crash. One need hardly add that money ran out on several occasions. Although he managed to complete the film (after all that, it had scant distribution), Boetticher returned to America to find his career in ruins. He made an unsuccessful film with Audie Murphy as star and co-producer in place of the now-retired Randolph Scott, and had plans for more when Murphy was killed in a private-plane crash. Boetticher did not film again for 15 years.

1944: The Missing Juror. One Mysterious

*Enfant terrible grows up. Peter **Bogdanovich** works out a scene during the making of Noises Off.*

*Night (GB: Behind Closed Doors). Youth on Trial. 1945: A Guy, a Gal and a Pal. Escape in the Fog. *The Fleet That Came to Stay. 1948: Assigned to Danger. Behind Locked Doors. 1949: Wolf Hunters. Black Midnight. 1950: Killer Shark. 1951: The Bullfighter and the Lady. The Sword of D'Artagnan (originally TV). The Cimarron Kid. 1952: Bronco Buster. Red Ball Express. Horizons West. 1953: City Beneath the Sea. Wings of the Hawk. East of Sumatra. The Man from The Alamo. Seminole. 1955: The Magnificent Matador (GB: The Brave and the Beautiful). 1956: The Killer is Loose. Seven Men from Now. 1957: Decision at Sundown. The Tall T. 1958: Buchanan Rides Alone. Westbound. 1959: The Rise and Fall of Legs Diamond. Ride Lonesome. 1960: Comanche Station. 1968: Arruza (D). 1969: A Time for Dying. 1984: Lusitano (D). 1985: My Kingdom For... (D).*

BOGDANOVICH, Peter 1939-

The nickname bestowed on this American director by night-club comedians – Peter-Bogged-Down-a-Bit – became all too apposite as a string of box-office misfires followed his early successes. He is still in there making films, but only just: nothing for the cinema since 1993. Bogdanovich was a well-known writer and critic, writing books on Dwan, Ford, Hawks, Hitchcock, Lang and Welles, before directing his first major film, *Targets*, an instant critical success which also attracted some public attention as one of the few 1960s Boris Karloff films worthy of the veteran horror star. Bogdanovich's next three films were all big mainline successes, none more so than *The Last Picture Show*. Made in black and white, the film is a powerful evocation of the stultifying, stagnant life in a dry, dusty Texas town in the early 1950s. Bogdanovich was nominated for an Oscar and possibly deserved the award over the actual winner, fellow-rising-star of the new American cinema, William Friedkin, for *The French Connection. Paper Moon*, also made in black and white, is not actually as enjoyable as its reputation, but *What's Up Doc?* is an entertaining, uncomplicated screwball comedy with some gloriously funny visual moments. At this time, Bogdanovich had already begun a personal and professional relationship with Cybill Shepherd (one of the stars of *The Last Picture Show*) and he showcased her talents in a rather underrated period piece of melancholia, *Daisy Miller*, and in a clodhopping musical, *At Long Last Love* which, like so many latter-day Hollywood musicals, was full of people who could neither sing nor dance. Bogdanovich again indulged his taste for nostalgia with, the flaccid *Nick-*

elodeon and, when that too was a flop, withdrew from film-making for three years. He returned as a sharper and leaner filmmaker with the critically rated but publically ignored *Saint Jack*, and enjoyed great triumph a few years later with *Mask*, the story of a boy born with a form of dysplasia, which deformed his face to an alarming degree. The story of his fight for a normal life is told with a great deal of tender loving care by the director, albeit draped in a tough exterior. Bogdanovich has not hit the same heights since, and his sequel to *The Last Picture Show, Texasville*, lacked all the poignancy of the original.

1966: †Voyage to the Planet of the Prehistoric Women. 1968: Targets. 1970: Directed by John Ford (D). 1971: The Last Picture Show. 1972: What's Up, Doc? 1973: Paper Moon. 1974: Daisy Miller. 1975: At Long Last Love. 1976: Nickelodeon. 1979: Saint Jack. 1981: They All Laughed. 1985: Mask. 1988: Illegally Yours. 1990: Texasville. 1992: Noises Off. 1993: The Thing Called Love. 1995: †Picture Windows (cable TV). 1996: To Sir With Love II (TV). 1997: Rescuers of Courage – Two Women (TV).

BOLESLAWSKI, Richard

(Boleslaw Ryszart Srzednicki) 1889-1937

There is a theory that this Polish director was just hitting his stride in the Hollywood of the 1930s when he collapsed on the set of *The Last of Mrs Cheyney* (the film was completed by George Fitzmaurice) and died shortly afterwards. He had studied under (and was later to write about) the famous drama teacher Stanislavsky at the Moscow Arts Theatre while still a teenager and had a long and sporadic career in the cinema and theatre, partly as actor, partly as director, interspersed with a return to Poland for military service against the Bolsheviks, before ending up in America in 1923 and becoming a successful Broadway director. His subsequent Hollywood ventures are of little note until 1933, when his Russian background was obviously considered a good reason for M-G-M to hand him *Rasputin and the Empress*, with the three Barrymores, Ethel, John and Lionel, after they considered it necessary to drop the original director, Charles Brabin (*qv*), from the project. Boleslawski was then able to tackle a really wide range of subjects, including the epic action of *Clive of India*, the screwball comedy of *Theodora Goes Wild*, and the western sentiment of the first sound version of *Three Godfathers*, later to be remade with John

Wayne. He also directed Greta Garbo in an interesting if rather stately screen treatment of Somerset Maugham's *The Painted Veil*. The film for which he will probably be remembered most, however, if only because its lush colour has propelled it on to our television screens, is *The Garden of Allah*, a strange, extraordinarily plush, but finally quite persuasive story of love in the desert, with Marlene Dietrich and Charles Boyer. By this time, Boleslawski had certainly done enough to suggest that he would probably have stayed around until the end of the studio system in the mid-1950s, probably most beneficially with Twentieth Century-Fox.

*1915: Tri Vstrechi/Three Meetings. 1918: †Chleb/Bread. 1919: Bohaterstwo Polskiego Skavto. 1920: Cud Nad Wisla/The Miracle of the Vistula. 1930: The Grand Parade (musical numbers only). *Treasure Girl. The Last of the Lone Wolf. 1931: The Gay Diplomat. Woman Pursued. 1933: Rasputin and the Empress (GB: Rasputin – The Mad Monk). Storm at Daybreak. Beauty for Sale (GB: Beauty). 1934: Fugitive Lovers. Men in White. Operator 13 (GB: Spy 13). †Hollywood Party (uncredited). The Painted Veil. 1935: O' Shaughnessy's Boy. Metropolitan. Clive of India. Les Misérables. 1936: Three Godfathers. The Garden of Allah. Theodora Goes Wild. 1937: †The Last of Mrs. Cheyney.*

BONDARCHUK, Sergei 1920-

No man who has made a 507-minute version of *War and Peace* is ever likely to be forgotten. However, the truth is that Bondarchuk was always more engrossing as an actor and, while he has a magnificent visual sense that produced awe-inspiring battle scenes in *War and Peace* and *Waterloo*, inspiration is less in evidence when it comes to the direction of his fellow players. Bondarchuk started acting with Russian stock companies in his teens, and made his screen debut in 1948 (in *The Young Guard*) as the Russian film industry got going again after the war. It was 1959 before he directed his first film, *Destiny of a Man*, and it was a notable debut, taking a realistic and down-to-earth look at people fighting to carry on normal lives during wartime. Bondarchuk was not to surpass this film, despite the Oscar won by the four-part *War and Peace* in 1968 as best foreign language film. Bondarchuk took leading roles in both films; but, as *Waterloo* was an international venture, he took no acting part in it, plumping instead for well-known names from many countries. Coming at

It goes like this... John **Boorman** (left) directs Powers Boothe during the making of *The Emerald Forest*.

the end of the fashion for immense epics, and overbalanced by the gale-force performance of Rod Steiger as Napoleon, the film was not a tremendous success, despite its brilliantly staged battlefields, black plumes of smoke, flames and red uniforms creating a Hell on Earth. Bondarchuk's subsequent films have not been widely seen outside his native Russia, and it seems now that his international reputation will rest on his earlier work.

1959: *Sudba Cheloveka (GB: Destiny of a Man. US: Fate of a Man). 1965: War and Peace, I: Andrei Bolkonski. War and Peace II: Natasha Rostova. 1966: War and Peace III: Borrodino. 1967: War and Peace IV: Pierre Bezuhov (English-language version of these four films shown in two parts and shortened to 373 mins in US and 357 mins in GB). 1970: Waterloo. 1974: They Fought for Their Country. 1976: The Peaks of Zelengore. 1978: The Steppes. 1982: Ten Days That Shook the World/Red Bells/Mexico in Flames. 1986: Boris Godunov. 1989: Il placido Don.*

BOORMAN, John 1933-

There is little doubt that this British-born director would have made it as a painter. His films, though sparsely scattered through the 1960s and 1970s, are, without exception, among the most striking visually in the modern cinema. The images in his films are as haunting as they are handsome, and some, like the final shot of the hand rising from the water in *Deliverance*, may disturb your dreams. Mystery, mythology and allegory are things which interest him, and there

are elements of these even in his seemingly more straightforward action films. When it comes to total impact, his films are much more variable. *Catch Us If You Can* is tricksy, full of surface things which catch the eye and a copybook exercise in editing – but quite empty inside. Admittedly, this is a vehicle for a pop star (Dave Clark) and wasn't meant to be much more, but it has nowhere near the impact of Richard Lester's Beatles film *A Hard Day's Night*. After that Boorman burst into the colour he uses so masterfully in what are still my favourite Boorman films – Point *Blank*, quite the cleverest and sharpest crime film an English director ever made in America, and the much-underrated *Hell in the Pacific*, which features Lee Marvin (also the star of *Point Blank*) and Toshiro Mifune as American and Japanese soldiers coming to terms with each other on a Pacific island. Since then, his films have lapsed into tedium and pretentiousness, although *Deliverance,* the best of them, has moments of great power. In 1981, Boorman, having been thwarted in his plans to make a live-action version of *Lord of the Rings,* unveiled another fondly cherished project, the Arthurian saga *Excalibur*. The resulting 140-minute tale of blood and sorcery is always the handsomest of films to behold, but it was perhaps unfortunate that we had so recently seen *Monty Python and the Holy Grail,* for all too often the spectre of that film sits gleefully on *Excalibur*'s shoulders. nowhere more so than in some strange and over-emphatic portrayals from some of the leading players. One thing we can rely on: a Boorman film will always be

worth *looking* at. In *Hope and Glory* , the best of his more recent work, the cinematography does full justice to the many and varied settings in this flavoursome memoir of his own wartime childhood, wittily scripted by Boorman himself. Since then Boorman, never the most prolific of film-makers, has seemed to struggle to set up new projects.

1965: *Catch Us If You Can (US: Having a Wild Weekend). 1967: Point Blank. 1968: Hell in the Pacific. 1970: Leo the Last. 1972: Deliverance. 1974: Zardoz. 1977: Exorcist II: The Heretic. 1981: Excalibur. 1985: The Emerald Forest. 1987: Hope and Glory. 1990: Where the Heart Is. 1995: *Two Nudes Bathing. Beyond Rangoon. 1998: The General.*

BOROWCZYK, Walerian 1923-

It seems a pity that this Polish-born director (his name is pronounced Boroffchick), once Europe's leading animator, then a maker of strikingly offbeat, poetical live-action films, should have trodden the same slippery downhill path slithered along by Pasolini in his later years. Rustic sexploitation is the name of the game, and one is soon hard put to recall one set of naughty nuns or copulating cowherds from another. Rapes also figure high on Borowczyk's later offerings, especially in the blood-splattered *Les Heroines du mal.* It may seem a little too unkind to describe Borowczyk's work since 1974 as 'up-market sex films', but certainly richly dark interiors, memorable pastel colouring and often extremely convoluted plots are not enough to keep boredom at bay. After the splendours of *Goto, Island of Love* and the unique evocation of mediaeval madness in *Blanche* (in both of which Borowczyk was given invaluable assistance by the performances of his real-life wife, the pale, stick-like, haunting Ligia Branice), the disappointment of such later crudities as *The Beast* (one expected Sylvia Kristel to come pouting into the scene at any moment here, and indeed Borowczyk directed her in his next film), is all the more intense. His films have continued to decline in recent years, although he has been inactive in the cinema since 1988. Following his early collaboration on cartoons with another fine Polish animator, Jan Lenica (1928-), Borowczyk moved to Paris, where he has lived since 1958.

1953: *Glows/The Head. 1954: *Atelier de Fernand Léger. *Photographies vivantes. 1955: Jesien/Autumn. 1957: *Once Upon a Time (c). *Love Rewarded (c). †*Striptease (c). 1*Dni Oswiaty (c). †*Sztandar Mlodych. 1958: †*House (c).*

*School (c). 1959: †*Les astronautes (c). *Terra Incognita (c). 1962: *Concert (c). 1963: *Holy Smoke (c). Renaissance (c). *Les stroboscopes. * Les bibliothèques (c). *Les écoles (c). *L'écriture (c). 1964: *Les jeux des anges (c). La fille sage (c). *Le musée (c). Gancia (c). 1965: *Le petit poucet (c). *Le dictionaiaire de Joachim (c). *Un été torride (c). 1966: Rosalie. 1967: *Diptyque. Le théâtre de Monsieur et Madame Kabal (c). *Gavotte. 1968: Goto, I'le d'amour (GB & US: Goto, Island of Love). 1969: *Le photographe (c). 1971: Blanche. 1974: Contes immoraux (GB & US: Immoral Tales). 1975: La bête (GB & US: The Beast). Dzieje Grzechu (GB & US: Story of a Sin). 1976: La marge (GB & US: The Streetwalker). 1977: Interno d'un convento (GB: Behind Convent Walls. US: Sex Life in a Convent). 1978: Les heroines du mal (GB: Three Immoral Woman. US: Heroines of Evil). 1980: Lulu. 1981: The Strange Case of Dr Jekyll and Mrs Osbourne/Dr Jekyll and the Women. 1982: Ars amandi/Art of Love. 1986: Emanuelle 5. 1987: Tout disparaitra. 1988: Cérémonie d'amour.

(c) Cartoon

BORZAGE, Frank 1893-1962

Humphrey Bogart once made a (not very good) film called Two Against the World. The phrase could serve as a theme for Borzage's work, during his peak period from 1924 to 1940 when, he made films of unabashed romantic lyricism that celebrated simple human values and found lovers looking the Depression (and each other) straight in the face. Born in Utah of Italian immigrant parents, Borzage came to Hollywood in 1912 as an actor, but had turned director by 1916. He began with a variety of westerns, dramas and comedies and, although Humoresque (1920) was the first of the dry-eyed weepies in which he would shortly specialize, it was not until 1924 that his reputation in the genre really began to build. That was the year he made Secrets, which he would remake nine years later as Mary Pickford's last film. In earlier years, Richard Barthelmess and Lillian Gish would have been ideal lovers for Borzage to celebrate. But the attention of audiences had moved from the country to the city and Borzage found Janet Gaynor and Charles Farrell as the working-class lovers in Seventh Heaven, Lucky Star and Street Angel. For Seventh Heaven (1927), Borzage was awarded the first-ever Best Director Academy Award. Love in times of trouble was also the theme of such films as Man's Castle, Little Man, What

Now? Hearts Divided, The Shining Hour, The Mortal Storm and even A Farewell to Arms, which is streets ahead (and half the length) of the 1957 remake and, by concentrating on the intimacy of a great love affair, exudes a powerful integrity which not even Hemingway's original possesses to such a degree. During this gleaming period of his career, such actors as Margaret Sullavan, Spencer Tracy, Jean Arthur, Charles Boyer and James Stewart, not forgetting Helen Hayes and Gary Cooper in Arms, gave a strong feeling of truth and a rich emotional appeal to the romantic fabrics Borzage wove. With the realism engendered in films by the war, Borzage moved away to unsuitable material. There were signs in his later 1940s' films that there was life (love and tears) in Borzage yet, until this most 'innocent' of directors somehow contrived to fall foul of the McCarthy blacklist and did not make another film until near the end of his life. He died from cancer.

1916: *†Mammy's Rose. †Life's Harmony. Immediate Lee. The Silken Spider. Nell Dale's Menfolks. The Forgotten Prayer. Nugget Jim's Partner. Land o' Lizards. Pride and the Man. Dollars of Dross. The Code of Honor. That Gal of Burke's. The Courting of Calliope Clew. The Demon of Fear. Enchantment. 1917: †Wee Lady Betty. Flying Colors. The Ghost Flower. Until They Get Me. The Curse of Iku. 1918: The Gun Woman. Shoes That Danced. Innocent's Progress. An Honest Man. Who is to Blame? The Atom. Society for Sale. 1919: Prudence of Broadway. Toton. Whom the Gods Would Destroy. Ashes of Desire. 1920: Humoresque. 1921: The Duke of Chimney Butte. Get-Rich-Quick Wallingford. 1922: Hair Trigger Casey (re-edited version of Immediate Lee). Back Pay. The Good Provider. Silent Shelby (re-edited version of Land o' Lizards). Billy Jim. The Valley of Silent Men. The Pride of Palomar. 1923: The Nth Commandment (GB: The Higher Law). Children of Dust. The Age of Desire. 1924: Secrets. 1925: The Lady. Lazybones. Daddy's Gone a-Hunting. Wages for Wives. The Circle. 1926: Marriage License? (GB: The Pelican). The Dixie Merchant. Easy to Wed. The First Year. 1927: Seventh Heaven. 1928: Street Angel. The River. 1929: Lucky Star. They Had to See Paris. 1930: Song o' My Heart. Liliom. 1931: Doctors' Wives. Young As You Feel. Bad Girl. 1932: Young America (GB: We Humans). After Tomorrow. A Farewell to Arms. 1933: Secrets. Man's Castle. 1934: Little Man, What Now? Flirtation Walk. No Greater Glory. 1935: Stranded. Shipmates Forever. Living on Velvet. 1936: Hearts

Divided. Desire. 1937: Green Light. History is Made at Night. Mannequin. Big City. 1938: Three Comrades. The Shining Hour. 1939: Disputed Passage. 1940: The Mortal Storm. Strange Cargo. Flight Command. 1941: Smilin' Through. The Vanishing Virginian. 1942: Seven Sweethearts. 1943: Stage Door Canteen. His Butler's Sister. 1944: Till We Meet Again. 1945: The Spanish Main. 1946: Magnificent Doll. I've Always Loved You (GB: Concerto). 1947: That's My Man (GB: Will Tomorrow Ever Come?). 1948: Moonrise. 1958: China Doll. 1959: The Big Fisherman. 1961: †Atlantis the Lost Continent (uncredited).

BOULTING, John 1913-1985 and Roy 1913-

Lean, lanky, bespectacled British twin brothers who created trends in the British cinema for 25 years before being overtaken by others. They proved astute judges of box-office possibilities at given times and if there is a theme that runs through their work it is that of the ordinary man triumphing comically or dramatically against the odds. Roy was the first of the twins to get a film career under way, contributing to a screenplay at 19 and progressing to assistant director at 23. Together the brothers formed Charter Films in 1937 on John's return from the Spanish Civil War where he had been an ambulance driver for government forces. The years that followed were full of impressive, often innovative films. Roy's first large-scale success – with each twin already adopting their lifetime procedure of producing the film his brother directed – was Pastor Hall, a story of Nazi oppression in the early 1930s. This was followed by one of the biggest critical triumphs of his career – Thunder Rock, a strange but very compelling film about a writer-turned-lighthousekeeper sorting out his life with the help of some ghosts. War service split the twins, with Roy opting for the Army, where he won an Academy Award for his documentary Desert Victory, and John for the RAF. After the war came the epic drama of Fame is the Spur, then The Guinea Pig, an enormously popular film which had 25-year-old Richard Attenborough playing a 14-year-old schoolboy and getting away with it, and two tense and hard-hitting thrillers, Seven Days to Noon and High Treason. Best of all their immediate post-war product was a film directed by John, Brighton Rock, again with Richard Attenborough, but this time in a very different role, as a vicious young criminal (America gave the film an evocative new title: Young Scarface). Attenborough was again to the fore, by this time playing character roles, when the Boultings embarked in the mid-1950s on a series of anarchic, institution-knocking comedies which the public took to their heart. The guiding light in most of these (*Private's Progress*, *Brothers in Law*, *Lucky Jim* etc) was Ian Carmichael as the hapless upper-class bungler completely bemused at first by the low cunning of the company into which he has stumbled, but finally victorious because of it. At this time Roy also made the very exciting *Run for the Sun*, a variation on *The Hounds of Zaroff*. Post-1960 work showed that the brothers' touch for comedy had deserted them, but Roy's later output includes a pleasing provincial comedy drama, *The Family Way* and, the underrated thriller *Twisted Nerve*, a jumpy melodrama in the Hitchcock tradition. The star of these last two films was Hayley Mills, to whom Roy was married from 1971 to 1977, one of his six wives.

John: *1945: Journey Together. 1947: Brighton Rock (US: Young Scarface). 1950: Seven Days to Noon. 1951: The Magic Box. 1954: †Seagulls over Sorrento (US: Crest of the Wave). 1955: Private's Progress. 1957: Lucky Jim. 1959: I'm All Right, Jack. 1960: †Suspect (US: The Risk). 1963: Heavens Above! 1965: Rotten to the Core.*
Roy: *1938: *Seeing Stars (D). *Ripe Earth (D). Consider Your Verdict. The Landlady. 1939: Trunk Crime (US: Design for Murder). 1940: Inquest. Pastor Hall. 1941: *Dawn Guard. 1942: Thunder Rock. *They Serve Abroad (D). 1943: Desert Victory (D). †Tunisian Victory (D). 1944: *Minefield! (D). 1945: Burma Victory (D). 1947: Fame is the Spur. 1948: The Guinea Pig. 1951: High Treason. 1953: Single-Handed (US: Sailor of the King). 1954:†Seagulls over Sorrento (US: Crest of the Wave). 1955: Josephine and Men. 1956: Run for the Sun. Brothers in Law. 1957: Happy is the Bride! 1958: †Carlton-Browne of the F.O. (US: Man in a Cocked Hat). 1960. †Suspect (US: The Risk). A French Mistress. 1966: The Family Way. 1968: Twisted Nerve. 1970: There's a Girl in My Soup. 1971: †Mr Forbush and the Penguins (uncredited. US: Cry of the Penguins). 1973: Soft Beds, Hard Battles (US: Undercovers Hero). 1979: The Number/The Last Word.*

BOX, Muriel (née Baker) 1905-

Screenplay writer who became Britain's foremost woman director during the 1950s. She began as a script-girl working for British Instructional Films from 1927. It was 1935 before her first screenplay

was accepted (for *Alibi Inn*). From then, however, she rapidly became one of Britain's most prolific writers, turning out dozens of one-act plays with her husband Sydney (married 1935, divorced 1969), brother of producer Betty Box. In 1945 Muriel again turned her attention to the cinema and Sydney was her producer and often co-writer. They won an Academy Award (Best Original Screenplay) for *The Seventh Veil*, and Muriel turned director in 1952. Although her films never touched great heights, most of them are solidly crafted entertainment within the demands of the times. The best examples of her work, always polished and often lifting ordinary subjects above the average, are *Street Corner*, a study of British women police; *The Beachcomber*, with Robert Newton, a remake of Laughton's *The Vessel of Wrath*; *Simon and Laura*, a lively, satirical look at television and its most perfect couple (in private life they fight like cat and dog); and *Rattle of a Simple Man*, an underrated and winning version of a stage play about the encounter between a naive northerner and a London prostitute.

*1952: The Happy Family (US: Mr Lord Says No!). 1953: Street Corner (US: Both Sides of the Law). *A Prince for Cynthia. 1954: To Dorothy a Son (US: Cash on Delivery). The Beachcomber. 1955: Simon and Laura. 1956: Eyewitness. 1957: The Passionate Stranger US: A Novel Affair). 1958: The Truth About Women. 1959: Subway in the Sky. This Other Eden. 1960: Too Young to Love. 1962: The Piper's Tune. 1964: Rattle of a Simple Man.*

BOYLE, Danny 1957 -

It's strange to find that Britain's hottest wunderkind film-maker is actually a father of three in his early forties. From a working-class Manchester family, Boyle spent his twenties and early thirties directing for the theatre. After catching the attention with episodes of the popular TV series *Inspector Morse* and the offbeat *Mr Wroe's Virgins*, Boyle found it relatively easy to secure the minimum £1 million budget for his first film *Shallow Grave*. A grisly and violent thriller on the theme of thieves falling out, it was directed with some flair by Boyle, but its impact was nothing compared to that of his second, *Trainspotting*, a vivid and harrowing look at heroin addicts in Edinburgh, complete with stomach-churning fantasy sequences, that took the world by storm. It portrayed an unappetising lifestyle that the film, despite its graphic depiction of it, comes close to glorifying, thanks partly to

the very successful vein of scabrous comedy that runs through it. And it was ferociously well acted in a clutch of star-making performances, although the same could not be said for the next, *A Life Less Ordinary*. This also had its share of fantasy, but this time it seemed superfluous to the theme of a kidnap plan in which the victim takes over the kidnapper's demands. Poorly received, it might cause Boyle to fight shy of lightweight stuff for several years.

1994: Shallow Grave. 1996: Trainspotting. 1997: A Life Less Ordinary.

BRABIN, Charles J. 1883-1957

Now perhaps unfortunately known both as the man who wooed and won Theda Bara, the Hollywood goddess who said she would never marry, and the man who was controversially fired from two films in the later stages of his career, Brabin, born in Liverpool, England, of Irish ancestry, made some fine films in Hollywood from 1918 to 1925, a period when he was one of the film capital's most prominent and popular directors. He had emigrated to America at the turn of the century and, after various jobs, became an actor, in stage productions from 1905 and films (with the Edison company) from 1908. Edison gave him his first chance to direct in 1912, and he gradually progressed to more prestigious films, especially those which showcased the talents of such exotic stars as Elinor Glyn and Theda Bara. His usual flamboyant visual style was occasionally muted to great effect, especially in the backwoods melodrama *Driven*. After he directed Bara in *La Belle Russe* and *Kathleen Mavourneen*, the two became constant companions. She, much quieter in real life than in her exotic screen roles, said later 'I didn't want to be married. I hadn't ever cared about getting married'. Reader, she married him. And they remained married until her death in 1955. But meanwhile things were going wrong for the tall, genial Brabin. After scoring a big success with an early version of the classic weepie *So Big*, he was asked by M-G-M to direct their mighty *Ben-Hur*. Brabin began shooting in Italy, but after several weeks, and countless looks at what they considered disappointing footage, the M-G-M hierarchy dismissed him and brought in Fred Niblo (*qv*). Brabin's projects sank in prestige after that, but M-G-M re-employed him with the advent of sound, and he rewarded them with two fascinating 1932 films. *The Mask of Fu Manchu* had Boris Karloff in the leading role, and Brabin was able to show the chilly side of his mastery of exotic detail. In contrast, *Beast of the City*, is a vicious crime melodrama with Walter Huston in trenchant form as the police captain who goes too far in his passion to rid the city of racketeers, and an early, and very effective appearance by Jean Harlow, just before she made *Red Dust*. Brabin started work on *Rasputin and the Express* (GB: *Rasputin – The Mad Monk)*, with the three Barrymores, in 1933, but was again sacked, this time by Irving Thalberg, and replaced by Richard Boleslawski (*qv*). Shortly afterwards, Brabin left Hollywood and moved to New York – and out of the film business.

1912: *The Awakening of John Bond. *A Soldier's Duty. *The Unsullied Shell. 1913: *The Flood Tide. The Man Who Disappeared (serial). 1914: *The Best Man. *The Birth of Our Saviour. *The King's Move in the City. *The Letter That Never Came Out. *The Long Way. *The Midnight Ride of Paul Revere. The Man in the Street. *The President's Special. *The Price of the Necklace. *A Question of Identity. 1915: *An Invitation and an Attack. *The Stoning. The Raven. The House of the Lost Court. 1916: *The Price of Fame. *The Regeneration of Margaret. That Sort (GB: That Sort of Girl). 1917: Red, White and Blue Blood. The Secret Kingdom (serial). Mary Jane's Pa. The Sixteenth Wife. Babette. Persuasive Peggy. The Adopted Son. 1918: Breakers Ahead. Social Quicksands. A Pair of Cupids. Buchanan's Wife. The Poor Rich Man. His Bonded Wife. La Belle Russe. 1919: Kathleen Mavoureen. Thou Shalt Not. 1920: While New York Sleeps. Blind Wives. 1921: Footfalls. 1922: The Broadway Peacock. The Lights of New York. 1923: Driven. Six Days. 1925: So Big. Stella Maris. 1926: Twinkletoes. 1927: Mismates. 1927: Hard-Boiled Haggerty. Framed. The Valley of the Giants. 1928: The Whip. 1929: The Bridge of San Luis Rey. 1930: Ship from Shanghai. The Call of the Flesh. 1931: The Great Meadow. Sporting Blood. 1932: New Morals for Old. The Beast of the City. Washington Masquerade (GB: Mad Masquerade). The Mask of Fu Manchu. 1933: The Secret of Madame Blanche. Stage Mother. Day of Reckoning. 1934: A Wicked Woman.*

BRAHM, John (Hans Brahm) 1893-1982

German-born director who worked in the theatre for nearly 20 years before trying his hand at films. After an initial venture in Britain, Brahm went to Hollywood where he became an efficient director of a variety of routine mid-budget films until

1944/45, when he made two splendid gaslight thrillers, *The Lodger* and *Hangover Square*. Both of these featured the immense Laird Cregar looming out of the fog to menace pretty turn-of-the-century maidens, and were full of atmosphere and a sense of imminent danger. Unfortunately, and most surprisingly, Brahm failed to make anything else that was really worthwhile in the rest of his career. The best of the catalogue are the unfairly dismissed *The Miracle of Our Lady of Fatima*, which peddles quietly effective religious sentiment and is beautifully photographed in subdued colours by Edwin DuPar, and *A Death of Princes*, featuring Eli Wallach, a hard-edged crime piece originally part of television's *The Naked City*, series, but shown in cinemas outside the United States. From the mid-1950s, Brahm worked almost entirely in television, mainly on suspense thriller material, but never again finding his earlier inspiration. He married the German actress Dolly Haas, who starred in his first film, *Broken Blossoms*, which was made in Britain.

1936: Broken Blossoms. 1937: Counsel for Crime. 1938: Girls' School. Penitentiary. 1939: Let Us Live. Rio. 1940: Submarine Zone. 1941: Wild Geese Calling. 1942: The Undying Monster (GB: The Hammond Mystery). 1943: Tonight We Raid Calais. Wintertime. 1944: Guest in the House. The Lodger. 1945: Hangover Square. 1946: The Locket. 1947: The Brasher Doubloon (GB: The High Window). Singapore. 1950: The Thief of Venice (released 1953). 1952: †Face to Face. A Star Shall Rise. The Miracle of Our Lady of Fatima (GB: The Miracle of Fatima). 1953: The Diamond Queen. 1954: The Mad Magician. 1955: Bengazi. Special Delivery/Von Himmel gefallen. Die goldene Pest. Laura (TV GB: cinemas). 1957: So Soon to Die (TV). 1960: A Death of Princes (TV. GB: cinemas). The Hero (TV). 1964: Hot Rods to Hell/52 Miles to Terror (released 1967).

BRENON, Herbert C. 1880-1958

Brenon loved working in Hollywood silents and, although his rapturous visual sense should have enabled him to adapt perfectly well to talking pictures, the will within him to make great films seems to have died with the silent era. He was born in Dublin, Ireland, but had found his way to America before the turn of the century where, after a brief acting career with stock companies, he became a script man with the infant Imp company in New York. Once begun, Brenon's career as a director skyrocketed. Although the material he chose was usually proven in some

source or another, it did not always look sure-fire box-office until Brenon got hold of it. Critics and public soon began to refer to 'the Brenon touch' as they would later to 'the Lubitsch touch', although the two men's styles were very different and Brenon shied away from comedy. Among his many successes were early versions of *The Kreutzer Sonata, Ivanhoe, The Passing of the Third Floor Back, Peter Pan, Beau Geste, The Great Gatsby*) and *Sorrell and Son*, each showing that he knew how to milk an important scene for its maximum impact without asking for more than it would give. He also directed Nazimova in *War Brides* and Lon Chaney (Senior) in *Laugh, Clown, Laugh*, two of his best and most profitable pictures. Brenon did not relish the sound revolution, and only grudgingly began making talkies in the early 1930s when it was evident that they had come to stay. It was soon apparent that he was no longer the same force, and, in 1935, he went to England (where he had been happy filming on previous occasions) and made several middle-range pictures there before retiring at 60. He was nominated for the first directorial Academy Award in 1928 for *Sorrell and Son*.

1912: †All for Her. The Clown's Triumph. Leah the Forsaken. The Long Strike. The Nurse. 1913: Ivanhoe. Kathleen Mavourneen. The Angel of Death. The Anarchist. Absinthe. Time is Money. 1914: The Secret of the Air (US: Across the Atlantic). Neptune's Daughter. 1915: The Two Orphans. The Soul of Broadway. Sin. The Kreutzer Sonata. The Heart of Maryland. Whom the Gods Would Destroy. The Clemenceau Case. 1916: The Bigamist. War Brides. A Daughter of the Gods. The Marble Heart. The Ruling Passion. The Governor's Decision. *Bubbles. Love, or an Empire. The Missing Witness. *The Voice Upstairs. 1917: The Eternal Sin/Lucretia Borgia. The Lone Wolf. Empty Pockets. The Fall of the Romanoffs. 1918: The Passing of the Third Floor Back. Victory and Peace (US: The Invasion of Britain). 1919: 12.10. La principessa misteriosa. A Sinless Sinner. 1920: Chains of Evidence. Beatrice. Sorella contro sorella (US: Sister Against Sister). 1921: The Passion Flower. The Sign on the Door. The Wonderful Thing. 1922: A Stage Romance. Moonshine Valley. Any Wife. Shackles of Gold. 1923: The Spanish Dancer. The Custard Cup. The Rustle of Silk. The Woman with Four Faces. 1924: The Side Show of Life. Shadows of Paris. The Breaking Point. Peter Pan. The Alaskan. 1925: Street of Forgotten Men. The Little French Girl. 1926: A Kiss for Cinderella. The Great Gatsby. The Song* *and Dance Man. Dancing Mothers. God Gave Me Twenty Cents. Beau Geste. 1927: The Telephone Girl. Sorrell and Son. 1928: Laugh, Clown, Laugh. 1929: The Rescue. 1930: The Case of Sergeant Grischa. Lummox. 1931: Beau Ideal. Transgression. 1932: Girl of the Rio (GB: The Dove). 1933: Wine, Women and Song. 1935: †Royal Cavalcade (US: Regal Cavalcade). Honours Easy. 1936: Living Dangerously. Someone at the Door. 1937: The Dominant Sex. The Spring Handicap. The Live Wire. 1938: Housemaster. Yellow Sands. 1939: Black Eyes. The Flying Squad.*

BRANAGH, Kenneth 1960-

Belfast-born actor-director long resident in England who has followed Sir Laurence Olivier's footsteps in attempting to bring Shakespeare to the masses, Although Shakespeare's leading characters have more down-to-earth qualities under Branagh's control, his films, with the exception of *Mary Shelley's Frankenstein*, have yet to break out of the art house circuit. On the other hand, Branagh himself, sometimes uneasily cast in his own movies, would, one feels, be well at home with the regional ribaldry of such films as *The Full Monty*. Disillusioned with the Royal Shakespeare Company, whose atmosphere he felt 'resembled the self-obsessed world of drama school at its worst,' Branagh formed the Renaissance Theatre Company, and quickly made himself a reputation with innovative Shakespeare adaptations that were often directed by well-known actors. His first attempt to put the Bard on screen, *Henry V,* won him Oscar nominations as actor and director. Although it does not compare with Olivier's 1944 version, its battle scene is staged with pace and imagination by the director who also offers a delightful coda featuring Henry's courtship of the French princess, played by Emma Thompson, who would become his wife from 1989 to 1995. *Dead Again* was a disastrously overheated attempt to mimic the Hitchcock-style Hollywood thriller, but Branagh was on safer ground with *Peter's Friends,* the story of a reunion of university friends, which has a delightful and funny first half before dramatically going rather too far over the top. One wonders, in fact, whether Branagh's forte may be comedy, as it's the comic elements in his other Shakespearian jaunts, *Much Ado About Nothing* and *Hamlet*, that work the best. That said, his adaptation of *Mary Shelley's Frankenstein* was, apart from his own miscasting as Frankenstein, an impressive piece of work, with some vivid set-pieces and stunningly stylish

moments that suggest Branagh may rely less on Shakespeare's inspiration in the years to come.

*1989: Henry V. 1991: Dead Again. 1992: Peter's Friends. *Swan Song. 1993: Much Ado About Nothing. 1994: Mary Shelley's Frankenstein. 1995: In the Bleak Midwinter. 1996: Hamlet.*

BRESSON, Robert 1907-

Despite the paucity of his output – only 14 films in 50 years – critics feel impelled to write reams about Bresson. Pages, indeed, where well-known Hollywood professionals might rate only half a column. The middle-of-the-road cinemagoer may well be baffled by all this, yet Bresson is not an easy director to define and most writers have obviously found it difficult to convey plainly their enthusiasm for his work in less than a few thousand words. Certainly his three 1950s' films are very fine, in their different ways. The quality of the rest of his work is more open to debate. Born in central France, he began his working life as a painter, then photographer in Paris. Truffaut has said that Bresson's subsequent work as a film director is closer to painting than photography, and this is probably true, especially in his fastidious but fascinating attention to detail, by which the viewer has a complete picture of character and situation built up without realising it. As Bresson himself puts it: 'Each shot means nothing by itself . . . but is given its meaning by its context'. His very special, timeless style was not really evident until 1943, although he had made one 45-minute film, and written or collaborated on several screenplays before World War II. The five films he made from this date are; generally accepted as being the *crème de la crème*, with opinions on the director's masterwork being equally divided between *Diary of a Country Priest* and *Pickpocket*. Personally I prefer the film which Bresson made in between these two – *A Man Escaped* – if only because it succeeds on every level. Based on a sensational escape by a Frenchman from an impregnable Gestapo fortress only hours before he was due to be executed in 1943, and on Bresson's own experience of imprisonment by the Germans during World War II, it is a suspenseful, intricately worked out and totally absorbing story which keeps the viewer glued to the screen every second of the way, right down to the moment when two of the escapers gradually vanish from sight behind the smoke of a steam engine puffing its way across a bridge. *Pickpocket,* if less successful commercially, also compels

total belief, although about life on the other side of the tracks, culminating in the memorable sun-shafted railroad scene where a pride of pickpockets hurry and scurry about their nefarious business with deadly precision. Although Bresson has remained his own man and his films have stayed unmissable, he has not quite recaptured these formidable highpoints of a distinguished career.

1934: Les affaires publiques. 1943: Les anges du péché (US: Angels of the Street). 1945: Les dames du Bois de Boulogne (US: Ladies of the Park). 1950: Journal d'un curé de campagne (GB & US: Diary of a Country Priest). 1956: Un condamné à mort s'est échappé (GB & US: A Man Escaped). 1959: Pickpocket. 1962: Procès de Jeanne d'Arc (GB & US: The Trial of Joan of Arc). 1966: Au hasard, Balthazar (GB & US: Balthazar). 1967: Mouchette. 1969: Une femme douce (GB & US: A Gentle Creature). 1971: Quatre nuits d'un rêveur (GB & US: Four Nights of a Dreamer). 1974: Lancelot-du-Lac. 1977: Le diable probablement (GB & US: The Devil, Probably). 1983: L'argent.

BRETHERTON, Howard
See Keighley, William

BREST, Martin 1951-

Despite a successful career in critical and box-office terms, this Bronx-born American director has hardly played fair by his fans by making only five mainstream films in 22 years – paltry rations even by modern standards. His several cameo appearances as an actor have hardly provided compensation. Brest's films tend to be modern-day urban thrillers with comedic elements. The first he directed for a studio, *Going in Style*, also has the most humour. Not surprising, as George Burns, Art Carney and Lee Strasberg are in fine form as the trio of old stagers who decide to carry out a bank robbery to relieve their boredom. After getting himself sacked from *WarGames* following disagreements with the producers, Brest delivered the perfect answer with the worldwide Eddie Murphy hit *Beverly Hills Cop*. And the combination of mirth and mayhem was repeated (albeit four years later) in *Midnight Run*, an extremely engaging and stylishly directed account of a bounty hunter's attempt to bring a wily embezzler back to face justice, in the face of opposition from several dangerous factions, not least of them the law. One might have expected Brest to work prodigiously in similar vein through the late 1980s and 1990s, but there have been only two films since. *Scent of a Woman*, a rather overblown version of a French success, but with some charming individual sequences, saw Al Pacino win an acting Oscar after several unsuccessful tries, and Brest nominated as best director. An even longer gap – six years – followed before *Meet Joe Black*, still in the thriller vein, but with a Satanic slant. No chance of this entry not being up to date; at this rate another Brest isn't due along until 2005: almost like waiting for Halley's Comet.

1974: *Hot Dogs for Gauguin. 1977: Hot Tomorrows. 1979: Going in Style. 1984: Beverly Hills Cop. 1988: Midnight Run. 1992: Scent of a Woman. 1998: Meet Joe Black.*

BRIDGES, James 1931-1993

Actor, writer and director, Bridges only managed to make eight films in his 19-year career, most of which failed to live up to their initial publicity promise. However, all of them have their supporters, especially *The China Syndrome*. Further opportunities for Bridges were cut short by his early death from intestinal cancer. Born in America's mid-west, he had laboured as an actor for many years, making his screen debut in *Johnny Trouble* (1957) and working all the while on his secondary career as a writer: he subsequently wrote, or had a hand in, most of the screenplays for his films. He was nearly 40 before he got to direct a film of his own, but it was worth waiting for. *The Baby Maker*, about a free-living girl who agrees to have a baby by the husband of a childless couple because the wife is barren, is warm, vibrant, amusingly well-observed and of great emotional appeal. It also contains Barbara Hershey's most glowing performance in the leading role, one of the very few times one has been really able to warm to one of her characters on screen. It's noticeable that Bridges has been particularly successful with actresses: no surprise, perhaps, that Jane Fonda is so good in *The China Syndrome*, an otherwise less-than-believable pot-boiler, but then Debra Winger, whose previous experience had largely been in exploitation pictures, turned out to be easily the most memorable thing in the otherwise flaccid *Urban Cowboy*. The pattern was repeated in *Perfect* (Jamie Lee Curtis) and *Bright Lights, Big City* (Dianne Wiest). Neither film was of much note apart from this, and they were to prove the last Bridges would make.

1970: *The Baby Maker. 1973: The Paper Chase. 1977: 9-30-55 (GB: TV, as September 30, 1955). 1978: The China Syndrome. 1980: Urban Cowboy. 1982: Mike's Murder (released 1984). 1985; Perfect. 1988: Bright Lights, Big City.*

BROOKS, Albert (A. Einstein) 1947-

Brooks the director, like Brooks the actor (and the two often go together), makes amusing and inventive little comedies about the anxieties of modern man that very few people outside his audience of core fans seem willing to pay money to see. Like Woody Allen, whose themes he sometimes parallels, Brooks is usually rewarded only by decent critical reviews. Like his sweating newsman in *Broadcast News*, he has never quite moved into the big time. But then his own mixture of humour and social comment was practically guaranteed not to have mass appeal. Nonetheless, there is much gentle amusement to be had from Brooks' work, mostly scripted by himself even if it all too often, and especially in the case of *Mother*, a series of fine phrases in search of a film. Engaging and inoffensive, his films only occasionally have enough bite to attract a wider audience. Still, in 1995, Brooks was honoured with a retrospective of his work by the American Film Institute, at the US Comedy Arts Festival and will doubtless continue to encourage us to smile at characters in which we will inevitably find bits of ourselves.

1979: *Real Life/Real People. 1981: Modern Romance. 1985: Lost in America. 1991: Defending Your Life. 1996: Mother. 1999: The Muse.*

BROOKS, James L. 1940-

Brooks' success with the few films he has

Putting it on the air. Director James L **Brooks** making *Broadcast News*.

directed has tended to obscure the greater part of his career as a hugely successful writer-producer of hit TV series. After beginnings as a TV newswriter, the New Jersey-born Brooks moved to Los Angeles where he created and/or produced a whole string of popular shows, including *Room 222, The Mary Tyler Moore Show, The Associates* and *Cheers*. He was 43 before he found time to make his first film, *Terms of Endearment*. Despite one critic describing it as an 'outsize sitcom', this story of an embattled and somewhat eccentric mother and daughter won several Oscars, including best director for Brooks and best picture. There were

Mel **Brooks** calls for a moment of madness during the making of *High Anxiety*.

more Oscar nominations (although this time no awards) for the next, *Broadcast News*, which, like *Terms*, was written and directed by Brooks, but this time reflecting his own beginnings in show business. A sharp starter, the film loses its way in the latter stages, developing into a sort of romantic mini-series with no like-able characters, although Jack Nicholson, who has appeared in three of the four Brooks films to date, steals the show as a shark of the news room. Nicholson was absent (fortunately for him) from *I'll Do Anything*, a survey of a single-parent actor father torn, between showbiz ambitions and caring for his young daughter. This started as a musical but, even with the songs deleted, no audience could be found for it. Brooks returned to critical approval (and Nicholson) three years later with *As Good As It Gets*.

1983: Terms of Endearment. 1987: Broadcast News. 1994: I'll Do Anything. 1997: As Good As It Gets.

BROOKS, Mel (Melvin Kaminsky) 1926 -

The nice thing about Mel Brooks is that, however crude and vulgar his hit-and-miss comedies become, he always *looks* (being his own star performer) as if he is having a wonderful time. This enthusiasm is his greatest asset as a comic actor, as finesse is not exactly his strong suit, either before or behind the camera. His comedy is the comedy of outrage – musical numbers built around Hitler's Germany or the Spanish Inquisition, streams of four-letter words in ancient Rome. The majority of his jokes concern bodily functions and whole sequences are likely to be constructed around single punchlines. Starting his career as a stand-up comic, Brooks soon switched to writing (first film as writer: *New Faces in* 1954) and finally direction. His appearance on the film scene in the late 1960s was like a breath of fresh air (Brooks himself would probably prefer to describe it as an injection of foul wind) in in industry beginning to tire of Jerry Lewis and not yet in tune with Woody Allen. *The Producers* was a hit with the critics, but it would be six years before Brooks conquered the world's box-offices with *Blazing Saddles*, bringing to the screen a unique blend of hit-and-miss coarseness and zaniness. He followed up rapidly with *Young Frankenstein* (craftily shot in black and white) which contains the best scene in any Brooks film: the uproarious encounter between the Frankenstein creature (Peter Boyle) and the blind hermit (an unbilled Gene Hackman). Since then his films have not reached the heights of which Brooks, at least as a writer, has shown himself capable and, with *History*

of the World Part I, tailed dismally down to, and below the sledgehammer level of the worst of the *Carry On* films. As a director, Brooks stages his larks well, but shows little idea of camera movement. And one regrets that he has not indulged more in the visual sense of humour that can produce great belly laughs in the midst of otherwise barren sequences. He has long been married to actress Anne Bancroft, who co-starred with him in the 1983 remake of *To Be Or Not to Be* (which he didn't direct) and played a cameo role in one of his most recent costume romps, *Dracula: Dead and Loving it*. His films continue to amuse intermittently, but have not looked like regaining the consistency of his earlier work.

1967: The Producers. 1970: The Twelve Chairs. 1974: Blazing Saddles. Young Frankenstein. 1976: Silent Movie. 1977: High Anxiety. 1981: History of the World Part I. 1987: Spaceballs. 1991: Life Stinks. 1993: Robin Hood: Men in Tights. 1995: Dracula: Dead and Loving It.

BROOKS, Richard 1912-1992

American writer-director who so consistently mixed the good with the mediocre that it became quite impossible to know what to expect from him next. After beginning his career as a sports reporter (and later commentator), Brooks worked regularly as a Hollywood screenwriter (working on novels in his spare time) from 1942 until 1950. One of his books, *The Brick Foxhole* was, although drastically restructured, made memorably into *Crossfire*. Brooks' first experience of directing one of his own screenplays, *Crisis*, was achieved through the influence of the star of the film, Cary Grant. It did not provide him with an auspicious start to a directorial career, and the most enjoyable of his early films are *Take the High Ground*, flag waving but well-made and highly entertaining stuff about the training of US Infantry recruits, and *Deadline USA*, a newspaper story which benefits from a realistic atmosphere and the strength of its leading players, Humphrey Bogart, Kim Hunter and Ethel Barrymore. With *Blackboard Jungle*, an uncompromising look at teenage violence in schools, Brooks became one of the front-rank Hollywood directors. As he went on, the harder his films hit, the more successful they were; and the gentler they were, the less effective. Thus, the Brooks films which have the greatest impact after 1955 are *Something of Value*, *Cat on a Hot Tin Roof*, *Elmer Gantry* (which won him an Academy Award for screenplay), *Sweet Bird of Youth*, *In Cold Blood* and *The*

Richard **Brooks** welcomes author Truman Capote to the set of *In Cold Blood*, based on Capote's best-selling book.

Happy Ending. But there were exceptions either way in the later 1970s, firstly with *Bite the Bullet*, a nostalgically constructed look at a marathon horse-riding contest in the old West, and then the disastrously overheated *Looking for Mr Goodbar*, which is redeemed only by the brilliant performance of Diane Keaton in the leading role. These two films probably show nothing more than that Brooks had mellowed with age, but remained unpredictable to the end. His second wife (from 1961) was the actress Jean Simmons. The marriage broke up in 1977. He died from congestive heart failure.

1950: Crisis. 1951: The Light Touch. 1952: Battle Circus. Deadline USA (GB: Deadline). 1953: Take the High Ground. 1954: Flame and the Flesh. The Last Time I Saw Paris. 1955: Blackboard Jungle. 1956: The Catered Affair (GB: Wedding Breakfast). 1957: Something of Value. 1958: The Brothers Karamazov. Cat on a Hot Tin Roof. 1960: Elmer Gantry. 1962: Sweet Bird of Youth. 1964: Lord Jim. 1966: The Professionals. 1967: In Cold Blood. 1969: The Happy Ending. 1971: $ (GB: The Heist). 1975: Bite the Bullet. 1977: Looking for Mr Goodbar. 1982: Wrong is Right (GB: The Man with the Deadly Lens). 1985: Fever Pitch.

BROWN, Clarence 1890-1987

Although this American director is not one about whom books have been written, he was one of the top men behind the camera at M-G-M for 25 years. His sense of pictorial composition, gained during his long apprenticeship as assistant director with the distinguished Maurice Tourneur, elevated many a tear-drenched epic into a gentle classic of the screen. This discreet but sure touch earned him the reputation of being a woman's director. He worked five times with Joan Crawford, but the actress with whom he is most associated is Greta Garbo. Who can say how much of the impact of his seven Garbo films, *Flesh and the Devil, A Woman of Affairs, Anna Christie, Romance, Inspiration, Anna Karenina* and *Conquest*, is owed to their director? From international romantic sagas, Brown gradually turned his career to Americana, with films which occasionally had something to say about simple, straightforward values and which could be heightened by his assured use of striking visuals. These powerfully persuasive pieces of entertainment include *Ah! Wilderness, Of Human Hearts, The Human Comedy, The Yearling* and *Intruder in the Dust*. One or two of these later films, especially The *Yearling* and *National Velvet*, are notable for their rich use of the early Technicolor process to create atmospheres that glow with warmth and a surface realism thick enough to be penetrated only by the truly cynical. After *Intruder,* the only one of Brown's last films to be reckoned as very much is *Plymouth Adventure*, making a disappointing post-war ending to a truly professional career. He had been trained as an engineer, working for some years in the car industry before trying to break into films, first as a humble general assistant, but later as editor, title writer and assistant director. From 1930, he was six times nominated for an Academy Award without winning. He died from kidney failure.

1919: †The County Fair. 1920: †The Last of the Mohicans. The Great Redeemer. 1921: †The Foolish Matrons (GB: Is Marriage a Failure?). 1922: The Light in the Dark. 1923: Don't Marry for Money. The Acquittal. 1924: Butterfly. Smouldering Fires. The Signal Tower. 1925: The Goose Woman. The Eagle. 1926: Kiki. 1927: Flesh and the Devil. 1928: †The Cossacks (uncredited). A Woman of Affairs. The Trail of '98. 1929: Navy Blues. Wonder of Women. 1930: Romance. Anna Christie. 1931: A Free Soul. Inspiration. †This Modern Age (uncredited). Possessed. 1932: The Son-Daughter. Letty Lynton. 1933: Looking Forward (GB: Service). Night Flight. 1934: Sadie McKee. Chained. 1935: Ah! Wilderness. Anna Karenina. 1936: Wife Vs. Secretary. The Gorgeous Hussy. 1937: Conquest (GB: Marie Walewska). 1978: Of Human Hearts. 1939: Idiot's Delight. The Rains Came. 1940: Edison, the Man. 1941: Come Live With Me. They Met in Bombay. 1943: The Human Comedy. 1944:

National Velvet. The White Cliffs of Dover. 1946: The Yearling. 1947: Song of Love. 1949: Intruder in the Dust. 1950: To Please a Lady. 1951: †It's a Big Country (episode deleted from print issued outside United States). Angels in the Outfield (GB: Angels and the Pirates). 1952: When in Rome. Plymouth Adventure.

BROWNING, Tod (Charles Browning) 1880-1962
Browning was a child of the night – and what music he made in a twilight world between living and dying, fear and terror. This American director who would become an acknowledged master of the grotesque and macabre, a Bosch in black and white, was born in Kentucky and ran away from home at 16. He joined carnivals, sideshows and riverboats, where he would raise gullible gooseflesh in a variety of ingenious disguises, as a 'living corpse' or a 'lizard-man'. Later, he entered vaudeville as a contortionist. A lifetime insomniac, Browning disliked the daylight hours and open spaces and cannot have been happy making the westerns with which he started his directorial career after entering films as an actor in 1913. Having met Lon Chaney in 1919, the master of deformity known as 'the man with 1,000 faces', Browning entered into his own kingdom of darkness, a world of massive drapes and shadowed stairways and corridors, where rats and bats scuttled and

squeaked as the only creatures to disturb centuries-old cobwebs. Browning and Chaney made ten films together before Chaney's death in 1930, in most of which misshapen beings were up to nefarious deeds in life's darker corners. Notable among these remarkably dark chillers were *The Blackbird, The Unholy Three, The Unknown* and *West of Zanzibar*. After Chaney's death from cancer of the throat, Browning might have been forgiven for a lapse into the alcoholism which he had conquered in the early 1920s. Instead, even without his great star, he went on make two classics of the horror film – *Dracula*, with its magnificently chilling scene-setting first reel, and *Freaks*, a story of wronged circus freaks taking grisly revenge on 'normal' people, which was banned for 30 years outside America. Two other mid-1930s films, *Mark of the Vampire*, full of rust and rot and without a trace of tongue in cheek, and *The Devil-Doll*, with its miniature murderers, in which Lionel Barrymore plays a part that might well have been written for Lon Chaney, both have splendid sequences. The last years at M-G-M were frustrating ones for Browning and, after failing to persuade the studio to buy the rights of *They Shoot Horses Don't They?* for him to film (it would be memorably made – and a box-office success – 25 years later) he retired to Malibu. In his eighties, he learned that he had cancer of the throat,

Director Tod **Browning** (in beret) and cinematographer James Wong Howe go for a sinister set-up with Bela Lugosi and Carol Borland on *Mark of the Vampire*.

the condition which killed Chaney, although ultimately he died from a stroke.

*1915: *The Lucky Transfer. *The Living Death. *The Highbinders. *The Burned Hand. *The Slave Girl. *An Image of the Past. *The Story of a Story. *The Spell of the Poppy. *The Electric Alarm. *The Woman from Warren's. *Little Marie. 1916: *The Fatal Glass of Beer. *Everybody's Doing It. *Puppets. 1917: †Jim Bludso. †A Love Sublime. †Hands Up! The Jury of Fate. Peggy, the Will o' th' Wisp. 1918: The Legion of Death. Which Woman? Revenge. The Deciding Kiss. The Eyes of Mystery. The Brazen Beauty. Set Free. 1919: The Unpainted Woman. The Wicked Darling. The Exquisite Thief. Bonnie, Bonnie Lassie. A Petal on the Current. 1920: The Virgin of Stamboul. 1921: Outside the Law. No Woman Knows. 1922: Under Two Flags. The Wise Kid. The Man Under Cover. 1923: The Day of Faith. Drifting. White Tiger. 1924: The Dangerous Flirt (GB: A Dangerous Flirtation). Silk Stocking Sal. 1925: Dollar Down. The Mystic. The Unholy Three. 1926: The Blackbird. The Road to Mandalay. 1927: The Unknown. The Show. London After Midnight (GB: The Hypnotist). 1928: The Big City. West of Zanzibar. 1929: Where East is East. The Thirteenth Chair. 1930: Outside the Law (remake). Dracula. 1931: The Iron Man. 1932: Freaks. 1933: Fast Workers. 1935: Mark of the Vampire. 1936: The Devil-Doll. 1939: Miracles for Sale.*

BRUCKMAN, Clyde 1894-1955

Seldom can one man have worked with so many of the great Hollywood comedians as this writer-director from California. Bruckman directed Buster Keaton, Laurel and Hardy, Harold Lloyd and W.C. Fields, and wrote stories and scripts for Lloyd, Keaton, Leon Errol, Andy Clyde and The Three Stooges. A journalist by profession, he came to Hollywood in 1919, providing gags and story ideas for any number of two-reelers. In 1923, he met Buster Keaton and started a profitable association which led to collaboration on the scenarios for most of Keaton's best silent comedies, including *Our Hospitality, Sherlock Junior, The Navigator, Seven Chances* and *The Cameraman*. In 1926, Bruckman and Keaton made *The General* together, with Bruckman co-writing and co-directing. He went on to make some of Laurel and Hardy's most uproarious and best constructed silent shorts, including *The Battle of the Century, Leave 'Em Laughing* and *The Finishing Touch*. Harold Lloyd saw Bruckman's work and put him in charge of three classic Lloyd comedies, *Welcome Danger, Feet First* and *Movie Crazy*. Bruckman was also involved in Lloyd's last 1930s' feature, *Professor, Beware!* He concentrated on writing from 1935, but, by the end of the decade, his kind of movie comedy had gone underground. The comic geniuses with whom he had worked had all passed their peak and Bruckman spent most of his remaining years writing for Columbia two-reelers, chiefly those featuring The Three Stooges. He was still working on them by the mid-1950s, but behind the laughlines there lurked despair. In 1944, Bruckman had returned to writing features with Universal, perhaps thinking of working with Olsen and Johnson. But his script for *Her Lucky Night* (1945) was so much like his work for Harold Lloyd that Lloyd sued Universal successfully on a charge of plagiarism. Bruckman never wrote for another feature film. One day in 1955 Bruckman, beset by alcohol and marital problems and disillusioned with his career, went into a restaurant, ordered and ate a sumptuous meal, downed his coffee and brandy, pulled out a revolver and shot himself.

*1926: †The General. 1927: A Perfect Gentleman. Horse Shoes. *Love 'Em and Feed 'Em. *Call of the Cuckoo. *Putting Pants on Philip. *The Battle of the Century. 1928: *The Finishing Touch. *Leave 'Em Laughing. 1929: Welcome Danger. 1930: Feet First. 1931: Everything's Rosie. 1932: Movie Crazy. 1933: *The Fatal Glass of Beer. *Too Many Highballs. *The Human Fish. 1934: *Horses' Collars. 1935: Spring Tonic. The Man on the Flying Trapeze (GB: The Memory Expert).*

BRUNEL, Adrian 1892-1958

British director who, although he displayed a talent both for satire and sensitive romantic drama, was handed few important assignments in the British cinema. It has been suggested that Brunel upset the powers-that-be around 1930, while directing *Elstree Calling*; certainly he spent three years in the wilderness after that and was only given minor films until giving up direction after 1940. He had started as a singer, then actor, before becoming interested in direction and forming Minerva Films with the young Leslie Howard. Under the Minerva banner, Brunel made a fistful of satirical shorts (Howard making early screen appearances in a couple of them) between 1920 and 1926. When asked to work on inferior material from 1933, Brunel's work shows the same enthusiasm but little of his talent gleams through the dross, the best of these films being *Badger's Green*. After quitting direction, Brunel worked again with Howard (as production consultant) on *The First of the Few* (US: *Spitfire*) and *The Gentle Sex*, before joining the film department of the Ministry of Information. After World War II, he concentrated on writing books, including *Nice Work*, an amusing collection of reminiscences about his film career.

*1917: The Cost of a Kiss. 1920: *The Bump. *Five Pounds Reward. *Bookworms. *Twice Two. 1921: The Temporary Lady. *Too Many Cooks. 1922: *Sheer Trickery. 1923: *The Shimmy Sheik. *Yes, We Have No - - - -. *Two-Chinned Chow. *Moors and Minarets. *Lovers in Araby. The Man without Desire. 1924: *Crossing the Great Sagrada. *The Pathetic Gazette. *The Boy Goes to Biska. 1925: *Battling Bruisers. *So This Is Jollygood. *Cut It Out. *The Blunderland of Big Game. *A Typical Budget. 1926: *Money for Nothing. Love, Life and Laughter at Swaythling Court. 1927: Blighty. The Vortex. 1928: The Constant Nymph. A Light Woman (US: Dolores). 1929: *In a Monastery Garden. The Crooked Billet. 1930. †Elstree Calling. 1933: Taxi to Paradise. I'm an Explosive. Follow the Lady. The Laughter of Fools. Two Wives for Henry. Little Napoleon. 1934: Important People. Badger's Green. Menace (US: While London Sleeps). Variety. The City of Beautiful Nonsense. 1935: Vanity. Cross Currents. While Parents Sleep. 1936: Prison Breaker. Love at Sea. The Invader (US: An Old Spanish Custom). 1938: †The Rebel Son/Taras Bulba (uncredited). 1939: The Lion Has Wings. The Girl Who Forgot. 1940: *Food for Thought. *Salvage with a Smile.*

BUCQUET, Harold S. 1891-1946

Genial British director who, after stage experience in his native London first as stage manager, then producer of plays, went to America in 1934, and worked for Metro-Goldwyn-Mayer for the rest of his life. He had begun as an actor, and did time as an extra when he first left Britain for America. From 1935, he was attached to Metro's short subjects unit, and directed several interesting two-reelers, including several in the 'Crime Does Not Pay' series. He will be remembered though, from his feature film period, which began in 1938, as the man, who made a great many of the Dr Kildare and Dr Gillespie films; in fact nine of the first ten in the series, which proved so popular from 1938 to 1944, were well crafted in Bucquet's hands with little corner-cutting, and proved a valuable training ground for sev-

"Please don't touch the set..." director Luis **Bunuel** lays down the law.

eral of the studio's most promising young stars-to-be. Bucquet then returned to his native Britain to direct Robert Donat in the mildly successful *The Adventures of Tartu*. On his return to M-G-M's Culver City headquarters, Bucquet co-directed the striking *Dragon Seed* with Katherine Hepburn, and then piloted her again, with Spencer Tracy, in *Without Love*. Bucquet was developing into one of the studio's most reliable directors, and there were signs that his straightforward visual style was taking on interesting touches of sophistication, but he died in February 1946 at 54.

1935: *Windy. *Little People. 1937: *It May Happen to You. *Soak the Poor. *Behind the Criminal. *Torture Money. 1938: *What Price Safety? *Come Across. *They're Always Caught. Young Doctor Kildare. 1939: Calling Dr Kildare. On Borrowed Time. The Secret of Dr Kildare. 1940: We Who Are Young. Dr Kildare's Strange Case. Dr Kildare Goes Home. Dr Kildare's Crisis. 1941: The Penalty. The People Vs Dr Kildare (GB: My Life is Yours). Dr Kildare's Wedding Day (GB: Mary Names the Day). Kathleen. 1942: Calling Dr Gillespie. The War Against Mrs Hadley. 1943: The Adventures of Tartu (US: Tartu). 1944: †Dragon Seed. 1945: Without Love.

BUÑUEL, Luis (L.B. Portolès) 1900-1983

Spain's greatest director, Buñuel has said that a religious education and Surrealism marked him for life. Throughout the turbulent years of his long career, his prime target remained the church, and Surrealism the weapon of his satire. He met the artist Salvador Dali while both were at Madrid University and, after Buñuel had worked as assistant director on several Spanish silent films (including a version of *The Fall of the House of Usher*), the two men collaborated on the shockingly memorable symbolism of *Un chien andalou* and *L'âge d'or*, films whose unique and sometimes horrifying images shook but made an indelible impression on the bastions of world cinema. After one more film, the surrealistically tinged *Las hurdes*, a pity-provoking account of the poverty of peasant life, Buñuel was amazingly not to make another major film for nearly 20 years – an appalling waste of talent in the richest years of its development. Fortunately, he re-emerged at the top in 1950 with *Los Olvidados*, but the regret remains, for by this time Buñuel was 50. The wasted years were spent in fruitless visits to Hollywood and uncredited direction of unimportant films in Spain. Although Buñuel made some haunting films in the early 1950s – most notably *El Bruto and El*, the richest period of his work runs from 1958 to 1970, years in which Buñuel produced a series of shattering works that could almost all claim to be considered masterpieces of the cinema. These superbly made, striking, thought-provoking and extremely literate films included *Nazarín, Viridiana, The Exterminating Angel, Diary of a Chambermaid, Simon of the Desert, Belle de jour* and, most brilliant of all, *Tristana*, in which Catherine Deneuve's hauntingly enigmatic beauty was put to its greatest effect. As the 1960s progressed, there was some dilution of Buñuel's satirical bile; although unmistakably his work, the edges that shot out from the film and bit into their targets were not so sharp. But he did win an Oscar for making the best foreign-language film with *The Discreet Charm of the Bourgeoisie* in 1972. In his 1970s films, Buñuel seemed more fascinated by the cinema itself than interested in erasing the bitter memories of the past.

1928: Un chien andalou (US: An Andalusian Dog). 1930: L'âge d'or (US: The Golden Age). 1932: Las hurdes (GB & US: Land without Bread). 1935: †Don Quintin el Amargo. †La hija de Joan Simón. 1936: †Quién me quiere a mi? †Centinela Alerta! 1937: Madrid 36 (uncredited). 1941: El Vaticano de Pio XII. 1946: Tampico/Gran Casino. 1949: El gran calavera (US: The Great Madcap). 1950: Los olvidados (GB & US: The Young and the Damned). Susanna (GB & US: The Devil and the Flesh). 1951: La hija del engaño (US: Daughter of Deceit). Una muja sin amor. Subida al cielo (US: Mexican Bus Ride). 1952: El bruto. The Adventures of Robinson Crusoe. El (US:

This Strange Passion). 1953: La ilusión viaja en tranvía. Cumbres borrascosas (US: Wuthering Heights). 1954: El rio y la muerte (US: Death and the River). 1955: La vida criminal de Archibaldo de la Cruz (GB & US: The Criminal Life of Archibaldo de la Cruz). Cela s'appelle l'aurore. La muerte en este jardina (GB: Evil Eden. US: Death in the Garden). 1958: Nazarín. 1959: Los Ambiciosos (US: Republic of Sin). 1960: La joven (GB: Island of Shame. US: The Young One). 1961: Viridiana. 1962: El angel exterminador (GB: The Exterminating Angel). 1963: Le journal d'une femme de chambre (GB & US: Diary of a Chambermaid). 1965: Simon del desierto (GB & US: Simon of the Desert). 1967: Belle de jour. 1968. La voie lactée (GB & US: The Milky Way). 1970: Tristana. 1972: Le charme discret de la bourgeoisie (GB & US: The Discreet Charm of the Bourgeoisie). 1974: Le fantôme de la liberté (GB: The Phantom of Liberté. US: The Phantom of Liberty). 1977: Cet obscur objet de désir (GB & US: That Obscure Object of Desire).

BURTON, Tim 1960-

A Hollywood local boy (born in Burbank, California), Burton has made his name in the past 15 years with dark fantasies, putting a comic slant on things that go bump in the night, and creating weird worlds of his own. A teenage cartoonist, he won a Disney fellowship at 18 and began working for the studio on such early 1980s cartoon features as *The Fox and the Hound* and *The Black Cauldron*. Here, his skills as an animator were very swiftly combined with budding directorial talents in his award-winning short *Vincent*. The story of a young boy who wanted to be just like horror star Vincent Price, the film was Burton's homage to his favourite actor and his own childhood fascination with horror movies. Burton's subsequent live-action films all contain cartoon-like elements. *Frankenweenie*, a short about a boy who restores his beloved dog to life, led to Burton's feature debut with *Pee-wee's Big Adventure*, a riot of colour and absurdity and certainly the funniest film puppet-like comedian Paul Reubens ever made. Burton's imagination continued unbridled in *Beetlejuice*, a vivid black comedy about newly-deads and their relationship with a bio-exorciser (a virtuoso role for Michael Keaton). Keaton was rather less at ease in the title role of Burton's next *Batman* and its sequel *Batman Returns*. It was inevitable that Burton would emphasise the Goth in Gotham City, but its dark and forbidding environs were at odds with the original comic franchise which, despite increasing budgets, has never really led to successful cinema in any of its incarnations over a 35-year period. Despite leaving the direction to someone else, Burton's touches were all over the puppet animation film *The Nightmare Before Christmas* (aka *Tim Burton's Nightmare Before Christmas*) but *Ed Wood*, filmed in black and white, was a different kettle of fish. Still, there were plenty of Burton's treasured graveyards in the bizarre story of bad film-maker Ed Wood Jr, which won Martin Landau an Oscar for his portrayal of dying horror star Bela Lugosi, another of Burton's childhood idols. Burton's early years were also reflected in the sci-fi spoof *Mars Attacks*, a lively transference of comic book to screen. Something darker, though, surely beckons: Burton looks set to entertain his fans with walks on the weird side for some time.

1982: *Vincent. 1984: *Frankenweenie. 1985: Pee-wee's Big Adventure. 1988: Beetlejuice. 1989: Batman. 1990: Edward Scissorhands. 1992: Batman Returns. 1994: Ed Wood. 1996: Mars Attacks! 1999: Sleepy Hollow.

BUTLER, David 1894-1979

Although it has become fashionable to deride his work as journeyman middle-of-the-road Hollywood, it is also true that this American director made bright, happy films, many of them (and there *were* a lot of them) with a warm, keen sense of affection for a specific period, and the majority solid box-office hits. His work with Shirley Temple, Bob Hope and Doris Day came when each of these stars was a top box-office attraction and Butler's canny handling of familiar elements helped to keep them there. He had begun as an actor – his first film appearance seems to have been in a 1914 short called *The Death Lock* – and worked consistently for such directors as D. W. Griffith, Tod Browning, John Ford, Fred Butler and King Vidor before turning director himself in 1927. His first big success was the Janet Gaynor/Charles Farrell Depression musical *Sunny Side Up* two years later, and he showed a subsequent talent for fantasy in *Just Imagine*, *A Connecticut Yankee* and *Down to Earth*. In 1934, Butler was introduced to Fox's biggest box-office star: he was 40, she was six. 'To her,' Butler later said of Shirley Temple, 'movies were a wonderful game. She was just playing make-believe.' With him, the child star was always perfectly relaxed on set, and they made a string of huge hits together: *Bright Eyes*, *The Little Colonel*, *The Littlest Rebel* and *Captain January*. Years later, they would combine on her last film, *The Story of Seabiscuit*, but neither could recapture the old magic. Bob

Hope had Butler in the chair for *Caught in the Draft*, *Road to Morocco*, *They Got Me Covered* and *The Princess and the Pirate*. Later, Butler's gleeful sense of fun helped make a successful musical-comedy team out of Dennis Morgan and Jack Carson, in *Two Guys from Milwaukee*, *Two Guys from Texas* and funniest of all, *It's a Great Feeling*, in which Carson plays the studio ham no-one will act with, and Butler comes on as himself and refuses to direct him. Butler stayed with Warners to direct a series of musicals with Doris Day and/or Ray Bolger, mostly caringly made period pieces that made ideal family entertainment. In *Calamity Jane* and *Where's Charley?* respectively, Day and Bolger give their best, most zestful film performances. These films were the last of the typical Butler output and, although *The Command* and *King Richard and the Crusaders* are exciting hokum, he only made a few more films before retirement. Journeyman director he may have been, but if you've gained half the enjoyment from the films of your favourite Continental director as I have had from watching the work of David Butler, you haven't done badly.

1927: High School Hero (GB: Just Lads). 1928: Prep and Pep (GB: Tiger's Son). The News Parade. Win That Girl. 1929: †Masked Emotions. Chasing through Europe. Fox Movietone Follies of 1929 (GB: Movietone Follies of 1929). Sunny Side Up. 1930: Just Imagine. High Society Blues. 1931: Delicious. Business and Pleasure. A Connecticut Yankee (GB: A Connecticut Yankee at King Arthur's Court). 1932: Down to Earth. Handle with Care. 1933: Hold Me Tight. My Weakness. 1934: Have a Heart. Handy Andy. Bottoms Up. Bright Eyes. 1935: The Little Colonel. The Littlest Rebel. Doubting Thomas. 1936: White Fang. Captain January. Pigskin Parade (GB: The Harmony Parade). 1937: You're a Sweetheart. Ali Baba Goes to Town. 1938: Kentucky Moonshine (GB: Three Men and a Girl). Kentucky. Straight, Place and Show (GB: They're Off!) 1939: East Side of Heaven. That's Right, You're Wrong. 1940: You'll Find Out. If I Had My Way. 1941: Playmates. Caught in the Draft. 1942: Road to Morocco. They Got Me Covered. 1943: Thank Your Lucky Stars. 1944: Shine On, Harvest Moon. The Princess and the Pirate. 1945: San Antonio. 1946: The Time, the Place and the Girl. Two Guys from Milwaukee (GB: Royal Flush). 1947: My Wild Irish Rose. 1948: Two Guys from Texas (GB: Two Texas Knights). 1949: John Loves Mary. Look for the Silver Lining. It's a Great Feeling. The Story of Seabiscuit (GB: Pride of Kentucky).

1950: The Daughter of Rosie O'Grady. Tea for Two. 1951: Lullaby of Broadway. Painting the Clouds with Sunshine. 1952: Where's Charley? April in Paris. 1953: By the Light of the Silvery Moon. Calamity Jane. 1954: The Command. King Richard and the Crusaders. 1955: Jump into Hell. Glory. 1956: The Girl He Left Behind. 1960: The Right Approach. 1967: C'mon, Let's Live a Little.

BUZZELL, Edward 1895-1985

This Brooklyn-born performer was a musical comedy star for years in Broadway revues before coming to films, where he later directed various light films for M-G-M, including two with the Marx Brothers, *At the Circus* and *Go West*. These are not the best of the Marxes' films, but they do reveal Buzzell's liking for freewheeling, firecracker comedy, a field in which he evidently felt relaxed. Certainly his sympathies are with Lucille Ball and Keenan Wynn, rather than Esther Williams and Van Johnson, in his best film *Easy to Wed* (1946), a remake of the comedy classic *Libeled Lady*, with the result that Ball and Wynn give really eye-catching performances. Outside the comedy spots, in fact, Buzzell could be really quite dull. One detects a certain lack of enthusiasm in many of his films, and few directors can have made as little out of Piper Laurie, although *Ain't Misbehavin'* was one he co-scripted himself. There wasn't much after that. He starred in several of the comedy shorts he directed in the early thirties.

1930: *Hello Thar. *Keeping Company. *The Royal Four Flusher. *The Crystal Gazer. *Hard Boiled Yeggs. *Hot and Bothered. *The Prodigal Daughter. Then Came the Pawn. 1931: *Blonde Pressure. Check and Rubber Check. *Chriss-Crossed. *Kings or Better. *The Last of the Moe Higgins. *The Lone Star Stranger. *Red Men Tell No Tales. *Soldier of Misfortune. *She Served Him Right. *Wine, Women But No Song. 1932: *The Wolf in Cheap Clothing. *The Gall of the North. *Love, Honor and He Pays. Hollywood Speaks. The Big Timer. Virtue. 1933: Ann Carver's Profession. Child of Manhattan. Love, Honor and Oh! Baby. 1934: Cross Country Cruise. The Human Side. 1935: Transient Lady (GB: False Witness). The Girl Friend. 1936: The Luckiest Girl in the World. Three Married Men. 1937: As Good As Married. 1938: Paradise for Three. Fast Company. 1939: At the Circus. Honolulu. Go West (GB: Marx Brothers Go West). Married Bachelor. The Get-Away. 1942: The Omaha Trail. Ship Ahoy. 1943: Best Foot Forward. The

Youngest Profession. 1945: Keep Your Powder Dry. 1946: Easy to Wed. Three Wise Fools. 1947: Song of the Thin Man. 1949: Neptune's Daughter. 1950: Emergency Wedding (GB: Jealousy). A Woman of Distinction. 1953: Confidentially Connie. 1955: Ain't Misbehavin'. 1961: Mary Had a Little...

CABANNE, Christy
(William C. Cabanne) 1888-1950

Although Cabanne gained a reputation as one of the most prominent directors of the silent era, able to handle such contrasting stars as Lionel Barrymore, the Gish sisters, Douglas Fairbanks, Mae Murray and Harry Carey, he was a man of action, keen on sports, and was best at directing rousing adventure films. Born in America's Mid-West, Cabanne was already an officer in the Marines at 22 when hired by D.W. Griffith as Marine Consultant on his film *The Unchanging Sea* in 1910. Then and there he decided to throw up his military career and became Griffith's assistant. From 1912, he began to direct films himself, sometimes under Griffith's 'personal supervision', which may have meant Griffith co-directed. Cabanne quickly made his name as a director of exciting, sometimes cliff-hanging action scenes, also as an iron fist in the velvet glove, capable of handling difficult stars. His handsome, moustachioed looks (he was, for a short while, an actor himself) would have qualified him ideally for playing the heroes of the guns-blazing, hooves-drumming kind of films he loved. He made four consecutive westerns with Harry Carey in 1918 and, with the coming of sound, after which his star never burned so bright, a series of middle-budget action films starring Preston Foster or Richard Arlen. In a rare departure from all this he-man stuff, Cabanne directed the five Scattergood Baines comedies at RKO in the early 1940s, with Guy Kibbee as the do-gooding small-town busybody. Up to the mid-1920s, Cabanne was often credited as William Christy Cabanne or Wm Christy Cabanne. He died from a heart attack.

*1912: *Drink's Lure. *The Detective's Stratagem. *Neptune's Daughter. *Father's Lesson. *The Daylight Burglar.*

*The Adopted Brother. *The Blue or the Gray. *The Woman in Black. *The Dilemma. *For the Cause. *A Chance Deception. *The Girl Across the Way. Best Man Wins. *Black and White. *An Adventure in the Autumn Woods. *The Gipsy Talisman. *Gentleman or Thief? *The Ranchero's Revenge. 1913: The Vengeance of Galora. *So Runs the Way. *The Suffragette Minstrels. *The Fatal Wedding. *Mister Jefferson Green. *Gangsters of New York. *Sapho/Sappho. *The Sorrowful Shore. *The Well. *His Inspiration. *The Iron Master. *The Wife. *For Those Unborn. *By Man's Law. *The Conscience of Hassan Bey. *Moths. 1914: *The Hunchback. *The Quicksands. *The Rebellion of Kitty Belle. *A Question of Courage. *Carmen. *Her Awakening. *The Odalisque. *The Sisters. *The Smugglers of Sligo. *The Dishonored Medal. *Arms and the Gringo. *The Suffragette Battle of Nuttyville. *A Lesson in Mechanics. *Granny. *The Saving Grace. *The Better Way. Dope. The Great Leap. §The Life of General Villa. §The Second Mrs Roebuck. 1915: The Martyrs of the Alamo. The Lost House. §The Absentee. The Failure. Enoch Arden (GB: As Fate Ordained). Double Trouble. The Lamb. 1916: The Great Secret (serial). §The Flying Torpedo. Daphne and the Pirate. Sold for Marriage. Reggie Mixes In (GB: Mysteries of New York). Diane of the Follies. Flirting with Fate. The Sawdust Ring. 1917: Miss Robinson Crusoe. Cheerful Givers. The Great Secret. One of Many. That's All American. Soul Triumphant. The Pest. 1918: The Slacker. Draft 258. Cyclone Higgins D.D. A Regular Fellow. Fighting Through. God's Outlaw. The Mayor of Filbert. 1919: The Beloved Cheater. The Triflers. 1920: The Notorious Mrs Sands. Life's Twist. Burnt Wings. The Stealers. 1921: What's a Wife Worth? Live and Let Live. The Barricade. At the Stage Door. 1922: Beyond the Rainbow. Till We Meet Again. 1923: The Average Woman. 1924: The Sixth Commandment. The Spitfire. Lend Me Your Husband. Youth for Sale. Is Love Everything? 1925: The Midshipman. The Masked Bride. 1926: Monte Carlo (GB: Dreams of Monte Carlo). Altars of Desire. 1927: Restless Youth (GB: Wayward Youth). 1928: Driftwood. Nameless Men. Annapolis (GB: Branded a Coward). 1930: Conspiracy. The Dawn Trail. 1931: Convicted. The Sky Raiders. Graft. Carne de cabaret. 1932: The Midnight Patrol. The Western Limited (GB: The Night Express). Hotel Continental. Hearts of Humanity. The Unwritten Law. Red-Haired Alibi. 1933: The Eleventh Commandment. Daring Daughters. Midshipman Jack. The World Gone Mad (GB:*

The Public Be Hanged). 1934: When Strangers Meet. Money Means Nothing. Jane Eyre. Girl of the Limberlost. 1935: Behind the Green Lights. Storm over the Andes (and Spanish version). Another Face (GB: It Happened in Hollywood). Rendezvous at Midnight. One Frightened Night. The Keeper of the Bees. 1936: The Last Outlaw. We Who Are About to Die. 1937: Annapolis Salute (GB: Salute to Romance). Criminal Lawyer. Don't Tell the Wife. You Can't Beat Love. The Outcasts of Poker Flat. The Westland Case. 1938: Everybody's Doing It. This Marriage Business. Night Spot. Smashing the Spy Ring. 1939: Legion of Lost Flyers. Man from Montreal. Danger on Wheels. Mutiny on the Blackhawk. Tropic Fury. 1940: Alias the Deacon. Black Diamonds. The Mummy's Hand. Hot Steel. The Devil's Pipeline. 1941: Scattergood. Baines. Scattergood Pulls the Strings. Scattergood Meets Broadway. 1942: Timber. Top Sergeant. Scattergood Rides High. Drums of the Congo. Scattergood. Survives a Murder. 1943: Cinderella Swings It. Keep 'Em Slugging. 1944: Dixie Jamboree. 1945: The Man Who Walked Alone. Sensation Hunters. 1946: Scared to Death. 1947 Robin Hood of Monterey. King of the Bandits. 1948: Silver Trails. Back Trail.

CACOYANNIS, Michael
(Mikhalis Kakogiannis) 1922-

It's a pity that *Zorba the Greek*, a film showered with Academy Awards even though it only occasionally escapes from tedium or overkill into the real Greece, should remain Cacoyannis' best-known film. For all his best work was done earlier. He was born in Cyprus of Greek parentage and, following a period studying law, became an actor and writer instead. He was not successful in finding directing assignments in Britain (where he had studied and acted) or America, so returned to Greece, where he eventually got a directorial career started in 1953. His early films stay in the mind: black, haunting hotbeds of emotion, three of them, *The Girl in Black, A Matter of Dignity* and *The Wastrel*, gaining in impact from the sad vulnerability of Ellie Lambetti (never as effective for other directors), one of them, *Stella*, introducing Melina Mercouri to films, and several of them sensitively photographed by Walter Lassally in heavily contrasted black and white, underlining the country's actual poverties, and richnesses of spirit. *Zorba the Greek* was a watershed for Cacoyannis; since then, nothing much has worked for him, certainly not the babble of *The Trojan Women*. And his one attempt at directing for American television has not been seen outside the United States.

1953: Windfall in Athens. 1954: Stella. 1955: The Girl in Black. 1957: A Matter of Dignity. 1959: Eroica/Our Last Spring. 1960. The Wastrel. 1961: Electra. 1964: Zorba the Greek. 1967: The Day the Fish Came Out. 1971: The Trojan Women. 1974: The Story of Jacob and Joseph (TV). 1975: Attila 74 (D). 1977: Iphigenia. 1985: Sweet Country. 1989: Zoe. 1999: The Cherry Orchard

CAHN, Edward L 1899-1963

Pluck a dozen cult drive-in, fantasy and science-fiction films of the Fifties from your memory and the odds are that Cahn will have directed one of them. At the time, indeed, it seemed that he and Roger Corman were responsible for 50 per cent of the market. Cahn himself made almost 50 of these black-and-white programme fillers between 1955 and his early death in 1963 – a prodigious rate of one every two months, enough to send today's directors screaming to the psychiatrist's couch. Although he left an interesting legacy. Cahn's stop-start directorial career at one time promised more. To supplement his studies at UCLA, he had taken a job as a film cutter – his entry to the film world. At 27, he rose to chief film editor at Universal, getting his first chance to direct five years later. His best film came early – a terrific western, *Law and Order*, unseen now for many years, based on the Earps and Clantons and starring Walter Huston and Harry Carey. Cahn's handling of a script co-written by John Huston led to the emergence of one of the most realistic of early westerns with a tremendous, fiery climax. Cahn's directorial career did not progress in the direction it might have after this, and he spent much of the next two decades in the production and editing departments, occasionally emerging to direct bottom-budget second-features, especially following his departure from Universal. The films he directed in the Fifties and Sixties are plentiful but almost all poor. Occasional exceptions include *It! The Terror from Beyond Space*, the prototype for *Alien* more than 20 years later, complete with the elements of an alien aboard, and two female members of a crew gradually eliminated by the slavering enemy.

1931: †The Homicide Squad (GB: Lost Men). 1932: Radio Patrol. Law and Order. Afraid to Talk. 1933: Emergency Call. Laughter in Hell. 1935: Confidential. 1937: Bad Guy. 1941: Redhead.

1944: Main Street After Dark. 1945: Dangerous Partners. 1947: Born to Speed. Gas House Kids in Hollywood. 1948: The Checkered Coat. Bungalow 13. 1949: Prejudice. I Cheated the Law. 1950: The Great Plane Robbery. Destination Murder. Experiment Alcatraz. 1951: Two Dollar Bettor (GB: Beginner's Luck). 1955: The Creature with the Atom Brain. Betrayed Women. 1956: Flesh and the Spur. Shake, Rattle and Rock. Girls in Prison. The She-Creature. Runaway Daughters. 1957: Zombies of Mora-Tau (GB: The Dead That Walk). Voodoo Woman. Dragstrip Girl. Motorcycle Gang. Invasion of the Saucer Men (GB: The Invasion of the Hell Creatures). 1958: Jet Attack (GB: Through Hell to Glory). It! The Terror from Beyond Space. Suicide Battalion. Hong Kong Confidential. Guns, Girls and Gangsters. The Curse of the Faceless Man. 1959: Invisible Invaders. Riot in Juvenile Prison. Pier 5 – Havana! Vice Raid. Inside the Mafia. The Four Skulls of Jonathan Drake. 1960: Gunfighters of Abilene. The Walking Target. A Dog's Best Friend. Oklahoma Territory. Twelve Hours to Kill. Cage of Evil. The Music Box Kid. Three Came to Kill. The Gambler Wore a Gun. Noose for a Gunman. Operation Bottleneck. 1961: Frontier Uprising. Police Dog Story. Five Guns to Tombstone. You Have to Run Fast. When the Clock Strikes. The Boy Who Caught a Crook. Gun Street. Secret of Deep Harbor. 1962: The Clown and the Kid. Incident in an Alley. 1963: Beauty and the Beast.

CAIN, Christopher (Bruce Doggett) 1943-

South Dakota-born director of mainly youth- or child-oriented films. Formerly a music arranger and background session singer, Cain switched to acting in the late 1970s, and made appearances on several high-profile TV series before directing his first film in 1976 – *Elmer*, a little-seen boy-and-dog story. He first attracted critical attention in 1984 with the release of *The Stone Boy*, a poignant piece about a kid who accidentally shoots the older brother he worships. Characterised by glowing pictorial values and concerned treatment, Cain's studies of youth continued with the more mainstream *That Was Then... This is Now* and *Young Guns*, both with Emilio Estevez. Rather more interesting, though, was the film in between, *Where the River Runs Black*, a *Wild Child*-like drama beautifully filmed on location in Brazil, and concerning an orphan boy snatched from his jungle habitat and brought to 'civilisation'. In recent years, Cain has returned to blander family fare; his work needs a tougher edge if it is to

ever to combine critical and box-office approval.

1976: Elmer. 1978: The Buzzard. 1980: Sixth, Sixth and Main. 1974: The Stone Boy. 1985: That was Then... This is Now. 1986: Where the River Runs Black. 1987: The Principal. 1988: Young Guns. 1990: Wheels of Terror. 1992: Pure Country. 1994: The Next Karate Kid. 1995: The Amazing Panda Adventure. 1997: Gone Fishin'. 1999: Keeping Time.

CAMERON, James 1954-

James Cameron makes big films. Skilful editing, pounding action and dazzling effects, often on huge budgets, are trademarks of his work, in which he seems determined to outdo himself with each succeeding film. It's a career that certainly no one would have predicted after Cameron's first disastrous attempt at directing in 1981. But, with the budgets and technicians he requires at his disposal, Cameron has shown he has few peers in making exciting entertainments the public will flock to see. Born near Ontario, Canada, the son of an engineer, Cameron broke into film-making at 26 with New World Pictures as a special effects man and, later, as an art director and production designer. His first film as director, the Dutch-made *Piranha II Flying Killers* (aka *Piranha II: The Spawning*) is a sci-fi horror so inept that its monsters look as if they are being run

James **Cameron** presides over more action and spectacle during the difficult shooting of *The Abyss*.

by clockwork. Three years later, Cameron rebounded with *The Terminator*, a sleeper hit which rates an 'A' in filmcraft in every scene. And as star he had an Arnold Schwarzenegger still at that time mired in epics about *Conan the Barbarian*. If this was good the next, *Aliens*, was better: it had 300 per cent more action and 100 per cent more logic than its predecessor, *Alien*. And, under Cameron's command, like the aliens it kept coming at you at a pace that never let up. Cameron's fascination with the sea, which would later produce *Titanic*, was also responsible for the one flop in the major part of his career *The Abyss*, an over-ambitious combination of science-fiction and deep-sea adventure. Small wonder that Cameron returned to safer ground with the mega-expensive *Terminator 2 Judgment Day*. The twists and turns of logic and time it offered are almost as amazing as its 'liquid metal' effects and highway chases. Schwarzenegger was again Cameron's star (and scored his last major success to date) in Cameron's *True Lies*, which is like a James Bond movie (with a Mrs Bond at home), complete with even more sensational effects. The effects were awe-inspiring in Cameron's most recent film to date, *Titanic*, a much-feted, three-hours-plus reconstruction of the disaster that befell the 'unsinkable' liner in 1912. Although the accompanying storyline is trite, its action hammers along, and some of the performances are more haunting than in anything Cameron had previously done. It won him the best director Oscar.

1981: *Piranha II Flying Killers/Piranha II: The Spawning*. 1984: *The Terminator*. 1986: *Aliens*. 1989: *The Abyss*. 1991: *Terminator 2 Judgment Day*. 1994: *True Lies*. 1997: *Titanic*.

CAMPBELL, Martin 1944-

Following a career spent largely toiling away at episodes of admittedly popular television series, it's only in the past ten years that this New Zealand-born director has really made an impact on the world of mainstream movies, especially when chosen to helm Pierce Brosnan's first James Bond movie *GoldenEye*. Yet at one time it seemed recognition of Campbell's potential could have come much earlier. Moving to the United Kingdom in 1966, he began his career there as a video cameraman. In 1974, the chance came to direct one of the many soft-porn sex comedies being made by the British film industry of the time, most of them of very poor quality. This one, though, was different. Itself a satire on the Soho soft-core market, *Eskimo Nell* was, thanks to fren-

zied direction and a sly script from co-star Michael Armstrong, actually quite often funny – certainly the best of its kind produced in the decade. Perhaps craving respectability, Campbell moved into television, directing multiple episodes of three of the most popular long-running crime series – *The Professionals*, *Shoestring* and *Minder*. Acclaimed for his direction of the award-winning crime-and-corruption series *Edge of Darkness*, Campbell moved to America, scoring a modest success with a well-acted, if overlong serial-killer thriller *Criminal Law*. His subsequent career there was fairly low-key until *GoldenEye* brought him back to Britain. Its action was all well-shot and made the film a big blockbuster at the box-office. Campbell moved on to more big-budget action with *The Mask of Zorro*. This revived the Hollywood star career of Antonio Banderas as Zorro's dashing protégé.

1974: *Eskimo Nell*. 1988: *Criminal Law*. 1989: *Defenseless (released 1991)*. 1991: *Cast a Deadly Spell (cable TV)*. 1994: *No Escape*. 1995: *GoldenEye*. 1998: *The Mask of Zorro*.

CAMPION, Jane 1954-

This New Zealand-born director makes long, beautiful and impressive films, but the characters in them are hard to get close to. She had originally studied anthropology at university, but then went an art college in Australia, where she studied surrealist painting and began her film career. There are surrealist-influenced images in most of Campion's subsequent works, which attracted attention from the beginning. Her first short film, *Peel*, won the Palme d'Or in its section at the Cannes Film Festival. Campion continued making award-winning shorts for the next seven years until venturing into features with *Sweetie*. As with many woman filmmakers, Campion's central characters are almost always women. None are more disturbing than the heroine of *Sweetie*, played by Campion favourite Geneviève Lemon. About a demanding young woman and her relationship with her submissive family, it provides, like all Campion films, little light and shade for those who like humour to leaven their drama. *An Angel at My Table* is often even more depressing, although finally uplifting in its true story of a novelist who spent eight years in psychiatric hospitals after being misdiagnosed a schizophrenic. Campion's first international film, *The Piano*, immediately brought her wider acclaim, together with a best screenplay Oscar. An unusual erotic drama with some striking

visual moments, the film took Campion back to her native New Zealand and also won an Oscar for its star, American Holly Hunter, as a strong-willed but mute Scottish widow who travels across the world in the 19th century to fulfil what turns out to be a loveless arranged marriage to a local landowner. New Zealand-born Anna Paquin also won an Oscar as Hunter's daughter. 'I have enjoyed writing characters,' says Campion, 'who don't have a 20th-century sensibility about sex. They have nothing to prepare themselves for its strength and power.' This was certainly true of her next protagonist, the heiress played by Nicole Kidman in Henry James' *The Portrait of a Lady*, although the film itself was less successful. There are moments of tedium in most of Campion's films, but it's only here that they overwhelm the drama, as Campion keeps the emotions of the story too cramped and confined. No doubt, though, her characters will continue to suffer to some effect. Oscar nominee for *The Piano*.

1982: **Peel*. 1983: **A Girl's Own Story*. 1984: **Passionate Moments*. 1985: **After Hours*. 1986: *Two Friends (TV)*. 1989: *Sweetie*. 1990: *An Angel at My Table*. 1993: *The Piano*. 1996: *The Portrait of a Lady*. 1999: *Holy Smoke*.

CAPRA, Frank 1897-1991

This Sicilian-born Hollywood director looked at the world through rose-coloured glasses and believed, rightly, that thousands of other people all over the world wanted to look at it the same way. He also believed that goodness and virtue, even in the humblest of people, could triumph over insuperable odds in the end, and his most famous films were celebrations of the common man *par excellence*, an idealized but immensely pleasurable figure. Of course, it was never true, much as Capra made us like it, that the world's nasties of life always repent and confess their misdeeds, but the climaxes to his greatest films, however little they might have to do with real life, are constructed with superb skill and can still bring a lump to the throat. These latter films run from 1933 to 1941, a period when Capra won three Best Director Oscars. He made some excellent films before this, especially *Dirigible*, *The Miracle Woman* and *The Bitter Tea of General Yen*, but these are in a more poetic, very different style. In post-war years, public tastes changed. Capra's best film, *It's a Wonderful Life*, was not well-liked at the box office, and his magnificent self-confidence gradually ebbed away. He had come to America at the age of six. Trained as a chemical engi-

Running all the way to the Oscars. Frank **Capra** (left) with Claudette Colbert and Clark Gable, the stars of his Academy Award-winning *It Happened One Night.*

ation. *The Donovan Affair.* 1930: *Ladies of Leisure. Rain or Shine.* 1931: *Dirigible. Platinum Blonde. The Miracle Woman.* 1932: *Forbidden. American Madness.* 1933: *The Bitter Tea of General Yen. Lady for a Day.* 1934: *Broadway Bill* (GB: *Strictly Confidential*). *It Happened One Night.* 1936: *Mr Deeds Goes to Town.* 1937: *Lost Horizon.* 1938: *You Can't Take It with You.* 1939: *Mr Smith Goes to Washington.* 1941: *Meet John Doe.* 1942: *Prelude to War* (D). §*The Nazis Strike* (D). 1943: §*Divide and Conquer* (D). § *Tunisian Victory* (D). *Arsenic and Old Lace.* 1944: §*The Battle of China.* 1945: *War Comes to America.* §*Know Your Enemy: Japan.* **Two Down and One to Go!* 1946: *It's a Wonderful Life.* 1948: *State of the Union* (GB: *The World and His Wife*). 1950: *Riding High.* 1951: *Here Comes the Groom.* 1959: *A Hole in the Head.* 1961: *Pocketful of Miracles.* 1964: **Rendezvous in Space.*

CARDIFF, Jack 1914-

Britain's finest exponent of colour photography in the post-war years, Cardiff turned to direction with initially pleasing results. Later, his films became progressively less interesting and more flatly performed, and he returned to photography in the 1970s. He began his work in cinematography as camera operator on *Wings of the Morning* (1937), the first British full-colour film. He gained his first solo credit on an Italian documentary short in the same year, and soon became acknowledged as one of the foremost Technicolor experts in films. His location work on *The Four Feathers* was much praised (although Cardiff was initially uncredited) and, from 1943, he was given sole charge of the photography in some of Britain's most breathtaking Technicolor undertakings, among them *A Matter of Life and Death, Black Narcissus, The Red Shoes, Scott of the Antarctic, The Black Rose* and *The African Queen.* He won an Academy Award for his work on *Black Narcissus.* He was now working on Hollywood-financed films shot outside America and, after photographing *The Vikings* for Richard Fleischer, Cardiff decided to turn director. His first ventures, oddly, were all in black and white. *Intent to Kill* and *Beyond This Place* were promising dramas and then came *Sons and Lovers,* a corrosive, touching, excellent version of D.H. Lawrence's story. Ironically, the only Oscar won by this, Cardiff's best film was for its black and white photography, in this case lensed by Freddie Francis (who would also turn director). The rest of Cardiff's directorial career was one disappointment after another, apart from

neer, he could find no work in that field, and drifted into films almost by chance, his lively mind earning him employment as a gag writer for silent comedies, latterly with Mack Sennett. It was in slapstick vein that he began his career as a feature film director with two comedies starring chalk-faced Harry Langdon. However, the two men quarrelled – a tragedy for Langdon, whose career went downhill, but a blessing in disguise for Capra, who was pitched more quickly than he might have wished into a wide variety of films. Capra's touches of realism and cleverness in presenting character had his audiences sharing both agonies and triumphs in *Submarine, Flight* and *Dirigible;* he was to become expert in manipulating their emotions to such an extent that his 1930s' and early 1940s' films influenced the lives and beliefs of a nation, as they followed the efforts of Longfellow Deeds, Jefferson Smith and John Doe to take on corruption and win, not without coming heart-rendingly close to failure. Capra took his Academy Awards for direction of *It Happened One Night* (which also won Best Picture, Columbia's first such award), *Mr Deeds Goes to Town* and *You Can't Take It with You,* although the last is now his most resistible film from this period.

After making flagwaving wartime documentaries, Capra returned with the magnificent *It's a Wonderful Life,* when James Stewart's character, on the verge of suicide, is visited by an angel who shows him what life in his town would have been without him; this is Hollywood whimsy at its very best. Capra's *Riding High,* a 1950 remake of his 1934 film *Broadway Bill,* has some scenes which better the original – but he was already losing his touch. Nowadays, the mere mention of Capra's name is enough to make literate and learned film-writers dip their pens in bile. But when, between director and actor, you actually pump the breath of life into impossibly idealized Everymen, as Gary Cooper, James Stewart or Barbara Stanwyck did, a powerful emotional current is given out from the screen. The fact that they have nothing to do with the real world has absolutely no bearing on that.

1922: **Fultah Fisher's Boarding House.* 1926: *The Strong Man.* 1927: *Long Pants. For the Love of Mike.* 1928: *The Matinee Idol. That Certain Thing. The Way of the Strong. So This is Love. Say it with Sables.The Power of the Press. Submarine.* 1929: *Flight. The Younger Gener-*

Young Cassidy, although this was begun by John Ford, and it is impossible to say how much he influenced the finished product. Eventually Cardiff returned to what he liked doing best: *Death on the Nile* for example, is sumptuously photographed in exotic locations in his best travelogue style.

1958: Intent to Kill. 1959: Beyond This Place (US: Web of Evidence). 1960: Scent of Mystery (GB: Holiday in Spain). Sons and Lovers. 1961: My Geisha. 1962: The Lion. 1963: The Long Ships. 1964: Young Cassidy). 1965: The Liquidator. 1967: The Mercenaries (US: Dark of the Sun). 1968: Girl on a Motorcycle (US: Naked Under Leather). 1973: Penny Gold. 1974: The Mutations/The Freakmaker.

CARNÉ, Marcel 1909-1996

This Paris-born French director was a man for his time – the immediate pre-war years. His films gripped then with their pessimistic fatalism and, with the help of Alexandre Trauner's extraordinary set designs – cluttered rooftops and grimy narrow cobblestoned streets that careered claustrophobically between characterless lodging-houses – Carné proved himself a master at creating a moody, doomy atmosphere inside a studio. Few careers have suffered such total eclipse since those halcyon days. Maybe it was the loss of Trauner (from 1951), screenplay writer Jacques Prévert (from 1948) and his other collaborators from the 1930s that hastened Carné's decline. More likely, just like Frank Capra, he could not move with the times, and the time for his bitter-sweet, low-life romantic dramas and theatrical approach certainly was over. Then again, so little that was good came out of the French cinema from 1945 to 1959 that it may be small wonder that his work slid downhill. He began his film career as a camera assistant at the age of 20 in 1929 with Jacques Feyder, with whom he worked for many years; he finally got a chance to direct a film, *Jenny,* when Feyder left for England to direct Marlene Dietrich in *Knight without Armour.* From this first film, a fairly commonplace affair of romantic entanglements against a nightclub background, it became apparent that, given good actors, Carné could extract memorable performances. This talent reached its high point with the work of his actors – Jean Gabin, Michèle Morgan, Jean-Louis Barrault, Louis Jouvet, Michel Simon and Pierre Brasseur among them – in his other 1930s' films, *Drôle de drame, Quai des brumes, Hôtel du nord* and *Le jour se lève.* These are all classics, the last of them lingering in the memory longer even than Carné's acknowledged masterpiece, *Les enfants du Paradis.* These mood pieces create a world of their own, of waterfront cafés, shabby furnished rooms and characters only half struggling to escape a tragic end which inexorably embraces them. In *Le jour se lève* Gabin gave his most charismatic and powerful performance as the man trapped by circumstance, and the police, in his tatty, upper-storey bedsit. Finally, he shoots himself. This is real flesh-and-blood stuff, as opposed to the spiritual passion and stylized drama of the haunting *Les enfants du Paradis,* which contains another unforgettable acting performance, this time by that distinctive actress Arletty. By now, France itself had been trapped, cornered and all but blown away (by the Germans) and, when the smoke cleared, the heart and soul which Carné had poured into his pre-war work were no longer fashionable. Unlike Capra, he kept going, but never recaptured critical or public acclaim.

*1929: *Nogent, Eldorado du dimanche. 1936: Jenny. 1937: Drôle de drame (US: Bizarre, Bizarre). 1938: Hôtel du nord. Quai des brumes (US: Port of Shadows). 1939: Le jour se lève (GB and US: Daybreak). 1942: Les visiteurs du soir (US: The Devil's Enemy). 1945: Les enfants du Paradis (US: Children of Paradise). 1946: Les portes de la nuit (US: Gates of the Night). 1948: La fleur de l'âge (uncompleted). 1949: La Marie du Port. 1950: Juliette ou la clé des songes. 1953: Thérèse Raquin (US: The Adulteress). 1954: L'air de Paris. 1956: Le pays d'où je viens. 1958: Les tricheurs (GB & US: The Cheaters). 1960: Terrain vague. 1962: Du mouron pour les petits oiseaux. 1965: Trois chambres à Manhattan. 1968: Les jeunes loups (GB & US: The Young Wolves). 1971: Les assassins de l'ordre. 1974: La merveilleuse visite. 1976: La Bible (D, originally for TV). 1980: The Immortal Heritage (originally for TV). 1993: Mouche.*

CARPENTER, John 1948-

It isn't easy for a young American director to make it to the top in the modern-day film world. His first film efforts have to be solidly-entertaining, eye-catching and original – and yet made on a shoestring. Carpenter, after winning an Academy Award for a short film in 1970, did it three times over, with a trio of films that cost less than a million dollars between them. *Dark Star,* the first and lowest-budgeted, was enjoyable, way-out science-fiction along *Alien* lines (but much more jokey), with the cracks just about pasted over in the sets Carpenter and his crew had built in their homes. Carpenter's next

John **Carpenter,** with long-time partner Debra Hill.

film is still his best – *Assault on Precinct 13.* The 'Cavalry fort besieged by Indians' theme is tautly transferred to the big modern American city, with the inhabitants of a police station besieged by what seems like the entire underworld. From science-fiction, Carpenter, by now a man in some demand, moved on to outright horror with *Halloween,* a maniac-on-the-loose story with supernatural touches (made for $300,000, it grossed over $12 million), and *The Fog.* Carpenter is a director who likes to get his audience on the edge of their seats, then make them jump off it. He continued to be mighty successful at it too, although in the early 1980s his films were insufficiently progressive – one longed for more variety in his work. Things have got no better in recent times. *Starman* was Carpenter's last film of any real note. He struggled badly with fantasy comedy in *Memoirs of an Invisible Man* and his other 1990s films have been poor imitations of better earlier films in the chiller, fantasy and horror genres. He was formerly married to the actress Adrienne Barbeau.

*1966: *Firelight. 1970: *The Resurrection of Bronco Billy. 1974: Dark Star. l976: Assault on Precinct 13. 1977: Someone's Watching Me (TV). 1978: Halloween. 1979: The Fog. Elvis (TV. GB: cinemas). 1981: Escape from New York. 1982: The Thing. 1983: Christine. 1984: Starman. 1986: Big Trouble in Little China. 1987: Prince of Darkness. 1988: They Live. 1991: Memoirs of an Invisible Man.*

1993: †Body Bags (TV). 1994: In the Mouth of Madness. 1995: Village of the Damned. 1996: Escape from L.A. 1998: Vampires/John Carpenter's Vampires.

CARSTAIRS, John Paddy
(J. Keys) 1910-1970

British writer, director and author of humorous novels, several of them autobiographical. Carstairs, after beginning as an assistant cameraman, worked steadily along the safe middle lines of the commercial British cinema for 30 years. He began writing screenplays with *Honeymoon Adventure*, in 1931, and directing in 1934. Most of his films as director were modest, middle-budget successes, with *Lassie from Lancashire* (1938) and *The Chiltern Hundreds* (1949) the most attractive and original. In 1953, for no particular commercial reason, Carstairs was put in charge of the first major Norman Wisdom comedy, *Trouble in Store*. The film was a massive box-office success in its native country, and Carstairs suddenly found himself a man with a reputation for steering new comic talent to success on the screen. Besides making several Wisdom comedies, he was also put in charge of early vehicles for Frankie Howerd, Ronald Shiner, Tommy Steele, Charlie Drake and Bob Monkhouse. The quality of these comedies was variable but, with the help of canny advertising, especially on the Rank films, they were nearly all money-makers for their producers. Carstairs quit films in 1962 to concentrate on writing and painting, but died at 60. His brother is the screenplay writer John Elder (Anthony Nelson Keys, 1912-). Their father was the silent screen comic actor and later character comedian of sound films, Nelson Keys (1886-1939).

*1934: Paris Plane. 1936: Holiday's End. 1937: Night Ride. Incident in Shanghai. Missing Believed Married. Double Exposures. 1938: Lassie from Lancashire. 1939: The Saint in London. The Second Mr Bush. Meet Maxwell Archer (US: Maxwell Archer Detective). 1940: Spare a Copper. *Telefootlers. *Dangerous Comment. *Now You're Talking. *All Hands. 1941: He Found a Star. 1946: Dancing with Crime. 1948: Sleeping Car to Trieste. 1949: Fools Rush In. The Chiltern Hundreds. 1950: Tony Draws a Horse. 1951: Talk of a Million. 1952: Treasure Hunt. Made in Heaven. 1953: Trouble in Store. Top of the Form. 1954: One Good Turn. Up to His Neck. 1955: Jumping for Joy. Man of the Moment. 1956: Up in the World. The Big Money. 1957: Just My Luck. 1958: The Square Peg. 1959: Tommy the Toreador. 1960: Sands of the Desert. 1961: A Weekend with Lulu.*

1962: Im Namen des Teufels (GB & US: The Devil's Agent).

CASS, Henry 1902-1989

This British director was really a man of the stage, and insisted from time to time on returning to that medium throughout his life. He took up an acting career there in the early 1920s, and turned director/producer a decade later. Very much his own man, Cass tackled any subject that interested him. Consequently his films, as well as the plays he directed, are a varied lot, and there is no consistent pattern to them. His first film, *Lancashire Luck*, in 1937, was also Wendy Hiller's film debut. Cass's period of greatest success in the cinema, however, came after World War II, when he made six films, most of them based on slender premises, but all of them successful and skilfully spun together. The first two, *The Glass Mountain*, with the help of some very popular music, and *No Place for Jennifer*, in which Janette Scott broke a million hearts as the little girl torn apart by her parents' divorce, were huge commercial successes. The others, *Last Holiday, Young Wives' Tale, Father's Doing Fine* and *Castle in the Air*, all made the maximum use of fairly unpromising material and featured Cass's own brand of gentle, clean, relaxed and just slightly dotty light comedy. The first of these, although archly contrived, also gave Alec Guinness the opportunity to contribute a virtuoso performance as the dying man who changes a great many lives in his last few weeks. When Cass returned in 1955 from working in the theatre, he was offered only routine second features. He did with them what he could, but his interest in the cinema was clearly waning with the 1950s and the last clutch of pictures he made were all for the Moral Rearmament organization.

*1937: Lancashire Luck. 1941: HMS Minelayer (D). 1942: *Ask the C.A.B. (D). *Free House (D). 1943: *Common Cause (D). *Danger Area (D). 1944: *Jigsaw (D). *Catholics in Britain (D). 1945: *The Great Game (D). *Macbeth. 29 Acacia Avenue (US: The Facts of Life). 1948: The Glass Mountain. 1949: No Place for Jennifer. 1950: Last Holiday. 1951: Young Wives' Tale. 1952: Castle in the Air. Father's Doing Fine. 1955: The Reluctant Bride (US: Two Grooms for a Bride). Windfall. No Smoking. 1956: Bond of Fear. Breakaway. The High Terrace. 1957: The Crooked Sky. Booby Trap. Professor Tim. 1958: Blood of the Vampire. 1959: Boyd's Shop. 1960: The Hand. The Man Who Couldn't Walk. 1966: Mr Brown*

Comes Down the Hill. 1967: Give a Dog a Bone. 1969: Happy Deathday.

CASSAVETES, John 1929-1989

Everyone suffered in a Cassavetes film, audience and players alike. These films, long, strong and powerful, are probably the nearest an American director has come to the world of angst. Not for Cassavetes – at any rate, until *Gloria* in 1980 – the finer points of cutting and editing, panning and scanning. His cameras slam full frontal on to the characters, often played by his wife Gena Rowlands, himself, or his friends Peter Falk and Ben Gazzara, as they plough their way to or from some kind of breakdown. American-born of Greek extraction, Cassavetes is probably still best known as an actor whose characters were mainly as tormented as those he would later show as a director. His one scene in his first film, *Fourteen Hours* (1951), ended up on the cutting room floor, but his intense acting style soon made him familiar. It was his earnings from a very successful television series, *Johnny Staccato*, that enabled him to make his first film as director, *Shadows*, an account of a poverty row love affair that was highly compelling in spite of (or because of its improvised dialogue and hand-held camerawork. After a brush with the commercial cinema, which left him somewhat embittered (although his *Too Late Blues* is a much underrated film), it was some years before Cassavetes embarked on a series of films that ripped their characters raw in front of the camera. *Gloria* was something else, a racily exciting thriller, full of telling little scenes, with Gena Rowlands as the gun-toting protector of a small boy. It brought with it the exciting possibility that Cassavetes might have found a way to come to terms with Hollywood main-line product at last. That prospect receded, though, with subsequent films, and was ended by his early death at 59 from complications arising from cirrhosis of the liver. His son Nick filmed his last screenplay, *She's So Lovely*, in 1997.

1959: Shadows. 1961: Too Late Blues. 1962: A Child is Waiting. 1968: Faces. 1970: Husbands. 1971: Minnie and Moskowitz. 1974: A Woman under the Influence. 1976: The Killing of a Chinese Bookie. 1977: Opening Night. 1980: Gloria. 1983: Love Streams. 1986: Big Trouble.

CASTLE, William (W. Schloss) 1911-1977

When only 21, New York-born Castle directed Bela Lugosi in a Broadway production of *Dracula*. Perhaps that gave him a taste both for showmanship and the impact of shock. At any rate, after 15 years as a director of co-features in Hollywood, only a few of which (*When Strangers Marry, Johnny Stool Pigeon, The Saracen Blade, New Orleans Uncensored*) are even worthy of note, Castle suddenly found his niche as a kind of Alfred Hitchcock of the 'Z' movie, a carnival barker who invited (literally, as he often appeared in trailers and promotional shorts) his audience to step right up and be scared to death. Every film carried a gimmick, whether it was an insurance policy against death by fright (*Macabre*), a 'system' called Emergo in which skeletons whistled over the audience at strategic points (*House on Haunted Hill*), or a 'fright break' in which the audience could flee the cinema. And, although history credits direction of *Chamber of Horrors*, with its 'Fear Flasher' and 'Horror Horn', to Hy Averback, one can hardly believe that Castle had nothing to do with it. The films themselves are cheap and cheerful; but at least Castle made something of them, and they never stop coming at you. One or two of them, notably *The Tingler*, are actually quite frightening. Later Castle, who once said that he modelled his entire career on that of the famous showman P.T. Barnum, produced Polanski's *Rosemary's Baby*. That was, ironically, more distinguished and more frightening that anything Castle ever did himself. Never mind; he was one hell of a salesman, as exemplified by the title of his autobiography: *Step Right Up! I'm Gonna Scare the Pants Off America*. He died from a heart attack.

1943: *Mr Smug. The Chance of a Lifetime. Klondike Kate. 1944: Betrayed/When Strangers Marry. The Whistler. She's a Soldier, Too. The Mark of the Whistler (GB: The Marked Man). 1945: Voice of the Whistler. The Crime Doctor's Wanting (GB: The Doctor's Warning). 1946: Just Before Dawn. Crime Doctor's Manhunt. The Mysterious Intruder. The Return of Rusty. 1947: The Crime Doctor's Gamble (GB: The Doctor's Gamble). 1948: The Gentleman from Nowhere. Texas, Brooklyn and Heaven (GB: The Girl from Texas). 1949: Undertow. Johnny Stool Pigeon. 1950: It's a Small World. The Hollywood Story. 1951: The Fat Man. Cave of Outlaws. 1953: Fort Ti. Serpent of the Nile. Conquest of Cochise. Slaves of Babylon. Charge of the Lancers. Drums of Tahiti. 1954: Battle of Rogue River. The Law versus Billy the Kid. Jesse James vs the Daltons. Masterson of Kansas. The Americano. The Saracen Blade. The Iron Glove. 1955: The Gun That Won the West. Duel on the Mississippi. New Orleans Uncensored (GB: Riot on Pier 6). 1956: The Houston Story. Uranium Boom. 1957: Macabre. 1958: House on Haunted Hill: 1959: The Tingler. 1960: Thirteen Ghosts. 1961: Homicidal. Mr Sardonicus (GB: Sardonicus). 1962: The Old Dark House. Zotz! 1963: 13 Frightened Girls. 1964: Strait-Jacket. 1965: The Night Walker. I Saw What You Did. 1966: Let's Kill Uncle. The Busy Body. The Spirit is Willing. 1967: Project X. 1974: Shanks.*

CAVALCANTI, Alberto 1897-1982

Globe-trotting Brazilian director, often credited simply as 'Cavalcanti', who made his most interesting films in England. He studied architecture in Geneva as a youth, before moving into films as an art director, then making a start to his directorial career in France. These French films offer pleasing pastoral images and reveal how suited Cavalcanti was to John Grierson's famous GPO Film Unit in England. Cavalcanti accepted Grierson's invite to join the unit in 1934, and worked on such films as *Pett and Pott* and *Coalface*, before taking over as head of the unit (shortly to become the Crown Film Unit) upon Grierson's departure in 1937. He also had a hand, mainly as producer, in such memorable 1930s' documentaries as *Night Mail* and *North Sea*. In 1940, he moved to Ealing and fiction. While most of his films there are interesting re-creations of a set period, his masterwork is only part of a film: the ventriloquist's dummy sequence, featuring Michael Redgrave, from *Dead of Night*, in which the doll gradually takes possession of its master. Cavalcanti rams home the full horror of the situation, with the help of Redgrave's brilliant, highly charged performance, right up to the final shot as the camera approaches poor Redgrave in his hospital bed, seeing him struggle to speak, but inevitably producing only the voice of the dummy. Over 30 years later, Richard Attenborough tried to open the story out into a full-length feature, but at best with only partial success. Cavalcanti returned to his native Brazil in 1949, but left three years later, after a brush with the authorities over his political affiliations. Subsequently, he made films in Italy, Israel, Britain (again), Austria and Romania.

1925: *Rien que les heures. Le train sans yeux. 1927. En rade (US: Sea Fever). Yvette. *La p'tite Lili. 1928: *La jalousie du barbouillé. Le capitaine Fracasse. 1929: Le petit chaperon rouge. Vous verrez la semaine prochaine. A mi - chemin du ciel. 1930: Dans une île perdue. Toute sa vie (and Portuguese version). Les vacances du diable. 1931: *Tour de chant (D). 1932: *En lisant le journal. *Le jour du frotteur. *Revue Montmartroise. *Nous ne ferrons jamais de cinéma (D). Le truc de brésilien. Le mari garçon. 1933: *Plaisirs défendus. Coralie et Cie. 1934: *S.O.S. Radio Service (D). Pett and Pott (D). *New Rates (D). 193S: *Coalface (D). 1936: *Men of the Alps (D). *Message from Geneva (D). 1937: *Line to the Tschierva Hut (D). *Who Writes to Switzerland (D). *We Live in Two Worlds (D). *Roadways (D). 1938: *Four Barriers (D). *The Chiltern Country (D). 1939: *A Midsummer Day's Work (D). Alice in Switzerland (D). The Warning (D). 1940: *La cause commune/Factory Front (D). Caesar (US: The Heel of Italy). 1941: *Young Veteran (D). *Mastery of the Sea (D). 1942: Film and Reality (D). Went the Day Well? (US: 48 Hours). 1943: *Watertight (D). 1944: Champagne Charlie. *Trois chansons de la resistance. 1945: Dead of Night. 1947: They Made Me A Fugitive (US: I Became a Criminal). Nicholas Nickleby. 1948: The First Gentleman (US: Affairs of a Rogue). 1949: For Them That Trespass. 1950: §Caicara (uncredited). 1952: Simao o Caolho (GB & US: Simon the One-Eyed). 1953: O Canto do Mar (GB & US: The Song of the Sea). 1954: Mulher de Verdade (GB & US: A Real Woman). 1955: Herr Puntila und sein Knecht Matti. 1956: †Die Windrose. 1957: Castle in the Carpathians. 1958: La prima notte/Les noces vénitiennes. 1960. The Monster Of Highgate Ponds. 1962: Yerma. 1967: Herzl.*

CATON-JONES, Michael 1958-

Scottish-born director who, despite moving into the big league, has not yet quite fulfilled his initial promise. His best film has been one which took him back to his native country: *Rob Roy*. At 17, Caton-Jones moved from Glasgow to London, where his first short film at the National Film School, *Liebe Mutter*, was named best film at the European Film Students' Awards. His second project, *The Riveter*, was picked up by BBC Television, but it was another British webcaster, Channel 4, that offered him professional opportunities, culminating in his first feature film, *Scandal*. A whitewashed version of a famous British political sex scandal, it was followed by the rather more enjoyable *Memphis Belle*, a crowd-pleasing war film concerning the 25th and final mission of a famous US-crewed World War Two bomber. Since then, the director's work has been mildly disappointing, only *Rob Roy* being man enough to pull in its desired audience. A mix of old-fashioned and graphically modern elements, the film has some spirited action scenes, stunning scenery and a splendidly hateful villain in Tim Roth, who was nominated for an Oscar in his role. Unfortunately it was followed by a poor remake of Fred Zinnemann's thriller *The Day of the Jackal*, which Caton-Jones, despite contributing some blasting action, could make no less unbelievable than it was. At 40, though, time is still on his side.

*1978: *Liebe Mutter. 1979: *The Riveter. 1988: Lucky Sunil. 1989: Scandal. 1990: Memphis Belle. 1991: Doc Hollywood. 1993: This Boy's Life. 1995: Rob Roy. 1997: The Jackal.*

CAYATTE, André 1909-1989

A former lawyer, Frenchman Cayatte turned from writing novels to writing for films at 28, becoming a director four years later. A skilful film-maker, strong on images if somewhat lacking in depth, Cayatte used the medium to express his own deeply held opinions. Thus many of his movies are courtroom dramas skilfully critical of weaknesses and anomalies in the French judicial system. Capital punishment, the jury system, juvenile delinquency, sexual discrimination and euthanasia are only some of the contentious subjects that have come before his courtroom cameras. In the process

The erratic but sometime brilliant Claude **Chabrol** at work in the 1970s.

Cayatte, a good-looking man with deep-set eyes, made some good movies as well, most notably *Justice est faite*, *Nous sommes tous les assassins*, *Le dossier noir* and *Verdict*. Outside legal drama, Cayatte was also successful with *Les amants de Vérone*, a modernised and revamped version of *Romeo and Juliet*. Although one-sided, many of these films were engrossing through the sheer force of the director's storytelling abilities. Cayatte enjoyed ten years' retirement before dying from a heart attack at 80.

1942: La fausse maîtresse. Au Bonheur des Dames (US: Shop Girls of Paris). 1943: Pierre et Jean. 1944: Le dernier sou (released 1946). 1945: Sérénade aux nuages. Roger-la-Honte. 1946: La revanche de Roger-la-Honte. 1947: Le chanteur inconnu. Le dessous des cartes. 1948: Les amants de Vérone. 1949: †Retour à la vie. 1950: Justice est faite. 1952: Nous sommes tous des assassins. 1954: Avant le déluge. 1955: Le dossier noir. 1956: Oeil pour oeil (GB and US: An Eye for an Eye). 1958: Le miroir à deux faces (GB and US: The Mirror Has Two Faces). 1960: Le passage du Rhin (US: Tomorrow is My Turn). 1962: Le glaive et la balance/Two Are Guilty. 1963: La vie conjugale: mes jours avec Jean-Marc. La vie conjugale: mes nuits avec Françoise. 1965: Piège pour Cendrillon (GB and US: A Trap for Cinderella). 1967: Les risques du métier. 1969: Les chemins de Khatmandou. 1970: Mourir d'aimer. 1972: Il n'y a pas de fumée sans feu (US: Where There's Smoke). 1974: Verdict. 1977: A chacun son enfer. 1978: La raison d'état. Justices. 1979: L'amour en question.

CHABROL, Claude 1930-

Chabrol has been called a French Alfred Hitchcock, although his films are far less direct and are concerned, albeit with death in many cases, with guilt and subconscious motives rather than suspense, effects and intricacies of plot. Although credited with starting the *nouvelle vague*, and with being one of France's most distinguished directors, Chabrol's record is far less consistent than that of Hitchcock (about whom he wrote a book in 1957), his films coming in clutches of fascinatingly good and unbelievably bad. The former are usually tightly knit tales of passion and deceit penetrating the veneer of the French middle-class; the latter international co-productions which are far more crudely made and in which Chabrol seems to have less interest. His father and grandfather were pharmacists, but Chabrol became a writer and critic before

directing his first film, *Le beau Serge*. He did not spring to international attention until ten years later but then proceeded to make a group of brilliant psychological drama-thrillers, including *Les biches*, *La femme infidèle*, *Que la bête meure*, *La rupture* and *Le boucher*. Most of these featured Stéphane Audran, the actress who became Chabrol's second wife in 1964. For several years after *La rupture*, Chabrol seemed to have lost his touch, especially with actors who, French and American alike, all seemed to over-emote under his guidance. *Docteur Popaul*, with Jean-Paul Belmondo and Mia Farrow, was a particular disaster. But Chabrol's supporters' patience was rewarded in 1978 when he made *Violette Nozière*, the true story of a French girl in the 1930s- who poisoned her mother and stepfather-to-be, which found him right back on his best form. Chabrol's mainstream successes continued in the 1980s, notably with two popular *policiers*, *Poulet au vinaigre* (*Cop au Vin*) and *Inspecteur Lavardin*. At about the same times he made the enigmatic *Masques*, a thriller in which no one is exactly what they seem: in the exposition, however, Chabrol proves more interested in duels of wit and words than in concealing the core of the mystery. The marriage to Audran came to an end in the late 1980s, since when Chabrol's work has lacked distinction. Doubtless he still has time to surprise us again.

1958: Le beau Serge. 1959: Les cousins. A double tour (GB: Web of Passion. US: Leda). 1960: Les bonnes femmes. Les godelureaux. 1961: The Seven Deadly Sins. L'oeil du malin (US: The Third Lover). 1962: Ophelia. Landru (GB & US: Bluebeard). †Les plus belles escroqueries du monde (US: Beautiful Swindlers). 1964: Le tigre aime la chair fraîche (GB & US: The Tiger Likes Fresh Blood). †Paris vu par... (GB & US: Six in Paris). 1965: Le tigre se parfume à dynamite (GB & US: An Orchid for the Tiger). Marie-Chantal contre Dr Kah. 1966: Le scandal (and English language version: The Champagne Murders). La ligne de démarcation. 1967: La route de Corinthe (GB: The Road to Corinth. US: Who's Got the Black Box?). 1968: Les biches (US: The Does). La femme infidèle. 1969: Que la bête meure (GB: Killer! US: The Beast Must Die/This Man Must Die). Le boucher (US: The Butcher). 1970: La rupture (US: The Breakup). 1971: Juste avant la nuit (GB & US: Just Before Nightfall). La décade prodigieuse (and English language version: Ten Days' Wonder). 1972: Docteur Popaul (GB: Scoundrel in White). 1973: Les noces rouges (GB: Red Wedding. US: Wedding in Blood). De Grey. Le banc de désolation. 1974: NADA (US: The Nada Gang). Une partie de plaisir. Les innocents aux main sales (and English language version: Innocents with Dirty Hands). 1975: Les magiciens. Deux et deux font quatre (TV). 1976: Folies bourgeoises (and English language version: The Twist). Alice, ou la dernière fugue. 1977: Blood Relatives. 1978: Violette Nozière (US: Violette). 1979: Les menteurs. 1980: Le cheval d'orgeuil. 1981: Les fantômes du chapelier. 1983: Le sang des autres. 1984: Le poulet au vinaigre (GB and US: Cop au Vin). 1986: Inspecteur Lavardin/Partage de minuit. 1987: Masques. Le cri du hibou (US: The Cry of the Owl). 1988: Une affaire de femmes. Alouette, je te plumerai. 1989: Le beau Serge. 1990: Doctor M/Club Extinction. Jours tranquilles à Clichy (US: Quiet Days in Clichy). 1991: Madame Bovary. 1992: Sam suffit. 1993: Betty, l'oeil de Vichy. 1994: L'enfer. 1995: L'analphabète. 1996: La cérémonie. 1997: Rien ne va plus. 1998: La couleur du mensonge.

CHAFFEY, Don 1917-1990

Although he tried a number of other genres, both in Britain and Hollywood, British-born Chaffey always returned in the end to what he did best: making films far or involving children. These juvenile entertainments have a freshness and appeal that entirely escapes Chaffey's other work, although it is admittedly hard to shine in the exploitation genres he chose. He was an art director with the fading Gainsborough Studios in 1949, when he made his first film, a thriller for children. When it won a medal at the Venice Film Festival the following year, Chaffey felt encouraged enough to go on as a director, breaking into mainline feature films in the mid-1950s. He made nothing of note, however, until an association with the Disney studio began in 1961. Immediately, his flair for pleasing a family audience without playing down to them or insulting their intelligence made itself apparent: *Greyfriars Bobby* and *The Three Lives of Tomasina* are sly, beguiling Scottish-based entertainments full of unforced charm, featuring, respectively, a dog and a cat and the same impish child actor, Matthew Garber. *The Prince and the Pauper* is probably the best version of Twain's story and *The Horse without a Head* exciting Saturday morning serial stuff that also makes above-average Disney. During this period, he also made *Jason and the Argonauts*, still one of the best of the Dynamation features, and *A Jolly Bad Fellow*, an often delightful Ealing-style vehicle for Leo McKern as a university don who murders his way to the

top. After this, Chaffey sank into prehistoric pot-boilers for Hammer, and other, even more forgettable ventures. He only returned to form in 1976 with Disney's Australian venture *Ride a Wild Pony*. He stuck with holiday viewing: *Pete's Dragon* (also for Disney) and *The Magic of Lassie* were not completely successful, but showed that Chaffey still had the talent to raise a cheer and a tear from junior film fans. He married actress Paula Kelly in 1985.

*1949: The Mysterious Poacher. 1951: The Case of the Missing Scene. 1952: *Bouncer Breaks Up. 1953: *A Good Pullup. *Watch Out. Skid Kids. 1954: Time is My Enemy. 1955: *Dead on Time. 1956: The Secret Tent. 1957: The Girl in the Picture. The Flesh is Weak. 1958: A Question of Adultery. The Man Upstairs. 1959: Danger Within (US: Breakout). 1960: Dentist in the Chair. 1961: Nearly a Nasty Accident. A Matter of WHO. Greyfriars Bobby. 1962: The Prince and the Pauper. The Webster Boy. 1963: The Horse without a Head (TV GB: cinemas). Jason and the Argonauts. A Jolly Bad Fellow (US: They All Died Laughing). 1964: The Three Lives of Thomasina. The Crooked Road. 1966: One Million Years B.C. 1967: The Viking Queen. 1968: A Twist of Sand. 1970: Creatures the World Forgot. 1971: Clinic Xclusive. 1972: Charley-One-Eye. 1974: Persecution (US: The Terror of Sheba). 1976: Ride a Wild Pony. 1977: Pete's Dragon. 1978: The Magic of Lassie. The Gift of Love (TV). 1979: C.H.O.M.P.S. Lassie: the New Beginning (TV). 1985: International Airport (TV).*

CHAPLIN, Sir Charles 1889-1977

Chaplin, British-born and raised and Hollywood-sharpened, offered the world an image – and was its own best salesman. As an actual film director, he was not of the first rank, but as an ideas man and a showcaser of his own talents, he was almost without peer. He endowed his tramp character with, besides toothbrush moustache, bowler hat and cane, such contrasting characteristics as narcissism, shyness, pitiability, vindictiveness, courage and petulance – all topped off with a funny walk. The public swallowed the image whole, and his skill with mimicry and long sequences which may depend on 20 or 30 pieces of comic timing made him the idol of millions. He had come to Hollywood films after several years as an attraction on the London music-halls, archetypally as a drunk. Within a year, he was directing his own films, in sole charge, as he was to be of almost every department, especially script and music, for the rest of his career. From 1920, a

streak of pathos began to mar his work, but his innovative (and ingenious) comedy routines, especially those in *The Gold Rush*, are priceless. Sound came along, but Chaplin stuck to silents, with music track added, until 1940 and *The Great Dictator*, when seriousness first began to get the upper hand, and Chaplin's great sense of pace, both as actor and director, started to desert him. *Monsieur Verdoux* seven years later was a black comic masterpiece, but it was the last golden shot from the crossbow and Chaplin was also falling from public favour. He had survived a morals scandal in the the 1940s when assailed by a paternity suit, but a brush with the House of Un-American Activities Committee was the signal for the United States to refuse him re-entry from Britain, and he fled to Switzerland. His last film, *A Countess from Hong Kong* is (like the other which he directed and where he only appears in a cameo role, *A Woman of Paris* (1923)) among his least interesting. It was inevitable that he should eventually be restored to public favour and, in 1972, he returned to America for the first time in 20 years to receive a special Oscar to add to the one he had won in 1928. He also took an Oscar in 1952 for his music for *Limelight*. The third of his four wives was the actress Paulette Goddard. They were married in 1936 (some sources say 1933, although no announcement of the marriage was made until 1940) and divorced in 1942. Chaplin was knighted in 1975.

1914: †Caught in a Cabaret. †Her Friend the Bandit. †Mabel's Busy Day. †Mabel's Married Life. †The Fatal Mallet. Caught in the Rain. Laughing Gas. The Property Man. The Face on the Bar-Room Floor. Recreation/Spring Fever. The Masquerader. His New Profession. The Rounders. The New Janitor. Those Love Pangs. Dough and Dynamite. Gentlemen of Nerve. His Musical Career. His Trysting Place. Getting Acquainted. His Prehistoric Past. 1915: His New Job. A Night Out. The Champion. In the Dark. A Jitney Elopement/Married in Haste. By the Sea. The Tramp. Work. A Woman. The Bank. Shanghaied. A Night in the Show. =Carmen/Charlie Chaplin's Burlesque on Carmen. 1916: Police! The Floorwalker. The Fireman. The Vagabond. One A.M. The Count. The Pawn Shop. Behind the Screen. The Rink. 1917: Easy Street. The Cure. The Immigrant. The Adventurer. 1918: The Bond. A Dog's Life. Triple Trouble. =Shoulder Arms. Charles Chaplin in a Liberty Loan. Appeal. 1919: Sunnyside. A Day's Pleasure. 1920: =The Kid. 1921: The Idle Class. 1922: Pay Day. Nice and Friendly. 1923: =The Pilgrim.

=*A Woman of Paris*. 1925: =*The Gold Rush*. 1926: =*A Woman of the Sea*. 1927: =*The Circus*. 1931: *City Lights*. 1936: *Modern Times*. 1940: =*The Great Dictator*. 1947: *Monsieur Verdoux*. 1951: =*Limelight*. 1957: =*A King in New York*. 1966: =*A Countess from Hong Kong*.

All shorts except (=) features

CHRISTENSEN, Benjamin 1879-1959

Denmark's master of the silent scream had a vivid visual sense which produced many memorable images of shock – especially in his best-remembered film *Häxan/Witchcraft Through the Ages*, which took him three years to make. The Americans saw this startling work, belatedly, and asked him to join their clan of chiller-makers in 1925. He soon proved a match for Julian, Leni, Browning and other fright-makers working in Hollywood in the last few years of the silent era, once let loose in old dark houses where his own sense of bizarre black beauty and comedies of terror brought fresh life to ghosts, ghouls and long-leggity beasties in such titles as *The Devil's Circus*, *The Haunted House*, *Seven Footprints to Satan* and *The House of Horror*. Christensen, it seems, was unwilling or unable to cope with sound, and the few films he made a decade later, before becoming a cinema manager, are unremarkable. One is left with silent Scandinavian images: the almost mediaeval murk of *The Mysterious X*; the horror of unknown, half-seen faces at windows in the sinister house of *Night of Revenge*, the blueprint for much of his Hollywood work; and above all the cruel cavortings of the witches in *Häxan*, a film years ahead of its time. Here was the use of the cinema as a medium of visual power, with mobile camera work, sophisticated use of light and shade to heighten impact and set off one's worst fears, and a feeling for weird, surrealistic backgrounds which provide part of the feel of the story that was only matched for its time by Wiene in *The Cabinet of Dr Caligari*. The film was banned in some countries for years because of the sadism and nudity depicted in some of its scenes. Christensen was a perfectionist who took months to complete any film, an unheard-of practice in the early silent days; but anyone who has seen these films will testify that the wait was worth it. Credited on his Hollywood films as Benjamin Christiansen.

1913: *The Mysterious X*. 1915: *Night of Revenge*. 1921: *Häxan/Witchcraft through the Ages*. 1922: *Unter Juden*. 1923: *Seine Frau die Unbekannte (US: His Mysterious Adventure)*. 1925: *Die Frau mit dem schlechten Ruf (GB & US: The Woman Who Did)*. 1926: *The Devil's Circus*. 1927: *Mockery*. 1928: *The Haunted House*. **The Hawk's Nest*. 1929: *Seven Footprints of Satan*. *The House of Horror*. 1939: *Children of Divorce/Skilsmissens Børn*. 1940: *The Child/Barnet*. 1941: *Gaa med mig Hjem/Come Home with Me*. 1942: *Damen med de Lyse Handsker/The Lady with the Coloured Gloves*.

CHRISTIAN-JAQUE (C. Maudet) 1904-1994

France has produced a number of directors of genius who made comparatively few films and a great many directors who made a few undistinguished films and disappeared for good. But there are not many main-liners like Christian-Jaque, who maintained a high work rate over 40 years, always kept one eye on the box-office and was France's most successful commercial director from 1950 until 1961, with films exhibited in man-in-the-street cinemas all over the world. These big successes were mostly costume extravaganzas whose costumes were as lush as the ladies' cleavage. Jaque worked with many of the world's most voluptuous actresses, including Gina Lollobrigida, Sophia Loren, Brigitte Bardot, Claudia Cardinale, Melina Mercouri and, on several occasions, Martine Carol, who became the fourth of his five wives. He began as an art director in the films of André Hugon and Julien Duvivier (after coming into the industry as a poster designer following a brief bout of film journalism). The eye for opulent designs that he brought to this work is reflected in his later work as director, especially the post-war films. He churned out films at a prodigious rate in the 1930s, but it was ten years on, as the great directors of the previous decade fell from favour, that his films began to be really popular. One of them, *Fanfan la Tulipe*, with Gérard Philipe and Gina Lollobrigida, a period adventure comedy of tremendous dash and charm, won him the best director award at the Cannes Film Festival, the only major prize he ever won. Ironically it was one of the last films he made in black and white, the rest of his big international successes being in splashy colour, charting the discreetly scandalous goings-on of historical heroines.

1931: *Le bidon d'or*. 1932: †*Adhémar Lampiot*. *Le tendron d'Achile/Achilles' Heel*. 1933: *Ça colle*. *Le boeuf sur la langue*. *La montre*. 1934: *Vilaine histoire*. *Atroce menace*. *Le père Lampion*. *Compartement pour dames seules/Ladies Only*. 1935: *Sous la griffe*. *La sonnette d'alarme*. *Voyage d'agrément*. *La famille Pont-Biquet*. *Sacré Léonce*. 1936: *La maison d'en face (US: The House Across the Street)*. *On ne roule pas Antoinette*. *L'é-

Desperate comeback...for Michael **Cimino,** after the disaster of *Heaven's Gate.* Here he directs Kelly Lynch in *Desperate Hours.*

cole des journalistes. Un de la Légion. Rigolboche. Monsieur Personne/Mr Nobody. Josette. 1937: †Les perles de la couronne (GB & US: The Pearls of the Crown). Les digourdis de la onzième. A Venise, une nuit. Les pirates du rail. Francis the First. 1938. Les disparus de Saint-Agil (US: Boys' School). Ernest le Rebelle. Raphaël le Tatoué. 1939: Le grand élan. L'enfer des anges. 1940: L'assassinat du père Noël (GB: The Killing of Santa Claus. US: Who Killed Santa Claus?). 1941: Premier bal. 1942: La symphonie fantastique. Carmen (released 1945). 1943: Voyage sans espoir. 1944: Sortilèges (US: The Bellman). 1945: Boule de suif. 1946: Un revenant (US: A Lover's Return). 1947: La chartreuse de Parme. 1943: D'homme à hommes. 1949: Singoalla (GB: The Wind is My Lover. US: The Mask and the Sword). *Barrières. 1950: Souvenirs perdus (GB: Lost Property). 1951: Barbe-Bleue (GB & US: Bluebeard). Fanfan la Tulipe. 1952: Adorables créatures. Lucrezia Borgia. 1953: †Destinées (GB: Love, Soldiers and Women. US: Daughters of Destiny). 1954: Madame Du Barry. 1955: Nana. 1956: Si tous les gars du monde... 1958: Nathalie/Nathalie agent secret (GB & US: The Foxiest Girl in Paris). La loi/La loi... c'est la loi (GB: Where the Hot Wind Blows. US: The Law is the Law). 1959: Babette s'en va-t-en guerre (GB & US: Babette Goes to War). 1960: †Love and the Frenchwoman. 1961: Madame Sans-Gêne (GB & US: Madame). 1962: Marco Polo (unfinished). 1963: Les bonnes causes (US: Don't Tempt the Devil). La tulipe noire (GB: & US: The Black Tulip). 1964: Le gentleman de Cocody (GB: Ivory Coast Adventure). Le repas des fauves. 1965: †The Dirty Game. 1966: La seconde vérité. Le Saint prend l'affût (GB: The Saint versus...). 1967: Two Tickets to Mexico/Dead Run. 1968: Lady Hamilton – zwischen Smach und Liebe (GB & US: Emma Hamilton). 1970: Don Camillo et les contestaires (unfinished). 1971: Les pétroleuses (GB & US: The Legend of Frenchie King). 1975: Dr Justice. 1978: La vie parisienne. 1980: Carné: l'homme à la caméra.

CIMINO, Michael 1940-

Breadth of vision or delusions of grandeur? This American director is a man of contradictions as evidenced by his first film Thunderbolt and Lightfoot, which tried to convert itself halfway, from a laconic and likeable adventure into a violent and dislikable thriller. One would say that Cimino does not give enough consideration to the effect of a film as a whole were it not for the way he handled the complex structure of The Deer Hunter, which won him the best director Oscar, as well as an Academy Award as best picture. But after the disaster of Heaven's Gate, which took 18 months to complete, hardly ran 18 days anywhere it played, was slaughtered by the critics and eventually by the director himself who took over an hour out of it, Cimino seemed to be left with nowhere to go. He has managed to make a few films in the ensuing years, but the quality has been largely poor and the content uninteresting in view of the paucity of his product. Desperate Hours was a better thriller than most critics allowed, but it seems certain now that Cimino's reputation will rest on the impact of his best film. A pity this, as it did seem at one time that Cimino had a rare talent for bringing home the true realities of a situation.

1974: Thunderbird and Lightfoot. 1978: The Deer Hunter. 1980 : Heaven's Gate. 1985: Year of the Dragon. 1987: The Sicilian. 1990: Desperate Hours. 1996: The Sunchaser.

CLAIR, René (René-Lucien Chomette) 1898-1981

Charm, lyricism and a keen understanding of the underlying rhythm of a film were the keys to the success of this French film-maker who made his name on the Continent with his very first film, after a short apprenticeship as an actor. Clair was brought up in Paris's market district, and a feeling for the ordinary people and places of the city permeates almost all of his work in his native country. There is something of the flavour of 1930s' Capra in Clair's hymns to the spirit of the ordinary Parisian, except that these stories could never be set in America. Clair accepted the coming of sound with reluctance, but with it came the films that established the Clair Touch, and enhanced his worldwide reputation: Sous les toits de Paris (in which Clair's initial use of everyday sights and sounds greatly intensifies the atmosphere, and really draws us into his world), Le million, A nous la liberté! and Quatorze juillet. These are films about camaraderie and remarkable events in the lives of unremarkable people. Satire (especially to be observed in A nous la liberté! which may have given Chaplin the inspiration for his Modern Times), was never so gentle as in Clair's hands, coated with the delightful visual sparkle that was later to distinguish some of his British and American work. Clair's cameras move in relaxed and unhurried fashion, from terrasses to attic pensions, eavesdropping on conversations (he always wrote his own screenplays) in group scenes that knitted together to produce a picture that whether happily (almost always) or sadly concluded, gave immense pleasure. His touch of the light fantastic buoys up the best of his English-speaking films – The Ghost Goes West, made for Korda in Britain, and (in Hollywood) I Married a Witch and It Happened Tomorrow. The post-war films back in France are always interesting, occasionally even outstanding, but less recognizably René Clair.

1923: Paris qui dort (GB & US: The Crazy Ray). 1924: *Entr'acte. Le fantôme du Moulin Rouge. 1925: Le voyage imaginaire. 1926: La proie du vent. 1927: Un chapeau de paille d'Italie (GB: The Italian Straw Hat. US: The Horse Ate the Hat). 1928: Les deux timides. *La tour. 1930: Sous les toits de Paris (US: Under the Roofs of Paris). 1931: Le million. A nous la liberté! 1932: Quatorze juillet (US: July 14th). 1934: Le dernier milliardaire. 1935: The Ghost Goes West. 1937: Break the News. 1941: The Flame of New Orleans. 1942: I Married a Witch. 1943: †Forever and a Day. 1944: It Happened Tomorrow. 1945: And Then There were None (GB: Ten Little Niggers). 1947: Le silence est d'or (US: Man About Town). 1949: Le beauté du diable (GB: Beauty and the Beast. US: Beauty and the Devil). 1952: Les belles de nuit (US: Beauties of the Night). *Le rouge est mis. 1955: Les grands manoeuvres (US: The Grand Maneuver). 1957: Porte des lilas (US: Gates of Paris). 1960: †Love and the Frenchwoman. 1961: Tout l'or du monde (GB & US: All the Gold in the World). 1962: Les quatres vérités (GB & US: Three Fables of Love; shortened version of original film). 1965: Les fêtes galantes.

CLARK, Bob (Benjamin Clark) 1941-

Louisiana-born director who began in horror films, enjoyed huge success with lowbrow comedies and more recently changed direction entirely to become a potent purveyor of Americana and nostalgia. An outstanding football player in his youth, Clark became a semi-pro on leaving college but turned down an offer to go fully professional with the Detroit Lions to act and direct in the theatre. Deciding to become a film director, Clark made a false start with a movie made in Florida that was never released. Re-locating to Canada, the director raised independent financing for what was to the first of several horror movies, the best of which is Black Christmas, very much a forerunner of the teenagers-in-peril movie that would soon become so popular. This one, though, is atmospheric, frightening and superior in all departments. That was also true of a Sherlock Holmes mystery, *Murder by Decree*, but Clark seemingly tired of chilling spines and tried tickling funny-bones with the 'adult' schoolboy humour of *Porky's*, which was a world-wide hit, and a sequel, which wasn't. Even as *Porky's II* flopped, Clark was already turning his hand to a glowingly observed past in *A Christmas Story*, the first of several pieces of Americana which have latterly included several TV movies.

1968: The Emperor's New Clothes (unreleased). 1970: Children Shouldn't Play with Dead Things, 1972: Dead of Night/Deathdream. 1974: Black Christmas. 1976: Breaking Point. 1978: Murder by Decree/Sherlock Holmes in Murder by Decree. 1980: Tribute. 1982: Porky's. 1983: Porky's II: The Next Day. A Christmas Story. 1984: Rhinestone. 1985: Turk 182! 1987: From the Hip. 1990: Loose Cannons. 1993: The American Clock (TV). 1994: My Summer Story/It Runs in the Family. 1995: Forbidden Memories (TV). Fudge-a-Mania (TV). Derby (TV). 1996: The Ransom of Red Chief (TV). 1998: I'll Remember April (TV)

CLAYTON, Jack 1921-1995

This British director of very meagre output gradually lost prominence following the impact of his first big feature film, *Room at the Top*. Two critical and popular successes *(Room and The Innocents)* were followed by two films that succeeded critically but not at the box-office – *The Pumpkin Eater* and *Our Mother's House*. Then came a long gap of seven years, and a version of *The Great Gatsby*, which succeeded with neither faction; then silence until 1983. Despite the impact of *Room at the Top*, which won two Oscars (although Clayton lost out to William Wyler for *Ben-Hur*) and started both a wave of kitchen-sink films and a whole new era in movie censorship, it seems to me that Clayton tended to make empty films – with the exception of the *The Innocents*. This is ghost story telling with a vengeance and, aided by brilliant black-and-white photography from Freddie Francis (who had also shot *Room at the Top*), Clayton demonstrated a rare talent for inducing the maximum terror from a story by use of suggestion and fleeting but highly disturbing images. He had gone into films at the age of 15, working his way up from third assistant director (or, as he put it, 'general dogsbody') to production manager and first assistant director, during a 13-year spell with Alexander Korda's London Films, interrupted by war service with the RAF Film Unit. The faintly unsettling quality

that he subsequently brought to *The Innocents* characterized all his films, but he did not find enough use for it to make a real impact on an audience and his later films remain at a distance from us.

*1944: *Naples is a Battlefield. 1955: The Bespoke Overcoat. 1958: Room at the Top. 1961: The Innocents. 1964: The Pumpkin Eater. 1967: Our Mother's House. 1974: The Great Gatsby. 1983: Something Wicked This Way Comes. 1987: The Lonely Passion of Judith Hearne. 1992: Memento Mori (TV).*

CLEMENS, William 1905-

Despite my general admiration for the Hollywood 'B' film directors who worked within the system through the 1930s and 1940s, there is very little to get enthusiastic about in Clemens' brief but prolific career at Warner Brothers. He had come to the studio as an editor with the first flush of enthusiasm for sound, and graduated to direction by 1936. Most of the films he made are minor mysteries, including all the Nancy Drew series. Of his other movies, his Boris Karloff vehicle *Devil's Island* is not exceptional, despite promising material. Perhaps Clemens was just not able to excel with the 65-minute structure within which he almost always worked. After leaving Warners in 1942, he worked at Paramount and RKO, making the best of the Tom Conway Falcon series, *The Falcon and the Co-Eds*. But he also directed a couple of average entries from the same series, and was out of films by the end of the decade.

1936: The Law in Her Hands. Down the Stretch. Man Hunt. Here Comes Carter (GB: The Voice of Scandal). The Case of the Velvet Claws. 1937: The Case of the Stuttering Bishop. Once a Doctor. Talent Scout. Footloose Heiress. The Missing Witness. 1938: Torchy Blane in Panama. Accidents Will Happen. Mr Chump. Nancy Drew – Detective. 1939: Nancy Drew Reporter. Nancy Drew — Trouble Shooter. The Dead End Kids on Dress Parade. Nancy Drew and the Hidden Staircase. 1946: Calling Philo Vance. King of the Lumberjacks. Devil's Island. 1941: She Couldn't Say No. The Night of January 16th. 1942: A Night in New Orleans. Sweater Girl. 1943: The Falcon in Danger. Lady Bodyguard. The Falcon and the Co-Eds. 1944: Crime by Night. The Falcon Out West. 1947: The Thirteenth Hour.

CLÉMENT, René 1913-1996

It's a long way down from *La bataille du*

rail to *Wanted: Baby Sitter*, but this French director haplessly lost his way in films and sadly disappointed us in later years. Until the 1960s, however, he did many interesting things in a commendable variety of genres, following beginnings as a documentary director who travelled the world (recovering from typhoid in Tunisia) in search of unusual material. These early films served him in good stead when it came to making his first feature *La bataille du rail*, a gripping and meticulously accurate account of the exploits of the French Resistance during World War II. The film has always brought affection within his own country and he followed it up with an excellent crime thriller *Les maudits*, and then two films which each took a Best Foreign Film Academy Award *The Walls of Malapaga* and *Les jeux interdits*. The latter is probably Clément's best, and certainly most affecting film, the story of two children, a boy of 11 and a girl of five (played by Brigitte Fossey, still acting in films) adrift in World War II, who build up a cemetery for dead animals. These were followed, after a two-year interval, by *Knave of Hearts*, which could well have been made by René Clair – a Frenchman's view of life and love in London. Clément changed direction again to provide *Gervaise*, a doomy period melodrama adapted from Zola's novel, and *Purple Noon/Plein Soleil*, a first-rate thriller adapted from another of Patricia Highsmith's novels about ordinary men trapped by circumstance. The films Clément has made since then are almost all below average by anyone's standards. *Is Paris Burning?* was an overblown war film, carrying nothing like the taut authenticity of *La bataille du rail*, while *Rider on the Rain* was a miserable, leaden attempt by the director to recapture his touch with the *noir* thriller. Awarded a César in 1984 for life achievement, he died from heart trouble.

*1931: *César chez les gaulois (D). 1936: *Soigne ton gauche. 1937: L'Arabie interdite (D). *Paris la nuit (D). 1938: *Flèche d'argent (D). 1939: *La Bièvre (D). *Energie électrique. *Histoire du costume. 1940: *Le triage (D). 1942: *Ceux du rail (D)). *Toulouse (D). 1943: *Chefs de demain (D). *La grande pastorale (D). 1944: *Mountain (D). 1945: La bataille du rail. 1946: Le père tranquille (US: Mr Orchid). Les maudits (GB & US: The Damned). 1949: The Walls of Malapaga/Au-delà des grilles. 1950: Le château de verre. 1952: Les jeux interdits (GB: Secret Games. US: Forbidden Games). 1954: Knave of Hearts (US: Lovers, Happy Lovers). 1955: Gervaise. 1958: The Sea Wall (US: This Angry Age).*

1959: *Plein soleil (GB & US: Purple Noon)*. 1961: *Quelle joie de vivre*. 1962: *Le jour et l'heure (GB & US: The Day and the Hour)*. 1964: *Les félins (GB: The Love Cage. US: Joy House)*. 1965: *Is Paris Burning?* 1969: *Rider on the Rain*. 1971: *La maison sous les arbres (GB & US: The Deadly Trap)*. 1972: *La course du lièvre à travers les champs (GB & US: And Hope to Die)*. 1975: *Wanted: Baby-Sitter*.

CLIFFORD, Graeme 1937-

Following 13 years as an assistant director and leading film editor, often on projects for Robert Altman and Nicolas Roeg, Australian-born Clifford turned director himself. After initial success with *Frances*, however, Clifford has struggled to make a mark in the competitive international film-making field. Clifford had originally studied medicine at Sydney University, but then worked for some years in British and Canadian TV. It was in Canada that he struck up a relationship with Robert Altman that resulted in his first film work, as assistant editor and assistant director on Altman's *That Cold Day in the Park*. After editing Bob Rafelson's version of *The Postman Always Rings Twice* in 1981, Clifford decided to strike out with his own films. The first, *Frances*, was a grim and unrelenting biography of lovely rebel Thirties film star Frances Farmer – a solidly crafted piece of work that won Academy Award nominations for Jessica Lange (as Frances) and Kim Stanley. Clifford returned to his native Australia three years later to make *Burke and Wills*, a sprawling historical adventure drama based on the story of an ill-fated exploration of the continent in 1860. Although fascinating, the overlong film was only marginally entertaining. Overlength was also a problem for Clifford's skateboarding thriller *Gleaming the Cube*, and the best of his more recent work has been for television, working with restricted running times both on a pocket version of Henry James' *The Turn of the Screw* and a TV movie called *Past Tense*, which has Scott Glenn as a police detective who writes novels by night. Inevitably, in a film like this, his two worlds become confused. The signs from Clifford's career to date are that he needs disciplined input from his production and writing teams to produce his best work.

1982: *Frances*. 1985: *Burke and Wills*. 1988: *Gleaming the Cube*. 1989: *The Turn of the Screw (TV)*. 1992: *Ruby Cairo/Deception*. 1993: *Past Tense (TV)*.

CLINE, Edward F. 'Eddie' 1892-1961

This American director, trained with Mack Sennett, worked with some of Hollywood's funniest men on some of their funniest films. And, although his credit is often that of co-director, it can't be just coincidence that the films he made with Buster Keaton, W.C. Fields, Olsen and Johnson and Wheeler and Woolsey are among the zaniest and most surrealistic they ever made – Cline's Sennett background coming home to roost with a vengeance. He had joined Sennett as a comic actor. For some months, he cavorted as a Keystone Cop before becoming one of Sennett's assistants on the other side of the camera. After four years of directing two-reelers for the studio, several of them featuring the Sennett bathing beauties, Cline became friends with Buster Keaton, and the two men collaborated on many of Keaton's craziest, but most inventive comedies of the 1920s, including *The Haunted House, The Boat, Cops, The Frozen North*, and the classics *The Balloonatic* and *The Electric House*. Cline returned to Sennett in 1924 and it would be 15 years before he hit the comedy headlines again, when Universal hired him to direct W.C. Fields' last three big comedies, *My Little Chickadee, The Bank Dick* and *Never Give a Sucker an Even Break*. Universal kept him on to direct Olsen and Johnson comedies, the first of which, *Crazy House*, lived up to its name, as the comics wreak havoc in their own film studio. The team's second film with Cline, *Ghost Catchers*, is also fast and furious fun, but the third, *See My Lawyer*, gave them too little to do. It was the last major comedy film Cline was to handle; Universal also had Abbott and Costello under contract, but they were hardly suited to Cline's style. After shoestring Jiggs and Maggie comedies for Monogram, and collaboration on the screenplays for two more, Cline got out of the business in 1950.

1916: *The Winning Punch. *His Busted Trust. *Sunshine. *His Bread and Butter. *Her First Beau. *Bubbles of Trouble. 1917: *The Dogcatcher's Love. *The Pawnbroker's Heart. *A Bedroom Blunder. *That Night. *Villa of the Movies. 1918: *The Kitchen Lady. *Those Athletic Girls. *His Smothered Love. *The Summer Girls. *Hide and Seek, Detectives. *Whose Little Wife Are You? *Cupid's Day Off. 1919: East Lynne with Variations. *Hearts and Flowers. *When Love is Blond. *A Schoolhouse Scandal. 1920: Sheriff Nell's Comeback. *Mary's Little Lobster. *Training for Husbands. *Monkey Business. *Ten Nights without a Barroom. †*One Week. †*Convict 13.

†*The Scarecrow. †Neighbors. 1921: †*The High Sign. †*The Haunted House. †*Hard Luck. †*Who's Who? *His Meal Ticket. *Singer Midget's Scandal. *Singer Midget's Side Show. †*The Golfer. †*The Boat. †*The Paleface. 1922: †*Cops. *The Frozen North. My Wife's Relations. *Daydreams. †*The Electric House. 1923: †*The Balloonatic/Balloonatics. *Room 23. †The Three Ages. Circus Days. The Meanest Man in the World. *The Love Nest. 1924: Captain January. When a Man's a Man. Little Robinson Crusoe. *Galloping Bungalows. *Off His Trolley. *The Plumber. Good Bad Boy. Along Came Ruth. 1925: *Bashful Jim. *Cold Turkey. *Beloved Bozo. *Love and Kisses. *Tee for Two. *Dangerous Curves Behind. *The Soapsuds Lady. *Hotsy Totsy. The Rag Man. Old Clothes. 1926: *A Love Sundae. *Goose Land. *Puppy Lovetime. *When a Man's a Prince. *Smith's Vacation. *The Gosh-Darn Mortgage. *Flirty Four-Flushers. *Spanking Breezes. *The Ghost of Folly. *Alice Be Good. *Smith's Baby. *A Harem Knight. *A Blonde's Revenge. 1927: *Hold That Pose. *The Girl from Everywhere. *The Jolly Jilter. Let It Rain. Soft Cushions. 1928: Ladies' Night in a Turkish Bath (GB: Ladies' Night). *Love at First Flight. The Head Man. Broadway Fever. The Crash. Vamping Venus. 1929: His Lucky Day. The Forward Pass. 1930: Leathernecking (GB: Present Arms). *Don't Bite Your Dentist. *Take Your Medicine. In the Next Room. Sweet Mama (GB: Conflict). The Widow from Chicago. Hook, Line and Sinker. 1931: *In Conference. *No, No, Lady. *Shove Off. *Mlle Irene the Great. The Girl Habit. Cracked Nuts. 1932: *The Door Knocker. *His Weekend. *The Mysterious Mystery. *The Rookie. Million Dollar Legs. 1933: *Detective Tom Howard of the Suicide Squad. *Uncle Jake. So This is Africa. Parole Girl. 1934: *Girl Trouble. *Not Tonight Josephine. *Morocco Nights. The Dude Ranch. Peck's Bad Boy. 1935: When a Man's a Man. It's a Great Life! The Cowboy Millionaire. 1936: *Love in September. F-Man. 1937: On Again – Off Again. Forty Naughty Girls. High Flyers. 1938: Breaking the Ice. Hawaii Calls. Go Chase Yourself. Peck's Bad Boy with the Circus. 1940: My Little Chickadee. The Villain Still Pursued Her. The Bank Dick (GB: The Bank Detective). 1941: Cracked Nuts. Meet the Champ. Hello Sucker. Never Give a Sucker an Even Break (GB: What a Man). 1942: Private Buckaroo. Snuffy Smith, Yard Bird (GB: Snuffy Smith). What's Cookin'? (GB: Wake Up and Dream). Behind the Eight Ball (GB: Off the Beaten Track). Give Out, Sisters. 1943:

Moonlight and Cactus. He's My Guy. Crazy House. Swingtime Johnny. 1944: Ghost Catchers. Hat Check Honey. Penthouse Rhythm. Night Club Girl. Slightly Terrific. 1945: See My Lawyer. 1946: Bringing Up Father. 1947: Jiggs and Maggie in Society. 1948: †Jiggs and Maggie in Court.

CLOUZOT, Henri-Georges 1907-1977

This French director was so beset by poor health throughout his career that it seems almost remarkable that he actually lived to be 69. Certainly his output was much truncated by illness, but he has managed to leave behind several black suspense thrillers which have hardly a good character between them. Illness had already entered his young life when he was forced to leave Naval Academy (poor eyesight was a factor also). After various jobs, including a spell in journalism, Clouzot found employment with Alphonse Osso's film company, working as writer, assistant director and associate director in turn, and even directing one short film in 1931. Ill-health again laid him low in 1934, and he spent the next four years in a Swiss sanatorium. In 1938, he returned to a career as a screenplay writer, and directed his first feature film three years later. His second, *Le corbeau* (remade eight years later in Hollywood as *The Thirteenth Letter*) caused something of a scandal; its story of poison-pen letters tearing asunder a small French provincial town was seen as pro-Nazi and anti-French and Clouzot was virtually banned from film-making for several years. He regained favour with *Quai des Orfèvres*, perhaps the lightest of all his thrillers and just about the only one with any humour in it. But it was the early 1950s before Clouzot conjured up the two films on which his reputation largely rests. The first of these was the immensely successful *The Wages of Fear*, which in Britain became the first foreign-language film to gain a major circuit release without even the benefit of a second feature. It was, needless to add, the top money-making French film of all time in terms of overseas box-office, a record held until the advent of *Un homme et une femme* 15 years later. The nail-biting story, concerning the efforts of four derelicts, driving two rickety trucks, to transport a dangerous cargo of nitroglycerine over equally dangerous Brazilian jungle roads, was remade unsuccessfully by Hollywood 25 years later. Clouzot's *Les diaboliques*, which also enjoyed wide release outside Europe, is a film of fright whose horrifying sequences – especially one concerning a body in a bath – have been much copied by chiller filmmakers ever

since. Clouzot's later years were greatly hampered by bad health, and he never again attained the success these two films brought him. His wife, the Brazilian actress Vera Amado (1921-1960; they married in 1950), appeared in several of his films as Vera Clouzot, most notably as the hapless victim in *Les diaboliques*.

*1931: *La terreur des Batignolles. 1932: =Chanson d'une nuit. 1933: =Tout pour l'amour. =Caprice de Princesse. =Chateau de rêve. 1941: L'assassin habite au 21 (US: The Murderer Lives at Number 21). 1943: Le corbeau (GB & US: The Raven). 1947: Quai des Orfèvres (US: Jenny Lamour). 1948: Manon. 1949: Miquette et sa mère. †Retour à la vie. 1953: The Wages of Fear. 1954: Les diaboliques (GB: The Fiends. US: Diabolique). 1956: Le mystère Picasso (GB & US: The Mystery of Picasso). 1957: Les espions. 1960: La vérité (GB & US: The Truth). 1968: La prisonnière (GB: Women in Chains. US: The Female Prisoner). 1969: Messa da Requiem.*

= as 'associate director' (French-language versions of German films)

COCTEAU, Jean 1889-1963

A French poet who became a film-maker in his forties, Cocteau proceeded to create films on fantastic themes, with great pictorial beauty, full of haunting, memorable images and distinctly other-worldly, almost ethereal performances from his own little company of actors that included his great friend Jean Marais. Cocteau once said that a film 'permits one to give the appearance of reality to the non-real' and that is exactly what his most famous films do – draw their audience into Cocteau's own gossamer web of fantasy, permitting the watcher to enjoy a child-like participation in the darkly poetic adventures of Beauty, Orphée and others conjured up by Cocteau's fertile imagination. Although, besides writing poetry, Cocteau was also a painter, novelist and playwright, it was in the realm of film-making that he was most completely successful. His films are totally unlike those of anyone else and, in their use of his own obsessions, memories, beliefs and fantasies, close to an autobiographical catalogue of his own life. The friend of composers, dancers and other leaders of French intellectual society in the early part of the 20th century, Cocteau became addicted to opium in the mid-1920s, but was eventually cured and wrote a book about his addiction. His influence on other film directors, from Luis Buñuel through to André Delvaux and Georges

Brainy brothers behind some big critical hits of the 1980s and 1990s, director Joel **Coen** (right) and his writer-producer brother Ethan.

Franju, is unmistakable and understandable: Cocteau's films, even at their most down-to-earth, are never less than stimulating. *Orphée* is certainly one of the most remarkable films ever made, with natural settings brilliantly disfigured by light and shade to suggest mythical regions. Cocteau has also written screenplays for a number of films which he did not direct, but which are all bathed in his influence. These include *La comédie de bonheur* (1940), *L'éternel retour* (1943), *Ruy Blas* (1947) and, most notably, *Les enfants terribles* (1949), based on his novel, on which Cocteau also directed one day's shooting when the director, Jean-Pierre Melville (*qv*), was taken ill.

*1925: *Jean Cocteau fait du cinéma. 1930: Le sang d'un poète (US: The Blood of a Poet. Released 1932). 1945: La belle et la bête (US: Beauty and the Beast). 1947. L'aigle à deux têtes (GB: The Eagle Has Two Heads. US: Eagle with Two Heads). 1948: Les parents terribles (US: The Storm Within). 1949: Orphée (GB & US: Orpheus). 1950: *Coriolan. 1952: La villa Santo-Sospir. 1956: †8 X 8. 1959: Le testament d'Orphée (US: Testament of Orpheus).*

COEN, Joel 1955-

Bespectacled, wild-haired maverick of the American cinema who, with his brother Ethan as producer and co-writer, has produced a fistful of award-winning films in his first few years as a film-maker. Coen's best films are the dark thrillers. His off-centre black comedies all have moments of inspiration but have, on the whole, been less successful. The brothers were film buffs from childhood. Joel attended New York University's Film School and then began a career in the industry, initially as an assistant editor on such cult low-budget horror films as *The Evil Dead*, In 1983, Joel and Ethan struck out on their own with *Blood Simple*, which, on a tiny budget, took the accepted *film noir* elements of adulterous couple, vengeful, dislikeable husband and corruptible private eye and moved them slowly and deliberately towards their destinies. Blood is black here, but fear and agony seem real: the film appeared in several top ten lists for the year, made the brothers' reputations and, as the icing on the cake, starred Frances McDormand, whom Joel married. It was followed by the first Coen comedy, *Raising Arizona*, a flaky film with charmless characters but some very funny moments. Since then, the Coens have scanned various sections of the American landscape for their work, most notably Minnesota in *Fargo*, a grim black comedy about two inept hit-men that featured an Oscar-winning role for Joel's wife Frances as a pregnant police chief. Also of note is *Miller's Crossing*, set in the 1920s: a well-nigh perfect gangster film, it's beautifully written and scored and full of studied scenes. The flawlessly planned plot is crammed with darkness, an element at which the Coens have proved masters: even the light relief in their films is corrosive and uncompromising. Academy Award nomination for *Fargo*.

1983: Blood Simple. 1987: Raising Arizona. 1990: Miller's Crossing. 1991: Barton Fink. 1994: The Hudsucker Proxy. 1996: Fargo. 1998: The Big Lebowski. 1999: La Brava.

COHEN, Larry 1938-

This American film-maker had a 15-year career as a writer, before beginning a distinctive career as a director. Since then, only one of his films, *The Private Files of J. Edgar Hoover,* has reflected his previous work, which had been largely in the realms of criminal investigation and the workings of the law in criminal cases. Suddenly, in 1972, Cohen emerged, as the maker of uncompromising, rough-edged chillers and thrillers that steamrollered their way through an audience; you may not think that Cohen's films are great masterpieces of the cinema, but on the other hand, you don't forget them easily. He does not go in for frills or furbelows but presents the material – he writes all his own screenplays – boldly, usually eliciting disturbingly naturalistic performances from his actors, no matter into what age range they fall. He made his first big impact with *It's Alive!*, the story of a man-eating baby, with a brilliantly pathetic per-

formance from John P. Ryan, an actor usually confined to minor heavies, as the father determined to protect his demon offspring. Like his actors, Cohen shows a great belief in his material, however trite it seems. At the beginning of the 1970s, he made two hard-hitting crime films. After a series of shockers, he returned to the genre by scripting a new version of Mickey Spillane's *I, the Jury;* he had begun to direct it, but gave way to Richard T. Heffron. In the 1980s and 1990s, Cohen continued to shy away from the mainstream. You get the impression that he's the kind of guy that values his independence and would have been happy working for American-International in the 1950s. Some of his rough diamonds have inevitably been failures, others distinctive and haunting oddities. The little-known *The Ambulance,* from 1990, for example, concerns a girl who is carried off by a mysterious ambulance but fails to turn up at any local hospital, setting the scene for a dreamlike black thriller.

1972: Bone/Beverly Hills Nightmare/ Housewife (GB: Dial Rat for Terror). 1973: Black Caesar GB Godfather of Harlem). Hell Up in Harlem. 1974: It's Alive! 1976: Demon/God Told Me To. 1977: The Private Files of J Edgar Hoover. 1978: It Lives Again! 1980: Mamma the Detective (TV). 1981: Full Moon High. 1982: 'Q' – The Winged Serpent. See China and Die (TV). 1984: Special Effects. 1985: Blind Alley/Perfect Strangers completed 1983). The Stuff 1987: It's Alive III: Island of the Alive. †Deadly Illusion. Return to Salem's Lot. 1988: Wicked Stepmother. 1989: Into Thin Air (TV). 1990: The Ambulance. 1991: The Heavy. The Man Who Loved Hitchcock. 1992: The Apparatus. 1995: As Good As Dead (cable TV). 1996: Original Gangstas.

COLLINSON, Peter 1936-1980

This British director brought a TV commercial-maker's eye to feature films and won attention, if not critical approval, with his first four films. *The Penthouse,* dealing with rape, and *The Long Day's Dying,* an intimate but muddy and messy war film, raised a certain amount of controversy (the latter was also a festival award-winner), as did *Up the Junction,* for different reasons as it broadened and coarsened a unique TV original. *The Italian Job,* an amusing caper comedy about a mastermind (Noël Coward) who organizes a huge gold bullion robbery while still serving a prison sentence, was Collinson's most successful commercial film, although its popularity owed much

to a spectacular car chase sequence actually staged by second-unit director Phillip Wrestler. Collinson subsequently developed a frenetic, all-stops-out style of film-making as, without the benefits that studio control might have brought him, the dangers signalled in the earlier films were allowed to develop unchecked into full-scale deficiencies. These were particularly apparent in the chillers he made, although at least *Fright* and *Straight on Till Morning* (both greatly aided by the bravura performances of their female leads, Susan George and Rita Tushingham respectively) never let up. But his two remakes of 1945 suspense classics, *And Then There were None* and *The Spiral Staircase,* are flatly done, with all the tension of worn-out elastic. He hit an all-time low with two films involving Oliver Reed, *The Sell Out* and *Tomorrow Never Comes,* the former of which contains a car sequence somewhat after the one in *The Italian Job;* here alas, the only object seems to be to aim the vehicle at every object in sight on the pavement. The intricacies of *The House on Garibaldi Street* gave some evidence of hope for a more caring director; but then cancer killed him at 44.

1967: The Penthouse. Up the Junction. 1968: The Long Day's Dying. 1969: The Italian Job. 1970: You Can't Win 'Em All. 1971: Fright. 1972: Straight on Till Morning. Innocent Bystanders. 1973: The Man Called Noon. 1974: Open Season. And Then There Were None. 1975: The Sell Out. The Spiral Staircase. 1976: Tigers Don't Cry. 1977: Tomorrow Never Comes. 1979: The House on Garibaldi Street (TV. GB: cinemas). 1980: The Earthling.

COLUMBUS, Chris 1959-

Pennsylvania-born Columbus has already known considerable box-office success in a career largely devoted to youth-oriented and family fare. He sold his first screenplay while still at university, and had penned numerous hits – among them *Gremlins, The Goonies* and *Young Sherlock Holmes* – before turning director at 28. Since then, comedy has been his stock in trade. Most of his films have warmly amusing moments even if few of them are consistently successful. Visual comedy, sometimes of the violent kind, has also figured prominently in his work – and, in *Home Alone* and *Mrs Doubtfire,* he conjured up two of the biggest comedy hits of the 1990s. Ours not to reason why a Mr and Mrs Columbus would actually call their son Christopher, but to date the boy hasn't done badly.

1987: Adventures in Babysitting (GB: A Night on the Town). 1988: Heartbreak

Hotel. 1990: Home Alone. 1991: Only the Lonely. 1992: Home Alone 2: Lost in New York. 1994: Mrs Doubtfire. 1995: Nine Months. 1998: Stepmom.

COMFORT, Lance 1908-1967

After an an apprenticeship as a photographer with medical films, and as a cameraman at Ealing, this British film-maker made a brilliant start to his directorial career with *Hatter's Castle*, a melodramatic but spectacularly effective story of a ruthless Scottish businessman who eventually gets his come-uppance. After this high point, Comfort's career very gradually declined over the years, although he always rose to the occasion when the material with which he was working, however minor, was above average of its kind. Lesser films tended to be pretty dreary in his hands, and his camera was never the most mobile. Thus, after a run of poor films in the 1940s, he fell into second-features. But, ironically, some of these contain his best work. Comfort was quite good at drawing emotional performances from volatile, brittle, intense performers, and the tension and anguish seems very real in such thrillers as *Eight O'Clock Walk*, *Pit of Darkness*, *Tomorrow at Ten* and *Blind Corner*. During the last ten years of his life, he was also a prolific director of half-hour dramas for television, many of them in the *Douglas Fairbanks Presents* series.

1938: *Sandy Steps Out. 1939: *Judy Buys a Horse. 1941: Hatter's Castle. Penn of Pennsylvania (US: The Courageous Mr Penn). 1942: Those Kids from Town. Squadron Leader X. 1943: Escape to Danger. When We Are Married. Old Mother Riley, Detective. 1944: †Hotel Reserve. 1945: Great Day. 1946: Bedelia. 1947. Temptation Harbour. 1948: Daughter of Darkness. 1949: Silent Dust. 1950: Portrait of Clare. 1953: The Girl on the Pier. The Genie. 1954: Bang! You're Dead (US: Game of Danger). Eight O'Clock Walk. 1956: The Man in the Road. 1957: Face in the Night. The Man from Tangier (US. Thunder over Tangier). At the Stroke of Nine. 1959: The Ugly Duckling. Make Mine a Million. 1961: The Breaking Point (US: The Great Armored Car Swindle). Rag Doll (US: Young, Willing and Eager). Pit of Darkness. The Painted Smile (US: Murder Can Be Deadly). 1962: The Break. Tomorrow at Ten. 1963: Touch of Death. Live It Up (US: Swing and Swing). Blind Corner (US: Blind Corner in the Dark). 1964: Devils of Darkness. 1965: Be My Guest.*

CONWAY, Jack 1887-1952

It is hard to understand the low esteem in which this American director is generally held today. I haven't yet found a book on film directors that will even give him space, and publications that do briefly discuss his career dismiss him as, at best, 'a dependable workhorse'. There is surely evidence for a retrial. He had gone to California in 1909 as an actor, becoming a film regular from 1911 then falling under the spell of D.W. Griffith, for whom he worked as an assistant director on *The Birth of a Nation*. By this time (1915),

Conway had already embarked on a directorial career of his own, mostly in two-reelers. Conway, who had much in common with Howard Hawks both as a man and as a director (later they were to co-direct *Viva Villa!* in strange and unhappy circumstances), soon gained a reputation as a director of action films that were technically equal to many similar movies with higher budgets. Joining M-G-M, where he was to stay for the remainder of his career, Conway quickly began to reveal the range of which he was capable. He had already piloted a Joan Crawford vehicle, *Our Modern Maidens*, and directed Lon Chaney twice, first in *While the City Sleeps*, then on Chaney's first and only talkie, a remake of his earlier success *The Unholy Three*. But 1932 was Conway's watershed year and the start for him on a splendid decade of films. *Arsene Lupin* showed for the first time, but not the last, his talent for expressing camaraderie and semi-friendly rivalry between men of the world, in this case played by John Barrymore and his brother Lionel. In the years that followed, Conway worked often with Clark Gable – they were two of a kind, and the empathy showed on screen – Myrna Loy, William Powell and Jean Harlow. He directed four of the fastest, craziest and most acidly witty comedies ever made – *Red-Headed Woman*, *Libeled Lady*, *Love Crazy* and *Too Hot to Handle*, the latter showing again his facility with action-comedy whose characters, however tritely scripted, in Conway's hands radiated warmth and humanity. There are also *Viva Villa!*, with Wallace Beery in rampaging form in what is almost a hymn to the frightening violence within the central character; *A Tale of Two Cities*, by far the best version of Dickens' novel, in which Conway's understanding of masculine make-up helps Ronald Colman create a portrait of doomed destiny not captured by other portrayers of Sydney Carton; and such popular big-scale entertainments as *A Yank at Oxford*, *Boom Town* (the male rivalry theme again, in an epic setting) and *Honky Tonk*. There was also the rather extraordinary *Dragon Seed* (co-directed with Harold S. Bucquet, *qv*) in which Katharine Hepburn poisons what seems like half the officers in the Japanese army in an eye-opening final tableau. After the war Conway seemed, like Gable, changed and tired. He made four more films, all flops, then retired. The case rests.

1914: Captain McLean. 1915: *The Old High Chair. *The Way of a Mother. *The Price of Power. *The Mystic Jewel. The Penitentes. 1916: The Social Buccaneer.

Chris **Columbus** takes the long view while making his smash-hit comedy *Home Alone* in 1990.

The Silent Battle. The Main Spring. Mary, Keep Your Feet Still. The Beckoning Trail. The Measure of a Man. 1917: A Jewel in Pawn. Her Soul's Inspiration. Come Through. The Bond of Fear. Little Mary-Fix-It. Polly's Redhead. The Little Orphan. The Charmer. Because of a Woman. 1918: Her Decision. Little Red Decides. Royal Democrat. You Can't Believe Everything. Lombardi Limited. A Diplomatic Mission. Desert Law. 1919: Restless Souls. 1920: Riders of the Dawn/The Desert of Wheat. The Dwelling Place of Light. Servant in the House. The U.P. Trail. Lure of the Orient. The Money Changers. 1921: The Spenders. The Rage of Paris. The Killer. The Millionaire. A Daughter of the Law. The Kiss. 1922: Across the Deadline. Don't Shoot! Another Man's Shoes. The Long Chance. Step on It! 1923: Trimmed in Scarlet. The Prisoner. Sawdust. What Wives Want. Quicksand. Flaming Passion. Lucretia Lombard. 1924: The Trouble Shooter. The Roughneck (GB: Thorns of Passion). The Heart Buster. 1925: The Hunted Woman. The Only Thing. 1926: Soul Mates. Brown of Harvard. 1927: Twelve Miles Out. The Understanding Heart. 1928: Bringing Up Father. The Smart Set. While the City Sleeps. 1929: Alias Jimmy Valentine. Untamed. Our Modern Maidens. 1930: The Unholy Three. †They Learned About Women. New Moon. 1931: †Five and Ten (GB: Daughter of Luxury. Uncredited). The Easiest Way. Just a Gigolo (GB: The Dancing Partner). 1932: But the Flesh is Weak. Red-Headed Woman. Arsene Lupin. 1933: Hell Below. The Solitaire Man. The Nuisance (GB: Accidents Wanted). 1934: The Girl from Missouri (GB: 100 Per Cent Pure). †Viva Villa! The Gay Bride. †Tarzan and His Mate (uncredited). 1935: One New York Night (GB: The Trunk Mystery). A Tale of Two Cities. 1936: Libeled Lady. 1937: Saratoga. A Yank at Oxford. 1938: Too Hot to Handle. 1939: Lady of the Tropics. Let Freedom Ring. 1940: Boom Town. 1941: Honky Tonk. Love Crazy. 1942: Crossroads. 1943: Assignment in Brittany. 1944: †Dragon Seed. 1947: †Desire Me (uncredited). High Barbaree. The Hucksters. 1948: Julia Misbehaves.

COOK, Fielder 1923-

No-one could accuse this American director of having a dull career. A drama of big business; a brooding action film set in the wilds of Ireland; an offbeat western; a Feydeau farce; a thriller set in Hollywood; a Napoleonic drama; the story of a mentally retarded teenager; a Christmas weepie; a wild west whodunnit; a study of judicial injustice; a baseball romance; a

modern comedy; an adventure about a man undertaking a marathon trip in a wheelchair; and even a version of *Beauty and the Beast*. And there's more. Cook is a man who directs actors well (although you might not realize it if *Prudence and the Pill* was the only one of his films you had seen). His best films *(Patterns, A Big Hand for the Little Lady, How to Save a Marriage . . .)* are meatily enjoyable and incisively scripted. But his output became more uneven in the 1970s and, while continuing to work steadily in television, he has not gained the reputation as a top director in the cinema that one had thought possible after his first film. Perhaps Cook, who began his career in television as a producer following World War II, has been a little too much his own man. He can be earnestly dull, although his best work stands up well to the passage of time. It seemed that he had given up on movie making after 1987. Then, ten years later, he unexpectedly re-emerged with a new and poignant version of *The Member of the Wedding*; more like this could give TV movies a good name.

1956: Patterns (GB: Patterns of Power). 1959: Home is the Hero. 1966: A Big Hand for the Little Lady (GB: Big Deal at Dodge City). 1967: How to Save a Marriage... and Ruin Your Life. 1968: †Prudence and the Pill. 1969: Teacher, Teacher (TV). 1970: Eagle in a Cage. 1971: Sam Hill: Who Killed the Mysterious Mr Foster?(TV). The Price (TV) Goodbye Raggedy Ann (TV). The Homecoming (TV). 1972: The Hands of Cormac Joyce (only shown on TV). 1973: Miracle on 34th Street (TV). From the Mixed-Up Files of Mrs Basil E.

Frankweiler (GB: The Hideaways). 1974: The West was Never Like This/This is the West That Was (TV). 1975: Miles to Go Before I Sleep (TV). 1976: Judge Horton and the Scottsboro Boys (TV). Beauty and the Beast (TV. GB: cinemas). 1977: A Love Affair: The Eleanor and Lou Gehrig Story. 1978: I Know Why the Caged Bird Sings (TV). 1979: Gauguin the Savage. Too Far to Go (TV). 1981: Family Reunion (TV). 1984: Why Me? (TV). 1986: Seize the Day (originally for TV). 1987: A Special Friendship (TV). 1997: The Member of the Wedding (TV).

COOLIDGE, Martha 1946-

What started as an extremely offbeat career by this Connecticut-born director, with a string of documentaries that won awards at festivals, had by the late 1990s flattened itself out into an average mainstream Hollywood career. But at least Coolidge has kept working – and every now and again she scores an a unexpected hit. After film school studies, Coolidge has worked in the industry since she was 18, Many of her films since she started commercial work in the early 1980s have suffered from poor script quality, if always professionally made. Her biggest hit, critically and commercially, came with *Rambling Rose*, the story of a young nymphomaniac in the Southern States of America in the mid 1930s, which turns into a lyrical coming-of-age drama that won Academy Award nominations (the first ever for a mother and daughter in the same year) for Diane Ladd and Laura Dern. That launched Coolidge into a more popular category of film, but her efforts in the field failed to find favour with the public until she combined with

A bearded Francis **Coppola** directs Brat Packers Matt Dillon (right), C Thomas Howell and (back to camera) Ralph Macchio in his cult movie *The Outsiders*.

old-timers Walter Matthau and Jack Lemmon to make one of the more salty of their 1990s' ventures, *Out to Sea*.

1972: David Off and On (D). 1973: More Than a School (D) 1974: Old-Fashioned Girl (D). 1976: Not a Pretty Picture (D). 1978: Bimbo (D). 1979: The Trouble Shooters. 1980: The City Girl (released 1983). 1982: Valley Girl. 1984: Joy of Sex. 1985: Real Genius, 1988: Plain Clothes. 1989: Trenchcoat in Paradise (TV). The Friendly. 1990: Bare Essentials (TV). Rope Dancing. 1991: Rambling Rose. 1992: Crazy in Love (TV). 1993: Lost in Yonkers/Neil Simon's Lost in Yonkers. Angie. 1995: Three Wishes. 1997: Out to Sea. 1999: Dorothy Dandridge (Cable TV)

COOPER, Merian C.
See Schoedsack, Ernest B.

COPPOLA, Francis Ford 1939-
Of all the American 'wonder-boys' of the post-1960 period, Coppola consolidated his position best, and could be said to be the senior citizen of the movement. Despite an unpromising start as director of soft-core sexploitation films, then still very much an underground genre in America, Coppola soon injected himself into the mainstream of film-making after catching the eye with a low-budget horror film. The rest of his 1960s movies did well with the critics, but were only partial box-office successes. Then came the dam-buster, in the shape of Coppola's two *Godfather* films, black, powerful, gripping, bloody and entertaining gangster dramas about the battle for power within the Mafia hierarchy, with hammer-hard performances from Al Pacino and Robert De Niro and a showy performance from Marlon Brando that won him his second Academy Award. The films also showed Coppola's talent as a writer, beautifully structuring the sprawling work of Mario Puzo into fascinating, lucid, literate, strong cinema. Three of his four Oscars have been for shared screenplay work, on *Patton* and the two *Godfather* films. His single individual Oscar is for the direction of *The Godfather, Part II*. In *The Conversation*, Coppola made intriguing entertainment out of a difficult subject – a professional 'bugger' or eavesdropper, played by Gene Hackman, who ultimately finds himself the biter bit. Coppola finally overreached himself in both literary and filmic ambition with *Apocalypse Now*. Despite good sequences, it was beyond even his talents to convert Joseph Conrad's vast novel *Heart of Darkness* into an equally vast parallel film about Vietnam. But the film had its supporters, did respectably well at the box-office and

Roger **Corman** prepares the scene as Alan Napier and Hazel Court deem Ray Milland (in coffin) to be more dead than alive in *The Premature Burial.*

little damage to Coppola's reputation. Since then, he has largely stuck to lighter, character-driven fare. His bigger films have been largely disappointing, notably *The Godfather Part III*, in which Coppola's dynamism is considerably diminished.

*1960: *Ayamonn the Terrible. Bellboy and the Playgirls/The Belt Girls and the Playboy. 1961: *The Peeper. Tonight for Sure. 1962: Come On Out. 1963: Dementia 13 (GB: The Haunted and the Hunted). 1968: Finian's Rainbow. 1969: The Rain People. 1972: The Godfather. 1974: The Conversation. The Godfather Part II. 1979: Apocalypse Now. 1981: One from the Heart. 1983: Rumble Fish. The Outsiders. 1984: The Cotton Club. 1985: *Captain Eo. 1986: Peggy Sue Got Married. 1987: Gardens of Stone. 1988: Tucker: The Man and His Dream. 1989: †New York Stories. 1990: The Godfather Part III. 1993: Bram Stoker's Dracula. 1996: Jack. 1997: The Rainmaker.*

• Coppola also directed some sequences (uncredited) in Roger Corman's films *The Young Racers* and *The Terror*, both 1963.

CORMAN, Roger 1926-
Although this American film-maker became a powerful and innovative independent producer, forever encouraging new young talent to the American cinema, for most of us he will remain the man who directed all those tremendously enjoyable, and increasingly good 'Edgar Allan Poe' horror films of the 1960s, the inhabitants of whose coffins never rested in peace and whose heroines tottered tremulously across the CinemaScope screen, brushing aside the Pathecolor cobwebs and doing the very things liable to end them up on a slab at the mercy of some madman, just as Fay Wray had been doing 30 years earlier. At the beginning of his career, Corman quickly became known as the 'King of the Z-Movies', making exploitational subjects that abounded in black humour, had often been rushed out in less than a week in front of cardboard scenery, and almost all made money. Corman had completed postgraduate studies in English literature at Oxford University, where he first became a Poe aficionado. Before the Poe period in his film career, however, he had already worked up a minor cult for such poverty-budget horror films as *Not of This Earth, Attack of the Crab Monsters, A Bucket of Blood, Wasp Woman* and *The Little Shop of Horrors*. Then came the cycle of tales of terror, made as vehicles for Vincent Price (with the exception of *The Premature Burial*, which was less successful) which made enormous profits from minimal budgets.

The films were stylish, confidently made and full of eye-popping moments of shock: mists rise from the ground, shrieks come from coffins, waves pound upon the shore and vague shapes move behind the windows of castles gone to the bad, while retribution reaches out from the past to claim the protagonists of the tales. The last two films in the series, *The Masque of the Red Death* and *The Tomb of Ligeia*, were made in England to combat rising costs. With *Ligeia*, Corman produced his masterwork, as near perfect an example of a horror film in the Poe/Lovecraft genre as one is ever likely to see. Weakened only by the casting of the heroine (Barbara Steele would have been the best choice), the story, of a nobleman hypnotized by the memory of his dead first wife, is very literate, very frightening and immaculately staged, especially in the scene where the heroine is lured into the bell tower by a black cat. The horror is blended skilfully with a sense of characterization and period. Corman made some interesting films after this, but nothing remotely as striking.

1954: *Five Guns West*. 1955: *Apache Woman*. *The Day the World Ended*. 1956: *The Oklahoma Woman*. *Gunslinger*. *Swamp Women*. *It Conquered the World*. *The Undead*. 1957: *Not of This Earth*. *Naked Paradise*. *Teenage Doll*. *Carnival Rock*. *Rock All Night*. *Viking Women and the Sea Serpent* (GB: *Viking Women*). *Sorority Girl* (GB: *The Bad One*). *She-Gods of Shark Reef* (GB: *Shark Reef*). *Attack of the Crab Monsters*. 1958: *I, Mobster* (GB: *The Mobster*). *War of the Satellites*. *Last Woman on Earth*. *Teenage Caveman* (GB: *Out of the Darkness*). 1959: *A Bucket of Blood*. *Wasp Woman*. 1960: *The Little Shop of Horrors*. *Atlas*. *Creature from the Haunted Sea*. *Ski Troop Attack*. *House of Usher* (GB: *The Fall of the House of Usher*). 1961: *The Intruder* (GB: *The Stranger*). *The Pit and the Pendulum*. 1962: *Poe's Tales of Terror* (GB: *Tales of Terror*). *The Premature Burial*. *Tower of London*. 1963: *The Young Racers*. *The Raven*. *The Terror*. *The Haunted Palace*. 1964: *The Masque of the Red Death*. *The Secret Invasion*. *The Tomb of Ligeia*. 1966: *The Wild Angels*. 1967: *The Trip*. *The St Valentine's Day Massacre*. 1969: *How to Make It* (GB: *Target Harry*). *Bloody Mama*. 1970: *Gas-s-s-s – or It Became Necessary to Destroy the World in Order to Save It*. 1971: *Von Richthofen and Brown* (GB: *The Red Baron*). 1990: *Frankenstein Unbound*.

CORNELIUS, Henry 1913-1958
South Africa-born film-maker who spent many years as an editor before blossoming in post-war years with two peerless comedy classics. Initially an actor, then journalist, he became involved with the film industry while studying at the Sorbonne in Paris. French director René Clair was his idol and Cornelius followed him when he went to England to work for London films on *The Ghost Goes West* in 1935. The studio boss Alexander Korda was impressed with Cornelius' work and he stayed on with them as an editor, working on some of Korda's best films, including *The Drum* and *The Four Feathers*. During World War Two Cornelius returned to South Africa, and began his directing career there on a series of documentaries for General Smuts' Propaganda Unit. Joining Ealing Studios back in Britain after the war, Cornelius hit the jackpot for them with his first film, *Passport to Pimlico*, which he co-wrote with the great T.E.B. Clarke. An explosion in the London suburb of Pimlico reveals documents that lead the inhabitants to declare independence, putting up barbed wire and keeping out officialdom until an honourable settlement is reached. With a script full of a funny incidentals and chucklesome characters, *Pimlico* is brilliantly executed by its director. Cornelius' two remaining successes are in similar comedy vein: that is, the underdog triumphing against the odds. Both were made for his own production company, but both are much in the Ealing mould. In *The Galloping Major*, the title character buys a racehorse that proves to have no speed but an ability to jump sure-footedly. He enters it in the Grand National and is, at the last moment, forced to ride it himself. All the other horses fall and it wins. Also a winner was *Genevieve*, a huge box-office success about the 'old crocks rally' to Brighton and back which roared to success on the backs of a whimsical script by Reginald Rose and two new box-office stars in Kenneth More and Kay Kendall. Ironically, More also starred in Cornelius' last film *Next to No Time!* But the director's light touch appeared to have deserted him – and there was no time to regain lost ground.

1940: **Northwards/Noordwaarts* (D). 1942: **Who Me?* (D). **Libya* (D). *We of Velddrift* (D). 1949: *Passport to Pimlico*. 1951: *The Galloping Major*. 1953: *Genevieve*. 1955: *I Am a Camera*. 1958: *Next to No Time!*

COSMATOS, George Pan
(Yorgo Pan Cosmatos) 1941-
This Greek-born international film director seems to have produced such a steady output of mainly popular films for so long that it comes as a surprise to find he's actually directed so few. Originally planning a career in the diplomatic service, Cosmatos read law at university but switched careers and attended the London Film School instead. After working in various capacities in the industry including art direction on *Zorba the Greek*, he made an inauspicious beginning as a director with *The Beloved/Restless*, a Raquel Welch vehicle that sent its audiences to sleep. Cosmatos soon revealed, though, that his major talent lay in shooting thundering action at often, though, a stylishly even pace. All too sadly the scripts of his films have not matched the visuals. But when the story and characters have been credible as in *The Cassandra Crossing* or the more recent *Tombstone*, then Cosmatos scores a popular hit.

1970: *The Beloved/Restless* (GB TV, as *Sin*). 1973: *Rappresaglia/Massacre in Rome*. 1976: *The Cassandra Crossing*. 1978: *Escape to Athena*. 1983: *Of Unknown Origin*. 1985: *Rambo: First*

Costa-Gavras at work on one of the best of his documentary-style thrillers, *Missing*.

Blood Part II. 1986: Cobra. 1989: Leviathan. 1993: Tombstone. 1996: The Shadow Conspiracy.

COSTA-GAVRAS

(Konstantinos Costa-Gavras) 1933-
Costa-Gavras is an angry director whose passion sometimes overrides his cinematic sense and whose films club away at their audience in much the same way as Yves Montand is attacked in Z. He was born in Greece, of Russian-Greek parentage, and moved into film direction in the most usual manner, that is to say, film studies followed by progression up the ladder from general assistant to second assistant director to first assistant director. In 1962, he undertook his first independent project, a documentary set in the Arctic Circle. After several months shooting in Greenland, the project was abandoned. His first fictional feature film is still in many ways his best. The Sleeping Car Murder is a superb thriller, set on board a train and shot in black-and-white. It introduced Costa-Gavras to the actor Yves Montand, who was to star in almost all his subsequent films. In 1966, the political side of Costa-Gavras' nature began to make itself apparent in Shock Troops and, in 1969, he bombshelled the world with Z, a gripping, violent and horrifying political thriller clearly based on the Greek colonels and their oppressive regime. The film was a success, and won an Academy Award as best foreign-language film. It was followed by The Confession (Montand had the central role in both these films) which also received worldwide distribution and commented bitterly on brainwashing tactics allegedly employed by Communists in Czechoslovakia. Costa Gavras' subsequent cries against political injustice were less successful, and in the late 1970s, he changed course, to make two poignant films with women as the central figures. In 1981, he re-emerged as a political animal with his first American movie, Missing, a drama clearly set against the possibly American-backed coup in Chile in 1973. Universal boldly backed the venture, and the result was an affecting and absorbing film, showing its director as dedicated as ever to making films which entertain while crying out against politically motivated injustices throughout the world. Although Missing remains the best of his later films, his work has retained its characteristic intensity. A naturalised Frenchman since 1956, he is married to the former war correspondent Michèle Ray.

1965: Compartiment tueurs (GB & US: The Sleeping Car Murder). 1966: Un homme de trop (GB & US: Shock Troops). 1968: Z. 1969: L'aveu (GB & US: The Confession). 1972: Etat de siège (GB & US: State of Siege). 1975: Section spéciale (GB & US: Special Section). 1977: La vie devant soi (GB & US: Madame Rosa). 1979: Clair de femme. 1981: Missing. 1983: Hanna K. 1986: Conseil de famille. 1988: Betrayed. 1990: Music Box. 1992: Contre l'oubli. 1993: La 199, petite apocalypse. 1995: †A propos de Nice. Lumière et cie. 1997: Mad City.

CRABTREE, Arthur 1900-1975

This British director was an excellent cameraman who, when he turned to direction, made superficial, artificial, stilted, showy period melodramas that just happened to be highly exploitable. Thus he flourished briefly at Gainsborough Studios in the late 1940s with films that, with the post-war public still seeking extravagance and escapism, flew in the face of critical disapproval to romp home at the box-office. The remainder of Crabtree's films did less well, but he worked prolifically in television, directing scores of half-hour action films. Before retiring, he also made two especially nasty horror films in the wake of a Hammer-induced resurgence of interest in the genre. Best film: Dear Murderer.

1944: Madonna of the Seven Moons. 1945: They Were Sisters. 1946: Caravan. 1947: Dear Murderer. 1948: †Quartet. The Calendar. 1949: Don't Ever Leave Me. 1950: Lilli Marlene. 1952: Hindle Wakes (US: Holiday Week). 1953: The Wedding of Lilli Marlene. Stryker of the Yard (TV. GB: cinemas). 1956: West of Suez (US: Fighting Wildcats). 1957: Death Over My Shoulder. Morning Call (US: The Strange Case of Dr Manning). 1958: Fiend without a Face. 1959: Horrors of the Black Museum.

COX, Alex 1954-

Britain's Alex Cox talks a great film. Few directors actually know more about the art of making movies, what makes them tick, and where they go wrong (or right). The sad thing is that, after great beginnings, Cox has all too often had trouble putting theory into practice. Following film studies in Britain and the US, he went to Hollywood where, at first unable to find work, he spent a short spell with a car repossession company. This gave him the idea for his first feature, Repo Man, a black fantasy comedy that became a huge cult hit. Cox returned to Britain for Sid and Nancy, an exceptionally well-made study of the rise and fall of a punk rocker, with amazingly naturalistic performances. It seemed that Cox could write his own ticket after these two successes, but unfortunately they let him do it. Straight to Hell was a surrealistic, self-indulgent spaghetti Western, which few people understood, or wanted to. Walker, in which Cox turns a historical epic (set in 1855 Nicaragua) into an absurdist farce, was another flop, and Cox looked in other directions, among them writing and commenting on films for British TV. Four years later he went to Mexico to make another film. 'It's amazing what a director can do,' he said, 'when he is freed from the traditional limitations imposed on him by Hollywood films.' Hmm. The resultant film, Highway Patrolman, though not without interest, wasn't shown in the UK until 1994. Again, few people saw it. Cox has filmed more regularly in recent times, although there were problems with The Winner, a jumbled mess about girls and gambling, from which Cox tried (unsuccessfully) to withdraw his name after it was re-cut by the producers. It seems that Cox's nihilistic style is suited only to a few screen subjects, but he is still likely to stun us all again one of these days.

1984: Repo Man. 1986: Sid and Nancy. 1987: Straight to Hell. Walker. 1991: Highway Patrolman/El Petrullero (released 1994). 1995: Death and the Compass. 1996: The Winner. 1998: Three Businessmen.

CRAVEN, Wes (Wesley Craven) 1939-

After years of producing and directing gruesome horror movies which sometimes ran into censorship problems, Ohio-born Craven has achieved mainstream success in more recent times by making horror films that are fast-moving, slightly less objectionable than those with which he started and spoofy in a cunningly stylish way. Brought up by strict Baptist parents, Craven didn't even see a film until he was in college, where he excelled in studies. Becoming a university professor (he taught humanities) with a formidable set of educational qualifications, Craven shocked his parents by switching careers at 30 and moving into films. After several films as editor, writer or assistant producer, he directed his first movie, Last House on the Left, in 1972. It contained graphic torture scenes with teenage girls at the mercy of a trio of sadists, and set the pattern for a career spent almost entirely in sometimes repulsive, sometimes notorious horror. Financing problems meant that the next, The Hills Have Eyes, was five years in coming, but with its hillbilly hellions terrorising hapless travellers, it probably remains the

Wes **Craven,** now more famous for films in the Scream and Nightmare on Elm Street series conjures up a little terror in the night for *Shocker.*

director's most controversial. After these two grisly (some would say disgusting) numbers, Craven went rather quiet in a fairly fallow period, during which he was unwise enough to make a sequel to *The Hills Have Eyes* that is by some way his worst film. He did not re-emerge as a high profile shockmaster until 1984, when his film *A Nightmare on Elm Street* created a franchise of seven episodes that would eventually be ended by Craven himself. In dream-stalking bogeyman Freddy Krueger, Craven created one of the memorable figures of cinematic horror, but again failed to capitalise on his success by making poor films for major studios, until returning to the Krueger character ten years later in ingenious fashion. After five sequels from other hands Craven turned the formula on its head by having Krueger invade the dreams of the actors who had created parts in the series. This was almost as scary, jolting and nail-biting as *Poltergeist*, but after a poor vehicle for Eddie Murphy, Craven did even better at the box-office with *Scream* and *Scream 2*, spoof horrors written by the talented Kevin Williamson that had more in-references to horror movies and the way they're made than corpses. The one-time *enfant terrible* of the horror genre is now in danger of becoming its grand old man. He calls his movies 'an allowable insanity. They bleed off America's capacity for violence and help us exorcise our demons.'

1972: *Last House on the Left.* 1977: *The Hills Have Eyes.* 1978: *Summer of Fear/Stranger in Our House (TV).* 1981: *Deadly Blessing.* 1982: *Swamp Thing.* 1983: *The Hills Have Eyes Part II.* 1984: *Invitation to Hell (TV).* A *Nightmare on Elm Street.* 1985: *Chiller (TV).* 1986: *Deadly Friend.* 1988: *The Serpent and the Rainbow.* 1989: *Shocker.* 1991: *The People Under the Stairs.* 1994: *Wes Craven's New Nightmare.* 1996: *Scream.* 1997: *Scream 2.* 1998: *Bad Moon Rising.* 1999: *50 Violins.*

CRICHTON, Charles 1910-

A British director who turned out to be one of the sturdiest products of Ealing Studios, Crichton proved himself equally at home handling whimsical comedy or sentimental drama. He also brought a fresh, straight-from-the-streets quality to the portrayal of children on screen. He worked increasingly for television after the final closure of Ealing in 1959, and was almost entirely lost from films to that medium. His first film work was in the cutting rooms of London Films, where he rose from assistant editor to be one of London's most valuable editors by the mid-1930s. In 1939, he joined Ealing in the same capacity, turning director in 1944. The success that made him a major director there was *Hue and Cry*, about a band of London street urchins (led by Harry Fowler, who had already worked for Crichton on *Painted Boats*) who bring a gang of dockside crooks to book. Not for the first time, Crichton shot on real locations, an innovative practice in the British cinema in 1947. His two best films were both made in 1951: *The Lavender Hill Mob*, a fast, furious and very funny comedy, crammed with incident and amusing little vignettes, about a mild bank clerk (Alec Guinness) who plans a huge bullion robbery; and *Hunted*, a forerunner of *Tiger Bay* in its study of the relationship between a child, in this case a runaway boy, and a murderer on the run. *The Battle of the Sexes* and *He Who Rides a Tiger* (an underrated, in-depth look at the criminal mind), are the best of Crichton's later films. In addition to the films listed below, some sources indicate that he also directed a short, *Young Veteran*, for Ealing in 1941, although this is credited on screen to Alberto Cavalcanti (qv), with Crichton credited as editor. In 1988, he emerged vigorously from retirement to earn an Oscar nomination for his direction of the hit comedy *A Fish Called Wanda*, which carried raunchier and more ribald echoes of his Ealing days.

1944: *For Those in Peril.* 1945: *Painted Boats (US: The Girl on the Canal).* †*Dead of Night.* 1947: *Hue and Cry.* 1948: *Against the Wind. Another Shore.* 1949: †*Train of Events.* 1950: *Dance Hall.* 1951: *The Lavender Hill Mob. Hunted (US: The Stranger in Between).* 1953: *The Titfield Thunderbolt.* 1954: *The Love Lottery. The Divided Heart.* 1956: *The Man in the Sky (US: Decision Against Time).* 1958: *Law and Disorder. Floods of Fear.* 1959: *The Battle of the Sexes.* 1960: *The Boy Who Stole a Million.* 1964: *The Third Secret.* 1965: *He Who Rides a Tiger.* 1968: **Tomorrow's Island.* 1970: **London–Through My Eyes (D).* 1983: **Perishing Solicitors.* 1988: *A Fish Called Wanda.*

CRICHTON, Michael 1942-

A fast-writing, best-selling American novelist who decided to make some of his own films instead of watching other people make them from his original stories. Crichton has nonetheless still made too few films, considering that the first four were extremely good entertainment. After starting his career writing paperback thrillers, Crichton turned to science-fiction (the most interesting films made from his books which he did not direct are both in this genre – *The Andromeda Strain* and *The Terminal Man*). Crichton continued vaguely in this vein for his own directorial debut, the fascinating and finally breathtakingly exciting *Westworld*, concerning a holiday paradise peopled by robots which eventually turn against the holidaymakers. Also exciting was *Coma*, a thriller which combined elements of science-fiction with Crichton's own medical background (he was an honours graduate in medicine from Harvard) and had a girl, gutsily played by Genevieve Bujold, as its central character. Full of excitement and suspense, it really had one on tenterhooks: the few films that he has made show Crichton as one of the most skilful manipulators of an audience on the Hollywood scene. A big box-office hit would be a deserved event and do the impetus of his directorial career no harm at all. Since 1988, however, he has again concentrated on writing and become one of the world's richest authors via the success of *Rising Sun, Disclosure* and the *Jurassic Park* books; all four of these were made into successful films.

1972: *Pursuit (TV).* 1973: *Westworld.* 1977: *Coma.* 1978: *The First Great Train Robbery.* 1981: *Looker.* 1984: *Runaway.* 1988: *Physical Evidence.*

CROMWELL, John
(Elwood Cromwell) 1887-1979
Despite making 45 films, Ohio-born Cromwell was really only a migrant visitor in Hollywood's golden summer, flying back to his first love, the stage, when the film capital's vintage years were over. He had already been a stage director for nigh on 20 years when sound brought him to films, following an appearance in one, *The Dummy* (1929), as an actor. Cromwell worked a lot with David O. Selznick, and seems largely to have been content to follow the powerful producer's instructions, although he was always loath to allow too much sentimentality into his films, one thing on which he and Selznick always argued. Still, there were some films into which Cromwell undoubtedly managed to insert personal

touches of acerbity; his pictures were extremely polished, fluid and well-edited. Notable among his successes were *Of Human Bondage, Banjo on My Knee, The Prisoner of Zenda, Algiers, Abe Lincoln in Illinois* and *Since You Went Away,* in which Cromwell's understanding of relationships and flair for enlivening even dull actors helped to lift the basic material above itself. The duel scene in *Zenda* is, of course, among the finest of its kind. In post-war years, and away from Selznick, a grittier, tougher Cromwell was revealed, especially in *Dead Reckoning, Caged* and *The Racket.* These are harder and certainly less good-humoured films, in keeping with the times; but in 1951 he fell out with RKO's Howard Hughes and returned to the stage. The three films he made some years afterwards formed an unnecessary coda to his cinema career. In the late 1970s Cromwell was seen as a very elderly character player in the Robert Altman films *Three Women* and *A Wedding.*

1929: †*The Dance of Life.* †*Close Harmony. The Mighty.* 1930: *The Texan (GB: The Big Race). For the Defense. Street of Chance. Tom Sawyer.* 1931: *The Vice Squad. Scandal Sheet. Unfaithful. Rich Man's Folly.* 1932: *The World and the Flesh.* 1933: *Double Harness. Sweepings. The Silver Cord. Ann Vickers.* 1934: *This Man is Mine. Spitfire. The Fountain. Of Human Bondage.* 1935: *Village Tale. Jalna. I Dream Too Much.* 1936: *To Mary – with Love. Little Lord Fauntleroy. Banjo on My Knee.* 1937: *The Prisoner of Zenda.* 1938: *Algiers.* 1939: *In Name Only. Made for Each Other.* 1940: *Abe*

The calm behind the storm... David **Cronenberg,** director of such controversial items as *Crash, Naked Lunch, The Fly* and *Dead Ringers.*

Lincoln in Illinois (GB: Spirit of the People). Victory. 1941: *So Ends Our Night.* 1942: *Son of Fury.* 1944: *Since You Went Away.* 1945: *The Enchanted Cottage.* 1946: *Anna and the King of Siam.* 1947: *Dead Reckoning. Night Song.* 1949: †*Adventure in Baltimore (GB: Bachelor Bait. Uncredited).* 1950: *Caged. The Company She Keeps.* 1951: *The Racket.* 1958: *The Goddess.* 1959: *The Scavengers.* 1960: *De Sista Stegen (GB & US: A Matter of Morals).*

CRONENBERG, David 1943 -

Canadian director who has been drawn to the gruesome and controversial throughout his career. Attracting anger and admiration in equal proportions, he has, like the protagonists of his 1996 film *Crash,* seemed to seek out some new, more macabre and painful-looking sensation with each new venture. Sometimes it seems that the phlegmatic Cronenberg is hoping each fresh film will out-gross the last in more ways than one. At any rate, his movies continue to absorb his fans and disgust his detractors. Since the mid-1980s, however, their quality has, on the whole, been disappointing. He had studied science at Toronto University and made two minor films before the idea for his breakthrough movie, *The Parasite Murders,* came to him. It took him three years to obtain the finance to make it, but the end product was devastating. Cronenberg burst on the film scene with the same power as his parasite creatures, which erupted to sick-making effect from the bodies of the humans in whom they had grown. The best of his early films, *The Parasite Murders, Rabid* and *Scanners,* all tend to echo *Invasion of the Body Snatchers. Rabid* especially captures with commendable imagination the atmosphere of a city under siege by an enemy it can't quite envisage. In *Scanners,* the subject matter (people who can literally blow the minds of others) remains fascinating to the end, and the effects are exceptional especially in the blowing-up of a head and the bulging and splitting of veins in a duel to the death between two 'scanners'. Cronenberg continued to dwell on parts of the human body splitting and mutating. The best of the grotesque abnormalities that have resulted from this theme has been *The Fly,* a remake of Kurt Neumann's 1958 film in which a man and a fly get their genes mixed in a teleportation chamber. Tailor-made for a director of Cronenberg's leanings, to be sure, and yet the subject and its treatment have a humanity that many of his other projects lack. *Dead Ringers* the next, had its supporters as well as a *tour de force* perfor-

mance by Jeremy Irons as twin surgeons, the battier of whom (by a whisker) strives to create steel implements for operating on mutant women. How Cronenberg eyes must have gleamed at that. Not many, though, went to see the next, *M. Butterfly* (a failed change of pace) or *Naked Lunch,* a morose adaptation of William S Burroughs' book in which an insect exterminator becomes hooked on his own bug powder and, hallucinating, imagines typewriters that turn into cockroaches with talking orifices, or gooey monsters with phallic appendages on their heads. Cronenberg got himself back into the headlines in 1997 with *Crash,* a viewer-unfriendly movie about people turned on by car crashes and their wounded victims. There seems little place left for Cronenberg to go, but no doubt he'll find somewhere.

1966: **Transfer. *From the Drain (student films).* 1969: *Stereo.* 1970: *Crimes of the Future.* 1974: *The Parasite Murders (GB: Shivers. US: They Came from Within).* 1976: *Rabid.* 1978: *Fast Company.* 1979: *The Brood.* 1980: *Scanners.* 1982: *Videodrome.* 1983: *The Dead Zone.* 1986: *The Fly.* 1988: *Dead Ringers.* 1991: *Naked Lunch.* 1993: *M. Butterfly.* 1996: *Crash.* 1999: *EXistenZ.*

CROSLAND, Alan 1894-1936

Crosland was a sophisticated, man-about-town Hollywood director. Today he is remembered mainly as the man who made the first feature-length part-talkie, *The Jazz Singer.* Yet his strength really lay in costume melodrama, where his light touch and vivid imagination could come into its own. Formerly an actor, he had joined the Edison company in 1912, initially working in the publicity department, and later contributing to the scripts of short subjects. One he would presumably have liked to forget was titled *Santa Claus versus Cupid.* He began directing in 1917, but his films were routine until he signed a contract with William Randolph Hearst to make big-budget period epics, with lots of romance and action. Through such films as *The Enemies of Women, Under the Red Robe* and *Romance of a Queen,* Crosland's reputation grew, until Warners hired him in 1926 to direct their spectacular version of *Don Juan,* with John Barrymore and Mary Astor. Crosland duly produced the goods – the kind of high-gloss, tasteful hokum for which he was noted, and subsequently worked again with Barrymore on *The Beloved Rogue. Don Juan* happened also to be the first full-length film feature with synchronized music, so it was natural that, when Warners came to make *The Jazz Singer*, with its musical interludes in full sound, Crosland was their choice to direct. In fact, Crosland's theatrical style of direction was unsuited to a film like *The Jazz Singer*, and it looks extremely static and tedious today. His sound films are a varied bunch, some not without interest, but none memorable: he was essentially a man of the silent era, both in personality and style. Crosland barely survived a horrendous car crash at the height of his fame in 1925: 11 years later, he was involved in a second automobile smash-up. This time he was killed.

1917: *Friends, Romans and Leo. Chris and the Wonderful Lamp. Knights of the Square Table. The Apple-Tree Girl. Kidnapped. Light in Darkness. The Little Chevalier. The Story That the Keg Told Me. 1918: The Unbeliever. The Whirlpool. 1919: The Country Cousin. 1920: The Flapper. Greater Than Fame. The Point of View. Youthful Folly. Broadway and Home. 1921: Worlds Apart. Room and Board. Is Life Worth Living? 1922: The Prophet's Paradise. Why Announce Your Marriage? Slim Shoulders. The Snitching Hour. Shadows of the Sea. The Face in the Fog. 1923: Under the Red Robe. The Enemies of Women. 1924: Miami. Three Weeks (GB: The Romance of a Queen). Unguarded Women. Sinners in Heaven. 1925: Compromise. Contraband. Bobbed Hair. 1926: Don Juan. When a Man Loves (GB: His Lady). 1927: The Beloved Rogue. Old San Francisco. The Jazz Singer. 1928: Glorious Betsy. The Scarlet Lady (GB: The Scarlet Woman). 1929: On With the Show. General Crack. 1930: Viennese Nights. Captain Thunder. Song of the Flame. The Furies. Big Boy. 1931: Children of Dreams. The Silver Lining/Thirty Days. 1932: Week-Ends Only. 1933: Massacre. 1934: Midnight Alibi. The Personality Kid. The Case of the Howling Dog. 1935: Mister Dynamite. It Happened in New York. The White Cockatoo. Lady Tubbs (GB: The Gay Lady). King Solomon of Broadway. 1936: The Great Impersonation.

CROWE, Cameron 1957 -

A teenage writing prodigy whose talent has taken a long time to flower, Crowe hit the big time at last in 1996 with *Jerry Maguire*. But, since Crowe's films are character-driven rather than depending on action and special effects, his late emergence in today's cinema is perhaps no surprise. A writer for the magazine *Rolling Stone* at 15, he had written a best seller, *Fast Times at Ridgemont High*, in his early twenties, also contributing the

screenplay to the film version in 1982. Crowe continued to write occasionally for the cinema until making his own debut as director with *Say Anything*. Still a teen drama but one with a difference, its story is about people with feet of clay, and, like Crowe's other films, it makes uplifting rather than dispiriting watching for younger audiences. *Singles*, though it has a cult following, is less successful, mainly thanks to its lack of interesting characters, an accusation that could never be levelled at *Jerry Maguire*, which proved that Crowe had learned valuable lessons from his previous script. The tremendous emotional build at the end of this comedy-drama about a man looking for the better part of himself, coupled with a great Tom Cruise speech, sent audiences home elated – and won the film a huge slice of box-office glory. Crowe looks set to prove himself a welcome shaft of dramatic light in a nineties' cinema rather lacking in variety. His brother, Christopher Crowe, has also directed films, among them *Saigon/Off Limits* (1988) and *Whispers in the Dark* (1992).

1988: Say Anything. 1992: Singles. 1996: Jerry Maguire.

CROWE, Christopher

See CROWE, Cameron

CRUZE, James (Jens Cruz Bosen) 1884-1942

A prominent American director of silent films, who did not adjust too well to sound (and left Hollywood in 1938), Cruze was hypnotized by scale and visual effect. Thus his best films – *The Covered Wagon, Beggar on Horseback, Old Ironsides* – are often breathtaking to watch, the work of a brilliant screen draughtsman. But they do lack character and character development, a fault he was no longer able to conceal with the coming of sound, which he did not welcome. Much of his inventive visual work, however, greatly influenced action films of the 1930s. He was born in Utah, of Danish Mormon parents, and had become an actor in vaudeville by 1906. He joined the Thanhouser film company in 1911 as an actor and stuntman, gaining a reputation for surviving a large variety of extremely daring and dangerous stunts unscathed. Ironically, in 1918, he badly broke a leg – by stepping in a gopher hole. This accelerated his desire to turn to direction, and he was soon recognized as a prolific and efficient craftsman, although it was 1923 before he moved into the front rank of Hollywood directors with *The Covered Wagon*. The

sweeping panoramas – covered wagons trekking across plains, crossing the River Platte or winding through a massive box-canyon – and meticulous re-creation of the period (1848) won wide praise for the film and its director. Today, the film still retains this pioneer documentary air. In the next three years, Cruze directed some remarkable films, among them *Hollywood, Ruggles of Red Gap, Merton of the Movies, Old Ironsides*, another western, the fast-moving *The Pony Express*, and the almost surrealistic *Beggar on Horseback*. All these were thoughtful, beautifully photographed movies, packed with detail. By 1927, Cruze was the highest paid director in the world ($7,000 a year). But his career was already in decline, a situation exacerbated by sound. His best 1930s pictures are two with Will Rogers, *Mr Skitch* and *David Harum*, but in 1935 Rogers died in a plane crash before the association could be furthered. Seven years later Cruze, already out of films, followed him in death. He was married to actresses Marguerite Snow (1913-1924) and Betty Compson (1924-1930).

1918: Too Many Millions. The Dub. 1919: You're Fired! Alias Mike Moran. Valley of the Giants. An Adventure in Hearts. Hawthorne of the USA. The Roaring Road. The Love Burglar. The Lottery Man. 1920: The Sins of St Anthony. Terror Island. A Full House. Always Audacious. Mrs Temple's Telegram. What Happened to Jones. Food for Scandal. The Charm School. 1921: The Dollar-a-Year Man. Crazy to Marry. Gasoline Gus. The Fast Freight. 1922: Leap Year/Skirt Shy (unreleased). Is Matrimony a Failure? The Dictator. Thirty Days. One Glorious Day. The Old Homestead. 1923: To the Ladies. The Covered Wagon. Hollywood. Ruggles of Red Gap. 1924: Merton of the Movies. The Fighting Coward. The Enemy Sex. City That Never Sleeps. The Garden of Weeds. 1925: Welcome Home. Wake Up the Town. Beggar on Horseback. The Pony Express. Marry Me. The Goose Hangs High. 1926: Old Ironsides (GB: Sons of the Sea). Mannequin. The Waiter from the Ritz. 1927: On to Reno. We're All Gamblers. The City Gone Wild. 1928: Excess Baggage. The Mating Call. The Red Mark. 1929:The Great Gabbo. The Duke Steps Out. A Man's Man. 1930: Once a Gentleman. She Got What She Wanted. 1931: Salvation Nell. 1932: †If I Had a Million. Washington Merry Go-Round (GB: Invisible Power). Racetrack. 1933: I Cover the Waterfront. Sailor Be Good. Mr Skitch. 1934: Their Big Moment (GB: Afterwards). Helldorado. David Harum. 1935: Two-Fisted.

Director George **Cukor** tells a press conference how he overcame all obstacles to bring home the Oscar-winning *My Fair Lady*.

1936: *Sutter's Gold.* 1937: *The Wrong Road.* 1938: *Gangs of New York. Prison Nurse. Come On Leathernecks!*

CUKOR, George 1899-1983
Up to his death Hollywood's oldest working director, Cukor, despite an obvious predilection (and talent) for extracting the maximum warmth and character from major female stars, stubbornly resisted the attempts of many critics to pigeonhole his talent. He created many films with characters one cares about, despite an often artificial setting, and all of his pictures were major studio (mostly M-G-M) productions. He worked in the theatre from 1919, initially as stage manager, then as director from 1923. Brought to Hollywood in 1929 more or less as a dialogue director, Cukor's reputation as a 'woman's director' began in 1932 with *What Price Hollywood?* a scathing look at the film capital with Constance Bennett (later remade as *A Star Is Born* with Cukor himself directing the 1954 musical version) and *A Bill of Divorcement.* The latter film introduced Katharine Hepburn, beginning an association between director and star that continued to flower, apart from a hiccough in 1972 when she

refused to star in his *Travels with My Aunt.* Subsequent Cukor films in which the Hepburn persona is used to best advantage include *Little Women, Holiday, Adam's Rib, The Philadelphia Story, Pat and Mike* and *Love Among the Ruins.* There were one or two misfires from the partnership, notably the dismal *Sylvia Scarlett,* which required Hepburn to spend most of the film dressed as a boy. Although it was a flop in its day, it has been somewhat mysteriously revered by some critics in recent times. Cukor also extracted above-average performances from Jean Harlow (in *Dinner at Eight),* Claudette Colbert (in *Zaza),* Joan Crawford (in *A Woman's Face,* the film that started her 1940s suffering), Ingrid Bergman (in *Gaslight),* Judy Holliday (in *Born Yesterday),* Judy Garland (in *A Star Is Born)* and Sophia Loren (in *Heller in Pink Tights),* while in *The Women* he had many of Hollywood's foremost actresses in one film. Cukor also made some delightful comedies, usually with Hepburn, Holliday or Spencer Tracy involved, but from the mid-1950s his films were less consistent. It was a surprise when he at last took an Oscar in 1964 for *My Fair Lady,* by no means one of his best films, nor even one containing a great female

performance, as Audrey Hepburn unexpectedly struggled with the role of Eliza Doolittle. Just when Cukor seemed to be fading from the film scene, a distinguished career behind him, he re-emerged late in 1981 with *Rich and Famous,* a remake of *Old Acquaintance.* Alas, it showed that only the basic *metteur-en-scène*'s skills remained.

1930 : †*Grumpy.* †*The Royal Family of Broadway.* †*The Virtuous Sin (GB: Cast Iron).* 1931: *Tarnished Lady. Girls About Town.* 1932: †*One Hour with You (Uncredited. Directed French version).* †*The Animal Kingdom (GB: A Woman in His House. Uncredited). What Price Hollywood? A Bill of Divorcement. Rockabye.* 1933: *Our Betters. Dinner at Eight. Little Women.* 1935: *David Copperfield. Sylvia Scarlett.* 1936: *Romeo and Juliet. Camille.* 1938: *Holiday (GB: Free to Live/Unconventional Linda).* 1939: *The Women. Zaza.* 1940: *The Philadelphia Story. Susan and God (GB: The Gay Mrs Trexel).* 1941: *Two-Faced Woman. A Woman's Face.* 1942: *Her Cardboard Lover. Keeper of the Flame.* 1943: *Resistance and Ohm's Law.* 1944: *Gaslight (GB: The Murder in Thornton Square).* †*I'll Be Seeing You (uncredited). Winged Victory.* 1947: †*Desire Me (uncredited). A Double Life.* 1949: *Edward, My Son. Adam's Rib.* 1950: *A Life of Her Own. Born Yesterday.* 1951: *The Model and the Marriage Broker.* 1952: *The Marrying Kind. Pat and Mike.* 1953: *It Should Happen to You. The Actress.* 1954: *A Star Is Born.* 1956: *Bhowani Junction.* 1957: *Wild is the Wind.* †*Hot Spell (uncredited). Les Girls.* 1960: *Heller in Pink Tights.* †*Song without End (uncredited). Let's Make Love.* 1961: *The Chapman Report.* 1962: *Something's Gotta Give (uncompleted).* 1964: *My Fair Lady.* 1969: *Justine.* 1972: *Travels with My Aunt.* 1975: *Love Among the Ruins (TV. GB: cinemas).* 1976: *The Blue Bird.* 1978: *The Corn is Green (TV).* 1981: *Rich and Famous.*
• Cukor also directed two scenes in the 1939 *Gone With the Wind* before being replaced by Victor Fleming.

CUMMINGS, Irving 1888-1959
New York-born Cummings' best years as a director were spent mining a rich vein of escapism with Twentieth Century-Fox from 1935 to 1945. As the demand for such pleasing, colourful but artificial light entertainment faded with the end of World War II, so Cummings disappeared from the Hollywood scene. He had begun his career as an actor in the early 1900s, with a stage company headed by Lillian

Russell, a popular and striking blonde actress about whom he was to make a major film biopic in 1940. Tall and dark, with brooding good looks, Cummings entered films in 1909, and by 1912 was a popular leading man in strong drama. By the early 1920s, however, his appeal was on the wane (and his hair was thinning) and he turned his talents to direction, initially with Universal, and became known as an efficient director of action films without ever becoming a major filmmaker. Possibly his best-known silent picture was the *The Johnstown Flood*, which starred rugged George O'Brien and gave a first feature-film lead to Janet Gaynor. Ironically, Gaynor was soon to become the first of the 'Fox girls' who saw the studio successfully through two decades. Cummings worked with all of them – Gaynor, Shirley Temple, Alice Faye, Carmen Miranda and Betty Grable, on frequent occasions. These 'Fox-gal' films have a light, sparkling touch to them, an air of brightness, optimism and joie-devivre. The earlier ones with Shirley Temple – *Curly Top, Poor Little Rich Girl, Just Around the Corner* and *Little Miss Broadway* – show especially deft direction, and Cummings found himself with a new reputation as a maker of musicals. Some of the later films, from *Hollywood Cavalcade* onwards, also contain some of the lushest Technicolor photography (mostly by Ernest Palmer) ever to come from Hollywood: Fox's (and Cummings') own tribute to the peaches-and-cream complexions of their box-office blondes. Cummings only made one film in postwar years – *Double Dynamite*. It flopped at the box-office in a way unthinkable for a Cummings picture in the late 1930s and early 1940s. He never made another film.

1922: The Man from Hell's River. Paid Back. Broad Daylight (GB: In Broad Daylight). The Jilt. Environment. Flesh and Blood. 1923: Broken Hearts of Broadway. The Drug Traffic. East Side West Side. Stolen Secrets. 1924: In Every Woman's Life. The Dancing Cheat. Fools' Highway. Riders Up. The Rose of Paris. 1925: The Desert Flower. As Man Desires. Just a Woman. One Year to Live. Infatuation. 1926: The Midnight Kiss. Bertha the Sewing Machine Girl. The Country Beyond. Rustling for Cupid. The Johnstown Flood (GB: The Flood). 1927: The Brute. Port of Missing Girls. 1928: Dressed to Kill. Romance of the Underworld. 1929: Behind That Curtain. Not Quite Decent. †In Old Arizona. 1930: A Devil with Women. Cameo Kirby. On the Level. 1931: A Holy Terror. The Cisco Kid. 1932: Night Club Lady. Attorney for the Defense. Man

Against Woman. 1933: The Mad Game. Man Hunt. The Woman I Stole. 1934: The White Parade. I Believed in You. Grand Canary. 1935: It's a Small World. Curly Top. 1936: Girls' Dormitory. Nobody's Fool. Poor Little Rich Girl. White Hunter. 1937: Vogues of 1938. Merry-Go-Round of 1938. 1938: Little Miss Broadway. Just Around the Corner. 1939: Everything Happens at Night. The Story of Alexander Graham Bell (GB: The Modern Miracle). Hollywood Cavalcade. 1940: Down Argentine Way. Lillian Russell. 1941: That Night in Rio. Louisiana Purchase. Belle Starr. 1942: Springtime in the Rockies. My Gal Sal. 1943: Sweet Rosie O'Grady. What a Woman! (GB: The Beautiful Cheat). 1944: The Impatient Years. 1945: The Dolly Sisters. 1951: Double Dynamite.

CURTIS, Dan 1928-

A rare example of a long-time producer turning director, this American film-maker worked in television for some time before turning out the successful spoof horror series *House of Dark Shadows*. He made his feature debut with a film from the series' theme, showing an interest in pictorial compositions and effects with colour, and offering a sympathetic treatment of its vampire hero. Curtis went on to prove himself a great stylist, with ambitions to make a major horror film. This he did not quite manage, despite atmospheric opening scenes in *Dracula* (a remarkably restrained performance from Jack Palance) of black trees rising by a gloomy lake that suggest a particularly forbidding painting. Visually, Curtis's snappily edited *Kolchak* series for TV, with Darren McGavin as the reporter forever (but convincingly) becoming involved with werewolves, vampires and other things that bump you off in the night, was also impressive, suggesting that with a good script, he had the finesse to achieve his ambition. His principal cinema film, *Burnt Offerings*, was, despite good individual moments, especially from Karen Black (who had starred in his TV three-decker *Trilogy of Terror*) something of a disappointment. Since then Curtis has stayed with television, and turned to other genres, with varying results. He spent much of the 1980s shooting the massive mini-series *The Winds of War* and its sequel *War and Remembrance*.

1970: House of Dark Shadows. 1971: The Night Stalker (TV). 1972: The Night Strangler (TV). 1973: The Norliss Tapes (TV). Dracula (TV. GB: cinemas). 1974: Scream of the Wolf (TV). The Turn of the Screw (TV). Melvin Purvis: G-Man (TV.

GB: cinemas as The Legend of Machine Gun Kelly), The Great Ice Rip-Off (TV). 1975: Trilogy of Terror (TV). The Kansas City Massacre (TV). 1976: Burnt Offerings. 1977: Curse of the Black Widow (TV). Dead of Night (TV). 1978: When Every Day Was the Fourth of July (TV). 1979: Supertrain/Express to Terror (TV). Mrs R's Daughter (TV). 1980: The Last Ride of the Dalton Gang (TV). 1992: Intruders (TV). 1994: Me and the Kid (TV). 1998: The Love Letter.

CURTIZ, Michael
(Mihály Kertész) 1888-1962

Despite never mastering the English language, Hungarian-born Curtiz became one of the finest and most reliable directors of Hollywood's golden years. Although something of an autocrat on set, not greatly liked by most actors and technicians, Curtiz extracted performances from his stars that have left some of the most indelible impressions on our minds from the 1930s and 1940s: Flynn and Rathbone, duelling it out against vast shadows on the castle walls in *The Adventures of Robin Hood*; a doomed Spencer Tracy saying goodbye to Bette Davis at the end of *20,000 Years in Sing Sing*. Davis drifting away from the boxing hall (again at the end) in *Kid Galahad*; Cagney going to the chair a coward in *Angels with Dirty Faces*; Cagney again, dancing across stage and up the wall in *Yankee Doodle Dandy*; Joan Crawford's great liquid eyes suffering their way to an Oscar in *Mildred Pierce*; Edward G. Robinson's maniacal gaze piercing the fog in *The Sea Wolf*; Bogart and Bergman giving each other up in *Casablanca*, the film for which Curtiz won his only Oscar. What other director can boast a range of images as potent as these? He was already a veteran of dozens of films in Hungary, Denmark, Germany and Austria – billed as Mihály Kertész (or Kertész Mihály as Hungarian custom has it), Michael Courtice or Michael Kertesz, largely dependent on which country he was working in – before studio boss Jack Warner saw one of his Austrian films and brought him to Hollywood and the Warner Brothers studio, where he was to work until 1953, creating a whole range of worlds, countries and periods of history on the studio backlot. At first, inevitably the darker side of Curtiz's Magyar-Germanic flair was expressed in horror films. But he soon proved adept at all genres popular at the studio and his gift for orchestrating crowd scenes was never put to better use than in his films with Errol Flynn, which began properly with *Captain Blood* (although the two men had met on *The Case of the*

Curious Bride). The action scenes here and in subsequent Flynn-Curtiz films that involve hundreds of men fighting on screen at once have a hypnotic rhythm of which Busby Berkeley would have been proud. No other big-scale action sequences have ever matched them. The contrasting natures of the two men – about the only thing they had in common was their stubbornness over what each wanted – regrettably split the partnership in 1941. Flynn began to slide, but Curtiz remained at his peak as a director until the end of the 1940s. After this, there are only a few above-average films to speak of – Trouble Along the Way, We're No Angels, The Best Things in Life Are Free and The Proud Rebel – and little more to say except that this formidable little man remained a working director to the end.

1912: Az Utolsó Bohém. Ma és Holnap. 1913: Rablélek. Hazasodik Az Uram. 1914: Princess Pongyola. Az Ejszaka Rabjai. Aranyáso. A Kölcsönkert Csecsemök. Bánk Bán. A Tolonc. 1915: Akit Ketien Szereinek. 1916: The Black Rainbow. The Doctor. A Magyar Föld Ereje. Az Ezust Kecske. Farkas/The Wolf. The Carthusian. A Medikus. Seven of Clubs. 1917: A Föld Embere. A Kuruzslo. A Béke Utja. A Vörös Sámson/The Red Samson. A Senki Fia. A Szentjóbi Erdö Titka. Arendás Zsidó. Az Utolsó Hajnal. Az Ezredes. Halálcsengö. Master Zoárd. Egy Krajcár Története. Tatárjárás. Tavasz a Telben. 1918: A Csunya Fiu. Szamárbor. The Scorpion. Judás. Lulu. †Alraune. Napraforgos Hölgy. A Wellington Rejtély. Az Ördög. Ninety Nine. Lu, the Coquette. Varázskeringö. The Merry Widow. 1919: Jön az Öcsem. Liliom (unfinished). Die Dame mit dem schwarzen Handschuh. 1920: Die Gottesgeisel. Boccacio. Die Dame mit den Sonnenblumen. Der Stern von Damaskus. 1921: Mrs Tutti Frutti. Cherchez la femme. Frau Dorothys Bekenntnis. Wege des Schreckens. 1922: Sodom und Gomorrha, Part I. Sodom und Gomorrha, Part II. 1923: Die Lawine (US: Avalanche!). Namenlos/Der Scharlatan. Der junge Medardus. 1924: Harun el Raschid. Die Sklavenkönigin (US: Moon Over Israel). 1925: Das Spielzeug von Paris (US: Red Heels). 1926: Fiaker Nummer 13. Der goldene Schmetterling (US: The Road to Happiness). The Third Degree. 1927: The Desired Woman. A Million Bid. Good Time Charley. 1928: Tenderloin. Noah's Ark. 1929: The Gamblers. Madonna of Avenue A. Glad Rag Doll. Hearts in Exile. 1930: The Matrimonial Bed (GB: A Matrimonial Problem). Mammy. Under a Texas Moon. Bright Lights. A Soldier's Plaything. River's End. 1931: †Dämon

des Meeres (German-language version of Moby Dick). God's Gift to Women (GB: Too Many Women). The Mad Genius. 1932: The Strange Love of Molly Louvain. The Woman from Monte Carlo. Doctor X. Cabin in the Cotton. †Alias the Doctor. 20,000 Years in Sing Sing. 1933: The Mystery of the Wax Museum. Private Detective 62. †Female. Keyhole. Goodbye Again. The Kennel Murder Case. 1934: The Key. Mandalay. Jimmy the Gent. British Agent. 1935: Front Page Woman. The Case of the Curious Bride. Little Big Shot. Captain Blood. Black Fury. 1936: The Charge of the Light Brigade. Mountain Justice. The Walking Dead. 1937: Stolen Holiday. Kid Galahad. The Perfect Specimen. 1938: Gold Is Where You Find It. The Adventures of Robin Hood (begun by William Keighley). Four Daughters. Four's a Crowd. Angels with Dirty Faces. 1939: *Sons of Liberty. Daughters Courageous. Dodge City. The Private Lives of Elizabeth and Essex. Four Wives. 1940: Virginia City. Santa Fé Trail. The Sea Hawk. 1941: The Sea Wolf. Dive Bomber. 1942: Captains of the Clouds. Yankee Doodle Dandy. Casablanca. 1943: Mission to Moscow. This is the Army. 1944: Passage to Marseille (GB: Passage to Marseilles). Janie. 1945: Roughly Speaking. Mildred Pierce. 1946: Night and Day. 1947: The Unsuspected. Life with Father. 1948: Romance on the High Seas (GB: It's Magic). 1949: My Dream Is Yours. The Lady Takes a Sailor. Flamingo Road. 1950: Bright Leaf. Young Man with a Horn (GB: Young Man of Music). The Breaking Point. 1951: Force of Arms. Jim Thorpe – All American (GB: Man of Bronze). I'll See You in My Dreams. 1952: The Story of Will Rogers. 1953: Trouble Along the Way. The Jazz Singer. 1954: The Boy from Oklahoma. The Egyptian. White Christmas. 1955: We're No Angels. 1956: The Scarlet Hour. The Vagabond King. The Best Things in Life Are Free. 1957: The Helen Morgan Story (GB: Both Ends of the Candle). 1958: King Creole. The Proud Rebel. 1959: The Hangman. The Man in the Net. 1960: The Adventures of Huckleberry Finn. A Breath of Scandal. 1961: Francis of Assisi. The Comancheros.

CUTTS, Graham (Jack G. Cutts) 1885-1958
Britain's most prestigious director of the mid-1920s, Cutts lost his place in the order of things after leaving Gainsborough, the company he helped to found. But he made some big box-office successes during his brief stay there, notably those which highlighted the magnetic visual appeal of the Welsh-born matinee idol Ivor Novello. Cutts began his career

as a marine engineer, but had become a film exhibitor by 1909. He moved into direction in 1922 and, in his few years at the top of the tree, was associated with some of the most prominent figures in the industry at the time, notably Victor Saville, Alfred Hitchcock, Herbert Wilcox, Adrian Brunel (all qv) and Michael Balcon. His work with the photogenic and delicately talented American actress, Mae Marsh, in three films, Flames of Passion, Paddy-the Next-Best-Thing and The Rat, led to a revival of her popularity in Britain, where she stayed for some years. The Rat, which also starred Novello as the scurrilous but lovable Apache dancer of Paris, gave rise to two popular sequels, projecting Novello in Valentino-style light as the skilful seducer who sometimes meets his match in spirited ladies of the aristocracy. These are expensive-looking productions designed to rival the best romantic adventure stories of the time from Hollywood and Cutts handles their sometimes exciting, sometimes wittily amusing developments with considerable flair, making it surprising that he quickly became such a pedestrian director when the 1930s came along. Cutts, it seems, was not a popular man with his fellow-workers. In the words of one, 'he was jealous of all other directors under contract to Gainsborough. He seemed to see them as a threat'. Hitchcock and Brunel were two to suffer from this apparent attitude, although Hitchcock, once Cutts' assistant, was soon in charge of his own films. Cutts, like another prominent director of the 1920s, George Pearson, ended his career making short documentary films. His daughter was the actress Patricia Cutts, also known as Patricia Wayne.

1922: While London Sleeps. The Wonderful Story. Flames of Passion (US: Tides of Passion). 1923: Paddy-the-Next-Best-Thing. Woman to Woman. 1924: The White Shadow. The Prude's Fall. The Passionate Adventure. 1925: The Blackguard. The Rat. 1926: The Sea Urchin. The Triumph of the Rat. 1927. The Rolling Road. Confetti. The Queen Was in the Parlour. 1928: God's Clay. 1929: Glorious Youth. The Return of the Rat. 1931: The Temperance Fete. 1932: The Sign of Four. Love on the Spot. Looking on the Bright Side. 1933: As Good As New. Three Men in a Boat. 1935: Oh Daddy! †Car of Dreams. 1936: Aren't Men Beasts! 1937: Let's Make a Night of It. Over She Goes. 1939: Just William. She Couldn't Say No. 1940: *Miss Knowall. 1945: *Air Transport Support (D). 1946: *Combined Operations (D). Our Daily Bread (D). 1947: The 9.2 inch Gun (D).

D

DAHL, John 1956-

Dial Dahl for darkness. The Montana-born director who has put the *noir* back in *film noir* began his show business career as a singer and drummer in a rock 'n' roll band! Before long, however, he was studying art and drama, and combined his several talents to make his first film, a rock 'n' roll short called *Here Come the Pugs*. Later he combined first with writer-producer David Warfield and later with his own brother Rick Dahl to launch a career writing major screenplays. It was 1989 before Dahl got to direct his first film, *Kill Me Again*, a classically structured private eye/femme fatale thriller, whose direction and story combined to make it an impressive imitation of an 'A' quality film from 40 years earlier. Dahl moves the yarn doomily along without much wasted footage, and shows some nice touches with the inevitable cross and double-cross at the end. It was three years before Dahl offered another journey into his world of danger and duplicity in *Red Rock West*, a heady, fatalistic brew of hired killers, lovers trapped by circumstance and,

Dark glasses, film noir... Black thriller specialist John **Dahl** on the set of one of his most highly-praised films *The Last Seduction*.

inevitably, the woman no one can trust. The characters are cold and passionless, oblivious till the last moment that fate is closing in on them all. The *femme fatale* assumed central position in his next film, which many consider his peak achievement to date. *The Last Seduction* opens on a shot of a great stone eagle – a heartless bird of prey like its central character, a duplicitous dame played by Linda Fiorentino, who also figured, to much less

effect, in Dahl's only disappointment to date, the ill-named *Unforgettable*, an unhappy venture into unfamiliar territory, the world of science fiction. Surely, though, Dahl's nihilistic style and noir sensibilities can assure us of more enjoyable trips down those mean streets of his imagination in the future.

*1982: *Here Come the Pugs. 1984: The Death Mutants. 1989: Kill Me Again. 1992: Red Rock West. 1993: The Last Seduction. 1996: Unforgettable. 1998: Rounders.*

Terror in Panavision. Highly successful modern director Joe **Dante** lines up a low-angle shot for his segment of *Twilight Zone – The Movie*.

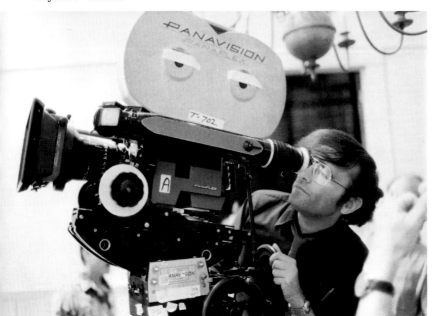

DANTE, Joe 1947-

American director of effects-driven fantasies, comedies and horror films. A lifetime fan of horror films – 'not the gory ones; my favourite is *The Innocents*' – he got together with a friend when both were 20, and edited together scores of clips from science-fiction and chiller films into a seven-hour entertainment called *The Movie Orgy*, which they hawked around to cinema clubs, college campuses and repertory cinemas. Later he worked at Roger Corman's New World studios, where he did some acting, made trailers and edited such epics as *Street Girls* and *Grand Theft Auto*. In 1978, Dante directed his first solo film: inevitably it was a horror movie, *Piranha*. Swimming in on the tail of *Jaws*, but with teeth firmly in cheek, it proved both an enjoyable story in its own right and an amusing skit on fishy disaster tales. Also fun was *The Howling*, a spoof werewolf movie but

Much-travelled director Jules **Dassin** was in Canada for *Circle of Two*, which proved to be his last film. Here he shows Tatum O'Neal what he wants her to do.

nious little touches and notable for the extended central robbery sequence, filmed entirely without dialogue. He returned to America in 1961 and made the heady melodrama *Phaedra* and the 'caper' drama *Topkapi*, which won Peter Ustinov a Best Supporting Actor Academy Award. Some of his films since then have taken renewed aim at corruption in those who hold power (a subject dear to Dassin's heart as long ago as *Brute Force*), but *Topkapi* remains the last critical or commercial success of his career.

1941: **The Tell-Tale Heart. 1942: Nazi Agent. The Affairs of Martha (GB: Once Upon a Thursday). Reunion/Reunion in France (GB: Mademoiselle France). 1943: Young Ideas. 1944: The Canterville Ghost. 1946: A Letter for Evie. Two Smart People. 1947: Brute Force. 1948: The Naked City. 1949: Thieves' Highway. 1950: Night and the City. 1952: *Million Dollar Trio. 1954: Rififi. 1957: Celui qui doit mourir (GB & US: He Who Must Die). 1958: La loi (GB: Where the Hot Wind Blows). 1960: Never on Sunday. 1961: Phaedra. 1964: Topkapi. 1966: 10.30 pm Summer. 1968: Survival 1967 (D). Uptight. 1970: Promise at Dawn. 1974: The Rehearsal (D. Unreleased). 1977: A Dream of Passion. 1980: Circle of Two.*

with advanced special effects, including an amazing transformation scene. More monsters of an only vaguely scary kind were on the menu in *Gremlins*, a huge success in which Dante's direction doesn't miss a trick, blending humour, sentiment, excitement and horror as, in between eating people, Dante's gremlins stop the traffic, smoke and gamble in the local bars and enjoy a showing of *Snow White and the Seven Dwarfs*. Dante was now on a roll: also a success was the fantasy thriller *InnerSpace*, in which a miniaturised man is injected into another's body. Very entertaining, the film seamlessly mixes sci-fi, comedy and thrills. A career misstep was rejecting *Beetlejuice* to do *The 'burbs*, but Dante made amends by bringing out a sequel to *Gremlins* that threw in everything but the kitchen sink. Dante's been pretty quiet since then, although he had a modest success with *Matinee*, about 1950s' monster movies and the mogul who makes them. Dante's boyish enthusiasm for the cinema of his childhood is still evident.

1976: †*Hollywood Boulevard. 1978: Piranha. 1979: †Rock 'n Roll High School. 1980: The Howling. 1983: †Twilight Zone The Movie. 1984: Gremlins. 1985: Explorers. 1986: †Amazon Women on the Moon. 1987: InnerSpace. 1989: The 'burbs. 1990: Gremlins 2 The New Batch. 1993: Matinee. 1994: Runaway Daughters (TV). 1997: The Second Civil War. 1998: Small Soldiers.*

DASSIN, Jules (Julius Dassin) 1911-
American-born of Russian parents, Dassin was a globe-trotting wanderer before becoming a film-maker. It seemed that he had found his forte in the late 1940s with humourless, hard-hitting social-conscience thrillers shot on genuine locations. The best of his earlier films is *The Canterville Ghost*, although this ghost comedy is kept afloat more by the deft performances of Charles Laughton and little Margaret O'Brien than by Dassin's direction. His talents undoubtedly lay with more powerhouse stuff. *Brute Force* is one of the toughest and seemingly authentic of prison thrillers, and it was followed by *The Naked City*, one of the most exciting and blood-pounding of all actuality crime thrillers, a murder hunt in which prolonged tracking shots keep pace with the killer (Ted de Corsia) as he flees through the thronged streets of New York, finally trapped and falling to his death from the parapet of a bridge across the river. Little more than a year after this tremendous film, the McCarthy blacklist halted Dassin's career in Hollywood, and he spent the next ten years making films elsewhere, eventually getting a reputation as an entirely different sort of director, one of full-blooded melodramas giving full rein to the talents of his second wife, Greek actress Melina Mercouri. Only one of these films, *Never on Sunday*, was an international success, but, before this, Dassin had made *Rififi*, one of the tautest robbery thrillers on record, full of inge-

DAVES, Delmer 1904-1977
The reputation of this American director actually rests on a very few good films. He really did make quite a lot of utter tosh, some of which, such as *To the Victor, Susan Slade, Youngblood Hawke* and *The Battle of the Villa Fiorita*, would all be in strong contention for the worst films of their year. The good films are the ones in which Daves keeps a straight face – and a splendid control of rhythm – in spite of highly unlikely material. He began as an actor (after studying civil engineering and law), but was already contributing to screenplays as a writer by 1929 and continued to write for many of his own films once his directorial career got under way with the tensely commendable *Destination Tokyo* in 1943. His career otherwise in the 1940s was undistinguished, apart from the extraordinary *The Red House*, with Edward G. Robinson at the helm of some heady rural melodrama, and *Dark Passage*, a slightly unbelievable but still compelling vehicle for Bogart and Bacall, chiefly notable for the frightening portrayal of the villainess by Agnes Moorehead. In 1950, Daves directed his first western, the trail-blazing *Broken Arrow*, the first film for many years not to treat the Indian as screeching can-

non-fodder for the Cavalry. Daves' sympathetic treatment of the Indians, which made the film unpopular in some quarters, reflected to an extent that portion of his boyhood which had been spent living with the Hopi and Navajo Indian tribes. Other good westerns followed, notably *Jubal*, the suspenseful *3:10 to Yuma* (splendidly shot in black-and-white and only marred by Glenn Ford's inability to be really nasty; but still a memorable film, magnificently climaxed and with an excellent performance by Leora Dana) and *Cowboy* which took a (fairly) realistic look at a long cattle drive. From 1959, Daves became involved for the remainder of his career with teenage love epics, at first very popular at the box-office (*Parrish, A Summer Place*) but eventually merely mawkish and even ridiculous. He wisely gave up after 1965, and spent most of his remaining years lecturing on the cinema, a medium which he had served in so many different capacities.

1943: Destination Tokyo. 1944: The Very Thought of You. Hollywood Canteen. 1945: Pride of the Marines (GB: Forever in Love). 1947: The Red House. Dark Passage. 1948: To the Victor. 1949: A Kiss in the Dark. Task Force. 1950: Broken Arrow. 1951: Bird of Paradise. 1952: Return of the Texan. 1953: Treasure of the Golden Condor. Never Let Me Go. 1954: Demetrius and the Gladiators. Drum Beat. 1956: Jubal. The Last Wagon. 1957: 3:10 to Yuma. 1958: Kings Go Forth. Cowboy. The Badlanders. 1959: The Hanging Tree. A Summer Place. 1961: Parrish. Susan Slade. 1962: Rome Adventure (GB: Lovers Must Learn). 1963: Spencer's Mountain. 1964: Youngblood Hawke. 1965: The Battle of the Villa Fiorita.

DAVIES, Terence 1946-

British director best known for painful – and painstaking – portraits of childhood. Davies' own harrowing experiences at the hands of an abusive father colour and infuse all his portraits of a working-class Britain. Nonetheless, these are flavoursome, if slow – sometimes to the point of inertia – nostalgia pieces: their atmosphere is 100 per cent redolent of Davies' upbringing in a disease-ridden Liverpool slum area, the youngest of ten children. As a non-practising homosexual and lapsed Catholic, Davies often cuts a rather sad figure. But his films, for all their horrors, exude warmth, and there may be some comfort in that. A cinema enthusiast from early boyhood Davies completed his first film script, inevitably autobiographical. Its backers, the British Film Institute,

thought he should direct as well, and so he did: two more shortish films followed, which have become known collectively as the Terence Davies trilogy. Davies continued his story of the sometimes unpalatable realities of family life with his best film *Distant Voices/Still Lives*, a somewhat harsher version of *This Happy Breed*: Pete Postlethwaite's forthright performance brought him to the forefront of British character stars. Despite its portrait of brutal domestic repression the film's innate humanity reaches the heart. Davies' pictorial mastery was even more in evidence in *The Long Day Closes*, another self-portrait, although one that it is at times wilfully slow, and emphasises Davies' weakness for holding individual shots far too long. Perhaps too glamorous and glowing a view of the north country working classes, it nonetheless encouraged Davies to go to America, where he made *The Neon Bible*. Booed off the screen at the Cannes Film Festival, the film actually isn't all that bad, with good performances from Jacob Tierney as the inevitable boy, and from Gena Rowlands as his eccentric aunt. Once again, though, Davies takes the story at much too slow a pace and his habit of focussing on fabric seriously impairs its impact.

1976: Children. 1980: Madonna and Child. 1983: Death and Transfiguration. 1988: Distant Voices/Still Lives. 1992: The Long Day Closes. 1994: The Neon Bible.

DAVIS, Andrew 1942-

An American cinematographer of many years' experience, who unexpectedly blossomed into a director of big-budget action films in the 1960s. From an acting family, Davis chose journalism instead as a profession, becoming a reporter and photojournalist before moving across to films as an assistant cinematographer in the late 1900s. He moved up to principal cinematographer by the early 1970s. His first film *Island*, about a group of rhythm 'n' blues performers, attracted critical attention, even if comparatively few members of the public saw it. But the low-budget, independent movie was not the way Davis' career was destined to go. The blockbuster phase of his career began when he was put in charge of a Chuck Norris vehicle, *Code of Silence*. Although padded to reach feature length the film did show that Davis could orchestrate action. He made a similarly styled film for Steven Seagal, *Above the Law*, followed by his first high-profile project, *The Package*, a very efficient thriller with Gene Hackman, and with Tommy Lee Jones,

who would later win an Oscar in Davis' *The Fugitive*. Davis now entered the period of his greatest success, which included Seagal's biggest box-office hit, *Under Siege*, a thoroughly entertaining story of one man against the bad guys on a nuclear warship. *Steal Big, Steal Little* proved outside Davis' range, but he had more success on the action front with Keanu Reeves in *Chain Reaction*, before directing Michael Douglas and Gwyneth Paltrow in the big-budget thriller *A Perfect Murder*. It's a field in which Davis looks set to the stay for the remainder of a rewarding career.

1978: Stony Island/My Main Man from Stony Island. 1981: Campsite Massacre/The Final Terror/Three Blind Mice/Carnivore. 1985: Code of Silence. 1988: Above the Law (GB: Nico). 1989: The Package. 1992: Under Siege. 1993: The Fugitive. 1995: Steal Big, Steal Little. 1996: Chain Reaction. 1998: A Perfect Murder.

DAVIS, Desmond 1927-

With only a few films to his credit, this British director may hardly seem worth including here, but one cannot help remarking how strange it is that anyone who could have directed such a delicate, touching and brilliantly acted film as *Girl with Green Eyes*, with its affecting sense of character, place, time and emotion, could have subsequently lost his way so thoroughly in the cinema. There followed two flawed but interesting films which proved of no interest whatsoever to the great mass of the money-paying public; and then two attempts at making a commercial film which only showed how good Davis had been at capturing small, enclosed, dangerously confined worlds. Both were flops. Since then he has been lost to television, while making some exceptionally good filmed plays, notably *The Withered Arm*, an adaptation of an M.R. James chiller in which Davis extended his range while still playing to his strengths. From 1948, following training with the Army Film Unit, Davis was a cameraman, most notably on films by Tony Richardson: A *Taste of Honey, The Loneliness of The Long Distance Runner* and *Tom Jones*. It had begun to seem unlikely that he would direct another feature film, but in 1981, he was behind the cameras once more, hopefully on his own terms. He should not be confused with another Desmond Davis (1907-1959), also British, a writer-director active mainly on TV, but also in the British cinema from 1946 until 1954.

*1964: Girl with Green Eyes. The Uncle. 1965. I Was Happy Here (US: Time Lost and Time Remembered). 1967. Smashing Time. 1969: A Nice Girl Like Me. 1979: *Night Flight. 1981: Clash of the Titans. 1983: The Sign of Four. 1984: Ordeal by Innocence. Camille (TV). 1988: Freedom Fighter (TV).*

DAY, Robert 1922-
An exciting British talent who sank deep into the trough of mediocre TV movies, Day was another cameraman who turned to direction. In the 1950s, the signs were all good. He achieved fine atmospheric effects amid believable high melodrama in three bloodcurdlers, and showed a nice, sense of crazy comedy in the gut-busting *Two-Way Stretch*, the apogee of all Peter Sellers' British comedies. There was Tony Hancock's funniest comedy, *The Rebel* and also *Tarzan the Magnificent*, the best Tarzan film since the 1930s. But television was already reaching out its tentacles. There were a few more Tarzan films, good at first then indifferent, in all senses, and the disastrous *She*, in which Day seemed to have lost all his flair for atmosphere and chills —and in a Hammer film too! By this time he was making countless episodes of TV series, at first in Britain (*Danger Man/Secret Agent*) then America (*The FBI, A Man Called Ironside, Cade's County, Tenafly and McCloud*, among many others). There have been only a few films since, all very minor, and a whole run of poor TV movies, of which *Twin Detectives* is possibly the nadir (even with Lillian Gish in the cast). Occasionally, though, even in a TV movie, Day reminded us not to write him off. *Ritual of Evil* really chilled and, a bit later, the suspense in *Murder By Natural Causes* did bite home. Day now seems to have retired, but signed off on a high note with a first-rate frontier western *The Quick and the Dead* – by no means to be confused with the Sharon Stone western of the same title. He has been married to the former actress Dorothy Provine since 1969.

1956: The Green Man. 1957: Strange Meeting. 1958: First Man into Space. Grip of the Strangler (US: The Haunted Strangler). Corridors of Blood. 1959: Life in Emergency Ward 10. Bobbikins. 1960: Tarzan the Magnificent. Two-Way Stretch. 1961: The Rebel (US: Call Me Genius). 1962: Operation Snatch. 1963: Tarzan's Three Challenges. 1965: She. 1966: Tarzan and the Valley of Gold. 1967. Tarzan and the Great River. 1968: †The House on Greenapple Road (TV). 1969: Ritual of Evil (TV). 1971: Banyon (TV).

In Broad Daylight (TV). Mr and Mrs Bo Jo Jones (TV). The Reluctant Heroes (TV. GB: The Reluctant Heroes of Hill 656). 1972: The Big Game. The Great American Beauty Contest (TV). 1974: Death Stalk (TV). 1975: †Sunshine Part II (TV GB: cinemas as My Sweet Lady). The Trial of Chaplain Jensen (TV). Switch (TV). A Home of Our Own (TV). 1976: Twin Detectives (TV). Kingston: The Power Play (TV). Having Babies (TV). 1977: Logan's Run (TV). Black Market Baby/Don't Steal My Baby (TV). 1978: The Initiation of Sarah (TV). The Grass is Always Greener Over the Septic Tank (TV). 1979: Murder by Natural Causes (TV. Walking Through the Fire (TV). 1980: The Man with Bogart's Face. 1981: Scruples (TV). 1983: China Rose (TV). Cook and Peary: The Race to the Pole (TV). Running Out (TV). 1985: The Lady from Yesterday (TV). Love, Mary (TV). 1986: Diary of a Perfect Murder (TV). 1987: Celebration Family (TV). The Quick and the Dead (TV).

DEAN, Basil 1888-1978
A theatrical producer and director who became involved with the British cinema during the 1930s, Dean will be remembered for two things: pushing two music-hall stars from the north of England, Gracie Fields and George Formby, forward into becoming two of Britain's most popular attractions; and founding the company which led to the construction of the studio – Ealing – where so much good work was done for the British cinema in the 1940s and 1950s. Apart from the Fields and Formby vehicles, those films which he directed himself for the studio, several of them starring his then-wife Victoria Hopper, were less successful. *The Constant Nymph* and *Autumn Crocus* proved most popular with the public, but they were followed by some expensive failures. Dean had become interested in the cinema when sound came along, coincidental with a visit to America he was making to direct his old friend Clive Brook as the screen's latest Sherlock Holmes. The following year, he returned to England, forming A.T.P. (Associated Talking Pictures) and making a deal with Radio Pictures (later RKO Radio) for worldwide distribution of British films. A second contract with Radio enabled Dean to build Ealing Studios in 1931, but he severed relations with his American associates when he found that they (not unreasonably) expected him to turn out 'quota quickies' (low-budget films made to fulfil statutory requirements) as well as the 'A' features he wanted the studio to make. Fortunately, Fields (from 1931) and

Formby (from 1934) came along, and the studio remained solvent, with Fields the highest paid star in Britain by 1937 at £40,000 a film. Dean's hectic direction of her films (on some he was producer only) helped paper over the rough edges, although some of them are hard to sit through today. In 1938, he resigned from the company after an argument over financial control and Michael (later Sir Michael) Balcon took over. Dean's own last film, *21 Days*, was released in 1940, three years after it had been made. Despite starring Vivien Leigh and Laurence Olivier, it was not a success, partly because the screenwriter (Graham Greene, his first screenplay) had had to emasculate the original story by John Galsworthy (in which suicide played an integral part) to placate the censors. During World War II, Dean organized forces' entertainment with ENSA.

1928: †The Constant Nymph (uncredited). 1929: The Return of Sherlock Holmes. 1930: Birds of Prey (US: The Perfect Alibi). Escape. 1932: Nine Till Six. The Impassive Footman (US: Woman in Chains). Looking on the Bright Side. 1933: Loyalties. The Constant Nymph (remake). 1934: Autumn Crocus. Sing As We Go. 1935: Lorna Doone. Look Up and Laugh. 1936: Whom the Gods Love (US: Mozart). 1937: The Show Goes On. 21 Days (US: 21 Days Together. Released 1940).

DEARDEN, Basil (B. Dear) 1911-1971
Like Launder with Gilliat, Wintle with Parkyn, and Boulting with Boulting, Dearden is one of those figures of the British cinema that one visualizes in harness – in this case with Michael Relph *(qv)*, with whom he worked from 1947 until 1968. The generally held opinion today seems to be that Dearden was a plodding journeyman director, superficial and devoid of originality or initiative. It is not one that I share. Although his work after 1952 is less even in quality, he remained a master of lighting techniques and his uses of shadow and camera angles could still heighten the suspense in a film as late as *The Man Who Haunted Himself*. From 1931, Dearden had worked closely with Basil Dean at A.T.P. (lengthening his name from Dear to avoid confusion), sometimes as writer, sometimes as assistant director and various other uncredited capacities on Dean's films. When Dean left in 1938, Dearden stayed with the studio (by then Ealing Studios) and made the move into direction in 1941, co-directing several Will Hay comedy vehicles with the star himself. After *The Goose Steps Out*, Dearden stepped

out on his own, and some interesting films followed. There was *The Bells Go Down*, an inventively made story of firemen in wartime, and three almost ghost stories, *Halfway House*, *They Came to a City* and the classic *Dead of Night* in which Dearden, as well as making 'The Hearse Driver' episode, directed the superbly sinister framework story. *The Captive Heart* was a moving, almost elegiac treatment of a P-o-W story; *Frieda* high old melodrama rightly given its head; and *Saraband for Dead Lovers* a stylishly florid period piece which gave Dearden rein for his 'shadow' penchant in the superb Flynn-inspired duel scene between Stewart Granger and Anthony Quayle. Dearden rounded off the decade with *The Blue Lamp*, a real thriller on genuine locations which immortalized Jack Warner's PC George Dixon when he was gunned down by Dirk Bogarde's flashy desperado. Dearden now entered into his 'co-director' period with partner Michael Relph. The most interesting films from this time are the social-conscience dramas – *I Believe in You*, *Sapphire*, *Victim* and *Life for Ruth*. There were also two very funny comedies – *Who Done It?* and *The Smallest Show on Earth* – and a highly civilized comedy-thriller, *The League of Gentlemen*, as well as rather too many typically mediocre mainline British films of the 1950s. In his later years, Dearden showed a tendency to go over the top, especially with melodramatics. But he could still extract fine performances from some of his actors, particularly in *A Place to Go*, *Woman of Straw* and *Khartoum*. Even Roger Moore seemed more mobile under Dearden's direction in 1970, but unfortunately there were no more movies after that. At 60, Dearden was killed in a car crash. He was married (from 1947) to actress Melissa Stribling. His son James Dearden turned film director in 1983. His latest film is *Rogue Trader* (1998).

1941: †*The Black Sheep of Whitehall*. 1942: †*The Goose Steps Out*. 1943: *The Bells Go Down*. †*My Learned Friend*. 1944: *They Came to a City*. *Halfway House*. 1945: †*Dead of Night*. 1946: *The Captive Heart*. 1947: *Frieda*. 1948: *Saraband for Dead Lovers* (US: *Saraband*). 1949: †*Train of Events*. *The Blue Lamp*. 1950: *Cage of Gold*. *Pool of London*. 1951: *I Believe in You*. 1952: *The Gentle Gunman*. 1953: *The Square Ring*. 1954: *The Rainbow Jacket*. 1955: *Out of the Clouds*. *The Ship That Died of Shame* (US: *PT Raiders*). 1956: *Who Done It?* 1957: *The Smallest Show on Earth*. 1958: *Violent Playground*. 1959: *Sapphire*. *The League of Gentlemen*. 1960: *Man in the Moon*. 1961: *The Secret Partner*. *Victim*.

All Night Long. 1962: *Life for Ruth* (US: *Walk in the Shadow*). 1963: *The Mind Benders*. *A Place to Go*. 1964: *Woman of Straw*. *Masquerade*. 1966: *Khartoum*. 1968: *The Assassination Bureau*. *Only When I Larf*. 1970: *The Man Who Haunted Himself*.

DE BONT, Jan 1943-

Dutch director of photography who proved a useful orchestrator of action and special effects when he turned director at the late age of 51. He had begun shooting the early Dutch films of Paul Verhoeven in the early 1970s. He preceded Verhoeven to Hollywood, but a reunion between the two, on *Flesh and Blood* in 1985, signalled De Bont's elevation to higher-profile films. In the next few years, he photographed such hits as *The Jewel of the Nile*, *Ruthless People*, *Die Hard*, *Black Rain* and *The Hunt for Red October*, before securing his first film as director with *Speed*. De Bont showed he had editing and directing skills as well as those in cinematography in the story of a mad bomber (Dennis Hopper) attempting to collect several million dollars by placing hostages in a life-threatening situation. The film went like the bomb Hopper plants on a speeding bus, made millions of dollars and gave Reeves a new image as an action hero. Its grosses, however, were exceeded by De Bont's next film, *Twister*, an effects-driven action yarn with devastatingly effective 'twister' sequences as scientists go in search of impending tornados and record valuable data concerning their structure. If *Speed* had indeed, as the posters promised, been the ride of your life, *Speed 2 Cruise Control* was a bit of a grind, and there was little De Bont could do to prevent the waterborne (but waterlogged) epic from sinking without trace.

1994: *Speed*. 1996: *Twister*. 1997: *Speed 2 Cruise Control*. 1999 *The Haunting of Hill House*

DE BROCA, Philippe 1933-

Born in Paris, de Broca did army service as a cameraman in Africa where he helped to shoot documentaries for the French armed forces: perhaps the locations here fired his enthusiasm for the madcap exotic adventures he was later to make. *Breathless* may be a film by another distinguished French director, but the title exactly sums up both de Broca's work and the usual audience reaction to it. His first three films were fast-paced bedroom frolics, all with Jean-Pierre Cassel, the ideal actor for such civilized versions of sexploitation. The swashbuckling, colour

and costumes of *Cartouche* were the cue for de Broca to change his leading actor to Jean-Paul Belmondo and to create a series of frenetic comedies in which our hero did a Pearl White around the world, leaping through windows, jumping from cars, swinging on ropes and escaping death and the villains by a hairsbreadth. The pace of these adventures was exhilarating, and the first two of them, *That Man from Rio* and *Chinese Adventures in China/Up to His Ears* were worldwide successes. A return to the formula seven years later (with *Le magnifique*) showed that its international appeal had worn thin. Since then, de Broca has cast around for other box-office formulae, and found one in the delectable shape of Annie Girardot as a lady police officer in *Tendre poulet* (later abysmally reprised by an American TV movie, *Dear Detective*). Since then de Broca and Girardot have filmed again together in *Le cavaleur* and *On a volé la cuisse de Jupiter*, for more hectic adventures half-way across the world. De Broca may never make a masterpiece, but he has entertained a lot of people in his helter-skelter search for success. In his sixties, his enthusiasm for fantasies and swashbuckling adventures remained undiminished.

1954: **Salon nautique*. 1955: **Opération Gas-Oil*. **Sous un autre soleil*. 1959: *Les jeux de l'amour* (GB & US: *The Love Game*). 1960: *Le farceur* (GB & US: *The Joker*). 1961: †*The Seven Deadly Sins* (US: *Seven Capital Sins*). *L'amant de cinq jours* (US: *The Five-Day Lovers*). 1962: †*Les veinards*. *Cartouche* (GB: *Swords of Blood*). 1964: *L'homme de Rio* (GB & US: *That Man from Rio*). *Un monsieur de compagnie* (US: *Male Companion*). 1966: *Les tribulations d'un Chinois en Chine* (GB: *Up to His Ears*. US: *Chinese Adventures in China*). *Le roi de coeur* (GB & US: *King of Hearts*). 1967: †*The Oldest Profession*. 1968: *Le diable par le queue* (US: *Devil by the Tail*). 1969: *Les caprices de Marie* (GB & US: *Give Her the Moon*). 1971: *Le poudre descampette* (US: *Touch and Go*). 1972: *Chère Louise*. 1973: *Le Magnifique/Comment détruire la réputation du plus célèbre agent secret du monde* (GB: *How to Destroy the Reputation of the Greatest Secret Agent*). 1975: *L'incorrigible*. 1977: *Julie Pot-de-Colle*. *Tendre poulet* (GB: *Dear Detective*. US: *Dear Inspector*). 1978: *Le cavaleur*. 1979: *On a volé la cuisse de Jupiter*. 1980: *Psy*. 1982: *L'Africain*. 1983: *Louisiana*. 1985: *Le crocodile*. 1986: *La gitane/The Gypsy*. 1988: *Chouans!* 1990: *Scheherazade*. 1994: *Le jardin des plantes/ Jardin de plantes* (US: *Tales from the Zoo*). 1997: *Le bossu/The Hunchback/On Guard!*

DE CORDOVA, Frederick 1910-

If you want to know who directed most of the lightest films at Warners and Universal-International in those flashy double-feature years from 1945 to 1953, the answer's probably Frederick De Cordova. There were others who did an eastern here, a fol-de-rol there, but De Cordova always seemed to get the silliest. He was working in Broadway when Warners hired him as a dialogue director in 1944, promoting him to director in the summer of 1945. He made winsome Joyce Reynolds-Robert Hutton comedies and the odd medium-budget thriller with Zachary Scott or Sydney Greenstreet. His films were polished and professional, but depth was hardly his strong suit. Universal-International was the obvious company for his talents, and he duly went there in 1948, soon becoming immersed in tales of Monte Cristo, buccaneers' girls, gals who took the west and sagas of desert derring-do. There were also light family comedies, including the two films about Bonzo the chimpanzee. The best of these lighter films was *Finders Keepers*, a zany comedy made pleasantly amusing by the frenetic playing of Tom Ewell. After sailing the seven seas with Jeff Chandler and cutting Indians down to size with Audie Murphy, De Cordova turned to television and hundreds of episodes of half-hour light situation-comedy shows. He re-emerged unexpectedly in the mid-1960s for two typically lightweight offerings that were limper than his 1950s fare, then returned to television.

1945: Too Young to Know. 1946: Her Kind of Man. 1947: That Way with Women. Love and Learn. Always Together. 1948: For the Love of Mary. Wallflower. The Countess of Monte Cristo. 1949: Illegal Entry. The Gal Who Took the West. 1950: Peggy. Buccaneer's Girl. The Desert Hawk. 1951: Bedtime for Bonzo. Katie Did It. Little Egypt (GB: Chicago Masquerade). Finders Keepers. 1952: Here Come the Nelsons. Bonzo Goes to College. Yankee Buccaneer. 1953: Column South. 1965: I'll Take Sweden. 1966: Frankie and Johnny.

DE COURVILLE, Albert 1887-1960

Despite the French-sounding name, de Courville was London born and bred, raised on a diet of London plays that fired his ambition to stage spectacular productions in the theatre. His subsequent successful career in revue was interrupted by a severe nervous breakdown and, during the 1930s, he devoted himself almost entirely to making middle-range films, mainly for Michael Balcon's Gaumont-British studio, before returning to the stage. Sir Michael later remembered de Courville as a man 'of extraordinary if erratic charm' and he could certainly be a tartar on set, although his films were always on schedule and under budget. Among them were the two comedy films, *There Goes the Bride* and *The Midshipmaid*, that set Jessie Matthews on the way to stardom. Miss Matthews was a stage star and de Courville had quickly learned how to make that kind of magic sparkle on the screen. John Mills, who had made his debut in *The Midshipmaid*, later made a rather lesser de Courville musical called *Charing Cross Road*. By this time, de Courville, who had also directed the young Margaret Lockwood in one of her first films, *The Case of Gabriel Perry*, was beginning to lose interest in a medium in which he could not see himself emerging as a leading light. Then he made his best film – *Seven Sinners*. This was a train-set thriller with Edmund Lowe and Constance Cummings which foreshadowed Hitchcock's *The Lady Vanishes*, perhaps not surprisingly in that both films were principally written by Frank Launder and Sidney Gilliat. There are echoes of other Hitchcock films – notably *Secret Agent* and *The 39 Steps* – and some nicely calculated set-pieces before the plot about gun-runners and murder in pre-war Paris twists and turns to its conclusion.

1930: Wolves (US: Wanted Men) 1931: 77 Park Lane. Night Shadows. 1932: There Goes the Bride. The Midshipmaid (US: Midshipmaid Gob). 1933: This Is the Life. 1934: Wild Boy. Things Are Looking Up. 1935: The Case of Gabriel Perry. Charing Cross Road. 1936: Strangers on a Honeymoon. Seven Sinners (US: Doomed Cargo). 1937: Clothes and the Woman. Oh Boy. 1938: Star of the Circus. Crackerjack. The Rebel Son/Taras Bulba. 1939: The Lambeth Walk. An Englishman's Home (US: Madmen of Europe).

DEL RUTH, Roy 1895-1961

Yet another of those good Hollywood directors who weren't quite individual enough to make the topmost layer, but still turned out many first-class films. Del Ruth made four films in the early 1930s (and one more much later) with James Cagney. The two men went well together, and there are certain similarities between the way Cagney acted and the way Del Ruth made movies. His films are pacy, punchy, confident affairs, showing a proficiency with musicals in between the fast-moving black-and-white Warners' melodramas for which his keen visual sense so suited him. He had begun as a journalist, joining Mack Sennett as a gagman and scriptwriter from 1915, directing by 1920. These early films are mainly two-reel comedies starring Ben Turpin, Billy Bevan, Harry Langdon *(Shanghaied Lovers)* and other silent stalwarts. Critics first became aware of Del Ruth with two early sound musicals, *Gold Diggers of Broadway* (featuring Winnie Lightner, whom Del Ruth married) and *The Desert Song*. But he came into his own in drama: *Three Faces East*, a spy story which reaches out and grabs its audience by the throat, showed that Del Ruth had already mastered the use of shadows and low-angle camerawork which distinguished many of his 1930s films, and it consolidated Erich Von Stroheim's position as 'the man you love to hate'. Del Ruth's unjustly neglected 1931 version of the *The Maltese Falcon* actually sticks closer to Hammett's original than either subsequent version and the intensity of the relationship between Ricardo Cortez (Sam Spade) and Bebe Daniels (Miss Wonderly) is equal to that between Bogart and Mary Astor ten years later. Of the Cagneys, the most interesting are *Blonde Crazy*, with Cagney and Joan Blondell as master con-artists who trick their way to the top after starting as bellboy and chambermaid, and *Taxi!* with Cagney (as later in *The Roaring Twenties*) as an aggressive cab-driver who becomes involved in cabland gang-war and nearly loses both wife (Loretta Young) and life in the process. The Eddie Cantor vehicle *Kid Millions* brought Del Ruth back to musicals. He subsequently directed a number of quite innovative musicals for Warners and M-G-M, including several with the Powells (Eleanor and Dick -- though never together), as well as a couple of skilfully assembled Sonja Henies at Fox and one of the better Bing Crosby vehicles, *My Lucky Star*, an early musical biopic. Perhaps the best of these song-and-dance shows of the 1930s are *Born to Dance*, *On the Avenue* and the oddball *Thanks a Million*, in which Dick Powell plays a singer aspiring to be a top politician. In the 1940s, Del Ruth made *Topper Returns*, a splendidly scatty ghost comedy, the best of the three very funny *Topper* films, but there was nothing else of special note until a last clutch of musicals at Warners, this time mainly in colour, one of them with Cagney (who did a guest shot in *Starlift*) and several with Doris Day. The snappy, happy, enjoyable films of this period also include the vastly underrated *About Face* and a non-musical, *Stop You're Killing Me*, featuring Broderick Crawford in a richly humorous remake of Damon Runyon's *A Slight Case of Murder*. If TV were to run a retrospective of Del Ruth films today, the chances are that no-one would ever have heard of him. But they certainly would enjoy the films.

1920: *†The Heart Snatcher. *†Hungry Lions and Tender Hearts. *Should Dummies Wed? *Through the Keyhole. *Farmyard Follies. *His Noisy Still. *A Lightweight Lover. *The Jazz Bandits. *Chase Me. 1921: *Love and Doughnuts. *Hard Knocks and Love Taps. *Be Reasonable. 1922: *The Duck Hunter. *Oh Daddy! *On Patrol. *When Summer Comes. *By Heck! *Gymnasium Jim. *Ma and Pa. 1923: *Nip and Tuck. *Flip Flops. *Asleep at the Switch. 1924: *The Cat's Meow. *A Deep Sea Panic. *The Hollywood Kid. *The Masked Marvel. *Shanghaied Lovers. *His New Mamma. *A Nip of Scotch. 1925: *†House of Flickers. *The Mysterious Stranger. *Head over Heels. Eve's Lover. Hogan's Alley. Three Weeks in Paris. 1926: Footloose Widows (GB: Fine Feathers). The Man Upstairs. The Little Irish Girl. Across the Pacific. 1927: Wolf's Clothing. The First Auto. Ham and Eggs at the Front. If I Were Single. 1928: The Terror. Powder My Back. Five and Ten Cent Annie (GB: Ambitious Annie). Beware of Bachelors. 1929: Conquest. The Hottentot. The Desert Song. The Aviator. Gold Diggers of Broadway. 1930: The Life of the Party. Hold Everything. The Second Floor Mystery. Three Faces East. Divorce Among Friends. 1931: Side Show. My Past. The Maltese Falcon. Blonde Crazy (GB: Larceny Lane). 1932: Beauty and the Boss. Taxi! Winner Takes All. Blessed Event. 1933: Employees' Entrance. The Little Giant. The Mind Reader. Captured! Bureau of Missing Persons. Lady Killer. 1934: Upperworld. Bulldog Drummond Strikes Back. Kid Millions. 1935: Folies Bergère (GB: The Man from the Folies Bergère). Broadway Melody of 1936. Thanks a Million. 1936: It Had to Happen. Private Number (GB: Secret Interlude). Born to Dance. 1937: On the Avenue. Broadway Melody of 1938. 1938: Tail Spin. Happy Landing. My Lucky Star. 1939: The Star Maker. Here I Am a Stranger. 1940: He Married His Wife. 1941: The Chocolate Soldier. Topper Returns. 1942: Maisie Gets Her Man (GB: She Got Her Man). 1943: Broadway Rhythm. DuBarry Was a Lady. 1944: Barbary Coast cent. †Ziegfeld Follies (released 1946). 1947: It Happened on Fifth Avenue. 1948: The Babe Ruth Story. 1949: Red Light. Always Leave Them Laughing. 1950: The West Point Story (GB: Fine and Dandy). 1951: Starlift. On Moonlight Bay. 1952: Stop, You're Killing Me. About Face. 1953: Three Sailors and a Girl. 1954: Phantom of the Rue Morgue. 19S9: The Alligator People.

1960: Why Must I Die? (GB: 13 Steps to Death).

DeMILLE, Cecil B.
(Cecil Blount de Mille) 1881-1959

DeMille (he preferred it spelled that way, although born de Mille in Massachusetts) sold the public morality and religion under the brown paper wrappings of sex and sin. Although he made dozens of films, his most famous remain the Biblical and historical spectaculars, with their casts of thousands, and their magnificent costumes, sets and effects. DeMille spared no expense, expected 110 per cent from cast and crew alike and believed passionately in the films he made. Although the butt of many jokes, his films made millions at the box-offices of the world. DeMille's judgment of what the public would pay to see hardly ever failed him, and those who reviled him were often those whose careers went down the drain long before DeMille's was over. He spent a fortune, but unlike some of today's free spenders, knew exactly what he was doing. His last film, The Ten Commandments, cost $13,500,000 – but made nearly $50,000,000. An ex-actor, he had arrived in Hollywood in 1913, directed his first film in 18 days, and three years later formed, with Adolph Zukor, Sam Goldwyn and Jesse Lasky, the Famous Players-Lasky organization that shortly became Paramount Pictures. DeMille by this time was already making his first full-blown epic, Joan the Woman, with opera singer Geraldine Farrar and a cast of a thousand players. His taste for the historical pageant with its contemporary moral implications was evident when, at the slightest excuse, and occasionally with none at all, he would insert a flashback to ancient times in a modern drama. His first version of The Ten Commandments was made in 1923 (then it cost one-and-a-half million dollars), with some scenes, including a parting of the Red Sea, hardly less impressive than the one in 1956, in two-colour Technicolor. After a clash with Zukor, by then head of Paramount, over production costs, DeMille left the studio. He continued making the epics which were by this time his trademark, but of the non-Paramount films, only The King of Kings, in 1927, was a really big success. Returning to Paramount in 1932, DeMille found that Zukor had restricted the budget of his new epic, The Sign of the Cross, to 650,000 dollars. DeMille brought the film in under budget, with Claudette Colbert as Poppaea and a barnstorming Charles Laughton as Nero, and it was an enormous success. He never left Paramount again. The years that followed

brought not only more historical epics, but the pioneering adventures – The Plainsman, Union Pacific, Northwest Mounted Police and Unconquered – which are in some ways DeMille's best films: there is a warmth and a feel for people in them that is often missing from such films as the 1934 Cleopatra, memorable though its set pieces, especially those aboard Cleopatra's barge, might be. Nowadays, any DeMille retrospective, especially from 1919 on, would be as welcome, in cinema or television, as it would be fascinating and entertaining: a kaleidoscope of what pulled Joe Public in. Only one DeMille film took a best picture Oscar, and its title was appropriate. For truly his was The Greatest Show on Earth.

1913: †The Squaw Man (GB. The White Man). 1914: †Brewster's Millions. †The Master Mind. †The Only Son. †The Man on the Box. †The Ghost Breaker. The Virginian. Rose of the Rancho. The Call of the North. The Girl of the Golden West. †What's His Name? The Man from Home. 1915: †The Goose Girl. The Captive. The Warrens of Virginia. The Arab. Kindling. Temptation. The Cheat. The Unafraid. The Wild Goose Chase. Chimmie Fadden. Carmen. Chimmie Fadden Out West. 1916: The Trail of the Lonesome Pine. The Dream Girl. Maria Rosa. The Heart of Nora Flynn. The Golden Chance. Joan the Woman. 1917: A Romance of the Redwoods. The Little American. Lost and Won. The Woman God Forgot. The Devil-Stone. 1918: We Can't Have Everything. The Whispering Chorus. Till I Come Back to You. Old Wives for New. Don't Change Your Husband. The Squaw Man (remake. GB: The White Man). 1919: For Better, For Worse. Male and Female (GB: The Admirable Crichton). 1920: Why Change Your Wife? Something to Think About. 1921: Forbidden Fruit. Fool's Paradise. The Affairs of Anatol (GB: A Prodigal Knight). 1922: Manslaughter. Saturday Night. 1923: Adam's Rib. The Ten Commandments. 1924: Triumph. Feet of Clay. 1925: The Golden Bed. The Road to Yesterday. 1926: The Volga Boatman. 1927: The King of Kings. 1928: The Godless Girl. 1929: Dynamite. 1930: Madam Satan. 1931: The Squaw Man (further remake. GB: The White Man). 1932: The Sign of the Cross. 1933: This Day and Age. 1934: Four Frightened People. Cleopatra. 1935. The Crusades. 1936: The Plainsman. 1938: The Buccaneer. 1939: Union Pacific. 1940: Northwest Mounted Police. 1942: Reap the Wild Wind. 1944: The Story of Dr Wassell. The Sign of the Cross (re-release of 1932 film with added footage). 1947: Unconquered. 1949: Sam-

Cheerful at the helm is director Jonathan **Demme**, here making the documentary *Cousin Bobby*.

It was followed by the equally quirky *Married to the Mob*, and an Oscar nomination for Dean Stockwell, before Demme joined the upper echelon of Hollywood film-makers in the grand manner with *The Silence of the Lambs*, which won Academy Awards for Best Film, Best Director, Best Actor (Anthony Hopkins) and Best Actress (Jodie Foster). Scary stuff turned screw-tight by the director, it was followed by the AIDS drama *Philadelphia* and yet another Best Actor Oscar, this time for Tom Hanks. As Demme's cameras focus on Hanks' dying countenance, he describes his love of opera in a scene which represents the highpoint of the actor's career to date. Once again, though, Demme disappointed his followers by deserting the cinema for several years, returning only with a documentary on performance artist Robin Hitchcock, underlining the three loves of his life, 'people, imagery and sound'.

1972: †*Gidgette Goes to Hell*. 1974: *Caged Heat*. 1975: *Crazy Mama*. 1976: *Fighting Mad*. 1977: *Citizen's Band/Handle With Care*. 1978: *Columbo: Murder Under Glass* (TV). *Last Embrace* (shown outside US with additional footage and re-copyrighted 1979). 1979: *The Hot Box*. 1980: *Melvin and Howard*. 1981: *Who Am I This Time?* (TV). 1984: *Stop Making Sense* (D). *Swing Shift*. 1985: *The Perfect Kiss*. 1986: *Something Wild*. 1987: *Swimming to Cambodia*. 1988: *Married to the Mob*. *Haiti: Dreams of Democracy* (D). 1991: *The Silence of the Lambs*. 1992: *Cousin Bobby* (D). 1993: *Philadelphia*. 1997: *Storefront Hitchcock* (D). 1998: *Beloved*.

(D) Documentary

DEMME, Jonathan 1944-
One of Hollywood's most successful directors over the past decade, Demme has baffled his admirers by frequently taking time out from a commercial career to make documentaries about musicians and people he has admired. Demme describes these projects as 'ego trips' and, although they lend an unusual facet to his career, they have denied his fans, sometimes for several years, some of the mainstream films he might have made. Demme initially worked as a cameraman, but was earning a living as a salesman when he met independent movie mogul Roger Corman in 1969. Within Corman's New World organization, he was gradually promoted from small assignments to scriptwriter and producer, before his first major feature, *Caged Heat,* an exploitation movie made to cash in on the 'girl gang' syndrome, but with a style which transcended its origins. It also had Erica Gavin, just about the most animated actress Russ Meyer (qv) ever used, and the extraordinary Barbara Steele as the villainess. Demme made the most of the personalities of the actors involved, as he did with *Crazy Mama*, which gave Cloris Leachman and Ann Sothern the chance of a shoot-out with the cops at the end and was full of touches that consistently pushed it into a higher grade than its standard *Bloody Mama*-type situations

warranted. Demme's films of this period did not prove popular (or travel much) outside America and, good as some of them are, it isn't difficult to see why: almost all of them deal with specifically American situations. The only exception is *Last Embrace* which, even so, failed to get a showing outside America for three years after being made. This dark thriller (that non box-office actress Janet Margolin is frighteningly good as the psychotic killer) pays extensive homage to Hitchcock – the climax at Niagara Falls is a particularly nice variation on Hitch's 'falling' themes – and is generally so much cleaner, wittier and better than De Palma's similar attempts in the same direction that Demme was doubtless quite content to move on to another genre. With the advent of CB radio in Britain, Demme's 1977 film *Citizen's Band* also finally arrived in Britain in 1981, as did *Crazy Mama*, and *Melvin and Howard*, made in 1980. *Band* and *Howard* both have especially likeable series of characters in them. There are touches of Capra here, and in the situations in which the characters find themselves. The films are charming, funny and gutsy by turn. Mary Steenburgen took an Oscar in *Melvin and Howard*. Unfortunately, there was little of note for some years after this, until *Something Wild*, a nightmare comedy which made rare good use of the distinctive talents of Melanie Griffith, but found its greatest fun in incidental characters and details – the soundtrack music, for example, ends when Griffith switches off her car radio.

DEMY, Jacques 1931-1990
Demy was more of a stage manager than a director, but, as Gilbert and Sullivan would have put it, 'a good one too'. He arranged his characters, his settings, with loving care, then tracked around them with fluid and caressing camera. Demy created fairy-tale worlds in miniature, whether in actual fairytales, like *The Pied Piper*, or modern fables set to music (mainly by Michel Legrand). Either way, his keying of pastel shades is unique in the cinema. Apart possibly from Franco Zeffirelli (qv), no-one made films as *prettily* as Demy. Born in France, he studied cinematography in Paris before getting his first job as an assistant to cartoonist Paul Grimault in 1952. The make-believe worlds of cartoon and Hollywood musical were obviously great influences on Demy and, after a distinguished start to his career

son and Delilah. 1952: *The Greatest Show on Earth*. 1956: *The Ten Commandments*.

with *Lola* (a theme and character he subsequently pursued in other films) and *La baie des anges*, he made the two films for which he is best known internationally, *Les parapluies de Cherbourg* and *Les demoiselles de Rochefort*, the first a love story lovingly photographed and told entirely in song, the second more of the same but with dance added. *Parapluies* is both beautifully organized and refreshingly different. In *Demoiselles*, the charm seems less unforced, the dancers (Gene Kelly and George Chakiris) straining a trifle too hard to produce laughing *joie-de-vivre*. After that, Demy only filmed occasionally, two of his movies being fairy tales proper, as beautiful to look at as the pages of a superbly illustrated book. But their pace is stately and generally they fall between child and adult appeal. Demy was married to the Belgian-born director Agnès Varda (1928-) from 1962. He died from a cerebral haemorrhage brought on by leukaemia.

*1955: *Le sabotier de Val de Loire*. 1957: *Le bel indifférent*. 1958: †*Le musée Grévin (D). 1959: †*La mère et l'enfant. *Ars. 1961: Lola. †The Seven Deadly Sins (US: Seven Capital Sins). 1962: La baie des anges (GB & US: Bay of Angels). 1964: Les parapluies de Cherbourg/The Umbrellas of Cherbourg. 1967. Les demoiselles de Rochefort/The Young Girls of Rochefort. 1968: Model Shop. 1970: Peau d'âne (GB: The Magic Donkey. US: Donkey Skin). 1971: The Pied Piper. 1973: L'évènement le plus important depuis que l'homme a marché sur la lune (GB & US: The Slightly Pregnant Man). 1978: Lady Oscar. 1982: Une chambre en ville. 1985: Parking. 1988: Trois places pour le 26.*

DE PALMA, Brian 1940-

This imitative American director is a would-be Hitchcock for the modern generation. De Palma has some fascinating basic ideas, but has made a habit of dwelling on their more sordid sideshoots. His shock sequences are like vaguely recalled memories from past thrillers, remade with the accent on gasp-provoking effect, but on most occasions without finesse. Thus his films, though most have moments which indicate that De Palma has a fine cinematic sense that sometimes emerges from the blood and viscera, are ugly and unpleasant toads, pervaded with sex and blood. The 'period' scene that opens *Carrie* is one of the most nastily unnecessary in all of cinema, even though some might argue that it fits the film's theme; and the rest of the movie an oratorio of overkill. *Obsession* is an ingenious

and potentially brilliant double identity thriller. But De Palma's habit of never using a stiletto where a chain-saw will do snaps one's patience and makes it seem monumentally silly and tiresome in the end. *Dressed to Kill*, which was, jointly with *Carrie*, De Palma's greatest box-office hit, is outwardly another *homage* to Hitchcock; but the Master might well shift uneasily in his grave at the long-drawn-out tension, the flashy sex scenes and the four-letter words used not in context but for shock effect. The screenplay, also by De Palma, is full of unnecessary sexual detail, like the work of the graduate film-maker, which De Palma was, not fully grown up. All this said, the mechanics of suspense are worked quite well by the director and may frighten the easily scared quite badly. De Palma can be innovative (his early shorts won several awards) and effective, too: the ending of *Carrie* is the stuff that heart-attacks are made of. His vehicles, however, have continued to suffer from directorial overstatement in more recent times. *Scarface* and *The Bonfire of the Vanities* would be low-points in any director's career. On the other hand, there are striking individual sequences in two of his more popular films, *The Untouchables* and *Mission Impossible*. Sean Connery's performance in the former (which won him an Oscar) and the considered portrayals of Sean Penn and Michael J Fox in the underrated *Casualties of War* showed that De Palma could be an actors' director when the right stars came along.

*1960: Icarus. 1961: *660124, the Story of an IBM Card. 1962: *Wotan's Wake. 1965: *The Responsive Eye (D). 1966: †The Wedding Party. 1967: Murder à la Mod!. 1968: Greetings. 1969: Hi, Mom! 1972: Get to Know Your Rabbit. Sisters (GB: Blood Sisters). 1974: Phantom of the Paradise. 1975: Obsession. 1976: Carrie. 1978: The Fury. 1979: Home Movies. 1980: Dressed to Kill. 1981: Blow Out. 1983: Scarface. 1984: Body Double. 1986: Wiseguys. 1987: The Untouchables. 1989: Casualties of War. 1990: The Bonfire of the Vanities. 1992: Raising Cain. 1993: Carlito's Way. 1996: Mission Impossible. 1998: Snake Eyes.*

DERAY, Jacques (J. Deray-Desrayaud) 1929-

This French director makes French gangster movies and thrillers. That's about all there is to it. Deray makes commercial films, and seems happy in his work – with the occasional departure from genre such as Sagan's *Un peu de soleil. . .* – and probably wouldn't find himself in this book were it not for the international suc-

cess of *Borsalino*. He describes his crime melodramas (Alain Delon has starred in eight of them to date) as 'first-degree films, straightforward, clear, precise, based on an atmosphere, a continual tension'. He has been, and continues to be, tremendously successful in his own country, but the internationally inclined films that followed *Borsalino* – *The Outside Man* and *Borsalino & Co* – seemed dehydrated copies of the original, and Deray must have been glad to get back to the flesh and blood of French mainline film-making. He was a small-part actor in French films before moving to the other side of the camera, working as assistant director to such film-makers as Luis Buñuel, Jules Dassin, Henri Verneuil and (on several occasions) Gilles Grangier. He made his first solo film in 1959, but it was the second, *Rififi à Tokyo*, that set the pattern for the rest of his career. He first teamed with Delon in *La piscine* and two years later had Delon and Belmondo together for *Borsalino*, an irresistible story of brotherly gangsters in the Marseilles of the 1930s. Deray may not ever make a masterpiece, nor even step into the shoes of Jean-Pierre Melville (he's too lightweight for that). But doubtless his films will continue to keep French box-offices in a healthy state.

1959: Le gigolo. 1961: Rififi à Tokyo (GB & US: Rififi in Tokyo). 1963: Symphonie pour un massacre. 1964: Par un beau matin d'été. 1965: L'homme de Marrakech (GB: Our Man in Marrakesh. US: That Man George). 1966: Avec la peau des autres. 1968: La piscine (GB: The Sinners. US: The Swimming Pool). 1970: Borsalino. 1971: Doucement les basses! (GB: Easy Down There!). Un peu de soleil dans l'eau froide. 1972: The Outside Man. Un homme est mort. 1974: Borsalino & Co. (GB: Blood on the Streets). 1975: Flic Story. 1976: Le gang. 1977: Un papillon sur l'épaule. 1980: Trois hommes à abattre. 1983: Le marginal. 1985: On ne meurt que deux fois (US: He Died With His Eyes Open). 1987: Le solitaire. 1989: Les bois noirs. 1991: Netchaiev est de retour. 1994: L'ours en peluche/L'orso di peluche (US: The Teddy Bear).

DE SICA, Vittorio 1894-1974

Although his detractors have argued that shallowness was never far away, it still seems unbelievable that the man who produced four consecutive masterpieces, which told us more about the plight and conditions of postwar Italians than any other films, could later have turned out such vapid and dispiriting stuff as *Boc-*

caccio 70, *Marriage Italian Style*, *Yesterday, Today and Tomorrow* and *Woman Times Seven*. In fact Cesare Zavattini, who wrote most of this later flotsam, was also responsible for the earlier neo-realist films which made De Sica Italy's most noted immediate post-war director, ahead even of Rossellini. De Sica was equally well known as an actor, initially playing charming leading men in Italian films of the 1930s. Later, while taking a break from direction in the 1950s, he established himself as a silver-haired character player, at first in the *Bread, Love and . . .* films, but subsequently in undistinguished roles which required little more than his presence before the camera, looking avuncular and faintly rakish. He began directing in the war years, working with Zavatini from 1942. The first of their films to attract attention was The *Children Are Watching Us* which, like all of their movies to 1952, takes a compassionate but realistic look at Italy's endemic social problems in these war-ravaged years, and, like the later films, has a downbeat ending which may offer a glimmer of hope for the future, but no more. Children were again involved in *Shoeshine* and *Bicycle Thieves*, moving films which both won Oscars as best foreign film, a feat De Sica repeated years later for *Yesterday, Today and Tomorrow* (bafflingly: *Two Women* would have been more appropriate) and, more understandably, for *The Garden of the Finzi-Continis*. *Shoeshine* looks at the economic conditions which lead to two boys being sent to a young persons' prison and rails at the apathy and inefficiency of those in office, which finally leads to the tragic ending (one of the boys, feeling betrayed, kills the other). *Bicycle Thieves*, though no less touching and rather more approachable as entertainment, is a more patchwork affair, taking sidelong glances at various injustices, on its way through the story of a man who loses the bicycle without which he cannot work, or live (a theme vaguely echoed years later by John Guillermin's underrated *Never Let Go*). Nor had De Sica finished: *Miracle in Milan* looked at the poor of all ages in an industrial world. While this had skipped backwards and forwards over the border between fantasy and reality, *Umberto D* was total realism, a study of old age, and the final coming to terms with senility and poverty, that has no exact parallel in the cinema. These films, which study how sometimes human dignity can survive the worst life can hurl, but sometimes how even this last inner resort disintegrates, are mostly performed by non-actors, people who live the roles rather than copy them from life. Of De Sica's later work,

The Condemned of Altona and *Una breve vacanza* are also worthy of mention.

1940: †*Rose scarlatte/Due dozzine di rose scarlatte. Maddalena zero in condotta.* 1941: *Teresa Venerdi (US: Doctor Beware).* 1942: *Un garibaldino al convento.* 1943: *The Children Are Watching Us.* 1944: *La porta del cielo (released 1946).* 1946: *Shoeshine.* 1948: *Bicycle Thieves (US: The Bicycle Thief).* 1950: *Miracle in Milan.* 1952: *Umberto D.* 1953: *Stazione Termini (GB: Indiscretion. US: Indiscretion of an American Wife).* 1954: *Gold of Naples.* 1956: *Il tetto (US: The Roof).* 1961: *La ciociara (GB & US: Two Women). Il giudizio universale (US: The Last Judgment).* 1962: †*Boccaccio 70.* 1967: *The Condemned of Altona. Il boom.* 1964: *Yesterday, Today and Tomorrow. Marriage Italian Style.* 1965: *Un mondo nuovo.* 1966: *After the Fox.* †*The Witches.* 1967: *Woman Times Seven.* 1968: *Amanti/A Place for Lovers.* 1969: *Sunflower.* 1970: †*Le coppie.* 1971: *The Garden of the Finzi-Continis.* 1972: *Lo chiamaremo Andrea.* 1974: *The Voyage (GB: The Journey).*

DE TOTH, André
(Mihaly Endre Tóth Sásvrái) 1910-
One-eyed Hungarian-born director who, after visits to Hollywood and Britain, went to Hollywood permanently (or at least until 1960) when the London Films unit with which he was working went there to complete *The Thief of Baghdad*. De Toth's 20 years in Hollywood represent the major part of his output – mostly vigorous westerns and hard-hitting crime and suspense thrillers. The best of the early American films are *None Shall Escape*, about a Nazi war criminal, and *Dark Waters*, an atmospheric suspense drama with Merle Oberon in deadly danger in bayou country. There was also *Pitfall*, a useful thriller in which Dick Powell is ensnared by predatory Lizabeth Scott. By this time De Toth was stormily married to Paramount star Veronica Lake; after making *Slattery's Hurricane* together, their careers foundered, and they declared joint bankruptcy in 1951, divorcing a year later after eight years of marriage. De Toth's directorial career did get going again, mainly at Warners in westerns, although his several films with Randolph Scott are among the star's least distinguished, the best of them being *Carson City*, which had the benefit of Raymond Massey as a stylish villain. Away from Warners, however, De Toth did make the pulsatingly exciting *Last of the Comanches* which, frame for frame, must

be one of the most nail-biting cavalry-and-Indians films ever shot, with a good cast headed by Broderick Crawford. *Crime Wave* was a solid thriller and *Monkey on My Back* gained a lot of attention as one of the earliest and least sentimental looks at drug-taking. Apart from these, little distinguished the later stages of De Toth's career apart from the first big 3-D success *House of Wax*, an unusual assignment, admittedly, for a man with only one eye, but one from which De Toth (and Vincent Price) made a giant box-office hit. Although one tends not to get involved with the characters in a De Toth film – exceptions are *Dark Waters*, *Last of the Comanches* and *Monkey on My Back* – the movies often contain long action sequences which, stylishly realized and skilfully edited, convey genuine high excitement to an audience. The five Hungarian films listed below all appear to be copyrighted in 1939, although De Toth worked on and off in the Hungarian cinema from 1931, and it seems unlikely in fact that he would have made all five films in the same year.

1939: *Ot Ora 40. Balalaika/Toprini Nász. Ket Lány az Utcán. Hat Hét Boldogság. Semmelweiss.* 1943: *Passport to Suez.* 1944: †*Since You Went Away (uncredited).* †*Guest in the House (uncredited). Dark Waters. None Shall Escape.* 1947: *Ramrod. The Other Love.* 1948: *Pitfall.* 1949: *Slattery's Hurricane.* 1951: *Man in the Saddle (GB: The Outcast).* 1952: *Springfield Rifle. Carson City. Last of the Comanches (GB: The Sabre and the Arrow).* 1953: *The Stranger Wore a Gun. House of Wax. Thunder over the Plains. Crime Wave (GB: The City is Dark).* 1954: *Riding Shotgun. Tanganyika. The Bounty Hunter.* 1955: *The Indian Fighter.* 1957: *Monkey on My Back. Hidden Fear.* 1958: *The Two-Headed Spy.* 1959: *Day of the Outlaw.* 1960: *Man on a String (GB: Confessions of a Counter-Spy).* 1961: *Morgan the Pirate. The Mongols.* 1962: *Gold for the Caesars.* 1968: *Play Dirty.* 1988: *Thane.*

DEUTCH, Howard 1957-
American comedy director much associated in his earlier days with director-producer-writer John Hughes. The son of a music publisher, Deutch cut his teeth on music videos and film trailers, before forming a three-year association with Hughes in which he directed three of his scripts, *Pretty in Pink, Some Kind of Wonderful* and *The Great Outdoors*. The first of these three proved a seminal teenage movie of the 1980s, but the other two were less successful, and Deutch branched out on his own with a series of

anarchic comedies, beginning with the undervalued *Article 99*, an attack on harsh and self-serving authorities in the guise of a black comedy set in a big city hospital. Deutch's subsequent comedies have had fewer teeth, and latterly he has worked with that veteran double-act Jack Lemmon and Walter Matthau. He is married to actress Lea Thompson, who has appeared in several of his films.

1986: Pretty in Pink. 1987: Some Kind of Wonderful. 1988: The Great Outdoors. 1991: Article 99. 1994: Getting Even With Dad. 1996: Grumpier Old Men. 1998: The Odd Couple 2: Travelin' Light.

DEXTER, Maury 1927-

If Roger Corman (*qv*) directed 'Z' movies, what should one call the movies that Maury Dexter made? Sub-Zs, perhaps. Yet there is talent at work even this far down in the Hollywood caverns. This American film-maker was hired by Twentieth Century-Fox in 1959 to work for their newly formed second-feature unit, the last such unit run by a Hollywood studio. Although shot in CinemaScope, most of the films the unit produced were in black-and-white and between 60 and 70 minutes, to go on double bills with the 100-plus-minute studio main features. Dexter made 15 of these films himself, supervised the work of others and produced several more. Leading lights in his repertory company of stars were Willard Parker and Merry Anders, both of whom starred in several of his films, as, later, did Ken Scott and Patty McCormack. Dexter's films are full of unsettling images and touches; one never feels comfortable within one of these little dramas, always that something unpleasant is about to happen. Not surprisingly, the two most effective films from this interesting period are those that swing most conclusively over into horror film territory: *The Day Mars Invaded Earth* and *House of the Damned*. *Mars* is an uncompromising piece of science-fiction that owes small debts to *War of the Worlds* and *It Came from Outer Space*, but the ambience is pure Dexter, right down to the kick in the ending. Although Dexter was only able to employ minor stars, those he has here, including Kent Taylor and Marie Windsor, are efficient players who had proved elsewhere that they were capable of raising 'B' features above the average if the base material was there and the director was at all inventive. The same applies to Merry Anders who fits snugly into the uneasy atmosphere of *House of the Damned*, one of the few films anywhere to follow in the footsteps of *Freaks*. After the Fox unit

disbanded in 1966, Dexter worked with bigger budgets, and with colour, on American-International's youthsploitation movies. The results lacked his distinctive individual touches, and he has made nothing more for the cinema since 1970.

1960: The High-Powered Rifle. Walk Tall. 1961: The Purple Hills. Womanhunt. 1962: The Firebrand. Air Patrol. The Day Mars Invaded Earth. 1963: Young Guns of Texas. Police Nurse. House of the Damned. Harbor Lights. The Young Swingers. 1964: Surf Party. Raiders from Beneath the Sea. 1965: The Naked Brigade. Wild on the Beach. 1967: Maryjane. 1968: The Mini-Skirt Mob. The Young Animals. 1969: Born Wild. 1970: Hell's Belles.

DICKINSON, Thorold 1903-1984

Not so much a film-maker, more a film scholar who was occasionally asked to make pictures – fortunately for cinemagoers. British-born Dickinson's career was as distinguished as it was sporadic, and forever globe-trotting at the behest of a friend or charitable organization – he was a passionate believer in any case in shooting on location. His best films (and they are very good), *Gaslight*, *The Next of Kin* and *The Queen of Spades*, insist that, despite the worthiness of many of his other projects, the forte of this boyish, learned-looking director was the good old-fashioned shiver-down-the-spine. But Dickinson would never have been happy to stay with one genre, any more than he could stay in one place for more than a short time. He had joined the movie business in 1925, following studies at Oxford University. By the following year, he had graduated to assistant director on films made by George Pearson (*qv*). After working as editor on more than a score of British films in the 1930s (one of which he completed when the director fell ill), Dickinson went to West Africa (for *The High Command*) and Spain, where he was involved in two shorts about the Civil War. The imminence of war brought him back to England, where he made *Gaslight*, a little too lionized in subsequent years after M-G-M had had the negative destroyed, but still more a match for their own workmanlike version with Ingrid Bergman. Madness, treachery and men driven to kill were themes that obviously interested Dickinson. They made *Gaslight* a disturbing chiller, *The Next of Kin* far more disquieting than the film about careless talk the army intended Dickinson to make, and *The Queen of Spades* a baroque masterpiece. Again it starred Anton Walbrook, so effective with

deadly madness in *Gaslight*, this time as the Russian officer who tries to wrench from Edith Evans' countess the secret of winning at cards: a genuine screen nightmare. Dickinson's last British film, *Secret People*, was too downbeat to be a critical or popular success and its failure seems to have effectively ended his career in the British cinema. He was involved with, but not asked to direct, *Malta Story* in 1953, then went to Israel to make the harrowing and moving *Hill 24 Doesn't Answer*. In 1956, he became Chief of Film Services to the United Nations and later, fed up with the British film situation throughout the fifties, opted for teaching film at the University of London. There were no further features. A pity: Dickinson could well have thrived in the British cinema of the mid-1960s. One wonders what he might have made, for example, of *Night Must Fall*.

*1934: †Java Head (uncredited). 1937: The High Command. 1938: *Spanish ABC (D). *†Behind the Spanish Lines (D). 1939: The Arsenal Stadium Mystery. 1940: Gaslight (US: Angel Street). *Yesterday is Over Your Shoulder (D). *Westward Ho! 1941 (D). 1941: The Prime Minister. 1942: The Next of Kin. 1946: Men of Two Worlds (US: Kisenga, Man of Africa). 1948: The Queen of Spades. 1951: Secret People. 1954: *The Red Ground. 1955: Hill 24 Doesn't Answer.*

DIETERLE, William (Wilhelm Dieterle) 1893-1972

Considering that the 1939 version of *The Hunchback of Notre Dame* is just about my favourite film, it is a bitter pill to swallow that its German director, William Dieterle, also made a fair percentage of outright clinkers, especially in his later years, his films from 1953 vying with each other for awfulness. But in the Warners years Dieterle's dark, Germanic nature was in full flight and he made some weird and wonderful variations on standard genres there before becoming immersed in the studio's passion for biopics. A stage actor from 1909, Dieterle was a handsome, if slightly forbidding leading man of German silents throughout the 1920s, not turning full-time to direction until 1928. He was in Hollywood by 1930, at first directing a few German-language versions of American films, but quickly settling into the Warners' mainstream. His dramas were either made in the grand manner, especially the extraordinarily erotic (for the 1930s, even in pre-Hays days) *Scarlet Dawn*, or very slick, like his two Bette Davis films, *Fog over Frisco* (full of wipes and almost suicidally paced), and *Fashions*. The biopics which followed, from 1935, are now seen as ponderous and dull by most observers. Yet they are very persuasively made, usually rise to a crescendo of emotion, and were a revelation at the box-office, where the lives of such as Pasteur and Zola had previously been considered poison to be avoided at all costs. As late as 1943, M-G-M were still very successfully milking the vein with *Madame Curie*. Between the biopics, Dieterle made *Hunchback*, at RKO Radio. This is a towering film, with a set (Notre Dame Square) to match. Charles Laughton is moody, moving and magnificent as Quasimodo the deformed bellringer, and Maureen O'Hara touching as Esmeralda. To a flawless backcloth of teeming mediaeval life, scene after scene is a *tour de force*, from the subterranean kingdom of beggars to the heartrending finale in the belltower. Dozens of directorial touches linger in the mind, in what is undoubtedly Dieterle's finest hour. The 1940s revealed an unexpected softer side to his nature when he teamed with David O. Selznick and Jennifer Jones to make *Love Letters* and, especially, the haunting *Portrait of Jennie*. This delicate fantasy, about a man who gradually realizes that he girl with whom he is falling in love may be a ghost, had very evocative black-and-white photography by Joseph August, although it was the special effects team that won the film's only Academy Award. It was the last really good film Dieterle was to make. Although of the later films *Rope of Sand*, *Dark City* and *The Turning Point* all have some merit, they are the best of a poor bunch. Dieterle returned to Germany in 1958.

1923: Der Mensch am Wege. 1925: †Die Gesunkenen (US: The Sunken. Uncredited). 1927: Das Geheimnis des Abbé X (US: Behind the Altar). 1928: Die Heilige und ihr Narr. Geshlecht in Fesseln – die Sexualnot der Gefangenen (US: Sex in Fetters). 1929: Ich lebe für Dich (US: Triumph of Love). Frühlingsrauchen. Das Schweigen im Walde. Ludwig II, King of Bavaria. 1930: Eine Stunde Gluck. Der Tanz geht weiter (GB: The Dance Goes On). Die Maske fällt. Kismet (German language version). 1931: †Dämon des Meeres/Moby Dick. The Last Flight. Her Majesty, Love. 1932: The Crash. Man Wanted. Six Hours to Live. Scarlet Dawn. Jewel Robbery. Lawyer Man. 1933: The Devil's in Love. Grand Slam. From Headquarters. †Female (uncredited). Adorable. Fashions of 1934 (GB: Fashion Follies of 1934). 1934: The Firebird. The Secret Bride (GB: Concealment). Madame DuBarry. Fog over Frisco. †Dr Monica (uncredited). 1935: †A Midsummer Night's Dream. Dr Socrates. The Story of

Louis Pasteur. 1936: The White Angel. Satan Met a Lady. 1937: The Great O'Malley. Another Dawn. The Life of Emile Zola. 1938: Blockade. 1939: Juarez. The Hunchback of Notre Dame. 1940: Dr Ehrlich's Magic Bullet (GB: The Story of Dr Ehrlich's Magic Bullet). A Dispatch from Reuter's (GB: This Man Reuter). 1941: All that Money Can Buy/The Devil and Daniel Webster. 1942: Tennessee Johnson (GB: The Man on America's Conscience). Syncopation. 1944: Kismet. I'll Be Seeing You. 1945: This Love of Ours. Love Letters. 1946: The Searching Wind. 1948: Portrait of Jennie (GB: Jennie). 1949: The Accused. Rope of Sand. Volcano. 1950: Dark City. Paid in Full. September Affair. 1951: Peking Express. Red Mountain. 1952: Boots Malone. The Turning Point. 1953: Salome. Elephant Walk. 1955: Magic Fire. 1957: Omar Khayyam. 1958: Dubrovsky. 1959: Die Herrin der Welt I. Die Herrin der Welt II (released as one film in England and America: Mistress of the World). 1960: Die Fastnachtsbeichte. 1964: The Confession (GB: TV as Quick! Let's Get Married).

DMYTRYK, Edward 1908-

Canadian-born of Ukrainian emigré parents, Dmytryk made tight, taut black-and-white thrillers in the early part of his Hollywood career. But his subsequent brushes with Congress, political entanglements, imprisonment and painful reinstatement seem to have sapped his desire to make good films and in fact he made only one of any note after 1954. Still, he kept working and the title of his autobiography probably sums it all up: *It's a Hell of a Life But Not a Bad Living*. Dmytryk had worked in film studios, initially in various menial capacities since he was 15, graduating to editor with the coming of sound. Although he first directed in 1935, it was not until 1942 and the beginning of the years with RKO Radio that he began to make his mark. *Seven Miles from Alcatraz* and *Hitler's Children*, two wartime flag-wavers, were both a lot better than their titles suggested. But the film that was to push his name towards the front rank at the studio was *Murder, My Sweet*, an adaptation of Raymond Chandler's *Farewell My Lovely* which completed Dick Powell's transition from baby-faced crooner to sour-mouthed tough guy and remains the best screen Chandler to date. Dmytryk and Powell combined on a second *film noir*, *Cornered* (also well worth sitting up for if it comes on your TV screens late at night). Two years later there was *Crossfire*, a terse (77 minutes) and very punchy story of racial discrimi-

nation masquerading (very well) as a crime thriller. In the same year (1947), Dmytryk was hauled before the Senate Un-American Activities Committee and cited for contempt of Congress as one of the Hollywood Ten. He was fired by RKO and spent three years in England before returning to America to serve a six-month jail sentence, then 'recanting' in the second round of hearings in 1951 and giving evidence which is said to have mentioned several of his ex-colleagues. In work again, he at first started well, with the lively swashbuckler, *Mutiny*, and some good social-conscience thrillers for Stanley Kramer, including the highly regarded *The Sniper* which foreshadowed Bogdanovich's *Targets*. His political experiences, however, seemed to weigh heavily upon him and, after *The Caine Mutiny* and *Broken Lance*, which contain memorable performances from two of Hollywood's top veteran actors, Humphrey Bogart and Spencer Tracy, Dmytryk's direction became increasingly leaden and devoid of inspiration. Only *The Young Lions* is free of this heavy-handed treatment: such potential successes as *The Mountain*, *Warlock* and *Mirage* are frankly spoiled by the quality of the direction. Ironically Dmytryk's last film, *The 'Human' Factor* showed a slight upswing: the hard-driving performance he extracted from George Kennedy was the best in a Dmytryk film for many years. He married (second) actress Jean Porter.

*1935: The Hawk. 1939: †Million Dollar Legs (uncredited). Television Spy. Emergency Squad. 1940: Mystery Sea Raider. Golden Gloves. Her First Romance. 1941: Sweetheart of the Campus (GB: Broadway Ahead). The Devil Commands. The Blonde from Singapore (GB: Hot Pearls). Under Age. Secrets of the Lone Wolf (GB: Secrets). 1942: Confessions of Boston Blackie (GB: Confessions). Counter-Espionage. Seven Miles from Alcatraz. 1943: Hitler's Children. Captive Wild Woman. Behind the Rising Sun. The Falcon Strikes Back. Tender Comrade. 1945: Murder, My Sweet (GB: Farewell, My Lovely). Back to Bataan. Cornered. 1946: Till the End of Time. 1947: Crossfire. So Well Remembered. 1949: Obsession (US: The Hidden Room). Give Us This Day (US: Salt to the Devil). 1952: Mutiny. Eight Iron Men. The Sniper. 1953: The Juggler. *Three Lives. 1954: The Caine Mutiny. Broken Lance. The End of the Affair. 1955: Soldier of Fortune. *Bing Presents Oreste. The Left Hand of God. 1956: The Mountain. 1957: Raintree County. 1958: The Young Lions. 1959: Warlock. The Blue Angel. 1962: The Reluctant Saint. A Walk on the*

Wild Side. 1963: *The Carpetbaggers.*
1964: *Where Love Has Gone.* 1965:
Mirage. 1966: *Alvarez Kelly.* 1968: *The
Battle for Anzio* (US: *Anzio*). *Shalako.*
1972: *Bluebeard.* 1974: *He is My Brother*
(unfinished). 1975: *The Human Factor.*

DONALDSON, Roger 1945-

Australian-born director who made his
reputation in New Zealand before going
to Hollywood in his late thirties. Originally a stills photographer, Donaldson began
to make films from 1975, and scored an
international hit six years later with
Smash Palace, a study of a man whose
marriage is falling apart faster than the
cars in the scrapyard of the title. Once in
America Donaldson's films continued to
veer between action and character as their
driving force. *The Bounty* was a moderate
remake of the famous story of mutiny on
the high seas, in spite of a formidable cast
that included Mel Gibson, Anthony
Hopkins, Laurence Olivier, Liam Neeson
and Daniel Day-Lewis. But Donaldson
then unveiled a string of films that were
either good or popular: indeed he has yet
to combine the two elements with complete success. These films usually possess
intelligence as well as impact; no Donaldson film is without the sort of scene that
sticks in the memory. The best of then,
although among the least popular, is
White Sands, such a nicely made, devious
thriller that it's a shame that, from start
to finish, you haven't a clue as to what's
going on. The CIA and a couple of arms

Director Roger **Donaldson** homes in the shopfront
action of *Cadillac Man*.

Musical maestro Stanley **Donen,** awarded an honorary Oscar in 1998.

dealers are in here somewhere, but it's the
thrill of the chase that counts. You can
see Donaldson's mind ticking over as he
gives us a mobile shot of star Willem
Dafoe taking a gun from the glove compartment of his car, a timesaving, pace-
setting device that sums up the tempo of
the whole plot and shows a director giving his audience quality service.

1975: *Nutcase.* 1977: *Sleeping Dogs.*
1981: *Smash Palace.* 1984: *The Bounty.*
1985: *Marie – A True Story.* 1987: *No
Way Out.* 1988: *Cocktail.* 1990: *Cadillac
Man.* 1992: *White Sands.* 1994: *The Getaway.* 1995: *Species.* 1997: *Dante's Peak.*
1998: *Everest.*

DONEN, Stanley 1924-

Another American director who has made
little of note since the mid-1960s. Before
then Donen had proved his talent in other
genres beside the musicals that had made
his name. He was a dancer to begin with,
on Broadway at 16, but already with
ambitions to become a choreographer.
Joining M-G-M in 1943, he moved from
assistant choreographer to choreographer
the following year, working with Gene
Kelly for the first time in films (although
they had appeared on stage together in
Pal Joey and *Best Foot Forward*) in *Cover
Girl* (1944). Five years later, Donen and
Kelly co-directed a film together for the
first time, and it was clear that exhilaration was the keystone of Donen's credo.
The musical numbers in *On the Town*
(well, some of them) were shot on location, the freshness, exuberance and dazzling dancing scattered through *Cover
Girl* were brought to sustained musical

perfection, the film is full of self-confidence and its performances are overwhelmingly winning, especially from
Kelly, Ann Miller and Vera-Ellen. If the
songs are less than memorable, perhaps
that's because only two numbers from the
original stage show were used, and so
Donen's part of the affair shines all the
brighter. For the next ten years, Donen
was king of Hollywood musicals. The
brightest and best of them are *Singin' in
the Rain, Seven Brides for Seven Brothers,
It's Always Fair Weather, Funny Face* and
The Pajama Game. These films contain
some of the most brilliantly staged musical numbers of all time, snap, crackle and
pop unsurpassed until 1972 when Bob
Fosse (*qv*), who had worked as a choreographer for Donen on *The Pajama Game*
and *Damn Yankees,* won an Academy
Award for *Cabaret.* Donen reproduced
this directorial drive fully only once outside the musical genre: on *Charade,*
although that sparklingly sophisticated
comedy-thriller did have, as well as
Donen's stylish direction, Cary Grant,
Audrey Hepburn, Walter Matthau and
James Coburn, plus the best script Peter
Stone ever wrote. Donen's direction was
hardly less effective if rather more tricksy
on the follow-up *Arabesque:* but the other
ingredients simply weren't there. Since
then, *Two for the Road* was admired by
some, but truthfully Donen was struggling
in one of the few scenes in which he has
never excelled: the intimate drama. *Movie
Movie* was likeable, and its musical numbers nostalgically *almost* as good as of
old, but other Donen films were disappointingly heavy-handed, and too few to
show if the magic had really gone. Perhaps if someone gave him a film adapta-

tion of a stage success it might reappear, but he now seems to have settled into retirement. Donen married actress Yvette Mimieux in 1972.

1949: †On the Town. 1950: Royal Wedding (GB: Wedding Bells). 1951: Love is Better Than Ever (GB: The Light Fantastic). 1952: Fearless Fagan. †Singin' in the Rain. 1953: Give a Girl a Break. 1954: Deep in My Heart. Seven Brides for Seven Brothers. 1955: †It's Always Fair Weather. †Kismet (uncredited). 1956: Funny Face. 1957: †The Pajama Game. Kiss Them for Me. 1958: †Damn Yankees (GB: What Lola Wants). Indiscreet. 1959: Once More, with Feeling! 1960: Surprise Package. 1961: The Grass is Greener. 1963: Charade. 1966: Arabesque. Two for the Road. 1967: Bedazzled. 1969: Staircase. 1974: The Little Prince. 1975: Lucky Lady. 1978: Movie Movie. 1980: Saturn 3. 1983: Blame it on Rio.

DONNER, Clive 1926-

Busy British director who has worked equally hard in films, television and the theatre, and is very much a visual stylist. Donner's attempts at making films on a grand scale have not been successful, and his television work has shown that he benefits from a smaller, more intimate atmosphere. An assistant cutter at 16 with Denham Studios, Donner worked his way through the ranks to editor in nine years,

editing such successful films as *Scrooge, The Card, Genevieve* and *The Purple Plain*. His first film as a director was the low-key *The Secret Place*, which showed what a good dramatic actress Belinda Lee might have been had she not decided to go in for continental costume frolics. Donner also made the touching and atmospheric *Heart of a Child*, but his three best films came close together in the early 1960s. These were *Some People, The Caretaker* and the only really first-rate film of his career, *Nothing But the Best*. The last is a black comedy which is virtually *Room at the Top* played for laughs. Alan Bates was a splendidly amoral hero and Denholm Elliott played for the first time his seedy black sheep-of-the-family character which he was to repeat throughout the next two decades. Colours were beautifully keyed throughout, Donner using blends of colour to express certain moods in the film. None of his subsequent work for the cinema has been so enjoyable, but he was successful many years later with a trio of period adventures made for television, which cleverly evoked the values and attitudes of the era to add a certain raw and ingenuous excitement to the often unlikely proceedings. There was also a very good stage version of *The Picture of Dorian Gray*. The feature films he made from 1965 to 1980 are a dismal collection, but his other work proves that Donner has not lost his (rather aesthetic) talent, given

the right ambience. And his 1980s TV versions of such old favourites as *Oliver Twist, A Christmas Carol* and *The Scarlet Pimpernel* are all striking, well-cast pieces of work. Not much, though, for the past decade.

*1957: The Secret Place. 1958: Heart of a Child. 1960: Marriage of Convenience. 1961: *Weekend in Paris. The Sinister Man. *The Purple Stream. 1962: Some People. 1963: The Caretaker (US: The Guest). 1964: Nothing But the Best. 1965: What's New Pussycat? 1967: Luv. Here We Go Round the Mulberry Bush. 1969: Alfred the Great. 1973: *Fly Me to the Bank. 1974: Vampira (US: Old Dracula). 1975: *Jenny's Diary. 1976: Rogue Male (TV). 1977: Spectre (TV). The Three Hostages (TV). 1978: She Fell Among Thieves (TV). The Thief of Baghdad (US: TV). 1980: The Nude Bomb. Charlie Chan and the Curse of the Dragon Queen. 1982: Oliver Twist (TV. GB: cinemas). 1983: The Scarlet Pimpernel (TV). Arthur the King/Merlin and the Sword (TV). 1984: To Catch a King (TV). A Christmas Carol (TV. GB: cinemas). 1986: Dead Man's Folly/Agatha Christie's Dead Man's Folly (TV). Babes in Toyland (TV). 1988: Stealing Heaven. 1992: Black Wedding/Terror Stalks the Class Reunion.*

DONNER, Richard 1930-

Few directors have hit the big time so late in life after labouring so long in the bowels of show business. But this New York-born film-maker quickly showed that his 1976 flight to directorial stardom with *The Omen* was no fluke success. Donner began his career as an actor, firstly in the theatre, later in small television and film parts. In 1958, he began directing TV commercials, industrial films and documentaries, making his 'fictional' bow later the same year with an episode of Steve McQueen's television series *Wanted – Dead or Alive*. From then on, Donner was constantly engaged on episodes of TV series, mostly detective thrillers, although he made some interesting episodes of *Twilight Zone*, a chiller series, which foreshadowed his later work in the fantasy genre. There was a film in 1961, called *X-15*, a slick, well-shot but routine flying drama. The cast, headed by Charles Bronson and Mary Tyler Moore, looks good now but was little-known then. Two movie flops at the end of the 1960s seemed to have consigned Donner to television for the rest of his days. Then along came the box-office-blasting *The Omen*, followed by Donner's highly successful direction of *Superman*, the best of the strip-cartoon epics, with Christopher

Richard **Donner**, at work on the first of the 'Superman' films in 1978.

Reeve blossoming in all directions under Donner's sympathetic helm: the film was great fun but never too much tongue-in-cheek. There was some acrimony when Donner was told he was not required for *Superman II*, having shot half of it at the same time as the first film. But he hit back with *Inside Moves*, a story of disabled people coming to terms with themselves and their disabilities, for which the young actress Diana Scarwid was nominated for an Oscar. Since then, Donner has concentrated on big-budget action movies with major box-office stars, with the exception of *Radio Flyer*, an unsalvageable project which he unwisely agreed to try and rescue in 1992. His most successful films in recent times have been the *Lethal Weapon* thrillers of which even more may be in the offing.

1961: X-15. 1968: Salt and Pepper. 1969: Twinky (US: Lola). 1974: Lucas Tanner (TV). Senior Year (TV). 1975: Sara T: Portrait of a Teenage Alcoholic (TV). Bronk (TV). Shadow in the Streets (TV). 1976: The Omen. 1978: Superman. 1980: †Superman II (uncredited). Inside Moves. 1982: The Toy. 1984: LadyHawke. 1985: The Goonies. 1987: Lethal Weapon. 1988: Scrooged. 1989: Lethal Weapon II. 1992: Radio Flyer. Lethal Weapon 3. 1995: Assassins. 1997: Conspiracy Theory. 1998: Lethal Weapon 4.

DOUGLAS, Gordon 1908-1993

Anyone writing about Gordon Douglas' career in 1967 could have been forgiven for consigning him to the utterly routine, and asking how he had lasted so long: a typically American director in the years when Hollywood was gradually running down, an accomplished technician with little personal flair. And then Douglas makes a film like *The Detective*. . . 'I can't believe Gordon Douglas directed that,' remarked a colleague as we left the preview cinema in 1968. Well, he did and not only is this a very good police film, brilliantly underplayed in its quieter moments (by Frank Sinatra and Lee Remick) but it is exceptionally well directed. The direction is affectionate, complementary to the moods of the film, yet unequivocally square-on at moments of impact, drawing the last ounce from already painfully well-drawn characters and never missing an opportunity to lift this absorbing story into a very high grade of adult entertainment. It's enough to make one look again for uncut diamonds glittering in the general dross of Douglas's earlier directorial career. He had been in show business since early childhood, appearing as a toddler in films

from 1912. From 1930, he was employed by the Hal Roach studio, often as gagman, bit-part player and assistant director in Laurel and Hardy comedies and other two-reel farces. He graduated to director on Our Gang shorts, which he made for four years. The bulk of the remainder of his career is made up of eight years with Columbia (1942-1950) and 11 years at Warners (1950-1961). The films at these studios are almost all well-made, a few quite pacy and exciting: *The Doolins of Oklahoma*, for example, is an above-average Randolph Scott western about a real-life group of western outlaws, *Them!* is doom-laden science fiction about giant ants (a big box office success of its time), *The Charge at Feather River* a pulsatingly thrilling cavalry-and-Indians western (with an attractive range of characters) which 3-D for once enhanced and *Follow That Dream* a quirky and likeable Elvis Presley vehicle, one of the few distinctive films the Pelvis made. That's a very small percentage of his output, of course, and none of these titles comes anywhere near measuring up to *The Detective*. But it does suggest Douglas cared about his material, and sometimes put more into it than it deserved. With all that said, there is still an awful lot of dull mediocrity: the Alan Ladd films are particularly lifeless. Douglas' Our Gang short *Bored of Education* won an Academy Award in 1936. He died from cancer.

1935: *Lucky Beginners. *The Infernal Triangle. 1936: *Bored of Education. *Pay As You Exit. *Spooky Hooky. *Two Too Young. †General Spanky. *Reunion in Rhythm. 1937: *Three Smart Boys. *Glove Taps. *Mail and Female. *Roamin' Holiday. *Rushin' Ballet. *Hearts Are Thumps. *Night 'n' Gales. *Fishy Tales. *The Pigskin Palooka. *Framing Youth. *Our Gang Follies of 1938. 1938: *Came the Brawn. *Canned Fishing. *Hide and Seek. *Feed 'Em and Weep. *Bear Facts. *The Little Ranger. *Aladdin's Lantern. 1939: Zenobia (GB: Elephants Never Forget). 1940: Saps at Sea. 1941: †Road Show. Broadway Limited. Niagara Falls. 1942: The Great Gildersleeve. The Devil with Hitler. 1943: Gildersleeve on Broadway. Gildersleeve's Bad Day. 1944: The Falcon in Hollywood. A Night of Adventure. Gildersleeve's Ghost. Girl Rush. 1945: Zombies on Broadway (GB: Loonies on Broadway). First Yank into Tokyo (GB: Mask of Fury). 1946: San Quentin. Dick Tracy vs Cueball. 1948: If You Knew Susie. The Black Arrow (GB: The Black Arrow Strikes). Walk a Crooked Mile. 1949: †Mr Soft Touch (GB: House of Settlement). The Doolins of Oklahoma (GB:

The Great Manhunt). 1950: Rogues of Sherwood Forest. Kiss Tomorrow Goodbye. The Nevadan (GB: The Man from Nevada). Fortunes of Captain Blood. Between Midnight and Dawn. The Great Missouri Raid. 1951: I Was a Communist for the F.B.I. Come Fill the Cup. Only the Valiant. 1952: Mara Maru. The Iron Mistress. 1953: She's Back on Broadway. So This is Love (GB: The Grace Moore Story). The Charge at Feather River. 1954: Them! Young at Heart. 1955: Sincerely Yours. The McConnell Story (GB: Tiger in the Sky). 1956: Santiago (GB: The Gun Runner). 1957: Bombers B-52 (GB: No Sleep Till Dawn). Fort Dobbs. The Big Land (GB: Stampeded!). 1958: The Fiend Who Walked the West. 1959: Up Periscope! Yellowstone Kelly. 1960: The Sins of Rachel Cade. 1961: Gold of the Seven Saints. Claudelle Inglish (GB: Young and Eager). Follow That Dream. 1963: Call Me Bwana. 1964: Robin and the Seven Hoods. Rio Conchos. 1965: Sylvia. Harlow. 1966: Stagecoach. Way ... Way Out. 1967: In Like Flint. Chuka. Tony Rome. 1968: Lady in Cement. The Detective. 1969: Skullduggery. 1970: Barquero. They Call Me MISTER Tibbs! 1971: †Skin Game (uncredited). 1973: Slaughter's Big Rip-Off. 1975: Nevada Smith (TV). 1977: Evel Knievel.

DOVZHENKO, Alexander 1894-1956

Ukraine-born Dovzhenko was a poet on celluloid. Once seen, the landscapes and images from his films will be with you for a lifetime. If the propagandist element in his films is occasionally intrusive (he was made head of Kiev Studios after pleasing Stalin with *Shchors* in 1939), the best of his works are pastoral masterpieces whose greatness is undeniable. Dovzhenko captured the backbone of the country, its real life, in a way that directors in few other countries even attempted (only *The Southerner*, *The Good Earth* and *The Grapes of Wrath* from Hollywood's vast output spring to mind). Dovzhenko is also concerned with the effects of war, the futility of fighting wrong-headed causes and the brutalities wars bring in their wake. These are conventional themes, but the poetic, sometimes elliptical treatment of them is not. The treatment is occasionally simplistic, but unvaryingly effective and moving, at times even horrifying, while the compositions have not been surpassed in the 60 years that have elapsed since Dovzhenko's most remarkable movies were made. Dovzhenko's passions were a reflection of his own upbringing. The son of a farmer, he studied natural science, physics, biology and economics before service on the Polish front in

World War I. He also studied painting and worked as a commercial artist before entering films in his early thirties. This reflects itself in the use of montage and abstract symbolism in his work, especially in *Earth* and *Aerograd*, and underscores a slight weakness in his approach – that his films are least likely to be appreciated by the people they portray. Younger audiences also may find his films difficult and become fidgety but even they will discover Dovzhenko's images exert a powerful, hypnotic magic as the films progress. With age, Dovzhenko grew to look like a cross between a Russian chess-master and British Labour politician Michael Foot – he was not one for sartorial splendour – and never quite recaptured the power of his earlier work. After his death from a heart attack his widow, the actress Yulia Sointseva, using his shooting scripts and draft screenplays, herself directed his planned trilogy on Ukrainian village life, and made two further films using his unfilmed material as a basis.

*1926: *Love's Berries. †Vasya the Reformer. 1927: The Diplomatic Pouch. 1928: Zvenigora. 1929: Arsenal. 1930: Earth. 1932: Ivan. 1935: Aerograd. 1939: Shchors. 1940: Liberation. 1943: The Fight for Our Soviet Ukraine (screenplay/'artistic director' only). 1945: Victory in the Ukraine (US: Ukraine in Flames). 1948: Michurin (US: Life in Bloom).*

DREIFUSS, Arthur 1908-1993

Arthur Dreifuss made miniscule musicals. Not for him, in these cut-budget 1940s frolics, the likes of Gene Kelly, Frank Sinatra, Cyd Charisse, Kathryn Grayson or Debbie Reynolds, or the pre-eminence of a Stanley Donen or Vincente Minnelli. Dreifuss had charge of striptease queen Ann Corio, Mary Beth Hughes, Ina Ray Hutton, Jinx Falkenberg, Jean Porter, Gloria Jean, Ray McDonald, Peggy Ryan or, if he got lucky, Ann Miller. But he entertained wartime audiences with what he had, even if his night-club sets seemed to be constructed in a corner of the studio about 20ft square. When the 1940s were over, he went back to Broadway. Dreifuss had been a child pianist and teenage conductor in his native Germany, before coming to America and working on Broadway musicals as choreographer and later producer. He came to Hollywood in 1935 as a dance director but rarely worked for the major studios. When the rash of wartime mini-musicals and teen-swing sessions started, Dreifuss was to be found eking out his budgets at Monogram, PRC, Eagle-Lion and Columbia. While M-G-M unleashed the purse-strings on their Tech-

nicolor musicals, Dreifuss remained on emergency rations. One of the best of the Dreifuss offerings, not surprisingly, was *Eadie Was a Lady*, with Ann Miller in tremendous high-kicking form as the college student who is a burlesque queen when school is out, a shameless revamping of the James Thurber play *The Male Animal*, later made into another musical (*She's Working Her Way Through College*) at Warners with Virginia Mayo in the Miller role. There were also four films in a row with pretty Jean Porter (who later married director Edward Dmytryk) and four more with peppy June Preisser. Dreifuss liked petite dancer-comediennes with plenty of personality and they gave good performances for him. One hardly expected to see him back in films again, but he turned up in the 1950s, in between Broadway assignments, on jukebox musicals with whose low budgets he must have been all too familiar. There were also a few youthsploitation films in the late 1960s and, most peculiarly, sandwiched in between, an adaptation of Brendan Behan's play *The Quare Fellow*. One couldn't imagine a less Dreifuss-like subject and not surprisingly the limp and downbeat result was not a box-office hit. He died on New Year's Eve.

*1937: *Frozen Affair. *Murder in Swingtime. 1939: *A Night at the Troc. Double Deal. *Yankee Doodle Home. 1940: Mystery in Swing. 1941: Reg'lar Fellers. 1942: Baby Face Morgan. Boss of Big Town. The Payoff. 1943: Melody Parade. Campus Rhythm. Sarong Girl. Nearly Eighteen. 1944: Ever Since Venus. *Dancing on the Stars. *Smoke Rings. The Sultan's Daughter. 1945: Eadie Was a Lady. Boston Blackie Booked on Suspicion (GB: Booked on Suspicion). Boston Blackie's Rendezvous (GB: Blackie's Rendezvous). The Gay Senorita. Prison Ship. 1946: Junior Prom. Freddie Steps Out. High School Hero. Betty Co-Ed (GB: The Melting Pot). 1947: Vacation Days. *Follow the Music. Little Miss Broadway. Sweet Genevieve. Two Blondes and a Redhead. 1948: Glamour Girl (GB: Night Club). Mary Lou. I Surrender Dear. An Old-Fashioned Girl. 1949: Manhattan Angel. Shamrock Hill. There's a Girl in My Heart. 1958: Life Begins at 17. The Last Blitzkrieg. 1959: Juke Box Rhythm. 1962: The Quare Fellow. 1967: The Love-Ins. Riot on Sunset Strip. 1968: A Time to Sing. For Singles Only. The Young Runaways.*

DREYER, Carl Theodor 1889-1968

Although he was sometimes austere and ponderous, Dreyer's vision and drive for perfection made him the greatest director

Denmark has ever produced. Unfortunately, the commercial failure of most of his films and his own perfectionism meant that his output was extremely limited. Dreyer brought with him to the cinema, after a period in journalism, an admiration for the films of D.W. Griffith and a strict Lutheran upbringing. His cinematic world is one of pastors, witches, superstitions, repression, the emotions of women as central figures in a narrative and the juxtaposition of human and religious love. It's very much the world of Hawthorne's *The Scarlet Letter,* for which Dreyer would have been the perfect director. As it was, *Leaves from Satan's Book,* an historical look at the Devil and all his works, with its leanings on *Intolerance,* was his first big success. But *The Parson's Widow,* although commercially less successful, understandably, is a better film which laid the foundations for his great works of later years. These range from the intimate and heart-searching drama *Michael* to the soaringly powerful *The Passion of Joan of Arc,* with its dynamic use of close-up, and the misty unease of *Vampyr,* a classic horror film whose reputation has grown with the years, although surprisingly it was poorly received in its time. Filmed on French locations – the Europe-trotting Dreyer had already filmed in Norway, Sweden and Germany as well as his native Denmark – it is notable for its use of light and the paleness that this creates, befitting all too well the anaemia that would be caused by a vampire's blood-sucking activities. This dream-like ambience, in which evil is sensed rather than seen, was created by reflecting lights off gauze screens back into the camera lens. In box-office terms, *Vampyr* was an expensive failure, and Dreyer found himself unable to obtain backing for further projects, including a life of Christ. He took up journalism again for ten years, returning in the war years with more films about pastors and witches, including the striking *Day of Wrath;* turning his hand to documentary shorts; and ending his career with a reprise of earlier themes in *Gertrud,* the story of a middle-aged woman who decides to live her life alone rather than stay with men (first a husband, then younger lover) who are unwilling to commit themselves totally to her. Dreyer was a film-maker before his time, even if his habit of using amateur players on occasions could work against his films. Nowadays he would find the world's film climate much more to his liking and would no doubt be allowed the artistic and financial freedom he always desired.

1919: The President. Leaves from Satan's Book. 1920: Prästänkan (GB: The Par-

son's Widow. US: The Witch Woman).
1921: Die Gezeichneten (GB and US:
Love One Another). 1922: Once Upon a
Time. 1924: Michael/Mikaël (US:
Chained). 1925: Du Skal aera din Hustru
(GB & US: Master of the House). The
Bride of Glomdal. 1927: The Passion of
Joan of Arc. 1932: Vampyr/The Strange
Adventure of David Gray (US: Castle of
Doom). 1942: *Good Mothers (D). 1943:
Day of Wrath. 1945: Two People. 1946:
*Water from the Land (D). 1947: *The
Danish Village Church (D). *De Gamle
(D). *The Struggle Against Cancer (D).
1948: *They Caught the Ferry. 1949:
*Thorvaldsen (D). 1950: *The Storstrøm
Bridge. 1954: *A Castle within a Castle
(D). 1955: Ordet (GB & US: The Word).
1964: Gertrud.

DUIGAN, John 1949-

Hard-working English-born, Australian-
raised director who started as an actor.
Rites of passage and primitive eroticism
are recurring themes in his always stunningly shot films. Although the treatment
and execution of these themes often
verges on the banal, Duigan is undeniably
a significant figure in the modern Australian cinema. After starring in student
productions while studying philosophy at
Melbourne University, Duigan began acting for films in his early twenties, perhaps
most significantly as the star of Bonjour
Balwyn (1979), which he also co-wrote.
Within two years, however, he had moved
to the other side of the camera, gradually
directing more significant films with such
leading native actors as Bryan Brown and
Judy Davis. The breakthrough to critical
recognition didn't really come until
Duigan made The Year My Voice Broke
in 1987. This film about growing up
became a big international hit, and gave
rise to a slightly less even but equally popular sequel, Flirting, which, as well as the
original actor, Noah Taylor, featured such
stars-to-be as Nicole Kidman and Thandie
Newton. After a gap of three years,
Duigan aimed for wider audiences with a
series of ambitious films of erotic content
and exotic locations, before returning to
the theme of a difficult childhood – by
this time working in America – with
Lawn Dogs in 1997. The Year My Voice
Broke won an Australian Oscar as best
picture.

1975: The Firm Men. 1976: The Tres-
passers. 1978: Mouth to Mouth. 1979:
Dimboola. 1981: The Winter of Our
Dreams. 1982: Far East. 1984: One Night
Stand. 1987: The Year My Voice Broke.
1989: Romero. Flirting. 1992: Wide Sar-
gasso Sea. 1994: Sirens. 1995: The Journey of August King. 1996: The Leading
Man. 1997: Lawn Dogs. 1998: Molly/Res-
cue Me.

DUNNE, Philip 1908-1992

This tall, bespectacled, very American-
looking writer and director, a native New
Yorker, made one or two good films for
Twentieth Century-Fox after a long career
writing screenplays, but probably started
directing too late in his life and went back
to writing after the mid-1960s. Dunne
began writing stories for The New Yorker
in the early 1930s, and was busy with this
occupation and co-writing screenplays
until 1941, when he went solo on a film
script for only the second time (the first
was the fast-moving thriller Lancer Spy,
made in 1937). Thereafter he usually
worked on his own, contributing such
screenplays as How Green was My Valley,
The Ghost and Mrs Muir, Pinky, Way of a
Gaucho (in whose supervision he also had
a hand, as three directors came and went)
and The Robe. Dunne was Chief of Film
Production for the overseas branch of the
Office of War Information in the war
years, and also wrote many political
speeches, notably for John F. Kennedy
and Adlai Stevenson. He directed his first
film, Prince of Players, rich in good acting
but notably uncommercial, in 1955, followed by eight more for Fox, the best of
which were Ten North Frederick, a soul-
searching family drama with Gary
Cooper, for which Dunne also wrote the
screenplay, and the absorbingly exciting
The Inspector, a prolonged chase drama
with a good variety of characters.

1955: Prince of Players. The View from
Pompey's Head (GB: Secret Interlude).
1956: Hilda Crane. 1957: Three Brave
Men. 1958: Ten North Frederick. In Love
and War. 1959: Blue Denim (GB: Blue
Jeans). 1961: Wild in the Country. 1962:
The Inspector (US: Lisa). 1965: Blindfold.

DUPONT, E.A. 1891-1956

Although this German-born director had
a painter's eye for vividly memorable
images, dramatically he was less effective.
His Teutonic temperament seemed to
bring a heavy hand to bear on scenes
which leaned on dialogue rather than
visuals, and not surprisingly his career
floundered when he went to America. The
European in his nature was quite unable
to cope with the Hollywood scene of the
1930s and, despite two very striking early
German films which impressed critics
round the world, he was only ever successful with Continental (or British) technicians and players. Christened Eward

Andreas (later known as André) Dupont,
he worked for a while in journalism
before coming into films as a writer in
1916, then director (at first of shorts)
from the following year. His notable successes are all in the silent period, and
include Die Spione, Die Geier-Wally,
Baruch and the film that made his name
around the world, Variété. Dupont
brought his hectic visual touch to Britain
in 1928, with some success, on Moulin
Rouge, Piccadilly and Atlantic in particular. His direction of the sombre Cape Forlorn was also praised. He went to America in 1933, where his over-elaborate style
only irritated critics and audiences alike.
His assignments became progressively less
interesting, and he was out of the business
for 11 years after an argument with the
Dead End Kids over the filming of Hell's
Kitchen in 1939. He came back to films in
1950 but only in the first production,
The Scarf, does one gain the impression
that Dupont had any real interest left.
Dupont had strong players (Emlyn
Williams, John Ireland, Mercedes
McCambridge) who must have suited
him, and his use of visuals, although
again rather laid on with trowel, did create an atmosphere laden with tension and
menace. Thereafter some of his projects
verged on the lunatic and only The Steel
Lady, a good, straightforward, exciting
war story, is worthy of attention.

1917: *Der ewige Zweifel. *Das Perlen-
halsband. *Durchlaucht Hyperchonder.
*Die schwarze Schachdame. Die Japaner-
in. 1918: Der Schatten. Der Teufel.
Europa Postlagernd! Das Geheimnis des
Amerika-Docks. Mitternacht. 1919:
†Alkohol. Das Derby. Das Grand Hotel
Babylon. Die Maske. Der Würger der
Welt. Die Spione. Die Apachen. 1920:
Whitechapel. Der Mord ohne Täter.
Herzstrumpf. Die weisse Pfau. 1921: Die
Geier-Wally. Kinder der Finsternis.
Kinder der Finsternis II. 1922: Sie und
die Drei. 1923: Die grüne Manuela. 1924: Der
Demütige und die Sängerin. 1925: Variété
(GB: Variety. US: Vaudeville). 1928: Love
Me and the World is Mine. Moulin
Rouge. 1929: Piccadilly. Atlantic (plus
French and German versions). 1930: Two
Worlds (plus French and German ver-
sions). Cape Forlorn (plus French and
German versions. US: The Love Storm).
1931: Salto Mortale (GB & US:
Trapeze). 1932: Peter Voss, der Mil-
liondieb. 1933: Der Läuer von
Marathon. Ladies Must Love. 1935: The
Bishop Misbehaves (GB: The Bishop's
Misadventures). 1936: Forgotten Faces. A
Son Comes Home. 1937: On Such a
Night. Night of Mystery (GB: The

Greene Murder Case). Love on Toast. 1939: †*Hell's Kitchen. 1951: The Scarf.* †*Pictura, An Adventure in Art (D). 1953: Problem Girls. The Neanderthal Man. The Steel Lady (GB: Treasure of Kalifa).* †*Miss Robin Crusoe (uncredited). 1954: Return to Treasure Island.*

DUVIVIER, Julien 1896-1967

One of France's foremost directors in the great 1930s, Duvivier does not seem to have retained his reputation to the extent of René Clair and Jean Renoir (both *qv*). This is probably justifiable in view of his later work, in spite of his success with the *Don Camillo* films. All the same, to an admirer of his best films, it comes as something of a surprise to find how many modern writers think so little of him. He began as an actor around the beginning of World War I and, by the end of it, had graduated, via scriptwriting – he wrote, or co-wrote nearly all of his films – to direction. His silent films are of little major worth, although *L'abbé Constantin* was a popular success, and it is the 1930s which hold the treasures that turn up so often at film theatre revival seasons. These are elegant, civilized, persuasive films, made by a discreet director who never went over the top, even given such an extravagant subject as *Pépé Le Moko*, which, innovative at the time with its spectacular overhead shots of the seething Casbah, looks a little dated today. The best of Duvivier from that decade would include *Poil de Carotte, Maria Chapdelaine* and *Un Carnet de bal*, which last film Duvivier was to recycle, during his wartime Hollywood stay, as *Lydia*. The Hollywood films are all quite enjoyable, especially *The Great Waltz*, which has an exquisite performance from Luise Rainer, and the multistory films *Tales of Manhattan* and *Flesh and Fantasy*. There was no great decline in the post-war years, but equally no masterpieces, and Duvivier's British-made *Anna Karenina* (1948) is especially dull. His *La chambre ardente*, perhaps the least personal of his later films, is a weird puzzle that contains some breathtakingly bizarre moments.

1919: Halcedama, ou: le prix de sang. 1920: La réincarnation de Serge Renaudier. 1922: Les Roquevillards. L'ouragan sur la montagne. Der unheimliche Gast. 1923: Le reflet de Claude Mercoeur. Credo, ou: la tragédie de Lourdes. 1924: L'oeuvre immortelle. Coeurs farouches. †*La machine à refaire la vie (D). 1925: L'abbé Constantin. Poil de carotte. 1926: L'agonie de Jérusalem. L'homme à Hispano. 1927: Le mariage de Mademoiselle Beulemans. Le mystère de la Tour Eiffel.*

1928: La vie Miraculeuse de Thérèse Martin. Le tourbillon de Paris. La divine croisière. 1929: Maman Colibri. Au bonheur des dames. 1930: David Golder. 1931: Les cinq gentlemen maudits (and German version). Hallo Hallo! Hier spricht Berlin! 1932: Poil de carotte (remake). La tête d'un homme. 1933: †*La machine à refaire la vie (D. Sound version). Le petit roi. 1934: La paquebot 'Tenacity'. Maria Chapdelaine (GB & US: The Naked Heart). La bandera (GB & US: Escape from Yesterday. 1936: L'homme du jour. La belle équipe (US: They were Five). The Golem. Pépé Le Moko. 1937: Un carnet de bal. The Great Waltz.* †*Marie Antoinette (uncredited). 1939: La fin du jour. La charrette fantôme. 1940: Untel père et fils (US: The Heart of a Nation). 1941: Lydia. 1942: Tales of Manhattan. 1943: Flesh and Fantasy. 1944: The Imposter. 1946: Panique/Panic. 1948: Anna Karenina. 1949: Au royaume des cieux (GB & US: The Sinners). 1950: Blackjack (US: Captain Blackjack). Sous le ciel de Paris. 1951: The Little World of Don Camillo. 1952: La fête à Henriette (US: Henrietta's Holiday). 1953: The Return of Don Camillo. L'affaire Maurizius (GB & US: On Trial!). 1954: Marianne et ma jeunesse. 1955: Voici le temps des assassins (GB & US: Deadlier Than the Male). 1956: L'homme à l'imperméable. Pot-Bouille (GB: The House of Lovers). 1958: La femme et la pantin. 1959: Marie-Octobre. Das Kunstseidene Mädchen/La grande vie. 1960: Boulevard. 1961: La chambre ardente (GB & US: The Curse and the Coffin). 1962: The Devil and the 10 Commandments. 1963: Chair de poule (US: Highway Pickup). 1967: Diabolically Yours.*

DWAN, Allan (Joseph Aloysius Dwan) 1885-1981

For years the last surviving link with Hollywood's earliest days, Canadian-born Dwan liked making 'nice, simple pictures' and he did just that – around 400 of them, one of the longest lists in this book. It is clear from the many interviews he gave through the years that he never ceased to enjoy making films, was rarely assertive or difficult and even got a kick out of working for smaller studios such as Republic and RKO Radio by thinking up ways and means to beat the restrictions of his budgets and so make better pictures. He especially enjoyed action films and was good at them; he also liked making musicals, a genre in which he often made silk purses out of sows' ears. He worked initially as an engineer, writing in his spare time. His connections with the revolutionary mercury vapor arc lamps –

invaluable to cinematographers in getting clear views of close-ups – brought him to Essanay Studios in 1909. Through connections made there, he sold them several of his story ideas and gave up engineering when they offered him a position as a scenario editor in 1910. Later he joined the Flying A Film Company as chief scenario editor and became a director almost by accident when the man supposed to shoot a two-reel western variously called *Branding a Bad Man* and *Brandishing a Bad Man* failed to show up. Dwan proved a director who liked to move along with the action – as early as 1915 he is said to have invented the dolly shot – and not surprisingly was soon in charge of Douglas Fairbanks pictures, an association which reached its apogee with *Robin Hood*, with its incredible sets and stirring action. He also proved himself a capable comedy director, especially on *Manhattan Madness*, again with Fairbanks, a spoof about a cattleman in New York (years later, Dwan was to use a reverse situation for the splendid *Trail of the Vigilantes*) as well as *Zaza and Manhandled*. The gangster story *Big Brother* (later remade as *Young Donovan's Kid*, with Wallace Beery) was another silent highlight, as was the comedy-drama *Stage Struck*, another with Gloria Swanson, the star of *Manhandled* and *Zaza*. Dwan ended the silent era and entered sound, again in the company of Fairbanks, with *The Iron Mask*, the oft-filmed Musketeers story. After a first big talkie success with *While Paris Sleeps*, Dwan made a few films in England, where he is said to have discovered the 18-year-old Ida Lupino on *Her First Affaire*. His three biggest commercial successes were *Suez*, a massive historical epic about the building of the Suez Canal, and two charming Shirley Temple vehicles, *Heidi* and *Rebecca of Sunnybrook Farm*. There were some fast and furiously funny middle-budget 1940s comedies, notably *Trail of the Vigilantes, Up in Mabel's Room* and *Getting Gertie's Garter*, before Dwan signed up with Republic. By far his biggest box-office film for them was *Sands of Iwo Jima*, a well-organized, flag-waving war film starring John Wayne, which nearly gave tight-fisted studio chief Herbert J. Yates a heart attack by costing over a million dollars; but it emerged as a handsome profit-maker for the studio. Most of Dwan's final work at RKO Radio was remarkable considering the crumbling state of the studio. There were a couple of turkeys which the veteran Dwan admits to playing for laughs, but also some very respectable westerns that really packed a punch, especially *Silver Lode, Cattle Queen of Montana* and *Tennessee's Partner*, in which

Dwan elicited one of the best performances of Ronald Reagan's career. 'I suppose if I did make any mistakes', he said, 'they lay in accepting anything I was offered. One way or another, it was always a challenge.' With a list of 400 films to his credit, there's no arguing with that either way.

1911: *Branding a Bad Man Brandishing a Bad Man. *A Western Dream. *A Daughter of Liberty. *A Trouper's Heart. *Rattlesnakes and Gunpowder. *The Ranch Tenor. *The Sheepman's Daughter. *The Sagebrush Phrenologist. *The Elopements on Double-L Ranch. *$5,000 Reward, Dead Or Alive. *The Witch of the Range. *The Cowboy's Ruse. *Law and Order on the Bar-L Ranch. *The Bronco Buster's Bride. *The Yiddisher Cowboy. *The Hermit's Gold. *The Sky Pilot's Intemperance. *The Actress and the Cowboys. *A Western Waif. The Call of the Open Range. *The Ranch Chicken. *The Schoolma'am of Snake. *Cupid in Chaps. *The Outlaw's Trail. *The Ranchman's Nerve. *When the East Comes West. *The Cowboy's Deliverance. *The Cattle Thief's Brand. *The Parting Trails. *The Cattle Rustler's End. *Cattle, Gold and Oil. *The Ranch Girl. *The Poisoned Flume. *The Blotted Brand. *The Brand of Fear. *Auntie and the Cowboys. *The Western Doctor's Peril. *The Smuggler and the Girl. *The Cowboy and the Artist. *Three Million Dollars. *The Stage Robbers of San Juan. *The Mother of the Ranch. *The Gunman. *The Claim Jumpers. *The Circular Fence. The Rustler Sheriff. *The Love of the West.

The man who shot 400 films. An early 1920s picture of Allan **Dwan** in the days when he had his own production company — and even a monogrammed megaphone.

ALLAN DWAN PROD.

*The Miner's Wife. *The Land Thieves. *The Cowboy and the Outlaw. *Caves of La Jolla (D). *Three Daughters of the West. *The Horse Thief's Bigamy. *The Lonely Range. *The Trail of the Eucalyptus. *The Stronger Man. *The Water War. *The Three Shell Game. *The Mexican. *The Eastern Cowboy. *The Way of the West. *The Test. *The Master of the Vineyard. *Sloppy Bill of the Rollicking R. *The Sheriff's Sisters. *The Angel of Paradise Ranch. *The Smoke of the Forty-Five. *Santa Catalina – Magic Isle of the Pacific (D). *The Last Notch. *The Gold Lust. *The Duel of the Candles. *Bonita of El Cajon. *A Midwinter Trip to Los Angeles (D). *The Misadventures of a Claim Agent. *Bronco Busting for Flying A Pictures (D). 1912: *The Winning of La Mesa. *The Locket. *The Relentless Law. *Justice of the Sage. *Objections Overruled. *The Mormon. *Love and Lemons. *The Best Policy. *The Real Estate Fraud. *The Grubstake Mortgage. *When Broadway Meets the Mountains. *An Innocent Grafter. *Society and Chaps. *The Leap Year Cowboy. *The Land Baron of San Tee. *An Assisted Elopement. *The Broken Ties. *After School. *A Bad Investment. *The Full Value. *The Tramp's Gratitude. *Winter Sports and Pastimes of Coronado Beach (D). *The Maid and the Man. *The Cowboy Socialist. *The Ranchman's Marathon. *Checkmate. *The Coward. *The Distant Relative. *The Range Detective. *Driftwood. *The Eastern Girl. *The Pensioners. *The End of the Feud. *The Wedding Dress. *Mystical Maid of Jamasha Pass. *The Other Wise Man. *The Haters. *The Thread of Life. *The Wandering Gypsy. The Reward of Valor. *The Brand. *The Green Eyed Cloister. *Cupid Through Padlocks. *For the Good of Her Men. *The Simple Lore. *Fifty Mile Auto Contest (D). *The Weaker Brother. *The Wordless Message. *The Evil Inheritance. *The Marauders. *The Girl Back Home. *Under False Pretences. *Where There's a Heart. *The Vanishing Race. *Point Loma – Old Town (D). *The Fatal Error. *The Tell Tale Shells. *San Diego (D). *Indian Jealousy. *The Canyon Dweller. *It Pays to Wait. *A Life For A Kiss. *The Meddlers. *The Girl and the Gin. *The Battle-Ground. *Bad Man and the Ranger. *The Outlaw Colony. *The Land of Death. *The Bandit of Point Loma. *The Jealous Rage. *The Greaser and the Weakling. *The Stranger at Coyote. *The Dawn of Passion. *The Vengeance That Failed. *The Fear. *The Foreclosure. *White Treachery. *Their Hero Son. *Calamity Anne's Ward. *Father's Favorite. *Jack of Diamonds/Queen of Hearts. *The Reformation of Sierra Smith. *The Promise. *The New Cowpuncher. *The Best Man Wins. *Mountain Kate. *One Two Three. *The Wanderer. *Maiden and Men. *God's Unfortunate. *Man's Calling. *The Intrusion at Lompoc. *The Thief's Wife. *The Would-Be Heir. *Jack's Word. *Her Own Country. *Pals. *The Animal Within. *The Law of God. *Nell of the Pampas. *The Daughters of Señor Lopez. *The Power of Love. *The Recognition. *Blackened Hills. *Loneliness of Neglect. *The Fraud That Failed. *Another Man's Wife. 1913: *The Horse Thief. *Calamity Anne's Inheritance. *Their Masterpiece. *His Old Fashioned Mother. *Where Destiny Guides. *The Silver-Plated Gun. †*A Rose of Old Mexico. *Building the Great Los Angeles Aqueduct (D). *Women Left Alone. *Andrew Jackson. *Calamity Anne's Vanity. *The Fugitive. *The Romance. *The Finer Things. *Love is Blind. *When the Light Fades. *High and Low. *The Greater Love. *The Jocular Winds. *The Transgression of Manuel. *Calamity Anne, Detective. *The Orphan's Mine. *When a Woman Won't. *An Eastern Flower. *Cupid Never Ages. *That Sharp Note. *Calamity Anne's Beauty. *The Renegade's Heart. *Matches. *The Mute Witness. *Cupid Throws a Brick. *Suspended Sentence. *Woman's Honor. *In Another's Nest. *The Ways of Fate. *Boobs and Bricks. *Calamity Anne's Trust. *Oil on Troubled Waters. *The Road to Ruin. *The Brothers. *Human Kindness. *Youth and Jealousy. *Angel of the Canyons. *The Great Harmony. †*Her Innocent Marriage. *Calamity Anne Parcel Post. *The Ashes of Three. *On the Border. *Her Big Story. *When Luck Changes. *The Wishing Seal. †*Hearts and Horses. *The Reward of Courage. *Soul of a Thief. *The Marine Law. *The Spirit of the Flag. *In Love and War/The Call to Arms. *The Powder Flash of Death. *Women and War. *The Picket Guard. *Mental Suicide. *Man's Duty. *The Animal. *The Wall of Money. *The Echo of a Song. *Criminals. The Restless Spirit. *Jewels of Sacrifice. *Back to Life. *Red Margaret, Moonshiner. *Bloodhounds of the North. *He Called Her In. *The Menace. *The Lie. 1914: *The Honor of the Mounted. *Remember Mary Magdalen. Discord and Harmony. *The Menace to Carlotta. *The Embezzler. The Lamb, the Woman, the Wolf. *The End of the Feud. *The Tragedy of Whispering Creek. *The Unlawful Trade. The Forbidden Room. The Hopes of Blind Alley. *The Great Universal Mystery. Richelieu. Wildflower. The County Chairman. The Small Town Girl. A Straight Road. The Conspiracy. The Unwelcome Mrs Hatch. 1915: The

Dancing Girl. David Harum. The Love Route. The Commanding Officer. May Blossom. Pretty Sister of José. A Girl of Yesterday. The Foundling. Jordan is a Hard Road. 1916: Betty of Greystone. The Habit of Happiness (GB: Laugh and the World Laughs). The Good Bad Man (GB: Passing Through). An Innocent Magdalene. The Half-Breed. Manhattan Madness. Fifty-fifty. Panthea. 1917: Fighting Odds. A Modern Musketeer. Superstition (released 1922). 1918: Mr Fix-It. Bound in Morocco. He Comes Up Smiling. 1919: Cheating Cheaters. Getting Mary Married. The Dark Star. Soldiers of Fortune. The Luck of the Irish. 1920: The Forbidden Thing. 1921: A Perfect Crime. A Broken Doll. The Scoffer. The Sin of Martha Queed (GB: Sins of the Parents). In the Heart of a Fool. 1922: The Hidden Woman. Robin Hood. 1923: The Glimpses of the Moon. Lawful Larceny. Zaza. Big Brother. 1924: A Society Scandal. Manhandled. Her Love Story. Wages of Virtue. Argentine Love. Night Life of New York. Coast of Folly. Stage Struck. 1926: Sea Horses. Padlocked. Tin Gods. Summer Bachelors. 1927: The Music Master. *West Point. The Joy Girl. East Side, West Side. French Dressing (GB: Lessons for Wives). 1928: The Big Noise. 1929: The Iron Mask. Tide of Empire. The Far Call. Frozen Justice. South Sea Rose. 1930: What a Widow! Man to Man. 1931: Chances. Wicked. 1932: While Paris Sleeps. Her First Affaire. 1933: Counsel's Opinion. I Spy (US: The Morning After). 1935: Black Sheep. Navy Wife. 1936: Song and Dance Man. Human Cargo. High Tension. 15 Maiden Lane. 1937: Woman-Wise. That I May Live. One Mile from Heaven. Heidi. 1938: Rebecca of Sunnybrook Farm. Josette. Suez. 1939: The Three Musketeers (GB: The Singing Musketeer). Frontier Marshal. The Gorilla. 1940: Sailor's Lady. Trail of the Vigilantes. Young People. 1941: Look Who's Laughing. Rise and Shine. 1942: Friendly Enemies. Here We Go Again. 1943: Around the World. 1944: Up in Mabel's Room. Abroad with Two Yanks. 1945: Brewster's Millions. Getting Gertie's Garter. 1946: Rendezvous with Annie. 1947: Calendar Girl. Northwest Outpost (GB: End of the Rainbow). Driftwood. 1948: The Inside Story. Angel in Exile. Montana Belle (released 1952). 1949: Sands of Iwo Jima. 1950: Surrender. 1951: Belle Le Grand. The Wild Blue Yonder (GB: Thunder Across the Pacific). 1952: I Dream of Jeanie. 1953: Sweethearts on Parade. The Woman They Almost Lynched. 1954: Flight Nurse. Silver Lode. Passion. Cattle Queen of Montana. 1955: Escape to Burma. Pearl of the South Pacific. Ten-

nessee's Partner. 1956: Slightly Scarlet. Hold Back the Night. 1957: The River's Edge. The Restless Breed. 1958: Enchanted Island. Most Dangerous Man Alive.

EASON, B. Reeves 'Breezy' 1886–1956
Action galloping across the screen was this American director's stock-in-trade – so much so that, in addition to making numerous small-scale westerns and action films himself, he was responsible, as second unit director, for some of the most spectacular action scenes ever produced, within films directed by other people. In view of this specific talent, his work as second unit director is also listed below. He had come to Hollywood as an actor, after experience in stock, and played in dozens of two-reel action films before turning to direction in 1915. His wife, Jimsy Mayo, and son, Breezy Eason Jr, sometimes acted in his films, but tragedy entered the Easons' life in 1921 when Breezy Jnr was killed in an accident while working on one of his father's film. Eason himself went on to make scores of few-reel action films whose titles, such as *Flashing Spurs* and *Border Justice*, were almost interchangeable. He also directed a number of fast-moving serials, some of which were later released as features and animal adventures, featuring, among others, Rin-Tin-Tin and Rex the Wonder Horse. In more detail, his second-unit work includes the cavalry charge at the end of *The Charge of the Light Brigade*, the chariot race from the 1925 version of *Ben-Hur*, the burning of Atlanta sequence from *Gone with the Wind*, the wild horse fight and train crash sequences from *Duel in the Sun* and the land rush from the 1930 *Cimarron*. His solo work was forgotten soon after it was shown, but for these second-unit scenes Eason will be remembered. At the time of his death, he was doing what he had been doing on and off for 40 years – making short-length westerns, in this case in the guise of 25-minute segments of *The Lone Ranger* series for television.

1915: *She Walketh Alone. *Competition. *A Good Business Deal. *To Melody a Soul Responds. *The Newer Way. *The Poet of the Peaks. *The Day of Reckoning. *Mountain Mary. *The

Honor of the District Attorney. *After the Storm. *The Exile of the Bar-K Ranch. *The Assayer of Lone Gap. *Drawing the Line. *The Spirit of Adventure. *In Trust. *A Question of Honor. *The Barren Gain. *The Little Lady Next Door. *Hearts in Shadow. *Profit from Loss. *The Blot on the Shield. *The Wasp. *The Smuggler's Cove *To Rent – Furnished. *The Bluffers. *The Silver Lining. *A Broken Cloud. *The Solution of the Mystery. *Yes or No? *The Substitute Minister. 1916: *Time and Tide. *Viviana. *Matching Dreams. *A Sanitarium Scandal. *Shadows. *The Head of the House. 1918: *Nine-Tenths of the Law. *The Fighting Heart. *The Four-Bit Man. 1919: *Jack of Hearts. *The Tell Tale Wire. *The Crow. *The Fighting Line. *The Kid and the Cowboy. *The Prospector's Vengeance. 1920: *Hair Trigger Stuff. *Held Up for the Makins. *The Rattler's Hiss. *The Texas Kid. Human Stuff. Blue Streak McCoy. Pink Tights. Two Kinds of Love. †The Moon Riders (serial). 1921: Colorado. The Big Adventure. Red Courage. The Fire Eater. 1922: When East Comes West. Roughshod. Pardon My Nerve! The Lone Hand. †Adventures of Robinson Crusoe (serial). 1923: His Last Race. Tiger Thompson. †Around the World in 18 Days (serial). 1924: Trigger Finger. Women First (GB: The Turf Sensation). Flashing Spurs (GB: Spider's Web). Vanishing Frontier (uncompleted). 1925: Border Justice. The Texas Bearcat. Fighting Youth. Fighting the Flames. The New Champion. The Shadow on the Wall. A Fight to the Finish. 1926: Lone Hand Saunders. The Test of Donald Norton. The Sign of the Claw. 1927: The Denver Dude. The Prairie King. Painted Ponies. †Johnny Get Your Hair Cut. Through Thick, and Thin. Galloping Fury. 1928: The Flyin' Cowboy. Riding for Fame. A Trick of Hearts. Clearing the Trail. 1929: The Lariat Kid. The Winged Horseman. 1930: †Troopers Three. Roaring Ranch. Trigger Tricks. Spurs. †King of the Wild (serial). 1931: The Vanishing Legion (serial). The Galloping Ghost (serial). †Bimi (feature version of King of the Wild). 1932: The Sunset Trail. Honor of the Press (GB: The Scoop). Cornered. The Heart Punch. Behind Jury Doors. The Last of the Mohicans (serial). 1933: Revenge at Monte Carlo (GB: Mystery at Monte Carlo). Alimony Madness. Her Resale Value. Dance Hall Hostess. Neighbors' Wives. 1934: Hollywood Hoodlum (GB: What Price Fame?). †The Law of the Wild (serial). †Mystery Mountain (serial). 1935: †The Phantom Empire (serial). †The Miracle Rider (serial). †The Adventures of Rex and Rinty (serial). †The

Fighting Marines (serial). 1936: †Darkest Africa (serial. GB: Hidden City). Red River Valley. Undersea Kingdom (serial). 1937: *Give Me Liberty. Land Beyond the Law. The Kid Comes Back (GB: Don't Pull Your Punches). Empty Holsters. Prairie Thunder. Sergeant Murphy. 1938: Daredevil Drivers. †Call of the Yukon. 1939: Blue Montana Skies. Mountain Rhythm. *Wild West Days. 1940: *Young America Flies. *Service with the Colors. Sockeroo. *March on Marines. *Meet the Fleet. *Take the Air. †Men with Steel Faces (GB: Couldn't Possibly Happen. Feature version of 1935 serial The Phantom Empire). †Radio Ranch (feature version of 1934 serial Mystery Mountain). 1941: *Wings of Steel. *The Tanks Are Coming. *Soldiers in White. 1942: *Maybe Darwin was Right. *Men of the Sky. Murder in the Big House (GB: Human Sabotage). Spy Ship. 1943: Truck Busters. *The Fighting Engineers. *Oklahoma Outlaws. *Mountain Fighters. *Wagon Wheels West. The Phantom (serial). Murder on the Waterfront. 1944: The Desert Hawk (serial). 1946: North of the Border. 'Neath Canadian Skies. 1948: †Return of the Mohicans (feature version of 1932 serial). 1949: Rimfire. 1952: The Singapore Story. Kamong Sentosa. 1953: Paper Tiger. Jungle Justice.
As second-unit director: 1925: Ben-Hur. 1930: Cimarron. 1932: The Shadow of the Eagle (serial). 1936: The Charge of the Light Brigade. 1938: Army Girl (GB:

The Last of the Cavalry). The Adventures of Robin Hood. 1939: Man of Conquest. Gone with the Wind. 1941: Sergeant York. They Died with Their Boots On. 1942: The Spoilers. 1945: The Spanish Main. Salome, Where She Danced. 1946: Duel in the Sun. 1947: Black Gold. 1948: Northwest Stampede. 1950: Dallas. 1951: Ma and Pa Kettle at the Fair. 1952: The Half-Breed.

EASTWOOD, Clint 1930-

Eastwood the director is infinitely more interesting than Eastwood the superstar, but his films are less predictable. Quite how the man who made Play 'Misty' for Me and The Outlaw Josey Wales could also make The Eiger Sanction and The Gauntlet is a little baffling. But one gets the impression, to echo T.S. Eliot, that 'he will do as he do do, and there's no doing anything about it!' It's also difficult to gauge the contribution made by his cameraman Bruce Surtees, whose lyrical photography decorates most Eastwood films and reached its highpoint to date in Josey Wales. 'Misty', Eastwood's directorial debut, is a lively shocker almost worthy of Hitchcock, and he elicits a career-best performance by Jessica Walter as the unbalanced girl responsible for all the mayhem. High Plains Drifter is a rather bizarre homage to Sergio Leone, whose Italian 'Dollars' spaghetti westerns made Eastwood a star, but Breezy, The Eiger

Portraying the west as it was. Clint **Eastwood** lines up a shot for his Oscar-winning Unforgiven.

Sanction and *The Gauntlet* revealed that Eastwood was able to add little to straightforward subjects. *Josey Wales* is his best film to date, a romantic western of epic structure and beautiful compositions in which Eastwood builds up a lovely relationship between himself and the ancient Indian actor Chief Dan George. Born in San Francisco, Eastwood spent a nomadic childhood during the American Depression, travelling with a father who pumped gasoline up and down the California coast. Although a star basketball player at school, Eastwood did not take the game up professionally, and led an unsettled life – lumberjack, swimming instructor, garage worker and stoker and, after taking a business-administration course, small-part actor in Hollywood. His 1980 film, *Bronco Billy*, about the rigours of a travelling rodeo-circus, reflects something of the restlessness in his early life. The films that have followed this, almost all of them featuring the director also as star, have spotlighted loners – one man against the odds, sometimes a blue-collar worker taking on a white-collar world. Eastwood the director, however, seemed on a downward course until he returned to the western with *Unforgiven*. Only a whit behind *Josey Wales* in stature, it was given the recognition denied the earlier film with the award of Best Picture and Best Director Oscars. The film featured a rich array of characters in a more realistic view of the Old West than was ever allowed in Eastwood's 'Dollars' westerns. Eastwood's films since then have not reached the same standard, though they remain pieces to be reckoned with. Perhaps one more return to the western...

1971: Play 'Misty' for Me. 1972: High Plains Drifter. 1973: Breezy. 1975: The Eiger Sanction. 1976: The Outlaw Josey Wales. 1977: The Gauntlet. 1980: Bronco Billy. 1982: Firefox. 1983: Honkytonk Man. Sudden Impact. 1985: Pale Rider. 1986: Heartbreak Ridge. 1988: Bird. 1990: White Hunter, Black Heart. The Rookie. 1992: Unforgiven. 1993: A Perfect World. 1995: The Bridges of Madison County. 1997: Absolute Power. Midnight in the Garden of Good and Evil. 1999: True Crime.

EDWARDS, Blake (William B. McEdwards) 1922-
One hangs on to the likings of one's youth and loyalties to stars and directors whose work caught one's attention at that formative time. However, this American director has long since lost me, his career shored up by the continuing box-office success of the Pink Panther films, and the fortuitous, Bo Derek-inspired success of

Men in white hats. Bruce Willis (left) and director Blake **Edwards** on the set of *Sunset*.

the tedious '10'. As a young actor (from 1942 to 1948), Edwards was tall, fair, handsome and not terribly successful. His writing career, which had started in 1948 on medium-budget westerns, got going properly in 1952, when he began to make, with Richard Quine (*qv*), who initially directed, a series of ingenuously entertaining musicals and comedies-with-music for Columbia, initially in Supercinecolor, but later in Technicolor, featuring such as Frankie Laine, Billy Daniels and Mickey Rooney. Besides the credits below, they include the Quine-directed *Sound Off, Rainbow 'Round My Shoulder, All Ashore, Cruisin' Down the River* and *My Sister Eileen*, all of which Quine and Edwards co-scripted. This last film also started an association with Jack Lemmon (see article on Quine) whom Edwards was later to direct in *Days of Wine and Roses*. The best of Edwards' early solo films as director is *He Laughed Last*, which he also co-wrote, a Damon Runyon-style comedy with music, almost entirely stolen by Jesse White as a gangster called Max, and full of funny lines. Edwards' major reputation was deservedly made between 1961 and 1963. First, he made the joyously different *Breakfast at Tiffany's*, with Audrey Hepburn in sparkling form, an enchanting cat and the famous finale in the rain, one of those silly Hollywood sequences that works so perfectly as to tug the tear ducts automatically open. This was followed by a genuinely frightening thriller, *Experiment in Terror*, in a genre to which Edwards has never returned, and then the hilarious *The*

Pink Panther, after which Peter Sellers' inept Inspector Clouseau – everything he touches turns to ashes – became a worldwide institution. Since then, there have been many more hit-and-miss Pink Panther comedies, some wildly unsuitable vehicles for his second wife (since 1969) Julie Andrews, as she made increasing efforts to escape the typecasting of *Mary Poppins*, some tedious and overlong action films and some overblown comedies (excepting *The Party*, uneven, but, thanks to Sellers, with some side-splitting moments). Then came '10', the sexploitation comedy of a veteran imitating a distasteful genre, followed by *S.O.B.*, another bore in which Edwards hit out pettishly at the philistine executives he has apparently had to suffer through the years, and the transvestite 'comedy' *Victor/Victoria*, overlong but buoyed up by Robert Preston's excellence. As a director of his own dialogue, there's no doubt Edwards knows what he's about. His pacing of visual fun is much less sure, but, with his sound knowledge of the mechanics of cinema, one just wishes he'd try more thrillers before one throws the fan club card away for good. But the dreadful *Son of the Pink Panther* has the distinct ring of a last shot in the locker.

1955: Bring Your Smile Along. 1956: He Laughed Last. Mister Cory. 1958: This Happy Feeling. The Perfect Furlough (GB: Strictly for Pleasure). 1959: Operation Petticoat. 1960: High Time. 1961: Breakfast at Tiffany's. 1962: Experiment in Terror (GB: The Grip of Fear). Days of

Wine and Roses. 1963: The Pink Panther. 1964: A Shot in the Dark. 1965: The Great Race. 1966: What Did You Do in the War, Daddy? 1967: Gunn. 1968: The Party. 1969: Darling Lili. 1971: Wild Rovers. 1972: The Carey Treatment. 1974: The Tamarind Seed. 1975: The Return of the Pink Panther. 1976: The Pink Panther Strikes Again. 1978: Revenge of the Pink Panther. 1979: '10'. 1981: S.O.B. 1982: Victor/Victoria. The Trail of the Pink Panther. 1983: Curse of the Pink Panther. 1984: The Man Who Loved Women. Micki † Maude. 1985: A Fine Mess. 1986: 'Blake Edwards' That's Life!'. 1987: Blind Date. 1988: Sunset. Justin Case (TV). 1989: Skin Deep. Peter Gunn (TV). 1991: Switch. 1993: Son of the Pink Panther.

EGOYAN, Atom 1960-

Egyptian-born, Canadian-raised director of Armenian parentage, who has been turning out art-house fare since he was 19. After almost 20 years of a seemingly deliberate avoidance of mainstream cinema, Egoyan embraced a more general audience with the poignant *The Sweet Hereafter*. Unashamedly appealing to a highbrow audience he has said: 'I like to think of the audience participating in my films. I ask them to engage their minds on an active level and go through periods where they may not know what's going on and wonder why they're watching.' It would be easy to be sarcastic about such sentiments, except that Egoyan's films are, on the whole, rather interesting fare. Egoyan's parents moved to Canada when he was three, having blessed him with the name Atom because 1960 was the year of Egypt's first atomic reactor. It is a cross he has had to bear ever since. Before he was 20, though, the bespectacled, good-looking Egoyan had written two plays and already started making short films. His first feature, *Next of Kin* – a popular title in the film world – reflected, as did others, his Armenian roots in its story of an alienated and bored young man who becomes fascinated by a video of an Armenian family. The film owes something to Egoyan's own life, as well as to an ironic sense of humour which streaks through most of his subsequent work. *Family Viewing* spreads this dysfunctionality to an entire family, in its surreal study of a young man attempting to solve the disappearance of his mother. Egoyan reached a wider audience with *Exotica*, a weird but compelling kettle of fish set in a strip club, where a bizarre set of characters mires itself in angst, desire and murky pasts. He was Oscar-nominated for the award-winning *The Sweet Hereafter*, a tightly observed portrait of a community

Russian director Sergei **Eisenstein** at work in the cutting-room in the 1930s.

in shock after the death of most of its children when their bus crashes into a frozen lake. Nothing in an Egoyan film is quite straightforward and you may have problems with the time scale here – the story is conducted on three different time levels at once – but there's no mistaking the grief and poignancy of the situation. Egoyan's wife, Arsinée Khanjian, has played roles in all his feature films.

*1979: *Howard in Particular. 1980: *After Grad with Dad. 1981: *Peep Show. 1982: *Open House. 1984: Next of Kin. 1985: *Men: A Passion Playground. *In This Corner. 1987: *The Final Twist. Family Viewing. 1988: *Looking for Nothing. 1989: Speaking Parts. 1991: The Adjuster. 1992: +Montreal vu par... 1993: Gross Misconduct (TV). Calendar. 1994: Exotica. 1995: *A Portrait of Arshile. 1997: The Sweet Hereafter. 1998: Sarabande. 1999: Felicia's Journey.*

EISENSTEIN, S.M. 1898-1948

That the Russian Sergei Mikhailovitch Eisenstein was a genius at the art of montage is indisputable. Whether he was also a genius of the cinema, in the manner of his compatriot Dovzhenko, is more open to doubt. One film, the magnificent *Alexander Nevsky*, with its unforgettable battle on the ice, suggests that he was. But, while lamenting the paucity of output that limited Eisenstein to a handful of completed films and a handful of uncompleted projects, one should also remember that he was an ambitious egotist and

propagandist largely responsible for his own misfortunes at a time when he could have been in his most prolific period. Without doubt, the images and techniques from his most successful film, *The Battleship Potemkin*, influenced a generation; although, away from its individual sequences, the film as a whole cannot live up to one's anticipation. Eisenstein was born in Riga, capital of Latvia, which was part of Russia when he was born and when he died, although independent from 1918 to 1940. In his early twenties, he became a set and costume designer in the theatre in Moscow, getting interested in films when making a filmed insert in 1923 for one of his stage productions. In short order, he had become a passionate, perfectionist film-maker. His immense eight-episode project *1905* failed to materialize (much footage had to be abandoned) but did lead to the films *Strike* and *The Battleship Potemkin*, which spectacularly put the Russian cinema on the map with their visions of anguish, violence and collective revolution. For a while Eisenstein was fêted everywhere and, although his country's authorities forced him to work at a frenzied pace on features, he felt he was still on course to achieve his life's goals. The 1930s, however, changed all that. A trip to Hollywood proved a singularly unhappy experience and Eisenstein's contract there was cancelled at the end of 1930. He journeyed south to make a massive Mexican documentary, but nine months after he had begun shooting the backers withdrew their support, and, amid charges of profligacy and extravagance, Eisenstein returned to Eastern Europe, never to re-emerge. A nervous breakdown followed in 1933, and there were uncompleted or unstarted projects before *Alexander Nevsky* was triumphantly made, aided by an imposing score by Prokofiev, in 1938. It was, however, the last great work. *Ivan the Terrible*, made under difficult wartime circumstances, turned out to be suffocatingly ornate, and also ran into trouble with the authorities, who suppressed Part II altogether until 1958, long after Eisenstein's death. Eisenstein did not live to complete the third part of his *Ivan* trilogy: indeed it was barely started. He had suffered one major heart attack in 1946 and a second in 1948 killed him, after he had returned to work on his trilogy against doctors' orders. If his films sometimes lack the human touch, he remains a master of the organization of images within the frame in such a way as to make the maximum impact on his audience.

1923: *Glumov's Film-Diary. 1925: Strike. The Battleship Potemkin (US: Potemkin). 1928: †October (US: Ten Days that Shook the World). 1929: †The Old and the New/The General Line. 1932: †Que Viva Mexico! (unfinished). 1937: Bezhin Meadow (unfinished). 1938: †Alexander Nevsky. 1939: Ferghana Canal (unfinished. Later, material re-edited and issued in 1940 as Mighty Stream). 1944: Ivan the Terrible Part I. 1946: Ivan the Terrible Part II: The Boyars' Plot.* The following films were made from material shot by Eisenstein in the making of *Que Viva Mexico!: 1933: Thunder Over Mexico. Eisenstein in Mexico. 1934: *Death Day. 1939: Time in the Sun. 1941: Mexican Symphony. 1955: Eisenstein's Mexican Film – Episodes for Study.*

ELDRIDGE, John 1917-1960

A British director whose films distinguished themselves by their very Englishness. Eldridge's documentaries and semi-documentaries have a poetic quality rarely found elsewhere. They are the sons and daughters of the British documentary movement of the 1930s and indeed Eldridge's three feature films, all with rural or coastal settings, were made for pioneer documentarist John Grierson's all-too-short-lived Group 3 Productions. Eldridge started in films as an assistant editor, but had begun making documentaries under his own steam by 1939. The first of these to come into the national spotlight was *Our Country* (1944), which received a big première at one of London's largest cinemas and immediately

polarized critical opinion. But the Britons, along with the Russians, have always been among the foremost poets of the cinema, and, in this remarkable picture of his country, Eldridge was aided in the fulfilment of his aims by the commentary of a 'real' poet, Dylan Thomas, sympathetic and uplifting music by William Alwyn and admirable black-and-white photography by Jo Jago. Eldridge's style was to make rounded characters from real people – more difficult than it sounds – but achieved with real skill, from dancing West Indians, to Scots trawlermen, cockney hop-pickers in Kent and Welsh schoolchildren. Eldridge also caught the eye with *Three Dawns to Sydney*, which transcended the bounds of normal travelogue in its story of the countries flown over by an aeroplane bound from England to Australia. After casting his poet's eye at Tyneside *(North East Corner)* and Edinburgh *(Waverley Steps)*, Eldridge moved into features, wisely choosing Grierson's unit as the one in which his talents would be best employed. These are gently humorous films, the first, *Brandy for the Parson*, about liquor-smugglers on the Kent coast; the next, *Laxdale Hall*, back to *Whisky Galore!* country, as Hebridean islanders cannily do battle with bureaucracy; and the third and best, *Conflict of Wings*, with script co-written by the poet John Pudney and sparkling Eastman Colour photography by Arthur Grant, slightly more serious fare about a bird sanctuary, carefully acted and thought out and a credit to all concerned, deservedly released as a main feature in its native Britain. Unfortunately, Eldridge was already in poor health, and it was to be his last film. Like other talents nurtured in the thirties and early forties, he might have found nowhere to go in the industry, as it progressed, but into television documentary. That we shall never know.

1939: S.O.S. (D). 1940: The Story of Michael Flagherty (D). 1942: *Young Farmers (D). 1943: New Towns for Old (D). Ashley Green Goes to School (D). 1944: Our Country (D). Tank Patrol (D). Fuel for Battle (D). 1945: Conquest of a Germ (D). A City Reborn (D). 1946: North East Corner (D). *†Civil Engineering. 1947: Three Dawns to Sydney (D). 1948: Waverley Steps (D). 1951: Brandy for the Parson. 1952: Laxdale Hall (US: Scotch on the Rocks). 1954: Conflict of Wings (US: Fuss over Feathers).*

ELVEY, Maurice (William Folkard) 1887-1967

The most productive British director in history, Elvey had an eye for what would make a commercial film, an instinct

which only began to fail him towards the very end of his long career. Some of his films, although rarely grand critical successes, were extremely popular with the public, especially in the late 1920s and early 1930s, when such films as *The Flag Lieutenant, Hindle Wakes. The Flight Commander, Quinneys, Balaclava, Sally in Our Alley* and *The Lodger* helped lay the foundations of the popular British cinema for the next decade. Elvey was a product of the impoverished north-east of England in the late 19th century. He was out at work, after minimal education, before the century was over, but bettered himself as an actor at 17. After becoming a stage director, he turned to films with the boom in the industry which took place in 1912-13. Elvey made some of the earliest British feature-length movies – such as *The Great Gold Robbery, The Suicide Club* and an early version of the old barnstormer *Maria Marten*. He was at one time married to the prominent film and stage actress Isobel Elsom – they met on *The Wandering Jew* (1923) – and shortly after this went to Hollywood where he gained valuable experience directing several medium-budget films. Years later, Miss Elsom was also to go to Hollywood where she became a character star. As the years rolled by, Elvey piled up a huge list of credits making films for all occasions and decades. Even in the 1950s, when his films were doing poorly at the box-office, the lowbrow farces that he made actually anticipated the craze for Carry On films by only a few years – showing that Elvey had not altogether lost touch with the public. Only the loss of an eye and failing health brought about his retirement at the age of 70.

1913: *The Fallen Idol. *Bridegrooms Beware. The Great Gold Robbery. *Popsy Wopsy. Maria Marten. *Inquisitive Ike. The Cup Final. 1914: *Lest We Forget. Black-Eyed Susan. The Suicide Club. The Loss of the Birkenhead. The Bells of Rheims. Her Luck in London. *The White Feather. It's a Long Way to Tipperary. *The Sound of Her Voice. *There's Good in Everyone. The Idol of Paris. Beautiful Jim. 1915: *Gilbert Gets Tiger-Itis. *Gilbert Dying to Die. A Honeymoon for Three. Midshipman Easy. London's Yellow Peril. Florence Nightingale. From Shopgirl to Duchess. Her Nameless Child. Grip. A Will of Her Own. Home. Charity Ann. Love in a Wood. 1916: Meg the Lady. Esther. *Money for Nothing. Driven. Vice Versa. Motherlove. When Knights were Bold. *Trouble for Nothing. The Princess of Happy Chance. The King's Daughter. 1917: Smith. The Grit of a Jew. The Woman Who Was Nothing. Flames. Mary*

Girl. The Gay Lord Quex. Justice. Dombey and Son. Goodbye. 1918: Hindle Wakes. Adam Bede. Nelson. The Life Story of David Lloyd George. Bleak House. 1919: Keeper of the Door. Comradeship (US: Comrades in Arms). The Rocks of Valpré. The Victory Leaders. God's Good Man. Mr Wu. The Swindler. 1920: The Elusive Pimpernel. The Amateur Gentleman. At the Villa Rose. The Hundredth Chance. A Question of Trust. The Tavern Knight. 1921: Innocent. The Fruitful Vine. The Hound of the Baskervilles. *The Tragedy of a Comic Song. *The Dying Detective. *The Devil's Foot. *A Case of Identity. *Yellow Face. *The Red-Headed League. *The Resident Patient. *A Scandal in Bohemia. *The Man with the Twisted Lip. *The Bery Coronet. *The Noble Bachelor. *The Copper Beeches. Empty House. *The Tiger of San Pedro. *The Priory School. *The Solitary Cyclist. A Gentleman of France. A Romance of Wastdale. Man and His Kingdom. 1922: The Passionate Debt of Honour. Dick Turpin's Ride to York. Running Water. 1923: The Sign of Four. The Wandering Jew. Guy Fawkes. Sally Bishop. Royal Oak. Don Quixote. 1924: Henry, King of Navarre. Slaves of Destiny. The Love Story of Ailette Brunton. My Husband's Wives. 1925: The Folly of Vanity. Curly Top. She Wolves. Every Man's Wife. 1926: *Baddesley Manor. *Windsor Castle. *Glamis Castle. *Kenilworth Castle. *Tower of London. Woman Tempted. Human Law. The Flag Lieutenant. Mademoiselle from Armentières. 1927: Hindle Wakes (remake. US: Fanny Hawthorn). Roses of Picardy. The Flight Commander. The Glad Eye. Quinneys. 1928: Mademoiselle Parley Voo. Palais de Danse. You Know What Sailors Are. 1929: High Treason. 1930: †Balaclava (US: The Jaws of Hell). The School for Scandal. 1931: Honeymoon Adventure. Sally in Our Alley. Potiphar's Wife (US: Her Strange Desire). 1932: The Water Gipsies. †Diamond Cut Diamond (US: Blame the Woman). Frail Women. In a Monastery Garden. The Lodger (US: The Phantom Fiend). The Marriage Bond. 1933: The Lost Chord. I Lived with You. This Week of Grace. The Wandering Jew (remake). Soldiers of the King (US: The Woman in Command). 1934: Princess Charming. My Song for You. Road House. Love, Life and Laughter. Lily of Killarney (US: The Bride of the Lake). 1935: Heat Wave. The Clairvoyant. The Tunnel (US: Transatlantic Tunnel). 1936: Spy of Napoleon. The Man in the Mirror. 1937: Change for a Sovereign. Who Killed John Savage? A Romance in Flanders. Melody and Romance. 1938: Who Goes Next? The Return of the Frog. Lightning Conductor.

1939: Sword of Honour. The Spider. Sons of the Sea. 1940: Room for Two. *Goofer Trouble. For Freedom. Under Your Hat. 1942: Salute John Citizen. 1943: The Lamp Still Burns. †The Gentle Sex. 1944: Medal for the General (US: The Gay Intruders). Strawberry Roan. 1946: Beware of Pity. 1951: The Late Edwina Black (US: Obsessed). The Third Visitor. 1952: My Wife's Lodger. 1953: House of Blackmail. The Great Game. Is Your Honeymoon Really Necessary? 1954: What Every Woman Wants. The Harassed Hero. The Happiness of Three Women. The Gay Dog. 1955: You Lucky People. Room in the House. Fun at St Fanny's. 1956: Stars in Your Eyes. Dry Rot. 1957: Second Fiddle.

EMMERICH, Roland 1955-

West German film-maker who operated out of his native Stuttgart until the early 1990s, but then went to Hollywood and quickly built a reputation as a maker of box-office-busting megablasts of special effects-oriented action. 'Never mind the quality, feel the width' might be Emmerich's motto and, with record-breaking takings for his recent *Independence Day*, few film companies could argue with the logic, Emmerich's films were all praised for their effects (if little else) and their American casts disguised the fact that they were made in the then-West Germany. Emmerich moved to America and immediately made one of Jean-Claude Van Damme's most successful films, *Universal Soldier*, in which the plot, very derivative of *RoboCop*, deservedly plays second-fiddle to the non-stop, muscle-rippling action. When Emmerich's *Stargate*, about scientists teleported to a distant world, was an unexpected success, he was entrusted with a huge budget for the spectacular sci-fi action film *Independence Day*. Very silly, but tremendously enjoyable stuff, with adrenalin-rushing action that has you cheering for the world's forces against the aliens, the film scored a bullseye with the public and crushed box-office doubt by amassing $306 million in America, and $750 million worldwide, to burst into the top five financial hits of all time.

1985: Making Contact/Joey. 1988: Ghost Chase. 1990: Moon 44. 1992: Universal Soldier. 1994: Stargate. 1996: Independence Day. 1998: Godzilla.

ENDFIELD, Cy 1914-1995

South African-born director who initially made knockabout comedies in Hollywood, then switched to drama just as the McCarthy witch-hunts caught up with

him and forced him out of America. Working in Britain, at first under the double cloak of a pseudonym and the tag of 'supervising director', Endfield soon revealed taste – and talent – for raw, red-blooded action, whether it was on the battlefield or in a man-to-man fist-fights. His partnership with actor Stanley Baker produced some hard-man movies that culminated in the pulsating action of *Zulu*, as row upon row of Zulu attackers hurl spears and defiance at the red-coated defenders of Rorke's Drift. This was followed by *Sands of the Kalahari*, truly a primitive film red in fang and claw, but less successful both publicly and critically. Sadly, since then, Endfield has been far less active, although he did contribute the script to the *Zulu* 'prequel', *Zulu Dawn*, in 1979. On all his American films (1942-1952), he is credited as Cyril Endfield. On his British-based films, he is credited as C. Raker Endfield (when not using a pseudonym) between 1953 and 1959, and as Cy Endfield from 1960 on. The initial short films are part of M-G-M's 'Passing Parade' series. He also wrote screenplays, and sometimes co-wrote his own films. Died from cerebral vascular disease.

1942: *Inflation. 1944: *Tale of a Dog. *Radio Bugs. *†Nostradamus IV. Dancing Romeo. 1945: *The Great American Mug. *Magic on a Stick. 1946: *Our Old Car. Gentleman Joe Palooka. 1947: Stork Bites Man. 1948: The Argyle Secrets. 1949: Joe Palooka in the Big Fight. 1950: The Underworld Story. The Sound of Fury (GB: Try and Get Me). 1952: Tarzan's Savage Fury. 1953: †The Limping Man (uncredited). Colonel March Investigates. 1954: †Impulse (uncredited). **The Master Plan. 1955: The Secret. 1956: †Child in the House. 1957: Hell Drivers. 1958: Sea Fury. 1959: Jet Storm (US: The Killing Urge). 1961: Mysterious Island. 1963: Zulu. Hide and Seek. 1965: Sands of the Kalahari. 1969: †De Sade. 1971: Universal Soldier.

† as 'supervising director'
** as Hugh Raker

ENRIGHT, Ray 1896-1965

Another of the Randolph Scottsmen. Scott's filmography suggests that he felt more comfortable working with men he knew and liked (eight films for Budd Boetticher *(qv)*, seven for Edwin L. Marin *(qv)* whose death severed their association, and five for André de Toth *(qv)*. Indiana-born Enright directed Scott seven times between 1942 and 1948, and vies with Boetticher for the position of best

Scott helmsman. The films he made with Scott are vigorous and action-filled, and have memorable fist-fights that climb all over the screen. Enright followed Scott from RKO Radio to Paramount to Columbia and back to RKO again before the two men parted company. It is interesting that Enright made nothing of note thereafter. Strangely, he had made very few westerns before this, spending 15 years with Warner Brothers turning out a variety of products typical of the studio. The studio started him off on Rin Tin Tin vehicles, but the main part of his 1930s output is taken up with musicals and comedies, notably *Blondie Johnson, Dames, Swing Your Lady* (even though Humphrey Bogart once described it as his worst film), *Gold Diggers in Paris* and *On Your Toes*. A second film with Bogart, the circus melodrama *The Wagons Roll at Night* (a rather shapeless remake of *Kid Galahad*), came just before he left Warners and moved into the war films and westerns that were to dominate the remainder of his career. Enright blossomed with independence and almost all of his films in the 1940s have something to recommend them, especially the all-out battles between Scott and John Wayne in *The Spoilers* and between Scott and Robert Ryan in *Trail Street*. Enright began his career as an assistant editor on Chaplin comedies, then joined Mack Sennett as an ideas man and film editor; he became the studio's supervising editor after a career interruption for service in World War I with the American Expeditionary Force. This probably explains the uncompromising nature of his war films; perhaps a switch back to Warners in the 1950s, when war films were still being churned out in Enright's favoured black-and-white, might have halted the decline in his career.

*1921: *Verse and Worse. †*His Unlucky Job. 1927: Tracked by the Police. Jaws of Steel. The Girl from Chicago. 1928: Land of the Silver Fox. Domestic Troubles. The Little Wildcat. 1929: Kid Gloves. Stolen Kisses. Skin Deep. 1930: Dancing Sweeties. Song of the West. Golden Dawn. 1931: Scarlet Pages. 1932: The Tenderfoot. Play Girl. 1933: Blondie Johnson. Tomorrow at Seven. The Silk Express. Havana Widows. 1934: Twenty Million Sweethearts. I've Got Your Number. The St Louis Kid (GB: A Perfect Weekend). Dames. The Circus Clown. 1935: While the Patient Slept. Traveling Saleslady. We're in the Money. Alibi Ike. Miss Pacific Fleet. 1936: China Clipper. Snowed Under. Earthworm Tractors (GB: A Natural Born Salesman). Sing Me a Love Song (GB: Come Up*

*Smiling). 1937: The Singing Marine. Ready, Willing and Able. Slim. Back in Circulation. Swing Your Lady. 1938: Gold Diggers in Paris (GB: The Gay Imposters). Hard to Get. Going Places. 1939: Angels Wash Their Faces. Naughty, But Nice. On Your Toes. 1940: Teddy, the Rough Rider (D). An Angel from Texas. Brother Rat and a Baby (GB: Baby Be Good). River's End. *Throwing a Party (D). 1941: Thieves Fall Out. The Wagons Roll at Night. Law of the Tropics. Bad Men of Missouri. 1942: Wild Bill Hickok Rides. Men of Texas (GB: Men of Destiny). The Spoilers. Sin Town. 1943: *The Rear Gunner (D). †Destroyer (uncredited). Good Luck, Mr Yates. The Iron Major. Gung Ho! 1945: China Sky. Man Alive. One Way to Love. 1947: Trail Street. 1948: Albuquerque (GB: Silver City). Return of the Bad Men. Coroner Creek. 1949: Montana. South of St Louis. 1950: Kansas Raiders. 1951: Flaming Feather. 1953: Man from Cairo (GB: Crime Squad).*

EPHRON, Nora 1941-

She makes you laugh, she makes you cry. No doubt about it, the bitter-sweet romantic comedies of Nora Ephron are here to stay. The daughter of successful playwrights/screenwriters Phoebe and Henry Ephron, Nora was a journalist and novelist before venturing into films with a co-screenplay credit on *Silkwood*, which won her an Oscar nomination. She enjoyed further writing successes with the semi-autobiographical *Heartburn* and the Steve Martin comedy *My Blue Heaven*. Her directorial debut, *This is My Life*, has nice performances and good one-liners, but dislikeable characters, a fault Ephron rectified in style with *Sleepless in Seattle*, an unashamed romantic wallow, in which the whole point was that you fell in love with the plight of widower Tom Hanks and his small son and their search for the perfect girl – played by Meg Ryan, who had enjoyed such spectacular success with the Ephron-scripted *When Harry Met Sally...* in 1989. Ephron had her first flop with another Steve Martin romp, *Mixed Nuts*, but righted the ship with *Michael*, a comedy about an unconventional angel, before reuniting Hanks and Ryan in *You've Got Mail*.

1992: This is My Life. 1993: Sleepless in Seattle. 1994: Mixed Nuts. 1996: Michael. 1998: You've Got Mail.

FARROW, John 1904-1963

An Australian-born Hollywood director whose literary career was probably more distinguished than his films, Farrow arrived in Hollywood as a writer after service in the Merchant Navy and the US Marine Corps. While he was working on films with such titles as *Ladies of the Mob, A Dangerous Woman* and *Last of the Pagans*, Farrow was compiling a Tahitian-French-English dictionary, writing a treatise on the history of the Royal Canadian Navy, and publishing a play and a novel, a life of Sir Thomas More, a history of the Papacy and a biography of Damien the leper priest. In 1936, having made a couple of shorts, Farrow had his first taste of feature direction on *Tarzan Escapes*, but the film was completely reshot by another director after problems with the censors' office. However, Farrow did meet and marry the leading lady, the Irish-born actress Maureen O'Sullivan. They had seven children, including actresses Mia and Tisa Farrow. His directorial career proper got under way the following year, although his initial ventures were not of any great note and, on the whole, although fairly short, quite slowly paced. Farrow's solemnity, however, was gradually eroded by the Hollywood scene. In 1939, he had his first big success with *Five Came Back* which, although only 75 minutes long, soon won itself a high reputation and was released by RKO Radio as a main feature. Its gripping story of a planeload of passengers stranded in the jungle was remade by Farrow himself in 1956 as *Back from Eternity*, although to less effect, largely because 22 minutes (of talk) had been added to the running time. Farrow rejoined the Navy with the outbreak of World War II, but was invalided out within a few months, and with typhus for good measure. Immediately on recovery he made a fine war film. The stirring story of *Wake Island*, where a handful of US Marines held out against the Japanese Navy for 15 days before being wiped out, was told with guts and affection, and it won Farrow the New York Film Critics' award as best director of 1942. He was also nominated for an Academy Award — his only Oscar nomination as director.

Rainer Werner **Fassbinder** took the leading role in one of his best films, *Fox*. Consoling the unfortunate Fox is Christiane Martel.

The rest of Farrow's career was uneven, although there were two excellent films in 1948 — *Night Has a Thousand Eyes*, a psychological thriller with Edward G. Robinson as a fortune-teller, and *The Big Clock*, a very stylish crime melodrama, with Charles Laughton's famous fall down a lift shaft as its climax. The last highpoint of Farrow's career was the delightfully tongue-in-cheek, enjoyable Robert Mitchum-Jane Russell film *His Kind of Woman*, with rich parts for Vincent Price (as a ham actor) and Raymond Burr (the villain) and many quirky touches. Alas, Farrow had returned to dullness when a heart attack killed him a few days short of his 59th birthday. But he had shared an Oscar for the screenplay of *Around the World in 80 Days*.

1934: *The War Lord. *The Spectacle Maker. 1937: The Invisible Menace. Men in Exile. West of Shanghai. She Loved a Fireman. 1938: Little Miss Thoroughbred. My Bill. Broadway Musketeers. 1939: Sorority House (GB: That Girl from College). Women in the Wind. The Saint Strikes Back. Reno. Five Came Back. Full Confession. 1940: Married and in Love. A Bill of Divorcement. 1942: Wake Island. Commandos Strike at Dawn. 1943: China. 1944: The Hitler Gang. 1945: You Came Along. 1946. California. Two Years Before the Mast. 1947: Blaze of Noon. Easy Come, Easy Go. Calcutta. 1948: Night Has a Thousand Eyes. The Big Clock. Beyond Glory. 1949: Red, Hot and Blue. Alias Nick Beal (GB: The Contact Man). 1950: Copper Canyon. Where Danger Lives. 1951: His Kind of Woman. Submarine Command. †Red Mountain*

(uncredited). 1952: Ride, Vaquero! 1953: Botany Bay. Plunder of the Sun. Hondo. 1954: A Bullet is Waiting. 1955. The Sea Chase. 1956: Back from Eternity. 1957: The Unholy Wife. 1959: John Paul Jones.

FASSBINDER, Rainer Werner 1946-1982

Decadence and despair were recurring themes in the work of this prolific if unconventional Bavarian-born director of German films. After turning out films in the 1970s at a rate unheard of since the vintage years of Hollywood, he later seemed to be reaching for wider audiences in such films as *Die Ehe der Maria Braun* and *Lili Marleen*. The same actors and actresses crop up in most of his films: this obviously saved him some time in setting up films, and partially explains his tremendous output. After short films and theatrical experience during which he met most of the players who were to form the 'stock company' of his movies — Hanna Schygulla, Irm Hermann, Margit Carstensen, Harry Baer, Claus Holm and Ingrid Caven (to whom he was briefly married) – Fassbinder got down to making features in 1969. Although he almost always used 'shocking' themes – male homosexuality in *Fox*, lesbianism in *The Bitter Tears of Petra Von Kant*, the love of an old woman for a young man in *Fear Eats the Soul*, a man who massacres his own family in *Why Does Herr R. Run Amok?* — and used small, almost bare sets and often primitive sound, Continental audiences were attracted to his films in large numbers. From the mid-1970s, he began making considerable dents in the international market.

There is certainly something hypnotically fascinating in the way some of Fassbinder's characters destroy themselves; the films' action progresses swiftly and decisively as the characters move deeper into pits of their own making. By the late 1970s, Fassbinder no longer seemed to feel the need to shock people into coming to see his films, and moved towards the melodramatic framework favoured by the old-style Hollywood. *Lili Marleen*, for example, is a consummate piece of filmcraft, fine traditional cinema that encouraged one to hope that Fassbinder would continue to grow and enlarge his cinematic vocabulary without entirely blunting the rough maverick edges that brought him to the fore. He wrote or co-wrote the scripts for almost all of his pictures. He died from a mixture of drugs and cocaine.

*1965: *Der Stadtsreicher. 1966: *Das kleine Chaos. 1969: Liebe ist kälter als der Tod. Katzelmacher. Gutter der Pest (GB & US: Gods of the Plague). †Warum lauft Herr R. amok? (GB & US: Why Does Herr R. Run Amok?) 1970: Das Kaffeehaus. †Niklashauser Fahrt. Der amerikanische Soldat (GB & US: The American Soldier). Rio das Mortes. Pioniere in Ingolstadt. 1971: Whity. Warnung vor einer heiligen Nutte (GB: Warning of a Holy Whore. US: Beware the Holy Whore). Der Händler der vier Jahreszeiten (GB & US: The Merchant of Four Seasons). Wildwechsel (GB: Wild Game. US: Jail Bait). Die bitteren Tränen der Petra von Kant (GB & US: The Bitter Tears of Petra von Kant). Acht Stunden sind kein Tag (originally TV). 1973: Welt am Draht (originally TV). Martha. Nora Helmer (originally TV). Angst essen Seele auf (GB: Fear Eats the Soul. US: Ali). 1974: Fontane Effi Briest (GB & US: Effi Briest). 1975: Faustrecht der Freiheit (GB: Fox. US: Fox and His Friends). Mutter Kusters Fahrt zum Himmel (GB: Mother Kuster's Trip to Heaven. US: Mother Kusters Goes to Heaven). Angst vor der Angst. 1976: Satansbraten (GB: Satan's Brew). Chinese Roulette. Ich will doch nur, dass ihr mich liebt (TV). Bolwieser (TV. In two parts). 1977: Die Frauen in New York (TV). 1978: Despair. †Deutschland im herbst. Die Ehe der Maria Braun (GB & US: The Marriage of Maria Braun). In einem Jahr mit 13 Monden (GB: In the Year of Thirteen Moons. US: In a Year of 13 Moons). 1979: Die dritte Generation (GB & US: The Third Generation). Berlin Alexanderplatz (originally series for TV). 1980: Lili Marleen. 1981: Lola. 1982: Veronika Voss. Querelle de Brest.*

FEIST, Felix E. 1906-1965

A curiously haphazard career, considering its 24-year span. New York-born Feist was the son of the Felix Feist who was for many years general sales manager at M-G-M. Not surprisingly, Feist junior seemed to want to prove himself independent of senior's influence, and not one of his feature films was for his father's illustrious company, although he did make many shorts for them in the 1930s. By the late 1920s, he had already become a newsreel cameraman, and from 1929 to 1932 did work at Metro-Goldwyn-Mayer directing screen tests, and producing and sometimes photographing travelogue one-reelers. His best films, including some sombre crime dramas — notably *The Devil Takes a Ride* (with a typically grim performance by Lawrence Tierney), *The Threat* and *Guilty of Treason* — were for quality middle-budget studios, RKO-Radio and Eagle-Lion. Before his early death, Feist also made one of several film adaptations of Curt Siodmak's story *Donovan's Brain.* Feist's downbeat version, with the most penetrating of Lew Ayres' later performances, is the best. On the whole, however, he had few opportunities to shine, and his was an unfulfilled cinematic career.

*1932: Stepping Sisters. 1933: The Deluge. 1934: Strikes and Spares. My Grandfather's Clock. 1935: Prince, King of Dogs. *Football Teamwork. 1936: *How to Vote. *How to Be a Detective. *Every Sunday. *Hollywood Extra! *Hollywood — the Second Step. 1937: What Do You Think? (series). The Romance of Digestion. Golf Mistakes. Double Diving. *Give Till It Hurts. *Decathlon Champion — the Story of Glenn Morris. 1938: Follow the Arrow. The Magician's Daughter. 1939: *Radio Hams. *Culinary Carving. *Take a Cue. *Set 'Em Up. Let's Talk Turkey. *Happily Buried. *Prophet without Honor. 1940: *Dreams. *Pound Foolish. 1942: All By Myself. 1943: You're a Lucky Fellow, Mr Smith. 1944: Pardon My Rhythm. This is the Life. The Reckless Age. 1945: George White's Scandals. 1947: The Devil Thumbs a Ride. 1948: The Winner's Circle. 1949: The Threat. 1950: Guilty of Treason (GB: Treason). The Golden Gloves Story. 1951: Tomorrow is Another Day. The Man Who Cheated Himself. The Basketball Fix (GB: The Big Decision). 1952: The Big Trees. This Woman is Dangerous. 1953: The Man Behind the Gun. Donovan's Brain. 1955: Pirates of Tripoli.*

FEJOS, Paul (Pal Fejos) 1897-1963

One of a number of Continental directors who failed to come to terms with the Hollywood system, Fejos began by making films in his native Hungary, but seemed to turn his back on film-making in 1923, emigrated to America and used his medical qualifications to obtain a post with the Rockefeller Institute as a bacteriologist. In 1926, however, Fejos went to Hollywood and began writing screenplays. Two years later, he attracted attention with an experimental five-reel film *The Last Moment* about a potential suicide, evocatively photographed by the young Leon Shamroy. He was hired by Universal (and later M-G-M) and made the delightful *Lonesome* which, although less personalized, is a sensitive and engrossing film in many ways comparable with King Vidor's *The Crowd*, released in the same year. By 1930, however, the love affair between Fejos and Hollywood was over. He walked out on two films one after another following disagreements and, via France, returned to Hungary, refusing to go back to America despite demands from M-G-M who had him under contract. He made some intriguing films in Denmark, France and Austria — visually thoughtful dramas which concentrate on the problems of none-too-bright people trying to cope with harsh reality — before devoting the remainder of his film-making career to globe-trotting documentaries, often about primitive people. Fejos' travels took him to Madagascar, the Seychelles, the East Indies, Siam, New Guinea and Peru — no wonder such a restless talent could not settle in the Hollywood of the early 1930s. In later years, Fejos initiated his own foundation for anthropological research.

*1919: Hallucination. 1920: The Black Captain. Lord Arthur Saville's Crime. Pán. Prophecy. Reincarnation. 1921: Arsène Lupin's Last Adventure. 1922: Pique dame (GB: Sensation. US: The Queen of Spades). 1923: The Stars of Eger. 1928: The Last Moment. Lonesome. 1929: Broadway. Last Performance (GB: The Last Call). 1930: Big House (French version of The Big House). Menschen hinter Gittern. †Captain of the Guard (uncredited). †King of Jazz (uncredited). 1931: Fantômas. 1932: Marie, légende hongroise (and Hungarian version. GB and US: Marie). †L'amour à l'americaine. Storm at Balaton. 1933: Sonnenstrahl (and French version: Gardez le sourire). Frühlingsstimmen. 1934: Flugten fra millionerne (GB: Flight from the Millions. US: Millions in Flight). 1935: Prisoner Number One. The Golden Smile. 1937: *Danstävling i Esira (D). *Skonhetsvard a djungeln (D). *Världens mest användbara träd (D). *Djungeldansen (D). *Havets djävul (D). *Vara faders gravar (D). Black Horizons (US feature-length version of preceding six shorts). 1938: *Stammen lever an (D). *Bambualdern pa Mentawei (D). *Hovdingens son är död (D). *Draken på Komodo (D). *Byn vid den trivsamme brunnen (D). Tambora (D). †Att segla är nödvändigt. (D). 1939: Man och kvinna/En handfull ris (D). 1941: The Yagua (D).*

FELLINI, Federico 1920-1993

If this Italian film-maker had been restrained by a Hollywood studio system, one feels that his films might have pleased himself less, but pleased his audiences more. No doubt about it, Fellini was a brilliant creator of unforgettable images, the screen's nearest equivalent to a modern Spanish painter somewhere between Dalí and Miró. What might have happened if this talent had been harnessed, channelled into a recognizable shape? Then again, there is a body of opinion which suggests that such talent *should* be allowed to roam wild and free, without any sense of discipline, letting all its neuroses hang out to dry on screen *à la* Woody Allen. Either way, we shall never know what might have been best for Fellini. Writing and inventing sight gags for Italian comedy films even before the outbreak of World War II, he continued to write his own screenplays, usually in collaboration, throughout his career. His work as assistant director to Roberto Rossellini (qv) on *Paisà, Rome Open City* and *L'amore* seemed to have a formative effect. His early black and white films – apart from *The White Sheik* which stems from his experiences as a magazine cartoonist – are descendants of the neo-realist school as well as reflecting Fellini's own background. Several of them also star his wife, Giulietta Masina, a waif-like Italian Shirley MacLaine, whom he married in 1943. The best of these are *I vitelloni*, depicting the aimless street life of Fellini's teenage years, the stark *Il bidone* and the heart-rending *La strada* and *Le notti di Cabiria*, in both of which latter films Masina demonstrated her special gift of making an audience care for a pitiable character. After this, Fellini's films became increasingly autobiographical and idiosyncratic, as if he were tiring of telling recognizable stories and felt himself running out of time in which to express all his feelings and prejudices in dramatic form. Thus, *La dolce vita*, *8½* and *Juliet of the Spirits* remain potent, enjoyable entireties; but after this Fellini's films are entertaining only in their set-pieces, such as the giant liner looming out of the fog in *Amarcord*. Following a choking fit while eating cheese, Fellini suffered a stroke, from which he later died.

1950: *Luci del varietà (GB: Lights of Variety. US: Variety Lights)*. 1951: *Lo sceicco bianco (GB & US: The White Sheik)*. 1953: *I vitelloni (GB: Spivs. US: The Loafers)*. †*Amore in città*. 1954: *La strada (GB: The Road)*. 1955: *Il bidone (GB: The Swindlers. US: The Swindle)*. 1956: *Le notti di Cabiria (GB: Cabiria. US: Nights of Cabiria)*. 1959: *La dolce vita (US: The Sweet Life)*. 1962: †*Boccaccio 70*. 1963: *8½*. 1965: *Juliet of the Spirits/Giulietta degli spiriti*. 1967: *Il viaggio di G. Mastorna (unfinished)*. 1968: †*Histoires extraordinaires (Toby Dammit episode. GB: Tales of Mystery. US: Spirits of the Dead)*. 1969: *Fellini — Satyricon*. 1970: *The Clowns*. 1972: *Fellini's Roma*. 1973: *Amarcord*. 1976: *Fellini's Casanova*. 1979: *Orchestra Rehearsal*. 1980: *City of Women*. 1983: *And the Ship Sails On.../E la nave va*. 1985: *Ginger and Fred*. 1987: *The Interview/Intervista*. 1989: *La voce della luna*.

FENTON, Leslie 1902-1978

British-born director who, after more than 50 Hollywood films as leading man and character actor, decided to turn director in 1938 and made 14 largely interesting films before leaving the cinema in 1951. Fenton started with four well-produced second-features for M-G-M, the first of which was the excellent *Tell No Tales*, which benefited from a strong script by Lionel Houser, and in having Melvyn Douglas in the leading role as an editor whose hunt for a scoop uncovers a murder. Also worth watching were *Stronger Than Desire*, with Virginia Bruce and Walter Pidgeon, a remake of *Evelyn Prentice* that was better than the original (admittedly not difficult); and *The Golden Fleecing* (itself many years later remade by M-G-M as *The Honeymoon Machine*), a comedy with Lew Ayres and Rita Johnson. After working in his native Britain during the early war years, Fenton was given charge of the screen version of the powerful play *Tomorrow the World*, with Skippy (later Skip) Homeier repeating his frightening portrayal of the young Nazi. Fenton ended his short directorial career with four westerns. Two of these, *Lulu Belle* and *The Redhead and the Cowboy*, were merely average horse-operas. However, *Whispering Smith*, the exciting, fast-moving story of a railroad detective, was Alan Ladd's first starring western and helped shore up his sagging career at Paramount; and *Streets of Laredo* (a remake of *The Texas Rangers)*, which created real characters, brought out the best performance of Macdonald Carey's career as the smiling, treacherous villain who shoots William Bendix under the table,

Federico **Fellini** directs Tina Aumont in a scene from *Fellini's Casanova*

making entire audiences wince. Both of these films were photographed in blazing Technicolor by Ray Rennahan, a brilliant pioneer of colour photography (he shot the colour prologue for the 1923 *The 10 Commandments)* who shared Academy Awards for *Gone With the Wind* and *Blood and Sand*. From 1932 to 1946, Fenton was married to the actress Ann Dvorak.

1938: *Tell No Tales*. *Miracle Money*. *A Criminal is Born*. *Captain Kidd's Treasure*. *The Forgotten Step*. 1939: *Stronger Than Desire*. 1940: *The Man from Dakota (GB: Arouse and Beware)*. *The Golden Fleecing*. 1941: *The Saint's Vacation*. 1943: *Where's a Future in It*. 1944: '*Tomorrow the World*. 1946: *Pardon My Past*. 1948: *A Miracle Can Happen (later On Our Merry Way)*. *Saigon*. *Lulu Belle*. *Whispering Smith*. 1949: *Streets of Laredo*. 1950: *The Redhead and the Cowboy*.

FERRARA, Abel 1952-

A dealer in darkness and despair. Ferrara's films, the notorious *Bad Lieutenant* especially, have something to offend everyone. They are also moody and blackly atmospheric, their characters cold, humourless people who fail to connect with others, or deliberately hold themselves aloof. Characterised by visceral violence, Ferrara's work is on the whole neither very bad nor very good, with the odd exception either way, sometimes perhaps because, like the people in them, they fail to make a connection with those sitting watching them. One thing you can be sure of: you could recognise a Ferrara film after one reel; no doubt he will continue to thrill his followers and repel his detractors. Born in the Bronx area of New York, scene of so many of his gruelling tales, Ferrara began making short films in high school, often in collaboration with Nicholas St John, later to write many of his feature films. At first it seemed he would be a specialist in video nasties like *The Driller Killer*, banned in many countries. The urban sleaze and violence began with the star-studded but repellent *Fear City*, and has continued more or less unabated ever since. The best example of it is probably *The King of New York*. Although a gangster film, with all the modern violence, sex, drugs and bad language, you might expect, it's made very much in the style of the 1930s: straight, with no sideline issues, as one man shoots his way to the top, gunning down all those who stand in the way of his becoming crime czar of the city. As in other films from Ferrara, many of the main characters are dressed in black. *Bad Lieutenant*, the story of a totally corrupt cop, with a performance of typically fierce intensity from Harvey Keitel, was a lesser film, but caught the public imagination, seeming to take Ferrara into a different bracket as a film-maker. But he has not invaded the borders of the mainstream since, although a reasonable remake of *Invasion of the Body Snatchers* was probably intended for a wider distribution than it actually got. The titles (*The Addiction, The Funeral, The Blackout*) reverberate with the bleakness of their attitudes. *The Blackout*, his most recent at time of writing, is yet another of the director's savage tales of urban decay. Grainy photography and hand-held cameras enshroud a familiar farrago of drugs, booze, sleaze, porno movies, spaced-out gangsters and topless dancers. Welcome to the Terrordrome.

1979: The Driller Killer. 1980: Angel of Vengeance/Ms. 45. 1983: Fear City. 1986: The Gladiator (TV). Crime Story (TV). 1987: China Girl. 1988: Cat Chaser. 1989: The King of New York. 1992: Bad Lieutenant. 1993: Snake Eyes (GB: Dangerous Game). Body Snatchers. 1994: The Addiction. 1995: The Cure. 1996: The Funeral. 1997: The Blackout. 1998: New Rose Hotel.

FEUILLADE, Louis

See Feyder, Jacques

FEYDER, Jacques (J. Frédérix) 1885-1948

Belgian-born director, mainly of French films, all of them richly detailed and noted for their sympathetic direction of female stars. Feyder, in fact, was much associated with great actresses. He married the French star Françoise Rosay in 1917 and directed Garbo and Dietrich at various stages of his career. He was an actor until 1916, his best-known appearance being in *Les Vampires*, made in 1915/16 by the great French serial-director Louis Feuillade (1873-1925), who turned out more than 400 films. Feuil-

lade's dream-like, 'unreal' technique, which lent so much tension and disquiet to his *Fantômas* and *Judex* serials, undoubtedly influenced the young Feyder greatly in the matter of the control of images within the frame. Feyder began making short films himself in 1916, then short features — but with no great success until the arrival of *L' Atlantide* in 1921. This story of grand passion was set in the Sahara, like one of Feyder's later films, *Le grand jeu*. A glorious run of successes followed: *Crainquebille, Visages d'enfants, L'image, Gribiche, Carmen* and *Thérèse Raquin*, before the official banning of his 1928 film, *Les nouveaux messieurs*, persuaded Feyder to accept an already received invitation to direct for M-G-M in Hollywood. He remained there for three years, directing Garbo in her last silent film *The Kiss*, and in two foreign-language versions of her first talkie, *Anna Christie*. Finding himself without the freedom he craved, and with the dust settled in France, Feyder returned there to make three memorable films, each of which has its champions as being his best. *Le grand jeu* is again set in the desert, where a legionnaire meets the low-life double of the high-society woman he joined the Legion to forget; *Pension Mimosas* is a mood piece about the overriding passion (unspokenly incestuous) of the leading character for her no-good son; while *La kermesse héroïque*, probably his most famous film, is elaborately set in a 17th-century Flemish town under the heel of the Spanish. Basically a comedy, although with political undertones concerning contemporary France, Belgium and Germany, it was banned by Goebbels after the Nazi invasion, by which time Feyder had fled to Switzerland. These last three films were all co-written by Feyder and Charles Spaak (1903-1975), a Belgian writer who went on to work on other great French films of the 1930s, notably *La grande illusion*, and directed one film, *Le mystère Barton*, in 1949.

1916: †Monsieur Pinson, policier. Têtes de femmes, femmes de tête. *Le bluff. Le pied qui étreint (serial). *Un conseil d'ami. L'homme de compagnie. *Tiens, vous êtes à Poitiers? L'instinct est maitre. *Le frère de lait. 1917: *Le trouvaille de Buchu. *Le billard casse. *Le pardessus de demi-saison. Abrégeons les formalités! *Les vieilles femmes de l'hospice. Le ravin sans fond. 1919: Le faute d'orthographe. 1921: L'Atlantide. 1922: Crainquebille. 1924: Visages d'enfants. 1925: L'image. Gribiche. 1926: Carmen. 1927: *Au pays du roi lépreux. 1928: Thérèse Raquin (US: Shadows of Fear). Les nouveaux messieurs. 1929: The Kiss. 1930: Anna Christie (German-language version. And Swedish version). Le spectre vert (French-language version of The Unholy Night). Olympia. Si l'empereur savait ça (French-language version of This Glorious Night). 1931: Daybreak. Son of India. 1933: Le grand jeu. 1934: Pension Mimosas. 1935: La kermesse héroïque (GB & US: Carnival in Flanders). 1937: Knight without Armour. Fahrendes Volk (and French version). 1941: Une femme disparaît. 1942: La loi du nord (completed 1939).

FIGGIS, Mike 1949-

It isn't often (John Carpenter and Dario Argento are other rare examples) that a director has written the music, as well as the script for his films. Not only has Figgis, born in Kenya, but raised in Newcastle, in the north-east of England, from the age of eight, done just that, but, in at least three of his most memorable films — *Stormy Monday, Leaving Las Vegas* and *One Night Stand* — his own music has made a valuable contribution to the tone and atmosphere of the movie. Figgis studied music in London, and began his career as a jazz rock musician, touring for some time with a rhythm and blues band called Gas Board (which featured later-famous singer Bryan Ferry). Changing careers, Figgis turned to experimental theatre direction in his mid twenties with *The People Show*, going with them to Europe, the United States and South America. An application to enrol in Britain's National Film School was rejected, and Figgis returned to the stage. But he was determined to break into films and, after leaving *The People Show* in the early 1980s, eventually persuaded British webcaster Channel 4 to bankroll him for a short feature called *The House*. Three years later, *Stormy Monday* emerged, a sturdy *film noir* that takes full advantage of its Newcastle and jazz backgrounds, using both to give a smoky local edge to its story of a crooked American wheeler-dealer (Tommy Lee Jones) moving in on Tyneside. Figgis now went to Hollywood but *Internal Affairs* was an uncertain start: Figgis' direction was too flashy, but he did show an ability to extract the perfect performance — in this case from Richard Gere as a very crooked cop — a skill he would hone to perfection in the later *Leaving Las Vegas*, a downbeat but gripping drama of self-destruction which won its star, Nicolas Cage, a deserved Academy Award, and its director and leading lady, Elisabeth Shue, Oscar nominations. Figgis followed this with *One Night Stand*. The director attempts a most unusual kind of movie — a romantic tragi-comedy — and, with the inevitable help of his own jazzy score, he darned nearly pulls it off. Figgis subtly and successfully suggests here that his protagonists are more suited to each other than the partners they're with — typical of his 'audience subterfuge' approach, which practically guarantees you'll see his point of view by the end.

1984: The House. 1987: Stormy Monday. 1990: Internal Affairs. 1991: +Women & Men: Stories of Seduction (TV). +Women & Men 2: In Love There Are No Rules (TV). Liebestraum. 1993: Mr Jones. 1994: The Browning Version. 1995: Leaving Las Vegas. 1997: One Night Stand. 1998: The Death & Loss of Sexual Innocence.

FINCHER, David 1963-

Several directors working in today's cinema began their careers in commercials and music videos, but few have made as solid a start as Britain's David Fincher. After making award-winning commercials for top brand names, Fincher went on to direct videos for such pop performers as Madonna, Billy Idol, George Michael, Paula Abdul and Aerosmith. *Alien³* was an imposing and demanding start to his film career, although the results might have a discouraged a less determined film-maker; too much (shouted) dialogue and not enough action cripple this third chapter of the saga, which conveys less of a sense of evil and more of a simpler science-fiction menace. Fincher put that right, though, with his next film, *Se7en*. This grim and grisly serial killer thriller caught the public imagination, as Fincher outdid *The Silence of the Lambs*. Evisceration runs riot in the film as a maniac murderer picks out victims who exemplify one of the seven deadly sins and puts them to death in the most gruesome and revolting ways possible. Fincher followed up with the high-profile black comedy-thriller *The Game*; but this proved one of Michael Douglas' less successful ventures. Still, as one of the younger directors in today's Hollywood, Fincher's skill at conveying a sense of darkness and foreboding should stand him in good stead for some years yet.

1992: Alien³. 1995: Se7en. 1997: The Game. 1999: The Fight Club.

FISHER, Terence 1904-1980

There are four distinct stages to this British director's career, although now it is only as a creator of Hammer horrors that Fisher is remembered. He spent 13 years as an editor before directing, or co-directing, some stylish films for Rank. In the years 1952 to 1957, Fisher seemed to gain some kind of reputation as the best man to direct the regular influx of veteran American stars, most past their prime, in medium-budget British second-features for the quota market. In this way, George Brent, Tom Conway, Howard Duff, Paulette Goddard, Dane Clark, Richard Conte, Alex Nicol, Zachary Scott, Paul Henreid, Wayne Morris and Pat O'Brien all came under his auspices. These films alas were not terribly good, but Hammer Films rescued Fisher's career from this rut by hiring him to direct *The Curse of Frankenstein*, the first in what was to be a long series of colour remakes of Universal's classic black-and-white horror films of the 1930s. *Frankenstein* was an uneasy beginning, betraying Fisher's second-feature roots. Hammer paused: but then two years later, Fisher produced his masterwork, *Dracula*, and a new vein in British horror was fully opened. Fisher's *Dracula* is plush, scarifying, shot in rich, dark colours, and with a genuine sense of menace and evil. The night-time work is particularly good, and Christopher Lee's *Dracula* was never less laughable than here. The final disintegration of the vampire count has since been imitated many times in lesser films. Fisher stayed with the horror and chiller genres for the remainder of his career, although the rest of his work consists of films with moments. Those with most to commend them are *The Revenge of Frankenstein, The Hound of the Baskervilles, The Brides of Dracula* (with its splendidly lurid and shocking windmill climax), *The Stranglers of Bombay, The Gorgon, Island of Terror* and Fisher's underrated version of *The Phantom of the Opera*, with an equally undervalued performance by Herbert Lom in the title role. Fisher died of cancer.

1947: To the Public Danger. 1948: A Song for Tomorrow. Colonel Bogey. Portrait from Life (US: The Girl in the Painting). 1949: Marry Me. 1950: †The Astonished Heart. †So Long at the Fair. 1951: Home to Danger. 1952: The Last Page (US: Manbait). Stolen Face. Distant Trumpet. Wings of Danger (US: Dead on Course). 1953: Mantrap (US: Man in Hiding). Spaceways. Blood Orange. †Three's Company. Four Sided Triangle. 1954: The Stranger Came Home (US: The Unholy Four). Final Appointment. Face the Music (US: The Black Glove). Mask of Dust (US: Race for Life). Children Galore. 1955: Stolen Assignment. The Flaw. Murder by Proxy (US: Blackout). 1956: The Gelignite Gang. The Last Man to Hang? The Curse of Frankenstein. 1957: Kill Me Tomorrow. 1958: Dracula (US: The Horror of Dracula). The

Revenge of Frankenstein. 1959: The Hound of the Baskervilles. The Mummy. The Stranglers of Bombay. The Man Who Could Cheat Death. 1960: The Brides of Dracula. The Two Faces of Dr Jekyll (US: House of Fright). 1961: Sword of Sherwood Forest. The Curse of the Werewolf. 1962: The Phantom of the Opera. Sherlock Holmes und der Halsband des Todes (and English-speaking version: Sherlock Holmes and the Deadly Necklace). 1963: The Horror of It All. 1964: The Earth Dies Screaming. The Gorgon. 1965: Dracula — Prince of Darkness. 1966: Island of Terror. Frankenstein Created Woman. 1967: Night of the Big Heat (US: Island of the Burning Damned). 1968: The Devil Rides Out (US: The Devil's Bride). 1969: Frankenstein Must Be Destroyed. 1973: Frankenstein and the Monster from Hell.

FITZHAMON, Lewin

See Hepworth, Cecil

FITZMAURICE, George 1885-1941

Prominent directors from the silent era are, apart from the odd giant and pioneer, not much remembered, especially when, like Fitzmaurice, they died before their careers were properly over. But between 1923 and 1932, Fitzmaurice had few equals at projecting romantic idols of the screen, creating a smouldering, erotic atmosphere around his cooing pairs. He had much to do with moulding the Englishman Ronald Colman into the idol of millions, although he also directed Valentino, Garbo, Pola Negri, Vilma Banky, Joan Bennett and Loretta Young. Fitzmaurice was born in France of Irish parentage. Although trained as a painter, he became a journeying salesman for cotton, jute, hemp and other eastern products, spending several years in India, China, Japan and Egypt. Around 1907 he went to America and used his early training as a artist to gain employment as a set director, then set designer in the theatre. Fitzmaurice entered films as a title-card designer, then writer and finally director in 1914. The first of his films to catch the eye was *Arms and the Woman:* (1916), a potentially inflammatory piece that was considerably toned down outside America. It dealt with brother-and-sister Hungarian immigrants. The youth becomes involved with anarchists and the girl marries a wealthy steelman, whose factory is burnt down by her brother when it starts to manufacture arms for the war effort. Fitzmaurice demonstrated the pictorial flair that was to be expected from his training (and which, with added refinement, became one of his trademarks) and made innovative use of newsreel material in the telling of his story. It was not until the 1920s, however, that 'Fitzy' properly flowered as a confident storyteller of lush, exotic romantic material, with lavish attention both to detail and the appropriate ethnic background. He had a secure touch as far as the box-office was concerned, and some of his most commercial films were *The Cheat*, with Negri, the two Vilma Banky-Colman vehicles, *The Dark Angel* and *The Night of Love,* and Banky again, with Valentino, in *The Son of the Sheik.* Fitzmaurice also directed Colman in *Tarnish, A Thief in Paradise, His Supreme Moment, Raffles, The Devil to Pay* and *The Unholy Garden.* His two Garbo films, *As You Desire Me* (from Pirandello) and *Mata Hari* are among the most fascinating of her early talkies, but they were not the most successful films the actress has ever made, and Fitzmaurice began to slide into lesser assignments. The wave of realism headed by Warner Brothers swept Fitzmaurice's type of films out of fashion, although in 1936 he did direct Jean Harlow to surprisingly good effect in *Suzy.* He was married to the actress-writer Ouida Bergere (she later married Basil Rathbone) who wrote the scenarios for many of his most famous films. Fitzmaurice was killed by an acute streptococcal infection akin to erysipelas.

1914: *The Quest of the Sacred Gem. The Bomb Boy.* 1915: *The Commuters. Stop Thief! Who's Who in Society. Money Master. The Test. Via Wireless. At Bay.* 1916: *New York. Big Jim Garrity. Fifth Avenue. Arms and the Woman. Romantic Journey.* 1917: *The Hunting of the Hawk. Blind Man's Luck. The Iron Heart. The Recoil. The Mark of Cain. Sylvia of the Secret Service. The On-the-Square Girl.* 1918: *Innocent. The Naulahka. The Hillcrest Mystery. A Japanese Nightingale. The Cry of the Weak. Our Better Selves. The Narrow Path.* 1919: *Common Clay. The Witness for the Defense. The Avalanche. The Profiteers. A Society Exile. Counterfeit.* 1920: *On with the Dance. Idols of Clay. The Right to Love.* 1921: *Forever/Peter Ibbetson. Paying the Piper. Experience.* 1922: *To Have and To Hold. Three Live Ghosts. Kick In. The Man from Home.* 1923: *The Eternal City. Bella Donna. The Cheat.* 1924: *Cytherea. Tarnish.* 1925: *A Thief in Paradise. His Supreme Moment. The Dark Angel.* 1926: *The Son of the Sheik.* 1927: *The Tender Hour. The Night of Love. The Love Mart. Rose of the Golden West.* 1928: *The Barker. Lilac Time.* 1929: *The Locked Door. His Captive Woman. The Man and the Moment. Tiger Rose.* 1930: *The Bad One.* †*Raffles.* 1931: *Strangers May Kiss. The Devil to*

Pay. One Heavenly Night. The Unholy Garden. 1932: *Mata Hari. As You Desire Me.* 1934: *All Men Are Enemies.* 1936: *Petticoat Fever. Suzy.* 1937: *The Emperor's Candlesticks.* †*The Last of Mrs Cheyney (uncredited). Live, Love and Learn.* 1938: *Arsene Lupin Returns. Vacation from Love.* 1940: *Adventure in Diamonds.*

FLAHERTY, Robert 1884-1951

American film-maker and explorer who pioneered the 'contrived' documentary, poetic, lyrical and cleverly romanticized accounts of life in the wilds. His main thought was to capture the true, primitive spirit of the far-flung lands to which he travelled, and he was not above taking people back to their long-forgotten roots to do it. His documentaries are among the most pictorially beautiful films ever seen, especially those films that he managed to complete without interference of one kind or another. In the early days of the 20th century, Flaherty's father explored Canada in a search for iron ore, taking his son with him. Flaherty developed a longing to push further into the wilderness, and was commissioned in 1910 to set up his own expeditions to the far north, also for the pursuit of iron ore. In 1913, his patron, Sir William Mackenzie, suggested that Flaherty take a camera with him on his next expedition — and the legend was born. Flaherty's first film, or least such footage as he had assembled for a documentary on Eskimo life, was destroyed by fire, a fate that was also to overtake another Flaherty film, *Acoma the Sky City*, many years later. After exploration and mapping expeditions in the Hudson Bay area, notably to Belcher Islands (one of which is named after him), Flaherty decided to try his hand again at film-making. Ever the perfectionist, he was determined to put on film exactly what he wanted to, working for two to three years on a film, a pattern repeated more or less throughout his career which wore the patience of some of his bosses very thin. The result on this occasion was *Nanook of the North,* a magnificent portrait of the hardships of Eskimo life. Many of the experiences that followed this triumph were not entirely happy ones for Flaherty, but he did make *Moana*, about the Samoan people, on which he pioneered the development and use of panchromatic film; parts of *White Shadows in the South Seas* and *Tabu* (both set in Polynesia); *Man of Aran* off the west coast of Ireland; some beautiful background work for *Elephant Boy* in India; and back in America, the evocative *The Land* and *Louisiana Story,* both in their ways accounts of the uneasy truce between nature, man and machines.

1916: *Untitled documentary of Eskimo life* (D). 1922: *Nanook of the North* (D). 1925: **The Pottery Maker* (D). 1926: *Moana* (D). 1927: *The Twenty-Four Dollar Island* (D). 1928: †*White Shadows in the South Seas.* 1929: **Acoma the Sky City* (D. Unfinished). 1931: †*Tabu.* 1933: **Industrial Britain* (D). *The English Potter* (D). **The Glassmakers of England* (D). **Art of the English Craftsman* (D). 1934: *Man of Aran* (D). 1937: †*Elephant Boy.* 1941: *The Land* (D). 1948: *Louisiana Story.*

FLEISCHER, Richard 1916-

The son of pioneer American animator Max Fleischer (1889-1973), Fleischer had an uneven directing career. The only pattern one can establish is his liking for the reconstruction of famous murder cases, leavened with straight thrillers and comic-strip fantasies. The former has led him to film *The Girl in the Red Velvet Swing* (the Nesbit-Thaw case), *Compulsion* (the Leopold-Loeb case), *The Boston Strangler* and *10 Rillington Place* (the Christie murders in Britain). Fleischer's better films are often very good cinema, especially in a solid pursuance of a single theme, although his turkeys (notably *The Big Gamble, Ashanti, Doctor Dolittle, Che!, Mandingo* and *The Prince and The Pauper*) can be very lame birds indeed. He moved from the theatre to films (having given up medical studies) in 1942, quickly establishing himself as one of RKO's quality minor directors, especially with *Follow Me Quietly, Armored Car Robbery* and *The Narrow Margin.* This period contains another exceptionally good thriller, *Trapped*, with Lloyd Bridges, which Fleischer made for the high-quality, low-budget and short-lived studio Eagle-Lion. His first major film was Disney's *20,000 Leagues Under the Sea*, and he recalled its star, Kirk Douglas, for more Boys'-Own heroics in his second box-office success *The Vikings.* The 'famous murders' have been the strongest Fleischer films since then, although he has made two excellent films that did only average box-office business —*Blind Terror*, with Mia Farrow as the blind girl menaced by an unknown killer, and the science-fiction drama *Soylent Green*, a highly original project graced by both Edward G. Robinson's last performance and by a visual flair that one hardly suspected Fleiseher possessed. It is a splendidly realized portrait of a dismal future, shot with natural settings and only on a medium budget. But the films he has made since then have been mainly poor.

1943: * *This is America (D. series).* **Flicker Flashbacks (series).* 1944:

Still a handsome man in his mid-Fifties, *Gone With the Wind* director Victor **Fleming** is pictured here with his daughter Victoria in 1937.

Memo for Joe. 1946. Child of Divorce. 1947: Design for Death (D). Banjo. 1948: So This is New York. Bodyguard. 1949: The Clay Pigeon. Follow Me Quietly. †Make Mine Laughs. Trapped. 1950: Armored Car Robbery. 1951: The Narrow Margin. 1952: The Happy Time. 1953: Arena. 1954: 20,000 Leagues under the Sea. 1955: The Girl in the Red Velvet Swing. Violent Saturday. 1956: Between Heaven and Hell. Bandido. 1958: The Vikings. These Thousand Hills. 1959: Compulsion. 1960: Crack in the Mirror. The Big Gamble. 1961: Barabbas. 1966: Fantastic Voyage. 1967: Doctor Dolittle. Think 20th. 1968: The Boston Strangler. 1969: Che! 1970: †Tora! Tora! Tora! 10 Rillington Place. 1971: Blind Terror (US: See No Evil). The Last Run. 1972: The New Centurions (GB: Precinct 45 — Los Angeles Police). 1973: The Don is Dead. Soylent Green. 1974: Mr Majestyk. The Spikes Gang. 1975:

Mandingo. 1976: The Incredible Sarah. 1977: The Prince and the Pauper (US: Crossed Swords). 1979: Ashanti. 1980: The Jazz Singer. 1982: Tough Enough. 1983: Amityville 3D. 1984: Conan the Destroyer. 1985: Red Sonja. 1987: Million Dollar Mystery. 1989: Call from Space.

FLEMING, Victor 1883-1949

Best-known as a director of rugged action films, this American director made some of M-G-M's most successful entertainments. Well at home with men of action and sassy ladies, Fleming crowned a hugely successful decade at M-G-M by directing both *The Wizard of Oz* and (most of) *Gone With the Wind*. All the same, he did not make the top rank of feted Hollywood directors, and died a disillusioned and disappointed man after the considerable failure of his last two films. Fleming

was a rugged character in his own right, racing cars for a living until he retired from that dangerous profession and decided to go in for cinematography. By 1916, he had progressed to chief cameraman, mostly on films directed by John Emerson (1874-1956), who later became a producer, and Allan Dwan *(qv)*. After World War I service with the photographic section of the US Army Signal Corps, Fleming decided to move into direction. By the mid-1920s, he had started winning big star assignments, notably *Mantrap* and *Hula* (both with Clara Bow, with whom he was romantically involved at the time), *Wolf Song* and *The Virginian* (both with Gary Cooper), and *The Way of All Flesh* (with Emil Jannings). In 1932, he signed a contract with M-G-M and the next eight years with that studio contain all Fleming's best-known films. There were three with Jean Harlow, whom he showcased to good effect in *Red Dust*, *Reckless* and *Bombshell*. Fleming was also extremely compatible with M-G-M's two top male stars, Clark Gable and Spencer Tracy. All three men were stubborn masculine individualists, and both actors won Oscars under Fleming's direction. It was no surprise, then, when Fleming was called in to replace George Cukor on *Gone With the Wind*, because it was felt he would better handle both Gable and the demanding action sequences. Fleming won an Academy Award for *Gone With the Wind* after what was, surprisingly, his only nomination. He could not have guessed things would go so wrong thereafter. There were two failures with Ingrid Bergman, not Fleming's sort of woman at all, and disappointing further ventures with Gable and Tracy, of which only Tracy's *A Guy Named Joe* was at all successful. Fleming was an uncomplicated man, and his mistake was in trying to make complicated films and to catch moods which were outside his capabilities.

*1919: †When the Clouds Roll By. 1920: The Mollycoddle. 1921: *Mama's Affair. Woman's Place. 1922: Red Hot Romance. The Lane That Had No Turning. Anna Ascends. 1923: Dark Secrets. Law of the Lawless. To the Last Man. Call of the Canyon. 1924: Empty Hands. Code of the Sea. 1925: The Devil's Cargo. Adventure. A Son of His Father. Lord Jim. 1926: The Blind Goddess. Mantrap. 1927: The Rough Riders (GB: The Trumpet Call). The Way of All Flesh. Hula. 1928: The Awakening. 1929: Abie's Irish Rose. Wolf Song. The Virginian. 1930: Common Clay. Renegades. 1931: Around the World in Eighty Minutes. 1932: The Wet Parade. Red Dust. 1933: The White*

Sister. Bombshell (GB: Blonde Bombshell). 1934: Treasure Island. 1935: Reckless. The Farmer Takes a Wife. 1937: Captains Courageous. †The Good Earth. 1938: Test Pilot. †The Great Waltz. 1939: The Wizard of Oz. Gone With the Wind. 1941: Dr Jekyll and Mr Hyde. 1942: Tortilla Flat. 1943: A Guy Named Joe. 1945: Adventure. 1948: Joan of Arc.

FLICKER, Theodore J.
See Frawley, James

FLOREY, Robert 1900-1979

Despite reverential career studies by a number of writers in recent times, there is little concrete evidence to suggest that the French-born Florey was a great talent neglected by Hollywood almost throughout his 20 years there. Usually working with slightly higher budgets than, say, Edgar G. Ulmer, he does not achieve the same doom-laden atmosphere in his blacker dramas. And his most famous films, among them *Murders in the Rue Morgue* and *The Beast with Five Fingers*, while having some relishable visual moments, do not quite live up to their reputation. After making some short films in Switzerland, Florey went to Hollywood as correspondent for a French film magazine. After spending some years in public relations with Chaplin, Mary Pickford, Douglas Fairbanks and Rudolph Valentino — many years later, he was 'associate director' on Chaplin's *Monsieur Verdoux* — Florey drifted back·into film-making, variously as writer, assistant director (on major films) and director (on minor films). By 1929, he was in charge of Paramount's Long Island studios. W.C. Fields was coming to the end of his tenure there, but it was to be other comedians — the four Marx Brothers — who gave Florey his first big cinema success with their initial screen venture *The Cocoanuts*. For a while

Bryan **Forbes** at work in the 1960s, when he was one for the most respected of British directors.

after this, Florey was on the fringe of the big league, directing Claudette Colbert and Edward G. Robinson in their first sound film, *The Hole in the Wall*, and Gertrude Lawrence in *The Battle of Paris*. Neither film was especially successful and, on his return two years later from a spell working in his native Paris, Florey found himself handed second-feature assignments at Paramount and Warners which, for the next ten years, he entered into enthusiastically albeit with no great flair for directing actors. *Ex-Lady*, a stunningly awful Bette Davis film before she shunted herself into the big-time at Warners, is probably the nadir of this period, of which some of the later Paramount features, *King of Alcatraz* and *Parole Fixer* among them, are perhaps the best. There were some enjoyably vigorous thrillers from Florey in the 1940s, particularly *Roger Touhy, Gangster, The Face Behind the Mask, Lady Gangster* and *Rogues' Regiment*, before Florey became one of the first emigrés to television, and worked solidly on such series as *Twilight Zone, 'M' Squad* and *The Untouchables* before retiring in 1964.

*1919: Heureuse intervention. *Isadore sur le lac. *Isadore à la deveine. 1923: *Fifty-Fifty. *Valentino en Angleterre. 1926: †That Model from Paris (uncredited). 1927: One Hour of Love. The Romantic Age. Face Value. The Life and Death of 9413 — a Hollywood Extra. Johann the Coffin Maker. The Loves of Zero. 1928: *Skyscraper Symphony. *Bonjour New York! Night Club. 1929: *Lillian Roth and Her Piano Boys. *Eddie Cantor. Pusher-in-the-Face. The Cocoanuts. The Hole in the Wall. The Battle of Paris. 1930: †Le blanc et le noir. La route est belle. L'amour chante (and Spanish version). 1932: Murders in the Rue Morgue. The Man Called Back. Those We Love. 1933: Girl Missing. Ex-Lady. The House on 56th Street. 1934: Registered Nurse. Smarty (GB: Hit Me Again). Bedside. I Sell Anything. 1935: The Florentine Dagger. The Woman in Red. Don't Bet on Blondes. Ship Café. I Am a Thief! Going Highbrow. The Payoff. †Go into Your Dance (uncredited). 1936: †Rose of the Rancho (uncredited). Hollywood Boulevard. The Preview Murder Mystery. Till We Meet Again. 1937: Outcast. King of Gamblers. Mountain Music. This Way Please. Daughter of Shanghai (GB: Daughter of the Orient). 1938: King of Alcatraz (GB: King of the Alcatraz). Dangerous to Know. 1939: The Magnificent Fraud. Hotel Imperial. Disbarred. Death of a Champion. 1940: Parole Fixer. Women without Names. 1941: The Face Behind the Mask. Meet Boston Blackie. Two in a Taxi. 1942: Dangerously They*

Live. $Lady Gangster. 1943: †Bombers' Moon (uncredited). The Desert Song. 1944: Man from Frisco. Roger Touhy, Gangster (GB: The Last Gangster). 1945: God is My Co-Pilot. †Escape in the Desert (uncredited). Danger Signal. 1946. The Beast with Five Fingers. 1948: Tarzan and the Mermaids. Rogues' Regiment. 1949: The Crooked Way. Outpost in Morocco. 1950: Johnny One-Eye. The Vicious Years (GB: The Gangster We Made).

$ As Florian Roberts

FORBES, Bryan (John Clarke) 1926-

British actor and writer who turned director in 1961 and made delicate, sensitive and understated films that contain many moving moments. He proved very much an actors' director, and his best films, although there are only one or two duds in the lot, depend on strong central performances. He worked well in black-and-white and his colour films have on the whole been less effective, and certainly less successful. Born in London, Forbes was something of a child prodigy, becoming chairman of a 'Junior Brains Trust' quiz programme on radio when he was 16. He began writing seriously in his early twenties, publishing his first book in 1950, and gaining his first screen credit (co-writer on *Cockleshell Heroes*) five years later. His acting career had never been much more than moderate and writing was dominating his activities by the late 1950s. In 1961, he directed his first film, *Whistle Down the Wind*, about a group of farm children who take an escaped convict (Alan Bates) to be the reincarnation of Jesus Christ. A sincere, superb piece of film-making, it took hold of the emotions and didn't let go of them until the truly moving climax was over. With brilliant performances from the children and an impressive first leading role from Bates, *Whistle Down the Wind* has probably remained Forbes' best film, although it has since had strong competition from *The L-Shaped Room, Seance on a Wet Afternoon, King Rat, The Whisperers, The Madwoman of Chaillot* and *The Raging Moon*. These are all skilfully-made and caring films. But, after an ill-fated spell as head of production for Associated-British Studios (1969-1972), Forbes' work did not quite have the same strength. His second wife Nanette Newman has starred in several of his films to great effect; they have been married since 1954. His first wife (1951-1954) Constance Smith was also an actress. He continues to write both fiction and non-fiction and in 1977 published an excellent

biography of the British actress Dame
Edith Evans.

*1961: Whistle Down the Wind. 1962:
The L-Shaped Room. 1963: Seance on a
Wet Afternoon. 1965: King Rat. 1966:
The Wrong Box. The Whisperers. 1967:
Deadfall. 1969: The Madwoman of
Chaillot. 1970: The Raging Moon (US:
Long Ago Tomorrow). †I am a Dancer.
1974. The Stepford Wives. 1976: The
Slipper and the Rose. 1978: International
Velvet. 1980: †Sunday Lovers. 1981:
Jessie (TV). 1982: Ménage à trois. 1983:
The Naked Face.*

FORD, John

(Sean O'Fearna, later O'Feeney) 1895-1973
The American-born 13th child of Irish
immigrants, Ford became one of Hollywood's best-known, best-loved and most
sought-after directors. Of his many films

(a large proportion of them westerns),
almost 30 come into the four-star category, and he was four times honoured with
Academy Awards. The crude comedy content of some of his films — an unlovable
camaraderie which seems more of interest
to the director than the audience — is a
forgivable flaw in the light of such monumental achievement. Emotionalism is a
strong factor in many of Ford's films
which, in his later days, showed a nostalgic longing for things past and old values.
These may only have existed in Ford's
eyes or hazy recollection, but nonetheless
they make for skilfully appealing entertainment. As the newspaper owner in *The
Man Who Shot Liberty Valance* says:
'When the legend becomes fact, print the
legend' — and it could well have been
Ford's own philosophy. Although there
are other great Ford films, better than any
of the westerns, it was with two-reel
horse-operas that he started in Hollywood

as a young director of 22. Many of these
starred leathery old Harry Carey as the
good bad man reformed by the love of a
good woman, although Ford also directed
Hoot Gibson and Tom Mix. As early as
1920, Ford had directed a version of
Three Godfathers with Carey (in the role
later to be played by Ford's other
favourite star John Wayne), called
Marked Men. But his career did not take
significant steps forward until 1923, when
he changed his screen credit from Jack
Ford to John Ford and made a version of
the Mississippi riverboat drama *Cameo
Kirby*, with John Gilbert and Jean Arthur.
Two major westerns followed: *The Iron
Horse*, in 1924, about railroad pioneers
and shot in the fierce desert of Nevada (a
pointer to Ford's later penchant for location work in Monument Valley); and
Three Bad Men, in 1926, which strangely
was the last Ford western until *Stagecoach* in 1939. The determined vein of
Irishness in Ford's work that reached its
apogee in *The Informer* (1935) had
already made itself apparent when John
Wayne acted for him for the first time in
Mother Machree (1927). Wayne, like
Ford, was a straightforward man who
never changed the ideals of his youth, and
he was to star regularly for Ford after the
director rescued his career from 'B' westerns with *Stagecoach*. Ford made a rich
variety of films in the 1930s, but his
Oscar-winner, *The Informer,* now looks
over-melodramatic and has dated heavily
(only the Dublin street atmosphere keeps
its appeal) and his reputation rightly rests
on his work in the 1940s. *The Grapes of
Wrath, The Long Voyage Home, They
Were Expendable* and *My Darling
Clementine* all stamp their actions, images
and emotions in the memory: these are all
front-rank films. From the same decade,
Three Godfathers is a greatly underrated
remake of *Marked Men*, with stunning
Technicolor photography, *Fort Apache*
starts the Cavalry trilogy finished by *She
Wore a Yellow Ribbon* and *Rio Grande*,
and *Wagon Master* is probably the purest
Fordian western of all. *How Green Was
My Valley*, an idealized but evocative portrait of a life in a poor Welsh mining
town, won Ford his third Oscar (to follow *The Grapes of Wrath)*, and a return
to Irishness in 1952 in the rip-roaring *The
Quiet Man* produced a fourth, though
somewhat less deserved Academy Award.
Ford also developed the affecting habit of
framing characters in various openings
who were destined for death or lives of
loneliness outside a family group, and
having them ride or walk away from that
opening. The classic example of this is in
the otherwise overrated *The Searchers*,
although it happens as early as *My Dar-*

John **Ford** with two of his most stalwart stars, John Wayne (left) and Ben Johnson, who appeared together in several of his best Westerns. Here they relax off set in *She Wore a Yellow Ribbon.*

ling Clementine. Ford's later films tend to come back in a flood of tears and memories — The Long Gray Line is certainly a four-handkerchief movie caressingly made by Ford and lifted to greatness by the performance of Maureen O'Hara — but by and large they are films of moments: the laconic riverside exchange between James Stewart and Richard Widmark in the unjustly neglected Two Rode Together, for example, with Wayne and Stewart again, and Lee Marvin, in the double-angle shoot-out of The Man Who Shot Liberty Valance. Ford suffered throughout his life from poor eyesight. It finally forced him to give up film-work in 1970, three years before his death from cancer.

1917: The Tornado. The Scrapper. *Cheyenne's Pal. The Soul Herder. The Secret Man. Straight Shooting. A Marked Man. Bucking Broadway. 1918: Thieves' Gold. The Phantom Riders. Hell Bent. Wild Women. The Scarlet Drop (GB: Hill Billy). A Woman's Fool. Three Mounted Men. 1919: The Fighting Brothers. *By Indian Post. *The Rustlers. *Gun Law. *The Gun Pusher. Roped. A Fight for Love. Bare Fists. Riders of Vengeance. *The Last Outlaw. The Outcasts of Poker Flat. The Ace of the Saddle. The Rider of the Law. A Gun Fightin' Gentleman. 1920: Marked Men. The Prince of Avenue A. The Girl in No. 29. Hitchin' Posts. Just Pals. 1921: The Wallop. Action. Jackie. Desperate Trails. Sure Fire. The Big Punch. The Freeze-Out. 1922: †Silver Wings. The Village Blacksmith. Little Miss Smiles. The Face on the Barroom Floor (GB: The Love Image). 1923: Three Jumps Ahead. North of Hudson Bay (GB: North of the Yukon). Cameo Kirby. Hoodman Blind. 1924: The Iron Horse. Hearts of Oak. 1925: Lightnin'. Kentucky Pride. The Fighting Heart (GB: Once to Every Man). Thank You. 1926: The Shamrock Handicap. Three Bad Men. The Blue Eagle. 1927: Mother Machree. Upstream (GB: Footlight Glamour). 1928: Four Sons. Hangman's House. Riley the Cop. Napoleon's Barber. 1929: Strong Boy. †The Black Watch (GB: King of the Khyber Rifles). Salute. †Men without Women. 1930: †Born Reckless. †Up the River. 1931: †Seas Beneath. The Brat. Arrowsmith. 1932: Airmail. Flesh. 1933: Pilgrimage. Doctor Bull. 1934: The Lost Patrol. Judge Priest. The World Moves On. The Whole Town's Talking (GB: Passport to Fame). 1935: Steamboat 'Round the Bend. The Informer. 1936: The Plough and the Stars. The Prisoner of Shark Island. Mary of Scotland. 1937: Wee Willie Winkie. The Hurricane. 1938: Four Men and a Prayer. Submarine Patrol. 1939: Young Mr Lincoln. Stage-

Walter **Forde** (right) sits in as his leading lady, Carol Goodner, is made up for a scene in his 1931 movie The Ringer.

coach. Drums Along the Mohawk. 1940: The Grapes of Wrath. The Long Voyage Home. 1941: Tobacco Road. How Green Was My Valley. Sex Hygiene (D). 1942: *The Battle of Midway (D). *Torpedo Squadron (D). How to Operate Behind Enemy Lines. 1943: December 7th (D. And shorter version). *We Sail at Midnight (D). 1945: They Were Expendable. 1946: My Darling Clementine. 1947: The Fugitive. 1948: Fort Apache. Three Godfathers. 1949: She Wore a Yellow Ribbon. 1950: Wagon Master. Rio Grande. When Willie Comes Marching Home. 1951: This is Korea! (D). 1952: What Price Glory? The Quiet Man. 1953: The Sun Shines Bright. Mogambo. 1954: The Long Gray Line. 1955: †Mister Roberts. *The Red, White and Blue Line. 1956: The Searchers. 1957: The Rising of the Moon. The Wings of Eagles. *The Growler Story. 1958: The Last Hurrah. Gideon's Day (US: Gideon of Scotland Yard). 1959: Korea (D). The Horse Soldiers. 1960: Sergeant Rutledge. 1961: Two Rode Together. 1962: †How the West Was Won. The Man Who Shot Liberty Valance. 1963. Donovan's Reef. 1964: Cheyenne Autumn. †Young Cassidy. 1966: Seven Women. 1970. Chesty (D).

FORDE, Walter (Thomas Seymour) 1896-1984
Briefly regarded as Britain's foremost director in the early 1930s, Forde is today principally recalled as a man of comedy, which is perhaps less than completely fair. Certainly, Forde's background was almost totally in comic vein. A stocky, light-haired man who looked like a humorous Spencer Tracy, Forde hailed from York-

shire and was a music hall entertainer in the north of England at 18, initially as a pianist but gradually bringing more comedy into the act. He entered films at 25 and soon became Britain's only major silent-film comedian in a series of two-reeler shorts with such titles as Walter's Winning Ways and Walter's Worries. He always wrote his own scenarios and by 1928 was already trying his hand at direction with three silent features. An understanding of the effects that could be obtained by skilful movement and placing of the camera seems to have come naturally to him. He began his sound career with two minor comedies in which he himself starred, but swiftly moved on to a wider variety and a better class of film with major companies. With Hitchcock in the doldrums, Forde quickly established a place at the head of Britain's directors with his 1931 version of Edgar Wallace's The Ringer, in which his clever use of the camera tightened tension in the hoary old thriller. Two good comedies, Third Time Lucky and The Ghost Train (both from plays by Arnold Ridley, and the latter beginning Forde's profitable association with Jack Hulbert) were followed by the outstanding Rome Express, an archetypal train thriller in which Forde's direction was acclaimed by one critic as 'masterly'. Forde's reputation suffered slightly in 1934 with the failure of Chu Chin Chow, but he re-established himself with one of Hulbert's best comedies, Bulldog Jack, and with an exciting war film, For Ever England, that almost, and indeed should have, made a star out of John Mills several years before he actually hit the top. The best of Forde's remaining films are two drily amusing comedy-thrillers in the Inspector Hornleigh series with Gordon Harker and Alastair Sim, although *Kicking the Moon Around* is a bright musical. By the end of the 1930s, other British directors predictably had caught up with his mastery of sound techniques. Although he remained in demand until 1944, he was not the same force in post-war years, and took an early retirement.

1920: *The Handy Man. *Fishing for Trouble. *Never Say Die. 1922: +*Walter Wins a Wager. +*Walter's Trying Frolic. +*Walter Makes a Movie. +*Walter Wants Work. 1928: Wait and See. What Next? 1929: Would You Believe It! The Silent House. 1930: Red Pearls. You'd Be Surprised! The Last Hour. Lord Richard in the Pantry. Bed and Breakfast. 1931: The Ringer. Splinters in the Navy. Third Time Lucky. The Ghost Train. Condemned to Death. 1932. Lord Babs. Jack's the Boy (US: Night and Day). Rome Express. 1933: Orders is Orders. 1934: Chu Chin Chow. Jack Ahoy! 1935: Bulldog Jack (US: Alias Bulldog Drummond). Brown on Resolution (later: For Ever England. US: Born for Glory). King of the Damned. 1936: Land without Music (US: Forbidden Music). 1938: Kicking the Moon Around (US: The Playboy). The Gaunt Stranger (US: The Phantom Strikes). 1939: Inspector Hornleigh on Holiday. Let's Be Famous. The Four Just Men (US: The Secret Four). Cheer Boys Cheer. 1940: Saloon Bar. Sailors Three (US: Three Cockeyed Sailors). Charley's (Big Hearted) Aunt. Neutral Port. Gasbags. 1941: The Ghost Train (remake). Inspector Hornleigh Goes To It (US: Mail Train). Atlantic Ferry (US: Sons of the Sea). 1942: Flying Fortress. *Go To Blazes. The Peterville Diamond. 1943: It's That Man Again. 1944: Time Flies. 1947: Master of Bankdam. 1949: Cardboard Cavalier.

+ Co directed

FORMAN, Miloš 1932-

Czech-born director of limited but often striking output who has been making films in Hollywood since 1971. An orphan who lost both parents in wartime concentration camps, Forman rose to prominence with the last three films he made in Czechoslovakia before the Russian takeover of the country in 1968. This trio of films, still among his best, are wittily observed portraits of life laughing at little people. *The Fireman's Ball* is especially treasurable and full of funny moments — at the time, it was quite the most original Czech film in ages. The Hollywood films are 'bigger', dealing more with social consciousness and sublime innocents paying the price of their innocence. I have serious reservations about Forman's manipulation of genuine mental patients in the generally distasteful *One Flew Over the Cuckoo's Nest*, which nonetheless took all five major Academy Awards in its year, including one for Forman as best director. *Hair*, which followed, was an unsuccessful opening out of a stage musical. But in *Ragtime*, a downbeat, kaleidoscopic look at life in turn-of-the-century America, Forman skil- fully captured the spirit of a structurally complicated book that many people had thought unfilmable. He followed this with another best director Oscar, this time for *Amadeus*. This impressive screen rendition of Peter Shaffer's play about a clash of musical wills in 18th-century Vienna won seven other Academy Awards. Unexpectedly, though, it heralded a drying-up of Forman's work for the cinema. There have been only three films since: *Valmont* was a pale copy of *Dangerous Liaisons*, but Forman was back on form with *The People Vs Larry Flynt*, an absorbing and in-your-face account of the career of America's king of magazine pornography. It won Forman his third Academy Award nomination.

1958: †Laterna Magika. 1960: †Laterna Magika II. 1963: Konkurs/Competition/ Audition. Kdyby ty muziky nebyly/If It Weren't for Music. 1964: Cerný Petr (GB: Peter and Pavla. US: Black Peter). 1965: Lásky jedné Plavovlásky (GB: A Blonde in Love. US: Loves of a Blonde). 1967: Hori, má Panenko (GB: The Fireman's Ball. US: The Firemen's Ball). 1971: Taking Off. 1975: One Flew Over the Cuckoo's Nest. 1979: Hair. 1981: Ragtime. 1983: Amadeus. 1989: Valmont. 1996: The People Vs Larry Flynt. 1999: Man on the Moon.

FORSYTH, Bill 1946-

Scottish-born director whose career seems to have been washed away in the murky waters of Hollywood. The more recent stages of his career are far from its bright beginnings, when Forsyth brought his own laconic Glasgow humour across in two richly amusing features shot on minimal budgets. A first-year dropout from the National Film School, Forsyth was bogged down in assistant's jobs on documentaries when he decided he might as well strike out and make features for himself. The first one came about 'as a result of me meeting kids at the Glasgow Youth Theatre. It's basically both a comedy and a comment on the unemployment situation: if you like, a fairy-tale for the workless'. The film, *That Sinking Feeling*, turned out to be a riotous and always wittily written comedy about a group of teenage Glasgow unemployeds who decide there 'must be something more to life than committing suicide' and hatch a hare-brained scheme to steal several hundred stainless steel sinks. Great ensemble playing from the youthful cast confirms the promise of the direction. The film received cheers at festivals but little in the way of distribution. Forsyth solved that problem with *Gregory's Girl*. The freshest and fun-

Bill **Forsyth** had grown a beard but lost some of his freshness by the time he made the over-ambitious *Housekeeping.*

Innovative choreographer-director Bob **Fosse** on the set of his last film, *Star 80*.

niest school story from Britain for 25 years, it tells of a dishy girl soccer player who makes the school team, scoring not only goals, but with the deposed striker who has been relegated to goalkeeper. The film, fiercely funny about school life, saw Forsyth move into the field of commercial hits without discarding any of his unique native talents. Thus he was able to employ Hollywood's Burt Lancaster as the star of *Local Hero*, an Ealing-style fantasy comedy set on the Scottish coast, with typical Forsythian streaks of zaniness and irreverence. It won him a British Academy Award. After that, things went away from Scotland, and astray for Forsyth. There were two low-key features in Canada, strained by inexactitude in the central casting, then a major disaster, *Being Human*, an ambitious comedy featuring Robin Williams in five ages, from caveman to modern man. Costing 20 million dollars, the film was subject to numerous wrangles between Forsyth and Warner Brothers, and ended up taking only 1.5 million dollars. Forsyth has been recently quoted as saying: 'In many ways it doesn't matter to me if I never make another film.' This is sad, but then he started planning a long-delayed sequel to *Gregory's Girl*, so let's hope more quirky comedy set in Scotland isn't out of the question.

1979: That Sinking Feeling. 1981: Gregory's Girl. 1983: Local Hero. 1984: Comfort and Joy. 1987: Housekeeping. 1989: Breaking In. 1993: Being Human. 1999: Gregory's 2 Girls.

FOSSE, Bob 1927-1987

Fosse the dancer was an amazing whizzbang of a man, turning sensational cartwheels and capable of astounding acrobatics. As an actor he was unmemorable, hence both the cinema's thumbsdown on this part of his career, and the strengths and weaknesses of the films that Chicago-born Fosse later made. The musical sequences in *Sweet Charity* are full of aggression and fire, while those in *Cabaret* are simply the snappiest, most devastating examples of fast and accurate timing over a sustained period ever put on screen. Dramatically, these films are better than one could have expected from Fosse's own acting track record and *Cabaret*, although difficult to like, won an Academy Award. Subsequently, he elicited Valerie Perrine's finest (by a distance) acting performance in *Lenny*, which would have won an Oscar against any other competition than Ellen Burstyn in *Alice Doesn't Live Here Anymore* (Miss Perrine *must* have come second), and won a tour-de-musical-force from such an unlikely source as Roy Scheider in *All That Jazz*. His films lacked warmth. But a Fosse musical sequence remained an unmissable experience. Of vaudeville parents, Fosse was dancing professionally at 14, became a choreographer by 1954, received seven 'Tonys' for stage work and played *Pal Joey* twice on stage in 1961 and 1963. He married and divorced three times, including (third) actress-dancer Gwen Verdon. Three films he choreographed but not did direct are *My Sister Eileen (1955)*, *The Pajama Game (1957)* and *Damn Yankees* (GB: *What Lola Wants*. 1958). He died from a heart attack.

1968: Sweet Charity. 1972: Cabaret. 1974: Lenny. 1979: All That Jazz. 1983: Star 80.

FOSTER, Lewis R. 1899-1974

An American screenwriter who also dabbled in direction, Foster worked for the Hal Roach studio for many years, first as an inventor of gags, later as script supervisor. In 1929, he directed six Laurel and Hardy two-reelers, the funniest of which is *Bacon Grabbers*, in which the boys have to deliver a summons to Edgar Kennedy for repossession of a radio. It contains a marvellous triple-disaster climax. Although he made his debut as a feature film director in 1936, Foster's main interest continued to lie in writing, and his original story in 1939 for *Mr Smith Goes to Washington* won him an Oscar. His screenplays include *The Magnificent Brute* (1936), *The More the Merrier* (1943), *Can't Help Singing* (1944) and *I Wonder Who's Kissing her Now* (1947). The main clutch of Foster's directorial work dates from 1949 to 1954, when he was associated with the Pine-Thomas unit at Paramount. The best of these are his initial ventures with John Payne as star — *El Paso, Captain China* and *Passage West*. Later, there was a good prison break story, *Crashout*, with some white-hot action and William Bendix giving his best performance in years as the kill-crazy leader of the six escapees. With good support from Arthur Kennedy, Gene Evans, Luther Adler, William Talman and Marshall Thompson, this is Foster's best film, although *Dakota Incident* is a decent A-grade western and *The Bold and the Brave* a fierce war film that signalled Mickey Rooney's comeback in sour character roles.

1929: *Unaccustomed As We Are. *Double Whoopee. *Hotter Than Hot. Berth Marks. *Men o' War. *Bacon Grabbers. *Angora Love. *Loud Soup. *Movie Night. 1930: *The Setting Son. *Too Hot to Handle. *The Sleeping Cutie. Broken Wedding Bells. * Cash and Marry. *Dizzy Dates. *A Fall to Arms. *Knights Before Xmas. *The Land of the Sky Blue Daughters. *Pure and Simple. *Man Without Skirts. 1931: Blondes Prefer Bonds. *Dumbbells in Derbies. *Eventually But Not Now. *The Itching Hour. Lime Juice Nights. Second Hand Kisses. 1936: †Love Letters of a Star. 1937: †She's Dangerous. Armored Car. The Man Who Cried Wolf. 1948: The Lucky Stiff. 1949: Manhandled. El Paso. Captain China. 1950: The Eagle and the Hawk. 1951: Passage West (GB: High Venture). Thie Last Outpost. Crosswinds. Hong Kong. 1952: Tropic Zone. 1953: Jamaica Run. Those Redheads from Seattle. 1955: Top of the World. Crashout. 1956: Dakota Incident. The Bold and the Brave. 1958: Tonka. 1960: †The Sign of Zorro.

FOSTER, Norman
(N. Hoeffer) 1900-1976

Whatever merits one may place on Indiana-born Norman Foster as a director, he had a lot more talent on the unseen side of the camera. An actor until 1936, Foster was certainly one of the most colourless juveniles of the decade. His early films as director are minor thrillers, mostly lively entries in the Mr Moto and Charlie Chan series. An association with Orson Welles seems to have led to Foster's becoming interested in native cultures and American folk-history, and many of his later films reflect this side of his life. His Davy Crockett films, originally made for television, were immensely successful at box-offices all over the world a grateful Disney Organization kept him in work for most of the remainder of his career. Earlier Foster had collaborated with Welles on the fascinatingly stylized *Journey into Fear* (influences from which can be seen in his later thrillers, *Kiss the Blood Off My Hands* and the excellent *Woman on the Run)* and the abortive *It's All True*. Foster's career ended in the late 1960s — he was still fascinated by Indians and America's past, making television dramas about Custer's career for the Disney Studio. Foster was married to the actresses Claudette Colbert and Sally Blane.

1936: I Cover Chinatown. 1937: Fair Warning. Thank You, Mr Moto. Think Fast, Mr Moto. 1938: Mysterious Mr Moto. Walking Down Broadway. Mr Moto Takes a Chance. 1939: Charlie Chan in Reno. Charlie Chan at Treasure Island. Mr Moto's Last Warning. Mr Moto Takes a Vacation. 1940: Viva Cisco Kid. Charlie Chan in Panama. 1941: Ride Kelly Ride. Scotland Yard. 1942: †It's All True (unfinished). †Journey into Fear. 1943: Santa. 1944: Le Fuga. La hora de la verdad. 1945: El Ahijado de la muerte. 1946: El Canto de la Sireno (GB: Song of the Siren). 1948: Rachel and the Stranger. Kiss the Blood off My Hands (GB. Blood on My Hands). 1949: Tell It to the Judge. 1950: Father is a Bachelor. Woman on the Run. 1951: Navajo. 1952: Sky Full of Moon. Sombrero. 1954: Davy Crockett — King of the Wild Frontier. 1955: Davy Crockett and the River Pirates. 1959: The Nine Lives of Elfego Baca. 1960: †The Sign of Zorro. 1964: Indian Paint. 1967: Brighty of the Grand Canyon (GB: Brighty). The Legend of Custer (TV). 1968: †Custer's Last Fight (TV).

FRANCIS, Freddie 1917-

Although not in at the beginning of the British horror wave, this London-born ex-cameraman made as many distinctive contributions to it as anyone else in the field. Given half-way decent material — which he very rarely was — Francis proved that he could make some very stylish and compelling chillers. After studying engineering, the 19-year-old Francis was apprenticed to a stills cameraman, then found his way into the film industry at Gaumont-British studios, emerging as a camera assistant by 1939. War service inter-

rupted his career, and it was 1956 before he got his first solo credit as director of photography, on *A Hill in Korea* (US: *Hell in Korea)*. In 1960, Francis took an Oscar for his black-and-white camera-work on *Sons and Lovers* and two years later turned to direction, after filming additional scenes for *Day of the Triffids*. His early films as director are distinguished by their skilful use of black-and-white to heighten suspense and an air of the mysterious. Later, inevitably, Francis worked for Hammer, although his best films were all made away from that studio: parts of the multi-story *Dr Terror's House of Horrors, The Skull, The Psychopath, Torture Garden*, and (easily his best work) *The Creeping Flesh*. A great deal of mumbo-jumbo in this film — part-scientific about evil blood cells overcoming good ones, and part-legend about a rain god weeping — is handled with sufficient flair to keep the audience from dissecting its latent absurdities. But the film's secret lies in Francis's style, never flashy, but knitting together the complicated plot with considerable skill. It also benefits from his photographer's eye: the keyed colour blends oaty browns with blacks and off-whites, and fills the night with hidden horror, so enveloping us in its scheme of things that the flash of a mad woman's red dress stands out like a beacon. The feel of the woodland scenes is more Scandinavian than English, evoking a shiver from angle and shadow, as the great hooded figure of evil moves slowly and relentlessly through the mists in the background. *The Creeping Flesh* is a most reticent film to find in the midst of a horror boom that leans heavily on gore and sex, but it was the last thing of any note to be made by Francis to date. Three of his last seven films, indeed, did not even have a proper release. Since beginning to direct, he has returned to cinematography occasionally — on *Night Must Fall* (1964) and *The Elephant Man* (1980), both in his favourite black-and-white. But he won a second Oscar, for his (colour) cinematography on *Glory* in 1989.

1962: †Day of the Triffids (uncredited). Two and Two Make Six (US: The Girl Swappers). Vengeance (US: The Brain. And German version). Paranoiac. 1963: Nightmare. 1964: Hysteria. Traitor's Gate (and German version). The Evil of Frankenstein. Dr Terror's House of Horrors. 1965: The Skull. The Psychopath. 1966: The Deadly Bees. 1967: They Came from Beyond Space. Torture Garden. 1968: The Intrepid Mr Twigg. Dracula Has Risen from the Grave. 1969: Mumsy, Nanny, Sonny and Girly (US: Girly). 1970: Trog. 1971: Vampire Hap-

pening. 1972: Tales from the Crypt. The Creeping Flesh. 1973: Tales That Witness Madness. Craze. 1974: Son of Dracula/Count Downe. Legend of the Werewolf. 1975: The Ghoul. 1977: †Golden Rendezvous (uncredited). 1985: The Doctor and the Devils. 1987: Dark Tower.

FRANJU, Georges 1912-1987

French-born Franju was a maker of moments, a peddler of images and a creator of set-pieces that you will never forget. Although this purveyor of dark poetry was unable to run these moments together for long enough to make a masterpiece, still they are often worth more than the whole of other directors' films. Interested in films since his very early twenties — he was co-founder of the Cinémathèque Française in 1936 —Franju began making short, often rather bizarre documentaries in earnest from 1948. When he turned to fictional features a decade later, it was evident that his tastes wound somewhere around the serials of Feuillade, the fantasies of Cocteau and the conventional horror film. Blood, knives, windows and mirrors are themes that crop up time and again. Images are shattered, physically or mentally; and the favourite Franju settings are full of darkness and insecurity, whether they be threatening interiors, or the gardens, woods and forests that recur so often in his films. His efforts to illustrate the enigmatic qualities among his players — chiefly Pierre Brasseur and Edith Scob — increase one's uncertainty as to what will happen next, an essential ingredient of the fascination of his stories. Most of his films outstay their welcome, or step outside the closed world which gives them their strength, but still there are those moments... the dance where all the participants wear heads of birds in *Judex*, the dissection scenes, too gruesome to watch, too hypnotic to look away from, in *Eyes Without a Face*, the asylum gardens in *La tête contre les murs*, echoed years later in *La faute de l'Abbé Mouret*, the tree that 'guards' *Thérèse Desqueyroux* after she has attempted to poison her husband. The influence of the German film-makers of UFA is also evident in these chiaroscuro portraits of living hell, and, in the mid-1970s, to prove his enthusiasm still ran high, Franju made a whole series of such *films-fantastiques* for television, as if aware his career were due for re-appraisal, and determined to leave as much behind as possible.

*1935: †*Le métro (D). 1948: *Le sang des bêtes (D). 1950. En passant par La*

Lorraine (D). 1951: *Hotel des Invalides (D). 1952: Le grand Méliès (D). 1953: *Monsieur et Madame Curie (D). 1954: *Les poussières (D). Marine marchande (D). 1955: *A propos d'une rivière/Le saumon atlantique/Au fil de la rivière (D). *Mon chien (D) 1956. *Le Théâtre National Populaire (D). *Sur le pont d'Avignon (D). 1957: Notre Dame, cathédrale de Paris (D). 1958: *La première nuit (D). La tête contre les murs (GB & US: The Keepers). 1960: Les yeux sans visage (GB: Eyes without a Face. US: The Horror Chamber of Dr Faustus). 1961: Pleins feux sur l'assassin (US: Spotlight on Murder). 1962: Thérèse Desqueyroux (US: Therese). 1963: Judex. 1964: Thomas l'imposteur. 1965: *Les rideaux blancs. 1970. La faute de l'Abbé Mouret (GB: The Sin of Father Mouret. US: The Demise of Father Mouret). 1971: La ligne d'ombre (TV). 1973: Nuits rouges/L'homme sans visage (GB & US: Shadowman). 1974: La nuit du voleur de cerbeau (TV). Le masque de plomb (TV). Les tueurs sans âme (TV). Le mort qui rampait sur les toits (TV). 1975: La marche des spectres (TV). Le rapt (TV). Le sang accusateur (TV). Le secret des Templiers (TV). 1978: La discorde (TV). Le dernier mélodrame (TV).

FRANK, Melvin 1913-1988

A look at the joint credits of Melvin Frank and Norman Panama (qv), and then at their solo films, leaves one in little doubt as to where the chief talent lay. Frank's record includes The Facts of Life, and A Touch of Class, while about the best that Panama can muster is The Road to Hong Kong. Certainly, at their best these two Americans were very funny writers. They had teamed together as early as university days, and were writing scripts for Bob Hope's radio shows by the end of the l930s. Their first screen contribution was the script for one of Hope's (funniest) vehicles, My Favorite Blonde, filmed in 1941, but released early in 1942. For the rest of the decade, the cinema, and Paramount Pictures in particular, kept them very busy. Their scripts were full of fresh, belly-laugh gems, and included Road to Utopia, Monsieur Beaucaire and Mr Blandings Builds His Dream House. After that, apart from White Christmas in 1954, Panama and Frank wrote, produced and directed their own films, hitting a peak in the mid-1950s with two Danny Kaye vehicles, Knock on Wood, and then their funniest film of all, The Court Jester, with its classic routine in which knights Danny Kaye and Robert Middleton are too busy desperately trying to remember the location of the pellet

with the poison (was it in the chalice from the palace, the vessel with the pestle, or the flagon with the dragon, and which one held the brew that is true?) to concentrate on jousting in the arena. From 1957, the two men largely went their own ways, and after a rather uncharacteristic start with Lil' Abner and The Jayhawkers, Frank made the classic funny-sad Hope-Lucille Ball picture, The Facts of Life, following it with a series of films which, while not at the top of their class, nor earth-shakers at the box-office, gave out dozens of quirkily funny little touches. A Touch of Class, although it runs downhill after an hilarious opening two or three reels, put Frank (rather regrettably) into a different class of film-making and his work after that, even though I was one of the very few who quite liked The Duchess and the Dirtwater Fox, undeniably lacked some of its earlier sparkle.

1949: †The Reformer and the Redhead. 1951: Strictly Dishonorable. †Callaway Went Thataway (GB: The Star Said No!). 1952: †Above and Beyond. 1954: †Knock on Wood. 1955: †The Court Jester. 1956: †That Certain Feeling. 1959: Li'l Abner. The Jayhawkers. 1960: The Facts of Life. 1965: Strange Bedfellows. 1968: Buona Sera, Mrs Campbell. 1972: A Touch of Class. 1974: The Prisoner of Second Avenue. 1976: The Duchess and the Dirtwater Fox. 1979: Lost and Found. 1987: Walk Like a Man.

FRANKEL, Cyril 1921-

British director of variable output, whose best work was all done in his early years. But his competent professionalism was later put to good use by television, in which medium he directed scores of episodes, mostly thrillers, from the early 1960s. After wartime service, Frankel was employed by the documentary-making Crown Film Unit. Later he made documentaries of his own, notably the sincere and moving Man of Africa. The feature films that followed it were mostly unsuccessful, in terms of both critical reviews and box-office takings. However, there were one or two notable exceptions. It's Great To Be Young was a fresh, vital and funny school story-cum-musical, full of youthful joie-de-vivre. Equally refreshing, if less successful, were She Didn't Say No! with the invaluable Eileen Herlie as an unmarried mother-several times over, and Alive and Kicking about the adventures of three old ladies, engagingly played by Sybil Thorndike, Kathleen Harrison and Estelle Winwood. Frankel also scored a minor success with Never Take Sweets from a Stranger, in which the tension and repulsion milked

from the title should have put any child off taking sweets from anyone. This was the last truly original work from Frankel in the cinema and the promise of his later projects was dissipated in the execution.

1950: *Explorers of the Depths. *Eagles of the Fleet (D). 1951: *Wing to Wing (D). 1953: *The Nutcracker. Man of Africa (D). 1954: Make Me an Offer! Devil on Horseback. 1955: It's Great To Be Young! 1957: No Time for Tears. 1958: She Didn't Say No! Alive and Kicking. 1960: Scheidungsgrund: Liebe. Never Take Sweets from a Stranger (US: Never Take Candy from a Stranger). 1961: Don't Bother to Knock (US: Why Bother to Knock?). On the Fiddle (US: Operation Snafu). 1963: The Very Edge. 1966: The Witches (US: The Devil's Own). 1967: The Trygon Factor. 1975: Permission to Kill. 1985: Bold Steps (TV). 1990: Harry and Harriet.

FRANKENHEIMER, John 1930-

One could forgive a director almost anything after The Young Savages, The Manchurian Candidate and Birdman of Alcatraz, although in truth there has been rather a lot to forgive since this American director's heyday of the early l960s. Not until Steven Spielberg was there to be such a youthful graduate from television — Frankenheimer made his first film in 1957, with a dozen episodes of the Playhouse 90 series already behind him, some of which were shown outside America as feature films. He soon proved himself an expert at making high-powered thrillers with something to say: The Young Savages is both a juvenile delinquency story and a courtroom drama — and hard-hitting as either; The Manchurian Candidate is the dazzlingly persuasive story of a soldier brainwashed in Korea into becoming an automaton-assassin, and Birdman of Alcatraz the absorbing and finally heart-breaking true story of a man confined to prison all his life for murder, even though he became a world-acknowledged expert on birds; The Train is an exciting, if straightforward wartime thriller that moved along like the loco of its title. Three of these films starred Burt Lancaster, whose quality of massive strength beneath a too-calm surface was perfectly illuminated by Frankenheimer's direction, and who also appeared in one of the better of the director's later films, The Gypsy Moths. Just when Frankenheimer seemed to have established himself as one of the foremost directors in his field, he began trying to branch out and things went more than a little awry. Only when he returned to the thriller in the mid-1970s,

John **Frankenheimer** sizes up an exterior location for *52 Pick-Up*, a latter-day film on which he displayed some his old flair for narrative drive.

most notably with *French Connection II*, a sequel which for once outgunned an original, did one see with some relief that he could still make strong and fluid entertainments. Another sideward step, this time into horror with *Prophecy*, was inevitably unsuccessful. In *The Challenge*, Frankenheimer tried to combine the action of a kung fu/samurai film with the scale and spirit of a Kurosawa epic and fell heavily between the two stools into pretentiousness. Of the films since then, only *52 Pick-Up* and *Dead Bang* showed something of his old drive until he exploded back close to his best form in 1994 with *Against the Wall*, a cable TV film about the Attica prison riots, and *The Burning Season*, a docu-drama set in Brazil. After that, he unwisely accepted the reins on the disastrous remake of *The Island of Dr Moreau* after the original director had left.

1956: *Forbidden Area* (TV). *Eloise* (TV). *The Ninth Day* (TV). *The Family Nobody Wanted* (TV). *Rendezvous in Black* (TV). *The Comedian* (TV). 1957: *The Last Tycoon* (TV). *The Young Stranger. Winter Dreams* (TV). *Clash by Night* (TV). *A Sound of Different Drummers* (TV). *If*

You Knew Elizabeth (TV). *The Fabulous Irishman* (TV). *The Death of Manolete* (TV). *The Thundering Wave* (TV). *The Trouble Makers* (TV). 1958: *Days of Wine and Roses* (TV). *Bombers' Moon* (TV). *The Last Man* (TV). *The Violent Heart* (TV). *A Town Has Turned to Dust* (TV). *Rumors of Evening* (TV). *Old Man* (TV). 1959: *Face of a Hero* (TV). *The Blue Men* (TV). *For Whom the Bell Tolls* (TV). 1960: *Journey to the Day* (TV). 1961: *The Young Savages*. 1962: *All Fall Down. Birdman of Alcatraz. The Manchurian Candidate*. 1963: *Seven Days in May*. 1965: *The Train*. 1966: *Grand Prix. Seconds*. 1968: *The Extraordinary Seaman. The Fixer*. 1969: *The Gypsy Moths*. 1970: *I Walk the Line. The Horsemen*. 1973: *The Iceman Cometh. Impossible Object*. 1974: *99 and 44/100% Dead* (GB: *Call Harry Crown*). 1975: *French Connection II* (GB: *French Connection No. 2*). 1976: *Black Sunday*. 1979: *Prophecy*. 1982: *The Challenge*. 1985: *The Holcroft Covenant*. 1986: *52 Pick-Up*. 1989: *Dead Bang*. 1990: *The Fourth War*. 1991: *Year of the Gun*. 1994: *The Burning Season. Against the Wall* (cable TV). 1996: *The Island of Dr Moreau*. 1998: *Ronin*.

FRANKLIN, Sidney 1893-1972

California-born Franklin was a man of impeccable taste who made smooth box-office films with many of Hollywood's foremost female stars over a 20-year period, before turning producer after the death of his friend and patron at M-G-M, Irving Thalberg. His passion for pre-planning, elaborate detail and extended shooting schedules was eventually his undoing when he found two projects, *Marie Antoinette* and *Goodbye Mr Chips!*, taken away from him by M-G-M in the late 1930s. In retrospect, Franklin directed very little that was memorable, or would look less than dated today, and his calculated perfectionism is no longer as persuasive. His ability to stir the emotions of an audience, however, still creates some charge in such films as *Smilin' Through* (the 1932 remake) and *The Good Earth*, which won two Academy Awards. After another Oscar-winning film, *Mrs Miniver*, which he produced, Franklin was awarded a special Oscar (appropriately the Irving G. Thalberg award) for outstanding motion picture production. Franklin's career in the film industry had begun at the age of 20, in harness with his older brother Chester (1890-1949) — the co-directing credits below are all with Chester. After Chester was drafted for war service in 1918, the brothers split up, and Sidney quickly established a reputation for providing glossy vehicles for the best-known qualities of some high-powered actresses, among them Greta Garbo (with whom, apparently, he never got on), Norma Talmadge and her sister Constance, Marion Davies, Mary Pickford and, latterly, Norma Shearer.

1914: †*The Sheriff*. 1915: †*Little Dick's First Case*. †*The Baby*. †*Little Dick's First Adventure*. †*The Rivals*. †*Her Filmland Hero.*†*Pirates Bold*. *The Kid Magicians*. †*The Runaways*. †*The Little Cupids*. †*Dirty Face Dan*. †*A Ten Cent Adventure*. †*The Straw Man*. †*The Doll House Mystery*. 1916: †*The Children in the House*. †*The Little Schoolma'am*. †*Let Katie Do It*. †*Martha's Vindication*. †*Gretchen the Greenhorn*. †*A Sister of Six*. 1917: †*Jack and the Beanstalk*. †*Babes in the Woods*. †*Treasure Island*. †*Aladdin and His Wonderful Lamp*. †*Going Straight*. 1918: †*Ali Baba and the 40 Thieves*. †*Fan Fan. Six Shooter Andy. The Bride of Fear. Confession. The Safety Curtain. Her Only Way. The Forbidden City. The Heart of Wetona*. 1919: *The Probation Wife. The Hoodlum* (GB: *The Ragamuffin*). *Heart o' the Hills*. 1920: *Two Weeks. Unseen Forces*. 1921: *Not Guilty. Courage*. 1922:

Smilin' Through. East is West. The Primitive Lover. 1923: Brass. Dulcy. Tiger Rose. 1924: Her Night of Romance. 1925: Her Sister from Paris. Learning to Love. 1926: Beverly of Graustark. The Duchess of Buffalo. 1927: Quality Street. 1928: The Actress (GB: Trelawney of the Wells). 1929: Devil May Care. Wild Orchids. The Last of Mrs Cheyney. 1930: The Lady of Scandal (GB: The High Road). A Lady's Morals (GB: Jenny Lind). 1931: The Guardsman. Private Lives. 1932: Smilin' Through (remake). 1933: Reunion in Vienna. 1934: The Barretts of Wimpole Street. 1935: The Dark Angel. 1937: The Good Earth. 1956: The Barretts of Wimpole Street (remake).

FRAWLEY, James 1937-

American director with a surrealistic sense of humour. Frawley is also an actor and a photographer, and learnt his craft with Theodore J. Flicker (1930-), whose equally miniscule cinema output includes the brilliantly funny and inventive *The President's Analyst*. Frawley's first work as director was on many episodes of the TV series *The Monkees*, and the likeable zaniness that brought it success can largely be attributed to him. As a film-maker, Frawley has only brought home the bacon when his own personality has been allowed to dominate the flavour of the film, as it seems to have done on *Kid Blue* and *The Big Bus*. The former is a romantic western which puts entertainment before authenticity and is full of warmly quirky touches. *The Big Bus* is a mad spoof disaster epic in which the driver is under suspicion of once having eaten 116 passengers (his co-driver was responsible) and his new co-driver, who breaks a cardboard carton of milk on the bar and threatens people with it, gets blackouts at speed. The villain, intent on sabotaging bus H.Q, turns the lights *out* so that he can flash his torch. There are a lot more characters: these are only the sane ones. Even the film's asides and background lines are funny, while satires on scenes and climaxes from a dozen other movies are crammed into its 89 minutes. *Bus* raised great hopes for Frawley's future, but *Airplane!* has since stolen its thunder, and Frawley has done little else. *The Muppet Movie* and his TV films have suggested an inability to lift unfamiliar material, and one wonders if he will again come to the fore. Besides the list below, Frawley has also directed two feature-length episodes of TV's *Columbo* series — *Try and Catch Me* (1977) and *Make Me a Perfect Murder* (1978).

1971: The Christian Licorice Store. 1973: Kid Blue. 1975: Delancey Street (TV).

1976: The Big Bus. 1978: The Deadly Price of Paradise (TV. GB: Nightmare at Pendragon's Castle). 1979: The Muppet Movie. 1980: The Great American Traffic Jam (TV). 1984: The Outlaws (TV). 1985: Fraternity Vacation. 1987: Warm Hands, Cold Feet (TV). Assault & Matrimony (TV). 1988: Spies, Lies and Naked Thighs (TV). 1990: Runaway Heart (TV). 1994: Another Midnight Run (TV). Cagney & Lacey: The Return (TV). 1995: Harrison: Cry of the City (TV). 1997: On the 2nd Day of Christmas (TV).

FREARS, Stephen 1941-

British director who, after being near the forefront of several 'new waves' in British cinema, has unexpectedly carved himself an international career in the past ten years. Although his output has been uneven, it has also proved extraordinarily wide-ranging while rarely failing to highlight his ability to obtain crowd-pleasing performances from his principal players. He had begun as an assistant to such seminal figures of Britain's neo-realist movement of the 1960s as Karel Reisz and Lindsay Anderson but, after extensive experience directing popular regional TV series, had an immediate cinema hit of his own with *Gumshoe*, featuring Albert Finney, whose assistant director he had been on *Charlie Bubbles* in 1967. A spoof of forties' detective thrillers, it catches a winning mood and holds it. The film seemed to herald the arrival of a major new director on the British scene, but in practice Frears returned to television for more than a decade. Projects for Channel 4 and the BBC that were shown in cinemas outside Britain edged him back towards the movie scene. But his first film specifically for the cinema in 13 years, *The Hit*, belied its title and it took Channel 4 to come to the rescue with *My Beautiful Laundrette*, which combined Frears' traits of grittiness and scabrous humour in its treatment of a script that is funny, sexy, violent and perceptive by turns with in its observation of the central gay love story. Intended for TV, this instead proved a big success in cinemas, encouraging Frears to try his hand at bigger screen stuff, notably *Prick Up Your Ears*, a biopic of the gay and self-destructive playwright Joe Orton. The award-winning *Dangerous Liaisons* set Frears up for the international career that had long interested him, although his work within that framework has been rather more variable, from the underrated *The Grifters* and *Hero* (probably Frears' best mainstream film) to the grim (in all senses) *Mary Reilly*, from which he took a couple of years to recover. And there were

two Irish black comedy-dramas, the excellent *The Snapper* and the rather less successful *The Van*. A worthy career, if not quite yet an *auteur*'s one.

1967: The Burning. 1971: Gumshoe. 1979: Bloody Kids (TV. Released to cinemas in 1983). 1981: Going Gently (TV). 1982: Walter (TV. US: cinemas). 1983: Walter and June (TV. US: cinemas). 1983: Saigon — Year of the Cat (TV. US: cinemas). 1984: The Hit. 1985: My Beautiful Laundrette. 1986: Song of Experience (TV). 1987: Prick Up Your Ears. Sammy and Rosie Get Laid. 1988: Dangerous Liaisons. 1990: The Grifters. 1992: Hero (GB: Accidental Hero). 1994: The Snapper. 1996: The Van. Mary Reilly. 1998: The Hi-Lo Country.

FREDA, Riccardo 1909-

Egyptian-born director, working in Italian films from 1937, initially as a writer. Born at another time, in another place, Freda's reputation as a talented purveyor of highly original, richly decorated action films, historical epics, thrillers and horror movies would have been assured. In post-war Italy, however, the genres that Freda favoured were thought to be too imitative of Hollywood and dismissed by audiences and critics alike in spite of their often staggering visual flair. Thus some of Freda's best work appears under English-sounding pseudonyms, as he strove (quite successfully from the early 1950s) to ensure his films were shown on the international market. Not surprisingly, given his eye for depth of colour and detail, Freda started his professional career as an art critic for an Italian daily newspaper. Some bright swashbucklers attracted some attention in the early years of his directorial career, but it was ten years before he started hitting his target, the international scene. The first of his films to obtain a wide distribution outside his native Italy was *Theodora, Slave Empress*, followed by his version of the *Spartacus* story, made before *Theodora*, but seen abroad some time afterwards. From the mid-1950s, Freda's liking for colourful and imaginative scenes of shock began to make itself apparent, especially in such muscleman epics as *The White Warrior* and *Samson and the Seven Miracles of the World*, the latter with Gordon Scott, being one of the best vehicles of its kind Italy ever produced. In the early 1960s, Freda combined with that widest-staring of actresses, the British-born Barbara Steele, on two outright horror films which frightened audiences the world over: *The Spectre* and *L'orribile segreto del Dottor Hichcock*. *The Spectre* remains Freda's best film, its sombre Scotland-set exteriors giving way to darkly glowing interiors of red, brown, black and gold, which blend with the liquid brown eyes of the star — Steele giving one of her most eye-opening performances as the terrorized wife who will have the last, maniacal, dying laugh. This is horror sustained at fever pitch, shredding the viewer's nerves and never giving him a chance to relax, with virtuoso set-pieces and never the hint of a snigger. After that, Freda went sideways into James Bond-style thrillers — yet more imitation of international box-office success. Since 1972, he seemed to have been in retirement, but made a return with two welcome shockers. Still game in 1993, he prepared a new project, *D'Artagnan's Daughter*. Ill-health, however, forced him to abandon it, and it was eventually made by his friend Bertrand Tavernier (*qv*) a couple of years later.

1942: *Don Cesare de Bazan*. 1943: *Non canto più*. 1945: *Tutta la città canta*. 1946: *L'aquila nera* (GB: *The Black Eagle*). 1947: *Les misérables* (in two parts). *Il cavaliere misterioso* (US: *The Mysterious Rider*). 1948: *Guaranty*. *L'astuto barone*. *Tenore per forza*. 1949: *O cacoulha do barulho*. *Il Conte Ugolino* (US: *The Iron Swordsman*). *Il figlio di D'Artagnan* (GB: *Son of D'Artagnan*. US: *The Gay Swordsman*). 1950: *Magia a prezzi modici*. 1951: *Il tradimento*. *La vendetta di Aquila Nera* (GB: *Revenge of the Black Eagle*). 1952: *Vedi Napoli e poi muori* (US: *See Naples and Die*). *La leggenda del Piave*. *Spartacus* (GB: *Spartacus the Gladiator*. US: *Sins of Rome*). 1953. *Teodora, imperatrice di Bisanzio* (GB & US: *Theodora, Slave Empress*). *Mosaici di Ravenna*. 1955: *Da qui all'eredità*. *Beatrice Cenci*. 1956: *I vampiri* (GB: *Lust of the Vampire*. US: *The Devil's Commandments*). 1957: *Trapped in Tangiers*. 1959: *Agi Murad — il diavolo bianco* (GB & US: *The White Warrior*). *Caltiki— the Immortal Monster*. 1960: *The Giants of Thessaly*. 1961: *Caccia all'uomo*. *Maciste alla corte del Gran Khan* (GB & US: *Samson and the Seven Miracles of the World*). †*The Mongols* (uncredited). †*Marco Polo* (uncredited). 1962: *The Seventh Sword*. †*Alone Against Rome* (GB: *Vengeance of the Gladiators*. Uncredited). †*Seven Seas to Calais* (uncredited). †*Gold for the Caesars* (uncredited). *Maciste all'inferno* (GB & US: *The Witch's Curse*). *L'orribile segreto del Dottor Hichcock* (GB: *The Terror of Dr Hichcock*. US: *The Horrible Doctor Hichcock*). 1963: *The Spectre* (US: *The Ghost*). *The Magnificent Adventurer*. 1964: *Romeo and Juliet*. 1965: *Coplan FX 18 casse tout* (GB & US: *The Exterminators*). 1966: *Roger La Honte* (GB &

US: *Trap for the Assassin*). 1967: *Coplan III*. 1968: §*La morte non conta i dollari*. 1969: $*Double face* (US: *Puzzle of Horrors*). 1970: *Tamar... wife of Er*. 1971: **Liguana dalla lingua di fuoco*. 1979: *Superhuman*. 1980: *Unconscious*.

$ as Robert Hampton
§ as George Lincoln
** as Willy Pareto

FREELAND, Thornton 1898-

An American director at his best making elegant, sophisticated comedies and musicals, with here and there just a touch of the zany and the unexpected. During the silent years, Freeland was an actor, cutter, cameraman and assistant director, becoming a fully fledged director with the advent of sound. His early sound musicals are lively entertainments that move well (the best of them are *Whoopee!*, *Flying Down to Rio* and *George White's Scandals*). The second of these introduced Fred Astaire and Ginger Rogers as a team, but did not quite propel Freeland forward to the front rank, although his films remained for the most part fluid and entertaining. In 1934, he went to Britain and began an association with Astaire's British equivalent, the dry-voiced, dry-humoured Jack Buchanan: their initial collaboration was on a fast and funny version of *Brewster's Millions*. With the outbreak of war, Freeland went back to America, but returned to Britain in post-war years, signing off a modest, but not entirely undistinguished film career with a pleasing, star-studded version of Arnold Bennett's comedy novel, *Dear Mr Prohack*. Freeland married American actress June Clyde, who also made both Hollywood and British films.

1929: *Three Live Ghosts*. 1930: *Be Yourself! Whoopee!* 1931: *Six Cylinder Love*. *Terror by Night*. *The Secret Witness*. 1932: *Love Affair*. *Week-End Marriage*. *They Call It Sin* (GB: *The Way of Life*). *Unexpected Father*. 1933: *Flying Down to Rio*. 1934: *George White's Scandals*. *Brewster's Millions*. 1936: *Skylarks*. *The Amateur Gentleman*. *Accused*. 1937: *Paradise for Two* (US: *The Gaiety Girls*). *Jericho* (US: *Dark Sands*). *Over the Moon* (released 1940). 1938: *Hold My Hand*. 1939: *So This is London*. *The Gang's All Here* (US: *The Amazing Mr Forrest*). 1941: *Too Many Blondes*. *Marry the Boss's Daughter*. 1946: *Meet Me at Dawn*. 1948: *The Brass Monkey/Lucky Mascot*. 1949: *Dear Mr Prohaek*.

FREGONESE, Hugo 1908-1987

Argentinian director of stern but human

dramas, whose career began, and closed, in his native country. Fregonese's best films still remain as humourless but striking and uncompromising as they originally appeared. A former medical student, he entered films as a technical adviser in the Hollywood of the mid-1930s. Returning to Argentina, he spent years as an assistant director before being given his first chance by his mentor Lucas Demare on *Savage Pampas* (co-directed with Demare), which ironically Fregonese was to remake 23 years later when his vintage days were over. By 1950, he was in Hollywood (and marrying actress Faith Domergue; they divorced in 1954), venturing into *film noir* with an early James Mason vehicle, *One Way Street*. Fregonese liked employing strong, but unhandsome actors, and this black film makes good use of Dan Duryea, William Conrad, King Donovan and Jack Elam. There was also the sombre, haunting Val Lewton-produced western *Apache Drums;* and just about the only Fregonese film with any humour in it, *My Six Convicts*, a stylish and very winning story of an innovative prison warden and the six 'trusties' he tries to rehabilitate. This time Fregonese (wisely) employed Millard Mitchell, Gilbert Roland, John Beal, Regis Toomey and Charles Bronson and gets likeable performances from them all. *Man in the Attic* is a gripping, at times frightening if not wholly successful version of the Jack the Ripper story, with Jack Palance for once rather too subdued; and *The Raid*, brilliantly shot in colour by Lucien Ballard, a grim, real and vivid western about a determined band of Rebels planning to burn down a town in Vermont — this had another good cast headed by Van Heflin, Anne Bancroft, Richard Boone, Peter Graves, Lee Marvin and Claude Akins. Fregonese directed top box-office stars for the first time in *Blowing Wild* (Gary Cooper, Barbara Stanwyck) and *Black Tuesday* (Edward G. Robinson). Both veer off into the wild, stylized melodrama which doesn't exactly make a good film but sticks stubbornly in the memory. That, however, was about it, apart from good moments in *Harry Black*, which contains one of Stewart Granger's best performances as the weary white hunter, and a brilliant supporting portrayal by I.S. Johar. Fregonese died from a heart attack.

1939: *Bariloche*. *El Delta*. 1943: †*Savage Pampas*. 1946: *Donde Mueren las Palabras* (US: *Where Words Fail*). 1947: *Apeñas un Delincuente* (GB: *Live in Fear*. US: *Hardly a Criminal*). 1949: *De Hombre a Hombre*. 1950: *One Way Street*. *Saddle Tramp*. 1951: *Apache Drums*.

Mark of the Renegade. 1952: Untamed Frontier. My Six Convicts. Decameron Nights. 1953: Blowing Wild. Man in the Attic. 1954: The Raid. Black Tuesday. 1956: I girovaghi. 1957: La spada imbattibile. Seven Thunders (US: The Beasts of Marseilles). 1958: Harry Black (US: Harry Black and the Tiger). 1961: †Marco Polo. 1963: $Un aereo per Baalbeck. 1964: Old Shatterhand (GB: Apaches' Last Battle. US: Shatterhand). Die Todesstrahlen des Dr Mabuse. 1966: Savage Pampas (remake). 1970: †Blood of Frankenstein (US: Dracula Vs Frankenstein). 1973: La Mala Vida. 1975: Más Alla del Sol.

$ as 'supervising director'

FRENCH, Harold 1897-1997

London-born director who made very English entertainments for the cinema for years. French was also a prolific stage director, especially of the works of Terence Rattigan and Noel Coward. None of his films was quite a masterpiece, nor even a big box-office hit, but several of them, particularly those made between 1940 and 1955, remain pleasing, unassuming, skilful entertainment. French had begun his career as an actor, on stage (from 1912) and in films (from 1923), performing off and on until 1936. With the coming of sound, having already made a reputation on stage, he began to star regularly for the cinema, although hardly any of his 1930s' films are remembered today. With the coming of World War II, however, French emerged fairly suddenly as a front-rank director of the British cinema. *The House of the Arrow* was an exciting version of A.E.W. Mason's thriller; *Secret Mission* and *The Day Will Dawn* are two stiff-upper-lip but soberly presented war films, and *Dear Octopus* the first of several warm and cosily amusing portraits of middle-class British family life that would also include *English Without Tears* (earlier, French had directed the famous stage version of *French Without Tears*), *Quiet Weekend* and *Isn't Life Wonderful!* French also made some mild flights of fancy *(White Cradle Inn* and *The Dancing Years)* and some stodgy romantic dramas. But he had a solid box-office success with the cunningly contrived *My Brother Jonathan*, on the crest of the British vogue for provincial stories spread over a number of years, with triumph and tragedy coming out equal in their characters' lives. It is hard to imagine this most civilized of men turning his hand to rough-and-tumble action in glorious Technicolor, but he did in fact direct *Rob Roy the Highland Rogue* for the Disney Organization, before ending his film career with *The Man Who Loved Redheads*, another Rattigan comedy with a brilliant cast. French then turned back to writing (having penned several screenplays in the mid-1930s, including *Accused, Crime Over London,* and *Jump for Glory)*. In later years he turned his attention to the stage. Tragedy entered French's life in 1941 when his wife Phyllis was killed in a bombing raid.

1931: East Lynne on the Western Front. The Officers' Mess. Jealousy. The Star Reporter. 1932: The Callbox Mystery. A Safe Proposition. When London Sleeps. Tight Corner. 1933: Night of the Garter. Yes Madam. The Umbrella. I Adore You. Mannequin. 1934: Faces. Murder at the Inn. How's Chances? The Girl in the Crowd. 1935: A Fire Has Been Arranged (all as actor). *1937: Cavalier of the Streets. 1939: Dead Men Are Dangerous. 1940: The House of the Arrow. 1941: †Major Barbara. Jeannie. 1942: Secret Mission. Unpublished Story. The Day Will Dawn (US: The Avengers). 1943: Dear Octopus (US: The Randolph Family). 1944: English Without Tears (US: Her Man Gilbey). Mr Emmanuel. 1946: Quiet Weekend. 1947: White Cradle Inn (US: High Fury). 1948: The Blind Goddess. †Quartet. My Brother Jonathan. 1949: Adam and Evelyne. 1950: The Dancing Years. †Trio. 1951: †Encore. 1952: The Man Who Watched Trains Go By (US: Paris Express). The Hour of 13. 1953: Isn't Life Wonderful! Rob Roy the Highland Rogue. 1954: Forbidden Cargo. 1955: The Man Who Loved Redheads.*

FREND, Charles 1909-1977

A typical British directorial career of its time. Frend served as cutter, assistant editor and editor for several British studios through the 1930s, before becoming a reliable director of Ealing Studios' middle-range product from 1941 until the demise of the studio in the late 1950s. Frend's two best films are stories of drama and survival at sea in wartime. In the inspiring *San Demetrio London*, a crew abandons ship only to spot their own ship still afloat days later from their life-raft, reboard it and incredibly, against all odds and weather conditions, get it home (it was a true story, of course: no fiction could be so bizarre). *The Cruel Sea* was a great public and critical success, but it did not lead to the recognition of Frend as a major director, and he gradually subsided with his studio — although *The Long Arm*, a first-class thriller, held up the decline. By the 1960s, with Ealing gone for good, Frend was directing minor films, of which *Girl on Approval* is the most interesting, and much television, including several episodes of the Patrick McGoohan series *Danger Man*. Frend ended his film career as a second-unit director — for example, on the Disney Organization's *Guns in the Heather* and David Lean's *Ryan's Daughter*, an unworthy curtain for a man who also had the charming *The Magnet* and the adventurous Technicolor *Scott of the Antarctic* to his credit in earlier, happier days.

1941: The Big Blockade. 1942: The Foreman Went to France (US: Somewhere in France). 1943: San Demetrio London. 1944: Return of the Vikings (D). 1945: Johnny Frenchman. 1947: The Loves of Joanna Godden. 1948: Scott of the Antarctic. 1949: A Run for Your Money. 1951: The Magnet. 1952: The Cruel Sea. 1954: Lease of Life. 1956: The Long Arm (US: The Third Key). 1957: Barnacle Bill (US: All at Sea). 1960: Cone of Silence (US: Trouble in the Sky). 1961: Girl on Approval. 1962: Torpedo Bay. 1967: The Sky Bike.

FREUND, Karl 1890-1969

Brilliant, giant-sized Czech-born expressionist cinematographer who turned director in 1933, but made all too few films before returning to camerawork for good in 1936. Interested in photography from an early age (his family moved to Berlin while he was still a child), Freund began photographing film shorts from 1907, newsreels from 1908 and features from 1913. It was another ten years, however, before he began to acquire his never-lost reputation as a master of lighting, of the use of shape and shadow to heighten effects of menace and suspense. Murnau's *Der Januskopf* and Wegener's *The Golem* (both 1920) were landmark films for Freund, who went on to work with Fritz Lang on the second part of *Die Spinnen/The Spiders* and on *Metropolis*. He worked extensively with Murnau, Paul Czinner, Wegener, Richard Oswald and E.A. Dupont (being largely responsible for the daringly effective style of Dupont's *Variety)* before emigrating to America in 1929. His talent for creating unsettling images was put to effective use on *Dracula* and *Murders in the Rue Morgue*, but he soon established the reputation of being able to add a little extra to any film, and in 1937 won an Oscar for his distinctive work on *The Good Earth*. His directorial career consists of eight films only, but it includes *The Mummy, Madame Spy, The Countess of Monte Cristo* and, most extraordinarily, *Mad*

Director William **Friedkin** and star Ellen Burstyn confer on the set of Friedkin's ground-breaking *The Exorcist*, unseen for 25 years until a successful reissue in 1998.

Love. This last film is truly a scuttling creature from Hollywood's darkest corners, alive with threatening atmosphere, and with a memorably terrifying performance by Peter Lorre as the mad surgeon who grafts the hands of a murderer on to the arms of a classical pianist — a demented sideshoot of the Frankenstein theme. Alas, Freund decided he preferred cinematography and never returned to the director's chair. Of his later work, *Camille, Green Hell, Pride and Prejudice, The Seventh Cross, Undercurrent, Key Largo* and *Bright Leaf* show the big man's varied talents off to the best effect.

1933: The Mummy. Moonlight and Pretzels (GB: Moonlight and Melody). 1934: Madame Spy. The Countess of Monte Cristo. I Give My Love. Gift of Gab. Uncertain Lady. 1935: Mad Love (GB: The Hands of Orlac).

FRIEDKIN, William 1939-

Although at the head of the new wave of American directors following his sensational success in 1973 with *The Exorcist*, Friedkin had lost his place by the 1980s. He was always good at working out set pieces, like the extraordinary special effects in that film, and yet there was more (and is more, one hopes) to his talent than that. He worked his way up from the bottom from the age of 16 in the world of television, and was directing at 21. His first film, *Good Times*, in 1967, a vehicle

for the then-married musical team of Sonny and Cher, was followed by Friedkin's all-round best film, *The Night They Raided Minsky's*, a brilliant, amusing and finally moving evocation of the last days of American burlesque in the 1920s. The film version of the Broadway play about a group of homosexuals, *The Boys in the Band*, had an unpleasant aura, and inevitably only reached a limited audience, but Friedkin followed up by winning an Academy Award for *The French Connection*: his flair for stage management was never more evident than in the heart stopping car chase which is the film's *pièce de résistance* and indeed almost its *raison d'être*, as detective Gene Hackman suicidally drives his car along under an elevated railway in pursuit of a train carrying his suspect. If it weren't for *Minsky's*, the gimmicky success of *Exorcist* and *Connection* would have left one unsurprised at the failure of Friedkin's subsequent ventures. In the 1980s, Friedkin floundered: it almost seemed that the man had no shame, making just about anything on offer and ending the decade with a (bad) horror film about a man-eating tree. There were signs of a revival with a tough, nasty cable TV movie called *Jailbreakers*, one of a series based on 1950s' drive-in movies. There are echoes of *Pretty Poison* in a film that has no surplus footage and a devastating kick in the tail. Friedkin returned to cinema features, but the two that followed were overblown and uninteresting. He married/divorced actresses Jeanne Moreau and Lesley-Anne Down (fighting a bitter legal battle with Down over the custody of their son). Currently married to studio executive Sherry Lansing.

1967: Good Times. 1968: The Birthday Party. The Night They Raided Minsky's. 1970: The Boys in the Band. 1971: The French Connection. 1973: The Exorcist. 1977: Sorcerer (GB: The Wages of Fear). 1978: The Brink's Job. 1980: Cruising. 1983: Deal of the Century. 1985: To Live and Die in LA. 1986: Rampage (released 1992). CAT Squad/Stalking Danger (TV). 1988: CAT Squad: Python Wolf (TV). 1990: The Guardian. 1994: Jailbreakers (TV). Blue Chips. 1995: Jade. 1997: 12 Angry Men (TV). 1999 Rules of Engagement

FULLER, Samuel 1911-1997

Fuller's raw energy carried him on into the 1980s when many of his American contemporaries had fallen by the wayside. Perhaps the Joe McCarthy of Hollywood film-making, seemingly radically opposed to communism or anything that he saw as threatening the traditional

American way of life and the values it should have, Fuller was nonetheless much more considerable as a film-maker than, say, Russ Meyer, in whom one can see some similarities. Fuller's strongest and most fluid work lies in his war films, from *Steel Helmet* and *Fixed Bayonets!* (both featuring Gene Evans) all the way to the recent *The Big Red One*, including *Hell and High Water* (silly, but tremendously tense and exciting) and *Merrill's Marauders*. *Park Row* (again with Gene Evans) is interesting in that it reflects Fuller's own journalistic background (he was once supposed to be the youngest crime reporter in New York) and there are powerfully rough-edged moments in *Pick-Up on South Street* and *Underworld USA*, although nothing much else in Fuller's *oeuvre* is worthy of note. As it had been so long since Fuller had made a film of any merit, *The Big Red One*, filmed in 1978 but released in 1980, came as a splendidly welcome surprise. Boasting a most restrained performance by Lee Marvin, it's a good example of how Hollywood could have moved with the times had the studio system stayed intact. The film gains strength as it goes on, and shows a tremendous grasp of the story as a unit. One felt it would probably be Fuller's last film, but he pitched himself enthusiastically into fresh projects

The book of the film. Cigar-chewing American director Samuel **Fuller** consults the script of his 1982 venture, *White Dog*.

Canadian Sidney **Furie** pictured near the beginning of his directorial career, while making the Cliff Richard musical *The Young Ones* in 1961.

for Furie fans to shout about in recent years. After an interesting start in his native country, Furie hit a hot streak in the 1960s after coming to Britain. The unexpectedly big success of the first major Cliff Richard musical, *The Young Ones*, chock-full of youthful get-up-and-go, in which Furie's lively camera kept pace with the (considerable) tempo of the film, was its director's launching pad. He continued well with two portraits of teenage restlessness, *The Boys* and *The Leather Boys*, then hit it big at the box-office again with the first of the Harry Palmer thrillers, *The Ipcress File*. The international success of this film led Furie to go to America, where he made the much-underrated *The Appaloosa* (in Britain *Southwest to Sonora*) with its livid atmosphere and human values respectively intensified and uplifted by Russell Metty's brilliant Technicolor photography. During this film, Furie's penchant for shooting from behind, beneath or through various objects placed in front of the camera becomes noticeable for the first time. It was to mar most of his subsequent work, although one film noticeably free from such irritating trickery is *The Lawyer*, a stark, straightforward thriller on which Barry Newman's TV series *Petrocelli* was later based. Furie's films since then have been mainly poor, some going straight to video. Exceptions have been *The Entity*, a powerful story of the supernatural, whose sense of unease was suited to, and heightened by Furie's furtive camera; and the first two *Iron Eagle* films, distinguished by surging aeral action scenes, if not by Furie's dilogue, as he returned to the screenplaywriting with which he had dabbled earlier in his career.

in the 1980s, and continued to act with vigour in cameo roles in other directors' films. Married (second) actress Christa Lang.

1949: I Shot Jesse James. 1950: The Baron of Arizona. Steel Helmet. 1951: Fixed Bayonets! 1952: Park Row. 1953: Pick-Up on South Street. 1954. Hell and High Water. 1955: House of Bamboo. 1957: China Gate. Run of the Arrow. Forty Guns. 1958: Verboten! 1959: The Crimson Kimono. 1960: Underworld USA. 1962. Merrill's Marauders. 1963: Shock Corridor. 1964: The Naked Kiss. 1967: Shark! (released 1970). †The Meanest Men in the West (TV. Released to cinemas 1976). 1972: Dead Pigeon on Beethoven Street. 1980: The Big Red One. 1982: White Dog. 1984: Thieves After Dark. 1988: Street of No Return.

FURIE, Sidney J. 1933-

Although I stayed faithful to this small, dark, intense Canadian director when many critics had written him off, it must be admitted that there hasn't been much

1957: A Dangerous Age. 1959: A Cool Sound from Hell. 1960: The Snake Woman. 1961: Doctor Blood's Coffin. During One Night. Three on a Spree. The Young Ones (US: Wonderful to be Young). 1962: The Boys. 1963: The Leather Boys. 1964: Wonderful Life (US: Swingers' Paradise). 1965: The Ipcress File. 1966: The Appaloosa (GB: Southwest to Sonora). 1967: The Naked Runner. 1968: The Lawyer. 1970: Little Fauss and Big Halsy. 1972: Lady Sings the Blues. 1973: Hit! 1974: Sheila Levine is Dead and Living in New York. 1976: Gable and Lombard. 1977: The Boys in Company C. 1982: The Entity. 1984: Purple Hearts: A Vietnam Love Story. 1985: Iron Eagle. 1987: Superman IV: The Quest for Peace. 1988: Iron Eagle II. 1991: The Taking of Beverly Hills. 1992: Ladybugs. 1994: Star Legion. 1995: Iron Eagle IV. 1996: Hollow Point. The Rage. 1997: Top of the World. 1999: The Collectors

GANCE, Abel 1889-1981

Tremendously innovative, this French director was a pioneer of cinema techniques, with something of a 'Napoleon fixation'. An actor-writer in French films from 1909, he had formed his own production company by 1911, the year he made his first short films. By 1915, he was already experimenting with expanding the resources of the infant cinema, with the use of distorting lenses in fantasy scenes in *La folie du Docteur Tube*. In 1926, he patented Polyvision, a triple-image process used in his own mammoth *Napoléon*, which has recently been revived with great success. Further Gance ideas patented include Perspective Sonore (a forerunner of stereophonic sound) used in *Napoléon Bonaparte* (1934) and Pictographe, a unique illusion formula conveying the impression of spectacular sets. Gance, in fact, was ahead of the field in most things, especially movement of the camera, shooting action from moving trucks, the backs of horses, swinging pendulums, or motorized tripod-heads, or with cameras suspended from wires — all adding to the epic sweep of his more spectacular films and the intimate intensity of their action. But always he was subject to interference from the 'front-office' whose tenants doubted the box-office value of Gance's innovations; the doubters finally began to get on top of him with the coming of sound, when several of his films were released in versions other than he would have wished, and Gance was forced to work according to the studio's demands. But he kept on making films, often about his favourite subject, Napoleon Bonaparte, until the early 1970s. Before sound, Gance had already given the world his greatest films: the three-hour anti-war film *J'accuse*, the thriller *La dixième symphonie*, the fascinating railway-set *La roue* (the latter two films built up on Gance's capacity to use montage and tight editing to suggest events and atmospheres) and of course *Napoléon*. This is a film rich in cinematic power: not surprisingly, perhaps, it was years before all its subtler virtues were recognized, many of them concealed beneath the sensational impact made by Polyvision, which in retrospect adds less to the film's impact than Gance's own skills.

1911: *Le digue, ou: Pour sauver la Hollande. *Le nègre blanc. II y a des pieds au plafond. 1912: *Le masque d'horreur. *Le pierre philosophe. 1915: *Un drame au château d'acre, ou: Les morts reviennent-ils? *L'énigme de dix heures. *La folie du Docteur Tube. 1916: La femme inconnue. L'heroïsme de Paddy. La fleur des ruines. Le fou de la falaise. Ce que les flots racontent. Strass et Cie. Le périscope. Barbe-Rousse. Fioriture, ou: La source de la beauté. Les gaz mortels, ou: Le brouillard sur la ville. 1917: Le droit à la vie. La zone de la mort. Mater Dolorosa. 1918: La dixième symphonie (GB & US: The 10th Symphony). J'accuse. Ecce homo (unfinished). 1921: La roue. 1923: Au secours! 1926: Napoléon. 1928: *Marines. *Cristaux. 1930: La fin du monde. 1932: Mater Dolorosa (remake). 1933: Poliche. †Le maître de forges. 1934: †La dame aux camélias. Napoléon Bonaparte (abridged version of 1926 film, with sound added). 1935: Le roman d'un jeune homme pauvre. Lucrezia Borgia. Jerôme Perreau, héros des barricades (US: The Queen and the Cardinal). 1936: Le voleur de femmes (and Italian version). Un grand amour de Beethoven (US: The Life and Loves of Beethoven). 1937: J'accuse (remake. GB: L'Accuse. US: That They May Live). 1938: Louise. Le paradis perdu (GB: Paradise Lost. US: Four Flights to Love). 1939: *Profil de la France. Christophe Colomb (unfinished). 1940: La Vénus aveugle. 1942: Le capitaine Fracasse (and Italian version). 1944: Manolete (unfinished). 1953: *Le quatorze juillet. 1954: La tour de Nèsle. 1959: Austerlitz (GB: Battle of Austerlitz). 1962: Cyrano et D'Artagnan. 1965: Marie Tudor (TV). 1971: Bonaparte et la révolution (re-edited version of 1926 film with new prologue).

GARNETT, Tay (William Taylor Garnett) 1895-1977
Rugged American director whose films ranged far and wide, parallelling his own preoccupations with driving, flying and sailing — he once went round the world on his yawl Athene. The heroines in his films were usually sparky, and sometimes deadly; the men were virile but sometimes none too bright. Garnett was a craftsman and, if you might not rely on him to do things brilliantly, at least you knew that he'd do them well. His peak period was 1937 to 1948. There's nothing of great note outside this period, save for One Way Passage, and perhaps China Seas, but then the latter film did have Gable, Harlow, Beery and photography by Ray June. Garnett in his twenties was a flying instructor who wrote in his spare time, and did occa-

sional stunt work for silent comedies. Then in 1920 Hal Roach took him on as one of his legion of gag-men. He began contributing to scenarios from 1922, and turned director in 1928. Garnett soon proved himself an expert at rip-roaring action films with veins of humour and exotic locations, although comedies, romances – tears have seldom been jerked with such polish as in One Way Passage (suave criminal William Powell enjoying doomed romance with dying Kay Francis) or The Valley of Decision, a beautifully structured Greer Garson epic – and war films were also packed into his traveller's carpetbag. The Postman Always Rings Twice is the definitive version of James M Cain's heady noir tale – full of unforgettable images. A Connecticut Yankee in King Arthur's Court was directed with spirit, and tremendously enjoyable, especially when Bing Crosby, Cedric Hardwicke and William Bendix were singing Busy Doin' Nothin'. Surprisingly, it was the last good film Garnett made. The greatest triumph of his later years was his adaptation and direction of the stage play from Helene Hanff's book 84 Charing Cross Road. His first and third (of three, all divorced) wives were actresses Patsy Ruth Miller and Mari Aldon.

1928: Celebrity. The Spieler (GB: The Spellbinder). 1929: The Flying Fool. †Oh, Yeah! (GB: No Brakes). 1930: Her Man. Officer O'Brien. 1931: Bad Company. 1932: One Way Passage. Prestige. Okay America! (GB: The Penalty of Fame). 1933: †S.O.S. Iceberg. Destination Unknown. 1935: China Seas. Professional Soldier. She Couldn't Take It (GB: Woman Tamer). 1937: Love Is News. Slave Ship. Stand-In. 1938: Trade Winds. Joy of Living. 1939: Eternally Yours. 1940: Slightly Honorable. Seven Sinners. 1941: Cheers for Miss Bishop. 1942: My Favorite Spy. 1943: The Cross of Lorraine. Bataan. 1944: Mrs Parkington. 1945: The Valley of Decision. 1946: The Postman Always Rings Twice. 1947: Wild Harvest. 1948: A Connecticut Yankee in King Arthur's Court (GB: A Yankee in King Arthur's Court). 1950: The Fireball. Cause for Alarm! 1951: Soldiers Three. 1952: One Minute to Zero. 1953: Main Street to Broadway. 1954: The Black Knight. 1955: †Seven Wonders of the World. 1960: A Terrible Beauty (US: The Night Fighters). 1963: Cattle King (GB: Guns of Wyoming). 1970: The Delta Factor. 1972: Challenge To Be Free. 1973: Timber Tramp.

GILBERT, Lewis 1920-
Recent critics have been unkind to this

British director, railing at the lack of authenticity in his war films, which are the core of an interesting career. At any rate, such films as Reach for the Sky and Carve Her Name with Pride are winningly acted, thrilling and moving, whatever their deeper values, and they and several other Gilbert war films were a notable booster to buoyant box-office receipts for British films in the 1950s. It was noticeable that when, many years later, in times of the new cinema 'freedom', Gilbert did make a war film that was grimly authentic and only for those with strong stomachs (Operation Daybreak), it was neither very entertaining nor very successful. In fact, until he began to slip from 1970, Gilbert did make films that were generally popular with audiences and critics alike, and very good entertainment value. He was a child actor who became an assistant director at Denham Studios while acting there in the late 1930s. With war, he joined the RAF and was attached to the US Air Corps Film Unit. Invalided out in 1944, Gilbert joined the Gaumont-British Instructional Unit and began to direct short films, moving to features (via films for children) in the late 1940s. He only really ever made four kinds of films: thrillers; films about children and teenagers; war films; and one or two comedies. The thrillers run from the early 1950s to the James Bond extravaganzas of 25 years later. The comedies are very engaging, especially Time Gentlemen Please and The Admirable Crichton. These are sunny, agreeable films, a relaxation if you will from the rigours of war into which Gilbert plunged himself in 1953 with Albert RN, followed by The Sea Shall Not Have Then, Reach for the Sky, Carve Her Name with Pride, Sink the Bismarck! and Light Up the Sky, all within eight years. Of the 'youngster' films, Cosh Boy was a vicious thriller which gained some notoriety when it got an early 'X' certificate from the British censor, Johnny on the Run a likeable romp with real characters, and A Cry from the Streets, which looks far less realistic now than it did then, a sort of combination of the two — delinquent schoolchildren and well-meaning welfare offers. One film that stands apart from the rest, although it also involved teenagers, is The Greengage Summer, a beautiful (and beautifully photographed) drama about the pains of Growing Up. Alfie, another comedy, albeit with black undertones, was another monster success, but then Gilbert seemed to lose his touch. The Adventurers was deplorable rubbish and it was followed by three extremely drippy romances, amidst more Bondery. After a four-year pause, Gilbert unexpectedly regained his standing in the industry with the award-winning *Educating Rita*, about an ordinary woman searching for education. British Oscars went to Michael Caine and Julie Walters. Later in the decade, there was another winning performance from Pauline Collins in Gilbert's equally popular *Shirley Valentine*.

*1944: *Sailors Do Care (D). 1945: *The Ten Year Plan (D). 1946: *Arctic Harvest (D). *Under One Roof. (D. Released 1949). 1947: *Fishing Grounds of the World (D). The Little Ballerina. 1950: Once a Sinner. 1951: There is Another Sun (US: Wall of Death). It's a Small World. Scarlet Thread. 1952: Emergency Call (US: Hundred Hour Hunt). Cosh Boy (US: The Slasher). Time Gentlemen Please. 1953: Johnny on the Run. Albert R.N. (US: Break to Freedom). 1954: The Good Die Young. The Sea Shall Not Have Them. 1955: Cast a Dark Shadow. 1956: Reach for the Sky. 1957: The Admirable Crichton (US: Paradise Lagoon). 1958: A Cry from the Streets. Carve Her Name with Pride. 1959: Ferry to Hong Kong. Sink the Bismarck! 1960: Light Up the Sky. 1961: The Greengage Summer (US: Loss of Innocence). 1962: HMS Defiant (US: Damn the Defiant!). 1964: The Seventh Dawn. 1966: Alfie. 1967: You Only Live Twice. 1970: The Adventurers. 1971: Friends. 1974: Paul and Michelle. 1975: Operation Daybreak. 1976: Seven Nights in Japan. 1977: The Spy Who Loved Me. 1979: Moonraker. 1983: Educating Rita. 1984: Not Quite Jerusalem. 1989: Shirley Valentine. 1991: Stepping Out. 1995: Haunted.*

GILLIAM, Terry 1940-

Genial American-born cartoonist, animator and, latterly, film director whose affable exterior conceals a macabre sense of fantasy humour, as perhaps befits a former member of the Monty Python team. Beginning his career as an illustrator for advertising agencies, Gilliam relocated to London in his early twenties, working as art director and cartoonist for a number of magazines, on one of which he met comedian/actor John Cleese, with whom he moved to the BBC in 1969 to become part of the team producing the innovative comedy series *Monty Python's Flying Circus*, for which Gilliam became resident animator and sometime on-screen performer. When the Pythons moved into films, Gilliam's opportunity to direct soon presented itself. His typically zany flourishes added to the crazy medieval world depicted in *Monty Python and the Holy Grail* before he made his solo directorial debut on the semi-Python *Jabberwocky*.

Although the film's mud and blood get in the way of its fun, Gilliam's pictorial flair was rarely seen to better advantage than here. Canoes are silhouetted against sunsets, boats paddle silkily across stagnant, misty lakes, and the princess tiptoes towards her hero through a flutter of nuns' handkerchieves. Such visual sensitivity was clearly suited to the cinema, and Gilliam continued with Python alumni in the quirky *Time Bandits*, before bringing out the way-out Orwellian fantasy *Brazil*. This is a considerable achievement, its terrors leavened by typically Gilliamesque streaks of surrealist humour. There was visual imagination a-plenty, too, in *The Adventures of Baron Munchausen*, but not a little tedium too. The film's commercial failure prompted Gilliam to try something more conventional in cinematic terms with *The Fisher King*; its story of two vagrants, one a former history professor, the other an ex-disc jockey, won a supporting actress Oscar for Mercedes Ruehl and re-established Gilliam's reputation. He was thus able to return to more outlandish themes with the futuristic fantasy *Twelve Monkeys* which, despite a mixed critical reception, performed capably at the box-office.

*1975: †Monty Python and the Holy Grail. 1977: Jabberwocky. *The Miracle of Flight. 1981: Time Bandits. 1984: Brazil. 1987: The Adventures of Baron Munchausen. 1991: The Fisher King. 1995: Twelve Monkeys. 1998: Fear and Loathing in Las Vegas.*

GILLIAT, Sidney 1908-

British director who worked in harness with Frank Launder *(qv)*; at first they were writers, then producer-directors from 1942. They enjoyed a deserved run of success for more than a decade with a fascinating variety of largely indigenous entertainment, but from 1955, both men were making films on a lower plane. Strangely enough, both entered the film industry in 1928. Gilliat's first assignment was as junior assistant to Walter Mycroft (1891-1959), later to direct a few broad comedies but at that time scenario chief at British International Pictures. He was a title writer (as was Launder) within the year and a fully fledged screenplay-writer by 1931. He and Launder worked on the same film for the first time in 1933 with *Facing the Music*, just after Gilliat had written his best screenplay to date, for *Rome Express*. But the period of their greatest success starts with 1936; then they co-wrote *Seven Sinners*, following it with another train-based thriller, Hitchcock's *The Lady Vanishes*, which also saw

the felicitous invention by Launder and Gilliat of Charters and Caldicott (played by Basil Radford and Naunton Wayne), two upper-class bumbling Englishmen more interested in the state of the Test Match than a corpse in the corridor. The characters appeared in several subsequent films, including the partners' first two films together as co-directors, *Partners in Crime* (appropriately!) and *Millions Like Us*. After this, the two men branched out on their own as separate directors, although continuing to write together. Many of their films benefit from the presence of Alastair Sim, whom they had encountered in the 'Inspector Hornleigh' films (based on a successful radio series). Sim had a featured role in Gilliat's first solo effort, *Waterloo Road*, which featured a famous fist fight between John Mills and Stewart Granger. *The Rake's Progress* was long but cleverly made, and held together by the limpid performance of Lilli Palmer, while Sim was in his element as an idiosyncratic police inspector in *Green for Danger*. With *State Secret*, which is alive with atmosphere, *Danger* is probably Gilliat's best film from a directorial point of view. Dark deeds are afoot at a wartime London hospital, and few will avoid a shiver as the killer (and the camera) closes in on his next victim. It is, at the same time, a wry, classic example of the comedy-thriller, to some extent explored by Launder and Gilliat in their train films. Gilliat followed it with *London Belongs to Me* (Richard Attenborough in his deprived-youth guise), which teems with rich characterizations. After the thriller *State Secret*, Gilliat actually made Gilbert and Sullivan's dull life story and repetitive operettas entertaining, and rounded off the period with *The Constant Husband*, a sparkling comedy with Rex (Rake) Harrison as an amnesiac who discovers he appears to be married to several wives. A later highlight of Gilliat's too-sparse career as a director was the black comedy of would-be lechery, *Only Two Can Play*, with Peter Sellers as the randy Welsh librarian.

*1929: †*The Tryst. 1942: †*Partners in Crime. 1943: †Millions Like Us. 1944: Waterloo Road. 1945: The Rake's Progress (US: The Notorious Gentleman). 1946: Green for Danger. 1948: London Belongs To Me (US: Dulcimer Street). 1950: State Secret (US: The Great Manhunt). 1953: The Story of Gilbert and Sullivan (US: The Great Gilbert and Sullivan). 1954: The Constant Husband. 1956: Fortune is a Woman (US: She Played with Fire). 1959: Left, Right and Centre. 1961: Only Two Can Play. 1966: †The Great St Trinian's Train Robbery.*

Last-minute instructions from John **Gilling** to Oliver Reed while making *The Scarlet Blade* in 1963.

1972: Endless Night.

GILLING, John 1912-1984

There are some very bad films in this British director's record, and one can only regret in particular the years he spent working on upper-budget rubbish for Warwick-Columbia, finding his true metier late in his career — and too late, for the British horror cycle was already half-over — when he started to work for Hammer Studios in the 1960s. But he should have known: for Gilling started his screen credits as a prolific writer of screenplays (after working as a Hollywood stuntman, and as assistant director with England's B.I.P. Studios in the 1930s) and his most effective stuff is almost always sinister and shivery: *House of Darkness, The Man in Black, Guilt is My Shadow, Blackout*. As a director in the British cinema of the 1940s and 1950s, Gilling was a second-feature man. Most of these are par for the quota-quickie course, with only one or two — *No Trace, The Voice of Merrill, The Embezzler* — showing above-average touches.

Came the mid-1950s and the association with the Warwick Company: Cinema Scope and Technicolor slices of utter hokum he could do nothing with, although on one or two occasions he only had his own screenplay to blame. Things started looking up with *The Flesh and the Fiends*, about Burke and Hare, and *The Shadow of the Cat* was also good — very suspenseful, with a well-marshalled cat actor stealing the spotlight. Hammer took Gilling into their fear factory, and he co-wrote *The Gorgon*, then directed *The Night Caller* (not for Hammer), and — back-to-back, by the look of it; at least they share the same churchyard if not the same corpses — *The Reptile* and *The Plague of the Zombies*, in which genuine nerve-ends of horror are touched. In 1974, Gilling moved to Spain, and made only one film thereafter. Nephew of prolific silent and early sound director W.P. Kellino (W.P. Gislingham. 1873-1958).

1948: Escape from Broadmoor. 1949: A Matter of Murder. 1950: †Blackout (uncredited). The Quiet Woman. No Trace. 1952: The Frightened Man. Mother Riley Meets the Vampire (US: Vampire Over London). The Voice of Merrill (US: Murder Will Out). 1953: Recoil. Three Steps to the Gallows (US: White Fire). Deadly Nightshade. Escape by Night. 1954: Double Exposure. The Embezzler. †Destination Milan. The Gilded Cage. 1955: Tiger by the Tail. 1956: The Gamma People. Odongo. §Zarak. 1957: Interpol (US: Pickup Alley). High Flight. 1958: The Man Inside. 1959: Idle on Parade (US: Idol on Parade). The Bandit of Zhobe. The Challenge (US: It Takes a Thief). 1960: The Flesh and the Fiends (US: Mania). Fury at Smugglers Bay. 1961: The Shadow of the Cat. The Pirates of Blood River. 1963: The Scarlet Blade (US: The Crimson Blade). Panic. 1965: The Brigand of Kandahar. The Night Caller (US: Blood Beast from Outer Space). 1966: The Plague of the Zombies. The Reptile. Where the Bullets Fly. 1967: The Mummy's Shroud. 1974: The Devil's Cross.

§ As Associate Director

GODARD, Jean-Luc 1930-

Avant-garde, French-born (of Swiss parentage) film-maker, much idolized by the intelligentsia. Godard appears to have communicated the seemingly wilfully obscure narrative of many of his films to numbers of those who write about his work. It seems that so many people have tied themselves in knots trying to explain what makes Godard so distinctive a director that probably only the man himself really knows. Clearly he enjoys playing games with his audiences by juggling time, space and segments of the story, inserting scenes which seemingly fragment such plots as Godard films have, without adding anything to them. Nonetheless, whether he delights or irritates you, Godard sits securely in the front rank of screen originals, and it is good that he succeeded in rejoining the mainstream of French cinema in 1980 after more than ten years' self-exile to its fringes. He began writing on the cinema in 1950, contributing to the famous French film magazine *Cahiers du Cinéma* from 1952 until 1965. His films, although at first only shorts, aroused critical interest almost from the beginning. His first feature, *Breathless*, was a murder thriller centring on the characters of the killer (Jean-Paul Belmondo) and his girl (Jean Seberg) who betrays him. The misogyny implicit in this film was suggested in several later Godard pictures, even though he married (and later divorced) two of his leading ladies, Anna Karina and Anne Wiazemsky. His political views (communist but anti-Soviet) also make themselves noticed in some of his movies, especially *Le petit soldat*, *Les carabiniers* and *La chinoise*. In the midst of these, Godard made one of his most accessible and fascinating films, *Alphaville*, a science-fiction thriller (at least on the surface) with Eddie Constantine in his familiar screen persona of the dog-eared detective Lemmy Caution. Owing something to *Metropolis* and *1984*, the film is technically Godard's most skilful, anticipating Richard Fleischer's *Soylent Green* by some eight years in its use of present-day buildings as grey, impersonal monoliths of the future. Godard used colour brilliantly to convey the naked violence of *Pierrot le fou* (again with Belmondo) and the apocalyptic *Week-End*, but after an abortive trip to America to make an (unfinished) film, Godard retreated to the fringe cinema of heavy left-wing politics. He returned to mainstream film-making in 1980 after more than a decade away and won the best film award at the Venice Festival in 1983 for *Prénom: Carmen*. Nonetheless the quality of his films has been much more variable in recent times compared to his heyday of the 1960s, including a disastrous modernised sideshoot of *King Lear*. He was awarded a César for lifetime achievement in 1986.

1954: **Opération Béton*. 1955: **Une femme coquette*. 1957: **Tous les garçons s'appellent Patrick*. 1958: **Charlotte et son Jules*. †**Une histoire d'eau*. 1959: *A bout de souffle (GB & US: Breathless)*. 1960: *Le petit soldat (released 1963. GB: The Little Soldier)*. 1961: *Une femme est une femme*. †*The Seven Deadly Sins (US:*

Seven Capital Sins). 1962: *Vivre sa vie (GB: It's My Life. US: My Life to Live)*. †*RoGoPaG*. 1963: *Le mépris (GB & US: Contempt)*. *Les carabiniers (GB: The Soldiers)*. †*Les plus belles escroqueries du monde (episode: 'Le grand escroc', cut from film and shown separately)*. 1964: *Bande à part (GB: The Outsiders. US: Band of Outsiders)*. *Une femme mariée (GB: A Married Woman. US: The Married Woman)*. **Reportage sur Orly (D)*. †*Paris vu par (GB & US: Six in Paris)*. 1965: *Alphaville (subtitled. Une étrange aventure de Lemmy Caution)*. *Pierrot le fou*. 1966: *Masculin-Féminin. Made in USA*. 1967: *Two or Three Things I Know About Her/Deux ou trois choses que je sais d'elle*. †*The Oldest Profession. La chinoise*. †*Far from Vietnam. Week-End. Le gai savoir*. 1968: *Un film comme les autres. One Plus One/Sympathy for the Devil. One A.M. (unfinished)*. 1969: *Amore e rabbia/Vangelo 70 (Godard's episode made in 1967). British Sounds (US: See You at Mao)*. †*Pravda*. †*Le vent d'est (US: Wind from the East)*. †*Lotte in Italia (US: Struggle in Italy)*. 1970: *Jusqu'à la victoire (US: 'Til Victory)*. 1971: †*Vladimir et Rosa*. 1972: *Tout va bien. A Letter to Jane*. 1975: †*Comment ça va. Numéro deux*. †*Ici et ailleurs*. 1980: *Sauve qui peut/La vie/Every Man for Himself*. 1982: *Passion*. 1983: *Prénom: Carmen*. 1984: *Je vous salue, Mary (US: Hail, Mary)*. 1985: *Detective*. 1986: *Grandeur et décadence d'un petit commerce du cinéma (TV)*. 1987: *+Aria. King Lear. Soigne ta droite*. 1990: *Nouvelle vague*. 1991: *Allemagne neuf zéro*. 1993: *Hélas pour moi*. 1995: *Les enfants jouent à la Russie*. 1996: *Histoires du cinéma*. 1997: *For Ever Mozart*.

GODFREY, Peter 1899-1970

British-born actor and playwright who drifted into film direction almost by accident. After a career acting in British films of the 1930s (e.g. *Good Morning, Boys!* in 1936), he went to Hollywood as an actor (e.g. in *Blockade*, 1938). There, it was discovered that he had directed on stage in England and made two small films, so he was given one or two minor directorial assignments in between movie roles. In 1944, Warners gave him a contract as a director, and he worked for them for seven years, directing almost all of their second-string stars: Raymond Massey, Peter Lorre, Jane Wyman, Dennis Morgan and Jack Carson, Virginia Mayo, Alexis Smith, Ronald Reagan, David Brian, Faye Emerson, Eleanor Parker and Sydney Greenstreet. None of Godfrey's films is very good but some of them still lurk in the corners of one's memory, especially those

in which the heroine is pursued by an unknown evil, often a victim of the leading male character: *The Two Mrs Carrolls*, *Cry Wolf* and *The Woman in White*. Although often stilted and awkward, these films have an eerie ambience which could only stem from the director. Unfortunately, they were not well received at the time — Humphrey Bogart and Errol Flynn did not present popular public images as wife-killers, killing the box-office stone dead instead — and Godfrey did not get a chance to explore the vein further, save perhaps in his last film, *Please Murder Me!*, with Angela Lansbury and Raymond Burr, a minor but not unworthy swansong to a minor but not unworthy film career. He worked prolifically in television in the 1950s before retiring in 1964.

1930: *Thread o' Scarlet*. 1931: *Down River*. 1939: *The Lone Wolf's Spy Hunt (GB: The Lone Wolf's Daughter)*. 1941: *Unexpected Uncle*. 1942: *Highways by Night*. 1944: *Make Your Own Bed*. 1945: *Hotel Berlin. Christmas in Connecticut (GB: Indiscretion)*. 1946: *One More Tomorrow*. 1947: *The Two Mrs Carrolls. Escape Me Never. That Hagen Girl. Cry Wolf. The Woman in White*. 1948: *The Decision of Christopher Blake*. 1949: *One Last Fling. The Girl from Jones Beach*. 1950: *Barricade. The Great Jewel Robber. He's a Cockeyed Wonder*. 1952: *One Big Affair*. 1956: *Please Murder Me!*

GOLAN, Menahem 1929-

A pioneer of the Israeli film industry, if not among its greatest directors, Golan has, mostly in company with his cousin Yoram Globus, led an eventful and film-filled career. Born in then-Palestine, Golan served in the Israeli Air Force in its late forties' infancy, then studied directing in London, and, back in Israel, became a theatre director. Deciding to branch out into films, Golan studied film-making at New York University, then worked as an assistant director at Hollywood's New World Studios, before returning to Israel to direct his first film at the age of 34. The film, *El Dorado*, was a major success, as was its follow-up, *Sallah*. Golan's work in his native country at this period is among his best, including the ingratiating *Lupo*, a warm and witty comedy about a cart driver overwhelmed and overtaken by modern life. Early ventures into international filming, though, such as the Audie Murphy-George Sanders thriller *Trunk to Cairo*, and *What's Good for the Goose*, an embarrassing comedy for Norman Wisdom, were dismal failures. It was with exploitative action films, however, that the Golan-Globus partnership flour-

French director Jean-Luc **Godard,** shot against a background of French pop star Sylvie.

ished, first under their own steam, then as the major shareholders in Cannon Films, for whom Golan directed such simplistic adventure films as *The Delta Force*. From 1981, in fact, producing was to dominate his career. With and without Globus (they went their separate ways in 1989) he produced, co-produced or executive produced dozens of films between 1975 and 1990. Ventures into direction in this period were, on the whole, poorly received and performed disappointingly at the box-office. Golan, though, has continued to direct in recent times, his most impressive film being the unheralded *Silent Victim*, the true story of a pregnant woman whose husband sues her after her suicide attempt kills their unborn child.

1963: *El Dorado*. 1964: *Sallah*. 1966: *Trunk to Cairo*. 1968: *Tevye and His Seven Daughters*. 1969: *What's Good for the Goose*. *Margo*. 1970: *Lupo*. *Malkat hakvish*. 1971: *Aliza the Policeman*. *Queen of the Road*. 1972: *Habricha el Hashemesh*. *Escape to the Sun*. 1973: *Kazablan*. 1975: *Lepke*. *Diamonds*. 1977: *Entebbe: Operation Thunderbolt*. 1978: *Agenten kennen keine Tranen/The Uranium Conspiracy*. 1979: *The Magician of Lublin*. 1980: *The Apple*. 1981: *Enter the Ninja*. 1983: *Over the Brooklyn Bridge*. 1986: *The Delta Force*. 1987: *Over the Top*. 1988: *Hanna's War*. 1989: *Mack the Knife*. 1991: *Silent Victim*. 1992: *Hit the Dutchman*. 1997: *The Versace Murder*. 1998: *Armstrong*. *Breaking the Silence*.

GOLD, Jack 1930-

One thinks of Jack Gold as one of the better British directors of the 1960s onwards, although in truth, when one looks at his record, it is not as good as it might be. His first features were two strong but not-too-commercial vehicles for Nicol Williamson, and therein lies the weakness of those Gold films which aren't actually failures: the public just doesn't seem to have paid (very much, anyway) to see his work. Two of his films, *Who?* and *The Sailor's Return*, ended up on television; *Man Friday* and *The Medusa Touch* both lurched into the ridiculous, and the disappointing *Aces High* never carved its portraits of RAF heroes in flesh and blood. One is left with Gold's successful filming of that very funny black-comedy play *The National Health*, and his TV work, which is much more distinguished, including *Catholics* and the much-praised portrait of the flamboyant homosexual Quentin Crisp, *The Naked Civil Servant*, which won awards for both its director and star John Hurt. Later, though, Gold made a better version of *Little Lord*

Fauntleroy than one had any right to expect in this day and age, eliciting performances from Alec Guinness, Ricky Schroder and Connie Booth that are sincere enough to make the creaky old story actually work. This was originally made for American television — although it looks well enough on cinema screens — and it may be that Gold now has such a secure grasp on small-screen mastery that he could well stay in and around this medium. *Fauntleroy* was immensely successful in America, as *The Naked Civil Servant* had been. In the 1980s Gold received praise for the prestige TV movies *Murrow*, *Escape from Sobibor* and *The Tenth Man*. But subsequent offerings for TV were less successful and he has filmed only occasionally in more recent times.

1958: **Happy As Can Be (originally for TV)*. 1959: **The Visit*. 1960: *Living Jazz*. 1966: **The Snowdon Aviary (originally for TV)*. 1968: *The Bofors Gun*. 1969: *The Reckoning*. 1973: *Catholics (TV)*. *The National Health*. 1974: *Who?* 1975: *The Naked Civil Servant (TV)*. *Man Friday*. 1976: *Aces High*. 1978: *The Medusa Touch*. *The Sailor's Return (later TV)*. 1979: *Charlie Muffin (TV)*. 1980: *Little Lord Fauntleroy (TV) GB: cinemas)*. 1982: *Praying Mantis (TV)*. 1983: *Red Monarch (TV)*. *Good and Bad at Games (TV)*. 1984: *Sakharov*. 1985: *The Chain*. *Murrow (cable TV)*. 1987: *Escape from Sobibor (TV)*. 1988: *The Tenth Man (TV)*. *Stones for Ibarra (TV)*. 1989: *Ball Trap on the Côte Sauvage*. 1990: *The Rose and the Jackal (TV)*. 1991: *The Last Romantics (TV)*. 1994: *The Return of the Native (TV)*. 1997: *Mystery! Into the Blue (TV)*.

GOLDSTONE, James 1931-

Every time this American director seemed about to push his career up a notch or two, he blew it on the very next picture. Thus *A Man Called Gannon* and *Winning* were followed by *Red Sky at Morning* and *The Gang That Couldn't Shoot Straight* and some good TV movies in the mid-1970s by *Swashbuckler*. Goldstone seemed to have got it right in the late 1970s, when the very entertaining *Rollercoaster* was followed by his *Studs Lonigan*, by a long way the most interesting of television's 'Best Sellers' series. Then came *When Time Ran Out..*, a disaster movie that was truly a disaster for all concerned. His career had started with much promise: an assistant editor at 19 (he worked on Don Siegel's *Riot in Cell Block 11*), he was directing for television by 1957. He worked for most of the most successful series —including *The Fugitive*, *The Man from UNCLE*, *Rawhide* and

Perry Mason. Later he was entrusted with the pilot films for several series — *Star Trek* and *Ironside* among them —before making the move to feature films, notably *Winning* in 1969. He struck up a good working relationship with Paul Newman on that film, but it was unfortunate that the two men should have chosen to wait until *When Time Ran Out..*, to renew the teaming. The script was truly horrendous, and one cannot imagine how so many top stars agreed to appear in it, even for big money. In truth the direction was not all that much better, with Goldstone seemingly all at sea with camera placings and unable to make anything move with conviction (admittedly difficult with such cardboard, not to say risible characters). That was his last cinema film to date, and there have only been a few undistinguished TV movies since.

1966: *Scalplock (TV)*. 1967: *Code Name: Heraclitus (TV)*. *Ironside (TV)*. 1968: *Shadow over Elveron (TV)*. *Jigsaw (originally for TV)*. *A Man Called Gannon*. 1969: *Winning*. 1970: *Red Sky at Morning*. *Brother John*. *A Clear and Present Danger (TV)*. 1971: *The Gang That Couldn't Shoot Straight*. 1972: *They Only Kill Their Masters*. 1974: *Cry Panic (TV)*. *Dr Max (TV)*. *Things in Their Season (TV)*. 1975: *Journey from Darkness (TV)*. *Eric (TV)*. 1976: *Swashbuckler (GB: The Scarlet Buccaneer)*. 1977: *Rollercoaster*. 1980: *When Time Ran Out...* 1981: *Kent State (TV)*. 1983: *Rita Hayworth: The Love Goddess (TV)*. 1984: *Calamity Jane (TV)*. 1986: *Dreams of Gold: The Mel Fisher Story (TV)*. 1988: *Earth*Star Voyager (TV)*.

GOODWINS, Leslie 1899-1969

Any fan of Mexican Spitfire romps, Leon Errol comedies, or the farces of Wally Brown and Art Carney (Z-movie rivals to Abbott and Costello) will be familiar with the work of Leslie Goodwins. The British-born director was well at home in low-brow, low-budget comedies, having been a comedy performer himself, first on the London stage, then in Christie comedies when he went to Hollywood. His directing career only really stretches from 1936 to 1947, the heyday of the Hollywood second-feature: one is almost surprised that he didn't storm back to England in 1947, the year that country restarted its 'quota quickie' output. Goodwins' knockabout comedies and (occasional) thrillers were swallowed whole by wartime audiences; sometimes he even did wonders with shoddy material, as in *The Girl from Mexico* (the first of the 'Spitfire' series), *Pop Always Pays*, *Murder in the Blue Room* and *The Dragnet*. There were a few odds and ends after his RKO-Radio contract days were over, but most of them are pretty dire, and one is left with the conclusion that within the confines of a close-knit studio atmosphere, Goodwins was at least able to retain his enthusiasm, if only for the frenzied fun of the Spitfire vehicles, which one contemporary critic described as 'inspired slices of breakneck buffoonery'. Goodwins died at 69 after a bout with pneumonia, having worked prolifically in television after Hollywood had forgotten him.

1933: †*Thrown Out of Joint. *Heave Two. *Shakespeare — with Tin Ears. 1936: *One Live Ghost. *High Beer Pressure. *Dummy Ache. *Vocalising. With Love and Kisses. Deep South. *Framing Father. *Camp Meetin'. *Grandma's Boys. *Who's Looney Now? *Radiobarred. *Swing It! *A Wedtime Story. 1937: *Hillbilly Goat. *Lochs and Bonds. *Dumb's the Word. *Tramp Trouble. *Wrong Romance. *Should Wives Work? *Morning, Judge. *Edgar and Goliath. Anything for a Thrill. Headline Crasher. Young Dynamite. *Bad Housekeeping. *Harris in the Spring. *Mississippi Moods. *That Man Samson. 1938: *Ears of Experience. *False Roomers. *Kennedy's Castle. *Fool Coverage. *His Pest Friend. *The Jitters. Fugitives for a Night. Almost a Gentleman. Mr Doodle Kicks Off. Crime Ring. Tarnished Angel. *A Western Welcome. *Romancing Along. Twenty Girls and a Band. 1939: The Day the Bookies Wept. The Girl from Mexico. Sued for Libel. Mexican Spitfire. 1940: Millionaire Playboy (GB: Glamour Boy). Pop Always Pays. Mexican Spitfire Out West. Men Against the Sky. 1941: Let's Make Music. †They Met in Argentina. Parachute Battalion. Mexican Spitfire's Baby. 1942: Mexican Spitfire at Sea. Mexican Spitfire Sees a Ghost. Mexican Spitfire's Elephant. 1943: Ladies' Day. Silver Skates. The Adventures of a Rookie. Gals Inc. Mexican Spitfire's Blessed Event. Rookies in Burma. 1944: Casanova in Burlesque. The Singing Sherrif. Goin' to Town. Hi Beautiful (GB: Pass to Romance). Murder in the Blue Room. 1945: I'll Tell the World. The Mummy's Curse. What a Blonde! Radio Stars on Parade. An Angel Comes to Brooklyn. 1946: Genius at Work. Riverboat Rhythm. Vacation in Reno. 1947: The Dragnet. The Lone Wolf in London. 1948: *Pal's Return. *Bachelor Blues. 1949: *Put Some Money in the Pot. 1950: *Brooklyn Buckaroos. *Photo Phonies. 1951: *Punchy Pancho. *Lord Epping Returns. *Tinhorn Troubadors. *From Rogues to Riches. 1953: Gold Fever. 1954: Fireman Save My Child. †The Go-Getter. 1955: Paris Follies of 1956. 1965: *A Comedy

Tale of Fanny Hill. 1967: †Tammy and the Millionaire.

GORDON, Bert I. 1922-

Most makers of low-budget horror films with cheapish special effects are here today and gone tomorrow. The mystery and fascination of Bert I. Gordon is that he has been at it for so long. No matter how audiences stay away or critics sneer, Gordon just keeps on coming. And his films are favourites in the home movie market, now changing into the video boom. The titles are all catchpenny, of course, and one or two of the films Gordon has churned out over a near-30-year period are a little better than his other work might lead you to expect. The caverns in *The Spider* are actually dingy enough to make their hairy denizen seem quite revolting, and *Picture Mommy Dead* is a lively, ongoing shocker only spoiled by the central casting of Gordon's inexperienced daughter Susan. Gordon hasn't produced anything like a decent horror film since then, even though bigger stars are being attracted to feature in his films, which remain as saleable as ever to willing video buyers. Gordon has such lovely ideas, in fact, that one wonders what he might do if someone actually gave him sufficient money to see them properly brought to the screen. He sometimes also writes his own screenplays.

1955: King Dinosaur. 1957: The Beginning of the End. Cyclops. The Amazing Colossal Man. 1958: Attack of the Puppet People (GB: Six Inches Tall). War of the Colossal Beast (GB: The Terror Strikes). The Spider. 1960: The Boy and the Pirates. Tormented. 1962: The Magic Sword. 1965: Village of the Giants. 1966: Picture Mommy Dead. 1970: How to Succeed with Sex. 1972: Necromancy. 1973: The Mad Bomber. The Police Connection (later Detective Geronimo). 1976: The Food of the Gods. 1977: Empire of the Ants. 1981: The Coming. 1984: Let's Do It. 1986: The Big Bet. 1989: Satan's Princess. 1992: The Witching Hour.

GORDON, Michael 1909-1993

This American director was unlucky in that he fell foul of the McCarthy witch-hunt, but lucky in that he had a theatrical career to fall back on, and subsequently became one of the first unrepentent directors to regain favour, making some big box-office successes for the studio that had employed him ten years earlier. He began acting while at (Yale) university, but turned to direction on the stage after working on Broadway for a couple of years as actor/assistant stage manager.

Columbia gave him employment as dialogue director from 1939 and, in the war years, handed him a few second-feature thrillers to direct (which he did with some polish) before he returned to directing in the theatre for four years. On his return to the cinema, he directed some dark dramas and thrillers, bits of which still stick in the mind despite unsensational reviews. *The Web* had the benefit of Edmond O'Brien, Vincent Price, Ella Raines and William Bendix, while the brilliant *An Act of Murder* remains one of the cinema's great underrated films, almost unbearable in the pressure it puts on the viewer, who is hard put to keep watching the screen as Fredric March's fine acting and Gordon's intense direction turn the screw. The same team (Gordon, March and Florence Eldridge) combined on *Another Part of the Forest*, while *Woman in Hiding* and *The Lady Gambles*, although not as good as the March films, provide the opportunity for Ida Lupino and Barbara Stanwyck to play at the same kind of fever pitch. After all this high-pressure stuff, it was rather surprising to find Gordon making glossy comic battles-of-the-sexes for Universal when he returned to films in 1959. But *Pillow Talk* was a box-office blockbuster, and he found himself with more high-budget, high-polish entertainments. None was quite as successful, although *Boys' Night Out, For Love or Money, Move Over, Darling* (especially) and *A Very Special Favor* are all lively films with some funny moments. *Portrait in Black*, almost a spoof *film noir*, played straight, is the quintessential Universal/Ross Hunter/Lana Turner vehicle of its period. The neglected *Texas Across the River* is a very funny western comedy, but after the horrendous would-be comedy of *The Impossible Years* and *How Do I Love Thee?* Gordon did well to retreat to teaching the art of theatre, before such fond memories as we had left could fade away. He should not be confused with the English director Michael Gordon, whose only film was the Australian-made *Wherever She Goes* in 1949.

1942: Underground Agent. One Dangerous Night. Boston Blackie Goes Hollywood (GB: Blackie Goes Hollywood). 1943: Crime Doctor. 1947: The Web. 1948: Another Part of the Forest. An Act of Murder. 1949: The Lady Gambles. Woman in Hiding. 1950: Cyrano de Bergerac. 1951: 1 Can Get It for You Wholesale/Only the Best (GB: This Is My Affair). The Secret of Convict Lake. 1959: Pillow Talk. 1960: Portrait in Black. 1962: Boys' Night Out. 1963: For Love or Money. Move Over, Darling.1965: A Very Special Favor. 1966: Texas Across

the River. 1968: *The Impossible Years.*
1970: *How Do I Love Thee?*

GORDON, Stuart 1946-

American director who began making
films at 39, but quickly established himself in the horror field. His career followed much the same pattern as that of
his contemporary Brian Yuzna — science-
horror vehicles leaning heavily on ultra-
gory special effects. More recently, however, Gordon seems to be developing into
the more interesting director of the two:
his best films to date have been his first
and his last. Gordon had put himself on
the horror map with *Re-Animator*, an
outrageously gruesome but somewhat
stylish adaptation of a Frankenstein-style
story by H. P. Lovecraft about attempts to
revive the dead. Ironically it was Yuzna
who made the sequel (*Bride of Re-Animator*), while Gordon unfortunately made
From Beyond, a humourless and truly
tacky gorefest with a messy story about
brain-eating fish and sexual content that
qualified it more for the shady video market than anything else. Black humour and
yucky effects continued to mark Gordon's
work into the 1990s, although the more
interesting projects from his mind (both
of whose stories he co-wrote) were films
he didn't get to direct: *Honey, I Shrunk
the Kids* in 1989 and *Body Snatchers* in
1993. There were, however, two TV
chillers whose style made them more
engrossing than their content, suggesting
that Gordon was flexing his visual mus-

cles. The twin thrusts in his work reached
an interesting fusion in his 1996 burst of
galactic action, *Space Truckers*. Good-
natured and easily Gordon's best all-
round film, it's an all-action sci-fi comedy
(with awesome special effects) that careers
along like a runaway train. Sometimes
near the knuckle in typically dark Gordon
style, the whole film is still a blast — a
rocky but rewarding ride that makes you
wonder if Gordon might, after all, escape
his home on the video range.

1985: *Re-Animator.* 1986: *From Beyond.*
1987: *Dolls.* 1989: *Robot Jox/Robojox.*
1990: *Daughter of Darkness (TV).* 1991:
The Pit and the Pendulum. 1993:
Fortress. 1994: *Castle Freak.* 1995: *The
Sandkings (TV).* 1996: *Space Truckers.*

GOULDING, Edmund 1891-1959

London-born Goulding, who started as a
boy actor and emigrated to America after
service in World War I, became one of
Hollywood's finest showcasers of the talents of its leading actresses. His three
later Bette Davis vehicles in particular
show as deep an understanding of the
structuring of a story as of the structure
of a scene. All are tearjerkers and, thanks
to the director's subtle touches and his
skilful handling of the actresses involved,
all three are likely to make you weep
buckets. Goulding was a talented writer
and this proved his entree to Hollywood.
He wrote for over 30 films between 1919
and 1925 before making his directing

debut on *Sun-Up.* On his next, *Sally,
Irene and Mary,* he made the acquaintance of Joan Crawford, whom he was to
direct to great effect in the multi-star
Grand Hotel. Another star of that film
was Greta Garbo, whom Goulding had
also previously directed in her first version of the Anna Karenina story. The
Bette Davis association started on the
soapy *That Certain Woman* (1937),
Goulding's second film version of his own
story *The Trespasser,* which he had previously made under that latter title with
Gloria Swanson in 1929. But it is in *Dark
Victory, The Old Maid* and *The Great Lie*
that their partnership reached full flower.
These are consummate pieces of Hollywood craftsmanship that look deep into
human emotions and relationships — one
overlooks completely the rampaging
melodrama of their stories. Goulding later
directed the sensitive actress Dorothy
McGuire in the sentimental *Claudia* and
the beguiling *Mr 880.* But the 1940s were
times of changing tastes and, with the
post-war years, Goulding attempted
something different during his stay at
Twentieth Century-Fox in two Tyrone
Power vehicles, the suave *The Razor's
Edge,* and the black drama of sideshow
life *Nightmare Alley.* But he did not
achieve his ambition of winning a best
director Oscar nomination, even for *The
Razor's Edge,* which was actually nominated in the best film category.

1925: *Sun-Up. Sally, Irene and Mary.*
1926: *Paris (GB: Shadows of Paris).*
1927: *Women Love Diamonds.* 1928:
Love/Anna Karenina. 1929: *The Trespass-
er.* 1930: †*Paramount on Parade. The
Devil's Holiday.* 1931: *Reaching for the
Moon. The Night Angel.* 1932: *Blondie of
the Follies. Grand Hotel.* 1934: †*Holly-
wood Party (uncredited). Riptide.* 1935:
The Flame Within. 1937: *That Certain
Woman.* 1938: *White Banners. The Dawn
Patrol.* 1939: *Dark Victory. We Are Not
Alone. The Old Maid.* 1940: *'Til We Meet
Again.* 1941: *The Great Lie.* 1943: †*For-
ever and a Day. The Constant Nymph.
Claudia.* 1946: *The Razor's Edge. Of
Human Bondage.* 1947: *Nightmare Alley.*
1949: *Everybody Does It.* 1950: *Mr 880.*
1952: *We're Not Married.* 1953: *Down
Among the Sheltering Palms.* 1956:
Teenage Rebel. 1958: *Mardi Gras.*

GRAHAM, William A. 1928-

Although he has time and again produced
good work in the field of TV movies, this
American director has not achieved distinction with his films made for the bigger
screen, and his opportunities to establish
himself in the cinema now seem to have

Ready for the beheading. Director Stuart **Gordon** has fun with a prop from one of his gory horror films.

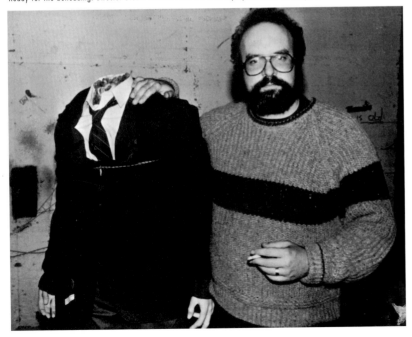

drawn to an end. The best of his work as seen by cinema audiences outside America, in fact, lies in those TV films that have been shown in cinemas. Graham studied to be a concert violinist for 12 years, but from the late 1950s began working on television, graduating to director by the early 1960s. He was soon at the top of his profession, being entrusted with many 'pilots' (introductory stories) for long-running series, including *The F.B.I.* and *The Big Valley*. There were also many episodes from such series as *Naked City, Route 66, The Fugitive, Ironside* and *The Name of the Game*. The latter, although running to 90 minutes (television time; actual time around 74 minutes) are not among Graham's best work as they were so frequently padded out to reach the required length. Of the TV movies shown in cinemas, *Police Story* is a fast-moving and absorbingly downbeat tale of police work, *Birds of Prey* had David Janssen, some spectacular helicopter work and a most unusual story, and *21 Hours at Munich* was better than almost anyone expected, Graham's fluid camerawork intensifying the suspense and excitement of the true-life hostage story, achieving some low-angle shots that really set the paces racing; he also got a rare attractive performance from Franco Nero. Of those TV movies by Graham that have remained confined to the small screen, the most interesting are *The Forgotten Man*, a poignant, well-made drama about a Vietnam veteran faced with more problems on his return than the men 25 years before in *The Best Years of Our Lives; Get Christie Love!*, a lively hokum thriller with an attractive black stuntwoman-heroine, Teresa Graves; and the two-part *The Amazing Howard Hughes* – one of the most impressive TV biopics – especially in its closing stages – yet made. The westerns – some of these also biopics – are among the most ambitious and interesting offerings of his later years.

1965: *The F.B.I.* (TV). *The Big Valley* (TV). 1966: *The Last Generation* (TV). *The Doomsday Flight* (TV. GB: cinemas). 1967: *The Intruders* (TV Shown in 1970). *The Outsider* (TV). *Waterhole No. 3* (GB: *Waterhole 3*). *Submarine X-1. The Legend of Custer* (TV). 1968: *Trial Run* (TV). *Perilous Voyage* (TV. Shown in 1976). 1969: *Then Came Bronson* (TV. GB: cinemas). *Change of Habit. Act of Piracy* (TV). 1970: *Marriage: Year One* (TV. Shown 1971). 1971: *The Forgotten Man* (TV). *Honky. Congratulations, It's a Boy!* (TV). *Thief* (TV). 1972: *Jigsaw* (TV). *Magic Carpet* (TV). *Cry for Me, Billy/Count Your Bullets* (GB: *Naked Revenge*). 1973: *Police Story* (TV. GB:

cinemas. Later shown on TV as The Stake Out). *Where the Lilies Bloom. Birds of Prey* (TV GB: cinemas). *Mr Inside, Mr Outside* (TV). *Shirts/Skins* (TV). 1974: *Get Christie Love!* (TV). *Larry* (TV). *Trapped Beneath the Sea* (TV). *Together Brothers*. 1975: *The Peach Gang* (TV). *Beyond the Bermuda Triangle* (TV). 1976: *Part 2 Sounder* (originally for TV). *21 Hours at Munich* (TV. GB: cinemas). *Shark Kill*. 1977: *Minstrel Man* (TV) *The Amazing Howard Hughes* (TV). *Contract on Cherry Street* (TV). 1978: *Cindy* (TV). *One in a Million: the Ron LeFlore Story* (TV). *And I Alone Survived* (TV). 1979: *Transplant* (TV). *Orphan Train* (TV). 1980: *Harry Tracy – Desperado/Dead or Alive*. 1981: *Deadly Encounter* (TV). 1982: *M.A.D.D: Mothers Against Drink Drivers* (TV). 1983: *The Last Ninja. Women of San Quentin* (TV). 1984: *Secrets of a Married Man* (TV). *The Calendar Girl Murders* (TV). 1985: *The Last Days of Frank and Jesse James* (TV). 1987: *Police Story: The Freeway Killings* (TV). 1988: *Street of Dreams* (TV). 1989: *Gore Vidal's Billy the Kid* (TV). 1990: *Montana* (TV). 1991: *Return to the Blue Lagoon*. 1992: *Bed of Lies* (TV). *Elvis and the Colonel: The Untold Story* (TV). 1993: *Appointment for a Killing* (TV).

GREEN, Alfred E. 1889-1960

Few writers seem concerned to list Green in books on prominent directors. Yet his near-40-year directorial career is one of the longest in Hollywood annals and contains a lively proportion of distinguished work. He worked in the cinema almost all of his life, becoming an actor, writer and assistant director with the Selig Polyscope company before World War I, and graduating to direction in his late twenties. In 1921, Mary Pickford chose him as co-director to her brother Jack on *Little Lord Fauntleroy* and *Through the Back Door*, and Green immediately moved into a classier grade of assignment. He handled vehicles for Thomas Meighan, Wallace Reid and John Barrymore, and there were four – *Sally, Irene, Ella Cinders* and *It Must Be Love* – with the elfin Colleen Moore. With the coming of sound, Green directed two performers to Academy Awards – George Arliss in *Disraeli* and Bette Davis in *Dangerous*. Another highlight of his 1930s career was *Baby Face*, in which Barbara Stanwyck slinks her way from the bottom of a firm to the top – via pretty well every male employee of any note. Riddled with dissolves and wipes, this sassy melodrama – with, or course, a moral ending – was one of the fastest-moving films of the early part of the decade. Green ended the

1930s with *The Gracie Allen Murder Case*. This is great fun, with Warren William as detective Philo Vance much beset by the scatterbrained Gracie, appearing for once without her husband and partner George Burns. Green's career went into decline with the end of the 1940s, and he was employed mainly on actional co-features, with the exception of a minor Edward G. Robinson vehicle, *Mr Winkle Goes to War*, and a very major musical – *The Jolson Story*. The public really took a liking to the film and broke Columbia's receipts record to the tune of seven-and-a-half million dollars. Green's direction had always been polished and craftsmanlike, carving out films that moved well and entertained the public. On *The Jolson Story* (the musical numbers were directed by Joseph H. Lewis: qv) that was more than enough: the story and the music did the rest. Much troubled with arthritis in his last years, Green nevertheless kept working on television series after retiring from the cinema.

1916: *The Temptation of Adam*. 1917: **Lost and Found. *For Reward of Service. The Princess of Patches. Little Lost Sister. The Lad and the Lion*. 1918: **The Friendship of Beaupère. *Trials and Tribulations*. 1919: *Love, Honor and Obey* (unreleased). *The Web of Chance. Right After Brown*. 1920: *A Double-Dyed Deceiver. Silk Husbands and Calico Wives. Just Out of College. The Man Who Had Everything*. 1921: *†Little Lord Fauntleroy. †Through the Back Door*. 1922: *Our Leading Citizen. Come On Over* (GB: *Darlin'*). *The Bachelor Daddy. The Ghost Breaker. The Man Who Saw Tomorrow. Back Home and Broke*. 1923: *The Ne'er-Do-Well. Woman-Proof*. 1924: *In Hollywood with Potash and Perlmutter* (GB: *So This is Hollywood*). *Pied Piper Malone. Inez from Hollywood* (GB: *The Good Bad Girl*). 1925: *Sally. The Talker. The Man Who Found Himself*. 1926: *Irene. Ella Cinders. The Girl from Montmartre. It Must Be Love. Ladies at Play*. 1927: *Two Girls Wanted. The Auctioneer. Is Zat So? Come to My House*. 1928: *Honor Bound*. 1929: *Making the Grade. The Five O'Clock Girl* (unreleased). *Disraeli*. 1930: *The Green Goddess. The Man from Blankley's. Sweet Kitty Bellairs. Old English*. 1931: *Smart Money. Men of the Sky. The Road to Singapore*. 1932: *The Dark Horse. Silver Dollar. Union Depot* (GB: *Gentleman for a Day*). *It's Tough to be Famous. The Rich Are Always with Us*. 1933: *Parachute Jumper. The Narrow Corner. I Loved a Woman. Baby Face*. 1934: *The Merry Frinks* (GB: *The Happy Family*).

Dark Hazard. Housewife. As the Earth Turns. Side Streets (GB: Woman in Her Thirties). Gentlemen Are Born. A Lost Lady. 1935: The Goose and the Gander. Sweet Music. Dangerous. The Girl from 10th Avenue (GB: Men on Her Mind). Here's to Romance. 1936: They Met in a Taxi. Colleen. More Than a Secretary. The Golden Arrow. Two in a Crowd. 1937: Mr Dodd Takes the Air. Let's Get Married. The League of Frightened Men. Thoroughbreds Don't Cry. 1938: Ride a Crooked Mile (GB: Escape from Yesterday). The Duke of West Point. 1939: King of the Turf. 20,000 Men a Year. The Gracie Allen Murder Case. 1940: South of Pago-Pago. Flowing Gold. Shooting High. East of the River. 1941: Adventure in Washington (GB: Female Correspondent). Badlands of Dakota. 1942: Meet the Stewarts. The Mayor of 44th Street. 1943: Appointment in Berlin. There's Something About a Soldier. 1944: Strange Affair. Mr Winkle Goes to War (GB: Arms and the Woman). 1945: A Thousand and One Nights. 1946: Tars and Spars. The Jolson Story. 1947: The Fabulous Dorseys. Copacabana. 1948: The Girl from Manhattan. Four Faces West (GB: They Passed This Way). 1949: Cover-Up. 1950: The Jackie Robinson Story. Sierra. 1951: Two Gals and a Guy. 1953: The Eddie Cantor Story. Invasion USA. Paris Model. 1954: Top Banana.

GREEN, Guy 1913-

Green carved out a path to the director's chair favoured by many other leading British directors of the 1940s and 1950s: from camera assistant to camera operator to photographer to director. His credits as a cameraman – he began his career as a portrait photographer – are remarkable, taking in many of the best British films of the period: *The Way Ahead, The Way to the Stars* (in America: *Johnny in the Clouds), Great Expectations, Oliver Twist, The Passionate Friends;* then, moving down a notch or two in quality, but into colour: *Captain Horatio Hornblower R.N, The Story of Robin Hood and His Merrie Men, Decameron Nights, The Beggars' Opera* and *For Better, For Worse.* His films as director are almost all heady romances or thrillers in which women are intricately involved. Thus his first, *River Beat,* has chirpy Phyllis Kirk doing most of the legwork investigating a smuggling racket. This was two cuts above the usual British second-feature standard of its time, and Green immediately moved up a step – employed by the Rank Organisation to make *Lost* (a weepie about a lost child) and *House of Secrets* (a thick-ear thriller), both A-fea-

Perfectionist Peter **Greenaway** strikes a typically authoritarian pose on the set of *Drowning by Numbers.*

tures in colour, and both effective entertainments. Green's reputation was made by *The Angry Silence,* a moving, poignant, well-scripted and always entertaining study of a man whose life is almost wrecked when he refuses to join a strike. *The Mark,* which followed, also tugged at the emotions, although its story deals with a man once convicted of child-molesting and it was, understandably, commercially less successful than *Silence.* But it contains Stuart Whitman's best film performance, and he was nominated for an Academy Award. Green then went to Hollywood and, apart from *A Patch of Blue,* the story of a blind girl, in which Shelley Winters, as the girl's sluttish mother, did win an Oscar, his film career became most surprisingly unsuccessful, *The Magus* perhaps being the worst of the lot although it has hot competition from several quarters. It was all most disappointing to those who had enjoyed watching Green's development through the 1950s, but suddenly almost everything he touched seemed to be overdone. In the late 1970s, he turned to weepies for television.

1954: River Beat. 1955: Portrait of Alison (US: Postmark for Danger). Lost (US: Tears for Simon). 1956: House of Secrets (US: Triple Deception). 1958: The Snorkel. Sea of Sand (US: Desert Patrol). 1959: S.O.S. Pacific. 1960: The Angry Silence. 1961: The Mark. Light in the Piazza. 1962: Diamond Head. 1965: A Patch of Blue. 1967: Pretty Polly (US: A Matter of Innocence). 1968: The Magus. 1969: A Walk in the Spring Rain. 1973: Luther. 1974: Once is Not Enough/Jacqueline Susann's Once is Not Enough. 1977: The Devil's Advocate. 1979: The Incredible Journey of Dr Meg Laurel (TV). Jennifer: a Woman's Story (TV). 1980: Jimmy B & André (TV). 1981: Inmates: A Love Story (TV). Isabel's Choice (TV). 1986: Strong Medicine (TV).

GREENAWAY, Peter 1942-

Expect a film by Peter Greenaway to both offend and impress you. You could equally be entering Greenaway's own private art gallery or the jaws of hell. The visual detail in Greenaway's work is amazing, be it after the style of Breughel or Bosch, although his narratives are spare and often elliptical. He has flirted with mainstream acceptance more than that other master of painterly, if often repellent images on film, Derek Jarman, but has always veered away again to the fringes of homo-erotic fantasy. Greenaway's menacing cameras prowl past visceral images revealing a fascination with, as well as the body and its functions, death and betrayal and their relation to such disparate things as food, sex, crime and architecture. The son of an ornithologist, Greenaway had begun his career appropriately as a painter, but it was not long before he was working as a film editor and making a string of enigmatic shorts, leading to his first feature in 1980. *The Draughtsman's Contract* opened doors for him, and, although regarded as too arid and puzzling in some quarters, was a conspicuous arthouse success that also reached the edges of a more general audience. He had less success over the next few years until *Drowning by Numbers* and, most notably, *The Cook, the Thief, His Wife and her Lover* brought him back to the fore. Both are greatly aided by the colour images of Greenaway's regular cinematographer Sacha Vierney. *Drowning* is almost a series of moving paintings that depict three women from the same family who all drown their husbands. As usual, artificiality reigns, and Greenaway lingers too long in the telling of the tale, but the film remains fascinating throughout. And the presence of 'name' stars undoubtedly enabled both it and *The Cook* to prove more accessible to audiences on either side of the Atlantic. The latter was undoubtedly among the most stylish and the most disgusting of its year. Vulgarity is its keynote and no opportunity is missed to underline it, from the continuous sex and violence, to the crass opulence of the restaurant where revolting gangster Michael Gambon holds court. Greenaway has searched in vain for its equal since, his more recent pictures lacking the pictorial inspiration which a Greenaway film once guaranteed.

1966: *Train. *Tree. 1967: *Revolution. *Five Postcards from Capital Cities. 1969: *Intervals. 1971: *Erosion. 1973: *H is for House. 1975: *Water. *Windows. *Water Wrackets. 1976: *Goole by Numbers. 1977: *Dear Phone. 1978: *1-100. *Vertical Features Remake. *A Walk Through H. 1980: The Falls. 1981: *Zandra Rhodes. *Act of God. 1982: The Draughtsman's Contract. 1983: *Four American Composers. 1984: *Making a Splash. A TV Dante – Canto 5. 1985: *Inside Rooms – The Bathroom. A Zed and Two Noughts. 1987: The Belly of an Architect. 1988: Drowning by Numbers. 1989: The Cook, The Thief, His Wife and Her Lover. 1991: Prospero's Books. 1993: The Baby of Mâcon. 1995: The Pillow Book. 1998: Eight and a Half Women.

GREENE, David 1921-

It comes as a shock to realise that this British-born director is over 70. It seems not that long ago that he was regarded as highly promising, which shows the dangers of starting a directorial career late in life, in days when fewer films each year are produced, even when considerable talent is undoubtedly there. Greene was an actor until the early 1950s, winning his spurs as a director with Canadian television. From television, and many episodes of series, he moved only cautiously into films. Some critics mysteriously saw signs of a great director emerging in his first feature *The Shuttered Room*. Perhaps they were the perceptive ones, for Greene followed up with the lively and original *Sebastian* and the strong *I Start Counting*. Now he did look set for the top, but *The People Next Door*, a wretched, hysterical X-certificate drama about drug-taking (one can't believe the TV original was that much better when Greene directed it for 'CBS Playhouse' in 1968) set his career back years. *Godspell* was a none-

too-successful transfer of the hit musical from stage to screen, *Madame Sin* merely jokey, and *The Count of Monte Cristo* a failure at every task it set itself, with Greene getting only one creditable performance (Kate Nelligan's) from his starry cast. It must be added on all of these projects that script rather than direction was at fault, a fact Greene underlined when making a very presentable suspense entertainment out of the only averagely scripted *Gray Lady Down*. But since then he has returned to TV fodder and minor films, although his *Fire Birds* (shown in Britain as *Wings of the Apache*) was an underrated action movie that really buzzed. He continued to work on good-quality TV material well into his seventies.

1960: A Shot in the Dark (originally for TV). 1966: The Shuttered Room. 1967: Sebastian. 1968: The Strange Affair. 1969: I Start Counting. 1970: The People Next Door. 1971: Madame Sin (TV. GB: cinemas). 1973: Godspell. 1974: The Count of Monte Cristo (TV in 1975, GB cinemas in 1976). 1975: Ellery Queen (TV). 1977: Lucan (TV). The Trial of Lee Harvey Oswald (TV). Gray Lady Down. 1979: Friendly Fire (TV. A Vacation in Hell (TV). 1981: Hard Country. World War III (TV). The Choice (TV). 1982: Rehearsal for Murder (TV). Take Your Best Shot (TV). 1983: Ghost Dancing (TV). Prototype (TV). 1984: Sweet Revenge (TV). Fatal Vision (TV). The Guardian (TV). 1985: Guilty Conscience (TV). This Child is Mine! (TV). Circle of Violence: A Family Drama (TV). 1986: Triplecross (TV). Broken Promise. Vanishing Act (TV). Miles to Go (TV). 1987: The Betty Ford Story (TV). After the Promise (TV). 1988: Inherit the Wind (TV). Liberace — Behind the Music (TV). 1989: Small Sacrifices (TV). Red Earth, White Earth (TV. GB: Snake Treaty). 1990: In the Best Interests of the Child (TV). Fire Birds (GB: Wings of the Apache). 1991: Whatever Happened to Baby Jane? (TV). Night of the Hunter (TV). In a Stranger's Hand (TV). 1992: The Penthouse (TV. Completed 1990). Willing to Kill: The Texas Cheerleader Story (TV). Honor Thy Mother (TV). 1993: Spoils of War (TV). Beyond Obsession (TV). 1995: Children of the Dust (TV). 1996: A Season in Purgatory (TV). 1997: Breach of Faith: A Family of Cops II (TV).

GRÉVILLE, Edmond T. 1905-1966

Gréville was a gadfly of a director, dodging from France to Holland to Britain. At his best in the 1930s, he spent the post-

war years (by now West Germany had been added to his much-stamped passport) making moody pot-boilers, mostly pretty gloomy and unpopular (with public and critics alike) but some of them with a certain raw grip. The son of a Protestant minister, Gréville acted as assistant director to E.A. Dupont (qv) and others while working on his own experimental short films in the late 1920s. At the same time, he began to make a name for himself as a novelist. The brooding, intense nature of his feature films *Remous/Whirlpool* and *Princesse Tam-Tam* led to an invitation to make films in Britain, but these were movies of a lighter nature not entirely suited to Gréville's peculiar talents, and his best work was done at the end of the decade – *Menaces*, for which Gréville, in Hitchcock style, shot two endings, and *Veertig Jaren*, a documentary made to celebrate the anniversary of Queen Wilhelmina of the Netherlands, which won a gold medal at the Venice Film Festival. These were the last highlights of Gréville's career which came to an end as sombre as most of his films when he committed suicide in 1966.

1927: *Un grand journal illustré. *Elle est Bicimidine. 1928: *24 heures de la vie d'un faux-col. 1929. *Més-estimations. *Le mystère de la villa rose. 1930: *La naissance des heures. 1931: *Le mariage de Sarah. *Moyse, marchand d'habits. *Le testament de Moyse. *La belle Madame Moyse. *Le tapis de Moyse. *Moyse et Cohen, businessmen. *Marius, amateur de cidre. *Un crime passionel. *La guerre aux sauterelles. La peau sur l'herbe (unfinished). Le train des suicidés. 1932: Plaisirs de Paris. Le rayon des amours. *Maître chez soi. *Je suis un homme perdu. *Berlingot. †Le triangle de feu. 1933: *Vacances conjugales. Remous/Whirlpool. 1934: La croix des cimes. 1935: Marchand d'amour. Princesse Tam-Tam. 1936: Gypsy Melody. 1937: Brief Ecstasy. Mademoiselle Docteur (English version only). What a Man! Secret Lives (US: I Married a Spy). 1938: Veertig Jaren (D). 1939: Menaces. 1941: Une femme dans la nuit. 1944: Cinq jours d'angoisse (1939 film with new ending). 1945: Dorothée cherche l'amour. 1946: Pour une nuit d'amour/Passionelle. 1947: Le diable souffle. 1948: Noose (US: The Silk Noose). But Not in Vain (and Dutch version). 1949: The Romantic Age (US: Naughty Arlette). 1950: Der Bildschnitzer vom Walsertal (unreleased). 1953: L'envers du paradise. 1954: Le port du désir (US: The House on the Waterfront). 1955: Tant qu'il y aura des femmes. 1956: Guilty? 1957: Quand sonnera midi. 1958: L'île au bout du monde (GB: Temptation Island. US: Temptation). 1959: Beat

Tom **Gries** lines up a shot from *Breakout* in 1975. Veteran cinematographer Lucien Ballard is just behind him.

Girl (US: Wild for Kicks). 1960: *The Hands of Orlac (and French version).* 1961: *Les menteurs (GB: The Liars. US: Twisted Lives).* 1963: *L'accident.* 1964: *Peril au paradis (TV).*

GRIES, Tom 1922-1977

The strange thing about this American director was that, although he never made another film as good as *Will Penny* — his first major motion picture — he didn't seem to want to, being content to churn out general entertainment films, some good, some bad, with the accent on he-man heroes. After service in the US Marines during World War II, Gries became a reporter for *Variety,* then a theatrical agent and publicist and finally producer — a most unusual way to gravitate towards a career directing films. He started directing for television in the mid-1950s, at the same time making a few minor films, then going back to TV and hundreds of episodes in such series as *I Spy, Route 66, The Monroes* and *Mission Impossible.* In 1967, Gries relaunched his feature-film career with *Will Penny,* an elegiac western about an ageing cow-puncher who becomes involved with a frontier woman and her son, and with a band of psychopathic cut-throats. The relationship between Charlton Heston, as Will Penny, and Joan Hackett as the woman to whom he forms his first attachment in years, is warm and real, and the uncompromising ending will leave all but the hardest misty-eyed. Gries followed this with a lively Jim Brown-Raquel Welch-Burt Reynolds western, *100 Rifles,* but his next two films were turkeys that hardly emerged outside America, took zilch at the box-office and sent Gries back to TV; there he revived his reputation with an Emmy award for the prison drama *The Glass House,* which had another popular leading actor in Alan Alda and another downbeat ending.

Gries's score was average after that, although *Breakheart Pass,* with Charles Bronson, was an exciting train-set western whodunnit and *Helter Skelter* attracted inevitable attention as being based on a real-life *cause célèbre—the* Manson murders. Gries died from a heart attack while playing tennis just after the completion of his last film *The Greatest,* the story of Muhammad Ali — but the film did not live up to its title, and is hardly the best testimony to Gries' undoubted talents which all too often lay hidden under a slew of action. Besides the list below, Gries was also writer/producer on the 1954 feature-length nature film, *Hunters of the Deep.*

1955: *Hell's Horizon.* 1956: *The Last Stop.* 1958: *The Girl in the Woods.* 1967: *Will Penny.* 1968: *100 Rifles.* 1969: *Number One.* 1970: *Fools. The Hawaiians (GB: Master of the Islands).* 1971: *Earth II.* 1972: *The Glass House (TV. GB: cinemas). Journey Through Rosebud.* 1973: *Lady Ice. Call to Danger (TV). The Connection (TV).* 1974: *The Migrants (originally for TV. QB VII (TV). The Healers (TV).* 1975: *Breakout. Breakheart Pass.* 1976: *Helter Skelter (TV. Shortened version shown in cinemas).* 1977: *The Greatest.*

GRIFFITH, D.W. 1874-1948

American pioneer of the silent cinema and of many of its more sophisticated techniques. Griffith is still generally regarded as the first great American director despite the failure of many of his later films; and, between 1914 and 1921, when his talent and confidence were in full flower, he was the maker of some of the most famous and exciting films in Hollywood history. David Wark Griffith spent his early years in show business, initially with the theatre but from 1907 principally in the cinema, taking acting chores while struggling to establish himself as a writer. In 1908, he sold several of his scenarios to Biograph and within a few months had not only become a fixture at the studio but started his incredibly prolific career as a director, soon assuming complete control of the material at his command, and rarely using any form of shooting script. The technical innovations which would raise the industry to an altogether higher level quickly began to flow from the screens of the now familiar white-hatted figure of Griffith and his trusty cameraman Billy Bitzer. In his very first film, *The Adventures of Dollie,* Griffith introduced the flash-back (or 'cut-back') to heighten the suspense of a child being swept towards a waterfall in a barrel. The same year, in

For Love of Gold, Griffith began using closer camera placements in relation to the shots immediately preceding and following, to obtain facial reaction and heighten dramatic effect. From this, he naturally built to dramatic use of close-ups (in *After Many Years*) and long- and medium-shots. He was experimenting with the camera as a means of conveying action and movement within an atmospheric landscape as early as *The Lonely Villa* (1909), while *The Politician's Love Story* in the same year contains the first aesthetic use of back-lighting as the sun shines through snow-filled trees and towards the camera. By the time of *The Lonedale Operator* (1911), Griffith was perfecting many of his experimental techniques, including sophisticated use of cross-cutting, extreme close-ups to improve narrative tension and a significant increase in action-speed within the shot. In between the popular sentimental dramas, featuring such players as Mary Pickford and Owen Moore, Griffith made several two-reel 'epics' of covered-wagon days, and several films, such as *The Battle, Fighting Blood, The House with Closed Shutters, Billy's Stratagem* and *The Battle of Elderbush Gulch,* which, in style and subject, anticipated his own monumental *The Birth of a Nation,* in 1915. In 1914 (completed in 1913) came *Judith of Bethulia,* a Biblical story that was America's first four-reel film (around 45 minutes). By this time (actually October 1913) Griffith had left Biograph, who were unhappy with his plans for longer, more expensive films, and joined Reliance-Majestic, releasing through Mutual. *The Birth of a Nation,* an epic story of the American Civil War, lasting three hours, was premiered in February 1915, to immediate critical and public acclaim, save for those sections of the community who criticized a racial (anti-negro) bias that now seems the film's weakest and only embarrassing element, For it remains highly watchable today, weaving its spectacular slice of history into more intimate drama involving Lillian Gish, who was to feature in almost all of Griffith's best films over the next few years. The sweeping panoramic stance of the camera, first adopted by Griffith as early as 1909, doubles the impact of the battle sequences, giving the impression of a vulture-like observer at an actual battlefield. The film made Griffith a worldwide celebrity, and his next film *Intolerance* was even bigger, with its immense Babylonian sets dwarfing even contemporary Italian epics. But it was a considerable flop at the box-office, actually putting Griffith into the red, and forcing him back into more intimate, though sometimes grand-structured dramas with Lillian Gish: *Hearts of the World, Broken Blossoms, True Heart Susie, Way Down East* and *Orphans of the Storm*. The exquisite acting of Gish in these films, the last of dozens she made for Griffith, their use of cross-cutting in the action sequences, their imaginative use of camera angles — notably the overhead shot of Gish trapped in a cupboard in *Broken Blossoms* — and their evocation of tender love affairs involving characters who ring totally true and whose fates one can sometimes hardly bear to watch, make them the highest dramatic achievement of Griffith's career even if *The Birth of a Nation* remains unrivalled for living spectacle. They are the culmination of his own love affair with heart-of-America sentiment and values. The public grew understandably tired of these values as the country moved into the Jazz Age — *Way Down East* was the last Griffith film to make significant amounts at the box-office — and the epic *America* sent him into the red for the second time, and effectively robbed him of his independence. He hardly worked after 1931 and died, proud, bitter and alcoholic, from a brain haemorrhage in his room at a Hollywood hotel. He had been awarded a special Oscar at the 1935 Academy Awards ceremonies 'for his distinguished creative achievements as director and producer and his invaluable initiative and lasting contributions to the progress of the motion picture arts'.

1908: *The Adventures of Dollie. The Fight for Freedom. The Tavern Keeper's Daughter. The Black Viper. The Red Man and the Child. The Bandit's Waterloo. A Calamitous Elopement. The Greaser's Gauntlet. The Man and the Woman. The Fatal Hour. For Love of Gold: a Story of the Underworld. Balked at the Altar. For a Wife's Honor. Betrayed by a Handprint. The Girl and the Outlaw. Behind the Scenes. The Red Girl. The Heart of O Yama. Where the Breakers Roar. A Smoked Husband. The Devil. The Stolen Jewels. The Zulu's Heart. Father Gets in the Game. The Barbarian — Ingomar. The Vaquero's Vow. The Planter's Wife. Romance of a Jewess. The Call of the Wild. Concealing a Burglar. After Many Years. The Pirate's Gold. The Taming of the Shrew. The Helping Hand. The Guerrilla. The Song of the Shirt. The Ingrate. A Woman's Way. The Clubman and the Tramp. Money Mad. The Valet's Wife. The Feud and the Turkey. The Reckoning. The Test of Friendship. An Awful Moment. Mr Jones at the Ball. The Christmas Burglars.* 1909: *One Touch of Nature. The Maniac Cook. Mrs Jones Entertains. The Honor of Thieves. Love Finds a Way. A Rural Elopement. The Sacrifice. The Criminal Hypnotist. Those Boys! Mr Jones Has a Card Party. The Fascinating Mrs Francis. The Welcome Burglar. Those Awful Hats. The Cord of Life. The Girls and Daddy. The Brahma Diamond. A Wreath in Time. Edgar Allan Poe. Tragic Love. The Curtain Pole. His Ward's Love. The Hindoo Dagger. The Joneses Have Amateur Theatricals. The Politician's Love Story. The Golden Louis. At the Altar. His Wife's Mother. The Prussian Spy. A Fool's Revenge. The Wooden Leg. The Roué's Heart. The Salvation Army Lass. I Did It, Mamma. The Lure of the Gown. The Voice of the Violin. 'And a Little Child Shall Lead Them'. The Deception. A Burglar's Mistake. The Medicine Bottle. Jones and His New Neighbors. A Drunkard's Reformation. Trying to Get Arrested. The Road to the Heart. A Rude Hostess. Schneider's Anti-Noise Crusade. A Sound Sleeper. The Winning Coat. Confidence. Lady Helen's Escapade. A Troublesome Satchel. The Drive for a Life. Lucky Jim. Twin Brothers. 'Tis an Ill Wind That Blows No Good. The Eavesdropper. The Suicide Club. One Busy Hour. The Note in the Shoe. The French Duel. A Baby's Shoe. The Jilt. Resurrection. Eloping with Aunty. Two Memories. The Cricket on the Hearth. Eradicating Aunty. †His Duty. What Drink Did. The Violin Maker of Cremona. A New Trick. The Lonely Villa. The Son's Return. The Faded Lilies. Her First Biscuits. Was Justice Served? The Mexican Sweethearts. The Peachbasket Hat. The Way of a Man. The Necklace. The Message. The Country Doctor. †Richelieu, or: the Cardinal's Conspiracy.*

Tender Hearts. The Friend of the Family. The Renunciation. Sweet and Twenty. Jealousy and the Man. A Convict's Sacrifice. The Slave. A Strange Meeting. The Mended Lute. They Would Elope. Jones's Burglar. The Better Way. With Her Card. His Wife's Visitor. Mrs Jones's Lover, or: 'I Want My Hat!' The Indian Runner's Romance. The Seventh Day. 'Oh Uncle!' The Mills of the Gods. Pranks. The Sealed Room. The Little Darling. Leather Stocking. 1776: Or, the Hessian Renegades. Comata, the Sioux. The Children's Friend. Getting Even. The Broken Locket. 1n Old Kentucky: a Stirring Episode of the Civil War. A Fair Exchange. The Awakening. Wanted: a Child. Pippa Passes/The Song of Conscience. Fools of Fate. The Little Teacher. A Change of Heart. His Last Love. The Expiation. In the Watches of the Night. Lines of White on a Sullen Sea. The Gibson Goddess. What's Your Hurry? Nursing a Viper. The Restoration. The Light That Came. Two Women and a Man. Sweet Revenge. A Midnight Adventure. The Open Gate. The Mountaineer's Honor: a Story of the Kentucky Hills. In the Window Recess. The Trick That Failed. The Death Disc. Through the Breakers. The Red Man's View. A Corner in Wheat. The Test. 1n a Hempen Bag. 1n Little Italy. To Save Her Soul. Choosing a Husband. A Trap for Santa Claus. 1910: The Rocky Road. The Dancing Girl of Butte. Her Terrible Ordeal. On the Reef. The Call. The Honor of His Family. The Last Deal. The Cloister's Touch. The Woman from Mellon's. The Course of True Love. The Duke's Plan. One Night and Then. The Englishman and the Girl. His Last Burglary. Taming a Husband.

In familiar white hat, the great D W **Griffith** works on *The Stuggle* in 1931, his last work of any note. The Russian-born photographer Joseph Ruttenberg, later to win four Oscars, is on the right of the shot.

The Final Settlement. The Newlyweds. The Thread of Destiny. In Old California. The Converts. The Man. Faithful. The Twisted Trail. Gold Is Not All. The Smoker. His Last Dollar. As It Is in Life. A Rich Revenge. A Romance of the Western Hills. Thou Shalt Not. The Tenderfoot's Triumph. The Way of the World. Up a Tree. The Gold Seekers. The Unchanging Sea. The Two Brothers. Love Among the Roses. Over Silent Paths. An Affair of Hearts. Ramona. A Knot in the Plot. The Impalement. In the Season of Buds. A Child of the Ghetto. A Victim of Jealousy. In the Border States. The Face at the Window. Never Again. May and December. The Marked Timetable. A Child's Impulse. Muggsy's First Sweetheart. The Purgation. A Midnight Cupid. What the Daisy Said. A Child's Faith. A Flash of Light. As the Bells Rang Out! Serious Sixteen. The Call to Arms. Unexpected Help. An Arcadian Maid. Her Father's Pride. The House with Closed Shutters. A Salutary Lesson. The Usurer: 'What Doth It Profit?' An Old Story with a New Ending. When We Were in Our 'Teens. The Sorrows of the Unfaithful. Wilful Peggy. The Modern Prodigal. The Affair of an Egg. †Muggsy Becomes a Hero. A Summer Idyll. Little Angels of Luck. A Mohawk's Way. In Life's Cycle. †A Summer Tragedy. The Oath and the Man: a Story of the French Revolution. Rose o' Salem-Town: a Story of Puritan Witchcraft. Examination Day at School. The Iconoclast. A Gold Necklace. That Chink at Golden Gulch. The Broken Doll. The Banker's Daughters. The Message of the Violin. Two Little Waifs. A Modern Fairy Tale. Waiter No. 5: a Story of Russian Despotism. The Fugitive. Simple Charity. Sunshine Sue. The Song of the Wildwood Flute. His New Lid. Not So Bad As It Seemed. A Plain Song. Effecting a Cure. †His Sister-in-Law. The Lesson. A Child's Stratagem. The Golden Supper. White Roses. Winning Back his Love. 1911: The Two Paths. When a Man Loves. The Italian Barber. His Trust. His Trust Fulfilled. Fate's Turning. The Poor Sick Men. A Wreath of Orange Blossoms. Three Sisters. Heart Beats of Long Ago. What Shall We Do with Our Old? Fisher Folk. His Daughter. The Diamond Star. The Lily of the Tenements: a Story of East Side of New York. The Heart of a Savage. A Decree of Destiny. Conscience. Was He a Coward? The Lonedale Operator. The Spanish Gypsy. The Broken Cross. The Chief's Daughter. Paradise Lost. Madame Rex. A Knight of the Road. His Mother's Scarf. How She Triumphed. The Two Sides. In the Days of '49. Crossing the American Prairies in the Early 'Fifties. The New Dress. The White Rose of the Wilds. A Romany Tragedy. A Smile of a Child. Enoch Arden. The Primal Call. Fighting Blood. Her Sacrifice. The Thief and the Girl. Bobby the Coward. Indian Brothers. The Last Drop of Water: a Story of the Great American Desert. Out from the Shadow. The Ruling Passion. A Sorrowful Example. The Blind Princess and the Poet. The Rose of Kentucky. Swords and Hearts. The Old Confectioner's Mistake. The Squaw's Love. The Revenue Man and the Girl. Her Awakening: the Punishment of Pride. The Making of a Man. Italian Blood. The Unveiling. Dan, The Dandy. The Adventures of Billy. The Long Road. Love in the Hills. The Battle. The Trail of Books. Through Darkened Vales. The Miser's Heart. Sunshine through the Dark. A Woman Scorned. The Failure. Saved From Himself. As in the Looking Glass. A Terrible Discovery. The Voice of the Child. 1912: A Tale of the Wilderness. The Eternal Mother. The Old Bookkeeper. For His Son. A Blot on the 'Scutcheon. The Transformation of Mike. Billy's Stratagem. Mender of Nets. Under Burning Skies: a Tale of the American Desert. The Sunbeam. A Siren of Impulse. A String of Pearls. Iola's Promise. The Root of Evil. The Girl and Her Trust. When Kings Were the Law. His Lesson. Home Folks. A Temporary Truce. The School Teacher and the Waif. The Spirit Awakened. Lena and the Geese. The Goddess of Sagebrush Gulch. The Punishment. Fate's Interception. The Female of the Species. Just Like a Woman. One is Business; The Other Crime. The Lesser Evil. The Old Actor. A Lodging for the Knight. A Beast at Bay. An Outcast Among Outcasts. Man's Lust for Gold. The Sands of Dee. Man's Genesis. Black Sheep. The Narrow Road. A Child's Remorse. The Inner Circle. With the Enemy's Help. A Change of Spirit. A Pueblo Legend. In the North Woods. An Unseen Enemy. The Massacre (released 1914). Blind Love. Two Daughters of Eve. Friends. So Near, Yet So Far. A Feud in the Kentucky Hills. The Chief's Blanket. In the Aisles of the Wild. The One She Loved. The Painted Lady. The Musketeers of Pig Alley. Heredity. The Informer. Brutality. The New York Hat. The God Within. My Hero. A Cry for Help. The Burglar's Dilemma. 1913: Three Friends. The Telephone Girl and the Lady. Mother Love. Pirate Gold. Oil and Water. Broken Ways. †Fate. The Sheriff's Baby. Little Tease. A Misunderstood Boy. The Lady and the Mouse. The House of Darkness. The Yaqui Cur. Just Gold. His Mother's Son. Brothers. An Adventure in the Autumn Woods. A Misappropriated Turkey. Drink's Lure. A Chance Deception. Love in an Apartment Hotel. The Unwelcome Guest. Near to Earth. A Welcome Intruder. The Hero of Little Italy. The Perfidy of Mary. The Left-Handed Man. The Wanderer. Olaf – an Atom. Death's Marathon. The Mothering Heart. The Ranchero's Revenge. A Timely Interception. Her Mother's Oath. The Sorrowful Shore. The Mistake. Two Men on the Desert. The Reformers, or: the Lost Art of Minding One's Business. The Primitive Man. 1914: The Battle at Elderbush Gulch (completed 1913). Wars of the Primal Tribes/In Prehistoric Days (completed 1913). $Judith of Bethulia (completed 1913). $The Battle of the Sexes. $The Escape. $Home, Sweet Home. $The Avenging Conscience, or: Thou Shalt Not Kill. 1915: $The Birth of a Nation (initially shown as The Clansman). 1916: †$Hoodoo Ann (uncredited). $Intolerance. A Day with Governor Whitman. A Day with Mary Pickford. 1917: $Her Condoned Sin (expanded, six-reel version of Judith of Bethulia). 1918: Buy Liberty Bonds. $Hearts of the World. $The Great Love. $The Romance of Happy Valley. $The Greatest Thing in Life. 1919: $The Girl Who Stayed at Home. $Broken Blossoms. $The Mother and the Law (mostly footage from Intolerance). $The Fall of Babylon (mostly footage from Intolerance). $True Heart Susie. The World at Columbus. $Scarlet Days. $The Greatest Question. 1920: $The Idol Dancer. $The Love Flower. $Way Down East. 1921: The Evolution of the Motion Picture. $Dream Street. $Orphans of the Storm. 1922: $One Exciting Night. 1923: $The White Rose. 1924: $America (GB: Love and Sacrifice). $Isn't Life Wonderful! 1925: $Sally of the Sawdust. $That Royle Girl. 1926: $The Sorrows of Satan. 1927: $† Topsy and Eva (uncredited). 1928: $Drums of Love. $The Battle of the Sexes. 1929: $Lady of the Pavements (GB: Lady of the Night). 1930: $The Birth of a Nation (1915 film with sound effects, music track and new prologue). $Abraham Lincoln. 1931: $The Struggle. 1936: $†San Francisco (some crowd scenes only). 1940: $One Million B.C. (GB: Man and His Mate. Supervisory capacity only).

All shorts except $ features

GRIFFITH, Edward H. 1894-*

This American director made comparatively few films (just over 50) considering that his 30-year career started in silent days, yet he was greatly favoured by many of the 1930s' most beautiful stars, who demanded his services to showcase their talents. Among them were Ann Harding, whom he directed four times,

Madeleine Carroll (six times), Loretta Young (twice), Constance Bennett, Margaret Sullavan, Simone Simon and Joan Crawford. Generally, the vehicles he created for them were quite successful, enhancing their images, and in Miss Harding's case prolonging her star status at RKO into the mid-1930s. It made Griffith something of a minor-league George Cukor: appropriately, he and Cukor co-directed No More Ladies for which Griffith crossed to M-G-M in 1935. Although born in Virginia, of wealthy parents, Griffith was educated in England and Germany, returning to America just before World War I broke out and working for a few months as a reporter. In 1915, he applied to the Edison company for work as a scenario writer, and was accepted, doing acting chores on the side. Two years later, he became a director on the adventure film Law of the North. Griffith now mixed writing and directing careers, but his films of the 1920s are a routine collection, and it is with his work for the major studios in the 1930s that chief interest lies. His association with Ann Harding, a cool, aristocratic blonde and then one of RKO's biggest drawing cards, began in 1929, with the screen adaptation of Paris Bound, a sparkling romantic comedy by Philip Barry (who also wrote Holiday, The Animal Kingdom and The Philadelphia Story). Miss Harding was teamed for the second time with Fredric March, and Griffith showed a keen cinematic sense in opening out the play successfully for the screen, even adding double exposures to show the characters' stream of consciousness. Horace Jackson's screenplay kept most of Barry's crackling dialogue intact, although he and Griffith greatly improved the story's pacing, wrapping it all up in 73 minutes! The Harding-Griffith-Jackson team took their time a bit more with their second venture with a Barry play, Holiday, which ran 99 minutes and cast its star in the role that was played by Katharine Hepburn in the 1938 Cukor version. Griffith's stylish direction greatly enhanced Miss Harding's reputation for tackling comedy as well as weepies. Griffith was upset when her prolonged shooting schedule on East Lynne prevented her from making his Rebound (Ina Claire substituted), but the Griffith-Harding-Jackson team did get together again, inevitably on another Barry play, The Animal Kingdom, a witty battle-of-the-sexes (Leslie Howard was leading man) which proved to be Ann Harding's last really big box-office hit. For the next two years, there was talk of Miss Harding and Griffith teaming again, on The Sun Also Rises, Alien Corn and The World Outside, but none of these materialized

and both their careers were declining when they combined for the last time on Biography (of a Bachelor Girl). Again the source material was a play, but this time not by Barry, and there was little Griffith could do to conceal the fact that the leading role was not ideally suited to his star's talents for creating sophisticated and slightly artificial characters. They never teamed again, although Griffith remained an 'A' feature director until drifting out of the cinema in the post-war years.

1917: *The Star-Spangled Banner. *In Love's Laboratory. *The Boy Who Cried Wolf. *Billy and the Big Stick. Law of the North. The Awakening of Ruth. One Touch of Nature. 1918: Fit to Fight. 1919: Fit to Win. The End of the Road. 1920: *A Philistine in Bohemia. *Thimble Thimble. The Garter Girl. Bab's Candidate. The Vice of Fools. 1921: Scrambled Wives. If Women Only Knew. The Land of Hope. Dawn of the East. 1922: Sea Raiders. The Go-Getters. Unseeing Eyes. 1924: Another Scandal. Week-End Husbands. 1925: Headlines. Bad Company. 1926: White Mice. Atta Boy! 1927: Alias the Lone Wolf. The Price of Honor. Afraid to Love. Hold 'Em, Yale! The Opening Night. 1928: Love Overnight. Captain Swagger. 1929: The Shady Lady. Rich People. Paris Bound. 1930: Holiday. 1931: Rebound. 1932: Lady with a Past. The Animal Kingdom (GB: The Woman in His House). 1933: Another Language. 1934: Biography (of a Bachelor Girl). 1935: †No More Ladies. 1936: Next Time We Love (GB: Next Time We Live). Ladies in Love. 1937: I'll Take Romance. Café Metropole. 1938: Café Society. 1939: Honeymoon in Bali (GB: Husbands or Lovers). 1940: Safari. 1941: One Night in Lisbon. Virginia. Bahama Passage. 1943: The Sky's the Limit. Young and Willing. 1946: Perilous Holiday.

* Believed deceased. Date of death uncertain

GRINDÉ, Nick (Harry Grindé) 1891-1979
An unfortunate name (although actually pronounced Grin-day), in view of the way in which this American director ground out second-features in the 1930s. Grindé's writing tastes, when he came to Hollywood in the early 1920s, were mainly for comedy. But his vehicles as director, apart from a few smart romantic comedy-thrillers in the early 1930s, were almost all action dramas or (quite sinister) thrillers. Grindé made sure there was no lack of conviction in these 65-minute assignments: the stocky, bespectacled director was a highly intelligent man and film-maker and,

considering the material he was given to work with, made fewer bad second-features than almost anyone else working in the B-genre at the time. His films for Columbia from 1939 to 1942 are the best group: the acting is good and most of them keep a grip on the interest tighter than their scriptwriters had a right to expect. Especially interesting are his three 'doomed medical ventures' with Boris Karloff. In The Man They Could Not Hang. Karloff is Dr Savaard, experimenting with mechanical hearts; in The Man with Nine Lives, he is Dr Kravaal, searching for a cure for cancer; while in Before I Hang, he plays Dr Garth, who discovers a serum to combat old age. (The last two Karloff 'mad doctor' films, The Ape and The Devil Commands, finding him dealing, respectively, with polio and brain-waves, were directed by William Nigh and Edward Dmytryk). Grindé and Karloff got on especially well, and the films skilfully skirt the more lurid possibilities of their plots, while providing horror fans with a good supply of skilful shocks. Grindé's subsequent career was a mishmash of the mediocre, especially the Republic films, and, in the post-war years, he left Hollywood and spent most of the remainder of his working life making commercials for televisions. One of several short films he directed, Robert Benchley's How to Sleep (1935), won an Academy Award. At one time he was married to actress Marie Wilson.

1925: Excuse Me. 1926: Upstage. 1928: Beyond the Sierras. Riders of the Dark. 1929: Morgan's Last Raid. The Desert Rider. 1930: †The Bishop Murder Case. †Remote Control. †Good News. *Bits of Broadway. *The General. Wu Li Chang. 1931: This Modern Age. *Ambitious People. *The Devil's Cabaret. *The Geography Lesson. 1932: Shopworn. Vanity Street. 1934: Stone of Silver Creek. *No More West. *Bum Voyage. *Vital Victuals. 1935: Ladies Crave Excitement. *How to Sleep. *The Great American Pie Company. Border Brigands. 1936: Public Enemy's Wife (GB: G-Man's Wife). Jailbreak (GB: Murder in the Big House). Fugitive in the Sky. 1937: White Bondage. *Under Southern Stars. The Captain's Kid. Public Wedding. Love is on the Air (GB: The Radio Murder Mystery). Exiled to Shanghai. 1938: Down in Arkansas. Federal Man-Hunt (GB: Flight from Justice). 1939: King of Chinatown. Sudden Money. The Man They Could Not Hang. A Woman is the Judge. 1940: The Man with Nine Lives (GB: Behind the Door). Scandal Sheet. Convicted Woman. Men without Souls. Girls of the Road. Before I Hang. Friendly Neighbors. 1941: Moun-

tain Moonlight (GB: Moving in Society). 1942: The Girl from Alaska. 1943: Hitler — Dead or Alive. We've Never Been Licked (GB: Texas to Tokyo). 1945: Road to Alcatraz.

GUEST, Val (Valmond Guest) 1911-
There has been little pattern to this British director's career since he switched from writing top comedies to the director's chair in 1942. But he has sometimes decidedly turned sow's ears into silk purses and had some very big commercial hits in the 1950s and early 1960s. Guest was an aspiring young actor in British films of the early 1930s; when this career foundered, he went to America as a film gossip journalist, working for *The Hollywood Reporter* and other chat-style publications. He proved to be a witty, readable contributor and, on his return to England in 1935, was hired by Gainsborough Films as a comedy writer. Here, working in collaboration with J.O.C. Orton, Marriott Edgar and others, Guest had the opportunity of working with the top British comedy stars at their peak, including The Crazy Gang, Arthur Askey and, most notably Will Hay, for whom he co-scripted eight films, from *Windbag the Sailor* (1936) to *Where's That Fire?* (1939), taking in the 1937 classic *Oh! Mr Porter*. Guest began directing light films for Gainsborough (including one with Askey) in 1942. *I'll Be Your Sweetheart*, a musical about three songwriters and the fight to establish copyright, is the best of these early films, although the 'Just William' comedies are lively uninhibited fare for juvenile audiences. In 1949, Guest met (and later married) the American actress Yolande Donlan, who gave sparkling performances for him in a number of bright comedies, most notably *Mr Drake's Duck*, as the city-girl farmer's wife whose duck starts laying uranium eggs. Guest supplied the screenplay, as he continued to do for most of his own films — and a number of other people's as well. There were more films with comedians: Bebe Daniels and Ben Lyon, in a couple of very popular lowbrow romps, Frankie Howerd in the moderate *The Runaway Bus*, Peter Sellers in *Up the Creek* and even a return to The Crazy Gang. After one or two poor shots at the thriller genre, Guest began to get this right too, notably with *Break in the Circle* and *Hell is a City*: He was also in the director's chair for the first two very profitable Quatermass horror films. His period of highest critical esteem runs from 1958 to 1963 and especially with *The Day the Earth Caught Fire* and *Jigsaw*, home-grown products which show an original and lively mind behind the camera. From

Conference between director John **Guillermin** (with pipe) and producer Dino De Laurentiis during the making of the 1976 *King Kong*.

the mid-1960s, Guest became increasingly involved in various lurid exploitation films: the titles — *Where the Spies Are, When Dinosaurs Ruled the Earth, Toomorrow, Au Pair Girls* and *Confessions of a Window Cleaner* speak all too loudly for themselves, and very ill-at-ease Guest seemed with them too. There was a belated return to form in 1980 with the delightful TV comedy-thriller *Dangerous Davies – the Last Detective*. This was much more in line with the work that had provided the roots of Guest's career (abetted by a charming performance from Bernard Cribbins).

*1942: *The Nose Has It. 1943: Miss London Ltd. 1944: Give Us the Moon. Bees in Paradise. 1945: I'll Be Your Sweetheart. 1947: Just William's Luck. 1948: William Comes to Town. 1949: Murder at the Windmill. Miss Pilgrim's Progress. 1950: The Body Said No! Mr Drake's Duck. 1952: Penny Princess. 1953: Life with the Lyons (US: A Family Affair). 1954: The Runaway Bus. The Men of Sherwood Forest. Dance Little Lady. They Can't Hang Me! Break in the Circle. The Lyons in Paris. The Quatermass Xperiment (US: The Creeping Unknown). 1956: It's a Wonderful World. The Weapon. 1957: Carry On Admiral (US: The Ship Was Loaded). Quatermass II (US: Enemy from Space). The Abominable Snowman. 1958: The Camp on Blood Island. Up the Creek. Further up the Creek. 1959: Life is a Circus. Yesterday's Enemy. Expresso Bongo. 1960: Hell Is a City. 1961: The Full Treatment (US: Stop Me Before I Kill!). The Day the Earth Caught Fire. 1962: Jigsaw. 1963: 80,000 Suspects. 1964: The Beauty*

Jungle (US: Contest Girl). 1965: Where the Spies Are. 1967: †Casino Royale. Assignment K. 1970: When Dinosaurs Ruled the Earth. Toomorrow. 1972: Au Pair Girls. 1974: Confessions of a Window Cleaner. 1975: The Diamond Mercenaries (US: Killer Force). 1980: Dangerous Davies — the Last Detective (TV). 1983: The Boys in Blue.

GUILLERMIN, John 1923-
The talent of this British director gradually emerged through a plethora of British second-features in the 1950s, but, despite subsequent employment on a number of big-budget international films from the mid-1960s to the late 1970s, he did not become a major, instantly identifiable name in the cinema. One can hardly look upon Guillermin as an *auteur* director, and perhaps he prefers it that way, although such general entertainment directors who don't hit the headlines are usually only as good as their last film as far as backers are concerned. Guillermin first went into the industry immediately after war service with the RAF, acting as assistant director on a number of short documentaries in France in the late 1940s, then gaining experience as co-writer and co-producer on the Z-grade comedies of Robert Jordan Hill, featuring rubber-necked Ben Wrigley. After making one (very boring) second-feature himself, Guillermin went to Hollywood in 1950 to study film-making methods, and a more positive approach was apparent on his return. He deservedly broke into the upper bracket in 1956 with *Town on Trial*, a creepy, edgy murder mystery, in which Guillermin not only got

a superior performance from John Mills (admittedly not difficult at that time) but showed a craftsmanlike touch in piling on the suspense in the murder scenes. Guillermin made several more good thrillers — *The Whole Truth*, *The Day They Robbed the Bank of England* and especially the undervalued *Never Let Go*, high-pressure stuff about a gang of car thieves which turned a 'B' plot into an 'A' feature in no uncertain fashion, and provided Peter Sellers, as the hard-cursing crook who imagines himself England's answer to Little Caesar, with his first real straight character role. Sellers starred for Guillermin again in the richly enjoyable, warmly observed *Waltz of the Toreadors*, which transformed lecherous farce into something lighter and altogether more likeable. In this period, Guillermin also made a good straightforward war film *I Was Monty's Double* (again with Mills) and one of the best-ever Tarzan features, *Tarzan's Greatest Adventure*. *The Blue Max* moved him on to high-budget stuff but disappointingly, apart from *The Towering Inferno*, *which was* amazingly successful, in view of a cast top-heavy with stars: its suspense really bit. But then that was always the game Guillermin knew best and, of an unrewarding crop of films since 1974, including a close-to-disastrous remake of *King Kong*, and a sequel that was even worse, the best – *P.J.* and *Death on the Nile* – are closest to that vein.

1949: Torment (US: Paper Gallows). 1951: Smart Alec. Two on the Tiles. Four Days. 1952: Song of Paris (US: Bachelor in Paris). Miss Robin Hood. 1953: †Strange Stories. Operation Diplomat. 1954: Adventure in the Hopfields. The Crowded Day. 1955: Dust and Gold. Double Jeopardy. Thunderstorm. 1956: Town on Trial!. 1957: The Whole Truth. 1958: I Was Monty's Double. 1959: Tarzan's Greatest Adventure. 1960: The Day They Robbed the Bank of England. Never Let Go. 1962: Waltz of the Toreadors. Tarzan Goes to India. 1964: Guns at Batasi. 1965: Rapture. 1966: The Blue Max. 1967: P.J. (GB: New Face in Hell). 1968: House of Cards. 1969: The Bridge at Remagen. 1970: El Condor. 1972: Skyjacked. 1973: Shaft in Africa. 1974: The Towering Inferno. 1976: King Kong. 1978: Death on the Nile. 1980: Mr Patman. 1983: Crossover. 1984: Sheena, Queen of the Jungle. 1986: King Kong Lives. 1988: The Tracker (TV).

GYLLENHAAL, Stephen 1949-

An American director who has often seemed on the verge of a breakthrough to directing top cinema material but has, to date, not quite made it. His films made for television have, oddly, been stronger titan those made for the cinema. Born and raised in a self-isolated Pennsylvania community run on the principles of 18th-century mystic Emanuel Swedenborg, Gyllenhaal was belatedly introduced to film at college. In the early 1970s, he became a production assistant on documentary films, then drove a cab for a while before landing a job making industrial films. He was in his mid-thirties, however, before he managed to put together his first fictional feature, *Certain Fury*, about two girls from disparate backgrounds on the run together. It was not well received, but Gyllenhaal built a reputation in quality TV movies, one of which, *Paris Trout*, an unrelentingly grim tale of racial and sexual repression, was shown in cinemas outside America to some acclaim, and led to a resumption of Gyllenhaal's film career. The results, however, were again not encouraging: *Waterland* was a picturesque nostalgia piece that is tedious when it should be poignant, *A Dangerous Woman* a sluggish story about a slightly retarded 30-year-old woman, and *Losing Isaiah* an overly simplistic account of the battle for a baby. Gyllenhaal's profile has been lower since then, but he continues to work at a steady pace and has made more strong TV movies in recent times. He is married to the Oscar-nominated screenwriter Naomi Foner.

1978: *Exit 10. 1985: Certain Fury. 1987: The Abduction of Kari Swenson (TV). 1988: Leap of Faith (TV). Promised a Miracle (TV). 1990: Family of Spies (TV) Killing in a Small Town (TV. GB: Evidence of Love). 1991: Paris Trout (cable TV. GB: cinemas). 1992: Waterland. 1993: A Dangerous Woman. 1995: Losing Isaiah. 1996: Shattered Mind (TV). 1997: Home Grown. 1998: Piece of My Heart. (TV).

The director directed. Dennis Hopper, who has himself made several forays behind the camera, takes instructions from the much younger Stephen **Gyllenhaal** while starring in *Paris Trout*.

HAAS, Hugo 1901-1968

Although principally a character actor, Haas turned to direction in his native Czechoslovakia after becoming a star in 1930s' comedies there, only to find World War II looming; he also directed a number of vehicles in Hollywood for himself – presumably despairing of getting star parts elsewhere. They are nearly all gloomy, turgid, moralizing dramas, telling of the hopeless infatuation of a shambling, working-class, middle-aged man for a brassy blonde in whom he sees qualities not discernible to the audience. Tragedy (usually accompanied by death) inevitably ensues. There is little to add, save that the early films with Beverly Michaels, a tall, cool blonde, are better than the later ones with the voluptuous Cleo Moore; and that *Edge of Hell*, which stars neither of them, is the best of the lot and actually does strike a few emotional cords. Most of them, too, do have a certain Z-grade earthiness all their own. An exception to all this Haas gloom is *Born To Be Loved*,

Cooling the heat. Director Taylor **Hackford** (centre) explains things to stars Jeff Bridges and Rachel Ward on hot desert locations for *Against All Odds*, an ill-advised remake of a classic *film noir*.

actually a well-characterized, nice little film, but there was more junk before and after. Haas was preparing to return to Czechoslovakia in 1968 when Russian tanks rolled in. He died shortly afterwards from heart failure, or, as friends put it 'from a broken heart'.

1937: †*Děvčata, nedějte se! Bila Nemoc.* 1938: *Co se Šepta.* 1939: *Our Combat.* 1951: *Pickup. Girl on the Bridge.* 1952: *Strange Fascination.* 1953: *Thy Neighbor's Wife. One Girl's Confession.* 1954: *Bait. The Other Woman.* 1955: *Hold Back Tomorrow.* 1956: *Edge of Hell.* 1957: *Hit and Run. Lizzie. Paradise Alley* (released 1962). 1959: *Night of the Quarter Moon. Born To Be Loved.* 1967: *The Crazy Ones.*

HACKFORD, Taylor 1944-

American director of many disappointments and occasional delights, whose greatest successes have been at the beginning of his directing career, and in the last few years. As often involved in the production side of films, Hackford had run his own company, New Visions, producing material for TV and films, before deciding to direct for the cinema. Encouraged when his first (short) film, *Teenage Father,* won an Oscar, Hackford moved on to make two of his best films. The first was *The Idolmaker,* a searing exposé of the rock music world, and of a promoter who lets nothing and no one stand in the way of his rise to the top. It was followed by the immensely popular *An Officer and a Gen-*

tleman, an abrasive, emotive and adrenalin-surging drama of officer recruits that won an Oscar for Louis Gossett Jr as the tough sergeant on their course. Hackford now seemed to be established, but instead he faltered. He continued with character-driven drama, but few people were interested in the characters from *Against All Odds*, a tepid remake of *Out of the Past*, *White Nights* and especially those from *Everybody's All American*, a downbeat drama about a star footballer whose life and career are going down the toilet, which probably damaged the career progress of its stars Dennis Quaid, Jessica Lange and Timothy Hutton. Hackford's fragmentary treatment never held one's attention and after it he withdrew from film-making to executive-produce major films for the company that had first led him to the cinema. *Bound by Honor* was an inauspicious return to direction five years later, but *Dolores Claiborne* was better and *The Devil's Advocate* better still, a cross between legal drama and satanic sci-fi with charismatic star performances from Al Pacino and Keanu Reeves. Hackford has been partners in life for many years with the British actress Helen Mirren, and it took their friends somewhat by surprise when they finally decided to marry on New Year's Eve 1997.

1978: **Teenage Father.* 1980: *The Idolmaker.* 1981: *An Officer and a Gentleman.* 1984: *Against All Odds.* 1985: *White Nights.* 1987: *Hail! Hail! Rock 'n' Roll! (D).* 1988: *Everybody's All American (GB: When I Fall in Love).* 1993:

Bound by Honor. 1995: *Dolores Claiborne.* 1997: *The Devil's Advocate.*

HALL, Alexander 1894-1968

When I think of this small, dapper American director, I immediately associate him with *Here Comes Mr Jordan*, that classic heaven-and-earth comedy remade years later with Warren Beatty as *Heaven Can Wait*. But in fact Hall made many other smooth, pleasant, entertaining films with above-average moments, mostly in musical sequences or scenes of high comedy. One suspected that, behind Hall's quizzical looks, there lurked an impish sense of humour and an inventive mind. He was a child actor whose budding adult career was interrupted by World War I service with the US Navy on board a submarine. After the war, Hall stayed in France gaining experience in various behind-the-scenes capacities with the Joinville Studios, as well as doing some acting. Returning to America in 1921, he took a couple of acting roles (one of them in Henry King's 1921 *Tol'able David*), then became an assistant director and editor for the remainder of the 1920s. There was very little time for humour in Hall's debut film as director, *Sinners in the Sun*, a 70-minute Carole Lombard vehicle which featured the young Cary Grant. The 1930s, in fact, was not a brilliant decade for Hall, who also continued his editing career on and off; but he did make the delightful *Little Miss Marker,* which provided Shirley Temple with her final boost to top stardom, and the Mae West film *Goin' to Town*, which is a lively, bubbly movie and probably says something about Hall's own brand of humour. Hall hit his stride at the beginning of the 1940s. Besides *Mr Jordan*, there were several lightweight entertainments highlighting the sophisticated comedy talents of Rosalind Russell, the best of them being *My Sister Eileen*, a bouncing bonanza box-office comedy hit, based on the stage success, with Janet Blair as Russell's kid sister. Hall's direction also sparkled on *Bedtime Story,* in which leads Loretta Young and Fredric March stood very little chance against what seemed like an entire supporting cast of inveterate scene-stealers, including Robert Benchley, Allyn Joslyn, Joyce Compton and Eve Arden. Hall was already beginning to climb down from the pinnacle of success but meantime there were some deliciously crazy touches in *The Heavenly Body, Once Upon a Time* (would you believe Cary Grant and Janet Blair in the story of a boy and his dancing caterpillar?), *The Great Lover* and *Love That Brute,* in which Paul Douglas is very funny indeed as a dim gangster. Hall's last two films were *Let's Do It Again*, with middle-ageing Jane Wyman and Ray Milland trying hard to pep up a semi-musical remake of *The Awful Truth*, and a disastrously fey vehicle for Lucille Ball and Desi Arnaz, *Forever Darling*. Hall was married to Lola Lane, one of the famous Lane sisters.

1932: Sinners in the Sun. †Madame Racketeer (GB: The Sporting Widow). 1933: †Midnight Club. †The Girl in 419. †Torch Singer (GB: Broadway Singer). 1934: Miss Fane's Baby is Stolen (GB: Kidnapped). Limehouse Blues. Little Miss Marker (GB: Girl in Pawn). The Pursuit of Happiness. 1935: Goin' to Town. Annapolis Farewell (GB: Gentlemen of the Navy). 1936: Give Us This Night. Yours for the Asking. 1937: Exclusive. 1938: There's Always a Woman. I Am the Law. There's That Woman Again (GB: What a Woman). 1939: Good Girls Go to Paris. The Lady's from Kentucky. The Amazing Mr Williams. 1940: The Doctor Takes a Wife. He Stayed for Breakfast. 1941: Bedtime Story. This Thing Called Love (GB: Married — But Single). Here Comes Mr Jordan. 1942: They All Kissed the Bride. My Sister Eileen. 1943: The Heavenly Body. 1944: Once Upon a Time. 1945: She Wouldn't Say Yes. 1947: Down to Earth. 1949: The Great Lover. 1950: Louisa. Love That Brute. 1951: Up Front. 1952: Because You're Mine. 1953: Let's Do It Again. 1956: Forever, Darling.

HALLER, Daniel 1928-

Los Angeles-born Haller's stylish contribution as art director on most of Roger Corman's Edgar Allan Poe films remains his outstanding achievement for the cinema, despite several interesting outings as a director since the mid-1960s. It now looks likely that Corman's handsome protégé will go down as an above-average maker of TV movies and occasionally striking director for the cinema. After studying set design at university, he worked as a designer for TV commercials until getting his break as art director and/or production designer on the low-budget horror films of Roger Corman, Bernard Kowalski and others releasing through American-International. Haller's handsome Gothic interiors on minimal budgets greatly enhanced the atmosphere and impact of such offerings as *The Fall of the House of Usher, The Pit and the Pendulum, The Premature Burial, Tales of Terror, Tower of London, The Terror, The Raven, The Haunted Palace* and *The Comedy of Terrors*. As Corman became successful, Haller was able to offer him more sophisticated sets and designs, notably for *The*

Masque of the Red Death. Haller began to direct on *Monster of Terror* in 1965, a disappointingly slack adaptation of H.P. Lovecraft's *The Color Out of Space*, but later showed a real feel for the horror genre in *The Dunwich Horror*, a tightly woven venture into the occult which uses camera angles to suggest evil and menace and is laudably reticent about actually showing any horror. But the demand for horror was slowing down and Haller moved into television, directing dozens of episodes of such series as *Night Gallery, A Man Called Ironside, Kojak* and *Charlie's Angels* before making TV movies, of which *Little Mo* is a real tear-jerker, *Buck Rogers in the Twenty-Fifth Century* a very enjoyable tongue-in-cheek pilot for the series, and *High Midnight* a serviceable thriller whose direction lifts it above the average TV crime yarn.

1965: Monster of Terror (US: Die, Monster, Die!). 1967: Devil's Angels. The Wild Racers. 1969: Paddy (US: Goodbye to the Hill). 1970: The Dunwich Horror. Pieces of Dreams. 1975: Khan (TV). Sunshine Part 11 (TV. GB cinemas as My Sweet Lady). The Desperate Miles (TV). 1978: Sword of Justice (TV). Little Mo (TV). 1979: Buck Rogers in the Twenty-Fifth Century (TV. GB: cinemas). High Midnight (TV). 1981: Follow That Car. Margin for Murder/Mickey Spillane's Margin for Murder (TV). Knight Rider (TV).

HAMER, Robert 1911-1963

One of the most brilliant, yet wayward directors ever produced by the British cinema, Hamer needed the stabilizing influence of a studio environment to create his best work. While he had that, with Ealing Studios, he made some of the finest and most distinctive films of the post-war years. But, as the Ealing product began to slip in the mid-1950s, so Hamer's confidence seemed to falter. He was a genius at creating atmosphere, and dialogue and characters that fitted into that atmosphere as if born there, whether in comedy or drama. And his *Kind Hearts and Coronets* is a landmark – and watershed – of British broad comedy, matched only by *The Ladykillers* (made by another director, Alexander Mackendrick *(qv)*, who eventually drifted away from films after the closure of Ealing). Hamer had entered the film industry straight from university, working his way up from assistant cutter to editor with London Films before joining Ealing in 1941. The studio gave him his first chance to direct in *Dead of Night*, on the 'haunted mirror' story. He followed this with two films starring Googie Withers, first as the (literally) poiso-

nous Brighton pub owner's wife of Victorian times in *Pink String and Sealing Wax*, then as the woman involved with a man on the run in post-war London in *It Always Rains on Sunday*. These are her two most striking performances, and both films found Hamer in superb control of his material. After *Kind Hearts and Coronets*, with Alec Guinness as the eight D'Ascoynes, all dying off rapidly, mostly at the hands of penniless would-be aristocrat Dennis Price, Hamer's work became more conventional, although all of his subsequent films (several again featuring Guinness) have their felicitous moments; none more so than *Father Brown*, a comedy-thriller based on G.K. Chesterton's clergyman detective, with Guinness perfectly cast in the title role, superbly abetted by Joan Greenwood, and by Peter Finch as the ubiquitous villain. Hamer's last film, *School for Scoundrels*, is also extremely funny in patches, but by this time alcoholism had all but drowned his talent. The only work he managed in the last few years of life, before death from a liver ailment, lay in contributions to the scripts of *55 Days at Peking* (1962) and *A Jolly Bad Fellow* (1963), the latter a black comedy of murder which Hamer in his heyday might have made a masterpiece to set alongside *Kind Hearts and Coronets*.

1945: †Dead of Night. Pink String and Sealing Wax. 1947: It Always Rains on Sunday. 1949: Kind Hearts and Coronets. The Spider and the Fly. 1951: His Excellency. 1952: The Long Memory. 1954: Father Brown (US: The Detective). To Paris with Love. 1958: The Scapegoat. 1959: School for Scoundrels.

HAMILTON, Guy 1922-

Hamilton remains the archetypal middle-range director of post-war British cinema. Tall, dark and austere, he worked for various famous masters as assistant director, received some critical praise for his terse direction of some good low-budget British 'A' movies of the 1950s, then seemed to dissipate his talent on big-budget spectaculars, of which he has been most successful with the James Bond films in his repertoire. Born in Paris of British parents, Hamilton started his film career as an apprentice with the Victorine Studios at Nice (he was fourth assistant director on Julien Duvivier's *(qv) Untel père et fils* in 1940). As the Nazis overran France, Hamilton crossed the Channel to England and joined the Royal Navy, serving until 1946. After demobilization, he learned the director's trade at the feet of various famous directors, including Carol Reed, Alberto Cavalcanti, Jean Negulesco and

John Huston (all *qv*). His first solo credit was the umpteenth adaptation of Edgar Wallace's hoary old story *The Ringer*, but Hamilton followed this with two attractively off-beat dramas, *The Intruder* (from Robin Maugham's story *Line on Ginger*, minus its homosexual element but none the worse for it) and *An Inspector Calls*, a film version of J.B. Priestley's story about a stuffy Edwardian family whose sins find them out via a 'ghost' detective. These were good enough to land Hamilton the direction of *The Colditz Story*, a cast-iron success from a best-selling book about prisoners of war escaping from an impregnable German fortress. Hamilton's skill with camera placements, which would only desert him in 1980 on *The Mirror Crack'd*, served him well in emphasizing the claustrophobic camaraderie of the prisoners and the tension of the escape scenes, and the acting strength and depth of the British cinema of the time produced a useful group of ensemble performances, especially from Eric Portman. This was the biggest success of Hamilton's early directing years; it was followed by a Max Bygraves musical vehicle, *Charley Moon*, that outstayed its welcome. *Manuela* was strong seafaring stuff about two men and a girl aboard a tramp steamer, with powerful performances from Trevor Howard and Pedro Armendariz, and a well-staged fire sequence. It remains the most original work of Hamilton's career, although his James Bond films, especially *Diamonds Are Forever* and *Live and Let Die*, are among the better ones in the series. After the disaster of *The Mirror Crack'd* — ironically the best part of this Agatha Christie thriller is the black-and-white film-within-a-film at the beginning — one thought he might reconsider films overloaded with stars and production values. But he continued along this track with another Christie multi-suspect mystery, *Evil Under the Sun*, his last film of any stature. He married the actresses Naomi Chance and Kerima.

1952: The Ringer. 1953: The Intruder. 1954: Au Inspector Calls. 1955: The Colditz Story. 1956: Charley Moon. 1957: Manuela (US: Stowaway Girl). 1959: The Devil's Disciple. A Touch of Larceny. 1961: The Best of Enemies. 1962: The Party's Over (released, abridged and with Hamilton's name removed by himself in 1965). 1964: Man in the Middle. Goldfinger. 1966: Funeral in Berlin. 1969: Battle of Britain. 1971: Diamonds Are Forever. 1973: Live & Let Die. 1974: The Man with the Golden Gun. 1978: Force 10 from Navarone. 1980: The Mirror Crack'd. 1982: Evil under the Sun. 1985: Remo Williams: The Adventure Begins (GB: Remo: Unarmed and Dangerous). 1989: Sauf votre respect/Try This On for Size.

HANSON, Curtis 1945-

Particularly adept at making movies that turn the well-ordered lives of their principal characters upside-down, Curtis Hanson has only gradually assumed real importance in the American cinema in his later years, and especially with the enormous critical success of *L.A. Confidential*. Originally a journalist, photographer and writer, he was editor of the influential *Cinema* magazine in his twenties and, ambitious to make, write and direct his own films, completed his first movie, *The Arousers*, at 25. Released in 1972, it was a complete flop at the box-office, although actually a powerful early study of a psychopathic serial killer who murders women when he finds himself unable to make love to them. Tab Hunter gave his finest film performance in the central role. Following its failure, Hanson devoted himself to a writing career for the next ten years, combining journalism with screenwriting. Not until 1980 did he try another film of his own, then three years later achieved a breakthrough with the rites-of-passage youth comedy *Losin' It*, which featured Shelley Long and an early starring role for Tom Cruise. Since then Hanson has concentrated on suspense and thrills, although there have only been five further films. All are of interest: *The Bedroom Window* is sub-Hitchcock but entertainingly done; *Bad Influence* was a fascinating if flawed study of evil; *The Hand That Rocks the Cradle*, a big box-office hit, was a traditional Hollywood shocker that caught the public imagination; and *The River Wild* had a typically dedicated performance by Meryl Streep and a crunchingly exciting last 20 minutes. An essay on big-city crime and corruption in the early 1950s, the award-winning *L.A. Confidential* placed Hanson firmly in the front rank of Hollywood directors. An engrossing, constantly hard-as-nails story, the film is conventional at heart, but crisp and atmospheric in the execution. Several characters interweave in one of those satisfying plots replete with darkness and violence, where all the pieces fall into place at the end. The pieces now seem to have fallen into place in Hanson's directing career, but the years when he wasn't making movies still remain a source of regret. Oscar nominee for *L.A. Confidential*.

1972: The Arousers/A Kiss from Eddie (GB: Sweet Kill). 1983: Losin' It. 1986: The Children of Times Square (TV).

Director Curtis **Hanson** wears one of his characteristic hats on location for *The Hand that Rocks the Cradle*.

1987: The Bedroom Window. 1990: Bad Influence. 1992: The Hand That Rocks the Cradle. 1994: The River Wild. 1997: L.A. Confidential.

HARLIN, Renny 1958-

Wild-haired Finnish director who settled in Hollywood in the mid-1980s, where he started making films with a horror slant, but soon showed a liking for big-budget action. From a medical family (his father was a surgeon), Harlin soon forsook this tradition in favour of films, becoming involved in his country's film industry before making commercials, industrial films, and then his first short in 1982. Disappointed with his efforts at getting funding for a feature film in Finland, he raised the money from America, and shot *Born American* mainly in Finland with American actors. It was hardly an auspicious start, but Harlin then went to Hollywood and showed a startling improvement in the technical quality of his work with *Prison*. A full-blooded chiller, it combined the toughest possible elements of the prison and horror genres, its effect-laden action scenes ingeniously contrived and staged with considerable panache. That landed Harlin an assignment with one of the *Nightmare on Elm Street* movies but it was the fluency and technical expertise he displayed in the making of *Die Hard 2* that jetted him into the big time. Thought not quite in the class of the original Bruce Willis thriller, this was a powerhouse of a film with some hammer-hard action sequences. Harlin now married American actress Geena Davis, and starred her in two action films: a messy pirate adventure, *CutThroat Island* and *The Long Kiss Goodnight*, a real crowd-pleaser (with Davis as a sort of Jane Bond) that did not ignite the box-office in the way that it might have, probably partially due to the failure of Davis and Harlin's previous high-profile venture together. The couple then parted and for a while Harlin was less active.

1982: *Hold On. 1986: Born American. 1988: Prison. A Nightmare on Elm Street 4: The Dream Master. 1990: The Adventures of Ford Fairlane. Die Hard 2. 1993: Cliffhanger. 1995: CutThroat Island. 1996: The Long Kiss Goodnight. 1999: Deep Blue Sea.

HARLOW, John 1896-

British director, mostly of lowbrow thrillers. Harlow was a former concert-party actor with yearnings to be a writer. In the mid-1920s, he went to Elstree to contribute to scenarios, and had become an assistant director there by 1927. The major part of Harlow's career as a director began in the 1940s, when the absence of other talents in wartime gave him the opportunity to establish himself and he made several strong downbeat dramas and thrillers between 1941 and 1947. These films promoted the career of David Farrar, who proved an extremely effective Sexton Blake in *Meet Sexton Blake* and *The Echo Murders*, and also featured in Harlow's *Headline* and *The Dark Tower*. Harlow was also a key man in changing the course of William Hartnell's career from comedy to drama, thanks to his gritty, high-pressure performances in *Headline, The Dark Tower* and especially *The Agitator* and *Appointment with Crime*, for which last film Hartnell changed his credit from Billy to William. Harlow's films were mostly sombre stuff, but, apart from the very silly Jessie Matthews misfortune, *Candles at Nine*, he was doing well, until a change of direction brought him into the broad comedy of the Old Mother Riley films, and his career took a nosedive. He returned to thrillers, but was able to obtain only very minor second-features, and was gone from the cinema scene by the mid-1950s, spending the remainder of his working years in TV. Harlow's specific talents should have taken him further, had he not seemed to make the wrong decisions at the wrong time. For most of his better films, he also wrote or co-wrote the screenplays.

1928: *Phototone Reels (series). 1933: Songbirds. My Lucky Star. 1934: Master and Man. Bagged. 1941: Spellbound (US: The Spell of Amy Nugent). 1942: This Was Paris. 1943: Headline. *One Company. The Dark Tower. 1944: Candles at Nine. Meet Sexton Blake. The Agitator. 1945: The Echo Murders. 1946: Appointment with Crime. 1947: Green Fingers.

1948: While I Live. 1949: Old Mother Riley's New Venture. 1950: Old Mother Riley Headmistress. 1952: Those People Next Door. 1953: The Blue Parrot. 1954: Dangerous Cargo. Delayed Action.

HARRINGTON, Curtis 1928-

Despite some interesting ventures into the field of horror, one feels sure that this ambitious American director has not achieved the targets he must have set for himself, when making the transition from 'underground' to commercial film-making in the early 1960s. As well as the horror genre, Harrington's interests include the films of Josef von Steinberg *(qv)* and the Japanese cinema, and visual influences from these masters are evident in his own work. Despite some critical attention, however, especially for *Night Tide* and *Games*, his work has become increasingly lurid, and he now seems entrenched in television. Harrington began making short films for himself at the age of 14. He continued making independent films, usually creepy shorts, well into the 1950s, combining this with a career in film journalism. From 1956 to 1962, Harrington worked for Twentieth Century-Fox, mostly as associate producer, on such films as *Peyton Place, The Long Hot Summer* and *The Stripper*. Then he moved to features as director: *Night Tide* was an interesting dream-like first effort, and it was followed by Harrington's best period to date, from 1966 to 1973, which included *Planet of Blood, Games, What's the Matter with Helen?* and the telefeatures *How Awful About Allan* (this having splendidly enigmatic performances from Anthony Perkins and Julie Harris) and *The Cat Creature*. These were characterized by tight, urgent direction, which kept the audience on edge awaiting the sudden shock, and by particularly high colour values. But, especially in view of its paucity, Harrington's output was extremely disappointing in its last ten years.

1942: *The Fall of the House of Usher. 1943: *Crescendo. 1944: *Renaissance. 1946. *Symbol of Decadence (later Fragment of Seeking). 1948: *Picnic. 1949: *On the Edge. 1952: *Dangerous Houses (unreleased). 1953: *The Assignation. 1955: *The Wormwood Star (released 1957). 1961: Night Tide (released US 1963. Released GB 1966). 1964: *Images of Productivity. 1966: †Voyage to the Planet of the Prehistoric Women/Voyage to a Prehistoric Planet (American version of Russian film Cosmonauts on Venus). Planet of Blood/Queen of Blood. *The Four Elements. 1967: Games. 1970: How Awful About Allan (TV). 1971: What's the

Matter with Helen? Whoever Slew Auntie Roo? (US: Who Slew Auntie Roo?). 1973: The Cat Creature (TV). The Killing Kind. 1974: Killer Bees (TV). 1975: The Dead Don't Die (TV). 1977: Ruby. 1979: Devil Dog: The Hound of Hell (TV). 1983: Mata Hari (released 1985).

HART, Harvey 1928-1989

Canadian Harvey Hart was the man you *would* have put your money on to make the grade in 1965. That was the year of *Bus Riley's Back in Town*, Hart's second film (the first was a 58-minute 'B' feature) which had some critics shouting his virtues and might well have had others doing the same if Universal had promoted it a bit more. *Bus* is about a man (Michael Parks: the film should have got him bigger leading roles but didn't) who arrives back home after two years in the Navy. His former girl-friend (Ann-Margret) has married for money to an older man often away on business trips. The film is concerned with Bus's attempts to find himself a job, disentangle himself from her spell and adjust to a new life. Things to remember about this often charming and very intimate film include the warm home atmosphere of the Rileys. The dialogue (written by William Inge under the pseudonym Walter Gage) is very sensitive, very understanding, and Hart's low-key handling ensures a set of beautifully underplayed performances. I note that I wrote at the time that it was a film which left one fascinated as to what its director might go on to achieve. Well, watch fascination turn to horror. It seems a harsh judgment to say that Hart's career thereafter is a catalogue of disaster, but most of the films it contains are not even moderate. One looks in vain for something good in reviews of the odd Hart film one has not seen. All one can come up with are one or two serviceable TV movies: *Can Ellen Be Saved?* and *Panic on the 5.22*. Any revival hopes were snuffed out when Hart succumbed to a heart attack at 61.

1965: Dark Intruder. Bus Riley's Back in Town. 1967: †Sullivan's Empire. The Sweet Ride. 1969: The Young Lawyers (TV). 1971: Fortune and Men's Eyes. 1973: The Pyx. 1974: Can Ellen Be Saved? (TV). Murder or Mercy (TV). Panic on the 5.22 (TV). 1976: Street Killing (TV). Shoot. 1977: The City (TV). Goldenrod (originally for cinemas but only shown on TV. The Prince of Central Park (TV). Captains Courageous (TV). 1978: WEB (TV). Standing Tall (TV). 1979: Like Normal People (TV). 1980: The High Country. The Aliens Are Coming (TV). 1981: Utilities. This is Kate

Bennett (TV). 1982: *Born Beautiful* (TV). 1983: *Party Animal. Massarati and the Brain* (TV). 1984: †*Master of the Game* (TV). 1985: *Reckless Disregard* (TV). 1986: *Beverly Hills Madam* (TV). 1987: *Murder Sees the Light* (TV). *Stone Fox* (TV).

HARTFORD-DAVIS, Robert 1923-1977

Despite the fact that he was mostly involved with exploitation subjects, Hartford-Davis was an interesting director who loved camera movement, taking a schoolboy's delight in zooms, crane shots, tracking shots and all the rest of the mobility at the camera s command. Apart from *Saturday Night Out*, which has a tender love story and some spectacular crane work woven into its multiple-story structure, Hartford-Davis's best work lies in the field of the horror film, and his use of colour in *The Black Torment* is delicate and imaginative. One recalls the scene where a bride on a black horse chases the hero through a forest of grey trees (another of Hartford-Davis's favoured tracking shots) with an echoing cry of 'Murderer!' Hartford-Davis had Desmond Dickinson behind the colour cameras on *Incense for the Damned*, a rather troubled version of Simon Raven's vampire novel *Doctors Wear Scarlet*, which, though finally released two years later with the director using a pseudonym, still proves to be a striking and quite faithful adaptation of the book, which deserved wider distribution than it was given. After entering films briefly in 1939, then picking up the threads in the post-war years, Hartford-Davis worked mostly on documentaries before becoming caught up in rather lurid exploitation films that constituted the Compton-Cameo group's efforts to move into big-time distribution and production. *That Kind of Girl* was 'social problem' drama, while *The Yellow Teddybears* was a nymphet-schoolgirl forerunner of the sexploitation film. Later, Hartford-Davis unwisely tried comedy, but *The Sandwich Man* was little more than a series of pier-end sketches, and *Press for Time* the weakest of the Norman Wisdoms — up to that time. Hartford-Davis should have stuck to the literate, elegant, intelligent chiller in which he had proved his ability. Instead, he went to America, and there were a couple of violent crime thrillers which hardly surfaced in Britain, before he vanished from the scene.

1952: *City of Contrast* (D). 1953: †*Dollars for Sale* (uncredited). 1955: *Man on the Cliff* (D). 1960: *A Christmas Carol. 1961: *Crosstrap. 1962: *That Kind of Girl. 1963: The Yellow Teddybears. Saturday Night Out. 1964: The Black Torment. 1965: Gonks Go Beat. 1966: The Sandwich Man. Press for Time. 1967: Corruption. 1969: The Smashing Bird I Used to Know. 1970: $Incense for the Damned. 1971: Nobody Ordered Love. The Fiend. 1972: Black Gunn. 1974: The Take.

$ As Michael Burrows

HARTLEY, Hal 1959-

Still hovering on the fringes of American cinema after ten years, festival favourite Hartley makes quirky black romantic dramas with undertones of (rarely seen) violence. The influence of Jean-Luc Godard is there for all to see in Hartley's films, which favour, as central figures, female protagonists played by such offbeat actresses as Adrienne Shelly and Parker Posey. After studying painting as the Massachusetts College of Art, Hartley found little initial outlet for his talents, ending up selling cameras and TV sets in a department store. In his spare time, he made small films on Super-8 stock, one of which won him acceptance to a film school, where he studied for three years before beginning his career as a film director with several medium-length shorts around half an hour long. He was 30 before scraping together the finance for his first feature, completed in only a couple of weeks. *The Unbelievable Truth* was a bizarrely plotted story about a model obsessed that nuclear holocaust and the end of the world are at hand. As with many of Hartley's films, the performances are rather more persuasive than the plot, suggesting that this could be a more interesting director if he were in charge of someone else's material. This was certainly true of *Trust*, where Hartley's subtle and understated direction helps performers Adrienne Shelly and Martin Donovan make the most of some rather pretentious dialogue as two losers who, seemingly set for a lifetime of unhappiness, touch each other's lives and make them better. As the 1990s have progressed, Hartley has flattered only to deceive. His most recent film at time of writing, *Henry Fool*, described by one work contemporary critic as 'the whole nine yards on Hal Hartley in one movie', ran out rather longer than nine yards at two hours 21 minutes. Sometimes amusing and sometimes poignant, in the now-established Hartley style, the film's dialogue, although more witty and sophisticated than in previous Hartley ventures, runs out of steam after the first hour.

1985: *Kid. 1986: *The Cartographer's Girlfriend. 1987: *Dogs. 1989: The Unbelievable Truth. 1990: Trust. 1991: Surviv-ing Desire. 1992: Simple Men. 1994: Amateur. 1995: Flirt. 1997: Henry Fool. 1998: The Book of Life.

HARVEY, Anthony 1931-

One might have expected Harvey to become one of Britain's most prominent directors after *The Lion in Winter*, but in the event this has not quite happened. Over-impressed, perhaps, by the success of that film, for which he was nominated for an Oscar, he has gone in for rather portentous (sometimes pretentious) subjects whose solemnity has outweighed their entertainment value. Harvey was a child actor who gradually progressed to editing through working in libraries, cutting rooms, laboratories and for G.B. Instructional. He learned his trade mainly in films by the Boulting Brothers (although also editing Kubrick's *Lolita* and *Dr Strangelove*) and edited some of Britain's best films from the late 1950s and early 1960s. His first film was a low-budget black-and-white affair about racial violence on the New York subway, with a lot of raw energy and power. His second, *The Lion in Winter*, remains his best, a richly enjoyable story about verbal warfare between Henry II, his exiled wife, Eleanor of Aquitaine, and their thoroughly dislikeable sons. Some brilliantly waspish dialogue by James Goldman was chewed over with relish by Katharine Hepburn (an Oscar-winner for her role) and Peter O'Toole in one of his most controlled performances. Harvey's cameras lingered appreciatively over this royal meal, showing again that he knew when to let his players have their heads if it was of benefit to the film. After this, however, he strayed into the field of critical but not commercial successes; *The Abdication*, another sad misfire in Liv Ullmann's ill-fated international career, was neither. Since then, *Eagle's Wing* had certain primitive strengths, but *Richard's Things*, another venture with Liv Ullmann, did not begin to work, and was sloughed off into television instead of the cinemas for which it was intended. Harvey's output has been disappointingly sparse in recent years.

1966: *Dutchman*. 1968: *The Lion in Winter*. 1971: *They Might Be Giants*. 1973: *The Glass Menagerie* (shown only on television). 1974: *The Abdication*. 1976: *The Disappearance of Aimee* (TV). 1978: *Eagle's Wing*. 1979: *Players*. 1980: *Richard's Things* (shown only on television). 1981: †*An Act of Love* (TV). *The Patricia Neal Story* (TV). 1983: *Svengali* (TV). 1984: *The Ultimate Solution of Grace Quigley* (GB: *Grace Quigley*). 1993: *This Can't Be Love* (TV).

HASKIN, Byron 1899-1984

This American director made such vivid adventure films that it seems rather a pity that he chose to make the greater part of his career as photographer and special effects man. It's no surprise that he was a newspaper cartoonist in his youth, for many of his films have the vigour and dash of strip-cartoon thrillers. Haskin was an assistant cameraman in the employ of Lewis J. Selznick (father of David O. Selznick) by 1919. Selznick's empire was soon to crumble but, just before it did, in 1922, Haskin had established his first solo credits as director of photography. He continued as cameraman until 1936 (with a few brief ventures into direction in the late 1920s) but, from 1932, was increasingly devoting his time to special effects, usually with Warner Brothers, and most often in the films of Michael Curtiz, Lewis Seiler, Raoul Walsh, Lloyd Bacon, William Keighley and John Huston (all *qv*). He returned permanently to direction at the Paramount studio in 1947, his first film being the grim gangster drama *I Walk Alone*. His reputation as a director of virile action was established by his colourful 1950 version of *Treasure Island* for the Disney studio. There were some good, vigorous westerns for the Pine-Thomas unit, especially *Denver and Rio Grande* with its spectacular train crash, although *Silver City* also had some tense train footage towards the end. *War of the Worlds* revealed Haskin's liking for the science-fiction genre and his talent for the effects involved. All of his subsequent ventures into the field are worthwhile, the next being the high-grossing *Conquest of Space*. His last three films are all sci-fi, in fact, and unfailingly inventive and exciting. *Captain Sindbad*, in jewel-bright colour, has a fabulous nine-headed monster and other equally good trick effects, easily outpointing the later efforts by Ray Harryhausen. *Robinson Crusoe on Mars* is a truly ingenious and splendidly realized space-age version of Defoe's yarn, great fun for boys from five to 85. *The Power* is a chilling and compelling thriller about a man with a super-powerful mind. It was much copied, especially by TV movies, in ensuing years. There are a few low spots in Haskin's career, particularly in the period from 1957 to 1962, but the last films revive one's faith in his ability. Mention should also be made of *The Boss*, a tough, sombre thriller well in the *I Walk Alone* mould. He died from cancer.

1927: *Irish Hearts. Matinee Ladies. The Siren. Ginsberg the Great* (GB: *The Broadway Kid*). 1930: $*Rookery Nook* (US: *One Embarrassing Night*). $*Canaries Sometimes Sing*. 1931: $*Plunder*. 1947: *I Walk Alone*. 1948: *Man-Eater of Kumaon*. 1949: *Too Late for Tears*. 1950: *Treasure Island*. 1951: *Warpath. Silver City* (GB: *High Vermilion*). *Tarzan and the Jungle Queen* (GB: *Tarzan's Peril*). 1952: *Denver and Rio Grande. War of the Worlds*. 1953: *His Majesty O'Keefe. The Naked Jungle*. 1954: *Long John Silver. Conquest of Space*. 1956: *The Boss. The First Texan* 1958. *From the Earth to the Moon*. 1959: *Jet Over the Atlantic. The Little Savage*. 1960: *September Storm*. 1961: *Armored Command*. 1963: *Captain Sindbad*. 1964: *Robinson Crusoe on Mars*. 1967: *The Power*.

$ as supervisor/technical supervisor

HATHAWAY, Henry (Henri de Fiennes) 1898-1985

One of the most professional of Hollywood journeyman directors, making films for more than 40 years, most of them for Paramount and Twentieth Century-Fox, the majority of them good (apart from a little clutch in the late 1950s), and some superbly entertaining. A child actor from 1908, Hathaway gradually became interested in the other side of the camera at first (from 1916) as property man, then (from 1923) as assistant director. He gained his baptism as a director on Paramount's 'Zane Grey' westerns, mostly featuring Randolph Scott, and a thundering good job he did on these middle-budget action films. The western would reoccur in Hathaway's career, but for the moment he concentrated on widening his range: *Now and Forever* was a cute romantic trifle that pushed Shirley Temple's career forward another notch, *The Lives of a Bengal Lancer* rousing 'North West Frontier' stuff with Gary Cooper, and *Peter Ibbetson* Cooper again in a rather rarefied romantic fantasy. Hathaway was now established, especially with the success of the early Technicolor western, *The Trail of the Lonesome Pine*. There was a series of rural dramas in the early 1940s, but he entered one of his most fruitful periods working for Fox on their realist thrillers of the middle years of the decade. These five films, made between 1945 and 1947, are perhaps the cornerstone of Hathaway's work. The best of them is *Call Northside 777*, a totally absorbing story, based on fact, of a reporter's efforts to prove the innocence of a man jailed for a murder he didn't commit. The underworld was also examined in *Kiss of Death* (with Richard Widmark's debut as the giggling killer) and *The Dark Corner*, which provided Clifton Webb with more suave villainy, while espionage was the name of the game in *The House on 92nd Street* and *13 Rue Madeleine*. Hathaway's remaining years at Fox were a time of ups and downs; almost all of the 'ups' were in the thriller genre, notably *Fourteen Hours*, *Niagara* (in which Hathaway brilliantly launched Marilyn Monroe, with the help of her own talent, some teasing camera angles and a massive publicity campaign), and *Seven Thieves*. Now in his sixties, Hathaway still had the vigour to make some fiery westerns, mainly with John Wayne; they included *North to Alaska*, *The Sons of Katie Elder*, *Five Card Stud* – an oddball but rather successful western for Agatha Christie fans – and Wayne's Oscar-winning *True Grit*. Hathaway himself was only once even nominated for an Oscar, but his films themselves are testimony to his ability to heighten narrative tension and shoot action so exhilarating it made the adrenalin run.

1932: *Wild Horse Mesa. Heritage of the Desert*. 1933. *Men of the Forest. Under the Tonto Rim. To the Last Man. The Thundering Herd. Sunset Pass*. 1934: *The Last Round-Up. Come On Marines! Witching Hour. Now and Forever*. 1935: *The Lives of a Bengal Lancer. Peter Ibbetson*. 1936: *Go West, Young Man. I Loved a Soldier* (unfinished). *The Trail of the Lonesome Pine*. 1937: *Souls at Sea*. 1938: *Spawn of the North*. 1939: *The Real Glory*. 1940: *Brigham Young — Frontiersman* (GB: *Brigham Young*). *Johnny Apollo*. 1941: *The Shepherd of the Hills. Sundown*. 1942: *China Girl. Ten Gentlemen from West Point*. 1943: †*A Lady Takes a Chance* (uncredited). 1944: *Wing and a Prayer. Home in Indiana*. 1945: *Nob Hill. The House on 92nd Street*. 1946: *The Dark Corner. 13 Rue Madeleine*. 1947: *Kiss of Death. Call Northside 777*. 1949: *Down to the Sea in Ships*. 1950: *Rawhide/Desperate Siege. The Black Rose. USS Teakettle* (later *You're in The Navy Now*, recopyrighted as 1951). 1951: *Fourteen Hours. The Desert Fox* (GB: *Rommel — Desert Fox*). 1952: *Diplomatic Courier*. †*Red Skies of Montana* (uncredited). †*O Henry's Full House* (GB: *Full House*). 1953: *The Coronation Parade. White Witch Doctor. Niagara*. 1954: *Prince Valiant. Garden of Evil*. 1955: *The Racers* (GB: *Such Men Are Dangerous*). 1956: *The Bottom of the Bottle* (GB: *Beyond the River*). *23 Paces to Baker Street*. 1957: *Legend of the Lost*. 1958: *From Hell to Texas* (GB: *Manhunt*). 1959: *Woman Obsessed. Seven Thieves*. 1960: *North to Alaska*. 1962: †*Rampage!* (uncredited). †*How the West Was Won*. 1964: †*Of Human Bondage* (uncredited). *Circus World* (GB: *The Magnificent Showman*). 1965: *The Sons of Katie Elder*. 1966: *Nevada Smith*.

This studio portrait of Howard **Hawks** dates from around 1940, one of the few unsmiling pictures of a humorous "man's man".

1967: *The Last Safari*. 1968: *Five Card Stud*. 1969: *True Grit*. 1971: *Shoot Out. Raid on Rommel*. 1973: *Hangup*.

HAWKS, Howard 1896-1977

It's appropriate that alphabetical order should throw Hawks and Henry Hathaway together, for these two American directors had a lot in common besides the same initials. They were both rugged, outdoorsy types. Both made John Wayne westerns — Hathaway's are slightly better films, Hawks' more effective celebrations of the Wayne persona — and strongly characterized action dramas boiling with atmosphere, featuring gutsy women and virile male camaraderie. But Hawks is slightly more into the nitty-gritty of life: his characters are always letting their hair down, to tremendous effect. Hathaway made no comedies, whereas Hawks' screwball farces are riotous masterpieces, so crisp that they might fall apart — but Hawks has raced on another couple of scenes before you could think about that. Women pursue, and men steer clear of marriage — but Hawks gives his ladies the last laugh with almost all the sharpest lines in the man-woman crossfire in his films. Katharine Hepburn, Lauren Bacall, Rosalind Russell, Paula Prentiss and Ann Sheridan were never funnier or more cutting than under Hawks' direction. A very tall, rangy man, he served as an officer in the US Army Air Corps in his younger days, before becoming a designer in an aircraft factory. But he soon longed to

return to the film business where he had briefly worked as a prop boy five years earlier. After using his own money to back an epic western, *Custer's Last Stand/Bob Hampton of Placer*, Hawks made contacts that enabled him to join the script department of Famous Players-Lasky. He wrote his first screen story, *Quicksands*, in 1923, followed by his first bona-fide screenplay, *Tiger Love*, in 1924. He started directing in 1926, but the Hawks classics really begin with sound: *The Dawn Patrol* has a wonderful feel for early aviation (not surprisingly in view of Hawks' own career) and *The Criminal Code* is a strong and trail-blazing prison drama that gave Boris Karloff the eye-catching featured role that led to him being asked to play the creature in *Frankenstein*. Hawks coaxed fierce performances from Paul Muni in *Scarface* and Edward G. Robinson in *Tiger Shark* to consolidate his reputation as one of Hollywood's leading directors. The fast and furious Hawks comedies began with Carole Lombard and John Barrymore feuding and fighting aboard the *Twentieth Century*. Almost all of his films in this vein are original and exceptionally funny, but perhaps especially *Bringing Up Baby, His Girl Friday, I Was a Male War Bride* and *Monkey Business* (and no coincidence that all four employed the deft, wide-eyed comedy talents of Cary Grant). Meanwhile, Hawks continued to make his brawling action films, teeming with atmosphere and life: *Barbary Coast, Ceiling Zero, Only Angels Have Wings*. In the 1940s, they got a bit more serious, as Hawks moved into war and crime: *Sergeant York, Air Force, To Have and Have Not, The Big Sleep* — but their impact was just as strong. Perhaps unsurprisingly with his devil-may-care approach, Hawks was never nominated for an Academy Award, but a shamefaced Hollywood finally gave him one in 1974 as 'a giant of the American cinema whose pictures taken as a whole represent one of the most consistent, vivid and varied bodies of work in world cinema'.

1926: *The Road to Glory. Fig Leaves*. 1927: *Paid to Love. The Cradle Snatchers. Fazil*. 1928. *A Girl in Every Port*. †*The Air Circus*. 1929: *Trent's Last Case*. 1930: *The Dawn Patrol*. 1931: *The Criminal Code*. 1932: *Scarface. The Crowd Roars. Tiger Shark*. 1933: *Today We Live*. 1934: *Twentieth Century*. 1935: *Ceiling Zero. Barbary Coast*. 1936: *The Road to Glory*. †*Come and Get It*. 1938: *Bringing Up Baby*. 1939: *Only Angels Have Wings*. 1940: *His Girl Friday*. 1941: *Sergeant York. Ball of Fire*. 1943: *Air Force*. †*Corvette K-225* (GB: *The Nelson Touch*.

Uncredited). 1944: *To Have and Have Not*. 1946: *The Big Sleep*. 1947: *Red River. A Song is Born*. 1949: *I Was a Male War Bride* (GB: *You Can't Sleep Here*). 1951: †*The Thing from Another World* (uncredited). 1952: *Monkey Business. The Big Sky*. †*O. Henry's Full House* (GB: *Full House*). 1953: *Gentlemen Prefer Blondes*. 1955: *Land of the Pharaohs*. 1958: *Rio Bravo*. 1962: *Hatari!* 1964: *Man's Favorite Sport?* 1965: *Red Line 7000*. 1967: *El Dorado*. 1970: *Rio Lobo*.

HAYERS, Sidney 1921-

The cinema may owe the presence of this chunky, bespectacled British director in its annals to his being invalided out of war service in 1942, after being wounded while serving as a pilot in the RAF. The young Hayers became involved with the production of a film about RAF men, *One of Our Aircraft is Missing*. After its completion, he joined up with the film's makers, Michael Powell and Emeric Pressburger, as a sound engineer and apprentice editor. He worked steadily as a film editor in the post-war years on a fairly undistinguished bunch of pictures, the best of which were Jack Lee's *A Town Like Alice* and Roy Baker's *Passage Home* and *The One That Got Away*. It was Baker who gave Hayers his first taste of direction when he allowed him to direct some scenes in *A Night to Remember* in 1958, the year Hayers decided to branch out on his own. His first few films were moderate second-features, but almost all of his films from *Circus of Horrors* to *The Southern Star* (the best of the lot) were minor 'A' class entries that were better than one would have expected. Besides *The Southern Star*, an immensely enjoyable, and very slightly dotty African adventure story for schoolboys of all ages, mention should also be made of *Night of the Eagle*, a genuinely frightening witchcraft chiller in which Hayers eschews almost all use of overt horror; *The Trap*, a touching love story in the snowy wilds of Canada; and *Three Hats for Lisa*, in which Hayers fashioned a rather charming musical from the most unlikely material. His 1970s' films were largely disappointing, but the middle-bracket market in which Hayers had made his mark was quickly disappearing, and it was not surprising when in the late 1970s, he chose to work in America on mini-series for television. These included *The Seekers, The Last Convertible* and *Condominium* (GB: *When the Hurricane Struck*). Unfortunately, these show every evidence that Hayers' best work will remain in the 1960s. Besides the credits below, he worked as second-unit director on Richard Attenborough's *A Bridge Too Far* in 1977.

1958: Violent Moment. 1959: The White Trap. 1960: The Malpas Mystery. Echo of Barbara. Circus of Horrors. 1961: Payroll. 1962: Night of the Eagle (US: Burn, Witch, Burn). 1963: This is My Street. 1965: Three Hats for Lisa. 1966: The Trap. Finders Keepers. 1969: The Southern Star. Mister Jerico (TV. GB: cinemas). 1970: The Firechasers (US: TV). Assault. 1971: Revenge. All Coppers Are . . . 1974: Deadly Strangers. Diagnosis: Murder. What Changed Charley Farthing? 1975: One Away. 1980: †Conquest of the Earth (TV. GB: cinemas). 1981: Jack Flash (TV).

HEISLER, Stuart 1894-1979

This American director made fewer films that one would expect from a 20-year career (not counting his lone 1960s' movie) and a look at his record suggests that by and large he was choosy about what he made. His television record from 1958 to 1963 (almost entirely in westerns) is highly-rated by TV buffs and gives the same impression. His best films — *The Biscuit Eater, Among the Living, The Glass Key, Smash-Up, Tulsa, The Star* and *This is My Love* — are all strong stuff of their kind. The lesser films are mostly in lighter vein, and one can infer a lack of positive approach on the director's behalf — not that one can blame him in some instances, although his failure to make anything from the Bogart films or *I Died a Thousand Times* (the remake of *High Sierra*) is disappointing. He was obviously at home, though, with heady, dark emotions, and the intensity and depth of some of his work is very impressive. Heisler spent a lifetime in films (coming to Hollywood in 1913), working his way very slowly up the behind-camera hierarchy until he became an editor in 1924. It took him another 16 years to make an impact as a director, and when he did it was with a film that is today almost forgotten. But *The Biscuit Eater* (the only poor thing about this film is its title) paved the way for a whole host of boy-and-animal pictures to follow. Few, however, had such Flaherty-like qualities of photography and atmosphere (cameraman Leo Tover) as *The Biscuit Eater*, which was shot almost entirely on location in Georgia. Heisler was as successful with the 'frightening' aspects of the plot (a zombie-like negro steals the boy's dog and retreats with it into the swamp) as with a delightful dream sequence and an ending which steers skilfully between sen-

timentality and morbidity. Paramount gave him a couple of semi-horror 'B's after that, neither of which is bad: one, *Among the Living*, with Albert Dekker as twin brothers, one a killer, introduced Heisler to Susan Hayward, who was later to star for him with great spirit in *Smash-Up* (her first Oscar nomination) and *Tulsa*, a rousing story of blood and thunder in the Oklahoma oil-fields, fiercely shot in blazing Technicolor by Winton C. Hoch in the same year that he won his Oscar for colour photography on *She Wore a Yellow Ribbon*. But, before those, Heisler made a very good version of Dashiell Hammett's *The Glass Key*, a really tough thriller, full of memorable lines and moments, which confirmed Alan Ladd's stardom, and pushed William Bendix's standing forward to that of favourite featured player. Heisler's low-angle camerawork, repeated in *Smash-Up*, adds greatly to the film's feeling of raw violence. This is also true of the best of his later films, *This Is My Love*, a powerful, tragic drama with haunting theme music, a throbbingly true performance from Linda Darnell which had great impact, and a pathetically brilliant portrayal of an embittered cripple by Dan Duryea. Mention should also be made of the war film *Beachhead*, in which Heisler's skill with the thrills overcomes the artificiality of the story. But once Heisler saddled up with Warners, his TV work became more interesting than his few remaining efforts for the cinema.

1936: Straight from the Shoulder. †Poppy (uncredited). 1937: †The Hurricane (uncredited). 1939: †They Shall Have Music (GB: Melody of Love. Uncredited). 1940: The Biscuit Eater (GB: God Gave Him a Dog). 1941: The Monster and the Girl. Among the Living. 1942: The Glass Key. The Remarkable Andrew. 1944: The Negro Soldier (D). 1945: Along Came Jones. 1946: Blue Skies. 1947: Smash-Up, the Story of a Woman (GB. A Woman Destroyed). 1949: Tokyo Joe. Tulsa. 1950: †Vendetta (uncredited. Heisler's contribution filmed 1947). Dallas. Chain Lightning. Storm Warning. 1951: Journey into Light. 1952: Saturday Island (US: Island of Desire). 1953: The Star. 1954: Beachhead. This Is My Love. 1955: I Died a Thousand Times. 1956: The Burning Hills. The Lone Ranger. 1961: Hitler.

HELLMAN, Monte 1931-

American director whose wilful, almost self-destructive independence has kept him in a cinematic wilderness for most of the last 20 years. Hellman's world peruses the deserts, highways, byways, backstreets

and underbelly of American life. His stars are similarly independent-minded people, such as Jack Nicholson and Warren Oates. His films exude a raw power, even if they are rarely likeable and sometimes not even easily understandable. They are, however, by and large, experiences worth undergoing, if not to be repeated. In his younger days, Hellman was very much associated with director/producer Roger Corman *(qv)*, who produced his first film. Since the two desert westerns, *Ride the Whirlwind* and *The Shooting*, in which Hellman brought strange, allegoric qualities to a standard exploitation script, he has remained a maverick, making films appreciated by the intelligentsia, but virtually ignored by the public. The trouble with the films of the 1970s is that their sense of alienation tends to communicate itself to the audience. It is all very well eschewing the easy approach to a subject, but the entertainment of those who will keep one in business to make more films must always be borne in mind. Hellman has not got this balance right since *The Shooting*, and even that is not an easily approachable film.

1959: The Beast from Haunted Cave. 1960: Creature from the Haunted Sea (pre-credits sequence only). 1962: †The Terror (uncredited). 1964: Back Door to Hell. 1965: Flight to Fury. 1966: The Shooting. Ride the Whirlwind. 1971: Two-Lane Blacktop. 1974: Cockfighter/Born to Kill. †Shatter (US: They Call Him Mr Shatter. Uncredited). 1978: China 9, Liberty 37/Gunfighters (US: Clayton and Catherine). †Avalanche Express (uncredited). 1988: Iguana. 1989: Silent Night, Deadly Night 3: Better Watch Out!

HEPWORTH, Cecil 1874-1953

One of Britain's earliest pioneer film-makers (although not notably a director until 1914), Hepworth became one of the most prominent figures of its cinema for 25 years, from 1898 to 1923, before unwise decisions led to his financial ruin. His best films make tremendously effective use of the English countryside as background and reflect a kind of gentle innocence only sometimes intruded upon by unhappy endings. To this end, he scorned artificial lighting wherever possible and forbade his players the use of make-up, making a stark contrast to most silents of the time. Under Hepworth's auspices, such players as Alma Taylor, Chrissie White, Henry Edwards and Stewart Rome became national institutions. But Hepworth, who had seemed (and indeed was) so innovative in pre-World War I times, very quickly appeared dated with the coming of the Jazz Age. His rural romances, although painstakingly made, seemed artificially constructed and no longer pleased the public. The son of the eminent lantern lecturer T.C. Hepworth, he followed very much in his father's footsteps, lecturing himself, selling projector lamps of his own design and, by 1898, becoming a cinematographer and setting up a company for film processing all within a few months. Hepworth's standing in the industry moved up rapidly, as he published the first ever book on cinematography, *Animated Photography,* then turned his film processing studio over to production of one-reel films. These were actuality shorts at first but, after Hepworth himself went over to a producer's role in 1904, his films (many of them directed by Lewin Fitzhamon; 1869-1961) soon became known for their early use of narrative: *Rescued by Rover,* made by Fitzhamon, who turned out over 600 films for Hepworth Films between 1904 and 1914, proved especially popular. In 1914, Hepworth returned to direction, spurred on by the determination to make 'English pictures, with the English countryside as background, and with English atmosphere and English idiom throughout'. He certainly stuck to his intent and, at least while war raged, the films were successful. Hepworth had soon moved into features, but made a fatal decision in 1919 when he expended over £100,000, a huge sum of money in those days, on the establishment of a new company with new premises. The outlay unhappily coincided with the beginning of a decline in his own fortunes as a film-maker. These later features, mostly starring Alma Taylor, were lovingly photographed in naturalistic settings, but moved slowly and often had stuffy and faintly amusing titles. They were far too redolent of the Victorian era for the public taste of the time, although Hepworth long considered the 1923 version of *Comin' thro' the Rye* to be his masterpiece. The drastic dip in box-office receipts for Hepworth's films caught him with insufficient financial support, and he was declared bankrupt in 1924, only directing one fictional film thereafter, and ending his film career making trailers and advertising shorts.

1898: *The Quarrelsome Anglers. Two Fools in a Canoe/Two Cockneys in a Canoe. *The Immature Punter. *The Oxford and Cambridge Boat Race (D). *The Interrupted Picnic. *Exchange is No Robbery. 1899: Express Train in a Railway Cutting (D). *Wiping Something Off the Slate. *The Conjuror and the Boer. *The Punter's Mishap. 1900: *The Gun-*

powder Plot. *The Egg Laying Man. *Clown and Policeman. *The Kiss. *The Explosion of a Motor Car. *Leapfrog As Seen by the Frog. *How It Feels to Be Run Over. *The Eccentric Dancer. *The Bathers. *The Sluggard's Surprise. *The Electricity Cure. *The Beggar's Deceit. The Burning Stable. *Topsy Turvy Villa. 1901: *The Glutton's Nightmare. The Funeral of Queen Victoria (D). *How the Burglar Tricked the Bobby. *The Indian Chief and the Seidlitz Powder. *The Comic Grimacer. *Interior of a Railway Carriage. *The Coronation of King Edward VII (D). 1902: *The Call to Arms. How to Stop a Motor-Car. 1903: Alice in Wonderland. *Firemen to the Rescue. The Absent-Minded Bootblack. *Saturday's Shopping. 1914: *The Hills Are Calling. *Blind Fate. *Unfit, or: the Strength of the Weak. The Basilisk. Time, the Great Healer. *His Country's Bidding. *The Quarry Mystery. *Morphia, the Death Drug. *Oh, My Aunt! 1915: The Canker of Jealousy. The Battle. *A Moment of Darkness. *The Passing of a Soul. Court-Martialled. The Baby on the Barge. The Man Who Stayed at Home. Sweet Lavender. The Golden Pavement. The Outrage. Iris. 1916: Trelawney of the Wells. Comin' thro' the Rye. A Fallen Star. Sowing the Wind. Annie Laurie. The Marriage of William Ashe. Molly Bawn. The Cobweb. 1917: The American Heiress. Nearer My God to Thee. 1918: The Blindness of Fortune. The Refugee. Tares. Broken in the Wars. The Touch of a Child. Boundary House. 1919: The Nature of the Beast. Sunken Rocks. Sheba. The Forest on the Hill. 1920: Anna the Adventuress. Alf's Button. Mrs Erricker's Reputation. Helen of Four

Gates. 1921: Tinted Venus. The Narrow Valley. Wild Heather. Tansy. 1922: The Pipes of Pan. Mist in the Valley. The Strangling Thread. 1923: Comin' thro' the Rye (remake). 1926: The House of Marney. 1933: Royal Remembrances (D).

HERZOG, Werner (W. Stipetic) 1942-
If William Wellman (qv) was the 'Wild Bill' of the American cinema in its vintage sound years, so the West German Werner Herzog is surely the Wild Bill of the contemporary European cinema — for his rugged locations and unorthodox methods. Sometimes Herzog almost seems to court death itself, but the eccentric nature of the man has resulted in some striking cinematic achievements, certainly on a wider plane than any of his fellow West German film-makers coming to the fore at more or less the the same time. His protagonists are often tortured, deformed, or deficient in some respect. At the same time, they are (sometimes tragically) true to their own lights, down no matter what path it leads, and the starkness of their lives is eased by Herzog's use of always fascinating and sometimes wild natural locations. His leading characters are never physically attractive, a number of them being played by Klaus Kinski, a post-war Peter Lorre, and Bruno S, a young street singer from Berlin discovered by the director. But their adventures (or, really, misadventures) have a morbid fascination that results from directorial skill. Brought up in a farmstead in a remote region of the Bavarian mountains, from which perhaps stems his love of desolate backgrounds, Herzog was raised to city life instead from the age of 12 by his divorced moth-

German director Werner **Herzog** on location for his 1987 film *Cobra Verde.*

er, and worked nights as a welder to supplement the family income. His brains, however, took him to university in Munich, then in Pittsburgh. While in America, he gained some experience by working for a television station. Returning to Munich, he worked briefly as a welder again, making the money to finance a second short film to follow the one he had made in 1962. Gradually Herzog won recognition by taking prizes at film festivals and, in 1967, received a grant from the West German government which enabled him to make his first full-length feature, *Lebenszeichen*. His most distinctive film to date has been *Aguirre, Wrath of God*, spectacularly shot in Peru, with Kinski as the adventurous 16th-century conquistador searching for El Dorado in the rivers and forests of South America. Herzog's only major failure so far has been with what should have been his most commercial film, the remake of Murnau's famous silent vampire film *Nosferatu*. It shows the perils of attempting to make a well-nigh faithful copy of the original (save that Herzog's film is 35 minutes longer). There are some startling images, but the film is very slow and its dialogue so risible as to have even sunk the Murnau film. Kinski is made up to look exactly like the original of Max Schreck, but his interpretation, although very creepy, tends to the over elaborate, and the film that surrounds him is a miss from the start. But both Herzog and Kinski regained lost ground with *Woyzeck*, their next film, and with the striking *Cobra Verde*, a wildly exotic summation of their work together. Herzog's interest in film seemed to slacken after Kinski's death in 1991.

*1962: *Herakles/Hercules (shown 1965). 1964: *Spiel im Sand. 1966: *Der beispiellose Verteidigung der Festung Deutschkreutz/The Unprecedented Defence of the Fortress Deutschkreutz. 1967: Letzte Worte/Last Words. Lebenszeichen (GB & US: Signs of Life). 1969: *Massnahmen gegen Fanatiker/Measures Against Fanatics (D). *Die fliegenden Arzte von Ostafrika/The Flying Doctors of East Africa (D). 1970: Auch Zwerge haben klein angefangen (GB & US: Even Dwarfs Started Small). Fata Morgana. Behinderte Zukunft/Handicapped Future (D). 1971: Land des Schweigens und der Dunkelheit/Land of Silence and Darkness. 1972: Aguirre, der Zorn Gottes (GB & US: Aguirre, Wrath of God). 1974: Jeder für sich und Gott gegen alle (GB: The Enigma of Kaspar Hauser. US: The Mystery of Kaspar Hauser). *Die grosse Ekstase des Bildschnitzers Steiner (GB: The Great Ecstasy of Woodcarver Steiner.*

*Wood Originally for TV). 1976: *How Much Would a Woodchuck Chuck? Herz aus Glas (GB & US: Heart of Glass). *Mit mir will keiner spielen. *La soufrière (D). 1977: Stroszek. 1979: Nosferatu: Phantom der Nacht (GB & US: Nosferatu the Vampyre). Woyzeck. 1982: Fitzcarraldo. 1984: Where the Green Ants Dream. 1985: Hanna von der Eisriesenwelt. 1986: Ballade vom kleinen Soldaten. 1987: Cobra Verde. 1989: Es ist nicht leicht ein Gott zu sein. 1990: Echos aus einem dusteren Reich (D). 1991: Herdsmen of the Sun (D). Schrei aus Stein. 1992: Lekionen in Finsternis (D). 1993: Bells from the Deep (D). 1997: Little Dieter Needs to Fly (D).*

HESSLER, Gordon 1925-

A career which should have produced more: this German-born Hollywood director did most of his best work in Britain and showed that, once given the material and budget to work with, he could produce first-rate films within the modern horror genre. Educated in England, Hessler worked as writer and editor in documentary films in the 1950s, then went to America in 1959 to work for television. In 1960, he became story editor for TV's *Alfred Hitchcock Presents. . .* and *The Alfred Hitchcock Hour*, progressing to associate producer and producer, and directing the occasional segment himself. It was undoubtedly here that he developed his taste for the macabre and the fantastic. His own first two directorial efforts, however, were terrible films — few competent directors can have made a worse start — and it was fortunate that he found a home with American-International, then still trailing in the glories of Corman's 'Edgar Allan Poe' series. Almost immediately, Hessler demonstrated a flair for claustrophobic horror, and the kind of twist 'just when you though the horror was over' endings that Corman had pioneered in *The Haunted Palace* and *The Tomb of Ligeia*. The best of an interesting quartet of horror movies that Hessler made for AIP is *Murders in the Rue Morgue*, stylish, baroque in effect and almost Cormanesque in its conception and execution. The only connection with Poe's story is that it is being enacted by a travelling company around which the plot — to do with an old murder and a man who's dead but won't lie down — revolves. Hessler sets out to shock, and shock he does by constantly edgy direction and intelligent use of a recurring dream sequence which fascinates, entertains and skilfully maintains the theme. The ending rewardingly explores further the territory touched on by the last few

frames of *Cry of the Banshee*. *The Golden Voyage of Sinbad* was a good average entry in the Harryhausen/Dynamation series, but by 1973, Hessler was back in American television, initially to good effect with *Scream, Pretty Peggy*, Bette Davis' first TV movie, in which Hessler's direction gives the grimly melodramatic proceedings quite a kick and the whole story an aura of menace. Since then, Hessler has worked in most genres, and on most series, his most distinctive work coming predictably in the 'menace' field, with Cloris Leachman in danger from a killer in *Hitchhike!* (a familiar situation, but tensely executed) and an episode of a series called *Kolchak: the Night Stalker* which involved a swamp creature. From the 1980s on, Hessler mixed production with direction, but never returned to the horror genre.

1964: Catacombs (US: The Woman Who Wouldn't Die). 1968: The Last Shot You Hear. 1969: The Oblong Box. Scream and Scream Again. 1970: Cry of the Banshee. 1971: Murders in the Rue Morgue. 1972: Embassy. 1973: Scream, Pretty Peggy (TV). The Golden Voyage of Sinbad. Medusa. 1974: †Shatter (uncredited). Skyway to Death (TV). Hitchhike! (TV). A Cry in the Wilderness (TV). Betrayal (TV). 1975: Profile in Evil (TV). 1977: The Strange Possession of Mrs Oliver (TV. 1978: Secrets of Three Hungry Wives (TV). KISS Meets the Phantom of the Park (TV). Puzzle (TV). 1980: The Secret War of Jackie's Girls (TV). 1983: Escape from El Diablo. 1985: Pray for Death. 1986: Rage of Honor. Akira: Pray for Death 2. 1987: Wheels of Terror/The Misfit Brigade. 1988: Out on Bail. The Girl on a Swing. 1991: Shogun Mayeda/Journey of Honor.

HIBBS, Jesse 1906-1985

Rather underrated American director who started directing very late in life, and only made a few films, 11 in all. Six of these were with Audie Murphy, which may not raise hopes very high. But in fact they are almost all among Murphy's best, strongest and most interesting work, and Hibbs' permanent defection to television in 1958 was a greater loss to the cinema than most people allow. Hibbs had worked as an assistant director for many years at Universal before moving forward to the director's chair in 1953 after making a short film that pleased the powers-that-be at the studio. His first feature film was innocuous, but with the second, *Ride Clear of Diablo*, he established a brand of action film that moved at a fast trot, had likeable characters and a strong vein of slightly grim humour. The next, *Rails into Laramie,* again had good acting from its principals (John Payne and Lyle Bettger instead of Audie Murphy and Dan Duryea) and its tensions were finely drawn. Hibbs was moving into first features, and the freshness and appeal of the non-violent outdoor film *Black Horse Canyon* attracted critical praise before Murphy asked for Hibbs as his director on the film of Murphy's true World War II exploits, *To Hell and Back.* Under Hibbs' guidance, Murphy's faintly unbelievable but moving memoirs of a war in which he won 28 medals made a vividly entertaining film that moved at a cracking pace with exceptionally well-shot battle sequences. Hibbs also directed Murphy in *World in My Corner,* a boxing yarn that only rarely rose above the routine, and in *Walk the Proud Land,* another excellent true-life story, this time about the first Apache agent. Hibbs' careful delineation of this character and Murphy's quiet, sincere playing ensured that the star dominated the film, even with such players as Anne Bancroft in the supporting cast. The sentiment inherent to the subject was also very well handled. Murphy was again in the thick of things, though not really at home in comedy, in the otherwise delightfully unusual and charmingly handled *Joe Butterfly,* a Japan-set comedy along *Teahouse of the August Moon* lines. Hibbs, though, seemed unsure quite how far to take the comedy and the film remains a likeable escapade instead of really reaching to the heart of things and tugging opposing emotions. Murphy and Hibbs were back on happier ground with Hibbs' last film *Ride a Crooked Trail,* another 'A' western, this time with Walter Matthau as the personable bad guy and a more than usually equivocal role for Murphy himself. In this same year, though (1958), Hibbs became entrenched in TV. There were numerous segments of such western series as *Wagon Train, Rawhide* and *Laramie,* as well as many episodes of *Perry Mason*'s courtroom charades, from 1961 to 1965 and the end of the series with, appropriately, *The Case of the Final Fadeout.* Hibbs himself faded from the entertainment scene entirely after 1967. He died from Alzheimer's Disease.

1953: *The World's Most Beautiful Girls. The All American (GB: The Winning Way). 1954: Ride Clear of Diablo. Rails into Laramie. Black Horse Canyon. The Yellow Mountain. 1955: To Hell and Back. The Spoilers. 1956: World in My Corner. Walk the Proud Land. 1957: Joe Butterfly. 1958: Ride a Crooked Trail.

HICKOX, Anthony
See HICKOX, Douglas

HICKOX, Douglas 1929-1988
Douglas Hickox's misfortune was to be born ten years too late. This very proficient British director, mostly of full-blooded action films, could have run up a catalogue of many more films had he begun directing for the Rank Organisation shortly after World War II. As it was, he was employed as a '30 bob a week office boy' at their Pinewood studios at the age of 17, rising to production assistant by 1949. But Army service intervened and after that, he never rose above assistant director until television commercial experience helped him push himself forward. 'I was never in the right place at the right time,' he explained with some regret. Nonetheless, he did finally manage to make a full-blown feature in 1969 with a film version of Joe Orton's black stage comedy *Entertaining Mr Sloane.* The spoof horror elements in this were assembled in more digestible fashion in *Theatre of Blood,* with Vincent Price on one of his contrived revenge binges, but Hickox proved that his work as a second-unit director had equipped him to provide stirring action scenes in big-budget films when he made *Sitting Target* and *Brannigan.* Whatever their deficiencies in the script department, these were sound jobs from a directorial point of view, although regrettably they did not lead to his constant employment in the cinema, and his only other film of merit proved to be *Zulu Dawn.* A prequel to *Zulu,* it shares many of the earlier film's virtues: narrative tension, pulsating excitement in the action scenes and a seething, vividly drawn background of native unrest. One feels that Hickox could have brought more life to some adventure films from the mainline British cinema of the 1950s than the men who actually made them. Alas, the British cinema never used his distinctive qualities with any consistency, and at 59 he was dead, from heart failure following bypass surgery. His son, Anthony Hickox (1957-) is a director of mainly video-oriented horror films. His work includes *Waxwork* (1988), *Sundown: The Vampire in Retreat* (90), *Waxwork II: Lost in Time* (91), *Hellraiser 3: Hell on Earth* (92), *Warlock: The Armageddon* (93), *Full Eclipse* (94), *Invasion of Privacy* (96) and *Prince Valiant* (97).

1959: †Behemoth the Sea Monster (US: The Giant Behemoth). 1962: *Four Hits and a Mister. 1963: *Telebox (series). *Take Six. It's All Over Town. 1964: Just for You. 1969: *Les Bicyclettes de Belsize.

Entertaining Mr Sloane. 1972: Sitting Target. 1973: Theatre of Blood. 1974: Brannigan. 1976: Sky Riders. 1979: Zulu Dawn. 1981: The Phoenix (TV). 1983: The Hound of the Baskervilles (originally for TV). 1985: Blackout.

HILL, George Roy 1922-
One of the most commercially successful American directors of the 1960s and 1970s, George Roy Hill found little favour with highbrow critics, although his films clearly had something that the public liked. Joy, perhaps, conveyed through the sheer zest for, and enjoyment in filmmaking that he clearly exhibits. There is a certain light-heartedness in Hill's approach to even the darkest of subjects, something akin to that demonstrated by Frank Capra *(qv),* although in most respects the two men are quite unalike in their treatments and techniques. At university, Hill had studied music but, after World War II service in the US Marine Corps, he tried working for a while as a reporter, switching to an acting career in 1948. This career was interrupted by a second bout of active service, this time as a pilot in the Korean War. Briefly continuing his acting career on demobilisation (he had a small role in the 1952 film *Walk East on Beacon* – in Great Britain, *Crime of the Century),* Hill turned increasingly to directing, both on the stage and in television, during the 1950s. His first screen effort, *Period of Adjustment,* was definitely in minor key, but his second, *Toys in the Attic,* is a greatly underrated drama, an adaptation of a play by Lillian Hellman, with superb performances by Geraldine Page and Wendy Hiller, a career-best showing by Dean Martin, most unusually cast, and another first-rate portrayal by that neglected actress Yvette Mimieux as his child bride. Hill pushes the drama home strongly and moves us as well. *The World of Henry Orient* and *Hawaii* both had some very good scenes, but were only partial successes. Much more of an entity was the delightful *Thoroughly Modern Millie,* with Julie Andrews more sparky than she ever was under Blake Edwards' direction. Its success, however, was quickly eclipsed by that of the legendary *Butch Cassidy and the Sundance Kid,* an often indulgent western parody that works magnificently thanks to witty, self-depreciating dialogue, a strong sense of *joie-de-vivre* and the warm rapport between its two stars, Paul Newman and Robert Redford, who repeated their partnership in Hill's next film, *The Sting,* for which he won an Academy Award. Since then, both actors have worked for Hill separately, and to

Then-newcomers Theolonius Bernard and Diane Lane share a first screen kiss under the watchful eye of George Roy **Hill** for his 1979 film, *A Little Romance.*

lesser effect. The best of his more recent films has been *A Little Romance,* an unlikely but fairly charming story of puppy love in Paris, with an emotionally effective ending that worked most audiences' tear-ducts overtime. One gets the impression that Hill's career was a long succession of finding different ways of having (and creating) fun. He may have manipulated the basic emotions of his audience, but box-office receipts all over the world confirmed that few of them were complaining.

1959: Judgment at Nuremberg (TV). 1962: Period of Adjustment. 1963: Toys in the Attic. 1964: The World of Henry Orient. 1966: Hawaii. 1967: Thoroughly Modern Millie. 1969: Butch Cassidy and the Sundance Kid. 1972: Slaughterhouse-Five. 1973: The Sting. 1975: The Great Waldo Pepper. 1977: Slap Shot. 1979: A Little Romance. 1982: The World According to Garp. 1984: The Little Drummer Girl. 1988: Funny Farm.

HILL, George (William) 1888-1934

Hill was a dynamic American director who made strong movies that hit home hard on the public. His mysterious death at his lonely beach house, apparently a suicide, cut short a career that would undoubtedly have continued to flourish at M-G-M, to whose product he brought some of the toughness of Warners early sound films. There is a certain quality of brooding violence about his best work that encompasses and constrains even so belligerent an actor as Wallace Beery, who

made four memorable appearances in Hill films. He had begun his career with D.W. Griffith, as set painter, stagehand and assistant cameraman, from 1908 on. By 1916, he had progressed to cinematographer, and directed his first film, from one of his own stories, in 1921. But his career really seems to have taken off after his marriage to the writer and sometime director Frances Marion (F.M. Owens 1887-1973) in 1925. The first of Hill's films for which she supplied the scenario, *Zander the Great,* is still reckoned by some writers to be his best, although others consider it unremarkable and wishy-washy in comparison to later Hill films. By 1928, he was well established and about to embark on a string of fine films that began with the silent *The Cossacks* (from another Marion script). With sound, Hill revealed a liking for naturalistic sound and detailed, atmospheric settings, as well as stories that dealt with the lower echelons of American life. *The Big House,* which won Marion a writing Oscar, was a scabrous exposé of prison life, and Hill's first film with Beery, who played the brutal prison kingpin. Hill then teamed Beery with Marie Dressler (who had clinched her comeback in another Hill-Marion film, *The Callahans and the Murphys*), in Hill's biggest financial success, *Min and Bill.* The stars played two rugged, impoverished dockside residents with hearts of pure gold, despite their continual verbal and sometimes even physical tussles. Despite the reputation of these two films, Hill's most powerful film is *The Secret Six,* with Beery again on the wrong side of the law as the slaughter-

house worker, who by sheer aggression and ruthlessness, sledgehammers his way to the top of the city's underworld, from which position crusading reporters Johnny Mack Brown (who dies in the attempt) and Clark Gable eventually manage to topple him, with a little help from Jean Harlow. This film is almost frightening in its raw power and menace, and Hill was never to equal it, although Beery starred again in his follow-up film, *Hell Divers,* with Gable by now promoted to co-star billing. Hill and Marion separated in 1933, an event which allegedly had a crushing effect on the director and, despite making preparations to shoot Pearl Buck's *The Good Earth* — eventually made by Sidney Franklin *(qv)* in 1937 — he was soon to die. In earlier films, he is sometimes credited as George William Hill, or George W. Hill.

1921: †Get Your Man. While the Devil Laughs. 1924: The Hill Billy. The Midnight Express. Through the Dark. The Foolish Virgin. 1925: The Limited Mail. Zander the Great. 1926: The Barrier. Tell It to the Marines. 1927: Buttons. The Callahans and the Murphys. 1928: The Cossacks. The Flying Fleet. 1930: The Big House. Min and Bill. 1931: The Secret Six. 1932: Hell Divers. 1933: Clear All Wires.

HILL, James 1919-1994

Although now indelibly associated with the animal film ventures of Virginia McKenna and Bill Travers, this British director in fact had a very varied career, dating back to his beginnings in documentary cinema of the late 1930s. His strong visual sense meant that his films usually catch the eye, even when there is little substance beneath the surface sparkle. And, in *Born Free,* he created the best animal tear-jerker (and with a scene-stealing heroine in Elsa the lioness) since Lassie left the film world. Hill began at 18 as an assistant with the GPO Film Unit. When World War II broke out, he joined the RAF Film Unit as a cameraman, and began making his own documentaries after being demobilized in 1945. He continued to make short films until 1966, one of the later ones, *Giuseppina,* winning him an Academy Award. Meanwhile, he had graduated to feature films through directing for the Children's Film Foundation — hour-long films and serials for showing at children's cinema clubs. His first *bona-fide* feature, *The Kitchen,* brought him under the wing of early 1960s' realism, but apart from *A Study in Terror,* a Sherlock Holmes-versus-Jack the Ripper horror thriller, with lurid murders, gaudy camerawork and edge-of-the-seat suspense, he soon renewed his acquaintance with entertainments for the younger generation, the odd pop musical and costume adventure mingling with lions, horses, foxes and elephants. *Born Free*, however, remains his triumph — Joy Adamson's best-selling book magnificently transferred to the screen. The way in which the stars romp with the three lionesses who play Elsa at various stages of her growth is near-miraculous. Direction and acting beautifully capture the acceleration of the story, and the desperately difficult process of getting Elsa (reared from a kitten) to adapt to the wild and fend for herself, taking months of effort, often in vain, is painstakingly, heartbreakingly reconstructed. The photography, as in all Hill's animal films, is clear and sunny. Forever in search of a similar film to equal its success, he never quite found it.

*1946: *Science Joins an Industry (D). 1947: *Journey for Jeremy. 1949: *Friend of the Family. 1952: *Britain's Comet (D). The Stolen Plans. 1953: Clue of the Missing Ape (US: Gibraltar Adventure). 1956: Peril for the Guy. 1957: *Cold Comfort. 1959: Mystery in the Mine (serial). 1960: *Giuseppina. 1961: *David and Golightly. The Kitchen. 1962: The Dock Brief (US: Trial and Error). Lunch Hour. 1964: *The Home-Made Car. Every Day's a Holiday (US: Seaside Swingers). 1965: A Study in Terror (US: Fog). Born Free. 1966: *The Specialist. The Corrupt Ones (GB: The Peking Medallion). 1967: The Lions Are Free (TV). 1969: Captain Nemo and the Underwater City. An Elephant Called Slowly. 1971: Black Beauty. The Lion at World's End (US: Christian the Lion). 1973: The Belstone Fox. 1976: The Man from Nowhere. 1984: The Young Visiters.*

HILL, Sinclair 1894-1945

While still in his twenties, Sinclair Hill became one of the most successful British directors of silent times. But his fortunes fluctuated with those of his company, Stoll, and he came to prominence just when the British cinema was about to go through a particularly difficult time. Keen on the burgeoning film industry from an early age, Hill got himself a job at 15 with a small English company called Tyler Films, beginning as an office boy. At the age of 17, he was hired by Savoia Films of Italy to act as English adviser at their Turin studios. He also did his first acting with the company. World War I ended Hill's Italian connection, and he returned to England. After war service, he resumed

his acting career, but it was as a writer that Stoll Films, then one of Britain's most prominent companies, hired him in 1920. By the end of the year, Hill was directing some of their most prestigious productions. The company made a fifth of all British productions in 1921, and Hill enjoyed great success, particularly with his two 1923 films, *The Indian Love Lyrics*, with Owen Nares, and *One Arabian Night*, a version of *Aladdin* with George Robey as Widow Twan-Kee. The following year, Hill wrote a script for Robey, *The Prehistoric Man*, his last screenplay for the cinema. By 1925, Hill's films had begun to look increasingly dated in their approach and Stoll, too, was failing. From 17 films in 1925, they slumped to five in 1926: one of these was a ponderous version of *Boadicea* by Hill, who nonetheless was made managing director of the company the next year in a desperate attempt to revive its flagging fortunes. He was now directing almost all of their limited output, including the best film of his last silent days, *The Guns of Loos*, an ambitious war film that was well-liked by the critics, showed Hill had improved his control of pace and action, and gave a first film role to the young Madeleine Carroll. But in 1928, Stoll abandoned production. Hill managed to sustain an independent career for a while as a middle-bracket director, including several popular films with the leer-lipped cockney star Gordon Harker, and *The Man from Toronto*, one of Jessie Matthews' earliest and least auspicious efforts. But he quit films altogether in 1938, seven years before his early death.

*1920: The Tidal Wave. 1921: *One Week to Live. Place of Honour. The Mystery of Mr Bernard Brown. 1922: Truants. Open Country. Half a Truth. The Experiment. The Lonely Lady of Grosvenor Square. The Nonentity. Expiation. Petticoat Loose. 1923: The Indian Love Lyrics. One Arabian Night/Widow Twan-Kee. 1924: The Conspirators. White Slippers. *The Acid Test. *The Drum. *The Honourable Member for Outside Left. 1925: The Squire of Long Hadley. The Presumption of Stanley Hay M.P. The Qualified Adventurer. The Secret Kingdom. 1926: Sahara Love. The Chinese Bungalow. Boadicea. 1927: A Woman Redeemed. The King's Highway. The Guns of Loos. 1928: The Price of Divorce. 1929: The Unwritten Law. *Mr Smith Wakes Up. *Peace and Quiet. Dark Red Roses. 1930: Greek Street. Such is the Law. 1931: A Gentleman of Paris. Other People's Sins. The Great Gay Road. 1932: The First Mrs Fraser. The Man from Toronto. 1933: Britannia of*

Billingsgate. 1934: My Old Dutch. 1935: Hyde Park Corner. 1936: The Cardinal. The Gay Adventure. 1937: Take a Chance. Midnight Menace. Command Performance. 1938: Follow Your Star.

HILL, Walter 1942-

This American director's largely bleak films dwell on the unfriendliness of surroundings, whether they be urban or naturalistic. His stories, mainly written or co-written by himself, portray characters influenced by, dwarfed by and sometimes menaced by their environment. His characters are loners, or men isolated by some series of events, waging a lone war, on either side of the law, against hostile forces. He has yet to match the impact of his first film, but there remains little doubt that few contemporary directors have as great a visual command of the medium. After spending his early twenties working in the oil and construction industries, Hill entered the cinema in 1967 as an assistant director, working on such films as *The Thomas Crown Affair* (1968) and *Take the Money and Run* (1969). But it was his work as a writer on, among others, *The Getaway* (1972), *The Thief Who Came to Dinner* and *The Mackintosh Man* (both 1973), that triggered his debut as a director with *Hard Times/The Streetfighter*. There's basically nothing out of the ordinary about this film (about a bare-knuckle fighter in the New Orleans of the 1930s), most of whose incidents are predictable enough. It is, however, carefully and economically made, and distinguished by some of the best colour cinematography (by Philip Lathrop) in a very long while. Hill's direction is firm and assured and occasionally — as in an overhead shot of two fighters battling it out in a netted arena where tiers of yelling onlookers clamour for blood — quite inspired. Nothing is over-emphasized, and the thud of fist on bone is allowed to speak for itself. And one can almost smell the night air at the stockyards in the perfect final scene. It was some time before Hill followed up, and when he did the buildings of the big cities loomed darker and more menacing than ever in *The Driver* and the cult success *The Warriors*. Since then, Hill has hit the great outdoors to less effect, in *The Long Riders*, which proved just another western, despite the novelty of having real-life acting brothers play such outlaw brothers as Frank and Jesse James and The Youngers, and *Southern Comfort*, in which Hill's skilful direction could not overcome the basic foolishness of script and situations. It was followed, however, by his biggest hit to date, *48 Hrs*. Since then, his films have not made huge amounts at the box-office, although the best of them – *Johnny Handsome*, *Trespass* and *Last Man Standing* – retain a certain primitive drive rarely to be found elsewhere in the cinema.

1975: *Hard Times (GB: The Streetfighter).* 1978: *The Driver (GB: Driver).* 1979: *The Warriors.* 1980: *The Long Riders.* 1981: *Southern Comfort.* 1982: *48 Hrs.* 198k: *Streets of Fire.* 1985: *Brewster's Millions.* 1986: *Crossroads.* 1987: *Extreme Prejudice.* 1988: *Red Heat.* 1989: *Johnny Handsome.* 1990: *Another 48 Hrs.* 1992: *Trespass/The Looters.* 1993: *Geronimo: An American Legend.* 1994: *Wild Bill.* 1996: *Last Man Standing.* 1998: *Icarus.* 1999: *Supernova.*

HILLER, Arthur 1923-

This Canadian-born director has had a sketchy, in-and-out career, although one of his lesser films, *Love Story*, was so successful that it has probably given him financial security for life. Hiller has been a director for most of his career, although it was only in the 1970s that he joined the big league. Even then, he seemed unable to please all of the people all of the time, although again and again he returned to comedy as his major preference. From the late 1940s, Hiller worked for the Canadian Broadcasting Corporation as a director, quitting in 1955 to try his luck in American television. That medium kept him busy until 1964, when he turned his attention full-time to the cinema after countless episodes of *Naked City, Ben Casey, Perry Mason* and *Route 66*. Most of his early films, nearly all of them comedies, suffer from poor scripts, partial exceptions being *The Wheeler Dealers* and *The Americanization of Emily*. But Hiller was very definitely a man in need of a hit when *Love Story* came along. Who could forecast that the mushy story of a dying girl – the sequel, *Oliver's Story*, is actually rather better, though it was nowhere near as successful – could take so many millions at the box-offices of the world and be serialized in so many newspapers and magazines? Hiller showed his mettle after that with two first-class films, the ferociously and hurtfully funny *The Hospital*, and the moving and greatly underrated musical *Man of La Mancha*. Hiller was well in control of both his subjects here, but there were traumatic times to follow, with the disasters of *The Crazy World of Julius Vrooder* and *W.C. Fields and Me*, and a hesitant treatment of what should have been a cast-iron hit (and was still enjoyable, thanks to Colin Higgins' script) with *Silver Streak*. *Making Love* was well received in some quarters, but

betrays a tentative approach to its subject (a husband falling in love with another *man*) that illustrates the lack of boldness in Hiller's later work: too often he now seems to settle for the safe option. Since the early 1980s, he has concentrated on comedy, again with varying results. His best efforts – *Outrageous Fortune* and *Taking Care of Business* – have been blessed with funny, slightly zany scripts with which Hiller seems to empathise.

1956: *Massacre at Sand Creek (TV).* 1957: *Homeward Borne (TV). The Careless Years.* 1962: *This Rugged Land (TV. GB: cinemas). Miracle of the White Stallions (GB: Flight of the White Stallions).* 1963: *The Wheeler Dealers (GB: Separate Beds).* 1964: *The Americanization of Emily.* 1965: *Promise Her Anything.* 1966: *Penelope. Tobruk.* 1967: *The Tiger Makes Out.* 1969: *Popi. The Out-of-Towners.* 1970: *Love Story. Plaza Suite.* **Confrontation.* 1971: *The Hospital.* 1972: *Man of La Mancha.* 1974: *Vrooder's Hooch/The Crazy World of Julius Vrooder.* 1975: *The Man in the Glass Booth.* 1976: *W.C. Fields and Me. Silver Streak.* 1979: *The In-Laws. Nightwing.* 1981: *Making Love.* 1982: *Author! Author!* 1983: *Romantic Comedy. The Lonely Guy.* 1984: *Teachers.* 1987: *Outrageous Fortune.* 1989: *See No Evil, Hear No Evil.* 1990: *Taking Care of Business (GB: Filofax).* 1991: *Married To It.* 1992: *The Babe.* 1996: *Carpool.* 1997: *$An Alan Smithee Film: Burn, Hollywood, Burn.*

$ As Alan Smithee

HILLYER, Lambert 1889-1984

One of the top Hollywood directors of westerns in silent days, Hillyer became entrenched in second-features with the coming of sound, although his work on minimal budgets is sometimes above-average, especially in the western and horror genres. Born in Indiana, Hillyer had been a reporter and short-story writer before coming to the cinema in 1914 as a writer, principally for D.W. Griffith, for whom he may also have done some uncredited direction. He remained ambitious to direct, and his meeting with the famous grim-faced western star William S. Hart enabled him to further that ambition. His first screenplay for Hart was on *The Desert Man* (1917) and the star, who had mainly directed his own films up until then, was soon entrusting many of the set-ups to Hillyer. It is difficult to decide which of the two men directed what at this transitional stage, but Hillyer was first credited as director on the 1917 film

The Narrow Trail. The association with Hart ended in 1922, and only *Tumbleweeds*, of Hart's later films, matches the work he did with Hillyer: the best of their films together is the affecting and exciting *The Toll Gate* in 1920 — it was also Hart's biggest moneymaker. After leaving Hart, Hillyer widened his experience in other genres, although, in the mid-1920s, he returned to the wide open spaces to make a series of well-liked westerns with Tom Mix *(The Lone Star Ranger* is probably the best of these), and a vigorous version of Rex Beach's famous western *The Spoilers*, with Noah Beery and Milton Sills; amazingly, the story had, even at this early time in western history, already been filmed once. In the early 1930s, there were some more westerns, this time with Buck Jones as star, but Hillyer's chances of becoming a prestige director were diminishing. He did make two good chiller-thrillers in 1936 for Universal, *Dracula's Daughter*, a much-underrated first sequel to the 1930 *Dracula*, and *The Invisible Ray*, with ingenious special effects, and sly use by Hillyer of stock footage (from the 1931 *Frankenstein)* and standing sets (from the serial *Flash Gordon).* After that, though, few of his films passed the 60-minute mark, and in the 1940s he was back to making westerns, though on a much reduced budgetary scale, with such riders of the range as Johnny Mack Brown, Charles Starrett, Jimmy Wakely and Whip Wilson. Hillyer made his last film in 1949, then went into television, where he made countless more half-hour horse-operas, notably many episodes of *The Cisco Kid* series between 1951 and 1955. A far cry indeed from the days of William S. Hart.

1917: *The Narrow Trail. An Even Break.* †*The Silent Man (uncredited).* 1918: †*Riddle Gawne (uncredited).* †*Branding Broadway (uncredited).* 1919: *Breed of Men. The Money Corral.* †*Square Deal Sanderson. Wagon Tracks. John Petticoats. The Poppy Girl's Husband (GB: Poppy Girl). Sand.* 1920: *The Toll Gate. The Cradle of Courage. The Testing Block. O'Malley of the Mounted.* 1921: *The Whistle. Three Word Brand. White Oak. Travelin' On.* 1922: *White Hands. Caught Bluffing. Skin Deep. The Altar Stairs. The Super-Sex.* 1923: *Scars of Jealousy. Temporary Marriage. The Shock. The Spoilers. The Lone Star Ranger. Mile-a-Minute Romeo. Eyes of the Forest.* 1924: *Idle Tongues. Barbara Frietchie. Those Who Dance.* 1925: *The Making of O'Malley. I Want My Man. The Knockout. The Unguarded Hour.* 1926: †*30 Below Zero. Her Second Chance. Miss Nobody.* 1927: *The War Horse. Hills of*

Peril. Chain Lightning. 1928: The Branded Sombrero. Fleetwing. 1930: Beau Bandit. 1931: One Man Law. 1932: The Fighting Fool. The Deadline. South of the Rio Grande. White Eagle. Hello Trouble. 1933: Dangerous Crossroads. The California Trail. The Forbidden Trail. The Sundown Rider. Unknown Valley. Police Car 17. Before Midnight. Master of Men. 1934: Once to Every Woman. The Fighting Code. *Hidden Evidence. *One Way Out. *The Professor Gives a Lesson. One is Guilty. The Man Trailer. Against the Law (GB: Urgent Call). The Defense Rests. The Most Precious Thing in Life. Men of the Night. 1935: Men of the Hour. Guard That Girl! The Awakening of Jim Burke (GB: Iron Fist). Behind the Evidence. In Spite of Danger. Superspeed. 1936: Dangerous Waters. The Invisible Ray. Dracula's Daughter. 1937: Speed to Spare. Girls Can Play. Women in Prison. 1938: My Old Kentucky Home. All-American Sweetheart. Extortion! 1939: Convict's Code. Should a Girl Marry? The Girl from Rio. 1940: The Durango Kid (GB: The Masked Stranger). The Pinto Kid (GB: All Square). Beyond the Sacramento (GB: Power of Justice). North from the Lone Star. The Wildcat of Tucson (GB: Promise Fulfilled). 1941: The Medico of Painted Springs (GB: Doctor's Alibi). Hands Across the Rockies. The Return of Daniel Boone (GB: The Mayor's Nest). The Son of Davy Crockett (GB: Blue Clay). Prairie Stranger (GB: The Marked Bullet). King of Dodge City. The Royal Mounted Patrol (GB: Giants A'Fire). Thunder over the Prairie. Roaring Frontiers. 1942: North of the Rockies (GB: False Clues). The Devil's Trail (GB: Rogues' Gallery). Vengeance of the West (GB: The Black Shadow). Prairie Gunsmoke. 1943: Batman (serial). *Gem Jams. *Radio Runaround. The Texas Kid. Fighting Frontier. Six-Gun Gospel. The Stranger from Pecos. Smart Guy (GB: You Can't Beat the Law). 1944: Law Men. Ghost Guns. Beyond the Pecos (GB: Beyond the Seven Seas). Smart Guy. Partners of the Trail. West of the Rio Grande. Land of the Outlaws. 1945: Flame of the West. Stranger from Santa Fé. South of the Rio Grande. The Lost Trail. Frontier Feud. Border Bandits. 1946: Under Arizona Skies. The Gentleman from Texas. Silver Range. Trigger Fingers. Shadows on the Range. Raiders of the South. 1947: Valley of Fear. Trailing Danger. Land of the Lawless. The Law Comes to Gunsight. The Hat Box Mystery. The Case of the Baby Sitter. Flashing Guns. Prairie Express. Gun Talk. Song of the Drifter. 1948: Overland Trails. Oklahoma Blues. Partners of the Sunset. Crossed Trails. Frontier Agent.

Range Renegades. The Fighting Ranger. The Sheriff of Medicine Bow. Outlaw Brand. 1949: Gun Runner. Haunted Trails. Gun Law Justice. Range Land. Riders of the Dusk. Trail's End.

HISCOTT, Leslie 1894-1968

Although London-born Hiscott made dozens of films at British studios in the 1930s, few of them are ever likely to be revived or even remembered, and the reason that so few have alternative American titles is that so few of them crossed the Atlantic. For Hiscott was master of the gentle art of the 'quota quickie', a film made to fill up cinema bills and to fulfil the conditions of the Cinematograph Act which required just over 30 per cent of all motion pictures shown in Britain to emanate from the home country. Many of Hiscott's resultant films were so short that they could comfortably be shown today in a television hour — commercials included. Yet, although he has been accused of giving British B-features the bad name they never lost over 30 years, in truth there were merits to some of his little films — especially the comedies and comedy-thrillers featuring Henry Kendall. Hiscott had been an actor in his early years, at one time in Italy. But in 1920, he returned to Britain as an assistant director and only rarely acted again. He had graduated to director by the late 1920s, at first making quite high-quality thrillers — there were three featuring Sherlock Holmes and two about Agatha Christie's Hercule Poirot. It was when he joined Julius Hagen's Real Art studio at Twickenham that the quickies really began — nearly 50 of them in six years before Hiscott quit Hagen to freelance. In the war years, Hiscott left the cinema to concentrate on writing, but came back in the mid-1950s as a favour to Richard 'Mr Pastry' Hearne, whom he had previously directed in The Butler's Dilemma. The two films that resulted, The Time of His Life and Tons of Trouble, were both better than their budgets and made a sympathetic character out of Pastry as well as raising some knockabout laughs. These films, as with all his post-Hagen work, were co-produced by Hiscott's wife Elizabeth. Though largely forgotten now, and not surprisingly, Hiscott remains a director of much historical interest.

1927: This Marriage Business. 1928: The Passing of Mr Quin. S.O.S. 1929: Ringing the Changes. The Feather. 1930: At the Villa Rose (US: Mystery at the Villa Rose). The House of the Arrow. The Call of the Sea. 1931: The Sleeping Cardinal (US: Sherlock Holmes' Fatal Hour).

Brown Sugar. Alibi. Black Coffee. A Night in Montmartre. 1932: The Missing Rembrandt (US: Sherlock Holmes and the Missing Rembrandt). Murder at Covent Garden. The Crooked Lady. Once Bitten. Double Dealing. A Safe Proposition. When London Sleeps. A Tight Corner. The Face at the Window. The Iron Stair. 1933: The Stolen Necklace. Out of the Past. The Melody Maker. Yes, Madam. That's My Wife. Cleaning Up. The Stickpin. Great Stuff. Strike It Rich. I'll Stick to You. Flat No. 3. 1934: The Man I Want. Passing Shadows. Keep it Quiet. Gay Love. Crazy People. 1935: The Big Splash. The Triumph of Sherlock Holmes. Annie, Leave the Room! Death on the Set (US: Murder on the Set). Three Witnesses. Inside the Room. Bargain Basement/Department Store. A Fire Has Been Arranged. She Shall Have Music. 1936: Fame. The Interrupted Honeymoon. Millions. 1937: Ship's Concert. Fine Feathers. 1938: *Take Cover. 1940: Tilly of Bloomsbury. 1941: The Seventh Survivor. 1942: Sabotage at Sea. The Lady from Lisbon. 1943: The Butler's Dilemma. 1944: Welcome Mr Washington. 1955: The Time of His Life. 1956: Tons of Trouble.

HITCHCOCK, Sir Alfred 1899-1980

British director, the 'master of suspense' who became the world's best-known filmmaker for 35 years. Hitchcock's innovatory techniques were all worked out at the planning stage, enabling him to make a film exactly as he saw it in his mind's eye, and achieve the maximum impact on his audience. Specific sequences from his films, shown again and again on television, are as legion (and as legendary) as his own guest appearances, which occurred in the majority of his pictures, his portly frame making him instantly recognizable, even when it was seen only in silhouette. He was a title designer and assistant editor with the British arm of Famous Players-Lasky at the beginning of his career, but soon moved into direction with producer Michael Balcon at Gainsborough. Hitchcock was a director of ideas — highly original ways of constructing a scene that soon brought him to the attention of critics and public, especially after The Lodger in 1926, which could also be called the first of his tension thrillers. It also has one of the first of his 'set-pieces' — the shot of the man upstairs pacing up and down, filmed through a glass floor. Hitchcock established his place at the fore of British thriller directors — his efforts outside the genre are much less distinguished — with Britain's first talking picture, Blackmail, and its sequence in which the repeated use of the word 'knife' jars into the brain of the heroine, who has just killed a man with one; with *Murder!*, one of the first whodunnits; and with *Number Seventeen*, an early 'chase' noteworthy for its use of cross-cutting to heighten the thrill of the pursuit. Hitchcock did not really hit his stride, however, until 1934, when he made the first of a brilliant series of thrillers with imminent danger as their theme. This was *The Man Who Knew Too Much*, and it was to be followed by *The Thirty-Nine Steps*, *The Secret Agent*, *Sabotage*, *Young and Innocent* and *The Lady Vanishes*. The first and last of these were probably the biggest box-office successes, and several of them involved, as had *Number Seventeen*, Hitchcock's favourite setting — a train. Hitchcock was encouraged to go to America, and promptly won a best picture Oscar for his first film there — *Rebecca*. A Hitchcock film was by now an event, and the remainder of his early 1940s films are full of lingering images — the glass of milk in *Suspicion*; the 'umbrella' assassination and Joel McCrea getting his raincoat caught in the machinery of a windmill in *Foreign Correspondent*; the spy falling from the Statue of Liberty in *Saboteur*; the small-town milieu and final falling from a train in *Shadow of a Doubt*; the key in Ingrid Bergman's hand that the camera zooms down on in *Notorious* (as it had on a twitching eye in *Young and Innocent*); the Dalí-inspired dream sequence and gun turning on its holder in *Spellbound*. From 1947, Hitchcock wavered. Only *Strangers on a Train* in the next seven years is in the classic Hitchcock mould, with its giddying fairground finale, and its murder reflected in the victim's dark glasses lying on the ground. But the master regained his touch with *Rear Window* in 1954 and followed this story of murder witnessed by a man in a wheelchair with a series of thrillers that are often quite daringly different, particularly *The Trouble with Harry*, *The Wrong Man*, *Vertigo*, *North by Northwest*, *Psycho* and *The Birds*. These are films from whose hypnotic and sometimes horrifying images one cannot take one's eyes; they have been much imitated. Of his later films, only *Frenzy* has touches really worthy of Hitchcock's uniquely agile mind, but he was in increasingly poor health during the 1970s, and it was a pleasant surprise when he managed one last, admittedly lightweight but still enjoyable suspense movie, *Family Plot*. Mere discussion of Hitchcock's films whets the appetite to see them again. His detractors will tell you that his deliberate planning is the antithesis of pure cinema, and that he

Sir Alfred **Hitchcock** amuses star Bruce Dern during location filming for Hitch's last picture, *Family Plot*.

is unable to see beyond a mechanical process of design and effect. Well, yes, and less fun for the actors perhaps. But why worry as long as it works? Hitchcock after all was working for an audience of average mentality, not a critic committed to a thousand words.

*1922: *Number 13 (unfinished). 1923: *†Always Tell Your Wife. 1925: The Pleasure Garden. 1926: The Mountain Eagle (US: Fear o' God). The Lodger (US: The Case of Jonathan Drew). 1927: Downhill (US: When Boys Leave Home). Easy Virtue. The Ring. 1928: The Farmer's Wife. Champagne. The Manxman. 1929: Blackmail (silent and sound versions). 1930: †Harmony Heaven. †Elstree Calling. Juno and the Paycock (US: The Shame of Mary Boyle). Murder! (and German-language version: Mary). *An Elastic Affair. 1931: The Skin Game. 1932: Rich and Strange (US: East of Shanghai). Number Seventeen. 1933: Waltzes from Vienna (US: Strauss's Great Waltz). 1934: The Man Who Knew Too Much. 1935: The 39 Steps. 1936: Secret Agent. Sabotage (US: The Woman Alone). 1937: Young and Innocent (US: The Girl Was Young). 1938: The Lady Vanishes. 1939: Jamaica Inn. 1940: Rebecca. Foreign Correspondent. 1941: Mr and Mrs Smith. Suspicion. 1942: Saboteur. 1943: Shadow of a Doubt. 1944: Lifeboat. Bon Voyage. *Aventure Malagache. 1945: Concentration (D. Unfinished). Spellbound. 1946: Notorious. 1947: The Paradine Case. 1948: Rope. 1949: Under Capricorn. 1950: Stage Fright. 1951: Strangers on a Train. 1952: I Confess. 1954: Dial M for Murder. Rear Window. 1955: To Catch a Thief. The Trouble with*

Harry. 1956: The Man Who Knew Too Much (remake). 1957: The Wrong Man. 1958: Vertigo. 1959. North by Northwest. 1960: Psycho. 1963: The Birds. 1964: Marnie. 1966: Torn Curtain. 1969: Topaz. 1972: Frenzy. 1976: Family Plot.

HIVELY, Jack 1910-1995

This American director probably wouldn't be worth an entry in this book were it not for his penchant for suddenly upping and making a film years after the last. He and his father George were film editors with RKO through the 1930s; Jack, however, was always anxious to direct and, at the end of the decade, producer Cliff Reid gave him the chance to direct some films for the studio's economy unit. These were mainly pinch-budget remakes of better films, or entries in the studio's 'Saint' series, with George Sanders, from the books by Leslie Charteris. Hively's first, *Panama Lady*, was one of his worst, and even Lucille Ball could not enliven it. But there were bright spots: *The Saint Takes Over* is among the best in its series, with bad girl Wendy Barrie actually getting shot down in the final gunfight, *Laddie* is a sincerely played (by Tim Holt and Virginia Gilmore) rural romance and *Four Jacks and a Jill* a bright musical with Anne Shirley, Ray Bolger, June Havoc and Desi Arnaz. Otherwise, the contemporary criticism applied to *They Met in Argentina* —'slight and trite' — could as well refer to the rest of Hively's RKO work. Leaving the studio, Hively did a good job on Paramount's *Street of Chance*, a well-written amnesiac thriller without a wasted scene, tightly acted by Burgess Meredith and Claire Trevor. But this did not lead to further assignments, and Hively did not direct again until Universal handed him the screen version of *Are You With It?* Hively kept the musical lively, with a bubbly assist from Donald O'Connor as the statistician who joins a travelling carnival. Again, however, there were no offers, and Hively returned to editing. Theoretically, this should have been the end of Hively's directing career. But nearly 30 years later he was suddenly back, still willing to give it a go, with a children's feature called *Starbird and Sweet William,* followed by a couple of folksy TV movies.

1939: Panama Lady. The Spellbinder. They Made Her a Spy. Three Sons. Two Thoroughbreds. 1940: The Saint's Double Trouble. The Saint Takes Over. Laddie. Anne of Windy Poplars (GB: Anne of Windy Willows). 1941: They Met in Argentina. The Saint in Palm Springs. Father Takes a Wife. Four Jacks and a Jill. 1942: Street of Chance. 1948: Are You With It? 1967: Lassie: Flight of the Cougar (TV). 1970: Handford's Point (TV). 1976: Starbird and Sweet William (TV). 1978: The Adventures of Huckleberry Finn (TV). 1980: California Gold Rush (TV).

HODGES, Mike 1932-

British director of extraordinarily varied experience. Hodges looked set for a solid career in urban drama after the success of his first film *Get Carter.* But his moves further afield both in terms of subject and location have not led to the full realisation of his potential. Hodges originally qualified as an accountant, but work for an American TV company's British offices prompted him to try his hand at writing. Five years editing and writing TV series followed, after which Hodges ventured into the documentary field as producer and director of the long-running TV news series *World in Action.* He moved closer to films with profiles of movie directors for TV arts series, and the successful direction of the TV thrillers *Suspect* encouraged him to try for the big screen. The result is still considered by many to be his best film: *Get Carter* was typical of the new gritty realism in British crime films of the 1970s and its Newcastle background, splendidly captured in steely colour photography, gave the harsh crime drama, with few if any likeable characters, an extra edge. Hodges stayed with its star, Michael Caine, for an uneven scattershot comedy *Pulp,* which attracted few people to cinemas, although more than the next, *The Terminal Man. Flash Gordon* was Hodges' contribution to the big-budget superfilm: like all Hodges' work, it was well-paced and never boring, but so far

over the top as to be largely ineffective in a field whose output needs to take itself with at least a modicum of seriousness. *Morons from Outer Space* proved that Hodges' forte was definitely not lunatic farce. The dramas that surrounded it were all of interest, but small beer at the box-office, and Hodges came to a grinding halt for several years after the last of them, *Black Rainbow,* a well-acted and directed, but only moderately written thriller about a medium who starts seeing deaths.

1971: Get Carter. 1972: Pulp. 1974: The Terminal Man. 1980: Flash Gordon. 1983: Missing Pieces (TV). Squaring the Circle. 1984: Buried Alive. 1985: Morons from Outer Space. 1986: Florida Straits (cable TV). Missing Pieces (TV). 1987: A Prayer for the Dying. 1989: Black Rainbow. 1998: The Croupier.

HOFFMAN, Michael 1955-

American director whose film career, begun in England, didn't amount to much until recent times. Heavily involved in student productions both at Boise University in Idaho and then Oxford University in England, the Hawaii-born Hoffman made his film debut while still at Oxford. The student production, *Privileged,* was not only released to cinemas, but contained three future stars in Hugh Grant, Imogen Stubbs and James Wilby. On leaving university, Hoffman made a bright comedy in Scotland, *Restless Natives,* about two workshy youths holding up tourists, but a return to American produced only two dull and pretentious films — although both had some good individual performances. *Soapdish,* a broad but inconsistent comic satire of daytime TV, gave Hoffman a higher profile, and he then set to work on his most ambitious film to date, *Restoration,* an adaptation of Rose Tremain's prize-winning story of corruption and decadence in the 17th century. It's a consistently impressive achievement, even if the amazing sets and production design all but dwarf the drama. As a break from such epic goings-on, Hoffman tried a romantic comedy – and quite successfully – with *One Fine Day,* one of those films where we know the protagonists are destined to end up with each other from the first reel. The trick is to keep us watching, and Hoffman pretty much pulls it off, with a plenty of good humour, a little genuine wit and a keen sense of pacing.

1982: Privileged. 1985: Restless Natives. 1987: Promised Land. 1988: Some Girls (GB: Sisters). 1991: Soapdish. 1995: Restoration. 1996: One Fine Day. 1999: A Midsummer Night's Dream.

HOGAN, James P. 1891-1943

With the advent of B-picture units at the major Hollywood studios in the 1930s, a whole new crop of resident directors appeared on the scene. Some came from the stage, others were promoted from the ranks of editors and assistant directors. Some, like James Hogan, found themselves recalled after being put out to an early pasture. Hogan had already proved himself a great professional at small-screen action in the silent days when, after beginning as a writer, he turned out nearly 30 low-budget films in the 1920s. Even so, after seven years pursuing a writing career, he must have been surprised when Paramount demanded his services for the cinema again in 1936. After formula westerns, they gave him some 'A' grade action films, but Hogan still proved best at the minor stuff — the westerns, the Bulldog Drummonds and the Ellery Queens. When presented with an all-star cast, as in *Last Train to Madrid* (which gave him Lew Ayres, Gilbert Roland, Anthony Quinn, Helen Mack, Dorothy Lamour, Lionel Atwill, Karen Morley, Robert Cummings, Olympe Bradna and Lee Bowman), *The Texans* or *Texas Rangers Ride Again,* Hogan somehow contrived to make the melodramatics stilted and unconvincing. But George Zucco was a splendid villain for him in *Arrest Bulldog Drummond* (the film in which, about to consign Drummond's colleagues to the deep, he says: 'Care to come and see the splash?') and *Ellery Queen and the Murder Ring.* By the time the latter film was made, Hogan had moved across to Columbia, later directing the excitement in the first of the Paramount Pine-Thomas action films (which would continue for 15 years), *Power Dive.* Hogan's last film is probably his best, despite being ridiculously titled *The Mad Ghoul.* It's a lively low-budget shocker from Universal which still looks stylish today. George Zucco delivered another good performance for Hogan as the mad doctor obsessed both with a deadly gas and (more understandably) Evelyn Ankers. The doctor finally succumbs to his own gas and Hogan rightly fades the whole film on the shot of the dying Zucco scrabbling away at the earth covering a grave, the heart of whose occupant might have saved him. Withdrawing from his next assignment, *Gypsy Wildcat,* because of failing health, Hogan succumbed to a heart attack at 52.

1920: The Skywayman (GB: The Daredevil). 1921: Bare Knuckles. 1922: †Where is My Wandering Boy Tonight? 1924: Unmarried Wives. Black Lightning.

Women and Gold. Capital Punishment.
1925: Jimmie's Millions. The Mansion of
Aching Hearts. S.O.S. My Lady's Lips.
Perils of the Sea. The Bandit's Baby. Steel
Preferred. 1926: King of the Turf. The
Isle of Retribution. Flaming Fury. 1927:
Mountains of Manhattan. The Final
Extra. The Silent Avenger. Finnegan's
Ball. 1928: Hearts of Men. Top Sergeant
Mulligan. The Broken Mask. Burning
Bridges. Code of the Air. The Border
Patrol. 1931: The Sheriff's Secret. 1936:
Desert Gold. The Accusing Finger. Ari-
zona Raiders. 1937: Arizona Mahoney.
Ebb Tide. Bulldog Drummond Escapes.
The Last Train from Madrid. 1938: The
Texans. Bulldog Drummond's Peril. Sons
of the Legion. Scandal Street. 1939:
Grand Jury Secrets. Arrest Bulldog Drum-
mond! Bulldog Drummond's Secret
Police. $1,000 a Touchdown. Bulldog
Drummond's Bride. 1940: Queen of the
Mob. The Farmer's Daughter. Texas
Rangers Ride Again. 1941: Power Dive.
Ellery Queen's Penthouse Mystery. Ellery
Queen and the Perfect Crime (GB: The
Perfect Crime). Ellery Queen and the
Murder Ring (GB: The Murder Ring).
1942: Enemy Agents Meet Ellery Queen
(GB: The Lido Mystery). 1943: No Place
for a Lady. The Strange Death of Adolf
Hitler. The Mad Ghoul.

HOLLAND, Agnieszka 1948-

One of the few prominent Eastern European directors of recent times to work also
in France, Britain and America (after a
feverish period of activity in her native
Poland, she went to live in Paris), Holland
has been least successful with her English-
language ventures and perhaps needs to
return to France, where she made the
intriguing *Olivier, Olivier* in 1992. The
daughter of journalists — her father died
under mysterious circumstances when she
was 13, probably at the hands of the secret
police — Holland was jailed for a brief
period herself for dissident work during
her time at the Prague Film Academy.
Learning quickly that discretion was the
better part of valour, she channelled her
anger into her film work, serving appren-
ticeships with leading Polish directors
Kryszstof Zanussi and Andrzej Wajda.
When she began her own career as director, however, her films were soon courting
controversy with their choice of politically
sensitive subjects. So persuasive was Holland's treatment, however, that, on their
eventual release, such films as *Provincial*
Actors and *A Woman Alone* went down
well with public and critics alike. She concentrated on writing from 1983 to 1985,
then returned to direction with *Angry Har-*
vest, a film that opened more doors for her

when it was nominated for the Best Foreign Film Oscar. This was a thrilling story
of a Jewish woman on the run from the
Nazis in World War Two after escaping
from a train bound for the death camps.
After contributing the screenplay towards
Sally Kirkland's Oscar-nominated performance in *Anna*, Holland made her first
English-language film as director, *Priest*, an
unconvincing true-life story of persecution
in Poland. She returned to the war and
Jewish persecution again in the remarkable
Europa, Europa, about a true-life teenage
boy who survives the war by acting as an
interpreter for the Germans. Equally interesting was *Olivier, Olivier*, the story of a
boy who disappears, then seems to have
returned years later. The question, as in
similar examples of such stories, is largely
one of whether the newcomer is an
imposter. Holland keeps us hopping as to
the outcome, but her films since then have
been less exceptional.

*1974: *Evening at Abdon's. 1975: *Sun-*
day Children. 1977: Screen Tests. 1979:
Provincial Actors. 1980: Fever. 1982: A
Woman Alone. 1985: Angry Harvest.
1988: To Kill a Priest/Le
complot/Popieluszko. 1990: Europa,
Europa. 1992: Olivier, Olivier. 1993: The
Secret Garden. 1995: Total Eclipse. †A
propos de Nice. 1997: Washington Square.
1999: The Third Miracle.

HOLT, Seth (James Holt) 1923-1971

One of the greater tragedies of the British
cinema. Holt was the brother-in-law of
director Robert Hamer, and it was ironic
that both their careers were blighted by
alcoholism. But as least Hamer made *Pink*
String and Sealing Wax, It Always Rains
on Sunday and *Kind Hearts and Coro-*
nets, whereas Holt never came anywhere
near achieving what some observers consider his full potential. His career is lit-
tered with uncompleted projects — films
never started or only half-finished. Those
he did manage to complete mostly suggest
a talent for nervy suspense of a quite
unusual kind. Born in Palestine of British
parents, Holt had joined Ealing Studios in
the war years as an assistant editor, at
Hamer's suggestion. Once graduated to
editor, he worked on many of the studio's
best films, including *The Spider and the*
Fly, The Lavender Hill Mob, Mandy, The
Titfield Thunderbolt and *The Ladykillers*.
Holt's first film as director was a stylish
and literate thriller, *Nowhere to Go*,
which dealt with the fate of a man on the
run and gave a first major screen role to
Maggie Smith. Three years later came *A*
Taste of Fear, a typical Hammer black-
and-white product of its time, with supe-

rior production and a deliberately obtuse
story crammed with twists, mysteries,
ambiguities and confusions of identities.
But it was genuinely frightening. After
another interval of three years, Holt made
Station Six — Sahara, a full-blooded imitation of a continental sex melodrama;
The Nanny, an excellent vehicle for Bette
Davis with suspense on high throughout;
and *Danger Route*, a thoroughly routine
thriller redeemed only by a unusually
bleak moments. There were more stops
and starts before, to great heralding of
trumpets, Holt returned to film-making
with another tale of the bizarre, from a
story by Bram Stoker. But cirrhosis of the
liver, the alcoholic's curse, killed him
before he could finish the film. Michael
Carreras completed the picture, titled
Blood from the Mummy's Tomb. The
signs are, though, that Holt would have
found only further frustration from the
atmosphere in the British film industry,
such as it was, in the 1970s.

1958: Nowhere to Go. 1961: A Taste of
Fear (US: Scream of Fear). 1963: Station
*Six — Sahara. 1964: *Wildlife in Danger*
(D). 1965: The Nanny. 1966: Diabolik
(unfinished; eventually made by Mario
Bava). 1967: Danger Route. 1968: Mon-
sieur Lecoq (unfinished). 1971: Blood
from the Mummy's Tomb.

HOOPER, Tobe 1943-

This Texas-born director's delight in surprising and shocking his audience could
well stem from the fact that, as a child, he
worked as a professional stage magician.
And so for a while he became the demon
king of horror film makers, with handsome box-office receipts from *The Texas*
Chainsaw Massacre to prove it. Hooper's
interest in films dates from high school
days, when he turned out an 8mm version
of *Frankenstein*. During the 1960s, he
earned money making pop documentaries
for television (including one on Peter, Paul
and Mary) and spent it making short
films in his spare time. His first feature,
Eggshells, was not widely distributed, but
the notoriety of the next, *The Texas*
Chainsaw Massacre, made his name, combining horrifying murders in gorily visceral detail with sharp, sophisticated camerawork. His next, *Eaten Alive*, had fewer
redeeming features, and was almost purely repellent. But *The Funhouse* showed
that he had gained both skill and
restraint. On this lively shocker, Hooper
combined traits of Roger Corman and
Dario Argento and just let rip on a story
of four youngsters who stay after closing
time at the funhouse for a dirty night out,
then find themselves fleeing round the

place pursued by the owner and his mutant son. Most of what follows is formula shock, although noisier, better-paced and better-edited than most: the sort of film William Castle might have been making had he lived. The finale in the engine-room is really imaginative and throws in everything but the kitchen sink, and the pace leaves no-one time to go to the loo. Hooper refers to his grisly offerings as horror-comics, and his good TV horror film, *Salem's Lot*, though still in his chosen genre, is perhaps a step up in literacy. *LifeForce* was an excellent vampire/alien movie that careered through its ludicrous script like a runaway train and gave us a stunning tableau of London reeling under a veritable plague of vampirism. Since then, Hooper has kept driving the train but somehow the wheels have come off. Lately, it seems that the director has even forgotten his talent for thundering films along. Certainly, it was still well in evidence in *Poltergeist*, which under the joint auspices of Hooper and Steven Spielberg *(qv)*, the latter acting as writer-producer, turned out to be the most sensational ghost story since Wise's *The Haunting*. If your nerves can stand the pounding Hooper gives them in this film, they'll be up to anything. With one superbly engineered shock after another, the film also has tremendous special effects that make it a really frightening experience.

1965:. *The Heiress. 1966: *Down Friday Street. 1967: *A Way of Learning. 1970: *The Heisters. 1972: Eggshells. 1974: The Texas Chainsaw Massacre. 1976: Eaten Alive (GB: Death Trap). 1979: Salem's Lot (TV). 1980: The Funhouse. 1982. Poltergeist. 1985: LifeForce. Invaders from Mars. 1986: The Texas Chainsaw Massacre 2. 1988: Robbie Zenith and the Pig of Knowledge (video). 1989: Spontaneous Combustion. 1990: I'm Dangerous Tonight (TV). 1993: †Body Bags (TV). Tobe Hooper's Night Terrors. 1995: The Mangler.

HOPPER, Jerry 1907-1988

Oklahoma-born Hopper came to the fore as a director of 90-minute Technicolor glossies just in time to ensure his steady employment by television after the 1950s and their boom for middle-budget co-features were over. But Hopper's short movie career was not without its highlights, and warmth and action were two things that his films often projected convincingly from the screen. Although a writer working on scripts for radio plays through the 1930s, Hopper switched to the technical side of things after war service, and became a film editor. The Pine-Thomas

unit at Paramount gave him his first chance at directing, but his films for them, although attractively set, all-action subjects, such as *Hurricane Smith* and *Secret of the Incas*, were not particularly distinguished. Then Hopper crossed to Universal, and immediately proved himself at home on more intimate subjects, especially those with veins of sentiment and/or comedy. *Naked Alibi* was a gritty thriller that attracted critical attention and *Smoke Signal* a fresh, brightly photographed western that provided further evidence that Piper Laurie was becoming more than a pretty face. The best film from Hopper's Universal (-International) period, though, is *The Private War of Major Benson*, a comedy about the relationship between a martinet commander and a very small cadet at a military academy. The film was a definite attempt to do something unusual, especially for Universal, and to his credit Hopper pulled it off. Charlton Heston, who had starred twice before for Hopper, displayed a subtle comedy touch that made him seem perfect for the part, and Tim Hovey did admirably as the boy: heart-warming laughter was the result. Little Hovey appeared twice more in Hopper films, but never to such effect. *The Missouri Traveler*, a glowing piece of *Huckleberry Finn*-style entertainment, with a winning performance from Lee Marvin, was the best of Hopper's later films before he became entrenched in television. He died from heart problems.

1952: The Atomic City. Hurricane Smith. 1953: Pony Express. 1954: Alaska Seas. Secret of the Incas. Naked Alibi. 1955: Smoke Signal. One Desire. The Private War of Major Benson. The Square Jungle. 1956: Never Say Goodbye. Toy Tiger. The Sharkfighters. Everything But the Truth. 1958: The Missouri Traveler. 1961: Blueprint for Robbery. 1962: †The Bull of the West (TV). 1970: Madron.

HORNER, Harry 1910-1994

Czech-born art director and production designer who had a brief fling at direction in the 1950s. Horner studied under Max Reinhardt in Germany, and followed him to Hollywood when he went there in 1935 to work on *A Midsummer Night's Dream*. He stayed to become production designer on several distinguished films, such as *Our Town*, *The Little Foxes* and *The Heiress*, the last of which won him him an Academy Award. Encouraged by this, Horner became a freelance director. His few films are all good looking, the style helping to disguise their low budgets (Milton Krasner photographed *Vicki*, and

Stanley Cortez *The Man from Del Rio*). The feeling of impending danger, of terrible violence throbbing below the surface, also runs through several of Horner's films. Perhaps the best of them is *Man from Del Rio*, which features one of Anthony Quinn's favourite roles (and rightly so) as the gunslinger tormented by too many memories of death in his past. It's an unusual, intense film with a tailed-away but very satisfying ending. But Horner and Quinn combined to much less effect on their next film, *The Wild Party*, which is little more than savage and unpleasant, and Horner was discouraged enough to return to production design, in which field he won a second Oscar, for *The Hustler*, in 1961. In the late 1960s, he became a producer-director of television series. He died from pneumonia.

1952: Red Planet Mars. Beware My Lovely. 1953: Vicki. 1954: New Faces of 1954. 1955: A Life in the Balance. 1956: Man from Del Rio. The Wild Party.

HOUGH, John 1941-

The impetus given to this British director's career by his first major film, *Eyewitness*, now seems to have drained away. The thoughtfulness and intelligence he put into relatively small-scale chillers and thrillers has been soaked up by fatuous and clichéd international projects. His work on episodes of *The Avengers* TV series of the late 1960s was smart and stylish and earned him his feature film chance. After a film for children, he seized his first major opportunity with *Eyewitness*, an ordinary-looking thriller on the boy-who-cried-wolf premise, which Hough shot in Malta and turned into one long, breathtaking slew of chases, tension and shock moments. The whole thing is immaculately edited and enough to leave an audience physically exhausted. Hough followed with *Twins of Evil*, one of the best of the later Hammer horrors and his last wholly satisfactory film, with stylish use of colour, a genuine sense of fright and menace and a firm grip on the Gothic set-pieces. Since then, Hough has filmed largely in America, but with progressively more lacklustre results. His 1980 film, *Incubus*, was back in the chiller vein, so one hoped for the best but it turned out to be objectionably bloodsoaked, and with a giggle-ridden script. Hough continued to disappoint in the 1980s and l990s, with a mixture of flaccid historical romances for TV, offbeat misfires and poor sequels to earlier films.

1969: Wolfshead — The Legend of Robin Hood. 1970: Eyewitness (US: Sudden Ter-

Ron **Howard** (left) on location for his first major success *Night Shift* with stars Shelley Long, Henry Winkler and Michael Keaton.

ror). 1971: *Twins of Evil. The Practice.* 1972: *Treasure Island.* 1973: *The Legend of Hell House.* 1974: *Dirty Mary, Crazy Larry. Escape to Witch Mountain.* 1978: *Brass Target. Return from Witch Mountain.* 1980: *Incubus.* 1981: *The Watcher in the Woods.* 1983: *Triumphs of a Man Called Horse.* 1984: *The Black Arrow (TV). A Distant Scream (TV. Released on US video as The Dying Truth).* 1986: *Biggles.* 1987: *American Gothic. A Hazard of Hearts (TV).* 1988: *Howling IV —The Original Nightmare.* 1989: *The Lady and the Highwayman (TV).* 1990: *Duel of Hearts (TV). A Ghost in Monte Carlo (TV).* 1997: *Something to Believe In.*

HOWARD, Ron 1953-

A fair-haired (later balding and moustachioed) American child actor, teenage and youth player (a huge hit on TV as Richie Cunningham of *Happy Days*) who turned to direction and became one of Hollywood's most reliable helmers of big-budget action movies. As a director, Howard lends an old-fashioned entertainment surge to his projects that often provokes an emotional reaction from the audience, helping to gloss over script deficiencies in some of his films. From an acting family, Howard appeared on stage with his parents at two and had made his film debut later the same year. As a child actor, his highest-profile roles were in *The Music Man* and *The Courtship of Adie's Father*, but his only major hit as a young man, before going into TV, was as one of the stars of George Lucas' seminal rites-of-passage film *American Graffiti*. As *Happy Days* neared the end of its run, Howard was already branching out into direction. He had a sleeper hit with *Night Shift*, with his *Happy Days* co-star Henry Winkler as a mortuary attendant embroiled in hare-

brained money-making schemes by Michael Keaton. This was little seen, however, outside America, and the film that put Howard into the international big time did the same for stars Tom Hanks and Daryl Hannah: *Splash*. This mermaid comedy had some funny lines, amusing dialogue and a leading trio of actors (completed by John Candy) who were constantly fun to be with. Howard continued to trip the light fantastic with the even more successful *Cocoon*, showing the lightest of touches in a story of a group of old codgers rejuvenated by alien influences. Drifting away from comedy after *Parenthood* (another major box-office hit) in 1989, Howard has gradually seen a greater critical acceptance of his work, particularly with *The Paper* and *Apollo 13*, in which his control of ensemble casts resulted in a string of impressive performances.

1969: *Deed of Derring-Do.* 1977: *Grand Theft Auto.* 1979: *Cotton Candy (TV).* 1980: *Through the Magic Pyramid (TV).* 1981: *Skyward (TV).* 1982: *Night Shift.* 1984: *Splash.* 1985: *Cocoon.* 1986: *Gung Ho.* 1988: *Willow.* 1989: *Parenthood.* 1991: *Backdraft.* 1992: *Far and Away.* 1994: *The Paper.* 1995: *Apollo 13.* 1996: *Ransom.* 1999: *Ed TV.*

HOWARD, William K. 1899-1954

Howard was a talented director who should have gone further. But he was also in many ways his own worst enemy. Intolerant of advice, he was a maverick who could not settle at a major studio, lived life to the full and was subject to bouts of alcoholism which his long-time associate, master cameraman James Wong Howe, would later say gradually ruined his career. He did make a few exceptionally good films, and there were chances to

regain lost ground, but he rarely accepted them. Much has been written about Howard, and he does seem to be generally regarded as one of the cinema's neglected masters. Yet if you actually give his long list of films a close inspection, not many of them are actually very good, and some are below par considering the talent involved. But, at his best, Howard was a great stylist. After serving in World War I, he headed for Hollywood and was at one time a cinema manager and film salesman before becoming an assistant director in 1920. After graduating to solo direction the following year, Howard found himself mainly assigned to action films, typically several in Paramount's Zane Grey western series. In a number of these, he put the mobile camera to good use in generating excitement. By now, he had become a great fan of the German expressionists, and used what he had learned to make his first major cinematic mark with *White Gold*, a heavily atmospheric landmark of the American silent cinema that enabled him to move on to bigger assignments. He continued his own striking approach to films, building up dark, shadowy atmospheres, in *The Valiant, Surrender* and *Transatlantic*. But perhaps his biggest success of the early sound years was *The Power and the Glory*, with Spencer Tracy. The two men had played polo together, both had rugged approaches to life and got on well. Under Howard's direction, Tracy gave perhaps his first great film performance, although, at the time, Howard was quick to give all the credit to the actor. His next few big-budget studio movies, however, were a disappointing crop. His reputation might have been restored by *The Princess Comes Across*, a zany comedy-thriller with Carole Lombard, with whom Howard also got along. But during the completion of the film, Howard ordered a Paramount supervisor from the set (an early use of a right won by the Screen Directors' Guild) and was practically black-listed by the major studios as a result. Anxious to work, Howard signed a contract with Alexander Korda's London Films in England and sailed in 1936. There was a fluent semi-epic, *Fire Over England*, and two decent, typically dark thrillers, but Howard's attachment to the whisky bottle on set won him few friends and, on his return to America in 1939, he found himself starved of opportunities to set up major productions. *Back Door to Heaven* was an above-average second-feature but it was really the last shot in the barrel, and Howard gave up the unequal struggle against the establishment at the end of 1945, after completing the unfortunately titled *A Guy Could Change*.

1921: †Get Your Man! Play Square. What Love Will Do. 1922: †Deserted at the Altar. Extra! Extra! Lucky Dan. Captain Fly-by-Night. †The Crusader. †Trooper O'Neil. 1923: The Fourth Musketeer. Let's Go! Danger Ahead. 1924: The Border Legion. East of Broadway. 1925: The Thundering Herd. Code of the West. The Light of Western Stars. 1926: Red Dice. Bachelor Brides. Volcano. Gigolo. 1927: The Main Event. White Gold. 1928: A Ship Comes In (GB: His Country). The River Pirate. 1929: Love, Live and Laugh. The Valiant. Christina. 1930: Good Intentions. Scotland Yard (GB: 'Detective Clive' — Bart). 1931: Transatlantic. Don't Bet on Women. Surrender. 1932: The Trial of Vivienne Ware. The First Year. Sherlock Holmes. 1933: The Power and the Glory (GB: Power and Glory). 1934: The Cat and the Fiddle. This Side of Heaven. Evelyn Prentice. 1935. Vanessa: Her Love Story. Rendezvous. Mary Burns — Fugitive. 1936: The Princess Comes Across. Fire Over England. 1937: The Squeaker (US: Murder on Diamond Row). †The Green Cockatoo (US: Four Dark Hours). †Over the Moon (released 1940). 1939: Back Door to Heaven. 1940: Money and the Woman. 1941: Bullets for O'Hara. 1942: Klondike Fury. 1943: Johnny Come Lately (GB: Johnny Vagabond). 1944: When the Lights Go On Again. 1945: A Guy Could Change.

HUDSON, Hugh 1940-

A contemporary and friend of Ridley Scott, Hudson's film output has been disappointingly thin since a stunning debut in 1981. The gestation periods on his new

British director Hugh **Hudson** has searched in vain for a successful follow-up to his breakthrough film *Chariots of Fire.*

films often rival those of David Lean but, since *Chariots of Fire*, the results have been nowhere near as rewarding. The eldest son of a wealthy landowning family, he was raised in London, Shropshire and Scotland, completing his education in the rarefied atmosphere of Eton before joining a London ad agency as head of its casting department. Six months later, Hudson landed a position as editor with a small film company in Paris. After two years pursuing French girls and escargots', Hudson returned to London to found his own agency for producing commercials. Teaming with Scott in 1970 in a new company, he embarked on an award-strewn five years of prizewinning commercials, breaking into films in 1978 as second-unit director on *Midnight Express*. With the help of producer David Puttnam, Hudson set up the film *Chariots of Fire*, about Olympic runners in 1919 confronted by hidebound authority. Its sweeping, adrenalin-rushing approach won it four Academy Awards, and Hudson himself was nominated for an Oscar as best director. The next, *Greystoke The Legend of Tarzan Lord of the Apes*, a $33 million version of the jungle classic, was much troubled in the making, and only partially successful, with the leading actress's voice being dubbed in the final reckoning. It was, however, a gem compared to *Revolution*, an epic of a different colour (American Independence), which found Hudson's fine visual style adrift in a ludicrous script with huge moments of incoherence. Even the visual touch had gone in *Lost Angels*, a dated piece about juvenile problems. It took Hudson some years to regroup, but he did so with two more films in the late 1990s. They have not so far, however, restored him to his former eminence.

1981: Chariots of Fire. 1984: Greystoke The Legend of Tarzan Lord of the Apes. 1985: Revolution. 1989: Lost Angels (GB: The Road Home). 1996: Durand. 1998: My Life So Far (The World of Moss).

HUGHES, John 1950-

A prodigious talent in his younger days, Hughes' career has followed very much along the lines of that of Roger Corman in the 1950s and 1960s: an intensive burst of film-making on a particular theme (in Hughes' case, the problems of modern youth), followed by a move into production to the complete destruction of his directorial career. After working as an advertising copywriter, Hughes, who, in his twenties, was already turning out dozens of (mainly unpublished) stories, novels and articles, joined the magazine *National Lampoon*. He soon became involved in the

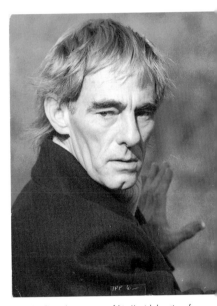

Ken **Hughes**, here on one of his Munich locations for 1974's *The Internecine Project.*

film side of his new company's business, his biggest success being the screenplay for *National Lampoon's Vacation*, although in the same year (1983), he also wrote the popular *Mr Mom*. From 1984 to 1989, Hughes entered into a burst of furious activity, writing and directing his own films. Typically, these are 'Wizard of Oz'-type films about misfits, with a teenage slant, that is to say its protagonists look in one way or another for a better life, only to find that happiness lies in their own backyard, and that fitting in is better than dropping out. The most popular of these are *The Breakfast Club* and, particularly *Ferris Bueller's Day Off*, in which Matthew Broderick plays the irrepressible Ferris, who will go to any lengths to play truant from college. Irreverent attitudes, character sassiness, lots of rock music and all the familiar Hughes ingredients are here, as the director presents his teenagers' feeling of superiority to adults being totally justified. He branched out with some success with *Planes, Trains and Automobiles*, a vehicle for comic actors Steve Martin and John Candy that proved both funny and touching, but, since the failure of the Shirley Temple-style heart-tugger *Curly Sue*, Hughes has concentrated on writing and production, notching up his biggest hits with the *Home Alone* series, the first two of which were directed for him by Chris Columbus.

1984: Sixteen Candles. The Breakfast Club. 1985: Weird Science. 1986: Ferris Bueller's Day Off. 1987: Planes, Trains and Automobiles. 1988: She's Having a Baby. 1989: Uncle Buck. 1991: Curly Sue.

HUGHES, Ken 1922-

British director who made crime thrillers of varying standards, then graduated to equally variable main features. A man of interesting ideas within a tight framework, Hughes was not without his minor triumphs in the earlier stages of his career. But, after winning praise for his first major project, *The Trials of Oscar Wilde*, the last 20 years of his film-making career proved almost totally without success. Born in Liverpool, he won an amateur film-making contest when only 14. He was a radio sound engineer before war service, made military training films, then joined World Wide Films as a writer and director of documentaries. He turned to fiction in 1952, but the early films, many of them featurettes in the *Scotland Yard* series, are mostly no more than programme-fillers, although one, *The Dark Stairway*, was gripping and above-average. Hughes began attracting attention with *The House Across the Lake*, a thriller which he adapted from his own novel *High Wray*. It had another of American actress Hillary Brooke's strong bad girls, the first of several forceful female performances in Hughes films, in which men put their lives on the line for love of a *femme fatale*. These seething melodramas are among Hughes' best work. There were two more well-made mid-1950s black-and-white pot-boilers, *Confession* and *Joe Macbeth*. The latter of these, with Paul Douglas and Ruth Roman (never better than in this part that suited her perfectly) as a modern-day Macbeth and Lady Macbeth, pushed Hughes into the big-time. But there were a few misfires before he came up with his best film to date, *The Trials of Oscar Wilde*, strikingly shot in Technicolor by Ted Moore, incisively written by Hughes himself, and attractively performed by Peter Finch (as Wilde), John Fraser, James Mason and Nigel Patrick. Of the succeeding Hughes films, *The Small World of Sammy Lee*, from Hughes' own TV play, was tightly done and nicely performed, but bad news at the box office. *Chitty Chitty Bang Bang* was just the opposite, flabby and overlong, but a great popular hit. *Drop Dead, Darling* had moments of sublime farce, but there was nothing sublime about the talky, tedious and very disappointing *Cromwell*, and Hughes' last few projects only got worse.

1944: *Soho (D). 1945: *The Burning Question (D). 1946: *Beach Recovery (D). *Those Nuisances (D). 1947: *The Mystery of the White Handkerchief. The Man on the Flying Trapeze. If the Cap Fits (D). 1952: Wide Boy. 1953: *The Drayton Case. *The Missing Man. *The Candlelight Murder. Black 13. *The Dark Stairway. 1954: *The Blazing Caravan. *The Strange Case of Blondie. *Passenger to Tokyo. The Brain Machine. The Little Red Monkey (US: The Case of the Little Red Monkey). The House Across the Lake (US: Heatwave). 1955: *Night Plane to Amsterdam. *Murder Anonymous. Confession (US: The Deadliest Sin). Timeslip (US: The Atomic Man). Joe Macbeth. 1956: Wicked As They Come. 1957: The Long Haul. 1959: Jazzboat. 1960: In the Nick. The Trials of Oscar Wilde (US: The Man with the Green Carnation). 1962: The Small World of Sammy Lee. 1964: †Of Human Bondage. 1966: Drop Dead, Darling (US: Arrivederci, Baby!) 1967: †Casino Royale. 1968: Chitty Chitty Bang Bang. 1970: Cromwell. 1974: The Internecine Project. 1975: Alfie Darling (US: Oh! Alfie). 1977: Sextette. 1980: Terror Eyes (later Night School).

HUMBERSTONE, H. Bruce 1903-1984

There was always plenty going on in this American director's films. Humberstone certainly knew how to keep an audience's attention, whether it was in the Charlie Chan thrillers or brightly Technicolored musicals. He worked for Fox and its successor, Twentieth Century-Fox, for 14 years and, although his basic direction was sometimes flat and uninspired, his films were almost all crowd-pleasers, and sometimes a bit more. Fox's pert blondes all shone under his guidance, and Alice Faye, Betty Grable, June Haver, Sonja Henie and Vera-Ellen all appeared in Humberstone films more than once. Darryl F. Zanuck thought enough of his talents to entrust the entire $1,800,000 fire sequence at the end of *In Old Chicago* to Humberstone, even though the rest of the film was directed by Henry King (qv). After entering films as a script clerk in 1919, Humberstone served for many years as an assistant director, working with such directors as Allan Dwan, Edmund Goulding and King Vidor (all qv) before deciding to take the plunge into solo direction. Fox kept him busy on series films — *Charlie Chan at the Opera* is one of the most enjoyable of the oriental sleuth's adventures — but Humberstone may have convinced them he was worthy of bigger things when he made *I Wake Up Screaming* in 1941. This moody thriller has a uniquely brooding, doomy atmosphere and a notable performance by Laird Cregar as the psychopathic detective in love with the memory of a murdered model. It was quite some way removed from Humberstone's usual lightweight stuff, but the studio then pitched him into some garish musicals. It was away from Fox that Hum-

berstone had his biggest critical and popular success, when he made the Danny Kaye vehicle *Wonder Man* for Samuel Goldwyn. Humberstone's dextrous handling of Kaye and a flimsy plot about a man and the ghost of his brother should again have earned him some reward, but Fox put him back on routine fodder. His later musicals are lacklustre as well as seeming silly and his only decent film in the 1950s was the lively Tony Curtis swashbuckler *The Purple Mask*, made seven years after he had left Fox for good. Known to his friends as 'Lucky'. He died from cancer of the stomach.

1932: Strangers of the Evening (GB: Who Killed Frank Daniels?). The Crooked Circle. †If I Had a Million. 1933: †King of the Jungle. Goodbye Love. 1934: The Merry Wives of Reno. The Dragon Murder Case. 1935: Ladies Love Danger. The Silk Hat Kid. 1936: Charlie Chan at the Racetrack. Three Live Ghosts. Charlie Chan at the Opera. 1937: Checkers. Charlie Chan at the Olympics. 1938: †In Old Chicago. Rascals. Time Out for Murder. Charlie Chan in Honolulu. While New York Sleeps. 1939: Pack Up Your Troubles (GB: We're in the Army Now). Pardon Our Nerve. 1940: Lucky Cisco Kid. The Quarterback. 1941: Tall, Dark and Handsome. I Wake Up Screaming (GB: Hot Spot). Sun Valley Serenade. 1942: Iceland (GB: Katina). To the Shores of Tripoli. 1943: Hello, Frisco, Hello. Pin Up Girl. 1945: Within These Walls. Wonder Man. 1946: Three Little Girls in Blue. 1947: The Homestretch. 1948: Fury at Furnace Creek. 1949: South Sea Sinner (GB: East of Java). 1951: Happy-Go-Lovely. 1952: She's Working Her Way Through College. 1953: The Desert Song. 1954: Ten Wanted Men. 1955: The Purple Mask. 1956: Tarzan and the Lost Safari. 1958: Tarzan's Fight for Life. Tarzan and the Trappers. 1961: Madison Avenue.

HUNT, Peter 1928-

For many years an excellent editor before he moved across to the director's chair, this British film-maker has always proved himself most at home with the maximum of action and the minimum of words. Thus he was in retrospect a perfect choice to direct one of the James Bond films, a series which he had served so faithfully and well as an editor. Neither is it a surprise that by and large the stars of his films are not the world's greatest actors, but rather proven rugged heroes of pounding action dramas. Strangely for one so skilled at producing explosive and colourful action on the screen, Hunt studied the violin as a teenager, then the history of art at university (in Rome). But he quickly turned to the film world in which he worked for almost 40 years, becoming an editor in the mid-1950s. It is unlikely that the acting in a film by Hunt will ever touch your heart; it is equally unlikely that you will ever be bored for long — as action, from South Africa *(Gold)* to Switzerland *(On Her Majesty's Secret Service)*, to Zanzibar *(Shout at the Devil)*, to the Arctic wastes *(Death Hunt)* and even to the fantasy land of *Gulliver's Travels*, thunders, pounding and gutsy, across the screen.

1969: On Her Majesty's Secret Service. 1974: Gold. 1976: Gulliver's Travels. Shout at the Devil. 1978: The Beasts Are on the Streets (TV). Flying High (TV). 1979: When She Was Bad... (TV). 1980: Death Hunt. 1981: Rendezvous Hotel (TV). 1983: Life on the Mississippi (TV). 1984: It Came Upon the Midnight Clear (TV). The Last Days of Pompeii (TV). Sins of the Past (TV). 1985: Wild Geese II. 1986: Hyper Sapiens People from Another Star. 1987: The President's Wife (TV). Assassination.

HUNTINGTON, Lawrence 1900-1968

British writer and director who made serviceable 'A' features from 1941 to 1955, before drifting out of the mainstream of British film-making. Many of these were in the thriller vein, several of them distinguished by their use of working-class London backgrounds (a city in which Huntington himself was born) and several also carrying a genuine charge of tension. In his early twenties, Huntington mixed writing and musical careers, becoming a dance-band musician by 1925 while continuing to write short stories and, eventually, screenplays. Not until the mid-1930s did he fling himself whole-heartedly into films, where his vigorous low-budget crime thrillers gradually grew in stature, reaching co-feature level by 1941 with *This Man is Dangerous*, a silly but enjoyable thriller with James Mason. In post-war years, Huntington was responsible for some thoughtful entertainments, including Mason's last British film before he left for Hollywood, *The Upturned Glass*, as well as *Night Boat to Dublin*, *Man on the Run* (about a deserter, with a star-studded cast-of-the-future including Laurence Harvey and Kenneth More), *The Franchise Affair* and particularly *Mr Perrin and Mr Traill*, a fascinating study (based on a book by L.A.G. Strong, whose work was popular film material at the time) of how jealousy can eat away at a man until it makes him do something quite out of character. In 1952, Huntington reunited husband-and-

wife team Michael Denison and Dulcie Gray from *The Franchise Affair* in *There Was a Young Lady* (which he also wrote), a delightful comedy-thriller that remains just about the only film to allow the piquant Dulcie Gray to show an impishly sexy side to her nature. It was not, however, a commercial success, and Huntington turned the remainder of his career to making numerous half-hour films for television, plus a few minor thick-ear thrillers for the cinema, none of which is very distinguished. Besides the films he directed himself, Huntington also wrote screenplays for movies made by other people, including *I Killed The Count* (1939), *Impulse* (1954), *A Question of Suspense* (1961) and *The Oblong Box* (1969), the last-named his final work for the cinema.

1929: After Many Years. 1934: Romance in Rhythm. 1936: Full Speed Ahead. Café Mascot. Strange Cargo. Two on a Doorstep. Bad Boy. 1937: Screen Struck. Passage to London. The Bank Messenger Mystery. 1938: Dial 999. Twin Faces. 1940: Flickers (D). 1941: This Man is Dangerous (later The Patient Vanishes). The Tower of Terror. 1942: Women Aren't Angels. Suspected Person. 1943: Warn That Man. 1945: Night Boat to Dublin. 1946: Wanted for Murder. 1947: When the Bough Breaks. The Upturned Glass. 1948: Mr Perrin and Mr Traill. 1949: Man on the Run. 1951: The Franchise Affair. 1952: There Was a Young Lady. 1955: Contraband Spain. 1959: Deadly Record. 1962: Stranglehold. The Fur Collar. 1963: Death Drums Along the River. 1966: The Vulture.

HURST, Brian Desmond 1895-1986

Irish director who went to Hollywood to learn at the feet of John Ford, then came to Britain and directed steadily, but did not hit his peak until the post-war boom in British films. His 1951 *Scrooge* remains the definitive film version of the story. Born in Southern Ireland (one source gives the year as 1892, but this seems very unlikely), Hurst was an art student in Paris before his trip to America where he worked for several years as one of Ford's assistants. Directing in Britain from the early 1930s, Hurst made an impression with a version of Edgar Allan Poe's *The Tell-Tale Heart*, later entering into an association with Alexander Korda's London Films. His late 1930s' chores included some abortive pre-production work on a version of *Lawrence of Arabia* and a salvage job on a film called *Prison without Bars*. Hurst's career got a boost in the early 1940s, though, when he made *Dangerous Moonlight*, a flying drama about a Polish pianist who loses his

memory during the Battle of Britain. Its popularity was increased by the success of its theme music, Richard Addinsell's 'Warsaw Concerto'. Hurst's next film, *Alibi*, a thriller with Margaret Lockwood and James Mason, was also a popular hit, and its direction was praised by critics; but Hurst spent the rest of the war years working on shorts and documentaries to boost the war effort, although, towards the end of the fighting, he became involved in directing some scenes for Gabriel Pascal's ponderous *Caesar and Cleopatra*. Hurst took some time to adjust to post-war tastes and both *Hungry Hill* and *The Mark of Cain* were too gloomy for their time. *Trottie True*, bedecked in early Technicolor, brought his work back to popularity and, after producing a successful version of *Tom Brown's Schooldays* in 1950, he made *Scrooge*, *Malta Story* and *Simba*, three contrasting films which all made big money at the box-office, especially *Simba*, with its strong star cast (Dirk Bogarde, Virginia McKenna, Donald Sinden) and topical subject — Mau-Mau atrocities in Africa — even if its atmosphere seemed faintly artificial. Strangely, it proved to be Hurst's last film of any weight and his career petered out disappointingly in the early 1960s.

*1934: Irish Hearts (US: Norah O'Neale). The Tell-Tale Heart (US: Bucket of Blood). 1935: Riders to the Sea. 1936: †Ourselves Alone (US: River of Unrest). The Tenth Man. Sensation. 1937: Glamorous Night. 1938: Prison Without Bars. 1939: †The Lion Has Wings. On the Night of the Fire (US: The Fugitive). 1940: *Miss Grant Goes to the Door. *A Call for Arms. 1941: Dangerous Moonlight (US: Suicide Squadron). 1942: Alibi. A Letter from Ulster (D). 1944: The Hundred Pound Window. 1945: Theirs is the Glory (D). †Caesar and Cleopatra. Men of Arnhem (D). 1946: Hungry Hill. 1947: The Mark of Cain. 1949: Trottie True (US: Gay Lady). 1951: Scrooge (US: A Christmas Carol). 1953: Malta Story. 1954: Simba. 1956: The Black Tent. 1957: Dangerous Exile. 1958: Behind the Mask. 1960: His and Hers. 1962: The Playboy of the Western World.*

HUSTON, John 1906-1987

Tall, craggy, individual American director whose lifestyle was as eccentric as some of the men he portrayed in his latter days as an extravagant character actor. Every year or so, though, he continued to emerge from his jungle retreat to surprise us with another film, often in some quite unexpected genre. He had made his name with grainy, hard-hitting thrillers and melodramas, after working as a screenplay writer

Happy to be making films into old age, John **Huston** completed his last film in the year of his death.

from 1932. He broke through in 1941 when at last allowed to direct one of his scripts — *The Maltese Falcon*, a classic detective thriller (from a book by Dashiell Hammett), which brought other careers to the fore, notably those of Humphrey Bogart and Sydney Greenstreet, who were both with Huston again on his next assignment, *Across the Pacific*, enjoyable wartime hokum that bounded with confidence. Huston then entered the US Signal Corps (he rose to major) and substantiated his reputation with three typically gritty documentary films as well as winning a Legion of Merit for 'courageous work under battle conditions' on several fronts. On his return from war in 1946, Huston chose the mysterious B. Traven's study of greed, *The Treasure of the Sierra Madre*, as his next project, but nearly drove studio chief Jack L. Warner to distraction (and close to abandoning the film) as he slowly filmed the action through the Mexican heat of 1947. When the film was unveiled early in 1948, however, even Warner had to admit the wait had been worthwhile. Not only did it please the public, and give Bogart one of his first real chances to show his range as an actor, but it won Huston twin Oscars for direction and screenplay. There were two more classic gangster thrillers — *Key Largo* and *The Asphalt Jungle* — before Huston began to enlarge his repertoire, most notably with *The African Queen* (Bogart again, and winning his only Oscar as the rough-and-ready World War I riverboat skipper), *Moulin Rouge* (which won Oscars for costume design and art direction), the moving *Heaven Knows, Mr Allison*, *The Misfits* (with last, great performances by Gable and Monroe) and the enormous fun of *The List of Adrian Mes-*

senger. Huston's output was less powerful from the mid-1950s, and he himself took more and more parts as an actor. Such 'experimental' films as *Reflections in a Golden Eye* and *A Walk with Love and Death* were not only not terribly successful in themselves, but box-office duds of the first order. Huston satisfied his admirers in the 1970s, though, with *Fat City*, a downbeat, uncommercial but strong drama of a fading boxer and people trying, in the words of its theme song, to 'make it through the night' and *The Man Who Would Be King*, a spectacular *and* commercial filming of Kipling's story of the north-west frontier — again, as with so many Huston dramas, with a theme of greed. Huston's skill as a director was always that the emotions in his films, whether love, fear, hatred, determination, holiness, greed or desperation, seemed genuinely felt, and he extracted some extraordinarily deep performances from actors not previously noted for extreme mobility. The third of his four wives (1946-1950) was actress Evelyn Keyes, and his daughter is the actress Anjelica Huston (1952-). He died from pneumonia.

1941: *The Maltese Falcon.* 1942: *Across the Pacific. In This Our Life.* 1943: *Report from the Aleutians (D).* 1945: *The Battle of San Pietro (D). Let There Be Light (D. Not released until 1980).* 1948: *The Treasure of the Sierra Madre. Key Largo.* 1949: *We Were Strangers.* 1950: *The Asphalt Jungle.* 1951: *The African Queen. The Red Badge of Courage.* 1952: *Moulin Rouge.* 1953: *Beat the Devil.* 1956: *Moby Dick.* 1957: *Heaven Knows, Mr Allison.* 1958: *The Barbarian and the Geisha. The Roots of Heaven.* 1959: *The Unforgiven.* 1960: *The Misfits.* 1962: *Freud (GB: Freud — the Secret Passion).* 1963: *The List of Adrian Messenger.* 1964: *The Night of the Iguana.* 1966: *The Bible. . . in the beginning.* 1967: †*Casino Royale. Reflections in a Golden Eye.* 1968: *Sinful Davey.* 1969: *A Walk with Love and Death. The Kremlin Letter.* 1971: *Fat City.* 1972: *The Life and Times of Judge Roy Bean.* 1973: *The Mackintosh Man.* 1975: *The Man Who Would Be King.* 1976: **Independence (D).* 1979: *Wise Blood.* 1980: *Phobia.* 1981: *Escape to Victory (US: Victory).* 1982: *Annie.* 1984: *Under the Volcano.* 1985: *Prizzi's Honor.* 1987: *The Dead.*

HUTTON, Brian G. 1935-

This American director has still not surpassed the quality of his first film and it seems unlikely that he will. From 1956 to 1963, Hutton was an actor (first film *Fear Strikes Out*, last one *The Interns*), but in

1964, he directed *Wild Seed* (shown in Britain as *Fargo*). This is a delicate, haunting black-and-white study of a teenage girl, running away from her foster-parents, who is befriended by a young drifter, hitches rides in railway trucks and searches for happiness. Hutton got a captivating performance from Celia Kaye and an understated portrayal from Michael Parks that, for intensity, reminded one of the young Brando. It was followed by another offbeat subject, *The Pad (and how to use it)*, but its impact was somewhat vitiated by the use of a stage actor, Brian Bedford, in the leading role. Thereafter, Hutton veered off into the world of big-budget, big-star movies. *Where Eagles Dare* proved that he could handle big-scale action, and was one of the best of the several films from novels by Alistair MacLean, while *Kelly's Heroes* was more wartime adventure with its tongue usefully in its cheek. But somehow Hutton faltered and, after three flops which bore only the occasional touch of directorial skill (Frank Sinatra's stalking of his quarry around the flapping cellophane tunnels of a building site in *The First Deadly Sin*, for example), it seemed that he had failed to cash in the vogue for the big-budget action movie at which he could have excelled in recent times. *High Road to China*, a well-handled Tom Selleck adventure, marked a partial return to form but, disappointingly, there has been nothing since.

1964: *Wild Seed (GB: Fargo).* 1966: *The Pad (and how to use it).* 1967: *Sol Madrid (GB: The Heroin Gang).* 1968: *Where Eagles Dare.* 1970: *Kelly's Heroes.* 1971: *Zee and Co (US: X, Y and Zee).* 1973: *Night Watch.* 1980: *The First Deadly Sin.* 1983: *High Road to China.*

HYAMS, Peter 1943-

Often his own director of photography, this New York-born director has throughout his career clung to the refreshingly old-fashioned belief that actions speak louder than words. His two Jean-Claude Van Damme films of the mid-1990s are better than anyone else's work with the same star, particularly those who want to make him look as though he can act. Hyams is under no such illusions. He simply puts Van Damme in the heart of the action where his fans will pay to see him and lets rip. He began as a newscaster with CBS, going on to make a documentary about Vietnam and embarking on a writing career in 1970. His first screenplay (which he did not direct) was *T.R. Baskin* (1971. GB: *Date with a Lonely Girl*) which he felt — rightly —was unsatisfactorily realized, and resolved to direct

Action specialist Peter **Hyams** takes pains lining up a shot in the making of his 1983 thriller The Star Chamber.

his own material. The results of this resolution were two TV movies. *The Rolling Man* was another small-screen success for the wily Dennis Weaver, a well-characterized drama which casts him as an ex-convict looking for his children, while *Goodnight My Love* remains one of the best-ever movies for television. Set unusually – but immaculately – in 1947, most of its action takes place at night, and its characters are constantly set in corners, or cramped, confined conditions, such as narrow stairways. Its heroes are two fairly down-at-heel detectives, played by rugged Richard Boone and the dwarf actor Michael Dunn, a contrast which gives rise to some crackling dialogue (written, of course, by Hyams). Its 'heroine' is a double-dealing, Lauren Bacall-style blonde, who eventually gets shot to death in a tense scene inside a cinema; the central character, in a plot more complicated, if anything, than *The Big Sleep*, is Julius Limeway (Victor Buono), a fat, white, luminous slug of a man, forever sitting at the same corner table of his plush nightclub and consuming endless quantities of snails. Clearly, there was a vivid imagination at work in this film (topped, perhaps, by a scene in which Dunn stands behind a door through which bullets are expected to come, and do, over his head) and Hyams was soon in big-screen action with *Busting*. This is almost *Goodnight My Love*, 1973-style, with Elliott Gould and Robert Blake as two street cops out to beat the system. The film has some sparklingly sarcastic dialogue and a brilliant tracking chase through streets and supermarket which leaves one breathless. Since then, Hyams has made two more films which contain climactic cat-and-mouse chases — the unusual *Capricorn One* and a science-fiction thriller *Outland*, a space-set remake of *High Noon*, with characterful portrayals by Sean Connery and Frances Sternhagen. *Capricorn One*, however, remains Hyams' best film to date. The story of a bogus Mars mis-

sion, its developments may be predictable, but they're shunted along with such verve by their writer-director that you don't much care. Hyams' work was less effective through most of the 1980s, but in the following decade he set his sights slightly lower with some interesting results. *Stay Tuned* was a zany comedy about a couple who fall into a TV hell of their own making, and *Narrow Margin* was a train-set thriller only a notch below the original RKO classic, the suspense given an added boost by stars Gene Hackman and Anne Archer doing much of their own stuntwork on top of a speeding train. It was typical of Hyams' attitude of what you see is what you get and like most of his action films, thundered along at a blasting pace.

1972: The Rolling Man (TV). Goodnight My Love (TV). 1973: Busting. 1974: Our Time. 1975: Peeper. 1978: Capricorn One. 1979: Hanover Street, 1981: Outland. 1982: Death Target. 1983: The Star Chamber. 1984: 2010. 1986: Running Scared. 1988: The Presidio. 1990: Narrow Margin. 1992: Stay Tuned. 1994: Timecop. 1995: Sudden Death. 1996: The Relic. 1999: End of Days

I

ICHIKAWA, Kon   1915-

Observers have found this Japanese director a difficult butterfly to pin down, since he rarely makes several films in the same genre or with the same underlying theme. And, after some memorable films between 1955 and 1965, his work declined dramatically in quality, seemingly in the search for a big commercial success. Still, the impact of his best films, *The Burmese Harp, The Punishment Room, Fires on the Plain, Conflagration, Her Brother, An Actor's Revenge, Alone on the Pacific* and *Tokyo Olympiad* (all within the same decade) will not be forgotten by those lucky enough to have seen them. Ichikawa was an animator and director of puppet films at the beginning of his career; not surprisingly, his visual sense remains his strongest asset. Often, the pictures in his films speak more poignantly and sometimes horrifyingly than any dialogue could. A very black vein of humour, sometimes almost cynicism, runs through many of his films, at first, as in *The Bil-*

lionaire, fairly contained, but later in full blossom. His grimmest films are *The Burmese Harp*, about a soldier who takes it as his mission in life to bury the war-killed unburied; the relentless *Fires on the Plain*, in which war is carried to its ultimate desperation — cannibalism; and *Conflagration*, in which a young man burns down a temple, which he sees as irretrievably tainted by tourists, soldiers and pollution. Ichikawa's most flamboyant work is *An Actor's Revenge*, almost a Japanese *No Way to Treat a Lady*, in which a Kabuki female impersonator dons his drag to kill off his parents' murderers without retribution; and his most accessible to western eyes are *Alone on the Pacific*, a simple tale of a single-handed crossing of the Pacific by a young Japanese sailor, and *Tokyo Olympiad*, a magnificent record of the muscle and effort expended at the Tokyo Olympic Games. Not quite what the commissioning authorities intended, it remains a splendid memorial to Ichikawa's sense of humour. Here is a Japanese director who can make western audiences laugh out loud – and cry as well.

1946: Musume Dojoji/A Girl at the Dojo Temple (puppet film. Unreleased). 1947: †Toho Senichi-Ya/A Thousand and One Nights. 1948: Hana Hira ku/A Flower Blooms. Sanhyaku-Roku-Jugo Ya/365 Nights (in two parts). 1949: Ningen Moyo/Design of a Human Being. Hateshi-naki Jonetsu/Endless Passion. 1950: Ginza Sanshiro/Sanshiro at Ginza. Net-sudei-Chi/The Hot Marshland Akatsuki no Tsuiseki/Pursuit at Dawn. 1951: Ye-Rai-Shang/Deadly Nightshade. Koibito/The Lover. Mukokuseki-Sha/Man without a Country. Nosumareta Koi/Stolen Love. Bungawan Solo/River Solo Flows. Kekkon Koshin-Kyoku/The Wedding March. 1952: Lucky San/Mr Lucky. Wakai Hito/The Young Generation. Ashi ni Sawatta Onna/The Woman Who Touched the Legs. Ano Te, Kono Te/This Way, That Way. 1953: Aoiro Kakumei/The Blue Revolution. Pu San/Mr Poo. Seishun Zenigata Heiji/The Youth of Henji Zenigata. Ai-Jin/Two Lovers. 1954: Watashi no Subete O/All of Myself. Okuman Choja/The Billionaire. Josei ni Kansuru Juni Sho/Twelve Stories About Women. 1955: Seishun Kaidan/The Youth's Ghost Story. Kokoro/The Heart. 1956: Shokei no Heya/The Punishment Room. Biruma no Tategoto/The Burmese Harp. Nihon-Bashi/ Bridge of Japan. 1957: Ana/The Hole. Manin Densha/The Crowded Train. Tohoku no Zunmu-Tachi/The Men of Tohoku. 1958: Enjo (GB: Conflagration. US: Flame of Torment). Money and Three Bad Men.

1959: *Kagi* (GB: *Odd Obsessions*. US: *The Key*). *Nobi/Fires on the Plain*. *Sayonara Konnichiwa/Goodbye and Good Day!* *Police and Small Gangsters*. 1960: *Bonchi*. †*Jokei* (GB: *Code of Women*. US: *A Woman's Testament*). *Ototo/Her Brother*. 1961: *Kuroi Junin no Onna/The Ten Black Women*. 1962: *Hakai* (GB: *The Outcast*. US: *The Sin*). *Watashi Wa Nisai/Being Two Isn't Easy*. 1963: *Yukinojo Henge* (GB: *An Actor's Revenge*. US: *The Revenge of Ukeno-Jo*). *Taiheiyo Hitoribotchi* (GB: *Alone on the Pacific*. US: *My Enemy the Sea*). 1964: *Zeni no Odori/Money Talks*. 1965: *Tokyo Olympiad*. 1966: *Aibo/Hey!Buddy!* (unfinished). *Topo Gigio e sei ladri* (Part-animation). 1968: **Kyoto/Tournament* (D). 1971: *Ai Futatabi/To Love Again*. 1973: *Matatabi/The Wanderers*. 1975: *Wagahai wa Neko de Aru/I Am a Cat*. 1976: †*Tsuma to Onna no Aida* (GB: *Between Women and Wives*. US: *Between Wife and Lady*). *Inugami-ke no Ichizoku/The Inugami Family*. 1977: *Akuma no Temari-uta/The Devil's Bouncing-Ball Song*. *Gokumonto* (GB: *Island of Horrors*. US: *The Devil's Island*). 1978: *Joobachi/Queen Bee*. 1979: *Hi no Tori/The Phoenix*. 1980: *Koto/Ancient City*. 1982: *Kofuku* (US: *Lonely Hearts*). 1983: *Sasamayeki/The Makioka Sisters/Fine Snow*. 1985: *Biruma no Tategoto/The Burmese Harp* (remake) *Ohan*. 1986: *Rokumekan/The Hall of the Crying Deer*. 1987: *Eiga Joyu/Actress*. *Taketori Monogatari/The Princess from the Moon*. 1991: *Tenkawa Densetsu Satsuji Jiken/Noh Mask Murders*. 1994: *Shijushichinin no Shikaku* (US: *47 Ronin*). 1996: *The Eight-Grave Village*.

INCE, Ralph 1887-1937

The brother of Thomas Ince, the pioneer producer of silent times (born 1882; died under mysterious circumstances 1924), this American film-maker was a cartoonist and actor before embarking on a prodigious directing career in 1912 — in contrast to his brother, who was more concerned with the progressive organization of a studio, and only directed a few shorts (including some with Mary Pickford) and a few features, including *The Battle of Gettysburg* and *Civilisation*. Not surprisingly, Ralph made most of his films for Thomas' companies, although there was a doomed attempt in 1917 to set up his own studio in partnership with a third brother, John Ince (1877-1947), who also directed some silent films. Ralph was tall and good-looking with a bush of crinkly fair hair. His looks made him an ideal leading man, and he loved acting; indeed, he never really gave up his acting career and led something of a Jekyll-and-Hyde existence, the Hyde (or

actor) in him often seeming more interesting than the director, with several screen portraits of Abraham Lincoln and a forthright rendition of Jack London's Wolf Larsen in *The Sea Wolf*. Although he had directed around 75 films by 1926, Ince's reputation never equalled that of his brother, and with the changeover to sound, he gradually returned whole-heartedly to acting, at first in his own films, but soon as a character player in films for other people; in 1932 alone, he appeared in 15 films. Around this time, Ince picked up the opportunity to direct again, and, early in 1934, surprised many people by accepting an invitation from Warner Brothers to direct low-budget 'quota quickies' for them at Teddington Studios in England. He probably hoped, with some justification, that these little films would be the launching-pad for his return to bigger things with the studio in America. Ince's work in the genre turned out to be superior to most of his competitors'— craftsmanlike crime films that were no disgrace in harness with a major film from Warners across the Atlantic. Several well-known players made very early appearances in Ince films, including Margaret Lockwood, Esmond Knight, Lilli Palmer and a young Australian actor, Errol Flynn, whom Ince recommended to Warners in America after his appearance as the leading man in *Murder at Monte Carlo* in 1934. There was also a promising young blonde actress, Lesley Brook, who starred in a number of films for Ince to such good effect that Warners actually put her under contract: she pursued her career with modest success until 1950. Ince could well have become a mid-range figure at Warners in the 1940s, but fate was not kind to the Ince family, and in April 1937, on a London street, Ralph was killed in a car accident.

1912: *The Godmother*. 1913: **The Treasure of Desert Isle*. **Why Am I Here?* **The Wreck* (and 1919 feature version). **The Right and the Wrong of It*. **His Second Wife*. **The Lost Millionaire*. **The Lucky Elopement*. **Mister Fixit*. **Peggy's Burglar*. **A Prince of Evil*. **Fatty on the Job*. **Diana's Dress Reform*. **Fatty's Affair of Honor*. **His Last Fight*. *A Million Bid*. *The Call*. *A Regiment of Two*. **Bingle's Nightmare*. 1914: **Two Women* (and 1919 feature version). **Uncle Bill*. **Wife Wanted*. **Midst Woodland Shadows*. **The Painted World* (and 1919 feature version). **Fatty's Sweetheart*. 413. **The Girl from Prosperity*. **He Danced Himself to Death*. **He Never Knew*. **Shadows of the Past* (and 1919 feature version). *Lincoln the Lover*. *The Goddess* (serial). **Back to Broadway*. 1915: **Some White Hope*. **Count 'Em*. **The Sort-of-Girl Who Came*

from Heaven. **From Headquarters*. *The Ninety and Nine*. **His Phantom Sweetheart*. *The Awakening*. *The Juggernaut*. 1916: **His Wife's Good Name*. **The Thorn and the Rose*. *The Destroyers*. *Conflict*. *The Combat*. *My Lady's Slippers*. 1917: *The Argyle Case*. *Today*. *The Co-Respondent*. 1918: *Tempered Steel*. *Fields of Honor*. *The Panther Woman*. *Her Man*. *The Eleventh Commandment*. 1919: *The Wreck*. *Two Women*. *The Painted World*. *Virtuous Men*. *Too Many Crooks*. *A Stitch in Time*. *The Perfect Lover*. *Sealed Hearts*. *Out Yonder*. *Shadows of the Past*. *The Sins of the Mothers*. 1920: *From Headquarters*. *The Land of Opportunity*. **His Wife's Money*. *Red Foam*. *The Law Bringers*. *Out of the Snow*. 1921: *After Midnight*. *The Highest Law*. *Wet Gold*. *Tropical Love*. *The Last Door*. *A Man's Home*. *Remorseless Love*. 1922: *Channing of the Northwest*. *A Wide-Open Town*. *The Referee*. *Reckless Youth*. 1923: *Success*. *Homeward Bound*. †*Counterfeit Love*. *The Moral Sinner*. 1924: *The House of Youth*. *The Uninvited Guest*. *Dynamite Smith*. *The Chorus Lady*. 1925: *Alias Mary Flynn*. *Playing with Souls*. *Smooth As Satin*. *Lady Robin Hood*. 1926: *Bigger Than Barnum's*. *Breed of the Sea*. *The Lone Wolf Returns*. *The Sea Wolf*. *The Better Way*. *Yellow Fingers*. 1927: *Home Struck*. *Wandering Girls*. *Molders of Men*. *Not for Publication*. *Shanghaied*. 1928: *Hit of the Show*. *South Sea Love*. *Coney Island*. *Chicago After Midnight*. *Danger Street*. *The Singapore Mutiny* (GB: *The Wreck of the Singapore*). 1929: *Hurricane*. *Hardboiled* (GB: *A Real Girl*). 1932: *Men of America* (GB: *Great Decision*). 1933: *Lucky Devils*. *Flaming Gold*. 1934: *No Escape*. *A Glimpse of Paradise*. *What's in a Name?* *Murder at Monte Carlo*. 1935: *Crime Unlimited*. *Blue Smoke*. *Black Mask*. *Mr What's-His-Name*. *Rolling Home*. 1936: *It's You I Want*. *Jury's Evidence*. *Jail Break*. *Twelve Good Men*. *Fair Exchange*. *Hail and Farewell*. *The Vulture*. 1937: *Side Street Angel*. *It's Not Cricket*. *The Perfect Crime*. *The Man Who Made Diamonds*.

INCE, Thomas H.

See Ince, Ralph

INGRAM, Rex

See Lachman, Harry

IRVIN, John 1940-

British-born director with a long background in films. Although Irvin has occasionally shown himself adept with intimate character drama, his attempts at big-scale action films have, although techni-

Britain's John **Irvin** has made several action pictures in Hollywood. Here he is on the set of *Next of Kin*.

cally highly competent, not found the scripts to rise above the routine. While he has commendably tackled an extremely wide range of subjects – often about action heroes facing huge odds – his best film remains the delightfully eccentric *Turtle Diary*, which he made in the mid 1980s. Irvin was still in his teens when he entered the industry as an apprentice cutter with the Rank Organisation, in the days when their studios were still producing a sizeable number of films each year. From there he moved to British Transport Films as an assistant director. Then, after receiving a grant from the British Film Institute, he spent five years making short documentaries and drama films. Irvin was also film adviser to the Jamaican government from the mid 1960s and worked extensively in television before making an explosive feature film debut in 1980 with *The Dogs of War*, an adaptation of a best-seller by Frederick Forsyth about mercenaries in Africa. *Ghost Story*, an underrated horror yarn with veteran Hollywood talent, preceded Irvin's two best films, both with English backgrounds. *Champions* was a poignant and sometimes exciting true-life story of a steeplechase jockey who makes a courageous recovery from cancer. But the jewel in Irvin's crown is undoubtedly *Turtle Diary*. Armed with an endearingly naturalistic screenplay by Harold Pinter, Irvin creates an eccentric but everyday, incident-filled world centred on the seedy milieu of the boarding-house where divorced bookshop assistant Ben Kingsley lodges with people as lonely as himself. There's not a false note throughout as (explaining the title), Kingsley and fellow crank Glenda Jackson steal three turtles from a zoo and return them to the sea. Irvin's films have not had the same inspiration since then, although *City of Industry*, a study of seedy criminals, is one of his more interesting, with a well-achieved and over-riding feeling of heat, even in the hours of darkness, that permeates the whole film. *Widows Peak*, a sparkling comedy with undertones of mystery, is also of note.

1963: *Gala Day. *Inheritance. 1964: *The Malakeen. *Carousella. 1965:*Pedro Cays. *John Arden - Playwright. *Exile. *Strangers. 1966: *The 26. *The North-westerners. *Go Go Go Said the Bird. 1967: *Mafia No! *Bedtime. 1980: The Dogs of War. 1981: Ghost Story. 1983: Champions. 1985: Turtle Diary. 1986: Raw Deal. 1987: Hamburger Hill. 1989: Next of Kin. 1990: Eminent Domain. 1991: Robin Hood (cable TV. GB: cinemas). 1993: Freefall. 1994: Widows Peak. 1995: A Month by the Lake. 1997: City of Industry. 1998: When Trumpets Fade:

IVORY, James 1928-

Elegance, taste, care and an eye for the re-creation of times past drape almost all the work of this American-born director who has ranged from India to England and back to America depicting the moods, manners, milieu and morals of enclosed societies whose members are pinned like butterflies and ruthlessly dissected for our inspection. After years of work in this field of human entomology, Ivory produced two master-works in the early 1990s. After studying fine arts at university, Ivory's first intention was to become a set designer – small wonder that the production design of his films is always so aesthetically pleasing – but later studied film, made some independent shorts (one of which was about Indian art objects) and then undertook a career-forming journey to India in 1960, initially to make a documentary there. He became fascinated by the Indian way of life, and by the collision between eastern and western cultures there. His films have expressed this clash of directions, although *Shakespeare-Wallah*, set against the adventures of a rather down-at-heel group of British strolling players, was undoubtedly the most accessible to western eyes. Ivory managed to probe deep into the qualities of Indian life, without coming to such down-to-earth, even cynical terms with them as Satyajit Ray *(qv)*, the native Indian director whose work Ivory so much admired. Since 1972, Ivory has spent more and more time back in America. His films, it seems predetermined by exhibitors, are not for the box-office masses there, or elsewhere come to that. Perhaps, in view of the unhappy failure of *The Guru* and *The Wild Party*, they are right. But such Ivory offerings as *Autobiography of a Princess* and *Roseland* are well worth seeking out. Later, some of his films received their initial showing on television, a medium to whose intimacy Ivory's style seems ideally suited. *The Europeans* though, a graceful film full of richness and delicacy and the best expression of Henry James' work on screen, catching exactly the flavour and intimations of James' writing,

remains best seen in a cinema. But critics expressed disappointment with Ivory's next cinema offering, *Quartet*. He was soon to turn the tables on them. After his three chosen paths – India, the nostalgic past and the literary – collided in the hypnotic *Heat and Dust*, Ivory hit a magic ten-year run which included Academy Award nominations for *A Room with a View*, *Howards End* and *The Remains of the Day*. The first two were both adaptations from the work of E.M. Forster, and won several acting Oscars, while the latter, an exquisite study of repressed emotions, is possibly his best film. He has fallen a little from those peaks since, but his work remains pictorially stunning.

1953: *Four in the Morning. 1957: †*Venice: Theme and Variations (D). 1959: *The Sword and the Flute (D). 1963: Gharbar (GB & US: The House-holder). 1964: *The Delhi Way (D). 1965: Shakespeare-Wallah. 1968: The Guru. 1970: Bombay Talkie. 1971: Adventures of a Brown Man in Search of Civilisation (D). 1972: Savages. Mahatma and the Mad Boy. 1973: Helen — Queen of the Nautch Girls. 1974: The Wild Party. 1975: Autobiography of a Princess. 1976: Sweet Sounds. 1977: Roseland. 1978: Hullabaloo over Bonnie and Georgie's Pictures (TV. US: cinemas). 1979: The 5:48 (TV). The Europeans. 1980: Jane Austen in Manhattan (TV. US: cinemas). 1981: Quartet. 1983: Heat and Dust. †Courtesans of Bombay (TV). 1984: The Bostonians. 1985: A Room with a View. 1987: Maurice. 1988: Slaves of New York. 1990: Mr & Mrs Bridge. 1991: Howards End. 1993: The Remains of the Day. 1995: Jefferson in Paris. 1996: Surviving Picasso. 1998: A Soldier's Daughter Never Cries.

An immaculate reconstructor of time and place, director James **Ivory** is seen evoking the era of the Thirties in *Mr & Mrs Bridge*.

JACKSON, Pat 1916-

Sensitive British director at his best with documentaries. Unfortunately, he never seemed to get the chance to bring this distinctive touch to his post-war work. As an editor and co-director with the trail-blazing GPO Film Unit in the mid-1930s, Jackson had the opportunity to work with John Grierson, Basil Wright, Alberto Cavalcanti, Harry Watt and others. But his reputation was really made with the wartime semi-documentary *Western Approaches*, which mixed genuine footage with clever mock-up work in Pinewood Studios, photographed in luxurious Technicolor by Jack Cardiff, to catch all the intensity of war at its height for the merchant seaman. Alas, Jackson remained promising for far too long. There was an abortive period under contract to Alexander Korda, and an almost equally abortive visit to M-G-M in Hollywood, where he made just one film in two years, the moody melodrama *Shadow on the Wall*, which cast Ann Sothern against type as a vindictive murderess, but was nothing special. From 1951, Jackson flittered about the fringes of the British film industry, hopping from producer to producer, studio to studio to independent. He kept fairly busy directing for television, but there were sometimes considerable gaps between his films. From 1958, Jackson hit his best patch. *Virgin Island* was a real-life story of considerable charm about a young couple starting out in life on an uninhabited West Indian island. It was followed by a telling little second-feature, *Snowball*, with Gordon Jackson; *What a Carve-Up!*, a very lively comedy-thriller send-up of *The Old Dark House* type of film (and not the sort of film one would have suspected Jackson had in him); *Seven Keys*, another good second-feature with Jeannie Carson and Alan Dobie; and the creepy, compelling *Don't Talk to Strange Men*. But they were small peaks, and did not lead to greater things. Jackson returned to television.

*1936: †*Book Bargain* (D). 1937: †*Big Money* (D). *Men in Danger* (D). 1938: *†Happy in the Morning* (D). *The Horsey Mail* (D). 1939: *†The First Days* (D). 1940: *Health in War* (D). *†Welfare of the Workers* (D). 1941: *Ferry Pilot* (D). 1942: *The Builders* (D). 1944: Western Approaches (US: The Raider). 1947: Patent Ductus Arteriosus (D). 1950: Shadow on the Wall. 1951: †Encore. White Corridors. 1952: Something Money Can't Buy. 1956: The Feminine Touch (US: The Gentle Touch). 1957: The Birthday Present. 1958: Virgin Island/Our Virgin Island. 1960: Snowball. 1961: What a Carve-Up! (US: No Place Like Homicide). 1962: Seven Keys. Don't Talk to Strange Men. 1964: Seventy Deadly Pills. 1965: Dead End Creek (serial). 1969: On the Run.*

JACKSON, Peter 1961-

Anarchic New Zealand-born director who has made a virtue of the title of his first film — *Bad Taste*. A few years earlier his films might have been condemned in a body as video nasties — but festival and critical approval has brought recognition and (almost) respectability to Jackson's charnel-house work, a world in which slicing someone's head off with a meat cleaver represents a tame demise. Born appropriately on Halloween, Jackson spent his childhood making films with his parents' Super-8 camera. Later, in between working as a photo engraver, he started to make a science-fiction comedy short that eventually became 75 minutes of a feature called *Bad Taste*. The New Zealand Film Commission ultimately bankrolled him to polish and complete the film, whose final emergence in 1987 sent audiences around the world racing for the sick-bags. A quite disgusting, but brilliantly made version of *Independence Day*, it features aliens descending on earth to savour their new fast food sensation – human flesh. That was a tough gorefest to outgross but Jackson did his best with *Meet the Feebles*, which featured puppets, deviates, sex, drugs, the usual quota of repellent violence – and a couple of musical numbers. After fulfilling his ambition to make a zombie movie absolutely oozing with special effects in *Braindead*, Jackson began to spread his wings with subtler stuff. *Heavenly Creatures*, an offbeat and fascinating examination of a real-life New Zealand murder case, brought the gore-happy kiwi an Academy Award nomination for best screenplay and made an international star of Kate Winslet. Undeservedly less successful was *The Frighteners*, a thunderingly paced horror comic made in New Zealand with a largely American cast. Jackson's special effects techniques here assume new sophistication, as a cowled 'soul collector' swoops over the town seeking some fresh victim. A number of plot threads are neatly tied together by Jackson in a story that, in an unreal way, and with characters straight out of *Twin Peaks*, makes perfect sense. Effects are right on the mark, as walls, mirrors and ceilings bulge, the dead rise and ectoplasmic masses seep away in search of escape. Lord knows where Jackson goes from here, but it's going to be an exciting ride.

1987: Bad Taste. 1989: Meet the Feebles. 1992: Braindead (US: Dead Alive). 1994: Heavenly Creatures. 1995: Forgotten Silver (originally for TV. Released 1997). 1996: The Frighteners.

JANCSÓ, Miklós 1921-

Hungarian director noted for his visual strengths, impressive control of camera movement, and for bringing across a feeling for the roots of his native land. Jancsó is generally acknowledged as the finest Hungarian post-war director — although his own ex-wife, Márta Meszáros (1931-), must be running him close; his most impressive films have been those made in, and involving, his native land. Those he has made in Italy and Yugoslavia, especially in recent years, seem to bring his sincerity into question. *Figures in a Landscape* is not a Jancsó film, but it sums up the basis of all his most compelling work. *The Round Up, The Red Psalm, Agnus Dei, Sirokko, The Red and the White* and more are dominated by great Hungarian plains, stunning visual set-ups and massive travelling shots; you could fill a picture gallery with stills from Jancsó films. The protagonists are dream-like puppets, usually embarking on some kind of interracial struggle: Jancsó holds out no more hope for one side than the other, and often his sympathies, such as they are, seem evenly divided. His images, if a shade deliberate, still stamp themselves on the memory. After studying film in post-war Hungary, Jancsó began making newsreels, then short films, from 1951 on. It was some time before he turned to features but, after the success of *Cantata*, he devoted himself to elaborately shot historical documents. *The Round-Up* made him an international figure, but he has not made a first-class film now since *Red Psalm*, and the worries of his critics that he may have become a painter rather than a thinker seem to be well-founded. Perhaps a return to roots is called for, and would bring a few last great films, of which he is surely still capable. But time is running short...

1951-1958: Co-directed or directed 23 short films. First solo directing credit on A Nyolcadik Szábad Majus 1 (1952). 1958: A Harangok Romaba Mentek/The

An uncharacteristically relaxed shot of individualistic film-maker Derek **Jarman** on the set of his typically offbeat version of *Edward II*.

sexuality is central to his work, which, as well as anachronisms in period pieces, is full of full-frontal naked men, whose presence may or may not be superfluous to the main action. The male form, in fact, has dominated Jarman's cinema and probably prevented it reaching a wider public. As a one-of-a-kind film-maker, however, he has earned his niche in history. Sex and sidelong glances are major players in Jarman's films; but there are few smiles in his aggrieved and aggressive work, which emphasises style and content to the exclusion of entertainment. The most interesting and accessible of his films are those from the late 1980s, especially *Caravaggio*, his first to encourage acting roles and narrative, *The Last of England*, a lament for a country ravaged by some nameless disaster (AIDS?) and *War Requiem*, a surrealistic, dialogue-free vision of World War II, using poetry and music to express emotions. A talented painter and costume designer, he died from AIDS.

1971: *Journey to Avebury. *Miss Gaby. 1972: *Tarot. *The Garden of Luxor. *Andrew Logan Kisses the Glitterati. 1973: *Sulphur. 1974: *Ula's Fire Island. *Reworking the Devils. *Duggie Fields. 1975: *Picnic at Ray's. Ula's Fete. 1976: Sebastiane. *Sloane Square. *Gerald's Film. *Houston Texas. 1977: *Jordan's Dance. *Every Woman for Herself and All for Art. 1978: Jubilee. 1979: The Tempest. *Broken English. 1980: In the Shadow of the Sun. 1981: T.G: Psychic Rally in Heaven. 1982: *Pontormo and Punks at Santa Croce. 1983: *Waiting for Waiting for Godot. 1984: Imagining October. *The Dream Machine. *Catalan. 1985: †Aria. The Angelic Conversation. 1986: Caravaggio. 1987: The Last of England. 1988: *Inspirazione. 1989: War Requiem. 1990: The Garden. 1991: Edward II. 1992: Blue/Derek Jarman's Blue. 1993: Wittgenstein.

Bells Have Gone to Rome. 1959: *Halhatatlanság. Izotópok a Gyógyaszatban. 1960: *As Éledés Müvészete. †Hamom Csillag/Three Stars. 1961: *Az Idö Kereke. *Alkonyok és Hajnalok. *Indián Történet. 1962: Oldás és Kötes/Cantata. 1963. *Hej, te Eleven Fu. 1964: Igy Jöttem/My Way Home. 1965: *Jelenlét. Szegenylegenyek/The Round Up. 1966: *Közelröl a Ver. 1967: Csillagosok Katonak/The Red and the White. Csend es Kiáltás/Silence and Cry. 1968: Fényes Szelek/The Confrontation. 1969: Sirokko (GB: Winter Sirocco. US: Winter Wind). 1970: *Füst. 1971: Agnus Dei. La pacifista/The Pacifist. La tecnica e il rito. 1972: Még Kér a Nép/And the People Still Ask (GB: Red Psalm. US: Red Song). 1973: Roma rivuole Cesare/Rome Wants

Another Caesar. 1974: Szerelmem Elektra/Elektreia. 1976: Vizi privati, pubbliche virtü (GB: Private Vices and Public Virtues. US: Private Vices — Public Virtue). 1977: Masterwork. 1979: Hungarian Rhapsody. 1980: Allegro Barbaro. 1981: Il cuore del tirrano/Boccaccio in Hungary. 1983: Omega, Omega... 1984: Muzsika. 1985: Budapest (D). L'aube. 1986: Szörnyek Evadya (US: Season of Monsters). 1989: Jesus Krisztus Horoszkóya. 1992: The Blue Danube Waltz.

JARMAN, Derek (Michael D. Jarman) 1942-1994
British film-maker with a vivid pictorial sense (as befits a painter), but little enthusiasm for narrative. Jarman's own homo-

JARMUSCH, Jim 1953-
Semi-underground American film-maker whose bleak, if often noisy films and characters offer the lie to E.M. Forster's famous advice: 'Only connect...' Jarmusch's characters are loners, outsiders, criminals and rebels. The actors he has attracted to his work make a formidable list, but if you see a few of the films then, whatever you may think of their merits, you will understand why Jarmusch remains (probably happily) on the fringes of the mainstream. Blighted landscapes, both urban and rural, form the backcloths to his stories, in which alienated protagonists stare glumly out of the screen until their nemesis, or their destiny arrives.

Innovative but rarely entertaining, Jarmusch's films form the back of beyond of American life: a slice of life, yes, but one quite alien to ordinary people.

1980: *Permanent Vacation*. 1982: **New World*. 1984: *Stranger Than Paradise*. 1986: *Down by Law*. 1989: *Mystery Train*. 1991: *†Night on Earth*. 1996: *Dead Man*. 1997: *Year of the Horse* (TV). 1999: *Ghost Dog*.

JARROTT, Charles 1927-

A charming children's film, a couple of faintly stuffy historical pageants with good individual performances, the fresh-air romance of *The Dove* and the dreaded musical remake of *Lost Horizon*: not much on which to peg a long career, film-wise, but the evidence suggests that this British-born director is good with actors, if not always with the actual films. Three of his performers were nominated for Oscars from *Anne of the Thousand Days* and another from *Mary, Queen of Scots*, while the performances in *Escape from the Dark*, from the children to Alastair Sim, are enchanting. Jarrott began his career as an actor, but had moved to the other side of the camera by the mid-1950s, working extensively in television, winning awards for some of his productions, then living for some time in Canada, where he built up a solid reputation on stage and television. Since that enormous white elephant *The Other Side of Midnight*, however, with Marie-France Pisier battling gamely through 166 minutes of X-certificate soap opera, Jarrott has worked on less prestigious projects and TV mini-series. His Disney film *Condorman* was a lively and enjoyable romp, and suggested a talent for helming films that needed a light touch. He married the actress Katharine Blake.

1962: *Time to Remember*. 1968: *The Strange Case of Dr Jekyll and Mr Hyde* (TV). 1969: *Anne of the Thousand Days*. 1971: *Mary, Queen of Scots*. 1973: *Lost Horizon*. 1974: *The Dove*. 1976: *Escape from the Dark* (GB: *The Littlest Horse Thieves*). 1977: *The Other Side of Midnight*. 1980: *The Last Flight of Noah's Ark*. 1981: *Condorman*. 1982: *The Amateur*. 1985: *The Boy in Blue*. 1987: *Poor Little Rich Girl* (Feature version of TV mini-series). 1990: *Night of the Fox* (Feature version of TV mini-series). 1991: *Lucy and Desi: Before the Laughter* (TV). 1994: *Treacherous Beauties* (TV). 1997: *The Sex Life of Algernon*. 1998: *Byron*.

JASON, Leigh (L. Jacobson) 1904-1979

Apart from a brief period in the late 1930s when he was riding high at RKO, this American director was a man who handled slipping stars. Trained in electrical engineering, Jason was a keen spare-time writer, and entered Hollywood as an electrician in 1924 with a view to eventually getting into scripting there. He succeeded after two years and continued writing throughout the next ten years, occasionally being given the opportunity to direct his own work as well. It was in 1936 that Jason found himself hired by RKO as a director of screwball comedy and light romantic entertainments. His first, *The Bride Walks Out*, with Barbara Stanwyck, was a sizeable success and established his reputation for steering some of Hollywood's best-liked and most durable ladies to pleasurable performances. Stanwyck revelled in a rare opportunity to play comedy, with Jason's direction ever subtle and some sharp dialogue from screenplay writer P.J. Wolfson and Philip G. Epstein. But the Wolfson-Epstein-Jason-Stanwyck combination was somewhat less successful in 1938 with a similar venture, *The Mad Miss Manton*, even though Henry Fonda was leading man. Before that, Jason had given Lucille Ball's career a boost when she outsparkled the stars in his *That Girl from Paris*. With the end of the 1930s, screwball comedy began to die away, and RKO went in different directions. So, to his detriment, did Jason, directing the fading Joan Blondell in three progressively inferior comedies in 1941. Columbia celebrated Jason's liking for ladies by giving him ten of them to direct in the eccentric thriller *Nine Girls* — they included Ann Harding, Evelyn Keyes, Anita Louise, Jinx Falkenberg, Shelley Winters and several other Columbia contractees. Jason also got to direct Columbia's biggest musical attraction, the energetic Ann Miller, in the semi-A musical *Carolina Blues*. In the postwar years, Jason found that there were fewer and fewer directing opportunities for a man with his special gifts. He was totally unsuited to the stolid war film *Okinawa*, with another fading star, Pat O'Brien, but by this time he had already become one of the first directors to turn to television, working busily on half-hour situation comedy.

1928: *The Price of Fear*. *The Tip-Off* (GB: *Underworld Love*). 1929: *Wolves of the City*. *The Body Punch*. *Eyes of the Underworld*. 1932: **Apples to You*. **Bubbling Over*. 1933: **A Preferred List*. *High Gear* (GB: *The Big Thrill*). 1934: **Everybody Likes Music*. **If This Isn't Love*. **The Knife of the Party*. **Nifty Nurses*. **Roamin' Vandals*. **Super Stupid*. 1935: **Hail Brother!* **Metropolitan Nocturne*. **A Returned Engagement*. **The Spirit of 1976*. 1936: *Love on a Bet*. *The Bride Walks Out*. *That Girl from Paris*. 1937: *New Faces of 1937*. *Wise Girl*. 1938: *The Mad Miss Manton*. 1939: *Career*. *The Flying Irishman*. 1941: *Model Wife*. *Three Girls About Town*. *Lady for a Night*. 1943: *Dangerous Blondes*. 1944: *Nine Girls*. *Carolina Blues*. 1946: *Meet Me on Broadway*. 1947: *Lost Honeymoon*. *Out of the Blue*. *Man from Texas*. 1952: *Okinawa*. 1954: *†The Go-Getter*.

JENNINGS, Humphrey 1907-1950

This book has largely skirted clear of documentarists, but Jennings is unskirtable. His films are so much a part of the British wartime cinema scene that they cannot be ignored; besides which, they remain the finest cinematic achievements of the World War II period in Britain. Many of the scenes in his masterwork, *Fires Were Started*, about the horrendous work of London's wartime firemen, are amazing, mouth-opening, agonizing pieces of montage. The sweat, the grime, the burns, the blood, are all horrifyingly real. A horse gallops through the smoke and away from the flames; a fireman dangles from his lifeline after falling from a blazing building. Beams crackle, crack and crash; the heat and the danger blaze intensely from the screen. Above all, the film inspires a feeling of patriotism, as did all Jennings' wartime work. Poet and painter, Jennings was a master of placing scenes together in a pattern which would have the maximum emotional impact on his audience. The images have worn better than the sounds; the dialogue in these films sometimes seems portentous, even too facile, although it did not appear so at the time. A brilliant scholar, writer and critic, Jennings had joined the famous GPO documentary unit in 1934 as a designer and editor. It was not long before he was making his own very individual short documentary films. After contributing some work on *Coalface*, he stepped out on his own with *Locomotives*, some parts of which anticipate the more famous *Night Mail*. But the war truly brought out the inspiration in Jennings. Sometimes, as in *S.S. Ionian*, his images were misplaced, but the pure visual poetry of such films as *The First Days*, *London Can Take It*, *Words for Battle*, *Listen to Britain* and *A Diary for Timothy* struck chords in the hearts and minds of the British people that no other film-maker could find. Jennings' films were just as skilled, though slightly less interesting – after all, who could match wartime fervour? – in the post-war years. As he hurtled helplessly to his death from a Greek cliff in 1950 while

Specialist in polished comedy Norman **Jewison**.

scouting locations for his next film, Britain lost its most remarkable film-maker of the period.

1934: *Locomotives (D). *Post Haste (D). 1935: *The Story of the Wheel (D). 1936: *†The Birth of a Robot (D). 1938: *Penny Journey (D). *Her Last Trip/S.S. Ionian (D). Speaking from America (D). *Design for Spring (D). *English Harvest (D). 1939: Spare Time (D). †*The First Days (D). *Spring Offensive/An Unrecorded Victory (D). 1940: *†Welfare of the Workers (D). †*London Can Take It (D). 1941: *Heart of Britain (D. Longer US version: This is England). †*Words for Battle (D). 1942: †Listen to Britain (D). 1943: Fires Were Started (Semi-D. US: I Was a Fireman). The Silent Village (Semi-D). 1944: The True Story of Lilli Marlene (Semi-D). *The 80 Days (D). 1945: A Diary for Timothy (D). 1946: A Defeated People (D). 1947: Cumberland Story (D). 1949: Dim Little Island (D). 1950: Family Portrait (D).

JEWISON, Norman 1926-
Canadian director who has made some effective big-screen dramas, but has proved at his happiest in comedy. After 1968, Jewison lavished great attention on the visual content of his films, but all too often to the detriment of entertainment value. A pity, as he had begun so well. Entrenched in Canadian and American television for many years, often directing variety and comedy specials, Jewison was 36 before he ventured into film-making. At first, he seemed a real find. 40 Pounds of Trouble was an often delightful latter-day Hollywood excursion into comedy

involving an established star (in this case Tony Curtis) with a scene-stealing child actor. It was followed by two Doris Day comedies which are full of quirky fun and unexpected belly-laughs. The appearances of Dick Van Dyke and Edward G. Robinson respectively helped Jewison to make something of The Art of Love and The Cincinnati Kid, before he made his best film, The Russians Are Coming, the Russians Are Coming. A really funny kaleidoscope of misadventure, it has countless little cameo scenes and marvellous visual touches that keep the laughter flowing throughout. The self-conscious artiness of The Thomas Crown Affair, with its multiple screens, flashy camerawork and pretentious dialogue marked a regrettable downswing after the tight cinematic tension of In the Heat of the Night, Jewison's previous film, which had given Rod Steiger an Oscar (as well as winning one for best film) and Sidney Poitier a meal-ticket in the shape of the detective Virgil Tibbs. Jewison's screens remain cluttered and imprecise, and several of his films have been major disappointments — Fiddler on the Roof, Jesus Christ Superstar and Rollerball among them. Nor should he be lulled into a false sense of security by some high critical praise for the hysterical ...And Justice for All. Jewison regained some lost ground with the unabashedly romantic Moonstruck, which won him an Academy Award nomination, and the poignant, underrated In Country. His fluffy romantic fantasy Only You also has its supporters.

1962: 40 Pounds of Trouble. 1963: The Thrill of It All. 1964: Send Me No Flowers. 1965: The Art of Love. The Cincinnati Kid. 1966: The Russians Are Coming, the Russians Are Coming. 1967: In the Heat of the Night. 1968: The Thomas Crown Affair. 1969: Gaily Gaily (GB: Chicago, Chicago). 1971: Fiddler on the Roof. 1973: Jesus Christ Superstar. 1975: Rollerball. 1978: F.I.S.T. 1979: ... And Justice for All. 1982: Best Friends. 1984: A Soldier's Story. 1985: Agnes of God. 1987: Moonstruck. 1989: In Country. 1991: Other People's Money. 1994: Only You. 1995: †Picture Windows (cable TV). 1996: Bogus. 1999 Lazarus and the Hurricane

JOFFÉ, Roland 1945-
British director, mainly of epic subjects. Joffé's meagre output for the cinema makes it all the more surprising that to date he has turned out three pretty wonderful movies and two near-disasters. But Joffé's strong visual sense and evident excitement in the film medium can sometimes be undercut by inadequacies in the

script. Since being nominated for Academy Awards on his first two major cinema films, Joffé has not quite held his place at the top level. After a long career directing first for the theatre then television, Joffé made his film debut in a big way with The Killing Fields. Winner of three Academy Awards, the uncomfortably penetrating film dealt with the true story of the friendship between an American war correspondent in Cambodia and his local confederate. Also an account of the survival of the human spirit against all odds, the film is full of striking, graphic, unforgettable moments, dictating a strong emotional response from the viewer. The same was true of the even more ambitious The Mission, a Palme d'Or winner at Cannes. A story of Spanish and Portuguese oppression in 18th-century South America, this is a breathtaking spectacle packed with action and thought-provoking dialogue, with a heartbreaking ending to match that in The Killing Fields. It was a graphic monument to the madnesses and atrocities committed in the pursuit of progress, a theme continued to some extent in Joffé's next, Fat Man and Little Boy, the title referring to the two atomic bombs dropped by America on Japan at the end of World War II. A dully-written film (unfortunately co-written by Joffé himself) in which almost nothing happens, it was a sore disappointment. Joffé had the good sense to use Oscar-nominated writer Mark Medoff for the next, City of Joy, and the result was an emotional bullseye with a story of poor and oppressed peasant workers in Calcutta. Though necessarily simplistic, the film did bring home much of the poverty of the city. It was not, however, a major box-office success, and Joffé's next, The Scarlet Letter, proved a bodice-ripping travesty of Nathaniel Hawthorne's classic novel.

1978: The Spongers (TV. US: cinemas). 1984: The Killing Fields. 1986: The Mission. 1989: Fat Man and Little Boy (GB: Shadow Makers). 1992: City of Joy. 1995: The Scarlet Letter. 1998: Goodbye Lover.

JOHNSON, Lamont 1920-
Another American director who seems to have left his best films behind him. Still, there are enough treasures along the way for Johnson's decision to switch from acting to directing to be applauded. He was one of the young 'beefcake' stars under contract to Universal-International in the 1950s, but didn't exactly make the Tony Curtis grade, and began directing episodes of TV series in the early 1960s. The Kirk

Douglas-Johnny Cash western *A Gunfight* brought him some attention, if only for the novelty of its idea of two gunfighters shooting it out before a paying audience, but a return to television was to provide a major boost to his career. In 1972, he combined for the first time with rising actor Martin Sheen (whose career was also bolstered by TV movies) on *That Certain Summer*, the first TV film to deal exclusively, and tastefully with homosexuality. Hal Holbrook gives a painfully poignant portrayal of a married homosexual whose 14-year-old son discovers his secret. Johnson then went on to make three excellent and widely differing cinema movies: *The Groundstar Conspiracy*, a tension-charged science-fiction thriller; *You'll Like My Mother*, a skilful, dark horror-comic; and *The Last American Hero*, one of the cleanest, best-moving films to come from America in some time, with Jeff Bridges as a champion stock-car racer from the sticks. Better than all of these was the next Johnson-Sheen TV movie, made in 1974. This time Sheen had top billing in *The Execution of Private Slovik*, which more than ever demonstrated the director's flair for making 'difficult' subjects watchable, touching and entertaining. Tightly edited and lovingly made, the film is heartrending to watch. The next TV movie, *Fear on Trial*, an account of one man's McCarthy blacklisting, was also interesting, if a little shapeless, but Johnson overreached himself with *Lipstick*, a lurid story of rape and its effects. Quite simply, he has not made a good film since. *Somebody Killed Her Husband* was an off-centre comedy-thriller that didn't *quite* work, while *Cattle Annie and Little Britches* was the first of his films actually to make you want to tear up your membership card of the Lamont Johnson Cheer-Leaders Club. He has continued to work on into his seventies, mainly in the field of concerned TV movies, most notably *Unnatural Causes*, about the plight of Vietnam veterans, and *The Broken Chain*, a period action story focussing on the role taken by native Americans during the American Revolution.

1966: A Covenant With Death. 1967: Kona Coast (originally for TV). 1969: Deadlock (TV). 1970: My Sweet Charlie (TV). The Mackenzie Break. 1971: A Gunfight. 1972: That Certain Summer (TV). The Groundstar Conspiracy. You'll Like My Mother. 1973: The Last American Hero. 1974: Visit to a Chief's Son. The Execution of Private Slovik (TV). 1975: Fear on Trial (TV). 1976: Lipstick. 1977: One by One. 1978: Somebody Killed Her Husband. 1980: Cattle Annie and Little Britches. Crisis at Central High (TV). 1981: Off the Minnesota Strip. Escape from Iran

(TV). 1982: Dangerous Company (TV). Beatrice (TV). 1983: Spacehunter: Adventures in the Forbidden Zone. 1984: Ernie Kovacs: Between the Laughter (TV). 1986: Unnatural Causes: The Agent Orange Story (TV). 1988: Gore Vidal's Lincoln (TV). 1990: Escape. 1992: Crash Landing: The Rescue of Flight 232/A Thousand Heroes (TV). 1993: The Broken Chain (TV). 1995: The Man Next Door (TV).

JOHNSON, Nunnally 1897-1977

What made Johnson suddenly decide to direct after so many years of service as a writer and producer at Twentieth Century-Fox? Whatever it was, it brought a varied handful of films in the 1950s that provide an interesting footnote to Johnson's distinguished career. He was for many years a reporter and short-story writer (notably for *The Saturday Evening Post*). Indeed, if his literate screenplays, which rarely fell below a certain high standard and never descended to the banal, have a fault, it lies in their oversimplification of their source works, often best-selling novels. His first solo screenplay credit came in 1934 on *The House of Rothschild*, and among those that followed were *Kid Millions, The Prisoner of Shark Island, Banjo on My Knee, Jesse James, The Grapes of Wrath, Tobacco Road, Roxie Hart, Life Begins at 8:30, The Moon is Down, Holy Matrimony, The Woman in the Window, The Keys of the Kingdom, The Dark Mirror, The Mudlark, The Desert Fox, My Cousin Rachel* and *How to Marry a Millionaire*, a record that shows a willingness to tackle a great variety of genres, invariably with success. He continued to write the screenplays of most of the films he directed himself. Of these, the movies with Gregory Peck are worthy but dull, rather like the actor himself, and the most interesting are a vivid, feisty whodunnit *Black Widow*; the schizophrenia drama *The Three Faces of Eve*, which won Joanne Woodward an Academy Award; and *Oh Men! Oh Women!*, a madcap comedy which is best when it gives Tony Randall his head. During the war years, Johnson briefly left Fox to start up International Pictures, but the venture was not a success and he returned to the fold after the new company was merged with Universal. After giving up direction, he wrote a few more screenplays, most notably *The Dirty Dozen*. He was married to former leading lady Dorris Bowdon, whom he met when she was starring in *The Grapes of Wrath*.

1954: Night People. Black Widow. 1955: How to Be Very, Very Popular. 1956: The

Man in the Gray Flannel Suit. 1957: The Three Faces of Eve. Oh Men! Oh Women! 1959: The Man Who Understood Women. 1960: The Angel Wore Red.

JONES, Harmon 1911-1972

This Canadian director was only 60 when he died, but the cinema had long since lost him to television. A pity, for most of the films he made between 1951 and 1956 were of above-average interest, considering the limited resources with which he was apparently working. A stage director in Canada before World War II, he joined Twentieth Century-Fox in 1946 as a film editor, working on a good crop of films that included *Anna and the King of Siam, Gentlemen's Agreement, Boomerang, Sitting Pretty* and *Pinky*. He directed his first film in 1951, a delightful 'A' grade comedy called *As Young As You Feel*, which featured a complete cast of scene-stealers, including Monty Woolley, Constance Bennett, Thelma Ritter, David Wayne and Marilyn Monroe. *The Pride of St Louis* was the entertaining real-life story of a baseball hero and *Bloodhounds of Broadway* Jones' best film, a wholly enjoyable gangster musical from a Damon Runyon story, sparklingly played, danced and sung by Mitzi Gaynor, brilliantly Technicolored (photography: Edward Cronjager) and with a whole gallery of delightful Runyon types. It didn't lead to bigger things at Fox for Jones, although *City of Bad Men* was an unusual western spun around the Corbett-Fitzsimmons heavyweight boxing championship and *Gorilla at Large* an amazingly star-studded horror film (originally in 3-D), which had Cameron Mitchell, Lee J. Cobb, Anne Bancroft, Raymond Burr, Lee Marvin and some dry dialogue nicely handled by Jones and his cast: only the gorilla was unconvincing. Jones' films were almost always bright and lively and this is especially true of *A Day of Fury*, a superior western made for Universal-International and a major if belated boost to Jock Mahoney's career as the villain. There wasn't much else, although *Wolf Larsen* is an adequate remake of *The Sea Wolf*; one just wishes Jones had been handed more assignments like *As Young As You Feel* and *Bloodhounds of Broadway*.

1951: As Young As You Feel. 1952: The Pride of St Louis. Bloodhounds of Broadway. 1953: The Silver Whip. City of Bad Men. The Kid from Left Field. 1954: Gorilla at Large. Princess of the Nile. 1955: Target Zero. 1956: A Day of Fury. Canyon River. 1958: Bullwhip! The Beast of Budapest. Wolf Larsen. 1966: Don't Worry, We'll Think of a Title.

Irish director Neil **Jordan** on the set of his ghost comedy *High Spirits*. The supporting cast seems to have seen better days.

JORDAN, Neil 1950-

Irish director who has made a variety of international movies in between return visits to his native country to direct films that often have a fantasy slant and are constantly of a controversial and confrontational nature. A musician in his younger days, Jordan played guitar and saxophone in a band that travelled all over Ireland, although less to the north after members of one band were shot and killed there by Protestant extremists. Turning to writing short stories, then nov-

els, Jordan became involved with the film industry in his early thirties after working as script consultant on John Boorman's *Excalibur*. Jordan made a documentary about his experiences and decided he would like to write and direct for the medium. His first, *Angel*, the first of six Jordan films to star the lugubrious Irish actor Stephen Rea, was a contemporary black thriller that reflected Jordan's own musical past, in that its hero (Rea) was a saxophonist who becomes involved in avenging the murders of two friends. A

formidable debut, it was like a slice of Raymond Chandler within a particularly desperate and abrasive Irish context. Rea was also in *The Company of Wolves*, a bold fantasy horror tale that crosses werewolf films with *Red Riding Hood*. Jordan was uncommonly successful here in creating a fairy-tale horror environment. Jordan's visual style was again almost a character by itself in *Mona Lisa*, a crime yarn in which the director turns London's underbelly into a garish and nightmarish hell on earth. Jordan was unable to repeat the impact of these films in subsequent years, until the unexpected success of *The Crying Game*, an IRA drama with an ingenious sex twist to its central story. Rea was again involved in this, as he has been in all Jordan's most recent films. *Interview with the Vampire* was a largely disappointing version of Anne Rice's novel, albeit with some striking moments, and the director has since returned to his roots, with *Michael Collins*, (which was about the IRA again) and *The Butcher Boy*, which wasn't. The latter again combines Jordan's worlds of fantasy and reality in a striking and fast-moving account of a tearaway Irish boy's descent from mischief into mayhem and murder.

1982: Angel (US: Danny Boy). 1984: The Company of Wolves. 1986: Mona Lisa. 1988: High Spirits. 1989: We're No Angels. 1991: The Miracle. 1992: The Crying Game. 1994: Interview with the Vampire. 1996: Michael Collins. 1997: The Butcher Boy. 1998: In Dreams/Blue Vision.

JULIAN, Rupert 1879-1943

One of those directors who fascinates because of his very elusiveness, Julian had a hand — albeit in somewhat chequered fashion in each case — in two of Hollywood's great silent films before vanishing from view. He was born and raised on a New Zealand farm, the son of a sheep rancher. When he was 18, his parents sent him to college to train for the Catholic priesthood. But, with the outbreak of the Boer War in South Africa two years later, Julian ran away from the college and enlisted with the New Zealand forces serving in the South African war. Captured and imprisoned by the Boers, Julian escaped and somehow evaded recapture, journeying through hostile country to reach the coast, boarding a tramp steamer and eventually rejoining his troops. He later received a battlefield commission as a lieutenant. Julian served some years with the army, but later resigned his commission, and decided to become a stage actor. He arrived in America in 1913. A hefty leading man with strong, fair-haired, blue-eyed features, and a dominant personality, Julian soon found himself in demand for parts in Hollywood silents, notably an early (1914) version of *The Merchant of Venice*. In 1916, he played Scrooge in *Marley's Ghost* and the lead in *The Bugler of Algiers*, one of his most popular films. But the role in which he came to be remembered was *The Kaiser, the Beast of Berlin* (1918), a portrayal he would be called on to repeat in other films. Julian also directed this film, having started as a director in 1915. He worked steadily in this capacity at Universal, revealing some talent for the sinister in his work on *Hungry Eyes*, *Midnight Madness* and *Creaking Stairs*. When Erich Von Stroheim's budget exceeded all bounds on *Merry-Go-Round*, and the Austrian was fired by studio boss Irving Thalberg, Julian was called into pick up the pieces. That film starred Norman Kerry and the appealing Mary Philbin, and both were together again, in support of Lon Chaney, when Julian was asked to direct *The Phantom of the Opera*. By all accounts, Julian had now become eccentric and temperamental, quarrelling with everyone. In any case, Chaney and he did not see eye to eye on how the film should be made, and this time it was Julian who was fired, although he had shot all but the final chase. Much of his direction is moody, atmospheric and fraught with edginess, making his rage at only getting co-director's credit on the final print the more understandable. This touch of unease is evident in some of his later 1920s' work, notably *Three Faces East*, *The Leopard Lady* and *The Cat Creeps*. But he seems not to have welcomed sound and, after 1930, the next mention of him anywhere comes 13 years later. He had a stroke on Christmas Day 1943, and died two days afterwards.

1915: **The Water Clue*. **The Underword*. *Jewel*. 1916: **John Pellet's Dream*. **Little Boy Blue*. **The Marriage of Arthur*. *The Right To Be Happy* (GB: A Christmas Carol). *The Turn of the Wheel*. *The Evil Women Do*. *We French*. *Naked Hearts*. *Bettina Loved a Soldier*. *The Bugler of Algiers*. *The Blackmailer*. 1917: *The Mysterious Mr Tiller*. *A Kentucky Cinderella*. *Mother o' Mine*. *The Gift Girl*. *The Circus of Life*. *The Desire of the Moth*. *The Door Between*. *The Savage*. 1918: *Hungry Eyes*. *The Kaiser, the Beast of Berlin*. *Hands Down*. *Midnight Madness*. 1919: *The Sleeping Lion*. *Creaking Stairs*. *The Fire Flingers*. *Millionaire Pirate*. 1920: *The Honey Bee*.

1922: *The Girl Who Ran Wild*. 1923: *†Merry-Go-Round*. 1924: *Love and Glory*. *Hell's High Road*. 1925: *†The Phantom of the Opera*. 1926: *Three Faces East*. *Silence*. 1927: *The Yankee Clipper*. *The Country Doctor*. 1928: *The Leopard Lady*. *Walking Back*. 1930: *Love Comes Along*. *The Cat Creeps*.

JURAN, Nathan 1907-

Born in Austria, but in America since childhood, Juran was an architect who turned art director on films in the mid-1930s, winning an Academy Award for his work on *How Green Was My Valley* in 1941. Universal-International gave Juran a chance to achieve his ambition to become a director by offering him several of their middle-budget action co-features of the early 1950s. The best of these is *Tumbleweed*, an offbeat western with Audie Murphy, Chill Wills and a personable white horse. But Juran's most striking work as a director stems from his partnership with Ray Harryhausen, the Dynamation man, a specialist in the art of stop-frame animation where models are moved a fraction at a time to give the impression of life and movement. The director on such films is more important than he might at first seem, since he must spend sometimes long hours getting his actors to do exactly the right thing to combine them with the 'Dynamation' effects. Thus Juran and effects men must at least share the credit for the success of *The Seventh Voyage of Sinbad*, *Jack the Giant Killer* and *First Men in the Moon*. On his own, Juran made the fresh and dashing *Siege of the Saxons*, some less satisfactory action films and finally a horror curiosity, *The Boy Who Cried Werewolf*, which reunited him with Kerwin Mathews, who starred in several of the early Dynamation films. Juran provided brisk, uncomplicated entertainment for more than 20 years.

1952: *The Black Castle*. *Gunsmoke!* 1953: *Law and Order*. *The Golden Blade*. *Tumbleweed*. 1954: *Highway Dragnet*. *Drums Along the River*. 1955: *The Crooked Web*. 1956. *The Deadly Mantis*. 1957: *Hellcats of the Navy*. *Twenty Million Miles to Earth*. *†Le imprese di una spada leggendaria*. *‡The Brain from Planet Arous*. 1958: *‡Attack of the 50ft Woman*. *The Seventh Voyage of Sinbad*. 1959: *Good Day for a Hanging*. 1960: *Flight of the Lost Balloon*. 1961: *Jack the Giant Killer*. 1963: *Siege of the Saxons*. 1964: *East of Sudan*. *First Men in the Moon*. 1969: *Land Raiders*. 1973: *The Boy Who Cried Werewolf*.

‡ As Nathan Hertz

KADÁR, Ján (János Kadár) 1918-1979

Czech director who made two outstanding films before being forced out of his native country by the Russian invasion of 1968. There were a few films in America before his early death, but he was never the same force. A previous invasion — by the Germans at the outset of World War II — had interrupted Kadár's studies at the Bratislava Film School. He was interned in a prison camp for most of the war and, when it was over, started his film career by making a moody documentary about starting life afresh in Czechoslovakia. He was a writer and co-writer of screenplays for the Barrandov company in Prague until 1950, when he started directing features. From 1952 until 1968, he worked in collaboration with Elmar Klos (1910-), making feature films and documentaries notable for their emotional appeal; not surprisingly, Kadár and Klos soon found themselves fighting a running battle with the authorities. Things ran a little more smoothly when some of their films began picking up awards at festivals, and in 1965, their 1964 film *Obchod na Korze* won the Academy Award as best foreign film of the year. This heartrending film is one of the most effective statements ever made about racism, bigotry and the decent forces that fight them. Tightly set in a small Jewish community in Nazi-occupied Czechoslovakia, it tells of a Slovak carpenter who protects an elderly Jewess by running her button shop, but pays a heavy price. Veteran Russian actress Ida Kaminska was actually nominated for a best actress Oscar (extraordinary for an actress in a Czech film) for her richly detailed account of the shopkeeper, although Josef Kroner is as deeply moving as her frightened but determined benefactor. Kadár and Klos brought the full bitter impact of the story across, which has a great deal of charm before tragedy begins to dominate, in fine style. After considerable difficulties, Kadár finally finished his next film (with Klos as associate director), *Adrift*, a very different but no less haunting film. Its almost macabre story is set on an island in what might be the bayou of America, but is in fact part of Czechoslovakia. A fisherman and his family rescue a naked woman from the water and revive her. As he begins to desire her, the fisherman comes to question his whole way of life. It's not the subject, though, but Kadár's treatment which lifts the film into greatness. One striking colour image piles incredibly on another: the three strange inquisitors, who wander in and out of the film; a mist-enshrouded church regatta; the swirling river, viscous, entrancing; a floating funeral; and, perhaps most memorable of all, a lantern swinging in the prow of a boat as, behind it, the fisherman struggles to kill a handsome, but half-blind stranger he suspects has made love to the girl. Again the performances are faultless, especially Milena Dravic, self-effacing as the fisherman's pretty wife. Two rare films, not to be repeated.

1946: *Life is Rising from the Ruins* (D). 1950: *Katka/Katya.* 1952: †*Unos/Kidnapped/The Kidnap.* 1953: †*Music from Mars.* 1955: †*Young Days.* 1956: †*The House at the Terminus.* 1957: †*Three Wishes.* 1959: †*Magic Lantern II.* 1960: †*Mládí/Time of Youth* (D). †*Spartakiade* (D). 1962: †*Death is Called Engelchen.* 1963: †*Obžalovaný* (GB: *The Accused.* US: *The Defendant*). 1964: †*Obchod na Korze* (GB: *A Shop on the High Street.* US: *The Shop on Main Street*). 1969: *Hrst Plná Vody/Zmitaná/Adrift.* 1970: *The Angel Levine.* 1975: *Lies My Father Told Me.* 1978: *The Other Side of Hell* (TV). 1979: *Freedom Road* (TV. GB: *cinemas*).

KANE, Joseph/Joe 1894-1975

It's unlikely that you'll find Kane in any esoteric books on major film-makers. Yet he directed 115 films in a career that, including his apprenticeship, spanned over 50 years. All but four movies were for that home of action pictures, Republic. Kane once said 'I love making westerns. I like the scenery and the outdoors. The sense of excitement. The horses and the cowboys.' To prove the truth of it, he made over 100 of them, working his way up from singing cowboys in 60-minute shenanigans to become the studio's top house director, making their 'De Luxe' grade pictures at half a million dollars a throw which, for Republic, was a big budget. The action that galloped across the screen under Kane's direction, backed by Hollywood's finest team of stuntmen, thrilled millions through three decades. In his early days, Kane had thoughts of becoming a cellist. But by 1920, he was a title card writer. In the early 1920s, he occasionally gained experience as an assistant director and moved into editing by 1926. His move from Paramount to Republic in 1935 was a happy chance as

far as his ambitions to direct were concerned, for his new studio were looking for someone to direct their new series of Gene Autry westerns. Kane carried on making these 'oaters', with Autry, Roy Rogers, Ken Maynard and other cowboy stars, by the fistful, until studio chief Herbert J. Yates gave him a Christmas present at the end of 1944: promotion to directing the studio's 'A' grade westerns with John Wayne (whom he had previously directed in some minor horse-operas of the 1930s) and Bill Elliott. Many of the vehicles Kane directed from this time to the beginning of the Republic decline some ten years later are solidly entertaining, and better than comparable fare from other studios, but most notable are *Dakota, The Plainsman and The Lady, Wyoming, Hoodlum Empire* (a rare non-western), *San Antone, Timberjack* and *The Road to Denver.* Besides the credits below, Kane was also second-unit director on a number of films, including *Dark Command* (1940), *Tobruk* (1967) and *In Enemy Country* (1968). From 1959 to 1965, he turned out dozens of western episodes for the TV series *Rawhide, Laramie, Cheyenne* and *Bonanza.*

1935: *Tumbling Tumbleweeds. Melody Trail. The Sagebrush Troubadour.* †*Fighting Marines* (serial). 1936: †*Darkest Africa* (GB: *Hidden City.* Serial). †*Undersea Kingdom* (serial). *The Lawless Nineties. King of the Pecos. The Lonely Trail. The Old Corral* (GB: *Texas Serenade*). *Guns and Guitars. Oh, Susanna! Ride, Ranger, Ride.* 1937: *Paradise Express. Git Along, Little Dogies* (GB: *Serenade of the West*). *Ghost Town Gold. Round-Up Time in Texas. Come On, Cowboys! Gunsmoke Ranch. Public Cowboy No. One. Yodelin' Kid from Pine Ridge* (GB: *The Hero of Pine Ridge*). *Boots and Saddles. Springtime in the Rockies.* 1938: *The Old Barn Dance. Born to Be Wild. Arson Gang Busters. Arson Racket Squad* (GB: *Fire Fighters*). *Under Western Skies. Man from Music Mountain. Billy the Kid Returns. Gold Mine in the Sky. Come On, Rangers! Shine On, Harvest Moon.* 1939: *Rough Riders' Round-Up. Frontier Pony Express. Southward Ho! In Old Caliente. Wall Street Cowboy. The Arizona Kid. Days of Jesse James. In Old Monterey. Saga of Death Valley.* 1940: *Young Buffalo Bill. The Carson City Kid. The Ranger and the Lady. Young Bill Hickok. The Border Legion. Colorado.* 1941: *Robin Hood of the Pecos. In Old Cheyenne. Sheriff of Tombstone. The Great Train Robbery. Nevada City. Rags to Riches. Bad Man of Deadwood. Jesse James at Bay. Red River Valley.* 1942: *The Man*

from Cheyenne. South of Santa Fé. Sunset on the Desert. Romance of the Range. Sunset Serenade. Sons of the Pioneers. Heart of the Golden West. Ridin' Down the Canyon. 1943: *King of the Cowboys. Idaho. Song of Texas. Silver Spurs. The Man from Music Mountain* (no connection with 1938 film of same title). *Hands Across the Border.* 1944: *The Cowboy and the Señorita. The Yellow Rose of Texas. Song of Nevada.* 1945: *Flame of the Barbary Coast. Dakota. The Cheaters.* 1946: *In Old Sacramento. The Plainsman and the Lady.* 1947: *Wyoming.* 1948: *Old Los Angeles. The Gallant Legion. The Plunderers.* 1949: *The Last Bandit. Brimstone.* 1950: *Rock Island Trail* (GB: *Transcontinent Express*). *The Savage Horde. California Passage.* 1951: *O, Susanna! Fighting Coast Guard. The Sea Hornet.* 1952: *Hoodlum Empire. Ride the Man Down. Woman of the North Country.* 1953: *San Antone. Fair Wind to Java. Sea of Lost Ships.* 1954: *Jubilee Trail. Hell's Outpost.* 1955: *Timberjack. The Road to Denver. The Vanishing American.* 1956: *The Maverick Queen. Thunder over Arizona. Accused of Murder.* 1957: *Duel at Apache Wells. Spoilers of the Forest. The Last Stagecoach West. The Crooked Circle.* 1958: *Gunfire at Indian Gap. The Notorious Mr Monks. The Lawless Eighties. The Man Who Died Twice.* 1966: *Country Boy.* 1967: *Search for the Evil One. Track of Thunder.* 1971: *Smoke in the Wind* (released 1975).

KANIN, Garson 1912-

One doesn't know whether to applaud this American film-maker's decision to switch from direction to writing after World War II, or to express disappointment, for he was equally entertaining in both capacities. Alas, when he returned as writer-director in the late 1960s after a long absence, it was obvious that he was a spent force in the cinema. In the 1930s, Kanin had been in turn a jazz musician, burlesque comedian and legitimate actor before directing his first play in 1937 and being put under contract to RKO the following year. His first film was a low-budget success, *A Man to Remember*, a remake of another RKO 1930s' film, *One Man's Journey*, about the life of a small-town doctor. After *The Next Time I Marry*, a pocket version *of It Happened One Night*, which had nothing much except Lucille Ball's personality, Kanin really hit his stride in the screwball comedy genre. *The Great Man Votes* is a delight, with moments of drama and pathos amid the laughs and a last great performance from John Barrymore, admittedly as a drunken professor. *Bache-*

lor Mother is a sparkling vehicle for Ginger Rogers (later remade, with sugar, by the studio as *Bundle of Joy*) and it was followed by *My Favorite Wife*, the original version of the wife returning from the 'dead' just as her husband is about to re-marry, here with Irene Dunne, Cary Grant, and many delightful little touches. After the moody eroticism of *They Knew What They Wanted* and another Ginger Rogers romp, *Tom, Dick and Harry*, Kanin became a maker of World War II documentary films, some of them of great emotional impact. When he returned from the war, the screwball comedy was virtually dead and RKO had changed. Kanin opted out of directing and went in for screenwriting with his wife Ruth Gordon. Most notably, there were *The Marrying Kind* and *It Should Happen to You* for Judy Holliday and *Pat and Mike* for Tracy and Hepburn; while all three were together on *Adam's Rib*. These were post-war equivalents of the madbrain comedy, with witty battle-of-the-sexes dialogue supplied by the Kanins. After this, Kanin concentrated largely on the theatre, although he did script the warm and world-weary *The Rat Race* (1960), which has Tony Curtis and Debbie Reynolds near their best. The two films of the late 1960s are so dire that one can only stand and wonder. Best to remember the Kanin films that gave so much pleasure.

*1938: A Man to Remember. The Next Time I Marry. 1939: The Great Man Votes. Bachelor Mother. 1940: My Favorite Wife. They Knew What They Wanted. 1941: Tom, Dick and Harry. *Night Shift. (D). 1942: Fellow Americans (D). Ring of Steel (D). 1943: *Night Stripes (D). †German Manpower (D). 1944: †Salut à la France (D). 1945: †The True Glory (D). 1969: Where It's At. Some Kind of a Nut.*

KAPLAN, Jonathan 1947-

This American director makes films with heart. Whatever their merits, there is some point where a Kaplan film reaches out and grabs your emotions — mostly in support of someone battling against the odds. This ability to get you on the side of his protagonist has resulted in Kaplan making some popular films out of seemingly difficult subjects. But it has been an up-and-down career and predictably his biggest success was followed almost immediately by one of his biggest flops. The son of actress Frances Heflin and composer Sol Kaplan (and nephew of Hollywood star Van Heflin), Kaplan was expelled from university, but subsequently joined the NYU Film School, where he was tutored by,

among others, Martin Scorsese. Beginning work at 24 with Roger Corman's New World studio on soft-core sexploitation films — 'I made a conscious decision to make as many films as I could in as short a time as possible' — Kaplan moved into the mainstream at 30 with the underrated *Mr Billion*, a light-hearted action romp about a garage mechanic who comes into a fortune. The film was a 4-F: fast, furious, fun and a failure. All of the films that followed it were well-directed and well-received, even if they hardly pulled in the public in droves: *Over the Edge*, which gave a screen debut to Matt Dillon, is a tautly made study of alienated youth, *Heart Like a Wheel* has a showcase performance by Bonnie Bedelia as a woman racing-driver, and *Project X* (both these last two went unreleased outside America) is a cunningly contrived story of the rescuing of laboratory chimps. Kaplan, though, bounced back with *The Accused*, a powerful rape drama which won an Oscar for its leading actress, Jodie Foster, and has a typically adrenalin-charging Kaplan ending. Unfortunately, it was followed by the wimpish adoption drama *Immediate Family*, and since then Kaplan has struggled, resuming a familiar pattern of his best work (*Love Field* with Michelle Pfeiffer) not attracting the paying public.

1972: Night Call Nurses. 1973: Student Teachers. The Slams. 1974: Truck Turner. 1975: White Line Fever. 1977: Mr Billion. 1979: Over the Edge. 11th Victim (TV). 1980: The Hustler of Muscle Beach (TV). 1981: The Gentleman Bandit (TV). 1983: Heart Like a Wheel. 1987: Project X. 1988: The Accused. 1989: Immediate Family. 1992: Unlawful Entry. Love Field. 1993: Reform School Girl (cable TV). 1994: Bad Girls. 1995: †Picture Windows (cable TV). 1996: In Cold Blood (TV). 1998: Brokedown Palace.

KARLSON, Phil (Philip Karlstein) 1908-1985

This Chicago-born director had an extra-ordinary career, in that all of the films he made from *The Texas Rangers* (1951) to *The Secret Ways* (1961) are rousingly good entertainment, whether or not they have deeper values. Yet you will look in vain outside this decade of film-making for more than one or two films of quality from Karlson. Many of the films from this splendid period are hard-hitting crime dramas, often based on real-life incidents. They move swiftly and incisively, with strong, gritty performances, tough action scenes and effective use of close-ups to add punch at the appropriate moment. Karlson was studying law at university at the beginning of the 1930s when he took

a part-time job with Universal to supplement his income. Law gradually faded into the background as Karlson trod pretty well every step on the Hollywood ladder, dishwasher, prop-boy, cutter, gagman, editor, associate producer and assistant director among them. In this last capacity, he worked on several of the most successful early Abbott and Costello comedies, and the story goes that it was Lou Costello who bankrolled Karlson for his first film as director, the dismal *A Wave, a WAC and a Marine*, with a young (and unfunny) Henny Youngman. Fortunately, the film was released through poverty-row merchants Monogram — 'I was lucky' Karlson said: 'They didn't realize how bad it was!' — who promptly hired him to make some of their bottom-budget pictures, including some shoestring musicals and Charlie Chan thrillers. Karlson showed his possibilities for the first time on *Black Gold*, which also gave a first major role to Anthony Quinn as an impoverished Indian who eventually strikes oil on his land. Quinn later showed his gratitude by playing the villain in Karlson's two swashbucklers, *Mask of the Avenger* and *The Brigand* by this time, Karlson had moved to Columbia (having briefly worked there in the 1940s). *Lorna Doone* was an unpromising start, but *The Texas Rangers* packs enough action in its 75 minutes to fill a dozen westerns and the dark thrillers begin with *Scandal Sheet*. Several of them — *Kansas City Confidential*, *Hell's Island* and *99 River Street* — teamed Karlson with star John Payne, with whom he enjoyed a beneficial working relationship, the two often working on the scripts as well. The best of this amazingly consistent group of 17 films is probably *Tight Spot*, with Ginger Rogers in fine form as a gangster's moll preparing to turn state's witness and Brian Keith giving the performance of his career as a crooked cop. Terrific stuff, this packs a mighty impact from first to last. Mention should also be made of *They Rode West*, a highly intelligent western, *The Phenix City Story*, a true-life corruption exposé related to the Fox postwar realist films (a 'B' movie which consistently received 'A' feature bookings) and *Key Witness*, a fascinating early foray into the mugging menace. After walking off *The Secret Ways* just before the end of shooting, following a disagreement with star Richard Widmark, Karlson faltered. *Kid Galahad* is one of the better Elvis Presleys, and *The Silencers* an entertaining start to the silly Matt Helm series. But the rest is disappointing. He died from cancer.

1944: A Wave, a WAC and a Marine. There Goes Kelly. 1945: G.I. Honey-

moon. *The Shanghai Cobra. Live Wires. 1946: Swing Parade of 1946. Dark Alibi. The Missing Lady. Behind the Mask. Bowery Bombshell. Wife Wanted (GB: Shadow of Blackmail). 1947: Kilroy Was Here. Black Gold. Louisiana. 1948: Rocky. Adventures in Silverado (GB: Above All Laws). Thunderhoof (GB: Fury). Ladies of the Chorus. 1949: Down Memory Lane. The Big Cat. 1950: The Iroquois Trail (GB: The Tomahawk Trail). 1951: Lorna Doone. The Texas Rangers. Mask of the Avenger. Scandal Sheet (GB: The Dark Page). 1952: The Brigand. Kansas City Confidential (GB: The Secret Four). 1953: 99 River Street. 1954: They Rode West. 1955: Hell's Island. Tight Spot. Five Against the House. The Phenix City Story. 1957: The Brothers Rico. 1958: Gunman's Walk. 1959: The Scarface Mob (TV. GB: cinemas). 1960: Key Witness. Hell to Eternity. 1961: The Secret Ways. The Young Doctors. 1962: Kid Galahad. Rampage! 1966: The Silencers. 1967: †A Time for Killing (GB: The Long Ride Home). 1968: The Wrecking Crew. 1970: Hornets' Nest. 1972: Ben. 1973: Walking Tall. 1975: Framed.*

KASDAN, Lawrence 1949-

After a storming start, this American writer-director's career has drifted disappointingly downhill. His examinations of relationships, at first so effective, have latterly tended to the dull and unbelievable. For a while, though, Kasdan's rise was meteoric. He began his career writing copy for commercials, but was determined to break into the screenwriting business. The sixth screenplay he submitted, *The Bodyguard*, was the first to be purchased, and he also sold *Continental Divide* (although ultimately directing neither of these), before coming to the attention of Steven Spielberg, who asked him to write the script for *Raiders of the Lost Ark*. Lucas also got Kasdan to co-script with him on the last two Star Wars films, *The Empire Strikes Back* and *Return of the Jedi.* Armed with these credentials, Kasdan had little difficulty setting up his first film as writer-director, *Body Heat*. In a real *film noir* for the 1980s, Kasdan fires the ashes of *Double Indemnity* and fashions a new wife-and-lover-plot-to-kill-husband story that has only that basic situation in common with its carnal forefather. The twists and triple twists that follow the actual murder are ingenious in the extreme. And Kasdan's dialogue for lethal lovers William Hurt and Kathleen Turner is terse, loaded and beautifully delivered under his direction. *The Big Chill* also featured Hurt, and marked the beginning of an association with Kevin Costner, ironic in view of the fact that the actor's role ended on the cutting-room floor. Although the film was a cult success, and contains many nice touches, human moments and fragments of natural comic dialogue, it did in small ways mark the beginning of a slow decline in the standard of Kasdan's work. *Silverado* was entertaining, made it up to Costner with a leading role, and is credited by some with renewing interest in the western. *The Accidental Tourist*, though, another vehicle for Hurt, was less entertaining — downright tedious in parts — despite winning an Oscar for Geena Davis. Since then, Kasdan has made little of note, and his last two movies, *Wyatt Earp* and *French Kiss,* have performed poorly with critics and public alike, the former proving a big money-loser which miscalculated its audience to an alarming degree. It was perhaps unfortunate that Kasdan did not direct *The Bodyguard*, although its massive success at box-offices worldwide will at least have done his reputation as a writer no harm.

1981: *Body Heat.* 1983: *The Big Chill.* 1985: *Silverado.* 1988: *The Accidental Tourist.* 1990: *I Love You to Death.* 1991: *Grand Canyon.* 1994: *Wyatt Earp.* 1995: *French Kiss/Paris Match.* 1999: *Mumford.*

KAUFMAN, Philip 1936-

Much has been written about this American director who tends to make films about outsiders bucking the system — rebels, pioneers, outlaws and refugees — although his output, if more sporadic than most, is as much up and down in quality as most Hollywood directors of his time. He does make very long films, though strangely the two longest of all have been the best. His early career was a struggle. His first two films, both satires of no great quality, were much delayed

The man's side of the story. Director Lawrence **Kasdan** (front with beard) with the male half of the cast in his film *The Big Chill*: Tom Berenger, Jeff Goldblum, Kevin Kline and William Hurt.

Philip **Kaufman** pictured on the set of one of his most successful films, *The Right Stuff*.

(and cut) in release. Also rejigged (by its star and producers) was *The Great Northfield Minnesota Raid*, a Western about the James and Younger gang. Then, after the brilliantly photographed but meandering adventure yarn *The White Dawn*, came more trouble. After two weeks' shooting, Kaufman left direction of his co-scripted epic western *The Outlaw Josey Wales* to its star, Clint Eastwood, citing 'stylistic differences... I just didn't want to operate in a situation where there are really two directors.' Then he was set to direct the first movie version of *Star Trek*. The project was cancelled (only to be resurrected later without Kaufman).There were happier times ahead: *Invasion of the Body Snatchers*, a decent remake of classic sci-fi, *The Wanderers*, a cult study of alienated youth, *The Right Stuff* and *The Unbearable Lightness of Being* all had merit and distinctive feels of their own. Although *The Right Stuff* is overlong at more than three hours, there are some great moments in its story of early astronauts and aviation pioneers. Creditable performances from a long star cast bolster a film of enough inspired sequences to make it linger in the memory. Even more haunting in a different way was *The Unbearable Lightness of Being*, which brought Daniel Day-Lewis into the public eye as young brain surgeon in late 1960s Czechoslovakia, who has a way with women, but finds himself also caught up in political turmoil that

results in him becoming a refugee from authority. Technically Kaufman's best film, it catches the smell of history in the making and its extraordinarily bold sexual sequences did its box-office prospects no harm. Sex was also a key theme of the much less successful *Henry & June*, a period piece of erotica based on the Anaïs Nin diaries and, in its way, a central element of perhaps Kaufman's most blatantly commercial film *Rising Sun*, a fiendishly inventive thriller about what videotape evidence may or may not tell detectives on a murder case against a backdrop of Japanese-American business competition in LA. Once again the outsider figure familiar in Kaufman's work is here, in the presence of Sean Connery, as the loner cop with the know-how to penetrate the Japanese community.

1963: Goldstein (released 1965). 1964: Fearless Frank (released 1969). 1972: The Great Northfield Minnesota Raid. 1974: The White Dawn. 1978: Invasion of the Body Snatchers. 1979: The Wanderers. 1983: The Right Stuff. 1987: The Unbearable Lightness of Being. 1990: Henry & June. 1993: Rising Sun.

KAURISMAKI, Aki 1957-

Finnish festival favourite of forthright opinions. Kaurismaki has said that his favourite line in films is 'Isn't life a disappointment?' His films, though, even if they're not always as good as the director thinks, don't often reflect that outlook. The director's ironic sense of humour lends his best work a wacky, off-the-wall quality. Forming a production company in 1981 with his brother Mika (who has also directed several films), he quickly made a name for himself with witty, irreverent, almost comic-strip-style adventures, comedies and melodramas, plus one or two revisionist versions of famous dramas *(Crime and Punishment, Hamlet Goes Business)*, which paid a little, if not much more attention to the story. His *Leningrad Cowboys Go America*, about a Finnish polka band touring the United States, proved popular with film societies, arthouse cinemas and late-night minority channels on TV. Kaurismaki reached for a wider audience with the international co-production *I Hired a Contract Killer*, which sets up an amusing Orwellian lifestyle for the hero, welded to the familiar plot of the man who hires someone to kill him then changes his mind. Unfortunately, Kaurismaki seems unable to take his twin themes forward in any rewarding direction, perhaps unsurprising in view of his lack of love for narrative drive in itself. His best film to date is probably the

lower-profile *Ariel*, about a miner who loses his job and embarks on a sometimes disastrous, but finally life-affirming trek across the country. Finland, in Kaurismaki's cameras, is cold, melancholy but beautiful. Other countries seem alien and hostile by comparison.

1981: +The Salmaa Gesture. 1983: Crime and Punishment. 1985: Calamari Union. 1986: Shadows in Paradise. *Rocky VI. 1987: Hamlet Goes Business. *Thru the Wire. *Rich Little Bitch. 1988: Ariel. 1989: Dirty Hands (TV). Leningrad Cowboys Go America. The Match Factory Girl. 1990: I Hired a Contract Killer. 1991: *Those Were the Days. 1992: La vie de l'homme. *These Boots. 1993: Take Care of Your Scarf, Tatjana. Total Balalaika Show. 1994: Leningrad Cowboys Meet Moses. 1995: +A propos de Nice. 1996: Kauas pilvet karkaavat/Drifting Clouds.

KAZAN, Elia (E. Kazanjoglou) 1909-

Turkish-born of Greek parentage, this Hollywood director made excellent and sometimes controversial films for 17 years before his career unaccountably fell apart. It's hardly likely that he will now make any more films. Yet from 1945 to 1961, Kazan was one of the giants of the American cinema, surviving even the odour that clung after he 'named names' to the House Un-American Activities Committee in the early 1950s. After being brought to America at the age of four, Kazan studied drama at university and acted on and off through the 1930s, working also as stage manager and, from 1935, director. Apart from a couple of documentary films, Kazan continued to build his reputation as a Broadway director until 1944, when Twentieth Century-Fox lured him to Hollywood to make the screen version of A *Tree Grows in Brooklyn*. The film, premiered in February 1945, won veteran actor James Dunn an Oscar and Kazan a place with Fox for the next nine years. His early 'problem' pictures for them have lost some of the impact they had then, although at the time *Gentleman's Agreement*, about racial prejudice, won him an Academy Award for direction and also an Oscar as best picture. *Pinky* was rather flawed by its too-timid approach and the central casting of Jeanne Crain, which made one feel uncomfortable, but those films conceived in an action vein — *Boomerang, Panic in the Streets, Viva Zapata!* and *On the Waterfront*, which won Kazan his second Oscar — still retain much of their original power. And *East of Eden* and *Baby Doll* were both smouldering dramas that did well with critics and public. Kazan's next two films, *A Face in*

Woe is me. It all went wrong for Elia **Kazan** in the later stages of his career. Here he looks as though he wishes he were somewhere else, instead of making his third-last film *The Arrangement*.

the Crowd* and *Wild River*, did less well at the box-office, although the latter, a time-taking, bleakly picturesque and oddly affecting drama, concerning the Tennessee Valley Authority's plans to flood the countryside and build dams at the end of the Depression, is considered by some to be his best film. After *Splendor in the Grass*, a heartrending, beautifully shot story of young lovers in Kansas just *before* the Depression, with an exquisite performance from Natalie Wood, the question was: where might Kazan go next? The answer, sadly, was downwards. Kazan met his Waterloo in the form of *America, America*, an enormously long film based on the memories of his own childhood and youth as an immigrant to the States. Some outstanding moments were quite lost in the film's general undisciplined mass. After that Kazan made three increasingly distressing failures; he was a man of his time, rooted in the best of Hollywood's post-war years. Married (second of three) actress/director Barbara Loden.

1934: †*Pie in the Sky. 1937: *People of the Cumberland (D). 1941: It's Up to You (D). 1945: A Tree Grows in Brooklyn.

1946: The Sea of Grass. 1947: Boomerang. Gentleman's Agreement. 1949: Pinky. 1950: Panic in the Streets. 1951: A Streetcar Named Desire. 1952: Viva Zapata! 1953: Man on a Tightrope. 1954: On the Waterfront. 1955: East of Eden. 1956: Baby Doll. 1957: A Face in the Crowd. 1960: Wild River. 1961: Splendor in the Grass. 1963: America, America (GB: The Anatolian Smile. 1969: The Arrangement. 1972: The Visitors. 1976: The Last Tycoon.

KEIGHLEY, William 1889-1984

Pennsylvania-born Keighley was a charming and likeable man who occasionally made very enjoyable films. But he was never more than one of Warner Brothers' middle-bracket directors through the 1930s and 1940s. His best films are the thrillers and gangster movies; in other genres he was polished but often ineffectual, being taken off the filming of Errol Flynn's *The Adventures of Robin Hood* (after completing half) for not putting enough steel into it. He was an actor before establishing a solid reputation as a Broadway director in the 1920s. With the coming of sound, he gravitated to Hollywood, being given a few assignments as assistant director — ironically once to Michael Curtiz, the man who was years later to replace him on *Robin Hood*. After co-directing two films with Howard Bretherton (1896-1969), who was to spend almost his entire career making low-budget westerns, Keighley was allowed to strike out on his own. But it was 1935 before he scored his first big success — with *G-Men*, the gangster film that set James Cagney on the right side of the law. Keighley followed this by putting another mobster figure on the straight and narrow — Edward G. Robinson as an undercover cop in *Bullets or Ballots*, a film full of shadows and unseen menace, with the staggering, snarling stairway shoot-out between Robinson and Humphrey Bogart. After the *Robin Hood* fiasco, Keighley had a mild, if admittedly built-in success with the film version of the stage hit *Brother Rat*, a comedy about hijinks at a military academy. He was notably back on form, though, with *Each Dawn I Die*, the famous prison film in which Cagney, as a crusading reporter, is framed by the mob and sent to a jail where the kingpin convict is George Raft. This is an uncompromisingly black and bitter film that anticipates Cagney's later incarceration in *White Heat*. There were a couple more Cagneys in lighter vein, and then Keighley's best film outside the crime milieu — *The Man Who Came to Dinner*. The play's full biting wit came across on

film, and made a character career for beady-eyed Mary Wickes after her delightful portrayal of bewheelchaired Monty Woolley's nurse. Keighley's best 1940s' film was made away from Warners, at Fox. The film, *The Street with No Name*, was predictably a crime number about an undercover cop (Mark Stevens) working to bust the bank hold-up gang run by Richard Widmark. Keighley's low-key direction keeps the tension edgy throughout. Undeterred by his *Robin Hood* experience years earlier, Keighley made two more films with a tiring Errol Flynn, before retiring to Paris with his wife, ex-actress Genevieve Tobin (they married in 1938). These included a fast-moving and exciting version of Stevenson's *The Master of Ballantrae*, with some especially well-directed action scenes. He died following a stroke.

1932: †The Match King. 1933: †Ladies They Talk About. Easy to Love. 1934: Journal of a Crime. Dr Monica. Big-Hearted Herbert. Kansas City Princess. Babbitt. 1935: Mary Jane's Pa (GB: Wanderlust). The Right to Live (GB: The Sacred Flame). G-Men. Special Agent. Stars Over Broadway. 1936: †Green Pastures. The Singing Kid. Bullets or Ballots. 1937: God's Country and the Woman. The Prince and the Pauper. Varsity Show. 1938: Secrets of an Actress. †The Adventures of Robin Hood. Brother Rat. Valley of the Giants. 1939: Yes, My Darling Daughter. Each Dawn I Die. 1940. The Fighting 69th. Torrid Zone. No Time for Comedy. 1941: Four Mothers. The Bride Came C.O.D. The Man Who Came to Dinner. 1942: George Washington Slept Here. 1944: Target for Today (D). 1947: Honeymoon. 1948: The Street with No Name. 1950: Rocky Mountain. 1951: Close To My Heart. 1953: The Master of Ballantrae.

KELLER, Harry 1913-1987

Keller is an interesting figure, in that he worked in films for 15 years before turning director, then made low-budget westerns (at a time when the genre had almost vanished) before reappearing two years after the last of these as a director of 'A' movies and co-features at Universal in the last years of the studio's double-feature programmes. Then in the 1960s, he became a producer, sometimes of surprisingly good fare. Most of his Universal films, too, are unexpectedly strong and sharp. Keller came to Hollywood in 1934 — almost the boy next door, as he was born in Los Angeles — and had advanced to editor two years later. He got his chance to direct at Republic, where all the best 'B' movie cowboys rode the range. His westerns with Allan 'Rocky' Lane are quite lively little numbers and there was also an interesting colour western for Fox, *Rose of Cimarron*, featuring a female central character played with plenty of bite by Mala Powers. It seemed that with the end of the 'B' western in 1954, Keller's career might be short-lived. But in 1956, he was taken on at Universal and remained there for eight years. There are two gripping, offbeat dramas in this period – *Man Afraid* contains George Nader's best performance, as a clergyman menaced by the father of a youth he was forced to kill; and *Voice in the Mirror* is a satisfying story about alcoholism with surprisingly good portrayals from Richard Egan and Julie London and one from Arthur O'Connell that might have seen him nominated for best supporting actor, the year before he actually was – in *Anatomy of a Murder*. The westerns are rather a mixed bunch – *Quantez* and *Day of the Badman* are quite good, but not tight enough nor the best of the 1950s' Fred MacMurray horse-operas – but *Seven Ways from Sundown* benefits from a very personable performance from Barry Sullivan. Keller seemed to find weakness, villainy and ambivalence more interesting than straightforwardness, which perhaps explains why his directorial career sank slowly under 'Tammy' films. As a producer, he had better luck, his successes including *Send Me No Flowers*, *Mirage*, *Texas Across the River* and *Skin Game*. Latterly, he kept busy in TV. He died from heart complications.

1949: The Blonde Bandit. 1950: Tarnished. 1951: Fort Dodge Stampede. The Desert of Lost Men. 1952: Leadville Gunslinger. Thundering Caravans. Black Hills Ambush. Rose of Cimarron. 1953: Marshal of Cedar Rock. Savage Frontier. Bandits of the West. El Paso Stampede. Red River Shore. 1954: The Phantom Stallion. 1956: The Unguarded Moment. 1957: Quantez. Man Afraid. 1958: The Female Animal. Voice in the Mirror. The Day of the Bad Man. Step Down to Terror (GB: The Silent Stranger). 1959: Stampede at Bitter Creek (TV. GB: cinemas). 1960: Seven Ways from Sundown. Geronimo's Revenge (TV. GB: cinemas). 1961: Tammy Tell Me True. 1962: Six Black Horses. 1963: Tammy and the Doctor. The Brass Bottle. 1964: Kitten with a Whip. 1967: In Enemy Country.

KENNEDY, Burt 1922-

Ninety per cent of this American director's films have been westerns, good, bad and indifferent in equal proportions. On the whole, the standard has declined since 1971, but there seems no hard-and-fast rule with Kennedy horse-operas. Some of his comedy-westerns, for example, are delightful — others disastrous. His best films on the whole seem to be those affectionate gallops down the Wild West's Memory Lane that do not tip over into farce, project likeable characters and have a backbone of truth somewhere deep inside. Kennedy's parents were burlesque artists known as The Dancing Kennedys. But their son always had a penchant for writing and, after war service, pursued this career on radio, appropriately scripting westerns. His speciality brought him to the attention of film western makers, notably (both *qv*) Andrew V. McLaglen (from 1955) and Budd Boetticher (from 1956). Kennedy contributed several screenplays to the splendid series of Boetticher-Randolph Scott westerns in the late 1950s, including *Seven Men from Now*, *The Tall T*, *Ride Lonesome* and *Comanche Station*, all stories of greed, revenge and destiny played out in the west's barren scrubland. His first western as director, *The Canadians*, about the Mounties always getting their men, showed up his inexperience, and he moved for a while into television, making episodes of *Lawman*, *The Virginian* and *Combat*. When he returned to the cinema in 1963, his direction was much more self-assured. *Mail Order Bride*, *The Rounders* and *Welcome to Hard Times* are all, in their different ways, about real frontier people, and the last of them Kennedy's most brutal and personal film — a mixture of his Boetticher scripts and his late multi-character stories. Between them, *The Money Trap* is a flawed but fascinating thriller, of interest not least because of the nostalgic re-teaming of Glenn Ford and Rita Hayworth. Later came the two tremendously enjoyable spoof westerns with James Garner, *Support Your Local Sheriff!* and *Support Your Local Gunfighter*, which depended heavily on strong, sparky, spunky female characters (Joan Hackett and Suzanne Pleshette, ideal actresses to choose) and on the engaging amiability of their character-full supporting casts. But Kennedy has made some total duds – *Return of the Seven*, *Dirty Dingus Magee*, *The Deserter*, *Hannie Caulder* – which are muddled, objectionable, dull or disastrous and occasionally all four. Nor does he seem very happy in his handling of major stars. But, at least, unlike Boetticher, he continued to work, albeit mainly in broadly spoof TV movie westerns, into his late sixties. He seemingly signed off uncharacteristically with the pleasantly zany Hulk Hogan sci-fi romp, *Suburban Commando*.

1961: The Canadians. 1963: Mail Order Bride (GB: West of Montana). 1964: The Rounders. 1965: The Money Trap. 1966: Welcome to Hard Times (GB: Killer on a Horse. Return of the Seven. 1967: The War Wagon. La Chica del Lunes/Monday's Child. 1968: Support Your Local Sheriff! 1969: Young Billy Young. The Good Guys and the Bad Guys. 1970: La Spina Dorsale del Diavolo/The Deserter. Dirty Dingus Magee. 1971: Support Your Local Gunfighter. Hannie Caulder. 1973: The Train Robbers. Shootout in a One Dog Town (TV). 1974: Sidekicks (TV). All the Kind Strangers (TV). 1975: The Killer Inside Me. 1976: †How the West Was Won (TV). 1977: The Rhinemann Exchange (TV). 1978: Kate Bliss and the Ticker Tape Kid (TV). 1979: The Wild Wild West Revisited (TV). Concrete Cowboys/Ramblin' Man (TV). 1980: More Wild, Wild West (TV). Wolf Lake (released 1984). 1985: Trouble at the Royal Rose/Trouble With Spys/The Trouble With Spies. 1987: The Alamo: 13 Days to Glory (TV). Down the Long Hills (TV). Once Upon a Texas Train (TV). 1988: Where the Hell's That Gold?!!? (TV). 1989: Big Bad John. 1991: Suburban Commando.

KENTON, Erle C. 1896-1980

One of Hollywood's most prominent and regularly employed 'B' film directors for nearly 30 years. Kenton made his mark for posterity too – with a couple of very atmospheric horror films and three of the funniest wartime Abbott and Costello comedies. It was no surprise when Kenton, already under contract to Universal at that time, was handed the assignment with Bud and Lou, for he had begun his Hollywood career (in 1914) as actor, gagman and odd-job-man with Mack Sennett, progressing up the Sennett ladder for five years until directing his first film in 1919. Nearly all Kenton's silent films were in comedy vein; it was only with the coming of sound that he began to direct a much tougher kind of film. He was with Paramount when they offered him a version of H.G. Wells' story *The Island of Dr Moreau*. Horror was an uncommon departure for the studio, but they were buoyed by their success with the Oscar-winning *Dr Jekyll and Mr Hyde* and willing to look to new horizons. The film Kenton turned in, *Island of Lost Souls*, is streets ahead of the 1977 and 1996 remakes, especially in terms of shivery scene-setting, the approach to the island somewhat foreshadowing the beginning of *King Kong*. Kenton's skilful use of black-and-white also ensures a greater sense of animal menace, with Bela Lugosi as the

Sayer of the Law, Alan Ladd allegedly under one of the animal skins and a bravura central performance from Charles Laughton as Dr Moreau, attempting to transform animals into human beings. This did not lead to a series of macabre ventures for Kenton: he was really at the wrong studio for that. Instead he returned to comedy when Paramount gave him the chance to direct W.C. Fields in one of his most priceless comedies, *You're Telling Me*, which includes the running battle with his living-room curtains as well as the famous climactic golf sketch. Kenton left Paramount in 1935 and, after spells with Columbia and RKO, joined Universal in 1941. His second film for Universal was *The Ghost of Frankenstein*, a tremendously underrated monster movie and the last fully fledged member of the Frankenstein series. Kenton extracted great moments of terrifying power from the dialogue, especially when the creature first speaks with the mad shepherd Ygor's voice after the brain-transplant operation, and a sympathetic performance from Lon Chaney Jr (one of his best for Universal) that was well in the Karloff tradition. Then Abbott and Costello came into Kenton's sphere and he directed them in *Who Done It?*, *Pardon My Sarong* and *It Ain't Hay*, before splitting from the team after an argument with Lou Costello during the making of *Hit the Ice*. Kenton then made two progressively limper Frankenstein films – *House of Frankenstein* and *House of Dracula* – but would have still seemed the ideal choice to direct Abbott and Costello when they met the Universal monsters in a 1948 film. However, he had left the studio two years earlier after the spooky *The Cat Creeps* and the only work he could find after that was on a couple of moral rearmament/social guidance movies. In the 1950s, he moved to directing half-hour episodes of comedy shows for television, retiring in 1961. He died from Parkinson's Disease.

*1919: Down on the Farm. *†Among Those Present. *A Lady's Tailor. *†No Mother to Guide Him. *†Salome vs. Shenandoah. 1920: *Dabbling in Art. *Fickle Fancy. *Movie Fans. †Love, Honor and Behave. Married Life. 1921: *She Sighed by the Seaside. A Small Town Idol. *A Perfect Villain. *Business is Business. 1922: *Splitting Hairs. *False Alarm. *The Haunted House. *The Landlord. *Laughing Gas. *The Piper. *A Poor Fish. 1923: *Dance or Die. *Hello Pardners. *The Income Tax Collector. *The Roaring Lion. *The Three Gun Man. *The Wise Cracker. Tea — with a Kick. 1924: *Fight and Win (series). Danger Signal. 1925: Red Hot Tires. A Fool*

and His Money. 1926: The Palm Beach Girl. The Love Toy. The Sap. Other Women's Husbands. 1927: The Girl in the Pullman (GB: The Girl on the Train). Wedding Bill$. The Rejuvenation of Aunt Mary. 1928: Golf Widows. Bare Knees (GB: Short Skirts). Name the Woman. The Companionate Marriage (GB: The Jazz Bride). The Side Show. Nothing to Wear. The Sporting Age (GB: The Stronger Love). The Street of Illusion. 1929: Father and Son. Trial Marriage. The Song of Love. 1930: Mexicali Rose (GB: The Girl from Mexico). A Royal Romance. 1931: The Last Parade. Lover Come Back. Leftover Ladies (GB: Broken Links). X Marks the Spot. 1932: Stranger in Town. Guilty As Hell (GB: Guilty As Charged). Island of Lost Souls. 1933: From Hell to Heaven. Big Executive. Disgraced! 1934: Search for Beauty. You're Telling Me. 1935: The Public Menace. Grand Exit. Best Man Wins. Party Wire. 1936: The Devil's Squadron. Counterfeit. End of the Trail (GB: Revenge!). 1937: Racketeers in Exile. The Devil's Playground. She Asked for It. 1938: The Lady Objects. Little Tough Guys in Society. 1939: Everything's On Ice. Escape to Paradise. 1940: Remedy for Riches. Petticoat Politics. 1941: Melody for Three. Naval Academy. They Meet Again. Flying Cadets. The Ghost of Frankenstein. 1942: Frisco Lil. North to the Klondike. Pardon My Sarong. Who Done It? 1943: How's About It? It Ain't Hay (GB: Money for Jam). †Hit the Ice (uncredited). Always a Bridesmaid. 1944: She Gets Her Man. House of Frankenstein. What are We Fighting For? (D). 1945: House of Dracula. 1946: Little Miss Big. The Cat Creeps. 1948: The Story of Bob and Sally (GB: Should Parents Tell?). 1951: One Too Many (GB: Killer with a Label).

KERSHNER, Irvin (I. Kerschner) 1923-
This American director has intermittently shown signs of a most intriguing talent during his 33 years as a director, during which time he has made only 17 films. The lower the budget, or the more offbeat the concept, the better results Kershner has produced. He clearly does not benefit from working with big budgets on surefire projects and yet he has tried it several times. That suggests an indecision as to how to get into a position of autonomy which he did not attain. So he may go back to out-of-the-way projects with admirable results but too little acclaim — it seems to be a Catch 22 situation, yet he has already left more good work behind than some directors who have made four times as many movies. After studying film at university, Kershner went to the Middle

East to make documentaries for the U.S. Information Service. At 35, he finally broke into feature films, making teenage Z-movies. Unlike other teenage Z-movies, though, Kershner's were remarkably good. The tension in *Stakeout on Dope Street* and *The Young Captives* is fresh and real. And their young leading players — Yale Wexler and Steven Marlo — gave performances of dramatic intensity that they did not match in later years. Kershner's 'breakthrough' film, *The Hoodlum Priest*, is in fact rather less than its reputation, but he followed it with *A Face in the Rain*, shot in Italy and one of several films that Rory Calhoun made at this time, showing him in a light different from his accepted image. The film is tense and touching by turns, firmly set in the World War II period, and has a tenderly observed performance by Marina Berti. Kershner continued to make good films: the bleak *The Luck of Ginger Coffey*, an early triumph for Robert Shaw; *A Fine Madness*, a comedy of amorality with dark undertones; and *The Flim Flam Man*, a riotous character comedy which cooks a snook at anyone who thinks George C. Scott incapable of being funny. Kershner followed these with *Loving*, a hurtful black comedy considered by many to be his best film. George Segal and Eve Marie Saint were the ideal players to bring out the full hilarious pain of the situations, and the film attracted a great deal of critical praise. Since then, things have gone awry for Kershner. He did presentable jobs on *Raid on Entebbe* (especially considering the haste) and *The Empire Strikes Back*, but the bite and emotional appeal of his earlier years has not been recaptured since that 1970 peak.

*1958: Stakeout on Dope Street. 1959: The Young Captives. 1961: The Hoodlum Priest. 1963: A Face in the Rain. 1964: The Luck of Ginger Coffey. 1966: A Fine Madness. 1967: The Flim Flam Man (GB: One Born Every Minute). 1970: Loving. 1972: Up the Sandbox. 1974: S*P*Y*S. 1976: The Return of a Man Called Horse. Raid on Entebbe (TV. GB: cinemas). 1978: Eyes of Laura Mars. 1980: The Empire Strikes Back. 1983: Never Say Never Again. 1989: Travelin' Man (cable TV). 1990: Robocop 2.*

KIESLOWSKI, Krzysztof 1941-1996
It seems that most Eastern European directors of the past 30 years have been rebels of one kind or another, and Kieslowski was certainly no exception. Since his films tend to be about poor people with few prospects, he suffered from varying forms of censorship from successive

governments and unions. To the Western eye, Kieslowski's films offend less against the system than those of some of his contemporaries. And, although in life he was something of a pessimist, his films do not always reflect that attitude. Their characters are constantly faced with making moral decisions and often find the right endings for their lives. Kieslowski's roots lie in documentary work, and he would tell interviewers that 'I don't know how to narrate fiction.' This, however, was not entirely true, particularly of the last few films of his career, where narrative threads are skilfully entwined to come to an ending that brings an appreciative smile to the lips for the director's skill. His interest in cinema was perhaps unexpected. His father was an engineer who suffered from tuberculosis, and the family moved from town to town. Kieslowski recalled that they were too poor to go to the cinema, so he and friends would climb up local picture-houses and peer through holes in the roof. An uncle who ran a technical school for theatre sparked his interest in the field and, after studies there, he got into the Lódz Film School at his third attempt. He started making documentaries while still there, in 1966, including a rather unflattering portrait of Lódz itself. While continuing to shoot documentaries, he began making feature films a decade later. He attracted particular attention in 1988 with *Dekalog*, ten hour-long films for TV based on the 10 Commandments. Two of these were expanded for the cinema, successfully in the case of *A Short Film About Killing* and rather less successfully with *A Short Film About Love*. An ailing Kieslowski rounded out his career with the much praised 'colours' films, the last of which, *Red*, is probably the best and most fully rounded work of his career. Similar in structure to Claude Lelouch's romantic films about *un homme* finally meeting *une femme*, after just missing each other throughout the story, it's vastly superior in the writing (co-scripted by Kieslowski) and in the central theme. Flawless filmmaking of a very high order, it was nominated for a best film Academy Award. He died from heart failure at 54.

1966: *The Office (D). *The Tram. 1967: *Concert of Requests. 1968: *From the City of Lódz (D). 1969: *The Photograph (D). 1970: *I Was a Soldier. *Factory (D). 1971: *Before the Rally (D). Workers '71: Nothing About Us Without Us (D). 1972: *Refrain (D). *Between Wroclaw and Zielona Góra (D). 1973: *Mason/Bricklayer (D). 1974: *X-Ray (D). *Love Story (D). 1975: Life Story/Curriculum Vitae. Personnel (TV). 1976:* *Slate. The Scar. *Hospital. Calm Before the Storm (TV). 1977: *Night Porter (D). I Don't Know. 1978: *Seven Women of Different Ages (D). 1979: Camera Buff. 1980: *Station (D). *Talking Heads (D). 1981: Blind Chance. Short Working Day. 1984: Without End. 1988: Dekalog (TV). A Short Film About Killing. A Short Film About Love. 1991: The Double Life of Véronique. 1993: Trois couleurs: blanc/White. Trois couleurs: bleu/Blue. 1994: Trois couleurs: rouge/Red.*

KIMMINS, Anthony 1901-1964

An efficient comedy director who knew just what the public wanted in times of economic depression, and how to make it, this British film-maker also revealed himself as a useful, sometimes striking director of drama when given the chance. He pursued a naval career for 15 years, although when he left the service and became a writer, actor and later director, the only sea story he ever had any connection with was *Midshipman Easy* (1935), for which he wrote the screenplay. Ealing Films took him on as an actor in 1933 and he directed a few films for them as well before deciding to concentrate on his writing career. But when Monty Banks (Mario Bianchi, 1897-1950) decided to quit the George Formby comedies after making *No Limit* (1935) and *Keep Your Seats Please* (1936) to helm comedy-musicals with his star-wife Gracie Fields, Kimmins was invited to take over. Having written the screenplay for *Keep Your Seats Please*, and watched Formby at work, Kimmins knew the simple guileless approach required, the close-ups of Formby's shy, north-country, but highly individual personality, especially while singing his catchy little ditties with their undercurrents of postcard-smut, that would make audiences of the 1930s smile knowingly and lovingly. Under Kimmins' tight guidance, Formby became the second-biggest box-office attraction (after Fields) and the highest-paid star in Britain. Kimmins also wrote the screenplays. He had just finished a screenplay for something different – a Jack Buchanan comedy called *Under Your Hat* – when war service took six years out of his career. When Kimmins returned to civilian life, he found that Formby's film career was finished and comedies no longer in demand. But he re-established himself with the stylish *Mine Own Executioner*, a psychological thriller with Burgess Meredith at his most controlled and affecting and a career-best performance from Kieron Moore as the disturbed war veteran he tries to save from himself. Kimmins deserved – and got – high praise for his decision to stylize the tension-racked climax. Kimmins' subsequent film dramas were mediocre by comparison and success eluded him until he returned to comedy – *Who Goes There?*, *Aunt Clara* (a glorious teaming of Margaret Rutherford and Ronald Shiner) and *The Captain's Paradise* were all winners. And one of Kimmins' last films, *Smiley*, a simple comedy-drama about the adventures of a little Australian boy, warmly photographed in colour by Ted Scaife and Russ Wood, was his biggest box-office hit since the last of the Formby films.

1934: By-Pass to Happiness. How's Chances? 1935: Once in a New Moon. His Majesty and Co. All at Sea. 1937: Keep Fit. 1938: I See Ice. It's in the Air (US: George Takes the Air). 1939: Come on George. Trouble Brewing. 1947: Mine Own Executioner. 1948: Bonnie Prince Charlie. 1951: Flesh and Blood. Mr Denning Drives North. 1952: Who Goes There? (US: The Passionate Sentry). 1953: The Captain's Paradise. 1954: Aunt Clara. 1956: Smiley. 1958: Smiley Gets a Gun. 1962: The Amorous Prawn.

KING, George 1899-1966

British director who vied with Leslie Hiscott *(qv)* in the 1930s for title 'King of the Quota Quickies' — but the name gave him an additional qualification! Like Hiscott, King had sufficient basic skill to prolong his career after that decade when the demand for 60-minute programme-fillers had passed. He also became a useful producer, on such disparate films as *Maria Marten* (1935), *The First of the Few* (1942) and *Eight O'Clock Walk* (1954), the latter his last work for the cinema. In 1919, King had quit medical studies to plunge into the film industry, where he became a jack of all trades — actors' agent, exhibitor, title-card writer (from 1921), assistant director (from 1922) and screenplay writer (from 1927). With the coming of sound, his wide experience saw him swiftly promoted to the director's chair. His very first film, *Too Many Crooks*, featured a young stage actor called Laurence Olivier, who was also making his film debut. Never again would King have quite such a distinguished player under his command. Once launched from routine thrillers into quota quickies – those films made to fill the bottom of the cinema bill and fulfil the regulations under which a certain percentage of all films shown in Britain had to be British-made – King made the usual array of lightweight comedies, romances and thrillers. The thrillers gradually became increasingly lurid and at the end of the decade King teamed several times with the barnstorming Tod Slaughter to make a number of rough-edged crime dramas. Quota quickies died with the outbreak of war (they returned, in allegedly 'improved' form, in 1947) and King directed some distinctly up-market war movies, most successful of which was *Candlelight in Algeria*. A vehicle for the popular James Mason, it garnered King the best reviews of his career. One contemporary reviewer described it as 'a British film which has the slickness and tense pace of many American productions, plus a restraint and beauty of its own'. He was also successful with *The Shop at Sly Corner* (which had another screen newcomer in Diana Dors), offering a characteristically charismatic performance from Oscar Homolka as the shopkeeper and an unsettling portrayal from Kenneth Griffith. The latter reappeared in King's last film *Forbidden*, a useful multishadowed thriller with Douglass Montgomery, Hazel Court and a suspenseful *Vertigo*-like climax.

1930: *Too Many Crooks. Leave It to Me.* 1931: *Midnight. Deadlock! Number, Please. The Professional Guest.* 1932: *Self-Made Lady. Two Way Street. Men of Steel. To Brighton — with Gladys.* 1933: *Matinee Idol. Too Many Wives. High Finance. Beware of Women. Mayfair Girl (US: Society Girl). Enemy of the Police. Smithy. Her Imaginary Lover. I Adore You.* 1934: *The Silver Spoon. Murder at the Inn. The Office Wife. To Be a Lady. Get Your Man. Guest of Honour. Nine Forty Five. The Blue Squadron. Adventure Limited. Oh No, Doctor. The Little Stranger.* 1935: *The Man without a Face. Full Circle. Windfall. Gay Old Dog.* 1936: *Sweeney Todd, the Demon Barber of Fleet Street. The Crimes of Stephen Hawke. Reasonable Doubt.* 1937: *Wanted. Merry Comes to Town. Under a Cloud. The Ticket of Leave Man. Silver Top.* 1938: *Sexton Blake and the Hooded Terror. John Halifax Gentleman.* 1939: *The Face at the Window. The Chinese Bungalow (US: The Chinese Den).* 1940: *Crimes at the Dark House. The Case of the Frightened Lady (US: Frightened Lady). George and Margaret. Two for Danger.* 1942: *Tomorrow We Live (US: At Dawn We Die).* 1943: *Candlelight in Algeria.* 1946: *Gaiety George (US: Showtime). The Shop at Sly Corner (US: The Code of Scotland Yard).* 1948: *Forbidden.*

KING, Henry 1888-1982

King has probably given as much pleasure to people in the cinema as any other American director. That he did not win an Academy Award (only two nominations) was one of Hollywood's deeper miscalcu-

lations. Although his films do show a falling-away in the 1950s, the previous 30 years are studded with high achievement. There were times when he was swamped by grandeur, pomp or literariness, pitfalls into which he seemed doomed periodically to fall. But when he returned to Americana, the simple rural qualities of America in times past, he was well-nigh unbeatable. King's most consistent period was the 1920s, and the films he made then are forgotten now by all but a few. *Tol'able David*, at the beginning of the decade, was a typically American rural romance that made his name, and has long been considered one of the films that made the maximum use of the resources of the silent cinema. It featured one of the best examples of Richard Barthelmess's charismatic gentility, forced in the end to take on his own Goliath. Barthelmess and King, who had formed Inspiration Pictures to make the film, subsequently combined again on *Sonny* and *Fury*. King eloquently directed Barthelmess' *Broken Blossoms* and *Way Down East* co-star Lillian Gish in two Italian-made films opposite Ronald Colman, *Romola* and *The White Sister*. These are vivid, fullblown romantic hardbacks. King returned to an Italian setting in *The Magic Flame*, with Colman this time starring opposite Vilma Banky, who had played for King in *The Winning of Barbara Worth*, which gave Gary Cooper his first major film role, appropriately in a western. Mention should also be made of King's powerful and finally heartrending 1925 version of *Stella Dallas*. The 1930s was a period of retrenchment for King, although *State Fair* (1933), with its homespun sentiment and down-to-earth values, reflected, in its effect on an audience, all that was best about King's work from that time on. Despite the fairly unprofitable association with the Tyrone Power-Alice Faye-Don Ameche group, these were sentiments that King returned to constantly, always with notable success, but especially in *Ramona*, Alice Brady's Oscar-winning performance for *In Old Chicago*, *Maryland* and the quite charming *Margie*, featuring Jeanne Crain before she became self-conscious. King's other peak achievement in the field of glowing, nostalgic Americana is the immensely underrated *Wait 'Til the Sun Shines, Nellie*, the reminiscences of a small-town barber, his loves, hates, triumphs and tragedies. This is a film which, had it featured a major star (which is not to say David Wayne does not give a very fine performance) might have gone down as an American classic. Both these films were glowingly bathed in colour, *Margie* by Charles Clarke and *Nellie* by Leon Shamroy. Also worth attention are the

films in which King examines the cracks and flaws beneath the dull surface of the Gregory Peck persona, most notably *The Gunfighter* and *Twelve O'Clock High* and, to a lesser degree, *The Snows of Kilimanjaro*. Amid his 1950s failures, he did make a moving film out of *Carousel*. Few American directors could have made such sentimental situations ring so true.

1915. *The Brand of Man. Who Pays (serial).* 1916: *Little Mary Sunshine. The Oath of Hate. The Sand Lark. Shadows and Sunshine. Joy and the Dragon.* 1917: *Vengeance of the Dead. Told at Twilight. Twin Kiddies. Souls in Pawn. The Unafraid. The Climber. Sunshine and Gold. The Bride's Silence. The Upper Crust. The Mainspring. Scepter of Suspicion. Southern Pride. A Game of Wits. The Mate of the Sally Ann.* 1918: *Beauty and the Rogue. Mademoiselle Tiptoes. King Social Briars. The Locked Heart. Up Romance Road. The Ghost of Rosy Taylor. Powers That Pray. Hearts or Diamonds. All the World to Nothing. Hobbs in a Hurry. When a Man Rides Alone.* 1919: *Some Liar. Brass Buttons. Where the West Begins. A Sporting Chance. Six Feet Four. This Hero Stuff. A Fugitive from Matrimony. Haunting Shadows. 23 ½ Hours Leave.* 1920: *The White Dove. Uncharted Channels. One Hour Before Dawn. Dice of Destiny. Help Wanted — Male.* 1921: *Mistress of Shenstone. When We Were 21. Salvage. Sting of the Lash. Tol'able David.* 1922: *The Seventh Day. The Bond Boy. Sonny. Fury.* 1923: *The White Sister.* 1924: *Romola.* 1925: *Any Woman. Sackcloth and Scarlet. Stella Dallas.* 1926: *Partners Again. The Winning of Barbara Worth. The Magic Flame.* 1928: †*The Woman Disputed.* 1929: *She Goes to War. Hell Harbor.* 1930: *The Eyes of the World. Lightnin'.* 1931: *Merely Mary Ann. Over the Hill.* 1932: *The Woman in Room 13.* 1933: *State Fair.* †*I Loved You Wednesday.* 1934: *Carolina (GB: The House of Connelly). Marie Galante.* 1935: *One More Spring. Way Down East.* 1936: *The Country Doctor. Ramona. Lloyds of London.* 1937: *Seventh Heaven.* 1938: *Alexander's Ragtime Band. In Old Chicago.* 1939: *Jesse James. Stanley and Livingstone.* 1940: *Little Old New York. Maryland. Chad Hanna.* 1941: *Remember the Day. A Yank in the RAF.* 1942: *The Black Swan.* 1943: *The Song of Bernadette.* 1944: *Wilson.* 1945: *A Bell for Adano.* 1946: *Margie.* 1947: *Captain from Castile.* 1948: *Deep Waters.* 1949: *Prince of Foxes. Twelve O'Clock High.* 1950: *The Gunfighter.* 1951: *I'd Climb the Highest Mountain.* 1952: *The Snows of Kilimanjaro.* †*O Henry's Full House (GB: Full House). Wait 'Til the*

Sun Shines, Nellie. 1953: King of the · Khyber Rifles. 1955: Untamed. Love is a Many-Splendored Thing. 1956: Carousel. 1957: The Sun Also Rises. 1958: The Bravados. 1959: This Earth is Mine. Beloved Infidel. 1961: Tender is the Night.

KING, Louis 1898-1962

The brother of Henry King (qv), Louis King was expert in bringing the freshness and unspoiled beauty of the American outdoors to the screen. King loved stories about horses from the early days of the Buck Jones westerns, and returned to the theme in most picturesque and winning fashion in folksy Fox family films of the 1940s, most of them sumptuously shot in Technicolor by the ubiquitous Charles Clarke. Like his brother's, King's very beginnings in films were as an actor, but he was directing briefly in 1923 and regularly by 1927, if in humbler surroundings than Henry, all of his films being very low-budget westerns. He began, unusually, by making a series of pocket westerns featuring an equally pocket-sized star, the 13-year-old (in 1927, when the series began) Buzz Barton. Little Buzz was a brilliant rider, could act a bit and had an engaging personality, and the action films King fashioned around him were fresh and winning. The Buzz-craze lasted through three years and close to 20 films, most of them directed by King. King then drifted across to Columbia (from RKO) and Buck Jones westerns. As the 1930s progressed, he started to mix outdoor adventures with series thrillers, including several serviceable Bulldog Drummond films. Although King did not direct the original *My Friend Flicka* (it was Harold Schuster), he made virtually all the films that followed from the Fox stable in similar vein. Like the films he made until the end of his cinema career in 1956, these were strong on scenic values and natural, unforced performances. Saturday morning matinee audiences thrilled to King pictures years after they were made, and they still look fresh, charming, true-to-life and pleasing to the eye. You can almost smell the clean air in a Louis King film.

1923: Sun Dog Trails. Peaceful Peters. Devil's Door Yard. Spawn of the Desert. Law Rustlers. 1927: Is Your Daughter Safe? The Boy Rider. The Slingshot Kid. Wizard of the Saddle. 1928: The Pinto Kid. The Little Buckaroo. The Bantam Cowboy. The Fightin' Redhead. Young Whirlwind. Rough Ridin' Red. Terror Mountain (GB: Tom's Vacation). Orphan of the Sage. 1929: The Freckled Rascal. The Vagabond Club. The Little Savage.

Pals of the Prairie. 1930: The Lone Rider. Shadow Ranch. Men Without Law. 1931: The Fighting Sheriff. Border Law. Desert Vengeance. The Deceiver. 1932: County Fair. Fame Street. Police Court (GB: Son of Mine). Drifting Souls. Arm of the Law. 1933: Robbers' Roost. Life in the Raw. 1934: Murder in Trinidad. Pursued. Bachelor of Arts. La Ciudad de Carton. 1935: Julieta Compra un Hijo. Angelita. Charlie Chan in Egypt. 1936: Special Investigator. Road Gang (GB: Injustice). Song of the Saddle. Shadow Ranch. Bengal Tiger. Draegerman Courage (GB: The Cave-In). 1937: That Man's Here Again. Wild Money. Bulldog Drummond Comes Back. Melody for Two. Wine, Women and Horses. Bulldog Drummond's Revenge. 1938: Tip-Off Girls. Prison Farm. Hunted Men. Illegal Traffic. Bulldog Drummond in Africa. Tom Sawyer — Detective. Persons in Hiding. 1939: Undercover Doctor. 1940: Seventeen. Typhoon. The Way of All Flesh. Moon Over Burma. 1942: Young America. 1943: Chetniks (GB: Underground Guerillas). 1944: Ladies of Washington. 1945: Thunderhead — Son of Flicka. 1946: Smoky. 1947: Thunder in the Valley (GB: Bob, Son of Battle). 1948: Green Grass of Wyoming. 1949: Will James's Sand (GB: Sand). Mrs Mike. 1950: Frenchie. 1952: The Lion and the Horse. 1953: Powder River. Sabre Jet. 1954: Dangerous Mission. 1956: Massacre.

KLEISER, Randal 1946-

After a series of perceptive and poignant portraits of problems at either end of the age scale in often award-winning TV movies, this American director rather lost his way following the success of his first cinema film, *Grease*. In more recent times, however, he has partially re-established his reputation as a sensitive portrayer of critical periods in human lives. Graduating from the USC Film School, Kleiser brought with him his masters thesis film, *Peege*, a study of old age that did well at film festivals and was taken up by TV channels on both sides of the Atlantic. With its help Kleiser quickly launched a career in US television, directing numerous episodes of such popular series as *Starsky and Hutch* and *Marcus Welby MD*, before branching out into TV movies from 1975. One of these, *The Boy in the Plastic Bubble*, about a youth with immunity deficiency, featured a young John Travolta, who went on to become the star of the immensely popular *Grease*, a bouncy pastiche of 1950s' college musicals. Two sagas of sun, sand and sex fared less well after that, and Kleiser found his status sliding as he vainly looked for another hit. A visit to Britain went some

way to putting him back on the right road, with the appropriately titled *Getting It Right*. A pleasant comedy with some sharp performances (notably from Helena Bonham Carter), it had the right feel about its settings and some wickedly funny lines in its portrait of a shy 31-year-old bachelor still looking for the right girl. Kleiser followed up with an excellent new version of Jack London's animal yarn *White Fang*, but it was 1995 before he made perhaps his best film, *It's My Party*, a painfully unflinching study of a man dying from AIDS, who decides to hold a night, day and night party before a quiet and dignified suicide. Kleiser's gently understated direction recalls the best of his early TV movies and many stars worked for small fees on the film, including Kleiser's old *Grease* alumnus, Olivia Newton-John.

1970: Peege. 1975: All Together Now (TV). 1976: The Boy in the Plastic Bubble (TV). Dawn — Portrait of a Teenage Runaway (TV). 1977: The Gathering (TV). 1978: Grease. 1980: The Blue Lagoon. 1982: Summer Lovers. 1984: Grandview USA. 1986: Flight of the Navigator. 1988: Big Top Pee-wee. 1989: Getting It Right. 1990: White Fang. 1992: Honey, I Blew Up the Kid. 1995: It's My Party. 1998: Reasonable Doubt.

KNOWLES, Bernard 1900-

Brilliant British cinematographer who made a fine start to his directorial career, but very quickly tailed off into the routine and spent most of this side of his career making half-hour stories for television. Knowles began his career as a newspaper photographer, at one time going to America to work for the *Detroit News*. On his return to England in 1922, Gainsborough took him on as an assistant cameraman, and he soon became a lighting cameraman, a pioneer of sophisticated camera techniques and an ace at conjuring up an atmosphere by use of black and white cinematography. Knowles' work was particularly noteworthy on *Dawn* (1928), *For Ever England* (US: *Born for Glory*, 1935), *The 39 Steps* (1935), *King Solomon's Mines* (1937) and *Gaslight* (US: *Angel Street*, 1940). After World War II, Knowles decided to forsake photography for direction and made a fine start with the delicate ghost story *A Place of One's Own*. The film was described by C.A. Lejeune, a critic not customarily given to superlatives as 'a fine piece of work ... gripping, marvellous, outstanding, eerie, perky, beautiful, lovely and different'. Unfortunately, the same reviewer dismissed his next film, *The Magic Bow*, with Stewart Granger playing

Paganini, and several people helping Granger to play the violin, in one word: 'Fiddlesticks'. The decline into mediocrity continued, with the reservation that Knowles' films always looked every bit as good as those of an ex-cinematographer should, especially his two ventures in Technicolor, *The Man Within* and *Jassy*. Unlike Jack Cardiff, Knowles never returned to cinematography, which was unfortunate.

1945: *A Place of One's Own*. 1946: *The Magic Bow*. 1947: *The Man Within (US: The Smugglers)*. *Jassy*. *The White Unicorn (US: Bad Sister)*. *Easy Money*. 1949: *The Lost People*. *The Perfect Woman*. 1950: *The Reluctant Widow*. 1953: *Park Plaza 605 (US: Norman Conquest)*. 1955: *Barbados Quest (US: Murder on Approval)*. *Handcuffs, London*. 1963: †*Hell is Empty (released 1967)*. 1964: *Frozen Alive*. 1965: *Spaceflight IC-1*.

KONCHALOVSKY, Andrei

(A. Mikhalkov-Konchalovsky) 1937-

Brother of another Russian director, Nikita Mikhalkov (they agreed to split the family name between them), Konchalovsky was a prize-winning film-maker in his own country, and eventually went to Hollywood. After a start of some promise, his work here proved uncharacteristic and disappointing and he was making films in Russia again by the 1990s. The son of poets, Konchalovsky originally had ambitions to become a concert pianist, but gave up ideas of a music career after three years of study and enrolled instead at Moscow's State Institute of Cinematography. Entering the industry as a writer – he continued writing for other people's films until 1976 – after having won awards for his thesis short, *The Boy and the Pigeon*, he began to make his own films in 1965. These were largely

Andrei **Konchalovsky** steering the *Runaway Train* in the days when his Hollywood career was still on track.

character-driven dramas that sometimes ran into trouble with the Soviet authorities. He moved to America in the early 1980s after the award-winning success of his three-and-a-half hour epic *Siberiade*, spanning the fortunes of two Russian families from 1900 to 1960. English-speaking films, however, provided an unhappy period in Konchalovsky's life, apart from the thundering action of *Runaway Train*, a film that won an Oscar nomination for its star, Jon Voight. He left his last Hollywood film, *Tango & Cash*, unfinished, and it was completed by another director, Albert Magnoli. Konchalovsky returned to his native country but has not yet regained his former reputation.

1961: **The Boy and the Pigeon*. 1965: *The First Teacher*. 1967: *The Happiness of Asya (banned in Russia until 1988)*. 1969: *A Nest of Gentlefolk*. 1971: *Uncle Vanya*. 1974: *Romance for Lovers*. 1978: *Siberiade*. 1982: *Split Cherry Tree (TV)*. 1984: *Maria's Lovers*. 1985: *Runaway Train*. 1986: *Duet for One*. 1987: *Shy People*. 1988: *Homer & Eddie*. 1989: *Tango & Cash*. 1991: *The Inner Circle/The Projectionist*. 1994: *Kourotchka Riaba (US: Ryaba My Chicken)*. 1997: *The Odyssey*.

KORDA, Sir Alexander

(Sándor Kellner) 1893-1956

Hungarian-born film-maker, later a studio magnate and possibly for a while the most influential figure in the British cinema. Settling in Britain in 1932, Korda came to love the country and its history, which he saw as the basis for making films that would break into the international market and challenge Hollywood at its own game — a burning ambition especially after his own dismal experiences as a director there. A journalist in Hungary in his early years, he worked at Pathé Studios in Paris as a jack-of-all-trades in 1911-12, returning to Hungary and writing, then directing films from 1914. From 1917 he became his own producer and in the 1920s moved to Vienna, then Berlin. In 1927, Korda went to Hollywood with his first wife, Maria Corda (real name: Maria Fargas), an actress whose career was terminated by the coming of sound. Korda's own films as director, for First National, Fox and others, rarely rose above the ordinary and he fled to Paris after a disagreement with Fox executives over his treatment of their films. Here he regained much of his reputation, especially with *Marius*, and came to Britain to work for Paramount-British, leaving them in 1932 and founding his own company, London Films. Korda was to produce well over 100 films for the

company before his death 24 years later from a heart attack, but direct only a few. But it was one of those he did direct himself, *The Private Life of Henry VIII*, that provided the breakthrough to Hollywood sooner than imagined. The film, with a central performance by Charles Laughton that made him the second British actor to win an Academy Award, really captured the public's imagination and won Korda a distribution link in America through United Artists. He was made a full partner in the company in 1935, almost bought it outright in 1938, became its temporary head in 1941 and relinquished his interests in 1946. Meanwhile, Korda followed *Henry VIII* with other 'lives' (including his own best film, *Rembrandt*, a critical if not public success which again starred Laughton, and brought a great painter vividly to life as a human being) and forays into the history of the British Empire and its struggles. By 1938, Korda was having struggles of his own: Denham Studios, his pride and joy, was taken away from him, and he spent the rest of his career up to his neck in financial juggling. But he also made a few more films himself, most notably *Perfect Strangers*, a touching and penetrating film about the pressures that wartime service put on a previously dull but stable marriage. Korda himself was married three times, his second wife being actress Merle Oberon, from 1939 to 1945. Among the more distinguished films that he produced or 'presented', but did not direct were: *The Scarlet Pimpernel* (1934), *Sanders of the River* (1935), *Things to Come* (1936), *The Drum* (1938), *The Four Feathers* (1939), *The Thief of Bagdad* (1940), *To Be or Not To Be* (1942), *The Fallen Idol* (1948), *The Third Man* (1949), *The Sound Barrier* (1952), *Hobson's Choice* (1954), *Summer Madness/Summertime* (1955) and *Richard III* (1956).

1914: †*A Becsapott Ujságiró/The Duped Journalist*. †*Tutyu and Toto*. †*Orhaz a Karpatokban/Watch-Tower in the Carpathians*. 1915: †*Lyon Lea*. \$*A Tiszti Kardbojt/The Officer's Sword*. 1916: *White Nights/Fedora*. *A Nagymama/The Grandmother*. *Mesek az Irógépröl/Typewriter Tales*. *A Kétszivü Férfi/ The Man with Two Hearts*. As *Egymillió Fontos Bankó/The Million Pound Note*. *Ciklámen*. *Vergödö Szívek/Fighting Hearts*. *A Nevetö Szaszkia/Laughing Saskia*. *Mágnás Miska/Miska the Magnate/Miska the Great*. 1917: *Szent Peter Esernyöje/St Peter's Umbrella*. *A Gólyakalifa/The Stork Caliph*. *Mágia/Magic*. *Harrison and Barrison*. 1918: *Faun*. *Az Aranyember/ The Man with the Golden Touch*. *Mary Ann*. 1919: *Ave Caesar!* *Fehér Rósza/The*

White Rose. Yamata. Se Ki, Se Be/Not In — Or Out. Number 111. 1920: Seine Majestät das Bettelkind (GB: The Prince and the Pauper). 1921: Herren der Meere (GB & US: Masters of the Sea). 1922: Eine versunkene Welt/Vanished World. Samson and Delilah. 1923: Das unbekannte Morgen (GB: The Unknown Tomorrow). 1924: Jedermanns Frau/Everybody's Woman. Tragödie im Hause Hapsburg (GB & US: Mayerling). 1925: Der Tanzer meiner Frau (GB: Dancing Mad). 1926: Madame wünscht keine Kinder (GB: Madame Wants No Children). 1927: Eine Dubarry von heute (GB: A Modern Dubarry). The Stolen Bride. The Private Life of Helen of Troy. 1928: Yellow Lily. Night Watch. 1929: Love and the Devil. The Squall. Her Private Life. Lilies of the Field. 1930: Women Everywhere. †The Princess and the Plumber. 1931: Rive gauche/Die Männer um Lucie (French and German versions of Laughter). Marius (and German version). Service for Ladies (US: Reserved for Ladies). 1932: Wedding Rehearsal. 1933: The Girl from Maxim's (and French version). The Private Life of Henry VIII. 1934: The Private Life of Don Juan. 1936: Rembrandt. 1940: †The Thief of Bagdad (uncredited). 1941: That Hamilton Woman (GB: Lady Hamilton). 1945: Perfect Strangers (US: Vacation from Marriage). 1947: An Ideal Husband.

Note: All films from 1914 to 1919, as Sándor Korda

$ as József Neumann

KORDA, Zoltán (Z. Kellner) 1895-1961

Hungarian-born director with a talent for wide-ranging adventure stories, bringing across the atmosphere of the country in which they were set, and a feeling for the oppressed indigenous peoples of the world that added a bite and poignancy to much of his work. Working with his brothers Alexander (the studio chief) and Vincent, a production designer and art designer, for London Films in the Britain of the 1930s, Zoltán made two outstanding 'British Empire' films — The Drum and The Four Feathers. By and large, he followed his brother Alex's footsteps, working with him in Hungary and later in Britain and Hollywood. Although plagued by tuberculosis in the middle part of his life, Zoltán kept working, mostly as a writer, until Alexander called him to Britain in 1932, following the founding of London Films. At first Zoltán worked on routine projects, but was delighted when asked to make Sanders of the River in 1933, although the film, from inception to completion, took two years to bring to

the screen, a situation that was repeated with much irony when Zoltán, of all people, was called in 'rescue' Robert Flaherty *(qv)* when he was thought to be taking too long to make *Elephant Boy. Sanders* was a great commercial success, principally on account of the music and the appeal of Paul Robeson, although from then on Zoltán and Alexander had many fierce battles over the extent to which native populaces should be portrayed as people: Alexander's coarser view (and seniority) usually won. Zoltán liked India and Africa as much as he liked tales of high adventure, and he returned to the locales time and again, although his masterwork, *The Four Feathers,* was made as early as 1939. This is a magnificent film, its Technicolor photography beyond anything Hollywood had achieved up to that time, its parched landscapes brilliantly captured. And Zoltán obtains an awesomely good performance from Ralph Richardson as Durrance, especially when blinded and lost in the heat of the desert. He went to Hollywood with his brother in the early 1940s, and stayed there when Alexander returned to Britain. Although he never made anything approaching *The Four Feathers,* there are some interesting films, especially *Sahara,* another desert-set war story, this time with Humphrey Bogart and based on a Russian film, *The 13;* and *A Woman's Vengeance,* a not inconsiderable version of Aldous Huxley's story *The Gioconda Smile.*

1918: †Karoly-Bakák. 1933: †Men of Tomorrow. Cash (US: For Love or Money). 1935: Sanders of the River (US: Bosambo). 1936: Forget-Me-Not (US: Forever Yours). †Conquest of the Air (first shown 1938, briefly released 1940, re-released abridged 1944). 1937: †Elephant Boy. 1938: The Drum (US: Drums). 1939: The Four Feathers. 1940: †The Thief of Bagdad (uncredited). 1942: Jungle Book. 1943: Sahara. 1945: Counter-Attack (GB: One Against Seven). 1947: The Macomber Affair. 1948: A Woman's Vengeance. 1951: Cry the Beloved Country (US: African Fury). 1955: †Storm Over the Nile.

KORTY, John 1936-

American director who has done some impressive work on television since 1970, but seems not to have found the right subject to make a big impact in the cinema. But his best TV movie, *The Autobiography of Miss Jane Pittman,* aroused considerable interest when it was shown in cinemas outside America. Korty is something of a jack-of-all-trades, having worked, since beginning to make amateur

films in the early 1950s, as editor, cameraman, animator, writer, producer and director, sometimes in several different capacities on the same film. He began by making animated TV commercials; later his cartoon *Breaking the Habit,* about trying to give up smoking, was nominated for an Academy Award. His documentary film *Language of Faces* also won attention — and several honours at film festivals. Korty finally won an Academy Award for his full-length documentary *Who Are the De Bolts ... and Where Did They Get 19 Kids?* in 1977. Before this, Korty had made several interesting films, especially *Riverrun,* set in a part of California where he ran his own early one-man film laboratory, and full of haunting images of countryside and sea. These films, however, with offbeat subjects and little-known casts, did not reach wide audiences, and Korty moved into TV. His projects remained just as individual, but were now watched by millions. *The People* was a thoughtful, gentle, science-fiction film with Kim Darby, and *Go Ask Alice* a disturbing survey of teenage drug-takers. Korty won an Emmy in 1974 for *Jane Pittman,* with Cicely Tyson (also winning an Emmy), about a 110-year-old black woman, the turbulent times she has lived through and her final triumph at drinking from a water fountain previously reserved for whites. Seldom has the spirit and conviction of the civil rights movement in the 1960s been brought across with better dramatic force. In 1978, Korty made a rare foray into the commercial cinema with *Oliver's Story,* actually making this follow-up to *Love Story* more palatable than the original. But his career has not quite made the strides one had hoped for since the mid-1970s. Korty is plainly determined to go his own way; since 1985, he has been firmly entrenched in the field of mainly high-quality, concerned TV movies.

*1963: *Language of Faces (D). 1965: Crazy Quilt. 1967: Funnyman. 1968: Riverrun. 1969: *Breaking the Habit (c). 1970: *Imogen Cunningham — Photographer (D). 1971: The People (TV. 1973: Go Ask Alice (TV). Class of '63 (TV). 1974: The Autobiography of Miss Jane Pittman (TV GB: cinemas). 1975: The Silence (GB: TV). 1976: Farewell to Manzanar (TV). Alex and the Gypsy (later Love and Other Crimes). 1977: Who Are the De Bolts... And Where Did They Get 19 Kids? (D). 1978: Oliver's Story. 1980: A Christmas Without Snow (TV). 1983: The Haunting Passion (TV). +Twice Upon a Time. 1984: Second Sight: A Love Story (TV). The Ewok Adventure/Caravan of Courage. 1986: A Deadly Business (TV).*

Resting Place (TV). 1987: Baby Girl Scott (TV). Eye on the Sparrow (TV). 1988: Winnie (TV). 1989: The Diane Martin Story (TV). Cast the First Stone (TV). 1990: Blind Hate (TV). A Son's Promise (TV). 1991: Long Road Home (TV). Keeping Secrets: Suzanne Somers in Her Own Story (TV). 1993: They/They Watch (TV). 1994: Getting Out (TV). 1995: Redwood Curtain (TV). 1997: Ms Scrooge (TV). 1998: Oklahoma City: A Survivor's Story.

(c) cartoon

KOSTER, Henry (Hermann Kosterlitz) 1905-1988

German-born Koster was obviously a popular man who got on well with actors. He had a deft touch with light comedy that brought pleasing, individual characteristics to the fore, and several stars, among them Deanna Durbin, James Stewart, Betty Grable, Loretta Young and Clifton Webb, were happy to have Koster behind the cameras on more than one occasion in their careers. He was a reporter and critic who began writing screenplays in 1927 and had turned director by 1932, turning out light fare in similar vein to the frolics he would later make in Hollywood. Fleeing the Nazis, he arrived in America in 1936, soon teaming up with his old producer Joe Pasternak at Universal. Koster was in on the Deanna Durbin musicals from their inception *(Three Smart Girls, 100 Men and a Girl)* and they started a run of success that lasted, with occasional hiccups — even Koster could not make Diana Barrymore an actress — until the early 1950s. Under Koster's careful direction, Deanna Durbin was fresh, perky and attractive and the six films she made with him contain most of her best work, topped by the hilariously crazy *It Started with Eve,* with its unlikely pairing of Durbin and Charles Laughton. In 1943, Koster moved across to M-G-M, to make musicals with June Allyson (two; he also directed her much later in the remake of *My Man Godfrey)* and Margaret O'Brien (two), before spending the major part of his Hollywood career with Twentieth Century-Fox. Besides more musicals, there are several comedies of considerable, if slightly fey charm: *Come to the Stable, The Luck of the Irish, The Bishop's Wife* (a lovely family film, funny and touching by turns) and *Harvey,* the latter with James Stewart as the fuddled alcoholic with an invisible six-foot white rabbit for a friend. Koster and Stewart teamed again, to great effect, on the more serious *No Highway,* with Stewart as the boffin convinced that a passenger plane will crack up after it has flown a certain number of hours. Koster captured the rising tension to great effect.

On location in Prague, Ted **Kotcheff** tries to make a point to muscleman star Dolph Lundgren for *The Shooter.*

There was also a pleasing series of films with Clifton Webb, even if they did not quite give us Webb at his waspish best. With the advent of *The Robe,* Koster lost the spring in his step and seemed overtaken by staidness and solemnity. Of the later films, only the underrated remake of *My Man Godfrey* gives anything like the carefree pleasure of the Koster of old. He married Hollywood actress Peggy Moran.

1932: Das Abenteuer der Thea Roland (GB: Thea Roland). 1933: Das hässliche Mädchen. Peter. 1934: Kleine Mutti/Little Mother. 1935: Katharina die Letzte/Catherine the Last. Das Tagebuch der Geliebten/Marie Baschkirtzeff. 1936:

Three Smart Girls. 1937: 100 Men and a Girl. 1938: The Rage of Paris. 1939: Three Smart Girls Grow Up. First Love. 1940: Spring Parade. 1941: It Started with Eve. 1942: Between Us Girls. 1944: Music for Millions. 1946: Two Sisters from Boston. 1947: The Unfinished Dance. The Bishop's Wife. 1948: The Luck of the Irish. 1949: The Inspector-General. Come to the Stable. 1950: Wabash Avenue. Harvey. My Blue Heaven. 1951: Elopement. No Highway (US: No Highway in the Sky). Mr Belvedere Rings the Bell. 1952: †O. Henry's Full House (GB: Full House). Stars and Stripes Forever (GB: Marching Along). My Cousin Rachel. 1953: The Robe. 1954:

Desirée. 1955: A Man Called Peter. The Virgin Queen. Good Morning, Miss Dove. 1956: The Power and the Prize. D-Day the Sixth of June. 1957: My Man Godfrey. 1958: Fraulein. 1959: The Naked Maja. 1960: The Story of Ruth. 1961: Flower Dram Song. 1962: Mr Hobbs Takes a Vacation. 1963: Take Her, She's Mine. 1965: Dear Brigitte... The Singing Nun.

KOTCHEFF, Ted (William Theodore Kotcheff) 1931-

I find myself in somewhat of a quandary over this Canadian director, since I have liked almost all his work from 1962 to 1982 save the film which is generally acknowledged to be his best — *The Apprenticeship of Duddy Kravitz*. Generally speaking, though, Kotcheff's films are anything but bland, in an age of blandness, and remain entertaining even when, which is quite often, they have something to say as well. After serving his apprenticeship in Canadian TV, Kotcheff came to Britain in the late 1950s and broke through to feature films with *Tiara Tahiti*. Although his direction here is a shade deliberate, it brings across well the contrasting personalities of James Mason and John Mills as they wage a class war on a paradise island. The most memorable of Kotcheff's other films are *Outback*, a black and brutal thriller set in Australia with nature red in tooth and claw; *Fun with Dick and Jane*, with George Segal and Jane Fonda teaming up delightfully as a married couple who take to robbery to beat their overdraft; *North Dallas Forty*, a penetrating study of the bone-shaking life of an American professional footballer, with a stand-out performance from G.D. Spradlin as the coach; and *First Blood*, a well crafted box-office hit for Sylvester Stallone that led to the Rambo films. Subsequently, *Last River to Cross* and *The Butcher's Boy* were announced for Kotcheff but not made by him, although they might have been better than most of the films he has made in the 1980s and 1990s and certainly better than his shameful contributions to the soft-porn 'Red Shoe Diaries' in the early 1990s. Not that much better than the rest of that dismal run, but a huge hit at the box-office was *Weekend at Bernie's*, a scatty black comedy whose success Kotcheff failed to repeat in an embarrassing sequel. Certainly a varied career: perhaps too varied in recent times.

1962: $Tiara Tahiti. 1965: Life at the Top. 1968: Two Gentlemen Sharing. 1970: Outback/Wake in Fright. 1973: Billy Two Hats. 1974: The Apprenticeship of Duddy Kravitz. 1976: Fun with Dick and Jane. 1978: Who is Killing the Great Chefs of Europe? (GB: Too Many Chefs). 1979: North Dallas Forty. 1981: Captured! (later Split Image). 1982: First Blood. 1983: Uncommon Valor. 1985: Joshua Then and Now. 1987: Switching Channels. 1988: Winter People. 1989: Weekend at Bernie's. 1992: Folks! 1993: Red Shoe Diaries 3: Another Woman's Lipstick. Weekend at Bernie's II. 1994: The Shooter. 1995: +Red Shoe Diaries 5: Weekend Pass. A Family of Cops (TV). 1996: Hidden Assassin. A Husband, a Wife and a Lover/A Strange Affair. 1997: Dog Eat Dog. 1999: The Populist.

$ As William T Kotcheff

KRAMER, Stanley 1913-

Poor Stanley Kramer's reputation has taken such a nosedive in recent times that this New York-born film-maker has even been deliberately excluded from some books on major film-makers while obscure cultist darlings take his place. Such demotion is undeserved, even if only *Oklahoma Crude* of Kramer's post-1960 films has anything like the strength of his earlier work. Kramer was an enterprising independent producer *(Champion, Home of the Brave, The Men, High Noon)*, whose successes encouraged Columbia to come to an arrangement with him for making low-budget, high-prestige films. Most of these films are quite unusual —one remembers the sharpness of *The Sniper*, the zaniness of *The 5000 Fingers of Dr T.* (ruined by front-office interference), the delightful two-hander *The Four Poster* (a farewell to the partnership, and marriage, of Lilli Palmer and Rex Harrison) and the warmth and humour of *My Six Convicts*. Many of these though, received only a restricted release, and all of Kramer's productions for Columbia with the exception of *The Caine Mutiny* lost money. Freed by Columbia, Kramer struck out on his own as a director with *Not As a Stranger* (fine stuff, the cinematic equivalent of a good read); *The Pride and the Passion* (silly, miscast and dull); and *The Defiant Ones*, a solidly acted early indictment of colour prejudice, exciting, affecting and far less embarrassing than Kramer's later Poitier film *Guess Who's Coming to Dinner*. In 1961, after the elephantine but intermittently compelling *Judgment at Nuremburg*, Kramer was given a special Oscar for 'consistently high quality in film making' but it seemed to affect his own judgment. There were one or two semi-successful 'message' pictures (as producer only) that did badly at the box-office, the vastly overblown – although again with some enjoyable moments – *Ship of Fools* and *It's a Mad, Mad, Mad, Mad World; Guess Who's Coming to Dinner*, a painfully naive fable almost totally redeemed by the sincerity of Katharine Hepburn and Spencer Tracy; and then a series of overheated disasters, relieved only by the relative crispness, sparseness and power of *Oklahoma Crude*.

1955: Not As a Stranger. 1956: The Pride and the Passion. 1958: The Defiant Ones. 1959: On the Beach. 1960: Inherit the Wind. 1961: Judgment at Nuremberg. 1963: It's a Mad, Mad, Mad, Mad World. 1965: Ship of Fools. 1967: Guess Who's Coiming to Dinner. 1969: The Secret of Santa Vittoria. 1970: RPM. 1971: Bless the Beasts and Children. 1973: Oklahoma Crude. 1976: The Domino Killings (released 1978). 1979: The Runner Stumbles.

KUBRICK, Stanley 1928-

Immensely talented American film-maker with a sure visual sense. Perhaps, though, led astray by the (deserved) success of *Spartacus*, Kubrick's later films are the best possible proof that bigger does not necessarily mean better. Since the mid-1960s, Kubrick has become a maker of films for effect and has lost much of the narrative drive that once distinguished his work. A staff photographer with an American magazine until he was 22, Kubrick made three shorts before his first independent feature venture, *Fear and Desire*, featuring Virginia Leith, who later went on to a middling career with Twentieth Century-Fox. His next but one, *The Killing*, was a fascinating mood piece about a racetrack robbery, full of tension and detail and with terrific supporting performances from Elisha Cook and Marie Windsor. *Paths of Glory*, an

Stanley **Kramer** in the days of his greatest success. Here he gets behind the camera for *Inherit the Wind*.

Stanley **Kubrick** (right) on a very chilly-looking location for shooting the final sequences in *The Shining*.

absorbing and bitter, if slightly overrated, World War I story, projected him towards financial independence, an advance consolidated by *Spartacus*, the only occasion Kubrick has really ventured into the Hollywood mainstream, and his outstanding film. In fact, *Spartacus* is a top film in its category by anyone's standards, an exciting, moving, brilliantly photographed spectacle whose characters are vividly brought to life as real human beings. Kubrick had never shown special interest before (or afterwards) in people as opposed to things (even the mechanics of the robbery are studied in more detail than its participants in *The Killing*, but in *Spartacus* this facet of his personality is triumphantly reversed. Literately written dialogue (by Dalton Trumbo) is seized on by the actors to create a touching series of portraits of people, all with strengths and weaknesses, and especially by Charles Laughton, conveying more by the movement of an eyelid than some actors could in an entire film, although the film's best-supporting-actor Oscar went to Peter Ustinov. There was a rather joyless version of *Lolita* and the spasmodically hilarious *Dr Strangelove*, then Kubrick struck out into the realms of grandiosity. *2001* is an imposing piece of science-fiction with a serious lack of story development which makes it seem tedious when seen today. *A Clockwork Orange* was ugly and unnecessary. *Barry Lyndon*, on the other hand, was undeniably beautiful, although little else and very long: a film in a vacuum. Kubrick's *The Shining*, the best of his later films, is also too long, but stronger on atmosphere and performances, and has an intensity missing from the disappointing 1987 war film *Full Metal Jacket*. With gaps ever widening between Kubrick films, it looks as

though *Eyes Wide Shut*, his most recent to date, may well be his last.

*1951: *Day of the Fight* (D). *Flying Padre* (D). 1953: *The Seafarers* (D). Fear and Desire. 1955: Killer's Kiss. 1956: The Killing. 1957: Paths of Glory. 1960: Spartacus. 1962: Lolita. 1963: Dr Strangelove, or: How I Learned to Stop Worrying and Love the Bomb. 1968: 2001: a Space Odyssey. 1971: A Clockwork Orange. 1975: Barry Lyndon. 1980: The Shining. 1987: Full Metal Jacket. 1998: Eyes Wide Shut.*

KULIK, Buzz (Seymour Kulik) 1922-1999
Kubrick or Kulik? Both come from New York City and started working in films in the early 1950s, but there the comparison ends. Counting his individual TV episodes, Kulik has five times as many screen stories to his credit. The odds are that a retrospective of his credits would be less imposing than those of Kubrick but perhaps more entertaining. Typically, he has shown himself at his most efficient with fast-moving private-eye thrillers, but generally his work just misses that extra edge that would carry it into the top class; a possible exception being his TV movie *Brian's Song*, about a young football player dying of cancer, which has a perceptive script and James Caan in his only TV film in the leading role. From 1954, Kulik directed dozens of episodes in such series as *Perry Mason, Have Gun – Will Travel, Naked City, The Defenders* and *Twilight Zone*. He opened his cinema account in 1961 with *The Explosive Generation*, aimed at the still-buoyant teenage market but with some care in the screenplay (and direction) of a story about a teacher kicked out for teaching sex education to his teenage students. From then on,

although he concentrated on films for a few years, his output is less distinctive. *Warning Shot* and *Shamus* are serviceable thrillers, though they might well be TV movies, while *Riot* is a striking, violent but impersonal prison story. Numerous series and 22 TV movies later, Kulik was still having occasional tries at cinema films. Obviously he felt he could have been a success in the medium, but it now seems too late for him to hit the big-time. Of his films for television, *Vanished, Bad Ronald, The Lindbergh Kidnapping Case* and *Ziegfeld: the Man and his Women* are the most watchable. Kulik, for all his proficiency, never quite developed a personal style. At least one can hardly say that about his predecessor in the alphabet. The last decade of his busy working life also included such epic TV mini-series as *From Here to Eternity* (1979), *George Washington* (1984) and, in 1989, *Around the World in 80 Days*.

1961: The Explosive Generation. 1963: The Yellow Canary. Sergeant Ryker (TV. Released to cinemas in 1968). 1964: Ready for the People (TV). 1966: Warning Shot. 1968: Villa Rides! Riot. 1970: Vanished (TV). 1971: Brian's Song (TV). Owen Marshal, Counselor at Law (TV). To Find a Man. 1972: Shamus. 1973: Incident on a Dark Street (TV). Pioneer Woman (TV). 1974: Remember When? (TV). Bad Ronald (TV). 1975: Cage Without a Key (TV). Matt Helm (TV). Babe (TV). 1976: The Lindbergh Kidnapping Case (TV). The Feather and Father Gang (TV). 1977: Corey: for the People (TV). Kill Me If You Can/The Caryl Chessman Story (TV). 1978: Ziegfeld: the Man and His Women (TV). 1980: The Hunter. 1981: The Pursuit of D.B. Cooper/Pursuit (TV). 1986: Women of Valor (TV). 1987: Her Secret Life/One for the Dancer/Code Name: Dancer (TV). 1988: Too Young the Hero (TV). 1991: Miles from Nowhere (TV).

KUROSAWA, Akira 1910-1998
The titles of this Japanese director's films mean more to the western filmgoer than those of anyone else from Japan. In his own country, he may now be rated below Oshima, Ozu, Mizoguchi, Ichikawa and even others, and his reputation eclipsed by the rise of younger talent. In commercial terms, however, no Japanese director has ever made films that the general public in other countries found to be as entertaining as Kurosawa's. His samurai 'westerns' were copied not only in America (which made *The Magnificent Seven* out of *Seven Samurai* and *The Outrage* out of *Rashomon*) but also in Italy, where Sergio

Leone made *A Fistful of Dollars* from *Yojimbo*, and Kurosawa's style was the biggest single influence on the spaghetti western. He had come into the business after replying to an advertisement for assistant directors and in five years (by 1941) had worked his way through the ranks from dogsbody to screenwriter. After directing action sequences for two of the films of Kajiro Yamamoto (1910-1993), Kurosawa decided it was time to direct his own films. Almost immediately, he demonstrated his flair for thrilling action scenes and in 1950 *Rashomon*, with its powerful atmosphere and striking visual effects, made him a name outside Japan. The samurai films began with *Seven Samurai* in 1954, and Kurosawa's success in the genre continued with *Throne of Blood* (his version of *Macbeth*), *The Hidden Fortress*, *Yojimbo*, *Sanjuro* and *Kagemusha*. These are fiercely-charging, uncompromising films. Smiles are rare and savagery abundant. Toshiro Mifune is usually at their heart. Yet there was a quieter side to Kurosawa's nature, expressed most succinctly in *Living*, *The Lower Depths* and especially the medical drama *Red Beard*. These films express a concern for the quality of life; oppressed people are never far from Kurosawa's mind, even in the samurai films, and *Dodes 'Ka-Den* is an extraordinary allegory about them. One of his least well-known but most enjoyable films is *The Bad Sleep Well*, a Japanese transposition of an Ed McBain detective novel. Happily, a suicide attempt in 1970 was soon safely in the past and, in 1975, Kurosawa's epic tale of adventure in turn-of-the-century Siberia, *Dersu Uzala*, beautifully photographed in colour, took the Oscar as best foreign film, an honour that had surprisingly eluded him until then. He died following a stroke.

1943: Sugata Sanshiro/Judo Saga. 1944: Ichiban Utsukushiku/The Most Beautiful. Zoku Sugata Sanshiro/Judo Saga II. 1945: Torano-o/They Who Tread on the Tiger's Tail. 1946: †Asu o Tsukuru Hitobito/Those Who Make Tomorrow. Waga Seishu ni kui Nashi/No Regrets for Lost Youth. 1947: Subarashiki Nichiyobi (GB: Wonderful Sunday. US: One Wonderful Sunday). 1948: Yoidore Tenshi/Drunken Angel. 1949: Shizukamaru Ketto/The Silent Duel. 1950: Skyanduru/Shubun/Scandal. Rashomon (US: In the Woods). 1951: Hakuchi/The Idiot. 1952: Ikiru (GB: Living. US: To Live/Doomed). 1954: Seven Samurai. 1955: Ikimono no Kiroku/I Live in Fear. 1957: Kumonosu-Jo (GB: Throne of Blood. US: Cobweb Castle). Donzoko/The Lower Depths. 1958. Kakushi Toride no San-Akunin/The Hidden Fortress. 1960: Warui Yatsu Hodo Yoku Nemuru (US: The Bad Sleep Well). 1961: Yojimbo (US: The Bodyguard). 1962: Sanjuro. 1963: Tengoku to Jigoku (GB: High and Low. US: Heaven and Hell). 1965: Akahige/Red Beard. 1970. Dodes 'Ka-Den. 1975: Dersu Uzala. 1980: Kagemusha/The Shadow Warrior. 1985: Ran. 1990: Akira Kurosawa's Dreams. 1991: Rhapsody in August. 1993: Madadayo.

L

LA CAVA, Gregory 1892-1952

American director who handled comedies and weepies with equal facility while the genres were at their most popular, in the 1930s. But, with the coming of the next decade, La Cava quickly faded from the movie scene. He had begun in films as an animator, working with Walter Lantz, who would later find fame with the Woody Woodpecker cartoons. La Cava began to direct live-action films from 1922, although some people unkindly suggested that they were still constructed like cartoons. La Cava soon proved himself in the field of comedy, however, directing W.C. Fields in the marvellous *So's Your Old Man*, which Fields would later rework as *You're Telling Me*. This is the story in which he plays a wacky inventor who meets up with a princess. Director and star re-teamed for the second and last time on *Running Wild*, which has Fields as a henpecked man hypnotized into becoming the dominant kind. It suffers more than most of Fields' silent films from lack of dialogue and is, incidentally, remarkably similar to the British comedy *Will Any Gentleman?*, made 25 years later. Came the 1930s and La Cava trotted from RKO to Paramount to M-G-M, directing epic Fannie Hurst tear-jerkers and screwball farces by turns. The most tear-drenched of the soapers is probably *Symphony of Six Million*, with Irene Dunne, and undeniably the best of the comedies is *My Man Godfrey*, with Carole Lombard and William Powell, about a madcap millionaire and his equally manic family who engage a tramp as their butler. In 1937, the New York film critics voted La Cava director of the year for his handling of *Stage Door*. Katharine Hepburn, Ginger Rogers, Lucille Ball and Eve Arden all sparkled in this acid dissection of life in a theatrical boarding house for ladies. Around this time, it was said that La Cava was directing many of his scenes in 'ad lib' fashion, encouraging his players to enact the scenes with whatever came into their heads to supplement the dialogue provided. He had also become the drinking companion of the set led by John Barrymore and W.C. Fields, and subsequent La Cava films were delayed or abandoned because of his 'recurrent

Akira **Kurosawa** (left) discusses progress on *Kagemusha* with his two executive producers — the prominent American directors Francis Ford Coppola and George Lucas (both *qv*).

illnesses'. La Cava and Miss Dunne combined again twice in the early 1940s, but the inspiration had gone, the time had gone, and the films were both clinkers. So was his next film, *Living in a Big Way*, which followed after a gap of several years, and ended his cinema career. He was nominated for an Oscar in two consecutive years, in 1936 and 1937.

1917: **Der Kaptain's Valet. *Der Kaptain is Examined for Insurance. 1920: *Judge Rummy in Bear Facts. 1922: His Nibs. 1924: Restless Wives. The New School-teacher. 1925: Womanhandled. 1926: Let's Get Married. Say It Again. So's Your Old Man. 1927: Paradise for Two. Running Wild. The Gay Defender. Tell It to Sweeney. 1928: Feel My Pulse. Half a Bride. 1929: Big News. Saturday's Children. 1930: His First Command. 1931: Smart Woman. Laugh and Get Rich. 1932: Symphony of Six Million (GB: Melody of Life). The Age of Consent. The Half-Naked Truth. 1933: Gabriel Over the White House. Bed of Roses. Gallant Lady. 1934: The Affairs of Cellini. What Every Woman Knows. 1935: Private Worlds. She Married Her Boss. 1936: My Man Godfrey. 1937: Stage Door. 1939: Fifth Avenue Girl. 1940: Primrose Path. 1941: Unfinished Business. 1942: Lady in a Jam. 1947: Living in a Big Way.*

LACHMAN, Harry 1886-1975

A painter who found himself drawn into making films, American-born Lachman became a globe-trotting director for 15 years before he tired of the medium and returned to life as a painter. During his stay in the Hollywood of the 1930s he did direct one masterly Laurel and Hardy comedy, *Our Relations*, as well as the notable *Dante's Inferno*. From his middle twenties Lachman, although born in Illinois, had lived in Paris, drawing and painting, gradually gaining a reputation as one of the more interesting post-Impressionists and eventually getting exhibitions of his work. In the early 1920s, though, to earn the living he was only barely scraping through art, Lachman took a job as a set designer at the Nice Studios. Three years later Rex Ingram (Reginald Hitchcock, 1892-1950), the Irish-born director of such silent films as *The Four Horsemen of the Apocalypse* (1921), *The Prisoner of Zenda* (1922) and *Scaramouche* (1923) and a keen spare-time artist and sculptor, noted Lachman's eye for composition on film, and engaged him as assistant director on his *Mare Nostrum* (1926). It was Ingram who encouraged Lachman to go to England in 1927 as Technical Supervisor at Elstree

Studios, and he swiftly became one of that studio's more interesting directors. After a spell directing films in France, Lachman accepted an offer to return to his native country and direct for Fox. It was for this company that he made *Dante's Inferno*, which featured a young Spencer Tracy, but is remembered for its vivid, seething, writhing depiction of Hell; almost any frame would be a worthy addition to one of Lachman's exhibitions. The film also had a spectacular fire, touched off by a whirling Spanish dancer played by Rita Hayworth (then still Rita Cansino). There was nothing very spectacular, though, about the rest of Lachman's Hollywood career. It was mostly 'B' pictures, Charlie Chans and the like. After a disappointing attempt at a life of Edgar Allan Poe, Lachman decided to call it a day. Today, his work still hangs in the galleries and museums of several different countries, including, of course, America and France.

1928: *†The Compulsory Husband. Weekend Wives. 1929: Under the Greenwood Tree. 1930: Song of Soho. The Yellow Mask. 1931: The Love Habit. The Outsider. 1932: Aren't We All? Insult. Down Our Street. La belle marinière. Mistigri. La couturière de Laneville. 1933: Face in the Sky. Paddy the Next Best Thing. 1934: Nada mas que una mujer. Baby Take a Bow. †George White's Scandals. 1935: Dressed to Thrill. Dante's Inferno. 1936: Charlie Chan at the Circus. The Man Who Lived Twice. Our Relations. 1937: The Devil is Driving. It Happened in Hollywood (GB: Once a Hero). 1938: No Time to Marry. 1940: They Came by Night. Murder Over New York. 1941: Dead Men Tell. Charlie Chan in Rio. 1942: Castle in the Desert. Dr Renault's Secret. The Loves of Edgar Allan Poe.*

LAMONT, Charles 1895-1993

San Francisco-born Lamont spent 18 years at Universal directing dozens of medium-budget films, with a few excursions over to Republic. It's hard today to see what qualities the studio found in his work, since very few of his films are more than moderate. There are post-war action films of little character, jitterbugging teen musicals with Donald O'Connor, Peggy Ryan and Gloria Jean, some awful sword, sand and sandal stuff (unkindly referred to by some as boobs, bangles and beads movies) and broad, lowbrow comedies with Abbott and Costello, Ma and Pa Kettle, Joan Davis and Judy Canova. None of them is among the best work of the artists concerned. Yet Lamont had been in regular employ as a director since

1923, after switching from acting. He made shorts for Mack Sennett, Buster Keaton, Harry Langdon, Lupino Lane and Al Christie, as well as 'show business' shorts, light documentaries, in fact almost anything, it seems, that he could lay his hands on. He is also credited with discovering Shirley Temple in 1932. He broke into features, after seeming destined to spend his career as a short-subject director, by making low-budget thrillers for the poverty-row Chesterfield company — 16 of them in two years. After more shoe-string work for Progressive, Republic and Grand National, Lamont was hired by Universal in 1939, his light-hearted approach to life being reflected in almost all his films for them. He was, however, a craftsman who always brought his films in on time and inside the budget, even when dealing with such recalcitrant artists as the comedian Lou Costello (the fat half of the Abbott and Costello team) from whom, by all accounts, Lamont would stand very little nonsense. Some of his films are revered by some critics who have detected tongue-in-cheek undertones to such turkeys as *Slave Girl* and *Salome, Where She Danced*. However, if you are looking for gems in Lamont's career, then *The Merry Monahans* is the best of the O'Connor musicals (brought to a halt by O'Connor's army service), with zippy numbers and touches of pathos nicely under-played by O'Connor, Jack Oakie, Ann Blyth and Peggy Ryan; *The Runaround* is a well-paced action-comedy about a runaway heiress and the two beefy but none-too-bright guys hired to track her down; and *Curtain Call at Cactus Creek* offers O'Connor again in an at times wildly funny romp about a group of travelling players in the old west joined by a gang of outlaws, with priceless supporting performances from Walter Brennan, Eve Arden and Vincent Price. By the end of his career at Universal, as the studio's long double-bill period neared its end, Lamont seemed to have done about every routine chore except direct a comedy with Francis the Talking Mule. So, just for good measure, he did one — *Francis in the Haunted House* — as his final film assignment for the studio. But Donald O'Connor had at long last said 'no more' to the series and, even with Mickey Rooney as the mule's master, the formula was played out. So was Lamont's long film career. He died from pneumonia at 98.

1923: **Hollywood Bound. 1924: *Almost a Husband. *Big Game. *Built on a Bluff. Clear the Way. A Diving Fool. *Make It Snappy. *The Midnight Watch. *Raising Cain. Sailing Along. *Tin Can*

Alley. *Tourists de Luxe. 1925: *Accidents Can Happen. *Al's Troubles. *Baby Be Good. *Cupid's Victory. *Dog Daze. *Educating Buster. *In Deep. *Helpful Al. *Love Sick. *Maid in Morocco. Married Neighbors. Piping Hot. *Paging a Wife. *Puzzled by Crosswords. *A Rough Party. A Winning Pair. 1926: *Bachelor Babies. *Bear Cats. *Close Shaves. *Excess Baggage. *Going Crazy. *Her Ambition. *Jane's Honeymoons. *My Kid. *Open House. *Open Spaces. *Sea Scamps. *Thanks for the Boat Ride. *By George! *A Yankee Doodle Duke. 1927: *Atta Baby. *Brunettes Prefer Gentlemen. *Funny Face. *Grandpa's Boy. *A Half-Pint Hero. *Kid Tricks. *Live News. *Monty of the Mounties. *Naughty Boy. *Scared Silly. *Shamrock Alley. *She's a Boy. *Wedding Yells. *Who's Afraid? 1928: *Angel Eyes. *Chilly Days. *Circus Blues. *Come to Papa. *Companionate Service. *Follow Teacher. *Girlies Behave. *The Gloom Chaser. *Hot Luck. *Kid Hayseed. *Ladies Preferred. *Making Whoopee. *Misplaced Husbands. *Navy Beans. *No Fare. *The Quiet Worker. *Wildcat Valley. 1929: *Auntie's Mistake. *The Crazy Nut. *Fire Proof. *The Fixer. *Ginger Snaps. *Helter Skelter. *Joy Tonic. *Only Her Husband. *Sole Support. *Top Speed. 1931: *All Excited. *Divorce à la Carte. *Fast and Furious. *The Gossipy Plumber. *Hollywood Half Backs. *Hot and Bothered. *Models and Wives. *One Hundred Dollars. *Out-Stepping. 1932: *Foiled Again. *The Hollywood Handicap. *Hollywood Runaround. *Hollywood Kids. *The Marriage War. *The Pie-Covered Wagon. *Running Hollywood. *War Babies. 1933: *The Big Squeal. *Blue Blackbirds. *Git Along, Little Wifie. *Glad Rags to Riches. *Keyhole Katie. *Kid 'n Hollywood. *The Kids' Last Fight. *Trimmed in Furs. *Merrily Yours. *A Pair of Socks. *Polly-Tix in Washington. *Techno-Crazy. *Two Black Crows in Africa. 1934: *Allez Oop. *Educating Papa. *Managed Money. *No Sleep on the Deep. *Pardon My Pups. *Plumbing for Gold. *Hello, Prosperity. *Half Baked Relations. *The Gold Ghost. *Palooka from Paducah. The Curtain Falls. Tomorrow's Youth. 1935: *The Captain Hits the Ceiling. *Choose Your Partners. *His Last Fling. Knockout Drops. *Tramp Tramp Tramp. *Alimony Aches. *Restless Knights. *One Run Elmer. *Hayseed Romance. *Tars and Stripes. *The E Flat Man. Son of Steel. The World Accuses. False Pretenses. Gigolette (GB: Night Club). A Shot in the Dark. The Girl Who Came Back. Circumstantial Evidence. Happiness C.O.D. The Lady in Scarlet. 1936: *Grand Slam Opera. *Oh,

Duchess! *Three on a Limb. *Knee Action. Ring Around the Moon. Little Red School House (GB: Schoolboy Penitentiary). Below the Deadline. August Week-End. The Dark Hour. Lady Luck. Bulldog Edition (GB: Lady Reporter). Lucky Corrigan. 1937: *Jail Bait. *Ditto. *Love Nest on Wheels. *The Wrong Miss Right. *Calling All Doctors. *He Done His Duty. *Sailor Maid. *Community Sing (and others in this series, through 1938 and 1939). *Fiddling Around. *Playing the Ponies. *My Little Feller. *New News. Wallaby Jim of the Islands. 1938: *A Doggone Mix-Up. International Crime. Shadows Over Shanghai. Slander House. Cipher Bureau. The Long Shot. 1939: Verbena Trágica. Pride of the Navy. Panama Patrol. Inside Information. Unexpected Father (GB: Sandy Takes a Bow). Little Accident. 1940: Oh, Johnny, How You Can Love! Love, Honor and Oh Baby! Sandy is a Lady. Give Us Wings. 1941: San Antonio Rose. Sing Another Chorus. Moonlight in Hawaii. Melody Lane. Road Agent. 1942: Don't Get Personal. You're Telling Me. Almost Married. Hi, Neighbor! Get Hep to Love (GB: She's My Lovely). When Johnny Comes Marching Home. It Comes Up Love (GB: A Date with an Angel). 1943: Top Man. Mr Big. †Hit the Ice. Fired Wife. 1944: Chip Off the Old Block. Her Primitive Man. Bowery to Broadway. The Merry Monahans. 1945: Salome, Where She Danced. That's the Spirit. Frontier Gal (GB: The Bride Wasn't Willing). 1946: She Wrote the Book. The Runaround. 1947: Slave Girl. 1948: The Untamed Breed. Ma and Pa Kettle. 1949: Bagdad. Ma and Pa Kettle Go to Town (GB: Going to Town). I Was a Shoplifter. Curtain Call at Cactus Creek (GB: Take the Stage). 1950: Abbott and Costello in the Foreign Legion. 1951: Abbott and Costello Meet the Invisible Man. Comin' Round the Mountain. Flame of Araby. 1952: Abbott and Costello Meet Captain Kidd. Ma and Pa Kettle on Vacation (GB: Ma and Pa Kettle Go to Paris). 1953: Abbott and Costello Go to Mars. Abbott and Costello Meet Dr Jekyll and Mr Hyde. 1954: Ma and Pa Kettle at Home. Untamed Heiress. Ricochet Romance. 1955: Carolina Cannonball. Abbott and Costello Meet the Keystone Kops. Lay That Rifle Down. Abbott and Costello Meet the Mummy. 1956: The Kettles in the Ozarks. Francis in the Haunted House.

LANDERS, Lew

(Louis Friedlander) 1901-1962
In 20 years, Landers galloped his way through around 130 films, almost none

of them exceeding 80 minutes in length and most of them under 70. They have nearly all vanished into the mists of time now. Night waitresses in border cafés; Boston Blackie smashing the rackets; girls from Havana and La Conga nights; redheads from Manhattan and murders in Times Square; enemy agents, conspiracies and The Whistler defying the law of the underworld. These were the films that you missed half of if you couldn't get the bus or underground in time. And, since Landers saw to it that they all moved at a rattling clip, you had probably missed most of the plot as well. For they were 'B' movies, every one of them, the ones that you sat through while waiting for the big film to start. It would be nice to record that Landers' output as one of the most prolific directors in the field is studded with undiscovered treasures. But either the purse-strings were too tight, or the talent too slight. A few of the bargain-basement horrors have a certain hypnotic fascination: The Raven, The Return of the Vampire, The Ghost That Walks Alone, The Mask of Diijon. Landers' methods and approach were set at the beginning of his career when, after varied early experience, this New York-born director got into making serials with Universal, the first of them, Tailspin Tommy, requiring the minimum of acting and new footage and any amount of stock shots from such early aviation successes as Hell's Angels. Landers directed four more serials (he used his real name up to and including Parole!, which has a brief early appearance by Anthony Quinn as a convict who gets stabbed in the back) before the studio moved him on to features, and he began his long conveyor-belt career. Towards the end of his film-making days, Landers became involved with all kinds of frivolities in a variety of weird colour processes, everything from SuperCinecolor to Color by the Color Corporation of America. The titles spoke for themselves: Hurricane Island, Captain Kidd and the Slave Girl, When the Redskins Rode, Last of the Buccaneers, Blue Blood, The Magic Carpet, Barbary Pirate, The Enchanted Forest, Aladdin, and His Lamp and Captain John Smith and Pochahontas. Whatever their merits, they all went like a whirlwind — as did Man in the Dark, a 3-D thriller with rollercoaster rides courtesy of cameraman Floyd Crosby. Perhaps Landers' most important film was California Conquest, with Cornel Wilde and Teresa Wright. Typically, Landers brought it in at 79 minutes. From 1955 until his early death in 1962, Landers was extremely busy in TV, turning out hour-long episodes of series within the week. Many of his TV films in the 'Kit Carson' series were shown as second-feature films outside the United States. As one studio executive once put it: 'When we had a film we wanted finished in two days, we called in Lew Landers'.

1934: *Tailspin Tommy* (serial). *The Red Rider* (serial). *The Vanishing Shadow* (serial). 1935: *The Call of the Savage* (serial). *Rustlers of Red Dog* (serial). *The Raven. Stormy.* 1936: *Parole! Without Orders. Night Waitress.* 1937: *They Wanted to Marry. You Can't Buy Luck. Border Café. The Man Who Found Himself. Flight from Glory. Living on Love. Danger Patrol.* 1938: *Condemned Women. Crashing Hollywood. Double Danger. Law of the Underworld. Smashing the Rackets. Blind Alibi. Sky Giant. Annabel Takes a Tour.* 1939: *Pacific Liner. Fixer Dugan (GB: Double Daring). Twelve Crowded Hours. The Girl and the Gambler. Bad Lands. Conspiracy.* 1940: *Ski Patrol. Honeymoon Deferred. Enemy Agent (GB: Secret Enemy). Sing, Dance, Plenty Hot (GB: Melody Girl). La Conga Nights. The Girl from Havana. Wagons Westward. Slightly Tempted.* 1941: *Lucky Devils. Ridin' on a Rainbow. Back in the Saddle. The Singing Hill. I Was a Prisoner on Devil's Island. Mystery Ship. The Stork Pays Off. Harvard, Here I Come (GB: Here I Come).* 1942: *Alias Boston Blackie. Canal Zone. The Man Who Returned to Life. Not a Ladies Man. Submarine Raider. Cadets on Parade. Atlantic Convoy. Sabotage Squad. The Boogie Man Will Get You. Smith of Minnesota. Stand By All Networks. Junior Army.* 1943: *After Midnight with Boston Blackie (GB: After Midnight). The Redhead from Manhattan. Power of the Press. Murder in Times Square. Doughboys in Ireland. The Deerslayer.* 1944: *Cowboy Canteen (GB: Close Harmony). Two-Man Submarine. Stars on Parade. Stars in Uniform. The Return of the Vampire. The Ghost That Walks Alone. The Black Parachute. U-Boat Prisoner (GB: Dangerous Mists). Swing in the Saddle (GB: Swing and Sway). I'm from Arkansas.* 1945: *Crime Inc. Power of the Whistler. Trouble Chasers. Follow That Woman. Arson Squad. The Enchanted Forest. Shadow of Terror. Tokyo Rose.* 1946: *Hot Cargo. The Mask of Diijon. A Close Call for Boston Blackie (GB: Lady of Mystery). The Truth About Murder (GB. The Lie Detector). Secrets of a Sorority Girl (GB: Secret of Linda Hamilton). Death Valley.* 1947: *Danger Street. Seven Keys to Baldpate. Under the Tonto Rim. Thunder Mountain. Devil Ship. The Son of Rusty.* 1948: *My Dog Rusty. Inner Sanctum.*

Adventures of Gallant Bess. 1949: *Stagecoach Kid. Law of the Barbary Coast. *I Found a Dog. Air Hostess. Barbary Pirate. Davy Crockett — Indian Scout (GB: Indian Scout).* 1950: *Dynamite Pass. Girls' School (GB: Dangerous Inheritance). Tyrant of The Sea. State Penitentiary. Beauty on Parade. Last of the Buccaneers. Chain Gang. Revenue Agent.* 1951: *Blue Blood. When the Redskins Rode. A Yank in Korea (GB: Letter from Korea). The Big Gusher. Hurricane Island. The Magic Carpet. Jungle Manhunt.* 1952: *Aladdin and His Lamp. Jungle Jim in the Forbidden Land. California Conquest. Arctic Flight.* 1953: *Torpedo Alley. Tangier Incident. Run for the Hills. Man in the Dark. Captain John Smith and Pocahontas (GB: Burning Arrows).* 1954: *Captain Kidd and the Slave Girl.* 1956: *The Cruel Tower.* 1958: *Hot Rod Gang (GB: Fury Unleashed).* 1962: *Terrified!*

Bearded directors are a popular breed in today's Hollywood. Here John **Landis** hides behind the whiskers just after making his reputation on *The Blues Brothers*.

LANDIS, John 1950-

Irreverence is the stock-in-trade of this American director, an ex-mailboy with Twentieth Century-Fox, whose sole aim at first seemed to be to stuff as many outrageous ideas into his films as possible. Sex, violence, four-letter words, lavatorial humour, car crashes and lowbrow satire all figure strongly in his early armoury. By and large, his films have been tremendously successful at the box-office, although one gets the idea that, if Landis were to make a film in 3-D, his first idea would be to have the characters throw up over the audience. *Schlock*, his first film, was horror satire with Landis himself as an ape-man and, after a gap, he followed it with *Kentucky Fried Movie*, off-off Broadway/late night TV skits transferred to the big screen with one or two nice ideas amid the manure. There were then two films with tubby John Belushi, a kind of scatological, latter-day Lou Costello destined to die at 33 — *National Lampoon's Animal House*, whose standard of humour matched the loutish students it depicted, and *The Blues Brothers*, a cataclysmic orgy of destruction in which Belushi and his lean partner, Dan Aykroyd, made their bid to be the anarchic, adult-audience Bud and Lou of the modern era. Full of senseless four-letter dialogue and tiresome violence up to the half-way mark, the film does improve as it goes on. Much as one might admire the stunt co-ordination work of Gary McLarty when the cars start crashing, one has to question whether this sort of farce should ever run 133 minutes and cost 30 million dollars. Landis' most impressive film to date for special effects has been *An American Werewolf in London*, a jokey horror film that's even funnier than it thinks it is, but has a really splendid transformation sequence and some enjoyable *homage* to the B-movie lycanthropy genre, even if still a bit strong on gore and full of non-sequiturs. 1983 was a landmark year for Landis. It was the year in which he made his best film, *Trading Places*, a bright, zesty comedy about a change of identities in the business world, but also the year of his omnibus project, *The Twilight Zone*. During filming of Landis' own segment, a helicopter crash killed actor Vic Morrow and two child actors. Landis was found not guilty of involuntary manslaughter after a lengthy trial, but still subjected to several lawsuits. Picking up the threads of his career, Landis began well with *Into the Night*, but after that the comedies got worse and worse, apart from the enjoyable *Coming to America*. *Innocent Blood* was a formula vampire spoof, but somehow Landis' reputation has continued to rise in spite of the spotty quality of his work.

1972: *Schlock*. 1977: *Kentucky Fried Movie*. 1978: *National Lampoon's Animal House*. 1980: *The Blues Brothers*. 1981: *An American Werewolf in London*. 1982: *Coming Soon* (TV). 1983: *Trading Places*. *The Twilight Zone* (GB: *Twilight Zone — The Movie*). 1985: *Into the Night*. *Spies Like Us*. 1986: *¡Three Amigos! Amazon Women on the Moon*. 1988: *Coming to America*. 1991: *Oscar*. 1992: *Innocent Blood*. 1994: *Beverly Hills Cop III*. 1996: *The Stupids*. 1998: *Blues Brothers 2000*. 1999: *Susan's Plan*.

LANFIELD, Sidney 1898-1972

Television's gain in 1953 was certainly Hollywood's loss. Lanfield's loss, too, since nothing this Chicago-born director did in his TV career between 1953 and 1965, when he retired, measured up to his work for the cinema. Schooled in slapstick, Lanfield proved only a little below the top class as a director of comedies and musicals. Once a musician in jazz clubs and burlesque, Lanfield settled in Hollywood in the mid-1920s, becoming a gag-writer for Fox and progressing to fully fledged screen stories and screenplays. Lanfield began directing in 1930, but his career really took off from 1936, when the studio put him in charge of the new series of romantic musicals starring skating champion Sonja Henie. The films, beginning with *One in a Million*, were enormously popular, as were Lanfield's concurrent comedies that cashed in on the radio 'feud' between commentator Walter Winchell and bandleader Ben Bernie. Lanfield made other musicals, including the pleasing *Swanee River*, with its lovely colour photography by Bert Glennon, while, in a departure from light-heartedness, he made *The Hound of the Baskervilles*, the first and one of the best of the Basil Rathbone Sherlock Holmes films. Lanfield quit Fox in 1940 and briefly sojourned at Columbia where he directed Rita Hayworth to stardom opposite Fred Astaire in *You'll Never Get Rich*. But, with his talent for the pacing of comedy and the placing and handling of throw-away laugh-lines, it was not surprising that he was soon handed meaty assignments with Jack Benny and Bob Hope. The Benny film is one of the zippiest comedies ever made, everything being tied up in exactly 59 minutes as Benny proves himself *The Meanest Man in the World*. The Hope vehicle *My Favorite Blonde* (the one with Madeleine Carroll and a talented penguin) was one of his biggest money-spinners. Lanfield stayed at Paramount for more movies, principally with Paulette Goddard or the suitably grateful Hope, who was still using the director as late as 1951 on *The Lemon Drop Kid*. The best of Lanfield's later films, however, was made at RKO — *Station West*, with Dick Powell, in his new tough-guy image as an 1880s Army undercover man. Lanfield had wanted Marlene Dietrich for the female lead; he got Jane Greer, who was much more suited to the part — and Agnes Moorehead, Burl Ives, Guinn 'Big Boy' Williams and Raymond Burr filled the film with character. But his TV work — almost 200 segments of various series — is disappointingly character*less*. Lanfield, who died from a heart attack, was married to actress Shirley Mason.

1926: †*Eight Cylinder Bull*. 1930: *Cheer Up and Smile*. *El Barbero de Napoleon*. 1931: *Hush Money*. *Three Girls Lost*. 1932: *Dance Team*. *Society Girl*. *Hat Check Girl* (US: *Embassy Girl*). 1933: *Broadway Bad* (GB: *Her Reputation*). 1934: *Moulin Rouge*. *The Last Gentleman*. 1935: *Hold 'Em Yale* (GB: *Uniform Lovers*). *Red Salute* (GB: *Arms and the Girl*). *King of Burlesque*. 1936: *Half Angel*. *Sing, Baby, Sing*. *One in a Million*. 1937: *Wake Up and Live*. *Thin Ice* (GB: *Lovely to Look At*). *Love and Hisses*. 1938: *Always Goodbye*. 1939: *The Hound of the Baskervilles*. *Second Honeymoon*. *Swanee River*. 1941: *You'll Never Get Rich*. 1942: *The Lady Has Plans*. *My Favourite Blonde*. 1943: *The Meanest Man in the World*. *Let's Face It*. 1944: *Standing Room Only*. 1945: *Bring on the Girls*. *The Trouble with Women* (released 1947). 1946: *The Well Groomed Bride*. 1947: *Where There's Life*. 1948: *Station West*. 1949: *Sorrowful Jones*. 1951: *The Lemon Drop Kid*. *Follow the Sun*. 1952: *Skirts Ahoy!*

LANG, Fritz 1890-1976

Trained as a fashion designer, painter and graphic artist in his native Vienna, Lang used his keen mind and painterly eye to the maximum effect, to become one of the world's great directors and foremost creators of atmospheres of menace, whether in actuality or suggestion. 'I always made films,' he once said, 'about characters who struggled and fought against the circumstances and traps in which they found themselves.' In doing so, Lang created living nightmares of both fact and fantasy. Sometimes his characters, usually 'the average man — because that made him easy to identify with' are caught web-like in nightmares of their own making. Sometimes, it is maniacs, master-criminals or psychopaths who do the trapping. Early in his career, after the move from Austria to the Decla company in Berlin in 1917 (he was invalided out of World War I after serving with distinction in the Austrian army), Lang worked out how studio sets and lighting could be used to create an atmosphere that would ensnare the audience in a world of fantasy. These early films are mostly tremendously imaginative journeys into the depths of human desperation, often with a science-fiction edge, and they are full of images that stay in the mind. As early as 1922 he dreamt up his fiendish master-criminal Dr Mabuse, whose exploits he would return to in two sound films. The other best-known films from his German period are *Metropolis*, a brilliantly conceived vision of a terrifying future, filled with huge, expressionist sets whose cost was almost the ruin of UFA, the company for which Lang was by now working; and *M*, by contrast set in the streets and byways of

Fritz **Lang** supervises a brief romantic idyll for couple-on-the-run Sylvia Sidney and Henry Fonda in his poignant 1937 thriller *You Only Live Once.*

the present-day city, the story of a child-murderer ultimately brought to light by the underworld, in which darkness and shadow are put to various highly effective uses. After the outright anti-Nazi propaganda of his second (memorably exciting) Dr Mabuse film in 1932, Lang fled, via France, to America. His wife and screenwriter Thea von Harbou supported the Nazi cause and stayed behind to make films for it; they divorced in 1934. The theme song to Lang's hauntingly different western *Rancho Notorious* tells continually of 'hate, murder and revenge' and these were themes that were to occupy Lang greatly during his 21 years as a filmmaker in Hollywood. Nowhere more so, either, than in his first film, *Fury,* a fiercely intense indictment of mob violence, with a searing performance by Spencer Tracy. After *You Only Live Once,* a typically poetic and atmospheric exploration of the *Bonnie and Clyde* theme, Lang experimented with colour on two westerns, *The Return of Frank James* and

Western Union, which have some of the most exciting action scenes ever shot. There are several expectedly very anti-Nazi war films during the war years, but also his two famous doomy melodramas with the Edward G. Robinson-Joan Bennett-Dan Duryea trio, *The Woman in the Window* and *Scarlet Street,* the latter a remake of Renoir's *La chienne.* Hate, murder and revenge indeed figure strongly in these brightly seedy portraits of low life, as they do also in the later Glenn Ford-Gloria Grahame pictures, *The Big Heat* (the film in which she has scalding coffee thrown in her face by Lee Marvin) and *Human Desire.* Besides *Rancho Notorious,* the best of Lang's later films are both uncharacteristic of him. *Clash by Night* relies on the strength of its actors for its power, while *Moonfleet,* the famous yarn about a small boy and 18th-century Dorset smugglers, is an excellent vehicle for Stewart Granger, with atmosphere and suspense well maintained throughout. As to be expected, Lang

makes skilful use of CinemaScope. His last films, at RKO, seemed passable thrillers at the time, but were made under unhappy circumstances — Lang was told to 'make them fast and make them cheap' — and look leaden seen on television today. They hastened Lang's departure for Germany, where he made one more Dr Mabuse film and a two-part film set in India, which carries some scenes of tremendous impact. Failing sight forced Lang to give up film-making in 1960. But his worlds of fear and helplessness live on in the darkest dreams of the wee small hours.

1919: Halbblut/The Half Breed. Die Spinnen/The Spiders — Part I: Der goldene See. Harakiri. 1920: Die Spinnen Part II: Das brillianten Schiff/The Diamond Ship. Das wandernde Bild/The Wandering Image. Vier um die Frau/Four Around a Woman. 1921: Der müde Tod (GB: Destiny. US: Between Two Worlds). 1922: Dr Mabuse, der Spieler/Dr Mabuse, the Gambler — Part I: Ein Bild der Zeit. Dr Mabuse, der Spieler — Part II: Inferno. 1923: Die Nibelungen — Part I:

Siegfrieds Tod/Death of Siegfried. 1924: Die Nibelungen — Part II: Kriemhilds Rache/Kriemhilde's Revenge. 1926: Metropolis. 1927: Spione (GB: The Spy. US: Spies). 1928: Frau im Mond (GB: The Girl in the Moon. US: By Rocket to the Moon). 1931: M. 1932: Das Testament von Dr Mabuse (GB: The Testament of Dr Mabuse. US: The Last Will of Dr Mabuse). 1933: Liliom. 1936: Fury. 1937: You Only Live Once. 1938: You and Me. 1940: The Return of Frank James. 1941: Western Union. Man Hunt. †Confirm or Deny (uncredited). 1942: †Moontide (uncredited). 1943: Hangmen Also Die. 1944: Ministry of Fear. The Woman in the Window. 1945: Scarlet Street. 1946: Cloak and Dagger. 1948: The Secret Beyond the Door. 1949: House by the River. 1950: An American Guerilla in the Philippines (GB: I Shall Return). 1951: Rancho Notorious. Clash by Night. 1952: The Blue Gardenia. 1953: The Big Heat. 1954: Human Desire. Moonfleet. 1955: While the City Sleeps. 1956: Beyond a Reasonable Doubt. 1958: Der Tiger von Eschnapur/The Tiger of Bengal. Das Indische Grabmal/The Indian Tomb. Journey to the Lost City (abridged single-film version of the preceding two titles). 1960: Die Tausend Augen des Dr Mabuse/The Thousand Eyes of Dr Mabuse.

LANG, Walter 1896-1972

It's doubtful whether the average cinema-goer has ever heard of Walter Lang. Yet this American director was responsible, especially from the late 1930s to the late 1950s, for some of Hollywood's most beguiling and joyous entertainments. After varied early experience — painter, fashion illustrator, graphic artist, clerk and amateur stage director — Lang became an assistant director with William Randolph Hearst's Cosmopolitan company in the early 1920s, and had progressed to director by 1925. Despite working mostly for minor companies, Lang gradually acquired a reputation as a man who made entertaining pictures, especially in romantic comedy with a touch of bite. But his career didn't really take off until he joined Twentieth Century-Fox in 1937, to work for them for 25 years. He began with *Wife, Doctor and Nurse*, a feisty little romantic triangle comedy, but really blossomed with two Technicolor vehicles for an ageing (all of 11 years old) Shirley Temple past her peak of popularity. These two films, *The Little Princess*, a Victorian riches-to-rags melodrama, and *The Bluebird*, an adaptation of Maeterlinck's famous fantasy about a little girl searching for the blue bird of happiness, are

quite remarkable in the way that they transport us into different worlds, without depriving the star of her individuality. Lang then became involved with the Betty Grable-Alice Faye studio musicals, but gave them welcome touches of warmth, gaiety and exhilaration. *Moon Over Miami*, for example, foreshadows *On the Town* (although the central characters are three golddiggers rather then three sailors) in the way its characters sing and dance through a blend of sets and locations with irresistible verve and energy. Tracking shots above and at ground level serve to heighten the pace of the enterprise, bursting with enthusiasm and zany comic touches. There was also the fondly remembered *State Fair*, bathed in a warm, nostalgic glow and with stacks of hummable Rodgers and Hammerstein songs. Lang's camerawork was perhaps less fluid here than before, but he was already moving in other directions. There was a four-handkerchief weepie, *Sentimental Journey*, then the wildly funny *Sitting Pretty*, with Clifton Webb carving out a whole new comedy career as the self-styled genius and babysitter, Lynn Belvedere. This is the one where the infant empties a bowl of porridge over Belvedere's head. Webb starred again for Lang in his second most successful film for the studio, *Cheaper by the Dozen*, as the Victorian-style father with 12 children who runs his home like a time-and-motion study. The film was a joy, as was the hilarious *The Jackpot*, with James Stewart as the hapless winner of a radio quiz game. *On the Riviera* is a much underrated Danny Kaye comedy, and the rest of Lang's Fox films were all big box-office winners, especially *With a Song in My Heart*, *Call Me Madam*, *There's No Business Like Show Business* and *The King and I*. He even made the Three Stooges seem entertaining in *Snow White and the Three Clowns*: it's their best film. Oscar nominations? Just one, for *The King and I*. Few Oscar nominees can be less well remembered.

1925: The Red Kimono. 1926: The Carnival Girl. The Golden Web. The Earth Woman. Money to Burn. 1927: By Whose Hand? The College Hero. Sally in Our Alley. The Satin Woman. The Ladybird. 1928: The Desert Bride. The Night Flyer. Shadows of the Past. 1929: The Spirit of Youth. Brothers (GB: Two Sons). 1930: The Big Fight. †Cock o' the Walk. Hello Sister. The Costello Case (GB: The Costello Murder Case). 1931: Command Performance. Hell Bound. Women Go On Forever. 1932: No More Orchids. 1933: The Warrior's Husband. Meet the Baron. 1934: The Mighty Barnum. The Party's Over. Whom the Gods Destroy. 1935:

Carnival (GB: Carnival Nights). Hooray for Love. 1936: Love Before Breakfast. 1937: Wife, Doctor and Nurse. Second Honeymoon. 1938: The Baroness and the Butler. I'll Give a Million. 1939: The Little Princess. 1940: Star Dust. The Bluebird. The Great Profile. Tin Pan Alley. 1941: Moon Over Miami. Week-End in Havana. 1942: Song of the Islands. The Magnificent Dope. 1943: Coney Island. 1944: Greenwich Village. 1945: State Fair. 1946: Sentimental Journey. Claudia and David. 1947: Mother Wore Tights. 1948: Sitting Pretty. When My Baby Smiles at Me. 1949: You're My Everything. 1950: Cheaper by the Dozen. The Jackpot. 1951: On the Riviera. 1952: With a Song in My Heart. 1953: Call Me Madam. 1954: There's No Business Like Show Business. 1956: The King and I. 1957: Desk Set (GB: His Other Woman). 1959: But Not for Me. 1960: Can-Can. The Marriage-Go-Round. 1961: Snow White and the Three Stooges (GB: Snow White and the Three Clowns).

LAUNDER, Frank 1906-1997

British director, in films from 1928 after writing two plays before he was 21. He teamed up with Sidney Gilliat *(qv)*, their first writing chore together coming with *Face the Music* (1933) and, after great success with such films as *Seven Sinners*, *The Lady Vanishes* and *Night Train to Munich*, they became producer-directors, at first with Gainsborough Pictures, later for their own company Individual Pictures. Launder's training in British films of the 1930s lay mainly in comedy. He wrote or co-wrote scripts for broad comedies starring Monty Banks, Max Miller, Ernie Lotinga, Leslie Fuller, Will Fyffe and Stanley Lupino. From 1936, he was script editor at Gainsborough, working on the Will Hay and Crazy Gang comedies. There are a few dramas, mostly quite interesting ones too, when he started out as his own director from 1943, but from 1950 he devoted his directorial labours entirely to comedy — and must notably the St Trinian's films. Before this series started, however, Launder made probably the funniest school comedy ever in *The Happiest Days of Your Life*. No two stars were ever more delightfully teamed together than Alastair Sim as the headmaster of a boys' school and Margaret Rutherford as the headmistress of the girls' school which descends, by ministerial error, on the premises of the hapless boys. Launder makes the most of this felicitous teaming, cramming an amazing amount of incident and comic business into the film's too-short 80 minutes. Some of its spirit survived into the enormously successful *The Belles of St Trinian's*, again with Sim, this time in a dual role as the headmistress and her bookmaker brother. The series continued, with diminishing laughter returns, into the 1960s, although with a small upsurge in *The Great St Trinian's Train Robbery*, which had some delightful vignettes. An attempt to revive the formula in 1980, however, was extremely ill-advised. See also the entry on Sidney Gilliat.

1942: †*Partners in Crime. 1943: †Millions Like Us. 1944: 2,000 Women. 1946: I See a Dark Stranger (US: The Adventuress). 1947: Captain Boycott. 1948: The Blue Lagoon. 1950: The Happiest Days of Your Life. 1951: Lady Godiva Rides Again. 1952: Folly to be Wise. 1954: The Belles of St Trinian's. 1955: Geordie (US: Wee Geordie). 1957: Blue Murder at St Trinian's. 1959: The Bridal Path. 1960: The Pure Hell of St Trinian's. 1965: Joey Boy. 1966: The Great St Trinian's Train Robbery. 1980: The Wildcats of St Trinian's.

LAVEN, Arnold 1922-

Television has a lot to answer for in pinching this very promising Chicago-born director to swell its ranks. Nearly 30 years after he, writer Jules Levy and producer Arthur Gardner founded Four-Star Television, Laven was still hard at it, making segments of series as *Police Woman, Six Million Dollar Man, Dog and Cat* and *Baretta*. In the early 1950s, the Levy-Gardner-Laven group had kicked off in feature films with three tight, no-nonsense, lowish-budget crime thrillers — *Without Warning* (about a maniac killer), *The Girl in Room 17* (Edward G. Robinson on the comeback trail after his brushes with the McCarthy blacklist) and *Down Three Dark Streets*, with three cases intertwining for detective Broderick Crawford. Laven's direction of all three is direct and hard-hitting, the qualities he would later bring to his handling of Sam Peckinpah's western script *The Glory Guys. The Rack* is again strong stuff; this time revolving round a court-martial, with Paul Newman, Edmond O'Brien and Lee Marvin. Unfortunately, Laven has always been more interested in television, acting as executive producer and oft time-director on such series as *The Rifleman, Law of the Plainsman* and *The Big Valley*. A big waste of a sharp talent, which only in later years betrayed a slacking-off of energy and enthusiasm. Laven's films came hard at you, and you enjoyed it. Alas, not for very long.

1952: Without Warning. 1953: Vice Squad (GB: The Girl in Room 17). 1954:

Down Three Dark Streets. 1956: The Rack. 1957: The Monster That Challenged the World. Slaughter on Tenth Avenue. 1958: Anna Lucasta. 1962: Geronimo. 1965: The Glory Guys. 1967: Rough Night in Jericho. 1969: Sam Whiskey. 1971: †Rex Harrison Presents Short Stories of Love (TV GB: Three Faces of Love).

LEACOCK, Philip 1917-1990

British documentarist who turned to feature films and became known for the charmingly natural performances he produced from children. Adult actors must have trembled in their boots at appearing in a Leacock film, knowing that under his gentle persuasion, the kids would steal every scene in which they appeared. Yet in 1963, Leacock threw it all up, and went to work for American television. So here is a man who has had three separate careers. At 18, he was an assistant director on short documentaries, much admiring the films from John Grierson's several documentary units. A year later he co-directed (with Harold Lowenstein) his first short documentary *Out to Play*. Already, the children of the city streets appear here at their most relaxed in front of Leacock's cameras. Leacock went on to make documentaries for the next 15 years, less five years' war service, but including several months in Spain assisting on the Civil War documentaries of Thorold Dickinson and Sidney Cole. After two semi-documentary features in the early 1950s, Leacock broke into feature-film-making proper, appropriately with Grierson's Group 3 Productions. *The Brave Don't Cry* is a grim, nail-biting reconstruction of a real-life mine disaster that reflects Leacock's documentary background, and *Appointment in London* a decent enough mainline war film with Dirk Bogarde, Dinah Sheridan and a thrilling climactic bombing raid. Leacock's breakthrough to nationwide recognition came with *The Kidnappers*, ironically made for Britain's major film distributor, Rank. The tremendous charm of this story of two Scottish youngsters who steal a baby and look after it made it an unexpected box-office success, not least engineered by the nation's critics, who covered the film with praise. For the next nine years, Leacock offered us children lovable, mischievous, harum-scarum, on-the-run and, latterly, affected or embittered by racial prejudice. Leacock worked in America after 1963 on such series as *Rawhide, Marcus Welby MD, Gunsmoke, Cannon, The FBI* and *Hawaii Five-O* (well over 50 episodes in all of sundry series) as well as making a fistful of indif-

ferent TV movies, of which only *Dying Room Only* has much of the individual sharpness and warmth of character that once distinguished his work. His brother is the cameraman and documentary filmmaker, Richard Leacock (1921-) who, born in the Canary Islands, has worked and lived largely in America since World War II.

1936: *†Out to Play (D). 1937: *Kew Gardens (D). 1939: †The Londoners (D). 1940: Island People (D). The Story of Wool (D). 1946: Riders of the New Forest (serial. Released 1949). 1947: Pillar to Post (D). 1951: Festival in London (D). Out of True. Life in Her Hands. 1952: The Brave Don't Cry. 1953: Appointment in London. The Kidnappers (US: The Little Kidnappers). 1955: Escapade. 1956: The Spanish Gardener. 1957: High Tide at Noon. 1958: Innocent Sinners. The Rabbit Trap. 1960: Let No Man Write My Epitaph. Hand in Hand. Take a Giant Step. 1962: 13 West Street. Reach for Glory. The War Lover. 1963: Tamahine. 1969: Adam's Woman. 1971: Baffled! When Michael Calls (TV). 1972: The Birdmen (TV. GB: cinemas as Escape of the Birdmen. First shown 1971, but copyrighted 1972). The Daughters of Joshua Cabe (TV). 1973: The Great Man's Whiskers (TV). Key West (TV). Dying Room Only (TV). 1977: Killer on Board (TV). 1978: Wild and Woolly (TV). 1980: Angel City (TV). 1982: The Wild Women of Chastity Gulch (TV).

LEACOCK, Richard

See Leacock, Philip

LEAN, Sir David 1908-1991

Brilliant, inventive British film-maker whose perfectionist nature gradually got the better of him as, after marvellous beginnings, he produced increasingly elephantine entertainments. Of particular regret are the 14 wasted years between 1970 and 1984, during which time Lean struggled to find and set up another subject for filming until *A Passage to India* finally got under way. 'It is hoped that shooting will begin next year' became the stock phrase when referring to his projects during this frustrating time. Perhaps it was that producers were fighting shy after *Ryan's Daughter*, not so much a white elephant as a white mammoth. And if Lean were not willing to compromise, surely his many fans remembering past glories would have been, rather than see nothing at all. For Lean was a double Oscar winner whose films filled British cinemas in the war and immediate post-

David **Lean** shows Sarah Miles the direction through the village her path must take, during the making of *Ryan's Daughter*.

Brief Encounter and the Dickens adaptations *Great Expectations* and *Oliver Twist* are alive with atmosphere, supreme examples of how to draw an audience into the story with strong characterization, intelligent use of lighting and technical effects and highly skilled use of cutting to increase tension, whether in a romantic, dramatic or a horrific situation. To some extent, Lean repeated this success with *Hobson's Choice*, especially in the scene where Charles Laughton, drunk as a lord, ends a long moonlight ramble by falling into a cellar. Lean continued to draw some extremely good performances from his players, although they tended to be dwarfed by the spectacle. Nonetheless, he took Academy Awards for *The Bridge on the River Kwai* and *Lawrence of Arabia*, and several acting and technical Oscars have also been won in his films.

1941: †*Major Barbara* (uncredited). 1942: †*In Which We Serve*. 1944: *This Happy Breed*. 1945: *Blithe Spirit. Brief Encounter*. 1946: *Great Expectations*. 1948: *Oliver Twist. The Passionate Friends* (US: *One Woman's Story*). 1950: *Madeleine* (US: *The Strange Case of Madeleine*). 1952: *The Sound Barrier* (US: *Breaking the Sound Barrier*). 1954: *Hobson's Choice*. 1955: *Summer Madness* (US: *Summertime*). 1957: *The Bridge on the River Kwai*. 1962: *Lawrence of Arabia*. 1965: *Doctor Zhivago*. 1970: *Ryan's Daughter*. 1979: †*Lost and Found — the Story of Cook's Anchor*. 1984: *A Passage to India*.

LeBORG, Reginald   1902-1988

Austrian-born LeBorg should have had a more distinguished career, after the promise of his first two years of filmmaking. Almost all other directors who made such bright beginnings in the war years on low-budget subjects — one thinks of Anthony Mann, Edward Dmytryk, Mark Robson or Robert Wise (*all qv*) — went on to become well-known. But LeBorg never rose above minor 'B' features, and became caught up in series which one would have thought were beneath his talent. Twenty years on, he was still working on these minor films, when the genre had almost vanished. Born in Vienna, LeBorg, after a spell in banking, made himself a stage career as actor, stage-manager and director before, like so many others, he moved to America as the Nazis rose to power, arriving there in 1935. He worked for Columbia, M-G-M and Universal in various behind-scenes capacities through the 1930s and early 1940s, notably staging musical sequences to be inserted into other directors' films.

war years when American competition was at its hottest. One of the secrets of his success was that his films appealed to all classes. But, from the time of his marriage (1949-1957) to Ann Todd, an inherently upper-class actress who appeared in three of his films, this gradually ceased to be true, and Lean moved towards more ambitious projects. Lean had become one of Britain's most skilful editors in the 1930s, after working as art editor on *Gaumont Sound News* (1930) and *British Movietonews* (1931-2). After he directed some scenes in Gabriel Pascal's *Major Barbara*, Noel Coward gave Lean his big chance by asking him to do the action sequences for *In Which We Serve*, his epic

story of the British navy under pressure in war. Lean clinched his new place in the front rank of British directors with the heartwarming *This Happy Breed*, the story of a London family between the wars, beautifully set, and glowingly photographed in Technicolor by Ronald Neame, who also used the process on Lean's next film, the captivating ghost comedy *Blithe Spirit*. Lean, in fact, has only used four photographers throughout his career. Guy Green took over from Neame on *Great Expectations*, and the others have been Jack Hildyard and Freddie Young, both noted colour specialists. Lean's best work, though, was created in black-and-white. The classic love story

Settling at Universal from 1941, he wrote the screenplay for *Heavenly Music*, a 1943 two-reeler which won an Academy Award, and began directing features in the same year. Several of these initial efforts were chillers in Universal's 'Inner Sanctum' series, almost all with Lon Chaney Jr. Perhaps LeBorg was handed the assignments on the grounds that his name *sounded* like that of a director of horror films. Whatever the reason, he would return to the genre from time to time throughout his career. Although not quite in the class of the shockers producer Val Lewton was making over at RKO at the same time, LeBorg's 'Inner Sanctum' films are almost all better than their tiny budgets warranted. Particularly striking is the first of them, *Calling Dr Death*, with Chaney as a doctor whose cheating wife is murdered — by him or one of her many paramours? LeBorg followed with *Weird Woman*, from a witchcraft story by Fritz Leiber *(Burn, Witch, Burn)*, which was remade in Britain in 1962 on a much higher budget as *Night of the Eagle*. In the same year (1944) saw his best film, in a completely different vein. Although *San, Diego — I Love You* was still a 'B', its running time was boosted to 83 minutes, giving LeBorg room to breathe life into an adroit and heart-warming comedy about a distinctly zany family who arrive in San Diego to sell their father's madcap inventions. The vivacious Louise Allbritton gives a delightful comedy performance as inventor Edward Everett Horton's daughter, especially in the sequence where she persuades bus driver Buster Keaton to take the entire family on a moonlight flip along San Diego beach. LeBorg achieves a tremendous air of naturalness, but the success of the film, very quickly discovered and boosted by contemporary pressmen, did him little good. In no time at all he was directing the first of the Joe Palooka (an amiably dim boxing champion) series in which he would become entrenched. He died from a heart attack. One critic described his last film as 'a classic of the late 60s' horror cycle'. LeBorg would have liked that.

*1936: *No Place Like Rome. *Swing Banditry. 1937: *A Girl's Best Years. 1941: *Campus Capers. *Dizzy Doings. *Jingle Belles. 1942: *Rhumba Rhythms. *Tune Time. *The Gay Nineties. *Reed Rapture. *Swingtime Blues. *Jivin' Jam Session. *Merry Madcaps. *Serenade in Swing. *Swing's the Thing. *Trumpet Serenade. 1943: *Swing Frolic. *Shuffle Rhythm. *Merry Madcaps. *Hit Tune Serenade. *Rainbow Rhythm. †Adventure in Music. She's for Me. Calling Doctor Death. 1944: The Mummy's Ghost. Weird Woman. Jungle Woman. Dead Man's Eyes. San Diego — I Love You. Destiny. 1945: Honeymoon Ahead. 1946: Little Iodine. Susie Steps Out. Joe Palooka — Champ. 1947: Fall Guy. The Adventures of Don Coyote. Joe Palooka in the Knockout. Philo Vance's Secret Mission. 1948: Port Said. Winner Take All/Joe Palooka in Winner Take All. Trouble Makers. Fighting Mad/Joe Palooka in Fighting Mad. 1949: Hold That Baby. Joe Palooka in the Counterpunch. Fighting Fools. 1950: Young Daniel Boone. Joe Palooka in the Squared Circle (GB: The Squared Circle). Wyoming Mail. 1951: G.I. Jane. Joe Palooka in Triple Cross (GB: The Triple Cross). 1952: Models Inc/Call Girl (later and GB: That Kind of Girl). 1953: The Flanagan Boy (US: Bad Blonde). Sins of Jezebel. The Great Jesse James Raid. 1954: The White Orchid. 1956: The Black Sleep. 1957: Voodoo Island. The Dalton Girls. War Drums. 1961: The Flight That Disappeared. 1962: Deadly Duo. 1963: Diary of a Madman. The Eyes of Annie Jones. 1969: Le sorelle/So Evil My Sister/Psycho Sisters.*

LEE, Ang 1954-

Taiwan-born director, in America since 1978. The oldest son of middle-class Chinese parents — 'film-making was not the most respectable career to choose,' he has said of their reaction — he studied at the Taiwan Academy of Arts before going to live in America, where he took drama at Illinois University and film at the University of New York. When the short film Lee had made for his graduation won a prize at the New York Film Festival, the future looked bright. But he then underwent six years of 'development hell', while his scripts (and their rewrites) were being rejected by various agents and studios. A return to his roots proved a crucial decision, when two prizewinning scripts were picked up by a small production company, Good Machine, and turned into Lee's first two features, *Pushing Hands*, which vanished without trace, and then *The Wedding Banquet*, which brought back 25 times its cost, and established Lee as a force to be reckoned with on the independent scene. A fast-paced comedy along the lines of *La Cage aux Folles*, as a gay estate agent decides to enter into a marriage of convenience to satisfy his parents, the film led Lee naturally into the next, *Eat Drink Man Woman* — another study of Taiwanese Americans clashing with more traditional-minded parents. Again, Lee blends comedy, drama and emotional insights in a gentle, but carefully planned way, in a story of a widowed master chef and his three daughters that combined Lee's interests in food and the persistence of a communal way of life. It seemed a far cry to the next, an adaptation of Jane Austen's *Sense and Sensibility*, but Lee steeped himself in the mores of the late 18th-century English upper classes and emerged with an elegant and literate film that was nominated for the best picture Oscar and actually won best screenplay for Emma Thompson. Curiously, Lee himself was not nominated. In recent times, his amiable image has toughened, and actors have expressed themselves unhappy with his lack of tact and excessive preparations (which include questionnaires for his casts). And, although *The Ice Storm* was stylishly presented, its characters generate less audience interest than in Lee's previous work.

*1984: *Fine Line. 1992: Pushing Hands. 1993: The Wedding Banquet. 1994: Eat Drink Man Woman. 1995: Sense and Sensibility. 1997: The Ice Storm. 1998: Ride With the Devil.*

LEE, Jack 1913-

British documentarist, war film-maker and useful director in general, stepping with facility from one genre to another, Jack Lee was lost to British films when he decided to emigrate to Australia. Once there, he busied himself with his own production company and did not re-emerge as a director. He had originally joined the famous documentary-making GPO Film Unit in the mid-1930s, and had progressed to associate producer with them by 1938. In 1940, he joined the equally noted Crown Film Unit as an editor, cutting the famous wartime documentary *London Can Take It* (1940) before moving on to films of his own. The best-remembered of his wartime documentaries is *Close Quarters*, a tense story of submarine warfare partly assembled from newsreel footage and partly staged at Pinewood Studios. Unfortunately, this suffered by comparison with Anthony Asquith's entirely fictional submarine drama *We Dive at Dawn*, which was issued in the same year (1943). Lee would have to wait until 1950 to make his mark, but again it was a war film, this time a prisoner-of-war escape thriller called *The Wooden Horse*, one of the first of its kind, and just the thing to pack in post-war audiences. Although its upper-crust accents and stiff upper lips seem phoney today, clever editing ensures that the film is packed with tension and the prisoners come across as genuine personalities, several British character actors of the post-war years making their first big impact in the film. Lee did not make many more films, but there was an adventure story, *South of Algiers*, with a typically abrasive performance by Eric Portman; a comedy, *The Captain's Table*; a women's-prison drama, *Turn the Key Softly*; an interesting attempt to film Rolf Boldrewood's story of Australian banditry, *Robbery under Arms*, made in Australia; and two more war films, *Circle of Deception* and the better-known *A Town Like Alice*, whose grim situations rang true, thanks to gritty performances by Peter Finch and Virginia McKenna, in spite of the fact that it was only as harrowing as Rank would allow Lee to make it at the time. In the mid-1970s, he was announced as the director of the Australian *Don's Party*, but it was eventually made in 1977 by Bruce Beresford. A pity: it would have represented yet another departure from formula in Lee's career.

1941: **The Pilot is Safe* (D). 1942: **†Ordinary People* (D). 1943: *Close Quarters* (D. US: *Undersea Raider*). 1944: *By Sea and Land* (D). 1945: *The Eighth Plague* (D). *V-1* (D). 1946: *Children on Trial* (D). 1947: *The Woman in the Hall*. 1948: *Once a Jolly Swagman* (US: *Maniacs on Wheels*). 1950: *The Wooden Horse*. 1952: *South of Algiers* (US: *The Golden Mask*). 1953: *Turn the Key Softly*. 1956: *A Town Like Alice* (US: *The Rape of Malaya*). 1957: *Robbery Under Arms*. 1958. *The Captain's Table*. 1960: *Circle of Deception*.

LEE, Rowland V. 1891-1975

American director who brought striking pictorial qualities to his films, mainly in the romance, horror and adventure genres, that still linger in the memory today. His work from 1929 to 1940 in particular has rightly brought him a certain 'cult' reputation. His use of semi-expressionist sets and settings to suggest a mood or an atmosphere is extremely rare in this period of American cinema, and at least a dozen of his films make fascinating late-night viewing on television; with the benefit of hindsight, we can discern qualities in Lee's films that seem to have been missed by most critics of the time. His parents were both stage actors, but their son, after some experience as a juvenile on Broadway, had a two-year spell in stockbroking before returning to the boards. He entered films in 1915 as an actor with Thomas Ince's NYMP productions, but served in World War I from 1917. When he returned to Ince in 1920, Lee expressed an interest in directing and began to combine the two careers,

although directing soon took over and he made his last major appearance as an actor in 1921. His silent films are mostly women's pictures, romances noteworthy only for their visual beauty. He attracted some attention with *His Back Against the Wall* in 1922 and later completed *Barbed Wire*, a pacifist film begun by Mauritz Stiller and starring Pola Negri. His special use of the potency of the haunting cinematic image, however, begins with his two Fu Manchu adventures, both featuring Warner Oland. Also of interest in this early sound period is *The Guilty Generation*, a doomy gangster version of *Romeo and Juliet*. Lee further enhanced his reputation with two films starring Gene Raymond. The first, *Zoo in Budapest*, is a delicate romance filled with dreamy images, backed by vivid use of sound and music effects. The second, *I Am Suzanne!*, is an equally gentle love story casting Raymond as a puppeteer who falls for a crippled acrobat. Lee also made a film in Britain, *Love from a Stranger*, but it did not revive Ann Harding's waning star career, despite the fact one reviewer claimed Lee had made the actress 'more human than in any other picture'. Lee's greatest year was 1939. He followed the release of *Son of Frankenstein* (completed in 1938) with *The Sun Never Sets* and *Tower of London* (all three starring Basil Rathbone), and with *The Son of Monte Cristo* coming early in 1940. All of these make extensive use of low-angle shooting, a favourite Lee device to heighten the impact of a scene, and of their imposing sets, although *The Sun Never Sets*, a jingoistic drama in pre-war spy-ridden West Africa, has worn less well than the others, all period films riddled with impressive set-pieces and distinctive, often sinister characters. In post-war years, Lee decided to take it easy, and his only film credit after 1945 is as co-writer and producer on Disney's religious epic *The Big Fisherman* in 1959. His brother, Robert N. Lee, sometimes contributed screenplays for his films. He died from a heart attack.

1920: *The Cup of Life*. 1921: *Blind Hearts*. *Cupid's Brand*. *The Sea Lion*. *The Dust Flower*. 1922: *Men of Zanzibar*. *His Back Against the Wall*. *Money to Burn*. *Mixed Faces*. *A Self-Made Man*. *Shirley of the Circus*. *Whims of the Gods*. 1923: *Desire*. *Alice Adams*. *You Can't Get Away with It*. *Gentle Julia*. 1924: *In Love with Love*. 1925: *Man without a Country*. *Havoc*. 1926: *The Silver Treasure*. *The Outsider*. 1927: *The Whirlwind of Youth*. *Barbed Wire*. 1928: *The Secret Hour*. *Doomsday*. *Three Sinners*. *The First Kiss*. *Loves of an Actress*. 1929: *Wolf of Wall Street*. *A Dangerous Woman*. *The Myste-

rious Dr Fu Manchu*. 1930: *†Paramount on Parade*. *A Man from Wyoming*. *The Return of Dr Fu Manchu*. *Ladies Love Brutes*. *Derelict*. 1931: *The Ruling Voice*. *The Guilty Generation*. 1932: *That Night in London* (US: *Overnight*). 1933: *Zoo in Budapest*. 1934: *I Am Suzanne!* *Gambling*. *The Count of Monte Cristo*. 1935: *Cardinal Richelieu*. *The Three Musketeers*. 1936: *One Rainy Afternoon*. 1937: *Love from a Stranger*. *The Toast of New York*. 1938: *Mother Carey's Chickens*. *Service de Luxe*. 1939: *Son of Frankenstein*. *The Sun Never Sets*. *Tower of London*. 1940: *The Son of Monte Cristo*. 1942: *Powder Town*. 1944: *The Bridge of San Luis Rey*. 1945: *Captain Kidd*.

LEE, Spike (Shelton Lee) 1957-

Leading American maker of street-level social dramas, whose narrative skills are sometimes undercut by seemingly racist (anti-white) attitudes. Having said that, Lee's films, in which he himself often plays featured roles, are frequently inspired by real events. Sometimes it seems that Lee is charting his version of black political American history. The son of a prominent jazz musician, Lee was a star pupil at film school in New York: his graduate feature, *Joe's Bed-Stuy Barbershop: We Cut Heads*, won an Academy Award for best student film of the year. Four years later, he established himself with *She's Gotta Have It*, a witty, raw, full-of-life sex comedy, with Lee himself as a kind of black Woody Allen. Comedy, however, featured less prominently in the films that followed, roughly at the rate of one a year, although the busy Lee has also found time to make commercials and many music videos, which 'keeps me sharp'. His films, to many of which jazz forms an important background ingredient, are challenging, thought-provoking and in-your-face, sometimes too simplistic, but never taking the easy option, nor offering any ready resolution to the racial oppression which Lee sees all over America. The best of them are *Do the Right Thing*, which won Lee an Oscar nomination for best screenplay, *Malcolm X* and *Clockers*. Even these, however, suffer from overlength, and it is interesting that Lee has not conquered markets outside America. His film company, 40 Acres and a Mule, is named after land and goods given to emancipated slaves in an 1865 treaty. His films are always headed 'A Spike Lee Joint'. Lee explains 'joint' in this context as 'a cool place for discussion of issues'. Anger drives him on; middle-age may bring the mellowness to drive his messages home with more considered force.

Spike **Lee** sets out on his mission to promote the black image in movies: from his first fictional feature film, *She's Gotta Have It.*

1977: *Last Hustle in Brooklyn. 1979: *Black College: The Talented Tenth. 1980: *The Answer. 1981: *Sarah. 1982: Joe's Bed-Stuy Barbershop: We Cut Heads. 1986: She's Gotta Have It. 1988: School Daze. 1989: Do the Right Thing. 1990: Mo' Better Blues. 1991: Jungle Fever. 1992: Malcolm X. 1994: Crooklyn. 1995: Clockers. 1996: Girl 6. 1997: 4 Little Girls (D). Get on the Bus. 1998: He Got Game. 1999: Summer of Sam.

LEE THOMPSON, J.
See Thompson, J. Lee

LEIGH, Mike 1943-
The title of this British director's first feature film, *Bleak Moments*, could sum up his work as a whole: it's full of bleak moments, which more often than not contribute to a well-rounded picture of working-class life, although they occasionally overwhelm the film. Critics and discerning audiences have flocked to Leigh's work almost since its inception, although the critic who wrote in the 1980s that 'in any other country apart front England, he would be an internationally established film-maker' was probably not only underestimating the Brits, but over-stating the international case. Pessimism runs all through Leigh's early work. He himself has admitted that 'there's not one of my

pieces before *High Hopes* that isn't somewhere along the way a lamentation for the awfulness of life.' Leigh studied acting at RADA, but was already a director and designer for stage productions by 1965. He worked with the Royal Shakespeare

Company in the late sixties and began directing films in 1971. Writing about Leigh, I was taken aback to think that I'd seen none of his work between *Bleak Moments* and *High Hopes* (1988) and then realised that there wasn't any. 'If

Do you see what I see? Director Mike **Leigh** (right) finds himself the subject of scrutiny by director of photography Roger Pratt. Off-set high jinks during the filming of *High Hopes.*

you'd said to me in 1971', Leigh has admitted, 'that I wouldn't make my next feature film until 1988, I'd have been more than somewhat appalled.' Never mind, there was lots of television, nearly all of it well received and some shown in cinemas outside the UK. *High Hopes*, which put him on the cinema map, is, although also a grim and biting satire of Thatcherite Britain, a film of considerable humour and instantly recognisable characters. Although *Naked*, a depressing, minimalist drama, is Leigh at his most resistible, he atoned with *Secrets and Lies*, a study of secret shames unnecessarily withheld from nearest and dearest, with some excellent scenes that stick in the memory. Leigh was nominated for an Oscar and, in his typical Eeyore fashion, managed to give the impression that he considered himself unlucky not to win. Long married to actress Alison Steadman, but the couple were divorced in 1996. One is sure that the old curmudgeon has lessons in store for us all yet.

1971: Bleak Moments. 1973: Hard Labour (TV). 1976: Nuts in May (TV. US: cinemas). 1977: The Kiss of Death (TV). Abigail's Party (TV. US: cinemas). 1978: Who's Who (TV. US: cinemas). 1980: Grown-Ups (TV. US: cinemas). 1982: Home Sweet Home (TV. US: cinemas). 1983: Meantime (TV. US: cinemas). 1984: Four Days in July (TV. US: cinemas). 1988: High Hopes. 1991: Life is Sweet. 1993: Naked. 1996: Secrets and Lies. 1997: Career Girls.

LEISEN, Mitchell 1897-1972

Although Leisen has acquired a high reputation as a romantic comedy stylist, those of his films which travel better through the years are the dramas and the weepies, each with qualities special to Leisen and to Paramount, that home of lavish sets and high-key lighting. Artistic to his fingertips — he was also a painter, sculptor and dressmaker — Leisen, the son of a Michigan brewery owner, became associated with Cecil B. DeMille's lavish productions from 1919, initially as costume designer, but later as set decorator and art director. His sense of design never let him down in his own films when he was creating some new elegant environment. Leisen gradually developed a desire to control the whole film, and not just its appearance: so he left DeMille after *The Sign of the Cross* was completed in 1932. His first two films for Paramount, the studio at which he was to remain for the next 19 years, were as associate director to Stuart Walker. Leisen's own contribution to these movies has been the subject of much dis-

cussion, but it is certain that he was a considerable influence on the visual aspects of *The Eagle and the Hawk*, a pacifist war film with any number of haunting moments and a very downbeat ending for its time — Fredric March, sickened by the war and its waste of life, commits suicide, but his fellow flyer Cary Grant makes it appear as though he died in action. *Death Takes a Holiday*, with March as Death, is a brittle, fondly remembered fable, although it looks a little creaky today. Far more time-resistant is the likeable thriller *Murder at the Vanities*, with all sorts of ingenious effects, such as the blood of the murdered (girl) private eye dripping down on to a showgirl from the flies of the theatre, and the killing of another showgirl by a bullet under the cover of stage machine-gun fire during a dance routine. Such effects reflect the confidence with which Leisen was directing, as shown by his next two, highly contrasted, assignments: *Four Hours to Kill*, another theatrical thriller, this time about a psychopathic hoodlum on the loose, and *Hands Across the Table*, the most sparkling of his romantic comedies, in which Carole Lombard (briefly glimpsed in *The Eagle and the Hawk*) and Fred MacMurray try to lure each other into marriage, each believing the other to be worth a mint. Leisen brought out Lombard's natural saltiness in a role which considerably advanced her career. From here on, Leisen began to acquire a reputation as a ladies' director, although I find his highly-rated late 1930s' and early 1940s' frolics difficult to settle to. One actress with whom he was most successful, though, was Olivia de Havilland, helping her to escape the Warner straitjacket of 'lady fayre' roles in two monumental, carefully structured and beautifully crafted weepies, *Hold Back the Dawn*, and *To Each His Own*, each with an ending guaranteed to crack the hardest of hearts. For the second of these, Miss de Havilland won an Oscar. Leisen's career tailed away in a post-war era not receptive to his glossy style of film-making, although he continued to work in television (including a delightful short film with the Marx Brothers) until retiring at 70.

1933: +Tonight is Ours. +The Eagle and the Hawk. Cradle Song. 1934: Death Takes a Holiday. Murder at the Vanities. 1935: Behold My Wife. Four Hours to Kill. Hands Across the Table. 1936: Thirteen Hours by Air. The Big Broadcast of 1937. 1937: Swing High, Swing Low. Easy Living. 1938: The Big Broadcast of 1938. Artists and Models Abroad (GB: Stranded in Paris). 1939: Midnight.

*Remember the Night. 1940: Arise My Love. 1941: I Wanted Wings. Hold Back the Dawn. 1942: The Lady is Willing. Take a Letter, Darling (GB: The Green-Eyed Woman). 1943: No Time For Love. 1944: Lady in the Dark. Frenchman's Creek. Practically Yours. 1945: Masquerade in Mexico. Kitty. 1946: To Each His Own. 1947: Suddenly It's Spring. Golden Earrings. 1948: Dream Girl. 1949: Bride of Vengeance. Captain Carey USA (GB: After Midnight). Song of Surrender. 1950: No Man of Her Own. 1951: The Mating Season. Darling, How Could You? (GB: Rendezvous). 1952: Young Man with Ideas. 1953: Tonight We Sing. 1955: Bedevilled. 1957: The Girl Most Likely. 1959: *The Incredible Jewel Robbery (TV). 1967: Spree! (completed 1963).*

+ As Associate Director

LELOUCH, Claude 1937-

This French director's rose-coloured romances, occasionally flawed by touches of coarseness, have travelled the world — and he has made some very winning entertainments, even if most of them are shallow stuff in which the style is everything. Every now and again, however, especially through such actors as Jean-Louis Trintignant and Lino Ventura, individual performances have produced something more deeply felt. But Lelouch has become more facile in recent years, and a season of his really good films would be almost totally confined to the years 1966 to 1973. From an Algerian family, Lelouch became passionately interested in films from a very early age, making his first (prize-winning) short film when only 13! His films began to be internationally shown from 1965, and he was a worldwide name the following year after the success of *Un homme et une femme*, with its beguilingly simple plot and persistent theme song — also an international success. Lelouch has rarely deviated from its formula since. His films are almost all focused basically on just two people, their coming together, parting and coming together again (and occasionally parting; but Lelouch is a lyrical film-maker not partial to unhappy endings). Most of them are only a touch above a live-action women's magazine romance, if cunningly put together in the cutting and music rooms. But a few are rather more than that, notably *Le voyou*, a very likeable high-gloss film about an equally likeable crook (Trintignant again) and *La bonne année*. In the latter, the performances of Lino Ventura and Françoise Fabian have a miraculous inner glow that stands up to the most minute inspection, and lifts the

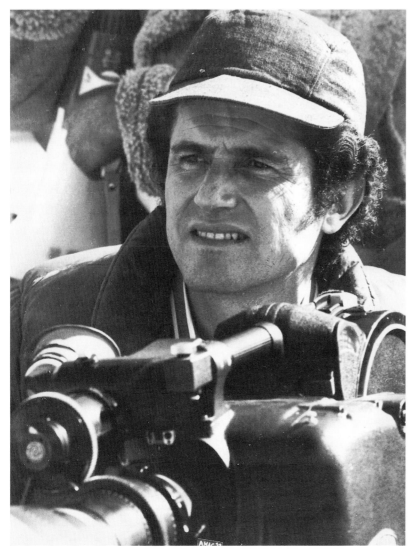

Claude **Lelouch** prepares a scene in his American-made 1977 film *Un autre homme, une autre chance.*

Money Money). **Iran (D). Smic, Smac, Smoc. 1973: †Visions of Eight (D). La bonne année (GB & US: Happy New Year). 1974: Toute une vie (GB & US: And Now My Love). 1975: Le chat et le souris (GB: Seven Suspects for Murder. US: Cat and Mouse). Mariage/Marriage. 1976: Si c'était à refaire (GB: Second Chance. US: If I Had to Do It All Over Again). Le bon et les méchants (US: The Good and the Bad). 1977: Un autre homme, une autre chance (GB: Another Man, Another Woman. US: Another Man, Another Chance). 1978: Robert et Robert. 1979: A nous deux (US: An Adventure for Two). 1981: Les uns et les autres/Bolero (US: The Ins and the Outs). 1983: Edith et Marcel. 1984: Viva la vie. 1985: Partir revenir. 1986: Les nouveaux bandits/Attention bandits. Un homme et une femme: 20 ans déjà. 1988: Itinéraire d'un enfant gâté. 1989: Une affaire de femmes. 1990: Il y a des jours... et des lunes. 1992: La belle histoire. 1995: Les Misérables du XXIème siècle/Les Misérables. 1996: Hommes femmes: mode d'emploi/Men, Women: Users' Manual. 1998: Hasards ou coïncidences.*

LENI, Paul 1885-1929

This German director's early death in Hollywood from blood poisoning probably robbed the cinema of what would have been one of its best directors of 1930s horror films. As it was, Tod Browning and James Whale assumed his mantle and wore it well; nevertheless Leni brought such a unique visual sense to his work that his loss has to be deeply regretted. Leni, like Mitchell Leisen, was a set designer at heart, and indeed began that way (in German films from 1914). But his eye went further, to how the sets could be used and manipulated in such a way as to affect an audience emotionally, to hold them fascinated or fill them with foreboding at some horrific event about to happen. One of his first films as director, *Das Rätsel von Bangalor*, starred Conrad Veidt, whose pale presence would inspire Leni twice more, and who also appeared in *The Cabinet of Dr Caligari*, the expressionist sets of which started Leni's vivid imagination working overtime. Its influence is clearly seen in *Hintertreppe/Backstairs*, with Fritz Kortner, as formidable an interpreter of the macabre as Veidt. The film that attracted the attention of Hollywood was *Das Wachsfigurenkabinett*, which featured a strong cast – Veidt, Emil Jannings, Werner Krauss, William Dieterle – in a Chamber of Horrors-type trilogy about three horrific waxwork figures, each with its own story, in the last of which the hero (in his nightmare) and

film triumphantly over the director's own mundane aspirations to make a marvellously affecting piece of entertainment. Lelouch's films are always very pretty, and there is undoubtedly no-one better than he at making romance to a high standard. *Un homme et une femme* gathered two Academy Awards — for best foreign film and best original story and screenplay, written, as always, by Lelouch himself. In recent times his films have travelled less widely, although he had an international success with *Les Misérables du XXIème siècle*, a 50-year epic loosely based on the Victor Hugo novel, whose three-hour running time leads to a typically Lelouchian resolution of triumph through hardship and adversity.

1951: *Le mal du siècle (D). 1956: *USA en vrac (D). *Une ville pas comme les autres (D). 1957: *Quand le rideau se lève (D). 1960: Le propre de l'homme (US: The Right of Man). 1962: *24 heures d'amants (D). 1963: L'amour avec des si. 1964: Une fille et des fusils (GB: The Decadent Influence. US: To Be a Crook). La femme spectacle (D. GB: Paris in the Raw. US: Night Women). 1965: *Pour un maillot jaune (GB: For a Yellow Jersey). Les grands innocents. 1966: Un homme et une femme/A Man and a Woman. 1967: Vivre pour vivre/Live for Life. †Far from Vietnam. 1968: †Treize jours en France (D. GB: Challenge in the Snow. US: Grenoble). 1969: La vie, l'amour, la mort/Life, Love, Death. Un homme qui me plaît (GB: A Man I Like. US: Love is a Funny Thing). 1970: Le voyou (GB: Simon the Swiss. US: The Crook/The Criminal). 1971: L'aventure c'est l'aventure (US: Money

heroine are relentlessly followed down shadowed streets and angled alleys by Krauss as Jack the Ripper. Leni continued to mix set design for other directors with his own films before Carl Laemmle, head of Universal, summoned him to Hollywood in 1927. Leni immediately proceeded to create a world of murk and darkness as shapes and shadows moved formlessly, clutching hands menaced the heroine, horrors lurked in and around every dingy corner and houses came alive with claustrophobic menace. He made a really creepy version of *The Cat and the Canary,* ironically flawed by the comic relief that would prove the box-office salvation of the Bob Hope version 12 years later, and followed it with the horrifying *The Man Who Laughs (*Veidt again, as a man whose face has been set in a hideous grin), *The Chinese Parrot,* an edge-of-seat mystery with the noted Chinese villain Sojin, and *The Last Warning,* in which the real central character is an allegedly haunted theatre. Leni was at the right studio at the right time: *Frankenstein* and *Dracula* were just over the horizon. Then suddenly, a rush to hospital, and he was dead: an ending more horrifying than any Leni film.

1916: Das Tagebuch des Dr Hartl. 1917: †Das Rätsel von Bangalor. 1918: Dornröschen. 1919: Die platonische Ehe. Prinz Kuckuck. 1920: Patience. 1921: Fiesco/Die Verschwörung zu Genua. Das Gespensterschiff. †Hintertreppe (GB & US: Backstairs). Komödie der Leidenschaften. 1924: Das Wachsftgurenkabinett (GB: Waxworks. US: Three Wax Men). 1927: The Cat and the Canary. The Chinese Parrot. The Man Who Laughs. 1929: The Last Warning.

LEONARD, Robert Z. 1889-1968

Chicago-born Leonard was directing a long time (perhaps too long), but he could project the images of high-class ladies with the best of them. One could hardly imagine Leonard at the helm of a Jean Harlow or Mae West vehicle. His glamour girls were mysterious, or unreachable, or both. And he glided smoothly through a series of high-gloss vehicles featuring Norma Shearer, Mae Murray (his own first wife), Gertrude Olmstead (his second), Marion Davies, Jeanette MacDonald, Luise Rainer, Greer Garson and Hedy Lamarr. A big, handsome man with red hair, Leonard was a leading man in silent films before beginning to direct in 1914. Two years later, he married Mae Murray, the blonde 'girl with the bee-stung lips', a former Ziegfeld dancer whom Leonard showcased in 24 films before their divorce

in 1925. No doubt impressed by such devotion to beauty, M-G-M hired him in the same year and began his long association with gleaming sets, ladies with faintly strained smiles and, at least until the early 1940s, some very popular films. His best film came in 1936 — the mammoth musical *The Great Ziegfeld,* which brought him his first and only Oscar nomination. Leonard was the ideal director for such an epic tribute to showmanship and glamour, assembling a sophisticated leading man (William Powell), two very classy leading ladies in Luise Rainer and Myrna Loy, massive sets, romantic dialogue and glitter, glitter everywhere. M-G-M's producers called him back for *Ziegfeld Girl* in 1941, after his cunningly crafted musicals with Jeanette MacDonald and Nelson Eddy, but this was his last big success, and not surprisingly his spirit did not prosper in the austere post-war years. *In the Good Old Summertime* is quite bouncy and enjoyable, bathed in a typical M-G-M warm Technicolor glow, but by and large these latter-day Leonard musicals lacked the bite required by less romantically inclined audiences, and his dramas are simply bland. From 1925 until 1941, though, no studio could have had a director better suited to its own image.

1914: The Master Key (serial). 1915: The *Silent Command. *A Boob's Romance. *Idols of Clay. *Little Blonde in Black. *Shattered Memories. Heritage. Judge Not. The Woman of Mona Diggins. The Crippled Hand. 1916: The Eagle's Wings. Little Eva Egerton. The Plow Girl. Secret Love. *The Silent Member. *The Boob's Victory. *The Evidence. *The Silent Man of Timber Gulch. *The Winning of Miss Construe. *The Woman Who Followed Me. 1917: *Christmas Memories. *Life's Pendulum. At First Sight. The Little Orphan. Princess Virtue. A Mormon Maid. The Primrose Ring. Face Value. 1918: Her Body in Bond. The Bride's Awakening. Danger — Go Slow. Modern Love. 1919: The Delicious Little Devil. The Big Little Person. What Am I Bid? The Way of a Woman. The Scarlet Shadow. Miracle of Love. April Folly. 1920: The Restless Sex. 1921: The Gilded Lily. Heedless Moths. Peacock Alley. 1922: Fascination. Broadway Rose. 1923: Jazzmania. The French Doll. Fashion Row. 1924: Circe the Enchantress. Mademoiselle Midnight. Love's Wilderness. 1925: Cheaper to Marry. Bright Lights. Time, the Comedian. 1926: Dance Madness. The Waning Sex. Mademoiselle Modiste. 1927: A Little Journey. The Demi-Bride. Adam and Evil. Tea for Three. 1928: Baby Mine. The Cardboard Lover. A Lady of Chance. 1929: Marianne. 1930:

In Gay Madrid. The Divorcee. Let Us Be Gay. 1931: The Bachelor Father. It's a Wise Child. Five and Ten (GB: Daughter of Luxury). Susan Lenox, Her Fall and Rise (GB: The Rise of Helga). 1932: Lovers Courageous. Strange Interlude (GB: Strange Interval). 1933: Peg o' My Heart. Dancing Lady. 1934: Outcast Lady (GB: A Woman of the World). 1935: After Office Hours. Escapade. 1936: The Great Ziegfeld. Piccadilly Jim. 1937: The Firefly. Maytime. 1938: The Girl of the Golden West. 1939: Broadway Serenade. 1940: New Moon. Pride and Prejudice. Third Finger, Left Hand. 1941: Ziegfeld Girl. When Ladies Meet. 1942: We Were Dancing. Stand By for Action! (GB: Cargo of Innocents). 1943: The Man from Down Under. 1944: Marriage is a Private Affair. 1945: Week-End at the Waldorf. 1946: The Secret Heart. 1947: Cynthia (GB: The Rich, Full Life). 1948: B.F.'s Daughter (GB: Polly Fulton). 1949: The Bribe. In the Good Old Summertime. 1950: Nancy Goes to Rio. Duchess of Idaho. Grounds for Divorce. 1951: Too Young to Kiss. 1952: Everything I Have is Yours. 1953: The Clown. The Great Diamond Robbery. 1954: Her Twelve Men. 1955: The King's Thief. Beautiful But Dangerous. 1957: Kelly and Me.

LEONE, Sergio 1921-1989

Although his spaghetti westerns led to a recovery in the popularity of 'horse-operas', western purists are inclined to wish that this Italian director had stayed away from their genre, even if he did revive the career of Clint Eastwood, almost instantly a world superstar on the strength of Leone's films. For Eastwood's success, much credit must go to the director: he saw and exploited untapped facets of the actor's make-up. Eastwood himself has been exploiting them most successfully ever since. The films themselves are bloodbaths, full of sound, fury and sadism. Bullets made round, black-edged holes, through which blood was seen to gush. People were hit by them in painful places. Characters were beaten, whipped, raped: the films were orgies of destruction of life and property, often with slow, deliberate showdowns, full of portentous close-ups of grime-encrusted faces. Leone's films are western skits done for real; but in the 1960s they struck a responsive chord in the hearts of the film-going public, who flocked to them in their millions, enabling Leone to make even longer westerns, with even longer, more elaborate showdowns. His specific achievement was to give the Italian western, in its brief burst of world-wide popu-

Sergio **Leone** explains a scene to Claudia Cardinale during the making of *Once Upon a Time in the West*.

larity, a character all its own — whatever one might think of that character. All of Eastwood's later westerns, and his 'Dirty Harry' films, and countless lesser international films besides, owe a considerable debt to Leone. In 1971, Leone even managed to make a fluid, witty and enjoyable film, *A Fistful of Dynamite*, with camerawork and performances that greatly improved upon the heavy-handed earlier work. But the film was comparatively unsuccessful, and Leone moved into production. A mayfly he might have been, but the beating of his wings was loud, influential and reverberates still. He died from a heart attack.

1961: The Colossus of Rhodes. 1962: †The Last Days of Sodom and Gomorrah/Sodom and Gomorrah (credited as second unit director only). 1964: A Fistful of Dollars. 1965: For a Few Dollars More. 1966: The Good, the Bad and the Ugly. 1968: Once Upon a Time in the West. 1971: Giù la testa (GB: A Fistful of Dynamite. US: Duck You Sucker). 1983: Once Upon a Time in America.

LeROY, Mervyn 1900-1987
LeRoy hovered just below the cream of Hollywood directors for more than 30 years, during which time he made some of its best-remembered and often-revived entertainments. His best films are very good indeed, but probably 50 per cent of his total output is only moderate. But, for the movies that show Hollywood at its

most influential or beguiling — *Little Caesar, Five Star Final, I Am a Fugitive from a Chain Gang, Gold Diggers of 1933, They Won't Forget, Random Harvest, Madame Curie, The Bad Seed* and *Gypsy* — LeRoy has well earned his place in the upper echelons of Hollywood's Hall of Fame. A child actor from 1912, and on vaudeville from 1916, LeRoy arrived in Hollywood in 1919 and slaved away on various unlikely jobs — wardrobe assistant, laboratory technician, assistant cameraman and extra — before a brief period as an actor in silents from 1920 to 1924. He began to write for films from 1925, notably several featuring Colleen Moore, and turned director at Warners, the studio where he was to make most of his best films, two years later. He made his name (and that of Edward G. Robinson in the title role) with *Little Caesar*, a rough-hewn gangster drama that now seems less stylish than its contemporary, *The Public Enemy*. Better films from a directorial point of view were two slightly later 'social reform' dramas, the biting exposé of unscrupulous, scoop-happy newspapers in *Five Star Final* (again with Robinson), and the haunting *I Am a Fugitive from a Chain Gang*. with Paul Muni as the unjustly imprisoned central character doomed in the end to be a shadowy figure forever on the run. *Three on a Match, Two Seconds, Big City Blues* and *Hard to Handle* are other forceful, fast-moving vehicles for such high-powered Warner stars as Robinson, Bette Davis and James Cagney, most of them quite pessimistic in

tone. Easily the best of LeRoy's later 1930s' films is *They Won't Forget*, a striking condemnation of lynch law, which did Claude Rains career no harm at all as the self-seeking prosecutor in the case of a murdered girl in a southern states town. Some of LeRoy's camera angles and lighting effects are exceptionally well organized and intelligent and the film, memorably bitter, hammers home its points to great effect. When LeRoy moved across to M-G-M in 1938, he seemed to undergo something of a personality change, at first turning producer (on, among other things, *The Wizard of Oz*), then making glossy, up-market entertainments; these did include *Random Harvest*, which is the Hollywood tear-jerker firing on all cylinders, and the skilfully crafted biography *Madame Curie*. In the latter, LeRoy's sympathetic direction made not the easiest of subjects — a life story that includes the discovery of radium — entertaining and moving. But, despite occasional highpoints after he returned to Warners in 1955, LeRoy never shook off this new, highly polished image. *The FBI Story* is a shadowy copy of earlier glories and his last film one of the blandest of all. His short film, *The House That I Live In*, took an Oscar in 1945, and LeRoy was given a special Oscar in 1975 for 'outstanding motion picture production'. He died from Alzheimer's Disease.

*1927: Her Primitive Mate/No Place to Go. 1928: Flying Romeos. Oh Kay! Harold Teen. Naughty Baby (GB: Reckless Rosie). 1929: Broadway Babies (GB: Broadway Daddies). Hot Stuff. Little Johnny Jones. 1930: Playing Around. Showgirl in Hollywood. Top Speed. Numbered Men. Little Caesar. 1931: Broadminded. Five Star Final. Gentleman's Fate. Too Young to Marry. Local Boy Makes Good. Tonight or Never. 1932: Heart of New York. High Pressure. Two Seconds. Big City Blues. Three on a Match. I Am a Fugitive from a Chain Gang. Hard to Handle. 1933: Elmer the Great. Tugboat Annie. Gold Diggers of 1933. The World Changes. 1934: Heat Lightning. Hi Nellie! Happiness Ahead. 1935: Page Miss Glory. I Found Stella Parish. Sweet Adeline. 1936: Anthony Adverse. Three Men on a Horse. 1937: The King and the Chorus Girl. They Won't Forget. The Great Garrick. 1938: Fools for Scandal. 1940: Waterloo Bridge. Escape. 1941: Blossoms in the Dust. Unholy Partners. Johnny Eager. 1942: Random Harvest. 1943: Madame Curie. 1944: Thirty Seconds over Tokyo. 1945: *The House That I Live In. 1946: Without Reservations. 1948: Homecoming. 1949: Little Women. Any Number Can Play. 1950: East Side,*

West Side. 1951: Quo Vadis? 1952: Love-
ly to Look At. Million Dollar Mermaid
(GB: The One Piece Bathing Suit). 1953:
Latin Lovers. 1954: Rose Marie. 1955:
Strange Lady in Town. †Mister Roberts.
1956: The Bad Seed. Toward the
Unknown (GB: Brink of Hell). 1958: No
Time for Sergeants. Home Before Dark.
1959: The FBI Story. 1960: Wake Me
When It's Over. 1961: The Devil at Four
O'Clock. A Majority of One. 1962:
Gypsy. 1963: Mary, Mary. 1965: Moment
to Moment.

LESTER, Richard 1932-

With his penchant for wild visual gags and
fragmented constructions, even in short
sequences, it's a wonder Lester ever got
any whole films made at all. He was the
man who brought the Goons of radio
fame (Peter Sellers, Spike Milligan and
Co.) to television in *A Show Called Fred*
and others, and he took this lovably zany
style of humour through several feature
films with such diverse performers as The
Beatles, Margaret Rutherford, Michael
Crawford, Phil Silvers and Rita Tushingham. Alas, he stayed too long at the fair,
until the comedies had become wilfully
obscure and their humour seemed anti-
quated. After a gap of four years, he
returned, prepared to direct a mixed bag
of general entertainment films with varying success, but with his own mischievous,
little boy's sense of the absurd often peeping out between cracks in the sober backcloths. Thus even the most disappointing
of his films is not without its moments of
joy. Born in Philadelphia, Lester sang,
played piano and composed music before
going to CBS, who gave him his first experience of direction. By 1956 he was in
England, where he was to stay, meeting
Sellers and Milligan and whirling around
behind the scenes of their TV show like
some bald, frenetic, camera-conscious
dervish, developing rapid-fire cutting techniques which often looked rough-edged in
these early days, but which he would later
hone almost to perfection. Lester began to
get a foothold in the British film industry
in the early 1960s. The foothold became a
secure niche after his first Beatles film *A
Hard Day's Night*, an exuberant, freewheeling and funny look at the penalties
of success, full of belly-laugh vignettes and
presenting the group as Merseyside Marxes. Lester followed it with the wildly funny
(and underrated) *Help!*, also with the Beatles, and the gleamingly modish, but still
enjoyable *The Knack... and How to Get
It*. He went dramatic with considerable
success in *Petulia*, although the film was
still quirkily his own. Its vein of sadism
was rather distasteful but has not been

repeated in Lester films. But meanwhile,
he was sliding with his comedies, which
remained too firmly rooted in the mid-
1960s, and lacked the joie-de-vivre that
had distinguished the earlier work. Lester
worked too little for too long, but yesterday's wonder boy struck back gloriously
in 1973 with the arrival of *The Three
Musketeers*, a richly enjoyable spoof of the
swashbuckling classic in which only the
action scenes are taken semi-seriously.
Lester got lovely comedy performances
from Raquel Welch, Spike Milligan and
Roy Kinnear and the only pity was that he
was encouraged to feel that mud-and-
grime and how-it-really-was-in-those-days
went marvellously with flashes of the
Lester humour, a theory he pursued with
rather mixed success in several other films.
Still, *Juggernaut* was a tense, straightforward, fast-moving thriller about a bomb
on board ship, with a palm-sweating performance by David Hemmings, and *Superman II* surprisingly surpassed the original
by keeping its tongue very firmly in its
cheek — with just one or two welcome
flashes of the old Lester sense of the idiotic. But after the misfired *Finders Keepers*
in 1984 which contained a cameo from
the young Jim Carrey (the prospect of
Lester and Carrey combining today is an
intriguing one), the director's interest in
the cinema seemed to wane.

*1960: *The Running, Jumping and Stand-
ing Still Film. 1962: It's Trad, Dad (US:
Ring-a-Ding Rhythm). 1963: The Mouse
on the Moon. 1964: A Hard Day's Night.
1965: Help! The Knack. . . and How to
Get It. 1966: A Funny Thing Happened on
the Way to the Forum. 1967: How I Won
the War. 1968: Petulia. 1969: The Bed-Sit-
ting Room. 1973: The Three Musketeers:
the Queen's Diamonds. 1974: Juggernaut.
The Four Musketeers: the Revenge of Mila-
dy. 1975: Royal Flash. 1976: Robin and
Marian. The Ritz. 1979: Butch and Sundance: The Early Days. Cuba. 1980:
Superman II. 1983: Superman III. 1984:
Finders Keepers. 1989: The Return of the
Musketeers. 1991: Get Back.*

LEVIN, Henry 1909-1980

If you had to pick an average 'A' feature
Hollywood director working between
1940 and 1970, with a good variety of
films to his credit and a certain talent
worth discussing, you couldn't do much
better than Henry Levin. Though never
quite in the directors' super-league, he
could often be relied on to give a project
that little spark, that little something
extra. A cheerful extrovert, Levin joined
Columbia as a dialogue director after
some experience as a director in the the-

atre. Some sources credit him with opening his account that same year (1943)
with the lively comedy-thriller *Dangerous
Blondes*, although he is credited only as
dialogue director. His first accredited
direction and only horror film was *Cry of
the Werewolf*, possibly his worst film. But
from then on, Levin constantly gave the
impression that he thought film-making
was fun and that he enjoyed what he was
doing. Even on Columbia's pinch-budgets,
there were solid minor successes: crime
films (*I Love a Mystery, Night Editor, The
Corpse Came C.O.D.*), swashbucklers
(*The Return of Monte Cristo, The Gallant
Blade*), comedies (*The Mating of Millie,
And Baby Makes Three*), adventure (*The
Bandit of Sherwood Forest*), a western
(*The Man from Colorado*), a prison
drama (*Convicted*) and one smash-hit,
Jolson Sings Again, which, to everyone's
surprise, proved every bit as good (and as
popular) as the original. Moving across to
Fox, and later freelancing, Levin made
two warmly nostalgic comedies (*Belles on
Their Toes, The Remarkable Mr. Pennypacker*), a psychological western (*The
Lonely Man*), musicals, comedies, fantasies and adventures. He also made an
epic, *Genghis Khan*, which proved one of
the first of its kind in which the characters sprang to life as real people: a spectacular with a rare human touch. Levin
had this facility: he worked well with
actors, so that they gave relaxed performances within the script's demands. This
is especially true of William Gargan and
Janis Carter in *Night Editor*; William
Holden and Glenn Ford in *The Man from
Colorado*; Lizabeth Scott and Edmond
O'Brien in the splendidly laconic *Two of a
Kind*; Jack Palance and Anthony Perkins
in *The Lonely Man*; Charlton Heston and
Susan Hayward in *The President's Lady*;
even Betty Grable and Dale Robertson in
The Farmer Takes a Wife. Heavy drama
was not Levin's thing. His skill lay in
unreeling his stories in a lively and entertaining way. It deserted him a little after
the late 1950s, a time when life was seep-
ing from traditional Hollywood cinema
itself.

*1943: +Appointment in Berlin. +Danger-
ous Blondes. 1944: Cry of the Werewolf.
The Fighting Guardsman. Sergeant Mike.
Dancing in Manhattan. 1945: I Love a
Mystery. 1946: The Unknown. The
Devil's Mask. Night Editor (GB: The
Trespasser). †The Bandit of Sherwood
Forest. The Return of Monte Cristo.
1947: The Guilt of Janet Ames. The
Corpse Came C.O.D. 1948: The Mating
of Millie. The Gallant Blade. The Man
from Colorado. 1949: Mr Soft Touch
(GB: House of Settlement). And Baby*

Makes Three. Jolson Sings Again. 1950: Convicted. The Petty Girl (GB: Girl of the Year). The Flying Missile. 1951: Two of a Kind. The Family Secret. 1952: Belles on Their Toes. 1953: The President's Lady. Mister Scoutmaster. The Farmer Takes a Wife. 1954: Three Young Texans. The Gambler from Natchez. 1955: The Dark Avenger (US: The Warriors). 1956: Let's Be Happy. 1957: The Lonely Man. Bernardine. April Love. 1958: A Nice Little Bank That Should Be Robbed. 1959: The Remarkable Mr Pennypacker. Holiday for Lovers. Journey to the Center of the Earth. 1960: Where the Boys Are. 1961: The Wonders of Aladdin. 1962: †The Wonderful World of the Brothers Grimm. If a Man Answers. Come Fly with Me. 1964: Honeymoon Hotel. 1965: Genghis Khan. 1966: Murderers' Row. Kiss the Girls and Make Them Die. 1967: The Ambushers. 1968: The Desperados. 1973: †That Man Bolt. 1977: The Thoroughbreds (later Treasure Seekers). 1980: Scout's Honor (TV).

+ as dialogue director

LEVINSON, Barry 1942-

An attention to close-knit relationships has marked the often distinguished work of this American director, together with an affection for his native Baltimore, the background for his striking directorial debut, to which he has returned several times in subsequent films. Levinson has also shown an ability to extract the maximum poignancy from prestigious but difficult subjects, succeeding notably in successive years with *Good Morning, Vietnam* and *Rain Man*, the second of which won him a best director Oscar. Levinson's early years, though, had been a time of struggle. While pursuing dilatory studies in broadcasting journalism (which sowed the seeds for his Vietnam film), Levinson also sold used cars (the background for his subsequent *Tin Men*), but decided eventually to pursue an acting career. That went by the board when he got a stint as a stand-up comedian which drew him to the attention of Mel Brooks, for whom he wrote (and played cameo roles) in the mid-1970s' frolics *High Anxiety* and *Silent Movie*. An Oscar nomination for *And Justice for All*'s screenplay drove Levinson towards directing his own work, initially because he wanted to put on screen in his own way his recollections of growing up in 1959 Baltimore. The result, *Diner*, drew warm reviews, and with an ensemble cast on top form, is, almost inevitably, a well-observed and affectionate portrait of American youth, their aspirations and disappointments. Although

the approach results in a portrait rather than a story, it's one that has frequent rewards for the discerning viewer. After a couple of shallow but colourful entertainment films established him on the Hollywood scene, Levinson returned to Baltimore for *Tin Men*, a sad, oddly touching and well-acted slice-of-life story with a vein of rather bitter humour, and dialogue by Levinson which carries the whiff of real life. Its low-key approach contrasted with the raucous Oscar-nominated performance of Robin Williams in Levinson's *Good Morning, Vietnam*, his biggest box-office success to date, but not as big as the next, *Rain Man*, a project Levinson took after four other directors had cried off. Certainly, the idea of a young hustler kidnapping his autistic savant brother because he's been left a bigger share of their inheritance doesn't seem like blockbuster material, but the scenes where the relationship between the brothers changes are raw and touching and, combined with the presence of stars Dustin Hoffman and Tom Cruise, Levinson's cultured approach made the film a major hit. Apart from more personal Baltimore history in *Avalon*, Levinson's later projects have been of varying quality, although he has always commanded major stars for leading roles. Financially, his biggest hit has been the controversial *Disclosure*, but there was also praise for the political satire *Wag the Dog*, which uncannily pinpointed the US presidential sex scandal of the late 1990s. In between film assignments, Levinson has also worked on the cult hit TV series, *Homicide: Life on the Streets*. The streets in question, needless to say, belong to Baltimore.

1982: Diner. 1984: The Natural. 1985: Young Sherlock Holmes/Young Sherlock Holmes and the Pyramid of Fear. 1986: Tin Men. 1987: Good Morning, Vietnam. 1988: Rain Man. 1990: Avalon. 1991: Bugsy. 1992: Toys. 1994: Jimmy Hollywood. Disclosure. 1996: Sleepers. 1997: Wag the Dog. 1998: Sphere. 1999: Liberty Heights.

LEWIN, Albert 1894-1968

This American producer's few films as director were about people who were jinxes on themselves or those around them, or possessed by strange, compelling forces. He has been accused of artiness and pretentiousness and these are certainly faults of his worst film, *Pandora and the Flying Dutchman,* but some of his other work, especially *The Moon and Sixpence* and *The Picture of Dorian Gray,* although experiences rather than movies, are not lightly to be dismissed.

Lewin, a fussy little man with a passion for accuracy of detail, was the ideal right-hand man for M-G-M's famous supervisor of production, Irving Thalberg: he had been an English teacher, film critic and screenwriter before accepting the post. When Thalberg died in September 1936, Lewin went to Paramount as a producer, but soon became restless for total control on projects of his own. The first of these was Somerset Maugham's *The Moon and Sixpence,* with George Sanders, based on the life of Gauguin the painter. Lewin brought a certain fresh beauty to the story of a stockbroker who abandons his dull life to become a painter in Tahiti. Sanders also featured in the elegant *The Picture of Dorian Gray,* still the best version of Wilde's tale of the ruthless Victorian who keeps an ageing portrait of himself in the attic while he stays forever young. Sanders would have seemed ideal casting for Gray, but he played Lord Henry Wotton, while the cruelly handsome Hurd Hatfield took the title role. Lewin's love of (sometimes lurid and horrifying) detail paid rich dividends in this picture but his next, *The Private Affairs of Bel Ami,* though again with Sanders, was less successful; *Pandora* really finished him as a major filmmaker, although today superstar directors seem to be allowed such massively boring aberrations. A word here, though, for the much-maligned and neglected *Saadia,* an exciting story set in Morocco, inevitably about a girl who brings bad luck to those who know her. Rita Gam and Mel Ferrer contribute sharply etched performances. Lewin's last film, *The Living Idol,* about a Mexican girl possessed by the spirit of the jaguar, had big production values, but died at the box-office. Lewin, who had contributed the screenplays to all six of his films, then concentrated on a writing career.

1942: The Moon and Sixpence. 1945: The Picture of Dorian Gray. 1947: The Private Affairs of Bel Ami. 1951: Pandora and the Flying Dutchman. 1954: Saadia. 1957: The Living Idol.

LEWIS, Jerry (Joseph Levitch) 1926-

Solely on his merits as a director, American comedian Jerry Lewis scarcely deserves a place in this book. Almost all of his best acting work was done for other directors, mainly Frank Tashlin. Directing himself, he is almost always self-indulgent, and one of the chief destroyers of his own cinema career. There is, however, one hilarious exception. This is *The Nutty Professor,* a Jekyll-and-Hyde project which Lewis had nurtured for ten years before getting it off the ground in 1963. Originally he had envisaged himself as the studious, girl-shy scientist and his ex-partner Dean Martin as the swinging Buddy Love into whom the scientist transmogrifies after drinking the inevitable potion. The partnership, however, had split up long before and Lewis ended up playing both roles — very successful in the part of the scientist, and a gallant try at the swinger. The pacing and plotting are faultless and there are one or two magnificent visual gags guaranteed to bring the house down: altogether a delightful evening's entertainment. Lewis could not profit from its success, however — nor from that of the hilarious madcap comedies fashioned for him by Tashlin. Later vehicles became more and more self-indulgent, and public patience with the Lewis comedies (and private backing) seemed to run out with the beginning of the 1970. The years that followed were full of unrealised or unreleased projects that Lewis directed, or planned to direct himself. Later, he resumed his directing career in France, where he is idolised by public and critics alike, but more recently he has preferred to grandstand on stage in a long-running revival of the musical *Damn Yankees*. Even in later days it was clear that Lewis never really understood, or even accepted his slide in popularity and the reasons for it. In a mid-1980s interview, he contended that 'a lot of people were hostile because I was a multi-faceted, talented, wealthy, internationally famous genius'. Modest with it, too.

1960: The Bellboy. 1961: The Ladies' Man. The Errand Boy. 1963: The Nutty Professor. 1964: The Patsy. 1965: The Family Jewels. 1966: †Three on a Couch. 1967: The Big Mouth. 1969: One More Time. 1970: Which Way to the Front? (GB: Ja, Ja, Mein General, But Which Way to the Front?). 1971: $The Day the Clown Cried. 1979: $That's Life. 1980: Hardly Working. 1983: Smorgasbord (completed 1981. Later: Cracking Up).

$ unreleased

LEWIS, Joseph H. 1900-

A thoughtful American director working almost entirely in 'B' movies, Lewis delighted in the mobility of the camera and often experimented with unusual ways of shooting a scene, sometimes with great success. There are unexpected and delightful subtleties to be found in the majority of his films, most of which are disappointing when taken as a whole.

Lewis' fragile talents have caused him to be somewhat overrated in recent years by 'auteur' theory critics (the theory that one man, the director, is responsible for everything in the film, especially its overall feel, and that it bears his distinctive stamp for all to see). Nevertheless, a reviewing of his films, especially the crime melodramas, is rarely completely unrewarding. A wiry, native-born New Yorker who could have passed for a sixth Marx Brother, Lewis had an interest in *mise-en-scène* and the varying effects of long takes for some scenes and crisp editing for others, together with variations on such familiar devices as tracking shots and overhead views, which stemmed from his own technical background — he broke into early sound films firstly as an assistant cameraman (with M-G-M) and later as an editor with Republic. He began directing in 1937, but his early films, mostly minor westerns, are quite unexceptional, although he does seem to be trying to impose an overall style on some of them; as he did, unsuccessfully, with a horror film, *The Mad Doctor of Market Street*, the *New York Times* commenting that 'the film seems to have been constructed from odd scraps of celluloid on the cutting-room floor'. Lewis hit his stride, however, with *My Name is Julia Ross*, one of the first films he actually chose to make, although he also had the advantage of personable performers in Nina Foch, George Macready and Dame May Whitty in a fog-enshrouded creepie about a kidnap victim whose very identity is threatened. Lewis moved further into the realms of psychological danger with *So Dark the Night*, in which the investigating detective (a rare and welcome leading role for Steve Geray) proves to be a schizophrenic and himself the murderer. Lewis was now in the middle of the best six years of his career; after directing the musical numbers for *The Jolson Story*, he made the exhilarating swashbuckler *The Swordsman* (again with Macready as the villain), full of fake Scottish accents, but visually stimulating, using fast tracking shots through woods and across streams and with unusually intelligent use of the very limited Cinecolor. The next two years brought a downbeat and finely detailed portrait of police detective work, *The Undercover Man*, (again with Foch); *A Lady Without Passport* (again with Macready and Geray), in which routine material about aliens in America is made unusually compelling by the intricate and subtle treatment; and *Gun Crazy*, his most famous film, a rural *amour fou* to place alongside Lang's *You Only Live Once* and Penn's *Bonnie and Clyde*. Lewis should have moved

upwards from here. But instead he slipped back. Among his later assignments, only *The Big Combo* and *7th Cavalry* have some worthwhile, haunting moments. Lewis spent the last eight years of his working career in television.

1937: †Navy Spy. Courage of the West. The Singing Outlaw. 1938: The Spy Ring. Border Wolves. The Last Stand. 1939: Two-Fisted Rangers (GB: Forestalled). 1940: Blazing Six-Shooters (GB: Stolen Wealth). Texas Stagecoach (GB: Two Roads). The Man from Tumbleweeds. Boys of the City. That Gang of Mine. The Return of Wild Bill (GB: False Evidence). Pride of the Bowery (GB: Here We Go Again). 1941: The Invisible Ghost. Criminals Within. The Arizona Cyclone. 1942: Bombs over Burma. The Silver Bullet. The Boss of Hangtown Mesa. The Mad Doctor of Market Street. 1943: Secrets of a Co-Ed (GB: Silent Witness). 1944: Minstrel Man. 1945: The Falcon in San Francisco. My Name is Julia Ross. 1946: So Dark the Night. 1947: The Swordsman. 1948: The Return of October (GB: Date with Destiny). 1949: The Undercover Man. Gun Crazy. 1950: A Lady Without Passport. 1952: Retreat Hell! Desperate Search. 1953: Cry of the Hunted. 1955: The Big Combo. A Lawless Street. 1956: 7th Cavalry. 1957: The Halliday Brand. 1958: Terror in a Texas Town.

LINKLATER, Richard 1961-

Texas-born director whose grinding studies of modern youth angst have won him something of a cult following. 'I was the product of a typical mediocre public education,' he has said. 'I didn't really learn anything until I left school and started studying on my own.' All the more surprising, perhaps, in view of this statement, that his films should largely portray people who are making nothing of their lives. His first film, *Slacker*, set the pattern: a bleached-out style of wierdos and layabouts hanging out in a Texas town where it seems no one has anything to do. *Dazed and Confused* and *SubUrbia*, although set largely at nighttime, continued the theme of wasted lives drowning in drugs and booze, but *Before Sunrise* was a departure although, its critics might contend, no less boring, being a poorly written and charmlessly played, if pretty romantic drama. It will be interesting to see, as seems likely, Linklater's nihilism clash with mainstream American cinema.

1991: Slacker. 1993: Dazed and Confused. 1995: Before Sunrise. 1997: SubUrbia. 1998: The Newton Boys.

LITVAK, Anatole

(Mikhail Anatol Litwak) 1902-1974
Like so many European emigrés, Litvak flourished in the Hollywood of the middle 1930s to the early 1950s, but not thereafter. He was most successful in maintaining a detailed, but fluid narrative structure with the emphasis on three-dimensional characters, an approach which makes his best films compelling from beginning to end. He specialized in films in which women played a central role, often caught in a web of circumstance not of their own making. Litvak began working in films in his native Russia at 21, but two years later, after directing one Russian film, moved his base to Germany. He began here as an editor of Pabst's Garbo film, *Die freudlose Gasse*, and it took him five years to break back into direction. With the rise of the Nazis, Litvak moved on to France, where he made several good films — notably *Coeur de lilas*, *L'équipage* and an internationally successful first account of the famous doomed royal romance of *Mayerling*, here with Charles Boyer and Danielle Darrieux. He found that this had given him a reputation for epic romances when he arrived in Hollywood (marrying actress Miriam Hopkins in 1937; they were divorced two years later) and he was handed several more, including two with Bette Davis — *The Sisters* and *All This and Heaven Too*, to which he brought qualities of realism that other Warners directors of the time might have disdained. They were strong on atmosphere too, as were his city-set films, teeming with life, with a firm working-class feel and sometimes menace, as the characters found themselves in the familiar Litvak tight corners. He collaborated on wartime documentaries with Frank Capra then returned to the 'beleaguered female' theme (after the flop of *The Long Night*), with two of his biggest successes: *The Snake Pit* had Olivia de Havilland as the woman unnecessarily committed to an insane asylum; but at least she got out of it at the end better than Barbara Stanwyck in *Sorry, Wrong Number* as the bedridden woman who hears her own murder being plotted over the phone. Litvak winds up the suspense nicely, at considerable cost to the audience's nerves. De Havilland and Stanwyck found themselves in Oscar competition for their roles, though both lost to Jane Wyman in *Johnny Belinda*. The remaining films of Litvak's career are a mixture of minor successes and minor disappointments. He did at last help one of his leading ladies to an Academy Award when Ingrid Bergman won for *Anastasia*; and he was still ensnaring

bewildered heroines in his last film, in this case Samantha Eggar in *The Lady in the Car with Glasses and a Gun*.

1924: **Tatiana. *Hearts and Dollars.* 1929: *$Dolly macht Karriere (GB: Dolly Gets Ahead. US: Dolly's Way to Stardom).* 1931: *$Nie wieder Liebe (GB & US: No More Love).* 1932: *Coeur de lilas (US: Lilac). Be Mine Tonight/Das Lied einer Nacht.* 1933. *Sleeping Car. Cette vieille canaille.* 1935: *L'équipage (US: Flight into Darkness).* 1936: *Mayerling.* 1937: *Tovarich. The Woman I Love (GB: The Woman Between).* 1938: *The Sisters. The Amazing Dr Clitterhouse.* 1939: *Confessions of a Nazi Spy. †The Roaring Twenties.* 1940: *Castle on the Hudson (GB: Years without Days). All This and Heaven Too. City for Conquest.* 1941: *Out of the Fog. Blues in the Night.* 1942: *This Above All. †Prelude to War (D).* 1943: *†The Nazis Strike (D). †Divide and Conquer (D). The Battle of Russia (D). Operation Titanic (D).* 1944: *†The Battle of China (D).* 1945: *War Comes to America (D).* 1947: *The Long Night.* 1948: *The Snake Pit. Sorry, Wrong Number.* 1951: *Decision Before Dawn.* 1953: *Act of Love.* 1955: *The Deep Blue Sea.* 1956: *Anastasia.* 1957: *Mayerling (TV).* 1959: *The Journey.* 1961: *Aimez-vous Brahms? (GB: Goodbye Again).* 1962: *Five Miles to Midnight.* 1966. *The Night of the Generals.* 1970: *The Lady in the Car with Glasses and a Gun.*

$ as Anatol Litwak

LLOYD, Frank 1888-1960

Despite two Oscars, this Scottish-born Hollywood director's career suffered a full eclipse in the late 1930s and early 1940s. Why it is difficult to say, save possibly that after the silent era ended Lloyd proved more effective with spectacle than people; but even then he should have been able to find sufficient suitable vehicles for his talents, as his final film, *The Last Command*, (a reworking of the Alamo theme more stirring than John Wayne's five years later) clearly showed. Following seven years' experience on the English stage, the young Lloyd emigrated to Canada in 1910, where he spent three years acting with touring companies before arriving in Hollywood in 1913. After a period as villains in Universal westerns, Lloyd expressed a desire to direct, soon showing a firm visual grasp of the silent-film medium and its requirements. He moved to Fox in 1915 and his prodigious output there included several literary-based titles that would frequently be remade by other hands, among them *A*

Tale of Two Cities, Madame X, Les Misérables, Riders of the Purple Sage, The Sea Hawk and a memorable 1922 version of *Oliver Twist* (which he also co-wrote) with Lon Chaney as Fagin and Jackie Coogan as Oliver. In the 1928/1929 Academy Award nominations, there were seven for best director, and Lloyd had three of them (for *The Divine Lady, Weary River* and *Drag*), a sign of the prestige he had accumulated within the industry. He was the winner, for *The Divine Lady*, with Corinne Griffith as Lady Hamilton. Another best-director Oscar followed a few years later for *Cavalcade*, although this looks rather static today, and he was widely tipped to make it three with the 1935 version *of Mutiny on The Bounty*. But he was unexpectedly pipped by John Ford with *The Informer* and never nominated again. Most of Lloyd's remaining films are rarely revived historical melodramas in which the leading players seldom seem at ease. The progression in his later career from studio to studio — M-G-M to 20th Century-Fox to Paramount to Columbia to Universal to RKO to United Artists to Republic — reflects his decline.

1914: **Billie's Baby. *For His Superior's Honor.* 1915: **From the Shadows. Eleven to One. Dr Mason's Temptation. An Arrangement with Fate. Jane. Fate's Alibi. The Bay of Seven Islands. A Double Deal in Pork. *Little Mr Fixer. In the Grasp of the Law. His Last Trick. The Little Girl of the Attic. The Pinch. The Prophet of the Hills. Paternal Love. Martin Lowe — Fixer. Their Golden Wedding. *10,000 Dollars. *The Toll of Youth. Trickery. The Source of Happiness. *To Redeem an Oath. *To Redeem a Value.* 1916: *The Call of the Cumberlands. The Gentleman from Indiana. The Tongues of Men. Madame President. An International Marriage. The Code of Marcia Gray. The Intrigue. The Making of Maddalena. Sins of Her Parents. The Stronger Love. David Garrick.* 1917: *The Price of Silence. The Heart of a Lion. American Methods. A Tale of Two Cities. When a Man Sees Red.* 1918: *The Kingdom of Love. Les Misérables. The Blindness of Divorce. True Blue. For Freedom.* 1919: *The Rainbow Trail. Riders of the Purple Sage. The Man Hunter. Pitfalls of a Big City. The World and Its Women.* 1920: *The Loves of Letty. Madame X. The Silver Horde. The Woman in Room 13. The Great Lover.* 1921: *A Tale of Two Worlds. Roads of Destiny. Voice in Dark. The Man from Lost River. The Invisible Power. The Sin Flood. The Grim Comedian.* 1922: *The Eternal Flame. Oliver Twist.* 1923: *Within the Law. Ashes of*

Vengeance. The Voice from the Minaret. 1924: Black Oxen. The Sea Hawk. The Silent Watcher. 1925: Winds of Chance. The Splendid Road. Her Husband's Secret. 1926: The Wise Guy. The Eagle of the Sea. 1927: Children of Divorce. 1928: Adoration. 1929: Weary River. The Divine Lady. Drag (GB: Parasites). Young Nowheres. Dark Streets. 1930: Son of the Gods. The Way of All Men (GB: Sin Flood). The Lash (GB: Adios). 1931: East Lynne. The Right of Way. The Age for Love. 1932: A Passport to Hell (GB: Burnt Offering). 1933: Cavalcade. Berkeley Square. Hoopla. 1934: Servants' Entrance. 1935: Mutiny on the Bounty. 1936: Under Two Flags. 1937: Maid of Salem. Wells Fargo. 1938: If I Were King. 1939: Rulers of the Sea. 1940: The Howards of Virginia (GB: The Tree of Liberty). 1941: The Lady from Cheyenne. This Woman is Mine. 1943: †Forever and a.Day. 1945: Blood on the Sun. 1954: The Shanghai Story. 1955: The Last Command.

LOACH, Ken 1936-

Once the stormy petrel of the British cinema, Loach is now its national institution. Still wearing his leftist social and political consciences firmly on his sleeve, Loach has now settled into a groove of film-making that has both given us a reassuring number of films and earned a wider acceptance from the discerning filmgoing public. The 1990s, in fact, were the decade in which Loach, while still standing on his soapbox, became an all-round entertainer. Born in Warwickshire, Loach read law at Oxford University, but decided to train as a director for TV. After cutting his teeth on the ground-breaking *Z Cars* series, Loach went on to direct a series of 'kitchen sink' dramas in the 'Wednesday Play' slot for the BBC that depicted working-class life and misfortunes in graphic detail with such plays as *Up the Junction* (1963) and *Cathy Come Home* (1966), which attracted huge viewing figures in spite of their controversial nature. The 'wasted lives' theme of these dramas was continued into Loach's films, aggressively realistic but somewhat soft-centred pieces such as *Poor Cow*, the award-winning *Kes* and the rather dreary *Family Life*. In the years that followed the failure of *Family Life*, Loach's work was disappointingly uneven. But *Hidden Agenda* — which courted controversy of a different kind: the role of the British government in the continuing Irish struggle — heralded a new sense of urgency in the old lion's work, perhaps helped on by his own advancing years. Thus *Raining Stones, Land and Freedom* and *Carla's*

Song, although polemical in part, have not only interesting characters but passages that are pure cinema. And, although Loach's other 1990s' films to date, *Riff-Raff* and *Ladybird Ladybird*, are too simplistic and one-sided in their attacks on society, they nonetheless attracted an audience. The present resurgence of British cinema is entirely suited to a film-maker of Loach's opinions and capabilities, and he now seems settled into its middle stream.

1967: Poor Cow. 1969: Kes. 1971: Family Life (US: Wednesday's Child). 1978: The Gamekeeper (TV. US: cinemas). 1979: Black Jack. 1981: Looks and Smiles. 1986: Fatherland. (US: Singing the Blues in Red). 1990: Hidden Agenda. Riff-Raff. 1993: Raining Stones. 1994: Ladybird Ladybird. 1995: Land and Freedom. 1996: Carla's Song. 1998: My Name is Joe.

LOGAN, Joshua 1908-1988

Texas-born Josh Logan was so much a man of the theatre for most of his life that it's amazing he actually made a real impact in the cinema with his few films as director. At 20 the director of the (rather unsuccessful) University Players group that also

included Margaret Sullavan, Mildred Natwick, Kent Smith, Henry Fonda and James Stewart, Logan studied direction in Moscow under the great drama teacher Stanislavsky, who had invented 'the Method'; he returned to America in 1932, mixing stage work with a mild flirtation with the cinema, in which he acted as dialogue director or co-director on a few independent films turned out by David Selznick and Walter Wanger. But in 1938, he had his first big Broadway success, directing *On Borrowed Time*, and the stage claimed him for 18 years, one collapse from mental exhaustion, and a string of enormous hits that included *Annie Get Your Gun, Fanny, Mister Roberts, Middle of the Night* and *South Pacific*. It wasn't until 1955 that Logan was able to turn his attention to the cinema, with a version of another of his stage successes, *Picnic*, but he immediately showed great understanding of the medium. With superb colour photography (by James Wong Howe) bathing it in a warm (but never sentimental) glow of nostalgia, *Picnic* is a striking, unusual and delightful film about aggression and repression that comes out as something between a comedy-drama and a love story —and pure cinema. Encouraged, Logan followed up with *Bus Stop*, another emotive film and one of the best of its year, with brilliant perfor-

*A young Ken **Loach** discusses a scene with Sandy Ratcliff in the harrowing Family Life (US: Wednesday's Child).*

Its a musical Josh: cheer up. Joshua **Logan** on the set of 1967's *Camelot.*

mances from Arthur O'Connell and (in patches) Marilyn Monroe, despite a southern-belle accent which at times sounds more like Australian. Logan was nominated for an Oscar for *Picnic* and again two years later for *Sayonara,* a long but touching story of American soldiers in love with Japanese girls at the time of the Korean War. A moving suicide scene, subtly handled by director and actors, helped win Academy Awards for both players concerned, Red Buttons and Miyoshi Umeki. There were no awards, however, for the inflated and slightly dull version of *South Pacific,* a film which signalled the end of the love affair between critics, public and

Logan, who, despite a few further half-cock films, soon returned to the theatre.

1938: †I Met My Love Again. 1955: Picnic. 1956: Bus Stop. 1957: Sayonara. 1958: South Pacific. 1960: Tall Story. 1961: Fanny. 1964: Ensign Pulver. 1967: Camelot. 1969: Paint Your Wagon.

LOSEY, Joseph 1909-1984

American film-maker who fell foul of the McCarthy blacklist soon after starting his feature-film career, and had to re-establish himself from a British base. The successes of his career were strikingly different films

that give pleasure by their very inventiveness and the director's facility for making entertainment out of unusual subjects. Losey's failures, however, were fairly massive. Although his supporters remained devoted to the cause of Losey as one of the world's great directors, he did not get on with the box-office after the 1960s. Losey did a little acting in his early days, and studied film in Russia under Eisenstein before directing on stage and working for the Rockefeller Foundation as the producer of dozens of industrial short films. His first commercial short was a marionette film, but his fourth, *A Gun in His Hand* (made for M-G-M's *Crime Does Not Pay* series which encouraged young directors) won an Academy Award. His early American films are a mixed bunch with the accent on problems of social conscience, and generally foreshadowed the up-and-down nature of Losey's career. *The Boy with Green Hair,* for example, is a charming fantasy with something relevant to say, and *The Big Night* as miserable as it is dire. In no time at all, however, the House Un-American Activities Committee saw to it that the newcomer was unemployable in his native country. He made a couple of presentable thrillers in Britain under assumed names, but was able to start using his own name again from 1957, at first on undistinguished films — *Time Without Pity* is almost as gloomy as *The Big Night* — but then chiefly in films with Stanley Baker, on vividly treated subjects that made the critics take up his cause. The best Losey film of this period is *The Servant,* in which a sinister, satanic butler gradually reverses positions with his weak, foppish master; it is a brilliantly acted film (the first of several with Dirk Bogarde) which illustrated Losey's preoccupation with the relationship between good and evil, in a deeper sense than that encountered in straightforward melodramas. Losey is on the side of good, but sorrowfully admits that evil seems to win through in the end. After that, the good films – *King and Country, Secret Ceremony, The Go-Between, Mr Klein* – were rather outnumbered by those in which, under rather pretentious treatment, tedium set in early. There were times when one wished Losey had had a rather more down-to-earth approach to his subjects — but then that might have robbed us of several very good films as well.

*1939: *Pete Roleum and his Cousins. 1941: *A Child Went Forth. *Youth Gets a Break. 1945: *A Gun in His Hand. 1948: The Boy with Green Hair. 1950: The Lawless. 1951: The Prowler. The Big Night. M. 1952: Stranger on the Prowl.*

*1954: $The Sleeping Tiger. 1955: *A Man on the Beach. 1956: **The Intimate Stranger (US: Finger of Guilt). 1957: Time Without Pity. The Gypsy and the Gentleman. 1959: Blind Date (US: Chance Meeting). 1960: The Criminal (US: The Concrete Jungle). *First on the Road. 1961: The Damned (US: These Are the Damned). 1962: Eve (US: Eva). 1963: The Servant. 1964: King and Country. 1966. Modesty Blaise. 1967: Accident. 1968: Secret Ceremony. Boom! 1970: Figures in a Landscape. The Go-Between. 1972: The Assassination of Trotsky. 1973: A Doll's House. 1974: Galileo. 1975: The Romantic Englishwoman. 1976: Mr Klein. 1978: Les routes du sud. 1979: Don Giovanni. 1982: The Trout. 1984: Steaming.*

$ as Victor Hanbury
** as Joseph Walton

LUBIN, Arthur 1899-1995

The pictures that this California-born director made were foolish but fun, their simple entertainment values disguising Lubin's meticulous approach, which involved long hours of preparation and an insistence on getting things just right. He was fortunate in becoming involved with two big money-making comedy series at their outset, but the weight of his career conceals quite a number of other small pleasures. Lubin began his career as an actor and – looking like a cross between Dub Taylor and Robert Morley – would probably have made an interesting character player. Someone, though, suggested to a minor studio, Monogram, that Lubin's experience might make him a useful director — and the pattern of his career was established. He joined Universal, his home off-and-on for more than 20 years, in 1936. Several of his early films for them were John Wayne adventure films. A couple of these, *California Straight Ahead* and *Adventure's End*, are well above average. In 1939, Lubin spotted Abbott and Costello performing their comedy routines at the New York World Fair, and recommended them to the studio. The following year, he found himself directing their first starring film, *Buck Privates*. Lubin had no great experience in comedy at the time, but helped highlight the new stars, talents in such a way that both they and the film were a wild success. Lubin directed all four of the Abbott and Costello films that followed — and never had basic 'B' movie comedies taken so much money. Universal found itself solvent again. But Lubin quit the series as his two stars were growing less and less agreeable, and their working habits more and more erratic. He put more money in the Universal coffers with a stylish new version of the old Lon Chaney success, *The Phantom of the Opera*, with spectacularly staged shocks. That old smoothie Claude Rains and Universal's tame songbird Susanna Foster brought a touch of sophistication to the hoary old yarn, which won two Oscars — for best colour photography and best colour art direction. In the late 1940s Lubin came up with a new winner for his studio in Francis the Talking Mule. Lubin's skill at getting laughs by clever cross-cutting turned a rather ordinary fantasy-comedy into a goldmine. *Francis* wasn't actually nearly as funny as the marvellous Lubin comedy *Rhubarb*, which is about a ferocious ginger cat that inherits a struggling baseball team. Of Lubin's later films, *Star of India* is a well-knit swashbuckler, faultless within its medium budget, *Queen for a Day* engaging sentiment and *The Incredible Mr Limpet* an enjoyable fantasy with cartoon inserts, about a man who turns into a fish. By this time Lubin was working hard in television — on *Mr Ed*, the comedy series about a talking horse. He died of complications from a stroke.

1934: A Successful Failure. 1935: Great God Gold. Honeymoon Limited. Two Black Sheep (later Two Sinners). Frisco Waterfront (GB: When We Look Back). 1936: The House of a Thousand Candles. Mickey the Kid (released 1939). Yellowstone. 1937: Mysterious Crossing. I Cover the War. Idol of the Crowd. California Straight Ahead. Adventure's End. 1938: Midnight Intruder. Secrets of a Nurse. The Beloved Brat (GB: A Dangerous Age). Prison Break. 1939: Risky Business. Big Town Czar. Call a Messenger. 1940: The Big Guy. Black Friday. Gangs of Chicago. I'm Nobody's Sweetheart Now. Meet the Wildcat. Buck Privates (GB: Rookies). Who Killed Aunt Maggie? 1941: San Francisco Docks. In the Navy. Where Did You Get That Girl? Hold That Ghost. Keep 'Em Flying. 1942: Ride 'Em Cowboy. Eagle Squadron. 1943: White Savage (GB: White Captive). The Phantom of the Opera. Ali Baba and the 40 Thieves. 1945: Delightfully Dangerous. 1946: Spider Woman Strikes Back. Night in Paradise. 1947: New Orleans. 1949: Impact. Francis. 1951: Francis Goes to the Races. Queen for a Day. Rhubarb. 1952: Francis Goes to West Point. It Grows on Trees. 1953: South Sea Woman. Francis Covers the Big Town. Star of India. 1954: Francis Joins the WACs. 1955: Footsteps in the Fog. Lady Godiva (GB: Lady Godiva of Coventry). Francis in the Navy. 1956: The First Traveling Saleslady. 1957: Escapade in Japan. 1960: The Thief of Baghdad. 1963: The Incredible Mr Limpet. 1965: Hold On! 1971: Rain for a Dusty Summer.

LUBITSCH, Ernst 1892-1947

German-born director of feather light comedies and comedy-musicals, a great stylist whose German films, often with Pola Negri, had already made him an international name before Hollywood beckoned in 1923. Once there, he quickly developed a reputation for making sex comedies in the subtlest, yet cheekiest way. Paramount was able to promote him as 'the man with the golden touch' and could guarantee enormous box-office returns from his films, especially those with Jeanette MacDonald and Maurice Chevalier, in which, as with most of his lighter films, he brought out the more impish comic possibilities of his principals. In Lubitsch's films, the actors seemed to be enjoying themselves in spite of the fact that, according to another well-known director, they actually had very little to do, as Lubitsch, like Hitchcock in another genre, had planned their every move down to the last detail. Alas for Hollywood, in real life its very own King Midas had a weak heart.... He was born in Berlin, and acting in his teens. At 19, he was already a member of Max Reinhardt's famous Deutsches Theater, beginning to appear in films from the following year (first appearance in *Das Mirakel*), making several comedies as a character called Meyer, which he may well have drawn from his own Jewish tailor father. He began directing in 1914 and scored his first big success four years later, after a series of comedies featuring the blonde Ossi Oswalda, a sort of Teutonic Mary Pickford, when Pola Negri, impressed by Lubitsch's subtle handling of character development, asked for him on her film *Die Augen der Mumie Mâ*. The film, a rather crude shocker, also featured Emil Jannings, and it was to Negri and Jannings that Lubitsch now turned for feature-length successes that would travel the world, while be continued to make the shorter Meyer and Oswalda comedies. These were mostly passionate historical melodramas which allowed Miss Negri's full-blooded style a free hand. In 1922, Mary Pickford invited Lubitsch to Hollywood to direct her in a film (perhaps she had seen the Oswalda comedies) and, although Lubitsch and Pickford proved not to get on, he never looked back. He soon modified his rather heavy German style to produce sophisticated satires involving sex and money. *Trouble in Paradise* is probably the most elegant, while the naughty-but-nice MacDonald-Chevalier films proved the most popular of all. He was director of production at Paramount in the 1930s, but it was an arid period as far as he himself was concerned. He made amends four times over in the 1939-1943 period, with Garbo's *Ninotchka* and the mittel-European *The Shop Around the Corner* (neither has dated well), plus *To Be or Not To Be*, a classic farce of pain, and *Heaven Can Wait* (a playboy telling his sins to Satan when he dies), neither of which has dated at all. After this, illness put a brake on Lubitsch's work, and he died from his sixth heart attack half way through a film (it was finished by Otto Preminger).

1914: *Fraulein Seifenschaum. 1915: *Blinde Kuh. *Auf Eis geführt. *†Zucker and Zimt. *Leutnant auf Befiel. 1916: *Wo ist mein Schatz? *Der schwarze Moritz. Als ich tot war. Schuhpalast Pinkus. *Der gemischte Frauenchor. *Der G.m.b.H. Tenor/Tenor, Inc. *Der erste Patient. 1917: *Ossis Tagebuch/Ossi's Diary. Der Blusekönig. *Wenn vier dasselbe tun. *Ein fideles Gefängnis. *Der Kraftmeyer. *Der letzte Anzug. *Prinz Sami. 1918: *Der Rodelkavalier. Der Fall Rosentopf/The Rosentopf Case. Ich möchte kein Mann sein. Die Augen der Mumie Mâ (GB: The Eyes of the Mummy. US: Eyes of the Mummy Mâ). *Das Mädel vom Ballet. Carmen (US: Gypsy Blood). *Führmann Henschel. *Marionetten. 1919: *Meier aus Berlin. Schwabenmädel. *Meine Frau, die Filmschauspielerin. Die Austernprinzessin/The Oyster Princess. Rausch/Intoxication. Madame Dubarry (US: Passion). Die Puppe/The Doll. 1920: Kohlhiesels Töchter/His Two Daughters. *Romeo und Julia im Schnee. Sumurun (GB & US: One Arabian Night). Anna Boleyn (GB: Anne Boleyn. US: Deception). 1921: Die Bergkätze (GB: The Mountain Cat. US: The Wildcat). 1922: Das Weib des Pharao (GB & US: The Loves of Pharaoh). 1923: Die Flamme (GB & US: Montmartre). Rosita. 1924: The Marriage Circle. Three Women. Forbidden Paradise. 1925: Kiss Me Again. Lady Windermere's Fan. 1926: So This is Paris. 1927: The Student Prince (in Old Heidelberg). 1928: The Patriot. 1929: Eternal Love. The Love Parade. 1930: Monte Carlo. †Paramount on Parade. 1931: The Smiling Lieutenant (and French-language version). 1932: Broken Lullaby (GB: The Man I Killed). †One Hour with You. Trouble in Paradise. †If I Had a Million. 1933: Design for Living. 1934: The Merry Widow (and French-language version). 1937: Angel. 1938: Bluebeard's Eighth Wife. 1939: Ninotchka. 1940: The Shop Around the Corner. 1941: That Uncertain Feeling. 1942: To Be or Not to Be. 1943: Heaven Can Wait. 1946: Cluny Brown. 1948: †That Lady in Ermine.

LUCAS, George 1944-

It is a distressing aspect of modern filmmaking that, no sooner has a young director had a huge success, than he seems to diversify. This has happened to an extent in more recent times with Quentin Tarantino (qv): Lucas, though, remains the most glaring example. Since his *Star Wars* in 1977, Lucas has become a Roger Corman-like figure, involved in everything from production and special effects to TV series and computer software. Not until

The team that made *The Empire Strikes Back*. Left to right: Irvin Kershner (director), Gary Kurtz (producer), George Lucas (executive producer) and Lawrence Kasdan.

1998 did he return to film-making with the first of three *Star Wars* prequels on which most of his fans had frankly given up. As a young student of film at the University of Southern California, Lucas made several short films, one of which was *THX-1138* (1965), which he would later expand into his first feature — a kind of cross between *1984, Star Wars* and *Westworld,* with Lucas showing off his mastery of the medium in terms of science-fiction entertainment. Surprisingly, the film was not a big commercial success, but that came two years later with *American Graffiti,* by far the best (because it created character and captured period at the same time) of a number of nostalgic films in the early 1970s set a few years in the past. A number of talented people made early appearances in this immensely profitable film, among them Harrison Ford, whom Lucas would later use in *Star Wars,* an outer-space pantomime which conveys its own sense of fun so well that audiences flocked in their millions. The unprecedented 21-year-gap that followed makes it extremely unlikely that Lucas will live to see his ambition of nine 'Star Wars' films fulfilled.

*1965: *THX-1138: 4 EB. 1967: *Herbie Anyone Lived in a Pretty Hometown. 1968: *The Emperor. 1970: THX-1138. 1973: American Graffiti. 1977: Star Wars. 1998/9: Star Wars Prequel 1.*

LUDWIG, Edward 1895-1982

As with many other actors who made a reasonable success of direction, hardly anyone now seems to remember that Ludwig began his career on the public side of the camera, mostly for Vitagraph in the early 1920s. Ludwig was born in Russia, but his family emigrated to America and later moved to Canada, where their son was educated. Ludwig first became a screenwriter when he gave up acting, but began directing in 1932. He soon showed a willingness to tackle a wide variety of genres, even if his output was not prodigious. There are few pictures more action-packed than Ludwig's adventure films and he showed an innate sense of pace which only deserted him once or twice in the early 1950s: *Big Jim McLain,* made then, is about his worst film, one of the few bad ones. As befits a wanderer in life, Ludwig roamed from studio to studio during his 30-year directing career — 11 of them, in all, including all the 'majors' and all the best-known 'minors'. Not that his work was so poor he had to keep on the move: if you were rating Ludwig films on a scale of one to four, I can't think of any that would get four, but quite a lot that would

merit three. There was an early role for Fred MacMurray in *Friends of Mr Sweeney;* a first starring vehicle for Claude Rains in the macabre *The Man Who Reclaimed His Head,* driving Edward G. Robinson to a pitch of intensity to match his *Little Caesar* in *The Last Gangster;* and bringing a breath of fresh air to the 1940 version of *Swiss Family Robinson.* The second of two action-filled war films – *They Came to Blow Up America* and *The Fighting Seabees* – brought Ludwig's first encounter with John Wayne, whom he subsequently directed on what remained Wayne's favourite Republic picture, *Wake of the Red Witch,* a seafaring adventure with an agonising, tragic climax, and an enormous budget by Republic standards of a million-and-a-quarter dollars. In the 1950s, Ludwig made several Technicolor action films for the Pine-Thomas unit at Paramount, of which *Caribbean* (glorious action fare about pirates and hidden treasure) and *The Vanquished,* a post-Civil War western, are the best. Ludwig's last film, *The Gun Hawk,* a thoughtful western with an amazing performance of almost Brando-like intensity from Rory Calhoun, confirmed Ludwig as the craftsmanlike director one had always suspected.

1932: Steady Company. 1933: They Just Had to Get Married. 1934: A Woman's Man. Let's Be Ritzy (GB: Millionaire for a Day). Friends of Mr Sweeney. 1935: The Man Who Reclaimed His Head. Old Man Rhythm. Age of Indiscretion. Three Kids and a Queen (GB: The Baxter Millions). 1936: Fatal Lady. Adventure in Manhattan (GB: Manhattan Madness). 1937: Her Husband Lies. The Barrier. The Last Gangster. 1938: That Certain Age. 1939: Coast Guard. 1940: Swiss Family Robinson. 1941: The Man Who Lost Himself. 1942: Born to Sing. 1943: They Came to Blow Up America. 1944: The Fighting Seabees. Three is a Family. 1947: The Fabulous Texan. 1948: Wake of the Red Witch. 1949: The Big Wheel. 1951: Smuggler's Island. 1952: Big Jim McLain. The Blazing Forest. Caribbean (GB: Caribbean Gold). 1953: Sangaree. The Vanquished. Jivaro (GB: Lost Treasure of the Amazon). 1955: Flame of the Islands. 1957: The Black Scorpion. 1963: The Gun Hawk.

LUMET, Sidney 1924-

This American film-maker used to be my favourite director. I was ecstatic over *12 Angry Men,* impressed by *The Pawnbroker* and trampled on by *The Hill;* and thought *The Deadly Affair* about the best thriller of its decade. Such worship makes

it all the more difficult to be objective, but I think disillusionment started about *The Group,* with its ragbag of disparate elements which Lumet made, as with many of his later films, so dislikeable as to alienate one from the movie itself. He began as an actor (only film: *One Third of a Nation* in 1939), but made his reputation as a director with CBS Television in the early 1950s. His first film, *12 Angry Men* (1957), has its detractors now, but in truth is a marvellous audience-manipulating jury-room drama which has not lost its grip over the years. It remains a power-charged piece of fuse-wire drama, with carefully studied performances. and a score of telling little moments that, under the director's thoughtful control, help to make it heartwarming and effective. This endistancing from effective performances served Lumet in good stead in the next ten years, especially on *The Fugitive Kind, Long Day's Journey into Night* and *The Deadly Affair,* powerful dramas tightly controlled. As befits one of the most personalized entries in this book, the Seventies Lumet films that I like are those that few others seem to: *The Anderson Tapes, Lovin' Molly* and *The Wiz,* films in which Lumet cannot let a 'statement' get in the way of the controlling theme. The real-life crime dramas, *Serpico, Dog Day Afternoon* and *Prince of the City* are fashioned (at length) to have the maximum impact (and *Dog Day* does have some stunning overhead work), but they simply aren't as interesting as Lumet thinks they are; while the much-lauded *Network* is simply unpleasant. No, he has become a rather flat director, although I will continue to go to a Lumet movie with high hopes, and *The Verdict* has some refreshingly old-fashioned virtues, while even the much-maligned *Guilty As Sin* has some electrifying moments that most critics seem to have missed. Three times nominated for an Oscar, the energetic Lumet continues to work into his seventies. He has been married four times, the first to actress Rita Gam.

1957: 12 Angry Men. 1958: Stage Struck. 1959: That Kind of Woman. 1960: The Fugitive Kind. 1961: A View from the Bridge. 1962: Long Day's Journey into Night. 1964: Fail Safe. 1965: The Pawnbroker. The Hill. 1966: The Deadly Affair. The Group. 1968: Bye Bye Braverman. The Sea Gull. 1969: The Appointment. Last of the Mobile Hotshots (GB: TV as Blood Kin). 1970: †King: a Film Record. . . Montgomery to Memphis (D). 1971: The Anderson Tapes. 1972: Child's Play. 1973: Lovin' Molly. Something Like the Truth (later The Offence). 1974: Serpico. Murder on the Orient Express.

Hollywood veterans Paul Newman and Sidney **Lumet** discuss a scene on their only film together, *The Verdict*.

1975: Dog Day Afternoon. 1976: Net-work. 1977: Equus. 1978: The Wiz. 1979: Just Tell Me What You Want. 1981: Prince of the City. 1982: Death-trap. The Verdict. 1983: Daniel. 1984: Garbo Talks. 1985: Power. 1986: The Morning After. 1988: Running On Empty. 1989: Family Business. 1990: Q & A. 1992: A Stranger Among Us/Close to Eden. 1993: Guilty As Sin. 1996: Night Falls on Manhattan. 1998: Critical Care. Gloria.

LUNA, Bigas (José Juan B. Luna) 1946-
Spanish director of up-market sex films, the thinking-man's Russ Meyer. Luna's films are spectacular in their vulgarity, but almost always stunningly well pho-tographed and containing driving doses of lifeforce. Not for the easily (or even not so easily) offended, the films, just like Meyer's, have built up a cult following on the European arthouse circuit. Narrative drive is not their strongpoint, but the atmosphere conjured up in various parts of Spain – 'My country fascinates me', Luna has written – and the tongue-in-cheek treatment of macho heroes and hot-

blooded women are distinctive trademarks of Luna's work. His career had begun in industrial and interior design, but, after examining the prospects of visual aspects of various sections of the media, Luna had settled on building a cinema career by his late twenties. After establishing a reputa-tion for avant-garde bestiality in comedies of the blackest hue, Luna made his first multi-award-winning film, *Anguish*, in which he toyed playfully with the conven-tions of the thriller in a plot about a mad-man with a mother fixation at large in a cinema whose audience is watching a film with a similar theme. Sexual activity con-tinued to be an overriding theme in Luna's films, which assumed higher profile with the success of *Golden Balls* and *Jamón, Jamón*, the latter strongly reminiscent of Meyer with its desert settings, macho bat-tles and frequent couplings. *The Tit and the Moon* was a step backwards, its embarrassing crudity and pretentiousness undermining the gentle earthiness aimed for and overwhelming such pleasing ele-ments as crystal-clear camerawork of the Catalan countryside. The critically-pasted *Bambola* is also best forgotten, but Luna regained lost ground with the stylish and

thoughtful *The Chambermaid of the Titanic* which, in drifting away from a Spanish setting, perhaps inevitably has a much cooler feel than Luna's previous work.

1976: Tatuaje. 1978: Bilbao. 1979: Caniche/Poodle. 1981: Renacida/Reborn. 1985: Lola. 1987: Angustia/Anguish. 1990: The Ages of Lulu/Las edades de Lulu. 1992: Jamón, Jamón. 1993: Golden Balls/Huevos de oro. 1994: The Tit and the Moon/La teta y la luna. 1996: Bam-bola. 1997: La femme de chambre du Titanic (GB: The Chambermaid of the Titanic. US: The Chambermaid and the Titanic). 1999: The Naked Maja. 1999: The Naked Maya

LYNCH, David 1946-
Although his cult star has waxed and waned, this American specialist in sublim-inal surrealism has always reasserted his grip on his followers with some new aspect of his own *ciné-fantastique*. Lynch makes puzzle pictures that no one is expected to solve, and jigsaw films whose pieces never quite fit together. And, just

to prove himself capable of making a 'normal' film, he made one on a very abnormal subject, *The Elephant Man*, and was nominated for an Academy Award in the doing. He was born in Montana, the son of an agriculture research scientist who 'was always in the woods'. Lynch studied painting, then lived rough for a while and did odd jobs before additional studies at the Philadelphia Academy of Fine Arts led to the commissioning of his first short film. Even at four minutes, this ends with a repulsive, blood-spattered image of the kind that runs through all his subsequent work. The film that put Lynch on the map, *Eraserhead*, took four years to make, and depicts a weird, nightmare, post-apocalyptic future where everyone receives a lobotomy at birth. Full of stomach-churning imagery, it attracted the curious, if not the critical. They went instead to *The Elephant Man*, which, even though Lynch's direction tends to the melodramatic, is a remarkable film about a grotesquely deformed man rescued from a freak show in Victorian times and subsequently sheltered by a brilliant surgeon. Lynch then declined *Return of the Jedi*, to which he might have made an interesting contribution, in favour of the impenetrable *Dune*, which proved a triumph of visual imagination, but a complete mishmash of storytelling. Lynch was back on home territory, though, with *Blue Velvet*, a cross between *film noir* and film bizarre whose dark doings command attention. His TV series *Twin Peaks* quickly built a large cult following after the quirky attractiveness of the pilot and following episodes, but all too soon the series became wilfully obscure and lost its following. Lynch, though, hit back with *Wild at Heart*, a 'road' movie unlike any other and a Palme d'Or winner at Cannes. Just when it seemed that the world was his (probably brain-eating) oyster, Lynch made a *Twin Peaks* spin-off film full of half-seen things, subliminal shots, pictures coming to life and not much sense. It died. It was four years before he tried again, with *Lost Highway*, which starts like a mystery horror film, but develops into a story in which Lynch plays hypnotically with parallel worlds, fused (and confused) identities and the occult. It would be impressive if it all made sense at the end, but, as ever, this is not Lynch's game. A partial explanation is offered, but the true sequence of events doesn't add up. Indeed it's not supposed to. To enter a Lynch film is to be welcome to a world where two and two are always five. His daughter Jennifer Lynch (1968-) directed the equally bizarre *Boxing Helena* (1993).

1968: *The Alphabet. 1970: *The Grandmother. 1976: Eraserhead. 1980: The Elephant Man. 1984: Dune. 1986: Blue Velvet. 1989: Industrial Symphony No.1: The Dream of the Broken-Hearted. Twin Peaks (TV). 1990: Wild at Heart. 1992: †Hotel Room (TV). Twin Peaks Fire Walk With Me. 1996: Lost Highway. 1999: The Straight Story.*

LYNCH, Jennifer
See LYNCH, David

LYNE, Adrian 1941-
British-born director, long in America, who makes eye-catching, controversial films that tend to either ignite or fizzle at the box-office, often in no proper relation to their merit. After seeming settled in a career making TV commercials, Lyne burst into films at 38, courting controversy from the start with *Foxes*. The story of teenage girls growing up in Los Angeles' San Fernando Valley, it came across as *Beach Party* meets *Valley of the Dolls*, its few sparks of joy unable to counter its overall depression. It was greeted with deserved apathy by the public, but not so the next one, *Flashdance*, which pulled them in at the box-office, despite being little more than a feature-length music video. The adrenalin surge of its dance routines (mainly performed by a stand-in for star Jennifer Beals) drew a vivid response from audiences. Joe Public, though, stayed away in droves from *9½ Weeks*, a seemingly surefire sexploitation

film with high-profile stars in Kim Basinger and Mickey Rourke, who proved in the long run to have all the sexual spark of two haddocks on the fishmonger's slab. But there was plenty of spark in *Fatal Attraction*, by far the director's biggest hit to date. A white-knuckle rollercoaster thriller with a good ration of jumpy moments, its unpleasantness and the intensity of the performances by stars Glenn Close and Michael Douglas gave the film such word-of-mouth appeal that the public were soon flocking in. Lyne then declined to direct *The Bonfire of the Vanities*, which was a wise decision, but did little better with the rather ponderous psychological thriller *Jacob's Ladder*, about a Vietnam vet suffering a series of horrific hallucinations. The controversial elements which might have made the film a success were rather negated by the downbeat treatment. Small wonder that Lyne seemed to go for an easier option next time round with *Indecent Proposal*, which was equally dull and unimaginative, but a much more commercial proposition, carrying as it did Robert Redford's proposal to spend one night with Woody Harrelson's wife Demi Moore for $1 million. Unconvincing stuff but, typical of Lyne, glossily dished up in such an attractive manner that the public swallowed it whole. They haven't had much chance though to savour his 1996 film *Lolita*.

1979: Foxes. 1983: Flashdance. 1986: 9½ Weeks. 1987: Fatal Attraction. 1990: Jacob's Ladder. 1993: Indecent Proposal. 1996: Lolita.

Maverick director David **Lynch** at work on *Twin Peaks Fire walk With Me*.

Director Jonathan **Lynn** (centre) looks like a character from one of his films, but comedy is obviously a serious business for stars Eric Idle and Robbie Coltrane in *Nuns on the Run.*

LYNN, Jonathan 1943-

Writer, producer, director and actor — few film-makers have as many strings to their bow as this king of comedy. For years Lynn, who started off as a percussionist in London revues, concentrated on dual career as a comic actor and director of stage plays. His co-writing and directing work on the enormously successful British TV series *Yes, Minister* (later *Yes, Prime Minister)* gave him a higher profile, and he moved into film direction with great success in the 1990s. The British-made *Nuns on the Run* led to a Hollywood entree and Lynn's most successful film, *My Cousin Vinny,* which featured a plum role for Joe Pesci as a 40-something embryo lawyer, and won an Oscar for Marisa Tomei as his tight-skirted, gum-chewing girlfriend. Lynn followed up well with *The Distinguished Gentleman,* a jolly and quite effective comedy vehicle for Eddie Murphy, as a

con-man elected to Congress where he finds himself, not unnaturally, quite at home. The fitted in well with Lynn's brand of what one might call farcical satire. Since then, this man of many talents' films have gone off the boil somewhat, although both *Sgt Bilko* and *Trial and Error* had more funny moments than their critics allowed and demanded, like much of Lynn's work, patience in getting to know the characters before they can really make you laugh. Perhaps a return to political comedy would be beneficial.

*1982: *Mick's People. 1985: Clue. 1990: Nuns on the Run. 1991: My Cousin Vinny. 1992: The Distinguished Gentleman. 1994: Greedy. 1996: Sgt Bilko. 1997: Trial and Error. 1999: The Ghost and Mrs Muir.*

MacDONALD, David 1904-1983

Scottish-born director of British films, trained in Hollywood. He made some good thrillers (and the occasional comedy) in the late 1930s and immediate post-war years, but seemed to lose his touch after the *Christopher Columbus* disaster in 1949. In his twenties he managed a rubber plantation in Malaya, but went to America in 1929, and became interested in film-making. Cecil B. DeMille *(qv)* hired him as a production assistant, but it would seem from MacDonald's subsequent career that he never developed the master's taste for films of epic stature. MacDonald went with DeMille on his return to Paramount in 1932, then came to Britain in 1936, making quota films for Paramount British. MacDonald's first big success came with a series of films, mainly comedy-thrillers, made with Barry K. Barnes, whose career would also disappoint in post-war years. The pattern of these was set by the first, *This Man is News*, with Barnes and Valerie Hobson, as a reporter and his girl-friend, tracking down a gang of jewel thieves. A briskly amusing script and MacDonald's snappy direction made this a very lively and entertaining film. The star trio, Barnes, Hobson and Alastair Sim, were reunited on the equally successful *This Man in Paris*, and the Barnes-MacDonald partnership continued through *Law and Disorder* (also with Sim), *Spies of the Air* and *The Midas Touch* before it was broken up by World War II. MacDonald joined the

Crown Film Unit for whom he made a stirring documentary, *Men of the Lightship*. As producer, he was also involved with Roy Boulting's award-winning documentaries, *Desert Victory*, and *Burma Victory*. MacDonald began the post-war years well enough, especially with *Snowbound*, a thriller of claustrophobic menace despite its Alpine setting, with Robert Nemton, Dennis Price, Stanley Holloway and Guy Middleton all in good form as men changed by greed, a theme to which MacDonald would return. 1949 produced three large-scale misfires, one of which, the wordy *Christopher Columbus*, sank under a surfeit of dialogue and practically took Fredric March's star career with it, although he continued as a star character player. MacDonald never recovered that lost ground, although the following year brought the interesting *The Adventurers*,

again about a group of men – this time Peter Hammond, Dennis Price (again), Jack Hawkins and Bernard Lee after, not gold as in *Snowbound*, but diamonds in South Africa. In both films, MacDonald's direction skilfully elicits sympathy for basically good men overcome by desire of riches. A lively swashbuckler, *The Moonraker*, was a small highlight in the last years of his film career, by which time he was already entrenched in television drama.

1936: Double Alibi. 1937: The Last Curtain. Riding High. It's Never Too Late to Mend. Death Croons the Blues. When the Poppies Bloom Again. 1938: Make It Three. Dead Men Tell No Tales. Meet Mr Penny. This Man is News. A Spot of Bother. 1939: Spies of the Air. This Man in Paris. The Midas Touch. 1940: Law

Director David **MacDonald** (right) and star Lee Patterson at work on a TV drama of the 1950s.

and Disorder. Men of the Lightship (D). †Crimes at the Dark House (uncredited). 1941: This England. *Lofoten (D). Left of the Line (D). 1947: The Brothers. 1948: Good Time Girl. Snowbound. 1949: Diamond City. Christopher Columbus. 1950: Cairo Road. The Adventurers (US: The Great Adventure). 1952: The Lost Hours (US: The Big Frame). 1953: Tread Softly. Operation Malaya (D). 1954: Devil Girl from Mars. §The Yellow Robe. §Three-Cornered Fate. §One Just Man. 1956: Alias John Preston. 1957: Small Hotel. 1958: The Moonraker. 1961: Petticoat Pirates. 1962: The Golden Rabbit.

§ TV segments strung together to make a feature film

MACKENDRICK, Alexander 1912-1993

How good a director was Mackendrick? All of his films except the last are brilliantly crafted entertainments with fascinating characters who, whether in comedy or drama, spring to life and hold one's attention throughout. Yet Mackendrick made only eight films in his 19 years as a director. Perhaps he had an increasingly hard task finding subjects that interested him, and the supply eventually ran out altogether. At any rate he did not add to his filmography after the late 1960s, when he was appointed Dean of the Film Department of the California Institute of the Arts. Born in America of Scottish parents, Mackendrick was raised in Scotland, and would return to that country twice for inspiration for his Ealing comedies. He began his career in films as an animator and scriptwriter for cartoons and, after documentary experience in wartime Italy with an army psychological welfare unit, he joined Ealing Studios as a sketch artist in 1946. His first film as director, Whisky Galore, kicked off several comedies in which 'intruders' are eventually confounded by traditional British values. These films – The Man in the White Suit, The Maggie and The Ladykillers are others – hold the interest because of the development of not one but several of the characters within its story. This holds good for such Mackendrick dramas as Sweet Smell of Success, Sammy Going South and his finest film, A High Wind in Jamaica. This last, an adaptation of Richard Hughes' novel about Victorian children on a pirate ship, has a sea voyage so believable one can almost taste the salt, and demonstrates again Mackendrick's marvellous skill with child actors, previously presented with Mandy Miller in The Man in The White Suit and Mandy, and Fergus McClelland in Sammy Going South. In

Jamaica, Deborah Baxter gives a performance of such gut-ripping intensity that it is small wonder she never approached half-way to matching it in a disappointing subsequent career. This intensity is the key to Mackendrick's successes. He had the ability to help actors reach emotional depths of which some would not have believed themselves capable.

1943: *Nero/Fiddling Fuel. 1949: Whisky Galore (US: Tight Little Island). 1951: The Man in the White Suit. 1952: Mandy. (US: Crash of Silence). 1954: The Maggie (US: High and Dry). 1955: The Ladykillers. 1957: Sweet Smell of Success. 1963: Sammy Going South (US: A Boy Ten Feet Tall). 1965: A High Wind in Jamaica. 1967: Don't Make Waves.

MacKINNON, Gillies 1948-

Scottish film director whose best work to date has been shot in his native country. MacKinnon, who often works in conjunction with his writer-producer brother Billy, originally studied mural painting at the Glasgow School of Art, then taught art in London, while boosting his income by working as a freelance cartoonist. Later, he began experimenting with short films, and got accepted on to a three-year course at London's National Film and Television School. When his graduation feature, Passing Glances, won several prizes and was broadcast on Channel 4, it was clear that MacKinnon had found his vocation. More films for Channel 4 and its rival, the BBC, followed, all of them festival successes, but especially The Grass Arena, the story of an alcoholic boxer who, in prison, discovers a life-saving interest in chess. Also of note (and much more fun) was Conquest of the South Pole, about five workless Edinburgh youths who re-create Amundsen's famous expedition to the South Pole in their own back yard. There was a rough-edged freshness and reality about these early films, but MacKinnon was slightly less successful with trips abroad. The Playboys, a 'tinker's tale' about a travelling carnival in Ireland, was not entirely unsuccessful in its old-fashioned, rather meandering way, but MacKinnon was unlucky with his first Hollywood assignment, A Simple Twist of Fate, based on George Eliot's Silas Marner, for which star Steve Martin had requested him. Unfortunately, Martin himself was completely unsuited to the central role and a dreary drama resulted, with nil returns at the box-office. For a while, MacKinnon struggled. He returned to his roots with Small Faces, a Glasgow tenement drama set in the 1960s. Although well per-

formed, it seemed oddly dated in approach. Still, it was more interesting than a return to Ireland with the dismal Trojan Eddie, but MacKinnon re-established his reputation for poignant human drama with Regeneration, a World War One story of shellshocked soldiers being prepared for a return to the front, at a Scottish mansion converted into a sanatorium. Armed with a screenplay by Allan Scott that strikes no false notes, MacKinnon produced a film that, despite its subject, was never less than gripping and entertaining. Graphic images of bodies half-buried on the battlefield are sufficient to bring the reality home without being over-used. After such perfection, one hopes MacKinnon can move forward with renewed confidence.

1986: Passing Glory. 1989: Conquest of the South Pole. 1990: Needle (TV). 1991: The Grass Arena (TV. Also shown in cinemas). 1992: The Playboys. 1994: A Simple Twist of Fate. 1995: Small Faces. 1996: Trojan Eddie. 1997: Regeneration. 1998: Hideous Kinky.

MAKAVEYEV, Dušan 1932-

Romances and comedies come no blacker than those made by this controversial Yugoslavian director: his films, though few in number, are almost guaranteed to give censors in all but the most liberated countries apoplexy, containing as they do blunt sexual visions seemingly calculated to shock, but in fact all part of the director's own darkly humorous approach to satire and political statement. His films are allied to those of Luis Buñuel (qv), but have more of a surface brightness. They mainly deal with female characters whose minds, bodies or lives are destroyed by pressures – especially Eva Ras in The Switchboard Operator, Milena Dravic in W.R and Susan Anspach in Montenegro. Naturally, such goings-on have been frowned upon in the Communist world, where some of Makaveyev's work has been banned. He is now past 60, and it seems unlikely that he will ever become a prolific film-maker, although he retains his own brand of cynical enthusiasm. It may be that, like other Eastern European refugee directors, Makaveyev could even end up in Hollywood. He has expressed enthusiasm for the American players with whom he has worked, and his work is well enough known in the United States: his Montenegro is the sort of film one would envision Frank Capra turning in if asked to make an X-rated movie, with the weirdest group of people one could imagine as well as Makaveyev's usual quota of blatant, faintly tongue-in-cheek sexual affront. His films remain true curiosities of the cinema and, as he is never likely to lose his individuality, will always offer a challenge to one's senses whether set in Belgrade, in Belgravia or on Hollywood Boulevard.

1953: *Jatagan mala. 1955: *Pečat/The Seal. 1957: *Antonijevo razbijeno ogledalo. 1958: *Spomenicima ne treba verovati. *Prokleti praznik/Feast of the Damned. *Slikovnica pcelara/The Beekeeper's Picture Book. *Boje sanjaju. 1959: *Sto j to radnicki savjet? 1961: *One Potato, Two Potato. *Pedagoska bojka. *Osmjeh 61. 1962: *Film o knjizi ABC. *Parade. *Dole platovi. 1963: *Miss Beauty 62. 1964: *Nova domaca životinja. *Nova igraćka. 1965: Covek nije tijka/Man is Not a Bird. 1967: Tragedija sluzbenice P.T.T. (GB: The Switchboard Operator. US: An Affair of the Heart/The Case of the Missing Switchboard Operator). 1968: Nevinist bez zastite (GB and US: Innocence Unprotected). 1971: W.R. Mysteries of the Organism. 1972: I Miss Sonia Henie. 1974: Sweet Movie. †Dreams of Thirteen (under pseudonym Sam Rotterdam). 1980: Montenegro, or: Pigs and Pearls. 1984: The Coca Cola Kid. 1988: Manifesto. 1993: The Gorilla Bathes at Noon. 1995: A Hole in the Soul.

MAKK, Karoly 1925-

Perceptive Hungarian director concerned both with the minutiae of life and portraits of people under pressure. Although never overwhelmingly acclaimed, even in his native country, Makk's steady output over a 50-year period has resulted in some well-acted and keenly observed films without any covert meanings, resulting in a flow of awards from film festivals. In a Makk film, what you see is pretty much what you get. As he said of one of his more recent works: 'Please do not look for any hidden philosophical depths or heights behind this seemingly complicated film.' Born into a small farming community, Makk grew up on a diet of Hollywood films fed to him by his father, who owned the local cinema. Makk himself began working in films soon after World War Two, but fell out with the authorities after the Communist takeover of 1949 and found himself packed off to a documentary film unit, not re-emerging to make his first feature until 1954. Subsequently, Makk's work introduced Hungarians to various 'problems' of society, including mid-life crises, juvenile crime, worklessness and housing shortages. The popular *Another Way* (1982) dealt with lesbianism and (much

more daring in Hungary) political repression, while *A Very Moral Night* (1977), set in a brothel, was an even bigger popular hit. Of Makk's other films, the most lauded by festivals has been *Love* (1970), a moving study of the relationship between two older women, one of whom has not long to live. And there has been the occasional international venture, such as *Lily in Love* (1983), a wise and witty adult comedy with plum roles for Maggie Smith and Christopher Plummer, and *The Gambler*, a story of Dostoyevsky, which marked a return to the screen for veteran Oscar-winning actress Luise Rainer after many years away.

1949: *Uttrk (D). 1951: *Colony Underground (D). 1954: Liliomfi. 1955: A 9-es korterem/Ward No. 9. 1956: Mese a 12 talalatrol/Tale of the 12 Points. 1958: Haz a sziklak alatt/The House Under the Rocks. 1959: A 39-es dandar/The 39th Brigade. 1960: Don't Keep Off the Grass. 1961: Megszallottak/The Fanatics. 1902: Elveszett paradicsom/Lost Paradise. 1963: Az utolso elotti ember/The Last But One. 1964: Mit csinatt felseged 3 tol 5/His Majesty's Dates/Where Was Your Majesty Between Three and Five? 1967: Bolondos vakacio/A Cloudless Vacation. 1968: Isten es ember elott/Before God and Men. 1970: Szerelem/Love. 1974: Macskajatek/Cat's Play. 1977: Egy erkolcsos ejszaka/A Very Moral Night. 1978: Philemon and Baucis. 1979: A teglafal matt/Behind the Brick Wall. 1980: Draga kisfiam! 1981: Die Jäger/Deadly Game. 1982: Another Way. 1983: Lily in Love/Jatsani kell/Fitz and Lily. 1980: Az utolso kezirat/The Last Manuscript. 1989: Hungarian Requiem. 1994: Positive. 1996: Hungarian Pizza. 1997: The Gambler.

MALLE, Louis 1932-1995

A critic remarked of one of Malle's last films that it was lovely to look at, but lacked narrative drive. That was not always true of the rich variety of work turned out by this French director, but it became increasingly so since the early 1970s. Malle had already been in filmmaking 20 years by then, from studying film at college to undertaking a series of voyages with the undersea explorer Jacques Cousteau that eventually resulted in the colour documentary *The Silent World*. Malle then struck out into film fiction with the gripping thriller, *Lift to the Scaffold*. In the succeeding years, Malle made a gloriously wide variety of films, underlining his own attempts to escape categorization and his denial of the 'auteur' theory. He ended this period with three of his best films – *Le feu follet, Viva*

Maria! and *Le voleur*. The first of these is a deeply moving study of an alcoholic drifting out of a hopeless life and towards suicide. A fine film, it contains Maurice Ronet's most deeply felt performance as the pitiable central character and was a sizeable international success. Even more so was *Viva Maria!* a firecracker of a movie firing off lunatic sight gags in all directions, and pairing Jeanne Moreau and Brigitte Bardot as a couple of amorous song-and-dance girls mixed up with revolutionaries in turn-of-the-century Latin-America. It didn't please many critics, but went down marvellously well with the general filmgoing millions. Malle veered off into another contrast with his next film, *Le voleur*, with its careful reconstruction of turn-of-the-century Paris, engrossing screenplay and one of Jean-Paul Belmondo's tightest performances in the title role. Malle then retraced his documentary roots by going to India, from which visit came a feature-length documentary and a TV series telescoped for cinemas as *Phantom India*. These brought home many of the less palatable aspects of impoverished Indian life (although not as well as the films of native Indian Satyajit Ray), but Malle seemed to return from his travels a changed man. The hand of Great Art now lay heavily on his shoulders and, although his films continued to explore a wide variety of themes, tedium often set in during the lyrical treatment of realism, and it appeared that Malle all too often was not achieving his own ambitious goals. Nevertheless, some of the later films, especially *Le souffle au coeur, Lacombe Lucien* and *Atlantic City, USA*, have their fervent admirers, and *Pretty Baby*, as well as making an international figure of Brooke Shields, brought its director another huge commercial success. In his last decade, however, Malle produced two films worthy of comparison with his best. First of these was *Au revoir les enfants*, a poignantly semi-autobiographical story about three Jewish boys hidden from the Nazis by the head of a Catholic boarding school. It was followed two years later by the quietly riotous and gently biting black comedy *Milou en mai*, a slightly shocking and utterly charming piece. Malle died at 63 from lymphoma complications. His second wife was the American actress Candice Bergen.

1955: *La fontaine de Vaucluse (D). *Station 307 (D). 1956: †Le monde du silence (GB: The Silent World). 1957: Ascenseur pour l'échafaud (GB: Lift to the Scaffold. US: Frantic). 1958: Les amants (GB & US: The Lovers). 1960: Zazie dans le Métro (GB & US: Zazie). 1962: Vie

Louis **Malle** at work on one of his English-speaking projects, *Atlantic City USA*, which won a best picture Academy Award nomination.

privée (GB & US: *A Very Private Affair*). *Vive le tour (D). 1963: *Le feu follet* (GB: *A Time to Live and a Time to Die*. US: *The Fire Within/Will o' the Wisp*). 1964: *Bons baisers de Bangkok* (D). 1965: *Viva Maria! Le voleur* (GB: *The Thief*. US: *The Thief of Paris*). 1968: †*Histoires extraordinaires* (William Wilson episode. GB: *Tales of Mystery*. US: *Spirits of the Dead*). 1969: *Calcutta* (D). *Phantom India* (D). 1971: *Le souffle au coeur* (GB: *Dearest Love*. US: *Murmur of the Heart*). 1972: *Humain, trop humain* (D. TV GB: *A Human Condition*). 1973: *Place de la République* (D). 1974: *Lacombe Lucien*. 1975: *Black Moon*. 1978: *Pretty Baby*. 1980: *Atlantic City, USA* (GB & US: *Atlantic City*. 1981: *My*

Dinner with André. 1983: *Crackers*. 1984: *Alamo Bay*. 1985: *God's Country* (D). 1986: *And the Pursuit of Happiness*. 1987: *Au revoir les enfants*. 1989: *Milou en mai* (GB: *Milou in May*. US: *May Fools*). 1992: *Damage*. 1994: *Vanya on 42nd Street*. 1996: *Marlene*.

MAMOULIAN, Rouben 1898-1987

Innovative Russian-born Hollywood director fond of orchestrating effects liable to make knowing audiences burst into applause. 'My aim,' he once said, 'was always rhythm and poetic stylization.' Perhaps this explains why some of his films, the less successful ones, are curiously lacking in flesh and blood, although striking to

behold, as with all Mamoulian's work. Any number of five-minute sequences from Mamoulian films could be (and hopefully are) shown to students as living examples of the largely lost art of cinema. These would certainly include the entire opening sequence of *Applause* (sights and sounds of the city apparently organized to the beat of a metronome), the camera discreetly observing Gary Cooper and Sylvia Sidney in *City Streets*, the 'remembering zis room' sequence by Garbo from *Queen Christina*, the remarkably intelligent use of colour in *Becky Sharp*, the duel between Tyrone Power and Basil Rathbone in *The Mark of Zorro* (a dance of death in a confined space), the transformation scene in *Dr Jekyll and Mr Hyde*, and big, densely populated musical set-pieces in *Love Me Tonight*, the underrated *High, Wide and Handsome* and the warmly nostalgic *Summer Holiday* that are as thrillingly assembled as the action scenes in any Michael Curtiz film. One of Mamoulian's most enjoyable films is his last, *Silk Stockings*, a musical remake of *Ninotchka* which Mamoulian packs with colour and humour and in which he brings winning performances from each one of his artists – a screen mixture of music, comedy and drama as only Mamoulian could make it. Mamoulian had come to America at 25, still very much a director of traditional Russian theatre. But his experience in opera led him on to the stage version of *Porgy and Bess*, and the formulation of the Mamoulian style, which held early sound audiences in thrall. Mamoulian was certainly among the liberators of the cinema, blending sound, visuals and camera movement with montage effects to capture the atmosphere of his setting and create the rhythm of his film – a world beyond the reach of most of his contemporaries. By the late 1950s, however, despite the success of *Silk Stockings*, the time for poets and innovators had sadly gone: Mamoulian was removed from two further films, *Porgy and Bess* and *Cleopatra* – ironically, both were critical and commercial failures – and did not set foot in cinematic waters again.

1929: *Applause*. 1931: *City Streets*. *Dr Jekyll and Mr Hyde*. 1932: *Love Me Tonight*. 1933: *Song of Songs*. *Queen Christina*. 1934: *We Live Again*. 1935: *Becky Sharp*. 1936: *The Gay Desperado*. 1937: *High, Wide and Handsome*. 1939: *Golden Boy*. 1940: *The Mark of Zorro*. 1941: *Blood and Sand*. 1942: *Rings on Her Fingers*. 1946: *Summer Holiday* (released 1948). 1951: †*The Wild Heart* (revised version of GB 1950 film *Gone to Earth*, with new material by Mamoulian). 1957: *Silk Stockings*.

MANKIEWICZ, Joseph L. 1909-1993

Despite winning four Academy Awards within a two-year period, this American director's films have not, on the whole, been among the foremost of Hollywood's achievements. After that initial golden period, indeed, Mankiewicz only had one or two minor successes, and soon gave up on film-making altogether. He made slow progress from being a writer (from 1929) and producer (from 1936), as if he liked these roles. Indeed, he often continued in these capacities when he became a director in the post-war years. It is in his strength as a writer of witty, urbane dialogue that his real talent lies – as a master of verbal in-fighting. No-one disputes the brilliance of the dialogue in his two Oscar-winning screenplays for *A Letter to Three Wives* and *All About Eve*. But the Directorial Academy Awards for the same two films are a little more surprising, since Mankiewicz has always been less concerned about how a film looks – something that undoes him, for example, in *The Barefoot Contessa* – than how it sounds. His interest in the cinema had begun while he was working as a correspondent for an American newspaper in Berlin in 1928. He made contacts at the U.F.A. Studios there, and was asked to translate title cards from German into English. On returning to America, Mankiewicz landed a job as a junior writer at Paramount and was put to work on title cards. With the beginning of sound, he was promoted to screenplays. These were mainly comedies and included *Million Dollar Legs, If I Had a Million* and *Diplomaniacs*. As a producer, his biggest successes included *Fury, The Shopworn Angel, The Philadelphia Story* and *Woman of the Year*. It is hard to believe that Mankiewicz did not have a hand in the smart dialogue of these last two Katharine Hepburn successes, but his initial efforts as a director were, strangely, in more dramatic vein. The best of these are the gripping and underrated amnesiac thriller *Somewhere in the Night,* one of the best-constructed of all Mankiewicz films, and the charming ghost fantasy, *The Ghost and Mrs. Muir.* In between the two Oscar-winning films, *House of Strangers* and *No Way Out* are both enthralling thrillers, and Mankiewicz followed on with the hugely successful spy suspense story *Five Fingers,* as suavely smooth and plausible as James Mason's roguish central scene-stealing character. After that it was largely a case of great expectations (and sometimes budgets) and small returns. Only *There Was a Crooked Man*, with its typically amoral protagonists, is really enjoyable in the old Mankiewicz style. He married (second of

three) actress Rosa Stradner She committed suicide in 1958.

1946: *Dragonwyck. Somewhere in the Night. The Late George Apley.* 1947: *The Ghost and Mrs Muir.* 1948: *Escape.* 1949: *A Letter to Three Wives. House of Strangers.* 1950: *No Way Out. All About Eve.* 1951: *People Will Talk.* 1952: *Five Fingers.* 1953: *Julius Caesar.* 1954: *The Barefoot Contessa.* 1955: *Guys and Dolls.* 1957: *The Quiet American.* 1959: *Suddenly Last Summer.* 1963: *Cleopatra.* 1964: *Carol for Another Christmas (TV).* 1966: *The Honey Pot.* 1970: *There Was a Crooked Man.* 1972: *Sleuth.*

MANN, Anthony
(E. Anton Bundesmann) 1906-1967

Working his way up one of the traditional routes of major American film-makers, through well-noticed minor thrillers, Anthony Mann made some remarkably good westerns, almost all with James Stewart, in the 1950s. Apart from a successful epic, *El Cid*, though, he seemed not to know where to go from there and his career had faltered when he died half-way through making what proved to be his final film. Mann worked in his chosen medium all his life, becoming a stage manager before he was 20, and directing Broadway plays, as Anton Bundmann,

Puffing the familiar pipe, the abrasive Oscar-wining Joseph L **Mankiewicz** is pictured at work in the 1950s.

through the 1930s. He directed screen tests for Selznick in the late 1930s and made his home permanently in the cinema from the early 1940s when he became an assistant director at Paramount, later moving across to RKO as a director of what would later become known as 'noir' thrillers. These gradually improved in quality, after a shaky start, to the point where *Desperate* and *Railroaded!* are actually quite compelling within their low-budget limitations. By the time he made the latter, Mann had moved across to the ambitious but short-lived quality low-budget surroundings of Eagle-Lion. It was here that he made the two crime thrillers that really got him noticed – *T-Men* and *Raw Deal*. These hard-hitting, dark and shadow-stylized crime thrillers were both photographed by John Alton and featured Dennis O' Keefe in semi-documentary stories about the cleaning-up of crime in the city. Two years later, Mann established his forte when he made *Winchester 73*, with James Stewart in the first of several roles as characters whose determination to stick to their guns would take them to the limits of their endurance. Stewart was often assisted in these first-class rugged westerns, which became big box-office draws, by Arthur Kennedy as the good-bad man who was initially friends with the hero, but usually had to die in the end. Others in this thoroughly enjoyable series included *Bend of the River*, *The Far Country*, *The Naked Spur* and *The Man from Laramie*. After the mid-1950s, Mann's hits came less frequently. But *The Tin Star* is one of his most powerful and stylish films, visually memorable in a way that harks back to his work of the 1940s (it was his last film in black-and-white) especially in the shot of the black carriage trotting back into town, a harbinger of tragedy. The best of Mann's later films is *El Cid*, a thinking man's epic with performances of great nobility from Charlton Heston and Sophia Loren, which finds beauty in all but its battles, these remaining bloody and undisciplined.

1942: Moonlight in Havana. Dr Broadway. 1943: Nobody's Darling. 1944: Strangers in the Night. My Best Gal. 1945: Two O'Clock Courage. The Great Flamarion. Sing Your Way Home. 1946: Strange Impersonation. The Bamboo Blonde. 1947: Desperate. Railroaded! T-Men. 1948: Raw Deal. †He Walked By Night (uncredited). 1949: Reign of Terror/The Black Book. Border Incident. 1950: Side Street. Devil's Doorway. Winchester '73. The Furies. 1951: The Tall Target. 1952: Bend of the River (GB: Where the River Bends). 1953: The

Naked Spur. Thunder Bay. The Glenn Miller Story. 1954: The Far Country. 1955. Strategic Air Command. The Man from Laramie. The Last Frontier. 1956: Serenade. 1957: Men in War. The Tin Star. 1958: Man of the West. God's Little Acre. 1960: Cimarron. 1961: El Cid. 1963: The Fall of the Roman Empire. 1965: The Heroes of Telemark. 1968: † A Dandy in Aspic.

MANN, Daniel (D. Chugerman) 1912-1991
Arriving in films late, after years on Broadway, this American director has had most success with (one would have thought, non-box-office) portraits of mid-dle-aged love affairs and some bright, colourful romps, faintly lunatic in a civi-lized way. After the mid-1960s, though, his choice of subjects often seemed less suited to his talents. In the beginning, Mann was successful in turning some unlikely vehicles into profitability. The first of these, almost inevitably, was a screen version of a stage success, featuring the debut of its middle-aged star Shirley Booth, whom Mann was to direct twice more in her very sporadic film career. The film *Come Back, Little Sheba* was highly publicized and, although it seems unduly turgid and gloomy today, much praised by the critics. Strangely, a lot of p people also went to see it, and suddenly Mann was a film director in some demand. His follow-up vehicle for Miss Booth, *About Mrs Leslie*, is actually rather more enjoy-able in its sad, romantic, affecting way, with more perceptive dialogue too, but it was less well liked. From the heady melo-drama of *The Rose Tattoo* and *I'll Cry Tomorrow* (yet another Susan Hayward bid for an Oscar) Mann moved unexpect-edly to *The Teahouse of the August Moon*. Again, this comedy about Ameri-can troops being indoctrinated into the Japanese way of life, with Marlon Brando in oriental guise, proved highly pro-motable and its success substantiated Mann's reputation as a man who got eye-catching (and often award-winning) per-formances from his stars. Paul Muni made a decent enough comeback in another Mann vehicle, *The Last Angry Man*, and then Elizabeth Taylor became the third actress (following Shirley Booth and Anna Magnani) to win an Academy Award in a Mann film when she starred in *Butterfield 8*. *Who's Got the Action?* and *Who's Been Sleeping in My Bed?* proved to be two unexpectedly bright and enjoyable vehicles for Dean Martin, although talented supporting actors such as Walter Matthau, Eddie Albert and Carol Burnett undoubtedly helped. *Our Man Flint* was also tremendously enjoy-

able, magnificent rubbish and the best of the sub-Bond films, with a cheetah-like hero in James Coburn (in true Mann style, the performance made him a star) and a great pace. Life after that was less successful for Mann, working mainly with fading stars. But *Willard* at least was a popular hit.

1952: Come Back, Little Sheba. 1954: About Mrs Leslie. 1955: I'll Cry Tomor-row. The Rose Tattoo. 1956: The Tea-house of the August Moon. 1958: Hot Spell. 1959: The Last Angry Man. 1960: The Mountain Road. Butterfield 8. 1961: Ada. 1962: Five Finger Exercise. Who's Got the Action? 1963: Who's Been Sleep-ing in My Bed? 1965: Judith. Our Man Flint. 1968: For Love of Ivy. 1969: A Dream of Kings. 1970: Willard. 1971: The Harness (TV). 1972: The Revengers. 1973: Interval. Maurie. 1974: Lost in the Stars. 1976: Journey into Fear. 1978: Matilda. 1980: The Incredible Mr Chad-wick. Playing for Time (TV). 1981: The Day the Loving Stopped (TV). 1987: The Man Who Broke 1000 Chains (cable TV).

MANN, Delbert 1920-
Coming to the cinema as its new white hope via a string of TV successes, this American director gradually dissipated that promise to the point where he was once again one of the most prolific direc-tors in American television, but working on routine TV movie projects. Sad, but it's true that through the years there has been a gradual decline in Mann's work, held up from time to time with highpoints that showed a director still interested in human values when the opportunity came along. He had worked his way from stage manager to director after World War II service as a bomber pilot, when the chance to work in television drama came in 1950. He handled the original versions of three Paddy Chayefsky plays, all of which he turned into interesting films. The first and most famous (even today it's probably still Mann's best-known film) was *Marty*, whose naturalistic dialogue fed a whole host of satirists. It hardly seemed Academy Award-winning stuff even in its time, even if Ernest Borgnine, Betsy Blair and Esther Minciotti were all very good, and the simple love story-cum-light comedy quite tellingly made. Still, it walked off with best film, best director, best actor (Borgnine) and best screenplay (Chayefsky) Oscars and Mann was on his way. *The Bachelor Party* was the second Chayefsky-Mann vehicle, a beautifully acted story of suburban aimlessness, but often boring and commercially unsuccess-ful. The third, *Middle of the Night*, was

both touching and had star value in Fredric March and Kim Novak. It did quite respectably, but not as well as *Separate Tables,* with David Niven deservedly winning an Oscar for his fake major, or the poignant *The Dark at the Top of the Stairs.* Mann then moved into a more commercial kind of cinema and for a while enjoyed great success, largely thanks to the good scripts on such Doris Day vehicles as *Lover Come Back* and *That Touch of Mink. Fitzwilly,* too, had the brightness and fun performances that distinguished these, but by the time he made it, in 1967, Mann's cinema career was definitely on the wane. He turned determinedly to adaptations of classic novels, for TV showing in America and cinemas elsewhere. These lack sparkle and flair, although his *Jane Eyre* is effectively made and played (by Susannah York and George C. Scott) apart from a dotty ending. Of the fistful of TV movies that followed, the best are *Francis Gary Powers* etc. which draws the acting maximum out of Lee Majors, and *Home to Stay,* featuring another of Henry Fonda's affecting portraits of the exigencies of old age.

1955: Marty. 1957: The Bachelor Party. 1958: Desire Under the Elms. Separate Tables. 1959: Middle of the Night. 1960: The Dark at the Top Of the Stairs. 1961: The Outsider. Lover Come Back. 1962: That Touch of Mink. 1963: A Gathering of Eagles. 1964: Dear Heart. 1965: Quick, Before It Melts. Mister Buddwing (GB: Woman Without a Face). 1967: Fitzwilly (GB: Fitzwilly Strikes Back). 1968: The Pink Jungle. Heidi Comes Home (US: TV as Heidi). 1970: David Copperfield (US: TV). Jane Eyre (US: TV). 1971: Kidnapped (US: TV). 1972: She Waits (TV). No Place to Run (TV). 1973: The Man without a Country (TV). 1975: A Girl Named Sooner (TV). 1976: Birch Interval. Francis Gary Powers: the True Story of the U-2 Spy Incident (TV). 1977: Tell Me My Name (TV). Breaking Up (TV). 1978: Love's Dark Ride (TV). Home to Stay (TV). Thou Shalt Not Commit Adultery (TV). 1979: Torn Between Two Lovers (TV. GB: cinemas). 1981: Night Crossing. 1983: The Member of the Wedding (TV). Brontë. The Gift of Love: A Christmas Story (TV). 1984: Love Leads the Way (TV). 1986: The Last Days of Patton (TV). Teddy: The Ted Kennedy Jr Story (TV). 1988: April Morning (TV). 1991: Ironclads (TV).

MARIN, Edwin L. 1899-1951

Competent, well-liked American director who worked reliably away on a variety of popular middle-range comedies, westerns and thrillers for 20 years until his early death at 52. Marin began in the business as a cameraman, but moved over to assistant director with the advent of sound films. A couple of small companies, Sono Art-World Wide and Monogram, gave him his first experience of direction and in 1934 he was lucky enough to be hired by M-G-M to direct some of their medium-budget co-features. M-G-M's were the cream of 'B' features and Marin was given the opportunity to work with better actors, technicians and production values than he would have got at other studios. A couple of Philo Vance mysteries were mixed with some minor screwball comedies and, towards the end of his M-G-M tenure, Marin inside the first four *Maisie* comedies with Ann Sothern. These leaned heavily on the peppy personality of their blonde star, and were really no great shakes, but pleased wartime audiences who made the films into a highly profitable series. In the latter stages of his career, Marin made a highly watchable John Wayne 'mystery western' *Tall in the Saddle,* and then six films with a failing George Raft and seven with a never-failing Randolph Scott. The best of the Scotts, all well plotted, slightly unusual adventures, several in Cinecolor, were *Abilene Town, Canadian Pacific, Fighting Man of the Plains* and *The Cariboo Trail.* Marin never managed to make a memorable film: even his decent treatment of *A Christmas Carol* was eventually eclipsed by the definitive British-made version 13 years later. But he had a sure visual eye that often produced pleasing results, notably in some of the Scott westerns. Perhaps he might have been more successful working with colour movies and outdoor settings rather earlier in his too-brief lifetime.

1932: The Death Kiss. 1933: The Avenger. A Study in Scarlet. The Sweetheart of Sigma Chi (GB: Girl of My Dreams). 1934: Bombay Mail. Affairs of a Gentleman. Paris Interlude. The Crosby Case (GB: The Crosby Murder Case). 1935: The Casino Murder Case. Pursuit. 1936: Speed. The Garden Murder Case. Moonlight Murder. I'd Give My Life. All American Chump (GB: Country Bumpkin). Sworn Enemy. 1937: Man of the People. Married Before Breakfast. 1938: Hold That Kiss. The Chase. Everybody Sing. A Christmas Carol. Listen, Darling. 1939: Fast and Loose. Society Lawyer. Henry Goes Arizona (GB: Spats to Spurs). Maisie. 1940: Florian. Hullabaloo. Gold Rush Maisie. 1941: Maisie Was a Lady. Ringside Maisie (GB: Cash and Carry). 1942: Paris Calling. A Gentleman After Dark. Miss Annie Rooney. Invisible Agent. 1943: Two Tick-

ets to London. 1944: Show Business. Tall in the Saddle. 1945: Abilene Town. Johnny Angel. 1946: Young Widow. Mr Ace. Lady Luck. Nocturne. 1947: Intrigue. Christmas Eve. 1948: Race Street. 1949: The Younger Brothers. Canadian Pacific. Fighting Man of the Plains. 1950: The Cariboo Trail. Colt. 45. Raton Pass (GB: Canyon Pass). 1951: Sugarfoot. Fort Worth.

MARION, Frances
See Hill, George (William)

MARSHALL, Garry (G. Marscharelli) 1934-

A one-time joke writer and stand-up comedian, Marshall's career as a director now seems to be on the downswing after reaching a crescendo in the 1987-1991 period with a run of four winning (in every sense) films which marked him out, however briefly, as the hottest director in Hollywood. Coming late (at 47) to direction after a writing and producing career, Marshall, the brother of director Penny Marshall, had begun his working life as a reporter for the *New York Daily News.* In his spare time, he played drums in a jazz group and bombarded well-known TV comedians with material for their shows. By the time he was 30, he had moved to a regular career in comedy writing; he was also executive producer of the consistently funny TV series of *The Odd Couple,* which ran for five years from 1970. The zany *Young Doctors in Love* provided his entry into film direction, and he scored a cult hit with *The Flamingo Kid* which he also co-wrote. An early hit for Matt Dillon, it also featured character actor Hector Elizondo in the first of eight films for Marshall, and was a perceptive look at beguiling immaturity and empty lives. Marshall now began directing high-profile stars in crowd-pleasing roles. *Overboard,* an underrated Goldie Hawn-Kurt Russell comedy, buzzing with incident and inbuilt pace, was merely an overture for the huge Bette Midler hit *Beaches,* a 24-carat gold weepie which builds to a tremendous climax you need at least two handkerchiefs to even see. Like *Overboard,* it has a terrific script, in this case by Mary Agnes Donoghue. Even this success was overshadowed by the next, *Pretty Woman,* which saw romantic comedy making a comeback in style and Julia Roberts jetting to stardom as the hooker ensnaring Richard Gere's millionaire wheeler-dealer. A warm and funny tale full of telling little moments, it benefited from Marshall's input, as well as his skill in showcasing the actors, who once again included Elizondo, here in his best turn for Marshall as the hotel manager.

Frankie & Johnny, again embellished with typical Marshall comedy touches, was almost a guaranteed success with Al Pacino and Michelle Pfeiffer as stars, but Marshall's directing career has dipped unexpectedly since then.

1982: Young Doctors in Love. 1984: The Flamingo Kid. 1986: Nothing in Common. 1987: Overboard. 1988: Beaches. 1990: Pretty Woman. 1991: Frankie & Johnny. 1994: Exit to Eden. 1996: Dear God. 1999: Runaway Bride.

MARSHALL, George 1891-1975

Impossible to encapsulate in a few words such a vast career, devoted mainly to westerns and comedies and, inevitably, comedy-westerns. Marshall directed for over 50 years, making close to 100 features and scores of one- and two-reelers. He had a certain, wry sense of what was funny and he was usually right. And many of his films, even the zaniest of the comedies, had a certain warmth that other directors wouldn't have achieved, heightening one's pleasure in the fun. Laurel and Hardy, W.C. Fields, Bob Hope, Jerry Lewis and many lesser film funnymen came under Marshall's warm and witty supervision. He began as an actor, (and was still playing small 'gag' roles in the 1930s), but was directing two-reel westerns by 1916. A gap in his amazing output, from 1926 to 1932, is explained by the fact that he was acting mainly in supervisory capacities during these years, notably from 1925 to 1928, when he was in charge of the Fox shorts programme. He did find time after this period, however, to direct two of the most delightful Laurel and Hardy two-reelers, *Their First Mistake* (in which they find and attempt to look after a baby) and the famous boat-painting comedy *Towed in a Hole*. Marshall's directing career really took off from 1939, when he made a Fields comedy, *You Can't Cheat an Honest Man* and the classic western romp, *Destry Rides Again*. Marshall would now remain a top Hollywood director for more than 20 years: he pushed Bob Hope's career forwards with the classic comedy-chiller *The Ghost Breakers* (later remade for Martin and Lewis by Marshall himself as *Scared Stiff*); teamed Alan Ladd and Veronica Lake profitably for the last time in *The Blue Dahlia*, making the most of that film's nocturnal settings; made a number of entertaining films with Fred MacMurray, the best of which is the black comedy *Murder He Says*; set Martin and Lewis on the road to success in *My Friend Irma*; directed Bob Hope again, to great effect, in *Monsieur Beaucaire* and *Fancy Pants*;

and scored a major box-office success, vaguely in *Destry* vein (and Marshall remade that one, too) with Glenn Ford and Shirley MacLaine in *The Sheepman*. His last nine films show a severe falling off to which a man in his late seventies who had directed so many funny movies was perhaps entitled.

*1916: *The Devil's Own. †*A Woman's Eyes. Love's Lariat. 1917: The Man From Montana. *Double Suspicion. *Bill Brennan's Claim. *Border Wolves. *The Comeback. *The Desert Ghost. *Casey's Border Raid. *The Honor of Men. *Meet My Wife. *The Raid. *Right-of Way Casey. *Roped In. *They were Four. *Won By Grit. 1918: *The Embarrassment of Riches. *Husband Hater. *The Fast Mail. 1919: The Adventures of Ruth (serial). Ruth of the Rockies (serial). Prairie Trails. 1920: A Ridin' Romeo. Hands Off. 1921: After Your Own Heart. The Lady from Longacre. The Jolt. 1922: *The Committee on Credentials. *West is West. Smiles Are Trumps. 1923: Why Trust Your Husband? Where is This West? Don Quickshot of the Rio Grande. The Haunted Valley. Men in the Raw. 1924: *The Fight. *The Hunt. *The Burglar. *Paul Jones, Jr. 1925: *A Parisian Knight. *The Sky Jumper. *A Spanish Romeo. *The Big Game Hunter. 1926: *It's a Pipe. *Two Lips in Holland. 1927: *Gentlemen Prefer Scotch. 1930: *He Loved Her Not. *Hey Diddle Diddle. 1931: *Practice Shots. 1932: *Their First Mistake. The Soilers. Strictly Unreliable. *A Firehouse Honeymoon. *The Old Bull. *Alum and Eve. *Big Dame Hunting. Pack Up Your Troubles. *Just a Pain in the Parlor. 1933: *Hip Action. *Husbands' Reunion. Knockout Kisses. *Position and Back Swing. *Sweet Cookie. *Towed in a Hole. *The Big Fibber. *Impact. *Caliente Love. *Down Swing. *Easy on the Eye. *Fine Points. 1934: Ever Since Eve. She Learned About Sailors. Wild Gold. 365 Nights in Hollywood. 1935: $10 Raise (GB: Mr Faintheart). Lift Begins at 40. In Old Kentucky. Music is Magic. Show Them No Mercy (GB: Tainted Money). 1936: A Message to Garcia. Can This Be Dixie? The Crime of Dr Forbes. 1937: Nancy Steele is Missing. Love Under Fire. 1938: The Goldwyn Follies. Battle of Broadway. Hold That Co-Ed (GB: Hold That Girl). 1939: Destry Rides Again. You Can't Cheat an Honest Man. 1940: When the Daltons Rode. The Ghost Breakers. 1941: Texas. Pot o' Gold (GB: The Golden Hour). 1942: Valley of the Sun. The Forest Rangers. Star Spangled Rhythm. 1943: True to Life. Riding High (GB: Melody Inn). 1944: And the Angels Sing. 1945:*

Murder, He Says. Hold That Blonde. Incendiary Blonde. 1946: The Blue Dahlia. Monsieur Beaucaire. 1947: Variety Girl. The Perils of Pauline. 1948: Tap Roots. Hazard. 1949: My Friend Irma. 1950: Never a Dull Moment. Fancy Pants. 1951: A Millionaire for Christy. 1952: The Savage. Off Limits (GB: Military Policemen). 1953: Scared Stiff. Houdini. 1954: Money from Home. Red Garters. Duel in the Jungle. Destry. 1955: The Second Greatest Sex. 1956: Pillars of the Sky (GB: The Tomahawk and the Cross). 1957: The Guns of Fort Petticoat. Beyond Mombasa. The Sad Sack. 1958: The Sheepman. Imitation General. 1959: The Mating Game. It Started with a Kiss. The Gazebo. 1961: Cry for Happy. 1962: †How the West Was Won. The Happy Thieves. 1963: Papa's Delicate Condition. Dark Purpose. Advance to the Rear (GB: Company of Cowards). 1966: Boy Did I Get a Wrong Number! Eight on the Lam (GB: Eight on the Run). 1968: The Wicked Dreams of Paula Schultz. 1969: Hook, Line and Sinker.

MARSHALL, Penny (Penelope Marscharelli) 1942-

Genial, fun-loving American actress turned director whose career behind the camera began with a bang, but has recently lost some of its impetus. She was on the road with her mother's dancing troupe as a teenager but had settled into comedy roles in TV series by her mid twenties. Her career breakthrough came in 1970 when her first starring show, *Laverne & Shirley*, soared to the top of the ratings at the beginning of its seven-year run. Marshall directed several episodes in the series, as well as episodes in the 1979 Michael Keaton-James Belushi series *Working Stiffs*, three of which were strung together for video release. Marshall was to have made her film directing debut on *Peggy Sue Got Married* but, when replaced by Francis Ford Coppola, she moved to the Whoopi Goldberg comedy *Jumpin' Jack Flash*. Although an uneven comedy spy thriller, the film was quite popular and Marshall was then offered *Big*, the most successful in a rash of age-reversal comedies at that time, which was in fact huge at the box-office, as well as winning an Oscar nomination for its star, Tom Hanks. Hanks would reappear in Marshall's baseball comedy *A League of Their Own*, but meanwhile she tackled more dramatic fare in *Awakenings*, perhaps her best film to date, a heartwarming and heartbreaking true story of catatonic patients revived temporarily by a caring doctor and a new drug. There is much to admire and touch the emotions throughout the film. This and *A League of Their*

Own, another film based on truth, this time about girls' baseball teams during World War II, were popular hits, but Marshall has perhaps since played too safe for her own god, particularly with *The Preacher's Wife*, a mistaken remake of a delicate fantasy classic, which led one to think that the director was in need of fresher material to revitalise her career. Her brother is the director Garry Marshall and her second (1971-79) husband was another director, Rob Reiner.

1979: Working Stiffs (video). 1986: Jumpin' Jack Flash. 1988: Big. 1990: Awakenings. 1992: A League of Their Own. 1994: Renaissance Man. 1996: The Preacher's Wife.

MARTON, Andrew (Endre Marton) 1904-1992

Hungarian film-maker, working internationally from the late 1920s, who became known both for his penchant for exotic and far-away settings in adventure films, and as a second-unit director of the highest calibre, often being called upon to film the action sequences for insertion into other directors' films. Marton certainly knew how to make the screen come alive with movement in an explosive and exciting way, but his few feature films as solo director provide some odd contrasts to this work, and include several animal films of some charm and warmth, shot on picturesque locations. Later he would reinforce this side of his career by directing many episodes of wild life-oriented TV series, such as *Daktari, Flipper* and *Sea Hunt*. Marton began his career as a film editor, working with Ernst Lubitsch in Germany and later Hollywood, where he directed his first film. After wandering half the world, making films with such backdrops as the North Pole, the Himalayas and Istanbul, Marton settled in Hollywood from 1940, and with M-G-M from 1944 until 1955, his most fruitful period of American film-making. This contains war films, adventure stories and animal films. Although Marton is probably best-known from his M-G-M tenure for his thundering jungle footage for *King Solomon's Mines*, for which he shot all the exterior scenes, his best work is his smallest film – another animal story called *Gypsy Colt*. This is an enchanting story of a horse which, when sold, keeps returning to its nine-year-old mistress. Beautifully photographed in Ansco Color, it's a delight to the eye, and also well paced by its director, who, not noted as an actors' man, draws the best performances in any of his films from Donna Corcoran (as the girl), Ward Bond and Frances Dee, portrayals which exude warmth and naturalness. His later films are competent and sometimes charming, but often cursed with dialogue which negates their pictorial values.

1929: Two o'Clock in the Morning (GB: The Hour of Fear). 1931: †Die Nacht ohne Pause. 1932: Nordpol Ahoi! (GB: S.O.S. Iceberg). 1934: Der Dämon der Berge (GB: Beast of the Himalayas. US: Demon of the Himalayas). 1935: Miss President. 1936: Wolf's Clothing. The Secret of Stamboul (US: The Spy in White). 1937: School for Husbands. 1940: A Little Bit of Heaven. 1945: Gentle Annie. 1946: Gallant Bess. 1950: †King Solomon's Mines. 1951: The Wild North. 1952: †Storm Over Tibet. The Devil Makes Three. 1953: Mask of the Himalayas (D). 1954: Gypsy Colt. Prisoner of War. Men of the Fighting Lady. Green Fire. 1956: †Seven Wonders of the World. 1958: Underwater Warrior. 1962: †The Longest Day. It Happened in Athens. 1964: The Thin Red Line. 1965: Crack in the World. Clarence the Cross-Eyed Lion. Around the World Under the Sea. 1966: Birds Do It. 1967: Africa – Texas Style!

MASON, Herbert 1891-1960

A nephew of the great Shakespearian actress Ellen Terry, this Briton was really a man of the theatre, but emerged unexpectedly as the director of several major British pictures in the late 1930s. An actor at 16, Mason later became an actor-manager and stage-managed many big London shows in the 1920s. With the coming of sound, he interested himself in the cinema, busying himself at varying tasks for Gaumont-British Studios, including production and assistant direction. In 1936, he made his first film, a crime thriller with the young John Mills, and was consequently put in charge of two of the last star vehicles of doyen British actor George Arliss, home from his Oscar-winning exploits in Hollywood, and soon to retire. Mason's revue experience stood him in good stead when he proved the most efficient director of a Jack Hulbert-Cicely Courtneidge musical comedy, *Take My Tip*, in which one or two of Hulbert's dance routines are beautifully staged and for precision almost rival those of Astaire. Perhaps Mason's most interesting film from this period, however, is *A Window in London*, a dark and disturbing circular drama, from a French original, about a man who thinks he sees a murder while travelling past a house on a train. The feeling of faint unease that Mason engenders throughout the film is very skilfully done. His films of the 1940s are on the whole of a lighter nature, including *Back Room Boy*, an amusing Arthur Askey comedy set in a lighthouse. Later Mason returned to production activities, notably with John Grierson's Group Three Productions, but it would have been more interesting to see him pursue the directorial career he gave up in his mid-fifties. Known to his friends as 'Werb'.

*1936: First Offence. East Meets West. 1937: His Lordship (US: Man of Affairs). Take My Tip. 1938: Strange Boarders. 1939: A Window in London (US: Lady in Distress). The Silent Battle (US: Continental Express). Dr O'Dowd. 1940: The Briggs Family. Fingers. 1941: *Mr Proudfoot Shows a Light. Once a Crook. 1942: Back Room Boy. 1943: Night Invader. It's in the Bag. 1945: Flight from Folly.*

MATÉ, Rudolph (Rudolf Matheh) 1898-1964

Polish-born film-maker whose career as a director, after a promising start, did not equal his impressive achievements as an innovative cinematographer. It was in the latter field that Maté began his cinema career as an assistant cameraman (in Hungarian films made by Alexander Korda (*qv*). Promoted to cinematographer by 1922, he experimented with many different ways of heightening effects in films and achieving different kinds of atmosphere and impact. Films in which his photography plays a noteworthy part include *Mikael (1924), Le passion de Jeanne d'Arc (1928), Vampyr (1932), Liliom (1933), Dante's Inferno (1935), Come and Get It (1936), Stella Dallas (1937), Foreign Correspondent (1940), Sahara (1943)* and *Gilda (1946)*. In America from 1935, Maté only started directing (for Paramount) in 1949, after one disastrous attempt at co-direction two years before. His first three films are corking thrillers: *The Dark Past*, a psychological drama, strongly and atmospherically made, is a remake of a much-lauded, unusual second-feature, *Blind Alley; D.O.A.* is the classic thriller that has Edmond O'Brien, dying from a slow-acting poison, trying to track down his killer before he himself dies; and, best of all, *Union Station* is a powerhouse of a film about the kidnap of a blind girl, with personable performances from William Holden (also in *The Dark Past*), Nancy Olson, Barry Fitzgerald and Jan Sterling, an electrifying study in psychotic villainy from Lyle Bettger and a brilliant, breathless climax in the tunnels beneath Union Station itself. At an economical and constantly tense 80 minutes, this is one of the best films of its kind ever made. Despite its success, Maté stayed in the middle range of film-making, sticking to action films, sometimes blackly violent, sometimes with an attractive vein of humour. The better ones include *Second Chance*, with Robert Mitchum and Jack Palance fighting it out in a cablecar in a film originally scaled for 3-D; *The Violent Men*, a western about bitterness, with performances from Barbara Stanwyck and Edward G. Robinson that cut deeper than usual in a Maté film; and *The Rawhide Years*, a very pleasing rambling western with another of Arthur Kennedy's smiling rogues. Maté films after the mid-1950s, although retaining a visual attractiveness, were increasingly disappointing, but he only lived to enjoy a year's retirement before his death from a heart attack.

1947: †*It Had To Be You. 1949: The Dark Past. D.O.A. 1950: Union Station. No Sad Songs for Me. Branded. The Prince Who Was a Thief. 1951: When Worlds Collide. The Green Glove. 1952: Paula (GB: The Silent Voice). Sally and Saint Anne. 1953: Mississippi Gambler. Second Chance. Forbidden. 1954: The Black Shield of Falworth. The Siege at Red River. The Violent Men (GB: Rough Company). 1955: The Far Horizons. 1956: Port Afrique. Miracle in the Rain. Three Violent People. The Rawhide Years. 1958: The Deep Six. 1959: For the First Time. 1960: Revak the Rebel (US TV: Rivak the Barbarian/The Barbarians). The Immaculate Road. 1961: Seven Seas to Calais. 1962: The 300 Spartans. 1963: Aliki (US: Aliki – My Love).*

MAYO, Archie 1891-1968

Although this American director left Warner Brothers in 1937, after joining them in 1929, his record there suggests that had he stayed his career would probably have lasted a few years longer than it did (he retired in 1946 at only 55); he might have directed Joan Crawford and others of the studio's ageing stars in their failing years of the early 1950s. Mayo had a crisp professional touch that makes some of his work unexpectedly abrasive; and he worked with almost all of Warners' biggest stars, including Humphrey Bogart, James Cagney, Bette Davis, Barbara Stanwyck, Olivia de Havilland and George Raft. He could sometimes drive his performers to fine heights of passion on screen – Davis and Paul Muni in the torrid *Bordertown* make a notable example and ironically one of his most famous films, *The Petrified Forest*, almost completely lacks any of his personal touches, and looks today dry and less than its reputation. The decision to stick so rigidly to the stage presentation was

praised at the time, but has made it a film which dates badly. Mayo had begun his career as an actor, after a few months as an extra. By 1917, he had begun mixing acting with direction of shorts, and, after 1923, devoted himself to directing entirely, moving on from shorts to features in 1926. Early highpoints of his career when sound came along were two strong Barbara Stanwyck vehicles, *Illicit* and *Ever in My Heart*, the first about a couple who live together then marry each other (disastrously), the second about an American woman who marries a German in 1910. Both were unusual subjects with downbeat endings – the second ends in a double suicide. Mayo tackled the unusual again later in his career, notably with Cagney in *The Mayor of Hell*, as the superintendent of a reform school, and Bogart in *Black Legion*, an early Ku Klux Klan film with an overhanging sense of menace. Most of Mayo's other films are fairly average of their kind, although after leaving Warners he had more success with lighter entertainment, especially a lively version of *Charley's Aunt* with Jack Benny; with the Glenn Miller Orchestra and some bitchy in-fighting in the *Orchestra Wives*; and a farcical finale in films, with a presentable Marx Brothers vehicle *A Night in Casablanca*, which had more pace and spirit than some of their later work.

1917: †*Double Dukes. *Kid Snatchers. *The Nurse of an Aching Heart. 1918: *Beaches and Peaches. 1923: *Don't Play Hookey. *Mama's Baby Boy. *A Man of Position. *Spring Fever. 1924: *Short Change. *High Gear. *Husbands Wanted. 1925: *Good Spirits. *The Imperfect Lover. *Off His Beat. *Oh Bridget. *A Rarin' Romeo. *Tender Feet. *Why Hesitate? 1926: *Weak But Willing. Christine of the Big Tops. Money Talks. Unknown Treasures.* †*Johnny Get Your Hair Cut. 1927: Dearie. Quarantined Rivals. Slightly Used. The College Widow. 1928: The Crimson City. On Trial. *The Foreigner. *Charles Rogers in The Movie Man. *Henry B. Walthall in Retribution. My Man. State Street Sadie (GB: The Girl from State Street). 1929: Sonny Boy. The Sap. The Sacred Flame. Is Everybody Happy? 1930: The Doorway to Hell (GB: A Handful of Clouds). Vengeance. Courage. Oh! Sailor, Behave! Wide Open. 1931: Svengali. Illicit. Bought. 1932: Under 18. The Expert. Street of Women. Two Against the World. Night After Night. 1933: The Mayor of Hell. The Life of Jimmy Dolan (GB: The Kid's Last Fight). Convention City. Ever in My Heart. 1934: Gambling Lady. Desirable. The*

Man with Two Faces. 1935: Go Into Your Dance. The Case of the Lucky Legs. Bordertown. The Petrified Forest. 1936: I Married a Doctor. Give Me Your Heart (GB: Sweet Aloes). Black Legion. 1937: Call It a Day. It's Love I'm After. 1938: The Adventures of Marco Polo. Youth Takes a Fling. 1939: They Shall Have Music (GB: Melody of Youth). 1940: Four Sons. The House Across the Bay. 1941: The Great American Broadcast. Confirm or Deny. Charley's Aunt (GB: Charley's American Aunt). 1942: Moontide. Orchestra Wives. 1943: Crash Dive. 1944: Sweet and Low Down. 1946: Angel on My Shoulder. A Night in Casablanca.

MAZURSKY, Paul 1930-

This American director flattered so often only to deceive that one became resigned to an uneven career. His films are usually boldly up-to-date and deal with fashionable subjects. Sometimes it seems that he almost seeks to start new trends, although not always with success. But he is a first-rate actors' director (he started his career as an actor at 20, and has pursued it sporadically ever since) and indeed the performances in his films are often better than the films themselves; he has made excellent use of such first-class performers as Natalie Wood, Donald Sutherland, Bette Midler, Anjelica Huston, Richard Dreyfuss, George Segal, Marsha Mason, Art Carney (who won an Oscar in Mazursky's *Harry and Tonto*) and Jill Clayburgh. The effect of real feelings coming through on screen only broke down in 1980 with the unsuccessful *Willie and Phil*. His acting performances include one as a young hoodlum in *Blackboard Jungle,* but in the early 1960s he began writing for television, mostly for comedy shows, and this led to his first co-screenplay credit on the Peter Sellers comedy *I Love You, Alice B. Toklas.* The following year, Mazursky directed his first film, the sensationally successful, if rather tiresome in parts, *Bob & Carol & Ted & Alice.* After this, though, Mazursky and box-office success fell out with each other, perhaps because his films were too downbeat, although they ranged from the ramblingly appealing *Harry and Tonto,* about the adventures of an old man and his cat, to the downright unpalatable *Next Stop, Greenwich Village,* which showed us aspects of Mazursky's early career we could have done without. *Blume in Love* was critically very successful, but the public did not take to it, and still don't, judging by the reaction to recent television showings. By the late 1970s, Mazursky was palpably in need of a commercial hit, and he reacted spectacularly with *An*

Unmarried Woman, with Jill Clayburgh producing one of her luminous and painfully real performances as the woman struggling determinedly to adjust to life without a man. But Mazursky was unable to make the ultramodern menage-à-trois-through-the-years situation of Willie and Phil anything but prolonged tedium, especially given the uncharismatic trio of stars cast in the leads. Since then, Mazursky has concentrated on rather dark comedies, with some success in the 1980s. But the following decade brought only evidence of a director whose creative powers were draining away.

1969: Bob & Carol & Ted & Alice. 1971: Alex in Wonderland. 1973: Blume in Love. 1974: Harry and Tonto. 1975: Next Stop, Greenwich Village. 1978: An Unmarried Woman. 1980: Willie and Phil. 1982: Tempest. 1984: Moscow on the Hudson. 1986: Down and out in Beverly Hills. 1988: Moon Over Parador. 1989: Enemies, a Love Story. 1991: Scenes from a Mall. 1993: The Pickle. 1996: Faithful. 1998: Winchell (TV).

McCAREY, Leo (Thomas L. McCarey) 1898-1969
Irreverence and a blithe, refreshing disregard for the conventions of a genre characterized the work of McCarey, one of America's golden men of the 1930-1945 period. Originally trained as a lawyer, he worked with most of Hollywood's most individual purveyors of humour – Laurel and Hardy, W.C. Fields, Mae West, Harold Lloyd, the Marx Brothers – with often side-splitting results, before proving he could make a comedy without comedians in The Awful Truth, and so winning the first of his three Oscars. He made wild comedies of character full of lovely telling moments – comic, touching or exciting – and even the weepies, although maudlin by today's tastes, brim with warmth and humour. Only his last five films failed, by his own standards, with critics and public alike. His irrepressible sense of humour soon drew him to silent slapstick and after a spell as an assistant director, he joined the Hal Roach studio in 1923 as a gagman and, soon, director of comedy shorts. From 1926 to 1929, he was supervisor on most Laurel and Hardy two-reelers, although credited as director on only three. His career as a feature director took off from 1932 when he made the Eddie Cantor vehicle The Kid from Spain, which was tremendously successful but has dated somewhat, and the Marx Brothers' zaniest film Duck Soup, which hasn't dated at all but at the time failed to do as well as their previous comedies and contributed to their moving

from Paramount to M-G-M. McCarey's big box-office hits began with Ruggles of Red Gap, the story of an English butler in America. That its characters spring to life so effectively, as they do throughout this period of McCarey's career, is due largely to his cashing in on his players' own personalities and giving them something of a free rein. Cary Grant and Irene Dunne (in The Awful Truth, a comedy of divorce melting into re-marriage), Charles Boyer and Irene Dunne (in Love Affair, a weepie McCarey later remade with Grant and Deborah Kerr as An Affair to Remember, the best of his last films), and Cary Grant and Ginger Rogers (in Once Upon a Honeymoon, a wartime spy comedy-thriller about allegiances) all seem perfectly matched partnerships; they win audience sympathy by bringing the warmth of mutual affection across from the screen, thanks to the director's fine balancing of traits and personalities. A word, too, for Make Way for Tomorrow, a daring (for the 1930s) story of old people deserted by those they need most, that had many handkerchieves out – because it was honest, and thus sad, rather than over-sentimental. The priestly parables of the 1940s with Bing Crosby are rather more glib, if a little less effective and for one of them, Going My Way, McCarey received two Oscars – for best direction and best original story. Many people have a superb sense of humour. McCarey's gift was that he could put his on celluloid, quite without offence, and make people share it. America's highest earner in 1945.

1921: Society Secrets. 1924: *All Wet. *Publicity Pays. *Young Oldfield. *Jeffries, Jr. *Stolen Goods. *A Ten Minute Egg. *Why Husbands Go Mad. *Sweet Daddy. *Seeing Nellie Home. *Outdoor Pajamas. *Why Men Work. *Too Many Mammas. *Sittin' Pretty. *The Poor Fish. *Bungalow Boobs. *Accidental Accidents. *The Royal Razz. *Fighting Fluid. *The Family Entrance. *Hello Baby. 1925: *Bad Boy. *Innocent Husbands. *Should Husbands Be Watched? *Plain and Fancy Girls. *Is Marriage the Bunk? *Hard Boiled. *Big Red Riding Hood. *What Price Goofy? *Looking for Sally. *No Father to Guide Him. *Isn't Life Terrible? *The Uneasy Three. *The Caretaker's Daughter. *His Wooden Wedding. 1926: *Crazy Like a Fox. *Dog Shy. *Be Your Age. *Charlie My Boy. *Mother Behave. *Long Fliv the King. *Mum's the Word. *Mighty Like the Moose. *Bromo and Juliet. *Tell 'Em Nothing. 1927: *Should Men Walk Home? *Why Girls Say No. *Eve's Love Letters. 1928: *We Faw Down (GB: We Slip Up). 1929: *Liberty.

*Wrong Again. Red Hot Rhythm. The Sophomore (GB: Compromised). 1930: Let's Go Native. Wild Company. Part-Time Wife. 1931: Indiscreet. 1932: The Kid from Spain. 1933: Duck Soup. 1934: Six of a Kind. Belle of the Nineties. 1935: Ruggles of Red Gap. 1936: The Milky Way. 1937: Make Way for Tomorrow. The Awful Truth. 1939: Love Affair. 1942: Once Upon a Honeymoon. 1944: Going My Way. 1945: The Bells of St Mary's. *Anybody's Kids. 1948: Good Sam. 1949: *You Can Change the World. 1952: My Son John. 1957: An Affair to Remember. 1958: Rally 'Round the Flag, Boys. 1962: Satan Never Sleeps (GB: The Devil Never Sleeps).

McLAGLEN, Andrew V. 1920-
If one hadn't seen Shenandoah, one would be likely to tag this British-born, American-raised son of actor Victor McLaglen as a director of vigorous action films of little individuality. Anyone who has directed as many TV western episodes as McLaglen – over 150 including many from the long-running Have Gun, Will Travel – is perhaps entitled to become a little cynical in his approach. Shenandoah, which came after all this TV work, is one of the very few McLaglen films to dig deeper than the surface of human emotions, and it shows that, given a script of the right quality – this one by James Lee Barrett, who also wrote McLaglen's Bandolero! and Fools' Parade – the director was capable of producing great cinema. It is also one of the few McClaglen films to deal with ordinary, in this case a family, heart-rendingly torn apart by the American Civil War. For once the action in a McLaglen film, although handled with the usual panache, is subsidiary to the main theme, and his direction benefits enormously , assuming a low profile at moments of great emotional stress. There is, too, the aching sincerity of James Stewart who (and it call be no mere coincidence) appears in all McLaglen's other best films, The Rare Breed, Bandolero! and Fools' Parade. The best of McLaglen's westerns with John Wayne are the first and last, McLintock! and Cahill – U.S. Marshall, although the former sparked off a run of Wayne westerns with McLaglen in which the formula is subservient to the personality of the star, and Chisum, for example, is a virtual re-run of McLintock! itself. McLaglen worked as an assistant director in the early and middle 1950s, mainly, on films by John Ford, William Wellman and Budd Boetticher. His second film was a western, and a good one at that, Gun the Man Down, with James Arness, soon to

star in another television western series of which McLaglen would direct many episodes, *Gunsmoke* (known for a time in Britain as *Gun Law*). McLaglen's talent for action kept him working on military and western projects through the 1970s and 1980s, although his product of this time was dispiriting to those who would have liked to have seen subtler talents re-emerge. Married to actress Veda Ann Borg from 1946 to 1957 (the second of his four wives), the husky McLaglen was once rejected for military service for being, at 6ft 7 in, too tall!

1955: *The Man in the Vault.* 1956: *Gun the Man Down.* 1957: *The Abductors.* 1960: *Freckles.* 1961: *The Little Shepherd of Kingdom Come.* 1965: *Shenandoah.* 1966: *The Rare Breed. Monkeys, Go Home!* 1967: *The Way West. The Ballad of Josie.* 1968: *Bandolero! The Devil's Brigade. Hellfighters.* 1969: *The Undefeated.* 1970: *Chisum.* 1971: *One More Train To Rob. Something Big. Fools' Parade* (GB: *Dynamite Man from Glory Jail*). 1973: *The Train Robbers. Cahill: United States Marshal* (GB: *Cahill*). 1974: *Log of the Black Pearl* (TV). 1975: *Stowaway to the Moon* (TV). *Mitchell.* 1976: *The Last Hard Men. Banjo Hackett.* 1977: *Murder at the World Series* (TV). 1978: *The Wild Geese.* 1979: *Breakthrough. North Sea Hijack* (US: *ffolkes*). 1980: *The Sea Wolves.* 1982: *Travis McGee* (TV). *The Shadow Riders* (TV). 1983: *Sahara.* 1984: *Fast Eddie* (unfinished). 1985: *The Dirty Dozen: Next Mission* (TV). 1989: *Return from the River Kwai.* 1991: *Eye of the Widow.*

McLEOD, Norman Z. 1898-1964

His own zany sense of comedy made this American director's film career one of contrasts. He loved working with comedians who had a sense of the absurd and his films with Bob Hope, The Marx Brothers, Danny Kaye, W.C. Fields and Ann Sothern are among their best work. Add the two 'Topper' films, though, and you have just about a complete list of McLeod's big successes. Outside this field, he proved strangely ineffectual, never seeming to summon up enough interest to impose his personality on these other films, some of which are really quite dull. In comedy, he could clearly see that it was important to play on the established personalities and character traits of his various stars, from Fields to the Charlie Ruggles-Mary Boland partnership, within differing situations to produce fresh, and sometimes inspired comedy. McLeod's own background was very much in visual lunacy, as he had begun his career immediately after World War I, firstly as an animator, then as gag writer for Christie comedies. His wartime experience as a fighter pilot with the Royal Canadian Air Force pushed him forwards towards direction when he worked on *Wings* (1927) and *The Air Circus* (1928), although this was a field to which he never returned after his directorial career had got positively under way by 1931. It was then that he encountered the Marxes, directing them in *Monkey Business* and *Horse Feathers*, two exercises in undiluted lunacy handled at lightning speed, as evidenced by the running times – at 77 and 68 minutes, they are two of the shortest Marx comedies, and the football match in the second is the funniest-ever such sequence. Still at Paramount, McLeod hopped over to W.C. Fields, their funniest film together being the classic *It's a Gift* – the one in which Baby LeRoy drops grapes in a sleeping Fields' mouth and a blind man wrecks his shop. McLeod plays this successfully as a comedy of character as opposed to farce. Mention should also be made of the three screwball comedies with Constance Bennett – *Topper, Merrily We Live* and *Topper Returns* – with which McLeod saw out the 1930s. The liaison with Bob Hope did not start until 1947, but it was immediately successful. Each time Hope's career looked like sagging a bit, a McLeod film revived it – notably with *The Paleface* and *My Favorite Spy*. They combined again on Hope's last really funny film, again a return to a proven formula, with *Alias Jesse James*, in which numerous film cowboys come to Hope's rescue at the end when all seems hopeless. It was also McLeod's swan song, a stroke in 1962 effectively ending his career. The 'Z' in his name stood for Zenos.

1928: *Taking a Chance.* 1930: †*Along Came Youth.* 1931: †*Finn and Hattie. Monkey Business. Touchdown* (GB: *Playing the Game*). *The Miracle Man.* 1932: *Horse Feathers.* †*If I Had a Million.* 1933: *Alice in Wonderland. Mama Loves Papa. A Lady's Profession.* 1934: *Melody in Spring. Many Happy Returns. It's a Gift.* 1935: *Redheads on Parade. Here Comes Cookie* (GB: *The Plot Thickens*). *Coronado.* 1936: *Early to Bed. Pennies from Heaven.* 1937: *Mind Your Own Business. Topper.* 1938: *There Goes My Heart. Merrily We Live.* 1939: *Topper Takes a Trip. Remember?* 1940: *Little Men.* 1941: *The Trial of Mary Dugan. Lady Be Good.* 1942: *Jackass Mail. Panama Hattie.* 1943: *The Powers Girl* (GB: *Hello! Beautiful*). *Swing Shift Maisie* (GB: *The Girl in Overalls*). 1946: *The Kid from Brooklyn.* 1947: *The Secret Life of Walter Mitty. Road to Rio.* 1948: *The Paleface. Isn't It Romantic?* 1950: *Let's Dance.* 1951: *My Favorite Spy.* 1952: *Never Wave at a WAC* (GB: *The Private Wore Skirts*). 1953: *Casanova's Big Night.* 1957: *Public Pigeon Number 1.* 1959: *Alias Jesse James.*

McTIERNAN, John 1951-

American director whose dynamic, hard-hitting action films have pulled in millions at box-offices worldwide. An expert at staging action and thrills, McTiernan has proved talented at concealing explosive endings to individual sequences until they arrive. Born in upstate New York, McTiernan studied both acting and filmmaking before receiving a fellowship and grant from the American Film Institute. His first efforts at directing were all in the horror genre, and none too successful at that. There were some signs that McTiernan was beginning to get a grip on his chosen profession in the spasmodically effective chiller Nomads, about a society of malevolent ghosts, and when he combined the genre with a major star (Arnold Schwarzenegger) in Predator, a violent, brutal and exciting sci-fi thriller, he broke through to the big time. McTiernan confirmed his ascension to blockbuster status with Die Hard, which few expected to be such a huge success. But its combination of suspense and dynamite action made the film irresistible and boosted Bruce Willis to major stardom. In his six films between 1987 and 1995, McTiernan now only used three big stars, Schwarzenegger, Willis and Sean Connery, who appeared in the overrated The Hunt for Red October, conspicuously lacking McTiernan's usual control of suspense, and the underrated Medicine Man, a well told ecological adventure set deep in the Brazilian jungle. Its elements of fun, sadness, drama and action blend into good medicine.

1982: *Watcher.* 1983: *The Demon's Daughter* (Unreleased). 1985: *Nomads.* 1987: *Predator.* 1988: *Die Hard.* 1990: *The Hunt for Red October.* 1991: *Medicine Man.* 1993: *Last Action Hero.* 1995: *Die Hard with a Vengeance.* 1998: *The Thomas Crown Affair.*

MEDAK, Peter 1937-

Hungarian-born director in British and American films, whose black comedies have on the whole been less successful than his more serious ventures. But then few directors have achieved opposite ends of the success and failure scale with such regularity. For every 'awful' in Medak's record, there's an 'amazing' too; a lot of his work, though, in one way or another, is pretty dark. Born in Budapest, Medak fled his homeland during the uprising of 1956 and landed in England, where he entered a long film industry apprenticeship that included work as sound editor, film editor, assistant director and second-unit director. He made his debut as a director in rather mannered style with the bizarre *Negatives*, which attracted some attention since its star, Glenda Jackson, was 'hot' on the British cinema scene. *A Day in the Death of Joe Egg* was an uneasy black comedy about a couple considering the mercy-killing of their child, but Medak had a much bigger commercial success with *The Ruling Class*, a very weird comedy about a British nobleman (Peter O' Toole) who thinks he's Jesus Christ. That seemed to fit Medak for a prime career in British and international cinema. In fact, the only 'amazing' film he made in the next decade came from Canada. *The Changeling* is a very superior example of the haunted house thriller whose horrors are never (well, only in flashback) seen. Its ghost lurks in narrow, confined spaces and age-old cobwebbed rooms, and Medak's cameras track relentlessly through these claustrophobic environs like an invader in some old and murky painting stirred almost to life. The result is quite the most frightening film since *The Haunting*, but it was followed by another decade of non-achievement, in which TV movies mingled with such cinematic turkeys as *Zorro, The Gay Blade* and *The Men's Club*. It took a trip back to Britain to return Medak to prominence with two real-life crime dramas. *The Krays* was a hard-as-ebony, extremely well set and strong reconstruction of the bloody careers of twin ganglords who ruled London's crime from East End to West End in the Fifties. But it was topped by '*Let Him Have It*', a reconstruction of a single criminal case from the same era, an emotive affair in which it seemed a miscarriage of justice might have been done. Medak's treatment of the affair is immaculate, and the acting couldn't be bettered. Since then, he has returned to America, where his work has assumed a lower profile. He has also made two cinematic records of stage productions starring his wife, opera singer Julia Migenes.

1968: *Negatives*. 1971: *A Day in the Death of Joe Egg. The Ruling Class*. 1973: *Third Girl from the Left* (TV). 1974: *Ghost in the Noonday Sun*. 1978: *The Odd Job*. 1979: *The Changeling*. 1980: *The Babysitter* (TV). 1981: *Mistress of Paradise* (TV). *Zorro the Gay Blade*. 1982: *Cry for the Strangers* (TV). 1986:

The Men's Club. 1990: *The Krays*. 1991: '*Let Him Have It*'. 1992: *Salomé. La voix humaine*. 1993: *Romeo is Bleeding*. 1994: *Pontiac Moon*. 1997: *The Hunchback of Notre Dame*. 1998: *Species II*.

MELVILLE, Jean-Pierre (J-P Grumbach) 1917-1973
After beginnings as a post-war forerunner of the '*nouvelle vague*', this French director, before his death at 55, left his mark in a very different way: as a purveyor of a certain kind of gangster film which, although retaining its essential Gallicism, took such actors as Alain Delon and Jean-Paul Belmondo closer to the world of the American *film noir* of the 1940s than any of their other (many) such forays. These are 'black-and-white in colour': Alan Ladd and Veronica Lake could easily inhabit this Melville world, with its night-time settings, shadowy corridors and avenging angels of death doomed from the opening reel, although it has a harsher grittiness even than, say, the desperate ambience of *The Blue Dahlia*. These films are compulsive viewing: switch on your television and, even if you get ratty with subtitles disappearing from the bottom of the screen, a Melville will compel you to see it through to the inevitable end. Powerful endings and memorable setpieces have a place in all Melville's work, even the earlier films, some of which are far removed from his later world of 'flics' and 'gangs', where the night-time photography glitters as cold and metallic as a gun barrel. After wartime service with the British army, Melville determined to turn his enthusiasm for the cinema into a career, and, unable to break into mainstream French film-making, founded his own production company and tiny studio. There was a fascinating version of Cocteau's *Les enfants terribles*, made with Cocteau's assistance; but the most striking film of this period, and indeed its last, is *Léon Morin, prêtre*, with Belmondo in the uncharacteristic role (but completely in character) of a priest, who strikes up a relationship with a worldly, although God-converted woman (radiantly portrayed by Emmanuelle Riva) which can sadly only end with fleshly temptation. The best of the thrillers is undoubtedly *Le samourai*, with Alain Delon perfect as the expressionless killer destroyed by one act of almost unknowing compassion – a success Delon has striven in vain to repeat in several subsequent films of the same genre, something that says much for Melville's singular talent.

1945: **Vingt-quatre heures de la vie d'un clown*. 1947: *Le silence de la mer*. 1949:

Les enfants terribles (US: *The Strange Ones*). 1952: *Quand tu liras cette lettre*. 1955: *Bob le Flambeur*. 1958: *Deux hommes dans Manhattan*. 1961: *Léon Morin, prêtre* (GB & US: *Leon Morin, Priest*). 1962: *Le Doulos* (GB: *Finger Man*. US: *Doulos, the Finger Man*). 1963: *L'aîné des Ferchaux* (US: *Magnet of Doom*). 1966: *Le deuxième souffle* (GB & US: *Second Breath*). 1967: *Le samourai* (GB: *The Samurai*. US: *The Godson*). 1969: *L'armée des ombres* (US: *The Shadow Army*). 1970: *Le cercle rouge* (GB: *The Red Circle*). 1972: *Un flic* (GB: *Dirty Money*).

MENDES, Lothar 1894-1974
Alphabetical order throws together two film-makers, Mendes and Menzies, who enjoyed their only major directorial success working for Alexander Korda. Mendes was a German who, like so many others of his generation, learned his trade with Max Reinhardt, beginning as an actor but turning to direction by 1921. He tackled a variety of film genres in Austria and Germany, going to Hollywood, where he was employed mainly making action scenes, often being credited as co-director with the dialogue director of early sound films. He remained at Paramount until 1933 – one of his better films there was Clara Bow's *Dangerous Curves*, a circus story – without making a distinctive mark, at which point he came to England to make *Jew Süss* with his old friend Conrad Veidt, whom he had previously directed in *Liebe macht blind*, while both were still in Germany. *Jew Süss*, although hard to sit through today, was a prestige British production of its time (it remains Mendes' second-best-remembered film) and its strength and professionalism brought his work to the attention of Korda who hired him to direct *The Man Who Could Work Miracles*, from the story by H.G. Wells, with whose *Things to Come* Korda had enjoyed great success. The result was a pleasing comedy-fantasy, with Roland Young in great form in the title role as a mild-mannered clerk suddenly given the power to work miracles by indulgent gods. The film was especially successful in America, but Mendes still refused to settle to a genre, or a country: there was a rather odd, semi-mystic vehicle for the talents of aged Polish pianist Paderewski and, back in America, a respectable comradely war film, *International Squadron*, starring James Stephenson, who died from a heart attack the same year (1941). Mendes' last few films were very moderate and unexciting, apart from the very last, *The Walls Came Tumbling Down*, a barely remembered but

well-written and suspenseful thriller about a reporter investigating the death of a priest. Although ambitious in his choice and variety of subjects, Mendes never quite consistently achieved the class of film to become a really distinguished director. He was at one time (1926-28) married to actress Dorothy Mackaill.

1921: Die Scheide des Todes. Der Abenteuer. 1922: Deportiert. 1923: S.O.S. – Insel der Tränen. 1925: Liebe macht blind/Love Blinds Us. 1926: Die drei Kuckucksuhren. The Prince of Tempters. 1927: †Convoy (uncredited). 1928: A Night of Mystery. †Interference. †The Four Feathers. 1929: Illusion. The Marriage Playground. Dangerous Curves. 1930: †Paramount on Parade. 1931: †Personal Maid. Ladies' Man. 1932: Strangers in Love. Payment Deferred. 1933: Luxury Liner. 1934: Jew Süss (US: Power). 1936: The Man Who Could Work Miracles. 1937: Moonlight Sonata. 1941: International Squadron. 1943: Flight for Freedom. 1944: Tampico. 1946: The Walls Came Tumbling Down.

MENZIES, William Cameron 1896-1957

Connecticut-born Menzies was an imaginative, hard-working art director: the few films he directed rarely reflected the full range of his talents. Menzies conjured up magnificent sets for those who could afford them, and made the positions of art director and production designer important ones in the film world: heaven knows what he might have done for Griffith's *Intolerance*, for example, had he been around a few years earlier. As it was, he contributed notably to several exotic silent subjects, among them the Fairbanks version of *The Thief of Bagdad* (Menzies would later be involved with the Korda remake in 1940) and Valentino's final three films, *Cobra, The Eagle* and *Son of the Sheik*. The background design to these films is rich in baroque splendour, and Menzies' fertile imagination carried him on after Valentino's death to films with John Barrymore – *The Beloved Rogue* and *Tempest*. For *Tempest* and *The Dove*, a vehicle for Norma Talmadge whose career was soon to be ended with the coming of sound, Menzies won an Academy Award. He was also director on Talmadge's last film, *Du Barry, Woman of Passion*, before beginning to branch out into writing and direction; the resulting films are of little stature except for *Things to Come*, for which he was brought to England by Alexander Korda. This is a tremendous realization of H.G. Wells' vividly pessimistic vision of the future, full of incident and staggering sets. In his own

brother Vincent Korda and his director Menzies, Korda had two of the most inventive minds in their fields working on the same film. The sets are comparable to those in Lang's *Metropolis*, although the overall effect has not quite the same flair. Apart from some work for Korda on *Conquest of the Air* and *The Thief of Bagdad*, Menzies then returned to production design, winning a second Oscar for his work on *Gone With the Wind* (he is said to have spent ages devising angles and effects to heighten the impact of Vivien Leigh's speech at the end of the first half). The best of his later films as director is a well-made little thriller, *Address Unknown*. As well as the films listed below, Menzies also directed some scenes, uncredited, on *Conquest of the Air* (1936, released briefly in 1938, then again in 1940), *The Thief of Bagdad (1940)* and *Duel in the Sun (1946)*. *The Green Cockatoo (US: Four Dark Hours)*, made in 1937, is credited to Menzies in all filmographies, but was at least partly directed by William K. Howard *(qv)*.

*1931: †The Spider. †Always Goodbye. 1932: †Chandu, the Magician. 1933: †I Loved You Wednesday. 1934: †Wharf Angel. 1936: Things to Come. 1937: †The Green Cockatoo (US: Four Dark Hours). 1944: Address Unknown. 1951: The Whip Hand. Drums in the Deep South. 1953: The Maze. Invaders from Mars. 1954: *Autumn in Rome. *Star Studded Ride.*

MEYER, Russ 1922-

American independent film-maker who somehow convinced a number of people over the years that his soft-core pornographic films have something to do with great art. They are pitched at hysteria level and, with one or two exceptions (notably *Vixen!* with Erica Gavin) they are mercilessly un-sexy. Over-developed girls cavort with plastic fellas whose blank expressions probably indicate that they are trying to remember their few lines; later Meyer films are packed with sadistic 'comedy', much of it alluding to long-surviving Nazis, and much bloodletting. Here is a director who believes that nothing succeeds like excess; he has been proved one hundred per cent right at the box-office. The endings of Meyer movies usually carry a moralizing message, meant to be tongue-in-cheek, but in effect is merely wearisome. However, Meyer has at least invented a genre all his own, and for that he deserves some credit. A former photographer of nude models, Meyer hit the financial jackpot with his first film, *The Immoral Mr Teas*, which returned

A roguish twinkle from the king of the skinflicks, Russ **Meyer**.

almost a million-dollar profit on a minimal investment. The year between *Vixen!* and *Cherry, Harry and Raquel!* marks the division between his old-style porno movies, largely with rural settings, and his later diversions; which have meaningless subliminal flashes with huge-breasted girls bouncing around deserts. For a few years, Meyer also worked on the periphery of the mainline American cinema, but the result, although made on much more lavish budgets, is merely bad movies, with far less of Meyer's own anarchic character in them. Although he has never been within a mile of making a good picture, Meyer is remorselessly his own man and it is not likely that movies will ever see anyone like him again.

1960: The Immoral Mr Teas. 1961: Eve and the Handyman. Erotica/Eroticon. 1962: The Immoral West and How It Was Lost/Naked Gals of the Golden West. 1963: Europe in the Raw. Heavenly Bodies. Steam Heat. 1964: Lorna. Kiss Me Quick! 1965: Fanny Hill. Motor Psycho. Mudhoney. 1966: Mondo Topless. Faster Pussycat! Kill! Kill! 1967: Good Morning and Goodbye! (GB: The Lust Seekers). Common Law Cabin. 1968: Finders Keepers, Losers Weepers! Vixen! 1969: Cherry, Harry and Raquel! 1970:

Beyond the Valley of the Dolls. 1971: *The Seven Minutes.* 1977: *Blacksnake/Sweet Suzy (GB: Slaves).* 1975: *The Super Vixens.* 1976: *Up!* 1979: *Beneath the Valley of the Ultra Vixens.*

MILES, Christopher 1939-

The brother of actress Sarah Miles, this British director has shown sincere good intentions in his film projects, even if the realization of them has often gone astray. A student of the French film school IDHEC, he began directing short subjects in 1962, and it was one of these, *The Six Sided Triangle*, which won a wide release, with its satire of film-making from various countries. His subsequent commercial films were unsuited to his quiet and liter-ate talents until *The Virgin and the Gypsy,* a version of the D.H. Lawrence story that captured much of the brooding atmosphere of the original. Miles' follow-up film also captured a period atmos-phere, but *Time for Living* was weaker dramatically, if always pretty to look at, like all Miles' films; his became a sporadic film career. In 1980, he tried again with Lawrence, this time on *Priest of Love, a* version of the last, harried years of the writer's life. Although the sights and sounds of a summer are sumptuously cap-tured, the lovely photography, and the director's fidelity to the truth do not sus-tain a 125-minute film which, in between its more interesting patches, tests both patience and endurance.

1962: **A vol d'oiseau.* 1963: **The Six-Sided Triangle.* 1964: **Rhythm 'n' Greens.* 1965: *Up Jumped a Swagman.* 1968: **The Rue Lepic Slow Race.* 1970: *The Virgin and the Gypsy.* 1971: *Time for Loving.* 1974: *The Maids.* 1975: *That Lucky Touch.* 1978: *Alternative 3 (TV).* 1980: *Priest of Love.*

MILESTONE, Lewis (Levis Milstein) 1895-1980

Milestone's niche in film history is secure with his Academy Award *for All Quiet on the Western Front.* Much of his other work has become devalued in recent years, many writers finding his approach flashy and facile. Milestone, however, was using what he felt were the best means at his disposal to express his own philoso-phies, about war in particular. Thus if the famous sideways tracking shots along the trenches in *All Quiet on the Western Front* have little to do with the way a bat-tle is fought, they have everything to do with Milestone's individual attempts 'to expose war for what it is and not to glori-fy it'. Whatever the merits of Milestone's method, they do bring home wars' full, sickening impact on the men who fight them. Although he often fell out with his producers over these chronicles of con-flict, and he made several other excellent films in different fields during the 1930-1950 period, Milestone persisted in show-ing war from the point of view of the ordinary soldier down through the years, taking in World War II and the Korean War as well, and it is on these films that his reputation rests. Milestone was born in the Ukraine, but emigrated to America at 18. He became an American citizen and from 1917 served in World War I, becoming an assistant director on Army training films. He spent several years as cutter, editor and writer before beginning to direct in 1925. With his fourth film, *Two Arabian Knights,* he won an Acade-my Award for best comedy direction, the only time this award was ever presented. Inevitably, the film had a war setting, with William Boyd and Louis Wolheim (the latter would appear in much more serious vein in *All Quiet)* as Flagg and Quirt-style soldiers. After his *All Quiet* Oscar, Milestone diversified into a num-ber of other genres, most notably with *The Front Page,* an archetypal newspaper story, and, Milestone claims on his own inspiration, one of the fastest-talking films ever made, with dialogue clattering across the screen like typewriter keys. There were three musicals, including the innova-tive *Hallelujah, I'm a Bum* about New York tramps; the extraordinary *The Gen-eral Died at Dawn,* compulsive viewing but almost overloaded with atmosphere;

Lewis **Milestone** goes through the script for his 1939 version of John Steinbeck's *Of Mice and Men.*

and a surprisingly very strong version of Steinbeck's *Of Mice and Men*, with career-best performances from Burgess Meredith and Lon Chaney, that was even liked by the author himself. Then war returned, and Milestone was in the thick of it, with a documentary and several fictional films, the best of which is *A Walk, in the Sun*, a starkly moving account of the events that befall one American army patrol. *The Purple Heart*, although melodramatic in overall effect, also has moments of extraordinary power. A few years later, , they were followed by the exciting, if uncharacteristically flag-waving *Halls of Montezuma* and in 1959, amid much feuding with star/producer Gregory Peck, a return to character with *Pork Chop Hill*. Milestone's last work was an episode of the TV series *Arrest and Trial* in 1964. He died following abdominal surgery.

1925: *Seven Sinners*. 1926: *The New Klondike*. *The Caveman*. 1927: *Two Arabian Knights*. 1928: *The Garden of Eden*. *The Racket*. 1929: *The Betrayal*. *New York Nights*. 1930: *All Quiet on the Western Front*. 1931: *The Front Page*. 1932: *Rain*. 1933: *Hallelujah, I'm a Bum* (later *Lazy Bones*. GB: *Hallelujah, I'm a Tramp*). 1934: *The Captain Hates the Sea*. 1935: *Paris in Spring* (GB: *Paris Love Song*). 1936: *Anything Goes*. 1937: *The General Died at Dawn*. 1939: *The Night of Nights*. *Of Mice and Men*. 1940: *Lucky Partners*. 1941: *My Life with Caroline*. 1942: †*Our Russian Front* (D). 1943: *Edge of Darkness*. *The North Star*. 1944: †*A Guest in the House* (uncredited). *The Purple Heart*. *Armored Attack* (reissue of *The North Star* with additional action footage). 1945: *A Walk in the Sun*. 1946: *The Strange Love of Martha Ivers*. 1948: *Arch of Triumph*. *No Minor Vices*. 1949: *The Red Pony*. 1950: *Halls of Montezuma*. 1952: *Kangaroo*. *Les Miserables*. 1953: *Melba*. *They Who Dare*. 1955: *Le vedova* (GB & US: *The Widow*). 1959: *Pork Chop Hill*. 1960: *Ocean's Eleven*. 1962: *Mutiny on the Bounty*.

MILLER, David 1909-1992

American director whose best pictures (although he has also had failures with the theme) have usually been portraits of women under pressure or threat. Miller got into the business at 21 as an assistant editor with Columbia, but by the mid-1930s had moved across to M-G-M, who allowed him to direct a variety of two-reelers, mainly sports shorts, before giving him his first feature, another version of *Billy the Kid* (1941), distinguished more

by the outstanding Technicolor work of Leonard Smith and William V. Skall than by any directorial qualities. After *Love Happy*, the final Marx Brothers feature and not actually as bad as most people would have you believe, Miller offered the first of several heroines trapped in her own claustrophobic world, with Joan Crawford in *Sudden Fear*, followed by the equally menaced Ginger Rogers in *Beautiful Stranger*, Heather Sears in *The Story of Esther Costello* and – the biggest commercial hit of the four – Doris Day in *Midnight Lace*. Miller's most highly rated film is the sad *Lonely Are the Brave*, with Kirk Douglas as one of the last old-style cowboys, ultimately confounded by modern machinery. A director with more flair, however, might have made this a more commercial venture without losing any of its aesthetic qualities, and several of Miller's films have been very drab, lacking the spark of real life that would make one believe in them. He died from cancer.

1935: *Trained Hoofs. *Let's Dance. 1936: *Crew Racing. *Table Tennis. *Racing Canines. *Aquatic Artistry. *Dare-Deviltry. *Hurling. *Dexterity. 1937: *Gilding the Lily. *Penny Wisdom. *Tennis Tactics. *Equestrian Acrobatics. 1938: *Fisticuffs. *The Great Heart. *It's in the Stars. *Modeling for Money. *Nostradamus. *La Savate. *Penny's Party. 1939: *Ice Antics. *Drunk Driving. 1940: *The Happiest Man on Earth. *The Flag Speaks. 1941: *More About Nostradamus. *Billy the Kid. 1942: *Further Prophecies of Nostradamus. *Sunday Punch. *Flying Tigers. 1949: *Top o' the Morning*. *Love Happy* (later *Kleptomaniacs*). 1950: *Our Very Own*. 1951: *Saturday's Hero* (GB: *Idols in the Dust*). 1952: *Sudden Fear*. 1954: *Beautiful Stranger* (US: *Twist of Fate*). 1955: *Diane*. 1956: *The Opposite Sex*. 1957: *The Story of Esther Costello* (US: *Golden Virgin*). 1959: *Happy Anniversary*. 1960: *Midnight Lace*. 1961: *Back Street*. 1962: *Lonely Are the Brave*. 1963: *Captain Newman M.D.* 1968: *Hammerhead*. 1969: *Hail Hero!* 1973: *Executive Action*. 1976: *Bittersweet Love*. 1979: *The Best Place To Be* (TV). *Goldie and the Boxer* (TV). 1981: *Love for Rent* (TV). *Goldie and the Boxer go to Hollywood* (TV).

MILLER, George (G. Miliotis) 1945-

In most of his movies a master of pace, Australia's George Miller, who made the 'Mad Max' films, has probably had too many fingers in too many pies in his 20 years in mainstream cinema, resulting in too few visits to the director's chair. Graduating at 25 as a doctor, he practised

medicine for 18 months in a big-city hospital. He quit to go into film production with partner Byron Kennedy (killed in a helicopter crash in 1983) but it was several years before, pooling all their savings, they came up with the small budget for their first major film, *Mad Max*. The international success of the film established Miller on the film scene. He made two sequels to the movie, both with star Mel Gibson. The last in the series, *Mad Max Beyond Thunderdome*, is a superior, well-crafted flight of the imagination, its action devastatingly well staged. Miller now went to Hollywood, where he made two modestly successful films, then returned to Australia, where his many films as producer included the phenomenally successful *Babe*. In 1998, Miller made a sequel to this first film, his first mainline movie for six years. He should not be confused with another George Miller (1943-), who has also worked in Australia and Hollywood and whose best-known films are *The Man from Snowy River* and *André*.

1972: *Violence in the Cinema Part 1*. 1973: *The Devil in Evening Dress*. 1979: *Mad Max*. 1982: *Mad Max 2* (US: *The Road Warrior*). 1983: †*Twilight Zone The Movie*. *The Dismissal* (TV). 1985: *Mad Max Beyond Thunderdome*. 1987: *The Witches of Eastwick*. 1992: *Lorenzo's Oil*. 1996: *40,000 Years of Dreaming*. 1997: *Heaven before I Die*. 1998: *Babe: Pig in the City*.

MILLER, Robert Ellis 1927-

This American director makes hard-shelled, soft-centred movies that have by and large not lived up to the promise of his early work. His looked a heartening talent at times in the late 1960s, but softness has gradually overtaken his work to the point where it is hard to feel for the characters in a Miller film: 'Twas not always thus: *Any Wednesday*, although severely truncated outside its native America, is a wise and witty comedy of words, delightfully played by Jane Fonda, Jason Robards, Dean Jones and Rosemary Murphy. Even better is the very affecting *The Heart is a Lonely Hunter*, in which Miller's cameras eavesdrop on a series of vignettes which poignantly establish the few highs and many lows in the life of a deaf mute: Alan Arkin (as the mute), Sondra Locke and Stacy Keach were never better than in this beautiful, haunting film. Since then, Miller has not been blessed with such sympathetic players (or, if he has, they have been past their best), but his own over-lyrical approach has not helped his career, and even Goldie Hawn

Liza **Minnelli** celebrates her fourth birthday (12 May 1950) on an MGM film set, with her father, Vincente Minnelli, and her mother, an ailing Judy Garland. A month later, Garland would attempt suicide.

could do little with the fuzziness of *The Girl from Petrovka*, hardly seen in cinemas. It seems unlikely that Miller will change his ways, now that his 70th birthday is behind him. Certainly he has worked more for TV than the cinema in the past 15 years.

1966: *Any Wednesday (GB: Bachelor Girl Apartment)*. 1968: *The Heart is a Lonely Hunter. Sweet November*. 1970: *The Buttercup Chain*. 1974: *The Girl From Petrovka*. 1976: *Just an Old Sweet Song (TV)*. 1978: *Ishi – the Last of his Tribe (TV)*. 1980: *Madame X (TV). The Baltimore Bullet. Short Cut to Haifa/Big Truck and Poor Clare*. 1983: *Reuben, Reuben*. 1984: *Her Life As a Man (TV)*. 1985: *Intimate Strangers (TV)*. 1987: *Brenda Starr released 1990)*. 1989: *Hawks*. 1990: *Bed and Breakfast*. 1992: *Killer Rules (TV)*. 1994: *Pointman (TV)*. 1995: *A Walton Wedding (TV)*.

MINGHELLA, Anthony 1954-

British writer-director, born in the Isle of Wight, who, after writing for TV, turned director in 1990 and took the world by storm six years later with his version of *The English Patient*, a book long thought unfilmable. Minghella's directing skills, in fact, very soon outstripped his writing abilities and, although, partly due to his meticulous preparation, his film output looks likely to be restricted to one movie every three years, he looks set for a high-profile film career. He first came to prominence as a playwright, voted most promising writer of the year in 1984 by the London theatre critics. He won the best new play award two years later for *Trade in Bangkok* and, hoping to see it filmed, turned it into a screenplay. When nothing came of that, nor of other aborted collaborations for the cinema, Minghella decided to direct his own material and, with the help of Channel 4, did just that in 1990 with *Truly Madly Deeply*, a romantic and funny ghost story which received huge critical acclaim. Minghella's facility with actors was already apparent: Juliet Stevenson gives a performance of great charm (her best for the cinema) and is well complemented by Alan Rickman as the dead lover who returns to haunt and comfort her. Minghella then made his first Hollywood movie, *Mr Wonderful*, which kept a fairly low profile at the box-office, despite some good reviews and sweet-natured performances from a strong ensemble cast that includes Matt Dillon, Annabella Sciorra, William Hurt, Mary-Louise Parker and Vincent D'Onofrio. The script had moments of weakness, which was also true of *The English Patient*, not that this stopped this sweeping epic from becoming a world-wide blockbuster, and deservedly so, for its performances are finely crafted with loving care. So it was most appropriate that Minghella should win the Oscar for best direction, but merely (!) a nomination for his rather wordy screenplay. The film also took the best picture award. The balding, beaming and bearded Minghella now moved forward to an adaptation of the same Patricia Highsmith novel, *The Talented Mr Ripley*, that had attracted Wim Wenders to make *The American Friend* in the late 1970s.

1990: *Truly Madly Deeply*. 1993: *Mr Wonderful*. 1996: *The English Patient*. 1999: *The Talented Mr Ripley*.

MINNELLI, Vincente 1903-1986

An artist rather than an author, Minnelli was responsible for some of the most dazzling Hollywood entertainments of the 1940s and 1950s and also some of the dullest. Minnelli was at his best with musicals and specifically those that were more or less screen originals. Asked to bring a popular hit such as *Brigadoon* or *Kismet* to the screen, he could make the results seem devoid of inspiration. Yet inspired he could be, in a vivid and breathtaking way. One film, *Meet Me in St Louis,* is pure gold – winning, warm, tuneful and beautifully made, with the songs perfectly integrated into the narrative. And, with set pieces in other musicals such as *Cabin in the Sky, Yolanda and the Thief, The Pirate, Ziegfeld Follies* (in which he directed three-quarters of the segments) and *The Band Wagon,* Minnelli becomes the Phineas T. Barnum of the screen, displaying all the goods in the window, but in an order no-one else would have dared dream of. A dancer and tumbler with the Minnelli family act at only three years old, he became stage manager, costume designer and set designer before tackling his first Broadway musical as director in 1935. M-G-M hired him in 1940, at first just to stage musical numbers, notably in *Strike Up the Band* and *Babes on Broadway,* but from 1943 as a full-time director. The next ten years contain much of his best work, with one or two films outside the musical field: *Undercurrent,* an absorbing psychological thriller; *Father of the Bride* and *Father's Little Dividend,* funny family comedies; and the totally hilarious *The Long, Long Trailer,* an enormous box-office triumph on the strength of Lucille Ball's success in the TV series *I Love Lucy* – her and Minnelli's comic timing is a joy. Around 1953, though, things began going a bit awry. *Brigadoon, Kismet, The Cobweb* (in which the cast seem to be performing behind glass and at the wrong tempo), *Tea and Sympathy* and *Designing Woman* combined to make a sizeable dent in Minnelli's glittering reputation. But he did recoup some lost ground with the teeming *Lust for Life,* which won Anthony Quinn his second Oscar, the wholly delightful *Gigi* (Minnelli himself taking one of eight Oscars here), *The Reluctant Debutante* (turned into the brightest of vehicles for the gossamer talents of Rex Harrison and Kay Kendall), and the powerful *Home from the Hill.* The only remaining rabbit in the magician's hat was the beguiling, if somewhat foreshortened *On a Clear Day You Can See Forever.*

1942: †*Panama Hattie (uncredited).* 1943: †*Thousands Cheer (uncredited). I Dood It (GB: By Hook or By Crook). Cabin in the Sky.* 1944: †*Ziegfeld Follies (released 1946). Meet Me in St Louis.* 1945: *Yolanda and the Thief. The Clock (GB: Under the Clock).* 1946: *Undercurrent.* †*Till the Clouds Roll By (uncredited).* 1948: *The Pirate.* 1949: *Madame Bovary.* 1950: *Father of the Bride.* 1951: *An American in Paris. Father's Little Dividend.* 1952: †*Lovely to Look At (uncred-*

ited). The Bad and the Beautiful. 1953: †*The Story of Three Loves. The Band Wagon. The Long, Long Trailer.* 1954: *Brigadoon.* 1955: *Kismet. The Cobweb.* 1956: *Lust for Life. Tea and Sympathy.* 1957: †*The Seventh Sin (uncredited). Designing Woman.* 1958: *Gigi. The Reluctant Debutante. Some Came Running.* 1960: *Home from the Hill. Bells Are Ringing.* 1961: *The Four Horsemen of the Apocalypse.* 1962: *Two Weeks in Another Town.* 1963: *The Courtship of Eddie's Father.* 1964: *Goodbye Charlie.* 1965: *The Sandpiper.* 1970: *On a Clear Day You Can See Forever:* 1976: *A Matter of Time.*

MIZOGUCHI, Kenji 1898-1956

Mizoguchi's graceful and uniquely Japanese brushes painted haunting portraits of tragic lovers: the beauty of the images on screen was rarely left untouched by the imminence of death. The earliest of Japan's great directors, Mizoguchi created a visual world quite unlike anything Western observers had seen before, with its characters' fates pursued inexorably by remarkably fluid camerawork that almost always avoided static set-ups. He was also concerned by the role of women in oriental society. This 'mission' reflected his own personal life. Born in Tokyo to poor parents, he saw his sister sold into the life of a geisha, and he himself lived with geishas for a considerable period of his comparatively short life. He left school at 13, to work successively in a hospital, and as a kimono designer, painter and newspaper layout artist. By the age of 21, though, he had moved into the Japanese cinema as an assistant director, and began to make his own movies in 1922. Most of his early films remain unseen to western eyes, the earliest of them to become available for general viewing being *The Story of the Last Chrysanthemums,* made in 1939. In this film, one can see for the first time his characteristic style by which characters, action, atmosphere and backcloth become unified under one 'roof' via a travelling-camera that takes in all the vital visuals while remaining at arm's length from the action. Mizoguchi's stories, however, are by no means toothless, but hard against oppression and injustice, usually with tragic endings which bring home some new and angry message. His 1950s films were more widely shown outside Japan than any others, and include such fine work as *Ugetsu Monogatari* (his first international success and possibly still his best-known film), *Sansho the Bailiff, The Empress Yang Kwei-Fei* – with its striking use of colour – and

The Life of Oharu. Each is a rich evocation of its own particular world that compels attention. Mizoguchi, who spent much of his life in physical pain from rheumatoid arthritis, died from leukaemia half-way through shooting another film, completed by his friend Kimisiburo Yoshimura.

1922: *Ai ni Yomigaeru Hi (US: The Resurrection of Love). Seishun no Yumeji (US: The Dream Path of Youth). Joen no Chimata (US: City of Desire). Furusato (US: Hometown). Rupimono. 813: The Adventures of Arsène Lupin. Haizan no Uta wa Kanashi (US: Failure's Song is Sad). Chi to Rei (US: Blood and Soul).* 1923: *Yoru (US: The Night). Kiri no Minato (US: Foggy Harbor/Anna Christie). Haikyo no Naka (US: In the Ruins). Kanto (D). Toge no Uta (US: Song of the Mountain Pass).* 1924: *Kanashiki Hakuchi (US: Song of the Sad Idiot). Gendai no Joo (US: The Queen of Modern Times). Josei wa Tsuyoshi (US: Women Are Strong). Schichimencho no Yukue (US: Turkeys in a Row). Samidare Zoshi (US: Chronicle of the May Rain). Jinkyo (US: This Dusty World). Musen Fusen (US: No Money, No Fight). Kanraku no Onna (US: Woman of Pleasure). Akatsuki no Shi (US: Death at Dawn).* 1925: *Kyokubadan no Joo (US: Queen of the Circus). Daichi wa Hohoemu (US: The Smiling Earth).* †*Akai Yuki no Terasarete (US: Shining in the Red Sunset). Furusato no Uta (US: The Song of Home). Ningen (US: The Man).* †*Gaijo no Sukechi (US: Street Sketches). Shirayuri wa Nageku (US: The White Lily Laments).* 1926: *Nogi Taisho to Kuma-San (US: General Nogi and Kuma-San). Doka O (US: The Copper King). Kamin-ingyo Haru no Sasayaki (US: A Paper Doll's Whisper of Spring). Shin Ono ga Tsumi (GB & US: My Fault). Kyoren no Onna Shisho (US: The Passion of a Woman Teacher). Kane (US: Money). Kaikoko Danji (US: Children of the Sea).* 1927: *Ko-On (US: The Imperial Grace). Jihi Shincho (US: Cuckoo).* 1928: *Hito no Issho – Parts I, II and III (US: The Life of Man).* 1929: *Tokyo-Koshinkyoku (US: Tokyo March).* †*Asahi wa Kagayaku (US: The Morning Sun Shines). Nihombashi. Tokai Kokyogaku (US: Metropolitan Symphony).* 1930: *Furusato (US: Hometown). Tojin Ikichi (US: Mistress of a Foreigner).* 1931: *Shikamo Karera wa Yuku – Parts I and II (US: And Yet They Go On).* 1932: *Toki no Ujigami (US: Man of the Moment). Mammo Kenkoku no Reimei (US: The Dawn of Mongolia).* 1933: *Taki no Shiraito (GB: The Water Magician. US: White Threads of the Waterfall). Gion Matsuru (US: Gion Festival).*

Kamikaze Ren. Jinpuren (US: The Jimpu Group). 1934: Aizo Togo (US: The Passing of Love and Hate). Orizuro Osen (GB: The Downfall. US: The Downfall of Osen). 1935: Maria no Oyuki (GB: Oyuki the Virgin. US: Oyuki the Madonna). Gubijinso (GB: The Field Poppy. US: Poppies). 1936: Naniwa Ereji (GB: Naniwa Elegy. US: Osaka Elegy). Gion no Shimai (GB & US: Sisters of the Gion). 1937: Aienkyo (GB & US: The Straits of Love and Hate). 1938: Aa Furusato (US: Ah, My Home Town). †Roei no Uta (US: Song of the Camp). 1939: Zangiku Monogatari (GB & US: The Story of the Last Chrysanthemums). 1940: Naniwa Onna (US: A Woman of Osaka). Geido Ichidai Otoko (US: The Life of an Artist). 1941: Genroku Chushingura – Part I (GB: The Loyal 47 of the Genroku Era. US: The Loyal 47). 1942: Musashi Miyamoto (GB: The Swordsman). Genroku Chushingura – Part II. 1944: Danjuro Sandai (US. Three Generations of Danjuro). 1945: Hisshoka. Meito Bijomaru (GB: The Sword/The Noted Sword. US: The Famous Sword Bijomaru). 1946: Josei no Shori (GB: The Victory of Women. US: Women's Victory). Utamaro o Meguro Gonin no Onna (GB: Five Women Around Utamaro. US: Utamaro and his Five Women). 1947: Joyu Sumako no Koi (GB: The Loves of Actress Sumako). US: The Loves of Sumako the Actress). 1948: Yoru no Onnatachi (GB & US: Women of the Night). 1949: Waga Koi wa Moeru (GB: My Love Has Been Burning. US: Flame of My Love). 1950: Yuki Fujin Ezu (GB: Portrait of Madame Yuki. US. The Picture of Madame Yuki). 1951: Musashino Fujin (GB: Madama Musashino/The Lady from Musashino. US: Woman of Musashino/Lady Musashino). Oyu-Sama (GB & US: Miss Oyu). 1952: Saikaku Ichidai Onna (GB & US: The Life of Oharu). 1953: Ugetsu Monogatari (US: Ugetsu). Gion Bayashi (GB: Gion Music Festival. US: A Geisha). 1954: Sansho Dayu (GB & US: Sansho the Bailiff). Chikamatsu Monogatari (GB & US: A Story from Chikamatsu). Uwasa no Onna (GB: A Woman of Rumour. US: The Woman in the Rumor). 1955: Yokihi (GB: The Empress Yang Kwei Fei. US: Yang Kwei Fei). Shin-Heike Monogatari (GB: New Tales of the Taira Clan. US: The Taira Clan). 1956: Agasen Chitai (GB & US: Street of Shame). 1957: †Osaka Monogatari.

MOLINARO, Edouard 1928-

Although critical judgments on his work have been remarkably varied, this French director seems to possess the common touch which has escaped many of his continental contemporaries. Most of his films in the last 20 years have found a wide international market and, if many of them have not been of the highest quality, who can argue with the commercial success of such films as A Pain in the A*** and La cage aux folles? Most of his recent work has in fact been in this broadly farcical vein, although his first feature film (after a background in short films for industry), Le dos au mur (distribution outside France with his first movie!) was a dramatic enough start. There were a couple of thrillers among the subsequent frolics but, despite a pretty dire Bardot vehicle, Une ravissante idiote, his first big success came with the frantically paced A Pain in the A*** in 1973 which, with Lino Ventura and Jacques Brel lending a certain Gallic fatalism, is actually funnier and certainly more successful than the Billy Wilder remake, Buddy Buddy, which followed eight years later. It was nothing, however, compared to the financial returns of La cage aux folles, which, despite angering the gay community with its old-fashioned, farcical, demeaning view of homosexual relationships, proved hilariously funny to most audiences, especially in America. Molinaro, ever with an eye to commercial possibilities, lost no time in providing his paying customers with a follow-up. After a brief and unhappy stay in Hollywood, Molinaro entered a rare fallow period. It seemed in the late 1980s that he might be ready to give up film-making, but he returned in dazzling form in 1996 with the well-received Beaumarchais l'insolent.

1957: Le dos au mur (GB: Evidence in Concrete. US: Back to the Wall). 1958: Un témoin dans la ville. 1959: Des femmes disparaissent (US: Road to Shame). 1960: Une fille pour l'été (GB: Girls for the Summer. US: A Mistress for the Summer). 1961: La mort de belle (GB & US: The Passion of Slow Fire). †The Seven Deadly Sins. 1962: Les ennemis. Arsène Lupin contre Arsène Lupin. 1963: Une ravissante idiote (GB & US: A Ravishing Idiot). 1964: La chasse à l'homme (GB: The Gentle Art of Seduction. US: Male Hunt). 1965: Les escrocs/Quand passent les faisans. 1967: Peau d'espion (GB & US: To Commit a Murder). 1968: Oscar. Hibernatus. 1969: Mon oncle Benjamin (GB: The Amorous Adventures of Uncle Benjamin). 1970: Le liberté en croupe. 1971: Les aveux les plus doux. 1972: Le Mandarine. 1973: Allez-vous perdre d'ailleurs. L'emmerdeur (GB & US: A Pain in the A***). Le gang des otages (US: The Hostages). 1974: L'ironie du sort. 1975: Le téléphone rose (GB & US: The Pink Telephone). 1976: Dracula père et fils. 1977: L'homme pressé (GB TV as The Hurried Man. US: Man in a Hurry). 1978: La cage aux folles (GB: La cage aux folles – Birds of a Feather). 1980: La cage aux folles 2. 1981: †Sunday Lovers. Pour cent briques on n'a plus rien. 1983: I Won't Dance (unfinished). 1984: Just the Way You Are. 1985: Palace. 1986: L'amour en douce (US: Love on the Quiet). 1987: Le prince Eric. 1988: L'amuse gueule. Enchanté. A gauche en sortant de l'ascenseur. 1996: Beaumarchais l'insolent (GB and US: Beaumarchais the Scoundrel).

MORA, Philippe 1947

French-born, Australian-raised director initially of confrontational documentaries, but later a specialist in fantasy, science-fiction and horror. Trained as a painter, Mora came to London to mount an exhibition of his paintings and stayed to make some high-profile and mainly narration-free documentaries, two of them about the Nazi regime before and during World War II. Returning to Australia via Canada and another feature-length documentary, the Depression Era study Brother, Can You Spare a Dime, Mora moved into mostly fantasy feature films, a vein of activity culminating in the literate, intelligent and climate delicate 'true life' story of an American writer (Mora's long-time friend Whitley Strieber) who really did see little blue men from outer space. Christopher Walken's performance as Strieber was remarkable, but the film marked the beginning of a period of inactivity from Mora on the film front. Continuing to work and paint both in Australia and America, he returned to film-making on a rather lower-profile basis in 1996 with the appropriately named Back in Business.

1969: Trouble in Molopolis (D). 1973: +The Double Headed Eagle (D). Swastika (D). 1975: Brother, Can You Spare a Dime? (D). 1976: Mad Dog Morgan (GB: Mad Dog). 1978: The Times They Are a-Changin' (D). 1982: The Beast Within. The Return of Captain Invincible. 1984: A Breed Apart. 1985: Howling II ... Your Sister is a Werewolf. 1986: Death of a Soldier. 1987: Howling III: The Marsupials. 1989: Communion. 1996: Back in Business. 1997: Burning Down the House/Snide and Prejudice. 1998: Thick and Thin.

MOXEY, John Llewellyn 1920-

Efficient British director who became rather more so with assignments that lean towards fantasy or horror. After 1967, he worked in America, making over 40 TV movies, some of them well above average. And when he has talented technicians – especially cameramen or art directors – to work with, his effects can be quite striking. An assistant director from 1946, television producer from 1950 and television director from 1955, Moxey (credited simply as John Moxey on all his British work) has always been a prodigious worker. He already had almost 30 90-minute television plays to his credit before his first film, *City of the Dead* in 1960. This is a massive dose of witchery-pokery, with very atmospheric black-and-white photography by Desmond Dickinson and Moxey proving for the first time but not the last that he could build some very chilly set-pieces. Unfortunately, although Moxey worked prolifically in TV on Plays of the Week and episodes of such series as *The Saint, The Baron* and *The Avengers*, the remainder of his British films are either disappointing or very minor. The TV movies are a mixed bunch, but they spring to life whenever Moxey gets hold of anything to do with fear – *The House That Would Not Die, A Taste of Evil, The Strange and Deadly Occurrence, Home for the Holidays* and especially *The Night Stalker*, a meeting of the old-style American crime film with a dose of modern vampirism, with a dogged central performance by Darren McGavin (the film led to a less successful series, also starring McGavin) and a brilliant climax in the killer's lair. There were too few chills in Moxey's casebook after that, although he continued directing shoals of TV movies, ending with the abysmal *Lady Mobster* in 1988.

1960: *City of the Dead (US: Horror Hotel). Foxhole in Cairo.* 1962: *Death Trap. The £20,000 Kiss.* 1963: *Ricochet. Downfall.* 1964: *Face of a Stranger.* 1965: *Strangler's Web.* 1966: *Circus of Fear (US: Psycho-Circus).* 1967: *Dial M for Murder (TV).* 1968: *Laura (TV). A Hatful of Rain (TV).* 1970: *The House That Would Not Die (TV). San Francisco International (TV. GB: San Francisco International Airport).* 1971: *Escape (TV). The Last Child (TV). A Taste of Evil (TV). The Death of Me Yet (TV).* 1972: *The Night Stalker (TV). Hardcase (TV). The Bounty Man (TV). Home for the Holidays (TV). Ghost Story (TV).* 1973: *Enter Horowitz (TV). Genesis II (TV).* 1974: *The Strange and Deadly Occurrence (TV). Where Have All the People Gone? (TV). The Day They Took the Babies Away (TV).* 1976: *Charlie's Angels (TV). Conspiracy of Terror (TV). Nightmare in Badham County (TV). Smash-Up on Interstate 5 (TV).* 1977:

Panic in Echo Park (TV). Tales of the Nunundaga (TV). Intimate Strangers (TV). 1978: *The President's Mistress (TV). The Courage and the Passion (TV).* 1979: *Sanctuary of Fear (TV). The Power Within (TV). The Solitary Man (TV).* 1980: *The Mating Season (TV). The Children of An Lac (TV).* 1981: *No Place to Hide (TV). Killjoy (TV).* 1982: *The Violation of Sarah McDavid (TV).* 1983: *The Cradle Will Fall (TV). Through Naked Eyes (TV).* 1985: *When Dreams Come True (TV). Blacke's Magic (TV).* 1987: *Sadie and Son/Detective Sadie and Son (TV).* 1988: *Lady Mobster (TV).*

MULLIGAN, Robert 1925-

Mulligan has never quite become the major American director that once seemed probable, and has been outstripped in reputation by his one-time producer/partner, Alan J. Pakula. Most of his films are gently observed and even the portraits of mental pressure – *Fear Strikes Out, Inside Daisy Clover* – are caringly made. However, many of his most promising projects, despite good casts and obviously thorough spadework by the director, have been less than successful: total conviction has evaded him since his early years in the cinema. He had originally thought of becoming a priest, but, after World War II service with the U.S. Marines, Mulligan joined CBS Television and by the mid-1950s had become one of their leading young directors. His first film, *Fear Strikes Out*, is a poignant and effective portrait of a son being forced to follow his father's profession (baseball) against his own wishes, with one of Anthony Perkins' most appealing performances and Karl Malden for once in the cinema put to good use as the father. Appealing portrayals were also the order of the day in *The Rat Race*, a story of hard-up show-business strugglers holding on to a kind of integrity. It had a relationship between Tony Curtis and Debbie Reynolds that should have been unbelievable but, thanks to tactful and selfless work by stars and director, actually convinces. This should have been the case with other Mulligan films, but he sometimes seems to hold back from pain and confrontation and thus *The Great Impostor, Love with the Proper Stranger, Inside Daisy Clover* and *Summer of '42* (though this last was extremely successful commercially) remain major but half-realized projects. *To Kill a Mockingbird* was more satisfying, thanks partly to Mulligan's skilful cutting and handling of children and settings to establish the feel of the piece. It also won an Academy Award for Gregory Peck in a showy part

that half a dozen actors could have played as well. After the uncharacteristic melodramatics of *Bloodbrothers*, Mulligan played safe with a successful enough, but unadventurous, adaptation of the hit stage play *Same Time, Next Year*. That, however, was better than his two most recent films which, although both boasting the odd tender and telling moment, failed to bring the required response from the cinemagoing public.

1957: *Fear Strikes Out.* 1960: *The Rat Race.* 1961: *The Great Impostor. Come September.* 1962: *The Spiral Road.* 1963: *To Kill a Mockingbird.* 1964: *Love with the Proper Stranger. Baby, the Rain Must Fall.* 1965: *Inside Daisy Clover.* 1966: *Up the Down Staircase.* 1968: *The Stalking Moon.* 1970: *The Pursuit of Happiness.* 1971: *Summer of '42.* 1972: *The Other.* 1974: *The Nickel Ride.* 1978: *Bloodbrothers. Same Time, Next Year.* 1982: *Kiss Me Goodbye.* 1988: *Clara's Heart.* 1991: *The Man in the Moon.*

MULCAHY, Russell 1953-

Australian director of glossy, high-profile, sometimes effects-driven, but largely disappointing action films. Mulcahy for some time worked in Britain as a director of music videos, but returned to his native country to make his first fictional feature, *Razorback*, an offbeat horror film about a giant hog terrorising the countryside. Its arresting visuals and crude energy put Mulcahy on the map, and he was able to get the backing for what proved to be his greatest success, *Highlander*. An ambitious fantasy adventure with impressive special effects, *Highlander* has some well-staged duels whose effectiveness owes much to Mulcahy's strong pictorial sense. It led to two sequels, the first of which was directed by Mulcahy himself, and a TV series. Mulcahy's subsequent films, despite major stars and big budgets with which to work, have not fulfilled their potential, and he has seemed less commanding with actors than with action.

1981: *Derek and Clive Get The Horn.* 1984: *Razorback.* 1986: *Highlander.* 1990: *Highlander II: The Quickening.* 1991: *Ricochet.* 1992: *Blue Ice.* 1993: *The Real McCoy.* 1994: *The Shadow.* 1996: *Silent Trigger/The Algonquin Goodbye.* 1998: *Talos the Mummy.* 1999: *Resurrection.*

MUNK, Andrzej 1921-1961

With Andrzej Wajda and Roman Polanski, Munk, whose career was cut short by his death in a car crash, was among the foremost Polish post-war film directors. His few features – he made many documentaries – are mostly about people persecuted or hunted in some particularly desperate way, and they exude cynicism and scepticism: obliquely, they have a lot to say about the state of Poland itself, which Wajda was to put in plainer terms. A graduate of the famous film school at Lodz, Munk was making documentaries while still studying, although his best and most famous, *A Walk in the Old Town,* vaguely reminiscent of Jennings' *Listen to Britain,* was not made until 1958. The 'town' is, of course, Warsaw and its sights and sounds come to us through the eyes and ears of a young girl violinist who sees and hears them in her own special image-orientated way. Munk's two best-known fictional features are both incomplete, one intentionally so, one sadly not. Parts of both films, *Eroica* and *Passenger,* are set in grim prisoner-of-war/concentration camps and catch hauntingly their desperation. *Eroica* is a two-part film originally intended as a trilogy: Munk was dissatisfied with the third episode and deleted it. He had finished less than two-thirds of his last film, *Passenger,* at his death. It was 'completed', using mainly stills, by a friend, Witold Lesiewicz and, although it runs little more than an hour, remains a devastating experience. Munk died young: but at least lie left his cries for his beloved country on film.

1949: Sztuka Mlodych/The Art of Youth (D). 1950: Zaczelo sie w Hiszpanii/It Started in Spain (D). 1951: Nauka Blizej Zycia/Closer to Life (D). Kierunek Nowa Huta/Direction – Nowa Huta (D). 1952: Poemat Symfoniczny 'Bajka' St Moniusky/Bajka (D). Pamietniki Chlopów/Diaries of the Peasants (D). Ursus/The Tale of Ursus. 1953: Kolejarskie Slowo/The Railwayman's Word (D). †Gwiazdy Musza Plonac/The Stars Must Shine (D). 1955: Niedzielny Poranek (D. GB: One Sunday Morning. US: Sunday Morning). Blekitny Krzyz (GB & US: Men of the Blue Cross). 1956: Czlowiek (US: Man on the Track). 1957: Eroica. 1958: Spacerek Staromiejski (D. GB: A Walk in the Old Town. US: A Walk in the Old City of Warsaw). 1959: Zezowate Szczescie (GB & US: Bad Luck). 1961: Pasazerka (GB & US: Passenger).

MURNAU, F.W. (F.W. Plumpe) 1888-1931

It was appropriate that Murnau should subtitle *Nosferatu,* one of his masterworks, *Eine Symphonie des Grauens.* For the films of this German director *were*

symphonies, composed in time and space, light and shade. If most critical assessments of him are conducted on a high level with complicated terms involving surfaces, lines, imaginary space, *découpage* and the architecture of the frame, these are no high-flown assumptions of something the director never intended. For it is clear from contemporary interviews that Murnau's own mind dwelt on just such planes, and that he was determined to stretch the cinema far beyond the limitations then prevailing. Enormously intelligent and far ahead of his time, Murnau worked to obtain new dramatic effects from the interrelation of fleeting shots in fragmented sequences – in other words, working in filmic jigsaws whose individual scenes are suddenly stunningly effective when the final piece is fitted. Using a combination of the real world and a skilful manipulation of the audience's imaginations, Murnau used the power of suggestion in new and amazing ways: thus the unseen and unspoken is constantly sensed by his audiences, no matter what their intelligence. He was briefly an actor in his early days, before World War I service as a combat pilot, although he sat out most of the war in Switzerland after crash-landing there. In 1919, he began directing films, most of his early efforts reflecting the general German preoccupation of the time with the macabre and fantastic, save that Murnau often used naturalistic backgrounds where others were using expressionist sets. Such films as *Satanas* (a fallen angel is offered a chance to regain his place), *Haunted Castle,* and a version of *Dr Jekyll and Mr Hyde,* all led up to *Nosferatu,* Murnau's film of the Dracula story; enough to chill anyone to the bone, it contains daring experiments with the camera which heighten the horror and deepen the sense of evil. Murnau's remarkable if often sinister visual adventures were continued in *Phantom, Tartüff* – a haunting chamber piece, and *Faust,* the remarkable pictorial backcloths of which recall the work of many painters, from Bosch through Rembrandt to Brueghel. Hollywood finally seized Murnau in 1927 and he made *Sunrise,* an upbeat hymn to humanity which won three Oscars, but shamefully not one for its director although there were only three Best Director nominees that year; the film did win an Oscar for best artistic quality of production. It was not, however, a commercial success – nor were Murnau's next two American films, the second of which, *Our Daily Bread,* was ultimately taken out of his hands by the studio. He regained his reputation by his brilliant work with Flaherty (*qv*) on the

sunflecked documentary *Tabu,* and was on the brink of taking up a new contract with Paramount when he was killed in a car crash.

1919: Der Knabe in Blau (US: Emerald of Death). Satanas. 1920: Sehnsucht/Bajazzo. Der Bucklige und die Tänzerin. Abend... Nacht . . . Morgen. Der Januskopf (US: Dr Jekyll and Mr Hyde). Der Gang in die Nacht. 1921: Schloss Vogelöd (US: Haunted Castle). Marizza, gennant die Schmugglermadonna. 1922: Der brennende Acker (US: Burning Soil). Nosferatu – Eine Symphonie des Grauens (GB & US: Nosferatu the Vampire). Phantom. 1923: Die Austreibung (US: Driven from Home). Die Finanzen des Grossherzogs. 1924: Der letzte Mann (GB & US: The Last Laugh). 1925: Tartüff (GB & US: Tartuffe). 1926: Faust. 1927: Sunrise – a Song of Two Humans (GB: Sunrise). 1928: Four Devils. 1930: Our Daily Bread (later City Girl). Die zwölfte Stunde – eine Nacht des Grauens (revised sound version of Nosferatu). 1931: †Tabu (D).

MURPHY, Geoff 1938-

New Zealand-born director much at home with rip-roaring action. He made some distinctive films in his native country, but became somewhat sucked into the Hollywood mainstream after going to America in 1990. He has, however, proved himself one of the rare latter-day makers of westerns, whose colour and vigour reflect some of the films he made in his earlier New Zealand days. The best of these are *Utu,* about a 19th-century Maori's quest for revenge on the British army members who slaughtered his family, and *The Quiet Earth,* in which a scientific researcher awakens one morning to find that all human and animal life has vanished from the face of the earth. His Hollywood career started brightly with *Young Guns II,* a western in the old style, with vividly rounded portraits of the characters involved. Most of his other films have had exciting moments, but his stature gradually slipped through the nineties and by the end of the decade he was working in TV.

1975: Wildman. 1979: Goodbye Pork Pie. 1982: Utu. 1985: The Quiet Earth. 1988: Never Say Die. 1989: Red King, White Knight (TV). 1990: Young Guns II/Young Guns II: Blaze of Glory. 1991: Freejack. 1992: Blind Side (cable TV). 1994: The Last Outlaw. 1995: Under Siege 2/Under Siege 2: Dark Territory. 1996: Don't Look Back (cable TV). 1997: The Magnificent Seven (TV). 1999: Fortress 2

MURPHY, Ralph 1895-1967

Efficient American director who made bright and breezy film fare, more or less resident at Paramount from the early 1930s until the middle 1940s. Several of his films were middle-budget musicals and light comedies. After leaving Paramount, Murphy developed a taste for making colourful adventure stories, directing several animal films and swashbucklers, usually filmed in splashy colour. With the coming of sound, he had moved from Broadway to Hollywood, becoming dialogue director on early talkies, and a fully-fledged director by 1931. His films never rose to any great heights, although he did direct Frank Sinatra in his first feature film, *Las Vegas Nights*, a typical Murphy 'semi-A' film. The outdoors adventures, *Mickey* and *Red Stallion in the Rockies*, are pleasant, easy-going entertainment and the three costume adventures with Patricia Medina and Louis Hayward in the early 1950s are lively and colourful enough for action double-bills. Murphy's career ended quietly with a couple of Lex Barker adventure films made in Italy, and he retired at 60. He was at one time married to actress Gloria Dickson, although they were divorced by the time (1945) she met a tragic death in a fire when only 30 years old.

1931: †*The Tip-Off (GB: Looking for Trouble). The Big Shot (GB: The Optimist).* 1932: *Panama Flo. 70,000 Witnesses.* 1933: *Strictly Personal. Golden Harvest. Song of the Eagle. Girl without a Room.* 1934: *The Great Flirtation. She Made Her Bed. Menace. Private Scandal. The Notorious Sophie Lang.* 1935: *McFadden's Flats. Men Without Names.* 1936: *Collegiate (GB: The Charm School). Florida Special. The Man I Marry.* 1937: *Top of the Town. Night Club Scandal.* 1939: *Our Neighbors, the Carters.* 1940: *I Want a Divorce. The Gay City. Hearts in Springtime.* 1941: *Las Vegas Nights. You're the One. Pacific Blackout.* 1942: *Mrs Wiggs of the Cabbage Patch.* 1943: *Night Plane from Chungking.* 1944: *The Man in Half Moon Street. The Town Went Wild. Rainbow Island.* 1947: *The Spirit of West Point.* 1948: *Mickey.* 1949: *Red Stallion in the Rockies.* 1950: *Stage to Tucson (GB: Lost Stage Valley).* 1951: *Never Trust a Gambler. The Lady and the Bandit (GB: Dick Turpin's Ride).* 1952: *Captain Pirate (GB: Captain Blood, Fugitive). Lady in the Iron Mask.* 1954: *Vendetta dei Thugs.* 1955: *Mystery of the Black Jungle (US: Black Devils of Kali).*

NARIZZANO, Silvio 1927-

Canadian-born director of offbeat films that either land square on target or miss by a mile. After experience in television, first in Canada, then in Britain where he gained a high reputation for his direction of human dramas, Narizzano turned to the screen in unlikely style with the lurid *Fanatic*, a far-fetched Hammer horror tale with a bravura performance by Tallulah Bankhead which the relatively inexperienced director proved unable to control. He was in splendid control, however, of his next – and best – film, *Georgy Girl*, in which he steered Lynn Redgrave (also in *her* best film) to a *tour-de force* as the loveless, lumpish teacher in a performance as funny and touching as the film. The rest of Narizzano's film career has been uneven to say the least, and it often seems that he has followed Miss Bankhead in over-heating his films to fever levels. But his film of Joe Orton's surrealist comedy *Loot* was quite well received, Narizzano's frenzied style being well-suited to the blackly funny goings-on. He also had some success with *Why Shoot the Teacher?* a moving school story made in Canada with Samantha Eggar; but it had little showing outside the American continent, and an attempt to strike again in the same vein with *The Class of Miss MacMichael*, made in Britain with Glenda Jackson and Oliver Reed, proved disastrous, and almost the end of his cinema career to date, although he has subsequently worked on successful TV adaptations of Agatha Christie's Miss Marple Mysteries with the indomitable Joan Hickson.

1960: +*Under Two Flags.* 1961: *24 Hours in a Woman's Life (TV).* 1965: *Fanatic (US: Die, Die, My Darling!).* 1966: *Georgy Girl.* 1968: *Blue.* 1972: *Redneck/Senza ragione.* 1975: *The Sky is Falling.* 1976: *Why Shoot the Teacher?* 1978: *The Class of Miss MacMichael.* 1981: *Choices.*

NAZARRO, Ray 1902-1986

Rousing action scenes were the stock-in-trade of this American director who spent practically his whole career with one stu-dio – Columbia. Almost all his films were low-budget westerns, with the occasional thriller or swashbuckler thrown in. He had come to Hollywood as an assistant director with the advent of sound, and joined Educational Pictures, who made principally two-reeler comedies. They gave him the chance to direct one of their 'Baby Burlesks' series with Shirley Temple, but nothing more came of it, and Nazarro joined Columbia in 1934. For 11 years he worked there as an assistant director and second-unit director, after starting with a few shorts. With the absence on war service of other studio directors, Nazarro was at last given the chance to make his own films in 1945, while continuing his second-unit work on the side. He made most of the Charles Starrett series of westerns, which lasted until 1952. After that he moved on to slightly bigger things, and there were a couple of vigorous colour westerns with George Montgomery, *Indian Uprising* and *Cripple Creek*, the latter boasting a good cast that included Jerome Courtland, William Bishop, Richard Egan, Karin Booth and John Dehner. Nazarro's best film is also from this period: *Southwest Passage* (in Britain, *Camels West*) an unusual, exciting and convincing western, faster-moving than most, predictably with lively action scenes, but less predictably with Grade A performances from Rod Cameron, John Ireland and Joanne Dru. After 1958, Nazarro, as the end of the double-feature programme loomed, made one or two films in Europe, but preferred to work largely in television – on westerns.

1932: *The Runt Page.* 1934: *The Superstition of the Black Cat.* *The Superstition of Three on a Match.* *The Superstition of Walking under a Ladder.* 1935: *The Superstition of the Rabbit's Foot.* 1945: *Outlaws of the Rockies (GB: A Roving Rogue). Song of the Prairie (GB: Sentiment and Song).* 1946: *Cowboy Blues (GB: Beneath the Starry Skies). The Desert Horseman (GB: Checkmate). Galloping Thunder (GB: On Boot Hill). Gunning for Vengeance (GB: Jail Break). Roaring Rangers (GB: False Hero). Heading West (GB: The Cheat's Last Throw). Singing on the Trail (GB: Lookin' for Someone). Throw a Saddle on a Star. Two-Fisted Stranger. Texas Panhandle. That Texas Jamboree (GB: Medicine Man). Terror Trail (GB: Hands of Menace).* 1947: *West of Dodge City (GB: The Sea Wall). Law of the Canyon (GB: The Price of Crime). The Lone Hand Texan (GB: The Cheat). Last Days of Boot Hill. The Buckaroo from Powder River. Rose of Santa Rosa.* 1948: *Phantom Valley. Six*

Gun Law. Song of Idaho. West of Sonora. Trail to Laredo (GB: Sign of the Dagger). Blazing Across the Pecos (GB: Under Arrest). El Dorado Pass (GB: Desperate Men). Quick on the Trigger (GB: Condemned in Error). 1949: Laramie. The Blazing Trail (GB: The Forged Will). Challenge of the Range (GB: Moonlight Raid). South of Death Valley (GB: River of Poison). Bandits of El Dorado (GB: Tricked). 1950: Outcasts of Black Mesa (GB: The Clue). Texas Dynamo (GB: Suspected). Hoedown. Trail of the Rustlers (GB: Lost River). Streets of Ghost Town. Frontier Outpost. The Palomino (GB: Hills of the Brave). David Harding Counterspy. The Tougher They Come. 1951: Fort Savage Raiders. The Kid from Amarillo (GB: Silver Chains). Cyclone Fury. Al Jennings of Oklahoma. Flame of Stamboul. War Cry. China Corsair. 1952: Indian Uprising. Montana Territory. Junction City. Cripple Creek. 1953: The Bandits of Corsica (GB: Return of the Corsican Brothers). Kansas Pacific. Gun Belt. 1954: The Lone Gun. The Black Dakotas. Southwest Passage (GB: Camels West). 1955: Top Gun. 1956: The White Squaw. 1957: The Phantom Stagecoach. The Domino Kid. The Hired Gun. Return to Warbow. 1958: Apache Territory. 1964: When Strangers Meet (US: Dog Eat Dog). 1967: Arriverderci, Cowboy.

NEAME, Ronald 1911-

The son of a director of early silents, in which his mother (actress Ivy Close) starred, this British director was one of Britain's best cinematographers in the 1930s and 1940s, most notably with his Technicolor work on *This Happy Breed* (1944) and *Blithe Spirit* (1945). When he turned to direction in 1947, after several years working in various capacities on David Lean films, there were a few movies in black-and-white, but after 1958 Neame worked entirely in colour. The quality of the colour in his films ever since has, without exception, been outstanding. The films as a whole have been somewhat less consistent, but they have usually done well at the box-office, through either their subject matter or the drawing power of two main stars. He was working in a film studio (Elstree) from the age of 16. By the time of Hitchcock's *Blackmail* in 1929, Neame was serving as clapper boy and camera assistant. He had progressed to director of photography by 1934 and, despite a brief period as a producer, it seemed inevitable that he should eventually direct. He took the initial step with *Take My Life*, a tense and very well made murder thriller which, considering its limitations, remains one of Neame's

most skilful achievements, with careful attention to detail and excellent photography by Guy Green, who had just won an Oscar on Lean's *Great Expectations*. Neame again used well-fashioned small sequences to build an absorbing whole in *The Card*, a deservedly popular adaptation of Arnold Bennett's story; Alec Guinness was never better than in this title role. Guinness and Neame worked successfully together again on the delightfully scabrous *The Horse's Mouth*, and the Technicolor photography on that one (by Arthur Ibbetson) was superb. However, Guinness lost by a whisker in an acting duel with John Mills in Neame's best film, *Tunes of Glory*, made the following year (1960). Neither of these two films might have looked secure commercially, but Neame's smoothly persuasive direction attracted the public to them. His biggest success of the 1970s was undoubtedly *The Poseidon Adventure*, with a highly sellable subject made extremely attractive by fast-paced direction and some spectacular special effects. Neame showed some of the best sense of camera positioning to date and also persuaded Gene Hackman to give a winning, straightforward performance as the priest who leads survivors to ultimate safety when a giant liner is capsized by a tidal wave. There have been lesser Neame films certainly – *The Seventh Sin, The Golden Salamander* and *The Chalk Garden* were notably lacking in dramatic tension – and some that have not quite come up to expectations. But it's a very respectable record.

1947: Take My Life. 1949: The Golden Salamander. 1951: The Card (US: The Promoter). 1953: The Million Pound Note (US: Man with a Million). 1956: The Man Who Never Was. 1957: The Seventh Sin. 1958: Windom's Way. 1959: The Horse's Mouth. 1960: Tunes of Glory. 1961: Escape from Zahrain. 1962: I Could Go On Singing. 1963: The Chalk Garden. 1965: Mister Moses. 1966: †A Man Could Get Killed. Gambit. 1968: The Prime of Miss Jean Brodie. 1970: Scrooge. 1972: The Poseidon Adventure. 1974: The Odessa File. 1979: Meteor. 1980: Hopscotch. 1981: First Monday in October. 1986: Foreign Body.

NEGULESCO, Jean 1900-1993

What a difference 13 years can make. In 1946, at Warners, Negulesco, producer Jerry Wald and star Joan Crawford were together for *Humoresque*, that classic, tragic melodrama where Crawford walks into the sea at the end for love of violinist John Garfield. Everything about the film was tight, strong and confident. The

story, even some of the dialogue ('She's as complex as a Bach fugue,' says one character of Crawford) was idiotic, but it worked. In 1959, at Twentieth Century-Fox, Negulesco, Crawford and Wald were together again for *The Best of Everything*, swamped in CinemaScope and De Luxe Colour, to make a hysterically pitched story of the tragedies that befall high-flying city girls. You should have laughed – and you did. For a start, one can only get away with such idiocy by concentrating on one woman and one storyline. However, the decline of Negulesco's work reflects even more than usually work the story of Hollywood's own decline from the late 1940s, as confidence in solid ability and talent was replaced by a desire to place something new and more extravagant before a public sapped away by television. Negulesco was born in Rumania, but made his name in Paris as a painter, also dabbling in stage sets. In America from the late 1920s, at first for exhibitions of his paintings, Negulesco gradually became interested in the cinema. He gained his first film experience as a second-unit director on the 1932 version of *A Farewell to Arms*, but spent a number of years in short subjects and as an assistant director; and it was not until 1944, when Warners offered him a five-year contract, that he got into his stride as a film-maker. Many of his films of this 1944-1948 period feature Sydney Greenstreet, Peter Lorre, Geraldine Fitzgerald, Ida Lupino and John Garfield and show a painter's control of chiaroscuro (the management of light and shade within the frame). His use of angled shots is also interesting, especially in *The Mask of Dimitrios*, in which Negulesco definitely made his mark visually. The change of studios in 1948 did not at first seem to affect Negulesco's work, especially when he made the smoky *Road House*, again with Lupino. Sentiment was kept reasonably at bay in *Under My Skin* (with Garfield, another Warner refugee), *Three Came Home, The Mudlark, Scandal at Scourie* (the last Garson-Pidgeon film) and *Titanic*. Strangely for one who studied under the tragic artist Modigliani as a teenager, Negulesco always seemed less assured with colour; although Edward Cronjager's Technicolor work in *Lure of the Wilderness* is attractive, one feels Negulesco would have been happier shooting the Okeefenokee Swamp in black-and-white. But it was CinemaScope and De Luxe that really got him. From 1954, and *Three Coins in the Fountain*, Negulesco's romantic wallows are almost unwatchable today.

1939: *Three and a Day. 1940: *The Flag of Humanity. *Alice in Movieland. *Joe

Reichman and His Orchestra. *Henry Busse and His Orchestra. *A Dog in the Orchard. 1941: *USC Band and Glee Club. *Carioca Serenaders. Jan Garber and His Orchestra. *Skinnay Ennis and His Orchestra. *Cliff Edwards and His Buckaroos. *Freddy Martin and His Orchestra. *Marie Green and Her Merrie Men. *Hal Kemp and His Orchestra. *Those Good Old Days. *At the Stroke of Twelve. Singapore Woman. 1942: *The Gay Parisian. *Spanish Fiesta. *California Junior Symphony. *A Ship is Born. *Leo Reisman and his Orchestra. *The Don Cossack Chorus. *The Spirit of West Point. *Richard Kimber and His Orchestra. *The Daughter of Rosie O'Grady. *Carl Hoff and His Band. *Six Hits and a Miss. *The Spirit of Annapolis. *Glen Gray and His Band. The Army Air Force Band. *The US Marine Band. *The Playgirls. 1943: *The Army Show. *Women at War. *The US Navy Band. *Over the Wall. *The US Army Band. *The Voice That Thrilled the World. *Ozzie Nelson and his Orchestra. *All American Band. *Childhood Days. *US Service Bands. *Sweetheart Serenade. *Cavalcade of the Dance. 1944: *Roaring Guns. *South American Sway. *Grandfather's Follies. The Mask of Dimitrios. The Conspirators. 1945: *All Star Melody Masters. *Listen to the Bands. *Borrah Minevitch and His Harmonica School. *The Serenaders. 1946: Three Strangers. Nobody Lives Forever. Humoresque. 1947: Deep Valley. 1948: Johnny Belinda. Road House. 1949: Britannia Mews (US: Forbidden Street). 1950: Under My Skin. Three Came Home. 1951: The Mudlark. Take Care of My Little Girl. 1952: Phone Call from a Stranger. O. Henry's Full House (GB: Full House). Lydia Bailey. Lure of the Wilderness. Scandal at Scourie. 1953: Titanic. How to Marry a Millionaire. 1954: Three Coins in the Fountain. Woman's World. 1955: Daddy Long Legs. The Rains of Ranchipur. 1957: Boy on a Dolphin. 1958: The Gift of Love. A Certain Smile. 1959: Count Your Blessings. The Best of Everything. 1961: Jessica. 1964: The Pleasure Seekers. 1969: The Heroes. The Invincible Six. 1970: Hello – Goodbye.

NEILAN, Marshall 1891-1958

Actors and actresses whose careers were affected by drink are not uncommon. Directors blighted by alcoholism are very infrequent. Only three or four spring readily to mind, but Neilan was one of these. Had he been able to continue his screen career, which stuttered on into the 1930s, but effectively ended with the 1920s, he would probably have become one of Hollywood's foremost purveyors of screwball comedy of the 1930s and the light romantic romps of the early 1940s. Neilan could also bring sentiment across in a sure, unsticky way, as he proved in a delightful series of Mary Pickford films around 1918 when he became her favourite director. A handsome, red-haired, outgoing man of Irish-American parentage, Neilan, known to his friends as Mickey, became an actor in typically flamboyant fashion after joining Biograph Studio as D.W. Griffith's chauffeur. He became a leading man in short order, playing opposite Pickford in several films, among them Rags and A Girl of Yesterday (both 1915), by which time he had also tried his hand at directing a few shorts. Allan Dwan gave him his first chance at making a five-reeler, The Cycle of Fate, in 1916, and the following year Neilan became Pickford's director with Rebecca of Sunnybrook Farm. Alas, Neilan's reputation as a man who lived to get off the film set and into a world of wine, women and song grew at much the same time as his value as a director who could bring charm and warmth to comedy and romance alike. As Dwan put it at a later date, Neilan 'ruined himself with liquor and indifference and the bitterness that came from the both of them'. There were parties that went on for days, 'courtesy' appearances by Neilan on the set of his films half-way through the day and a gradual drift from studio to studio. Failed projects and 'co-director' credits became more frequent with the years. Neilan was said to have been totally disenchanted with films at the advent of sound, although his skilful handling of some early sound shorts (quite a come-down from big-budget 'A' features, but a sign of what little he was then considered capable), especially those with Thelma Todd and ZaSu Pitts, suggests he could easily have adjusted to sound features. Pickford called him back for one last try with Secrets (1933) but, more in sorrow than anger, was forced to fire her former favourite when he proved too often inebriated to do a proper job. Neilan, who was said to have made and spent millions, was at one time married to silent-screen star Blanche Sweet. Ironically, despite spending later years in reduced circumstances, he eventually beat his drinking problem and made a small comeback as a character actor in the 1950s before his death from cancer at 67.

1913: *The American Princess. 1914: *Ham the Piano Mover. *Ham the Lineman. 1915. *The Come Back of Percy. *Spooks. The Chronicles of Bloom Center (series). 1916: *The Cycle of Fate. The Country God Forgot. The Prince Chap. 1917: The Bottle Imp. Those Without Sin. The Girl at Home. The Jaguar's Claws. The Tides of Barnegat. The Silent Partner. Freckles. Rebecca of Sunnybrook Farm. The Little Princess. 1918: Amarilly of Clothes Line Alley. Stella Maris. M'Liss. Hit-the-Trail Holliday. Out of a Clear Sky. Heart of the Wilds. 1919: Three Men and a Girl. Daddy Long Legs. The Unpardonable Sin. Her Kingdom of Dreams. 1920: In Old Kentucky. The River's End. †Don't Ever Marry. †Go and Get It. 1921: Bob Hampton of Placer. Bits of Life. The Lotus Eater. 1922: Penrod. Fools First. †Minnie. The Stranger's Banquet. 1923: †The Eternal Three. The Rendezvous. 1924: Dorothy Vernon of Haddon Hall. Tess of the D'Urbervilles. 1925: The Sporting Venus. The Great Love. 1926: Diplomacy. Everybody's Acting. Wild Oats Lane. Mike. The Skyrocket. 1927: Venus of Venice. Her Wild Oat. 1928: His Last Haul (GB: Pious Crooks). Three-Ring Marriage. Take Me Home. Taxi 13. 1929: Black Waters. Tanned Legs. The Awful Truth. The Vagabond Lover. 1930: Sweethearts on Parade. 1931: *Catch as Catch Can. *War Mamas. *Ex-Sweeties. 1933: †Secrets (uncredited). 1934: Chloe. Love Is Calling You. The Social Register. The Lemon Drop Kid. 1935: This Is the Life. 1936: Sing While You're Able. 1937: Swing It Professor (GB: Swing It, Buddy). Thanks for Listening (GB: Partly Confidential).

NEILL, Roy William

(Roland W.N. de Gostrie) 1886-1946
You won't find many comedies in the output of this Hollywood director (actually born on a ship off Dublin, to Franco-Irish parents) who spent a lifetime making serious and sometimes sombre 'B' movies, often very effectively. Thus it's all the more surprising that he was placed at the helm of some frantic Max Miller farces during his years in Britain as a director of quota quickies' for Warners. Nowadays, although he died at only 60, his name is probably more familiar to the public than that of any other Hollywood 'B' director, thanks to the frequent showing of his Basil Rathbone-Sherlock Holmes films on television. He was a journalist in the early part of his career and distinguished himself as a war correspondent in the Chinese Revolution of 1911/12. By 1915 he was in Hollywood as a title-writer and assistant director at the Inceville Studios of movie pioneer Thomas H. Ince. Neill moved forward to directing two years later and proved a diligent worker whose films were always professionally made and brought in within their budgets. At on time (around 1924) his own assistant was the mighty Josef von Sternberg (qv).

In later years, von Sternberg, with typical generosity, would say 'I learned nothing from him'. From the late 1920s, Neill worked mainly for Columbia, almost entirely on thrillers, but in 1937, Warners asked him to go to Britain to replace their contract director there, Ralph Ince (qv), ironically the brother of Neill's mentor of early days, who had just been killed in a car accident. After 14 British films in three years, Neill returned to America with the outbreak of war, and soon started on his series of second-feature Sherlock Holmes adventures which, despite their strange modernization (that was Neill's idea, along with the flag-waving messages always given by Basil Rathbone at the end, so that Nazis and spies could be dragged in as the bad guys), often engendered some very creepy atmosphere, contained performances from Rathbone and Bruce which only occasionally crept towards caricature at the end of the series, and boasted a splendid series of villains, including Lionel Atwill, Gale Sondergaard and George Zucco. The melodrama was kept full-blooded and the films never grew stodgy. One of Neill's most interesting films is his last, *Black Angel*, about an alcoholic searching for his wife's killer, with a splendidly grating atmosphere. No doubt Neill would have stayed happily grafting away at Universal-International black-and-whites (Neill only made one colour film) until the end of the studio system, had not untimely death intervened.

1916: The Criminal. A Gamble in Souls. A Corner in Colleens. 1917: The Price Mark. Love Letters. The Girl Glory. They're Off. The Mother Instinct. The Flame of the Yukon. 1918: The Mating of Marcella. The Kaiser's Shadow. Vive La France! Flare-Up Sal. Green Eyes. Love Me. The Tyrant Fear. 1919: Trixie from Broadway. Charge It to Me. Puppy Love. The Bandbox. The Career of Catherine Bush. 1920: Yes or No. Good References. The Inner Voice. The Woman Gives. Dangerous Business. 1921: Something Different. The Idol of the North. The Conquest of Canaan. The Iron Trail. 1922: What's Wrong with the Woman? 1923: Radio Mania. Toilers of the Sea. 1924: By Divine Right. Broken Laws. Vanity's Price. 1925: Greater Than a Crown. The Kiss Barrier. Percy (GB: Mother's Boy). Marriage in Transit. 1926: The City. Black Paradise. The Cowboy and the Countess. The Fighting Buckaroo. A Man Four Square. 1927: The Arizona Wildcat. Marriage. 1928: Lady Raffles. The Olympic Hero. San Francisco Nights (GB: Divorce). The Viking. *Cleopatra. *The Virgin Queen. *The Czarina's Secret. *The Heart of General Robert E. Lee. *The Lady of Victories. *Madame Dubarry. 1929: Behind Closed Doors. Wall Street. 1930: The Melody Man. †Cock of the Walk. Just Like Heaven. 1931: The Avenger. The Good Bad Girl. Fifty Fathoms Deep. 1932: That's My Boy. The Menace. 1933: The Circus Queen Murder. As the Devil Commands. Above the Clouds (GB: Winged Devils). Fury of the Jungle (GB: Jury of the Jungle). 1934: The Ninth Guest. Black Moon. Whirlpool. Blind Date. I'll Fix It. Jealousy. 1935: Mills of the Gods. The Black Room. Eight Bells. 1936: The Lone Wolf Returns. 1937: Doctor Syn. Gypsy. 1938: Quiet Please. Simply Terrific. The Viper. Double or Quits. Thank Evans. 1939: Many Tanks Mr Atkins. A Gentleman's Gentleman. Everything Happens to Me. The Good Old Days. Murder Will Out. Hoots Mon. 1940: His Brother's Keeper. 1942: Madame Spy. Sherlock Holmes and the Secret Weapon. Eyes of the Underworld. 1943: Sherlock Holmes in Washington. Rhythm of the Islands. Frankenstein Meets the Wolf Man. Sherlock Holmes and the Spider Woman (GB: Spider Woman). 1944: The Scarlet Claw. Pearl of Death. Gypsy Wildcat. 1945: The House of Fear. The Woman in Green. Pursuit to Algiers. 1946: Terror by Night. Dressed to Kill (GB: Sherlock Holmes and the Secret Code). Black Angel.

NEILSON, James 1918-1979

American director who spent most of his career working for television, but popped up in the cinema of the 1960s, directing, for a four-year period, some of the Disney studio's most prestigious live-action films, several of them shot on location in Britain. A stills photographer until World War II, Neilson was a combat cameraman during that conflict and later turned to TV, becoming a cameraman from the late 1940s and director from 1954. His most notable work in that medium in the 1950s consisted of several macabre episodes in the *Alfred Hitchcock Presents* series, a far cry front his next port of call at Disney. The films he made here are mostly quite enjoyable family fare, with a feel for the countryside both in the warmly nostalgic *Summer Magic* and the period adventures of Dr Syn and Young Dick Turpin. His fragmented and typically long Fred MacMurray comedy, *Bon Voyage!* is also worth having. On leaving Disney, he made an unusually harsh western, *Return of the Gunfighter*, originally for TV but shown in cinemas, but the remainder of his films are unsuccessful on their own terms and of little account. He did return to form (and the countryside) with a pleasing TV movie version of *Tom Sawyer* – one could almost feel the warmth of the summer and smell Aunt Betsy's cooking. Ill-health forced his early retirement in the mid-1970s.

1955: The Country Husband (TV. GB: cinemas). 1957: Night Passage. The Blackwell Story (TV. GB: cinemas). 1962: Moon Pilot. Bon Voyage! Summer Magic. 1963: Dr Syn Alias the Scarecrow. The Moon-Spinners. 1965: The Legend of Young Dick Turpin. The Adventures of Bullwhip Griffin. 1966: Return of the Gunfighter. 1967: Gentle Giant. Where Angels Go, Trouble Follows! 1968: The First Time (GB: You Don't Need Pyjamas at Rosie's). 1969: Flareup. 1973: Tom Sawyer (TV).

NELSON, Ralph 1916-1997

There were no half measures with this American director: he would pile sentiment on sentiment, action on action, or gore on gore. An actor before World War II service with the Army Air Corps, he continued often to play small roles in his own productions when he started directing for television in the 1950s. Attracting attention when given an Emmy for his direction of *Requiem for a Heavyweight* on American television, Nelson entered films with another version of the same story. This, like *Soldier in the Rain*, proved too offbeat to make much money, and obviously taught Nelson something about commercial viability. His next film, *Lilies of the Field*, unabashed sentiment about an itinerant black man helping a group of German nuns to build a chapel, was not only an unexpected success, but won its star, Sidney Poitier, an Oscar. Success alternated with flop through the remainder of the 1960s, although Nelson's direction was more than useful in *Father Goose* (with invaluable help from Cary Grant and Leslie Caron), *Duel at Diablo* (red meat for action-starved western fans, although criticized for torture scenes which were severely trimmed in some countries) and the underrated *tick...tick...tick...* in which racial tensions rise after the unlikely event of a black man being elected sheriff of a southern states town. Nelson then made his biggest box-office hit, *Soldier Blue*. The violence of its Indian massacres, in which seemingly every part of the male and female body was sliced off and blood fountained all over the screen, brought worldwide queues and much criticism in the Press. Nelson travelled the world to defend the film, insisting that it was sincerely meant and that the violence was utterly necessary. Despite the doubts that were still cast on his intentions, Nelson continued to bludgeon his audiences into submission in one field or another. Now, however, the films themselves were doing less well at the box-office, several of those from the late 1970s being hardly seen outside their countries of origin (one, *Because He's My Friend*, was made in Australia). Seeing the trend, Nelson returned to television, and a treacly reprise of his *Lilies of the Field* hit. In his younger days, he was very briefly (1938-1939) married to actress Celeste Holm.

1962: *Requiem for a Heavyweight* (GB: *Blood Money*). 1963: *Soldier in the Rain. Lilies of the Field.* 1964: *Fate is the Hunter. Father Goose.* 1965: *Once a Thief.* 1966: *Duel at Diablo.* 1967: *Counterpoint.* 1968: *Charly.* 1969: *...tick...tick...tick.* 1970: *Soldier Blue.* 1971: *Flight of the Doves.* 1972: *The Wrath of God.* 1974: *The Wilby Conspiracy.* 1976: *Embryo.* 1977: *A Hero Ain't Nothin' But a Sandwich.* 1978: *Because He's My Friend.* †*Lady of the House* (TV). 1979: *You Can't Go Home Again* (TV). *Christmas Lilies of the Field* (TV).

NEUMANN, Kurt 1906-1958

Another of the unsung band of Hollywood directors who slaved away seemingly quite happily in 'B' features, in Neumann's case for nearly 30 years. For most of that period, his films were sometimes quite fast-paced comedies, thrillers and dramas that rarely soared over a running time of 75 minutes. From the late 1940s until the mid-1950s, however, Neumann embarked on a series of films with unusual subjects and widely differing backdrops, all made with care and mostly well-received critically. Commercially, his biggest success came with the horror film *The Fly*, and his career was at the crossroads (with the end of the studio system in sight) at the time of his early death. Born in Germany, Neumann had some early experience as a writer before emigrating to America at 19. He soon entered the cinema industry, working for Universal from the beginnings of sound, as a director from 1931. Leaving Universal in 1935, Neumann directed for a number of studios, including M-G-M, Columbia, RKO and Paramount, before becoming associate producer (and director) on RKO's Tarzan series from 1945. This might have qualified him for transfer into television, but in 1948 poverty-row studio Monogram decided that he was one of the men they needed to direct their classier Allied Artists films which had begun the previous year. The third of Neumann's three films for them, *Bad Boy*,

which actually ran to 87 minutes, was the most successful, shooting Audie Murphy to stardom as a hardened young criminal reformed by the head of a boys' rehabilitation ranch. Neumann directed Murphy again to great effect as Billy the Kid in his next film, *The Kid from Texas*, then gave the tiny Lippert company one of its biggest profit margins with *Rocketship XM*, which, as the first postwar outer-space adventure (a rocket to the Moon ends up on Mars) really caught the public's imagination. Neumann had always elicited pleasant performances, even if his own direction of 'movement' scenes seemed sometimes a trifle heavy-handed, and his facility with actors was apparent in the portrayals of Joel McCrea and young Dean Stockwell in the gentle western *Cattle Drive*. The performances in *Carnival Story*, especially from Anne Baxter and Lyle Bettger, were first-class under Neumann, who also made a German version with Eva Bartok and Curt Jürgens. Neumann then became associated with Twentieth Century-Fox's co-feature unit, from which emerged *The Fly*. One of the first films to deal with telekinesis, it evoked such a collection of shrieks, squeals and shudders that two sequels followed in due course. They might have been better had Neumann been alive to direct them.

1930: *The King of Jazz* (Spanish and German versions only). 1931: **House of Mystery. *Sealed Lips. *Trapped.* 1932: *Fast Companions/Information Kid. *The Red Shadow. My Pal the King.* 1933: *The Big Cage. Secret of the Blue Room. King for a Night.* 1934: *Half a Sinner. Let's Talk It Over. Wake Up and Dream.* 1935: *Alias Mary Dow. The Affair of Susan.* 1936: *Let's Sing Again. *Violets in Spring. Rainbow on the River.* 1937: *Espionage. Hold 'Em Navy* (GB: *That Navy Spirit*). *Make a Wish.* 1938: *Wide Open Faces. Touchdown Army* (GB: *Generals of Tomorrow*). 1939: *Unmarried* (GB: *Night Club Hostess*). *Ambush. All Women Have Secrets. Island of Lost Men.* 1940: *Ellery Queen – Master Detective. A Night at Earl Carroll's.* 1942: *Brooklyn Orchid. About Face. The McGuerins from Brooklyn.* 1943: *Taxi Mister! Fall In. Yanks Ahoy! The Unknown Guest.* †*The Return of the Vampire.* 1945: *Tarzan and the Amazons.* 1946: *Tarzan and the Leopard Woman.* 1947: *Tarzan and the Huntress.* 1948: *The Dude Goes West. Bad Men of Tombstone.* 1949: *Bad Boy. The Kid from Texas* (GB: *Texas Kid Outlaw*). †*Two Knights in Brooklyn/Two Mugs from Brooklyn.* 1950: *Rocketship XM.* 1951: *Cattle Drive. Reunion in Reno.* 1952: *The Ring. Hiawatha. Son of Ali Baba.* 1953:

Tarzan and the She-Devil. 1954: *Carnival Story* (and German version: *Rummelplatz der Liebe/Carnival Story/Circus of Love*). 1955: *They Were So Young.* 1956: *Mohawk. The Desperadoes Are in Town.* 1957: *Kronos. The She-Devil. The Deerslayer.* 1958: *The Fly. Machete.* 1959: *Watusi. Counterplot.*
† combined GB version of *The McGuerins from Brooklyn/Taxi Mister!*

NEWFIELD, Sam (Samuel Neufeld) 1899-1964

One has a little mental picture of Newfield, megaphone in hand, dashing from set to set, or assembling stock footage in what seems like quick motion. For Newfield was one of the most prolific of all American directors, always working with rock-bottom budgets for shoestring studios. Someone once called Newfield a workhorse, and that he undoubtedly was. Nor is there any evidence to suggest that, given the chance, he could have risen to a higher grade of film. There was one film for Paramount, *Adventure Island* (Newfield must have thought he had strayed into the wrong studio, especially working with colour for the first and only time), and a couple of movies in Britain with fading Hollywood stars, but Newfield failed to make much of any of them. He had entered the film industry as a boy of 20, along with his older brother Sigmund, later to become an executive producer at PRC, the company for whom Newfield was to make so many 60-minute action films, several of them with Buster Crabbe, in the mid-1940s. Newfield had become a director of comedy shorts by 1926, making over 50 of those before moving on to features by 1933. He directed between 150 and 200 films between this time and 1958, but it is virtually impossible to tell whether the following list is complete: Newfield often used aliases, including 'Peter Stewart' and 'Sherman Scott', as well as directing under his real name. His nephew, Sigmund Neufield Jr, is a television director with several interesting episodes of *Kojak* to his name.

1926: **Jane's Engagement Party. *Jane's Predicament. *Which is Which? *Please Excuse Me. *What's Your Hurry?* 1927: **A Gym Dandy. *High Flyin' George. *Man of Letters. *George's School Daze. *Ask Dad. *Auntie's Ante. *Big Game George. *A Disorderly Orderly. *Jane's Sleuth. *My Mistake. *On Deck. *On Furlough. *Rushing Business. *Watch, George! *What An Excuse. *When George Hops.* 1928: *Newlyweds' Visit.. *Out at Home. *Sailor George. *She's My Girl! *Watch the Birdie. *Half Back Buster. *George's False Alarm. *Good*

Scout Buster. *Buster Minds the Baby. *Buster Trains Up. *Busting Buster. 1929: *Buster's Spooks. *Chaperons. *Night Owls. *This Way Please. *Too Many Women. 1930: *Peek-a-Boo. *She's a He. *Sid's Long Count. *The Beauty Parade. *French Leave. *Her Bashful Beau. *Fellow Students. *All Wet. 1933: Reform Girl. The Important Witness. Big Time or Bust (GB: Heaven Bound). Under Secret Orders. 1934: Marrying Widows. Beggar's Holiday. 1935: *You Can Be Had. Trails of the Wild (GB: Arrest at Sundown). Northern Frontier. Code of the Mounted. Racing Luck. 1936: Federal Agent. Burning Gold. The Lion's Den. Ghost Patrol. The Traitor. Timber War. Border Caballero. Lightnin' Bill Carson. Roarin' Guns. Aces and Eights. Go-Get-'Em Haines. Stormy Trails. 1937: The Gambling Terror. Trail of Vengeance. Guns in the Dark. Doomed at Sundown. Boot Hill Brigade. The Colorado Kid. Melody of the Plains. Bar Z Bad Men. †Roarin' Lead. Gun Lords of Stirrup Basin. A Lawman is Born. Arizona Gunfighter. Ridin' the Lone Trail. 1938: Paroled – to Die. The Feud Maker. Code of the Rangers. Desert Patrol. The Phantom Ranger. The Terror of Tiny Town. The Rangers' Roundup. Harlem on the Prairie. Thunder in the Desert. Two Gun Justice. Durango Valley Raiders. Frontier Scout. Lightnin' Carson Rides Again. 1939: Trigger Pals. Six-Gun Rhythm. §The Invisible Killer. §Goose Step (GB: Hitler – Beast of Berlin). 1940: **The Sagebrush Family Trails West. Secrets of a Model. §I Take This Oath. **Frontier Crusader. §Hold That Woman! §Marked Men. **Billy the Kid in Texas. **Billy the Kid's Gun Justice. 1941: The Lone Rider in Texas Justice (GB: The Lone Rider). The Lone Rider Rides On. The Lone Rider in Frontier Fury (GB: Frontier Fury). The Lone Rider Fights Back. **Billy the Kid's Range War. §Billy the Kid's Fighting Pals. The Lone Rider Crosses the Rio. The Lone Rider in Ghost Town. **The Texas Marshal. §Billy the Kid in Santa Fé. §Billy the Kid Wanted. The Lone Rider Ambushed. §Billy the Kid's Round-Up. 1942: The Lone Rider and the Bandit. §Billy the Kid Trapped. The Lone Rider in Cheyenne. §Billy the Kid's Smoking Guns (GB: Smoking Guns). The Mad Monster. Jungle Siren. Queen of Broadway. 1943: The Lone Rider in Border Roundup (GB: Border Roundup). Dead Men Walk. The Black Raven. §Law and Order (GB: The Double Alibi). **Along the Sundown Trail. **Prairie Pals. 1944: Frontier Outlaws. Thundering Gun Slingers. Nabonga (GB: The Jungle Woman). The Monster Maker. Valley of Vengeance (GB:

Vengeance). The Contender. Fuzzy Settles Down. Rustlers' Hideout. I Accuse My Parents. Swing Hostess. 1945: The Lady Confesses. Gangsters' Den. Stagecoach Outlaws. Apology for Murder. Border Badmen. Fighting Bill Carson. Prairie Rustlers. White Pongo (GB: Adventure Unlimited). 1946: Outlaw of the Plains. Lady Chasers. Overland Riders. Terrors on Horseback. The Flying Serpent. Lightning Raiders. Murder is My Business. Gentlemen with Guns. Ghost of Hidden Valley. Prairie Badmen. Larceny in Her Heart. Gas House Kids. Queen of Burlesque. Blonde for a Day. *Mantan Messes Up. 1947: Three on a Ticket. **Adventure Island. Raiders of Red Rock. Code of the Plains. 1948: **The Counterfeiters. Money Madness. 1949: **State Department – File 649 (GB: Assignment in China). Wild Weed (GB: The Devil's Weed). 1950: Radar Secret Service. Western Pacific Agent. Motor Patrol. Hi-Jacked. 1951: Leave It to the Marines. Three Desperate Men. Fingerprints Don't Lie. Mask of the Dragon. Skipalong Rosenbloom. The Lost Continent. Sky High. 1952: †Outlaw Women. Lady in the Fog (US: Scotland Yard Inspector). The Gambler and the Lady. 1954: †Desert Outpost (TV. GB: Cinemas). 1955: Thunder Over Sangoland. Last of the Desperados. 1956: The Wild Dakotas. Frontier Gambler. The Three Outlaws. 1958: Flaming Frontier. Wolf Dog.

§ as Sherman Scott ** as Peter Stewart

NEWELL, Mike 1942 -

British director whose wide-ranging output often centres on enclosed worlds and cold-hearted protagonists – although few of his films contain characters that are without a charm, and he has coaxed some remarkably charismatic performances from leading actors in his time. From parents whose enthusiasm for amateur theatricals fired his own enthusiasm to direct, Newell began his career as a TV news reporter, but had begun to direct at 23, initially on such popular soap series as Coronation Street, but soon on more prestigious 'Playhouse' type productions, of which he had made more than 20 at the time of his film debut in 1976. Newell's The Man in the Iron Mask, made for American TV but shown in cinemas elsewhere in the world, was a much more stylish and fluent version of the old Dumas chestnut than either of the two more recent films. And it's with intimate dramas and comedies that might just as beneficially have been shown on TV that he has had his greatest successes in the ensuing years. The first such hit was with

Dance with a Stranger, a stylish, claustrophobic account of the last days of Ruth Ellis, the last woman to be hanged for murder in Britain. The biting drama made a star of Miranda Richardson, who would later feature to good effect for Newell in another low-key hit, Enchanted April. Soursweet, a saga of an oriental couple struggling to make a go of life in England, and Into the West, an Irish boy-and-horse-tale of much incidental charm, were highpoints in the years that followed, if no great shakes at the box-office. If what Newell's career needed at this stage was a high-profile hit, it certainly received one with Four Weddings and a Funeral, a record-breaking comedy with some richly funny lines. With some concessions to the 1990s, this was somewhat in the traditions of such films established by the Boulting Brothers several decades earlier, but with a string of eye-catching performances from an enthusiastic cast headed by Hugh Grant, whose own career received an inestimable boost from its success. Grant also starred for Newell in An Awfully Big Adventure, a rather gloomy theatrical piece, before the director went to America to make the thriller Donnie Brasco, in which Newell coaxed Al Pacino's best performance in years as the veteran gangster wearing out his welcome with the Mob.

1976: The Man in the Iron Mask (TV. GB: cinemas). 1980: The Awakening. 1981: Bad Blood. 1983: Blood Feud (TV. Shortened version shown in cinemas). 1984: Dance with a Stranger. 1986: The Good Father. 1987: Amazing Grace and Chuck (GB: Silent Voice). 1988: Soursweet. 1991: Enchanted April (originally for TV). 1992: Into the West. 1993: Four Weddings and A Funeral. 1995: An Awfully Big Adventure. 1997: Donnie Brasco. 1999: Pushing Tin.

NEWMAN, Joseph M. 1909-

This American director has been the subject of critical reverence in recent years; having seen nearly all his films, I find it a little difficult to see quite why. The best of them are within the film noir genre: Abandoned, 711 Ocean Drive and The Human Jungle, seedy portraits of the underworld, drawn with careful conviction. Red Skies of Montana, about fighters of forest fires, is well worth seeing for its vivid action sequences. Asked to make a fairly major film, though, Newman tends to go dull, as in The Outcasts of Poker Flat, Dangerous Crossing, Kiss of Fire, The Gunfight at Dodge City and The Big Circus; in Kiss of Fire, Newman even damped the fires in Jack Palance and

Barbara Rush. Perhaps he needed the straitjacket shooting schedules of M-G-M's two-reel 'Crime Does Not Pay' series, in which he started as a director in 1938 (as Joe Newman), after some years as an assistant director. He had barely progressed to features when war service intervened. Serving as a major in the Signal Corps, Newman made numerous training films, as well as one first-class feature-length documentary, *Diary of a Sergeant*. Returning to films in 1947, he freelanced, and was briefly forced back into short subjects, before coming to an arrangement with Twentieth Century-Fox. His best work, however, was done for other studios, among them Universal, for whom he also made *This Island Earth*, a colourful outer-space fantasy well thought of in sci-fi circles. After the mid-1950s, Newman's films proved disappointing, and he does not appear to have directed anything after a little television from 1962 to 1965.

1938: *Man's Greatest Friend. 1939: *Money to Loan. *The Story of Alfred Nobel. *The Story That Couldn't Be Printed. 1940: *Maintain the Right. *Cat College. *Know Your Money. Women in Hiding. *Buyer Beware. 1941: *Respect the Law. *Triumphs Without Drums. *Coffins on Wheels. 1942: *Vendetta. Northwest Rangers. *Don't Talk! 1945: Diary of a Sergeant (D). 1947: *Luckiest Girl in the World. *The Amazing Mr Nordill. 1948: Jungle Patrol. 1949: The Great Dan Patch. Abandoned. 1950: 711 Ocean Drive. 1951: Lucky Nick Cain (GB: I'll Get You for This). The Girl Who Came Back. Love Nest. *Smoke Jumpers (D). 1952: The Outcasts of Poker Flat. Red Skies of Montana. Pony Soldier (GB: MacDonald of the Canadian Mounties). 1953: Dangerous Crossing. 1954: The Human Jungle. 1955: Kiss of Fire. This Island Earth. 1956: Flight to Hong Kong. 1957: Death in Small Doses. 1958: Fort Massacre. 1959: Gunfight at Dodge City. Tarzan the Ape-Man. The Big Circus. 1961: King of the Roaring Twenties (GB: The Big Bankroll). A Thunder of Drums. The George Raft Story (GB: Spin of a Coin). Twenty Plus Two (GB: It Started in Tokyo).*

NIBLO, Fred (Federico Nobile) 1874-1948
Although coming late to films, Nebraska-born Niblo directed some of the most exotic and flamboyant talents in Hollywood during his decade at the top. Such stars as Greta Garbo, Ramon Novarro, Rudolph Valentino, Douglas Fairbanks, Barbara La Marr, Lillian Gish, Vilma Banky, Ronald Colman and Norma Talmadge blossomed under his auspices. He

was a man with a flair for a certain kind of dashing, mysterious romance only available on the silent screen. It was no surprise that such a man could not adapt to sound, especially, in his mid-fifties. Niblo seems happy to have returned to acting in these closing years of his career. He had started as an actor, or more properly a vaudevillian, around 1892, becoming much associated with George M. Cohan, whose sister Josephine became his first wife. Around 1910, he seems to have settled down as a Broadway stage director, directing his first two films on a trip to Australia in 1915, then arriving in Hollywood as a 'producing director' in 1917. Niblo's first few films as director featured his own second wife, the Australian-born star Enid Bennett. His breakthrough film was Fairbanks' *The Mark of Zorro* in 1920. After that the major films dripped from his fingers: *The Three Musketeers* (Fairbanks), *Blood and Sand* (Valentino), *Thy Name is Woman* (Novarro), *The Red Lily* (Novarro), The *Temptress* (Garbo), *Camille* (Talmadge), *Two Lovers* (Colman and Banky) and, perhaps most famous and best-remembered, *Ben Hur*. Although the famous epic never recouped its six million dollars' cost, it was a tremendous public success around the world. Niblo stayed at M-G-M until 1930, before coming to Britain to make a couple of films which failed to revive his waning career. He died from pneumonia.

1915: Officer 666. Get Rich Quick Wallingford. 1918: The Marriage Ring. Fuss and Feathers. When Do We Eat? Happy, Though Married. 1919: The Haunted Bedroom. The Law of Men. Partners Three. The Virtuous Thief. What Every Woman Learns. Stepping Out. 1920: Sex. The Woman in the Suitcase. The False Road. Hairpins. Her Husband's Friend. The Mark of Zorro. Silk Hosiery. 1921: The Three Musketeers. Mother o' Mine. Greater than Love. 1922: The Woman He Married. Rose o' the Sea. Blood and Sand. 1923: The Famous Mrs Fair. Strangers of the Night. 1924: Thy Name is Woman. The Red Lily. 1925: Ben-Hur. 1926: †The Temptress. 1927: Camille. †The Devil Dancer. 1928: The Enemy. Two Lovers. The Mysterious Lady. Dream of Love. 1930: Redemption. Way Out West. 1931: Young Donovan's Kid (GB: Donovan's Kid). The Big Gamble. 1932: Two White Arms. †Diamond Cut Diamond. Blame the Woman.

NICHOLS, Mike (M. Peschkowsky) 1931-
German-born entertainer and director, in Hollywood from early childhood. After success as a satirist, Nichols moved into

film direction in 1966, and was straight-away nominated for an Oscar on his first film, *Who's Afraid of Virginia Woolf?* And he deservedly won the best director Academy Award the following year for *The Graduate*, a feat he found hard to live up to for many years afterwards. Nichols, though, is certainly a man of many talents. He began as an actor, studying the 'Method' under Lee Strasberg, then moving into cabaret in partnership with Elaine May. His comic duologues of the middle and late 1960s were enormously successful, records they made still being requested on radio programmes years later. When the partnership broke up, Nichols briefly returned to acting before becoming a Broadway director of repute, and making his screen bow with the film version of *Who's Afraid of Virginia Woolf* which won five Oscars. Nichols himself missed out (to Fred Zinnemann for *A Man for All Seasons*), but made up for it the following year with *The Graduate*, a far better and more original film, a freewheeling entertainment which struck pretty well every emotional chord. It was bright, slightly daring, and very skilfully made both in shooting and editing terms and in its manipulation of its audience; and it had two very attractive new stars in Dustin Hoffman and Katharine Ross. The decision to use the music of Simon and Garfunkel on the soundtrack was also a major plus, skimming the film along at a heady pace to a brilliantly staged, throat-lumping ending. Nichols seemed to have found a unique personal style, but he later appeared to abandon it for Great Cinema. Only the fine performances of Jack Nicholson and Ann-Margret in *Carnal Knowledge* really distinguish the remainder of his early films, and after the poor critical and commercial performance of the too-eager-to-please *The Fortune*, Nichols did not return to filming until the 1980s, when he began to build up an enviable record in mainstream film-making. The controversial *Silkwood* in 1983 was followed by a string of popular hits including *Working Girl, Wolf, The Birdcage* and probably best of all, the acerbic Hollywood memoir *Postcards from the Edge*. He has been four times married.

1966: Who's Afraid of Virginia Woolf? 1967: The Graduate. 1968: *Teach Me! 1970: Catch 22. 1971: Carnal Knowledge. 1973: The Day of the Dolphin. 1974: The Fortune. 1975: Bogart Slept Here (unfinished). 1980: Gilda Live. 1983: Silkwood. 1986: Heartburn. 1987: Biloxi Blues. 1988: Working Girl. 1990: Postcards from the Edge. 1991: Regarding Henry. 1994: Wolf. 1996: The Birdcage. 1998: Primary Colors.

NIMOY, Leonard 1931-

This long-serving *Star Trek* actor launched a briefly promising career as a director in the 1980s but his work on the other side of the camera has been insignificant apart from the massive comedy hit *3 Men and a Baby*. His two *Star Trek* films are okay, if not the best in the series, but the films that followed *3 Men and a Baby* were daunting failures that betrayed a fatal lack of spark and flair. The last, *Holy Matrimony*, was a pretty silly comedy-drama about a blonde showgirl who, to escape the law, finds herself marrying a 12-year-old boy in a remote religious community. Still, Nimoy can look back with pride at the titanic takings from *3 Men and A Baby*, one of the mightiest comedy hits of the 1980s. In truth, though, it is only a tolerable toddle through triteness, even though it turned into a bundle of box-office joy.

1984: Star Trek III: The Search for Spock. 1986: The Voyage Home: Star Trek IV. 1987: 3 Men and a Baby. 1988: The Good Mother/The Price of Passion. 1990: Funny About Love. 1994: Holy Matrimony.

NORMAN, Leslie 1911-1993

It was a pity that London-born Norman waited until he was 44 before effectively making his directorial bow. For in his short career as a director he made several excellent commercial films (always working in black-and-white) which stir the emotions in differing ways. Working in the industry at the age of 16, he became an editor at 19. After getting a fleeting taste of direction before World War II, he worked for Ealing Studios in post-war years in varying capacities, contributing some screenplays (notably *A Run for Your Money* and *Where No Vultures Fly*) and working as producer on some distinguished films that included *Eureka Stockade (US: Massacre Hill)*, *Mandy (US: Crash of Silence)* and *The Cruel Sea*. His effective debut as director was on *The Night My Number Came Up*, a tense thriller about a nightmare coming true, which holds one's attention all the way. Norman got particularly good performances from Denholm Elliott and Alexander Knox in this cleverly made, suspense-packed film. Norman then turned unexpectedly to the chiller genre with *X the Unknown*, which went round its native Britain in a very chilling double bill with Clouzot's *The Fiends*. Good acting is backed by Norman's edgy direction and brilliant photography by Gerald Gibbs. Norman returned twice to Australia (scene of *Eureka Stockade*), for *The Shi-*

ralee, in which he coaxed little Dana Wilson to a brilliant scene-stealing performance, and *Summer of the Seventeenth Doll*. Between these came his most disappointing film, *Dunkirk*, Ealing's massive reconstruction of the retreat of British forces from France in 1940. *Mrs Miniver* had depicted some of the same events 16 years before, far less accurately, but with more emotional tug. *Spare the Rod*, a likeable and sensitive early attempt to look at delinquent behaviour and methods of dealing with it in schools, was one of the few films Norman made in the 1960s before his departure for television. His son is the film writer and novelist Barry Norman. He died from throat cancer.

1939: †Too Dangerous to Live. 1955: The Night My Number Came Up. 1956: X the Unknown. 1957: The Shiralee. 1958: Dunkirk. 1959: Summer of the Seventeenth Doll (US: Season of Passion). 1960: The Long and the Short and the Tall (US: Jungle Fighters). 1961: Spare the Rod. Mix Me a Person. 1968: †The Lost Continent (uncredited).

NUGENT, Elliott 1899-1980

American actor and writer who became one of Hollywood's brightest directors of slightly zany comedy. A bout with alcoholism and a mental breakdown contributed to the early end of his film-directing career, but he happily recovered to write several books, including a very witty and readable autobiography in the 1960s. At college with humorist James Thurber, Nugent was a Broadway actor at 22 and soon established himself as a successful playwright as well. At 26, he made his film acting debut (in *Headlines)* but, even when he had progressed to leading roles by 1929, preferred to alternate between cinema and theatre. As a film director, he soon made his mark. *Three Cornered Moon* (1933) is a dated but delightful combination of romantic drama and screwball comedy about a *nouveau pauvre* American family of the Depression, while *Whistling in the Dark* (also 1933) is an innovative and immensely entertaining comedy-thriller, a foretaste of Nugent's greatest success in the genre with *The Cat and the Canary*. Nugent had already directed Bob Hope twice by the time of *Cat*, a consummate haunted-house chiller comedy, full of swirling mists, flickering shadows, clutching hands that menace the heroine and creepy corridors. With Hope as the nervous hero, Nugent had a number of familiar elements before him, but blended them superbly, rationing equally chuckles and chills to create a classic of its kind and make Hope a star. Nugent

directed Hope again in *Nothing But the Truth*, as a man sworn not to tell a lie for 24 hours (and later again in *My Favorite Brunette*), as well as finally getting on screen a very witty and amusing adaptation of the play he had written with Thurber, *The Male Animal*. Henry Fonda was perfectly cast as the college professor eventually stirred to jealousy, the part Nugent himself had played on Broadway. The theatre continued to keep Nugent busy, but there was time for *My Girl Tisa*, a delicate, very detailed period piece with Sam Wanamaker as a rabble-rousing lawyer in the 1890s, and a much underrated version of *The Great Gatsby*, very effective as cinema, although far less faithful to the book than the 1974 remake. Nugent had the enviable facility of communicating his own sense of fun and liking for cinema to an audience, in a very easy, relaxed fashion, which made it look as though everyone was having a good time. Among the diverse talents that passed under his control were Harold Lloyd, Danny Kaye, Alan Ladd, Mickey Rooney, Bing Crosby, Miriam Hopkins and Clifton Webb.

1932: †The Mouthpiece. †Life Begins (GB: The Dawn of Life). 1933: Whistling in the Dark (GB: Scared). Three-Cornered Moon. If I Were Free (GB: Behold We Live). 1934: Strictly Dynamite. Two Alone. She Loves Me Not. 1935: Enter Madame. Splendor. College Scandal (GB: The Clock Strikes Eight). Love in Bloom. 1936: And So They Were Married. Wives Never Know. 1937: It's All Yours. 1938: Professor Beware. Give Me a Sailor. 1939: Never Say Die. The Cat and the Canary. 1941: Nothing But the Truth. 1942: The Male Animal. 1943: The Crystal Ball. 1944: Up in Arms. 1947: Welcome Stranger. My Favorite Brunette. 1948: My Girl Tisa. 1949: The Great Gatsby. Mr Belvedere Goes to College. 1950: The Skipper Surprised His Wife. 1951: My Outlaw Brother. 1952: Just for You.

NOYCE, Phillip 1950-

Australian director whose best films almost all deal with small groups battling against the odds. He has also shown himself adept at vivid action set-pieces within the context of a film, and his eye for colour composition has added materially to the impact of some of his work even though that work has, through the years, lacked consistency. Following early years making shorts and short features, some of which enjoyed festival exposure, and dabbling in art direction, Noyce demonstrated that he was part of the new strength in Australian cinema by making first the

thriller with some exciting sequences if not much plot logic and, in a hearkening back to *Dead Calm*, ended with a waterborne climax. Noyce also directed the follow-up, *Clear and Present Danger*, a good story with lots of gun-rattling action. Noyce stages one of his most outstanding action scenes in this one, when Harrison Ford and his colleagues are trapped by machine-gunners in a network of narrow streets. In between and after the Clancy films, though, Noyce fired two decided blanks with *Sliver* and *The Saint*, and the general progress of his career continues to be erratic.

1968: **Better to Reign in Hell*. 1972: **Caravan Park*. 1973: **That's Showbiz*. 1974: *Castor and Pollux (D)*. 1975: *God Knows Why, But It Works (semi-D)*. 1977: *Backroads*. 1978: *Newsfront*. 1982: *Heatwave*. 1986: *Shadows of the Peacock/Echoes of Paradise*. 1988: *Dead Calm*. 1989: *Blind Fury*. 1992: *Patriot Games*. 1993: *Sliver*. 1994: *Clear and Present Danger*. 1997: *The Saint*. 1999: *The Bone Collector*.

O'CONNOR, Pat 1942-

Irish film-maker who has been most successful when filming in his native country. His American ventures have on the whole far less merit. Widely travelled in his younger days, O'Connor studied art and film in Canada and the United States before returning to Ireland as a producer and director of documentaries and dramas, winning a British Academy Award in 1982 for his TV drama *The Ballroom of Romance*. O'Connor stayed in Ireland for his debut film, *Cal*, a well-made early look at the problems of Northern Ireland which paints a probably justifiably bleak view of Belfast in the 1980s' Troubles. The abrasively scripted film remains watchable throughout. A trip to Hollywood in the late 1980s produced only two very disappointing films, but O'Connor did marry the star of the second, Mary Elizabeth Mastrantonio, who returned to Ireland with him to make a film about an earlier battle for Irish independence, *Fools of Fortune*. After a disastrous film for American cable TV, *Zelda*,

Looking *Dead Calm*, Phillip **Noyce** has moved from Australia to Hollywood in the past decade with some success.

powerful anti-racist *Backroads*, about black and white criminals, then *Newsfront*, a story of newsreel cameraman whose blood-surging immediacy enabled it to travel the world. Noyce himself, though, was to remain in Australia for another ten years until he made *Dead Calm*, a nail-biting high seas thriller in which a yachting couple fall victim to a psychopath. Noyce did a terrific job of keeping pace and tension cranked up, and the presence of three international stars in

Sam Neill, Nicole Kidman and Billy Zane gave it the platform for a world stage. Noyce now did go to America, where he started by making one of Rutger Hauer's more enjoyable star vehicles *Blind Fury*, in which Noyce keeps a strong sense of humour running through the mayhem. Though unlikely, the film is never silly and buoyantly lively throughout. After a patient wait, Noyce was handed his first major Hollywood assignment in *Patriot Games*, an adaptation of a Tom Clancy

O'Connor showed some of the form of his younger days in another return to Ireland for *Circle of Friends*, an adaptation of a Maeve Binchy novel in which O'Connor coaxed an amazing performance from Minnie Driver in the central role that provided her with the springboard to stardom. Still willing to give Hollywood a try, O'Connor achieved at least a partial success there with *Inventing the Abbotts*, which achieved a warm glow of nostalgia for a a time gone by and boasted a string of appealing performances. It was, however, somewhat hampered by O'Connor's old failing of slowness of pace.

1981: The Ballroom of Romance (TV). 1984: Cal. 1987: A Month in the Country. 1988: Stars and Bars. 1989: The January Man. 1990: Fools of Fortune. 1993: Zelda (cable TV). 1995: Circle of Friends. 1997: Inventing the Abbotts. 1998: Dancing at Lughnasa.

O'FERRALL, George More 1906-1982

O'Ferrall's decision to work in television from 1957 was one of the graver losses to a British cinema floundering in its efforts to maintain post-war impetus. After labouring for 18 years, less war service, as an assistant director in British films, O'Ferrall had made as decent a group of films as anyone else in Britain before the decision to quit. In most of his films, he manages to create a whole clutch of sympathetic characters, so that the audience is hooked and uplifted one way or another. His first, *Angels One Five*, made a star of John Gregson as a doomed pilot, and created queues everywhere in Britain. *The Holly and the Ivy* was a Christmas entertainment that was almost equally successful, with many good performances, including one of Margaret Leighton's most likeable screen portrayals. Of the remainder of O'Ferrall's (he was born in England, in spite of an Irish name and ancestry) tiny film output, *The Heart of the Matter*, *The Green Scarf* and *A Woman for Joe* were all highly rated by some contemporary critics, although the first of these, an adaptation from Graham Greene, was resoundingly unsuccessful in commercial terms. O'Ferrall subsequently tried one film in CinemaScope, then settled for much smaller horizons – and screens. He retired to Spain in the 1970s and died there.

1951: Angels One Five. The Holly and the Ivy. 1953: The Heart of the Matter. 1954: The Green Scarf. 1955: †Three Cases of Murder. The Woman for Joe. 1956: The March Hare.

OLMI, Ermanno 1931-

This Italian director's beginnings as a clerk, and his background in industrial documentaries, almost inexorably led him to make perceptive and caring films about the lives of ordinary working people. Most of these early documentaries revolve round various aspects of the Edison-Volta electrical plant at which he was employed in post-war years. Olmi made his name with his second feature film, *Il posto*, a beautiful, gently observed piece in which, as in all his pictures, Olmi lets his camera adopt the role of a silent spectator, observing from a distance the little human dramas that unfold – here in the story of a poor youth seeking employment in the big city (Milan) – yet missing nothing. This and the following film, *I fidanzati*, are the most satisfying and wholly pleasurable experiences in Olmi's too infrequent films, apart from his 1978 movie, *The Tree of Wooden Clogs*, a three-hour colour epic about peasant life in the Bergamo territory of Italy at the turn of the century. Its closeness to the roots of such life and its ability to communicate feelings and the tragedy of injustices are so much more real than in Bertolucci's *1900*, with which it invites comparison. One cannot substitute pictorial beauty for a genuine feel for peasant people and their humble lives; Olmi, so to speak, has a head start on most other film-makers in this respect. Yet Olmi's films do not do well in his native country, and consequently there have been too few of them; Italian audiences perhaps have a taste for the less ordinary things of life. To people outside that country, though, Olmi's films are never less than fascinating.

1954: *La diga del Ghiacciaio (D). 1954-1961: 37 more short documentary films, most notably Il pensionato and ending with Un metro è lungo. 1959: Il tempo si è fermato (GB & US: Time Stood Still). 1961: Il posto (GB: The Job. US: The Sound of Trumpets). 1963: I finanzati (GB: The Engagement. US: The Fiancés). 1964: E venne un uomo (GB: A Man Named John. US: And There Came a Man). 1969: Un certo giorno (GB & US: One Fine Day). 1970: I recuperanti (GB & US: The Scavengers. Originally for TV). 1971: Durante l'estate (GB & US: During the Summer. Originally for TV). 1974: La circostanza (GB & US: The Circumstance). 1978: L'albero degli zoccoli (GB & US: The Tree of Wooden Clogs). 1982: Cammina, cammina. 1983: Milano '83. 1987: Lunga vita alla signora! 1988: The Legend of the Holy Drinker. 1990: Lungo il fiume. 1993: Segreto del bosco vecchio. 1995: The Bible: Genesis.

OPHULS, Max (M. Oppenheimer) 1902-1957

German-born director, mostly of elegant romantic melodramas. Many of Ophuls' most memorable films contain a series of actions forming a logical chain, sometimes leading to a decisive and inevitable conclusion, but often – in a formula much beloved of film-makers – a chain of circularity. Ophuls' own tracking cameras – he was a master of movement – follow this line of thought, caressing in amorous moments, prowling in times of tension. There is little more thrilling in the cinema than sophisticated use of the mobile camera – Donen, Hitchcock and many other directors in Hollywood used it to advantage, though never with such skill, intelligence or imagination as Ophuls. He was a well-known stage director before becoming interested in films with the advent of sound. There were a few films in Germany, but Ophuls and his family left in the early days of the Nazi rise to power, and he became a naturalized French citizen in the 1930s. *Liebelei/Une histoire d'amour* is the most interesting film from this period, and the one which most precisely foreshadows Ophuls' preoccupation with the realities and caprices of 'l'amour'. In the post-war years, though a long time establishing himself in the Hollywood to which he had travelled following the fall of France in 1940, Ophuls made the films which have established his reputation. After the rather vapid romantic swashbuckler *The Exile*, there was the exquisitely delicate *Letter from an Unknown Woman*, dealing (as do other Ophuls films) with the sad and unfilled life of a lady, in this case one who falls in love at 14 with a rakish pianist in 1890 Vienna, and continues to love him through various encounters over the years, all insignificant for him until her premature death, when her last letter stirs some slight feelings in him. A 'woman's picture' perhaps, but a haunting and superior example. Ophuls' other American films are basically thrillers, although again women and obsessions play central roles: *Caught* is a *film noir* as only Ophuls could make it – a supremely graceful dance of death. *The Reckless Moment* (both these films starred James Mason) is slightly less effective, despite a good script. Scenes in a boathouse, however, suggest that Ophuls was relishing atmosphere created by light, shade, camera angles and faintly surreal scenery – with, of course, his own special tracking and dolly shots thrown in. Ophuls then returned to France: *La ronde* is a bit dull but then it always was a dull story and Ophuls' touches make his easily the best of several versions. Much richer in atmosphere are *Madame De. . .*, *Le plaisir* and,

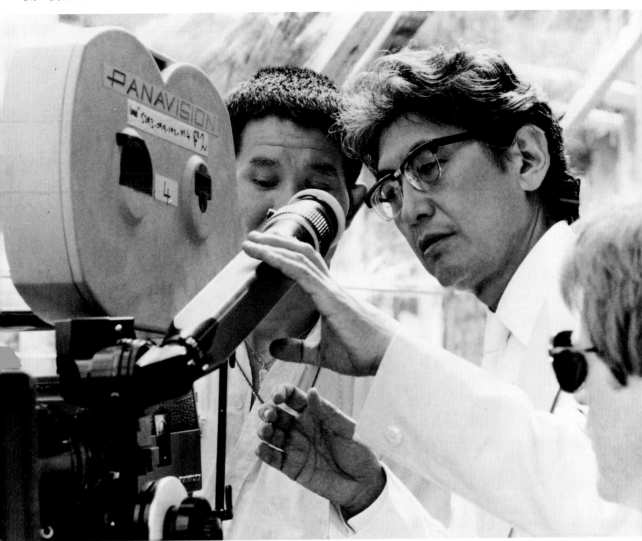

Snappily-dressed Japanese director Nagisa **Oshima** frames a scene from *Merry Christmas Mr Lawrence*. The film was a success, but Oshima's career has since waned.

just before his early death from rheumatic fever, the sumptuously sad *Lola Montès*, with its unique circus setting, masterly handling of colour (Ophuls had previously worked in black-and-white) and series of circular motifs that become more apparent in Ophuls' work than ever before. It is doubtful if he would have surpassed this work, but sad that we could not see him try.

1930: *Dann schön lieber Labertran.* 1931: *Die verliebte Firma.* 1932: *Die verkaufte Braut (GB & US: The Bartered Bride). Die lachende Erben. Liebelei.* 1933: *Une histoire d'amour (French-language version of Liebelei).* 1934: *On a volé un homme. La signora di tutti.* 1935: *Divine.* 1936: *Komedie om Geld.* **Ave Maria de Schubert.* **La valse brillante de Chopin. La tendre ennemie (US: Tender*

Enemy). 1937: *Yoshiwara.* 1938: *Le roman de Werther (GB & US: Werther).* 1939: *Sans lendemain (US: There's No Tomorrow).* 1940: *De Mayerling à Sarajevo (GB: Sarajevo. US: Mayerling to Sarajevo). L'école des femmes (unfinished).* 1947: *The Exile.* 1948: *Letter from an Unknown Woman.* 1949: *Caught. The Reckless Moment.* 1950: †*Vendetta (uncredited. Film completed 1947). La ronde.* 1952: *Le plaisir (US: House of Pleasure).* 1953: *Madame De... (US: The Earrings of Madame De).* 1955: *Lola Montès (GB: The Fall of Lola Montes. US: The Sins of Lola Montes).*

OSHIMA, Nagisa 1932-

This Japanese director started making films at about the same time as the early demises of the two great figures of early

Japanese cinema, Mizoguchi and Ozu (both *qv*) and, after establishing an international reputation toward the end of the 1960s, became the most prominent Japanese film-maker of his generation. His films are obsessively concerned with sex and death – rich, heavy, heady mixtures set in modern Japan, as vivid as they are usually lengthy. At university, Oshima had studied law, but quickly moved into the cinema, becoming an assistant director in 1954, and directing his first film five years later. He attracted attention in the western world from 1967, with *Death by Hanging, Boy* and *Diary of a Shinjuku Thief* in particular. A decade later, he again sprang to international prominence with his two sexually explicit films, *Empire of the Senses* and *Empire of Passion.* The former gained some notoriety when seized by the New York Customs and banned from showing in the city's film festival. Oshima's introduction to international cinema was the moodily fascinating and typically strange *Merry Christmas Mr Lawrence*. The next, however, *Max Mon Amour*, about a woman in love with a chimpanzee, was far too strange for both public and critical tastes and Oshima has not made a full-length feature since.

1959: *Ai to Kibo no Machi* (US: *A Town of Love and Hope*). 1960: *Seishun Zankoku Monogatori* (GB: *Cruel Story of Youth*. US: *Naked Youth*). *Taiyo no Hakaba* (US: *The Sun's Burial*). *Nihon no Yoru to Kiri* (GB & US: *Night and Fog in Japan*). 1961: *Shiiku* (GB & US: *The Catch*). 1962: *Amusaka Shiro Tokisada* (GB: *The Rebel*. US: *The Revolutionary*). 1964: *I'm Here, Bellett. A Child's First Adventure*. 1965: **Yunbogi no Nikki* (GB & US: *The Diary of Yunbogi*). *Etsuraku* (GB & US: *The Pleasures of the Flesh*). 1966: *Hakuchu no Torima* (GB & US: *Violence at Noon*). 1967: *Ninja Beugeicho* (GB & US: *Tales of the Ninja*). *Nihon Shunka-ko* (GB: *Sing a Song of Sex*. US: *A Treatise on Japanese Bawdy Songs*). 1968: *Daitoa Senso* (GB: *The Pacific War*). *Koshikei* (GB & US: *Death by Hanging*). *Kaeyyekita Yopparai* (GB & US: *Three Resurrected Drunkards*). 1969: *Shinjuku Dorobo Nikki* (GB: *Diary of a Shinjuku Thief*. US: *Diary of a Shinjuku Burglar*). *Shonen* (GB: *Boy*). *Mo Taku-To to Bunkadaika-Kumei*. 1970: *Tokyo Senso Sengo Hima* (GB: *The Man Who Left His Will on Film*. US: *He Died After the War*). 1971: *Gishiki* (GB & US: *The Ceremony*). 1972: *Natsu no Imoto* (GB: *Summer Soldiers*. US: *Dear Summer Sister*). 1976: *L'empire des sens/Ai no Corrida* (GB: *Empire of the Senses*. US: *In the Realm of the Senses*). 1978: *L'empire des passions* (GB: *Empire of Passion*. US: *Phantom Love*). 1982: *Merry Christmas Mr Lawrence*. 1986: *Max Mon Amour*. 1994: *†Erotic Tales*.

OSWALD, Gerd 1916-1989

The son of noted German director Richard Oswald (R. Ornstein. 1880-1963). Richard made almost 100 German films, but only three in Hollywood, where he had arrived with son Gerd in tow in 1938. Gerd was an assistant director for many years, firstly at Monogram, then Twentieth Century-Fox, before breaking into direction via Fox's television arm. They gave him a feature to direct, and it proved to be his best: *A Kiss Before Dying*, in which he coaxed a career-high performance from Robert Wagner as a psychopathic killer, and proved that Wagner, the blandest of actors, could actually be quite effective if one turned the coin and showed the darker side of his all-

American appeal. Joanne Woodward and Mary Astor also gave tensely effective performances in this – sometimes quite literally – cliff-hanger. *Crime of Passion*, another psychological study, had Barbara Stanwyck grimly dominant as the wife who pushes her husband up to, and over the top. And one of his German films, *Schachnovelle*, with Curt Jürgens as the chess-playing prisoner, is a model in tension. Oswald's teaming of Bob Hope and Fernandel in *Paris Holiday* was a great disappointment: obviously comedy was not his forte, and he stuck to drama after that. Oswald spent the greater part of the time between 1962 and 1970 working for television, directing episodes of such series as *Bonanza, Outer Limits, Star Trek, The Felony Squad, Nichols* and – a reunion with Robert Wagner – *It Takes a Thief*. He died from cancer.

1955: *The Ox-Bow Incident* (TV. GB: 1956: *A Kiss Before Dying. The Brass Legend*. 1957: *Crime of Passion. Valerie. Fury at Showdown*. 1958: *Screaming Mimi. Paris Holiday*. 1959: *Am Tag als der Regen kam* (US: *The Day It Rained*). 1960: *Schachnovelle* (GB: *Three Moves to Freedom*. US: *The Royal Game*). 1961: *Brainwashed*. 1962: †*The Longest Day* (uncredited). 1963: *Tempestà su Ceylon/Storm over Ceylon* (US: *The Scarlet Eye*). 1965: *Agent for H.A.R.M.* 1969: *80 Steps to Jonah*. 1971: *Bunny O' Hare*. 1975: *To the Bitter End*.

OSWALD, Richard
See Oswald, Gerd

OZU, Yasujiro 1903-1963

The British once made a film called *Millions Like Us* about ordinary working people: it could sum up all the work of this esteemed Japanese director. But, unlike Britain, where studies of the working-classes flourished from around 1932 to around 1955, Ozu's cameras observed the lives of the lower middle class of Japan – and in a more gentle, yet at the same time more painful way. Although the two men are dissimilar in almost all other respects, Ozu had something in common with Alfred Hitchcock (*qv*), in that his films were worked out to the last detail, blueprints which he and his scriptwriter, Kogo Noda, would construct during late-night drinking sessions. Unlike Hitchcock, though, Ozu hated to use 'stars', but chose his actors for the characteristics they projected. His films portray family life, and people coming to terms with the world (occasionally, even, choosing to go their own way, in defiance of

what seems like a predestined existence). Ozu's cameras are usually pitched at a lower level than in western – and indeed most eastern – films, at the point of view of a man sitting in the traditional Japanese position, cross-legged on the floor. Thus it becomes a passive observer, submitting, like the cast, to Ozu's view of things. Ozu had a rather unsettled childhood, his parents moving from place to place, while his father was away from home for long periods on business. Expelled from boarding school, he later had the opportunity to move to a good school in Kobe – but instead of going along for the interview, went to the pictures instead. Inevitably, the movie fanatic went into the film business, becoming an assistant director in 1923 and directing by 1925. He soon began to develop his own style, most noticeably in such films as *The Life of An Office Worker* (in which an anticipated sum of money ultimately never materializes) and *Tokyo Chorus*, about a man who loses his job and ends up as a sandwich man. Most of these early films are comedies rather than tragedies, although one can sense the hurt beneath the smiles. He later re-worked several of his earlier films into new ones, to reflect the changing times. His greatest international successes came in the 1950s, especially with *Tokyo Monogatari, The Flavour of Green Tea Over Rice*, the 'seasons' series, and two 'remakes', *Floating Weeds*, the story of a marriage break-up, and the charming *Good Morning!*, which examines the world of a child. Ozu was only 59 when he died from cancer.

1925: *Gakuso o Idete/Out of College*. 1927: *Zange no Yaiba/Sword of Penitence*. 1928: *Nyobo Funshitsu/Wife Lost. Kabocha/Pumpkin. Wakado no Yume/The Dreams of Youth. Nikutai bi/Body Beautiful. Hikkoshi-Fufu/Two on the Move*. 1929: *Wakaki hi/Day of Youth. Wasei Kenka Tomodachi. Takara no Yama. Daigaku wa Keredo/I Passed But.... Tokkan Kozo. Kaishain Seikatsu/The Life of an Office Worker*. 1930: *Kekkon-Gaku Nyumon. Hogaraka ni Ayume. Rakudai wa Shita Kereda/I Failed But ... Sono no yo Tsuma/That Night's Wife. Onryo. Ashi ni Sawatta Koun. Shukujo to Hige. Ojusan*. 1931: *Tokyo no Gassho/Tokyo Chorus. Bijin Aishu/Beauty's Sorrows*. 1932: *Haru wa Gofujin Kara. Umarete wa Mita Keredo/I Was Born But.... Sheishun no Yume ima Izuko. Mata au hi Made/Till We Meet Again*. 1933: *Tokyo no Onna/Woman of Tokyo. Hijosen no Onna/Dragnet Girl. Dekigokoro/Passing Fancy*. 1934: *Haha ko Kowazu-ya/A Mother Should Be Loved. Ukigusa Monogatari/A Story of Floating Weeds*. 1935:

Looking much like any western film-maker at work, this was one of Japan's most distinguished directors – Yasujiro **Ozu**.

earnest on a film-directing career, even though the star of his next, *Little Shop of Horrors*, was still not human, being a man-eating plant! The film, typical of the zaniness which, in Oz's hands, becomes good fun rather than irritating, introduced the director to manic comedian Steve Martin (he played a demon dentist), who starred in his next film *Dirty Rotten Scoundrels*. A very acceptable remake of the 1960s' comedy *Bedtime Story*, this is a cheerful comedy with gleamingly witty lines and riotous moments, its laughs coming at regular intervals. Oz moved on to the even funnier *What About Bob?*, his best performer at the box-office to date, with Bill Murray (another *Little Shop of Horrors* alumnus) in a variant on the story about the persistent patient who finally drives the psychiatrist round the bend. Under Oz's direction, delightfully wild performances from Murray and Richard Dreyfuss help us forget that this is little more than an anecdote and keep us happily chuckling away towards the climax. A further escapade with Martin, *HouseSitter*, was less successful, but Oz returned to winning ways with *In & Out*, a comedy about a teacher in his forties confronted by the fact that he may be gay. Although not as progressive as it thinks it is, the film hit a nerve with the paying public and earned co-star Joan Cusack an Oscar nomination – one of several performers who looked above-par under Oz's astute direction.

1982: †The Dark Crystal. 1984: The Muppets Take Manhattan. 1986: Little Shop of Horrors. 1988: Dirty Rotten Scoundrels. 1991: What about Bob? 1992: HouseSitter. 1995: The Indian in the Cupboard. 1997: In & Out. 1999: Bowfinger's Big Thing.

Hakoiri Musume/An Innocent Maid. Tokyo Yoi – toko/Tokyo is a Nice Place. Tokyo no Yado/An Inn in Tokyo. 1936: Daigaku Yoi toko/College is a Nice Place. Hitori Musuko/The Only Son. 1937: Shukujo wa nani o Wasuretaka/What Did the Lady Forget? 1941: Toda-ke no Kyodai/The Brothers and Sisters of the Toda Family. 1942: Chichi Ariki/There Was a Father. 1947: Nagaya no Shinshi Roku/Diary of a Tenement Gentleman. Kazi no naka no Mendori/A Hen in the Wind. 1949: Banshun/Late Spring. 1950: Munekata Shimei/The Munakata Sisters. 1951: Bakushu/Early Summer. 1952: Ochazuke no Aji/The Flavour of Green Tea Over Rice. 1953: Tokyo Monogatari/Tokyo Story. 1956: Soshun/Early Spring. 1957: Tokyo Boshoku/Twilight in Tokyo. 1958: Higanbana/Equinox Flower. 1959: Ohayo/Good Morning! Ukigusa/Floating Weeds. 1960: Akibiy-

ori/Late Autumn. 1961: Kohayagawa-ke no Aki/Early Autumn. 1962: Samma no Aji/An Autumn Afternoon.

OZ, Frank (F. Oznowicz) 1944-
Cheerful, British-born puppeteer, performer and latterly director of mainline comedy fare. He made his name with the children's ITV series *Sesame Street* and the more fully oriented *The Muppet Show*, both hugely popular in the 1970s. Oz also provided many of the voices for these shows, including two of the Muppets' biggest attractions, Miss Piggy and Fozzie Bear. He and Jim Henson were the lynchpins of *The Muppet Show* and, after Henson had made a couple of Muppet films, they co-directed the rather more adult *The Dark Crystal*. After the sheer joy of *The Muppets Take Manhattan*, the best of the Muppet films, Oz embarked in

P

PABST, G.W. 1885-1967
Born in Bohemia, later part of Czechoslovakia, of Austrian parents, Pabst's period of greatest achievement was only from 1925 to 1933. Few filmgoers today, while vividly recalling *Pandora's Box* and maybe one or two other Pabst classics, realize that he continued directing until 1956, and only gave up then after suffering a mild stroke. *Pandora* remains a

thing of beauty at each new viewing, illuminated by Louise Brooks' butterfly magnetism. But, as one who has actually fallen asleep during *The Threepenny Opera*, albeit at a late-night showing, I can testify that not all Pabsts wear so well. Perhaps the transient nature of much of his work helps to explain his decline, as well as the often traumatic life he lived. Raised and educated in Vienna, Pabst was in America as an actor from 1908, remaining there until 1914, by which time he was directing German-language plays in New York. On a return trip to Vienna, however, Pabst was trapped in France when World War I began, and detained by the French until 1918. He entered films in 1921 as an actor and assistant director, making his first film as solo director in 1923. From 1925, he entered a rich period in which the 'look' of his movies conveys their feel. His teaming of two stars at opposite ends of their careers – Asta Nielsen and Greta Garbo – in *Die freudlose Gasse* was sensationally effective, and for some years he enjoyed the reputation of getting the best out of a series of distinctive and perhaps difficult leading ladies, notably Brigitte Helm (of *Metropolis* fame), Valeska Gert and Louise Brooks. At the outset of the 1930s, he courted and won political controversy with his two pacifist films *Westfront 1918* and *Kameradschaft,* the first a war story, the second about a mining disaster, each designed to show the upsurge of comradely feelings between French and Germans at times of crisis. The mining film is facile, perhaps, but affecting and difficult to forget. These two films, coming on top of his other Louise Brooks film *Diary of a Lost Girl,* and the bleak beauty of *The White Hell of Pitz Palu,* confirmed Pabst's international reputation as a director of visual invention and impressiveness, but the 'pacifist statements' were uneasily received in Germany and, with the rise of the Nazis, Pabst moved to France. He tried Hollywood, too, in 1934, but unsuccessfully, and made more moderate French films before a fateful trip to Austria for family reasons produced a replica of his 1914 circumstances. He was held by the authorities, and compelled to stay in Germany for the duration of the war, making a few films there which would later get him reviled as a collaborator. But his post-war films, although disappointing in standard (his former hypnotic lustre being replaced by harsh luridness), were decidedly anti-Nazi and pro-Semitic. Circumstances were not kind to this film-maker who, as it were, 'only danced one summer'.

1923: Der Schatz (GB & US: The Treasure). Gräfin Donelli/Countess Donelli.

1925: Die freudlose Gasse (GB: The Joyless Street. US: Street of Sorrow). 1926: Geheimnisse einer Seele (GB & US: Secrets of the Soul. Man spielt nicht mit der Liebe (GB & US: Don't Play with Love). 1927: Der Liebe der Jeanne Ney (GB: Lusts of the Flesh. US: The Love of Jeanne Ney). 1928: Abwege (GB & US: Crisis). 1929: Die Büchse der Pandora (GB & US: Pandora's Box). †Die weisse Hölle vom Piz Palu (GB & US: The White Hell of Pitz Palu). Das Tagebuch einer Verlorenen (GB & US: Diary of a Lost Girl). 1930: Westfront 1918 (US: Comrades of 1918). Skandal um Eva. 1931: $Kameradschaft. $Der Dreigroschenoper (GB & US: The Threepenny Opera). 1932: Die Herrin von Atlantis (and French version: L'Atlantide). 1933: Don Quixote. Du haut en bas. 1934: A Modern Hero. 1937: Mademoiselle Docteur (US: Street of Shadows). 1938: Le drame de Shanghai. 1939: Jeunes filles en détresse. 1940: Feuertaufe (D). 1941: Komödianten. 1943: Paracelsus. 1945: Der Fall Molander (unfinished). 1947: Der Prozess (US: The Trial). 1949: Geheimnisvolle Tiefe. 1952: La voce del silenzio. 1953: Cose do pazzi. 1954: Das Bekenntnis der Ina Kahr (GB & US: The Confession of Ina Kahr). 1955: Der letzte Akt (GB: Ten Days to Die. US: The Last Ten Days). Es geschah am 20 Juli (GB: Jackboot Mutiny). 1956: Rosen für Bettina. Durch die Wälder, durch die Auen.

$ and French-language version

PAKULA, Alan J. 1928-1999

This American director has stuck to the theme of warm (though often difficult) human relationships, begun by the ex-partner, Robert Mulligan *(qv),* whom he has now overtaken in critical esteem. Originally an animator, he went to Paramount in 1951 as a production assistant,

In both physical and literal senses, giant-sized Alan J **Pakula** is one of Hollywood's biggest directors. Here he looks like a dead ringer for Raymond Burr of Perry Mason fame.

and it seems to have been coincidental that his first assignment as producer there, on *Fear Strikes Out* (1957), was also Mulligan's first film as director. In the early 1960s, they formed their own production company, and Pakula produced several Mulligan-directed films, from *To Kill a Mockingbird* (1962) to *The Stalking Moon* (1969). Pakula made an uncertain start to his own directorial career with *The Sterile Cuckoo*, a hopefully penetrating but in practice rather wishy-washy look at a college love affair. Pakula then unexpectedly struck gold with his second film, *Klute*, the deliberately unsettling account of the uneasy alliance between a call girl and a detective to catch a murderer. Noted for its prowling camerawork and early use of four-letter words, the film has an attractive performance in a difficult role by Donald Sutherland, although Jane Fonda rather overbalances this film — she was much better and more controlled in Pakula's later *Comes a Horseman*, one of his best films to date. In terms of box-office achievement, though, it was eclipsed by Pakula's film of the Watergate scandal, *All the President's Men,* where he explores to great effect a world as nightmarish as that groped through by the characters in *Klute.* The earlier film had won one Oscar (for Jane Fonda); this one took four, plus a nomination (his first) for its director. Pakula's films have usually been a success with the critics, but their popular impact remains variable. He has returned to the theme of stubbornly independent people struggling to come to terms with each other. In *Comes a Horseman*, in which Fonda and James Caan really convince as dog-eared western pioneers, determined to fight Jason Robards to the last, the theme is intermingled with action. In *Starting Over*, a funny-sad comedy with Jill Clayburgh and Burt Reynolds, it is the whole film; Pakula's efforts at making a charming movie seem a little calculated, but they work well enough much of the time. If one wanted to pin a title on Pakula's work, in fact, one could well take the name of one of his less successful films — *Love and Pain and the whole damn thing.* There was certainly a lot of pain in the harrowing and resolutely glum *Sophie's Choice,* which won an Oscar for its leading actress Meryl Streep. And dullness dominated Pakula's films until the 1990s, when he began to make more aggressively commercial movies, triggered off by the success of *Presumed Innocent,* a twisty legal thriller with highly exploitable elements and a cleverly concealed surprise ending. Pakula has not quite matched its impact since.

1969: *The Sterile Cuckoo* (GB: *Pookie*). 1971: *Klute*. 1973: *Love and Pain and the whole damn thing.* 1974: *The Parallax View.* 1976: *All the President's Men.* 1978: *Comes a Horseman.* 1979: *Starting Over.* 1981: *Roll-Over.* 1982: *Sophie's Choice.* 1985: *Dream Lover.* 1987: *Orphans.* 1988: *See You in the Morning.* 1990: *Presumed Innocent.* 1992: *Consenting Adults.* 1993: *The Pelican Brief.* 1996: *The Devil's Own.*

PAL, George (Georg Pál) 1908-1980

Hungarian-born puppeteer and special effects expert whose films have taken five Academy Awards for special effects. The filmography below lists only Pal's actual credits as director, but his influence on the worlds of science-fiction and fantasy in many other Hollywood movies is incalculable. He was a set designer for UFA in Berlin in the early 1930s, before moving into advertising films in Holland, where he also began to direct shorts from 1936. In 1939, he went to Hollywood and started the 'Puppetoon' series, which remained popular through the war years, brought stop-frame animation to delightful perfection and won Pal a special Oscar in 1943 'for the development of novel methods and techniques'. In post-war years, Pal turned his attention to visual effects in fantasy films. Many of these, including *The War of the Worlds, The Naked Jungle, Conquest of Space* and *The Power,* were directed by Pal's long-time friend and collaborator, Byron Haskin *(qv).* All show remarkably vivid use of colour and crisp editing in addition to their excellent special effects. The Academy Awards won by films either produced or directed by Pal (all for special effects) were for *Destination Moon* (1950), *When Worlds Collide* (1951), *The War of the Worlds* (1952), *tom thumb* and *The Time Machine.* Pal could well have won an additional award for the sparkling fairytale sequences which he himself directed in *The Wonderful World of the Brothers Grimm.*

1934: **Radio Valve Revolution.* 1935: **Ali Baba and the Forty Thieves. *The Magic Atlas. *In Lamplightland.* 1936: **On Parade. *Ether Symphony.* 1937: **Love on the Range. *What Ho! She Bumps. *De Reddingbrigade. *The Philips Broadcast of 1938.* 1938: **South Sea Sweetheart. *Sleeping Beauty. *Sky Pirates. *The Ballet of Red Radio Valves.* 1939: **Aladdin and the Magic Lamp. *Philips Cavalcade.* 1940: **Friend in Need.* 1941: **Gay Knighties. *Hoola Boola. *Dipsy Gypsy. *Rhythm in the Ranks. *Western Daze.* 1942: **Jasper and the Haunted House. *Jasper and the Watermelons. *The Sky Princess. *Strauss Takes a Walk. *Tulips Shall Grow.* 1943: **Bravo Mr Strauss. *Good Night, Rusty. *Jasper and the Choo-Choo. *The 500 Hats of Bartholomew Cubbins. *Jasper's Music Lesson. *The Truck that Flew. *The Little Broadcast. *Jasper Goes Fishing. *Good Night, Rusty. *Gooseberry Pie.* 1944: **A Package for Jasper. *A Hatful of Dreams. *And to Think I Saw It on Mulberry Street. *Hotlips Jasper. *Jasper's Paradise. *My Man Jasper. *Mr Strauss Takes a Walk. *Say 'Ah', Jasper. *Two Gun Rusty.* 1945: **Jasper and Beanstalk. *Jasper's Booby Trap. *Jasper's Minstrels. *Together in the Weather. *Jasper Tell. *Jasper's Close Shave/The Barber of Seville. *Jasper's Paradise.* 1946: **Jasper in a Jam. *A Date With Duke. *John Henry and the Inky Poo. *Jasper's Derby. *Shoeshine Jasper. *Olio for Jasper.* 1947: **Tubby the Tuba. *Romeow and Juliecat* (later included in *Variety Girl*). **Rhapsody in Wood. *Wilbur the Lion.* 1952: *†The War of the Worlds* (uncredited). 1958: *tom thumb.* 1960: *The Time Machine.* 1961: *Atlantis the Lost Continent.* 1962: *†The Wonderful World of the Brothers Grimm.* 1964: *7 Faces of Dr Lao.*

PANAMA, Norman 1914-

An entry to complete the record on the Panama-Melvin Frank partnership, for details of which see the entry on Frank. Panama's solo films as director have been mainly disappointing comedies with tiring stars. *The Trap* was a passable thriller with good use of colour, but Panama has not returned to the genre. *I Will... I Will... for Now,* with its relentless spate of *doubles entendres,* X-certificate style, smacked of desperation, and not even Elliott Gould, Diane Keaton, Paul Sorvino and Candy Clark could do anything with a screenplay co-written by Panama himself, whose frenetic direction of his cast only encourages them to fall back on such mannerisms as make them distinctive performers.

1949: *†The Reformer and the Redhead.* 1951: *†Strictly Dishonorable. †Callaway Went Thataway* (GB: *The Star Said No!*). 1952: *†Above and Beyond.* 1954: *†Knock on Wood.* 1955: *†The Court Jester.* 1956: *†That Certain Feeling.* 1958: *The Trap* (GB: *The Baited Trap*). 1962: *The Road to Hong Kong.* 1966: *Not with My Wife, You Don't!* 1969: *How to Commit Marriage. The Maltese Bippy.* 1973: *Coffee, Tea or Me?* (TV). 1975: *I Will... I Will... for Now.* 1971: *Barnaby and Me.*

Alan **Parker** (hands raised) times the start of a musical number from *The Commitments*. Bronagh Gallagher, Angeline Ball, Maria Doyle, Glen Hansard and (bottom) Andrew Strong prepare to burst into song.

PARKER, Alan 1944-

Following a delightful feature-film debut in 1976, this boundlessly enthusiastic London-born director is his own best publicist and has made each of his films an event, regardless of their success or failure. His movies either pulse with energy, or are punishing, harrowing affairs; and he has had particular success in his treatment of children. Even as a writer, Parker's first film credit was on the school romance *Melody* (later *S*W*A*L*K*). He also worked in television, at first making commercials, but later directing children again in *The Evacuees*, a lovely evocation of wartime childhood. His first feature film *Bugsy Malone* must have seemed a huge commercial risk — a musical about American gang wars in the prohibition era, played entirely by children (although adults rather incongruously provide the singing voices). In fact, the film was a critical and

commercial triumph. Perhaps anxious to be rid of the novelty tag, Parker turned to *Midnight Express*, an account of the horrendous incarceration by the Turkish authorities of a young American convicted of smuggling cannabis. Although bloody enough in its violence, the direction makes parts of the film too glossy for the subject. Parker moved from pre-teenagers to late-teenagers in his next film, *Fame*, which would have been marvellous as a gutsy TV documentary film about young New York musical hopefuls, complete with built-in musical blast finale, at around the running time (55 minutes) of Parker's 1976 *No Hard Feelings*, made for cinemas but shown on TV. Unfortunately, all the elements added to the basic idea seem to be working against the film, while its 135-minute running time makes it a drag for any age group — and such situations as there are to sustain it are only barely believable. Never-

theless, both films were well thought of in some quarters and made money. The barrage of four-letter words they contained was continued in *Shoot the Moon*, many of them from the children of the broken marriage that comes under Parker's scrutiny. Not enough variation in the film meant that it was all pitched on too overwrought a level. In the last 15 years, Parker has continued to make challenging films that have brought offence and disappointment to some and exhilaration to others. The strongest of them have been *Mississippi Burning*, a brilliantly acted portrait of racial violence that won Parker his second Oscar nomination, to follow *Midnight Express*; and *The Commitments*, a musically surging account of the rise and fall of an Irish band. Perhaps the most consistently successful of Parker's films have been those with a musical background — *The Commitments* following *Bugsy Malone* and *Fame*. This run was brought to an end, however, by the film version of the stage smash *Evita*, which starts well, looks great, but proved to have insufficient dramatic weight to pull in the paying public in the hoped-for numbers. For all his disappointments, though, Parker remains a director of much talent, with exciting and inventive camera control. If he'd only put the brake on the overkill, and settle down to make the fluid, keenly paced, affectionately observed film of which he is capable, we could all settle back and enjoy it. It might even be a masterpiece.

1973: *Footsteps. *Our Cissy. 1974: No Hard Feelings (TV). 1975: The Evacuees (TV). 1976: Bugsy Malone. 1978: Midnight Express. 1979: Thank You Very Much (TV). 1980: Fame. 1981: Shoot the Moon. 1982: Pink Floyd — The Wall. 1984: Birdy. 1987: Angel Heart. 1988: Mississippi Burning. 1990: Come See the Paradise. 1991: The Commitments. 1994: The Road to Wellville. 1996: Evita. 1999: Angela's Ashes.

PARRISH, Robert 1916-1995

A real child of Hollywood. The brother of actress Helen Parrish, who died from cancer at 37, Robert Parrish was an actor himself from the age of 12. Unsuccessful in acting as a late teenager, he turned to the other side of the camera, becoming an editor after spells as sound editor and assistant editor, notably in films directed by John Ford, for whom he had also acted. His films as director (since 1951) are mainly mirthless affairs. Parrish is not the man for comedy, as The Bobo and his section of Casino Royale go to prove. The more serious his work, though, the more successful it generally is. His first two films, Cry Danger and The Mob, are fast-moving, hard-hitting crime thrillers — the director tipping his hat to the fast-disappearing film noir of post-war years. Parrish continued to make good movies in between lesser works without becoming a major figure, or developing a personal style. Thus The Purple Plain is a vivid account of a nerve-shot pilot trying to get his wounded navigator back to safety through the Burmese jungles of World War II, with good acting performances and an excellent plane crash sequence. At this stage, though, Parrish had already begun wandering through as many countries as genres: France, Spain, Italy, Britain, Mexico and the West Indies — Parrish filmed in all of them. But Saddle the Wind is a fine, brooding western with a final showdown between brothers Robert Taylor and John Cassavetes. In the French Style worships Jean Seberg, on the way to giving the best performance of her sad life (one wanderer directing another) as a girl growing up mentally in

Paris. Up from the Beach is a suspenseful thinking man's war film with a cosmopolitan cast headed by Cliff Robertson and Françoise Rosay. That, however, was the last good film, and Parrish eventually wandered away from the cinema as well as Hollywood. He shared an Academy Award for his editing work on the 1947 film Body and Soul. He died from cardiac arrest.

1943: †German Manpower (D). 1951: Cry Danger. The Mob (GB: Remember That Face). †Ten Tall Men. 1952: The San Francisco Story. Assignment – Paris! †The Lusty Men (uncredited). My Pal Gus. 1953: Rough Shoot (US: Shoot First). 1954: The Purple Plain. 1955: Lucy Gallant. 1957: Fire Down Below. 1958: Saddle the Wind. 1959: The Wonderful Country. 1962: In the French Style. 1965: Up from the Beach. 1967: †Casino Royale. The Bobo. 1968: Duffy. 1969: Doppelganger (US: Journey to the Far Side of the Sun). 1971: A Town Called Bastard (US: A Town Galled Hell). 1974: The Marseille Contract (US: The Destructors). 1984: †Mississippi Blues.

PARROTT, James 1892-1939

This book has generally shied away from directors purely of short subjects, but Parrott could, were he still alive, lay claim to directing more films familiar to today's cinemagoers and TV viewers than any of his contemporaries, having made many of the best Laurel and Hardy two-reelers. Like his brother, Charley Chase – though Charley was a more successful comedian – Parrott was a writer, gagman, producer and comic from around 1912 onwards. Calling himself Poll Parrott (later Paul Parrott), he starred in his own two-reel comedy films from 1918 onwards. In the mid-1920s, he joined the Hal Roach 'all-stars' comedy two-reelers, directing some of them from 1927. He began directing Laurel and Hardy the following year, and his best films for them, in a six-year period of convulsive comedy, are: Should Married Men Go Home? which has Ollie flattening his own garden fence trying to emulate Stan's leap over it, and the famous golf-course finale; Two Tars, with its motorcar wrecking escalation; Perfect Day, with its accumulation of tiny variations on gags on getting into and starting a car; The Hoosegow, in which convicts Stan and Ollie have trouble with picks and ruin the prison governor's car; Blotto, with its famous final shot of the boys' taxi disintegrating when Stan's wife fires a rifle at it; Brats, where they play their own sons; Hog Wild, where they try to

erect a radio aerial; Helpmates, one of the funniest of all their films, in which their efforts to clear up the house for the imminent return of Mrs Hardy lead to one beautifully directed disaster after another, until Stan finally burns the house down; The Music Box, the great piano-moving farce and another exercise in amazingly sustained hilarity; and Twice Two, in which they play their own wives. Parrott also directed the duo in the short feature, Pardon Us. After 1934, most of the Laurel and Hardy features were directed by James W. Horne (1880-1942), who had also directed such shorts as Big Business and Laughing Gravy, while Parrott concentrated on scriptwriting, notably on Way Out West, Swiss Miss and Blockheads. But in May 1939, Parrott died from a heart attack at 46. A year later, his brother Charley Chase died from a heart attack at the same age. The Music Box was a 1932 Academy Award winner.

1920: Open the Bars. Squirrel Food. A Leaf from Nature's Book. 1924: Just a Minute. Powder and Smoke. A Perfect Lady. Hard Knocks. Love's Detour. Don't Forget. The Fraidy Cat. 1926: There Ain't No Santa Claus. Many Scrappy Returns. 1927: Never the Dames Shall Meet. The Way of All Pants (GB: The Way of All Dress). The Lighter That Failed. Are Brunettes Safe? A One Mama Man (GB: Watch It). Forgotten Sweeties. Bigger and Better Blondes. Fluttering Hearts. What Women Did for Me. Now I'll Tell One. Assistant Wives. Us. The Sting of Stings (GB: A Treat for the Boys). 1928: Their Purple Moment. Should Married Men Go Home? Two Tars. Habeus Corpus. All for Nothing. Blow by Blow. Ruby Lips. Chasing Husbands. 1929: Stewed, Fried and Boiled. Lesson Number 1. Furnace Trouble. Happy Birthday. Perfect Day. They Go Boom. The Hoosegow. 1930: Night Owls. Blotto. Be Big. Brats. The Laurel and Hardy Murder Case. Below Zero. Hog Wild (GB: Aerial Antics). Another Fine Mess. 1931: The Pip from Pittsburgh. $Pardon Us (GB: Jailbirds). $Rough Seas. $One of the Smiths. The Panic Is On. Skip the Maloo! What a Bozo! Helpmates. 1932: Young Ironsides. Girl Grief. Mr Bride. The Music Box. The Chimp. County Hospital. 1933: Now We'll Tell One. Twice Two. Twin Screws. 1934: Washee Ironee. Opened by Mistake. Benny from Panama. A Duke for a Day. Mixed Nuts. 1935: Treasure Blues. The Tin Man. Sing Sister Sing. The Misses Stooge.

All shorts except $ short features

PARRY, Gordon 1908-1981

Workmanlike British director, generally better with drama than with comedy. A late arrival on the directorial scene, Parry was at his best between 1951 and 1954. After that, television, and particularly the popular series *The Adventures of Robin Hood,* took up much of his time. He had originally studied to be an electrical engineer, but threw it up for acting in 1929. Two years later, he joined Gaumont-British as an assistant and by 1933 had progressed to assistant director. He also gained experience as an associate producer on some G-B films, before World War II came along and Parry became unit manager for propaganda shorts at the Ealing studios in London. During this period, he also worked as second-unit director for David Lean and Noel Coward on *In Which We Serve.* When he became a director in 1947, though, Parry showed no inclination to make war films, but

stuck largely to interior stories. The artificiality *of Bond Street* was an inauspicious beginning, but in the early 1950s, he had several popular successes in a row. *Tom Brown's Schooldays* was a well-presented remake of Thomas Hughes' classic; *Women of Twilight* a harsh and dark drama in the footsteps of *No Room at the Inn,* with an attention-grabbing performance from Freda Jackson; *Innocents in Paris* a pleasant compendium of the adventures of British innocents abroad, with a fine company of farceurs headed by Margaret Rutherford and Alastair Sim; and *Front Page Story* a hard-hitting newspaper yarn. It must also be said that all these promising subjects might have been better had they been made by a director of more flair. Without such good material, Parry floundered in the nether regions of British film-making for the remainder of the decade and, after years working in television, he retired to France, where he

eventually died from a heart attack at 72. One of his two daughters is the actress Natasha Parry.

1947: Bond Street. 1948: Third Time Lucky. 1949: Now Barabbas was a robber. . . . The Golden Arrow (US: Three Men and a Girl. Released 1952). 1950: Midnight Episode. 1951: Tom Brown's Schooldays. 1952: Women of Twilight (US: Twilight Women). 1953: Innocents in Paris. Front Page Story. 1954: Fast and Loose. 1955: A Yank in Ermine. 1956: Sailor Beware! (US: Panic in the Parlor). A Touch of the Sun. 1957: The Surgeon's Knife. 1958: Tread Softly Stranger. 1959: Friends and Neighbours. The Navy Lark.

PASOLINI, Pier Paolo 1922-1975

Italian poet, novelist and film-maker. Pasolini was obsessively concerned with the working-class and peasant people of his country, and almost all his films depict their conditions and lives, or employ non-actors from these classes for use as 'faces'.

Setting up a panoramic view for the 1969 film *Amore e rabbia*, a multi-episode movie. In the bottom foreground, looking pensive, is the director of this segment, Pier Paolo **Pasolini.**

His attitudes to Marxism, Catholicism and other prickly subjects in Italy reveal themselves in his films. Together with these elements, and their more overt content, which includes, as well as sex and violence, bestiality, masochism, sadism and cannibalism, Pasolini's films were certain targets for controversy. But many of them also have a rare beauty that renders their less digestible content more palatable. One writer remarked that a work written on Pasolini in 1969 still remained the best on the subject. It's an astute observation, for this is the watershed time in Pasolini's career when content overtook form. *Pigsty* is the last film where the latter is triumphant over the former. From then on, Pasolini's films became increasingly repulsive and difficult to sit through by turns. A published poet at 19, Pasolini had ventured into screenwriting by 1954, among his many credits being a collaboration on the script of Fellini's *Le notte di Cabiria* (1956). As a director, Pasolini never failed to court controversy even from his opening film, *Accattone!*, a reworking of his own novel *Una vita violenta*, a grimly convincing evocation of the slums of Rome, and the life of a pimp therein. The theme of prostitution was continued in Pasolini's *homage* to Anna Magnani, *Mamma Roma*. Its depiction of the squalid conditions of Rome's underworld was graphically real. But his reputation was really secured by *The Gospel According to St Matthew*, an acerbic and uncompromising, if fairly straightforward re-telling of the New Testament story, using only words and scenes from St Matthew's Gospel. Rough-edged and grindingly realistic, the film is spellbinding to watch and carries a heavy emotional impact. It remained Pasolini's best film, although *Oedipus Rex* and *Pigsty* are both remarkable in many ways, the first for its unique desert atmosphere that suggests primeval times, the second as a black comedy *tour-de-force* for adult tastes. *Theorem* (from another of his novels) is also well thought-of, although I personally find it disappointing. In November 1975, Pasolini's life came to a violent end when he was battered to death by a 17-year-old youth who alleged that the director had made homosexual advances to him.

1961: Accattone! 1962: Mamma Roma. †RoGoPaG. 1963: La rabbia, part I (unreleased). Sopraluoghi in Palestina. 1964: Comizi d'amore (D). Il vangelo secondo Matteo (GB & US: The Gospel According to St Matthew). 1966: Uccellacci e uccellini (US: Hawks and Sparrows). †Le streghe (US: The Witches). 1967: Oedipus Rex. 1968: Capriccio all'Italiana. Theorem. *Appunti per un film sull' India (D). 1969: †Amore e rabbia/Vangelo '70 (GB & US: Love and Anger). Pigsty. 1970: Medea. *Appunti per un' Orestiade Africana (D). 1971: The Decameron. 1972: †Dodici Dicembre (uncredited). The Canterbury Tales. 1973: Storie scellerate (GB: Bawdy Tales). 1974: Il fiore delle mille e una notte (GB: Arabian Nights. US: A Thousand and One Nights). 1975: Salò, or the 120 Days of Sodom.

PEARSON, George 1874-1973

Pioneer British film-maker whose most successful work was in the 1920s — he discovered golden-haired Betty Balfour when she was 17 and took her to the top of all popularity polls in British stars. From 1920 to 1926, they made 11 films together. What these pictures lacked in sophistication – Pearson was a forward-looking director but somewhat deficient in finesse – they made up for in their working-class appeal. Pearson's decline began ironically with possibly his best film – *The Little People*. Too innovatory for British audiences, it was a big flop, and with the 1930s, after some work in production for Michael Balcon, Pearson found himself directing 'quota quickies' for which he had little flair. A former teacher and headmaster, Pearson had been with the British film industry almost from its beginnings. Claiming that he saw the cinema as 'the teacher's true medium', he joined Pathé as a scriptwriter in 1912. Despite his late start, it was a medium in which he would lead a full life. He was instrumental in improving the primitive shooting conditions of films in Britain, freeing the camera from its initial rigid position (set on a capstan head bolted to the floor) and, by 1915, after his appointment as head of Gaumont, getting £30,000 spent on new studio premises at Shepherd's Bush. Most of his early films are documentaries, but he soon began to make important features, among them *The Fool*, *Sentence of Death*, *A Study in Scarlet*, *John Halifax Gentleman*, *Sally Bishop*, *The Better 'Ole* and *Garryowen*. His series of 'Ultus' thrillers, modelled after the serials of Louis Feuillade, were also popular. He first directed Betty Balfour on *Nothing Else Matters*, but his most successful films with her were the 'Squibs' series, casting her as a cockney flower-girl of spirit, involved in a series of low-life intrigues, romances and adventures. Pearson's eye for interior detail added authenticity to these rather melodramatic proceedings, although he could also make good use of location work, notably in *Squibs Wins the Calcutta Sweep*, and his use of cross-cutting — Griffith was his idol — gives his films an easy rhythm. Although his camerawork is never flashy, it seldom fails to show the little 'Pearson' touches which give his silent films such character, albeit perhaps the character of an Edwardian novelette. With sound, Pearson found his assignments drastically diminished in importance, although one, *The River Wolves*, was praised for its realistic waterfront atmosphere and settings. Like most of his films in the 1930s, it was a short-length thriller designed as a second-feature. Despite such a come-down, and advancing years, Pearson continued to direct. In 1939, he joined the G.P.O. Film Unit, and devoted himself for a short while to his old love — the documentary. In 1942, Pearson, a man of tremendous vigour, moved on to the Colonial Film Unit as its Head of Production, remaining there until his retirement at 81. Two years later he published his autobiography, *Flashback*.

1912: *Peg Woffington. *Fair Sussex (D). *In Dickens Land (D). 1913: *Rambles through Hopland (D). *Where History Has Been Written (D). *Kentish Industries (D). *Lynmouth (D). *Wonderful Nights of Peter Kinema (series). *A Lighter Burden. *Mr Henpeck's Dilemma. Heroes of the Mine. *A Fishergirl's Folly. The Fool. Sentence of Death. 1914: The Live Wire. A Study in Scarlet. *A Son of France. Incidents in the Great European War. The Cause of the Great European War. The Life of Lord Roberts VC. *Buttons. *For the Empire. *Christmas Day in the Workhouse. 1915: A Cinema Girl's Romance. The True Story of the Lyons Mail. Ultus — the Man from the Dead. John Halifax Gentleman. 1916: Ultus and the Grey Lady. Sally Bishop. Ultus and the Secret of the Night. 1917: *Canadian Officers in the Making (D). *The Man Who Made the Army (D). Ultus and the Three Button Mystery. 1918: The Better 'Ole. The Kiddies in the Ruins. Ultus and the Phanton of Pengate. 1919: *Hughie at the Victory Derby. 1920: Garryowen. Nothing Else Matters. 1921: Mary Find-the-Gold. Squibs. Mord Em'ly (US: Me and My Girl). 1922: The Wee McGregor's Sweetheart. Squibs Wins the Calcutta Sweep. 1923: Love, Life and Laughter. Squibs MP. Squibs' Honeymoon. 1924: Reveille. 1925: Satan's Sister. 1926: The Little People. Blinkeyes. 1927: Huntingtower. 1928: Love's Option. 1929: Auld Lang Syne. 1931: East Lynne on the Western Front. 1932: The Third String. 1933: A Shot in the Dark. The Pointing Finger. The River Wolves. 1934: Four Masked Men. Whispering Tongues. Open All Night. 1935: The Ace of Spades.

Just after his great success with *The Wild Bunch*, Sam **Peckinpah** (left) directed *The Ballad of Cable Hogue*. Here he discusses a scene with David Warner.

*That's My Uncle. Gentleman's Agreement. Once a Thief. Jubilee Window. Check-mate. 1936: The Secret Voice. Murder by Rope. Wednesday's Luck. 1937: The Fatal Hour. Midnight at Madame Tussaud's. 1938: *Souvenirs. *Old Soldiers. *Mother of Men. 1939: *British Made (D). 1940: *Land of Water (D). *Take Cover (D). *Rural School (D). *A British Family in Peace and War (D). 1941: *British Youth (D). *An African in London (D).*

PECKINPAH, Sam

(David S. Peckinpah)   1926-1984
American director who has made some of the most exciting gun duels and action scenes ever put on screen. Nor was it all

blood and thunder: the human spirit was never better celebrated than in some of Peckinpah's early work. Unfortunately, after *The Wild Bunch*, things did not develop quite as one would have hoped. One could have swallowed Peckinpah's explanations for the gushing blood and guts in *The Wild Bunch*, as showing that death was a violent and horrendous thing, and especially so in the old west, and that now he had cleansed all that from his system — had the same blood and guts not flowed ever more freely in successive Peckinpah assignments. Peckinpah, a westerner himself from ranchland in North Fork, California, had been steeped in western lore and legend from an early age and, after beginning his career as a

writer, was soon involved in television westerns at the peak of their popularity. From 1956, he wrote numerous episodes of *Gunsmoke!* and several other western series, directing these same series from 1958. He created two of these, *The Westerner* and, most popular, *The Rifleman*. Moving into films by 1961, Peckinpah made an immediate impression with his expert direction, losing no opportunity to lift *The Deadly Companions* above the average. However, this was nothing to the stir he created with his second, *Ride the high Country*, which, despite the subsequent impact of *The Wild Bunch*, remains Peckinpah's best film. It is an elegy to a dying breed of westerner, with career-best performances from Joel McCrea and Randolph Scott as the two veteran ex-lawmen hired to guard a consignment of gold through rugged territory. The final gunfight, as fierce and fine as anything the western has given us, really sets the adrenalin flowing, thoughtful details give the film a genuine whiff of life, and McCrea's death scene, as he lies looking at the beauty of the country, is as eloquent as anything in the genre. But there were traumatic times ahead for Peckinpah, first over the re-cutting of his *Major Dundee* which, even after its butchering, still remains a fine, if occasionally confused film, with colour images rarely matched in the western. The blood-letting returned in the exciting *Straw Dogs*, shot in England; having been rather less successful with the quieter, more reflective *Junior Bonner* (although the film was well-liked in some quarters) Peckinpah then concentrated on tougher-than-tough action, with heads and arms flying everywhere. His later films – *The Getaway*, though hokum, shows astute cinematic sense at times and is the best of them – rather lack the human touch. Died from a heart attack.

1961: The Deadly Companions. Ride the High Country (GB: Guns in the Afternoon). 1965: Major Dundee. 1966: Noon Wine (TV). 1969: The Wild Bunch. 1970: The Ballad of Cable Hogue. 1971: Straw Dogs. 1972: Junior Bonner. The Getaway. 1973: Pat Garrett and Billy the Kid. 1974: Bring Me the Head of Alfredo Garcia. 1975: The Killer Elite. 1977: Cross of Iron. 1978: Convoy. 1983: The Osterman Weekend.

PENN, Arthur 1922-

American director who has made an interesting variety of films, some of them very fine — but only 13 in 30 years. By and large his films have been more popular with the critics than with the public. The exception is his major triumph, *Bonnie and Clyde*, which not only won two Oscars and was nominated for several more, but proved to be Warner Brothers' biggest financial success of its decade. Since then, Penn has not proved to be a major figure at the box-office; his films are always fascinating, even exciting, in concept and casting, but sometimes lacking in fulfilment. Originally an actor – an occupation begun while still serving with the infantry in World War II – Penn had turned to directing TV plays by the early l950s. In 1958, he directed both his first play and his first film. The film was *The Left-Handed Gun*, with Paul Newman as Billy the Kid, and it started Penn off on a spasmodic film career. Violence plays an important role in all Penn's films save the most recent: it smoulders inside Newman in *The Left-Handed Gun;* breaks down the barriers

between teacher and child in *The Miracle Worker;* forms, with sex, the attraction between *Bonnie and Clyde;* lingers as a disturbing influence on the hippie commune of *Alice's Restaurant*, probably my favourite Penn film because, with *Bonnie and Clyde*, it is the most cinematic, capturing a quixotic but edgy mood in a series of skilfully etched vignettes; and can be the only arbiter in the running battle between Marlon Brando and Jack Nicholson in *The Missouri Breaks*. The violence reaches its apogee in the repulsive *The Chase*, a less attractive film even than the inaccessible *Mickey One*. These films, however, were followed by *Bonnie and Clyde*, simply a marvellous picture on all levels, garnished with glowing colour photography by Burnett Guffey which deservedly won an Oscar. Penn's thunder in his sympathetic treatment of the Indians in *Little Big Horn* was rather stolen by Dustin Hoffman's 120-year-old make-up. Penn had another go at the western with *The Missouri Breaks*, but one wonders what he, Brando and Nicholson ever saw in this very ordinary range-feud drama. There was a welcome return to form, however, in *Four Friends*, a story of the relationships between four people through the years, in which Penn's talent for gently persuading actors to perform above themselves was fully restored. He also added a new warmth to his work, even if the film itself rather loses its way in midstream. The remainder of Penn's output is of less account, although the chiller *Dead of Winter* saw him prove his efficiency in a genre he had not tried before. His prison movie for cable TV, the South Africa-set *Inside*, brought a fresh intensity to his style.

1958: The Left-Handed Gun. 1962: The Miracle Worker. 1965: Mickey One. 1966: The Chase. 1967: Bonnie and Clyde. 1969: Alice's Restaurant. 1970: Little Big Man. 1973: †Visions of Eight. 1975: Night Moves. 1976: The Missouri Breaks. 1981: Four Friends (GB: Georgia's Friends). 1985: Target. 1987: Dead of Winter. 1989: Penn and Teller Get Killed. 1996: Inside (cable TV).

PERRY, Frank 1930-1995

Nominated for an Oscar on his first film, this New York-born director continued to interest critics with his work while failing to break into the commercial big-time. His most noteworthy attempt to do so, with *Mommie Dearest* in 1981, was surprisingly not a success, despite an amazing impersonation of Joan Crawford by Faye Dunaway, who had previously worked for Perry on *Doc*. Perry had already shown his caring nature during

his apprenticeship in television, where he worked on 'social conscience' documentaries. His first film, *David and Lisa*, was a low-budget black-and-white movie about the movingly tentative relationship between two mentally disturbed adolescents. Full of haunting images, it has career-best performances from the two leads, Janet Margolin (since shamefully wasted by the cinema — only *Last Embrace* (1979) made anything like as interesting use of her), and Keir Dullea. Thanks to critical approval, the film gradually caught on with at least a section of the public, although Perry predictably lost the Academy Award to David Lean and *Lawrence of Arabia*, a triumph of might over right. Perry, working with his then-wife Eleanor (1933-1981) as scriptwriter, continued to tackle offbeat subjects, mostly for television, until he began a seven-year spurt of film-making in 1968. For all their qualities, the films of this period are unattractive in general terms, peopled by unpleasant or unapproachable characters. Having said that, let us add that *Last Summer* is a disturbing, even horrifying picture of adolescent violence lurking beneath the sunniest of skins; *Rancho De Luxe* a black and bitter look at the disintegration of the modern west, masquerading as a zany comedy, and the rarely seen *Play It As It Lays* a stark portrait of psychic breakdown in the life of a Hollywood actress, far too downbeat for general consumption, despite yet another acting *tour-de-force* from Tuesday Weld and disturbingly good support from Anthony Perkins, her companion-in-nightmare from *Pretty Poison*. After the mid-1970s, Perry, married to another writer, Barbara Goldsmith, turned with renewed vigour to the theatre and television. He found time, though, to make a few typically individual movies, notably the quirky comedy-thriller *Compromising Positions*. His 1992 documentary *On the Bridge* seemed a summation both of his life and his career.

1962: David and Lisa. 1963: Ladybug, Ladybug. 1968: The Swimmer (completed by Sydney Pollack: qv). 1969: Trilogy. Last Summer. 1970: Diary of a Mad Housewife. Doc. 1972: Play It As It Lays. 1974: Man on a Swing. Rancho DeLuxe. 1979: Dummy (TV). 1980: Skag/The Wildcatters (TV). 1981: Mommie Dearest. 1982: Monsignor. 1985: Compromising Positions. 1987: Hello Again. 1992: On the Bridge (D).

PETERSEN, Wolfgang 1941-

Since his international success with *Das Boot*, this German director has settled for

shortened version was shown in some countries and Petersen later released his own 'director's cut' of the film. He stayed based in Germany for a successful screen adaptation of Michael Ende's children's classic *The NeverEnding Story*, full of deadly swamplands, spooky woods and wondrous special effects, and for more fantasy of the science-fiction variety with the partially successful *Enemy Mine*. By the 1990s, Petersen had moved full-time to America, but his first film, *Shattered*, a long-cherished project, lacked the intricacy to make it a top shock thriller and, despite an all-star cast, proved a major disappointment. Petersen, though, soon put his Hollywood career back on course with *In the Line of Fire*, a solid thriller and perhaps his best American film, *Outbreak*, a hi-tech, high-velocity if jingoistic plague thriller which included a nerve-shredding dogfight between helicopters. There was more exciting action in *Air Force One*, but it was undercut by foolish plotting. Petersen may need to root his next film deeper into reality to keep his name to the fore.

1970: I Will Kill You (TV). 1973: Einer von uns beiden/One of Us Two. 1975: Smog (TV). 1976: Reifgezeugnis (TV. Re-copyrighted in 1982 and issued to cinemas as For Your Love Only). Vier gegen die Blank! Short Circuit. 1977: Die Konsequenz/The Consequence. Planubung. 1978: Schwarz und weiss wie Tage und Nächte/Black and White Like Day and Night. 1981: Das Boot/The Boat. 1984: The NeverEnding Story. 1985: Enemy Mine. 1991: Shattered. 1993: In the Line of Fire. 1995: Outbreak. 1997: Air Force One.

PETRIE, Daniel 1920-

A late starter to directing, Nova Scotia-born Petrie produced unexceptional cinema work, but has an ability to enhance attractive star performances. In the field of TV movies, however, he gradually acquired stature, sufficient at least for him to continue directing for the cinema until well into the 1980s. An actor until the 1950s, Petrie directed his first film in 1959, but swiftly showed a tendency to go over the top, failing rather badly with some interesting projects, although *Stolen Hours* is a pretty fair remake of *Dark Victory*, considering the heyday of such films had long passed, with Susan Hayward every bit as good as Bette Davis in the original role. It was perhaps the first sign of Petrie's talent to extract strong performances from his female stars, above and beyond their material. The theory was just about exploded by Jennifer Jones in *The*

One of the few modern German directors to make a successful transition to Hollywood is Wolfgang **Petersen.**

a profitable Hollywood career in action and adventure films with such major stars as Harrison Ford, Dustin Hoffman and Clint Eastwood. In his earlier years, however, Petersen had produced a very wide-ranging collection of films; fantasies, crime stories and social dramas among them. In all of these, he proved himself capable of crafting and editing his work to make the maximum impact. He had begun his career as an assistant stage manager with a Hamburg theatre company, but at 20 had already directed his first

play. Deciding on a sideways step, he studied at the Berlin Film and TV Academy for four years, and had begun directing dramas for television by 1970. Films followed in 1973 and Petersen was about to try his luck in Hollywood towards the end of the 1970s when he was offered *Das Boot*. This remarkable study of stress in war aboard a German submarine, marked by its suspense and intensity, won prizes all over the world and gained Petersen Oscar nominations both for direction and screenplay. A somewhat

Not many film directors can claim to hail from Nova Scotia. An exception is Daniel **Petrie,** seen here while shooting *Resurrection* in 1980.

Lonely Night (TV). 1971: The City (TV). A Howling in the Woods (TV). 1972: Moon of the Wolf (TV). Hec Ramsey/The Century Turns (TV). 1973: Trouble Comes to Town (TV). The Neptune Factor. 1974: Mousey (TV. GB: cinemas as Cat and Mouse). The Gun and the Pulpit (TV). Buster and Billie. 1975: Returning Home (TV). 1976: Lifeguard. Eleanor and Franklin (TV). Sybil (TV. GB: cinemas). 1977: The Quinns (TV). Eleanor and Franklin: the White House Years (TV). 1978: The Betsy. 1980: Resurrection. 1981: Fort Apache the Bronx. 1982: Six Pack. 1984: The Bay Boy. The Dollmaker (TV). 1985: The Execution of Raymond Graham (TV). 1986: Square Dance. 1988: Cocoon The Return. Rocket Gibraltar. 1989: My Name is Bill W (TV). 1991: Mark Twain and Me (TV). 1994: Lassie. 1995: Kissinger and Nixon (TV). 1996: Calm at Sunset (TV). 1997: The Assistant.

PEVNEY, Joseph 1920-

In 50 years in show business, over 40 of them as a director, New York-born Pevney racked up an impressively long list of credits. There was rarely a year from 1950 to 1980 when he wasn't working on several films, or numerous episodes of television series. His movies are mostly run-of-the-mill co-features, although he did move on to more important assignments towards the end of the 1950s, when he made his most lavish and best film, *Man of a Thousand Faces*. From a theatrical family, Pevney had his own song-and-dance act in vaudeville at 13 and was directing shows by the time he was 22. After army service in World War II, Pevney headed for Hollywood, at first as an actor (first film: *Nocturne*, 1946), but from 1950 as a director under contract to Universal. He began quite well: *Shakedown*, with a typical double-shaded performance from Howard Duff, and *Undercover Girl*, with Alexis Smith, are both watchable thrillers with intelligent use of a mobile camera and some good low angles. Pevney's next film was one of his most popular, the boxing picture *Iron Man*, with Jeff Chandler in the title role and the young Rock Hudson as one of his opponents in some good fight sequences. From then on, however, Pevney hits his worst period. It's surprising he still found work after such woefully weak vehicles as *Meet Danny Wilson*, *The Strange Door*, *Just Across the Street*, *Playgirl*, *Congo Crossing* and *Istanbul*. Thanks to Debbie Reynolds and a tuneful theme, he did have a big hit with *Tammy and the Bachelor*. And *Yankee Pasha* was exciting, colourful hokum. Restored to the crime genre in *The Midnight Story*,

Idol, but it began to work again once Petrie got his teeth into television, a medium for which he started working seriously in 1963. His edgy, actor-focused style here seems to encourage forceful performances from the ladies, while his actors tend to underplay their roles, often to quite good effect. Thus Shirley Jones in *Silent Night, Lonely Night*, Barbara Eden in *A Howling in the Woods*, Barbara Rush in *Moon of the Wolf* – very effective fun spine-chillers these last two – Joanne Woodward and Sally Field in *Sybil* and especially the fine Jane Alexander in the two Roosevelt films all catch the eye, while such actors as Lloyd Bridges, David Janssen and Edward Herrmann give self-effacing support. Encouraged by the critical reception of *Lifeguard* – another extremely effective female performance, here, by Kathleen

Quinlan – Petrie returned to the cinema. *The Betsy* was beastly, as disastrously overplayed as some of Petrie's earlier films, with only the admirable Miss Alexander shoring up the collapse. But Petrie has continued to try without producing anything as individual *(Fort Apache the Bronx* is the quintessence of every tough police movie you ever saw) as such TV movies as *Trouble Comes to Town, Eleanor and Franklin, The Gun and the Pulpit* and *My Name is Bill W*. His two sons, Donald (*Grumpy Old Men; Richie Rich*) and Daniel Jr (*In the Army Now; Toy Soldiers*) are also film directors.

1959: The Bramble Bush. 1961: A Raisin in the Sun. 1962: The Main Attraction. 1963: Stolen Hours. 1966: The Idol. The Spy with a Cold Nose. 1969: Silent Night,

Pevney did enough to be handed the Lon Chaney biopic, *Man of a Thousand Faces*. Even if the Cagney in James Cagney tends to come through, this is a very good movie, and Pevney got powerful performances from Dorothy Malone and Jane Greer, achieving an authentic whiff-of-greasepaint atmosphere with the help of some skilled black-and-white photography by Russell Metty, soon to become better known for his colour work. The best of the Pevney films that followed are *The Plunderers*, an edgy western with strong emotional appeal, again with Jeff Chandler, and *Portrait of a Mobster*, a continuation of Warners' short gangster cycle of the time, well-suited to Pevney's by-now bleak monochrome style. By this time, though, he was well entrenched in TV, on such series as *Wagon Train*, *The Big Valley*, *Alfred Hitchcock Presents*, *Star Trek*, *Marcus Welby*, *Petrocelli* and many, many others. Pevney was married to the former child star Mitzi Green from 1942 until her death from cancer at 48 in 1969.

1950: Shakedown. Undercover Girl. 1951: Iron Man. The Lady from Texas. The Strange Door. Meet Danny Wilson. Air Cadet (GB: Jet Men of the Air). Flesh and Fury. 1952: Just Across the Street. Because of You. 1953: It Happens Every Thursday. Desert Legion. Back to God's Country. 1954: Playgirl. Yankee Pasha. Three Ring Circus. 1955: Female on the Beach. Foxfire. Six Bridges to Cross. 1956: Away All Boats. Congo Crossing. 1957: Istanbul. Tammy and the Bachelor (GB: Tammy). The Midnight Story (GB: Appointment with a Shadow). Man of a Thousand Faces. 1958: Twilight for the Gods. Torpedo Run. 1959: Cash McCall. 1960: The Plunderers. The Crowded Sky. 1961: Portrait of a Mobster. 1966: Night of the Grizzly. 1973: My Darling Daughters' Anniversary (TV). 1975: Who is the Black Dahlia? 1977: The Cadaver in the Clutter (TV). 1979: Island of Sister Teresa/Mysterious Island of Beautiful Women (TV). 1984: Contract for Life: The S.A.D.D. Story (TV). 1985: Prisoners of the Sea.

PICHEL, Irving 1891-1954

A heavy, glowering man, Pennsylvania-born Pichel was in fact a gentle, serious-minded soul whose best work was concerned with old people, children, fantasy, laughter and tears. If it produced the desired emotional reaction in an audience, one would imagine that Pichel was pleased. He had begun in show business as an actor on the stage, and continued acting off and on, eventually in his own

films, until his death. He came to Hollywood with sound as a character actor of some weight, although he had already been there in the late 1920s, working as a scriptwriter for M-G-M. From his acting career, one remembers best his Fagin in the 1933 *Oliver Twist*, and his scowling heavy in *Dracula's Daughter*. By this time his directorial career was well established, if not yet at its height. He had started auspiciously, co-directing those favourite late-night TV fantasies, *The Most Dangerous Game* and *She*. But his other assignments remained minor, and only after he gave up acting for some years from 1940 did his career as a director enter an Indian summer between 1942 and 1947. There were two big-budget laughter-and-tears vehicles for Monty Woolley, three associations with the very young Natalie Wood, who recalled being fond of Pichel because he bought her lollipops, *Colonel Effingham's Raid*, a good comedy-drama vehicle for Charles Coburn who takes full advantage, and the massive tear-jerker *Tomorrow is Forever*, which has Orson Welles coming back from the dead to discover that his wife (Claudette Colbert) has married another. There was also a very tense and moving resistance drama, *The Moon is Down*, from Steinbeck's story: one of the best of its kind, it seemed wholly authentic at the time with the help of a cast of star character actors, including Cedric Hardwicke, Henry Travers and Lee J. Cobb, who aided one to identify with the people they played. Pichel veered away from sentiment with an extremely exciting Alan Ladd thriller *OSS* and an atmospheric but melodramatic piece called *They Won't Believe Me* (and you couldn't believe it when Robert Young managed to get to the courtroom window and throw himself out just before the jury brings in a verdict of Not Guilty). After the disaster of *The Miracle of the Bells*, Pichel tackled smaller assignments, one of which, *Destination Moon*, turned out to be an unexpected box-office success. But he retired from the commercial cinema at 60, and only returned to make a couple of religion-slanted films, before succumbing to a heart attack a few days after his 63rd birthday.

1932: †The Most Dangerous Game (GB: The Hounds of Zaroff). 1933: Before Dawn. 1935: †She. 1936: The Gentleman from Louisiana. Beware of Ladies. 1937: Larceny on the Air. The Duke Comes Back (GB: The Call of the Ring). The Sheik Steps Out. 1939: The Great Commandment (released 1941). 1940: Earthbound. The Man I Married. Hudson's Bay. 1941: Dance Hall. 1942: Secret

Agent of Japan. The Pied Piper. Life Begins at 8.30 (GB: The Light of HEart). The Moon is Down. 1943: Happy Land. 1944: And Now Tomorrow. 1945: Colonel Effingham's Raid (GB: The Man of the Hour). A Medal for Benny. Tomorrow is Forever. 1946: OSS. The Bride Wore Boots. Temptation. 1947: They Won't Believe Me. Something in the Wind. 1948: The Miracle of the Bells. Mr Peabody and the Mermaid. 1949: Without Honor. 1950: The Great Rupert. Quicksand. Destination Moon. 1951: Santa Fé. 1953: Martin Luther. 1954: Day of Triumph.

POLANSKI, Roman 1933-

People living on the ragged edge — or forced to live on it: this Polish (French-born) director's films are concerned with pressures, alienation and a succumbing to the evil nightmares lurking within us. There is a maniacal, macabre feeling about his early shorts, even those intended to make us laugh. One senses a bitterness in Polanski that the beauty of the images he often creates on screen can't gloss over. Polanski himself is no stranger to alienation and fear: his parents were interned in concentration camps during the war and he wandered the countryside hiding from German soldiers. After apprenticeship at the famous Lodz film school, Polanski made the first of several striking black-and-white features, *Knife in the Water*. He went to Britain to make *Repulsion*, a study of mental disintegration that is full of haunting if often derivative images, and *Cul-de-Sac*, a bizarre oddity that is derivative of nothing, unless it be the nihilistic work of certain contemporary English playwrights. Polanski had great success around the world with his first Hollywood film, *Rosemary's Baby*, a malevolent horror comic about the circumstances leading up to the birth of the Devil's child, with memorable performances from Mia Farrow, Sidney Blackmer and Ruth Gordon. His attempts to raise ghoulish giggles were less successful — the horror comedy *Dance of the Vampires* was simply too scary to be funny, and the sex comedy *What!* not zany enough to avoid tedium. His *Macbeth* is merely a rush of excesses to the head, but *Chinatown* is altogether more interesting, a fascinating puzzle film of the kind that Hollywood used to make, except that in this case the detective (Jack Nicholson), never looks really likely to come out on top. In 1969, Polanski hit the headlines when his pregnant wife, actress Sharon Tate, was murdered by the Manson gang. Eight years later, he was again news in, if possible,

Roman **Polanski** looks set to call for a charge as he organises a street chase sequence of his 1987 thriller *Frantic*.

even less pleasant circumstances, when he was accused of drugging and raping a 13-year-old girl. Polanski left America and has not returned, although he received a cautious welcome back into the film fold after the critical praise for *Tess*, a long and beautiful, if tiring film based on Hardy's classic *Tess of the D'Urbervilles*. This film, again, was about a character out on her own. Polanski brings home only too well his theme, which he has followed through life, that if you don't help yourself no-one else is likely to do it for you. Polanski married the French actress Emmanuelle Seigner in 1989. She had first starred for him in *Frantic*, and would go on to a key role in his disastrous *Bitter Moon*, reminiscent of his previous work, but with none of its conviction. Since then he has been unlucky with unrealised projects, and made a poor screen version of the stage success *Death and the Maiden*.

1957: *Rower/The Bicycle* (unfinished). 1958: **Morderstwo. *Rozbijemy Zabawe. *Lampa. *Two Men and a Wardrobe.* 1959: **Gdy Spadaja Anioly.* 1960: **Le gras et le maigre (US: The Fat and the Lean).* 1962: **Ssaki/Mammals. Knife in the Water.* 1963: *†Les plus belles escroqueries du monde (US: The Beautiful Swindlers).* 1965: *Repulsion.* 1966: *Cul-de-Sac.* 1967: *Dance of the Vampires (US: The Fearless Vampire Killers or Pardon Me But Your Teeth Are in My Neck).* 1968: *Rosemary's Baby.* 1971: *Macbeth.* 1973: *What!* 1974: *Chinatown.* 1976: *The Tenant.* 1979: *Tess.* 1985: *Pirates.* 1987: *Frantic.* 1992: *Bitter Moon.* 1994: *Death and the Maiden.* 1999: *The Ninth Gate.*

POLLACK, Sydney 1934-

This American director has usually made interesting and sometimes slightly offbeat star vehicles, notably for Burt Lancaster

and Robert Redford, although sometimes they lack that bite which would take them into the very top class. *The Scalphunters* is his most uninhibited and therefore most enjoyable film. Otherwise he seems to hold back just a little — perhaps the overwhelming influence of those big star personalities. On the other hand, there are few failures in Pollack's record, and he took an Academy Award for *Out of Africa*, following two unsuccessful nominations, for *They Shoot Horses, Don't They?* and *Tootsie*. Like so many directors of his generation, Pollack began as an actor. He had a star role in the film *War Hunt*, and so the association with Redford began. In the same year (1962), Pollack began to direct for television, at first on *Ben Casey*, a series in which he made more than a dozen appearances as an actor, then on single plays in such series as Kraft Suspense Theatre, Alfred Hitchcock Hour and Bob Hope Chrysler Theatre. His first film, *The Slender Thread*, attracted some praise, although it is not really sustained by its thin central situation, despite anguished and sincere performances from Anne Bancroft and Sidney Poitier as suicide and Samaritan on opposite ends of a telephone — better as a radio play, perhaps, with the participants unseen. Pollack has steered clear of interior dramas since then, and has concentrated notably on the quality of the colour work and the images it can produce, from *This Property is Condemned* (James Wong Howe) onwards. Thanks to the performances of Robert Redford and a glowing Natalie Wood, this adaptation of a Tennessee Williams play remains credible for much of its length, although Pollack cannot control the melodrama towards the end, which seems impossibly contrived. He was more successful with *They Shoot Horses, Don't They?* a roller-derby marathon (in all senses) that won its director an Oscar nomination. He combined well again with Redford on the mountain-man drama *Jeremiah Johnson;* and the political thriller *Three Days of the Condor,* but the Redford-Streisand 'chemistry' didn't begin to work in the languorous *The Way We Were.* However, the Pollack-Redford combination finally hit the jackpot with *The Electric Horseman,* in which Redford plays a has-been rodeo champion reduced to being on-air spokesman for a breakfast cereal, until he rides his horse out into the desert and freedom. The encounters between the rider and a newsgirl (Fonda) hot on his trail, and their subsequent adventure, provide under Pollack's careful handling the touching core of the film. More recently, he has had hefty box-office hits with *Tootsie* and with the Tom Cruise vehicle *The Firm.* Pollack has also renewed interest in his acting career, most notably with a leading role in Stanley Kubrick's long-in-the-making *Eyes Wide Shut.*

1965: The Slender Thread. 1966: This Property is Condemned. 1968: †The Swimmer (uncredited). The Scalphunters. 1969: Castle Keep. They Shoot Horses, Don't They? 1972: Jeremiah Johnson. 1973: The Way We Were. 1974: The Yakuza. 1975: Three Days of the Condor. 1977: Bobby Deerfield. 1979: The Electric Horseman. 1981: Absence of Malice. 1982: Tootsie. 1985: Out of Africa. 1990: Havana. 1993: The Firm. 1995: Sabrina. 1999: Random Hearts.

POLLOCK, George 1907-

For a few brief years, Pollock restored to the British cinemagoing public a world of spinster detectives, chintzy teas, dire deeds at the vicarage, shadows in the barn, even jolly jinks at the health resort, such as they hadn't seen since the 1930s — and made them love it. Although most of his films were comedies, some broader than others, this British director is chiefly remembered for his 'Miss Marple' detective comedy-thrillers, and here he had an admirable ally in the querulous, beady-eyed, multi-chinned form of Margaret Rutherford. Nothing like Agatha Christie's original conception of Jane Marple, she quickly made the part her own. The films themselves were exactly like light 'quota quickie' whodunnits of the 1930s, but done with more polish and professionalism, cunningly crafted by their director to celebrate the most-loved values of their time — and they had Dame Margaret. An assistant director since the early 1930s, Pollock only began to direct at 50. There was just an engaging comedy about an Irish dustman, *Rooney,* on the credit side before he discovered Miss Marple in 1961. In between her adventures, Pollock made a couple of comedies with Eric Sykes, one of which, *Kill or Cure,* is in much the same dated but entertaining vein as the Marple films. The Rutherford films came to an end with *Murder Ahoy!,* made in 1964, but released late in 1965 to space the series out; in it Dame Margaret assures the villain before the final spirited sword-duel: 'It won't be easy, you know: I was Roedean ladies' fencing champion of 1931!' After the failure of his next film, another Christie, *10 Little Indians,* Pollock, his niche in British screen history assured, wisely retired.

1957: Stranger in Town. Rooney. 1958: Sally's Irish Rogue (US: The Poacher's Daughter). 1959: A Broth of a Boy. Don't Panic Chaps! 1960: And the Same to You. 1961: Village of Daughters. Murder She Said. 1962: Kill or Cure. 1963: Murder at the Gallop. 1964: Murder Most Foul. Murder Ahoy! 1965: 10 Little Indians.

POST, Ted 1918-

It probably says something of the grinding routine of Ted Post's cinema work that his best film is still a little black-and-white western he made in 1959 called *The Legend of Tom Dooley,* virtually the only time Post's direction created people one cared about. Otherwise, he has directed Clint Eastwood many times. The impersonal nature of many of Eastwood's performances is matched only by his director's style. Post had in fact been directing for television since 1950, one of its earliest recruits. He started working on Eastwood's TV western series, *Rawhide,* in 1958, and directed 20 hour-long segments of it over the next six years. When Eastwood returned to America in 1967 draped in spaghetti stardom,

he called for Post, who dutifully made *Hang 'Em High,* in its style, as an American imitation of the Leone 'Dollars' films. There are one or two quite good things in Post's career before Eastwood called him back to make the second 'Dirty Harry' film, *Magnum Force,* in 1973. *Beneath the Planet of the Apes,* an underrated sequel, is more exciting than *Planet of the Apes* itself; *Dr Cook's Garden,* for television, casts Bing Crosby to quirky advantage in a horror plot; *Do Not Fold, Spindle or Mutilate* is an enjoyable matching of veteran talents, although Post allows Helen Hayes and Mildred Natwick to hog too much of the limelight at the expense of Myrna Loy and Sylvia Sidney; and *The Baby* is a shocker so sick as to be quite enjoyable. There isn't much more to add except that the man has shot an awful lot of film, and most of it hits you over the head to make sure you know it's there. After a series of unwelcome films in the 1970s, he did make *Cagney anal Lacy,* a crisp TV movie, bolstered by the personalities of Loretta Swit and Tyne Daly as two tough lady cops, which led to the famous series.

1956: The Peacemaker. 1959: The Legend of Tom Dooley. 1967: Hang 'Em High. 1969: Beneath the Planet of the Apes. 1970: Night Slaves (TV). Dr Cook's Garden (TV). 1971: Yuma (TV). Five Desperate Women (TV). Do Not Fold, Spindle or Mutilate (TV). 1972: The Bravos (TV). Sandcastles (TV). The Baby. 1973: The Harrad Experiment. Magnum Force. 1975: Whiffs (GB: C.A.S.H.). Columbo: A Matter of Honor (TV). Columbo: A Case of Immunity (TV). 1977: Good Guys Wear Black. Go Tell the Spartans. 1978: Diary of a Teenage Hitchhiker (TV). 1979: The Girls in the Office (TV). 1980: NightKill. 1981: Cagney and Lacey (TV). 1986: Stagecoach (TV). 1991: The Human Shield. 1996: Love Found.

POTTER, H.C. 1904-1977

New York-born 'Hank' Potter was primarily a man of the theatre, but filmgoers will, for the most part, be grateful that he managed to get in enough visits to Hollywood to make 20 films there between 1936 and 1957. Potter worked for most of the major studios, but seems to have been happiest at RKO Radio and Universal, where he made some of his most delightful comedies. Not coming to Hollywood with the advent of sound like many of his Broadway colleagues, Potter was eventually tempted into the film fold by Samuel Goldwyn's offer to direct *Beloved Enemy,* an Irish 'troubles' melodrama set in the early 1920s. He wandered around making two or three light films for other studios, but there was nothing memorable until his tear-drenched remake of *Shopworn Angel*, with Margaret Sullavan and James Stewart, proved just the thing for pre-war audiences, and boosted his rating. The softness of his images and lightness of his touch brought him to a stylish musical tearjerker, *The Story of Vernon and Irene Castle*, second-rate perhaps by Astaire and Rogers standards (they played real-life dancers and film stars: Vernon was killed in a plane crash in 1918) but first-class entertainment by anyone else's, with direction by Potter that makes the final reel true four-handkerchief stuff. After a second Astaire musical, *Second Chorus*, a minor Edward G. Robinson vehicle, *Blackmail,* and one of the Maisie comedies for M-G-M, Potter popped across to Universal for the film version of the crazy stage revue *Hellzapoppin'*. The studio wasn't willing to take a chance in putting all the heady chaos of the original on film, so the picture proved to be a rather watered-down version of Olsen and Johnson's stage riot. Even so, directed by Potter at a fine pace, it was still a barrel-load of laughs. Potter then returned to the stage for several years; he was not asked to direct the film version of his stage smash *A Bell for Adano*, but Hollywood, in the shape of RKO Radio, did recall him in 1947, firstly for the delightful *The Farmer's Daughter*, for which Loretta Young unexpectedly won an Academy Award, and then for his best film, *Mr Blandings Builds His Dream House*. This enchanting, sophisticated comedy has Cary Grant teamed with Myrna Loy as a city couple getting rooked left, right and centre by country folk — one of several marvellously funny films Grant made in the late 1940s, all for different directors. Potter made just a few more Hollywood films – *The Time of Your Life* is a fascinating oddity that bears re-viewing – before returning to stage work for good. The H and C stood for Henry Codman.

1936: Beloved Enemy. 1937: Wings over Honolulu. 1938: The Cowboy and the Lady. Romance in the Dark. Shopworn Angel. 1939: Blackmail. The Story of Vernon and Irene Castle. 1940: Second Chorus. Congo Maisie. 1941: Hellzapoppin'. 1943: Victory Through Air Power. Mr Lucky. 1947: The Farmer's Daughter. A Likely Story. 1948: Mr Blandings Builds his Dream House. The Time of Your Life. You Gotta Stay Happy. 1950: The Miniver Story. 1955: Three for the Show. 1957: Top Secret Affair (GB: Their Secret Affair).

POWELL, Michael 1905-1990

Highly individual British film-maker, responsible for some bizarre but beautiful entertainments over 44 years as a director, many of them showing remarkable use of colour. His films are intrinsically British, yet almost all of them tinged by the desire to do something different. Thus some of his work is refreshing, some exciting, some demanding and some stimulating. When some of these qualities meet, as in *A Matter of Life and Death*, *Black Narcissus* or *Peeping Tom*, he comes close, with his sense of opulent visual beauty, to creating a masterpiece that refuses pigeonholing into any particular genre. Powell was born and educated in the Kent city of Canterbury that was to form the backcloth to his talkative and rather too highbrow *A Canterbury Tale*. Tiring of his first job (in a bank), Powell obtained a job at the Nice studio of director Rex Ingram. By 1930, he had already worked as stills photographer, cameraman, cutter, editor, continuity man, actor, screenwriter and assistant director. The following year, he was hired in England to make 'quota quickies' – second-feature comedies and thrillers lasting an hour or less – and immediately, in *Two Crowded Hours* and *Rynox*, showed himself to be a man of invention and promise. He had to direct 24 of these films in six years before getting to make a film of his own choice. This proved to be *The Edge of the World*, a Grierson-like documentary set on the remote Scottish island of Foula. He met his long-time associate, the Hungarian Emeric Pressburger (1902-1988) when the latter was hired to write the screenplay of *The Spy in Black*. Powell was in full partnership with Pressburger from 1941, as a writer-producer-director team known as 'The Archers'. They made a series of films that either delighted or enraged critics, and had a similar mixed reception from the public. But *A Matter of Life and Death*, an enthralling and gripping fantasy about a fight for life between Heaven and Earth, *The Life and Death of Colonel Blimp*, with Roger Livesey – so good in *Life and Death* – as a bumbling war hero seen through 40 years of his life, and *Black Narcissus*, about a group of missionary nuns driven to extremes in the inhospitable Himalayas, were quirky, fascinating films, richly observed in colour (with Jack Cardiff ultimately winning an Oscar for the last of them). Powell's ballet and opera films are also strikingly coloured and *The Red Shoes*, featuring yet another in Powell's long line of red-headed heroines in Moira Shearer, has the most entertaining ballet sequence ever put on film. *Contraband, The Spy in*

Black, I Know Where I'm Going! and *The Small Back Room*, which contains a vivid hallucination sequence, are the best of Powell's black-and-whites, which often made effective use of wild parts of the British coastline. Later came *Peeping Tom*, Powell's most controversial film of all, about a photographer-killer who films his victims' death agonies as he transfixes them with a pointed tripod. Much reviled for its sadism, it seemed to me as an 18-year-old filmgoer just a rattling good nightmare thriller.

1931: Two Crowded Hours. Rynox. My Friend the King. The Rasp. The Star Reporter. 1932: Hotel Splendide. C.O.D. His Lordship. Born Lucky. 1933: The Fire Raisers. Red Ensign (US: Strike!). 1934: Something Always Happens. The Night of the Party (US: The Murder Party). The Girl in the Crowd. 1935: Lazybones. The Love Test. The Phantom Light. The Price of a Song. Some Day. 1936: Crown Vs. Stevens. The Man Behind the Mask. Her Last Affaire. The Brown Wallet. 1937: The Edge of the World. 1939: The Spy in Black (US: U-Boat 29). †The Lion has Wings. 1940: †The Thief of Bagdad. Contraband (US: Blackout). 1941: *An Airman's Letter to His Mother. 49th Parallel (US: The Invaders). 1942: †One of Our Aircraft is Missing. 1943: †The Volunteer. †The Silver Fleet. †The Life and Death of Colonel Blimp (US: Colonel Blimp). 1944: †A Canterbury Tale. 1945: †I Know Where I'm Going! 1946: †A Matter of Life and Death (US: Stairway to Heaven). †Black Narcissus. 1948: †The Red Shoes. 1949: The Small Back Room (US: Hour of Glory). 1950: †Gone to Earth (US: revised as The Wild Heart). †The Elusive Pimpernel (US: The Fighting Pimpernel). 1951: The Tales of Hoffman. 1955: †Oh Rosalinda! *†The Sorcerer's Apprentice. 1956: †The Battle of the River Plate (US: Pursuit of the Graf Spee). †Ill Met by Moonlight (US: Night Ambush). 1958: Honeymoon (released 1961). 1960: Peeping Tom. The Queen's Guards. 1964: Bluebeard's Castle. 1966: They're a Weird Mob. 1969: Age of Consent. 1972: The Boy Who Turned Yellow. 1974: Trikimia. 1978: Return to the Edge of the World.

PREMINGER, Otto 1905-1986

The post-1956 failures of this individualistic Austrian director, in Hollywood since 1935, were a source of great sadness to his followers who, used to his many ups and downs in an unpredictable career, were unprepared for so many downs in a row. Many critics have looked for themes

Otto **Preminger** gives Dorothy Dandridge her marching orders on the set of his trail-blazing all-black musical *Carmen Jones.*

said to have held up his directing career which only got away later while Zanuck was away on war service. Apart from *Laura*, these early films are fairly innocuous, but Preminger hit a good period from 1950 on, making *Whirlpool*, *Where the Sidewalk Ends*, *The Thirteenth Letter*, *Angel Face*, *River of No Return*, *Carmen Jones* and *The Man With the Golden Arm*; a commendable variety of highly coloured films, mostly for Fox, in many of which women are threatening or being threatened. In this period, he also gave his best-remembered acting performance (he had started as an actor, under Max Reinhardt, in Vienna), as the camp commandant in *Stalag 17*. The films hereafter are less even in quality, and strangely it is the black-and-whites which are usually best: *Anatomy of a Murder*, *Advise and Consent* (both cunningly crafted, long films, with several good performances in each case keeping the audience on tenterhooks), *Bunny Lake is Missing* (dingy photography here helping splendid cameos from Noel Coward and Martita Hunt) and, to a lesser extent, *In Harm's Way*. Although I found the zany *Skidoo* funnier than most people, there is no doubt that most of the remaining Preminger films are dismal and often stodgily acted. Three times married; the writer-producer Eric Lee Preminger is his son from an extra-marital relationship with the actress-stripper Gypsy Rose Lee.

1931: Der grosse Liebe. 1936: Under Your Spell. 1937: Danger — Love at Work. 1938: †Kidnapped (uncredited). 1943: Margin for Error. 1944: In the Meantime, Darling. Laura. 1945: A Royal Scandal (GB: Czarina). Fallen Angel. 1946: Centennial Summer. 1947: Forever Amber. Daisy Kenyon. 1948: †That Lady in Ermine (uncredited). 1949: The Fan (GB: Lady I Windemere's Fan). Whirlpool. 1950: Where the Sidewalk Ends. 1951: The Thirteenth Letter. 1952: Angel Face. 1953: The Moon is Blue. 1954: River of No Return. Carmen Jones. 1955: The Court-Martial of Billy Mitchell (GB: One-Man Mutiny). The Man With the Golden Arm. 1957: Saint Joan. 1958: Bonjour Tristesse. 1959: Porgy and Bess. Anatomy of a Murder. 1960: Exodus. 1962: Advise and Consent. 1963: The Cardinal. 1965: In Harm's Way. Bunny Lake is Missing. 1967: Hurry Sundown. 1968: Skidoo! 1969: Tell Me That You Love Me Junie Moon. 1971: Such Good Friends. 1975: Rosebud. 1979: The Human Factor.

in Preminger's work, but they are not easy to discern. Certainly, there are more than a few *femmes fatales*, a ready talent with darkly photographed *films noirs*, and an enviable facility for handling long jigsaw-puzzle pictures with tight and telling scripts. But Preminger has always been ready to tackle anything if needs be, and perhaps this brought about his downfall in the end. From 1944 to 1965, however,

there is a long series of compelling, sometimes enigmatic performances from his leading actresses, from Gene Tierney in *Laura* in 1944 to Carol Lynley in Preminger's last good film, *Bunny Lake is Missing* in 1965. He came to America to direct a play after making one film in Germany, and shortly afterwards became involved with Twentieth Century-Fox. Here disputes with Darryl F. Zanuck are

PRESSBURGER, Emeric
See Powell, Michael

PUDOVKIN, V. 1893-1953

The Russian Vsevolod Pudoykin was more of a theorist than a film-maker, a montage expert whose juggling of short scenes to produce various responses from the audience is a shade too emotionless. As much a blueprint director as Hitchcock or Ozu (both *qv*), Pudovkin, like Ozu, often used amateur actors. His visual effects, though expertly conveying such emotions as anguish and despair, are rather calculated compared with those of other Russian directors of the period, who seem to put more of their heart and soul into what are often historical passing parades. All the same, Pudovkin did make some very effective films, whose visuals still linger — notably *Storm Over Asia, The End of St Petersburg* and *Mother.* Pudovkin, following horrific experiences in World War I, when he was wounded and interned by the Germans from 1915, only escaping three years later, settled down in 1922 at the film workshop run by Lev Kuleshov (1899-1970), the father of the Soviet montage school, and proved his finest pupil. Directing in earnest from 1925, Pudovkin's eye for effect and his methodical approach soon brought him to the front rank of film directors. In 1934 he was badly injured in a car accident that killed his scriptwriter and long-time collaborator Nathan Zarkhi — it was four years before he was able to make another film. One senses a certain muffling of his later work by Soviet authorities, and one of his films, *Admiral Nakhimov,* was held up for well over a year. He wrote three instructional books: *Film Acting, Film Technique,* and *The Actor's Art in Film and Stanislavsky's 'Method'.*

1921: †*Golod... Golod... Golod.../Hunger... Hunger... Hunger (D).* 1925: †*Shakmatnaia Goriatchka/Chess Fever.* 1926: *Mat/Mother. Mekhanika Golovnogo Mozga/The Mechanics of the Brain (D).* 1927: *Konets Sankt Peterburga/The End of St Petersburg.* 1928: *Potomok Chingis-Khana/Storm Over Asia.* 1931: *Prosto Shuchai/A Simple Case.* 1933: *Dezerter/Deserter.* 1938: †*Pobeda/Victory.* 1939: †*Minin and Pozharsky.* 1940: *Twenty Years of Soviet Cinema (D).* 1941: *Suvorov/General Suvorov.* †*Pir v Zhirmunka/Feast at Zhirmunka (D).* 1942: †*Ubiitsy Vykhodyat no Dorogu/The Murderers Are Coming.* 1943: †*Volnya Rodini/In the Name of the Fatherland.* 1946: †*Admiral Nakhimov.* 1948: †*Tri Vstrechi/Three Encounters.* 1950: *Zhukovsky.* 1953: *Vozraschenie Vasilicia Bortnikova/The Return of Vasili Bortnikov.*

QUINE, Richard 1921-1989

What put the decline in Quine? This Detroit-born ex-actor's films were never great, but throughout the l950s they were light, bright, enjoyable and fun to be with. One could guarantee the company of any or several of Billy Daniels, Mickey Rooney, Jack Lemmon, Kim Novak, Judy Holliday and Ernie Kovacs, as Quine wheeled away at Columbia on happy-go-lucky musicals, zany comedies and even a couple of pacy, brooding thrillers in *Pushover* and *Drive a Crooked Road.* These were entertaining, solidly crafted films destined mainly for the top halves of double bills. Then along came Suzie Wong. After that, *The Notorious Landlady* (a return to Novak and Lemmon) and *Sex and the Single Girl* hold up the slide with some delightful sequences, but the rest is dull and very disappointing, although in 1978 Quine did raise a few more laughs with his Peter Sellers version of *The Prisoner of Zenda,* thanks to the welcome return of a touch of the zanies. The critics, however, hated it. The son of an actor, Quine made his screen debut as a child player in l932's *The World Changes.* Ten years later, while makinig *Tish,* he met and married actress Susan Peters, but she was paralysed from the waist down after a hunting accident in 1944 and they divorced in 1948. That was the year Quine began to turn towards direction, making his last appearance as an actor in 1950. Many of his early films were made in conjunction with Blake Edwards *(qv);* they are low-budget musicals or comedies around the 80-minute mark, but in Technicolor or Supercinecolor and breezy with it. Columbia were happy with the results and Quine began to move on to bigger projects after *Pushover,* which boasted another of Fred MacMurray's splendid feet-of-clay figures of authority. Quine's zestful musicals continued to zing across the screen with *So This is Paris* (sub–*On the Town*) and *My Sister Eileen* (Lemmon again, but this time outshone by an in-form Betty Garrett and Janet Leigh); there were more wacky comedies with an eye for the sudden belly-laugh (*Operation Mad Ball* and *It Happened to Jane*), two easy-to-like Judy Hollidays, *The Solid Gold Cadillac* and

Full of Life, the much-underrated, enchanting (literally!) *Bell, Book and Candle* (Lemmon yet again, James Stewart and Novak captivating as a witch) and Novak and Kovacs again, with Kirk Douglas, in the effective if slightly soapy *Strangers When We Meet.* Suzie Wong was probably Quine's biggest assignment: the results were dull, uninteresting and dispiriting. All the director's lightness had disappeared. In the distressing years that followed, only the occasional film displayed even touches of the old beguiling zaniness. Quine committed suicide by shooting himself in 1989.

1948: †*Leather Gloves (GB: Loser Take All).* 1951: †*Purple Heart Diary (GB: No Time for Tears).* *The Awful Sleuth. *Woo Woo Blues. Sunny Side of the Street.* 1952: *Rainbow 'Round My Shoulder. Sound Off.* 1953: *All Ashore. Cruisin' Down the River. Siren of Bagdad.* 1954: *Drive a Crooked Road. Pushover. So This is Paris.* *Extra Dollars.* 1955: *My Sister Eileen.* 1956: *The Solid Gold Cadillac. Full of Life.* 1957: *Operation Mad Ball.* 1958: *Bell, Book and Candle.* 1959: *It Happened to Jane. Strangers When We Meet.* 1960: *The World of Suzie Wong.* 1962: *The Notorious Landlady.* 1963: *Paris When It Sizzles.* 1964: *Sex and the Single Girl. How to Murder Your Wife.* 1965: *Synanon (GB: Get Off My Back).* 1966: *Oh Dad, Poor Dad, Mama's Hung You in the Closet and I'm Feeling So Sad.* 1967: *Hotel.* 1968: *A Talent for Loving.* 1970: *The Moonshine War.* 1972: *Columubo: Requiem for a Falling Star (TV). Columbo: Dagger of the Mind (TV. GB: cinemas).* 1973: *Columbo: Double Exposure (TV).* 1974: *W.* 1975: *The Specialists (TV). McCoy: Double Take (TV).* 1978: *The Prisoner of Zenda.*

RAFELSON, Bob 1933-

New York-born Rafelson's few films have largely remained out of the reach of the ordinary cinema-goer, and he has managed only nine full features in 30 years – strange for a man who, from 1960, was such a prolific writer for television. Rafelson's most interesting films, *Five Easy Pieces* and *The King of Marvin Gardens,* are chamber pieces made interesting by firm direction and solid ensemble playing, in the first instance by Jack Nicholson, Karen Black, Susan Anspach and Billy 'Green' Bush and in the second by Nicholson again, Bruce Dern, Ellen Burstyn and Julia Ann Robinson. Rafelson had been a musician and writer before breaking into television in the late 1950s. From 1960, he wrote more than 30 'Plays of the Week', before spending two years (1966-7) on episodes of the frantic pop comedy series *The Monkees*. It was Nicholson who co-scripted the Monkees feature film *Head* with which Rafelson broke into the cinema. With *Five Easy Pieces*, Rafelson won the New York critics' best director award and the film was nominated for four Academy Awards. *The King of Marvin Gardens* gives a far more dispiriting and unsettling portrait of Atlantic City than the Louis Malle film of that name, but the film is almost determinedly uncommercial. *Stay Hungry*, about body-builders, is more of a commercial attempt but it, too, stayed on the periphery of the big time. Rafelson looked to have cracked the mainstream, though, with *The Postman Always Rings Twice* (again with Nicholson), an over-visceral but popular remake of the Lana Turner/John Garfield original. It was six years before the next, *Black Widow*, a partially successful but engrossing thriller. Its public appeal, though, was limited, as was that of the handsome *Mountains of the Moon*, an equally absorbing account of the Burton-Speke exploration of the Nile. Since then, Rafelson has returned to Nicholson – and disappointments. People still stay away from his too few films in droves, and it seems that he has not been able to build up the core cult following of such British directors as Ken Loach and Mike Leigh (both *qv*).

1968: Head. 1970: Five Easy Pieces. 1972: The King of Marvin Gardens. 1976: Stay Hungry. 1980: †Brubaker (uncredited). 1981: The Postman Always Rings Twice. 1987: Black Widow. 1990: Mountains of the Moon. 1991: Man Trouble. 1994: †Erotic Tales. 1996: Blood and Wine. 1998: Poodle Springs (Cable TV).

RAFFILL, Stewart 1942-

English-born Hollywood director whose directorial touch looked fine as long as he was dealing with family adventure about groups of people battling the perils of nature, but deserted him when he tried other genres. Not surprisingly, Raffill's background was in animals and animal films. In his native country he studied animal husbandry at agricultural college, then came to America at 19 and worked

in films as an animal trainer, soon building up his own collection of 'film animals to rent'. After doing some second-unit directing for the Disney Studio and writing the screenplay for their film *Napoleon and Samantha*, Raffill made the popular *Adventures of the Wilderness Family* and *Across the Great Divide*, cleanly and strongly made family adventures with never a drop in pace and barely a concession to sentimentality as their characters, led by handsome Robert Logan and teenager Heather Rattray, battle for survival in the Wilderness. Logan and Rattray were also in Raffill's *The Sea Gypsies*, telling of five Pacific castaways who end up on an island off Alaska. While the stars went on to make *The Wilderness Family Part 2* and *Mountain Family Robinson*, directed, less securely, by other hands, Raffill diversified, with near-disastrous effects. Of his remaining films, only *The Philadelphia Experiment* is of interest, while *Mac and Me*, *Mannequin on the Move* and *Tammy and the T-Rex* were slaughtered by the critics. Chastened, Raffill wisely returned to action in the wide open spaces in the late 1990s.

1971: The Tender Warrior. 1974: When the North Wind Blows. 1975: Adventures of the Wilderness Family. 1976: Across the Great Divide. 1978: The Sea Gypsies (GB: Shipwreck!). 1981: High Risk. 1983: The Ice Pirates. 1984: The Philadelphia Experiment. 1988: Mac and Me. 1991: Mannequin on the Move/Mannequin Two: On the Move. 1993: Tammy and the T-Rex. 1997: Bear-boy. 1998: The Swiss Family Robinson.

RAIMI, Sam 1959-

Many directors of horror films have tried to make a name for themselves by sensational excesses of violence and special effects. For some, it has merely brought oblivion. For others, such as Tobe Hooper, Wes Craven (*qv*) and Raimi, it has provided the foundation for a career in mainstream horror. Raimi's technical wizardry in the editing and effects departments has ensured that his films are often more scary than many of his competitors, while moving at a heart-pounding rate. An enthusiast for the cinema from childhood, Raimi was making his own 8mm films as a teenager, with such titles as *The Bogus Monkey Pignut Swindle*, *A Pieing We Will Go*, *Flight of the Paper Eagle*, *The Sappy Sap* and *Six Months to Live*. Leaving university, he formed Renaissance Pictures with producer Robert Tapert and actor Bruce Campbell. They made a 30-minute sampler of a horror film Raimi wanted to

make and, hawking it around, got the necessary $500,000 to start up production. Completed in 1982, *The Evil Dead* took the 1983 Cannes Film Festival by storm and made Raimi a world figure at 24. Sensationally frightening, the film had effects that belied the low budget and moody camerawork that suggests the lurking presence of demons within the woods even when they and their machinations can't be seen. Seeking a wider audience, Raimi joined forces with Joel and Ethan Coen for a crime comedy called *Crimewave*. The results, however, were dreadful and Raimi quickly returned to the horror genre and *Evil Dead II*, which, though less intense than the first, is good, clean fun for horror fans who demand nothing more than a welter of blood, swivelling zombies and non-stop action. Raimi drew on *Phantom of the Opera* for the next, *Darkman*, and, although he and four others supplied an unintentionally laughable script and the film enjoyed mixed critical reaction, it was another money-spinner. *Army of Darkness*, which completed Raimi's *Evil Dead* trilogy, was considerably more ambitious than the first two, but was more of a horror comic sprung to life, and lacked their concentrated evil. To date, Raimi has yet to return to the genre.

*1981: *Within the Woods. 1982: The Evil Dead. 1985: Crimewave/Broken Hearts and Noses. 1987: Evil Dead II/Evil Dead II: Dead by Dawn. 1990: Darkman. 1992: Army of Darkness: Evil Dead 3/Army of Darkness: The Medieval Dead. 1995: The Quick and the Dead. 1998: A Simple Plan. 1999: For the Love of the Game.*

RAPPER, Irving 1898-

How strange that the director who produced the smoke-shrouded splendour of *Now, Voyager* should have turned his hand to such extraordinary, Z-grade projects in the twilight of his career. It just goes to show how much the average professional director could blossom in the rich hothouse of a studio environment, and how badly he could flounder outside it, gasping for air and withering away. So much for the detrimental effects of the much-reviled studio system. Rapper was born in England, but his parents emigrated to the United States when he was a child. He moved straight from New York University to directing for the stage, and was well established when Warners hired him in 1935 as a dialogue coach. He stayed in films, initially as an assistant director, but as full director from 1941. Almost from the beginning, Rapper worked with Max Steiner as his music composer. Steiner's sweeping scores work wonders for *The Gay Sisters*, with Barbara Stanwyck, and *One Foot in Heaven*, with Fredric March as a small-town Methodist minister. Jack Warner saw the handkerchieves out at the end of these films, and put Rapper (and Steiner) at the helm of the Bette Davis vehicle *Now, Voyager*. The story of a dowdy spinster who changes her image thanks to a kindly doctor, and finds a love that can never fully be hers, couldn't succeed today, even as a woman's magazine serial. But the film has become a classic through the sheer skill of the playing and Rapper's careful highlighting of it. Each angle seems right, whether for intimacy, alienation or simply the best possible impact (think of the contrasting low-level shots of Davis as a middle-ageing frump coming down the stairs, and as the fashionable woman, as yet unsure of herself, on the gangway of the ship that is to take her to romance). The railway station farewell, with superb swirling smoke and intelligent photography by Sol Polito, as well as the two-cigarette shot and the 'Why ask for the moon when we have the stars?' finale, are unforgettable weepy moments. Rapper also directed Miss Davis in *The Corn is Green* and, reunited with Rains and Henreid, in the magnificently silly *Deception*. Away from Warners' aegis, on *Another Man's Poison*, both Davis and Rapper went way over the top. But he was successful with two likeable light comedies, the witty *The Voice of the Turtle* and the frothy *Forever Female*. By the late 1950s, Rapper was fading fast. But who would have thought he would come to *Joseph and His Brethren*, *Pontius Pilate*, *The Christine Jorgensen Story* or *Born Again*? This was one voyager who should have stayed safe in his Burbank harbour.

1941: Shining Victory. One Foot in Heaven. 1942: The Gay Sisters. Now, Voyager. 1944: The Adventures of Mark Twain. 1945: Rhapsody in Blue. The Corn is Green. 1946: Deception. 1947: The Voice of the Turtle/One for the Book. 1949: Anna Lucasta. 1950: The Glass Menagerie. 1951: Another Man's Poison. 1953: Forever Female. Bad for Each Other. 1956: Strange Intruder. The Brave One. 1958: Marjorie Morningstar. 1959: The Miracle. 1960: Giuseppe venduto dei fratelli (GB: Sold into Egypt. US: Joseph and His Brethren). 1961: Pontius Pilate. 1970: The Christine Jorgensen Story. 1978: Born Again.

RATOFF, Gregory 1897-1960

It seems unlikely that an arm-waving Russian with fractured English could succeed as a director in Hollywood, but Ratoff maintained a very respectable average between 1936 and 1950 (and anyway the Hungarian Michael Curtiz's English was even worse), even if he is more remembered today for the excited foreigners he created in character roles than for the films he directed. Generally Ratoff made dull actors duller, and character stars even better. Thus *Lancer Spy*, with its unlikely combination of George Sanders, Dolores Del Rio, Peter Lorre, Joseph Schildkraut and Lionel Atwill, packs genuine excitement and a breathless climax: one can just imagine Ratoff jumping up and down urging the actors on. *Wife, Husband and Friend* (later remade equally amusingly as *Everybody Does It*) made unusual use of Loretta Young and had another good cast headed by Cesar Romero, Binnie Barnes, Warner Baxter and Eugene Pallette, while *Rose of Washington Square* was a big hit for the Alice Faye-Tyrone Power team (and Al Jolson, too), and established Ratoff as one of Fox's leading directors: he stayed with them, off and on, until 1947. He also made the two films which established Ingrid Bergman in Hollywood: *Intermezzo* and *Adam Had Four Sons*, and returned to the *Lancer Spy* style of pacing to make *The Corsican Brothers* a rousing swashbuckler, with a splendidly oily performance from Akim Tamiroff. He continued to direct Fox's blondes, with Betty Grable in the minor *Footlight Serenade*, June Haver in the really extraordinary Technicolor musical fantasy *Where Do We Go from Here?* (which packs in half of America's history, gag sequences and several songs in 77 minutes) and Peggy Cummins, with an appalling cockney accent she must have learned from Ratoff, in the otherwise excellent moody suspense piece *Moss Rose* with Vincent Price in great form as the policeman on the case. *Paris Underground* is an atmospheric Resistance vehicle for Gracie Fields and Constance Bennett and *Black Magic*, a vivid extravaganza, with Tamiroff again, and Orson Welles; in need of a lighter touch, it was not successful. There aren't many outright duds in Ratoff's entertaining catalogue, but *Song of Russia*, *Abdullah's Harem* and the Robert Morley *Oscar Wilde* must come near the bottom of the list. Despite his popularity at Fox, Ratoff never quite achieved the box-office 'clout' to set up as many projects as he would have liked. He died in Switzerland at 63.

1933: †Sins of Man. 1937: Lancer Spy. 1938: Wife, Husband and Friend. 1939: Rose of Washington Square. Barricade. Day-Time Wife. Intermezzo: a Love Story (GB: Escape to Happiness). Hotel for Women/Elsa Maxwell's Hotel for Women. 1940: I Was an Adventuress. Public Deb No. 1. 1941: Adam Had Four Sons. The Men in Her Life. The Corsican Brothers. 1942: Two Yanks in Trinidad. Footlight Serenade. 1943: Something to Shout About. The Heat's On (GB: Tropicana). 1944: Song of Russia. Irish Eyes Are Smiling. 1945: Paris Underground (GB: Madame Pimpernel). Where Do We Go from Here? 1946: Do You Love Me? 1947: Carnival in Costa Rica. Moss Rose. 1949: Black Magic. That Dangerous Age (US: If This Be Sin). 1950: My Daughter Joy (US: Operation X). 1953: Taxi. 1954: Abdullah's Harem (GB: Abdullah the Great). 1960: Oscar Wilde.

RAWLINS, John 1902-1997

Briefly a 'comer' at Universal in the war years, an exciting director of action scenes and a skilful displayer of the talents of exotic leading ladies, John Rawlins is now chiefly remembered by fans of the serial genre. Rawlins had a certain talent, but faded quite quickly in the post-war years. He had originally broken into films as a stuntman around 1926, playing in several serials in which he also had small roles. In the 1930s, he switched from acting to editing, for Columbia, but it was Universal that hired him to direct serials and minor action films in 1938. He continued to do just that for the next four years, making his first comedy in 1941, the extravagantly titled *Six Lessons from Madame La Zonga*, with the Lupe Velez-Leon Errol team from RKO's 'Mexican Spitfire' series. Rawlins also handled the first of Universal's new Sherlock Holmes series, but it was not very successful, and the rest of the films were made by Roy William Neill, a more suitable director. But, having already shown some talent for exotic adventure – *Bombay Clipper*, *Raiders of the Desert*, *Half Way to Shanghai* – Rawlins found himself handed *Arabian Nights*, the studio's first Technicolor picture. The result was a tremendous smash which packed wartime audiences in in their hundreds of thousands, chiefly to see the much-publicized charms of Maria Montez and Jon Hall. The action scenes were extremely well handled, giving the film something for everyone. It was followed by other films in similar vein, all of them, until near the end of the war, quite successful at the box-office, although the most flagrant hokum. Meanwhile, Rawlins went on to *We've Never Been Licked*, a big war film about the conflict in the Far East, and *Ladies Courageous*, another flag-waver in which the studio supported Loretta Young and Geraldine Fitzgerald with what seemed like its complete roster of contract actresses in a brisk and noisy, if not very believable story of girls getting war planes from one base to another for the U.S. Air Force. At this point, Rawlins unfortunately returned to the Montez-Hall duo at the time their popularity was slipping away. *Sudan* was a loser, a pale imitation of past idiotic glories, with not nearly enough action. Rawlins found himself returned to small-budget pictures. He left Universal and, although some of his later action films – especially *Massacre River, Fort Defiance, Rogue River* and *Shark River* – are colourful, exciting co-features, Rawlins' cinema career did not last beyond the 1950s. He died from pneumonia.

1933: *Sign Please. *They're Off! 1938: The Young Fugitives. The Missing Guest. State Police. Air Devils. 1940: †The Green Hornet Strikes Again (serial). †Junior G-Men (serial). The Leather Pushers. 1941: †Sea Raiders (serial). A Dangerous Game. Mutiny in the Arctic. Men of the Timberland. Raiders of the Desert. Six Lessons from Madame La Zonga. Mr Dynamite. 1942: †Overland Mail (serial). Bombay Clipper. Unseen Enemy. Mississippi Gambler. Half Way to Shanghai. The Great Impersonation. Sherlock Holmes and the Voice of Terror. Arabian Nights. 1943: We've Never Been Licked (GB: Texas to Tokyo). 1944: Ladies Courageous. 1945: Sudan. 1946: Strange Conquest. Her Adventurous Night. 1947: Dick Tracy's Dilemma (GB: Mark of the Claw). Dick Tracy Meets Gruesome (GB: Dick Tracy's Amazing Adventure). 1948: The Arizona Ranger. Michael O'Halloran. 1949: Massacre River. 1950: Rogue River. The Boy from Indiana (GB: Blaze of Glory). 1951: Fort Defiance. 1953: Shark River. 1958: Lost Lagoon.*

RAY, Nicholas (R.N. Kienzle) 1911-1979

A huge cult has grown around this American director in recent years, bigger than almost any film-maker, and certainly one of Ray's uneven output, could warrant. He was a curious figure, handsome and personable, once an architect, as restless as his cameras and so often in poor health that, although it seems cruel, one can only express surprise that he lived to be 68. His best films are clustered in his initial RKO Radio period – apart from *Rebel Without a Cause,* his only truly first-rate film outside that studio. Observers have professed to find various wonders in such later Ray films as *Hot Blood, The True Story of Jesse James, Bitter Victory* and others. I can only confess that their virtues escaped me at the time and, on a re-viewing, still do. To fail to accept that

Ray was as capable of making bad films as almost any other director, whatever slight redeeming qualities they may have had, seems to me to be blinding oneself to the truth. Having said that, there is much on the credit side. Ray wrote and directed material for radio in the mid-1930s: it would be another decade before he entered the film industry as an assistant director. Producer John Houseman, for whom Ray had worked on radio and in the theatre, gave him his first chance with *They Live by Night.* An adaptation of Edward Anderson's novel *Thieves Like Us,* this is far superior to Robert Altman's 1974 remake, which kept the title of the book. More sympathetic than that film, in spite of the harsh nature of its subject, it conveys the full tragedy of a doomed romance. Other highlights of Ray's RKO tenure included the neglected *A Woman's Secret,* a very unusual film *noir,* and two films with Bogart, *Knock on Any Door,* with John Derek as the misfit killer, and *In a Lonely Place,* a riveting psychological thriller which takes Bogey's screen persona and turns it inside out to show the dangerous undertones which could destroy such a man. *The Lusty Men* is also very good, an early rodeo drama, homing in on the smouldering restlessness of Susan Hayward. From the 1950s *Johnny Guitar* is a lurid western that lurches precariously along just this side of risibility, *Run for Cover* a good, solid horse-opera with effective action and John Derek still playing the maverick, *Rebel without a Cause* a feast of great acting and dynamic direction, and *Bigger Than Life,* a shaky shocker shored up by directorial touches and two fine central performances (from James Mason and Barbara Rush). As for the later work, there are striking moments in *The Savage Innocents, King of Kings* and *55 Days at Peking,* some of which was directed by Andrew Marton to help out an ailing Ray. One of the last films, *We Can't Go Home Again,* might well have reflected on Ray's own past glories; by this time, there is everything to suggest that the restless rebel had finally lost his way. From 1948 to 1952, he was married to the actress Gloria Grahame.

1948: The Twisted Road/They Live By Night. 1949: A Woman's Secret. Knock on Any Door. †Roseanna McCoy (uncredited). 1950: Born to Be Bad. In a Lonely Place. 1951: Flying Leathernecks. †On Dangerous Ground. †The Racket (uncredited). 1952: †Androcles and the Lion (uncredited). †Macao (uncredited). The Lusty Men. 1954: Johnny Guitar. 1955: Run for Cover. Rebel Without a Cause. 1956: Bigger Than Life. Hot*

Blood. 1957: The True Story of Jesse James (GB: The James Brothers). Bitter Victory. 1958: Wind Across the Everglades. Party Girl. 1959: The Savage Innocents. 1961: King of Kings. 1962: †55 Days at Peking. 1965: The Doctor and the Devils (unfinished). 1970: The Chicago Seven (D. Unfinished). 1973: We Can't Go Home Again. 1974: †Dreams of Thirteen. 1980: †Lightning over Water.*

RAY, Satyajit 1921-1992

Indian director of great perception and technical accomplishment. After a hard time getting his first film afloat, he painted a series of picturesque and affectionate, but often painful portraits of Indian village life. In later times, Ray (pronounced 'Rye') turned his attention to city life, and the corruption it engenders. In 35 years, his photographer's eye certainly snapped the inner core of the Indian soul, and sometimes not liked what it saw. For several years, Ray worked with an advertising company as artistic supervisor, but from 1950 began trying to raise the money to make a feature film. After many trials and heartbreaks the film, *Pather Panchali,* was finally shown in 1955, and was an immediate sensation. All the beauty and cruelty of nature, and life itself, were brought out in Ray's treatment of a young boy's growing-up in a country village, with a sister doomed to die in a terrifying storm sequence near the end of the film. The film is full of memorable images, and its characters are sharply etched, so that each stands out as an individual, good and bad mixed within him. It was followed by two more films about the boy, Apu, and his growing-up: the three films have come to be known as the Apu Trilogy. Ray had no difficulty holding his position at the forefront of Indian directors after that time; his films show great beauty and skill in construction, if some of the lesser works lack the all-pervading atmosphere of the Apu Trilogy. Ray also made mystic adventures based on Indian folklore but from the early 1970s became increasingly concerned with the problems of Indian society. *Company Limited,* for example, is a slow but perceptive and fascinating film whose quiet tone belies its bitterness and singularity of purpose. It takes Ray a while to get to the meat of it, although there are sundry rewards and subtleties involved in the deceptively casual build-up to the hero's final sell-out to the system. Ray continued this angry obsession in subsequent films, notably *Distant Thunder, The Adversary* and *The Middle-Man,* the latter continuing the theme of lost innocence, but taking its protagonist even fur-

A relaxed shot of one of India's greatest and most consistent directors, Satyajit **Ray.** Here he undergoes an interview for American TV.

ther into a darkening web of corruption. Ray's sole attempt to enter the international market, with the Ivory-like *The Chess Players*, was not a great success outside India, its atmosphere perhaps too rarefied for many other than high-caste Indians, of which Ray, of course, was one. Kept away from filming from 1982 by a series of heart attacks, Bay returned in 1989 to make, under doctors' supervision, three further films, before succumbing to a heart ailment shortly after receiving a special Academy Award in 1992. His screenplay for *Target* was directed by his son Sandeep in 1995.

*1955: Pather Panchali (US: Song of the Little Road). 1956: Aparajito (GB & US: The Unvanquished). 1957: Paras Pather (GB & US: The Philosopher's Stone). 1958: Jalsaghar (GB & US: The Music Room). 1959: Apu Sansar (GB & US: The World of Apu). 1960: Devi (GB & US: The Goddess). 1961: Rabindranath Tragore (D). Teen Kanya (GB & US: Two Daughters). 1962: Kanchenjunga. Abhijan (US: Expedition). 1963: Mahanagar (GB & US: The Big City). 1964: Charulata (GB & US: The Lonely Wife). 1965: *Two. Kahapurush-o-Mahapurush (GB: The Coward and the Holy Man. US: The Coward and the Saint). 1966: Nayak (GB & US: The Hero). 1967: Chiriakhana (US: The Zoo). 1968: Goopy Gyne, Bagha Byne (GB & US: The Adventures of Goopy and Bagha). 1969: Aranya Din-Ratri (GB & US: Days and Nights in the*

*Forest). 1970: Pratidwandi (GB & US: The Adversary). 1971: Seemabadha (GB: Company Limited). Sikkin (D). 1973: Ashani Sanket (GB & US: Distant Thunder). 1974: *The Inner Eye. 1975: Sonar Kella (GB & US: The Golden Fortress). Jana Aranya (GB: The Middle-Man. US: The Masses' Music). 1977: Shatranj ke Kilhari/The Chess Players. 1979: Joi Babs Felunath/The Elephant God. 1980: Hirok Rajar Deshe/The Kingdom of Diamonds. 1981: Sadgati/Deliverance (TV. US: cinemas). *Pikoo (TV). 1982: Ghare Baire/Home and the World. 1989: Ganashatsu/Enemy of the People. 1990: Shakha Prosakha/Branches of the Tree. 1991: Agantuk/The Stranger.*

REDFORD, Robert 1936-

An assiduous film-maker whose work sometimes reflects his care for the countryside, Redford's films as director are scarce but on the whole choice. As his acting days perhaps near a close, it is to be hoped he will spend more time on the other side of the camera. After a spectacular career as a star, Redford made an auspicious debut as director with *Ordinary People*, a searing but sympathetic portrait of a family in crisis. The film won several Academy Awards, including one for Redford as best director. After several years away from the cinema developing his Sundance Institute(now the location for the United States Film Festival) for training young film-makers, Redford returned to acting in 1984,

but not to directing until 1988, when he made *The Milagro Beanfield War*, perhaps this least appreciated and most ingratiating feature. A winning and whimsical allegory of one poor Mexican bean farmer's decision to cultivate land needed by outside developers and how it leads to a stand-off between the downtrodden community and big business, the film has a fistful of likeable characters and a lush score that won Dave Grusin an Oscar. Redford himself narrated *A River Runs Through It*, and his casting of rising hearthrob Brad Pitt gave a higher profile to a poetic tale of a Montana childhood in which the director obtains understated portrayals from his players and engages our emotions almost without our knowing it. *Quiz Show* was also well liked, although it was less interesting than other Redford-directed films and a mite overlong in its relation of a true scandal involving the 'fixing' of an American TV quiz show. After another sizeable pause, Redford then directed himself for the first time in an adaptation of the best-selling novel *The Horse Whisperer*.

1980: Ordinary People. 1988: The Milagro Beanfield War. 1992: A River Runs Through It. 1994: Quiz Show. 1998: The Horse Whisperer.

REED , Sir Carol 1906-1976

Distinguished British director, at his considerable best from 1939 to 1949. There's an inner excitement about the Reed films from this period, which stems partly from watching a film-maker turn talent into artistry, partly from seeing a good story told to great effect. Conditions after the mid-1950s were no longer suited to Reed's special abilities, and a certain decline from that point was inevitable. But, with the nine films from *The Stars Look Down* to *The Third Man*, with the exception of *The Young Mr Pitt*, Reed struck one of the richest and most rewarding runs in all British cinema. These are intelligent, deeply satisfying films, all in black-and-white, and often using the cream of British talent in acting, writing and technical departments. Reed had begun as an actor, and had some experience of stage management when he entered the film industry as a dialogue director at Ealing in 1932. He hit his stride almost from the outset, with a stirring version of *Midshipman Easy*, featuring Margaret Lockwood, who would appear in almost all his best films of the early 1940s. Reed's earlier films are, it seems, overdue for revaluation. *Bank Holiday* intertwines several stories around people on holiday in Britain: it is a microcosm of its time. By 1939, Reed was directing with great confidence, most of his films at this stage being scripted by Frank Launder and Sidney Gilliat, and several roughly in the vein of *The Lady Vanishes*, in which Miss Lockwood had also starred. In the racily enjoyable *A Girl Must Live*, she's a runaway taken under the wing of a gang of chorus girls; *The Girl in the News* teams her profitably with Barry K. Barnes (from *This Man is News*) in a spirited comedy-thriller about a nurse framed for murder; *The Stars Look Down*, a great success in the working-class idiom of *The Citadel* and *The*

Proud Valley, has her supporting miner Michael Redgrave's struggles to become an M.P.; while *Night Train to Munich* has her fleeing the Nazis again, with another Launder-Gilliat script and Naunton Wayne and Basil Radford rejoining her for good measure. *The Way Ahead* was an inspiring semi-documentary war film, *Odd Man Out* a rather stately thriller which nonetheless conveys much of James Mason's desperation as an Irish rebel on the run. The subtly engrossing *The Fallen Idol* is a beautifully observed picture of the relationship between a little embassy boy and the friendly butler he shields

because he thinks the police will arrest him for murder; here Reed's most sophisticated use of camera angles suggests the evil of Sonia Dresdel, and the prisonlike, inhospitable aspect of the embassy itself. *The Third Man* had Orson Welles pursued through a Vienna of fairs and ruins, shapes and shadows, and Reed's cameraman Robert Krasker deservedly winning an Oscar. Of the later films, *A Kid for Two Farthings* is a gentle fantasy of some charm, and *Our Man in Havana* a complex black comedy with Alec Guinness at his smoothest and a script by Graham Greene that drips with acid wit. Reed finally did win an Oscar for *Oliver!*, a musical version of *Oliver Twist*, but hardly one of his best films. He was married to actress Diana Wynyard from 1943 to 1947 and later to another actress, Penelope Dudley-Ward.

1935: †*It Happened in Paris. Midshipman Easy (US: Men of the Sea)*. 1936: *Laburnum Grove. Talk of the Devil.* 1937: *Who's Your Lady Friend?* 1938: *Bank Holiday (US: Three on a Week-End). Penny Paradise. Climbing High.* 1939: *A Girl Must Live. The Stars Look Down.* 1940: *Night Train to Munich (US: Night Train). The Girl in the News.* 1941: *Kipps (US: The Remarkable Mr Kipps). The Young Mr Pitt.* 1942: **A Letter from Home. *The New Lot.* 1944: *The Way Ahead (US: Immortal Battalion).* 1945: †*The True Glory (D).* 1946: *Odd Man Out.* 1948: *The Fallen Idol.* 1949: *The Third Man.* 1950: **National Playing Fields (D).* 1951: *Outcast of the Islands.* 1953: *The Man Between.* 1955: *A Kid for Two Farthings.* 1956: *Trapeze.* 1958: *The Key.* 1959: *Our Man in Havana.* 1963: *The Running Man.* 1968: *Oliver!* 1970: *Flap (GB: The Last Warrior).* 1971: *Follow Me (US: The Public Eye).*

REINER, Carl 1922-

This New Yorker couldn't have chosen a more appropriate title for his first film as director: *Enter Laughing*. Practically all of Reiner's show business life has been centred on comedy. Crazy, madcap ideas run through all his work, many of them wildly successful. Stringing them together into successful feature films has, though, proved another matter. After comedy turns with GI entertainment groups on the Pacific Front in World II, and a brief stint in repertory, Reiner's career remained small beer until he became part of the legendary early TV comedy/variety programme, *Your Show of Shows*, in 1950, supporting its star, Sid Caesar, for four riotous seasons. Reiner formed something of a partnership with one of the

Carol **Reed** working in then-West Berlin, filming *The Man Between* there in 1953. Star Claire Bloom has her back to the camera.

Burly Rob **Reiner** prepares Michael Douglas for a dinner sequence as he plays the title role in
The American President.

show's writers, the young Mel Brooks,
and together they created the popular
'2000-Year-Old Man' recordings. Reiner
also wrote a book, *Enter Laughing,* based
on his own early acting experiences, and
created and often wrote the wildly successful *The Dick Van Dyke Show* in the
early 1960s. When he decided to make
the move to films, *Enter Laughing* proved
an obvious source of material, especially
since Reiner had already converted his
book into a Broadway play. The film,
however, like most of Reiner's work,
would only find cult minority audiences.
The Comic and *Where's Poppa?* were also
well received (although the former, a bitter-sweet look at the silent-film era, failed
to find distribution outside America). It
took the broad George Burns comedy *Oh,
God!* to bring Reiner back into the limelight, and he then entered into an innovative series of films with a comedian new
to the movies, Steve Martin. All of these
have hilariously inventive and imaginative
moments, although the best is perhaps
Dead Men Don't Wear Plaid, which
mixes footage of old black-and-white
films with new monochrome material in
an endearing fashion, although, like most
of Reiner's movies, there are times when it

is just too broad and silly. After the Martin connection ended in 1984, with *All of
Me,* Reiner's films seemed to lack an overall strategy. His vehicle for the talented
English star Robert Lindsay – *Bert Rigby,
You're a Fool* – was a particular disappointment. His latest work at time of
writing, *That Old Feeling,* is a typical
mixture of slack scenes and wild ideas.
That's the story of his (comic) life. He's
the father of director Rob Reiner.

*1967: Enter Laughing. 1969: The Comic.
1970: Where's Poppa? 1977: Oh, God!
The One and Only. 1979: The Jerk. 1982:
Dead Men Don't Wear Plaid. 1983: The
Man With Two Brains. 1984: All of Me.
1985: Summer Rental. 1987: Summer
School. 1989: Bert Rigby, You're a Fool.
1990: Sibling Rivalry. 1993: Fatal
Instinct. 1996: That Old Feeling.*

REINER, Rob 1945-

Unlike his father Carl Reiner, who has
specialised in comedies, Rob Reiner has
made films on a much broader (and, it
has to be said, more successful) scale.
Reiner Senior must have watched with a
mixture of pride and envy his son's suc-

cess with such disparate films as *Stand By
Me, When Harry Met Sally... Misery, A
Few Good Men* and *The American President.* Big, balding and burly like his
father, Reiner combined writing for TV
comedy series with playing small, mostly
comic cameo roles in films, before his
biggest acting success came in 1974 with
the smash-hit TV series *All in the Family*
(the US version of Britain's *Till Death Do
Us Part*), in which he played the brainy,
liberal son-in-law of the central character,
ranting bigot Archie Bunker. His debut as
a director came in 1983 with *This is
Spinal Tap,* a huge critical and cult hit, a
spoof 'rockumentary' about an English
band on tour in America. Since the highpoint of *A Few Good Men,* a military
courtroom drama which was nominated
for the best film Oscar and brought Reiner the third of his three Directors' Guild
of America nominations as best director
of the year, Reiner's career has been on a
somewhat lower plane. He suffered his
first outright flop with *North,* an over-
ambitious and under-scripted fantasy. Significantly well-written screenplays had
been the bedrock of Reiner's work to that
time. Married/divorced actress-director
Penny Marshall.

*1983: This is Spinal Tap. 1985: The Sure
Thing. 1986: Stand By Me. 1987: The*

Princess Bride. 1989: When Harry Met Sally... 1990: Misery. 1992: A Few Good Men. 1994: North. 1995: The American President. 1996: Ghosts of Mississippi (GB: Ghosts from the Past). 1999: The Story of Us.

REIS, Irving 1906-1953

New York-born Reis didn't direct many films in his comparatively brief career, but they include one of the funniest and most delightful movies in all American cinema. *The Bachelor and the Bobby Soxer* (in Britain, *Bachelor Knight*) has any number of memorable moments, including Cary Grant taking on Rudy Vallee in the parents' sprint, and the famous 'Man of Power' duologue between Grant and Myrna Loy. It is a film even Hawks could have been proud of. It was surprising that Hollywood had not handed Reis bigger assignments from the start: he was one of radio's most prominent directors in the 1930s, and instrumental in giving Orson Welles his start in that medium. Reis came to RKO at roughly the same time as Welles, but was stuck directing Falcon adventures, only managing his first 'A' feature, *The Big Street,* just before war service. Lucille Ball got, and took, her first big screen chance in this rather endearing Damon Runyon oddity, as the gold-digging singer who changes her ways when crippled by her paramour. Reis' first assignment on return was the Pat O'Brien psychological thriller *Crack-Up,* not too well thought of at the time, but now a frequent late-night TV favourite, with a chilling sequence on board a train. Reis followed *Bachelor* with the sombre and strong *All My Sons,* with Edward G. Robinson taking on Burt Lancaster. *Enchantment,* a sentimental romantic confection with David Niven reliving past love, was extremely effective, as was the delightfully unusual semi-musical *Dancing in the Dark,* with William Powell in amusing form in one of the best of his later roles. *Three Husbands* was a surprisingly good role-reversal version of *A Letter to Three Wives,* and *The Four-Poster,* a still-stagebound version of Jan de Hartog's play, but almost entirely captivating thanks to Lilli Palmer's performance opposite then-husband Rex Harrison. There were some signs that Reis had reached a peak and passed it. But his early death was a tragedy all the same.

*1932: *Trout Fishing. 1940. One Crowded Night. I'm Still Alive. 1941: Footlight Fever. The Gay Falcon. Week-End for Three. A Date with the Falcon. 1942: The Falcon Takes Over. The Big Street. 1946: Crack-Up. 1947: The Bachelor and the Bobby-Soxer (GB: Bachelor Knight).*

1948: All My Sons. Enchantment. 1949: Roseanna McCoy. Dancing in the Dark. 1950: Three Husbands. 1951: †Of Men and Music. New Mexico. 1952: The Four-Poster.

REISNER, Charles F. (Chuck) · 1887-1962

A fascinating, colourful character from the middle range of American comedy directors, Chuck Reisner (quite frequently billed, oddly, as Riesner) was a boxer, singer and comedian before coming to Hollywood in 1915. He worked with Charlie Chaplin on four films, and directed many other famous names of comedy, although, oddly, all of them except Marie Dressler, only once. Among them were Buster Keaton, W.C. Fields, Lucille Ball, Jack Benny, Dressler, The Marx Brothers and Abbott and Costello. His job with Keystone and other studios during World War I days was mainly as a knockabout comic in slapstick two-reelers, but he became friendly with Chaplin, and was his assistant director on *A Dog's Life* in 1918. The following year, Reisner began directing two-reel comedy shorts for himself, although continuing to act, and to work with Chaplin: he was the little man's associate director, actually shooting much of the footage, on *The Kid* (1921), *The Pilgrim* (1923) and *The Gold Rush* (1925). After this date, he left Chaplin to make his own features. Reisner, however, had inherited none of Chaplin's careful, almost leisurely ways. He made films at incredible speed, always within their shooting schedules. His best silent comedy was Keaton's *Steamboat Bill Junior,* almost the Great Stone Face's last classic: the cyclone sequence at the end is legendary, full of marvellous sight gags and, like the film, moving at a tremendous lick. Keaton made a courtesy appearance in Reisner's *Hollywood Revue of 1929,* by which time the director was under contract to M-G-M, where he stayed until 1935. They recalled him in 1941 for the film that was intended to be the Marx Brothers' swan song in movies – *The Big Store.* This has marvellous long sequences involving Margaret Dumont and Douglass Dumbrille and the pacing throughout is beautifully controlled by the director. The rest of his second tenure at the studio was none too successful, apart from his Abbott and Costello film *Lost in a Harem.* Reisner apparently got on much better with the two comedians than most directors, and they seem happy to be enmeshed in a more traditional form of Hollywood comedy with running gags, zany moments and musical interludes. In post-war years Reisner tired of Hollywood, and was one of the first directors

to dive into situation comedy on television, making a couple of unnecessary returns to minor studios for moderate second-features which had little to do with his roots.

*1919: *Dog Days. 1920: *Dog-Gone Clever. *A Blue Ribbon Mutt. *The Laundry. *Happy Daze. *A Lyin' Tamer. *The Champion Loser. 1921: *His Puppy Love. *Stuffed Lions. *Won: One Flivver. *Milk and Yeggs. 1925: The Man on the Box. 1926: Oh! What a Nurse! The Better 'Ole. 1927: The Missing Link. What Every Girl Should Know. The Fortune Hunter. 1928: Fools for Luck. Steamboat Bill Junior. Brotherly Love. 1929: Hollywood Revue of 1929. Noisy Neighbors. China Bound. 1930: Chasing Rainbows. Caught Short. Love in the Rough. 1931: Reducing. Stepping Out. *Jackie Cooper's Christmas/The Christmas Party. Politics. Flying High. 1932: Divorce in the Family. 1933: The Chief (GB: My Old Man's a Fireman). 1934: Student Tour. The Show-Off. You Can't Buy Everything. 1935: It's in the Air. 1936: Everybody Dance. 1937: Murder Goes to College. Sophie Lang Goes West. Manhattan Merry-Go-Round (GB: Manhattan Music Box). 1939: Winter Carnival. 1941: The Big Store. 1942: This Time for Keeps. 1943: Harrigan's Kid. 1944: Meet the People. Lost in a Harem. 1948: In This Corner. The Cobra Strikes. 1950: The Traveling Saleswoman. L'ultima cena.*

REISZ, Karel 1926-

Czech-born film-maker, in Britain since boyhood. Very active on television, and a front runner in the 'free cinema' movement of the mid-1950s that led to his own *Saturday Night and Sunday Morning,* he has had a curiously spasmodic and unsatisfactory film career. In 1981, though, he made his best film for 15 years, *The French Lieutenant's Woman,* giving some grounds for hope for a revival in his film fortunes. A writer on film technique, Reisz began making documentaries in the 1950s, sometimes in collaboration with the other members of the Free Cinema Trio, Lindsay Anderson and Tony Richardson (both *qv*). These look dated now, but were effective in their time, especially *We Are the Lambeth Boys,* a study of a youth club catering for working-class teenagers. The raw energy in these documentaries is certainly evident in *Saturday Night and Sunday Morning,* a soaringly outspoken 'slice of life' which changed the face of the British cinema, pointed the way to a more uninhibited attitude to sex which would soon loosen the censor's grip, opened the doors to a whole slew of rebel working-class heroes from up and down the country, was entertaining with it, started Albert Finney's star career, and generally has a lot to answer for. Its director, though, soon faltered. *Night Must Fall* could not measure up to the Hollywood version of the 1930s, despite a brilliant supporting performance from Mona Washbourne, but *Morgan, a Suitable Case for Treatment,* a gleamingly voguish black comedy, was intermittently riotous, especially where David Warner's love of furry creatures is concerned. Reisz's elastic treatment of the case makes room for any number of amusing cameos, especially from Irene Handl as Morgan's Mum and Arthur Mullard as a wrestler called Danny the Gorilla – no wonder Morgan feels an affinity with him. Reisz's few subsequent films, however, seem clumsy and dull – even sometimes unpleasant. *The French Lieutenant's Woman,* though, if not a wholly acceptable translation to screen of John Fowles' strange novel, is a film of great beauty with a radiant, Oscar-nominated performance from Meryl Streep. Reisz assumed a lower profile with *Sweet Dreams,* a pleasing biography of country singer Patsy Cline, and a baffling one with *Everybody Wins,* his worst film since *The Gambler.*

1952: *Stars Who Made the Cinema (D). 1955: *†Mamma Don't Allow (D). 1959: We Are the Lambeth Boys. (D). 1960: Saturday Night and Sunday Morning.

1963: *Night Must Fall. 1966: Morgan, a Suitable Case for Treatment (US: Morgan). 1968: Isadora. 1974: The Gambler. 1978: Who'll Stop the Rain? (GB: Dog Soldiers). 1981: The French Lieutenant's Woman. 1985: Sweet Dreams. 1990: Everybody Wins.*

REITMAN, Ivan 1946-

Czech-born Hollywood director, something of a maverick in his younger days, noted for irreverent sex-and-action films and broad comedies. He has continued to enjoy mainstream hits in recent times when his work has shown signs of more subtlety, especially when armed with carefully-crafted scripts. Throughout his career, his films have been lightweight but entertaining with occasional comic inspirations and emotional highpoints. Fantasy, comedy and horror, three of the threads in his career, came together in his biggest hit to date, *Ghost Busters.* After studies at Canada's National Film Board, Reitman made a rather inglorious beginning to directing feature films by getting a year's probation for producing *Columbus of Sex,* based on a scandalous Victorian novel. Undaunted, he directed *Foxy Lady* and *Cannibal Girls,* which were hardly in better taste, the latter distinguished by some 'buzzer-and-bell' horror scenes to warn unsuspecting audiences to head for the sickbag or the exit. Perhaps tiring of flouting conventions, Reitman went into pro-

duction for several years, working on an assortment of comedy and horror films, including one of David Cronenberg's early stomach-churners, *Shivers.* The director in him re-emerged with the 'Second City'-style comedy films, *Meatballs* and *Stripes,* both of which marked early starring appearances for laconic Bill Murray, who made it three in a row for Reitman with *Ghost Busters,* the special effects-driven fantasy-comedy that put its director in the big league. Reitman now widened his horizons with the glossy Robert Redford-Debra Winger drama *Legal Eagles,* and two entertaining films with Arnold Schwarzenegger, *Twins* and *Kindergarten Cop.* The best, however, was yet to come in the form of *Dave,* a triumphant treatment of the old dual identity theme, with a dazzling script by Gary Ross that was Oscar-nominated. Reitman's skills in placing cameras at the perfect distance from the focal shot and in timing the sequence and editing of scenes were never better showcased than here. He then returned to comedy with the enjoyable *Junior* and the spasmodically funny *Fathers Day,* neither of which enjoyed the box-office success of some of his former work. Reitman continues to produce other directors' work on a regular basis, although his track record here is inferior to his own as director.

1968: Orientation. 1971: Foxy Lady. 1973: Cannibal Girls. 1979: Meatballs. 1981: Stripes. 1984: Ghost Busters. 1986:

On the set of *Everybody Wins* (1989). Left to right: Nick Nolte, Debra Winger, Arthur Miller and director Karel **Reisz**.

Happy in his twilight years...French director Jean **Renoir** busying about the set for *Le petit théâtre de Jean Renoir* in 1969.

Legal Eagles. 1988: Twins. 1989: Ghostbusters II. 1990: Kindergarten Cop. 1993: Dave. 1994: Junior. 1997: Fathers Day. 1998: Six Days Seven Nights.

RELPH, Michael 1915-

An entry to complete the file on the team of Relph and Basil Dearden (*qv*). Relph was working in films from the age of 17, firstly at Gaumont-British as an assistant art director, then as a fully fledged art director with Ealing Studios from 1943. He was an associate producer at the time of his first film with Dearden, *The Cap-*

tive Heart (1946), and the two men worked closely together from the following year until 1968. It was Dearden who supplied the creative directorial drive, while Relph (the son of actor George Relph) preferred to write and produce. However, they shared directing credit on several films, and Relph directed three films under his own steam before returning to his former chores. Of these, *Desert Mice* is an amusingly observed study of ENSA entertainers during World War II.

1952: †I Believe in You. †The Gentle Gunman. 1953: †The Square Ring. 1955:

†*Out of the Clouds.* †*The Ship That Died of Shame (US: PT Raiders). 1957: Davy. 1958: Rockets Galore (US: Mad Little Island). 1959: Desert Mice.*

RENOIR, Jean 1894-1979

The son of painter Auguste Renoir, Jean Renoir was perhaps the greatest of French directors, at his incomparable best during the 1930s, but somewhat less effective after the outbreak of World War II when he went to Hollywood. Before then, he made at least nine films which stand as classics. Time has not diminished their qualities, nor their appeal to the emotions. *La grande illusion*, for example, is still familiar, and welcome, around the world. People seem to look on its periodic reappearance, whether on television or in the cinema, as comparable to the visit of a favourite nephew. And perhaps that is not too facile a comparison, as Renoir's films, whether tragic, comic or just life-observed, are about people rather than events, although as a storyteller he is as delicate and skilled as any. His earliest films frequently star his first wife Catherine Hessling (also his father's last model) whom he had married in 1920, a few weeks after his father's death. Renoir also made acting appearances himself (he and Catherine would appear as the Big Bad Wolf and Red Riding Hood in a Cavalcanti film of 1930, the year before they split up) although none so important as in one of his greatest films, *La règle du jeu* (1939), in which he has the key role. This satire of French society, perhaps 20 years ahead of its time, is unlike any of Renoir's other 1930s' films: of these, *La chienne* and *La bête humaine* are urban tragedies and the haunting *Toni* a rural one, their murders kindled by temptresses. *Boudu sauvé des eaux* is a delightful black farce about a tramp saved from drowning who is ultimately forced to fake another drowning to regain his freedom, faintly reminiscent of *A nous la liberté*, if only in its very Gallic ending. *La grande illusion*, with memorable performances by Pierre Fresnay, Jean Gabin and Erich Von Stroheim in his spinal collar, is one of the great anti-war films, a heart-breaker in the way it shows war undercutting the finer qualities of life. Renoir was in Hollywood for seven years, but the only one of his films there that approaches the feel and intensity of his French work is the elegiac *The Southerner*, with its remarkably self-effacing performances from Zachary Scott and Betty Field. In post-war years Renoir wandered a while before returning to France. *The River* is a film I have never come to grips with, despite several attempts since my parents first walked out half-way through it in 1951, dragging me with them. No such problems with *French Cancan*, a fizzing, firecracker survey of that institution, with colours worthy of his father's paintings, a last great Renoir performance from Jean Gabin, and a spitfire show from Maria Felix. Of the later films, the risible *Le testament du Docteur Cordelier*, a Jekyll-and-Hyde story, is probably the only total disaster in the Renoir canon, while my own favourite is *Le caporal épinglé*, which brings Renoir's uniquely warm yet hardly rose-coloured view of humanity to the fore again; it concerns a prisoner-of-war whose determination to escape is almost light-hearted until his friend is killed. Renoir's cameras home in on such humanity, and let the audience do the rest. He was given an honorary Oscar in 1975.

1924: *Une fille sans joie* (later reissued, re-edited, as *Catherine*). *La fille de l'eau* (GB: *Whirlpool of Fate*). 1926: *Nana*. 1927: *Charleston* (unfinished; issued in three-reel form). *Marquitta*. 1928: *La petite marchande d'allumettes* (GB: *The Little Match-Seller*. US: *The Little Match-Girl*). *Tire-au-flanc*. 1929: *Le tournoi*. *Le bled*. 1930: *On purge Bébé*. 1931: *La chienne*. 1932: *La nuit du carrefour*. *Boudu sauvé des eaux* (GB & US: *Boudu Saved from Drowning*. 1933: *Chotard et cie*. 1934: *Madame Bovary*. *Toni*. 1935: *Le crime de Monsieur Lange*. 1936: *La vie est à nous* (US: *People of France*). *Une partie de campagne* (GB & US: *A Day in the Country*. Unfinished). 1937: *Les bas-fonds* (GB & US: *The Lower Depths*). *La grande illusion*. *La Marseillaise*. *Terre d'Espagne* (D). 1938: *La bête humaine* (GB: *Judas Was a Woman*). 1939: *La règle du jeu* (GB & US: *The Rules of the Game*). 1940: †*La Tosca*. 1941: *Swamp Water* (GB: *The Man Who Came Back*). 1943: *This Land is Mine*. 1944: **Salute to France* (D). *The Southerner*. 1946: *The Diary of a Chambermaid*. 1947: *The Woman on the Beach*. 1951: *The River*. 1952: *La carrozza d'oro* (GB: *The Golden Coach*). 1955: *French Cancan* (GB: *French Can Can*. US: *Only the French Can*). 1956: *Eléna et les hommes* (GB: *The Night Does Strange Things*. US: *Paris Does Strange Things*). **L'album de famine de Jean Renoir* (D). 1959: *Le Testament du Docteur Cordelier* (GB: *Experiment in Evil*. US: *The Doctor's Horrible Experiment*). *Le déjeuner sur l'herbe* (GB: *Lunch on the Grass*. US: *Picnic on the Grass*). 1962: *Le caporal épinglé* (GB: *The Vanishing Corporal*. US: *The Elusive Corporal*). 1968: **La direction d'acteur par Jean Renoir* (D). 1969: *Le petit théâtre de Jean Renoir* (originally for TV).

RESNAIS, Alain 1922-

Every critic and writer has his blind spots among the great directors of the world, and I confess that Resnais is mine. If I say that I think his best film is still the three-reeler *Night and Fog*, made as long ago as 1955, I am sure there will be a dozen willing pairs of hands eager to push me under the nearest subway train. It's not for want of trying: I sat resolutely in front of one of his more recent works, *Mon oncle d'Amérique*, but it is as miserable a film as you could wish to find. Having said that, I must also add that *Last Year in Marienbad* is generally considered to be one of the outstanding surrealist puzzle pictures of all time. Despite the infrequent appearances of his feature films, Resnais' early years are thickly populated with documentary shorts. He was always enthusiastic about films, even if perhaps in too cerebral a way, and began making 8mm 'home movies' while still at school, one of which is still in existence. After a course at the French film school IDHEC, he immediately embarked on a busy career as a maker of shorts, establishing a reputation by 1950. These documentaries soon began to assume the proportions of memories that haunt one, beginning a theme that Resnais would return to in his works of fiction, which are often dominated by a real-life or imaginary past. This led him to *Night and Fog*, an unforgettable treatment of the grim story of concentration camps, a true documentary in that it establishes both facts and atmosphere, telling us much more about the camps than simply showing piles of bodies, now almost too familiar a sight even to shock. There is more anger as Resnais shows us such real horrors as Himmler's greenhouse, Hitler's zoo or the commandant's symphony orchestra (recently given its own story in the TV movie *Playing for Time*), than in almost any of his bigger films. *Le chant du styrène* and *Toute la memoire du monde* are memorably inventive treatments of seemingly dry and dusty subjects, but at this point Resnais began to diversify. *Hiroshima Mon amour*, a somewhat stylized view of a Franco-Japanese love affair, was critically acclaimed, and led Resnais to the enigma of Marienbad. This was followed by his first feature film in (extremely good) colour, *Muriel*, a kind of high-level women's picture whose characters seem to exist in a vacuum. Since then, Resnais' most successful films have been *Je t'aime, Je t'aime* an experimental science-fiction work; *Stavisky*, one of his more popular and accessible films; *Providence*, another study of old age and memories which, despite a colossal score by Miklos Rosza, seems vulgar when it should be caring;

and *Mon oncle d'Amérique*, the first in a trilogy rounded off by *L'amour à mort*. The next, *Mélo*, has charm and is rather more accessible: it won a César for star Sabine Azéma, who also featured in multiple roles in Resnais' twin films *Smoking* and *No Smoking* which, at nearly 300 minutes in total, are are sufficient to test most people's staying power. But *On connait un chanson*, with 'dialogue' mostly composed of snatches of songs, was an innovation and no mistake. For me, however, Resnais' films lack humour and compassion: they do not seem to communicate with an audience in real terms.

1936: **L'aventure de Guy*. 1945: **Le sommeil d'Albertine*. *Schéma d'une identification*. 1946: *Ouvert pour cause d'inventaire*. 1947: **Visite à Lucien Coutaud* (D). **Visite à Félix Labisse* (D). **Portrait de Henri Goetz* (D). **Visite à Hans Hartnung* (D). **Visite à Oscar Dominguez* (D). *Visite à César Domela* (D). 1948: **La bague* (D). *L'alcoöl tue* (D). **Van Gogh* (D). 1949: **Chateaux de France* (D). **Malfray* (D). 1950: **Gauguin* (D). †*Guernica* (D). 1953: **†Les statues meurent aussi* (D). 1955: **Nuit et brouillard* (GB & US: *Night and Fog*. D). 1956: **Toute la mémoire du monde* (D). 1957: **Le mystère de l'atelier 15*. 1958: **Le chant du styrène* (D). 1959: *Hiroshima mon amour*. 1961: *L'année dernière à Marienbad* (GB: *Last Year in Marienbad*. US: *Last Year at Marienbad*). 1963: *Muriel*. 1966: *La guerre est finie* (GB: *The War is Over*). 1967: †*Loin de Vietnam/Far from Vietnam*. *Je t'aime, je t'aime*. 1972: †**L'an. 01* (uncredited). 1974: *Stavisky*. 1977: *Providence*. 1980: *Mon oncle d'Amérique*. 1983: *La vie est un roman* (US: *Life is a Bed of Roses*). 1984: *L'amour à mort* (US: *Love Unto Death*). 1986: *Mélo*. 1989: *I Want to Go Home*. 1993: *Smoking*. *No Smoking*. 1997: *On connait la chanson* (US: *Same Old Song*).

REYNOLDS, Burt (Burton A. Reynolds) 1936-

As a director/actor Reynolds is constantly trying to do something interesting, to bring across a whole range of atmospheres, feelings and statements, and enrich and deepen the characters in the story. This, to an extent, elevates his films above the screenplay. He has only made five films to date, but patently enjoys the challenge. In his first film, *Gator*, it is already evident that the director is endeavouring to do something different with each scene, with a large degree of success. There are nods to everyone from Hitchcock to Mel Brooks (both qv). But by and large, Reynolds remains his own man. His direction has style, a sense of humour and a sure touch

Burt **Reynolds** looks like the cigar-chewing directors of old as he directs for the first time in 1976. The belt round his waist gives away the title of the movie. It's *Gator*.

for the visual. His action scenes are first-class, and he gets uniformly good performances from his actors. His black comedy *The End*, about a man doomed to die ('It's the same thing Ali MacGraw had in *Love Story*, isn't it?' he howls), is so uneven one could almost imagine the director making the dud bits so bad that the more amusing scenes seem hilarious. At any rate, after a three-year gap, he was back to tough-guy action with *Sharky's Machine*, a very, very rugged thriller about cops, crime and corruption. Blood runs down the walls and people get blown away, but the director

still finds time for an extraordinarily obsessive non-contact love affair as the detective (himself) becomes infatuated by the girl he is keeping under surveillance (and who may be killed at any minute), and embittered by her profession (dancer-cum-high-class hooker); it reminds one of the relationships in *Laura* and *I Wake Up Screaming* (GB: *Hot Spot*, later remade as *Vicki*). All this is conveyed in visuals rather than words, revealing a director as obsessed with creating something of moment from a routine situation as the character in the film is with the girl.

1976: *Gator*. 1978: *The End*. 1981: *Sharky's Machine*. 1984: *Stick*. 1993: *The Man from Left Field*.

REYNOLDS, Kevin 1953-

Best known for his clashes with his long-time friend and frequent star Kevin Costner than under his own steam, Reynolds made some major action films, although none has quite hit its intended target. He and Costner now seem finally to have gone their separate ways. As a young man Reynolds earned degrees in history and law and practised law in Texas for several years before deciding to have a shot at making films. While at film school in California Reynolds made a student film, *Proof*, that attracted the attention of Steven Spielberg, who helped Reynolds get the money for a feature-length version of the film. That turned out to be *Fandango*, a would-be *American Graffiti* that starred a then-unknown Costner, who made as few ripples as the film. When the two re-teamed for *Robin Hood: Prince of Thieves* seven years later, both Reynolds' budget and Costner (as a very American Robin) had got much, much bigger. The end product looked as though the cast read the script and decided the best thing was to have a good time and enjoy themselves, probably not to the humourless Costner's liking, although between them, he and Reynolds managed to stage some reasonable action scenes, hopefully without coming to blows themselves. If *Rapa Nai*, Reynolds' next stop on a round-the-world action trip, set on a 17th-century Easter Island with very 20th-century dialogue, was over-ambitious, it was nothing compared to the next, *Waterworld*, whose $200 million plus budget, a record until *Titanic* appeared a couple of years later, was the subject of much controversy. A sort of *Mad Max* afloat, the film has a credibility problem that might not matter if could have kept up the blazing action of its first half hour. Reynolds and Costner were soon at loggerheads again on this one and, like some patrons, Reynolds left before the end, leaving Costner to finish and edit the film, which eventually broke even on its mammoth cost. Reynolds went off to something a little quieter, but *187* proved a sub-par ghetto school story.

1982: **Proof*. 1984: *Fandango*. 1988: *The Beast*. 1991: *Robin Hood: Prince of Thieves*. 1993: *Rapa Nui*. 1995: *Waterworld*. 1997: *187*.

RICH, David Lowell 1920-

A 'B' movie director born out of his era. The older brother of John Rich (born

Tony **Richardson** was at the top of his form when he made *Tom Jones* in 1963. His on-set visitor here is his then-wife Vanessa Redgrave.

1925), who made the films *Wives and Lovers*, *The New Interns*, *Roustabout*, *Boeing-Boeing*, *Easy Come, Easy Go*, then won an Emmy for *The Dick Van Dyke Show*, New York-born David Lowell Rich made 33 TV movies in 12 years, most of them well down to the standards of mediocrity set by the genre. He has rarely dealt with emotional subjects, or exciting on-location work, which is a pity, as the indications have been that he had talent in both of these directions. A director of live television in New York from the early 1950s, Rich worked prolifically on fictional series from 1956, beginning with *Big Town* and *M Squad*, and going on to *77 Sunset Strip*, *Wagon Train*, *Route 66* and *Naked City*. His early films are mostly teenage rip-offs, but he made a neglected and very effective version of the old chestnut *Madame X* in 1965, extracting an amazing performance from Lana Turner in

the title role, for once completely deglamorized in the closing stages of the film, which are real four-handkerchief stuff. Rich's other above-average film is *Eye of the Cat*, an intelligent chiller. Of the TV work, the location-set thrillers *Berlin Affair* and *Assignment: Munich* are the most interesting, *Adventures of the Queen* unexpectedly entertaining, and *Ransom for Alice!* an atmospheric and unusual western-type story, with personable performances from Gil Gerard and Yvette Mimieux. Many of the other TV movies, though, are all the more disappointing in view of the capabilities he has shown. He did, however, win an Emmy for his direction of *The Defection of Simas Kudirka* in 1978 and continued to work in the TV movie genre until the end of the 1980s.

1957: *No Time To Be Young* (GB: *Teenage Delinquents*). 1958: *Senior Prom*. 1959:

Hey Boy! Hey Girl! Have Rocket, Will Travel. 1964: *See How They Run* (TV. GB: cinemas). 1965: *Madame X*. 1966: *The Plainsman* (originally for TV). 1967: †*Three Guns for Laredo* (originally for TV. Rich's section filmed 1965). *Rosie! The Borgia Stick* (TV). *Wings of Fire* (TV). 1968: *A Lovely Way to Die* (GB: *A Lovely Way to Go*). 1969: *Marcus Welby MD* (TV). *Eye of the Cat*. 1970: *Berlin Affair* (TV). *The Mask of Sheba* (TV). 1971: *The Sheriff* (TV). *Assignment: Munich* (TV). 1972: *Lieutenant Schuster's Wife* (TV). *Northeast to Seoul/Northeast of Seoul*. *The Judge and Jake Wyler* (TV). *All My Darling Daughters* (TV). 1973: †*That Man Bolt*. *Set This Town on Fire* (TV. Filmed 1969 as *The Profane Comedy*). *Brock's Last Case* (TV). *The Horror at 37,000 Feet* (TV). *Crime Club* (TV). *Beg, Borrow or Steal* (TV). *Satan's School for Girls* (TV). *Death Race* (TV). *Runaway* (TV. GB: cinemas as *The Runaway Train*). 1974: *The Chadwick Family* (TV). *The Sex Symbol* (TV. GB: cinemas). *Aloha Means Goodbye*

(TV). 1975: *The Daughters of Joshua Cabe Return* (TV). *Adventures of the Queen* (TV). *You Lie So Deep, My Love* (TV). 1976: *Bridger – the Fortieth Day* (TV). *The Secret Life of John Chapman* (TV). 1977: *SST Death Flight/SST Disaster in the Sky* (TV). *Ransom for Alice!* (TV). *Telethon* (TV). 1978: *A Family Upside Down* (TV). *Defection of Simas Kudirka* (TV). *Little Women* (TV). 1979: *The Concorde – Airport '79* (GB: *Airport '80. . . the Concorde*). 1980: *Enola Gay: The Men, The Mission, The Atomic Bomb* (TV). 1981: *Chu Chu and the Philly Flash*. 1983: *Thursday's Child* (TV). *The Fighter* (TV). 1984: *The Sky's No Limit* (TV). *His Mistress* (TV). 1985: *The Hearst and Davies Affair* (TV). *I Want to Live!* (TV). 1986: *Choices* (TV). 1987: *Infidelity* (TV). 1989: *Convicted* (TV).

RICH, John

See Rich, David Lowell

RICHARDSON, Tony

(Cecil Antonio Richardson) 1928-1991

Whatever happened to Tony Richardson? Once the roars of approval, applause and glitter of the Oscar for *Tom Jones* died away, Richardson vanished from the limelight. Although he soldiered on in the cinema, his stage work was much more satisfactory. Almost all of his films since those heady days were unsuccessful and few of them even commercial.There are some who contend that Richardson never made a good film anyway. But this is far from true. Associated in the 1950s with Karel Reisz and Lindsay Anderson (both *qv*) in the Free Cinema movement, Richardson directed the jazz short *Mamma Don't Allow* with Reisz, then settled down to making films written by, or featuring people who had come in on the crest of the angry young wave of the late 1950s: John Osborne's *The Entertainer* (with early roles for Albert Finney and Alan Bates) and *Look Back in Anger*, Tom Courtenay in *The Loneliness of the Long-Distance Runner*, Rita Tushingham in *A Taste of Honey* and finally, triumphantly, Finney again in the Osborne-scripted version of Fielding's *Tom Jones*. The film took the Academy Award for 1963 and deservedly so: it was undoubtedly that year's best. Full of life and *joie-de-vivre*, it tells its rowdy tale at a rollicking pace, while the photography, art direction and production design brilliantly recreate Fielding's England and Richardson, in addition to drawing robustly enjoyable characterizations from Finney, Hugh Griffith and Edith Evans in particular, uses any number of conceits, such as freeze-frame or characters addressing the audi-ence, all of which come off in exhilarating style. Richardson also took an Academy Award. No doubt it was a hard act to follow, but in the event Richardson probably made a mistake in drifting away from England and his roots, into an altogether more mystic, oddball kind of international cinema. In 1977, he made an attempt to return to *Tom Jones* territory with *Joseph Andrews*, but the magic, freshness and inspiration had gone. At one time married to Vanessa Redgrave, and the father of actresses Natasha and Joely Richardson, he died from an AIDS-related illness.

1955: †*Mamma Don't Allow*. 1959: *Look Back in Anger*. 1960: *The Entertainer*. 1961: *Sanctuary*. *A Taste of Honey*. 1962: *The Loneliness of the Long-Distance Runner*. 1963: *Tom Jones*. 1965: *The Loved One*. 1966: *Mademoiselle*. *The Sailor from Gibraltar*. 1967: **Red and Blue*. 1968: *The Charge of the Light Brigade*. 1969: *Laughter in the Dark*. *Hamlet*. 1970: *Ned Kelly*. 1973: *A Delicate Balance*. 1974: *Dead Cert*. 1977: *Joseph Andrews*. 1978: *A Death in Canaan* (TV). 1981: *The Border*. 1984: *The Hotel New Hampshire*. 1986: *Phantom of the Opera* (TV). *Penalty Phase* (TV). 1990: †*Women & Men: Stories of Seduction*. 1991: *Blue Sky* (released 1994).

RIEFENSTAHL, Leni (Helene Riefenstahl) 1902-
This German-born director's beautiful images stir opposing emotions in us, for

Looking every inch her glamorous actress of the early career, the luminous Leni **Riefenstahl** went on to become one of Germany's most influential directors.

they form beautiful cinema, but in a horrendous cause. Even now, one cannot view her two crowning achievements, *Triumph des Willens* and *Olympische Spiele*, with wholehearted approval, albeit that parts of them so ennoble the human race. Extraordinary visual gifts lay hidden within a lithe blonde actress for several years. But, after she had made *The Blue Light* in 1932, Hitler selected her to make a short on the 1933 Nazi party rally, and his sponsorship and support was invaluable to her from then on. Her two big documentaries of the mid-1930s, one about the Nuremberg Rally, the other concerning the Berlin Olympics, are myth rather than reality, even if it is reality they purport to portray. The films are her triumph – and they were her downfall. After the fall of Germany in 1945, Riefenstahl found herself in turn imprisoned, itinerant, workless. She has not been able to complete a film satisfactorily since 1936. Had the Nazis prevailed, she would probably have become the greatest woman film director the world has known. But who could blame that world for denying her the opportunity?

*1932: Das blaue Licht (GB & US: The Blue Light). 1933: *Sieg des Glaubens/ Victory of the Faith (D). 1934: Triumph des Willens/Triumph of the Will (D). 1935: *Tag der Freiheit – Unsere Wehrmacht (D). 1936: Olympische Spiele/Olympia (GB: Berlin Olympiad. US: Olympia/The Olympic Games). 1953: Tiefland (D. Completed 1945). 1956: Schwarze Fracht/Black Freight (D. Unfinished). 1977: Nuba (D. Unreleased).*

RILLA, Wolf 1920-

German-born director of British films, in England since 1935 and writing for radio since 1942. He worked in the forefront of British cinema from 1956 to 1963, but his most prolific years before and after these dates have been spent working for television, where he began to make a name as writer and producer from the early 1950s. He made his first – minor – films from 1953: *The End of the Road*, a compassionate study of old age with a typical, appealingly cantankerous performance from Finlay Currie, attracted most praise. Rilla moved towards a larger scale with *The Blue Peter*, a most attractive film (Rilla's first in colour) about the rehabilitation of a shell-shocked naval hero (Kieron Moore's best performance since *Mine Own Executioner);* it confirmed his facility with actors. His most successful films in the ensuing years were *Bachelor of Hearts*, a light university comedy-romance which rode to box-office success

on the the strength of Hardy Kruger's popular appeal, *Village of the Damned*, a taut adaptation of John Wyndham's chilling science-fiction book *The Midwych Cuckoos* with some very suspenseful moments, and *Watch It Sailor! a* sequel to the smash-hit farce *Sailor Beware!* (US: *Panic in the Parlor).* After a couple of unsuccessful dramas, Rilla went back to television, only returning in the 1970s with a mild sexploitation film and an oddity that failed to find its niche. Perhaps his two most disappointing films were *Pacific Destiny,* a prestige production of the mid-1950s, and *The World Ten Times Over,* which cashed in on the then-popular appeal of June Ritchie and Sylvia Syms, and has a 'sisters' theme rare for its time. In both films, Rilla showed an interesting flair for visuals, but the weakest element in each case was the script – on the second film supplied by Rilla himself. Son of actor Walter Rilla.

1953: Glad Tidings. Marilyn/Roadhouse Girl. Noose for a Lady. The Large Rope. 1954: The Black Rider. The End of the Road. 1955: Stock Car. The Blue Peter. 1956: Pacific Destiny. 1957: The Scamp. 1958: Bachelor of Hearts. 1959: Witness in the Dark. 1960: Village of the Damned. Die zornigen jungen Männer. Piccadilly Third Stop. 1961: Watch It Sailor! Jessy (D). 1962: Cairo. 1963: The World Ten Times Over (US: Pussycat Alley). 1973: Secrets of a Door-to-Door Salesman (US: Naughty Wives). 1974: Bedtime with Rosie. 1980: Training Salesmen (D).

RIPLEY, Arthur 1895-1961

A rather mysterious and ill-defined character, New York-born Ripley only made a few feature films, yet quite a cult has grown up around his work in recent years. His background was in comedy, yet all his feature films are in dramatic vein, and there is precious little humour in them. Several of them are a little strange, like Ripley himself, who was once described by fellow-director Edgar G. Ulmer as 'not very normal ... a sick man ... mentally and physically'. Yet in the early years, Ripley was multi-talented and seemed destined for a busy career. In the film business from 14 (as a cutter), he soon had two separate strings to his bow, as an editor and a screenwriter. He also became a gag writer (one of the many) for Mack Sennett and wrote gags, stories and screenplays for Harry Langdon when Langdon was still at the peak of his powers in the middle and late 1920s. Later, Ripley would direct Langdon in several two-reel shorts in the years of his decline. As an editor, Ripley's most important

credit was probably on Erich von Stroheim's 1922 film *Foolish Wives.* Ripley began directing short comedies in 1933, starting with two classics with W.C. Fields, *The Barber Shop* and *The Pharmacist.* Further two-reel ventures featured Langdon, Edgar Kennedy and Robert Benchley, usually with a dual emphasis on verbal and visual humour, with Ripley continuing to supply many of the words. Ripley's most interesting feature films are *Voice in the Wind*, a haunting, moody tragedy about a Czech pianist tortured by the Nazis, with a memorable performance from the usually inflexible Francis Lederer, and *Thunder Road,* a thundering story of moonshine whisky runners which sometimes seems as out of control as the bootleggers' rickety lorries; it has a downbeat ending, but sticks in the mind. These rather rum films perhaps reflected the more serious side – in real life Ripley was a lugubrious-looking man with a mournful moustache – of one of the more bizarre entries in Hollywood's casebook.

*1933: *The Barber Shop. *The Pharmacist. 1934: *Counsel on de Fence. *Shivers. *The Leather Necker. *In the Dog House. 1935: *South Sea Sickness. *Edgar's Hamlet. *In Love at 40. *Gasoloons. 1936: *Happy tho' Married. *Will Power. *How to Behave. *How to Train a Dog. 1938: †I Met My Love Again. 1940: *Twincuplets. *Scrappily Married. 1942: †Prisoner of Japan. 1944: Voice in the Wind. 1946: The Chase. 1948: †Siren of Atlantis (uncredited). 1958: Thunder Road.*

RITCHIE, Michael 1938-

Superior American film-maker of persuasive, atmospheric entertainments, with an occasional penchant for bloodthirsty action. He has also taken a wry, searching look at an assortment of American institutions, and uses superstar actors to obtain charismatic performances at the centre of his stories. Ritchie was already attracting critical attention while still at university. His Harvard production of *Oh Dad, Poor Dad, Mama's Hung You in the Closet and I'm Feeling So Sad* was apparently better than the Broadway show and certainly than Richard Quine's ghastly film version. He joined television as an assistant director, but had graduated to full director by 1964 and directed his first film in 1969, being selected by Robert Redford for *Downhill Racer* after Redford had seen some of his television work. Even at this early stage, Ritchie showed an ability to etch action and character equally sharply and his films of the 1970s were all commercially successful, although *Prime Cut* was an uncharacteristically unpleasant Ritchie film much criticized for its violence. In more recent years, *The Island* would fall into the same category. Nor are these films generally as good as *Smile*, a witty satirical look at beauty contests, *The Candidate*, an uncompromising look at a meat market of a different nature, and *The Bad News Bears*, Ritchie's biggest box-office hit, in which he skilfully milks much good humour from the acerbic story of a team of no-hope, sub-teen baseball players, grouchily managed by Walter Matthau. In 1980, Ritchie came up with the best-yet version of a concert performance, as he surveyed Bette Midler in *Divine Madness*. Since then, he has made rather too many films that too few people have gone to see, the last highpoint being *Fletch*, a crowd-pleasing Bob Hope-style comedy-thriller vehicle for Chevy Chase. A sequel to this, however, was dismal.

1965: From Nigeria with Love (TV. Feature-length episode of Dr. Kildare). 1967: The Outsider (TV). Cry Hard, Cry Fast (TV. Feature-length episode of Run for Your Life). 1968: The Sound of Anger (TV). 1969: Downhill Racer. 1972: Prime Cut. The Candidate. 1974: Smile. 1976: The Bad News Bears. 1977: Semi-Tough. 1979: An Almost Perfect Affair. 1980: The Island. Divine Madness. 1983: The Survivors. 1984: Fletch. 1985: Wildcats. 1986: The Golden Child. 1987: The Couch Trip. 1989: Fletch Lives. 1992: Diggstown (GB: Midnight Sting). 1993: The Positively True Adventures of the Alleged Texas Cheerleader Murdering Mom (TV). 1994: The Scout. Cops and Robbersons. 1995: The Fantasticks. 1997: A Simple Wish.

RITT, Martin 1914-1990

Acting power is the key to this American director's films. Not surprisingly, Ritt once taught acting, at Lee Strasberg's 'Method' studio, where one of his pupils was Paul Newman, who later starred in several Ritt films. The films themselves gained a litter of Academy Award nominations, although only three Oscars were actually won – by Patricia Neal and Melvyn Douglas in *Hud*, and Sally Field in *Norma Rae*. Ritt had an extremely high record of consistency in 30 years of making films, bringing great strength and emotional force to visual scenes as well as extracting the most from his actors and, in Sally Field's case, an unexpected depth of performance. An actor since 1936, Ritt directed his first stage play ten years later and his first film, *Edge of the City*, ten years after that. Although a low-budget, black-and-white production, the film

immediately established Ritt in the industry. It was a punchy, dramatic, *On the Waterfront*-style drama, with a towering performance by Sidney Poitier. After this powerful debut, Ritt faltered for a while. The adaptations of Faulkner stories, *The Long Hot Summer* and *The Sound and the Fury*, signified very little and, despite several appearances by Newman, only *The Black Orchid*, underplayed with surprising delicacy by Anthony Quinn and Sophia Loren, was really a good movie – and that was not commercial – until the advent of *Hud*. About a clash of wills on a Texas ranch in desolate country, it is one of Ritt's least complicated films and has a string of strong portrayals, headed by Newman once more, this time as the selfish, arrogant eldest son of the ageing rancher (Douglas). Posters dubbed the character 'the man with the barbed wire soul'. Ritt scored great popular successes with *The Spy Who Came In from the Cold* and *Hombre* (Newman yet again, in his last Ritt film), although neither was wholly satisfactory given the source material. From 1969 to 1974, though, Ritt struck his best period, with *The Molly Maguires*, a much-underrated story of sabotage and unrest in the Pennsylvania coal-mines in the latter half of the last century, that showed the emotions of its participants gut-raw; *The Great White Hope*, a strong, fluid and very well-made story about black boxing champion Jack Johnson, with tremendous performances from James Earl Jones and Jane Alexander; *Sounder*, a compassionate portrait of the lives of black sharecroppers in the 1930s; and *Conrack*, a warmly human view of a white teacher's efforts to educate illiterate black children in South Carolina. At this point, Ritt was well into a social-conscience kick: *The Front*, about the McCarthy blacklistings, had its effectiveness blunted by the casting of Woody Allen, but *Norma Rae* was triumphant emotive cinema, a vindication of all that Ritt obviously believed in. He died from cardiac disease.

1956: Edge of the City (GB: A Man is Ten Feet Tall). 1957: No Down Payment. 1958: The Long, Hot Summer. 1959: The Sound and the Fury. The Black Orchid. Five Branded Women. 1961: Paris Blues. 1962: Hemingway's Adventures of a Young Man (GB: Adventures of a Young Man). 1963: Hud. 1964: The Outrage. 1965: The Spy Who Came in from the Cold. 1966: Hombre. 1968: The Brotherhood. 1969: The Molly Maguires. 1970: The Great White Hope. 1972: Sounder. Pete 'n' Tillie. 1974: Conrack. 1976: The Front. 1977: Casey's Shadow. 1979: Norma Rae. 1981: Back Roads. 1982: No

Small Affair. 1983: Cross Creek. 1985: Murphy's Romance 1987: Nuts. 1989: Stanley and Iris.

RIVETTE, Jacques 1928-

French film-maker whose movies are almost all unorthodox, beautiful to watch, long, and alternately rewarding or infuriating. Some film enthusiasts of my acquaintance would not go near a Rivette film. Others regard him as the greatest of living film-makers. Such polarization must at least denote director of some stature. His 1979 film *Merry-Go-Round*, sums up all the rest, in that the characters therein are on a roundabout and can't get off. Just as for *The Time Travelers* in Ib Melchior's 1964 fantasy, there is no escape in Rivette's world. The hope of a safe harbour at the end in the form of a denouement is continually undermined by a director determined to allow the viewer no easy solutions to his playful marathons. Reading some observations written by a fellow-critic on Rivette's *Paris nous appartient*, it occurs that the man could just as easily be writing about *Céline et Julie vont en bâteau*: that fact alone would probably give Rivette a satisfied chuckle. A cameraman and assistant director in the 1950s, Rivette worked with some of France's most distinguished directors, including Jean Renoir, François Truffaut and Eric Rohmer (all *qv*). He also began directing shorts. In 1960, he began his direction of what could, I suppose, be called 'longs': *Paris nous appartient* runs 141 minutes, *L'amour fou* 256 minutes, *Out One: Spectre* 260 minutes and *Céline et Julie* 192 minutes. The 'original' of *Out One: Spectre*, simply called *Out One*, at one time ran for nearly 13 hours. The lesson is clear: take a thinking cap and a pack of sandwiches – and be prepared for a stimulating evening or a battle against sleep, according to your disposition. Grumbled a *Variety* reviewer in 1995, on seeing Rivette's version of *Joan of Arc* (cut down from six hours to four): 'Someone should have told the director that good things come in small packages.' Bit late now.

*1950: *Aux quatre coins. 1951: *Le quadrille. 1952: *Le divertissement. 1956: *Le coup du berger. 1960: Paris nous appartient (GB: Paris is Ours. US: Paris Belongs to Us). 1965: Suzanne Simonin, la religieuse de Diderot (GB: La religieuse. US: The Nun). 1968: L'amour fou. 1971: Out One (unreleased). 1973: Out One: Spectre. 1974: *Essai sur l'agression. *Naissance et mort de Prométhée. Céline et Julie vont en bâteau (GB & US: Celine and Julie Go Boating).*

1976: *Duelle – les filles du feu.* 1977: *Noroît/Nor' West. La vengeresse.* 1979: *Merry-Go-Round.* 1980: *Paris s'en va* (unreleased). 1981: *Le pont du nord.* 1984: *L'amour par terre.* 1985: *Hurlevent/Wuthering Heights.* 1989: *La bande des quatre.* 1991: *La belle noiseuse.* 1994: *Jeanne la Pucelle/Joan of Arc.* 1995: *Haut bas fragile.* 1996: *Mystère/Secret Defence/Murder Mystery.* 1998: *Famille.*

ROBERT, Yves 1920-

French director of middle-brow romps and romantic comedies who made some very popular entertainments, while maintaining a parallel career as a bright and cheerful leading man. He made his first film in 1949 and two years later had already directed a short. A vehicle for frenetic comedian Louis De Funes, *Vive Monsieur Blaireau*, casting the star as a wily poacher, signalled the beginnings of Robert's real popularity as a director and he went on to make several light films that, like *Blaireau*, found international distribution. In 1956, he married the leading actress Danièle Delorme (born Gabrielle Girard) who co-produced some of his films, including *The War of Buttons*, a charming children's film remade three decades later in Britain. She also starred in the occasional Robert vehicle, most notably the witty sex frolic *Pardon Mon Affaire* and its sequel *Nous irons tous au Paradis/Pardon Mon Affaire Too*. Robert also made a sequel to his hit comedy *Follow the Man With One Black Shoe*, both films provoking massive hits in France and doing modestly well elsewhere. The crowning achievement of Robert's career was undoubtedly the two films he made from the memoirs of fellow-director Marcel Pagnol, *La gloire de mon père* and *Le chateau de ma mère*. Delightful, gentle, lyrical evocations of an idyllic childhood in the French countryside, these are wonderful films with stunning colour photography. Robert's rhythmically tracking cameras let the family's little exploits speak for themselves, in lovingly crafted extended vignettes, especially in the latter film when a canal keeper lends the family a key that enables them to take an adventurous short cut through chateau estates to their rented cottage.

1951: *Les bonnes manières.* 1954: *Les hommes ne pensent qu'à ça.* 1957: *Ni vu, ni connu* (GB: *Vive monsieur Blaireau*). 1959: *Signé Arsène Lupin.* 1960: *La famille Fenouillard.* 1961: *La guerre des boutons* (GB and US: *The War of the Buttons*). 1962: *Bébert et l'omnibus* (US: *The Holy Terror*). 1964: *Les copains.* 1965: *Monnaie de singe.* 1967: *Alexandre*

le bienheureux. 1969: *Clérambard.* 1972: *Le grand blond avec une chaussure noire* (GB: *Follow the Man With One Black Shoe.* US: *The Tall Blond Man With One Black Shoe*). 1973: *Salut l'artiste* (GB and US: *The Bit Player*). 1974: *Le retour du grand blond* (GB: *Return of the Tall Blond. The Return of the Tall Blond Man With One Black Shoe*). 1976: *Un éléphant ça trompe énormément* (GB and US: *Pardon Mon Affaire*). 1977: *Nous irons tous au Paradis* (GB and US: *Pardon Mon Affaire Too*). 1979: *Courage Fuyons.* 1984: *Le jumeau.* 1990: *La gloire de mon père/My Father's Glory. Le chateau de ma mère/My Mother's Castle.* 1992: *Le bal des casse-pieds.* 1994: *Montparnasse – Pondicherry.*

ROBERTS, Stephen 1895-1936

It may seem improbable that a pilot and stuntman could become a brisk director of light and polished Hollywood entertainments of the 1930s. But West Virginia-born Roberts managed the change with some style, and it was Hollywood's loss that he succumbed to a heart attack when only 40. His forte, the sleek crime comedy, would have stood him in good stead at least until the 1940s. He was also very successful in highlighting star personalities and bringing forward their most likeable traits. A 'Lafayette Escadrille' pilot of World War I, Roberts toured fairs and showgrounds on his return home, doing stunt aerobatics. In the 1920s, he entered films, performing flying and other stunts and doing stand-in work for action scenes. Later he obtained small acting roles, and became a familiar voice on radio. In 1923 he began a prolific career as a director of two-reel comedies, making close to 100 before Paramount gave him a chance to direct features in 1931. After opening with a Randolph Scott film, *Sky Bride*, he was soon in charge of fairly prestigious projects. *The Night of June 13th* was a crisp thriller, while Roberts gained a certain amount of notoriety with the watered-down version of *The Story of Temple Drake* (alias William Faulkner's *Sanctuary*), about an ultimately willing kidnap and rape victim. Roberts filmed the rape scene in almost total darkness, virtually the only lighting being the glow from Jack La Rue's cigarette. In contrast, *One Sunday Afternoon* was a charming period (1910) romantic comedy with Gary Cooper and Fay Wray. Cooper has never looked more at ease in this genre, and the film was later remade twice, once under the same title with Dennis Morgan (a musical version) and once, with James Cagney, Rita Hayworth and Olivia de Havilland, as *The Strawberry Blonde*.

Having directed Ginger Rogers in *Romance in Manhattan*, Roberts used her to much better advantage as William Powell's co-star in the *Thin Man*-style caper, *Star of Midnight*, a champagne cocktail of a film whose success he repeated with Powell and Jean Arthur in *The Ex-Mrs Bradford*. At the right studio in the right genre at just about the right time, Roberts looked set for a profitable run. Alas, the ex-air ace's heart failed him.

1923: †*Somebody Lied.* 1924: *Cheer Up. Poor Butterfly.* 1925. *Fair Warning. Fire Away. Waiting. Wild Waves.* †*Fares Please.* 1926: *Framed. Flaming Romance. Hanging Fire. High Sea Blues. Hold 'er Sheriff. Hold Your Hat.* †*The Jelly Fish. Kiss Papa. Light Housekeeping. Live Cowards. Much Mystery. Pink Elephants. The Radio Bug. Sky Bound. Solid Gold. The Tin Ghost. Who Hit Me? Who's My Wife?* 1927: *Ain't Nature Grand? Batter Up. Brain Storm. Fox Tales. High Spots. Hot Lightning. Jungle Heat. Nothing Flat. No Cheating. Queens Wild. Red Hot Bullets. Seeing Stars. Sure Cure.* 1928: *Call Your Shots. Stage Fright. Hot or Cold. Just Dandy. Kitchen Talent. Leaping Luck. The Last Laugh. Polar Perils. Racing Mad. Social Prestige. Wives Won't Weaken. Who's Lyin'?* 1929: *Beauties Beware. Cold Shivers. Going Places. Hot Times. Honeymooniacs. Hunting the Hunter. Look Out Below. The Madhouse. Parlor Pests. Smart Steppers. Studio Pests. The Talkies. Those Two Boys. Ticklish Business. What a Day. Whoopee Boys. Wise Wimmin.* 1930: *The Big Jewel Case. Dad Knows Best. French Kisses. Hail, the Princess. His Error. Hot – and How! How's My Baby? The Laugh Back. Love a la Mode. My Harem. Oh Darling. Romance De Luxe. Their Wives' Vacation. Western Knights.* 1931: *Arabian Knights. Here's Luck. Let's Play. Parisian Gaieties. The Royal Bluff.* §*Sky Bride.* 1932: §*The Night of June 13th.* §*Lady and Gent.* †§*If I Had a Million.* 1933: †*The Story of Temple Drake.* §*One Sunday Afternoon.* 1934: §*The Trumpet Blows.* §*Romance in Manhattan.* 1935: §*Star of Midnight.* §*The Man Who Broke the Bank at Monte Carlo.* 1936: §*The Lady Consents.* §*The Ex-Mrs Bradford.*

All shorts except § features

ROBSON, Mark 1913-1978

From 1949 to 1965, this American director, schooled by such giants as Orson Welles (*qv*) and Val Lewton, made 22 films, of which at least 16 are enjoyable or thought-provoking – and often both: an enviable record of consistency for one who entered the film industry as a property boy at the age of 18. Robson's better films tend not to have highs and lows, but to be continuously entertaining. A missionary in China, a Jewish refugee girl, a blind soldier struggling to rehabilitate himself, Nobel prizewinners, a Mexican boy accused of rape and the assassination of Mahatma Gandhi were unexpected subjects for commercial success all over the world, but under Robson's careful handling, relentless pacing and skilful balancing of fact and fiction, they all did very nicely. He had moved from Fox to RKO, where he was to spend his next 12 years, in 1935, soon progressing to assistant editor. Among the films he helped to edit were Orson Welles' *Citizen Kane, The Magnificent Ambersons* and *Journey into Fear.* But from 1942, Robson was much involved with the low-budget horror unit of producer Val Lewton, for whom, after editing *Cat People, I Walked with a Zombie* and *The Leopard Man,* he directed five films, including *Bedlam* and *The Seventh Victim. As* with all Lewton's 'horror' movies, these were intelligent and chilling, if somewhat slow-paced. In the late 1940s, Robson joined Stanley Kramer's independent unit releasing through Columbia, and straight away had his biggest commercial success to date with *Champion,* a gruelling boxing story ideally suited to the hard-driving style of Kirk Douglas in the title role. *Home of the Brave* and *Bright Victory* were well-intentioned 'social conscience' pictures which attracted much critical praise, although Robson was more successful commercially with *My Foolish Heart,* an early Susan Hayward vehicle of the type to which her fans would rapidly become accustomed. Robson struggled for a while after leaving the Kramer fold, although *Hell Below Zero* is the best of Alan Ladd's British-made films. But the director really hit a hot streak with *Trial,* nerve-wrangling courtroom stuff that made a powerful, disturbing and at times highly emotional film. This was followed by Bogart's last film, *The Harder They Fall* and a series of crowd-pullers that included *The Inn of the Sixth Happiness, Peyton Place, The Prize* and *Von Ryan's Express.* His Gandhi film, *Nine Hours to Rama,* is much underrated. In the late 1960s, his work did decline dramatically. His last film, *Avalanche Express,* was a jinx movie. Both Robson and the star, Robert Shaw, died from heart attacks in the year it was made.

1943: The Seventh Victim. The Ghost Ship. 1944: Youth Runs Wild. 1945: Isle of the Dead. 1946: Bedlam. 1948: Roughshod. 1949: Champion. Home of

the Brave. My Foolish Heart. 1950: Edge of Doom (GB: Stronger than Fear). Bright Victory (GB: Lights Out). 1951: I Want You. 1953: Return to Paradise. 1954: Hell Below Zero. Phffft! The Bridges at Toko-Ri. 1955: A Prize of Gold. Trial. 1956: The Harder They Fall. 1957: The Little Hut. Peyton Place. 1958: The Inn of the Sixth Happiness. 1960: From the Terrace. 1962: Nine Hours to Rama. 1963: The Prize. 1965: Von Ryan's Express. 1966: Lost Command. 1967: Valley of the Dolls. 1969: Daddy's Gone a-Hunting. 1971: Happy Birthday, Wanda June. 1972: Limbo. 1974: Earthquake. 1979: Avalanche Express.

RODRIGUEZ, Robert 1966-

Hollywood director who created a sensation with his first feature and more recently has been associated with fellow writer-director Quentin Tarantino. The third of ten children, Rodriguez developed an early interest in drawing and, while still in his teens, created a daily cartoon strip called *Los Hooligans,* based on his own large family. It ran in *The Daily Texan* for three years. At the same time, Rodriguez used his family to solve cast and crew problems on an endless series of videos which he eventually cut together to make an hour-long anthology he called *Austin Stories:* the video won him admission to the film programme at the University of Texas. His debut film was *El Mariachi,* a fresh and vigorous pastiche of spaghetti westerns (in a Mexican setting). The film's vivid action, raw energy and sheer nerve made it a darling of the festival circuit and earned it a general release in several countries. Rodriguez later wrote a book about its making: *Rebel Without a Crew: Or How a 23-year-old film-maker Became a Hollywood Player.* When Rodriguez went to Hollywood, he made a bigger, splashier version of the same film, complete with major Latino stars in Antonio Banderas and Salma Hayek. Predictably the original was better and had a cutting edge that couldn't be reproduced on a bigger budget. Linking up with Tarantino, Rodriguez made a segment of *Four Rooms,* then shot his friend's screenplay for *From Dusk Till Dawn,* which emerged as a thrashingly exciting crime-and-vampire story that almost never slackens its pace while not taking itself seriously for a minute. There were sequels to the film but by this time Rodriguez had moved on, while staying with TexMex-California locations for a remake of *The Mark of Zorro,* eventually made by Martin Campbell.

*1991: *Bedhead. 1993: El Mariachi. 1994: Road-racers (cable TV). 1995:*

+Four Rooms. Desperado. 1996: From Dusk Till Dawn.

ROEG, Nicolas 1928-

British cameraman, writer and director who makes stylish if sometimes infuriating entertainments that often deal with mental disturbance or other-worldly qualities. His first film as solo director, *Walkabout,* was justly acclaimed by the critics – and public – as a vividly different entertainment, but opinion has been divided on his work since then, and he remains a painstaking perfectionist, as his record – ten feature films in 23 years – demonstrates. He began his career as an apprentice editor with M-G-M British at 18 but, apart from writing the story for *A Prize of Arms* in 1961, stuck to improving his career as a cinematographer from the mid-1950s. He was second-unit photographer on *Lawrence of Arabia* in 1962, shooting desert action scenes, before winning praise for his colour camerawork on *The Masque of the Red Death* and *Nothing But the Best,* both made the following year. He was second unit director on *Judith* (1965), then photographed and co-directed the extraordinary *Performance* which, despite the sex and violence it contained, critics and public alike seemed to find unapproachable. The sun-drenched, nerve-frayed Australian desert of *Walkabout,* which also made rare good use of Jenny Agutter's special qualities, was followed by a contrastingly cold Venice as the setting of Roeg's supernatural thriller-cum-sex-ploitation film, *Don't Look Now,* whose surface tedium was occasionally disturbed by deliberately baffling visual references culminating in horrifying death. Though the film's reputation has grown among those who managed to stay awake, its principal attraction at the time was a widely publicised central sex scene between Julie Christie and Donald Sutherland. A very similar atmosphere – boredom, bafflement and a frisson of the unexpected, coupled with heavy sex scenes – pervaded *The Man Who Fell to Earth.* But the sex, storytelling and unease fell together in the right pattern for Roeg in *Bad Timing.* Its opening sequence looks like a suicide attempt by a girl, after a tiff with her boyfriend. But gradually, horrifyingly, Roeg prises the relationship apart to reveal her analyst lover as a psychopath to set alongside Norman Bates in *Psycho.* He has driven the girl to such a step by persistent misunderstanding ... and has worse in store for her. It's unpalatable, but brilliantly made. Roeg continued to challenge his audiences through the 1980s. At the end of the decade, he made his most commercially successful film in 15 years with a

In familiar cap and scarf, Britain's innovative Nicolas **Roeg** is pictured during the making of one of his biggest successes, *Don't Look Now.*

+Erotic Tales II.

truly delightful adaptation of Roald Dahl's children's story *The Witches*, maintaining a fevered pace in its battle between good and evil. His taste for bizarre erotica, though, rather seemed to run away with his career in the 1990s. Divorced from the British actress Susan Stephen, Roeg later married the Hollywood star Theresa Russell.
1970: *+Performance (completed 1968).*

*Walkabout. 1971: *The Glastonbury Fair. 1973: Don't Look Now. 1976: The Man Who Fell to Earth. 1979: Bad Timing (US: Bad Timing/A Sensual Obsession). 1982: Eureka. 1985: Insignificance. 1987: +Aria. 1988: Track 29. 1989: Sweet Bird of Youth (TV). The Witches. 1992: Cold Heaven. 1994: +Erotic Tales. Heart of Darkness (TV). Two Deaths. 1995: Full Body Massage (TV). 1997:*

ROGELL, Albert S. 1901-1988

Oklahoma-born director, notably of 'B' westerns, who brought new high standards to the series western in the late 1920s. His Ken Maynard and Art Acord films are especially of note. The younger brother of Sid Rogell (1900-1974) who was for many years with RKO, at one time as chief executive, he picked up his eye for visual effects from his early days as an assistant cameraman, moving from photographer to assistant director in the early 1920s and getting his first directorial assignment, *The Greatest Menace,* in the autumn of 1923. His career as an action director really got under way with assignments on five-reel westerns for First National and Blue Streak from the mid-1920s. Some of his vehicles for the riding skills of Ken Maynard gained remarkable notices for low-budget horse-operas. His use of close camerawork and cross-cutting, for example, in the 1926 seven-reeler *Señor Daredevil,* had critics reaching for comparisons with *Ben-Hur* and its chariot race, especially in a pounding finale as Maynard galloped to get a convoy of food supplies to a town cut off and besieged by the bad guys. Billed at this time as 'Al Rogell' (the 'Albert S.' came in when he left westerns in 1929), the director also won praise for *Red Raiders,* a larger-budget Maynard western with action on a grand scale and Indians biting the dust in their thousands. Rogell and his cameraman Sol Polito, later to pursue a distinguished career at Warners, achieved some remarkable effects, including a thrilling covered-wagon charge and an innovative backward-tracking shot, almost giving a three-dimensional effect as hundreds of cavalrymen, first seen on the skyline, thunder down the hill and towards the camera, getting closer and closer despite the camera's moving away from them. These panoramic action scenes were intercut with tight close-ups on Maynard performing spectacular feats of horsemanship. Theoretically, Rogell should have moved on to a career along similar lines to that of John Ford. Perhaps he was insufficiently ambitious, for he remained bogged down in second-features for the next 20 years. And most of them were thrillers. Two from 1941 (by which time Rogell was working at Universal), *Tight Shoes* and *The Black Cat,* have an atmosphere of cool hostility that places them above the run of the mill. Before going into TV, Rogell made a film in Britain that ranks as one of his best: *Before I Wake,* a sinister stepmother plot put over in style, with a tense duel of wits between Jean Kent and Mona Freeman.

1923: The Greatest Menace. 1924: The Mask of Lopez. The Silent Stranger. Fighting for Justice. Galloping Gallagher. North of Nevada. Thundering Hoofs. Lightning Romance. The Fighting Sap. The Dangerous Coward. 1925: Easy Money. Super Speed. Youth's Gamble. The Knockout Kid. The Goat Getter. The Snob Buster. The Circus Cyclone. Crack o' Dawn. Pals. The Fear Fighter. Triple Action. The Cyclone Cavalier. 1926: Lazy Lightning. Man of the West. The Unknown Cavalier. The Ridin' Rascal. Rustlers' Ranch. Fighting Fate. The Set Up. Red Hot Leather. Sky High Corral. Men of the Night. Wild Horse Stampede. Señor Daredevil. 1927: Overland Stage. Red Raiders. Western Whirlwind. Men of Daring. Western Rover. The Sunset Derby. Grinning Guns. The Devil's Saddle. Rough and Ready. Somewhere in Sonora. 1928: The Upland Rider. Shepherd of the Hills. Canyon of Adventure. The Glorious Trail. The Phantom City. 1929: Cheyenne. California Mail. The Lone Wolf's Daughter. The Flying Marine. 1930: Painted Faces. Mamba. 1931: Aloha (GB: No Greater Love). Sweepstakes. The Tip-Off (GB: Looking for Trouble). Suicide Fleet. 1932: Carnival Boat. The Rider of Death Valley. Air Hostess. 1933: The Wrecker. Below the Sea (later Hell's Cargo). East of Fifth Avenue (GB: Two in a Million). Fog. 1934: No More Women. The Hell Cat. Among the Missing. Fugitive Lady. Name the Woman. 1935: Air Hawks. Unknown Woman. Atlantic Adventure. Song of the Damned (later Escape from Devil's Island). 1936: Roaming Lady. Grand Jury. You May Be Next! (GB: Panic on the Air). 1937: Murder in Greenwich Village. Start Cheering. 1938: The Lone Wolf in Paris. City Streets. The Last Warning. 1939: Hawaiian Nights. For Love or Money (GB: Tomorrow at Midnight). Laugh It Off (GB: Lady Be Gay). 1940: Private Affair. I Can't Give You Anything But Love, Baby. Li'l Abner (GB: Trouble Chaser). Argentine Nights. 1941: Tight Shoes. The Black Cat. Public Enemies. 1942: Jail House Blues. Sleepytime Gal. Butch Minds the Baby. Youth on Parade. True to the Army. Priorities on Parade. 1943: Hit Parade of 1943. In Old Oklahoma (later War of the Wildcats). 1945: Love, Honor and Goodbye. 1946: Earl Carroll Sketchbook (GB: Hats Off to Rhythm). 1947: The Magnificent Rogue. Heaven Only Knows. 1948: Northwest Stampede. 1949: The Song of India. 1950: The Admiral Was a Lady. 1955: Before I Wake (US: Shadow of Fear).

ROHMER, Eric (Jean-Marie Maurice Scherer) 1920-

While he has kept a discreet distance – like so many, of his characters' attitudes to life – from the hurly-burly of French commercial cinema, the skilful and sustained accessibility of Rohmer's often charming and delicately performed comedies of manners has made him a safe bet at art houses throughout the world for over 25 years. In their own world, Rohmer's films are guaranteed to run and run. This may be because, although they are more or less conversation pieces, they are also cleverly constructed (he always writes his own screenplays) in such a way as to keep an audience's interest alive until matters dovetail at the end, by which time most of Rohmer's characters know more about themselves than when the film began. He himself describes his films as 'closer to a novel than any other art form'. After World War II, Rohmer became a journalist and then critic, at first under the name Maurice Scherer, but under his adopted name from 1955. Two years later, he became editor of the influential magazine *Cahiers du Cinéma*, for which he had worked since the early 1950s. He had begun making short films in 1950, and combined writing and film-making careers until 1963, by which time he had just embarked on his series of six 'contes moraux', which comprised *La boulangère de Monceau, La carrière de Suzanne, La collectioneuse, Ma nuit chez Maud* (possibly his most satisfying film), *Le genou de Claire* (a world-wide success as *Claire's Knee*) and *L'amour l'après-midi*. After the completion of this sextet, Rohmer's work was rather less satisfactory until he embarked on a new 'series', which this time he called 'comédies et proverbes', beginning with *La femme de l'aviateur* and *Un beau mariage*, films which again demonstrated Rohmer's adroitness at creating a narrative from the slightest of substance – something akin to the miracle of loaves and fishes, as the viewer is deceived, to his own delight, into believing the restricted rations he has devoured have comprised a rich meal. Rohmer continued his minute dissections of people's lives – often those on holiday – with a series of 'contes' which he completed in 1998.

*1950: *Journal d'un scélérat. 1951: *Charlotte et son steak/Présentation. 1952: †Les petites filles modèles (unfinished). 1954: *Bérénice. 1956: La sonate à Kreutzer (GB and US: The Kreutzer Sonata). 1958: *Véronique et son cancre. 1959: Le signe du lion (US: The Sign of Leo). 1962: *La boulangère de Monceau. 1963: La carrière de Suzanne. 1964: *Nadja à Paris. †Paris vu par ... (GB and US: Six in Paris). 1966: *Une étudiante*

d'aujourd-hui. La collectioneuse (US: The Collector). 1968: Fermière à Montfauçon. 1969: Ma nuit chez Maud (GB: My Night with Maud. US: My Night at Maud's). 1970: Le genou de Claire (GB and US: Claire's Knee). 1972: L'amour l'après-midi (GB: Love in the Afternoon. US: Chloë in the Afternoon). 1976: Die Marquise von O (GB and US: The Marquise of O). 1978: Percival le Gallois (US: Perceval). 1980: La femme de l'aviateur (GB and US: The Aviator's Wife). 1981: Un beau mariage (GB & US: A Good Marriage). 1983: Pauline à la plage. 1984: Les nuits de la pleine lune/Full Moon in Paris. 1985: Le rayon vert (GB and US: The Green Ray). 1986: L'ami de mon amie (GB: My Girlfriend's Boyfriend. US: Boyfriends and Girlfriends). 1987: 4 aventures de Reinette & Mirabelle. 1990: Conte de printemps (GB and US: A Tale of Springtime). 1992: Un conte d'hiver (GB and US: A Tale of Winter). 1995: Les rendezvous de Paris. 1996: Conte d'été (GB and US: A Summer's Tale). 1998: Conte d'automne/Autumn Tale.

ROMERO, Eddie (Enrique Romero) 1924-

Few people will have heard of Eddie Romero, yet most cinemagoers, and certainly those from the Fifties and Sixties, will have seen one of his vivid (some might say lurid) action or horror films. And, whatever the overall quality of these movies, no Philippines-born director has had more films shown in the international market. From a family of diplomats, Romero proved a prolific writer who penned his first film scripts at the age of 17. Following World War II he became the editor of a magazine before branching out into film direction at 23 and, from 1955, proving the founding father of English-language production in the Philippines. This in turn led to a lengthy period of co-production with American companies, during which time Romero saw his work widely distributed in both America and Britain, where his films were snapped up to provide fodder for the ailing double-feature bill. Working on tight budgets and producing atmospheric if stickily acted and sometimes risibly scripted works, Romero would have been well at home working for a Hollywood Poverty Row studio of the Forties. Many of his horror films, several of which star Hollywood exile John Ashley, are now keenly sought by collectors.

1947: Ang kamay ng diyos. 1948: Hindi kita malimot. Sa piling mo. 1949: Selosa. Apoy sa langit. 1950: Abogada. Always. 1951: Ang princesa at ang. †Pulubi. †Kasintalian s pangarap. 1952: †El Indo.

†*Barbaro.* †*Ang ating pag-ibig.* 1953: †*Maldita.* **Ang asawa kong amerikana. Buhay alamang. May isang tsuper ng taksi.* 1954: *Torpe. Iskandalosa. Takas.* 1955: *Golpe de gulat. May bakas ang lumipas. Maria Went to Town.* 1956: ***Huk! Huling mandirigma.* 1957: *Cavalry Command* (released 1965). 1958: *The Kidnappers.* 1959: +*Terror is a Man.* ***Surrender - Hell!* 1961: *Lost Battalion. Meet Johnny L.* 1962: *N.B.I. Raiders of Leyte Gulf. Pitong gabi sa Paris.* 1963: *Magtago ka na, binata.* 1964: *Moro Witch Doctor. The Walls of Hell. Amok. Simaron.* 1965: *The Ravagers. Cordillera.* +*The Brides of Blood Island/Brides of Blood/Brides of the Beast.* 1966: *The Passionate Strangers.* 1967: *Manila: Open City.* 1968: +*The Mad Doctor of Blood Island.* 1969: *Blood Devils.* 1970: *Beast of the Yellow Night.* 1971: *Twilight People.* 1972: *Woman Hunt.* 1973: *Black Mama, White Mama* (GB: *Hot, Hard and Mean*). *Beyond Atlantis.* 1974: *Savage Sisters.* 1975: *Sudden Death.* 1976: *As We Were.* 1977: +*Lahing Filipino. Banta ng kahapon. Sinong kapiling? Sinong kasiping?* 1979: *Palaban.* 1980: *Aguila.* 1981: *The Day Before Yesterday.* 1983: *The Return of Dr X.* 1984: *White Force.*

†As Enrique Moreno
**As John Barnwell

ROMERO, George A. 1939-

One of America's most effective directors of chillers and horror films from 1968 to 1988, Romero has dissipated his talents too much. Still, his *Night of the Living Dead*, made in black and white, remains one of the rare examples of true horror in recent Hollywood history. Romero, afflicted with a film-making urge since high school days (the first four films listed below are all on 8mm), admits to being strongly influenced by William Gaines' Entertaining Comics – horror picture stories which have influenced other film-makers as well. They offered no concession to light relief, and there was to be none in Romero's work until the late 1970s. After six years in TV commercials, following a failure to break into feature films, Romero made a stir with *Night of the Living Dead*, in which zombies plague the American countryside, leading to terrifying scenes when characters are trapped in houses. The shock moments are very skilfully done, and the horror presented uncomfortably head-on, with a total absence of humour. Romero was somewhat less successful with *Jack's Wife*, about a woman who feels that occult forces are driving her towards the unknown; *Martin*, a rough-edged vampire film with atmospheric black-and-white flashbacks; and *The Crazies*. But the second part of what Romero now claims as a horror trilogy, *Zombies*, is a first-class horror comic, sharply edited and zingily directed and much more polished and professional than his previous work. The secret of its suspense lies in not knowing which, if any, of the four main characters will survive, and their subsequent narrow escapes at the hands of the swarming, flesh-eating zombies, if at times overly contrived, provide nail-biting stuff for those with strong nerves and stomachs. This is where Romero's fast and skilful editing really comes into its own. His next film, *Knightriders*, a long, long miscalculation about modern knights on motorcycles travelling the countryside holding tournaments, could have done with even more editing than it had. Happily, Romero was soon back on more familiar ground with *Creepshow* and *Day of the*

This may be a crowd of zombie extras asking for a raise. Even so, horror ace George A **Romero** looks unfazed. A publicity shot for Romero's *Day of the Dead.*

Dead, the latter the last part of his zombie trilogy. There was an ominous gap to the nail-biting *Monkey Shines*, an original and progressively more exciting sci-fi thriller. Unfortunately it's also Romero's last work of note to date.

1954: **The Man from the Meteor.* 1955: **Gorilla.* 1956: **Earthbottom* (D). 1958: **Curly. *Slant.* 1962: *Expostulations (released 1965).* 1968: *Night of the Living Dead.* 1972: *There's Always Vanilla/The Affair.* 1973: *Jack's Wife (later abridged as Hungry Wives). The Crazies.* 1977: *Martin.* 1978: *Zombies (GB: Zombies – Dawn of the Dead).* 1981: *Knightriders.* 1982: *Creepshow.* 1984: *Day of the Dead.* 1988: *Monkey Shines.* 1990: *+Two Evil Eyes. +Tales from the Darkside: The Movie.* 1993: *The Dark Half.*

ROSEN, Phil/Philip E. 1888-1951

Another example of a Hollywood career fading very quickly into second-features with the coming of sound. Russian-born Rosen had emigrated to America at the turn of the century, and was established in the film industry as a cameraman with an eye for detail before World War I. In the 1920s, Rosen became one of the film capital's more prominent directors, with a taste for lavish and intricate detail that expanded on his reputation as a photographer. *The Young Rajah*, which he made late in 1922, is one of the most exotic of all Valentino's films, as opulent as only an affluent Hollywood could make it, with Valentino's appeal at its most smouldering in the famous sequence where he woos Wanda Hawley in what is possibly the world's most ornate small boat, complete with a prow composed of six carved snakes. Rosen also enjoyed great success with his biography of Abraham Lincoln, in which the title role was taken by George Billings, as famous for his silent interpretations of the role as Raymond Massey was to become with sound. Would that Rosen had had such lavish production values on his sound films. But by 1931, he was already making 'B' westerns, and the pattern for the remainder of his career was set. The 1940s contained a long string of increasingly dull, Rosen-directed Charlie Chan films – a sad finale to the career of a man once called by M-G-M to remake totally *The Exquisite Sinner*, the work of no less a director than Josef von Sternberg (*qv*).

1916: *The Beach Comber.* 1917: *California or Bust. In the First Degree.* 1919: **The Jay Bird.* 1920: **The Sheriff's Oath. *West is Best. The Road to Divorce. The Path She Chose. Are All Men Alike?*

1921: *Extravagance. The Little Pool. The Lure of Youth.* 1922: *The Bonded Woman. The World's Champion. The Young Rajah. Handle with Care. Across the Continent.* 1923: *A Wise Son. Lovers' Lane.* 1924: *The Dramatic Life of Abraham Lincoln/Abraham Lincoln. This Woman. The Bridge of Sighs. Being Respectable.* 1925: *The Heart of a Siren. The White Monkey. Wandering Footsteps.* 1926: *A Woman's Heart. Stolen Pleasure. Rose of the Tenements. The Adorable Deceiver. †The Exquisite Sinner.* 1927: *Closed Gates. Heaven on Earth. Salvation Jane. The Woman Who Did Not Care. The Cruel Truth. Thumbs Down. Stranded. Pretty Clothes. Cancelled Debts.* 1928: *Marry the Girl (GB: The House of Deceit). Burning Up Broadway. Undressed. Modern Mothers. The Apache.* 1929: *The Peacock Fan. The Faker. The Phantom in the House.* 1930: *Extravagance (remake). The Rampant Age. The Lotus Lady. Second Honeymoon. Worldly Goods.* 1931: *Arizona Terror. Range Law. The Two-Gun Man (GB: Two's Company). Alias the Bad Man. Branded Men. The Pocatello Kid.* 1932: *A Man's Land. Klondike (GB: The Doctor's Sacrifice). The Vanishing Frontier. Lena Rivers. Young Blood (GB: Lola). The Gay Buckaroo. The Texas Gun Fighter. Whistlin' Dan.* 1933: *The Sphinx. The Phantom Broadcast (GB: Phantom of the Air). Hold the Press. Black Beauty. Devil's Mate (GB: He Knew Too Much). Picture Brides. Shadows of Sing Sing. Self Defense.* 1934: *Beggars in Ermine. The Cheaters. Take the Stand (GB: The Great Radio Mystery). Dangerous Corner. Woman in the Dark. Little Men. West of the Pecos.* 1935: *Death Flies East. Born to Gamble. Unwelcome Stranger. The Calling of Dan Matthews.* 1936: *Missing Girls (GB: When Girls Leave Home). The Bridge of Sighs. The President's Mystery (GB: One for All). Easy Money. Ellis Island. Tango. It Couldn't Have Happened. Three of a Kind. The Brilliant Marriage.* 1937: *Roaring Timber. Jim Hanvey, Detective. Two Wise Maids. Youth on Parole. It Could Happen to You.* 1938: *The Marines Are Here.* 1939: *Ex-Champ (GB: Golden Gloves). Missing Evidence.* 1940: *Double Alibi. The Crooked Road. Forgotten Girls. Queen of the Yukon. Phantom of Chinatown.* 1941: *Murder By Invitation. Paper Bullets (later Gangs Incorporated). The Deadly Game. I Killed That Man. Spooks Run Wild. The Roar of the Press.* 1942: *Road to Happiness. The Man with Two Lives. The Mystery of Marie Roget.* 1943: *You Can't Beat the Law. A Gentle Gangster. Wings Over the Pacific. Prison Mutiny.* 1944: *Charlie Chan in the Secret*

Service. The Chinese Cat/Charlie Chan in the Chinese Cat. Return of the Ape Man (GB: Lock Your Doors). Black Magic. Call of the Jungle. The Jade Mask. Army Wives. 1945: *Captain Tugboat Annie. The Cisco Kid in Old New Mexico/In Old New Mexico. The Scarlet Clue. The Red Dragon.* 1946: *The Shadow Returns. The Strange Mr Gregory. Step by Step.* 1949: *The Secret of St Ives.*

ROSENBERG, Stuart 1925-

As one of the best television directors of the 1960s, it seemed that New York-born Rosenberg was prime material for a distinguished cinema career, especially after his debut with *Cool Hand Luke*, which won George Kennedy a best supporting actor Oscar. But perhaps he had stayed too long in television, for his subsequent film work hovered on the edge of mainstream cinema and took precious little at the box-office. In the late 1970s, however, he seemed to balance offbeat subjects with the right entertainment values, raising hopes that he had come to terms with the cinema at last. A former teacher, Rosenberg went into television in the mid-1950s and subsequently directed scores of segments of crime and mystery series, including *The Untouchables, Alfred Hitchcock Presents, Naked City, The Defenders* and *The Twilight Zone*. He has not gone back to TV since 1967 when he unwrapped *Cool Hand Luke*, with Paul Newman as the likeable guy determined to escape his life on the prison chain gang. Rosenberg's direction underlined the strength of the personalities involved, undercutting the less pleasant aspects of the film, and putting the focus squarely on Newman's winning performance. Director and star tried in vain to repeat the successful formula in three further films together, but *WUSA, Pocket Money* and *The Drowning Pool* did little for either of them. Rosenberg found himself on sounder commercial ground with *The Amityville Horror*, based on a supposedly true-life best-seller about a house possessed; and the harsh, oppressive ambience produced by his unrelenting treatment brought the film home a nail-biting winner. His career almost turned full circle in 1980 with *Brubaker* – back in prison with another charismatic leading man, this time Robert Redford as the crusading governor determined to reform the vilest and most violent jail farm in all America. If Redford is perhaps too good to be true, Rosenberg's direction sustains audience sympathy and ensures the emotional impact of the final scenes. Since then Rosenberg's output has been sporadic and unsatisfactory with the excep-

tion of his last film to date, *My Heroes Have Always Been Cowboys* a poignant and crowd-pleasing film about a rodeo rider retrieving his father from a retirement home.

1960: †*Murder Inc.* 1961: *Question 7.* 1965: *Memorandum for a Spy (TV. Reissued two years later, in slightly revised form, as a TV movie called Asylum for a Spy).* 1966: *Fame is the Name of the Game (TV). The Faceless Man (TV. Later expanded by another director into a feature, The Counterfeit Killer, released 1968).* 1967: *Cool Hand Luke.* 1969: *The April Fools.* 1970: *WUSA. Move.* 1972: *Pocket Money.* 1973: *The Laughing Policeman (GB: An Investigation of Murder).* 1975: *The Drowning Pool.* 1976: *Voyage of the Damned.* 1978: *Love and Bullets.* 1979: *The Amityville Horror.* 1980: *Brubaker.* 1984: *The Pope of Greenwich Village.* 1986: **Let's Get Harry.* 1991: *My Heroes Have Always Been Cowboys.*

*As Alan Smithee

ROSI, Francesco 1922-

Italian director, known as 'Italy's social conscience'. His films are principally outcries against the exploitation of the poor in one form or another, often told, as in *Salvatore Giuliano* or *Lucky Luciano*, in the guise of a gangster story. The former was the film that made Rosi's reputation in 1961, after years as an assistant director and sometime screenwriter. The pictorial imagery is relentlessly effective in the documentary-like reconstruction of the life of a Sicilian bandit who becomes to the peasantry – whose economic plight is detailed in all its misery – the same kind of folk-hero as Ned Kelly. From time to time, Rosi has used the brooding intensity of the American actor Rod Steiger, notably as the corrupt industrialist in *Hands over the City* and the gangster *Lucky Luciano*. In an extraordinary departure from style, Rosi also made a greatly successful fantasy, *Once Upon a Time*, with Sophia Loren and Omar Sharif, which invades Demy territory, but with somewhat more success than Demy himself. Rosi has disappointed the followers of his earlier work in recent years with what they consider stylistically elegant films devoid of meaningful content. On the whole, though, his films continue to attract both good reviews, and box-office profits. It was good to see him explore fresh fields away from a factual background, especially with a vivid version of *Bizet's Carmen*. But his films grew ever more scarce as he progressed into his seventies.

Herbert **Ross** at work on *The Turning Point* in 1977, which earned him an unenviable place in history. It was nominated for 11 Academy Awards, including best picture, but didn't win any – a record.

1952: †*Camicie rosse.* 1957: †*Kean, Genius or Scoundrel? (uncredited).* 1958: *La sfida (US: The Challenge).* 1959: *I magliari.* 1961: *Salvatore Giuliano.* 1963: *Manu sulla città/Hands over the City.* 1965. *Il momento della verità (GB & US: The Moment of Truth).* 1967: *Once Upon a Time (GB: Cinderella, Italian Style. US: More Than a Miracle).* 1970: *Uomini contro.* 1972: *Il caso Mattei (GB & US: The Mattei Affair).* 1973: *Lucky Luciano.* 1976: *Cadaveri eccellenti (GB & US: Illustrious Corpses).* 1979: *Eboli (GB: Christ Stopped at Eboli).* 1981: *Tre fratelli.* 1984: *Bizet's Carmen.* 1987: *Cronaca di una morte annunciata (GB & US: Chronicle of a Death Foretold).* 1990: *To Forget Palermo/Dimenticare Palermo/The Palermo Connection.* 1997: *La tregua/The Truce.*

ROSS, Herbert 1927-

American choreographer who, like his contemporary Bob Fosse, turned director in his early forties with some success. His films are mostly in colour with fairly substantial budgets, generally, but not always, more successful in a light rather than dramatic vein. For a dance director, Ross proved remarkably adept with actors, especially in bringing out their more endearing qualities, and three acting Academy Awards have so far been won in his films. Like Fosse, he began as a dancer, but had turned his attention to direction by the early 1950s. His first film as choreographer was *Carmen Jones;* later he came to Britain to devise the exhilarating dance routines on the first two Cliff Richard musicals, *The Young Ones* and *Summer Holiday*. By this time, Ross had also directed a number of Broadway musicals, including the 1960 production of *Finian's Rainbow*. His first foray into the cinema, *Goodbye Mr Chips*, was naturally in that mould, but he soon diversified, enjoying his first big success with a highly satisfactory film of Woody Allen's stage play *Play It Again, Sam*. Full of delightfully funny moments, the film and its performances gain an edge from Ross's calmly paced direction that it might not have received from Allen's own rather more frenzied style. Ross scored further successes in contrasting genres with *The Last of Sheila*, a jigsaw-puzzle whodunnit; *The Turning Point*, a film about ballet and the conflict in women's lives between home and career, with virtuoso roles for two strong actresses (filled by Shirley MacLaine and Anne Bancroft); and two Neil Simon scripts, *The Goodbye Girl* and the more variable *California Suite*. Ross also made *Funny Lady*, the sequel to *Funny Girl*, a film on which he himself had been choreographer. Seemingly at the height of his powers as a bankable box-office director, Ross struck out twice in a row with two equally lavish productions, *Nijinsky* and *Pennies from Heaven*, in each case opening out films which could have profited from the more intimate style he had used in some of his earlier work. Ross now played safe with another Neil Simon script on *Max Dugan Returns*. But the only substantial success of his later years has been *Steel Magnolias*, an adaptation of a successful play, with an often witty script and a heavyweight all-star female cast. Ross's facility with actresses was underlined in 1995 by the performances of Whoopi Goldberg, Drew Barrymore and Mary-Louise Parker in his last film to date, *Boys on the Side*.

1969: *Goodbye Mr Chips.* 1970: *The Owl and the Pussycat.* 1971: *T.R. Baskin (GB: A Date with a Lonely Girl).* 1972: *Play It Again, Sam.* 1973: *The Last of Sheila.* 1975: *Funny Lady. The Sunshine Boys.* 1976: *The Seven-Per-Cent Solution.* 1977: *The Turning Point. The Goodbye Girl.* 1978. *California Suite.* 1980: *Nijinsky.* 1981: *Pennies from Heaven.* 1982: *I Ought To Be in Pictures.* 1983: *Max Dugan Returns.* 1984: *Footloose. Protocol.* 1987: *Giselle. The Secret of My Success. Dancers.* 1989: *Steel Magnolias.* 1990: *My Blue Heaven.* 1991: *True Colors.* 1993: *Undercover Blues/Cloak and Diaper.* 1995: *Boys on the Side.*

ROSSELLINI, Roberto 1906-1977

Distinguished Italian film-maker, at his most forceful in the post-war years. Then, he took the world by storm with a series of dramatic and painful films depicting the horrifying aftermaths of war that were instrumental, together with films by Vittorio De Sica *(qv)* and others, in boosting the prestige of the Italian cinema. These films, *Rome: Open City, Paisà* and *Germany: Year Zero* are characterized by their use of actual backgrounds and non-professional players, the rough edges of their production (contrasting with the polish of Rossellini's first feature, *La nave bianca*) combining with these elements to produce a contemporary feel and newsreel-like harshness. Rossellini's prestige slumped following his much-publicized romance with – and eventual marriage to – Ingrid Bergman. The films they made together are often very intelligently done, but somehow seem to lack a driving force. After the divorce from Bergman, Rossellini regained some of his reputation (especially with the 1959 film *Il generale della revere*, with Vittorio De Sica in his element as the conman at large during World War II), but never took his place at the forefront of Italian and world cinema, having been overtaken by newer, younger talents. Born in Rome, the city whose tragedies he would later mourn, Rossellini became interested in the technical side of making films as a young man, inventing a new variety of camera, which he would later use in his own films, before beginning to make documentaries in 1936. One of his earliest, *Prélude à l'après-midi d'un faune*, was actually banned by the Italian censors as indecent. Close behind Luchino Visconti *(qv)* as a front-runner in the neo-realist school shunned by the authorities, Rossellini followed films with Anna Magnani by making several with Bergman of which *Stromboli, Europa 51* and *Viaggio in Italia*, though not liked at the time, have recently been re-evaluated and are now rated by some critics as Rossellini's best films. From the 1960s onwards, he made many historical documentaries for Italian and French television.

1936: **Daphne.* 1938: **Prélude à l'après-midi d'un faune. †Luciano serra pilota.* 1939: **Fantasia sottomarino. *Il tachino prepotente. *La vispa Teresa.* 1941: **Il ruscello di Ripasottile. La nave bianca.* 1942: *Una pilota ritorna.* 1943: *L'uomo della croce. †Desiderio.* 1945: *Roma, città aperta (GB: Rome, Open City. US: Open City).* 1946: *Paisà (US: Paisan).* 1947: *Germania, anno zero (GB & US: Germany: Year Zero).* 1948: *L'amore (GB:*

Ways of Love. US: Woman). 1949: *Stromboli.* 1950: *Francesco – giullare di Dio (US: Flowers of St Francis).* 1952: *Europa '51 (GB: No Greater Love. US: The Greatest Love). †The Seven Deadly Sins. †Siamo donne (GB: We the Women).* 1953: *Dov'è la libertà?* 1954: *Viaggio in Italia (GB: Journey to Italy/The Lonely Woman. US: Strangers). Joan of Arc at the Stake/Joan at the Stake. Fear. †Amori di mezzo secolo.* 1958: *India (D).* 1959: *Il generale della rovere (US: General Della Rovere)* 1960: *Era notte a Roma (GB & US: It Was Night in Rome). Viva l'Italia!* 1961: *Vanina Vanini (GB & US: The Betrayer). Torino nei centi'anni (D).* 1962: *Anima nera. †RoGoPaG.* 1964: *L'età del ferro (D. US: The Iron Age).* 1966: *La prise de pouvoir de Louis XIV (originally for TV).* 1967: *Idea di un'isola (D. Originally for TV).* 1968: *Atti degli apostoli (originally for TV. GB and US: Acts of the Apostles).* 1970: *Socrates (originally for TV).* 1971: *Blaise Pascal (originally for TV. US: Pascal).* 1972: *Agostino di Ippona.* 1973: *L'età di Cosimo de' Medici (originally for TV).* 1974: *Descartes (originally for TV).* 1975: *Anno uno (GB & US: Year One).* 1977: *Il messia/The Messiah.*

ROSSEN, Robert (R. Rosen) 1906-1977

The life and beliefs of this tortured figure from Hollywood's history are mirrored in many of his films: his early days as a boxer; his experience as a writer with Warners during the vintage years of their social protest films; his political ideals; and his obsession with (his own) illness. Despite his many self-doubts, however, Rossen also managed to make some of the most powerful entertainment films to come out of America in the 20 years following the war, and had it not been for the way his life progressed, including blacklisting at the hands of the McCarthy committee, might have made several more. Brought up on New York's rough East Side, Rossen forsook boxing for writing in his early twenties and went to Hollywood in 1936, contributing scripts for some of Warner's top stars. His earliest films as director (from 1947) *Johnny O'Clock* and *Body and Soul*, suffer a little from the artificiality of the director's approach, although both have hard-hitting moments and *Body and Soul*, a portrait of corruption in the boxing world, won an Oscar for best editing. Corruption was also at the heart of *All the King's Men*, a horrifyingly effective study of how absolute power corrupts absolutely, based on the career of a Southern United States politician. Aided, as always, by a script written by himself, Rossen homes tightly in on the drama, eliciting, not for the last time, strong performances from his entire cast. The film was a popular as well as a critical hit, and won the best picture Academy Award, as well as two acting Oscars, for Broderick Crawford and Mercedes McCambridge. Rossen was nominated as best director, but did not win. At this stage of his career, however, Rossen was blacklisted by the industry for his former Communist affiliations; two years later, he admitted his 'Red' past, 'named names' and was allowed to work again. Friends, however, said he was haunted by the experience and never recovered. Most of Rossen's remaining films are interesting partial failures, such as *They Came to Cordura*, a first-class drama which touches the raw nerve of human emotions, and the poetic *Lilith*. But, to his everlasting credit, there was also *The Hustler*, with Paul Newman as a backstreets pool-room equivalent of *The Cincinnati Kid*. Newman's was just one of four dynamic performances: Piper Laurie, Jackie Gleason and George C. Scott, most memorable of all as his hawk-cruel manager, were the other three, while the pool-room scenes themselves carry a rare charge of tension. Rossen's telling dialogue was perhaps the best he ever wrote, but the film, although nominated for nine Oscars, won only two, with Rossen missing out again.

1947: Johnny O'Clock. Body and Soul. 1949: All the King's Men. 1951: The Brave Bulls. 1955: Mambo. 1956: Alexander the Great. 1957: Island in the Sun. 1959: They Came to Cordura. 1961: The Hustler. 1964: Lilith.

ROUSE, Russell 1913-1987

There is something a little strange about most of the few films made by this New York-born writer and director. It's not just that most of them have a gimmick of some kind or another. *Wicked Woman* has been described as the most camp film ever made and *The Oscar* the worst film ever made; Rouse seems perverse enough to have done it just to get another entry in the *Guinness Book of Records*. *The Thief* is a film completely without words and *The Well* has to be the only film ever made about a black child down a well who can save someone from being hung if only she can be rescued. *D.O.A.*, written although not directed by Rouse and his longtime writer-producer partner Clarence Greene, concerns a man dying of a slow-acting poison trying to find his own murderer. *Thunder in the Sun* is the only western about a Basque wagon train; *House of Numbers* has Jack Palance as twins(!); *The Caper of the Golden Bulls*

must be the only robbery story staged against the running of the bulls in Pamplona. *The Fastest Gun Alive* has an orchestrated gun duel in which the participants are seen separately and *The House is Not a Home* a unique line-up of brothel girls that includes Raquel Welch and Edy Williams. Apart from *The Well* and *D.O.A.*, not many of these films are actually very good; but Rouse's other film *New York Confidential*, a crime film without a heart that portrays its central characters as family and businessmen, is very well acted by Broderick Crawford, Anne Bancroft and Richard Conte and pre-dates *The Godfather* by 17 years: in its way another first for Rouse. It must have been difficult for Rouse to find backing for some of these projects and if his direction had only matched his originality, he might have had a longer career. Rouse, who died from complications following a stroke, was married to actress Beverly Michaels. Rouse and Greene shared an Oscar for the story of *Pillow Talk* in 1959.

1951: †The Well. 1952: The Thief. 1953: Wicked Woman. 1955: New York Confidential. 1956: The Fastest Gun Alive. 1957: House of Numbers. 1959: Thunder in the Sun. 1964: A House is Not a Home. 1966: The Oscar. The Caper of the Golden Bulls (GB: Carnival of Thieves).

ROWLAND, Roy 1910-1995

A middle-line M-G-M stalwart for more than 20 years, this native New Yorker directed many competent films for the studio, although his most individual work came in the series of comedy shorts he made with the great Robert Benchley and in one of his rae films for another studio, *The 5,000 Fingers of Dr T*. Originally, he had intended to be a lawyer, but the booming sound industry of the early 1930s attracted him, and he became a script clerk, progressing to assistant director by 1932. He had his first taste of direction in 1934, and began to get regular work on two-reel shorts from 1936. He was put in charge of the undiluted wit of the Benchley films from 1937 and presided over some of the best in the series, including *How to Raise a Baby* and *The Courtship of the Newt*. Later, Rowland was moved to the 'Crime Does Not Pay' series, before making his first features in 1943. All of Rowland's films are worth a little, especially the three expert weepies with tiny Margaret O' Brien – *Lost Angel*, *Our Vines have Tender Grapes* and *Tenth Avenue Angel*. *The Outriders* is a rousing western with a

nice eye from outdoor visuals and a good villain role for Barry Sullivan, and *Scene of the Crime* a good quality low budget thriller. Others, however, are pretty routine by Metro standards, and some of Rowland's better work was done outside the studio. For Columbia the attractive Technicolor fantasy *The 5,000 Fingers of Dr T* (the title refers to the 500 boys imprisoned by the evil Dr T, forever being forced to play a monster piano in his bizarre castle of musical instruments) with splendidly realized dream sequences and a lunatic performance by Hans Conreid; for Warners, *Bugles in the Afternoon*, a thunderingly good western in the early 1950s' tradition, with some of the most exciting action scenes – between Indians and Cavalry – ever filmed; for United Artists, *Witness to Murder*, with Barbara Stanwyck hair-raisingly pursued in high places by the man she has seen commit a murder. In the mid-1950s, though, Rowland made some dullish films with veteran stars, and even his reputation for action finally ebbed away on the tide of some poor continental adventure films.

*1934: †Hollywood Party (uncredited). 1936: *Sunkist Stars at Palm Springs. 1937: *Song of Revolt. *Cinema Circus. *A Night at the Movies. *Hollywood Party in Technicolor. *How to Start the Day. 1938: *How to Figure Income Tax. *Music Made Simple. *An Evening Alone. *How to Raise a Baby. *How to Read. *How to Watch Football. *The Courtship of the Newt. *Opening Day. *Mental Poise. *How to Sub-Let. *An Hour for Lunch. 1939. *Dark Magic. *Home Early. *How to Eat. *Think First. 1940: *Please Answer. *Jack Pot. *You the People. 1941: *Sucker List. *Changed Identity. 1943: A Stranger in Town. Los Angel. 1945: Our Vines Have Tender Grapes. 1946: Boys' Ranch. 1947: The Romance of Rosy Ridge. Killer McCoy. 1948: Tenth Avenue Angel. 1949: Scene of the Crime. 1950: The Outriders. Two Weeks with Love. 1951: Excuse My Dust. 1952: Bugles in the Afternoon. 1953: The 5,000 Fingers of Dr T. Affair with a Stranger. The Moonlighter. 1954: Witness to Murder. Rogue Cop. 1955: Many Rivers to Cross. Hit the Deck. 1956: Meet Me in Las Vegas (GB: Viva Las Vegas). Slander. These Wilder Years. 1957: Gun Glory. 1958: The Seven Hills of Rome. 1963: The Girl Hunters. 1964: Gunfighters of Casa Grande. The Man Called Gringo. 1967: The Sea Pirate.*

RUBEN, Joseph 1951-

After inauspicious beginnings, this New York-born director has ultimately graduated to directing top stars in middle-range vehicles during the last decade. Of all his work to date, though, only two films, *Sleeping With the Enemy* and *The Stepfather*, have been truly successful in financial terms, and Ruben needs something like a huge action hit to move him into the big league. After film studies at the University of Michigan, Ruben had made an early start to his film career at 23 with *The Sister-in-Law*, an early vehicle for John Savage as a singer involved in narcotics smuggling. Alas, this was followed by a string of forgettable teen exploitation films, and it wasn't until 1983 that Ruben produced something of genuine interest in *Dreamscape*, which starred Dennis Quaid, who had, when unknown, featured in two previous Ruben ventures. Ruben's direction in this fantasy thriller is extremely

interesting, even if the script, written by Ruben and Chuck Russell, himself to later turn director, can hardly be taken seriously. The plot posits the idea that someone with telekinetic powers could project themselves into another's dreams and, if need be, frighten that person so much that they could die from a heart attack in their sleep. The dream sequences that result from this imaginative idea are, in Ruben's hands, almost worthy of the most macabre paintings of Bosch, with death and decay ruling over all. Ruben's precision direction also had a lot to do with the cult success of *The Stepfather*, a chiller that doesn't take itself seriously for a second longer than it it takes to make an audience jump. First-class editing – not a scene is held too long – and the splendidly nutty performance Ruben obtains from

star Terry O'Quinn also contribute substantially to the film's success. The editing of action scenes has been notably skilful in Ruben's other films, especially *Sleeping With the Enemy* and *Money Train*, although less successful elements have marred their overall impact.

1974: The Sister-in-Law. 1976: The Pom Pom Girls. 1977: Joyride. 1978: Our Winning Season. 1980: Gorp. 1983: Dreamscape. 1987: The Stepfather. 1989: True Believer/Fighting Justice. 1991: Sleeping With the Enemy. 1993: The Good Son. 1995: Money Train. 1998: Return to Paradise.

RUDOLPH, Alan 1943 –

Rudolph may be America's best known little-known director. His films have on the whole been critically well received, yet they lack something that will make mass audience go to see them, even when, as they often do, they contain major stars. Although they are full of stylish, quirkily attractive touches, Rudolph's films have no noticeable narrative flow. Nonetheless, pieces of them stick in the mind long after the entire film of a more mainstream director has been forgotten. He was born in the heart of the movie industry to character actor and later major-league director Oscar Rudolph. After briefly considering accountancy as a career, he enrolled in a directors' training programme in 1967, subsequently serving as an assistant director on numerous TV series and TV movies, plus the occasional feature film, such as *Riot* (1968). Quitting his work, he directed two totally untypical graphically violent horror films, before working with Robert Altman for four years, then returning to the director's chair with *Welcome to LA*, one of his more accessible films, if typically fragmented, and featuring several of the actors who would figure prominently in his films of the next few years, including Genevieve Bujold and Keith Carradine. 'Off centre' and 'unpredictable' are two of the phrases you could apply to the films that followed, most of which went to arthouses and on to minority television channels. From 1987, though, Rudolph assumed a slightly higher profile, although the film he directed that year, *Made in Heaven*, perhaps sums up some of his difficulties. As Rudolph said: 'The writer-producers said it was me they wanted, but it turned out they didn't want the darker touches I would have liked to add.' Also of interest was *The Moderns:* strong on atmosphere but less interesting in content, this is a skilful and elaborate evocation of Paris in the 1920s, or more properly its artists' quarter of the

Alan **Rudolph** has spent more than 20 years working on the fringes of the Hollywood mainstream. Here he issues instructions on the set of *The Moderns* in 1988.

time. It was followed up by *Love at Large*, a detective story that isn't. Deliberately artificial, with oblique dialogue and story threads that turn to comic stylism, the film is really about people looking for love rather than people looking for people. Like most of Rudolph's films, it never quite hits its target. They keep you watching though, and none more so than *Mrs Parker & the Vicious Circle*, another fascinating re-creation of a bygone era, with a newsreel immediacy that makes it hard to ditch.

1970: Premonition. 1973: Barn of the Living Dead/Nightmare Circus/Terror Circus. 1976: Welcome to LA. 1978: Remember My Name. 1980: Roadie. 1982: Endangered Species. 1983: Return Engagement (D). 1984: Choose Me. Songwriter. 1985: Trouble in Mind. 1987: Made in Heaven. 1988: The Moderns. 1990: Love at Large. 1991: Mortal Thoughts. 1993: Equinox. 1994: Mrs Parker & the Vicious Circle. 1997: Afterglow. 1999: Breakfast of Champions.

RUGGLES, Wesley 1889-1972

The brother of actor Charles Ruggles, this American director had already gained wide experience of show business when he arrived in Hollywood in 1914 to play Keystone Cops for Mack Sennett, having travelled with a minstrel show and acted with stock companies. His acting experience at Keystone included roles in several Charlie Chaplin shorts, but by 1917 Ruggles was directing two-reelers for himself, progressing to features within a few months. For the next 30 years, he proficiently and on occasions imaginatively directed many 'A' budget films. His best-regarded period is from 1927 to 1934, peaking in 1931 with the incisive and rather bitter *Are These Our Children?* and his most fondly remembered film, the sprawling western *Cimarron* with its magnificently shot land-rush sequence. This period also contains a Ronald Colman-Ann Harding vehicle *Condemned*, in which the atmosphere – Colman is sent to Devil's Island, a notorious penal colony – is more convincing than the stars; the only film Clark Gable and Carole Lombard made in tandem, *No Man of Her Own* – they play sublimely well together in a film which skilfully combines its elements of action and comedy; *I'm No Angel*, one of Mae West's biggest hits; and George Raft's *Bolero*. Ruggles did a brilliant job on the dance sequences in this last, a story of an ambitious New York night-club dancer, and the film was a tremendous hit. He made films less often and less well after

the mid-1930s. One of the later films, *Arizona*, was clearly an attempt to repeat the success of *Cimarron*, but the old sweep and verve seemed to have gone. From 1931 to 1937, he was married to the much-wed actress Arline Judge.

1917: *Bobby, the Pacifist. Bobby's Bravery. *Bobby, Philanthropist. *Bobby, Movie Director. For France. 1918: The Blind Adventure. 1919: The Winchester Woman. 1920: Sooner or Later. Piccadilly Jim. The Desperate Hero. Love. The Leopard Woman. 1921: The Greater Claim. Uncharted Seas. Over the Wire. 1922: Wild Honey. If I Were Queen. Slippery McGee. 1923: Mr Billings Spends His Dime. The Remittance Woman. The Heart Raider. 1924: The Age of Innocence. 1925: *Welcome Granger. *He Who Gets Rapped. *Merton of the Goofies. *The Great Decide. *The Fast Male. *The Covered Flagon. *Madam Sans Gin. *Three Bases East. *What Price Gloria? *Don Coo-Coo. *Miss Me Again. The Plastic Age. Broadway Lady. 1926: A Man of Quality. The Kick-Off. 1927: Beware of Widows. Silk Stockings. 1928: The Fourflusher. Finders Keepers. 1929: Scandal (GB: High Society). Street Girl. Girl Overboard. Condemned (GB: Condemned to Devil's Island). 1930: Honey. The Sea Bat. 1931: Cimarron. Are These Our Children? 1932: Roar of the Dragon. No Man of Her Own. 1933: The Monkey's Paw. College Humor. I'm No Angel. 1934: Bolero. Shoot the Works (GB: Thank Your Stars). 1935: The Gilded Lily. Accent on Youth. The Bride Comes Home. 1936: Valiant is the Word for Carrie. 1937: I Met Him in Paris. True Confession. 1938: Sing, You Sinners. 1939. Invitation to Happiness. 1940: Too Many Husbands (GB: My Two Husbands). 1941: Arizona. You Belong to Me (GB: Good Morning, Doctor). 1942: Somewhere I'll Find You. 1943: Slightly Dangerous. 1944: See Here, Private Hargrove. 1946: London Town (US: My Heart Goes Crazy).

RUIZ, Raúl 1941-

Although his work has often been savaged by mainstream critics, who find much of it not so much puzzling as indecipherable, Chilean-born Ruiz is undoubtedly an innovator – a surrealist at heart, and probably the biggest challenger of the rules since Luis Buñuel. One critic's description of one of Ruiz's more recent films as 'richly messy' probably sums a great many viewers' attitude to his work. Ruiz plays with absurdity and juggles with imagination. If his rule-bending sometimes leads him to drop the ball, he can, as few others

could claim, say that he has almost invented his own cinematic language. Many critics describe his work as labyrinthine but work your way through one of his mazes and you are likely to find yourself entering another. This director plays mischievous games with his audience but tends to make up the rules as he goes along. His second version of *Treasure Island* for example, involves characters from the book, and others, playing a game based on it. It's Robert Louis Stevenson, Jim, but not as we know it.

1960: *La maleta (unfinished). 1967: *El tango del viudo (unfinished). 1968: Tres triste tigres. 1969: *Militarismo y tortura. *La cate naria (unfinished). 1970: +Que hacer? 1971: La colonia penal. *Mapuches. *Ahora te vamos a llamar hermano. Nadie dijo nada. 1972: *Los minuteros/The Street Photographer. La expropiación. 1973: *Nueva canción Chilena. +Palomita blanca (unfinished). El realismo socialista. Palomilla brava/Bad Girl. *Abastecimiento. 1974: Dialogo de exilados. 1975: Mensch verstreut mit Welt verkehrt. 1976: *Sotelo. 1977: Colloque de chiens. 1978: L'hypothèse du tableau volé/The hypothesis of the Stolen Painting. *Les divisions de la nature. 1979: De grands evénements et des gens ordinaires. Petit manuel d'histoire de France. Images du débat. Rue des Archives '79. Jeux/Games. 1980: *Le jeu de l'oie/Snakes and Ladders. L'or gris/Grey Gold. *Teletests. *La ville nouvelle. *Fahlstrom. *Pages d'un catalogue. 1981: Le borgne (serial). The Territory. On Top of the Whale. 1982: Les trois couronnes du matelot. *Querelle des jardins/The War of the Gardens. *Les ombres chinoises. *Classification des plantes. 1983: Bérénice. Pointe de fuite. *Voyage autour d'une main. La ville des pirates. La présence réelle. 1985: L'éveillé du Pont de l'Alma. Richard III. Dans un miroir. 1986: Treasure Island. Regime sans pain. Mamame. 1987: La vie est un songe. La chouette aveugle. 1988: +Brise glace/The Icebreaker. 1989: Allegory. 1990: The Golden Boat. 1991: Treasure Island. 1993: Dark at Noon. 1994: Exit Girl. 1996: Three Lives and Only One Death. 1997: Généalogies d'un crime. 1998: Shattered Image. 1999: Le Temps retrouvé

RUSSELL, Charles or Chuck 1945-

A long-time writer, assistant director and line producer, this American's long background in exploitation films has resulted in his belated conversion to director, in some vivid and violent action films with a strong vein of humour. In the 1970s, Russell worked on many films for Roger Cor-

Hair typically flowing free, Ken **Russell** (left) sizes up the situation.

man's New World Films (including *Death Race 2000*) and Sunn Classics. His liking for thrills on the very edge of reality came with his script for the 1983 film *Dreamscape*, co-written with its director, Joseph Ruben. He got his start as a director with one of the *Nightmare on Elm Street* films, then made a much more effective contribution to the horror genre with a remake of *The Blob*, a rip-roaring version of the 1958 cult classic. Besides making his movies fun, Russell uses ominous camera angles, grating music, misty woods, silent streets and swirling sewers to create genuine areas of apprehension. There was a long gap to the even more successful *The Mask*, a special effects-driven action comedy that he cemented comic stardom for Jim Carrey. Pitched at a hectic pace, the film is studded with funny moments. Russell was then entrusted with an Arnold Schwarzenegger vehicle *Eraser*, a good

action film for the big man's fans, providing a megablast of mayhem with the occasional original touch, even if its whole central set-up fails to convince.

1986: A Nightmare on Elm Street 3: Dream Warriors. 1988: The Blob. 1994: The Mask. 1996: Eraser.

RUSSELL, Ken 1927-

British director, a former ballet dancer and photographer, who followed visually beautiful, if fictionalized and distinctly unorthodox TV biographies of famous composers with a film career that rarely operated below full throttle. Like or loathe his films, it isn't possible to ignore them. After a quirky comedy, *French Dressing*, and a formula thriller, *Billion Dollar Brain*, the climax of which Russell dressed up with an idea borrowed from *Alexander Nevsky*, he produced his mas-

sive (130-minute) rendition of D.H. Lawrence's *Women in Love*. With a fine cast setting up a smouldering erotic atmosphere, the film brilliantly captures the earthiness of the original story, about two English girls finding heavy sexual relationships in the 1920s, a period which is lavishly and carefully recreated. Boosted commercially by its much publicized male nude wrestling sequence involving Alan Bates and Oliver Reed, this was a breathtaking, passionate and vividly entertaining film, and it won a best actress Oscar for Glenda Jackson. Russell then went right over the top with *The Music Lovers* (about Tchaikovsky), *The Devils* and *Savage Messiah*, but *Mahler* tempered its power with vivid imagery, intelligently set to the composer's music and skilfully recounting the story of his life. *Tommy*, an almost all-singing story of a blind boy's rise to fame, with music by

The Who, was strong, faintly surrealistic and enjoyably flamboyant. But there was little to cheer about after that, save for avid Russell fans, although some liked his *Altered States*, an updating of the Jekyll and Hyde story, dressed up by Russell in pounding, eye-hurting, top-of-the-pops style. He drums home its shock value with the help of first-rate special effects, even if the ending finally reveals it as a film with nowhere to go. That's not normally Russell's trouble. He usually knows exactly where he's going and, if you don't like the direction, he'll drag you along by the hair. After a string of lurid misfires, though, Russell finally slowed his film work rate in the early 1990s.

1957: *Peepshow. 1958: *Amelia and the Angel. *Lourdes (D). 1962: Elgar (TV). 1964: Bartok (TV). French Dressing. 1965: The Debussy Film (TV). 1967: Billion Dollar Brain. 1968: Song of Summer (TV). 1969: Women in Love. 1970: Dance of the Seven Veils (TV). The Music Lovers. 1971: The Devils. The Boy Friend. 1972: Savage Messiah. 1974: Mahler. 1975: Tommy. Lisztomania. 1977: Valentino. 1978: William and Dorothy (TV). 1980: Altered States. 1984: Crimes of Passion/China Blue. 1986: Gothic. 1987: +Aria. 1988: Salome's Last Dance. The Lair of the White Worm. 1989: The Rainbow. 1990: Women & Men: Stories of Seduction (TV). 1991: Whore. Prisoner of Honor (cable TV/cinemas). 1994: +Erotic Tales. 1996: Uri. 1997: Dogboys (TV).*

RYDELL, Mark 1934-

Clean-looking, handsome American actor who developed into a director who often made slightly unusual demands on the abilities of strong star personalities. After training at the Actors' Studio, Rydell played a variety of minor leading roles, mostly on TV, with the occasional film, such as *Crime In the Streets* (1956). By 1962, he had begun directing for television, initially on the *Ben Casey* series, later helming episodes of *Gunsmoke, I Spy, The Wild, Wild West* and *The Fugitive*. His first film, *The Fox*, was a strong, erotic, visually impressive and enjoyable adaptation of a D.H. Lawrence story; Anne Heywood's unexpectedly striking performance in it revived a flagging career. *The Reivers* was a warmly mellow, brilliant evocation of a childhood at the turn of the century, exceptionally skilful in conveying its emotive qualities to an audience and allowing Steve McQueen to give a performance of considerable charm. This charm is noticeable, to a greater or lesser degree, in all of Rydell's

work, apart from the disastrous *Harry and Walter Go to New York* which, despite a tremendous cast – James Caan, Michael Caine, Elliott Gould, Diane Keaton and more – and a period setting, obstinately refuses to work, chiefly because of a pallid script. But Rydell regained lost ground when he directed Bette Midler to a virtuoso performance in her first major role in *The Rose*, although the film itself became, at 134 minutes, a little wearing. But Rydell returned from the sex and drugs of the pop world to the glow of nostalgia with *On Golden Pond*, a weepie but a superb one. Billy Williams' colour photography of menacing skies and sun-flecked water is quite flawless, and helps Rydell catch the mood of the piece (just as cameraman Richard Moore had done on *The Reivers*), a last fling, perhaps, for Hollywood's vintage years. Under Rydell's gently probing direction, Katharine Hepburn and Henry Fonda, as the elderly couple spending their 48th summer together by their holiday lake, are finally unbearably touching; both won Academy Awards. There were emotive moments too in the enjoyable *The River* but, after a long gap, Rydell has worked to much less effect in recent times.

1967: The Fox. 1969: The Reivers. 1971: The Cowboys. 1973: Cinderella Liberty. 1976: Harry and Walter Go to New York. 1978: The Rose. 1981: On Golden Pond. 1984: The River. 1991: For the Boys. 1994: Intersection. 1996: Crime of the Century (TV). 1999: Wild Horses.*

SAGAL, Boris 1923-1981

Russian-born Sagal's cinema career was disappointing — just like that of TV acting specialist David Janssen. And the men have more in common in that both worked very well on television expressing dourness and disillusion. Many of Sagal's TV movies have amazingly downbeat endings, often resulting in the death of one of the leading characters. Of his cinema films, only the underrated *The Omega Man* conveys the essence of his seemingly bleak view of life. He had been directing for TV since the mid-1950s, mainly in stories, straight or humorous, that dealt

with the darker side of things, from such series as *Twilight Zone, The Alfred Hitchcock Hour* and *Johnny Staccato*. His films, which began in 1963, are mostly fairly lifeless vehicles for second-line stars. But his TV movies soon began to demonstrate an unexpected disillusionment with such surface values. *The Movie Murderer* is a drily composed portrait of an arsonist (Warren Oates) with a fine study in fading womanhood by Nita Talbot. An even more bleak world is entered in *Destiny of a Spy* and the science-fiction *Hauser's Memory; Deliver Us from Evil* is a riveting study of greed and *The Harness* a bruisingly observed version of a John Steinbeck story about an ill-tempered and withdrawn farmer with an ailing wife. And there are no happy endings for the characters played by James Franciscus and Glenn Ford in *The Dream Makers* and *The Greatest Gift*, the former allowing Franciscus some scope for his rarely seen talent for emotional acting, as a teacher who becomes a big wheel in the pop music business. His world eventually collapses and he is reduced to driving a taxi and finally shot by a mugger. In the late 1970s, Sagal became embroiled in 'mini-series', such as *Rich Man, Poor Man, The Moneychangers* and *Ike*, which allowed him little scope for his special gifts. He also married Marge Champion, the dancer-actress long married to her stage and screen partner, Gower Champion. But for Sagal, like so many of his fictional protagonists, there was to be no happy ending. While scouting locations for a film, he walked into a moving helicopter blade and was killed.

1963: Dime with a Halo. Twilight of Honor (GB: The Charge is Murder). 1965: Girl Happy. 1966: Made in Paris. 1967: The Helicopter Spies (TV. GB: cinemas). The 1,000 Plane Raid (TV. GB: cinemas). 1968: Mosquito Squadron. 1969: †Night Gallery (TV). Destiny of a Spy/The Gaunt Woman (TV). U.M.C. (GB: Operation Heartbeat. TV). The D.A: Murder One (TV). 1970: The Movie Murderer (TV). Hauser's Memory (TV). Four-in-One (TV). 1971: The Harness (TV). The Omega Man. The Failing of Raymond (TV). McCloud: The Disposal Man (TV). 1972: Columbo: The Greenhouse Jungle (TV). Hitched (TV. GB: Westward the Wagon). 1973: Deliver Us from Evil (TV). Columbo: Candidate for Crime (TV). The Snoop Sisters: Fear is a Free Throw (TV). Madigan: The Lisbon Beat (TV). Madigan: The Naples Beat (TV). 1974: Indict and Convict (TV). Amy Prentiss (TV). The Greatest Gift (TV). A Case of Rape (TV). The Dream Makers (TV). Three for the Road (TV).*

1975: *Man on the Outside* (TV). *The Runaway Barge* (TV). 1976: *Mallory: Circumstantial Evidence* (TV). *Sherlock Holmes in New York* (TV). 1977: *Angela* (released 1984). 1978: *The Awakening Land* (TV). 1980: *Masada* (TV. GB: cinemas as *The Antagonists*). 1981: *When the Circus Came to Town* (TV).

SALE, Richard 1911-1993

American writer who married fellow-playwright Anita Loos and for 11 years became a director, mostly of his own scripts. A short story-writer and novelist from the early 1930s, Sale turned to direction in the immediate post-war years, at first for Republic, but soon at Twentieth Century-Fox, where he demonstrated a pleasing light touch in Technicolor musicals, especially in finding a warmer side of June Haver's personality than had been demonstrated before, in two charming films, *I'll Get By,* which has Miss Haver and Dennis Day in very good form, plus numerous guest stars, and the much neglected *The Girl Next Door,* which has cartoon inserts in its delightful story of a Broadway star falling for her cartoonist neighbour. *A Ticket to Tomahawk,* again with Dan Dailey, who would feature in *The Girl Next Door,* is a rousing comedy-western, also in Technicolor and with a tremendous cast including the young Marilyn Monroe. Sale, however, also had his fair share of misfires. *Gentlemen Marry Brunettes,* despite extremely good colour control and skilful use of the CinemaScope screen, simply didn't have principals who could sing or dance enough to carry a show and, after the uncharacteristic *Seven Waves Away,* a lifeboat drama, Sale stuck to writing. He died following two strokes.

1947: *Spoilers of the Forest.* 1948: *Campus Honeymoon.* 1950: *A Ticket to Tomahawk. I'll Get By.* 1951: *Half Angel. Let's Make It Legal. Meet Me After the Show.* 1952: *My Wife's Best Friend.* 1953: *The Girl Next Door.* 1954: *Malaga (US: Fire Over Africa).* 1955: *Gentlemen Marry Brunettes.* 1957: *Seven Waves Away (US: Abandon Ship!).*

SALKOW, Sidney 1909-

A Harvard law student, Salkow turned to the stage for his career, and later became a resourceful director of thrillers and action films, often making a film appear more lavishly produced than its modest budget could manage. His best films were in the early 1940s and it may have been that war service slightly altered the course of his career. Most of that career was

spent with Columbia, the studio Salkow joined late in 1939, after an apprentice-ship of fast-moving action films with Universal and Republic. At Columbia, he was put on to the studio's Lone Wolf thrillers, with suave Warren William as the Raffles-like character who once stole jewels but now catches crooks. Impressed with his work on these, the studio handed him two larger assignments, both featuring Glenn Ford — *The Adventures of Martin Eden* (from the Jack London novel) and *Flight Lieutenant.* Both films co-starred Evelyn Keyes, and were acceptably made, with good acting performances and punchy action scenes. After military service, Salkow made an attractive light comedy, *Faithful in My Fashion,* before entering his swashbuckling period. Titles such as *Sword of the Avenger, Shadow of the Eagle, The Golden Hawk, Prince of Pirates* and *Raiders of the Seven Seas* speak for themselves. The last three in particular have lively action scenes, and plenty of them; while *Prince of Pirates* has a lady swashbuckler — a rare extrovert role for Barbara Rush. Some of the films in this period were made on visits to England and Italy. *Sitting Bull* was a big-scale western but overlong and boring, and Salkow filled out the remaining 12 years of his film career with an assortment of low-budget (and not very good) thrillers and westerns; he also made a couple of horror films with Vincent Price, and worked extensively in television. His last film of all, *The Great Sioux Massacre,* returned him to the Sitting Bull story, but it was not much of an improvement on the earlier film.

1937: *Four Days' Wonder. Girl Overboard. Behind the Mike.* 1938: *That's My Story. The Night Hawk. Storm Over Bengal.* 1939: *Fighting Thoroughbreds. Woman Doctor. Street of Missing Men. Zero Hour. She Married a Cop. Flight at Midnight.* 1940: *Café Hostess. The Lone Wolf Strikes. The Lone Wolf Meets a Lady. Girl from God's Country.* 1941: *The Lone Wolf Keeps a Date. The Lone Wolf Takes a Chance. Time Out for Rhythm. Tillie the Toiler.* 1942: *The Adventures of Martin Eden. Flight Lieutenant.* 1943: *City Without Men. The Boy from Stalingrad.* 1946: *Faithful in My Fashion.* 1947: *Millie's Daughter. Bulldog Drummond at Bay.* 1948: *Sword of the Avenger.* 1949: *Fugitive Lady. La rivale dell'imperatrice.* 1950: *Shadow of the Eagle.* 1952: *Scarlet Angel. The Golden Hawk. The Pathfinder.* 1953: *Prince of Pirates. Raiders of the Seven Seas. Jack McCall – Desperado.* 1954: *Sitting Bull.* 1955: *Robbers' Roost. Las Vegas Shakedown. Toughest Man Alive.* 1956: *Gun*

Brothers. 1957: *The Iron Sheriff. Gun Duel in Durango. Chicago Confidential.* 1960: *The Big Night.* 1963: *Twice Told Tales.* 1964: *Blood on the Arrow. The Last Man on Earth. The Quick Gun.* 1965: *The Murder Game. The Great Sioux Massacre.*

SANDRICH, Mark 1900-1945

Pipe-smoking American director of comedies and musicals who worked out his pictures in fine detail, and made all of the best Astaire-Rogers musicals of the 1930s. A man with an inventive and agile mind, Sandrich had trained as a physicist. At 22, he visited the set of a film being made by his glamorous cousin Carmel Myers, solved a minor electrical problem there and found himself offered a job as electrics expert and assistant prop-man. Sandrich's warmly extrovert personality adapted itself naturally to the film world and by 1926 he was directing two-reeler shorts for, among others, Lupino Lane. After making a couple of features, Sandrich joined RKO in 1930. At first they put him back on two-reelers for the comedy team of Clark and McCullough but when one of his shorts, *So This is Harris,* which itself reflected the advances in musical techniques which Sandrich would perfect in the Astaire-Rogers films, won an Oscar, he found himself working on features again, at first with Wheeler and Woolsey, another comedy team popular at the time. Then came the opportunity to direct *The Gay Divorcee,* Ginger Rogers' and Fred Astaire's first musical as a starring team. Sandrich became part of a hard-working, hard-thinking team that included Astaire, dance directors Hermes Pan and Dave Gould, cameraman David Abel, art director Carroll Clark and writer Dwight Taylor. It was Sandrich's idea that the musical numbers should flow from dialogue just as Astaire and Rogers flowed as a dance team, and he advanced the 'playback' (filming action, songs and dances to a pre-recorded soundtrack) to help his players concentrate on the job in hand. The team went from success to success: *Top Hat, Follow the Fleet* and *Shall We Dance?* followed. Despite the success of these musicals, however, RKO was in a parlous financial state by 1938 and no longer able to give the films the production values Sandrich required. After a row over the penny-pinching on *Carefree,* Sandrich left RKO and set up his own unit at Paramount. The musicals here (he also directed some funny Jack Benny comedies) are more bland, although *Holiday Inn* reunited him with Astaire, and had Bing Crosby singing the million-seller *White Christmas.* While preparing another Astaire-Crosby musical *Blue Skies* in 1945 (made the following year by Stuart Heisler), Sandrich had a heart attack and died.

1926: *†*Jerry the Giant*. **Napoleon Junior*. 1927: **A Midsummer Night's Steam*. **Brave Cowards*. **Careless Hubby*. **First Prize*. **Hello Sailor*. **Hold Fast*. **Hold That Bear*. **Hot Soup*. **The Movie Hound*. **Night Owls*. **Shooting Wild*. **Some Scout*. 1928: **Bear Knees*. **A Cow's Husband*. **High Strung*. *†**Love is Blonde*. **A Lady Lion*. **Sword Points*. *Runaway Girls*. 1929: *The Talk of Hollywood*. **Two-Gun Ginsburg*. 1930: *Aunt's in the Pants*. **Barnum Was Wrong*. **General Ginsburg*. **Gunboat Ginsburg*. **Hot Bridge*. **Moonlight and Monkey Business*. **Off to Peoria*. **Razored in Old Kentucky*. **Society Goes Spaghetti*. **Talking Turkey*. **Trader Ginsburg*. 1931: **The County Seat*. **Cowslips*. **The Gay Nighties*. **Many a Sip*. **A Melon-Drama*. **Scratch As Catch Can*. **The Strife of the Party*. **The Way of All Fish*. **The Wife o' Riley*. **False Roomers*. 1932: **Ex-Rooster*. **A Hurry Call*. **The Iceman's Ball*. **Jitters, the Butler*. **The Millionaire Cat*. **A Slip at the Switch*. **When Summons Comes*. **So This is Harris*. 1933: **The Druggist's Dilemma*. **Hokus Focus*. **Private Wives*. **Thru Thin and Thicket, or, Who's Zoo in Africa*. *Aggie Appleby, Maker of Men* (GB: *Cupid in the Rough*). *Melody Cruise*. 1934: *Hips Hips Hooray*. *Cockeyed Cavaliers*. *The Gay Divorcee* (GB: *The Gay Divorce*). 1935: *Top Hat*. 1936: *Follow the Fleet*. *A Woman Rebels*. 1937: *Shall We Dance?* 1938: *Carefree*. 1939: *Man About Town*. 1940: *Buck Benny Rides Again*. *Love Thy Neighbor*. 1941: *Skylark*. 1942: *Holiday Inn*. 1943: *So Proudly We Hail!* 1944: *Here Come the Waves*. *I Love a Soldier*.

SANTELL, Alfred 1895-1981

Best-regarded in the 1920s, this American director remained in top features throughout his career. But his most-praised films now date badly, and are seldom shown today. To begin with, Santell specialized in hard-edged contemporary dramas. One of the most popular of these was the boxing film *The Patent Leather Kid*, a big crowd-puller of 1927. By the end of the 1920s though, Santell had settled into sentimentality and directed several high-budget weepies before attempting to diversify. It was 1913 when Santell first entered the industry, after training to be an architect. He was set decorator, comedy writer, then an occasional direc-

tor of two-reel comedies from 1917, making his first feature in 1921. At first, Santell continued to concentrate on the writing side, of which he had become fond, but by 1925 had become more recognized as a director, sometimes billed as Al Santell. His biggest money-makers were in the 1930s — *Daddy Long Legs*, *Polly of the Circus*, *Rebecca of Sunnybrook Farm* and *Tess of the Storm Country*, all simple, sentimental stories with such stars as Janet Gaynor and Marion Davies; they pleased the public even if they seemed to belong in the silent era. *The Right to Romance* and *The Life of Vergie Winters* were two three-handkerchief Ann Harding sob-stories, but Santell scored his biggest prestige success of the decade with his version of Maxwell Anderson's stage success *Winterset*. The film boosted Burgess Meredith to stardom, and has moodily atmospheric value, although what the critics saw as poetic looks, in much the same way as *The Petrified Forest* from the same time, merely arty today. *Internes Can't Take Money*, a fast-moving hospital drama that contains Santell's best directorial work, was the film that led to the Dr Kildare series, and *Having Wonderful Time* is a zany star-studded comedy that gave early chances to Red Skelton and Lucille Ball in support of Ginger Rogers. From there, however, Santell drifted into folksy melodrama and Dorothy Lamour pictures, and disappointed critics with his biography of Jack London and a version of Eugene O'Neill's play *The Hairy Ape*, despite good casting in Susan Hayward and William Bendix. Some of the shorts that are sometimes credited to Santell (for example *The Magic Jazzbo*, in 1917, and *Home James*, *Some Job* and *The Stolen Keyhole*, all from 1918) appear to have been made by a director called Albert A. Sautell.

1917: **My Valet*. **Out of the Bag*. 1918: **O Susie Behave!* **Main 1-2-3*. **Vamping the Vamp*. **At Swords' Points*. 1919: **Stop, Cease, Hesitate!* **As You Were*. **Seeing Things*. **Two Tired*. 1920: **Pills for Papa*. **Rings and Things*. **A Wild Night*. 1921: *It Might Happen to You*. 1922: **Rented Trouble*. **But a Butler*. *Wildcat Jordan*. 1923: *Lights Out*. 1924: *Empty Hearts*. *Fools in the Dark*. *Parisian Nights*. *The Man Who Played Square*. 1925: *Classified*. *The Marriage Whirl*. *Sweet Daddies*. *Subway Sadie*. *Just Another Blonde*. 1927: *The Gorilla*. *The Patent Leather Kid*. *Orchids and Ermine*. 1928: *Wheel of Chance*. *Show Girl*. *The Little Shepherd of Kingdom Come*. 1929: *Romance of the Rio Grande*. *This is Heaven*. *Twin Beds*. 1930: *The Arizona*

Kid. *The Sea Wolf*. 1931: *Body and Soul*. *Daddy Long Legs*. *Sob Sister* (GB: *The Blonde Reporter*). 1932: *Polly of the Circus*. *Rebecca of Sunnybrook Farm*. *Tess of the Storm Country*. 1933: *Bondage*. *The Right to Romance*. 1934: *The Life of Vergie Winters*. 1935: *People Will Talk*. *A Feather in Her Hat*. 1936: *Winterset*. 1937: *Breakfast for Two*. *Internes Can't Take Money* (GB: *You Can't Take Money*). 1938: *Cocoanut Grove*. *The Arkansas Traveler*. *Having Wonderful Time*. 1939: *Our Leading Citizen*. 1941: *Aloma of the South Seas*. 1942: *Beyond the Blue Horizon*. 1943: *Jack London*. 1944: *The Hairy Ape*. 1945: *Mexicana*. 1946: *That Brennan Girl*.

SANTLEY, Joseph (J. Mansfield) 1889-1971

Utah-born Santley was a minor-league Busby Berkeley. For 20 years, more than 50 per cent of Santley's output as a director was composed of light musicals, and he spent many hours trying to work out impressive effects and dance routines on fairly modest budgets. A child actor in the theatre, he became a famous stage Billy the Kid in 1907, then came to Hollywood to play in silent films. Marrying English-born singer and actress Ivy Sawyer, Santley appeared with her in musical comedies on stage, and developed an interest in the staging of musical numbers. When sound came to Hollywood, Santley was put in charge of a number of creaky one-reelers demonstrating the musical talents of various Broadway stars, such as Eddie Cantor, Ruth Etting and Rudy Vallee. He also directed the musical sequences in the Marx Brothers' *The Cocoanuts*, for which he received co-director credit. For a couple of years, he returned to the stage, but in 1932 went to Hollywood again to begin a long series of assembly-line musicals and comedies. The titles are almost indistinguishable: *Dancing Feet*, *Dancing on a Dime*, *Music in My Heart*, *Melody and Moonlight*, *Melody Ranch*, *Swing, Sister, Swing*, *Goodnight Sweetheart* and so on. Often these little numbers were enlivened by Santley's inventive touches, particularly in camera placements involving overhead or crane shots. Many of his later films were made for Republic, featuring such chirpy actresses as Jane Frazee or Ruth Terry, and he was also in the director's chair for several of the rural comedies of wide-mouthed Judy Canova. Santley ended his film days with two Frankie Laine-Billy Daniels musicals for Columbia, a series that would burst into colour and be taken over by Blake Edwards and Richard Quine (both *qv*). Santley himself went into television in 1951 and directed many early variety shows and musical specials before his retirement in 1959.

*1929: †The Cocoanuts. *High Hat.
*Hold Up. *Rudy Vallee and His Con-
necticut Yankees. *That Party in Person.
*Just One Word. *Ruth Etting. *Radio
Rhythm. *Raising the Roof. *All Ameri-
cans. *The Harmony Boys. *Tito Schipa.
*Tito Schipa Concert No. 2. Swing High.
1932: *Lambs' All-Star Gambler No. 3.
*Ladies Not Allowed. 1933: *The Poor
Fish. *Hear 'Em and Weep. *$50 Million
Can't be Wrong. *Peeping Tom. 1934:
The Loudspeaker. Young and Beautiful.
1935: Harmony Lane. Million Dollar
Baby. Waterfront Lady. 1936: Dancing
Feet. Her Master's Voice. Walking on Air.
The Smartest Girl in Town. We Went to
College (GB: The Old School Tie). The
Harvester. Laughing Irish Eyes. 1937:
Meet the Missus. There Goes the Groom.
1938: She's Got Everything. Swing, Sis-
ter, Swing. Always in Trouble. Blonde
Cheat. 1939: Two Bright Boys. Spirit of
Culver (GB: Man's Heritage). The Family
Next Door. Music in My Heart. 1940:
Melody and Moonlight. Behind the
News. Melody Ranch. 1941: Dancing on
a Dime. Rookies on Parade. Ice-Capades.
Sis Hopkins. Puddin' Head (GB: Joan
Goes to Town). Down Mexico Way.
1942: Yokel Boy (GB: Hitting the Head-
lines). A Tragedy at Midnight. Joan of
Ozark (GB: Queen of Spies). Remember
Pearl Harbor. Call of the Canyon. 1943:
Thumbs Up. Chatterbox. Sleepy Lagoon.
Shantytown. Here Comes Elmer. 1944:
Jamboree. Rosie the Riveter (GB: In
Rosie's Room). Goodnight Sweetheart.
Three Little Sisters. Brazil. 1945: Earl
Carroll Vanities. Hitchhike to Happiness.
1946: Shadow of a Woman. 1949: Make
Believe Ballroom. 1950: When You're
Smiling.*

SARAFIAN, Richard C. 1929-

When this American director (of Armenian descent) broke away from television in
1968, after ten hard-working years there,
it seemed at first as though he might
make the big league. He came to Britain
to make *Run Wild, Run Free*, a pleasing
boy-and-animal film with an exciting
mist-enshrouded climax, and underlined
his talent for location work, back in
America, with *Man in the Wilderness* and
The Man Who Loved Cat Dancing. The
wintry exteriors in these films were particularly pleasing. A big commercial hit,
however, eluded Sarafian; *The Next Man*,
although not all that bad, and starring
Sean Connery, has hardly been seen outside television. The nearest Sarafian came
to the big time was with *Vanishing Point*,
a hymn to speed and violence which did

have a theme attractive to the masses: an
ex-racing driver (Barry Newman) on the
run from the police across the Nevada
desert. Sarafian, though, was unable to
follow through, and *Lolly Madonna XXX*
and *Sunburn* were deadly indeed. He has
since returned to television, a medium for
which he started working in 1959, putting
in time on numerous series, including
Maverick, Lawman (several excellent
episodes from this), *Cheyenne, The Dakotas, 77 Sunset Strip, I Spy, The Wild, Wild
West, The Big Valley, Gunsmoke* and *The
High Chaparral* — a list which reflects
Sarafian's liking for the wide open spaces.
From 1980, he began mixing the direction
of straight-to-video titles with small acting assignments.

*1959: Terror at Black Falls. 1965: Andy.
1968: Shadow on the Land (TV. Original-
ly made for 'The Road West' series in
1966). 1969: Run Wild, Run Free. 1970:
Fragment of Fear. 1971: Vanishing Point.
Man in the Wilderness. 1973: Lolly
Madonna XXX (GB: The Lolly Madonna
War). The Man Who Loved Cat Dancing.
1975: One of Our Own (TV). 1976: The
Next Man. The African Queen (TV).
1977: A Killing Affair (TV). 1979: Sun-
burn. Disaster on the Coastliner (TV)
1981: less Gangster Wars (TV). 1984:
The Bear. 1986: Eye of the Tiger. 1988:
Street Justice. 1990: Solar Crisis (later
Starfire). 1992: Truk Lagoon.*

SARGENT, Joseph (Giuseppe Sargente) 1925-

After 15 years working for television, this
American director of Italian ancestry had a
brief stab at a cinema career. His work has
impact, and almost all of it is above average of its kind. After toying with careers as
a pianist and photographer, Sargent came
to Hollywood in the 1950s as an actor.
Gradually, though, via stage productions,
he developed a taste for direction, and
started making TV series episodes from
1961, cutting his teeth on *Lassie, Gunsmoke* and *The Man from U.N.C.L.E.* His
first TV movie, *The Sunshine Patriot*, is
without doubt the best of the earliest films
of the genre. Under Sargent's purposeful
direction (the personable performances he
obtained were to become a mark of his
work), this spy story creates and sustains
interesting characters and in fine style sus-
pends our disbelief. Two more of Sargent's
TV movies, *Tribes* and *Sunshine*, the latter
a weepie about a young woman dying
from bone cancer, were considered good
enough to release to cinemas outside
America, but actually better than either of
these was *Maybe I'll Come Home in the
Spring*, a touching story of daughters
struggling to come to terms with their par-

ents. Sargent also made two pilot films that
were well above the average: *Longstreet*,
which contains James Franciscus' best performance as the blinded insurance investigator, and the very dark *The Marcus-Nelson Murders*, which led to the series *Kojak*.
Hustling, a documentary-like story of prostitution, again highlighted Sargent's facility
for carving out touching human relationships, although he had two fine leading
actresses in Lee Remick and Jill Clayburgh.
His films include the box-office bullseye
The Taking of Pelham One-Two-Three;
MacArthur is generally underrated; but the
abysmal *Goldengirl* raised doubts about
his future until *Coast to Coast* confirmed
his ability to obtain charismatic characterizations (in this case from Dyan Cannon
and Robert Blake) given the right ambience. His execution of ideas, though, has
not always been as sharp, and his only
work for the cinema since 1985 has been
the abysmal *Jaws the Revenge*. On TV he
continues to be a force to be reckoned
with, directing mainly high-quality TV
movies, winning two Emmys for his work.
He also received high praise for the mini-
series *Streets of Laredo* in 1996.

*1965: One Spy Too Many (TV. GB: cine-
mas). 1966: The Spy in the Green Hat
(TV. GB: cinemas). 1967: The Hell With
Heroes. 1968: The Sunshine Patriot (TV).
1969: The Forbin Project. The Immortal
(TV). 1970: Tribes (TV. GB: cinemas, as
The Soldier Who Declared Peace). The
Man Who Died Twice (released 1973).
1971: Maybe I'll Come Home Again in
the Spring (TV). Longstreet (TV). 1972:
The Man. Man on a String (TV). 1973:
Wheeler and Murdoch (TV). White Light-
ning. The Marcus-Nelson Murders (TV).
Sunshine (TV. GB: cinemas). Emily and
Joe (TV). 1974: The Taking of Pelham
One-Two-Three. Man on a Swing. 1975:
Hustling (TV). The Night That Panicked
America (TV). Friendly Persuasion (TV).
1977: MacArthur (GB: MacArthur: The
Rebel General). 1979: Goldengirl. 1980:
Coast to Coast. 1982: Tomorrow's Child
(TV). Freedom (TV). 1983: Nightmares.
Memorial Day (TV). Choices of the
Heart: The Jean Donovan Story (TV).
1984: Terrible Joe Moran (TV). 1985:
Love is Never Silent (TV). Passion Flower
(TV). 1986: Of Pure Blood (TV). There
Must Be a Pony (TV). 1987: Jaws the
Revenge. 1988: The Karen Carpenter
Story (TV). 1989: The Kill. Incident (TV).
Day One (TV). 1990: Caroline? (TV).
The Last Elephant/Ivory Hunters (TV). A
Green Journey (TV). The Love She
Sought (TV). 1991: Never Forget (TV).
1992: Miss Rose White (TV). Somebody's
Daughter (TV). 1993: Skylark (TV).
1994: Abraham (TV). 1995: My Antonia*

Jessie Matthews (standing) and Victor **Saville** discuss backstage problems during the making of the "Millie the Non-Stop Variety Girl" episode of the portmanteau film *Friday the Thirteenth*.

(TV). 1997: *Miss Evers' Boys* (TV). *Mandela and de Klerk* (TV). 1998: *The Long Island Incident* (TV).

SAURA, Carlos 1932-

The father of modern Spanish cinema. Elements of Saura's innovative work are still reflected today in the films of such directors as Pedro Almodóvar and Bigas Luna. While some of his films are noted by their daring, vivid use of colour and symbolism, Saura has also proved adept at dramas of realism that exposed weaknesses in the prevailing social conditions. With the death of the old enemy, Franco, in 1975, Saura's films became less political and more recently have included a dazzling trio of dance films which, like almost all his work, are distinctively

Spanish. Initially a professional stills photographer, he was encouraged by his painter brother Antonio to think of a career in films and attended film school in Madrid. Saura's first few films attracted little attention and it was only with *The Hunt/La Caza* in 1966 that he established himself as a film-maker to watch. A tense drama about three Civil War veterans out hunting, it was followed by another thriller, *Peppermint frappé*, somewhat reminiscent of the British film *Stolen Face* as a doctor, rejected by a woman, remodels another's face to look just like her. The film starred Geraldine Chaplin, who became Saura's constant companion for more than a decade and bore him a son before they split in 1979. After numerous festival awards and hits at the Spanish box-office, Saura's career perhaps reached

its peak in 1990 in conjunction with one of the new icons of Spanish cinema, actress Carmen Maura. *Ay! Carmela* returns to Saura's old subject, the Spanish Civil War, welding it to the story of a troupe of travelling performers, who also happen to be Republican sympathisers. While ostensibly a comedy, the film has disturbing undercurrents throughout, and a devastating climax. We have been this way before, poking fun at unbending militarism, in such American films as *To Be Or Not to Be*. But they lacked the sense of real danger ever present in Saura's film.

1955: *Antonio Saura. 1957: *La tarde del Domingo/Sunday Afternoon. 1958: Cuenca. 1960: Los golfos/The Hooligans. 1964: Llanto por un bandido. 1966: La caza/The Hunt. 1967: Peppermint frappé. 1968: Stress es tres tres. 1969: La madriguera (US: The Honeycomb). 1970: El jardin de las delicias. 1973: Aña y los lobos (GB:*

Aña and the Wolves. US: Anna and the Wolves). 1974: Cousin Angelika. 1975: Cria cuervos (GB: Raise Ravens. US: Cria!). 1976: Elisa, vida mia. 1978: Los ojos vendados/Blindfold. 1979: Mama cumple cien años (GB: Mother Turns One Hundred. US: Mama Turns 100). 1980: Deprisa deprisa (GB: Fast Fast. US: Hurry Hurry). 1981: Bodas de sangre/Blood Wedding. 1982: Dulces horas/Sweet Hours. Antonieta. 1983: Carmen. 1984: Los Zancos/The Stilts. 1986: El amor brujo (US: Love the Magician). 1988: El Dorado. 1989: La noche oscura/The Dark Night. 1990: Ay! Carmela. 1992: Outrage! 1995: Flamenco. 1996: Taxi. 1997: Pajarico (US: Little Bird). 1998: Tango.

SAVILLE, Victor 1897-1979

The relative failure of this British director's films in Hollywood (where he spent most of the latter part of his career), coupled with his own self-effacing comments — 'I have never considered myself highly as a director. My one ambition has always been to produce' —has tended to obscure the fact that this modest, bespectacled man, with a sure sense of style and glamour, made some of the most beguiling entertainments to emerge from the British cinema of the 1930s, films that the alert, innovative and hard-working Saville ensured could meet Hollywood on its own terms. In his younger days, Saville was in turn salesman, production manager and writer, before going into partnership with Michael Balcon and Graham Cutts (qv) in 1923. The young Alfred Hitchcock (qv) was one of their early protégés, but Balcon and Saville, the production side of the team, parted company in 1926. From the beginning of sound, Saville was drawn more and more into direction, including the dazzling series of early Jessie Matthews musicals at Gaumont-British, and a variety of comedies, thrillers and musicals for his old partner Balcon at Gainsborough. These films are assured, polished, well-paced entertainments that clearly show Saville's dual skills. In every department – and especially in the overall production design and its use to maximum effect – they compare well with contemporary films from any other part of the world. The first of Saville's musicals was Sunshine Susie (1931), a British version of the German musical-comedy Die Privatsekretarin, with the tragic Renate Muller (to commit suicide at 30), the star of the original, and jaunty Jack Hulbert. Hulbert was also in Love on Wheels. Saville's films made a great deal of money at British box-offices and, with a few key figures – Balcon, Basil Dean (qv) and Hitchcock among them – he was certainly

instrumental in maintaining the buoyancy of the British film industry of the period, nowhere more so than with the Matthews musicals, Friday the Thirteenth, The Good Companions, Evergreen (their best-remembered collaboration), First a Girl and It's Love Again. Saville's hymns to this sexy brunette elf are shimmering, gossamer creations, full of good tunes, well-organized dance routines, high-key interiors which gleam with Paramount class, and atmospheric exteriors. He almost succeeded in co-starring her with Astaire in 1934, and it was a dark day for her when he departed to join Korda's London Films in 1937, making thrillers and flavoursome (if now dated) rural dramas such as Storm in a Teacup and South Riding. At this point, Saville achieved his ambition of becoming a producer with M-G-M, at first (The Citadel, Goodbye Mr Chips!) with notable success. He returned to direction from 1944 in spasmodic fashion: Tonight and Every Night is a fake but enjoyable portrait of Britain's Windmill Theatre in wartime, which surprisingly does more for Janet Blair than Rita Hayworth, and The Green Years is pleasant, tearful fare (from a novel by The Citadel's A.J. Cronin). But Saville's direction showed an increasing lack of assurance in America (although The Long Wait is a grippingly good thriller), and he eventually returned to Britain in the late 1950s.

1919: *The Story of Oil. *Liquid Sunshine. 1927: The Arcadians/Land of Heart's Desire. 1928: Tesha (US: A Woman in the Night). 1929: *Me and the Boys. *Armistice. Kitty. Woman to Woman. 1930: The W Plan. A Warm Corner. 1931: The Sport of Kings. Michael and Mary. Sunshine Susie (US: The Office Girl). Hindle Wakes. 1932: The Faithful Heart (US: Faithful Hearts). Love on Wheels. 1933: The Good Companions. Friday the Thirteenth. I Was a Spy. 1934: Evergreen. Evensong 1935: †The Love Affair of the Dictator/The Loves of a Dictator. First a Girl. The Iron Duke. Me and Marlborough. 1936: It's Love Again. 1937: Dark Journey. †Storm in a Teacup. †Action for Slander (credited as producer only). 1938: South Riding 1943: †Forever and a Day. 1944: Tonight and Every Night. 1946: The Green Years. 1947: Green Dolphin Street. If Winter Comes. 1949: Conspirator. 1950: Kim. 1951: Calling Bulldog Drummond. 1952: 24 Hours of a Woman's Life (US: Affair in Monte Carlo). 1954: The Long Wait. The Silver Chalice.

SAYLES, John 1950-

So what's the writer-director of America's most concerned social conscience dramas doing writing scripts for such films as Piranha and Clan of the Cave Bear? Well, Sayles' other activities obviously help him raise the funds for the films he really wants to make and, just for good luck, he also dabbles in acting, creates TV series and makes music videos. But the title of his book, Thinking in Pictures, gives a clue as to where his interests really lie. Extremely tall and gauntly handsome, Sayles has also played small roles in most of his own films. 'I've always wanted to do everything once,' he says of his show-business life. 'I've even reviewed books.' Sayles, the son of teachers, got his very first job as an attendant in a nursing home, but had already begun placing short stories in his early twenties. He came to the attention of Hollywood when his second novel was nominated for national awards and, by the late seventies, he was writing exploitation screenplays for Roger Corman's New World Films, of which Piranha was the first and Alligator and Battle Beyond the Stars probably the best. Sayles set out his stall as director with his debut film, Return of the Secaucus 7, the first in a long series of films propelled along by dialogue and situations rather than action, in this case about a group of angry young people on the verge of responsibility. Sayles' films are about people, politics, hardship and decision-making. Often their characters find that it's time to make a stand, in much the same way Gary Cooper did in the equally politically-minded High Noon. The settings in Sayles' films are often industrial or working-class. An exception is the true-life period baseball drama Eight Men Out, but Sayles' films are always pocked by patches of dullness, and here the drama succumbs altogether. More successful are Matewan and City of Hope; concern and sympathy for the oppressed drips from every frame of these painstakingly crafted films. With the remarkable Passion Fish Sayles, although still focusing on personalities rather than events (although both are essential to its theme), began to address a slightly wider audience. He also extracts Mary McDonnell's best screen performance as the paralysed and embittered woman who finds unlikely and lasting friendship with an equally emotionally damaged black companion. Overlength continued to be a problem in most of Sayles' films, and it still was in another of his most successful, Lone Star, a mostly absorbing modern western whose token murder plot scarcely conceals familiar Sayles themes of relationships, reconciliation and coining to terms with the past. The title and advertising campaign helped this one reach a considerable crossover audience despite its (slight) failings in pace.

1980: *Return of the Secaucus 7.* 1981: *Lianna.* 1982: *Baby It's You.* 1984: *The Brother from Another Planet.* 1987: *Matewan.* 1988: *Eight Men Out.* 1991: *City of Hope.* 1992: *Passion Fish.* 1994: *The Secret of Roan Inish.* 1995: *Lone Star.* 1998: *Men With Guns.* 1999: *Limbo.*

SCHAFFNER, Franklin J. 1920-1989

American director whose film career went radically wrong after he won an Academy Award for *Patton.* Only Schaffner's superb visual sense continued to remain from past glories. The gap between *The War Lord* and *Sphinx* seems too yawning for anyone to leap across, but poor Schaffner managed it. Born and raised in Japan, Schaffner came to America to study law, but World War II intervened and, following service in the U.S. Navy, Schaffner worked on the documentary film series *The March of Time* before joining CBS Television. In the next ten years, up to 1962, Schaffner became a drama director and won four Emmy awards, graduating to cinema films in 1962. For the next eight years, he made giant strides to the top, in a variety of films that showed, above all else, the ability to transmit from screen to audience an emotional charge from exchanges of dialogue. This is especially true of *The Best Man,* as gripping and involving a portrait of political chicanery as the American cinema ever produced, with a powerful ending, and *The War Lord,* a splendid evocation of Flemish medieval life, with pulsating action, sensitive performances from Charlton Heston and Rosemary Forsyth and magnificent colour photography by Russell Metty. After a clean, cool and exciting spy thriller, *The Double Man,* Schaffner and Heston combined again to produce something almost as unusual as *The War Lord.* This was the science-fiction adventure *Planet of the Apes,* a brilliant realization of a novel which even original author Pierre Boulle had thought unfilmable, and which kept its devastating sting-in-the-tail well hidden until the very end. *Patton,* although not Schaffner's best film, won him the Oscar the consistency of his work deserved, but what followed was heart-stoppingly disappointing; Five more films, each one worse than the last, culminating in *Sphinx,* a ludicrous archaeological thriller (like something out of Universal's 1940s' 'Mummy' films) with dialogue so execrable that Schaffner seemed to give up on everything but gor-

geous views of Egypt and the Middle East. In light of subsequent developments, some critics now feel that Schaffner was never as good as his material, but this is not true. Such films as *The Best Man* and *The War Lord* show craftsmanship of the highest order, plus skill in almost never allowing his players to step outside the established mood of the piece. It is precisely that mood that Schaffner seems subsequently to have misjudged. He died form cancer.

1958: *The Velvet Alley* (TV). *Seven Against the Wall* (TV)). 1962: *The Stripper* (GB: *Woman of Summer*). 1964: *The Best Man.* 1965: *The War Lord.* 1967: *The Double Man. Planet of the Apes.* 1969: *Patton* (GB: *Patton: Lust for Glory*). 1971: *Nicholas and Alexandra.* 1973: *Papillon.* 1976: *Islands in the Stream.* 1978: *The Boys from Brazil.* 1980: *Sphinx. Our Town* (TV). 1982: *Yes, Giorgio.* 1984: *The Chinese Bandit* (unfinished). 1987: *Lionheart.* 1989: *Welcome Home.*

SCHATZBERG, Jerry 1927-

One film every two years seems to be the rule rather than the exception for present-day American directors, and Schatzberg made exactly 11 films in 20 years. Some of his films attracted high critical praise, but it was only in 1981 that he had his first big box-office hit, with the release of *Honeysuckle Rose.* Schatzberg was a photographer for some years, specializing in fashion lay-outs. Not surprisingly, his first film, *Puzzle of a Downfall Child,* was about the life of a fashion model and her photographer. Cinematic know-how, however, was almost entirely lacking and, despite the presence of such stars as Faye Dunaway and Roy Scheider, the film barely emerged outside the United States, actually being shown as a second-feature in Britain. Schatzberg soon proved to have an interest in downbeat stories on the seamier side of life, although *The Panic in Needle Park,* which contained Al Pacino's first leading role, had considerable censorship problems before it emerged, being an unrelenting study of drug addiction in a New York ghetto. *Scarecrow* (Pacino again, with Gene Hackman) reached a wider audience – they were two hoboes, bumming across America – but *Dandy, the All-American Girl,* a much-troubled film, was not much seen outside the States. *The Seduction of Joe Tynan* was seen elsewhere, despite being about American politics, and continued Schatzberg's preoccupation with the slimy underbelly of American life. The characters in his films, though, tend to be

tedious and irritating and this highly praised film is no exception, albeit with Meryl Streep, Alan Alda and Barbara Harris at the head of its cast. Alda's own trite screenplay ensures that Schatzberg's battle to bring the drama across is seldom easy. *Honeysuckle Rose* had a solid-sell LP to back up its story of an ageing country-and-western star slipping off the straight and narrow country road with his girl guitarist, but again the characters, Dyan Cannon (as his wife) apart, are unattractive. If Schatzberg likes them that way, then fine. But he needs stronger scripts to attract our interest to them. His films and their abrasive characters continued to draw critical praise in the 1980s, but not the paying public. There were award-winning performances by Kathy Baker and Morgan Freeman in Schatzberg's *Street Smart* but, in the face of box-office indifference, he has not filmed since 1989.

1970: *Puzzle of a Downfall Child.* 1971: *The Panic in Needle Park.* 1973: *Scarecrow.* 1976: *Dandy, the All American Girl* (GB: *Sweet Revenge*). 1979: *The Seduction of Joe Tynan.* 1980: *Honeysuckle Rose.* 1983: *Misunderstood.* 1984: *No Small Affair.* 1987: *Street Smart.* 1988: *Blood Money/Clinton and Nadine.* 1989: *Reunion.*

SCHEPISI, Fred (Frederici Schepisi) 1939-

This Australian director seems to have gone a little astray of late, but up to the end of the l980s, his was a formidable record. After a repressive education at a Catholic boarding school, Schepisi, who would later use those experiences for his first major film, left school at 15, decided against a career in the priesthood, and eventually moved into the advertising world, first as a copy writer but by the early 1960s as a director of TV commercials. He had formed his own company, The Film House, by 1964. In the 1970s, Schepisi gradually veered towards feature films, winning several Australian Oscars with the first, *The Devil's Playground,* a somewhat oppressive but not easily shrugged aside semi-autobiographical portrait of the problems of both teachers and pupils at a boarding school not dissimilar from Schepisi's own. He followed that with the equally striking *The Chant of Jimmie Blacksmith,* a beautifully composed, skilfully made and finally very violent truth-based account of a turn-of-the-century Aborigine pushed too far by a succession of white masters. Schepisi went to Hollywood on the strength of it, but his career there was relatively uneventful until the latter half of the 1980s, when he produced *Roxanne*, an uncharacteristic but winning modern comedy remake of *Cyrano de Bergerac*, written by Steve Martin as a vehicle for himself and, in Schepisi's hands, almost always fun to be with. Schepisi returned to Australia for another big hit, *A Cry in the Dark*, a poignant if sometimes laborious account of the 'dingo baby' affair, in which Meryl Streep's casting as Lindy Chamberlain gathered the film international attention. Since then, Schepisi's films, despite inherent early promise, have proved disappointing, the best of them being the rather uncommercial *6 Degrees of Separation*, an elegant version of the stage play about a charismatic black youth who disrupts the routine lives of New York's upper class. Talky, but totally absorbing, the film had the fortune to secure the talents of the young Will Smith as the youth. The misfortune as far as the box-office was concerned was that it was before *Independence Day* and *Men in Black* made him famous.

*1966: People Make Papers (D). 1970: *The Party. 1973: 4-Libido. 1976: The Devil's Playground. 1978: The Chant of Jimmie Blacksmith. 1981: Barbarosa. 1984: Iceman. 1985: Plenty. 1987: Roxanne. 1988: A Cry in the Dark/Evil Angels. 1990: The Russia House. 1992: Mr Baseball/Tokyo Diamond. 1994: I.Q. 6 Degrees of Separation. 1997: +Fierce Creatures. 1999: The Shipping News.*

SCHERTZINGER, Victor 1880-1941

Although Schertzinger is remembered today only as the man who set Bing Crosby and Bob Hope on the Road to becoming millionaires before his sudden death, this American film-maker was a multi-talented man who had been writing songs, composing music and directing films since the early years of the century. Beginning his career as a violinist in 1898, Schertzinger had become a well-known conductor at 30, gradually drifting away from the field of classical music to musical comedy, for which he began to compose songs and scores. Thomas Ince, the film pioneer, hired Schertzinger in 1916 to compose scores for his films, the first of which was *Civilization*. The Pennsylvania-born Schertzinger became interested in other aspects of the film industry and, after beginning to direct films in 1917, pursued twin interests for the remainder of his career. Many of his silent films were popular rural dramas starring the boyish Charles Ray, but Schertzinger was naturally delighted with the advent of sound, for it gave his musical talents a fresh dimension. Working for Paramount at the time, Schertzinger

had by then become a familiar dapper character in the film capital, often dressed in white zipper jacket, white plus-fours, white shoes and fashionable white golf cap. One of his earliest sound films, *Redskin*, a remarkable film for its time, remains one of his finest achievements as a director. One of the first films to portray events from the Indian's point of view, it was largely photographed in Technicolor until Paramount became worried about the cost. Schertzinger turned the decision to film in black-and-white to the film's advantage — retaining the Indian scenes in colour, but filming the 'white man' scenes in monochrome, then giving them a yellow tint. Schertzinger moves the film's action along rapidly, without glossing over any of its less palatable aspects — the pain of a race forced to do things against its beliefs is clearly shown. The film, like Schertzinger's career, is surely due for reappraisal. Throughout the 1930s, Schertzinger composed music and songs for other people's films as well as his own; he was a very busy man. His films, almost all in light vein, seem to have a pleasant sense of rhythm which perhaps has something to do with his musical knowledge. He was a natural choice to direct light opera star Grace Moore in her biggest success, *One Night of Love*, and also made (and wrote and composed the songs for) the follow-up vehicle, *Love Me Forever*. Returning to Paramount in 1939 (he had left to freelance in 1932), Schertzinger directed Bing Crosby four times (including the best of the 'Road' films, *Road to Zanzibar*, and the memorable *Birth of the Blues)*, and Mary Martin twice. Schertzinger's films, like his music, were rarely dull.

1917: The Millionaire Vagrant. The Clodhopper. Sudden Jim. The Pinch Hitter. 1918: The Son of His Father. Hired Man. His Mother's Boy. The Family Skeleton. Playing the Game. His Own Home Town. The Claws of the Hun. A Nine O'Clock Town. 1919: Hard Boiled. Home Breaker. The Lady of Red Butte. Other Men's Wives. The Sheriff's Son. String Beans. Extravagance. Quicksands. The Peace of Roaring River. When Doctors Disagree. Upstairs. 1920: Pinto. The Jinx. The Blooming Angel. The Slim Princess. 1921: Made in Heaven. What Happened to Rosa. The Concert. Beating the Game. Mr Barnes of New York. Head Over Heels. Bootlegger's Daughter. Scandalous Tongues. 1923: The Lonely Road. The Scarlet Lily. Refuge. Dollar Devils. The Kingdom Within. The Man Next Door. Chastity. Long Live the King. The Man Life Passed By. 1924:

Bread. A Boy of Flanders. 1925: Thunder Mountain. Frivolous Sal. Man and Maid. The Wheel. The Golden Strain. 1926: Siberia. The Return of Peter Grimm. The Lily. 1927: Stage Madness. The Secret Studio. The Heart of Salome. 1928: The Showdown. Forgotten Faces. Manhattan Cocktail. 1929: Fashions in Love. The Wheel of Life. Redskin. Nothing But the Truth. The Laughing Lady. 1930: †Paramount on Parade. Safety in Numbers. Heads Up. 1931: The Woman Between (GB: Madame Julie). Friends and Lovers. 1932: Strange Justice. Uptown New York. 1933: The Constant Woman. The Cocktail Hour. My Woman. 1934: Beloved. One Night of Love. 1935: Let's Live Tonight. Love Me Forever (GB: On Wings of Song). 1936: The Music Goes 'Round. 1937: Something to Sing About. 1939: The Mikado. 1940: Rhythm on the River. Road to Singapore. 1941: Birth of the Blues. Road to Zanzibar. Kiss the Boys Goodbye. 1942: The Fleet's In.

SCHLESINGER, John 1926-

This British-born director has long been a trail-blazer in terms of public taste, with an almost infallible sense of what will go well at the box-office even when it seems daringly avant-garde, or even downright uninteresting. This and the fact that several Oscars have been won in his films have brought him a place among the world's leading directors; yet I have to confess that I find few of his films wholly satisfactory, although elements in most of them are totally admirable. An entertainer and magician during World War II, Schlesinger followed belated university education by taking up an acting career. When this proved unrewarding, he joined BBC Television to direct documentaries and his first major documentary for the cinema, *Terminus*, set in Waterloo railway station, was powerful enough to make a considerable reputation. Schlesinger's first feature film, *A Kind of Loving*, followed on the heels (perhaps the only time Schlesinger has followed rather than led) of *Saturday Night and Sunday Morning* as a portrait of the passionate side of the British working-class. Pursuing its own path with complete dedication, and making a star of Alan Bates, it still seems Schlesinger's most skilful film in many respects, including editing and camera movement and placement that would in later Schlesinger films seem suspect. Then again, its characters seem rooted in real life — this is only spasmodically true of his later work, although hardly the point with *Billy Liar!* about a working-class day-dreamer, a Walter Mitty of the slums,

Long-serving British director John **Schlesinger** working on one of the best of his more recent films, *Pacific Heights* .

brilliantly conveyed in the film by Tom Courtenay. Schlesinger took the female star of that film, Julie Christie, into the title role of his next, *Darling*, which won her an Academy Award, although even at the time the film seemed very empty and looks direly dated today. The same can be said of the frantically trendy *Sunday, Bloody Sunday*; better was *Midnight Cowboy*, with painfully real performances by Jon Voight and Dustin Hoffman — Schlesinger's recreation of these cellar-rats (a stud and his pimp) as pitiable, even attractive characters won Oscars for best film, best direction and best screenplay. Even Schlesinger could make little of the unapproachable people from *The Day of the Locust* or *Honky Tonk Freeway*, but in *Yanks* he gets well-sustained performances from all his principal players. There are many pleasurable things in this film, even if its dramatic content leaves one largely unsatisfied. Schlesinger directs with affection, and preserves a precise microcosm in time to perfection. Dark-

ness and paranoia have increasingly coloured his work in recent times, especially in *Pacific Heights*, one of his most commercially successful films, and *The Innocent*. The vein was lightened in 1995 by *Cold Comfort Farm*, a joyous rendition of Stella Gibbons' famous literary satire.

1950: *†*The Starfish*. 1956: **Sunday in the Park* (D). 1959: **The Innocent Eye* (D). 1960: *Terminus* (D). 1961: **The Class* (D). 1962: *A Kind of Loving*. 1963: *Billy Liar!* 1965: *Darling*. 1967: *Far from the Madding Crowd*. 1969: *Midnight Cowboy*. 1971: *Sunday, Bloody Sunday*. 1973: †*Visions of Eight*. 1975: *The Day of the Locust*. 1976: *Marathon Man*. 1979: *Yanks*. 1981: *Honky Tonk Freeway*. 1982: *Privileged (as consulting director)*. 1984: *Falcon and the Snowman*. 1987: *The Believers*. 1988: *Madame Sousatzka*. 1990: *Pacific Heights*. 1993: *The Innocent*. 1995: *Cold Comfort Farm (originally for TV)*. 1996: *Eye for an Eye*. 1997:

The Tale of Sweeney Todd (TV).

SCHLÖNDORFF, Volker 1939-

West German film-maker whose work is now reaching wider international audiences. Schlöndorff makes searching and often very unusual films with great insight into how the past affects the present, and the root causes of war, violence and corruption. An assistant director from 1961, at first in France, Schlöndorff branched out on his own with documentary war reports for television from Algeria and later Vietnam. His first feature film, *Young Törless*, was shown around the world to approval, and it seemed that Schlöndorff had joined the ranks of top continental directors in one stride. However, although he kept busy on such films as *Summer Lightning* (one of his sparest works, featuring his wife Margarethe von Trotta who has also collaborated with him on script and direction), little was heard from him by international audiences until 1975, when he made *The Lost*

Honour of *Katharina Blum*; by this time such fellow-countrymen as Fassbinder, Herzog and Wenders (all *qv*) had all become well-known. With *Blum* (a condemnation of yellow-press methods), as with all his films, Schlöndorff covered a wide variety of plot developments at a rare pace. His reputation was greatly enhanced in 1980 when his extraordinary film *The Tin Drum* was awarded the Oscar as best foreign-language picture. Once again, Schlöndorff races through an admirably coherent, though complicated narrative at a good rhythm, and the film never sags under its 142-minute running time in surveying 20th-century German history through the rather frightening gaze of a young boy who has stunted his own growth because he has decided not to grow up. Visually, it is Schlöndorff's most impressive film to date, showing colour control much improved from the days of *Michael Kohlhaas*; some memorably unsettling scenes which involve the boy, played by 12-year-old David Bennent, himself a case of arrested development, are often shot from the boy's own low-level point of view. Schlöndorff consolidated this success a couple of years

later with *Circle of Deceit*, which again questions the ethics of the Press, this time against a backcloth of civil warfare in the Lebanon of the mid-1970s. Since then his work, often US-based, has been sporadic and less satisfactory.

*1960: * Wenn Kummert's. 1966: Young Törless. Mord und Totschlag (GB & US: A Degree of Murder). 1969: Michael Kohlhaas. 1970: Baal. 1971: Rio das Mortes (TV). Der plötzliche Reichtum der armen Leute von Kombach/The Sudden Fortune of the Poor People of Kombach. 1972: Die Ehegattin (US: A Free Woman). Die Moral der Ruth Halbfuss. Strohfeuer/Summer Lightning. 1974: Ubernachtung in Tirol. 1975: †The Lost Honour of Katharina Blum. 1976: Der Fangschuss. 1977: Coup de grâce. 1978: †Deutschland im Herbst. Das zweite Erwachen der Christina Klage. 1979: The Tin Drum. 1980: Der Kandidat/Kaleidoscope. 1981: Circle of Deceit/Die Fällschung. 1983: +Krieg und Frieden (D). 1984: Swann in Love. 1985: Death of a Salesman (TV). 1987: A Gathering of Old Men/Murder in the Bayou (TV). +Vermischte Nachrichten (D. US: Odds and*

Ends). 1990: The Handmaid's Tale. 1991: Voyager. 1996: Der Unhold/The Ogre. 1998: Palmetto/Just Another Sucker.

SCHOEDSACK, Ernest B. 1893-1979

Although the comparison has been made before, the likeness between Schoedsack and the film director in his masterpiece *King Kong* (co-directed with Merian C. Cooper, 1893-1973), is inescapable: one hand in harmony with nature and exploration, the other firmly resting on the box-office till. A tall, rangy, pipe-smoking American, Schoedsack led an adventurous younger life before settling down in Hollywood. Beginning his career as a second cameraman with Mack Sennett, he applied to join the Signal Corps' photographic section when America entered World War II. After photographing action in France and Germany, Schoedsack also filmed the Polish intervention in Russia in 1919 and the Greco-Turkish war of 1921-1922. Later, he joined Cooper on an expedition to Singapore, Ceylon and Africa, where they made a short documentary together and formulated plans for their greatest documentary, *Grass*.

German director Volker **Schlöndorff's** English-language work has been largely disappointing. Here he is on *Voyager*.

Filmed under hazardous conditions in mountainous Kurdistan, *Grass* is the completely unstaged record of an epic trek by a tribe of Kurds to grassland. Shots of the tribes ascending and descending mountains are awe-inspiring and there is a horrifyingly exciting crossing of a river. The film was never completed to the makers' satisfaction, but released in feature form to great critical approval. After this, Cooper and Schoedsack worked for Paramount – their detractors accused them of 'going Hollywood' – making *Chang,* an exciting documentary about tigers in Thailand; and their first fictional feature, a version of *The Four Feathers.* Schoedsack then went alone to Sumatra to make *Rango,* a delightful documentary about an orangutan. Back in Hollywood, he stuck to exotic settings with a short but exciting, atmospheric and very influential thriller *The Most Dangerous Game.* Cooper, who co-produced this film (Irving Pichel – *qv* – co-directed) had by this time reached an executive position with RKO, who backed the next Cooper-Schoedsack project, *King Kong.* Here their documentary sense, and feel for unexplored places,

coupled with superb special effects by Willis O'Brien, paid rich dividends in the form of the greatest giant animal film ever made. The world was now Schoedsack's oyster, but he never again achieved such acclaim. The follow-up to *King Kong, Son of Kong,* was disappointing, and *The Last Days of Pompeii,* Cooper and Schoedsack's last big spectacle for RKO, was far too stilted in dramatic terms. At least the latter went out in a blaze of special effects glory: the eruption of the last ten minutes is a sequence which rivals that of the earthquake in M-G-M's *San Francisco,* made the following year. Of Schoedsack's later films, the most successful was *Dr Cyclops.* His first in Technicolor, it found him on happier ground in the South American jungle (albeit one filmed at Paramount) with the story of a mad scientist who miniaturizes his 'guests'. Schoedsack married Ruth Rose, who co-wrote the sceenplays for several of his films.

1924: **Golden Prince/The Lost Empire (D). 1926: †Grass (D). 1927: †Chang (D). 1929: †The Four Feathers. 1931: Rango (D). 1932: †The Most Dangerous*

Game (GB: The Hounds of Zaroff). 1933: †King Kong. Son of Kong. Blind Adventure. 1934: Long Lost Father. 1935: The Last Days of Pompeii. 1937: Trouble in Morocco. Outlaws of the Orient. 1940: Dr Cyclops. 1949: Mighty Joe Young. 1952: †This is Cinerama.

SCHRADER, Paul 1946-

This American director sees so much evil in the world that one sometimes fears for his state of mind. Blood, violence, sexual excess and psychotic conditions are his stock-in-trade. His films, whether as writer, director or both, exude dark power: one can almost smell the corruption and feel the despair of many of his characters. His scripts have their foundation stones in four-letter words, the dialogue of the urban backstreets where most of his stories are set. All this black bile could stem from his own restricted upbringing. His parents were strict Calvinists and he was not allowed to go to the cinema. While studying divinity, however, he became editor of a film magazine and, after a period in which he

Portrayer of urban paranoia, Paul **Schrader** works on a familiar background of city streets in *Light Sleeper.*

admits to great depressions, began to write screenplays. These mid-1970s' scripts are full of venom: *The Yakuza, Taxi Driver, Rolling Thunder* – the first and third of these written in collaboration – all have obsessed characters with violence at the back of their mind, while *Obsession* is a clever, dark whodunnit rather bungled in the telling by director Brian de Palma. It was no surprise that Schrader should want total control of his work. *Blue Collar* attacked Union corruption, but finds its greatest strength in its action scenes — a robbery planned by three car assembly workers. Schrader pursued the theme of urban menace in *Hardcore*, which hit at his own upbringing, as Calvinist George C. Scott tries to retrieve his daughter from the hell of featuring in gutter-level hardcore films. The film works less well than *American Gigolo*, a strong, dark, social thriller with Richard Gere as the all-American midnight cowboy made good: he pleases rich women for rich rewards. After working on the script for *Raging Bull*, Schrader made a departure from theme, if not from city streets, with *Cat People*, a (predictably visceral) remake of the 1942 RKO horror classic. The failure of the supernatural content and the effectiveness of Natassia Kinski's haunted Catwoman suggests that Schrader's forte will remain in producing hard-driving acting performances in unpalatable but compelling surroundings. For such a turner-over of stones one sometimes wonders if he doesn't show too much relish at what lies beneath. The underbelly of society continued to fascinate him through the 1990s, although there was an interesting departure with the cable TV film *Witch Hunt*, with Dennis Hopper in the role created by Fred Ward in the earlier *Cast a Deadly Spell* as the only 'straight' guy in a different postwar Los Angeles dominated by the black arts.

1978: *Blue Collar. Hardcore* (GB: *The Hardcore Life*). 1980: *American Gigolo*. 1982: *Cat People*. 1985: *Mishima: A Life in Four Chapters*. 1987: *Light of Day*. 1988: *Patty Hearst*. 1990: *The Comfort of Strangers*. 1991: *Light Sleeper*. 1994: *Witch Hunt* (cable TV). 1996: *Touch*. 1997: *The Affliction*.

SCHROEDER, Barbet 1941-

This Iranian-born director, based in Paris in his early days, but in Hollywood since 1985, mostly makes films about characters you would cross the street to avoid. Since his move to Hollywood, his films have been disappointing, but they have produced some memorably malignant characters — notably those played by Jennifer Jason Leigh in *Single White Female*, Jeremy Irons in *Reversal of Fortune*, Nicolas Cage in *Kiss of Death* and Michael Keaton in *Desperate Measures*. The son of a German geologist, Schroeder was an actor, photo-journalist, jazz entrepreneur and film critic (for the influential *Cahiers du Cinéma*) before settling down to produce, then direct films. His time as a photo-journalist led him to make some entertaining documentaries, and it was one on the writer Charles Bukowski that led him to begin his American career — with a semi-fictional account of Bukowski's early life, *Barfly*. Some of this was entertaining in a grimly funny way, but there are moments of tedium, which is also true of the much-fêted *Reversal of Fortune*, which contains some fine acting in its account of a real-life murder trial and won Schroeder an Oscar nomination, although he might have clinched the award but for the mistaken decision not to show the trial itself. This was not as popular, however, as *Single White Female*, which showed Bridget Fonda and Jennifer Jason Leigh in their most intense acting form, in the story of the flatmate from hell, who tries to take over the other girl's life. This was far more interestingly complex than Schroeder's subsequent films, which have opened to increasingly poor reviews.

1969: *More*. 1971: *Sing-Sing* (D). 1974: *Idi Amin Dada* (D). 1976: *Maîtresse*. 1978: *Koko the Talking Gorilla* (D). 1984: *Les tricheurs*. 1987: *Barfly*. 1990: *Reversal of Fortune*. 1992: *Single White Female*. 1994: *Kiss of Death*. 1995: *Before and After*. 1998: *Desperate Measures*.

SCHUMACHER, Joel 1939-

Tall, ascetic-looking American director, the stunning look of whose movies reflects his background in fashion and design. His films are mainly thrillers or ensemble pieces and include two in the 'Batman' series. Most of his work, although high-profile fare, hasn't quite fulfilled its potential. And, although he has specialised in the splashy and the fanciful, it's the smaller scale pictures, *Cousins* and *Falling Down*, that have achieved their targets and reached the emotions of their intended audience. In an unusual route to the film director's chair, Schumacher was a window dresser, boutique owner and clothes designer before entering films in his early thirties as a costume designer, then revealing talents as a screenwriter, mainly with lightly comic vehicles. His first film, *The Incredible Shrinking Woman*, is an underrated fantasy comedy, with Schumacher revealing a sure light touch that would later sometimes desert him. A Brat Pack ensemble angst drama, *St Elmo's Fire*, lifted Schumacher into a higher echelon of directors, although in truth its total was less than the sum of its parts, a fault that would bedevil other Schumacher projects. But, to be fair, he has attempted a wide variety of genres. *The Lost Boys* was a lively teen horror film with a good quota of amusing lines, *Cousins* a lushly romantic Hollywood adaptation of a French original, *Flatliners* a rather preposterous story of students experimenting with life after death, and *Dying Young* a dismal weepie. Despite this rather mixed record, although probably on the strength of *Falling Down*, a brilliant study of urban paranoia, Schumacher was entrusted with two John Grisham blockbusters, the dullish *The Client* and the far more successful *A Time to Kill*, as well as his two 'caped crusader' films, *Batman Forever* and *Batman and Robin*, which depended more on personalities than firepower for their impact. As the Batman franchise seemingly passed its expiry date, Schumacher turned to yet another different kind of movie in *8 Millimeter*.

1981: *The Incredible Shrinking Woman*. 1983: *DC Cab* (GB: *Street Fleet*). 1985: *St Elmo's Fire*. 1987: *The Lost Boys*. 1989: *Cousins*. 1990: *Flatliners*. 1991: *Dying Young*. 1993: *Falling Down*. 1994: *The Client*. 1995: *Batman Forever*. 1996: *A Time to Kill*. 1997: *Batman and Robin*. 1998: *8 Millimeter*. 1999: *Flawless*.

SCHUSTER, Harold D. 1902-1986

As a director, this American film-maker alternated simple, sentimental stories, often involving children and animals, with tough routine thrillers. A former cameraman himself, he proved an expert at colour control. As a name, he may be forgotten today, but some of his films still bring fond memories of childhood. Coming to Hollywood in the early 1920s, Schuster was an actor before turning to cinematography, then editing. He worked as editor on Murnau's *Sunrise* and Rowland V. Lee's *Zoo in Budapest*, among dozens of others for Fox and Twentieth Century-Fox, before moving to England to make his directorial debut on that country's first Technicolor film, *Wings of the Morning*. Lovely photography of the (largely Irish) countryside and exciting horse races complement appealing performances by Henry Fonda and Annabella, and the film established a pattern for the highpoints of Schuster's career. He stayed

Looking like a Mafia don from one of his own crime films, Martin **Scorsese** (who has since lost the moustache and beard) gets an overall view of a shot from his landmark boxing movie *Raging Bull*.

work reasserted itself in the last years of his cinema career, notably in *Dragoon Wells Massacre*, the best of his later films, with Jack Elam memorable as an ugly westerner who becomes friendly with a little girl; and in *The Courage of Black Beauty*, which returned Schuster to familiar pastures. The remainder of his working life was spent in television, often, predictably, working on segments of outdoor adventure series.

1937: Wings of the Morning. Dinner at the Ritz. 1938: Swing That Cheer. Exposed. Queer Cargo (US: Pirates of the Seven Seas). 1939: One Hour to Live. Framed. 1940: Ma! He's Making Eyes at Me. Zanzibar. South to Karanga. Diamond Frontier/A Modern Monte Cristo. 1941: Small Town Deb. A Very Young Lady. 1942: On the Sunny Side. Girl Trouble. The Postman Didn't Ring. 1943: My Friend Flicka. 1944: Marine Raiders. 1946: Breakfast in Hollywood (GB: The Mad Hatter). 1947: The Tender Years. 1948: So Dear to My Heart. 1952: Kid Monk Baron (GB: Young Paul Baron). 1953: Jack Slade (GB: Slade). 1954: Loophole. Security Risk. Port of Hell. 1955: Finger Man. The Return of Jack Slade. Tarzan's Hidden Jungle. 1956: Down Liberty Road. 1957: Dragoon Wells Massacre. Portland Exposé. 1958: The Courage of Black Beauty.

SCORSESE, Martin 1942-

This unpredictable American director has probably pleased everyone some of the time in his 11 years as a commercial filmmaker. Although his roots are in reality, he has tackled a commendably wide variety of genres in his handful of films, several of which have starred Robert DeNiro. Which of them you think brilliant and which disappointing depends on what you like to see in the cinema. But the quality, thoughtfulness and technical proficiency of his work, in an age of amateurs, is undeniable. He has also contributed screenplays, although not, in my view, to his best films. Giving up training for the priesthood after a year of study, Scorsese enrolled instead at New York University's Film School. He was to stay at the university for ten years, during which time he obtained his master's degree in film communications and made several prize-winning shorts and his first feature, later re-released when he had made the big league. He entered the commercial cinema in the early 1970s, making two strong, violent thrillers, *Boxcar Bertha* and *Mean Streets*. The film which made him a 'bankable' director, however, was *Alice Doesn't Live Here Anymore*,

with Britain and Annabella, this time joined by David Niven and Paul Lukas in *Dinner at the Ritz*, a likeable comedy-thriller. Back in Hollywood, he worked on medium-budget action films on exotic locations, or comedies that dealt with teenage teething problems. Then Fox handed him *My Friend Flicka*, about a boy and his horse. A big success for the studio, it spawned a host of similar films,

from both Fox and the minor studios. It was children and lambs in Disney's *So Dear to My Heart*, before a brush with the McCarthy committee left Schuster workless for several years. When he returned, it was to make some decent black-and-white thrillers *(Loophole, Finger Man)* and westerns *(Jack Slade* and its sequel), in which a new hard edge is evident. His talent with children and colour

which had a perceptive and saltily enjoyable script by Robert Getchell, and the female performance of the decade by Ellen Burstyn, as the mother who must forge a new life for herself and her troublesome son when her boorish husband is killed in a road accident. Scorsese followed up with the much blacker, but almost as good *Taxi Driver*. Robert DeNiro is the man whose revulsion at the pimps, prostitutes and general corruption in the streets eventually drives him to kill. Amazingly, Scorsese was not even nominated for an Academy Award for either of these two skilful films although, after a partial failure with the 1940s-set musical *New York, New York*, truncated outside its native America, he finally did make the Oscars nominations list for *Raging Bull*; here Robert DeNiro followed the trail blazed by Ellen Burstyn in winning an Oscar. The fight scenes have brutal authority to the point of squalor, but the boxer's disintegration towards the end raises no sympathy, and the film is less entertaining than Scorsese's previous

work. The Scorsese-DeNiro machine thundered on, however, tackling another new theme in 1982 with *The King of Comedy*. And Scorsese's continuing ability to produce powerful but commercial work saw the two men come full circle with the epic gangster dramas *GoodFellas* and *Casino*. Meanwhile Paul Newman won another acting Oscar in *The Color of Money*, a polished if slightly disappointing sequel to *The Hustler*. Despite several further nominations in the best director category, Scorsese himself has yet to win.

1964: **What's a Nice Girl Like You Doing in a Place Like This?* 1965: **It's Not Just You, Murray.* 1967: **The Big Shave.* 1968: *Who's That Knocking at My Door?* 1970: *Street Scenes 1970.* 1972: *Boxcar Bertha.* 1973: *Mean Streets.* 1974: *Italianamerican (D).* *Alice Doesn't Live Here Anymore.* 1976: *Taxi Driver.* 1977: *New York, New York.* 1978: *American*

Boy (D). The Last Waltz (D). 1980: *Raging Bull.* 1982: *The King of Comedy.* 1985: *After Hours.* 1986: *The Color of Money.* 1988: *The Last Testament of Christ.* 1989: *+New York Stories.* 1990: *GoodFellas.* 1991: *Cape Fear.* 1993: *The Age of Innocence.* 1995: *Casino.* 1997: *Kundun.* 1999: *Bringing Out the Dead.*

SCOTT, Ridley 1939-

A purveyor of vivid visual images, this ginger-haired British director has said 'I love most of all to film the past' which is surprising as his ventures there have been less successful than those set in the present and, particularly, the future. Stuck in television for many years, Scott was an art director turned drama series director before really making his name in the 1970s with a series of commercials whose style was so elegant and striking that their content seems almost an after-

Sigourney Weaver and Ian Holm look dubious about instructions issued by Ridley **Scott** (right) on the spaceship set of his box-office blockbuster *Alien*.

thought. And it was content, logic and pacing that were occasionally to let Scott down when he turned film director in 1977: his first film, *The Duellists*, is so beautiful to look at that it almost makes up for the oddity of the rest. Scott certainly added content and pacing to the bag in his worldwide hit *Alien*, even if logic was still a back marker. Super effects and breathtaking editing, plus an inventive advertising campaign, made this unlikely tale of astronauts being pursued round their spacecraft by a giant, slavering alien a tremendous popular hit. Scott directed it with numbing force. Staying with science-fiction, Scott then made *Blade Runner*. Again, the breathtaking effects and brilliant set design dominated a confusing story. But it seemed that Scott had been judged less than fairly after studio interference, and ten years later he brought out his own cut of the film to general acclaim. *Legend* was a different kind of fantasy and one that, even with Tom Cruise on board as star, the public didn't take to. Nor were they especially enthused by two thrillers, *Black Rain* and *Someone to Watch Over Me*. The feisty female characters that had served him so well in *Alien*, however, re-emerged in his two most successful films of the 1990s, *G.I. Jane* and especially *Thelma & Louise*, in which both his female stars, Susan Sarandon and Geena Davis, were nominated for Academy Awards, as holidaymakers who, through a chain of circumstance, become celebrated fugitives from the law.

1962: *Boy on a Bicycle. 1977: The Duellists. 1979: Alien. 1982: Blade Runner. 1985: Legend. 1987: Someone to Watch Over Me. 1989: Black Rain. 1991: Thelma & Louise. 1992: 1492 Conquest of Paradise. Blade Runner The Director's Cut. 1995: White Squall. 1997: G.I. Jane. 1999: I Am Legend.*

SCOTT, Tony 1944-

Although directing on a slightly lower artistic level than his brother Ridley, this British-born director has had an almost equal share of box-office success. Scott makes high-powered drive-in movies with major stars and his editing and technique can quite comfortably cover a lack of substance in a story. His career has followed a pattern similar to that of his brother. Education in art colleges, followed by a reputation founded on the making of slick and appealing TV commercials. Scott moved into features with the bizarre lesbian vampire movie *The Hunger*, but has since concentrated on much more mainstream fare with such

major stars as Tom Cruise (whom has directed twice), Kevin Costner, Denzel Washington, Gene Hackman, Val Kilmer, Christian Slater and Robert De Niro. Most of his films are little more than a blast of noise and action, but carried through with panache and style. To date the best of them have probably been *The Last Boy Scout*, a crime thriller which allows maximum space to Bruce Willis' own brand of world-weary humour, and *Crimson Tide*, a suspenseful submarine thriller. Driven thunderously along by the director, its tension really bites and its undersea action hammers home the thrills. It also demonstrates the emergence of something like a pictorial stylist in Scott, as he offers some fine shots of the submarine above water, puffing like a grampus as it plunges through and then beneath the waves.

1983: *The Hunger. 1986: Top Gun. 1987: Beverly Hills Cop II. 1989: Revenge. 1990: Days of Thunder. 1991: The Last Boy Scout. 1993: True Romance. 1995: Crimson Tide. 1996: The Fan. 1998: Enemy of the State.*

SEARLE, Francis 1909-

There can be few more dogged purveyors of programme-filler material than the British director Francis Searle. Beginning in 1936, he made one-reel 'Cinemagazine' shorts, two-reel documentaries, second-features from 1946 until well after their heyday was over, and then 30-minute colour comedies into the 1970s. He began his career as a layout artist in advertising, but had entered the film industry by the early 1930s as a camera assistant at Highbury Studios. After cutting his teeth on dozens of 'Cinemagazines', Searle moved to Gaumont-British where he joined their instructional unit and made documentaries. One of the earliest of these, released in both feature and one-reel versions, was *War Without End*, a detailed and commendably down-to-earth examination of work in a (then) modern hospital. Searle returned to the theme of hospital life in his 1944 film *Student Nurse*, and then went into the commercial cinema. His first film, *Girl in a Million*, is also the only 'A' feature he ever made. With the reintroduction of the 'B' film in Britain in 1947, Searle became a man in demand. Most of the small films he made in this category over the next 16 years are thrillers of minimal value, but one or two — *The Man in Black, The Rossiter Case, A Case for P.C. 49, Whispering Smith Hits London, Cloudburst* and *Gaolbreak* — are a little sharper than the rest. Some of them, especially such 1950s 'gems' as *Love's a Luxury, Wheel of Fate, Under-*

cover Girl and *Murder at 3 am.* — are among the worst of those tawdry little dramas that gave British 'B' features such a bad name. And, although Searle kept working, like the next entry in this book, he was never handed a major film. Searle ended his film career as he had begun 35 years earlier – directing shorts.

1936: *Ace Cinemagazine (series). *A Cornish Idyll (D). War Without End (D. And one-reel version). 1939: *English Oil Wells (D). 1941: *Sam Pepys Joins the Navy. 1942: *They Keep the Wheels Turning (D). 1943: *First Day on the Spot (D). 1944: *Student Nurse (D). 1946: Girl in a Million. 1948: Things Happen at Night. 1949: Celia. The Man in Black. 1950: Someone at the Door. The Lady Craved Excitement. 1951: The Rossiter Case. Cloudburst. A Case for P.C. 49. 1952: Whispering Smith Hits London (US: Whispering Smith Versus Scotland Yard). Never Look Back. Love's a Luxury. 1953: Murder at 3 am. Wheel of Fate. 1954: Profile. 1956: The Gelignite Gang (US: The Dynamiters). 1957: Day of Grace (D). Undercover Girl. 1959: *Music with Max Jaffa. Murder at Site Three. 1960: Trouble with Eve. Ticket to Paradise. 1961: Freedom to Die. 1962: Emergency. Gaolbreak. Dead Man's Evidence. Night of the Prowler. 1963: The Marked One. 1966: *Miss Mactaggart Won't Lie Down. 1968: *Gold is Where You Find It. *Talk of the Devil. 1969: *It All Goes to Show. *The Pale-Faced Girl. 1970: *Whole Lot of Trouble. *A Couple of Beauties.*

SEARS, Fred F. 1913-1957

In his few short years on the Hollywood scene, this human whirlwind became known as the 'King of the B Movie'. In just 11 years, Sears acted in 40 films and directed 52 more. It is hard to grasp such activity, all the more so since Sears died from a heart attack at only 44, but some of the 'cheapies' he made in his nine fevered years as a director are considerably better than one might expect. Born in Massachusetts, Sears had already had experience of both acting and direction on stage before war service interrupted his career. On his return to civilian life in 1946, he joined Columbia as an actor. Among his films for them in this capacity were *Down to Earth, The Corpse Came C.O.D., The Gallant Blade* and *Rusty Leads the Way*. But he never rose above minor roles, and started to direct for the studio when given the opportunity to take over the Charles Starrett horse-opera series from Ray Nazarro *(qv)*. Once described as 'a man of improbable humour and wild energy', Sears was soon well into his stride. He was no great shakes with actors to begin with, but the action in his films came fast and furious. The first of them that critics took any notice of was *Ambush at Tomahawk Gap*, a rugged little Technicolor number with tough performances from John Derek, John Hodiak and David Brian that suggested Sears was learning to handle stars. In the same year, Sears made possibly his worst western, *The Nebraskan*, probably bad enough to be anybody's worst western, and all the more ludicrous for being released flat instead of in the intended 3-D. The year 1955, though, brought Sears' first bona-fide 'A' feature, *Chicago Syndicate*, a good meaty crime thriller with solid performances from Dennis O'Keefe, Abbe Lane, Paul Stewart and Allison Hayes. The atmosphere seems authentic and the final chase, as one might expect from Sears, is tense and very thrilling. Unambitious, of its type it's faultless. Sears' biggest box-office success was undeniably his first musical, *Rock Around the Clock*. The film had youngsters rocking in the aisles all over the world and recovered its costs dozens of times over. It was Sears' last unexpected success although the sequel, *Don't Knock the Rock*, which he also directed, made a good deal of money too. The films of his last two years, though, were rather poor, and the signs were that, had he lived, this dynamo of a man would have expended his seemingly limitless energies making westerns for television.

1949: Desert Vigilante. Horsemen of the Sierras (GB: Remember Me). 1950: Across the Badlands (GB: The Challenge). Raiders of Tomahawk Creek (GB: Circle of Fear). Lightning Guns (GB: Taking Sides). Prairie Roundup. 1951: Ridin' the Outlaw Trail. Snake River Desperadoes. Bonanza Town (GB: Two-Fisted Agent). Pecos River (GB: Without Risk). 1952: Smoky Canyon. The Hawk of Wild River. The Kid from Broken Gun. Last Train from Bombay. 1953: Target — Hong Kong. The 49th Man. Ambush at Tomahawk Gap. Mission Over Korea (GB: Eyes of the Skies). The Nebraskan. Sky Commando. El Alamein (GB: Desert Patrol). 1954: The Miami Story. Overland Pacific. Massacre Canyon. The Outlaw Stallion. 1955: Wyoming Renegades. Cell 2455 — Death Row. Chicago Syndicate. Apache Ambush. Teen-Age Crime Wave. Inside Detroit. 1956: Fury at Gunsight Pass. The Werewolf. Miami Exposé. Rock Around the Clock. Earth vs. the Flying Saucers. Rumble on the Docks. Cha-Cha-Cha Boom! 1957: Don't Knock the Rock. Calypso Heat Wave. Utah Blaine. The

Night the World Exploded. The Giant Claw. Escape from San Quentin. Crash Landing. 1958: The World Was His Jury. Going Steady. Badman's Country. Ghost of the China Sea.

SEASTROM, Victor
See Sjöström, Victor

SEATON, George 1911-1979
Polished and professional American writer-director who occasionally rose well above his average standard and was twice rewarded with an Oscar for so doing. One would have hoped for a greater output, though, than his 20 films in nearly 30 years. But he could from time to time inspire well-above-average performances from his leading players, especially the ladies, and also proved adept with children. Seaton began his career as an actor, but his ambitions to write took him to Hollywood in 1933, and he had soon sold his first scripts. Working at Columbia in 1940 on the screenplay of *The Doctor Takes a Wife*, Seaton met William Perlberg (1899-1969), who was producing the film. The two men formed a partnership and Perlberg, a former personal assistant to Columbia chief Harry Cohn, was to produce all Seaton's films for the next 25 years. The pair of them also produced a few films that Seaton did not write and direct. Seaton and Perlberg went to Twentieth Century-Fox in the early 1940s and, after several fairly flat but popular light entertainments, they made *Miracle on 34th Street* (in Great Britain, *The Big Heart*), with Edmund Gwenn enjoying his finest hour (and an Academy Award) as the department store Father Christmas who has to prove to a disbelieving little girl (Natalie Wood, who later worked again for Seaton) that he is the real thing. The dialogue for Gwenn is among Seaton's best, and the final courtroom scene a real winner. There was rather more routine sentimentality in Seaton's subsequent films of the late 1940s and early 1950s (although Gwenn had another well-written role as the old professor contemplating suicide in *Apartment for Peggy*) and it is also at the root of his big 1954 success (by which time he and Perlberg had moved to Paramount), *The Country Girl*. But this story of a faded, alcoholic actor, adapted from a play by Clifford Odets, has the greatest dramatic impact of any Seaton film. Bing Crosby made a really pathetic figure of the grasping, blame-dodging, out-of-work actor, and Grace Kelly's excellent portrait of his dowdy, long-suffering wife, rang true enough to earn her an Oscar. Seaton also

took one for a script that skilfully mixed frankness and sentiment. Although Seaton had his share of failures in his later years, *Teacher's Pet* is an amusing comedy with Doris Day sparkling in the company of Clark Gable and Gig Young, *36 Hours* an unusual war film that has Seaton's most ingenious storyline, *Airport* a monster box-office success but overrated entertainment, and *What's So Bad About Feeling Good?* just as underrated, a nutty comedy that died the death with the public.

1945: Billy Rose's Diamond Horseshoe (GB: Diamond Horseshoe). Junior Miss. 1946: The Shocking Miss Pilgrim. 1947: Miracle on 34th Street (GB: The Big Heart). 1948: Apartment for Peggy. 1949: Chicken Every Sunday. 1950: The Big Lift. For Heaven's Sake. 1952: Anything Can Happen. 1953: Little Boy Lost. 1954: The Country Girl. 1956: The Proud and Profane. 1957: Williamsburg: the Story of a Patriot (D). 1958: Teacher's Pet. 1961: The Pleasure of His Company. 1962: The Counterfeit Traitor. 1963: The Hook. 1964: 36 Hours. 1968: What's So Bad About Feeling Good? 1969: Airport. 1973: Showdown.

SEDGWICK, Edward 1892-1953
American director of comedy films, with roots deep in circus and vaudeville comedy. With his background, Sedgwick was ideally suited to directing the great stone-faced silent comedian Buster Keaton, and he did, six times in the late 1920s and early 1930s, as the great man began to slide. Sedgwick too began to slide, though, like Keaton, he continued to work. But, as a purveyor of basic, knockabout comedy and the sudden belly-laugh, Sedgwick never entirely lost his touch, even in minor films. His parents, Edward Sedgwick Senior and his wife Josephine, were vaudevillians who took their three children, Edward and his twin younger sisters Eileen and Josie, into the act at an early opportunity. In 1915, all three younger Sedgwicks broke into films, Edward as a comic actor, the two girls as the heroines of numerous westerns and serials. Eileen (1893-1991) and Josie (1895-1973) continued their acting careers until towards the end of the silent era, but Edward was directing by 1921. At first he too specialized in westerns, notably those starring Tom Mix and Hoot Gibson, but from the middle 1920s, he began to establish himself as a comedy director. The collaboration with Keaton began with *The Cameraman* in 1928, which contains hilarious pantomime sequences as Keaton (a photographer in the film) tries to learn the trade of news cameraman. This was a silent film, as was the next, *Spite Marriage*, Keaton's last great film, in which

Since *Desperately Seeking Susan*, Susan **Seidelman** has been desperately seeking success in the cinema to little avail.

Sedgwick also obtains an eye-catching performance from Dorothy Sebastian as the actress who marries a trouser-presser (Keaton) to spite the man who jilted her. Proceedings escalate to a typically hectic Keaton finale, carried out with mind-boggling timing. Sedgwick and Keaton continued their association into the sound era but the magic soon faded when confronted with the new medium and Keaton's increasing personal problems. Sedgwick continued to direct routine comedy until the early 1940s, leaving films for a while after a particularly disastrous venture with a studio-bound Laurel and Hardy, *Air Raid Wardens*. In 1948, Sedgwick and Keaton improbably found themselves back in harness together, with Sedgwick direct-

ing and Keaton thinking up gags for the Red Skelton spoof western vehicle *A Southern Yankee* (in Great Britain, *My Hero*). Although it would have been even funnier with a vintage Keaton, the film was still one of Skelton's best and most inventive romps; in one memorable scene – thought up, naturally, by Keaton – Skelton has to pass between Confederate and Union forces and does so wearing a uniform blue on one side and grey on the other. Sedgwick died from a heart attack.

1920-21: Fantomas (serial). 1921: Bar Nothin'. Live Wires. The Rough Diamond. 1922: Boomerang Justice. The Bearcat. Chasing the Moon. Do and Dare. The Flaming Hour. 1923: The First

Degree. The Gentleman from America. Dead Game. Single Handed. The Ramblin' Kid. Out of Luck. Romance Land. Shootin' for Love. Blinky. The Thrill Chase. 1924: Ride for Your Life. Forty-Horse Hawkins. Broadway or Bust. Hook and Ladder. Hit and Run. The Sawdust Trail. The Ridin' Kid from Powder River. The Hurricane Kid. 1925: Let' Er Buck. The Saddle Hawk. Spook Ranch. Lorraine of the Lions. Two-Fisted Jones. †Phantom of the Opera. 1926: Flaming Frontier. Under Western Skies. The Runaway Express. Tin Hats. 1927: The Bugle Call. Slide, Kelly, Slide. Spring Fever. West Point. 1928: Circus Rookies. The Cameraman. 1929: Spite Marriage. 1930. Free and Easy. Doughboys (GB: Forward March). †Remote Control. 1931: Parlor, Bedroom and Bath (GB: Romeo in Pyjamas). A Dangerous Affair. Maker of Men. 1932: The Passionate Plumber. Speak Easily. 1933: What! No Beer? Horse Play. Saturday's Millions. 1934: Here Comes the Groom. I'll Tell the World. The Poor Rich. Death on the Diamond. 1935: Father Brown — Detective. The Virginia Judge. Murder in the Fleet. 1936: Mister Cinderella. 1937: Riding on Air. Pick a Star. Fit for a King. 1938: The Gladiator. 1939: Burn 'Em up O'Connor. Beware — Spooks! 1940: So You Won't Talk. 1943: Air Raid Wardens. 1948: A Southern Yankee (GB: My Hero). 1951: Ma and Pa Kettle Back on the Farm.

SEIDELMAN, Susan 1952-

Although this American director started out making abrasively zany romantic comedies, her ascension to mainstream Hollywood cinema resulted only in her making damply zany romantic comedies whose ambitions proved costly failures at the box-office. Although she may still be regarded as a feminist trailblazer and a role model for other women directors, she has not been given charge of a major project now for a decade. She had originally studied to be a fashion designer, but entered film school in 1974, and made several award-winning shorts there in her graduate year. None of the feature films she made thereafter is especially good, but the first two certainly attracted attention. She had some festival exposure (and success) with *Smithereens*, a gritty but alienating portrait of a punkette hustler, drifting through a lurid New York with vague dreams of managing a rock band, then hit the big time with *Desperately Seeking Susan*, a modish comedy of blurred identity with the dual advantage of Rosanna Arquette and Madonna at their most voguish. Seidelman now tackled three mainline comedy films, but showed a lack of finesse in timing and pacing in projects that were uninspired and uninvolving. Especially disappointing was *She Devil*, an adaptation of a biting TV black comedy that proved to have all its teeth removed by the time it reached the screen, where not even Meryl Streep could do anything with its blandness.

1977: **And You Act Like One, Too. *Deficit. *Yours Truly, Andrea G Stern. 1982: Smithereens. 1983: Desperately Seeking Susan. 1987: Making Mr Right. 1989: Cookie. She Devil. 1994: +Erotic Tales/Tales of Erotica. 1995: The Barefoot Executive (TV). 1999: Gaudi Afternoon.*

SEILER, Lewis 1891-1963

Although this New York-born director made movies for 35 years, directed Humphrey Bogart five times, and created a bright series of musicals for Twentieth Century-Fox in the 1940s, he only had one major success in his career: *Guadalcanal Diary* in 1943. Most of Seiler's career was to be spent in grim drama, but he had begun in lighter vein, working as a gagman and assistant director on two-reel comedies from 1919. By 1923, he was co-directing, with Ben Stoloff (1895-1960), a series of short animal comedies. Seiler remained largely a director of shorts until beginning a series of five-reel Tom Mix westerns late in 1926, including one of the most famous, *The Great K and A Train Robbery* — all for Fox, for whom Seiler worked until 1930. *Train Robbery* and another of Seiler's Mix films, *No Man's Gold,* are especially noteworthy for their action scenes and stuntwork, always a feature of Mix's westerns, but spectacularly exciting here. The first film has fights on top of moving freight trains while in the second our hero hurtles down on the villains' hideaway in a steel ore bucket suspended from a cableway. Seiler's career moved in stops and starts after he parted company with Fox. But Warners worked him hard after he joined them at the end of 1937, although none of his Bogart films is among the star's best, only *The Big Shot* being made after Bogey had become a top star at the studio. Seiler's most profitable film there was probably *Dust Be My Destiny,* with the Dead End Kids teamed with the still-popular partnership of John Garfield and Priscilla Lane. He also made a funny comedy called *You're in the Army Now,* with the oddball teaming of Phil Silvers, Jimmy Durante and Jane Wyman. Seiler's standing improved for a while after he left Warners in 1942: *Pittsburgh* was a successful star vehicle with Marlene Dietrich,

John Wayne and Randolph Scott (though it isn't terribly good), and then came *Guadalcanal Diary.* Based on the true Marine invasion of Guadalcanal in the South Pacific, it has action that really stirs the adrenalin and an impressive range of 'types' who ring true to life; an inspiring war film that sustains its credibility throughout. It seemed strange after this that Fox should put Seiler in charge of a trio of brightly-coloured Vivian Blaine-Perry Como-Carmen Miranda musicals. He handled them well enough, but did rather better with *Molly and Me,* with likeable performances from Gracie Fields as a maid and Monty Woolley as the crusty old employer whose life she reshapes. In the 1950s, Seiler worked out his career with second-features for Warners and Columbia, none of them very memorable. This signs are that he needed a good budget and high production values to come up with the goods, especially in the action scenes that made his name.

1923: *†*Circus Pals. †*School Pals. †*A Monkey Mix-Up. †*Jungle Pals. †*Monks a la Mode. †*The Monkey Farm. 1924: Darwin Was Right. *He's My Pal. †*Etiquette. †*The Cowboys. *Up on the Farm. *Westward Whoa. 1925: *The Butterfly Man. *A Cloudy Romance. *A Flying Fool. *A High Jinx. *On the Go. *The Sleepwalker. *Strong for Love. 1926: *Rah! Rah! Heidelberg! *The Reporter. No Man's Gold. The Great K and A Train Robbery. 1927: Tumbling River. Outlaws of Red River. The Last Trail. Wolf Fangs. 1928: Square Crooks. †The Air Circus. 1929: The Ghost Talks. Girls Gone Wild. A Song of Kentucky. 1932: No Greater Love (GB: Divine Love). *The Circus Show-Up. Deception. 1934: Frontier Marshal. Asegure a su Mujer. 1935: Ginger. Charlie Chan in Paris. Paddy O'Day. 1936: Here Comes Trouble. The First Baby. Star for a Night. Career Woman. 1937: Turn Off the Moon. He Couldn't Say No. 1938: Crime School. Penrod's Double Trouble. Heart of the North. 1939: King of the Underworld. The Kid from Kokomo (GB: The Orphan of the Ring). You Can't Get Away with Murder. †Hell's Kitchen. Dust Be My Destiny. 1940: Flight Angels. It All Came True. Tugboat Annie Sails Again. Murder in the Air. South of Suez. 1941: Kisses for Breakfast. You're in the Army Now. The Smiling Ghost. 1942: The Big Shot. *Beyond the Time of Duty. Pittsburgh. 1943: Guadalcanal Diary. 1944: Something for the Boys. 1945: Molly and Me. 1946: Doll Face (GB: Come Back to Me). If I'm Lucky. 1948: Whiplash. 1950: Breakthrough. 1951: The Tanks Are Coming. 1952: The Winning Team. Oper-*

ation Secret. 1953: The System. 1954: The Bamboo Prison. 1955: Women's Prison. 1956: Over-Exposed. 1957: The True Story of Lynn Stuart.

SEITER, William A. 1892-1964

The silent output of this bluff, genial American director is almost entirely routine. With sound, however, his personality began to express itself in his work, as he produced a series of lively, outgoing entertainments. In his peak period, from 1933 to 1948, he made some good musicals, several films with such moppet stars as Shirley Temple and Deanna Durbin, some strong action films and slightly offbeat comedies with a number of the screen's best-known comedy teams. Born in New York City, and educated with a view to a military career, Seiter was more interested in writing. Gaining employment with Mack Sennett as a Keystone Cop, he soon worked his way into the scenario department and became an assistant director by 1916. Two years later he began directing, at first a few short subjects, but from 1921 concentrating on feature films. He met and married actress Laura La Plante in 1926, and she starred in some of his silent features. The marriage, however, ended in 1932 and two years later Seiter married another actress, Marian Nixon. It was at Paramount that his distinctive comedy touch made itself felt in the episode of the multi-story *If I Had a Million* in which henpecked Charles Ruggles takes his pet rabbit to the china store where he is a downtrodden employee, and (having inherited the million dollars of the title) proceeds to let the animal smash everything in sight. Over at RKO, Seiter directed four comedies with Wheeler and Woolsey and five films featuring Ginger Rogers, easily the best of which is the elegant musical *Roberta*. He also nipped across to the Hal Roach lot for his only Laurel and Hardy comedy feature, *Sons of the Desert* (in Britain, *Fraternally Yours*) considered by many L and H buffs to be their best. Seiter also worked for Twentieth Century-Fox in the 1930s, notably making two of the most charming Shirley Temple vehicles, *Dimples* and *Stowaway* (the latter especially is one of her best films and dates hardly at all) and a Robert Taylor-Barbara Stanwyck romantic thriller about a presidential assassin, *This is My Affair* (in Britain, *His Affair*), which then-critic Graham Greene was moved to describe as 'the best American melodrama of the year'. As always, Seiter's sense of pace was an invaluable asset. Seiter continued to surprise with his versatility. There was a big John Wayne western, *Allegheny Uprising*, the Deanna

Durbin films (although *Nice Girl?* is one of her most overrated) and a reunion with Fred Astaire (from *Roberta*) this time opposite his new partner Rita Hayworth in *You Were Never Lovelier*. He also guided The Marx Brothers through *Room Service*, their only appearance in a vehicle not originally tailored for them. *Destroyer* was a gritty war film, but Seiter ended his film career at Republic with *Make Haste to Live*. Exciting at times, it was a bit sluggish overall, not usually a Seiter failing, and after it he retired. He died from a heart attack.

1918: *The Fly Ball. *Ain't It So? *All Fur Her. *The Fatal Flower. 1919: Tangled Threads. 1920: *The Little Dears. *The Sure Cure. The Kentucky Colonel. 1921: Hearts and Masks. Passing Through. Eden and Return. The Foolish Age. Boy Crazy. 1922: Gay and Devilish. The Understudy. Up and At 'Em. When Love Comes. The Beautiful and the Damned. 1923: Bellboy 13. The Little Church Around the Corner. 1924: Helen's Babies. Listen, Lester. Daddies. The White Sin. His Forgotten Wife. The Family Secret. The Fast Worker. 1925: The Mad Whirl. The Teaser. Dangerous Innocence. Where Was I? 1926: What Happened to Jones. Skinner's Dress Suit. Rolling Home. Take It from Me. 1927: The Cheerful Fraud. The Small Bachelor. Out All Night. Thanks for the Buggy Ride. 1928: Waterfront. Good Morning Judge. Happiness Ahead. Outcast. 1929: Synthetic Wife. Why Be Good? Smiling Irish Eyes. Prisoners. Footlights and Fools. Love Racket (GB: Such Things Happen). 1930: Strictly Modern. Back Pay. The Flirting Widow. Sunny. The Truth About Youth. Going Wild. 1931: Big Business Girl. Kiss Me Again (GB: Toast of the Legion). Too Many Crooks. Caught Plastered. Full of Notions. Peach O'Reno. Way Back Home (GB: Old Greatheart). 1932: Girl Crazy. Young Bride. Is My Face Red? †If I Had a Million. Hot Saturday. 1933: Hello Everybody! Diplomaniacs. Chance at Heaven. Sons of the Desert (GB: Fraternally Yours). Professional Sweetheart (GB: Imaginary Sweetheart). 1934: Rafter Romance. Sing and Like It. Love Birds. We're Rich Again. The Richest Girl in the World. 1935: The Daring Young Man. Roberta. Orchids to You. If You Could Only Cook. In Person. 1936: Dimples. The Moon's Our Home. Stowaway. The Case Against Mrs Ames. 1937: This is My Affair (GB: His Affair). The Life of the Party. Life Begins in College (GB: The Joy Parade). 1938: Sally, Irene and Mary. Three Blind Mice. Room Service. Thanks for Everything. 1939: Susannah of the Mounties. Allegheny Uprising (GB: The First Rebel). 1940: Hired Wife. It's a Date. 1941: Nice Girl? Appointment for Love. 1942: You Were Never Lovelier. Broadway. 1943: Destroyer. A Lady Takes a Chance. 1944: Belle of the Yukon. Four Jills in a Jeep. 1945: It's a Pleasure. That Night with You. The Affairs of Susan. 1946: Little Giant (GB: On the Carpet). Lover Come Back. 1947: I'll Be Yours. 1948: Up in Central Park. 1949: One Touch of Venus. 1950: Borderline. 1951: Dear Brat. 1952: The Lady Wants Mink. 1953: Champ for a Day. 1954: Make Haste to Live.

SEITZ, George B. 1888-1944

From 1916 to 1928 and the end of the silent era, this American film-maker was the king of the serial and the action film. Although writers criticized his melodramatic handling of intimate interiors, noone could deny his facility with action, whether it was a sharply edited cliffhanger, or a panoramic battle scene of breathtaking sweep. Only occasionally in the sound era – *The Last of the Mohicans, Kit Carson* – was Seitz allowed to make a subject suited to his talents, yet he continued to direct at as furious a pace as ever. Even as a writer of romantic plays and adventure novels (1906-1915), he ground out work at a tremendous rate. Entering films in 1913 as a screenwriter and actor, Seitz soon had his teeth into the world of serials and by 1919 was acknowledged as the best serial-maker in the world, even eclipsing France's equally prolific Louis Feuillade. Having already collaborated on the most famous serial of all, *The Perils of Pauline*, starring Pearl White, Seitz co-directed her 1916 serial *The Iron Claw*, and directed all her subsequent 'chapter plays'. After making 19 serials, Seitz devoted himself from 1925 exclusively to feature films. He was most successful with the western, scoring a notable hit in 1925 with *The Vanishing American*, Zane Grey's story of the oppressed Red Indians. In it, Richard Dix, as the chief Indian character, gives one of the subtlest and most affecting performances in any Seitz film – his death scene at the end is both understated and very moving – in addition to the expected action sequences, all of which inspired one contemporary reviewer to call it 'a picture that will live in one's memory'. Seitz also had a great success with *The Last Frontier* (1926), an epic western begun by Thomas Ince and his brother John, under the direction of B. Reeves Eason, two years earlier. But the project had been shelved at the time of Thomas Ince's sudden death; Seitz completed it in spectacular style. The overhead scenes of thousands of Indians galloping into battle were copied by Seitz 14 years later when he made his last western epic *Kit Carson*. The late 1920s, though, saw the end of this kind of western saga for a few years, and Seitz moved on to fast-moving action yarns such as *Woman Wanted* (1935), in which Joel McCrea and Maureen O'Sullivan seem to be on the run virtually throughout a film (they are fleeing a gang of crooks that has framed her for murder) that moves at a helter-skelter pace even for the 1930s, and includes a spectacular car crash that ends up virtually on top of the camera. *Kind Lady* (also 1935) is a rare Seitz venture into the macabre, but a very successful one, with Basil Rathbone spine-chilling as the clever criminal whose gang take over the home of a rich, middle-aged lady. Later in the decade, Seitz began working on the Andy Hardy series for M-G-M, of which he directed 12 (although hardly suitable material for the Seitz of his peak years) before his early death at 56. At his best, Seitz was a director of immense visual imagination. He was the brother of seventimes Oscar-nominated cinematographer John F Seitz. The B stood for Brackett.

1916: The King's Game. †The Iron Claw (serial). 1917: The Last of the Carnabys. The Hunting of the Hawk. The Fatal Ring (serial). 1918: The House of Hate (serial). The Lightning Raider (serial). Getaway Kate. The Honest Thief. 1919: The Black Secret (serial). Bound and Gagged (serial). 1920: Rogues and Romance. Pirate Gold (serial). Velvet Fingers (serial). 1921: The Sky Ranger (serial). Hurricane Hutch (serial). 1922: Go Get 'Em Hutch (serial). Speed (serial). 1923: Plunder (serial). 1924: Way of a Man (serial). Leatherstocking (serial). Galloping Hoofs (serial). Into the Net (serial). The 40th Door (serial. And feature version). 1925: Sunken Silver (serial). Wild Horse Mesa. The Vanishing American. 1926: Pals in Paradise. The Ice Flood. The Last Frontier. Desert Gold. 1927: Jim the Conqueror. The Blood Ship. The Great Mail Robbery. The Tigress. Isle of Forgotten Women (GB: Forgotten Women). The Warning. 1928: Ransom. Beware of Blondes. Hey Rube! (GB: High Stakes). Court-Martial. The Circus Kid. Blockade. 1929: Black Magic. Murder on the Roof. 1930: Midnight Mystery. Danger Lights. Guilty? 1931: Drums of Jeopardy. Arizona (GB: The Virtuous Wife). The Lion and the Lamb. Shanghaied Love. Night Beat. 1932: Sally of the Subway. Docks of San Francisco. Sin's Pay Day. Passport to Paradise. The Widow in Scarlet. 1933: Treason. The Thrill Hunter. The Women in His Life.

1934: *Lazy River. The Fighting Rangers.* 1935: *Only Eight Hours. Society Doctor. Shadow of Doubt. *Buried Loot. *Alibi Racket. *Desert Death. Kind Lady (GB: House of Menace). Times Square Lady. Calm Yourself. Woman Wanted.* 1936: *Absolute Quiet. The Last of the Mohicans. Exclusive Story. Mad Holiday. The Three Wise Guys.* 1937: *Under Cover of Night. A Family Affair. The Thirteenth Chair. Mama Steps Out. Between Two Women. My Dear Miss Aldrich.* 1938: *Judge Hardy's Children. You're Only Young Once. Out West with the Hardys. Yellow Jack. Love Finds Andy Hardy.* 1939: *Six Thousand Enemies. The Hardys Ride High. Thunder Afloat. Judge Hardy and Son.* 1940: *Sky Murder. Andy Hardy Meets Debutante. Kit Carson. Gallant Sons.* 1941: *Andy Hardy's Private Secretary. Life Begins for Andy Hardy.* 1942: *A Yank on the Burma Road (GB: China Caravan). The Courtship of Andy Hardy. Pierre of the Plains. Andy Hardy's Double Life.* 1944: *Andy Hardy's Blonde Trouble.*

SELANDER, Lesley 1900-1980

California-born Selander directed second-feature westerns for 33 years — if he could have broken into direction sooner, it would have been longer. I must admit I find almost all of his westerns tiresome, and seldom better than mediocre, but there are some exceptions, all of them falling in the years 1947 to 1954, when the easy-going, well-liked, fair-haired director obviously found some kind of inspiration. Interested in both the cinema and photography as a boy, Selander became a laboratory technician at 18, an assistant cameraman at 20, and full-fledged cinematographer by 1922. Such rapid progress was deceptive for, despite becoming an assistant director by 1924, Selander was unable at first to make the stride to direction; he only succeeded in doing so 12 years later, through the offices of Buck Jones, with whom he had struck up an acquaintance. Jones was the first of numerous western stars whose vehicles Selander was to direct. All of Selander's films up to 1947 are very minor, most, if not all, of them running under 65 minutes. From 1945, they also included a few non-westerns, but these are real C-grade movies, such as *The Vampire's Ghost.* The first Selander film to attract anyone but hardened western buffs for its own sake was *Red Stallion* (1947), a charming story about a boy and his horse; Selander's first film over 70 minutes, it had a pleasantly un-cute performance from popular child actor Ted Donaldson and some splendid outdoor scenery in colour. Battling with the defi-

ciencies of Cinecolor and Trucolor – Selander must have made more films in these two processes than any other director – made him something of an expert in colour photography, and his occasional films in Technicolor are striking indeed. Also of note is Selander's last 1947 film, *Panhandle,* his first for Allied Artists (the up-market end of Monogram Studios), starring Rod Cameron, with whom Selander was to make several other above-average horse-operas. A rugged, traditional, intelligent western, with well-made action scenes and crisp photography (by Harry Newman), it was followed, in similar vein, by *Stampede, Short Grass, Fort Osage* (rousing Cavalry and Indians stuff in very passable Cinecolor) and *Cavalry Scout,* all featuring Cameron, who had also been in Selander's two less inspired Fox westerns *Dakota Lil* and *Belle Starr's Daughter.* Also for Allied Artists was *Arrow in the Dust,* another Cavalry and Indian dust-rouser, with blazing action all the way through, excellent Technicolor and good performances from Sterling Hayden and Coleen Gray. For TV, Selander directed multiple episodes of such series as *Sergeant Preston of the Yukon, Lassie, Cannonball, Laramie, Frontier Circus* and *The Tall Men* before retiring in 1968.

1926: †**Jerry the Giant.* †**Napoleon Junior.* 1936: *Ride 'Em Cowboy. Empty Saddles. Sandflow. The Boss of Gun Creek/The Boss Rider of Gun Creek.* 1937: *The Left-Handed Law. Hopalong Rides Again. The Barrier. Smoke Tree Range. Black Aces. Partners of the Plains.* 1938: *Cassidy of Bar 20. The Heart of Arizona. Pride of the West. Bar 20 Justice. The Mysterious Rider. The Frontiersman. Sunset Trail.* 1939: *Silver on the Sage. Heritage of the Desert. Renegade Trail. Range War.* 1940: *Santa Fé Marshal. Hidden Gold. Stagecoach War. Knights of the Range. The Light of Western Stars. Three Men from Texas. Cherokee Strip (GB: Fighting Marshal).* 1941: *The Round Up. Doomed Caravan. Pirates on Horseback. Thundering Hoofs. Wide Open Town. Riders of the Timberline. Stick to Your Guns.* 1942: *Undercover Man. Bandit Ranger. Red River Robin Hood. Lost Canyon.* 1943: *Buckskin Frontier (GB: The Iron Road). Border Patrol. Bar 20. Colt Comrades. Riders of the Deadline.* 1944: *Forty Thieves. Call of the Rockies. Lumberjack. Bordertown Trail. Firebrands of Arizona. Sheriff of Sundown. Sheriff of Las Vegas.* 1945: *The Great Stagecoach Robbery. The Trail of Kit Carson. Cheyenne Wildcat. Three's a Crowd. The Vampire's Ghost. The Fatal Witness. Phantom of the Plains. Jungle

Raiders (serial).* 1946: *The Catman of Paris. Passkey to Danger. Traffic in Crime. Night Train to Memphis. Out California Way.* 1947: *The Pilgrim Lady. The Last Frontier Uprising/The Last Frontier. Saddle Pals. Robin Hood of Texas. Red Stallion. Blackmail. Panhandle.* 1948: *Guns of Hate. Belle Starr's Daughter. Indian Agent. Strike It Rich.* 1949: *Brothers in the Saddle. Rustlers. Stampede. The Mysterious Desperado. Masked Raiders. Riders of the Range. Sky Dragon.* 1950: *Storm over Wyoming. Dakota Lil. Rider from Tucson. Rio Grande Patrol. Short Grass. Law of the Badlands.* 1951: *Saddle Legion. I Was an American Spy. The Kangaroo Kid. Gunplay. Cavalry Scout. Pistol Harvest. Overland Telegraph. Flight to Mars. The Highwayman.* 1952: *Trail Guide. Road Agent. Desert Passage. The Raiders/Riders of Vengeance. Battle Zone. Fort Osage. Flat Top (GB: Eagles of the Fleet).* 1953: *Fort Vengeance. War Paint. Fort Algiers. Fighter Attack. Royal African Rifles (GB: Storm Over Africa). Arrow in the Dust.* 1954: *The Yellow Tomahawk. Return from the Sea. Dragonfly Squadron.* 1955: *Shotgun. Tall Man Riding. Desert Sands. Fort Yuma.* 1956: *The Broken Star. The Tomahawk Trail (GB: Mark of the Apache).* 1957: *Revolt at Fort Laramie. Outlaw's Son. The Wayward Girl. Taming Sutton's Gal.* 1958: *The Lone Ranger and the Lost City of Gold.* 1964: *War Party.* 1965: *Fort Courageous. Convict Stage. Town Tamer.* 1966: *The Texican.* 1967: *Fort Utah. Arizona Bushwhackers.*

SENNETT, Mack (Michael Sinnott) 1880-1960

Pioneer Canadian-born director (and later prolific producer) of slapstick shorts, known as the 'King of Comedy'. A child singing prodigy, Sennett had early hopes of a career in opera, but his voice proved to be unsuited to such ambitions as he grew to adulthood, although he played in several Broadway musicals as a 'chorus boy'. After some experience in vaudeville shows, Sennett joined Biograph Studios in 1908 as an actor, and soon became a leading man in quickie comedy shorts, also playing in straight dramas, sometimes under the direction of D.W. Griffith (*qv*), from whom Sennett gleaned much technical knowledge. He began to direct in December 1910 and in 1912, with two backers, started his own company: he called it Keystone. By 1914, Keystone was on top of Hollywood's silent comedy world: its roster of stars included 'Fatty' Arbuckle, Mabel Normand, Charlie Chaplin (who moved to another studio when Sennett refused to pay him $1000 a week), Slim Summerville, Mack Swain and Edgar Kennedy. Later, Sennett would 'discover' Ben Turpin, Harry Langdon, Gloria Swanson and Harold Lloyd. The frantic careless rapture of Sennett's comedy films, as stars and extras alike risked life and limb and cars seemed to miss each other by inches on every other corner of the Sennett lot, made them enormously popular with the paying public. The Keystone Kops, that hapless band of warriors who sat 20 deep in careering cars and hardly ever got their man, were introduced in 1913 and quickly became a national institution. The Sennett bathing beauties were scarcely less popular, and featured several embryo stars. Sennett's editing was masterly and his army of gag writers, who in time came to call him, with a mixture of affection and terror, The Old Ogre, worked around the clock. As a businessman, Sennett was somewhat less successful. He formed Triangle Films in 1915 with Griffith and Thomas Ince *(qv)*, but all three had left the company two years later. Sennett continued to make successful comedy films, but drifted from company to company in search of more independence. With the coming of sound, he was at once a lesser figure, although he carried on for a few years, actually directing some of his own comedies and two-reel musicals (some with the young Bing Crosby) for the first time in many years. He was semi-retired from 1935, although briefly working in an advisory capacity for Twentieth Century-Fox a few years later. The 1937 Oscar ceremonies saw Sennett deservedly given an honorary award: 'to the master of fun, discoverer of stars, sympathetic, kindly, understanding comedy genius, for his lasting contribution to the comedy technique of the screen, the basic principles of which are as important today as when they were first put into practice'. A wordy tribute to a man who never needed words to make people laugh.

1910: The Masher. The Lucky Toothache. 1911: Comrades. Cured. Cupid's Joke. Priscilla's April Fool. Priscilla and the Umbrella. Misplaced Jealousy. The Country Lovers. Curiosity. Dave's Love Affair. The Manicure Lady. A Dutch Gold Mine. Their Fates Sealed. Bearded Youth. Stubbs' New Servants. The Jealous Husband. The Delayed Proposal. The Wonderful Eye. The Ghost. Junks Joins the Temperance Club. The Beautiful Voice. An Interrupted Game. Mr Peck Goes Calling. The Dare Devil. The Diving Girl. $500,000 Reward. The Villain Foiled. The Lucky Horseshoe. The Baron. The Village Hero. A Convenient Burglar. When Wifey Holds the Purse-Strings. Mr Bragg, a Fugitive. Josh's Suicide. Too

Many Burglars. Trailing the Counterfeit. Through His Wife's Picture. The Inventor's Secret. Their First Divorce. Won Through a Medium. A Victim of Circumstances. Dooley's Scheme. Resourceful Lovers. Her Mother Interferes. Abe Gets Even with Father. Her Pet. Why He Gave Up. Taking His Medicine. A Mix-Up in Raincoats. Caught with the Goods. 1912: The Joke on the Joker. Brave and Bold. With a Kodak. Who Got the Reward? Did Mother Get Her Wise? Pants and Pansies. Lily's Lovers. Got a Match? A Near-Tragedy. The Fatal Chocolate. Priscilla's Capture. A Message from the Moon. The Engagement Ring. Hot Stuff. A Spanish Dilemma. A Voice from the Deep. Oh, Those Eyes! Those Hicksville Boys. Help, Help. Won By a Fish. Their First Kidnapping Case. The Brave Hunter. The Leading Man. The Fickle Spaniard. A Close Call. When the Fire Bells Rang. The Furs. Helen's Marriage. Tomboy Bessie. Algy, the Watchman. Katchem Kate. Neighbors. A Dash through the Clouds. The New Baby. Trying to Fool Uncle. The Speed Demon. One Round O'Brien. His Own Fault. The Would-Be Sinner. Willie Becomes an Artist. The Water Nymph. Cohen Collects a Debt. Riley and Schultz. The New Neighbor. Pedro's Dilemma. The Beating He Needed. Stolen Glory. The Ambitious Butler. The Flirting Husband. The Grocery Clerk's Romance. At Coney Island. Mabel's Lovers. At It Again. The Deacon's Troubles. A Temperamental Husband. The Rivals. Mr Fix It. A Bear Escape. A Desperate Lover. Pat's Day Off. Brown's Seance. A Family Mix-Up. A Midnight Elopement. Mabel's Adventures. Hoffmeyer's Legacy. The Drummer's Vacation. The Duel. Mabel's Stratagem. 1913: Saving Mabel's Dad. The Cure That Failed. For Lizzie's Sake. A Double Wedding. How Hiram Won Out. The Mistaken Masher. The Deacon Outwitted. The Elite Ball. Just Brown's Luck. The Battle of Who Run. The Stolen Purse. The Jealous Waiter. Mabel's Heroes. Her Birthday Present. Heinze's Resurrection. A Landlord's Troubles. Forced Bravery. The Professor's Daughter. A Tangled Affair. A Red Hot Romance. A Doctored Affair. The Sleuth's Last Stand. A Deaf Burglar. A Rural Third Degree. The Sleuths at the Floral Parade. A Strong Revenge. The Two Widows. Foiling Fickle Father. Love and Pain. The Rube and the Baron. The Man Next Door. The Chief's Predicament. A Wife Wanted. Jenny's Pearls. At Twelve o'Clock. Her New Beau. On His Wedding Day. Hide and Seek. The Land Salesman. Those Good Old Days. A Game of Poker. Father's Choice. All in the Balance. A Fishy Affair. The Bangville Police. The New Conduc-

tor. His Chum, the Baron. That Ragtime Band. His Ups and Downs. A Little Hero. Mabel's Awful Mistake. Cohen Saves the Flag. Their First Execution. †Hubby's Job. The Foreman of the Jury. The Gangster. Barney Oldfield's Race for Life. The Hansom Driver. The Speed Queen. Feeding Time. The Waiter's Picnic. Peeping Pet. A Bandit. His Crooked Career. For Love of Mabel. Safe in Jail. The Telltale Light. Love and Courage. Professor Bean's Removal. The Firebugs. Baby Day. Mabel's New Hero. The Gypsy Queen. Love Sickness at Sea. The Largest Boat Ever Launched Sideways. Rastus and the Game Cock. A Noise from the Deep. The Riot. Zuzu the Band Leader. Cohen's Outing. Mabel's Dramatic Career. The Fatal Taxicab. When Dreams Come True. The Bowling Match. A Healthy Neighborhood. Schnitz the Tailor. A Muddy Romance. The Gusher. A Bad Game. Some Nerve. Love and Dynamite. Too Many Brides. 1914: †In the Clutches of a Gang. A Bathing Beauty. 20 Minutes of Love. A Fatal Flirtation. The Knocker. Mabel's Latest Prank. He Loved the Ladies. The High Spots on Broadway. A Colored Girl's Love. Stout Hearts But Weak Knees. Washing Our Clothes. Tango Tangles. †A Rural Demon. †Across the Hall. The Fatal High C. Mack At It Again. †Love and Gasoline. A Busy Day. †Mabel's Strange Predicament. †Mabel at the Wheel. $Tillie's Punctured Romance. 1915: My Valet. For Better — But Worse. Those College Girls. A Favorite Fool. Only a Messenger Boy. The Little Teacher. Rascal of Wolfish Ways. Stolen Magic. 1921: †$Home Talent. 1922: †$Oh Mabel, Behave. 1928: $The Good-Bye Kiss. The Lion's Roar. 1929: The Old Barn. The Bride's Relations. Whirls and Girls. Broadway Blues. The Bees' Buzz. The Big Palooka. Girl Crazy. The Barber's Daughter. The Constabule. The Golfers. The Lunkhead. A Hollywood Star. The New Half-Back. 1930: Scotch. Match Play. Sugar Plum Papa. Honeymoon Zeppelin. Campus Crushes. Fat Wives for Thin. The Chumps. Grandma's Girl. Rough Idea of Love. Racket Cheers. 1931: Dance Hall Marge. A Poor Fish. Ghost Parade. Hold 'er Sheriff. Monkey Business in Africa. Fainting Lover. I Surrender Dear. Movie-Town. One More Chance. Speed. 1932: †$Hypnotized. 1935: $Way Up Thar. Ye Old Saw Mill. Flicker Fever.

All shorts except $ features

SEWELL, Vernon 1903-
British writer and documentarist who turned to a mixture of dark thrillers,

comedies and chiller films, and made dozens of second-features in the 1940s, 1950s and 1960s — by which time he was also working busily in TV. He often supplied his own screenplays, although these are not usually as strong as his direction, which at its best chills the spine. His 'B' features, however, were all too often at the very moderate level of the British cinema of the time. Trained in engineering, Sewell broke into the British film industry with the coming of sound, as an assistant cameraman at Walton Studios. He also worked as an art director and film editor in the early 1930s, and had already had experience of direction by the time he joined Gaumont British-Instructional in 1937, making several short documentaries for them. He began to turn to features in the 1940s, most notably with *The Silver Fleet*, a good war film with a typically fine performance from Ralph Richardson as a Dutch submarine manufacturer in the clutches of the Nazis. This was well written and tightly directed, as was *Latin Quarter* (a remake of his first film *The Medium*), which was hardly the musical its title might suggest, but a pre-Hammer horror-style movie about a demented sculptor who hides his victims in his work; the theme was much revamped in the peak years of the horror film, although few of the film's successors could manage as blood-curdling a climax. Most of Sewell's subsequent films are insignificant quickies, although some of them do make one regret that Sewell did not continue to gain major assignments. *Johnny You're Wanted* is a film of great charm about a runaway boy, while several of his early 1960s films – *House of Mystery, The Man in the Back Seat* and *Strongroom* among them – are thrillers that exert a grip tighter than their low budgets would seem to promise. Of the later films, *Curse of the Crimson Altar* is a big disappointment considering that Boris Karloff, Christopher Lee and Barbara Steele were all involved; but *The Blood Beast Terror* does have its moments, particularly in frightening, high-angle shots of a runaway coach at night-time. In life, Sewell has for many years been a keen yachtsman and some of his films reflect this interest, as well as his documentary training. In television, he directed many episodes of the trail-blazing series *The Avengers*.

1934: *The Medium.* 1935: **Facts and Figures (D). *Men Against the Sea (D).* 1937: **A Test for Love (D). *As We Forgive (D).* 1938: *Breakers Ahead. †What Men Live By.* 1943: *The Silver Fleet.* 1944: *The World Owes Me a Living* 1945: *Latin Quarter (US: Frenzy).* 1947:

Don **Sharp** (right) tells actor Richard Pasco how to get to grips with things while making *Rasputin The Mad Monk*.

The Ghosts of Berkeley Square. 1948: *Uneasy Terms.* 1949: *Jack of Diamonds.* 1950: *Trek to Mashomba.* 1951: *The Dark Light. Black Widow.* 1952: *Ghost Ship.* 1953: *Counterspy (US: Undercover Agent). The Floating Dutchman.* 1954: *Dangerous Voyage. The Radio Cab Murder.* 1955: *Where There's a Will.* 1956: *Soho Incident (US: Spin a Dark Web). Home and Away. Johnny You're Wanted.* 1957: *Rogue's Yarn.* 1958: *Battle of the V1 (US: V1/Unseen Heroes).* 1959: *Wrong Number.* 1960: *Urge to Kill.* 1961: *House of Mystery. The Wind of Change. The Man in the Back Seat.* 1962: *Strongroom.* 1963: *A Matter of Choice. Strictly for the Birds.* 1967: *Some May Live. The Blood Beast Terror.* 1968: *Curse of the Crimson Altar (US: Crimson Cult).* 1971:

Burke and Hare.

SHADYAC, Tom 1959-

A former stand-up comedian and once the youngest of Bob Hope's gag writers , this American film-maker has quickly established himself in recent times as the leading purveyor of broad megastar comedy, working in quick succession with Jim Carrey, Eddie Murphy and Robin Williams. Pacing, timing and a 'native' touch have enabled Shadyac to bring often quite crude comedy material home as laughter-raising stuff. After several years writing and performing comedy, Shadyac decided to make his own films and, to obtain the right grounding, enrolled in UCLA's film school. Following one short and one TV movie, he was handed control of Carrey's breakthrough feature, *Ace Ventura Pet Detective*, which proved a jolly lowbrow jape with a neat central idea and some pleasingly contrived incidentals. Shadyac's skill at comedic mise-en-scene also proved an immense boost to *The Nutty Professor*. Basically a one-joke comedy, it proved, in Shadyac's hands, to be a box-office colossus and a reversal of Eddie Murphy's fading fortunes. Next recipient of Shadyac's magic touch was Carrey who, after two mediocre box-office performers, found Shadyac steering him to his greatest success in *Liar, Liar*, a goofy and generally funny legal comedy that gets wilder and less resistible as it goes on.

1989: *Tom, Dick and Harry. 1991: Frankenstein: The College Years (TV). 1993: Ace Ventura Pet Detective. 1996: The Nutty Professor. 1997: Liar, Liar. 1998: Patch Adams.

SHARP, Don 1922-

Tasmanian-born director in British films. Starting as an actor-writer (and later director) in children's films, he achieved a reputation for action and chase sequences and a certain cult following for his work in horror films. But he never quite made the major league: his smaller films contain many delights, but the big-budget movies are almost always disappointing. In Britain from 1948, Sharp attracted a certain amount of attention with his acting and writing and (uncredited) co-direction of action scenes in the refreshing maritime entertainment *Ha'Penny Breeze*, but, although he contributed some well-thought-out and literate screenplays in the early 1950s, it was 1954 before his career as a director got under way in earnest. *The Blue Peter*, which he co-directed, was a thoughtful drama, again with a naval flavour, in which Kieron Moore gives the best of his 1950s' performances, as the shell-shocked officer who comes back to Britain to run a college for naval cadets. Warm, human and exciting, the film also has excellent colour photography, a notable feature of most of Sharp's work. He found critical favour in 1960 with *Linda*, a small-scale but touching and down-to-earth portrait of first love; but he was out of the limelight for a couple of years until starting his series of horror films, of which *Kiss of the Vampire* is the best-regarded, although I personally prefer *Witchcraft*, with its splendid graveyard scenes, swirling mists and generally chilly clutch. In the mid-1970s, Sharp forsook the horror genre and made two hard-hitting, no-nonsense thrillers, *Callan* (from

the successful TV series about a working-class secret agent), and *Hennessy*. His version of *The Thirty Nine Steps*, although much inferior to the Hitchcock film of 1935, has an expected zip about the action sequences, especially a frenzied wheelchair pursuit and the finale on the face of Big Ben which, silly though it is, proved remarkably suspenseful. Sharp did not make a major film after the disastrous *Bear Island*, in which he seemed not to be able to give much assistance to actors struggling with impossible accents. He also directed (uncredited) some very exciting action scenes in *Those Magnificent Men in Their Flying Machines* (1965) and *Puppet on a Chain* (1970). Mention should also be made of a beautiful documentary, *The Changing Years*, which he made in 1958, and of the twin TV miniseries, *A Woman of Substance* (1983) and its sequel *Hold the Dream* (1986).

1949: †Ha'penny Breeze (uncredited). 1954: †The Blue Peter. 1955: The Stolen Airliner. 1957: The Adventures of Hal 5. 1958: *The Changing Years (D). The Golden Disc (US: The Inbetween Age). 1960: The Professionals. Linda. 1962: Kiss of the Vampire (US: Kiss of Evil). †Two Guys Abroad. 1963: It's All Happening (US: The Dream Maker). The Devil Ship Pirates. 1964: Witchcraft. 1965: The Face of Fu Manchu. Rasputin the Mad Monk. The Curse of the Fly. †Those Magnificent Men in Their Flying Machines, or: How I Flew from London to Paris in 11 Hours and 25 Minutes (uncredited). 1966: Our Man in Marrakesh (US: Bang Bang You're Dead): The Brides of Fu Manchu. 1967: Jules Verne's Rocket to the Moon (US: Those Fantastic Flying Fools/Blast Off). 1968: Taste of Excitement. 1969: The Violent Enemy. 1970: †Puppet on a Chain (uncredited). 1972: Psychomania (US: The Death Wheelers). 1973: Dark Places. 1974: Callan. 1975: Hennessy. 1978: The Four Feathers (TV GB: cinemas). The Thirty Nine Steps. 1979: Bear Island. 1984: Secrets of the Phantom Caverns (later What Waits Below). 1985: Guardian of the Abyss (video). 1988: Tears in the Rain.

SHAVELSON, Melville 1917-

Humour and humanity are high on the priorities of this American film-maker, as one might expect from a genial Jewish wit (be once wrote a book called *How to Make a Jewish Movie*) born in the heart of Brooklyn. Many of his films are about real people, and show a clear affection for times and places past. He has a considerable talent for recapturing an atmosphere

in these films, but they remain muted in impact, partly because Shavelson and his long-time writer-producer partner Jack Rose (they worked together from 1940 to 1962) were not quite as skilful with dramatic dialogue as they were at fashioning wisecracks. Shavelson and Polish-born Rose had started working together on Bob Hope's radio show, and went on to supply gags and co-write screenplays for his films. Shavelson, whose first co-script credit was on *The Princess and the Pirate* (1944), also wrote for Danny Kaye *(Wonder Man, The Kid from Brooklyn)*. Both Hope and Kaye featured in Shavelson's films when he turned director, and his pictures with them are his most successful. Hope played two real-life characters, although, in *The Seven Little Foys*, he is still Bob Hope rather than Eddie Foy. But the film is likeable entertainment and the seven children are all charmers. Hope still seems to be wasting his talent in *Beau James*, a long, rambling story which never seems to come to grips with itself (or its audience). Nostalgic memories of New York, however, are excellently brought out in street scenes. A biopic of jazz trumpeter Red Nichols, *The Five Pennies*, was also pleasant, but slow at times and lacking in emotional impact. Shavelson wisely next used its star, Danny Kaye, in an out-and-out comedy, *On the Double*, maintaining a hectic pace and giving Kaye's flair for zany impersonation full rein. Shavelson's later films are disappointing, although he did make a TV movie biography of Rudolph Valentino, which remains the best work on the subject to date. Some writers seem born to direct their own material, but, on the evidence of his films, one can't honestly add Shavelson to that list.

1955: The Seven Little Foys. 1957: Beau James. 1958: Houseboat. 1959: The Five Pennies. 1960: It Started in Naples. 1961: On the Double. 1962: The Pigeon That Took Rome. 1963: A New Kind of Love. 1965: Cast a Giant Shadow. 1968: Yours, Mine and Ours. 1972: The War Between Men and Women. 1974: Mixed Company. 1975: The Legend of Valentino (TV). 1976: The Great Houdinis (TV). 1979: †Ike (TV mini-series). 1983: The Other Woman (TV). 1985: Deceptions (TV).

SHELTON, Ron 1943-

Sports-oriented American director whose work has cocked a snook at those who say that sports films never make money. Himself a distinguished basketball and baseball player, Shelton also studied painting and sculpture at university before attempting to make a go of baseball as a career. Giving up after five years playing in the minor leagues, he tried sculpting for a living before entering the film industry in his late thirties. After various work as associate producer, assistant director and screenwriter, Shelton went solo as a writer-director, hitting the mark immediately with, perhaps appropriately, a quasi-autobiographical drama about a baseball star who, over the hill, is hired to put new life into the failing Durham Bulls. An intelligent and sometimes subversive romantic comedy *Bull Durham* doesn't succeed on every level, but some of its attempted bitter-sweet feel does come across. In the only break from sport in his early directing years, Shelton then made *Blaze*, though his own script here isn't equal to the acting of Paul Newman and Lolita Davidovich in this freewheeling biopic of a state governor who falls for a stripper. Basketball was the sport referred to in the title of the very successful *White Men Can't Jump*, a buddy-buddy film about hustling in the backstreets courts of Venice, California. Shelton's direction remains on the ball, but again his difficult-to-hear, excessively foul-mouthed dialogue becomes tiresome before the end. He was executive producer on another crooked-basketball drama, *Blue Chips*, a flop that might have been a little better if he had directed it rather than William Friedkin. Instead, Shelton made *Cobb*, about a baseball hero with feet of clay. The film was not a success in America and was little seen elsewhere. Shelton turned to golf with much more success in *Tin Cup*. Kevin Costner had starred earlier for Shelton in *Bull Durham*, and *Tin Cup* is Costner's most enjoyable 1990s' film, an engaging account of a washed–up golf pro who gets his act together and wins the American Open. It's also Shelton's best script to date. He took a brief respite from ball games with *Mighty Joe Young*, although you could say that there could be few better bets for basketball stardom than a giant gorilla.

1988: Bull Durham. 1989: Blaze. 1992: White Men Can't Jump. 1994: Cobb. 1996: Tin Cup. 1998: Mighty Joe Young.

SHERMAN, Jim 1949-

A latecomer to the cinema, Dublin-born Sheridan has produced some quality work, although you could hardly say he's made up for lost time: four films in his first decade is poor reward for the millions of fans he made with *My Left Foot*. A man of the theatre like his father before him for his first 40 years, Sheridan toured with the Children's T Company, which he founded. Later Sheridan became artistic

director of arts centres, first in Dublin, then New York, during which time he took a film course at NYU and became interested in making movies. The four films that he has made have all had an Irish background, although the first, *My Left Foot*, which won Sheridan an Oscar nomination, remains the most rewarding, with its emotive account of the Irish writer Christy Brown, afflicted from childhood with cerebral palsy — a role that deservedly won Daniel Day-Lewis an Academy Award against strong competition. Sheridan's sensitive and sometimes wryly humorous tracking of the action grips audience sympathy to the poignancy of the situation. Sheridan extracted another great performance, this time from Richard Harris (Oscar-nominated), in the rather underrated *The Field*, a deep, very Irish tragedy. Although the story's plot twists take some swallowing, Sheridan's direction is expert, especially in the climactic action sequence. It was three years to the next (although in the meantime Sheridan did write the excellent screenplay for the charming *Into the West*), also with Day-Lewis, but *In the Name of the Father* proved less than dramatically gripping considering its emotive subject — the wrongful conviction of the 'Guildford Four'. Sheridan does make something of the film's central father-son relationship, but very little of the passing years which, despite a few explosive incidents, convey boredom rather than suspense. Ironically, Day-Lewis is released from jail at the start of *The Boxer* (the first in four years for both star and director), which did undeservedly poorly at the wickets, especially as the screenplay by Sheridan and Terry George (who had written another IRA film together, *Some Mother's Son*, the previous year), is nicely constructed and does bring home how tough it is for IRA peace negotiators to keep the lid on their militant elements.

1989: My Left Foot. 1990: The Field. 1993: In the Name of the Father. 1997: The Boxer.

SHERMAN, George 1908-1991

Another 'B' western director who graduated to the medium-budget range. His later films are in a rather higher class than those of directors with similar career patterns – for example, Lesley Selander *(qv)* – although not by very much. A small man of seemingly limitless energy, New York-born Sherman joined Republic on its inception in 1935 as an assistant director, working for three years under Republic's best western director, Joseph Kane *(qv)*. He began directing his own westerns at

the end of 1937, making a string of films with such Republic stalwarts as John Wayne, Gene Autry and Don 'Red' Barry. Sherman left Republic in 1945, according to one source because he wanted to make no more films with their thickly-spoken Czech leading lady Vera Ralston (Kane took over that chore) and moved to Columbia, where he worked in colour for the first time. From this point onwards, Sherman's work is marked by individual action set-pieces of considerable impact and by vivid, imaginative use of blazing Technicolor. In many of his films, there is evidence of a considerable cinematic intelligence at work, but he was rarely able to string his better scenes together to make an above-average film. Exceptions to this in his years with Columbia (1945-1948) and Universal-International (1948-1955) are *Renegades*, in which Larry Parks' good-bad guy pushed him forward to *The Jolson Story* and short-lived stardom, *Relentless*, *Larceny* and *The Battle at Apache Pass. Border River*, however, typifies Sherman's failings, in that it has an absolutely terrific climactic fight between Joel McCrea and Pedro Armendariz; but the rest of the film, especially in interiors, is very lacklustre. Going back to my notes on one of Sherman's more ambitious films, *Count Three and Pray*, I find myself writing that 'the action is good, but the dramatics never strike any heights'. Sherman did better with less pretentious stuff: *The Treasure of Pancho Villa*, just about his best film, is a sizzling Mexican adventure-drama with a magnificently exciting climax. Sherman also made two good, medium-budget, hard-hitting westerns with Guy Madison, *Reprisal!* and *The Hard Man*, both of which represent the darker side of the west that Hollywood was beginning to explore. Sherman spent the 1960s largely in television, but in 1971, John Wayne asked him to direct him in *Big Jake* (an old horse called back from the grazing land for one last run). This is the one in which people keep telling Wayne's character they thought he was dead. The film pays homage to Wayne's screen persona in an affectionately fun-taking way and predictably has a blazing climax.

1937: Wild Horse Rodeo. 1938: Outlaws of Sonora. The Purple Vigilantes (GB: The Purple Riders). Riders of the Black Hills. Pals of the Saddle. Heroes of the Hills. Overland Stage Raiders. Rhythm of the Saddle. Santa Fé Stampede. Red River Range. 1939: Mexicali Rose. The Night Riders. Wyoming Outlaw. Three Texas Steers (GB: Danger Rides the Range). Colorado Sunset. Cowboys from Texas. New Frontier. The Kansas Terrors. Rovin'

Tumbleweeds. South of the Border. 1940: Ghost Valley Raiders. Covered Wagon Days. One Man's Law. Rocky Mountain Rangers. The Tulsa Kid. Under Texas Skies. The Trail Blazers. Texas Terrors. Lone Star Raiders. Frontier Vengeance. 1941: Wyoming Wildcat. The Phantom Cowboy. Two-Gun Sheriff. Desert Bandit. Kansas Cyclone. The Apache Kid. Death Valley Outlaws. A Missouri Outlaw. Citadel of Crime (GB: Outside the Law). 1942: Stagecoach Express. Jesse James Jr. The Sombrero Kid. Arizona Terrors. The Cyclone Kid. London Blackout Murders (GB: Secret Motive). X Marks the Spot. 1943: The Mantrap. The Purple V. A Scream in the Dark. The West Side Kid. Mystery Broadcast. 1944: The Lady and the Monster (GB: The Lady and the Doctor). Storm over Lisbon. 1945: Crime Doctor's Courage (GB: The Doctor's Courage). 1946: †The Bandit of Sherwood Forest. Renegades. Talk About a Lady. The Gentleman Misbehaves. Secret of the Whistler. Personality Kid. 1947: Last of the Redmen (GB: Last of the Redskins). 1948: Larceny. Feudin', Fussin' and a-Fightin'. Relentless. Black Bart (GB: Black Bart, Highwayman). 1949: Red Canyon. Calamity Jane and Sam Bass. Sword in the Desert. Yes Sir, That's My Baby. 1950: Comanche Territory. Spy Hunt (GB: Panther's Moon). The Sleeping City. Tomahawk (GB: Battle of Powder River). 1951: Target Unknown. The Golden Horde (GB: The Golden Horde of Genghis Khan). The Raging Tide. 1952: Steel Town. The Battle at Apache Pass. Back at the Front (GB: Willie and Joe in Tokyo). Against All Flags. 1953: The Veils of Bagdad. Lone Hand. War Arrow. 1954: Border River. Dawn at Socorro. Johnny Dark. 1955: Chief Crazy Horse (GB: Valley of Fury). The Treasure of Pancho Villa. Count Three and Pray. 1956: Comanche. Reprisal! 1957: The Hard Man. 1958: The Last of the Fast Guns. Ten Days to Tulara. Son of Robin Hood 1959: The Flying Fontaines. 1960: The Enemy General. Hell Bent for Leather. The Wizard of Bagdad. For the Love of Mike (GB: None But the Brave). 1961: The Fiercest Heart. 1963: Panic Button. 1964: Murieta (GB: Vendetta). 1966: Smoky. Daniel Boone—Frontier Trail Rider (TV. GB: cinemas). 1971: Big Jake.

SHERMAN, Vincent 1906-

Remembering this American film-maker as one of the leading directors at Warners during their peak period, one is surprised to find that he has made less than 40 films. His use of camera angles and other pieces of cinema trickery to undermine an audience resistance to artificiality could turn paste into diamonds, especially in his two Bette Davis vehicles *Old Acquaintance* and *Mr Skeffington*. In both of these Sherman handled a complex narrative of epic proportions with great deftness, providing each with a satisfactory and emotional ending, effective and believable, though the scripts promised neither. The confidence born of working for a successful studio in its peak period certainly helped, and as that confidence ebbed away after the traumatic late 1940s, so did Sherman. He had been an actor, on Broadway (from 1929) and in Hollywood (from 1933), before joining Warners in 1937 as a scriptwriter. Given a chance to direct from 1939, he at first struggled to impose a personality on his work. His two films with Humphrey Bogart, *The Return of Dr X* and *All Through the Night*, are both fairly silly, but with *The Hard Way* (1942), considered by some to be one of the best films of the 1940s, Sherman made his presence felt. His control of a story structure that extends over several years, first hinted at in the rather maudlin *Saturday's Children*, is here seen fully established, as he effortlessly draws his audience along with the tale of hard-bitten Ida Lupino, pushing her naive young sister (Joan Leslie) out of the gutter and into a show business career. It develops into a black and bitter drama, with an uncharacteristically uncompromising ending for its time; Miss Lupino won the New York Film Critics' best actress award for her role. The splendid inter-bitchery of Bette Davis and Miriam Hopkins sparked off *Old Acquaintance* (when George Cukor remade it in 1981 he had to make do with Jacqueline Bisset and Candice Bergen) and Sherman capitalized on it. He also extracted one of Bette Davis' most varied performances in *Mrs Skeffington*, more nonsense put across with such style that it almost seemed like a great film. Ann Sheridan, too, blossomed under his direction in *Nora Prentiss* and *The Unfaithful*, but his three Joan Crawford vehicles, made at the end of his Warners tenure, were among her lesser films. He had a moving success with the British-made *The Hasty Heart*, in which his skill with players saw Richard Todd shoot to stardom as the dying soldier. After the early 1960s, Sherman vanished for a few years, and it seemed his directorial career might be over. Some years later, though, he re-emerged in television. Although his power was much diminished, his work in that medium still occasionally offered reminders of how they used to make 'em.

1939: The Return of Dr X. 1940: Satur-day's Children. The Man Who Talked Too Much. 1941: Underground. 1942: All Through the Night. The Hard Way. 1943: Old Acquaintance. 1944: In Our Time. Mr Skeffington. 1945: Pillow to Post. 1946: Janie Gets Married. 1947: Nora Prentiss. The Unfaithful. 1949: Adventures of Don Juan (GB: The New Adventures of Don Juan). The Hasty Heart. 1950: Backfire. Harriet Craig. The Damned Don't Cry. 1951: Goodbye My Fancy. 1952: Affair in Trinidad. Lone Star. †Assignment — Paris! (uncredited). 1955: Defendo il mio amore. 1957: †The Garment Jungle. 1958: The Naked Earth. 1959: The Young Philadelphians (GB: The City Jungle). 1960: Ice Palace. 1961: A Fever in the Blood. The Second Time Around. 1967: Cervantes (US: The Young Rebel). 1977: The Last Hurrah (TV). 1978: †Lady of the House (TV). 1979: Women at West Point (TV). 1980: Bogie (TV). 1982: Trouble in the High Timber Country (TV).

SHINDO, Kaneto 1912-

A master of atmosphere is this Japanese director who conjured up weird worlds of black-and-white, and burst on the world with three internationally distributed films in the 1960s. Shindo was the son of a farmer, and many of his films are set in the country, some concerning the people who live off the land, others in very different vein — tales of shiver and shock that took horror fans everywhere by storm. From 1934 to 1945, Shindo worked as an art director, but turned to writing in the post-war years, and directed his first film in 1951, as a tribute to his wife, who had died in her twenties. Another moving film was *Children of Hiroshima*, looking at life in his native town after the H-bomb of 1945. Shindo had to wait until 1960 for his next critical success. This was the wordless *The Island*, a grim, unrelenting but compelling portrait of impoverished Japanese rural life, perhaps a lament for Shindo's own father. Its remarkable pictorial imagery paved the way for the very different *Onibaba*, a shocking but hideously compelling story about two women who live in a shack in the midst of a forest of waving reeds by a river. The reeds make a symphony of black, white and silver as the women go about their ghastly work, in a film set mainly at night-time. Their 'work' is the murder of passing strangers for their clothes, their bodies being thrown into a deep pit. As *Onibaba* did not reach the western world until a couple of years after it was made, exhibitors were able to sell his next creepie, *Kuroneko*, again set mostly at night, as a kind of sequel, although it was made three years after *Onibaba*. In the early 1970s, *Onibaba* achieved some kind of additional distinction by becoming the first foreign-language film to be shown on the British independent television network. Some of Shindo's other films, though, with the emphasis on sex, found their way on to the exploitation market. In many ways, he is a forerunner of the foremost of Japan's 'New Wave' directors, Nagisa Oshima *(qv)*, with his obsessions with sex, death, horror and the interrelation of all three. Shindo almost always writes his own scripts and has contributed many screenplays to the films of others, an aspect of his career on which he has largely concentrated since 1977.

1951: Story of a Beloved Wife. 1952: Children of Hiroshima. Avalanche. 1953: Epitome. A Woman's Life. 1954: The Gutter. 1955: Wolves. A Geisha's Suicide. 1956: The Boat. 1957: Harbour Rats. 1958: Only Women Have Trouble. 1959: Lucky Dragon No. 5. The Bride from Japan. 1960: The Island. 1961: The Man. 1962: Ningen/Mother. 1964: Onibaba (GB: Onibaba — The Hole. US: The Demon). Manji/Passion. 1965: Conquest. 1966: Honno/Lost Sex. 1967: Libido. Kuroneko (US: The Black Cat). 1968: Operation Negligee. Heat Wave Island. 1969: Strange Affinity. 1970: Live Today — Die Tomorrow. 1975: My Way. The Life of a Film Director (D). 1977: Chikuzan (GB: The Life of Chikuzan. US: Chikuzan Travels Alone). 1982: Hokusai Manga. 1984: Chiheisen. 1995: Gogo no Yigonjo.

SIDNEY, George 1911-

A musical specialist who also made some useful swashbucklers, Sidney was one of M-G-M's best directors for 15 years. For sheer joy, verve and entertainment value, it would be hard to equal a fistful of his best films — say, *Anchors Aweigh, The Harvey Girls, Show Boat, Scaramouche, Kiss Me Kate* and *Pal Joey*. Sidney has his detractors, who find his work shallow and gaudy, but audiences of the 1940s and 1950s were beguiled by the dazzling perfection of his films' professionalism and timing, and found their exuberance and excitement infectious. Sidney made popular entertainments, for the most part supremely well. A former child actor (in films, among them Tom Mix westerns) and musician, Sidney joined M-G-M in the early 1930s, and worked as sound technician, film editor, assistant director and second-unit director, before beginning to direct two-reel documentaries in 1936. Two of Sidney's 20-plus shorts, *Quicker*

'n a Wink (1941) and *Of Pups and Puzzles* (1941), were Academy Award-winners, and the studio promoted him to features. His first musical was the multi-star war-effort *Thousands Cheer,* which offered him limited scope, but the next, *Bathing Beauty,* shot Esther Williams to stardom as the star of a series of glamorous aqua-musicals, all patterned on this one, the last of which, *Jupiter's Darling,* 11 years later, would ironically be again directed by Sidney. It was followed by the influential *Anchors Aweigh,* in which Gene Kelly dances with a little girl and a cartoon mouse (not at the same time), full of extrovert dance sequences and daring overhead camerawork that presaged *On the Town* with the same two stars, Kelly and Frank Sinatra. *The Harvey Girls* was a sunnily enjoyable period musical with a beautifully delivered stand-out number

'Atcheson, Topeka and the Santa Fé', and a rare and welcome performance by Ray Bolger. After a couple of none-too-happy adventures in drama, Sidney was restored to the musical with *Annie Get Your Gun,* then *Show Boat,* an unjustly neglected remake of the classic 1936 musical. Sidney delivered one of the screen's finest (and longest) duel scenes in *Scaramouche,* and actually made Kathryn Grayson seem sexy in the dazzling and exhilarating *Kiss Me Kate,* filmed with enormous dash and colour and originally made for 3-D. Then he moved to Columbia. His three films here with Kim Novak are more muted, but still successful popular entertainments. Ann-Margret was also in three films for him, but sadly there were no more Sidney specials after 1967.

1936: *Polo (D). 1937: *Pacific Paradise

Swinging advice from Don **Siegel** to child player Charlie Matthau, now a director himself. The film is *Charley Varrick,* in which Matthau's father Walter starred.

*(D). *Sunday Night at the Trocadero. 1938: *Billy Rose's Casa Mañana Revue. *Party Fever. *Men in Fright. *Football Romeo. *Practical Jokers. *Alfalfa's Aunt. 1939: Tiny Troubles. *Love on Tap. *Duel Personalities. *Clown Princes. *Cousin Wilbur. *Hollywood Hobbies. *Dog Daze. 1940: *What's Your I.Q No. 2. *Quicker 'n a Wink. *A Door Will Open. 1941: *Flicker Memories. *Willie and the Mouse. *Of Pups and Puzzles. Free and Easy. 1942: Pacific Rendezvous. 1943: Pilot No. 5. Thousands Cheer. 1944: Bathing Beauty. 1945: Anchors Aweigh. 1946: Holiday in Mexico. The Harvey Girls. 1947: Cass Timberlane. 1948: The Three Musketeers. 1949: The Red Danube. 1950: Key to the City. Annie Get Your Gun. 1951: Show Boat. 1952: Scaramouche. 1953: Kiss Me Kate. Young Bess. 1955: Jupiter's Darling. 1956: The Eddy Duchin Story. 1957: Jeanne Eagels. Pal Joey. 1959: Who Was That Lady? 1960: Pepe. 1963: Bye Bye Birdie. A Ticklish Affair. 1964: Viva Las Vegas (GB: Love in Las Vegas). 1966: The Swinger. 1967: Half a Sixpence.*

SIEGEL, Don 1912-1991

While my admiration for certain films made by this American director is unbounded, it must in all fairness be also suggested that no film-maker who turned out *Night Unto Night, The Duel at Silver Creek, A Spanish Affair, The Black Windmill* and *Telefon* can be all good. Every major director is entitled to his aberrations, but there have been rather too many in Siegel's career for comfort, and one never quite knew what to expect next from him. Perhaps it's what comes of being, like one of his characters, Charley Varrick, 'the last of the independents'. For all their variety, Siegel's films are about people rather than events: many of them concern loners or psychopaths. The films are lean and spare, like the loner heroes, and for the most part hard-hitting and enjoyable. Comic and romantic elements in Siegel's films are rare and usually unconvincing; by and large, his is a man's world, even if he allowed women to hit back in *The Beguiled*. But you can expect most Siegel films to bear an adult certificate, and be tough and uncompromising. His is a world where nice guys finish last or, at very best, hanging on in there by the skin of their teeth, living on nerve-ends. Siegel himself hung on in there waiting for 12 years for a chance to direct at Warners. From 1933, he worked in their film library, selecting action inserts, and later mounting entire montage sequences with such skill that the studio allowed him to organize his own department. In

this capacity, or as (uncredited) assistant director, or second-unit director, Siegel worked on dozens of Warner films between 1939 and 1945, being responsible for almost all of the newsreel action sequences in their war films. In 1945, they let him direct a couple of shorts, *Hitler Lives* and *Star in the Night*; both won Academy Awards. But Siegel only directed two features for the studio before he was off on his own: the richly enjoyable *The Verdict*, the fog-enshrouded thriller in which Peter Lorre and Sydney Greenstreet at one stage actually grasp each other by the lapels, and the dreary *Night Unto Night* (which the studio didn't release for two years). Siegel married its star, Viveca Lindfors, but they were divorced in 1953 and in 1956 he married another actress, Doe Avedon. Despite the limited success of *The Big Steal*, which had a delightful rapport between Robert Mitchum and Jane Greer and an exciting climactic chase, Siegel found the going hard and from 1952 was forced to direct such programmers as *The Duel at Silver Creek*, a dressed-up C-grade western, in which Audie Murphy and Stephen McNally tackle what looks like the oldest gang of outlaws in the west. But Siegel hit pay-dirt in 1954 with *Riot in Cell Block 11*, a realistic, exceptionally well-staged recreation of a prison riot. Eighteen months later, he confirmed his new status with *Invasion of the Body Snatchers*, an excellent, chilling shocker which never indulged in overdoses of overt horror, and kept up a high-pitched level of urgency throughout. Of Siegel's later films, the best is *The Shootist*, John Wayne's last film; it is quite simply one of the great films of our time, as well as a masterly summation of Wayne's own films and career. A moving 'indoor' western about a gunfighter dying of cancer, it contains Wayne's finest performance.

*1945: *Hitler Lives. *Star in the Night. 1946: The Verdict. 1949: Night Unto Night (completed 1947). The Big Steal. 1952: The Duel at Silver Creek. No Time for Flowers. 1953: Count the Hours (GB: Every Minute Counts). China Venture. 1954: Riot in Cell Block 11. Private Hell 36. 1955: Annapolis Story (GB: The Blue and the Gold). 1956: Invasion of the Body Snatchers. Crime in the Streets. 1957: A Spanish Affair. Baby Face Nelson. 1958: The Line-Up. The Gun Runners. 1959: Edge of Eternity. Hound Dog Man. 1960: Flaming Star. 1962: Hell is for Heroes! 1964: The Killers (originally for TV). The Hanged Man (TV. GB: cinemas). 1967: Stranger on the Run (TV). 1968: Madigan. Coogan's Bluff. 1969: †Death of a Gunfighter (uncredited). Two*

Mules for Sister Sara. 1970: The Beguiled. 1971: Dirty Harry. 1973: Charley Varrick. 1974: The Black Windmill. 1976: The Shootist. 1977: Telefon. 1979: Escape from Alcatraz. 1980: Rough Cut. 1982: Jinxed!

SILVER, Joan Micklin 1935-

Since her late, but auspicious debut in 1974 with *Hester Street*, this American director has quietly clocked up a record of consistency that must be the envy of many of her Jewish-feminist contemporaries. Although only occasionally venturing into heavy drama, her films touch real problems and emotions. And her unobtrusively skilful direction has created some magical moments in a generally uncommercial but rewarding career. She was born in Nebraska and had married and produced three daughters before she and her husband Raphael (who would produce her films) moved to New York, and she embarked on a sometime career writing for the *Village Voice* and educational film companies. Dissatisfied with her first experience of writing for a feature film (on 1972's *Limbo*), she determined to strike out on her own and came up with *Hester Street*, a major arthouse success about Jewish immigrants in Manhattan in the early 20th century, a flavoursome, detailed and sometimes poignant portrait of its community that won an Oscar nomination for leading actress Carol Kane. Although the films that followed this were rarely completely successful, they had attractively written screenplays by the director that were full of natural sounding dialogue that was amusing and perceptive without being at all showy. This aspect of her work was shown to its best advantage in her most commercially successful film *Crossing Delancey*, which contained a plum role for Amy Irving as the book-store girl from uptown horrified to find herself the victim of old-style matchmaking with Sam the pickleman from downtown. A romance of embarrassing moments, it leaves you hoping the heroine makes all the right decisions before the curtain falls. The next, *Lover Boy*, perhaps Silver's least characteristic film, was an undeserved failure, being a pizza delivery equivalent of *Shampoo* — a conventional but cute and often comic sex frolic, directed with some style and perhaps more verve than Silver's fans are accustomed to. Since the rather more deserved flop of her 1992 film, *Big Girls Don't Cry... They Get Even*, Silver has concentrated largely on sensitive, quality TV movies. Her daughter, Marisa Silver (born 1960) also ventured half-a-dozen times into film direction between 1984 and

1992.

1972: *Immigrant Experience: The Long Long Journey. 1974: Hester Street. 1976: Bernice Bobs Her Hair. 1977: Between the Lines. 1979: Head Over Heels/Chilly Scenes of Winter. 1984: Finnegan, Begin Again (cable TV). 1988: Crossing Delancey. 1990: Lover Boy. 1991: +Prison Stories: Women on the Inside (TV). 1992: Big Girls Don't Cry... They Get Even (GB: StepKids). A Private Matter (TV). 1997: In the Presence of Mine Enemies (TV). 1998: A Fish in the Bathtub.

SILVER, Marisa
See SILVER, Joan Micklin

SIMON, S. Sylvan 1910-1951
Let's hear it for the man who actually made Red Skelton seem funny. Much of this American director's work is routine, and he seemed to need the right material to produce the goods. On occasions, though, he scored notable successes and proved himself skilful at staging action scenes, whether comic or dramatic, to provide the maximum effect. Simon was a drama instructor before moving from the stage to the cinema in the mid-1930s. For a couple of years, Warners kept him busy making screen tests, and he strung several of them together in 1937 to make a fascinating two-reeler called *Hollywood Screen Test*. It was Universal, though, who gave him the chance to direct features, a mixture of light romantic comedies and thrillers, before he moved to M-G-M in 1938 for what would be a nine-year stay. His first big hit for them was *Whistling in the Dark*, the film that got Red Skelton's film career on the move and the kind of movie in which he would have been well-advised to stay, the tight, tailor-made comedy-thriller with side-splitting action-comedy sequences. Skelton and Simon made two sequels to the film, and the director also tried his hand, less successfully, with Abbott and Costello, who had a loan-out pact from Universal. *Grand Central Murder* was a good second-feature, and he couldn't really go wrong with *Son of Lassie* (the one in which the dog goes to war), but after 1946, Simon went over to Columbia, where he made three of his best films. These were *I Love Trouble*, a fast-moving comedy-thriller with a delightful performance from Janet Blair, whom Simon then teamed with Skelton (on loan from M-G-M) in the wildly funny *The Fuller Brush Man*. This not only took Skelton back to the formula of *Whistling in the*

Dark, but initiated a sequence of 'salesperson' comedies. All of them careered through a breathless series of hilarious situations, in which Simon (mainly as producer) teamed with Frank Tashlin (mainly as writer) and Lloyd Bacon (mainly as director): they also included *The Fuller Brush Girl* (in Britain *The Affairs of Sally*), *Miss Grant Takes Richmond* (in Britain *Innocence is Bliss)* and *The Good Humor Man*. Simon himself was now going over to production full-time, but there was one last film to direct, and it proved his best: *Lust for Gold*, a dramatic 'sleeper' which kept the trade buzzing for months and piles on the suspense in its story of the struggle for possession of the 'Lost Dutchman' mine. Fine performances by Glenn Ford and Ida Lupino complement Simon's careful angling of the story to highlight the corrupting effect of greed. Whether Simon would have returned to direction is doubtful, and will never be known. In 1951, he died suddenly, only 41 years old.

1937: *Hollywood Screen Test. A Girl with Ideas. Prescription for Romance. 1938: Nurse from Brooklyn. The Road to Reno. The Crime of Dr. Hallet. Spring Madness. 1939: Four Girls in White. These Glamour Girls. The Kid from Texas. Dancing Co-Ed (GB: Every Other Inch a Lady). 1940: Two Girls on Broadway (GB: Choose Your Partner). Dulcy. Sporting Blood. 1941: Keeping Company. Washington Melodrama. Whistling in the Dark. 1942: The Bugle Sounds. Rio Rita. Whistling in Dixie. Tish. Grand Central Murder. 1943: Salute to the Marines. Whistling in Brooklyn. 1944: Song of the Open Road. 1945: Abbott and Costello in Hollywood. Son of Lassie. 1946: The Thrill of Brazil. The Cockeyed Miracle (GB: Mr Griggs Returns). Bad Bascomb. 1947: Her Husband's Affairs. I Love Trouble. 1948: The Fuller Brush Man (GB: That Mad Mr Jones). 1949: Lust for Gold.

SIODMAK, Robert 1900-1973
The dark world of this German (American-born) director only really exists, despite his long years in the cinema, in the Hollywood of the 1940s. It is a world of night, of desperation, of menace, of murder and of despair. Yet, despite their morbid and downbeat qualities, these films are rivetingly entertaining, full of hypnotic set-pieces, edge-of-seat suspense, doomed central characters and startling climaxes. They are the films of a great stylist working in an atmosphere and a time (of the quality second-feature thriller and the incipient *film noir)* that ideally

suited him. His last really good film was made in 1949, and two years later, Siodmak (pronounced Shodmak) was on his way, via England and France, back to Germany. Siodmak, whose father was a banker in Leipzig. was said to have lost so much money on his own banking ventures in the 1920s that he was forced to take a menial job as a translator of title cards (having had a good education in English) on imported American and British films. Liking the business, he became a film editor and 1929 co-directed (with Edgar G. Ulmer) his first film, *People on Sunday*. In 1933, he went to France to continue his career. The best of his films there is *Pièges*, but his films outside the 1942-1949 period are barely worth discussing in comparison to those within it. During these eight years, Siodmak made 15 films which vary from good to outstanding, with only one failure *(Time Out of Mind)*. His beginnings in Hollywood, after an arrival in 1940, were inauspicious: Paramount handed him fairly insignificant and light-hearted assignments. *Fly by Night* was perhaps the first indication that Hollywood had an *auteur* for the 1940s on its hands. Paramount pushed the film hard after seeing the results from its gripping little story about a hospital trainee who, by a trick of fate, becomes enmeshed in espionage. Siodmak followed with the uncharacteristic and moving *Someone to Remember*, with stage star Mabel Paige as the old lady who becomes foster-mother to a group of college boys. *Son of Dracula*, played straight, has some remarkable night-time imagery, and *Cobra Woman* is the most bizarre of the Universal Maria Montez extravaganzas. Even so, they cannot compare with *Phantom Lady*, now acknowledged as a classic thriller, in which Siodmak set the pattern for the rest of his 1940s' work. The dark, rainwashed streets, the presence of Ella Raines, that steeliest of glamour girls, Elisha Cook's manic drummer and his later murder, are only a few highlights from a film that memorably sustains its mystery and suspense. These were years in which Siodmak seemed able to play on the qualities of his actors to lend atmosphere to his films. Thus the fly-like central characters (George Sanders, Charles Laughton) of *Uncle Harry* and *The Suspect*, caught in webs of their own making; the brooding, sub-surface menace of Burt Lancaster in *The Killers* and *Criss Cross;* the spectacular casting against type of Gene Kelly and Deanna Durbin in the edgy *Christmas Holiday*, largely successful in spite of Durbin's fight against Siodmak's treatment; the good-bad sisters of Olivia de Havilland in *The Dark Mirror* and, best of all, the terrifyingly vulnerable dumb girl of Dorothy McGuire, fleeing a mad killer in Siodmak's best film *The Spiral Staircase*. The 1975 remake is not even in the same league.

1929: †*Menschen am Sonntag* (GB & US: *People on Sunday*). 1930: *Abschied*. *Der Kampf mit dem Drachen*. 1931: *Der Mann, der seinen Morder sucht* (US: *Looking for His Murderer*). *Voruntersuchung* (US: *Inquest*). *Sturme der Leidenschaft* (*And French version. GB and US: Tempest*). 1932: *Quick*. 1933: *Brennendes Geheimnis* (US: *The Burning Secret*). *Le sexe faible* (GB & US: *The Weaker Sex*). 1934: *La crise est finie*. 1936: *La vie Parisienne*. *Mister Flow*. *Le chemin de Rio*/*Cargaisons blanches* (GB: *Woman Racket*. US: *Traffic in Souls*). 1937: *Mollenard* (US: *Hatred*). 1938: †*Ultimatum*. 1939: *Pièges* (GB: *Snares*. US: *Personal Column*). 1941: *West Point Widow*. 1942: *The Night Before the Divorce*. *My Heart Belongs to Daddy*. *Fly by Night* (GB: *Secret of G.32*). 1943: *Someone to Remember*. *Son of Dracula*. 1944: *Cobra Woman*. *Phantom Lady*. *Christmas Holiday*. 1945: *The Suspect*. *Uncle Harry*/*The Strange Affair of Uncle Harry*. *The Spiral Staircase*. 1946: *The Dark Mirror*. *The Killers*. 1947: *Time Out of Mind*. 1948: *Cry of the City*. 1949: *The Great Sinner*. *Criss Cross*. *Thelma Jordon* (GB: *The File on Thelma Jordon*). 1950: *Deported*. 1951: *The Whistle at Eaton Falls* (GB: *Richer Than the Earth*). 1952: *The Crimson Pirate*. 1954: *Le grand jeu* (US: *Flesh and the Woman*). 1955: *Die Ratten*. 1956: *Mein Vater der Schauspieler*. 1957: *Nachts, wenn der Teufel kam* (US: *The Devil Strikes at Night*). 1958: *Dorothea Angemann*. 1959: *The Rough and the Smooth* (US: *Portrait of a Sinner*). 1960: *Katia* (US: *The Magnificent Sinner*). *Mein Schulfreund*. 1961: *L'affaire Nina B.* 1962: *Tunnel 28* (GB: *Escape from East Berlin*). 1964: *Der Schutz* (US: *The Yellow Devil*). *Der Schatz der Azteken*. 1965: *Die Pyramide des Sonnengottes*. 1966: *Custer of the West*. 1968: *Der Kampf um Rom I*. 1969: *Der Kampf um Rom II*.

SIRK, Douglas
(Claus Detlev Sierk, later Hans Detlef Sierck) 1900-1987
Vast reams have been written on the work of this Danish-born Hollywood director, very little during his career. And that is not surprising for, having revisited the Universal 'classics', *Magnificent Obsession*, *All That Heaven Allows*, *Written on the Wind*, *Imitation of Life* and others, it is very difficult to see what the fuss is all about. True, Sirk did make some extremely valuable films, but hand

me *Has Anybody Seen My Gal*, *Sleep My Love*, *The Tarnished Angels* and *Battle Hymn*, while I drop some of the more prestigious work in the river. Sirk's early work, it must be admitted, does reflect his own magnificent obsessions. His German movies (from 1935) immediately showed a taste for lavish interiors and lovely but anguished women as central characters. Still, he was almost unknown when he arrived in Hollywood and, although employed by Columbia, given precious little to do. He did eventually make *Hitler's Madman*, which is very entertaining, if wildly inaccurate, and two films which played on George Sanders' persona as the rogue with feet of clay, *Summer Storm* and *A Scandal in Paris*. *Lured* and *Sleep My Love* were presentable thrillers, but Sirk was disappointed with his work at Columbia and returned to Germany. By the autumn of 1950, he was back in America working for Universal-International, although his assignments were hardly better. In 1952, though, Sirk was given his chance to show his rich understanding of colour in films when handed *Has Anyone Seen My Gal*, a wryly observed, but never sardonic portrait of life in a small American town of the 1920s, with Charles Coburn in splendid form as the crusty millionaire visiting distant and moderately impoverished relatives to see if they are worth leaving his fortune to. For pure, relaxed enjoyment, this remains the most enjoyable and least dated of Sirk's films, but it also marked the beginning of his love affair with glamour, both male and female, in the forms of Rock Hudson, Piper Laurie, Jane Wyman, Barbara Rush, Robert Stack, Dorothy Malone and others on Universal's cheesecake-and-beefcake payroll. In the meantime, however, it was followed by *Meet Me at the Fair* and *Take Me to Town*, two more vigorous and flowingly likeable evocations of a rosy past, both of which enhanced his reputation as a middle-budget colour director. Viewed today, the weepies that followed seem absurdly melodramatic with their earnest over-emoting, but in their time they were box-office gold, and *Written on the Wind* won an Oscar for Dorothy Malone and a nomination for Robert Stack. Much better was the stylish 1957 film that reunited them, *The Tarnished Angels* (based on William Faulkner's *Pylon*) and, in the same year, *Battle Hymn*, Sirk's last venture with Rock Hudson, an extremely interesting and unusual war film with more than a hint of *The Inn of the Sixth Happiness*, and every bit as good. Sirk was back to overwrought suffering amongst the rich with *Imitation of Life*,

another remake (like *Magnificent Obsession*) of a 1930s soaper. Unfortunately, ill-health at this stage induced him to give up his cinema career, although happily he lived a long life.

1935: *April, April*. *Das Mädchen vom Moorhof*. *Stutzen der Gesellschaft* (GB: *The Pillars of Society*). 1936: *Das Hofkonzert*. *Schlussakkord* (GB: *Final Accord*. US: *Ninth Symphony*). 1937: *La Habañera*. *Liebling der Matrosen*. *Zu neuen Ufern* (GB: *To New Shores*. US: *Life Begins Anew*). 1938: *Die Heimat ruft*. 1939: *Boef je* (US: *Wilton's Zoo*). 1942: *Hitler's Madman*. 1944: *Summer Storm*. 1946: *A Scandal in Paris*. 1947: *Lured* (GB: *Personal Column*). 1948: *Sleep My Love*. 1949: *Shockproof*. *Slightly French*. 1950: *Mystery Submarine*. *The First Legion*. 1951: *Thunder on the Hill* (GB: *Bonaventure*). *The Lady Pays Off*. *Weekend with Father*. 1952: *Has Anybody Seen My Gal*. *No Room for the Groom*. *Meet Me at the Fair*. 1953: *Take Me to Town*. *All I Desire*. 1954: *Taza, Son of Cochise*. *Magnificent Obsession*. *Sign of the Pagan*. *Captain Lightfoot*. 1955: *All That Heaven Allows*. 1956: *There's Always Tomorrow*. *Written on the Wind*. †*Never Say Goodbye* (uncredited). 1957: *Battle Hymn*. *The Tarnished Angels*. *Interlude*. 1958: *A Time to Love and a Time to Die*. 1959: *Imitation of Life*.

SJÖSTRÖM, Victor 1879-1960
It was fortunate that Sjöström, the greatest of Swedish directors in the silent era, should have decided to go to Hollywood in time to make nine films there before the advent of sound. Otherwise, he might have remained a fairly obscure footnote in professorial annals read only by the most devout movie enthusiasts. For Sjöström the director – he was also an actor and appeared in several of his own films – was a man made for the silent era, in his carving-out of stories in which characters and landscapes interweave in the deciding of destinies. When sound came, he hardly seemed interested and, apart from a couple of quite ordinary films in Britain and Sweden, returned full-time to acting. Again luckily, he found kindred souls in Hollywood with whom to work, in the persons of Lillian Gish and Lon Chaney; and there was also Lars Hanson, who had already worked for Sjöström — his name was anglicized to Seastrom on the credits of his English-speaking films. Sjöström's childhood was dominated by his tyrannically religious father, an aspect of his life that is brought out in several of his films, both Swedish and American. When his

father died, Sjöström decided to follow his late mother's profession – acting – and had become an established stage actor and director before entering the cinema in 1911. Sjöström directed, and appeared in, many Swedish films which you are never likely to see outside the premises of a film society, and then only if you are lucky. Opinions are sharply divided as to which of these has most worth, but he was evidently at his peak in his own land in the years 1917 to 1921, when he made stories that used Swedish landscapes as an integral character of the drama. Disappointed with his films in the early 1920s, and feeling he needed a fresh challenge, Sjöström accepted, early in 1923, an offer to go to Hollywood. At first daunted by the huge sets and vast studios, Sjöström quickly adapted himself to the new milieu and wrote his own ticket with *He Who Gets Slapped*. This was tailored to the talents of Lon Chaney as the scientist who, after losing everything he values in life, becomes a clown but gains revenge on those who had wrecked his life before he himself dies. The film also had a showy role for the young Norma Shearer, and Sjöström reunited them in *The Tower of Lies*, set in Sweden and adapted from a novel by favourite Swedish writer Selma Lagerlof. Sjöström had filmed her work before (the most famous adaptation of one of her stories, however, was *The Story of Gösta Berling*, directed by Sjöström's friend Mauritz Stiller; *qv*). These are films of extraordinary density and passion, but still not as good as Sjöström's two films with Lillian Gish. *The Scarlet Letter* and *The Wind*. The former is by the far the best version of Nathaniel Hawthorne's story of religious bigotry, and Miss Gish and Lars Hanson are perfect casting as the defiant Hester Prynne and the tormented Dimmesdale. *The Wind*, though, is the definitive achievement on the silent screen by a master of the medium. The story is set in the wilds of America where the wind covers everything with sand. It covers the body of the man Miss Gish has buried after accidentally killing him. And inevitably, it uncovers it again at the end, before her demented eyes. The star is magnetic, the film a masterpiece of wordless imagery. Small wonder Sjöström had so little relish for sound.

1912: Triädgardmästaren (US: The Gardener). Lady Marions Sommarflirt (US: Lady Marion's Summer Flirtation). En Sommarsaga (US: A Summer Tale). Et Hemligt Giftermål. Aktenskapsbyrån. 1913: Löjen och Tårar. Halvblod (US: The Half-Breed). Blodets Röst. †Livets Konflikter (US: Life's Conflicts). Ingeborg

Holm (GB: Give Us This Day). Prästen. 1914: Kärlek, Starkare än Hät (US: Love, Stronger Than Hate). Miraklet (US: The Miracle). Bra Flicka Reder Sig Själv (US: A Good Girl Should Solve Her Own Problems). Dömen Icke. Gatans Barn. Högfjällets Dotter (US: Daughter of the Mountain). Hjärten som Mötas (US: Hearts That Meet). Det Var i Maj (US: It Was in May). 1915: Strejken (US: Strike!). En av de Manga. Sonad Skuld. Skomakare Bliv Vid Din Läst (US: Cobbler Stick to Your Last). Judaspengar (US: Judas Money). Landshövingens Döttrar (US: The Governor's Daughters). Havsgamarna. 1916: I Prövningens Stund. Skepp som Mötas (US: Ships That Meet). Hon Segrade. Thérèse. Dodskyssen. 1917: Terje Vigen (GB & US: A Man There Was). Tosen fran Stormyrtorpet (GB: The Woman He Chose. US: The Girl from Stormy Croft). 1918: Berg-Ejvind och Hans Hustru (GB: Love the Only Law/The Outlaw and His Wife. US: You and I). 1919: Ingmarssönerna Parts I and II (US: The Sons of Ingmar). Hans nåds Testamente (GB: His Grace's Last Testament. US: His Grace's Will). 1920: Klostret i Sendomir (GB: Secret of the Monastery. US: The Monastery of Sendomir). Karin Ingmarsdotter (GB: God's War. US: Karin, Daughter of Ingmar). Mästerman (US: The Executioner). 1921: Körkarlen/The Phantom Carriage (GB: Thy Soul Shall Bear Witness. US: The Stroke of Midnight). 1922: Vem Dömer? (GB: Love's Crucible. US: Mortal Clay). Det Omringade Huset (US: This House Surrounded). 1923: Eld Ombord (GB: The Hell Ship. US: Fire on Board). Name the Man. 1924: He Who Gets Slapped 1925: Confessions of a Queen. The Tower of Lies. 1926: The Scarlet Letter. 1928: The Wind. The Divine Woman. The Masks of the Devil. 1930: A Lady to Love. 1931: Markurells i Wadköping (US: Father and Son). 1937: Under the Red Robe.

SKOLIMOWSKI, Jerzy 1938-

Polish director (also a pugnacious character star who resembles Hollywood's George Dzundza) whose films have gathered critical and festival plaudits, which has no doubt been considerable consolation for the fact that most of his work has failed to find a large audience. Stress and oppression are themes that run through his often starkly-lit stories – doubtless reflecting his own problems with the Polish authorities in the days before the old-style Communist regime was overthrown. After attempting to make his way as an author, publishing a collection of short stories and two volumes of poetry, the

young Skolimowski began contributing screenplays to films by such prominent Polish directors as Andrzej Wajda and Roman Polanski before making his own directorial debut with *Rysopis*, a film to which he also contributed screenplay, art direction and editing as well as acting in the film and producing it. Polish authorities soon took exception to his outspoken but considered portraits of the conflict between the old guard and the newer post-war generation and soon after his 1967 film *Hands Up!* was banned, Skolimowski was making films on a more international basis. The most successful of these, however, is still streaked with Polish sensibilities. *Moonlighting* is about a group of Polish workmen doing up a house in London, from whom the escalating events in Poland (as the Solidarity movement is suppressed) must be kept by their leader (Jeremy Irons) who is soon reduced to shoplifting to keep things going. It's an occupation at which, although he develops a naive cunning, he bears a charmed life. These escapades, both tense and amusing, prove the most entertaining part of this fascinating film, and convey an endearing desperation not sufficiently developed in the director's other work.

1963: Rysopis (US: Identification Marks: None). 1964: Walkover. 1965: Barrier. 1966: Le départ. 1967: Hands Up! 1968: Dialogue. 1969: The Adventures of Gérard. 1970: Deep End. 1972: Herzbube/King, Queen, Knave. 1978: The Shout. 1982: Moonlighting. 1984: Success is the Best Revenge. 1985: The Lightship. 1989: Torrents of Spring. 1991: 30 Door Key. 1992: Before and After Death. 1995: Individina.

SMIGHT, Jack 1926-

American director with a penchant for the bizarre and the macabre. He has also frequently dabbled in comic battles of the sexes with such conspicuous lack of success that one would have though he would have stuck to other genres. His detective story *Harper* was well-liked, and his excursions along the fringes of science-fiction have been interesting. He began working for television in the early 1950s, first as assistant director, graduating to director by 1957. After *Harper*, in 1966, Smight continued promising for a few years. *Kaleidoscope* was a quirky caper film with Warren Beatty, Susannah York and some very odd detective characters, while his taste for the faintly nauseating, dressed up extravagantly as entertainment, was first revealed in his best film, *No Way to Treat a Lady*, with obsessively Jewish policeman George Segal pursuing

Rod Steiger as a murderous master of disguise. A very black comedy, it was followed by more peculiarities in *The Illustrated Man* (Steiger again), a version of a Ray Bradbury science-fantasy yarn that only just fails to come off, and *The Traveling Executioner*, which one could describe as a folksy western with elements of rape, murder, electrocution, hanging, pimping and prostitution. At any rate, this story of an executioner with a wooden leg who carries his own electric chair around the old west does have rather a splendid climax, and one can almost envisage Smight, like some mad scientist, chuckling as he assembled its ingredients. The barely-released *Rabbit Run* seems to have put a temporary stop to his film career, but he continued an almost unhealthy attitude to decay and near-death in two TV movies, *The Screaming Woman* and *The Longest Night*, which are both, in different circumstances, about people being buried alive, and in *Frankenstein: the True Story*, an ambitious, but only partly successful attempt to transfer Mary Shelley's original story almost literally to the screen. At least, it does contain a spectacular death for James Mason, plus Michael Sarrazin's best screen performance as the pathetically decaying monster. After that Smight worked less effec-

tively: a big war film, one of the *Airport* series, unconvincing science-fiction and more tedious modern comedy.

1958: Eddie (TV). 1964: Strategy of Terror (TV. Later: cinemas). I'd Rather Be Rich. 1965: The Third Day. 1966: Harper (GB: The Moving Target). Kaleidoscope. 1967: The Secret War of Harry Frigg. No Way to Treat a Lady. 1968: The Illustrated Man. 1970: Rabbit Run. The Traveling Executioner. 1971: Madigan: the London Beat (TV). McCloud: A Little Plot in Tranquil Valley (TV). McCloud: Somebody's Out to Get Jenny (TV). 1972: Madigan: the Midtown Beat (TV). Banacek: Detour to Nowhere (TV). The Screaming Woman (TV). The Longest Night (TV). Banacek: Let's Hear It for a Living Legend (TV). 1973: Partners in Crime (TV). Double Indemnity (TV). Linda (TV). Columbo: Dead Weight (TV). Frankenstein: The True Story (TV. GB: cinemas). 1974: Airport 1975. 1976: Midway (GB: Battle of Midway). 1977: Damnation Alley. 1978: Roll of Thunder (TV). 1979: Fast Break. 1980: Loving Couples. 1982: Remembrance of Love (TV). 1984: For Whom the Bell Tolls (TV). 1986: Number One With a Bullet. 1987: +Braddock: Missing in Action III (uncredited). 1988: The Favorite/Intimate Power.

SMITH, Kevin 1970-
Precocious American film-maker who started with low-budget independent successes and is now moving towards the mainstream. A teenage entrepreneur, Smith became, in his early twenties, the owner of a comic-book store called Jay and Silent Bob's Secret Stash. He sold that to finance his first film, *Clerks*, an abrasive black-and-white youth comedy which, oddly enough, revolved round the lives of teens working in a store. Rudely funny and cuttingly observant, the film flew the flag for American independent cinema by making a vast profit on its $27,000 outlay. Smith bought back Jay and Silent Bob's Secret Stash, and has proceeded to play characters called Silent Bob in all his films. It seemed as though might be a one-hit wonder when he brought out *Mallrats*. The film was limp and unfunny, in spite of a star cast that included Shannen Doherty, Ben Affleck and Joey Lauren Adams. But Smith hit back with *Chasing Amy*, featuring Affleck, Adams and a comic-book background to the story of Affleck trying to get Adams into bed despite the fact that she's a lesbian. This was both a festival and cult success, and Smith now moved into overdrive, penning screenplays for *Superman Reborn* and *Fletch 3* and film-

Steven **Soderbergh** with some of the younger players in his critically-acclaimed period piece *King of the Hill*.

ing the drama *Dogma*, whose all-star cast included writing Oscar-winners Affleck and Matt Damon.

1994: *Clerks*. 1995: *Mallrats*. 1996: *Chasing Amy*. 1998: *Dogma*.

SODERBERGH, Steven 1963-
A talented American director who, after years of initial struggle, was nominated for an Oscar with his first film, *Sex, Lies and Videotape*. That was a cult success all over the world, but since then Soderbergh has struggled to repeat its impact. Although he has done some good work, none of his ensuing films has caught the public imagination in the same way. Failing in his first efforts to break into Hollywood, Soderbergh directed music videos to earn a living while making short films and working on screenplays. *Sex, Lies and Videotape*, which he wrote in eight days, might not be ideal cinematic material, but it exercises a curious, almost morbid fascination. And, despite its foul language and sombre approach to the eponymous items, it's a film which champions, in the end, all the traditional virtues of love and happiness. The next, *Kafka*, was an interesting paranoia thriller, somewhat reminiscent of Kafka's own *The Trial*, but it failed to find much of an audience. But *King of the Hill* was a little gem, a lovingly-made and slightly offbeat Depression Era rites of passage story in which a young boy must hold fast against overwhelming family tragedy. That met with unanimous critical approval, something Soderbergh's subsequent work has not achieved. But he is still young and well capable of coming back into the limelight.

1985: *Rapid Eye Movement*. 1987: *Winston*. 1989: *Sex, Lies and Videotape*. 1991: *Kafka*. 1993: *King of the Hill*. +*Fallen Angels* (TV). 1995: *The Underneath*. 1996: *Gray's Anatomy*. 1997: *Schizopolis*. 1998: *Out of Sight*. 1999: *The Limey*. 2000: *Leatherheads*.

SOFTLEY, Iain 1959-
British director whose background in music videos and documentaries not only led him into films, but obviously taught him a thing or two about pacing. Whatever their varying merits, Softley's three films to date have not been tedious. The first of them is *BackBeat*, an involving and well-acted study of the early life of superstar pop group The Beatles. Much less successful was Softley's first international venture, *Hackers*. An unconvincing computer-age thriller, it did have dazzling

effects and raised implications that were suitably frightening. Softley, however, moved into the big time with the award-laden *The Wings of the Dove*, a bold adaptation of a Henry James story long thought unfilmable. Softley's treatment expresses well the elegant, civilised decadence of Henry James' scheming aristocrats. And Softley must have been well pleased with the remarkable performance of Helena Bonham Carter, which brought her an Oscar nomination.

1994: *BackBeat*. 1996: *Hackers*. 1997: *The Wings of the Dove*.

SOLNTSEVA, Yulia
See DOVZENKO, Alexander

SONNENFELD, Barry 1953-
After a spectacular career as a director of photography, this New York-born filmmaker has made some very successful commercial ventures since turning director at the age of 38. Working for the Coen Brothers and other mainstream directors, Sonnenfeld's sometimes daring photography was a major factor in the success of such films as *Blood Simple*, *Compromising Positions*. *Raising Arizona*, *Throw Momma from the Train*, *Big*, *When Harry Met Sally...*, *Miller's Crossing* and *Misery*. He was second-unit director on the last one as well, a stepping stone to fully-fledged direction that he took with ease on the two 'Addams Family' films. *Get Shorty*, an acidic portrait of life in Hollywood's B stream, confirmed his status as one of Hollywood's leading 1990s' directors, and he launched his directing career into the stratosphere with two Will Smith vehicles, *Men in Black*, a

One of the most dynamic and versatile of today's woman directors is Penelope **Spheeris**, pictured here in the director's chair for *The Decline of Western Civilisation Part II: The Metal Years*.

A 23-year-old Steven **Spielberg** at work on one of his earliest assignments, the TV compilation *Night Gallery*. At the other end of her career was the star, melodrama queen Joan Crawford.

special effects extravaganza about agents hunting aliens – it became one of the ten most successful films of all time – and *The Wild, Wild West*. Sonnenfeld looks set to continue providing colourful, vivid semi-family entertainment into the next century.

1991: *The Addams Family*. 1993: *For Love or Money/The Concierge. Addams Family Values*. 1995: *Get Shorty*. 1997: *Men in Black*. 1999: *The Wild, Wild West*.

SPAAK, Charles
See FEYDER, Jacques

SPHEERIS, Penelope 1945-
One admires Spheeris greatly for overcoming a difficult and sometimes tragic early life to become a film director. Unhappily, it has to be said that, although her persistence is to be applauded, her work in the field has been fairly undistin-

guished, whether, like the earlier work, aimed at the youth market, or, latterly, big-budget family comedies, often based on successful formulas from the past. In between, she makes rather draining and unattractive documentaries on the more outlandish youth icons of our times, such as punk rockers and the heavy metal stars. There is, of course, one magic exception to all this in the supremely daffy *Wayne's World*, the jewel in Spheeris' rather battered crown. It is interesting, though, that she has consistently worked with musicians, comedians and non-professionals rather than star names. She was born in New Orleans, though it could have been anywhere, since her parents ran a travelling carnival and moved all round America. When she was seven, her father, who doubled as the carnival's strongman, was stabbed to death in a fight. Her nine-times married mother moved to California, where Spheeris would, ironically, eventually lose the father of her own daughter to a drug overdose. But she also went to university,

emerging with a master's degree in film, and began working and writing for the brilliant satirists of TV's *Saturday Night Live*. She also produced short films for the programme, gaining her entry to movies a few years later with the first of her confrontational rock documentaries. She made little of much worth, though, until *Wayne's World*, an endearingly silly tale of two all-American goofballs who broadcast a weekly TV show from the basement of a private home. The humour in this idiot's delight of a show proves very infectious, and the film became Spheeris' first major box-office success. It led to a hastily put-together sequel, which she didn't direct. But, although inferior, it would probably have been better than the seemingly promising pair she tackled next, *The Beverly Hillbillies* and *The Little Rascals*, although outtakes from the latter over the closing credits underlined the difficulties she had had in obtaining any sort of personable performances from her kindergarten cast. She mined much the same vein in *Black Sheep*, an inoffensive but not very funny vehicle for the soon-to-die heavyweight comedian Chris Farley, then returned to another of her counter-culture documentaries.

1980: *The Decline of Western Civilization*. 1983: *Suburbia/The Wild Side*. 1985: *The Boys Next Door*. 1986: *Hollywood Vice Squad*. 1987: *Dudes*. 1988: *The Decline of Western Civilization Part II: The Metal Years*. 1991: +*Prison Stories: Women on the Inside* (TV). 1992: *Wayne's World*. 1993: *The Beverly Hillbillies*. 1994: *The Little Rascals*. 1996: *Black Sheep*. 1998: *Senseless. The Decline of Western Civilization Part III*.

SPIELBERG, Steven 1946-
American director at his best with riproaring, superbly orchestrated adventure stories that career from crisis to crisis, sometimes with a trace of the macabre. Spielberg's sure sense of staging, editing and pacing placed him right at the top of the Hollywood tree in just a few years. But he showed he could bomb out with the best of them when he made the sprawling, undisciplined comedy *1941*. Very few directors, though, can boast a string of hits as gigantic as *Jaws, Close Encounters of the Third Kind, Raiders of the Lost Ark* and its sequels and the two *Jurassic Park* films. These captured the public imagination to such an extent that several of them have entered the lists of the ten most popular films of all time. Spielberg himself has been movie crazy since early childhood, making his first film at 14 (and winning prizes for it!). At

23, after another prize-winning film, the two-reeler *Amblin'*, he was taken on as a director by MCA, the television arm of Universal and, after only a couple of years, caught the eyes of the world with *Duel*, a simple but thunderingly effective film about a car pursued by a giant truck, whose driver the car-driver can never see, that was issued around the world as a feature film. A few years later came *Jaws*, which became the biggest money-maker of all time (although subsequently passed by *Star Wars*). Its scenes of man-versus-shark are for the most part horrifyingly effective, edge-of-seat stuff, greatly aided by insistent music by John Williams (who also scored *Star Wars*). *Close Encounters* was a dazzling adventure about extra-terrestrials, with formidable special effects, particularly in its last reel, and, after the thundering success of *Raiders of the Lost Ark*, a throw-back to old-fashioned Technicolor entertainment with hints of the serial (only made on a billion-dollar budget), filmgoers were offered two more adventures with its bullwhip-wielding hero Indiana Jones. Hints of seriousness and Oscar intent first appeared (and indeed made themselves rather too obvious) in *The Color Purple*. Nominated for 11 Academy Awards but winner of none, the film was more successfully followed by *Empire of the Sun*, a vivid account of an 11-year-old boy's flight from the Japanese in World War Two, and then by the phenomenal *Schindler's List*, a story of Nazi persecution that finally brought the best director Oscar home to Spielberg's mantelshelf. Spielberg continues to show delight in the cinema as a medium, and there are always brilliant individual moments in his films though none stronger than the graphic Normandy landings of *Saving Private Ryan*, which some saw as the greatest war film of all time. He married the actresses Amy Irving and (latterly) Kate Capshaw.

1960: *Escape to Nowhere*. 1963: *Firelight*. 1969: **Amblin'*. †*Night Gallery (TV)*. 1970: *Four in One (TV)*. 1971: *Columbo: Murder by the Book (TV)*. *Something Evil (TV)*. 1972: *Duel (TV. GB: cinemas)*. 1973: *Savage (TV)*. *The Sugarland Express*. 1975: *Jaws*. 1977: *Close Encounters of the Third Kind*. 1980: *1941. The Special Edition of Close Encounters of the Third Kind*. 1981: *Raiders of the Lost Ark*. 1982: *E.T. the Extra-Terrestrial* 1983: †*Twilight Zone – the Movie*. 1984: *Indiana Jones and the Temple of Doom*. 1985: *The Color Purple*. 1987: *Empire of the Sun*. 1989: *Indiana Jones and the Last Crusade*. 1991: *Hook*. 1993: *Jurassic Park*. *Schindler's List*. 1997: *The Lost World: Jurassic*

Park. *Amistad*. 1998: *Saving Private Ryan*. 1999: *Memoirs of a Geisha*.

SPOTTISWOODE, Roger 1943-

English-born editor and director who moved to Hollywood after working for Sam Peckinpah in the English-shot *Straw Dogs* in 1972. Since establishing himself as a director in America, Spottiswoode has made a number of capable entertainments. Despite one or two blemishes on his record, some of his films are exceptional of their kind, and he has shown an enviable facility for working with major stars, on very low-profile films and in cable TV originals. He got his first directing break in Canada on a horror film called *Terror Train*. It was above average of its Halloween-style kind, and Spottiswoode had soon followed it with one of his most distinguished films, *Under Fire*. This fine, raw film features Nick Nolte, Gene Hackman and Joanna Cassidy as roving war correspondents caught up in the Central American melting-pot that is the Nicaragua of 1979. Few of the horrors of the situation are spared us, and tension drips from every frame of such immaculately and intelligently reconstructed immediacy. Although Spottiswoode did eventually blot his copybook with the Sylvester Stallone comedy clinker *Stop! Or My Mom Will Shoot*, his hard-hitting cable TV movies, *Third Degree Burn* and *The Last Innocent Man*, are extremely well made and well worth catching, and *Turner & Hooch*, with Tom Hanks and an extraordinarily slobby dog, was a comedy that did work. In the late 1990s, Spottiswoode had another worldwide hit when he was entrusted with the direction on the second Pierce Brosnan James Bond film, *Tomorrow Never Dies*.

1980: *Terror Train*. 1981: *The Pursuit of D B Cooper/Pursuit*. 1983: *Under Fire*. 1986: *The Best of Times*. 1987: *The Last Innocent Man (cable TV)*. 1988: *Shoot to Kill (GB: Deadly Pursuit)*. 1989: *Turner & Hooch*. *Third Degree Burn (cable TV)*. 1990: *Air America*. 1991: *Time Flies When You're Alive*. 1992: *Stop! Or My Mom Will Shoot*. 1993: *And the Band Played On*. 1995: *The Spire*. 1997: *Tomorrow Never Dies*.

SPRINGSTEEN, R.G. 1904-1989

This American director seems to have been one of the most popular men around: but he made a lot of sluggish films. Springsteen's pictures were nearly all westerns, and it sure was a mighty slow ride through his pastures, pardners. But he also made two absolute gems, one

of them a frantic comedy, the other a sentimental drama. Known to his friends as Bud or Buddy, Springsteen had worked unambitiously as an assistant director since the advent of sound, and since 1935 with Republic, the studio for which he made all his films until 1957 (only Joseph Kane – *qv* – had a longer tenure with the outfit). As with Ray Nazarro *(qv)* and others, the studio gave Springsteen the chance to direct minor westerns in the years just before the end of World War II. These were 60-minute dust-rousers with Allan 'Rocky' Lane, Wild Bill Elliott and Monte Hale. Several of the Hale westerns were in Trucolor, or Magnacolor, as it was called at first, a cheap process developed by the studio and also used on Springsteen's biggest (and best) pre-1950 film, *Hellfire*, with Elliott and Marie Windsor. Republic put him on Judy Canova comedies in the 1950s, plus a few 'semi-A' action films, which he directed with his customary lethargy. But in 1954 there was *Geraldine*, an absolutely marvellous skit on pop music and sobbing songsters. Springsteen didn't miss the opportunity and the film is wildly funny entertainment, with Stan Freberg a standout as one of the aforementioned cry-baby merchants. Springsteen then made several thrillers in England with such fading Hollywood stars as Kent Taylor. On his return to America, the studio unexpectedly handed him *Come Next Spring*, a sentimental rural drama that no-one expected to amount to much, although its script had attracted Ann Sheridan, Steve Cochran, Sonny Tufts, Walter Brennan and Edgar Buchanan. If Springsteen had gathered a few critical laurels for *Geraldine* from those who managed to catch it, he found himself much more in the limelight when *Come Next Spring* came out in March 1956. Word of mouth soon spread about the 'nice little picture' and Republic chief Herbert J. Yates unexpectedly found himself with a nice little profit. The film, in fact, is so real, it makes the appealing storyline seem almost dull. Great care had obviously been taken by Springsteen with the down-to-earth melodrama, and even Trucolor seemed muted. This very pleasing picture came too late to further Springsteen's career, and the studio itself was dying. From 1958 until 1968, when he retired, Springsteen worked on TV westerns or films produced by A.C. Lyles: homes for ageing stars — and directors. He was credited in his first few films as Robert Springsteen. He died from heart failure.

1945: *Marshal of Laredo*. *Wagon Wheels Westward*. *Colorado Pioneers*. 1946: *California Gold Rush*. *Conquest of*

Cheyenne. Home on the Range. Santa Fé Uprising. Stagecoach to Denver. Sheriff of Redwood Valley. Sun Valley Cyclone. Man from Rainbow Valley. 1947: Vigilantes of Boomtown. Marshal of Cripple Creek. Along the Oregon Trail. Under Colorado Skies. Homesteaders of Paradise Valley. Oregon Trail Scouts. Rustlers of Devil's Canyon. The Main Street Kid. 1948: Heart of Virginia. Secret Service Investigator. Out of the Storm. Son of God's Country. Sundown in Santa Fé. Renegades of Sonora. 1949: Sheriff of Wichita. Death Valley Gunfighters. Flame of Youth. The Red Menace (GB: The Enemy Within). Hellfire. Navajo Trail Raiders. 1950: Singing Guns. Belle of Old Mexico. Harbor of Missing Men. The Arizona Cowboy. Hills of Oklahoma. Covered Wagon Raid. Frisco Tornado. 1951: Million Dollar Pursuit. Honeychile. Street Bandits. 1952: The Fabulous Senorita. Oklahoma Annie. Gobs and Gals (GB: Cruising Casanovas). Tropical Heat Wave. Toughest Man in Arizona. 1953: A Perilous Journey. 1954: Geraldine. Track the Man Down. 1955: Cross Channel. Secret Venture. Double Jeopardy. I Cover the Underworld. 1956: Come Next Spring. When Gangland Strikes. 1957: Affair in Reno. 1958: Cole Younger — Gunfighter. Revolt in the Big House. 1959: Battle Flame. King of the Wild Stallions. 1961: Operation Eichmann. 1963: Showdown. 1964: He Rides Tall. Black Spurs. Bullet for a Badman. 1965: Taggart. Apache Uprising. Johnny Reno. 1966: Waco. Red Tomahawk. 1967: Hostile Guns. 1968: Tiger by the Tail.

STAHL, John M. 1886-1950

Although in his earlier years, this American director made several 'social conscience' pictures –'torn from today's headlines' as the publicity boys frequently put it – he is best remembered as the man who made massive soap operas (four-handkerchief weepies of epic structure) in the 1930s. Most of them were remade by the studio (Universal) at decent intervals, but none of the versions that followed are as good, or as affecting, as the Stahl originals. These films (several of them starring Irene Dunne), Back Street, Only Yesterday, Imitation of Life, Magnificent Obsession and When Tomorrow Comes, contain luminously appealing performances by their leading ladies, and remarkably compel you to suspend disbelief in spite of their lavish foolishness. This is direction of high competence and confidence. Later Stahl diversified, although still retaining the epic feel and bringing a lump to one's throat, in such subjects as The Immortal Sergeant and The Keys of the Kingdom. Holy Matrimony was off his beat, but a delightful first teaming of Monty Woolley and Gracie Fields. He also made the extraordinarily black Leave Her to Heaven, with Gene Tierney vividly cast as the woman who will ruin anyone's life to achieve her own ends. Visually, the film is remarkable: it was Stahl's first in colour and he had just about the best possible ally in cinematographer Leon Shamroy. But he was 'removed' from Forever Amber, and the studio were probably right: Stahl would never have made the kind of film they wanted. His career suffered from that, but in any case he was already in his sixties, and destined to die three years later. For records of how emotional impulses can dominate and change lives, his films have few equals. Some sources indicate that Stahl, who entered the industry in 1913 as an actor, may have made short films prior to the list given below.

1917: *The Lincoln Cycle (series of seven). 1918: Wives of Men. Suspicion. 1919: Her Code of Honor. A Woman Under Oath. Greater Than Love. 1920: Women Men Forget. The Woman in His House. 1921: The Child Thou Gavest Me. Suspicious Wives. Sowing the Wind. 1922: The Song of Life. One Clear Call. 1923: The Wanters. The Dangerous Age. 1924: Husbands and Lovers. Why Men Leave Home. 1925: Fine Clothes. 1926: The Gay Deceiver. Memory Lane. 1927: Lovers? In Old Kentucky. 1930: A Lady Surrenders (GB: Blind Wives). 1931: Seed. Strictly Dishonorable. 1932: Back Street. 1933: Only Yesterday. 1934: Imitation of Life. 1935: Magnificent Obsession. 1937: Parnell. 1938: Letter of Introduction. 1939: When Tomorrow Comes. 1941: Our Wife. 1943: The Immortal Sergeant. Holy Matrimony. 1944: The Keys of the Kingdom. The Eve of St Mark. 1945: Leave Her to Heaven. 1947: The Foxes of Harrow. 1948: The Walls of Jericho. 1949: Father was a Fullback. Oh, You Beautiful Doll.

ST CLAIR, Malcolm 1897-1952

California-born St Clair, wildly successful in the Hollywood of the 1920s, was easily young enough to survive the coming of sound – but he didn't seem to want to. Either that, or he convinced himself that it was ruining his career. When he made up his mind to have a stab at it, it was too late. He spent much of his last 12 years in films in second-features, and by the look of them, most of his light touch had gone. At the beginning, it was all so different. He joined Mack Sennett as a gag writer and knockabout player at 18 and, when 22, was already directing two-reel comedies. Finding Sennett unwilling to soften his slapstick to allow touches of subtlety and sophistication, St Clair left him in 1921 and made several comedy shorts under his own steam, two of them co-directed with Buster Keaton. From 1923, St Clair made features, including two Rin-Tin-Tin adventures at Warners, but in 1925 he joined Paramount, clearly the studio most suited to his talents. Almost at once, he achieved a reputation for sleek handling of sophisticated romantic comedies and social satire, with the upper-class romances of Are Parents People? (with Adolphe Menjou and Betty Bronson, the film that established him), A Woman of the World and Good and Naughty, both the latter featuring Pola Negri, who in A Woman of the World played a tattooed countess! Menjou came back to St Clair for another slice of satirical sophistication, in the naughty-but-nice The Grand Duchess and the Waiter in 1926. In a nation-wide poll that year, St Clair was voted the third finest Hollywood director (and top American), after Ernst Lubitsch. Only Lubitsch at this stage could equal his skill at presenting intelligent, lavish comedy in visual terms. Anita Loos' Gentlemen Prefer Blondes was a natural for St Clair, and he duly made it – but it was his last big success. Sound was advancing fast and, after an unsuccessful move from Paramount to M-G-M – he would have been far better advised to stay put – St Clair left films altogether for a long holiday. He never regained his former footing, and did not return to Hollywood at all on a regular basis until 1936. The latter stages of this career are crowded with low-budget comedies, many of them featuring 'The Jones Family' and totally lacking the finesse of his best work. His films with Laurel and Hardy at Fox in the 1940s began quite promisingly with Jitterbugs, but soon petered out under relentless studio corner-cutting and suppression of independence and individuality. At the time of his early death at 55, he had not made a film of any kind for four years. Sometimes billed as Mal St Clair.

1919: *†The Little Widow. *†Rip & Stitch, Tailors. *†No Mother to Guide Him. 1920: *Don't Weaken. *Young Man's Fancy. *He Loved Her Like He Lied. *†Hungry Lions and Tender Hearts. 1921: *Bright Eyes. *Call a Cop. *†The Goat. *Sweetheart Days. *Wedding Bells Out of Tune. 1922: *†The Blacksmith. *Keep 'Em Home. *Christmas. *Rice and Old Shoes. *Their First Vacation. *Twin Husbands. *Entertaining the Boss. 1923: *Fighting Blood (series). George Washington. 1924: The Telephone Girl (serial).

Find Your Man. The Lighthouse by the Sea. 1925: After Business Hours. On Thin Ice. The Trouble with Wives. Are Parents People? A Woman of the World. 1926: A Social Celebrity. The Show-Off. The Grand Duchess and the Waiter. Good and Naughty. The Popular Sin. 1927: Breakfast at Sunrise. Knockout Reilly. 1928: Gentlemen Prefer Blondes. Beau Broadway. The Fleet's In/Sporting Goods. 1929: The Canary Murder Case. Side Street. Night Parade (GB: Sporting Life). 1930: The Boudoir Diplomat. Montana Moon. Dangerous Nan McGrew. †Remote Control. 1933: Goldie Gets Along. Olsen's Big Moment. 1936: Crack-Up. 1937: Time Out for Romance. She Had to Eat. Born Reckless. Dangerously Yours. 1938: Down on the Farm. A Trip to Paris. Safety in Numbers. Everybody's Baby. 1939: The Jones Family in Hollywood. The Jones Family in Quick Millions. †Hollywood Cavalcade. 1940: Young as You Feel. Meet the Missus. 1941: The Beautiful Bachelor. 1942: The Man in the Trunk. Over My Dead Body. 1943: Jitterbugs. Two Weeks to Live. The Dancing Masters. 1944: The Big Noise. Swing Out the Blues. 1945: The Bullfighters. 1948: Arthur Takes Over. Fighting Back.

STEVENS, George 1904-1975

Although this American director's reputation has plunged in recent decades, a look at the films he made in the 1930s and 1940s reveals him as one of the most versatile, talented and successful of Hollywood's younger directors of the time. He showcased many of the film capital's most prominent actresses to great effect, whether in comedy or drama — among them were Katharine Hepburn, Ginger Rogers, Irene Dunne, Joan Fontaine, Jean Arthur and Elizabeth Taylor, all of whom worked for him more than once. He also made several outstandingly entertaining films in various genres during this period, although he was only once nominated for an Oscar. After 1950, he suffered from a case of the David Leans, taking months to prepare a film, and months more to shoot it. Some of the results were very effective in a rather more grandiose and ponderous way than before, and Stevens was rewarded with two Academy Awards, for A Place in the Sun and Giant. Needless to say, they are not the best of his movies, but that's Hollywood. The child of acting parents, he was himself on stage at five, but his interest in photography led him to try his luck in films as an assistant cameraman. By the late 1920s, he had progressed to cinematographer, shooting many of Laurel and Hardy's classic silent comedies for Hal Roach, including Two

Tars. After making a start as a director on two-reelers from 1930, he made his way to RKO, where he directed more shorts and a couple of minor feature comedies, before making his first big impact with Alice Adams, a biting small town drama with good atmosphere and one of the most charismatic of Katharine Hepburn's earlier performances. Barbara Stanwyck also shone under his direction in Annie Oakley, after which the studio decided that Stevens was the man to alternate with Mark Sandrich (qv) on the Astaire-Rogers musicals. The first, Swing Time, is one of their best, but the partnership was getting on the nerves of both and Stevens found himself directing them separately in A Damsel in Distress (Astaire) and Vivacious Lady (Rogers). Neither was a great success, but Stevens recovered ground spectacularly by making his best film, Gunga Din, pulsating entertainment in which broad humour, action and pathos are blended into a most amusing and exciting mixture with a classic tear-jerker climax. Stevens' previous sentimental films had not been as successful as his lighter, more lively entertainments but, after three well-spiced comedies, including the classic first meeting of Hepburn and Spencer Tracy in Woman of the Year, Stevens scored a bullseye on the tear-ducts with I Remember Mama. By now he was back from war service with the film unit of the Signal Corps. Perhaps his wartime experiences affected his attitudes, for he was never able to recapture the lively, relaxed style of his earlier years, although the films, when they came, now at infrequent intervals, were still well-received. Shane is an overrated western, long and slow; Giant half a good film, with one of Elizabeth Taylor's best performances, but an awkward and pointless last 90 minutes; and The Greatest Story Ever Told, a moving and underrated, if over-inflated life of Christ, with the best-ever portrayal of Jesus by Max Von Sydow. Stevens' son, George Jr, was for many years Director of the American Film Institute.

1930: *Blood and Thunder. *Ladies Last. 1931: *Air Tight. *Call a Cop! *High Gear. *The Kick-Off. *Mama Loves Papa. 1932: *Boys Will Be Boys. *Who Me? *Family Troubles. 1933: The Cohens and Kellys in Trouble. *What Fur? *Grin and Bear It. *A Divorce Courtship. *Flirting in the Park. *Quiet Please. *Rock-a-Bye Cowboy. *Room Mates. *Should Crooners Marry? *Walking Back Home. 1934: *Bridal Bail. *Cracked Shots. *Ocean Swells. *Rough Necking. *Strictly Fresh Yeggs. *The Undie-World. Bachelor Bait. Kentucky Kernels (GB: Triple Trouble). 1935: Alice

Adams. Annie Oakley. 1936: Swing Time. 1937: Quality Street. A Damsel in Distress. 1938: Vivacious Lady. 1939: Gunga Din. 1940: Vigil in the Night. 1941: Penny Serenade. Woman of the Year. 1942: The Talk of the Town. 1943: The More the Merrier. 1948: I Remember Mama. 1951: A Place in the Sun. 1952: Something to Live For. 1953: Shane. 1956: Giant. 1959: The Diary of Anne Frank. 1965: The Greatest Story Ever Told. 1969: The Only Game in Town.

STEVENSON, Robert 1905-1986

Spindly, genial British director who made some popular entertainments in Britain in the 1930s. He went to Hollywood and worked uncertainly for a while, mixing weepies, melodramas and thrillers, before finding a home at Disney and making almost all of the studio's best-loved live-action films during a 20-year period, including Old Yeller, The Absent-Minded Professor, Mary Poppins, Blackbeard's Ghost, The Love Bug, Bedknobs and Broomsticks and One of Our Dinosaurs is Missing. Stevenson's films all move very fluently, some of them at a great pace, and his work seemed much more professional than that of most of his contemporaries working in the pre-war British cinema. Stevenson began his career as a journalist, but entered the British film industry as a screenwriter in 1930 (first film, Greek Street). He continued his writing career until 1937, notably on such Jack Hulbert vehicles as Sunshine Susie (in America, The Office Girl) and Love on Wheels. His first film as director was Hulbert's Happy Ever After, and he directed the jut-jawed entertainer twice more, in Falling for You and Jack of All Trades. After such popular successes as Tudor Rose, Owd Bob, King Solomon's Mines, Non-Stop New York and The Ware Case, Stevenson and his then-wife Anna Lee went to Hollywood, where he was put under contract to David O. Selznick without being given a chance to direct. Eventually, however, he did get to make a few interesting pictures, including a presentable remake of Back Street and a popular version of Tom Brown's Schooldays, and worked hand-in-glove with Orson Welles on a loweringly memorable Jane Eyre, still the best available film of Charlotte Bronte's book. The chiaroscuro photography is typical of Stevenson's 1940s' films (he had already worked with RKO photographic ace Nicholas Musuraca on Tom Brown's Schooldays) and he settled at RKO in 1948, immediately making To the Ends of the Earth, a trickily constructed, darkly shot and totally watchable story of the hunt for a dope-

The Disney Studios' most reliable purveyor of family entertainment over a 20-year period was British-born Robert **Stevenson**.

er and a Day. Jane Eyre. 1946: *The American Creed (D). 1947: Dishonored Lady. 1948: To the Ends of the Earth. 1949: I Married a Communist (GB: The Woman on Pier 13). 1950: Walk Softly Stranger. 1951: My Forbidden Past. 1952: The Las Vegas Story. 1957: Johnny Tremain. Old Yeller. 1958: Darby O'Gill and the Little People. 1960: Kidnapped. 1961: The Absent Minded Professor. 1962: In Search of the Castaways. 1963: Son of Flubber. The Misadventures of Merlin Jones. 1964: Mary Poppins. The Monkey's Uncle. 1965: That Darn Cat! 1966: The Gnome-Mobile. 1967: Blackbeard's Ghost. 1968: The Love Bug. 1969: My Dog the Thief. †The Mickey Mouse Anniversary Show. 1971: Bedknobs and Broomsticks. 1973: Herbie Rides Again. The Island at the Top of the World. 1975: One of Our Dinosaurs is Missing. 1976: The Shaggy D.A.

STILLER, Mauritz (Moshe Stiller) 1883-1928
Finnish-born director, a distinguished figure of the early Swedish cinema who had rather less luck in Hollywood than his great friend Victor Sjöström (qv). He is credited with discovering Greta Garbo; and his best films, one of which starred her and took them both on a fateful trip to Hollywood, are made in a wide variety of styles and genres. Erotikon, for example, hovers close to the early DeMille, while Sir Arne's Treasure has echoes of Eisenstein and Lang. Then again, Gunnar Hedes Saga and Gösta Berlings Saga, the Garbo film, are both basically weepies. The former could have been a vehicle for D.W. Griffith, with Richard Barthelmess, while the latter might have attracted the attention of John M. Stahl. These, and the earlier comedies, demonstrate a versatility, within the Swedish context, that makes it all the more surprising to discover how poorly Stiller fitted in Hollywood. It is also true that he was a snappy dresser who liked high living — an ideal make-up, one would have thought, for the film colony of the mid-1920s. But then there was Garbo. And thereby hangs a tale . . . Stiller, trained as a violinist (thus there are some autobiographical elements in Gunnar Hedes Saga, where the hero plays the violin), fled his native country when conscripted into the Czar's army and ended up in the infant Swedish film industry, making his first films in 1912. By 1919, he and Sjöström had established themselves as the leading figures in the Swedish cinema. It was in that year that Stiller made his most striking and haunting Swedish film, Sir Arne's Treasure, one of several he and Sjöström carved out from the works

smuggling ring, so cleverly made that you could miss the key to the plot in a blink. Stevenson's previous work did not exactly seem to qualify him for life with the Walt Disney studio, but he settled happily there from 1956. Some of his comedies, notably Blackbeard, Professor, The Love Bug and Dinosaurs are riotous triumphs of frenzied but even pacing, impeccable taste and a sense of what would make an audience laugh. He received his only Academy Award nomination for Mary Poppins, a film that did win five Oscars and made the studio over 30 million dollars. Stevenson's deftness of touch, and the charming portrayals he obtains from the children,

were typical of the man. The studio were understandably reluctant to let him go, but he finally managed to slip off to a well-earned retirement at 72.

1932: Happy Ever After. 1933: Falling for You. 1935: Jack of All Trades (US: The Two of Us). 1936: The Man Who Changed His Mind (US: The Man Who Lived Again). Tudor Rose (US: Nine Days a Queen). 1937: King Solomon's Mines. Non-Stop New York. Owd Bob (US: To the Victor). 1939: The Ware Case. Young Man's Fancy. Return to Yesterday. 1940: Tom Brown's Schooldays. 1941: Back Street. 1942: Joan of Paris. 1943: †Forev-

of Selma Lagerlof, something of a Swedish Edna Ferber in her day. This was a picturesque (and picaresque) 16th-century fantasy, with superbly atmospheric visuals and a vividly memorable icebound climax as the hero/villain and his two companions struggle to reach their ship and escape with the treasure, shielded by the heroine (dead, though their pursuers do not realize it). Garbo entered Stiller's life five years later. He made her lose weight for a plum role in the rather turgid *Gösta Berlings Saga*, and the performance brought her to the attention of Louis B. Mayer, head of M-G-M, who brought her to Hollywood, with Stiller in tow. Mayer and Stiller did not get on: the Scandinavian director was not given Garbo's first film and only offered her the second upon her insistence. After completing part of the film, he was removed by studio top brass who did not like the way the picture was being made. The same thing would happen to him twice at Paramount, whither he fled from Mayer. Now hampered also by a severe respiratory ailment, Stiller was advised to recuperate in Switzerland, but returned instead to Sweden, where he died from pleurisy a few months later. It is probably true that M-G-M wished to put their own stamp on Garbo, and that Stiller was in their way. Whatever the circumstances, the experiences left him a shattered man and cost the world a talented director.

1912: *Mor och Dotter/Mother and Daughter. De Svarta Maskerna/The Black Mask. Den Tyranniske Fästmannen.* 1913: *Vampyren/The Vampire. När Kärleken Dödar/When Love Kills. När Larmklockan Ljuder/When the Alarm-Bell Sounds. Barnet/The Child. Den Okända. Kammarjunkaren. Smugglarne/The Smugglers. Den Moderna Suffragetten/In Mrs Pankhurst's Footsteps. †Livets Konflikter (uncredited). Mannekängen (unfinished).* 1914: *Bröderna/Brothers. Far Sin Kärleks Skull. Stormfägeln/Storm-Birds. Skottet/The Shot. Det Röte Tornet/The Red Tower. När Konstnärer Alska. När Svärmor Regerar.* 1915: *Lekkamraterna. Hämnaren. Hans Hustru Förflutna. Hans Bröllopsnatt. Mastertjuven. Madame de Thèbes (GB: Son of Destiny). Minlotsen. Dolken.* 1916: *Lyckonälen. Kärlek och Journalistik (GB: Love and Journalism). Kampen om Hans Hjärta/The Battle for His Heart. Vingarne/Wings. Balettprimadonnan (GB: Anjala, the Dancer). Thomas Graals Bästa Film (GB: Wanted a Film Actress. US: Thomas Graal's Best Film). Alexander den Store (GB & US: Alexander the Great).* 1918: *Thomas Graals Bästa Barn (GB: Thomas Graal's Best Child. US: Thomas Graal's First Child).* 1919: *Sången om den Eldröda Blomman (GB: The Flame of Life. US: Song of the Scarlet Flower). Herr Arnes Pengar/Sir Arne's Treasure (GB: Snows of Destiny. US: Three Who Were Doomed).* 1920: *Fiskebyn (GB: Chains. US: The Fishing Village). Erotikon (GB: Bonds That Chafe).* 1921: *Johan. De Landsflyktige (GB: The Exiles. US: In Self Defense).* 1923: *Gunnar Hedes Saga (GB: The Judgment. US: The Blizzard).* 1924. *Gösta Berlings Saga (GB: The Atonement of Gosta Berling. US: The Legend of Gosta Berling).* 1926: *†The Temptress.* 1927: *Hotel Imperial. The Woman on Trial. †Barbed Wire.* 1928: *†The Street of Sin.*

STONE, Andrew L. 1902-

Filmgoers who know the name of this American film-maker from his series of on-location thrillers and disaster movies (before that genre became all the rage) in the 1950s may be surprised to find that he has been directing feature films since 1928, and probably also that he made fewer than 30 films in 45 years. The stories from this peak period are films that really make the adrenalin flow: cliffhangers and suspense dramas with an edge-of-seat thrill around every corner, many of them accentuated by the incisive editing of Virginia Stone, the director's wife. From 1952 to 1960 the Stones enjoyed their greatest success in this genre. On either side of it, Andrew tended to make light musicals with an emphasis on serious music, and over-inflated musical biopics. He had joined Universal at 16 as a property boy, but by 1927 was directing two-reel shorts, a couple of them early experiments with music. He stayed at Paramount until 1942, when he broke away to form Andrew L. Stone Productions. It was for his own company, through Twentieth Century-Fox, that he made his best musical, *Stormy Weather,* with some very imaginative sequences and an all-black cast headed by Lena Horne and Bill 'Bojangles' Robinson. Stone's entertainments continued in lighter vein through the 1940s, but the tough and brutal *Highway 301* changed the formula. At this point, he was making mostly co-feature thrillers, but *The Night Holds Terror,* a tense drama about a family held to ransom by three gunmen, in which the suspense was finely drawn, and the acting (principally from John Cassavetes and Vince Edwards) the best to date in a Stone film, attracted enough attention to enable him to expand his operations and increase his budgets. Stone virtually repeated the formula in *Cry Terror!,* cops and robbers with a high gloss, with terror as its keynote and one of Angie Dickinson's best performances as a bitchy criminal; then he attempted the disaster movie proper with the tremendously successful *The Last Voyage* in which, in typical Stone style, he actually bought an old liner and sank it before the camera's very eye. Later, the Stones separated and Andrew went back to his musicals, with poorly received biographies of Grieg and Strauss. But Universal remembered him in 1977 and called him back, at the age of 75, to help out with the disaster sequences and act as assistant director on other action scenes, in their *Rollercoaster.*

1927: **The Elegy. *Fantasy (GB: Applejoy's Ghost).* 1928: *Dreary House. Liebenstraum. *Frenzy. *Adoration.* 1929: *Sombras de Gloria.* 1932: *Hell's Headquarters.* 1936: *The Girl Said No.* 1937: *Stolen Heaven.* 1938: *Say It in French.* 1939: *The Great Victor Herbert.* 1941: *There's Magic in Music.* 1943: *Stormy Weather. Hi Diddle Diddle.* 1944: *Sensations of 1945. Bedside Manner.* 1946: *The Bachelor's Daughters (GB: Bachelor Girls).* 1947: *Fun on a Week-End.* 1950: *Highway 301.* 1952: *The Steel Trap. Confidence Girl.* 1953: *A Blueprint for Murder.* 1955: *The Night Holds Terror.* 1956: *Julie.* 1958: *Cry Terror! The Decks Ran Red.* 1960: *The Last Voyage.* 1961: *Ring of Fire.* 1962: *The Password is Courage.* 1964: *Never Put It in Writing.* 1965: *The Secret of My Success.* 1970: *Song of Norway.* 1972: *The Great Waltz.*

STONE, Oliver 1946-

Tall, dark and handsome enough to be an actor (at which he has also briefly dabbled), Stone has used his power in the American film industry to expose corruption and injustice, as well as to look at flawed figureheads in several different walks of life. He has also looked at the appalling side effects, both physical and mental, of war. A Vietnam veteran of some distinction, he subsequently made a trilogy of films centring on the conflict there, two of them, *Platoon* and *Born on the Fourth of July,* attracting considerable critical attention and winning him two of his three Academy Awards. His strong and confrontational films, at their peak of popularity in the late 1980s and early 1990s, are customarily based on his own screenplays. Dropping out of university, Stone had moved to Vietnam at 19, to become a teacher. With the onset of war, he joined the US marines there, then served with the infantry from 1967, winning a cluster of medals. Returning to America, and following film studies at New York University, he began to work

Director Oliver **Stone** looks happier with life than were many of his cast undergoing the gruelling war film *Platoon*.

(140), demonstrated. Later, *Nixon* would run even longer, although not to any great effect. The best of these later films is *JFK*, which, although flawed dramatically, is a fascinating and persuasive document. Blackness and gore dominate Stone's latter day 'crime' films, *Natural Born Killers* and *U Turn*. Although the former gained by far the greater notoriety, the latter is easily the more interesting, a nattily made, quirky *noir* thriller which piled its mountain of coincidences and double-crosses so high that it finally topples over — though its full-blooded performances keep it enjoyable.

1970: +*Street Scenes 1970*. 1974: *Seizure*. 1981: *The Hand*. 1985: *Salvador*. 1986: *Platoon*. 1987: *Wall Street*. 1988: *Talk Radio*. 1989: *Born on the Fourth of July*. 1990: *The Doors*. 1991: *JFK*. 1993: *Heaven & Earth*. 1994: *Natural Born Killers*. 1995: *Nixon*. 1997: *U Turn/Stray Dogs*. 1999: *On Any Given Sunday*.

STRAYER, Frank R. 1891-1964

A proficient and prolific American director of 'B' movies in the 1930s and 1940s. Originally trained for a military career, he left the US Navy after World War One and joined the Metro studio as an assistant director, serving in that capacity for six years before getting a chance to direct his own films. Although he made some good horror films (notably *The Vampire Bat*) and thrillers, he's best remembered today as the man who directed the first 14 'Blondie' comedies, a run that includes all the best films in the series. After directing so many dark little numbers, it was surprising Strayer should have been handed this assignment, but his razor-sharp editing techniques, honed on dozens of 60-minute dramas, proved invaluable to the pace and impact of this most successful series. After World War Two, he directed mainly for television, with the exception of a couple of religion-slanted features.

1925: *The Lure of the Wild*. *The Fate of a Flirt*. *An Enemy of Men*. 1926: *When the Wife's Away*. *Sweet Rosie O'Grady*. 1927: *Pleasure Before Business*. *Now We're in the Air*. *The Bachelor's Baby*. *Rough House Rosie*. 1928: *Partners in Crime*. *Just Married*. *Moran of the Marines*. 1929: *The Fall of Eve*. *Acquitted*. 1930: *Borrowed Wives*. *Let's Go Places*. 1931: *Caught Cheating*. *Murder at Midnight*. *Anybody's Blonde* (GB: *When Blonde Meets Blonde*). *Dragnet Patrol* (GB: *Love Redeemed*). *Soul of the Slums* (GB: *The Samaritan*). 1932: *The Crusader*. *Behind Stone Walls*. *Love in High Gear*. *Gorilla*

in the film industry as a photographer and assistant director from 1970. In his first few years as a director, he made horror films, but set out more serious intent with his screenplay for Alan Parker's *Midnight Express*, for which he won his first Oscar. In the early 1980s, Stone wrote some high-profile screenplays for other directors' films. Strangely, though, this work – which includes *Scarface*, *Conan the Barbarian* and *Year of the Dragon* – is among his least distinguished. Once he returned to the horrors of war, however, Stone was obviously a different force. *Salvador*, a grim exposé of the atrocities of the El Salvador civil war of the early 1960s, was unpleasant, depressing, angry and won an Oscar nomination for its leading actor, James Woods. It proved but a curtain-raiser for the film that made Stone's name as a director, *Platoon*. Within a familiar framework of good and evil, Stone brought a new brutality and realism to portraits of the Vietnam conflict — in a graphically violent account of the war as witnessed at first hand by its ordinary foot soldiers. If its characters were less than easy to relate to, Stone remedied that in *Wall Street*, based on the US ideology of 'Greed is good; greed works' – one of many quotable lines in a story of the sharks and dolphins of the New York financial world – another battlefield in which, it seems, only the strong survive, headed by corporate raider Gordon Gekko, a role that won Michael Douglas an Oscar. There was another best actor nomination (for Tom Cruise) in Stone's next Vietnam film, *Born on the Fourth of July*, although at 145 minutes the film is a bit of a grind whose one-note descent into a private hell puts an immense strain on our innate sympathy. The running timne, though, was par for the Stone course, as the following three, *The Doors* (141 mins), *JFK* (191) and *Heaven & Earth*

Ship. Tangled Destinies. Dynamite Denny (GB: Denny of the Railroad). Manhattan Tower. The Monster Walks (GB: The Monster Walked). 1933: The Vampire Bat. By Appointment Only. Dance, Girl, Dance. 1934: Fugitive Road. In The Money. In Love with Life. Twin Husbands. Fifteen Wives. Cross Streets. One in a Million. 1935: Death from a Distance. The Ghost Walks. Symphony of Living. Society Fever. Public Opinion. Port of Lost Dreams. Hitch Hike to Heaven (GB: Footlights and Shadows). 1936: Murder at Glen Athol. Sea Spoilers. 1937: Big Business. Hot Water. Off to the Races. Laughing at Trouble. 1938: Blondie. Borrowing Trouble. 1939: Blondie Meets the Boss. Blondie Brings Up Baby. Blondie Takes a Vacation. 1940: Blondie on a Budget. Blondie Has Servant Trouble. Blondie Plays Cupid. 1941: Blondie Goes Latin (GB: Conga Swing). Blondie in Society (GB: Henpecked). Go West, Young Lady. 1942: Blondie for Victory (GB: Troubles Through Billets). Blondie Goes to College (GB: The Boss Said 'No'). Blondie's Blessed Event (GB: A Bundle of Trouble). 1943: Footlight Glamour. It's a Great Life. The Daring Young Man. 1945: Senorita from the West. Mama Loves Papa. 1946: I Ring Doorbells. 1950: Messenger of Peace. 1951: The Sickle and the Cross.

STURGES, John 1911-1992

When it came to action films, especially in the 1950s and 1960s, this American director's were as vivid and exciting as any. He was particularly good at sustaining whole sequences at a high pitch for minutes on end, a legacy of the skills acquired as an editor. Best of all were his westerns: a brilliant sense of colour control backed an immense flair for blazing action. Thus some of the most thrilling scenes in all Hollywood's westerns come from Sturges movies. While he had not quite the visual sense or genuine feel for the genre that Ford or Peckinpah showed, Sturges' adventure films were just as likely to send you out of the cinema tingling. Outside of this field, he usually floundered, and one suspects that in the end he reluctantly acknowledged the fact and stuck to his thrills and spills. In the early 1930s, Sturges worked in RKO's cutting rooms, and had advanced to film editor by the time World War II broke out. He improved his techniques making many training films for the Army Air Corps, and co-directed a documentary, Thunderbolt, with William Wyler. Columbia got to hear of his work and, after the war, took him on as a director of second-features. The best of these is, predictably, a

western, The Walking Hills, with a tight script and a splendid cast headed by Randolph Scott, Arthur Kennedy, Ella Raines and John Ireland. Sturges came to recognize the strengths of such a cast in action films, and many of his movies carry half-a-dozen star names. At M-G-M from 1950, he made two useful thrillers, Mystery Street and Right Cross and a very good weepie, The Girl in White. Sturges recovered from a further bout of second-features to bounce conclusively into the big-time with Bad Day at Black Rock, a talky but tense modern western that proved a blockbuster at the box-office. From the mid-1950s, he began to freelance, with sporadic returns to M-G-M. The Law and Jake Wade contains some of the most pulsating combat scenes between white man and Indian ever shot, the last reel of Last Train to Gun Hill may have you falling out of the armchair still biting your nails, and The Magnificent Seven has drummingly exciting action sequences, much helped by Elmer Bernstein's music. The Hallelujah Trail showed that Sturges also had a facility for knockabout western comedy, but its formula was not repeated, while the all-star, all-incident film brought him his greatest popular success, the prisoner-of-war film The Great Escape, lifted at the box offices of the world by Steve McQueen's motor-cycle-riding escapee. In view of the enjoyment Sturges has given to action fans all over the world, it would perhaps be charitable to draw a veil over

The Old Man and the Sea, Never So Few, By Love Possessed, A Girl Named Tamiko and others with which he must have felt ill-at-ease: the old story of the clown wanting to play Hamlet and boring everyone in the process.

1946: The Man Who Dared. Shadowed. Alias Mr Twilight. 1947: For the Love of Rusty. †Thunderbolt (D. Completed 1945). Keeper of the Bees. 1948. Best Man Wins. The Sign of the Ram. 1949: The Walking Hills. 1950: The Capture. Mystery Street. Right Cross. 1951: The Magnficent Yankee (GB: The Man with 30 Sons). Kind Lady. The People Against O'Hara. It's a Big Country. 1952: The Girl in White (GB: So Bright the Flame). 1953: Jeopardy. Fast Company. Escape from Fort Bravo. 1954: Bad Day at Black Rock. 1955: Underwater. The Scarlet Coat. 1956: Backlash. Gunfight at the OK Corral. 1958: The Law and Jake Wade. The Old Man and the Sea. 1959: Last Train from Gun Hill. Never So Few. 1960: The Magnificent Seven. 1961: By Love Possessed. 1962: Sergeants 3. A Girl Named Tamiko. 1963: The Great Escape. 1964: The Satan Bug. 1965: The Hallelujah Trail. 1967: Hour of the Gun. 1968: Ice Station Zebra. 1969: Marooned. 1972: Joe Kidd. 1973: Valdez the Half-breed (GB: The Valdez Horses. US: Chino). 1974: McQ. 1976: The Eagle Has Landed.

Director John **Sturges** (right) prepares Robert Ryan and Spencer Tracy for a desert confrontation in Bad Day at Black Rock.

STURGES, Preston (Edmond P. Biden) 1898-1959
American director who made wild, weird and wonderfully lunatic comedies for the war years that are still fondly remembered today. The swift collapse of his talent after those years had gone is one of the screen's great sadnesses. Still, the inspired idiocy of his seven comedies between 1940 and 1944 is something to treasure, and perhaps it is greedy to expect more. Like many masters of insane humour, Sturges was, according to his contemporaries, 'a strange guy'. He was perhaps entitled that strangeness, after an unorthodox upbringing by eccentric socialites that culminated in his being asked to manage his mother's cosmetic firm at 16, at which point he invented a 'kiss-proof lipstick'; this was the first of numerous (some might say hair-brained) inventions from the gadfly Sturges brain that also included a 'Heath-Robinson' vertical takeoff flying-machine. From the late 1920s, Sturges concentrated his wild energies on a writing career. Surprisingly, he settled well into the middle range of Hollywood screenwriters, and typically engineered his own career turnabout when he offered one of his scripts, *The Great McGinty*, to Paramount, for ten dollars if they would let him direct it. They accepted, and the Sturges legend was born. The films that followed are almost indescribable. They have plots of sorts, though few of their characters are by any stretch of the imagination 'normal' and the action, just when you think you have it pinned down to some kind of level, is likely to whip off into spasms of manic buffoonery. Sturges characters are fun, and there are a lot of them, though perhaps none funnier than Trudy Kockenlocker in *The Miracle of Morgan's Creek*. All in a night, Trudy meets, marries and becomes pregnant by a G.I. whose name she remembers vaguely as Ratskywatsky – the family of Kockenlockers gravely discussing the unlikelihood of such a name is side-splitting in itself – she ends up marrying hapless Eddie Bracken (Bracken was later to be the 'hero' of Sturges' *Hail the Conquering Hero)* and giving birth to sextuplets to newspaper headlines of 'Canada protests' (a reference to the Dionne quintuplets) and 'Hitler demands recount'. But the best of these riotously undisciplined romps is *The Lady Eve* in which Henry Fonda superbly plays the disaster-prone, virginal target for predatory Barbara Stanwyck's attentions. There are a number of possible reasons for Sturges' fall from grace in the mid-1940s. Given his volatile temperament, however, it was always possible that Sturges would make a ghastly mistake and, with hindsight, the move from Paramount to the

auspices of Howard Hughes in 1945 was it. The confidence and dynamism all seemed to go at once and Sturges ended his days in exile in France, an embittered man making one last, awful film before an early death.

1940: *The Great McGinty (GB: Down Went McGinty). Christmas in July.* 1941: *Sullivan's Travels. The Lady Eve.* 1942: *The Palm Beach Story.* 1943: *The Great Moment.* 1944: *Hail the Conquering Hero. The Miracle of Morgan's Creek.* 1946: *The Sin of Harold Diddlebock (later and GB: Mad Wednesday).* 1948: *Unfaithfully Yours.* 1949: *The Beautiful Blonde from Bashful Bend.* 1956: *The Diary of Major Thompson (US: The French They Are a Funny Race).*

SUMMERS, Jeremy
See Summers, Walter

SUMMERS, Walter 1896-1973
One has the feeling that this unconventional British director had eternal longings to be another Ernest B. Schoedsack *(qv)* or Merian C. Cooper. But the quality of his work was not distinguished enough, nor could he find the support of a major studio in the same way on the British side of the Atlantic. In show business all his life, Summers was a child actor on stage and entered the British film industry in 1913, firstly as an actor, then assistant director and title-card writer for Cecil Hepworth *(qv)*. He had a dozen screenplays to his credit in 1922 and 1923, the year in which he began to direct. He burst into the limelight in the mid-1920s with a series of elaborate reconstructions of famous battles. A Fellow of the Royal Geographical Society, fascinated by travellers and explorers, and obsessed by deeds of courage in the face of the enemy or the elements, Summers made, in the midst of more mundane entertainment films, a strange, semi-improvised documentary in 1932 on the famous husband-and-wife flyers Amy Johnson and Jim Mollison, which has some extraordinary aerial photography. The following year, his studio, B.I.P., sent him to scout locations in North Africa for an adventure film called *Timbuctoo*. While there, Summers seized the opportunity to make a documentary, *Across the Sahara*, using tinted film and capturing unique footage of the wild terrain and desert townships. The studio, however, reacted unsympathetically, deleting much of his location and animal footage from the main film and releasing his documentary with a particularly inapt musical soundtrack. Thus

chastened, Summers returned to the commercial cinema, continuing to mix writing with direction, and displaying a taste for the macabre in such ghoulish offerings as *Dark Eyes of London*. His most successful entertainment film of the 1930s was *The Return of Bulldog Drummond*, with Ralph Richardson giving an immaculate interpretation of the famous sleuth. Summers was strong on atmosphere and meticulous in the background detail of his films, but he was born into an era in which his superiors were unable or unwilling to give him the sort of shooting schedules from which his work could have benefited. He did not return to the cinema after World War II. His son, Jeremy Summers (1931-) has directed around 15 films, from *Depth Charge* (1960) to *One Hour to Zero* (1976), as well as numerous episodes of television series. His most enjoyable film is the delightful *Crooks in Cloisters* (1963) about a gang of crooks hiding out in a monastery and disguised as monks.

1923: †*I Pagliacci.* †*Afterglow. A Couple of Down and Outs.* 1924: *The Unwanted. Who is the Man?* †*The Perfect Crime. The Cost of Beauty.* 1925: *Ypres (D).* 1926: *Mons (D. US: The Battle of Mons). Nelson.* 1927: *The Battles of the Coronel and Falkland Islands.* 1928: *Bolibar (US: The Betrayal).* 1929: *The Lost Patrol. Chamber of Horrors.* 1930: *Raise the Roof. The Man from Chicago. Suspense.* 1931: *The Flying Fool. Men Like These (US: Trapped in a Submarine).* 1932: **Dual Control (D). The House Opposite.* 1933: **Across the Sahara (D). Timbuctoo.* 1934: *The Return of Bulldog Drummond. The Warren Case. What Happened Then?* 1935: *McGlusky, the Sea Rover.* †*Music Hath Charms.* 1936: †*Ourselves Alone (US: River of Unrest). The Limping Man.* 1937: *The Price of Folly.* 1938: *Première.* 1939: *At the Villa Rose. Dark Eyes of London (US: Human Monster).* 1940: *Traitor Spy.*

SUTHERLAND, A. Edward 1895-1973
Tall, dark and handsome in a faintly owlish way, British-born Eddie Sutherland looked like an actor, and indeed was until his late twenties. He was fond of society life and great friends with such great lifters of the elbow as W.C. Fields and John Barrymore, both of whom he directed. His high living, however, appears not to have materially affected his career, although he was one of the first Hollywood directors to leave the film capital behind when the infant medium of television looked for experienced talent in the post-war years. Until then, Sutherland

had provided smooth, enjoyable entertainment for 20 years. He worked with most of the character comedians with pleasant enough results — Fields, Raymond Griffith, Wallace Beery and Raymond Hatton and, later, Laurel and Hardy and Abbott and Costello. A stage actor in England as a child, Sutherland moved to America in his teens, and got into Keystone comedies by the time he was 19. After World War I, he moved gradually towards direction: he was Chaplin's assistant on *A Woman of Paris* in 1923 and began directing his own films two years later. His first film with W.C. Fields was *It's the Old Army Game*, and Fields was appreciative of the skill Sutherland had already acquired in the mounting of sight gags. Sutherland married the leading lady of the film, Louise Brooks, but they were divorced two years later. Sutherland's two greatest successes both came in 1935: *Mississippi*, a sentimental comedy-musical with the unlikely combination of Fields, Bing Crosby and Joan Bennett; and *Diamond Jim*, which made a big star out of Edward Arnold, a rip-roaring period drama with a good script by Preston Sturges *(qv)*. Like all Sutherland's films, they bowled along at a goodly pace, and entertained the masses. Credited variously as A. Edward, Eddie or Edward Sutherland. The 'A' stood for Albert.

1925: Coming Through. Wild, Wild Susan. A Regular Fellow. 1926: Behind the Front. It's the Old Army Game. We're in the Navy Now. 1927: Love's Greatest Mistake. Figures Don't Lie. Fireman Save My Child. 1928: The Baby Cyclone. Tillie's Punctured Romance (GB: Marie's Millions). What a Night! 1929: †Close Harmony. †The Dance of Lifr. Fast Company. Pointed Heels. The Saturday Night Kid. 1930: The Social Lion. Burning Up. †Paramount on Parade. The Sap from Syracuse (GB: The Sap Abroad). 1931: Up Pops the Devil. Gang Buster. June Moon. Palmy Days. 1932: Mr Robinson Crusoe. Sky Devils. Secrets of the French Police. 1933: International House. Murders in the Zoo. Too Much Harmony. 1935: Diamond Jim. Mississippi. 1936: Poppy. 1937: Champagne Waltz. 1938: Every Day's a Holiday. 1939: The Flying Deuces. 1940: One Night in the Tropics. Beyond Tomorrow. The Boys from Syracuse. 1941: The Invisible Woman. Nine Lives Are Not Enough. Steel Against the Sky. 1942: Army Surgeon. Sing Your Worries Away. The Navy Comes Through. 1943: Dixie. 1944: Follow the Boys. Secret Command. 1945: Having Wonderful Crime. 1946: Abie's Irish Rose. 1956: Bermuda Affair.

SZWARC, Jeannot 1936-

The French-born director with the unpronounceable name (no, I'm not about to offer guidance) is included here on the grounds that *Somewhere in Time* at last proved what television buffs had been telling us for years — that this is a fine director of actors with a keen understanding of character and a first-class control of narrative drive. Working in TV since the mid-1960s, Szwarc became one of the driving forces behind the success of the *Ironside* series, before revealing a taste (and distinctive talent) for the macabre in numerous episodes of the *Night Gallery* series. He tried a feature film in 1972, but *Extreme Close-Up* meant nothing to anyone, in spite of a screenplay by Michael Crichton *(qv)*, also to become a director of repute. Szwarc moved into TV movies, sticking to shivers and shocks with *The Devil's Daughter* and *Night of Terror* and making a disturbing feature-length Kojak episode called *Shield for Murder*. *A Summer without Boys* revealed more of the 'actors' director', while more weirdies were foisted on cinema audiences in *Bug* and *Jaws 2*, the latter routinely exciting, but far more contrived and mechanical than its predecessor. The threads of Szwarc's career all came together, though, with *Somewhere in Time,* written by fantasy king Richard Matheson, but basically the kind of weepie that hadn't seen the light of day since Jane Wyman's time. Its time-travel story doesn't quite hang together under close inspection, but the immense fondness with which the director treats it sees it through. Under Szwarc's direction, Christopher Reeve shows great power to reach out and affect an audience, and Jane Seymour, too, is a revelation. The film didn't really do the trick for Szwarc in terms of international recognition and, after a period of unproductive work in the 1980s, he has spent recent years making films in his native France.

1972: Extreme Close-Up. The Devil's Daughter (TV). Night of Terror (TV). The Weekend Nun (TV). 1973: You'll Never See Me Again (TV). Lisa Bright and Dark (TV). A Summer Without Boys (TV). 1975: Bug. Crime Club (TV). Small Miracle (TV). 1976: Hazard's People (TV). 1977: Code Name: Diamond Head (TV). Jaws 2. 1980: Somewhere in Time. 1982: Enigma. 1983: Supergirl. 1985: Santa Claus. 1986: The Murders in the Rue Morgue (TV). 1988: Grand Larceny (TV). 1989: Honor Bound. 1994: La vengeance d'une blonde. 1996: Hercule et Sherlock. 1997: Les soeurs soleil.

TAMAHORI, Lee 1958-

New Zealand-born director who quickly went to Hollywood after making a tremendous impact with his first film in his native country. Tamahori had joined the film industry in the late 1970s as a boom operator, and worked in a number of bottom-of-the-ladder jobs before establishing himself as an assistant director in the 1980s. From here, he became an award-winning director of commercials, making more than 100 before branching out into feature film production. His debut, *Once Were Warriors*, was a searing account of a contemporary Maori family (Tamahori himself is half-Maori) and the mother's battle to regain her self-esteem and keep control of an alcoholic husband, and five kids, the eldest of whom has joined a street gang. Very violent and not at all pleasant, the film brought home the realities of the lives lived by such families who have left their rural roots to try to make a go of life in the city. Clutching a bagful of awards, Tamahori headed for America, where his first film was the ambitious *Mulholland Falls*. Impeccably set in the Los Angeles of the post-war years, it proved to be a gruff, thick-ear, tolerably entertaining jigsaw thriller with an amazing all star cast. Unfortunately, it was not what the public wanted to see, but Tamahori began to rebuild his reputation with *The Edge*, a solid suspense thriller about a battle for survival in the wilderness. He looks set to remain a distinctive film-maker for some time to come.

1994: Once Were Warriors. 1996: Mulholland Falls. 1997: The Edge.

TARANTINO, Quentin 1963-

This cult American director who looks like a stand-up comedian once sold videos for a living. Now his films sell videos in their millions. Tall, dark, lanky, lantern-jawed and his own best publicist, Tarantino was raised by a single-parent mother, and had soon left the video store to scrape a living as an actor. Between assignments, he would spend all his time writing, turning out several unproduced screenplays. As his acting is never likely to win him as many awards as his other talents, it was perhaps lucky that Tarantino hit on the idea of fashioning a screen-

Unmistakeably the features of Quentin **Tarantino,** here on his first film *Reservoir Dogs*. He's dressed for the supporting role of Mr Brown.

play with the deliberate idea of attracting backers. The ploy was instantly successful and the result was *Reservoir Dogs* which, although not released for a year after Tarantino completed it in 1991, shocked people with its graphic violence, and attracted acclaim from critics who compared it to the early Kubrick thriller *The Killing*, which Tarantino admitted had been his greatest influence while writing it. *Pulp Fiction*, though, was a much more polished effort, and its convoluted story deservedly won Tarantino the Oscar for best screenplay, although he ludicrously lost best director to Robert Zemeckis for the over-praised *Forrest Gump*. This inventively structured film about Tales from the Darkside in the big city has few weak links, although one of them is Tarantino's acting; fortunately, he was absent from the cast of *Jackie Brown*, a crime caper spun round an arms dealer and the $500,000 in cash he's planning to bring into the country. Despite a typically complicated Tarantino plot in which the director sometimes toys with us at too great a length, the film has a moody atmosphere all its own and a stunning array of veteran talent headed by Robert Forster (who won an Oscar nomination) and Pam Grier. It's certainly Tarantino's most complete film to date, but there isn't likely to be another one for a while. I'm

never going to be the director that makes a movie a year,' he says. 'I don't see how directors do that and live a life.' He should worry. His success instantly revived interest in his previously rejected screenplays: among those already filmed are *True Romance*, *From Dusk Till Dawn* and *Natural Born Killers*. All of them bore his hallmark of cataclysmic violence, although this element is muted in *Jackie Brown* — as if Tarantino is moving more towards the style of his hero, Clint Eastwood.

1991: Reservoir Dogs. 1993: Rock All Night (cable TV). 1994: Pulp Fiction. 1995: +Four Rooms. 1997: Jackie Brown.

TARKOVSKY, Andrei 1932-1986
Russian director of few, but long and challenging films that took him years to put together. He also wrote his own scripts. After feeling his way with two shorter films, Tarkovsky burst on the international scene with *Ivan's Childhood*, a moving yet horrifying account of a boy's determination to avenge his parents' death at the hands of the Nazi invaders, which took the Golden Lion at the Venice Festival. It was four years before Tarkovsky's next film *Andrei Rublev* was made and showing was delayed still fur-

ther by the first of many clashes Tarkovsky was to have with Soviet authorities. After his next film *Solaris*, though, there was no suppressing his reputation as a film-maker of international standing. A bleak and shivery piece of science-fiction pitched somewhere in the immense chasm between *Kubrick's 2001: a Space Odyssey* and Resnais' *Je t'aime, je t'aime*, it was really a plea for love and peace under its enigmatic surface; but it too failed to please the powers-that-be in the Soviet film industry, who claimed that it was too difficult for the average Russian audience to understand (probably correct, but hardly the point). Nor were they any happier with *Mirror*, a film as multi-faceted as *Citizen Kane:* one enthusiastic observer remarked that here Tarkovsky had come the closest yet to the filming of the human soul. Tarkovsky was on less secure ground with *Stalker*, slow-motion science-fiction which puts its viewer through the same kind of tunnel — or 'meatgrinder' as the sparse script nicknames it — as the fictional characters it creates. The film is so heavily burdened with its own significance that the immense running time, not previously a deficiency (or even noticeable) in Tarkovsky films, begins to tell. The film is still interesting though and, typical of Tarkovsky, enigmatic to the end. His last film, made when he was terminally ill with lung cancer, is less typical of his work as a whole.

1959: *Segodnya Otpuska Nye Budyet/There Will Be No Leave Tonight. 1961: Katok i Skripka (GB: The Steamroller and the Violin. US: Violin and Roller). 1962: Ivanovo Detsvo (GB: Ivan's Childhood. US: My Name is Ivan). 1965: Andrei Rublev. 1972: Solaris. 1974: Zerkalo (GB & US: Mirror). 1979: Stalker. 1983: Nostalgia. 1986: Offret/Offret Sacrificatio (GB and US: The Sacrifice).

TASHLIN, Frank 1913-1972

Tashlin was a cartoonist, gagman, writer and director responsible for some of the funniest and best-timed broad visual humour to come from the American cinema over a period of 22 years. There is some evidence to suggest that he made films less well than he set up sight gags, but no matter: in any or all of these capacities, few men made us laugh louder in the TV-depressed post-war years. For 18 years, Tashlin was a cartoonist, beginning with Max Fleischer, breaking away

briefly to become a gagman for Hal Roach, credited as 'Supervisor' on Warners' Merrie Melodies cartoons of the late 1930s (notably several Porky Pigs) and eventually director of cartoons. From the mid-1940s, his inventive brain was ever more frequently deployed in donating riotous moments to live-action films and he left cartoons for good in 1946 after providing gags for the Marx Brothers (including the house that falls down when Harpo stops leaning on it) in A Night in Casablanca. His writing credits over the next five years are almost all on middle-budget comedies that had 'em rolling in the aisles: The Fuller Brush Man, The Paleface, The Fuller Brush Girl, Kill the Umpire, The Good Humor Man, Miss Grant Takes Richmond. He turned director in 1951: Son of Paleface is a funny and likeable sequel to the Bob Hope original, although perhaps Tashlin's talents as a director had not yet caught up with his standards of writing, and of engineering such side-splitting moments as the leap

across the canyon. It was soon followed, though, by Susan Slept Here, probably Tashlin's best film purely as a director, with excellent use made of Dick Powell and Debbie Reynolds. It was still very funny, but in a more human way than Tashlin was to manage thereafter. There were two films with Jayne Mansfield, The Girl Can't Help It and Will Success Spoil Rock Hunter?, in which sight gags run wild and the players are enjoyably encouraged to mug it up. Tashlin's first films with Jerry Lewis had not been encouraging, but the two combined memorably from 1962, on It's Only Money, The Disorderly Orderly and Who's Minding the Store?, in which a string of zany situations were all the better for being handled by a director rather than the star. In the mid-1960s, Doris Day seemed a willing Pearl White in Tashlin's lunatic world, in Caprice fleeing the villain through doors whose surrounding walls have been blasted away, a gag that goes all the way back to Laurel and Hardy in Helpmates, and is distantly related to Tashlin's earliest gags in A Night in Casablanca. The list of films that follows does not include cartoons directed by Tashlin, for example A Tale of Two Mice (1945), and many more besides.

1951: †The Lemon Drop Kid (uncredited). The First Time. 1952: Son of Paleface. 1953: Marry Me Again. 1954: Susan Slept Here. 1955: Artists and Models. The Lieutenant Wore Skirts. 1956: Hollywood or Bust. The Girl Can't Help It. 1957: Will Success Spoil Rock Hunter? (GB: Oh! For a Man!) 1958: Rock-a-Bye Baby. The Geisha Boy. 1959: Say One for Me. 1960: Cinderfella. 1961: Bachelor Flat. 1962: It's Only Money. 1963: The Man from the Diners' Club. Who's Minding the Store? 1964: The Disorderly Orderly. 1965: The Alphabet Murders. 1966: The Glass Bottom Boat. 1967: Caprice. 1968: The Private Navy of Sergeant O'Farrell.

TATI, Jacques (J. Tatischeff) 1908-1982

This mournfully benign-looking Frenchman, forever identified with the pipe-smoking character of Monsieur Hulot, is more a director than an actor, in that he uses his fictional character to bumble through a series of wordless visual gems of his own devising. These are funniest of all in his first big success, the gently humorous Monsieur Hulot's Holiday, whose mood is wonderfully all-of-a-piece and contains some marvellously fresh belly-laughs (who could ever forget the rocket flying in through the open window during the fireworks display?). In his later films, Tati became increasingly obsessed

A big, serious-looking man who made funny films, Frank **Tashlin** (right) here discusses with Bob Hope on Son of Paleface.

by urban paranoias. These films are less consistently funny and sometimes tedious when he lets his much-loved long shots linger too long to set up an atmosphere. His own character, too, has become less human. None of which is enough, though, to lessen one's regret at the gradual drying up of his work. Tati was a considerable sportsman in his youth, playing rugby to a standard that brought him to the verge of the French national team. But he was always the clown off the field and, in his mid-twenties, built up a wordless little night-club act in which he mimicked various sporting activities. This led to a short film, *Oscar, champion de tennis*, which launched him on his new career. His first feature film as director-star, *Jour de fête*, did not come along until 1949. An amusing series of vignettes about the misadventures of a village postman, it was followed two years later by *Hulot*, which made Tati an international name. His last announced project, *Confusion*, in 1977, was all too aptly titled and failed to materialize.

1947: *†L'école des facteurs. 1949: Jour de fête. 1951: Monsieur Hulot's Holiday. 1958: Mon oncle/My Uncle. 1967: Playtime. 1971: Traffic. 1974: Parade (TV).

TAUROG, Norman 1899-1981

This chubby American director looked like one of the minor characters from his own films. Round-faced and blue-jowled, with the bee-stung lip that ran in the family (Jackie Cooper was his nephew), a wisp of hair and large, inquisitive eyes, Taurog could have sprung from the ranks of querulous minor gangsters in one of his comedies. In fact, he began life as a boy actor, before developing into a prolific and efficient director — of entertainers as opposed to actors, such as Larry Semon, Jackie Coogan, (inevitably) Jackie Cooper, W.C. Fields, Burns and Allen, Mickey Rooney, Wheeler and Woolsey, Bing Crosby, Ethel Merman, Amos 'n' Andy, Judy Garland, Mario Lanza, Martin and Lewis and (latterly and least successfully) Elvis Presley. The Presley vehicles are about the only dull spots in a career that began with countless comedy shorts through the 1920s. At first, Taurog found feature work hard to get, but, following an Academy Award for his direction of nephew Jackie Cooper in *Skippy*, the story of a boy from a good home who makes friends in the slums, he was recognized as a director of both comedy with established stars, and weepie-dramas with younger actors. He directed Jackie Coogan in *Huckleberry Finn* and seven years later made a good job of the

Selznick classic *The Adventures of Tom Sawyer*. That year (1938) was also the year of Taurog's best film, *Boys' Town*, with Spencer Tracy and Mickey Rooney giving eye-catching performances in the famous story of delinquent boys for which Tracy took his second Oscar. Taurog, who was nominated for an Academy Award but this time did not win, also directed the sequel, *Men of Boys' Town*, in 1941. Taurog made relaxed and popular entertainments for Paramount and M-G-M through the 1930s and 1940s, before making four very enjoyable comedies, all with sentimental streaks, in the 1950s: *Room for One More* is a delightful laughter-and-tears romp with Cary Grant, Betsy Drake and a lot of kids headed by George 'Foghorn' Winslow; *The Stars Are Singing* an archly but appealingly-contrived vehicle for two new songstresses and a comedian with a hilarious trick dog (Bob Williams and Red Dust); *The Birds and the Bees*, an enjoyable and underrated musical remake of *The Lady Eve*; and *The Stooge*. This last film, unjustly neglected and criticized because of its sentimental content, is in fact Martin and Lewis' best together, cleverly worked out and beautifully timed, showing Taurog's gentle technique at its most persuasive.

1920: *†The Fly Cop. *†The Suitor. *†The Stage Hand. *†School Days. 1921: *†The Fall Guy. *†The Hick. *†The Bakery. *†The Bell Hop. *†The Rent Collector. *†The Sawmill. 1922: *†The Show. *†A Pair of Kings. 1923: *†The Four Flusher. *The Mummy. 1924: *Pain As You Enter. *Rough and Ready. *Fast and Furious. * What a Night. 1925: *Below Zero. *Cheap Skates. *Going Great. *Hello Goodbye. *Hello Hollywood. *Motor Mad. *Pleasure Bound. *Spot Light. *Step Lightly. 1926: *Teacher Teacher. *Jolly Tars. *Careful Please. *Creeps. *Here Comes Charlie. *Honest Injun. *The Humdinger. *Mr Cinderella. *Move Along. *Movieland. *Nobody's Business. *Nothing Matters. *On Edge. 1927: *Up in Arms. *At Ease. *Kilties. *Breezing Along. *Drama De Luxe. *The Draw-Back. *Goose Flesh. *Her Husky Hero. *His Better Half. *Howdy Duke. *The Little Rube. *New Wrinkles. *Papa's Boy. *Plumb Dumb. *Somebody's Fault. 1928: *At It Again. *Blazing Away. *Always a Gentleman. *Blondes Beware. *Cutie. *A Home Made Man. *Listen Children. *Rah! Rah! Rah! *Slippery Road. The Farmer's Daughter. 1929: In Holland. The Diplomats. †Lucky Boy. †Troopers Three. *All Steamed Up. *Knights Out. *Detectives Wanted. Hired and Fired. *The Medicine

Men. 1930: *The Fatal Card. *Just a Pal. *Meet the Boyfriend. *Oh, Teddy. *The Patient. *Sing, You Dancers. *Song Service. Sunny Skies. Hot Curves. Follow the Leader. 1931: *Cab Waiting. *The Great Pants Mystery. *Simply Killing. †Finn and Hattie. Newly Rich (GB: Forbidden Adventure). Skippy. Huckleberry Finn. Sooky. 1932: †If I Had a Million. Hold 'Em Jail! The Phantom President. 1933: A Bedtime Story. The Way to Love. 1934: Mrs Wiggs of the Cabbage Patch. We're Not Dressing. College Rhythm. 1935: The Big Broadcast of 1936. 1936: Strike Me Pink. Rhythm on the Range. Reunion (GB: Hearts in Reunion). 1937: Fifty Roads to Town. You Can't Have Everything. 1938: The Adventures of Tom Sawyer. Boys' Town. Mad About Music. The Girl Downstairs. 1939: Lucky Night. 1940: Young Tom Edison. Broadway Melody of 1940. Little Nellie Kelly. 1941: Men of Boys' Town. Design for Scandal. 1942: Are Husbands Necessary? A Yank at Eton. 1943: Presenting Lily Mars. Girl Crazy. 1946: The Hoodlum Saint. 1947: The Beginning or the End? 1948: The Bride Goes Wild. Words and Music. 1949: That Midnight Kiss. 1950: Mrs O' Malley and Mr Malone. Please Believe Me. The Toast of New Orleans. 1951: Rich, Young and Pretty. Room for One More. 1952: The Stooge. Jumping Jacks. 1953: The Caddy. The Stars Are Singing. 1954: Living It Up. 1955: You're Never Too Young. 1956: The Birds and the Bees. Bundle of Joy. Pardners. 1957: The Fuzzy Pink Nightgown. 1958: Onionhead. 1959: Don't Give Up the Ship. 1960: Visit to a Small Planet. G.I. Blues. 1961: All Hands on Deck. Blue Hawaii. 1962: Girls! Girls! Girls! 1963: Palm Springs Weekend. It Happened at the World's Fair. 1965: Tickle Me. Sergeant Deadhead. Dr Goldfoot and the Bikini Machine (GB: Dr G. and the Bikini Machine). 1966: Spinout (GB: California Holiday). Double Trouble. 1968: Speedway. Live a Little, Love a Little.

TAVERNIER, Bertrand 1941-

Despite a career of much promise but only a modicum of fulfilment, Tavernier's work remains popular in his native France and is shown more widely abroad than that of many of his contemporaries. His films are carefully made with studious attention to detail and correctness but tend to lack spark and a consistent pace and suffer from lack of incident in rather long running times. The son of a writer and poet, Tavernier was himself a writer, publicist, interviewer, film-club owner and critic, before directing his first full feature film in 1973. The film, *The Watchmaker* of Saint Paul, which starred Philippe Noiret, the lugubrious French actor to feature in so many of Tavernier's films, made his reputation with its meticulous depiction of the life of a small-town tradesmen who has to reconsider his own values when it seems his son has committed a murder. He made a bid for international recognition with *Deathwatch*, a fascinating sci-fi idea about a man (Harvey Keitel) with a camera implanted in his head, but it buckled under a lack of tightness in editing and story control and failed to reach a wide audience. Although Tavernier's films continued to suffer from overlength, he achieved some success in the 1980s with *Clean Slate (Coup de torchon)*, a corrosive black comedy featuring Noiret as a law officer determined to clear out corruption in a 1938 French West African town, *Mississippi Blues*, a flavoursome docudrama co-directed with Robert Parrish, and *'Round Midnight*, an affectionate homage to jazz musicians and their world. He also had considerable international exposure with *D'Artagnan's Daughter*, although the film lacks real vigour and only condescends to burst into the expected action towards the end.

1964: +La chance et l'amour. 1965: +Les baisers. 1973: L'horloger de Saint-Paul (GB: The Watchmaker of Saint Paul. US: The Clockmaker). 1974: Que la fête commence (US: Let Joy Reign Supreme). 1975: Le juge et l'assassin (US: The Judge and His Hangman). 1976: Des enfants gâtés (US: Spoiled Children). 1978: Femmes fatales. 1979: La mort en direct/Deathwatch. 1980: Une semaine de vacances (US: A Month's Vacation). Coup de torchon (GB and US: Clean Slate). 1982: Philippe Soupault et le surréalisme (D). 1983: +Mississippi Blues/Pays d'Octobre. 1984: Un dimanche à la campagne. 1986: 'Round Midnight. 1987: La passion Béatrice (US: Beatrice). 1988: Lyon, le regard interieur (D). 1989: La vie et rien d'autre (US: Life and Nothing But...). 1990: Daddy nostalgie (GB: These Foolish Things). 1992: La guerre sans nom (D). 1994: La fille de D'Artagnan (GB and US: D'Artagnan's Daughter). 1995: L'appât (GB: The Bait). 1996: Capitaine Conan. 1999: De l'autre côté du periph.

TAYLOR, Don 1920-

Versatile American actor, director and writer who became a second-rank star in the 1950s before going over to direction and turning out a number of perfectly competent films and TV movies that were sometimes better than one might have expected from the source material. Although his films date only from 1961, he had begun directing for television in 1957, working on numerous episodes of *M Squad*, *Burke's Law*, *Alfred Hitchcock Presents* and *Night Gallery*. One of the last, *The Messiah of Mott Street*, is rather moving, a Christmas story with Edward G. Robinson making one of his rare television appearances as an old man literally battling against the Angel of Death for the sake of his grandson. Taylor's cinema career has been a bit 'in and out' although both *Escape from the Planet of the Apes* and *Damien: Omen II* were better than most sequels. On television, he won great praise for *A Circle of Children*, with one of Jane Alexander's typically resourceful performances as a socialite who tries to do her bit to help handicapped children. Taylor's direction is generally characterized by a lightness of touch and a freshness of approach that usually keeps proceedings light and lively — a notable exception was *The Great Scout and Cathouse Thursday*, a strong candidate for anyone's worst film of the year; in it, faced with a horrendous script, everyone concerned went over the top. However, it seem to do little harm to Taylor's career. His second wife is the former actress Hazel Court.

1961: Everything's Ducky. 1964: Ride the Wild Surf. 1967: Jack of Diamonds. 1968: Something for a Lonely Man (TV). 1969: The Five Man Army. The Man Hunter (TV). 1970: Wild Women (TV). 1971: Escape from the Planet of the Apes. 1972: Heat of Anger (TV). 1973: Tom Sawyer. 1974: Honky Tonk (TV). Night Games (TV). 1975: Echoes of a Summer (US: The Last Castle). 1976: The Great Scout and Cathouse Thursday. 1977: A Circle of Children (TV). The Island of Dr Moreau. 1978: Damien — Omen II. 1979: The Gift (TV). 1980: The Final Countdown. 1981: Broken Promise (TV). Red Flag: The Ultimate Game (TV). 1982: Listen to Your Heart (TV). A Change of Heart (TV). Drop-Out Father (TV). 1983: September Gun (TV). 1984: He's Not Your Son (TV). My Wicked, Wicked Ways – The Story of Errol Flynn (TV). 1985: Going for the Gold: The Bill Johnson Story (TV). Sexpionage (video). 1986: Classified Love (TV). 1987: Ghost of a Chance (TV). 1988: The Diamond Trap (TV).

TEAGUE, Lewis 1938-

After decades of hard work gradually moving up the film ladder, it looked as though, somewhere around the mid-1980s, Teague might have Hollywood at his feet. Somehow, that situation went astray, and the director who gave us *The Jewel of the Nile* has spent the last ten years of his career making some rather mediocre TV movies. The native New Yorker began his show business life as a film editor, working for many years in this capacity with Roger Corman's New World films. From 1974, he also began working as a second-unit director, most notably on Samuel Fuller's *The Big Red One*. Around the same time as that, Corman gave him his first real chance at direction with the Prohibition crime drama *The Lady in Red*. Aided by a terrific script from fellow-director John Sayles, Teague saw that the film rattled along in stylish fashion. He directed another Sayles script in *Alligator*, well above par for the monster movie course, and again a film of some style with well-staged storm-drain excitements. *Fighting Back* was smart thriller, but did not catch the public's imagination. However, that was not true of *Cujo*, a very popular demon dog story, after which Teague was assigned to a Stephen King fantasy, *Cat's Eye* which was more fun than most King films, with intelligent deployment of its feline stars. *The Jewel of the Nile* was in some ways better than its predecessor, *Romancing the Stone*, with some surging action sequences. Although it was not as well received as it might have been, few could have forecast that it would prove Teague's last film of any note.

1974: +Dirty O'Neil. 1979: The Lady in Red/Guns, Sin and Bathtub Gin. 1980: Alligator. 1982: Fighting Back (GB: Death Vengeance). 1983: Cujo. 1984: Cat's Eye. 1985: The Jewel of the Nile. 1988: Collision Course. 1989: Shannon's Deal (TV). 1990: Navy SEALS. 1991: Wedlock (later Deadlock). 1992: T Bone 'n' Weasel (TV). 1993: Time Trax. 1995: Tom Clancy's Op Center (TV). 1996: The Dukes of Hazzard Reunion! (TV).

TENNYSON, Pen

See Woods, Arthur B.

TETZLAFF, Ted (Theodore Tetzlaff) 1903-

This American film-maker was more interesting as a director of photography than as a director of films — although he does have one outstanding essay in suspense to his credit. In films from an early age, he worked in cinematography, in one capacity or another, from 1920, shooting several Frank Capra films in the late 1920s, as well as *Tol'able David* (1930 version), *My Man Godfrey*, *Easy Living*, *The Princess Comes Across*, *I Married a Witch*, *The Enchanted Cottage* and *Notorious*. On the last, Tetzlaff was said to have got rather grouchy over Hitchcock's insistence in getting angles, shapes and shadows exactly the way he wanted — probably because Tetzlaff had already started up in direction on his own account, with the 1941 comedy *World Premiere*. This is a very funny, lunatic comedy about two bumbling German agents sent to Hollywood to bring chaos to the entire movie industry. One of John Barrymore's last films, it also had Fritz Feld and Sig Rumann in inspired form as a kind of Teutonic Laurel and Hardy. Tetzlaff got back into direction after war service, at first with RKO, for whom he made several presentable Pat O'Brien films and *Johnny Allegro*, a sideshoot of *The Most Dangerous Game*, before he shot his masterwork, *The Window*, a brilliant second-feature on the boy-who-cried-wolf theme. Tension ran to a high level and stayed there as little Bobby Driscoll can make no-one believe he has seen a killer at work, while the murderer himself closes inexorably on the witness, finally pursuing him along a wooden beam in a memorable scene. In all departments, this was a fine job of film-making, and Driscoll (later to die in tragic circumstances at 31) won a special Oscar. Tetzlaff subsequently made a number of routine films, and even attempted to repeat *The Window* formula with the British-made *Time Bomb*, a low-budget suspense thriller with exactly the same terse running time (73 minutes). But he never again approached *The Window's* high quality and left films in 1960.

1941: *World Première*. 1947: *Riffraff*. 1948: *Fighting Father Dunne*. 1949: *A Dangerous Profession. Johnny Allegro (GB: Hounded). The Window*. 1950: *The White Tower. Under the Gun. Gambling House*. 1951: *The Treasure of Lost Canyon*. 1953: *Time Bomb (US: Terror on a Train)*. 1955: *Son of Sinbad*. 1956: †*Seven Wonders of the World*. 1959: *The Young Land*.

THOMAS, Gerald 1920-1993

How can one write 500 words about the man who directed 29 'Carry On' films and a few allied specimens? Everyone should run the movies for themselves and decide whether they are riotous, abysmal, historically important — or none of these things. The fact is that, for 12 years until their appeal began to flag, the 'Carry On' films as a group made the biggest single financial contribution to the British film industry. Their participants were allowed to exaggerate their own comedy styles, or 'camp it up' as the approach later came to be termed, and included such experienced *farceurs* as Sidney James, Kenneth Williams (the two most valuable members of the team), Kenneth Connor, Hattie Jacques, Bernard Bresslaw and Joan Sims. Thomas just pointed his cameras at them when they were about to deliver some particularly outrageous *double-entendre* and let the audience and Talbot Rothwell's scripts do the rest. The brother of Ralph Thomas *(qv)*, this most British of directors (actually born in Yorkshire) began his film career immediately after World War II, as an assistant editor, progressing to editing and second-unit direction before making a Children's Film Foundation drama, *Circus Friends* (starring Carol White, whom he would re-employ as a sexy teenager in *Carry On Teacher*) as his first solo feature. *Time Lock*, his second film, was a tense thriller with a small role for the young Sean Connery, but in no time at all, the 'Carry Ons' intervened and, to everyone's surprise in the industry, quickly became a fondly regarded national institution. For the record, the best of them are *Carry On Cleo, Carry On Cowboy, Carry On Screaming, Carry On Up the Khyber* – the dinner-party sequence at the end of

The team behind the "Carry on" comedies was director Gerald **Thomas** (left) and producer Peter Rogers.

the last is superbly orchestrated and the best individual scene in any of them – *Carry On Henry* and *Carry On Abroad*. The series always worked better in costume, though audiences seemed not to care about the 'story', however slapdash. Sometimes, as in *Carry On Abroad*, elements of genuine satire could be observed to be creeping in. Thomas' direction was rarely more than serviceable: it didn't have to be!

1956: Circus Friends. 1957: Time Lock. The Vicious Circle (US: The Circle). 1958: Chain of Events. The Solitary Child. The Duke Wore Jeans. Carry On Sergeant. 1959: Carry On Nurse. Carry On Teacher. Please Turn Over. 1960: Carry On Constable. Watch Your Stern. No Kidding (US: Beware of Children). 1961: Carry on Regardless. Raising the Wind (US: Roommates). 1962: Carry On Cruising. Twice Round the Daffodils. The Iron Maiden (US: The Swingin' Maiden). 1963: Nurse on Wheels. Carry On Cabby. Carry On Jack (US: Carry On Venus). 1964: Carry On Spying. Carry On Cleo. 1965: The Big Job. Carry On Cowboy. 1966: Carry On Screaming. Don't Lose Your Head. 1967: Follow That Camel. 1968: Carry On Doctor. Carry On Up the Khyber. 1969: Carry On Camping. Carry On Again, Doctor. 1970: Carry On Up the Jungle. Carry On Loving. 1971: Carry On Henry. Carry On at Your Convenience. 1972: Carry On Matron. Carry On Abroad. Bless This House. 1973: Carry On Girls. 1974: Carry On Dick. 1975: Carry On Behind. 1976: Carry On England. 1977: That's Carry On! (compilation plus new sequences). 1978: Carry On Emmannuelle. 1986: The Second Victory. 1992: Carry on Columbus.

THOMAS, Ralph 1915-

The older brother of Gerald Thomas *(qv)*, who made all the 'Carry On' films, this British director is more associated with mainstream British cinema of the post-war years, although he too has a successful comedy series to his name in the 'Doctor' films. These were also box-office till-breakers in their day, and must be recorded as Ralph Thomas' best-known achievement. In fact he made more dramatic films than his brother even if only a few of these were successful with critics and public alike. Generally speaking, Ralph Thomas had a good, light, breezy style and chose subjects that lent themselves to attractive publicity campaigns. From the late 1950s, however, the quality of his work began to decline along with the standards of stu-

Coming towards the end of his career with a slew of action films, J Lee **Thompson** lays down *Murphy's Law*.

dio-based commercial British cinema, and only *Quest for Love*, itself but a partial success, stands out as a minor gem in his later work. Very briefly a reporter, Thomas joined British Lion in 1934 and became an assistant editor before war service interrupted his career. He joined the Rank Organisation and, after cutting his teeth on trailers, began directing in 1949. He had some success with *The Clouded Yellow*, a very English version of a *film noir*, with a suspenseful climax, but had little subsequent success until *Doctor in the House* in 1953. This collection of old medical jokes, draped across a slim storyline about young trainee doctors, proved to be exactly what the public wanted, starting a run of medical comedies that continued unabated until the early 1970s. Thomas now entered his most successful period, making *Doctor at Sea* (it had Brigitte Bardot as heroine and was the best of the whole series, with razor-sharp comedy direction); a good war film, *Above Us the Waves*, with well-manoeuvred tension and exciting underwater sequences; continuing his profitable association with Dirk Bogarde, a Canada-set outdoor thriller, *Campbell's Kingdom*; a presentable version of *A Tale of Two Cities*, with Bogarde as Sydney Carton; and a moving weepie, *The Wind Cannot Read*, about a doomed romance between an RAF officer and a Japanese girl. But Thomas came unstuck when he attempted to out-Hitch the Master with a version of *The 39 Steps* which lacked flair and fluency, and, as the 1960s progressed, his comedies became broader

and less palatable, ending with the lamentable *Percy* films. But he did make *Quest for Love*, a beguiling piece of science-fiction about parallel worlds, with a tight grip on its subject in the first two and last two reels, but a bit of a sag in the middle. Thomas' career pattern was rather the opposite.

1949: Helter Skelter. Traveller's Joy. Once Upon a Dream. 1950: The Clouded Yellow. 1951: Appointment with Venus (US: Island Rescue). 1952: Venetian Bird (US: The Assassin). 1953: The Dog and the Diamonds. A Day to Remember. Doctor in the House. 1954: Mad About Men. 1955: Doctor at Sea. Above Us the Waves. 1956: Checkpoint. The Iron Petticoat. 1957: Doctor at Large. Campbell's Kingdom. 1958: A Tale of Two Cities. The Wind Cannot Read. 1959: The 39 Steps. Upstairs and Downstairs. 1960: Conspiracy of Hearts. Doctor in Love. 1961: No Love for Johnnie. No, My Darling Daughter! 1962: A Pair of Briefs. The Wild and the Willing. 1963: Doctor in Distress. Hot Enough for June (US: Agent 8¾). 1964: The High, Bright Sun (US: McGuire, Go Home!). 1965: Doctor in Clover (US: Carnaby M.D.). 1966: Deadlier Than the Male. 1968: Nobody Runs Forever. 1969: Some Girls Do. 1970: Doctor in Trouble. Percy. 1971: Quest for Love. 1972: The Love Ban. 1974: Percy's Progress (US: It's Not the Size That Counts). 1979: The Biggest Bank Robbery (TV).

THOMPSON, J. Lee 1914-

Despite the fact that he did nothing of real note after 1962, and had many depressing failures in the years between then and 1989, Thompson is still rightly remembered as a teenage prodigy who had a good track record in the British cinema from 1950 until 1961. It was perhaps his downfall that, fired by the success of *The Guns of Navarone*, he moved into the field of international spectaculars, at which point his direction seemed to lose its individuality and assume a sluggishness one hadn't noticed before. Thompson had two plays published and performed before he was 20, and contributed a fistful of screenplays to British films, from *Glamorous Night* (1937) to *For Them That Trespass* (1949), before tackling direction on the film version of one of his own plays, the four-hander *Murder Without Crime*. In the next ten years, Thompson surged to the forefront of pre-kitchen sink realism in the British cinema with a series of gloomy dramas, often with downbeat endings: *The Yellow Balloon*, *The Weak and the Wicked*, *Yield to the Night*, *Woman in a Dressing Gown* (from a celebrated TV play) and *No Trees in the Street*. Thompson got strong, sometimes even tortured performances from the principals in these sombre films. In lighter vein, he made a happy little comedy called *For Better, For Worse*, unhappily seldom revived today; it had a string of good individual performances and a warm, real and human feel despite its slapstick touches. *As Long As They're Happy* and *The Good Companions* were two semi-musicals with Janette Scott, the teenage star who had shot into the public eye after appearing in Thompson's screenplay *No Place for Jennifer* in 1949; *Companions* especially (a remake of Jessie Matthews' success of 1932) is full of youthful zest and carries a scintillating dance climax, as well as one of Eric Portman's best performances and commendable use of Technicolor: an unexpectedly enjoyable film. Thompson's easy way with young stars carried over on to his best film, *Tiger Bay*, a moving and exciting thriller, with an unforgettable performance by Hayley Mills on her debut. The film was splendidly paced as, for the most part, were Thompson's two big colour action films, *Northwest Frontier* and *The Guns of Navarone*, the latter a major blockbuster at the box-office. Mention should also be made of *Cape Fear*, a violent, tense and chilling black thriller with Gregory Peck and Robert Mitchum which, for sheer intensity, outdoes the Martin Scorsese remake of 1991. And so to the veil that must be drawn over most of what followed. Well, perhaps not quite: a TV movie in 1972, *A Great American*

Tragedy, was a return to the more intimate dramas with which Thompson made his name. It featured powerful performances by George Kennedy and Vera Miles as the couple whose cosy and comfortable life falls apart when he unexpectedly loses his job, and a perceptive, adult and believable script (by Caryl Ledner) adroitly handled by the director. There was a brief revival in the 1980s, with a feisty, underrated variant on *King Solomon's Mines* and a sober, well-acted political/action drama *The Ambassador*. Thereafter, the director's career subsided in a morass of slickly made but very middling vehicles for action stars Charles Bronson and Chuck Norris.

1950: *Murder Without Crime*. 1952: *The Yellow Balloon*. 1953: *The Weak and the Wicked* (US: *Young and Willing*). 1954: *For Better, For Worse* (US: *Cocktails in the Kitchen*). 1955: *As Long As They're Happy*. *An Alligator Named Daisy*. 1956: *Yield to the Night* (US: *Blonde Sinner*). 1957: *The Good Companions*. *Woman in a Dressing Gown*. 1958: *Ice-Cold in Alex* (US: *Desert Attack*). 1959: *No Trees in the Street*. *Tiger Bay*. *Northwest Frontier* (US: *Flame Over India*). 1960: *I Aim at the Stars*. 1961: *The Guns of Navarone*. 1962: *Cape Fear*. *Taras Bulba*. 1963: *Kings of the Sun*. 1964: *What a Way to Go! John Goldfarb, Please Come Home*. 1965: *Return from the Ashes*. 1966: *Eye of the Devil*. 1968: *Mackenna's Gold*. 1969: *The Chairman* (US: *The Most Dangerous Man in the World*). *Country Dance* (US: *Brotherly Love*). 1972: *Conquest of the Planet of the Apes*. *A Great American Tragedy* (TV. GB: *Man at the Crossroads*). 1973: *Battle for the Planet of the Apes*. 1974: *Huckleberry Finn*. *The Reincarnation of Peter Proud*. 1975: *Widow* (TV). *The Blue Knight* (TV). 1976: *St Ives*. 1977: *The White Buffalo*. 1978: *The Greek Tycoon*. *The Passage*. 1980: *Cabo Blanco*. 1981: *Happy Birthday to Me*. *Code Red* (TV). 1982: *10 to Midnight*. 1983: *The Evil That Men Do*. 1984: *The Ambassador*. 1985: *King Solomon's Mines*. 1986: *Murphy's Law*. *Firewalker*. 1987: *Death Wish IV: The Crackdown*. 1988: *Messenger of Death*. 1989: *Kinjite/Forbidden Subjects*.

THORPE, Richard (Rollo Thorpe) 1896-1991
This American director spent 33 years with the same studio, M-G-M. Anything lightish in weight was a possibility for Thorpe's talents: he was a man with a dry sense of fun who liked making escapist pictures. He was good at staging action sequences and among his best known films are all the M-G-M Tarzans following his

arrival at the studio in 1935, and a series of swashbuckling adventures in the early 1950s featuring Robert Taylor. Thorpe began his career as an actor, and it was in this capacity that he broke into films at the age of 25. By 1923, however, he had begun to direct two-reelers, mostly action-packed western featurettes. He continued directing minor westerns and thrillers when he moved into features in 1924 and did little of note before joining M-G-M in 1935. He was to become the longest-serving director in their history. In time he became known as the studio's 'one-take' specialist, replacing Woody Van Dyke (*qv*), previous holder of the title, because of his rapid shooting schedules. Thorpe made routine studio fare until the 1950s, when he was given more important assignments. His biggest money-maker to date was *The Great Caruso*, with Mario Lanza as the famous opera star: it made a four-and-a-half million-dollar profit. He then directed several big-budget productions with Robert Taylor. The most successful of these were three swashbucklers made in England: *Ivanhoe*, *Knights of the Round Table* and *Quentin Durward*, the last of which climaxes with a splendidly staged fight in a bell tower; but all of them have rousing action scenes, handled by Thorpe with great confidence. Thorpe's last big box-office success was Elvis Presley's *Jailhouse Rock*. He also worked briefly in television before retiring in 1968.

1923: **Three O'Clock in the Morning*. **That's That*. 1924: **Battling Buddy*. **Bringin' Home the Bacon*. **Hard Hittin' Hamilton*. **Fast and Fearless*. *Walloping Wallace*. *Gold and Grit*. *Rarin' to Go*. *Rough Ridin'*. 1925: **Double Action Daniels*. **On the Go*. **Fast Fightin'*. *The Desert Demon*. *Saddle Cyclone*. *Full Speed*. 1926: *Rawhide*. *The Bandit Buster*. *The Fighting Cheat*. *Double Daring*. *College Days*. *Josselyn's Wife*. 1927: *The Cyclone Cowboy*. *Between Dangers*. *The Desert of the Lost*. *The Soda Water Cowboy*. *White Pebbles*. *The First Night*. 1928: **The Flyin' Buckaroo*. *The Galloping Gobs*. *Valley of Hunted Men*. *Vultures of the Sea* (serial). *The Vanishing West* (serial). *The Cowboy Cavalier*. *Desperate Courage*. 1929: *The Fatal Warning* (serial). *King of the Kongo* (serial). *The Bachelor Girl*. 1930: *The Lone Defender* (serial). *The Dude Wrangler* (GB: *Feminine Touch*). *The Thoroughbred* (GB: *Riding to Win*). *Border Romance*. *Wings of Adventure*. *The Utah Kid*. *Under Montana Skies*. 1931: *King of the Wild* (serial). *Grief Street* (GB: *Stage Whispers*). *The Lawless Woman*. *The Lady from Nowhere*. †*Wild Horse*. *The Sky Spider*. *Neck and Neck*. *The Devil Plays*. 1932: *Cross Examina-*

tion. Forgotten Women. Murder at Dawn (GB: The Death Ray). Probation (GB: Second Chances). Midnight Lady (GB: Dream Mother). Escapade (GB: Dangerous Ground). Forbidden Company. Beauty Parlor. The King Murder. The Thrill of Youth. Slightly Married. 1933: Women Won't Tell. The Secrets of Wu Sin. Love is Dangerous (GB: Women Are Dangerous). Forgotten. Strange People. Notorious But Nice. I Have Lived. Man of Sentiment. Rainbow Over Broadway. 1934: The Quitter. City Park. Murder on the Campus (GB: At the Stroke of Nine). Stolen Sweets. Green Eyes. Cheating Cheaters. 1935: Secret of the Chateau. Strange Wives. Last of the Pagans. 1936: The Voice of Bugle Ann. Tarzan Escapes! 1937: Dangerous Number. Double Wedding. Night Must Fall. 1938: The First Hundred Years. Man Proof. Love is a Headache. The Toy Wife (GB: Frou Frou). Three Loves Has Nancy. The Crowd Roars. 1939: The Adventures of Huckleberry Finn. Tarzan Finds a Son! 1940: The Earl of Chicago. Wyoming (GB: Bad Man of Wyoming). Twenty Mule Team. 1941: Barnacle Bill. Tarzan's Secret Treasure. The Bad Man (GB: Two-Gun Cupid). 1942: Apache Trail. White Cargo. Tarzan's New York Adventure. Joe Smith, American (GB: Highway to Freedom). 1943: Three Hearts for Julia. Above Suspicion. Cry Havoc! 1944: Two Girls and a Sailor. The Thin Man Goes Home. 1945: Thrill of a Romance. What Next, Corporal Hargrove? Her Highness and the Bellboy. 1947: Fiesta. This Time for Keeps. 1948: A Date with Judy. On an Island with You. 1949: Big Jack. The Sun Comes Up. Challenge to Lassie. Malaya (GB: East of the Rising Sun). 1950: Black Hand. Three Little Words. 1951: †It's a Big Country. The Great Caruso. Vengeance Valley. The Unknown Man. 1952: Carbine Williams. Ivanhoe. The Prisoner of Zenda. 1953: The Girl Who Had Everything. All the Brothers Were Valiant. 1954: Knights of the Round Table. Athena. The Student Prince. The Flame and the Flesh. 1955: The Adventures of Quentin Durward (US: Quentin Durward). 1957: Ten Thousand Bedrooms. Tip on a Dead Jockey (GB: Time for Action). Jailhouse Rock. 1959: The House of the Seven Hawks. Killers of Kilimanjaro. 1960: The Tartars. 1961: The Honeymoon Machine. 1962: The Horizontal Lieutenant. 1963: Follow the Boys. Fun in Acapulco. 1964: The Golden Head. The Truth About Spring. 1965: That Funny Feeling. 1966: The Scorpio Letters (originally for TV). 1967: The Last Challenge (GB: The Pistolero of Red River).

TOKAR, Norman 1920-1979

One gets the feeling that this American director would probably have been at home directing the Marx Brothers. Although almost all of his films were made for the Walt Disney organisation, Tokar's wild sense of humour was allowed full play in several films which have plenty of belly-laughs for sophisticates. He also had a rich flair for colour composition, and the more dramatic of his films are speckled with memorable images. The funster in him was not immediately evident when he joined Disney in 1961 after a mixed career of acting, writing and directing. Of his first films, *Savage Sam* is a good blood-and-thunder western for youngsters with some splendid visual moments, and *Follow Me Boys!* an enjoyable and much-underrated piece of Americana with lovely colour composition, an amiable rambling story and invaluable supporting contributions from Charlie Ruggles, Lillian Gish and a talented ginger cat. There were a few clinkers in Tokar's record, too, notably *The Ugly Dachshund* and *The Horse in the Gray Flannel Suit,* but, from *The Boatniks* to *The Cat From Outer Space,* the fun fizzed fast and furious, with only *Where the Red Fern Grows* (not for Disney) and *No Deposit, No Return* missing out in Tokar's run of hits. The best and funniest of these films is *Snowball Express,* a sort of *Mr Blandings Builds His Dream House* on skis, full of delightful throwaway lines and with a priceless study in continual bewilderment from Dean Jones. Tokar's direction never lets up on the pace of the thing, and makes the most of the barrage of funny situations devised by his three screenwriters.

1962: Sammy the Way-Out Seal (TV. GB: cinemas). Big Red. 1963: Savage Sam. A Tiger Walks. 1964: Those Calloways. 1965: The Ugly Dachshund. 1966: Follow Me Boys! 1967: The Happiest Millionaire. 1968: The Horse in the Gray Flannel Suit. 1969: Rascal. 1970: The Boatniks. 1972: Snowball Express. 1974: Where the Red Fern Grows. The Apple Dumpling Gang. 1976: No Deposit, No Return. 1977: Candleshoe. 1978: The Cat From Outer Space.

TORRE NILSSON, Leopoldo 1924-1978

Argentina's only world-famous director, unless one counts the cosmopolitan Hugo Fregonese, Torre Nilsson made gloomy, sometimes socially critical dramas. Probably his prestige was at its highest in the early 1960s, when international audiences saw for the first time such films as *La Casa del Angel, La Caida* and *Fin de Fies-*

ta. These are intriguingly, plotted melodramas, full of fiercely black, brooding photography, usually written by the director's wife, novelist Beatriz Guido. But it is unwise (and easy) to overestimate these films, simply because they are from a part of the world not known for its cinematic achievements. In terms of technique and power, they do not compare to the best films from, say, Hollywood, France or Italy on similar subjects. When still a teenager, he was assisting his father, director Leopoldo Torres-Rios (1899-1960) and his first, faltering attempts at feature films were co-directed with Torre's-Rios. From the mid-1950s, though, he began to put his own stamp on films, the themes of which often dealt with disillusionment with people and causes, and absolute corruption through absolute power. The political climate of his native country was not helpful to the kind of films Torre Nilsson turned out, however, but he chose not to move outside Argentina, although internal pressures made him turn to other kinds of cinema from the late 1960s onwards. His reputation declined accordingly. To appreciate the impact he made when free to make films exactly the way he wanted, with their reminders of Buñuel and Welles, one should look principally at the Torre Nilsson films shot between 1957 and 1964. One can't help feeling that a move to, say, France or Mexico would have lent greater fulfilment to his career.

*1947: *La Mura. 1950. †El Crimen de Oribe. 1953: †El Hijo del Crack. 1954: Dias de Odio (GB & US: Days of Hate). La Tigra. 1955: Para vestir Santos. 1956: Graciela. El Protegido. 1957: La Casa del Angel (GB: House of the Angel. US: End of Innocence). 1958: El Secuestrador (GB & US: The Kidnapper). 1959: La Caida (GB: The Fall). 1960: Fin de Fiesta (US: The Party is Over). Un Guapo del 900. 1961: La Mano en la Trampa (GB & US: Hand in the Trap). Piel de Verano (GB & US: Summer Skin). 1962: Setenta Veces Siete (US: The Female. Seventy Times Seven). Homenaje a la Hora de la Siesta (GB: Four Women for One Hero). 1963: La Terrazza (GB & US: The Terrace). 1964: The Eavesdropper. 1966: Cavar un Fosso. 1967: Chica del Lunes/Monday's Child. Traitors of San Angel. 1968: Martin Fierro. 1970: El Santo de la Espada (US: Knight of the Sword). 1971: La Maffia. 1972: Guemes: la Tierra en Armas. 1973: Los Siete Locos (US: Seven Mad Men). 1974: Boquitas Pintadas (US: Painted Lips). 1975: Diario de la Guerra del Credo. Los Gauchos Judios. 1976: El Pibe Cabeza. 1977: Piedra Libre.*

TOURNEUR, Jacques 1904-1977

Given half-an-ounce of good material to work with, Tourneur would weave together a good movie. Tourneur liked to make colourful pictures, literally and figuratively and, although he is chiefly remembered as the director of some spine-chilling chillers reticent in their showing of overt horror, he worked with imagination in a number of other genres. His skill at editing a film and maintaining its rhythm, whether easy-going or tense, probably stemmed from his long apprenticeship with his father, Maurice (qv). They worked together in Hollywood, where Tourneur lived and worked from 1914 to 1928 and again from 1935 to 1964, and in France, where he was born and where he made his feature film debut in 1931. But he did not win widespread praise for his direction until he moved from M-G-M to RKO in 1942 and was chosen by producer Val Lewton (the two men had worked together on crowd scenes for the 1935 version of A Tale of Two Cities) to direct the initial ventures in a series of low-budget horror films which, unknown to the studio, were to be horrors of light, shade and suggestion, rather than blood and gore. When they saw rushes of Cat People, studio executives wanted Tourneur removed, but Lewton outsmarted them and Tourneur was allowed to complete the film, which became an unexpected success and ensured financial backing for the rest of the series. Tourneur and Lewton parted company after three films — the second, I Walked with a Zombie, is also very shivery in an atmospheric sort of way, being a zombie-oriented transportation of Jane Eyre to the West Indies. Tourneur later regretted the parting and it was some years before he created his next wholly successful film, Out of the Past, one of the best noir thrillers of the 1940s, with a sense of death and doom hanging over all. In the late 1940s, Tourneur began free-lancing for various studios: The Flame and the Arrow is a vivid and enjoyable swashbuckler from the heart of Burt Lancaster's acrobatic period; Anne of the Indies crisp and fast-moving with enough action for half-a-dozen pirate pictures; Way of a Gaucho an unusual semi-western, well-made and a last, blazing Technicolor tribute to the beauty of Gene Tierney; Great Day in the Morning (back at RKO) a western proper and a superior one at that, Tourneur carving out real characters; and Nightfall a fast-moving flashback thriller with nicely timed excitement, good acting and crisp black-and-white photography. In his later years, Tourneur made two returns to the horror field: there are some jumpy moments in

Night of the Demon, especially a flight through a forest, but the action and dialogue let it down time and again. The Comedy of Terrors, however, is priceless. A splendid cast headed by Boris Karloff, Vincent Price, Peter Lorre and Basil Rathbone go full tilt at a spoof horror film about two undertakers who drum up business for themselves. It is the best film of its kind ever made, and created within the kind of small set-up where Tourneur revealed himself to be happiest.

1931: Tout ça ne vaut pas l'amour. 1933: Pour être aimé. Toto. 1934: Les filles de la concierge. 1936: *Harnessed Rhythm. *The Jonker Diamond. *Killer-Dog. *Master Will Shakespeare. 1937: *What Do You Think? (series). *The Boss Didn't Say Good Morning. *The Grand Bounce. *The King Without a Crown. *The Man in the Barn. *Romance of Radium. *The Rainbow Pass. 1938: *The Face Behind the Mask. *The Ship That Died. *Strange Glory. *Think It Over. 1939: *Yankee Doodle Goes to Town. They All Come Out (semi-D). Nick Carter – Master Detective. 1940: Phantom Raiders. 1941: Doctors Don't Tell. 1942: *The Magic Alphabet. *The Incredible Stranger. Cat People. 1943: I Walked with a Zombie. The Leopard Man. Days of Glory. 1944: Experiment Perilous. 1946: Canyon Passage. 1947: Out of the Past (GB: Build My Gallows High). 1948: Berlin Express. 1949: Easy Living. Stars in My Crown. 1950: The Flame and the Arrow. 1951: Circle of Danger. Anne of the Indies. 1952: Way of a Gaucho. 1953: Appointment in Honduras. 1955: Stranger on Horseback. Wichita. Great Day in the Morning. 1956: Nightfall. 1957: Night of the Demon (US: Curse of the Demon). 1958: †Fury River. Timbuktu. The Fearmakers. 1959: †Frontier Rangers. Mission of Danger. The Giant of Marathon. 1963: The Comedy of Terrors. 1965: War Gods of the Deep (GB: City Under the Sea).

TOURNEUR, Maurice (M. Thomas) 1876-1961

The father of Jacques Tourneur (qv), this French director shared his son's talent for tales of mystery and imagination, including (in 1912) what must be the earliest version of Edgar Allan Poe's The System of Doctor Tarr and Professor Fether, the forerunner of the lunatics-running-the-asylum stories which have remained popular throughout the history of the cinema. Forced to retire only in 1949 after losing a leg in a car accident, Tourneur must have cursed himself for not being able to work in 3-D (be would have been an ideal director of Warners' Phantom of the Rue Morgue, based on another Poe story),

since he was obsessed with depth and pictorial beauty as a means to give life and atmosphere to a film. Clearly, he was the perfect director for Maeterlinck's The Blue Bird, which he made in 1918, with its picaresque adventures and its atmosphere of ethereal loveliness. His style of film-making was outdated by the 1920s; his films were still notable then for their fluid camerawork and ravishing pictorial style (especially Treasure Island, The Christian and Aloma of the South Seas) and carried A-budget production values, but seemed too slow for Jazz Age tastes. After a quarrel over the making of Mysterious Island in 1926, he left Hollywood after a 12-year stay there, and returned to France. Here he found his reputation undiminished, and the resentment engendered when he had gone to America in 1914, thus not having had to fight in World War I, had almost vanished. Tourneur settled down to making films at a less hectic rate than in Hollywood, many of them romantic historical spectacles. After his enforced retirement, he devoted his ever-active brain to the translation of American literature into French.

1912: Jean La Poudre. Le friquet. The System of Doctor Tarr and Professor Fether (US: The Lunatics). Figures de cire. Rouletabille, Pt I: Le mystère de la chambre jaune. Rouletabille, Pt II: La dernière incarnation de Larsan. 1913: Le denier pardon. Soeurette. Le puits mitoyen. Le camée. Le corseau rouge. Mademoiselle cents millions. Les gaîtés de l'escadron. La dame de Montsoreau. 1914: Monsieur Lecoq. Mother. The Man of the Hour. The Wishing Ring. The Pit. 1915: Alias Jimmy Valentine. The Cub. The Ivory Snuff Box. The Butterfly on the Wheel. Trilby. 1916: †Human Driftwood. The Pawn of Fate. The Hand of Peril. The Closed Road. The Rail Rider. The Velvet Paw. 1917: A Girl's Folly. The Whip. The Undying Flame. Exile. The Law of the Land. Barbary Sheep. The Pride of the Clan. Poor Little Rich Girl. The Rise of Jenny Cushing. 1918: Rose of the World. The Blue Bird. Woman. A Doll's House. Prunella. Sporting Life. 1919: The White Heather. The Broken Butterfly. The Life Line. Victory. 1920: †County Fair. My Lady's Garter. Treasure Island. The White Circle. The Great Redeemer. Deep Waters. †The Last of the Mohicans. 1921: †The Foolish Matrons. The Bait. While Paris Sleeps (released 1923). 1922: Lorna Doone. 1923: The Christian. Isle of Lost Ships. The Brass Bottle. Jealous Husbands. 1924: Torment. The White Moth. 1925: †Clothes Make the Pirate. Sporting Life (remake). Never the Twain Shall Meet. 1926: Old Loves and New. Aloma of the South Seas. †*Mysterious Island* (uncredited. Released 1929). 1927: *L'équipage* (GB: *The Crew*. US: *The Last Flight*). 1929: *Das Schiff der verlorene Menschen*. 1930: *Accusée — levez-vous!* 1931: *Partir. Maison de danses*. 1932: *Au nom de la loi. Les gaîtés de l'escadron* (remake). *Lidoire*. 1933: *Les deux Orphelines. Obsession*. 1934: *Le voleur*. 1935: *Justin de Marseilles*. 1936: *Koenigsmark* (and English version: *Crimson Dynasty*). *Samson. With a Smile*. 1937: *Le patriote* (US: *The Mad Emperor*). 1938: *Katia*. 1940: *Volpone*. 1941: *Péchés de jeunesse* (US: *Sins of Youth*). *Mam'zelle Bonaparte*. 1942: *La main du Diable* (GB: *The Devil's Hand*. US: *Carnival of Sinners*). 1943: *Le val d'Enfer*. 1944: *Cécile est morte*. 1947: *Après l'amour*. 1948: *L'impasse des deux anges*.

TRUFFAUT, François 1932-1984

This distinguished French film-maker was an extraordinary man to pin down, in that he almost never made the same kind of film twice, and his films varied infuriatingly from very good to mediocre. There are autobiographical elements in many of them, which are veined with ideas of childhood, loneliness, women, mothers and obsessional objects. Doubtless a lot of Truffaut was poured into his first big success, *The 400 Blows*, a splendidly evocative portrayal of a desolate childhood which made his name at 27, allowing him a lifetime to offer us different aspects on his love of the cinema. It was a story hard-earned, however. Sent to live with his grandmother until he was eight, he was a miserable, isolated child at school, spent a period in reform school in his early teens; joined the army but deserted. Writing and the cinema came to his rescue, and, after being a critic of the *nouvelle vague* school, he began making shorts from 1955. *The 400 Blows*, which won Truffaut the best director award at the Cannes Festival, was followed by four sequels, all about the same character. They are not, however, among Truffaut's strongest films, since the young star, Jean-Pierre Léaud, matured into a less interesting actor as an adult. Nonetheless, several Truffaut films still haunt the memory down the years, a sign of a very individual talent at work: *Fahrenheit 451*, though not liked by many, is a most unusual, vividly handled and bitingly edited piece of science-fiction; *Jules et Jim* a touching and tender love triangle luminously shot in black-and-white and delicately directed; *The Bride Wore Black* and *Une belle fille comme moi* multi-layered thrillers about vengeful women, both stacked with telling little moments; and *Day for Night*, perhaps his most popular film (about the ramifications of the actual making of a film), won the Academy Award that year (1974) for the best foreign-language picture. Truffaut has not quite matched it since. His films became a shade too self-conscious in their effects, and in 1975 he made his first totally tedious film in *The Story of Adele H.* But no matter: his immense talent made itself felt again when properly applied. Meanwhile he has left us with the definitive image of himself in *Day for Night*, a recurring vision which haunts the mind's eye of the director of the film-within-a-film, of a boy with a cane, padding alone down a dark street. Eventually it is seen that he is stealthily creeping up on the local cinema. He reaches it, steals all the front-of-house stills from *Citizen Kane* and runs away. One wonders if Truffaut, who found the affection the boy of the films and he himself craved, through his audience, kept the stills in his attic... A brain tumour killed him at 52.

A leading role in one of his own films for François **Truffaut** in *The Story of Adèle H.*

1955: *Une visite. 1957: *Les mistons (GB & US: *The Mischief Makers*). 1958: †**Une histoire d'eau*. 1959: *Les quatre cents coups* (GB & US: *The 400 Blows*). 1960: *Tirez sur le pianiste* (GB: *Shoot the Pianist*. US: *Shoot the Piano Player*). 1962: *Jules et Jim/Jules and Jim*. †*L'amour à vingt ans* (GB & US: *Love at Twenty*). 1964: *La peau douce* (GB: *Silken Skin*. US: *The Soft Skin*). 1966: *Fahrenheit 451*. 1967: *La mariée était en noir* (GB & US: *The Bride Wore Black*). 1968: *Baisers volés* (GB & US: *Stolen Kisses*). 1969: *L'enfant sauvage* (GB & US: *The Wild Child*). *La sirène du Mississippi* (US: *Mississippi Mermaid*). 1970: *Domicile conjugale* (GB & US: *Bed and Board*). 1971: *Les deux anglaises sur le continent* (GB: *Anne and Muriel*. US: *Two English Girls*). 1972: *Une belle fille comme moi* (GB: *A Gorgeous Bird Like Me*. US: *Such a Gorgeous Kid Like Me*). 1973: *La nuit américaine* (GB & US: *Day for Night*). 1975: *L'histoire d'Adèle H* (GB & US: *The Story of Adèle H*). 1976: *L'argent de poche* (GB & US: *Small Change*). 1977: *L'homme qui aimait les femmes* (GB & US: *The Man Who Loved*

Women). 1978: La chambre verte (US: The Green Room). 1979: L'amour en fuite (GB & US: Love on the Run). 1980: Le dernier métro (GB & US: The Last Metro). 1981: La femme d'à côté (GB & US: The Woman Next Door). 1983: Vivement dimanche (GB: Finally, Sunday! US: The Long Saturday Night).

TULLY, Montgomery (Geoffrey M. Tully) 1904-
One of the principal makers of 60- and 30-minute crime thrillers for the British cinema of the 1950s, this Irish director allowed little humour into his stern tales of murder and mystery, but could lift poor material into the mediocre, and fair material into a good film. A former journalist and writer (he continued to write for films until 1946), Tully joined Publicity Films, makers of industrial documentaries, from 1929, working at their Merton Park Studios, where, many years later, he was to make so many of his 'B' features. Although Tully worked on many documentaries for the company in collaboration with others, his first credit with them as director came on *From Acorn to Oak* in 1937, made for the Dunlop Tyre Company, with inventively staged historical sequences inset into its story of tyre development. Tully remained with Publicity until World War II. Then, from 1945, he struck out as a feature director. His first feature film, *Murder in Reverse*, was a crime thriller with William Hartnell and a good one, with an ingenious plot. *Boys in Brown* was a story of reform school boys, popular in its day but rather dated now, and made in 'independent frame' which blended natural background with studio foregrounds, supposedly more effective than mere back-projection but very short-lived as an experiment. From 1954, Tully became involved in the 'Scotland Yard' series of featurettes which examined the police force's forensic methods of solving crime. These little films were sometimes quite grisly in content and varied greatly in quality, some packing quite a punch for their size. Although they vary in length between 28 and 35 minutes, they have all been designated as short films in the list below. In the mid-1950s, Tully made several films with visiting American stars struggling to keep their careers going after the break-up of the studio system. One of these, *Dial 999*, with Gene Nelson and Mona Freeman, proved to be Tully's best film, and was widely praised by trade-paper and magazine reviewers (as a 'B' feature it was not shown to the national press). A taut thriller about a man on the run, it made its audience grip the sides of their seats in suspense, stretching their nerves tighter and tighter. In his later

years, Tully made a few simple comedies and another crime thriller with William Hartnell. But neither was at his best and the film, *Jackpot*, was no jackpot for anyone. The best of his later films is *The Third Alibi*, a well-acted, punchy thriller.

*1937: *From Acorn to Oak (D). 1940: *Behind the Guns (D). 1941: *Salute to the Farmers (D). 1945: Murder in Reverse. 1946: Spring Song. 1947: Mrs Fitzherbert. 1949: Boys in Brown. 1951: †A Tale of Five Cities (US: A Tale of Five Women). 1952: Girdle of Gold. 1953: Small Town Story. 1954: The Diamond (US: Diamond Wizard). Five Days (US: Paid to Kill). Devil's Point (US: Devil's Harbor). *Late Night Final. *The Silent Witness. 36 Hours (US: Terror Street). 1955: The Glass Cage (US: The Glass Tomb). Dial 999 (US: The Way Out). 1956: *Person Unknown. *Wall of Death. *The Case of the River Morgue. *Destination Death. *The Lonely House. *Inside Information. No Road Back. The Counterfeit Plan. 1957: *The Case of the Smiling Widow. *Night Crossing. *The White Cliff Mystery. The Hypnotist (US: Scotland Yard Dragnet). The Key Man. Man in the Shadow. *Print of Death. 1958: Escapement (later Zex. US: The Electronic Monster). Strange Awakening (US: Female Fiends). *The Crossroad Gallows. *Crime of Honour. The Long Knife. Man with a Gun. Diplomatic Corpse. I Only Arsked! 1959: Man Accused. 1960: Dead Lucky. Jackpot. The Price of Silence. The House in Marsh Road. The Man Who Was Nobody. 1961: The Middle Course. The Third Alibi. Two Wives at One Wedding. 1962: She Knows Y'Know! Out of the Fog. 1963: Master Spy. Clash by Night (US: Escape by Night). 1964: *Boy with a Flute. 1966: Who Killed the Cat? 1967: The Terrornauts. Battle Beneath the Earth. 1968: The Hawks.*

TUTTLE, Frank 1892-1963
American director of quality fare through three decades whose career was stopped in its tracks by the McCarthy witch-hunt in 1947 — even though he was a 'friendly' witness. Today, he is one of the most neglected of directors, though more than once his films were responsible for starting 'cycles' of popularity. Resident at Paramount for 24 years, Tuttle joined the studio in 1921 after a career in journalism. He soon began to direct, but continued to mix writing with direction until 1925: after that he only occasionally contributed to the screenplays of his own films. His films in the 1920s are mainly about working girls going places; they were almost all smart, pacy modern dra-

mas, hot on melodrama and sex appeal, with such stars as Clara Bow (six films), Bebe Daniels (four), Gloria Swanson, Louise Brooks, Evelyn Brent and Nancy Carroll. One of the Clara Bow films, *Kid Boots*, introduced Eddie Cantor to cinema audiences and, when talkies came, Tuttle directed the pop-eyed comedian again in one of his big Goldwyn comedy-musicals *Roman Scandals*. Paramount seemed to see it as their cue to shunt Tuttle on to a whole string of comedies with music, several of them featuring Bing Crosby. But he also made several innovative crime films for them, notably the first version of Dashiell Hammett's *The Glass Key*, with Edward Arnold, George Raft and Guinn 'Big Boy' Williams in the roles later filled by Brian Donlevy, Alan Ladd and William Bendix in 1942, just after Ladd had shot to stardom in Tuttle's own *This Gun for Hire*. Tuttle directed Ladd again in *Lucky Jordan* and, much later, in virtually the last of the hard-hitting old-style gangster movies — Warners' *Hell on Frisco Bay*, teaming Ladd with Edward G. Robinson, Joanne Dru, Paul Stewart and Fay Wray. Tuttle was not blacklisted after his 1947 testimony to the House Un-American Activities Committee, admitting his former Communist affiliations, but it was difficult for him to find work in Hollywood until Warners employed him in the mid-1950s for some television and a few films — by which time he was in any case close to retirement. But he had made an important contribution to the careers of several key Paramount stars, and his work, always lively and professional, should not be forgotten.

*1922: The Cradle Buster. 1923: Puritan Passions. Second Fiddle. Youthful Cheaters. 1924: *Peter Stuyvesant. Grit. Dangerous Money. *The Puritans. 1925: The Manicure Girl. A Kiss in the Dark. Miss Bluebeard. Lucky Devil. Lovers in Quarantine. 1926: The Untamed Lady. The American Venus. Kid Boots. Love 'Em and Leave 'Em. 1927: Blind Alleys. Time to Love. The Spotlight. One Woman to Another. 1928: Easy Come, Easy Go. His Private Life. Love and Learn. Varsity. Something Always Happens. 1929: Marquis Preferred. The Studio Murder Mystery. Sweetie. The Greene Murder Case. Men Are Like That. 1930: The Benson Murder Case. Only the Brave. True to the Navy. †Paramount on Parade. Love Among the Millionaires. Her Wedding Night. 1931: No Limit. It Pays to Advertise. Dude Ranch. This is the Night. 1932: This Reckless Age. The Big Broadcast. 1933: Dangerously Yours. Roman Scandals. Pleasure Cruise. 1934: Ladies Should Listen. Here is My Heart. Springtime for*

Henry. 1935: All the King's Horses. The Glass Key. Two for Tonight. 1936: College Holiday. 1937: Waikiki Wedding. 1938: Doctor Rhythm. 1939: Paris Honeymoon. I Stole a Million. Charlie McCarthy — Detective. 1942: This Gun for Hire. Lucky Jordan. 1943: Hostages. 1944: The Hour Before the Dawn. 1945: Don Juan Quilligan. The Great John L. (GB: A Man Called Sullivan). 1946: Suspense. Swell Guy. 1950: Le traqué (GB: Gunman in the Streets. US: Time Running Out). 1951: Magic Face. 1955: Hell on Frisco Bay. 1956: A Cry in the Night. 1959: Island of Lost Women.

ULMER, Edgar G. 1900-1972

Of all the directors of shoestring movies made for Hollywood 'Poverty Row' studios, none is more revered today than Austrian-born Edgar G. Ulmer. How Ulmer failed to become one of the major directors of the screen is among the cinema's great mysteries, although, in a way, he helped to dig his own grave. He was so good at making commercial, well-reviewed, profitable films out of the small change in the producer's pocket that he became trapped in that field. One senses from interviews that he enjoyed the challenge, yet regretted the opportunities that might be passing him by. His best films have an edge, a kind of intensity that carries them beyond the (severe) limitations of their budgets. Ulmer was a highly intelligent man with a vivid imagination, a caustic sense of humour and a brain that was forever ticking away on some new refinement to improve his work. He studied architecture at the Academy of Arts and Sciences in Vienna, went on to a philosophy course at Vienna University, and was a set decorator at 20, on such films as *Sodom and Gomorrah* and *The Golem*. He was first in America in 1923, as a set decorator for the great Max Reinhardt and, after periods in Germany, America, then Germany again, during which he co-directed – with Robert Siodmak (qv) – his first film, *Menschen am Sonntag*, he returned to Hollywood for good in 1930. Throughout the 1930s, while working as writer or production designer, Ulmer was struggling to obtain work as a director. For the 12 years until

he was offered regular employment by Hollywood's poorest studio (PRC), Ulmer made tiny westerns, films in Ukrainian, Yiddish and Mexican, obscure documentaries and films for black audiences. Scrape the films from the darkest corners of the cinema's vaults and you are bound to find an Ulmer among them. Most of his films were made in less than a week, yet they include: *Bluebeard*, with a restrained John Carradine as a mad puppeteer doing away with women in 19th-century Paris (Ulmer designed the sets too); *Detour*, a minimal murder melodrama with an overhanging sense of doom and first-person narration; *The Black Cat*, raw stylized Gothic with Karloff and Lugosi, the latter taking a rare turn on the side of good; *Murder is My Beat*, made for what looks like about ten dollars, but a good, meaty detective story, with a Chandleresque air about it; and *The Naked Dawn*, a fierce little western with Arthur Kennedy typically as a good-bad bandit. Ulmer once said that his left hand was entirely concerned with the box-office while his right was trying to create art and decency with a style. Although there were a few clinkers that defied even his quirky talents, few would deny that Ulmer served these dual masters to the best of his considerable ability. The list that follows does not include two-reel westerns that Ulmer is said to have made in 1925 and 1926. The Library of Congress copyright catalogues include no Ulmer credits for these years, although he may have worked under assumed names.

*1929: †Menschen am Sonntag (GB & US: People on Sunday). 1933: Damaged Lives. Mister Broadway. 1934: The Black Cat. †Thunder Over Texas. 1935: From Nine to Nine. 1937: Natalka Poltavka. †Greene Felde/Green Fields. 1938: Yankel dem Schmidt/The Singing Blacksmith. 1939: Die Klatsche/The Light Ahead. Zaprosh za Dunayem/Cossacks in Exile. Fishke der Drume/Fishke the Cripple. Moon Over Harlem. The Dobbin. 1940: Americaner Schadchen/American Matchmaker. *Cloud in the Sky (D). 1941: *Another to Conquer (D). *Let My People Live (D). 1942: †Prisoner of Japan. Tomorrow We Live (GB: The Man with a Conscience). 1943: My Son the Hero. Isle of Forgotten Sins. Girls in Chains. Jive Junction (GB: Swing High). 1944: Bluebeard. 1945: Out of the Night (GB: Strange Illusion). Club Havana. Detour. 1946: The Wife of Monte Cristo. Her Sister's Secret. The Strange Woman. 1947: Carnegie Hall. 1948: Ruthless. 1949: The Pirates of Capri/Captain Sirocco (GB: The Masked Pirate). 1951: St Benny the Dip (GB: Escape If You Can). The Man from Planet X. 1952: Babes in Bagdad. 1954: Murder*

Is My Beat. 1955: The Naked Dawn. 1957: The Perjurer. The Daughter of Dr Jekyll. 1959: Hannibal. 1960: The Amazing Transparent Man. Beyond the Time Barrier. 1961: †L'Atlantide (GB: Atlantis, the Lost Continent. US: Journey Beneath the Desert). 1964: The Cavern.

† as John Warner

UNDERWOOD, Ron 1953-

Light comedies, light romances and even light horror films make up the sparse movie output of this California-born director who made his name on television with some highly original children's entertainments including the award-winning *The Mouse and the Motorcycle*. He began his film career with *Tremors*, a creature feature with an endearing sense of humour: pretty exciting too once it hit its stride. *City Slickers*, a vehicle for Billy Crystal, also had its share of humour and excitement. Almost all of its story about three urban work hacks on a 'cowboy' holiday worked well, with an exciting sense of camera movement adding to the enjoyment. Since then, Underwood has hit slightly choppier waters with the romantic comedies *Heart and Souls* and *Speechless*, neither of which fulfilled their potential.

1990: Tremors. 1991: City Slickers. 1993: Heart and Souls. 1995: Speechless.

USTINOV, Peter 1921-

Ustinov has become an increasingly rare migrant to the director's chair and, with his entrenchment as Hercule Poirot in the all-star Agatha Christie mysteries of recent times, it is difficult to believe he will ever sit there again. A pity, for the comedies he has directed are full of hilarious moments and have a brisk surface sparkle (and occasionally very funny cameos from the director himself). Strangely, though, his best film, *Billy Budd*, is a drama and one in which Ustinov himself plays a leading role. A stimulating and engrossing sea story, it has a splendid portrait of evil by Robert Ryan, quite worthy of a best supporting actor Oscar (Ryan wasn't even nominated in the category, although co-star Terence Stamp was) which Ustinov has won twice himself, for *Spartacus* (deservedly) and *Topkapi* (rather less so). Born in London to Anglo-French-Russian parents, Ustinov was something of a teenage genius, making his acting debut at 16 and bringing his mellifluous tones and dry wit to the cinema from 1940. His first film as a director, *School for Secrets*, is his least satisfactory, but he hit form immediately afterwards with *Vice Versa*, a rollicking story about a

Roger **Vadim** returned to the title of one of his most successful early films when he made *And God Created Woman* in 1987.

father and his son (Roger Livesey and Anthony Newley) who exchange roles in life. Ustinov remained an occasional director after that, but, since the failure of *Hammersmith is Out* in 1972, has restricted himself to strolling through films like an amiable panda. *Memed My Hawk* was worse – but there were more Poirot vehicles to go back to. Ustinov has also written a number of screenplays, among them *The Way Ahead*, *School for Secrets*, *Billy Budd* and *Hot Millions*.

1946: *School for Secrets* (US: *Secret Flight*). 1947: *Vice Versa*. 1949: †*Private Angelo*. 1961: *Romanoff and Juliet* (US: *Dig That Juliet*). 1962: *Billy Budd*. 1965: *Lady L*. 1972: *Hammersmith is Out*. 1983: *Memed My Hawk*.

VADIM, Roger (R.V. Plémiannikov) 1927-
This French director who has moulded (and married) some of the world's most beautiful women was hot stuff at the box-offices of the western world from 1956 to 1963, initially with films starring his first wife, Brigitte Bardot. The films themselves were certainly torrid and if dramatically they were not so hot, few minded at that stage. Vadim went on to marry Annette Stroyberg and Jane Fonda and engage in a lengthy liaison with Catherine Deneuve. Fonda starred for him as the sex object in his outer-space fantasy *Barbarella*, a big international hit. Since then, his plots have declined into charades and, without erotic actresses of star quality to appear in them, have appeared increasingly tedious. Vadim learned his art, if that is the word for it, at the feet of another celebrant of beautiful women, Marc Allégret (*qv*), who directed Bardot in her earlier films, when she and Vadim were already married (from December 1952 to December 1957). Vadim took over for *And God Created Woman* and *Heaven Fell That Night*, the two films that confirmed her status as a sex goddess. Vadim's voyeuristic visions drew male audiences in their millions, pushed the frontiers of censorship away, and did the cause of the French cinema no harm, in their own way paving the road for the success of the *nouvelle vague* of the early 1960s. Such blood heat at the box-office could hardly last and in that decade, Vadim began to struggle to keep his place, most notably with a dispiriting version of *La Ronde*. The old chestnut was never really a good idea in the first place, but Vadim's version is infinitely inferior to that of Max Ophüls (*qv*) which at least gave it some atmosphere, quality and grace. Vadim's frequent contributions to his own screen-

plays have hardly been to his credit, but he did extract Angie Dickinson's sexiest performance on screen in *Pretty Maids All in a Row*, otherwise an unhappy venture in Hollywood cinema. After a bizarre last film with Bardot, Vadim returned to Hollywood in the late 1970s. His best work in America, however, has been in television, notably a striking version of *Beauty and the Beast* in 1983, featuring Susan Sarandon and Klaus Kinski.

1956: *Et Dieu créa la femme* (GB: *And Woman . . . Was Created*. US: *And God Created Woman*). 1957: *Sait-on jamais?* (GB: *When the Devil Drives*. US: *No Sun in Venice*). *Les bijoutiers du clair de lune* (GB: *Heaven Fell That Night*. US: *The Night Heaven Fell*). 1959: *Les liaisons dangereuses*. 1960: *Et mourir de plaisir* (GB & US: *Blood and Roses*). 1961: *La bride sur le cou* (GB: *Please, Not Now!*). †*The Seven Deadly Sins*. 1962: *Le vice et la vertu* (GB & US: *Vice and Virtue*). *Le repos du guerrier* (GB: *Warrior's Rest*. US: *Love on a Pillow*). 1963: *Château en suède* (US: *Naughty, Nutty Chateau*). 1964: *La ronde* (US: *Circle of Love*). 1966: *La curée* (GB & US: *The Game is Over*). 1967: *Histoires extraordinaires* ('Metzengerstein' episode. GB: *Tales of Mystery*. US: *Spirits of the Dead*). 1968: *Barbarella*. 1971: *Pretty Maids All in a Row*. 1972: *Hellé*. 1973: *Don-Juan 1973 ou si Don Juan était une femme* (GB: *Don Juan, or if Don Juan Were a Woman*. US: *Ms Don Juan*). 1974: *Charlotte*. 1976: *Une femme fidèle* (GB: *When a Woman in Love. . .*). 1979: *Night Games*. 1981: *The Hot Touch*. 1982: *Comeback*. 1983: *Surprise Party*. 1987: *And God Created Woman* (remake). 1991: *The Mad Lover*.

VAN DYKE, W.S. 1887-1943
Woodbridge Strong Van Dyke II, alias 'One Take Woody', was one of the most colourful characters from Hollywood's most adventurous and confident times. The speed at which he made his films (thus giving rise to his nickname) should not obscure the fact that he directed a great many fine, smoothly made pictures. He was equally at home with the far-flung, often location-shot adventures that dominated the earlier part of his career and with the sophisticated comedies, dramas and musicals that he made when his health forced him to become a studio-bound director in the 1930s. Those who consider Van Dyke to be of little significance should remember that *Barriers Burned Away*, *White Shadows in the South Seas*, *Trader Horn*, *Tarzan the Ape Man*, *The Thin Man* and *San Francisco* were all landmark movies in their day. In his youth a lumberjack, prospector and

gold-miner, Van Dyke came to Hollywood seeking work in 1916. He got himself hired as one of D.W. Griffith's many assistants on *Intolerance*, was taken on at the Lasky Studios for a time, and wrote some westerns for 'Bronco Billy' Anderson before directing minor westerns, making himself a reputation as a fast and efficient maker of serials, then going back to westerns, but on improved budgets and with such stars as Buck Jones and Tim McCoy. With the latter he made a series of 'thinking man's westerns' in the last days of the silents; they adopted positive attitudes on such subjects as the oppression of the Indian, while at the same time making use of natural locations. Van Dyke's interest in native peoples continued when he co-directed *White Shadows in the South Seas* with Robert Flaherty *(qv)*, a very successful Polynesian documentary filmed in difficult conditions, following it with *The Pagan* and *Trader Horn*, for which he went to East Africa (and caught malaria). Van Dyke stayed in the studio for *Tarzan the Ape Man*, with its lyrical photography and tender love story; this was easily the best Tarzan film ever made. Then he made his last film voyage, to the Arctic, to make *Eskimo*. By this time his health was suffering, and M-G-M agreed with his decision to make no more films in distant and inhospitable locations. Instead, he took on the world of the big city, from its slums *(Manhattan Melodrama, The Devil Is a Sissy)* to the skyscrapers with their cocktail-sipping inhabitants. The most personable and enduring product of the latter environment was *The Thin Man*, with William Powell and Myrna Loy as Nick and Nora Charles, verbal sparring-partners and sleuths extraordinary. The characters were so popular that Van Dyke directed three sequels (and was slated for a fourth at the time of his death), the first two almost as good as the initial venture. Van Dyke also showed a flair for the spectacular. Having recreated the great Chicago fire of 1871 in *Barriers Burned Away* (1924), he outdid his own exploits by re-staging, with the help of some brilliant editing and wonderful angled shots, the San Francisco earthquake of 1906 in *San Francisco* (1936). Van Dyke was into his second week of another epic, Pearl Buck's *Dragon Seed*, in 1943, when he was taken ill. He handed over the film to another director, but died from a heart attack soon afterwards. At 55, Van Dyke had done more than most men could hope to do in twice the time.

1917: *The Land of Long Shadows. The Range Boss. The Open Places. Sadie Goes to Heaven. Gift o' Gab. Men of the*

Desert. 1918: *The Lady of the Dugout.* 1919: *Daredevil Jack (serial).* 1920: *The Hawk's Trail (serial). Double Adventure (serial).* 1921: *The Avenging Arrow (serial). White Eagle (serial).* 1922: *According to Hoyle. The Boss of Camp 4. Forget-Me-Not. The Milky Way.* 1923: *The Little Girl Next Door/You Are in Danger. The Destroying Angel. The Miracle Makers. †Ruth of the Range (serial. Uncredited).* 1924: *Loving Lies. The Beautiful Sinner. Half-a-Dollar Bill. Winner Take All. The Battling Fool. Gold Heels. Barriers Burned Away (GB: The Chicago Fire).* 1925: *Hearts and Spurs. The Trail Rider. Timber Wolf. The Ranger of the Big Pines. The Desert's Price.* 1926: *The Gentle Cyclone. War Paint.* 1927: *Winners of the Wilderness. Heart of the Yukon. California. Eyes of the Totem. Foreign Devils. Spoilers of the West.* 1928: *Under the Black Eagle. Wyoming (GB: The Rock of Friendship). †The Adventurer (GB: The Gallant Gringo. Uncredited). †White Shadows in the South Seas.* 1929: *The Pagan.* 1931: *Trader Horn. Never the Twain Shall Meet. Guilty Hands. Cuban Love Song.* 1932: *Night Court (GB: Justice for Sale). Tarzan the Ape Man.* 1933: *Penthouse (GB: Crooks in Clover). The Prizefighter and the Lady (GB: Everywoman's Man).* 1934: *Laughing Boy. Eskimo (GB: Mala the Magnificent). Manhattan Melodrama. Hide-Out. †The Painted Veil (uncredited). The Thin Man. Forsaking All Others.* 1935: *Naughty Marietta. I Live My Life. †A Tale of Two Cities (uncredited).* 1936: *Rose Marie. His Brother's Wife (GB: Lady of the Tropics). San Francisco. The Devil is a Sissy (GB: The Devil Takes the Count). After the Thin Man. Love on the Run.* 1937: *Personal Property (GB: The Man in Possession). They Gave Him a Gun. †The Prisoner of Zenda (uncredited). Rosalie.* 1938: *Marie Antoinette. Sweethearts.* 1939: *Stand Up and Fight. It's a Wonderful World. Another Thin Man. Andy Hardy Gets Spring Fever.* 1940: *I Take This Woman. I Love You Again. Bitter Sweet.* 1941: *Rage in Heaven. The Feminine Touch. Dr Kildare's Victory (GB: The Doctor and the Debutante). Shadow of the Thin Man.* 1942: *I Married an Angel. Cairo. Journey for Margaret.* 1944: *†Dragon Seed (uncredited).*

VAN SANT, Gus (G. Van Sant Jr) 1953-
American director of faintly rough-edged dramas about small-town or small-time people. Many of these characters are not exactly likeable but they do tend to stick in the memory. Now, with his Oscar nomination for *Good Will Hunting*, Van Sant has moved to the forefront of American

independent directors. A producer of commercials and occasional assistant director at New World studios, Van Sant remained on the fringes of the film industry until he was in his mid-thirties. But he then made *Drugstore Cowboy*, a film of no great promise but much quiet achievement. Unexpectedly old-fashioned in construction and development the film's an effective little sermon tinged with wistful regretfulness about married drug-store robbers who, with two confederates, are happy with a lifestyle that 'just didn't pay off', as anti-hero Matt Dillon explains at the end. Van Sant was now able to explore offbeat themes without having to worry too much about distribution problems. *My Own Private Idaho* was an unusual and highly original road movie that covers the mixed fortunes of two gay street hustlers. Since they were played by teen idols River Phoenix and Keanu Reeves, the film enjoyed a wider audience than might have been anticipated. There was very little audience, however, for *Even Cowgirls Get the Blues*, Van Sant's only dud to date. But he was quickly back on track with *To Die For*, a black comedy with a virtuoso performance from Nicole Kidman as an airhead with ambition. This is a work of no small achievement with a terrific ending, with Kidman frighteningly icy as the Barbie doll from Hell. *Good Will Hunting* was a more readily commercial undertaking whose Oscar-winning script by two members of its cast (Matt Damon and Ben Affleck) presented plum acting opportunities that led to co-stars Damon and Minnie Driver receiving Oscar nominations, plus an Academy Award for Robin Williams. Van Sant was also nominated for his absorbing handling of the story of a rebellious 20-year-old genius.

1985: *Mala Noche.* 1987: *Five Ways to Kill Yourself. *Ken Death Gets Out of Jail. *My New Friends.* 1988: **Junior.* 1989: *Drugstore Cowboy.* 1991: *My Own Private Idaho.* 1993: *Even Cowgirls Get the Blues.* 1995: *To Die For.* 1997: *Good Will Hunting.* 1999: *He Won't Get Far.*

VARNEL, Marcel 1894-1947
Britain's king of comedy in the 1930s and 1940s was a small, dapper Frenchman previously best known for staging operettas. It seems an unlikely story. Yet under his guidance, such figures as Will Hay, Arthur Askey, The Crazy Gang and George Formby did 90 percent of their best work for the cinema. Varnel had a great sense of the overall concept of a scene, particularly when it involved elements of escalating disaster – such scenes in his work are always perfectly orga-

nized. He steered the comedy team of Will Hay, Moore Marriott and Graham Moffatt to its greatest successes from 1937 to 1939, encouraging Marriott (the doddery old fool) and Moffatt (the plump, cheeky youth) to stoop and scurry round the bespectacled, befuddled figure of Hay like terriers attacking the ankles of a postman. Varnel's small stature had enabled him to continue playing juveniles on the Paris stage well into his twenties (ironically, as Moffatt was to do under his direction). From 1922, though, Varnel began to direct musical comedies, and in 1925 was asked to come to Broadway, where he directed musicals and operettas (and later one or two straight plays). With the coming of sound, he made a couple of films in Hollywood, but preferred a more intimate working atmosphere and moved to Britain. Working at Ealing and Gainsborough studios, Varnel first teamed with Hay on *Good Morning, Boys* in 1936, and then produced a string of laughter

hits that included *Oh! Mr Porter, Convict 99, Ask a Policeman, Turned Out Nice Again, Where's That Fire?* and *Band Waggon.* The Hay films especially are a joy, and the priceless *Oh! Mr Porter* the gem in Varnel's comedy crown, with Hay and his cohorts dithering superbly at the dilapidated railway station of Buggieskelly, somewhere in Ireland – although one should not forget the hilarious street chaos in *Where's That Fire?* (caused by an enormously long firemen's pole), much of it achieved in long takes. If comedy is not to be improved through editing, then it must be superbly organised, and this is a supreme example. Varnel's early death in a car crash as a great loss to the British comedy scene, which floundered without him until the success of the first Norman Wisdom and 'Doctor' films in 1953. His son Max Varnel (born in Paris in 1925) proved only a routine director of 'B' feature crime films. Ironically, his best was a sentimental comedy, *A Taste of Money,*

made in 1960.

1932: †*Chandu, the Magician. The Silent Witness.* 1933: *Infernal Machine.* 1934: *Freedom of the Seas. Girls Will Be Boys.* 1935: *Dance Band. I Give My Heart. No Monkey Business.* 1936: *All In. Public Nuisance No. 1. Good Morning, Boys.* 1937: *Okay for Sound. Oh! Mr Porter.* 1938: *Convict 99. Alf's Button Afloat. Hey! Hey! USA. Old Bones of the River.* 1939: *Ask a Policeman. Band Waggon. The Frozen Limits. Where's That Fire?* 1940: *Gasbags. Neutral Port. Let George Do It.* 1941: *Hi! Gang. I Thank You. Turned Out Nice Again. The Ghost of St Michael's. South American George.* 1942: *King Arthur Was a Gentleman. Much Too Shy.* 1943: *Get Cracking. Bell Bottom George.* 1944: *He Snoops to Conquer.* 1945: *I Didn't Do It.* 1946: *George in Civvy Street. This Man is Mine.*

VERHOEVEN, Paul 1938-

Period dramas, science-fiction and modern-dress pieces about disreputable characters make up the movie output of this Dutch director, whose three contributions to the sci-fi genre are probably his beats films. Don't look for depth in a Verhoeven film, which often has a strong sexual element – but he is a master of big canvasses and some of his huge action scenes would make impressive paintings. At first a teacher of maths and physics, Verhoeven developed an interest in film-making while serving with the Royal Dutch Navy, where he made documentaries. His early films in Holland mainly deal graphically with both gay and straight sexuality and, although these films look rather tired today, they did attract the attention of Hollywood, who started Verhoeven off at the ripe old age of 47 with *Flesh and Blood*, a tenth-century mud-and-guts epic played with over-the-top relish by a cast headed by Dutch actor Rutger Hauer, who had featured a in a couple of Verhoeven's earlier films. Blood and gore also splattered all over the screen in the considerably more successful *Robocop*, an entertaining adult romp aimed at producing the maximum grievous bodily damage. It produced two sequels, by which time Verhoeven had moved on to *Total Recall*, another lively sci-fi thriller, this time about a man who has had his memory erased for purposes other than those he imagines. Special effects impressively run riot especially in the creation of a colony of mutants. And Verhoeven really hit the top rank in Hollywood with *Basic Instinct*, cannily maximising a minimal plot with hot sex scenes and provocative moments that recalled his early years in

Given his more serious early background, director Paul **Verhoeven's** Hollywood success with stylish, flashy mixes of sex and violence is perhaps surprising.

Holland. Verhoeven overreached himself with the abysmal *Showgirls*, and returned to the sci-fi genre for something of a comeback with *Starship Troopers*, comic-strip action reminiscent of the 1950s, as earth warriors take on a whole army of bugs from outer space in a violent, exciting, ultra-nasty and impressively staged movie for modern sci-fi fans, with some amazing digitally realized effects.

1960: **Ben hagedis taveel/A Lizard Too Much.* 1963: **Feest/Let's Have a Party.* 1966: **Het korps mariniers/The Dutch Marine Corps.* 1969: **De worstelaar/The Wrestler.* 1971: *Wat zien ik/Business is Business.* 1973: *Turks fruit/Turkish Delight.* 1975: *Keetje Tippel/Cathy Tippel/Katie's Passion.* 1977: *Soldaat van Oranja/Soldier of Orange/Survival Run.* 1980: *Spetters.* 1983: *The Fourth Man.* 1985: *Flesh and Blood/Flesh + Blood/The Rose and the Sword/The Sword and the Rose.* 1987: *RoboCop.* 1990: *Total Recall.* 1992: *Basic Instinct.* 1995: *Showgirls.* 1997: *Starship Troopers.*

VERNEUIL, Henri (Achod Malakian) 1920-
Turkish director working in France from 1946. Although not a film-maker of great repute among the intelligentsia, Verneuil's films have almost all been aimed squarely at the commercial market, and as such are probably more familiar to audiences of, for example, Britain and America, than those of many more prestigious continental directors. Verneuil believes in stories dealing with basic emotions, and in the use of big star names, whether from France, Hollywood or elsewhere. Thus the French actors most often used in his films include Jean Gabin, Alain Delon, Jean-Paul Belmondo and Fernandel, as well as such 'Europhiles' as Anthony Quinn, Charles Bronson, Dirk Bogarde, Ava Gardner and Omar Sharif. Since the beginning of the 1960s, he has worked solidly in brash international thrillers, with a couple of sentimental war films and a western thrown in. But his most successful films are the Fernandel comedies of the 1950s, especially *The Sheep Has Five Legs,* which co-starred the delectably sulky Françoise Arnoul, who first burst upon international audiences in another Verneuil film *Forbidden Fruit.* Considering their strong casts, Verneuil's later films are disappointingly slack, only the occasional well-staged set-piece such as Omar Sharif's death in a mountain of grain at the end of *The Burglars* relieving our disappointment. Verneuil, who was originally a journalist, has contributed to the scripts of most of his films. He seemed to have dropped out of the cinema after

1976, but in 1981 unexpectedly reappeared with yet another of his caper thrillers, *Mille milliards de dollars.*

1951: *Les tables aux crevés (US: The Village Feud).* 1952: *Fruit défendu (GB & US: Forbidden Fruit).* Brelan d'as. 1953: *Le boulanger de Valargue (GB & US: The Wild Oat).* Carnaval. *L'ennemi public numéro un (GB: Public Enemy No. 1. US: The Most Wanted Man).* 1954: *The Sheep Has Five Legs.* 1955: *Les amants du tage (US: Lovers' Net).* 1956: *Paris-Palace Hôtel (US: Paris Hotel).* 1957: *Une manche et la belle (US: What Price Murder?).* 1958: *Maxime. La vache et le prisonnier (GB & US: The Cow and I).* 1959: *L'affaire d'une nuit (US: It Happened All Night).* 1960: †*Love and the Frenchwoman.* 1961: *Le président. Les lions sont lâchés.* 1962: *Un singe en hiver (GB: It's Hot in Hell. US: A Monkey in Winter).* 1963: *Mélodie en sous-sol (GB: The Big Snatch. US: Any Number Can Win).* 1964: *Week-End à Zuydcoote (GB & US: Weekend at Dunkirk).* 1967: *The 25th Hour.* 1968: *Guns for San Sebastian. The Sicilian Clan.* 1971: *Le casse (GB & US: The Burglars).* 1973: *The Serpent.* 1975: *The Night Caller.* 1976: *Le corps de mon ennemi.* 1981: *Mille milliards de dollars.* 1984: *Les morfalous.* 1991: *Mayrig/Mother.* 1993: *588 Rue Paradis.*

VIDOR, Charles 1900-1959
Lushness was at the heart of everything this Hungarian-born Hollywood director did, as he moved from thrillers, dramas of deadly dames, musicals about composers, comedians and torch-singers and regal romances. Vidor stirred in his ingredients and just let fly. Occasionally, he got the formula just right, as in *Ladies in Retirement, Cover Girl* or, most spectacularly, *Gilda.* But he was just as likely to come up with such turkeys as *A Song to Remember, The Loves of Carmen* or *Rhapsody.* It's almost impossible to imagine Vidor among the low life at Warner Brothers and indeed they were one of the very few studios for whom he never worked. Trained to be a singer, Vidor developed a liking for films while working at the UFA studios in Berlin the early 1920s. Emigrating to America in 1924, he pursued a career as a Wagnerian opera star; but, with the coming of sound to the cinema, he used his savings from singing to finance a short film, *The Bridge.* M-G-M liked it enough to ask Vidor to tidy up *The Mask of Fu Manchu* (directed by Charles Brabin) and he gradually received other minor assignments, working as assistant director and editor the meanwhile. He scored a small success with the

macabre *Double Door,* the only film vehicle of doughty American stage actress Mary Morris, but there was nothing else of note until Vidor moved to Columbia in 1939, and directed a good psychological crime film, *Blind Alley,* and the lushly folksy Jean Parker melodrama, *Romance of the Redwoods.* Columbia boss Harry Cohn, whose rugged language constantly alienated the sensitive Vidor, nonetheless put the newcomer on his 'A' picture rota. Vidor's films for the studio were a mixture of genres, of variable quality: *Ladies in Retirement* is a gripping, sharp-edged drama with a typically strong performance from Ida Lupino, but *The Desperadoes* is a dull western, drowning in its own Technicolor. Then came Rita Hayworth, and great success for Vidor firstly in an energetic musical, *Cover Girl,* with Gene Kelly carving out prototypes for many of his successful M-G-M routines of later years. Miss Hayworth's second film for Vidor, *Gilda,* is his most famous, though few now remember the name of its director. The film has an intense, nightmarish quality, as the characters in it glide inexorably to their destinies. Miss Hayworth's dance to *Put the Blame on Mame, Boys,* made her the definitive post-war pin-up, and she seldom seemed as uninhibited as under Vidor's direction. Alas, she had fewer good films left in her than her director, who made a mixed bag in his last few years. Of these 1950s' efforts, *Hans Christian Andersen* is an underrated musical fantasy with a delightful score, *Love Me or Leave Me* a rough-riding musical biopic, very good despite having Doris Day (though she never acted better) in a part more suited to Hayworth in her prime, *The Swan* a delicate love story held together by the acting of Alec Guinness and Grace Kelly, and *The Joker is Wild* back in *Love Me or Leave Me* country with Frank Sinatra in the true story of the night-club entertainer who has his vocal chords slashed by gangsters.

1931: **The Bridge.* 1932: †*The Mask of Fu Manchu* (uncredited). 1933: *Sensation Hunters.* 1934: *Double Door. Strangers All.* 1935: *The Arizonian. His Family Tree.* 1936: *Muss 'Em Up (GB: House of Fate).* 1937: *A Doctor's Diary. The Great Gambini. She's No Lady.* 1939: *Romance of the Redwoods. Those High Gray Walls (GB: The Gates of Alcatraz). Blind Alley.* 1940: *My Son, My Son! The Lady in Question.* 1941: *Ladies in Retirement. New York Town.* 1942: *The Tuttles of Tahiti.* 1943: *The Desperadoes.* 1944: *Cover Girl. Together Again.* 1945: *A Song to Remember. Over 21.* 1946: *Gilda.* 1948: *The Loves of Carmen.* 1951: †*It's a Big Country.* 1952: *Hans Christian*

Andersen ... and the Dancer. Thunder in the East. 1954: *Rhapsody.* 1955: *Love Me or Leave Me.* 1956: *The Swan.* 1957: *The Joker is Wild. A Farewell to Arms.* 1960: †*Song Without End.*

VIDOR, King 1894-1982

There are some writers who believe Vidor to be the greatest of Hollywood directors. Certainly, up to 1945, he gave them plenty of evidence for their case. His themes deal with man's heartbreak, and sometimes triumph, in waging a lone battle against the enemy, the elements, society or even life itself. Born in Texas, Vidor was a projectionist and freelance newsreel cameraman before going to Hollywood in 1915. He struggled on for four years as script clerk, extra and (unsuccessful) writer, before breaking through to direction by making two-reelers and a couple of films for a Christian Science consortium. He also directed several films for his own shoestring studio, but his stock was greatly boosted by his tactful handling of veteran actress Laurette Taylor in *Peg o' My Heart*, and M-G-M hired the fledgling director without further ado. He rewarded them with one of the great war films of the silent era, *The Big Parade*, memorable for its depiction of the confusion of battle (especially in a scene in a wood) and the despair of the ordinary man and woman involved. Vidor directed its star, John Gilbert, twice more, in *La Bohème* (with a dominant Lillian Gish) and *Bardelys the Magnificent*. The second of these anticipated the last of Vidor's great silent successes, *The Crowd*, not only in its theme, but in that they have the same leading lady, Eleanor Boardman (soon to become the second Mrs Vidor). *The Crowd* is a story of ordinary people, of ambition, disappointment and compromise. It didn't equal the five-million-dollar profit of *The Big Parade*, but it was a deserved critical success, for its sincere treatment of simple sentiments and its thrillingly innovative use of mobile camera. Vidor explored similar themes with slightly less impact in *Street Scene* and *Our Daily Bread*. These films did not catch the public imagination. But Vidor had meanwhile chalked up the first of his five Oscar nominations for *Hallelujah*, a rare all-negro picture, and they queued in their thousands for *Show People, Cynara, Billy the Kid* (a violent western foreshadowing Vidor's Waterloo in *Duel in the Sun*) and most of all for *The Champ*, which won two Academy Awards and is infinitely superior to the 1978 remake by Franco Zeffirelli (*qv*). Vidor's most successful films of the late 1930s were his remake of the epic weepie *Stella Dallas*, with a finely-shaded performance from Barbara Stanwyck, and the British-made *The Citadel*, with Robert Donat as the doctor fighting poor conditions, but almost losing his way in life. Ralph Richardson's supporting performance is one of the best in any Vidor film, but it was to be topped by the gritty and greatly moving portrayal of Spencer Tracy in *Northwest Passage*, a stirring semi-western saga of human endurance. *H.M. Pulham Esq* and *An American Romance* are skilfully structured stories that provide one with a satisfying two hours' cinema, but Vidor came a terrible cropper with *Duel in the Sun*, an immensely over-long and over-heated western, and was not recognizable as the same director afterwards. In 1979, Vidor was awarded an honorary Oscar, having so narrowly missed the real thing on previous occasions.

1913: †*Hurricane in Galveston.* 1914: *Sugar Manufacture. *In Tow.* 1915: *Fort Worth Robbery.* 1917-18: *Judge Brown's Justice (and ensuing series).* 1919: *The Turn in the Road. Better Times. The Other Half. Poor Relations.* 1920: *The Family Honor. The Jack-Knife Man.* 1921: *The Sky Pilot. Love Never Dies. The Real Adventure.* 1922: *Woman, Wake Up! Dusk to Dawn. Conquering the Woman. Peg o' My Heart.* 1923: *The Woman of Bronze. Three Wise Fools.* 1924: *Wild Oranges. Happiness. The Wine of Youth. Wife of the Centaur. His Hour.* 1925: *Proud Flesh. The Big Parade.* 1926: *La Bohème. Bardelys the Magnificent.* 1928: *The Crowd. The Patsy (GB: The Politic Flapper). Show People.* 1929: *Hallelujah.* 1930: *Not So Dumb. Billy the Kid.* 1931: *The Champ. Street Scene.* 1932: *Bird of Paradise. Cynara.* 1933: *The Stranger's Return.* 1934: *Our Daily Bread (GB: The Miracle of Life).* 1935: *The Wedding Night. So Red the Rose.* 1936: *The Texas Rangers.* 1937: *Stella Dallas.* 1938: *The Citadel.* 1939: †*The Wizard of Oz (a few scenes only).* 1940: *Northwest Passage. Comrade X.* 1941: *H.M. Pulham Esq.* 1944: *An American Romance.* 1946: *Duel in the Sun.* 1948: *A Miracle Can Happen (later On Our Merry Way).* 1949: *The Fountainhead. Beyond the Forest.* 1951: *Lightning Strikes Twice.* 1952: *Japanese War Bride. Ruby Gentry.* 1954: *Man Without a Star.* 1956: *War and Peace.* 1959: *Solomon and Sheba.* 1964: *Truth and Illusion: an Introduction to Metaphysics (D).*

VIGO, Jean (J. de Vigo) 1905-1934

French film-maker who, after a traumatic childhood, made three feature films which, though unsuccessful in their day, have had a profound effect on directors all over the world. Vigo's father was an anarchist who was in jail more often than he was out, and was found strangled in his prison cell (whether by murder or suicide was never established) when his son was 12. A sickly youth (no doubt his health was not improved by the filthy conditions of his home and the oppressive atmosphere of the boarding schools he was later to satirize in *Zéro de conduite*), Jean Vigo moved to Nice in his teens and, after starting a cinema club there, became interested in making his own films. It took him a long time, but he did eventually manage to get under way in 1929 with *A propos de Nice*, a dream-like look at his home city, not without affection, despite the bitter contrast between the lives of the rich and the poor, and sometimes almost looking as if L.S. Lowry, slightly under the influence of the early Luis Buñuel (*qv*) had taken his brushes to France. *Zéro de conduite*, his next feature, is much more acerbic, a bizarre black comedy set in a boarding school for boys, and in every way the begetter of *If...* some 35 years later, even to the final mutiny, although Vigo's is slightly more in touch with reality. He had moved to Nice to improve his health, in the hope that the air might help his tubercular condition. But on his return to Paris to make what proved to be his last two films, his health again began to fail. By the time of *L'Atalante*, in 1934, leukaemia had been added to his pulmonary problems, and Vigo was dying even as the film was being prepared for showing. No doubt he was additionally distressed by the fact that it was being cut against his wishes. Even so, *L'Atalante* is a luminously memorable love story, so real that one can almost smell the swirling fog and the lapping river, not to mention the stinking cabin of Père Jules (Michel Simon) on board the barge which is the home of the newly-wed Jean and Juliette, he almost losing her when she is tempted to run away to the bright lights of Paris. It is a film dominated by atmosphere, and one which creates its own tiny world, peopled by just a few characters. There is little doubt that Vigo would have gone on to become one of the dominant figures of the French cinema had he lived. His wife died, also of tuberculosis, five years later.

1929: *A propos de Nice.* 1931: *Taris, champion de natation/Taris, roi de l'eau.* 1933: *Zéro de conduite.* 1934: *L'Atalante.*

VISCONTI, Luchino
(Count Don Luchino Visconti di Modrone) 1906-1976
This Italian director offered strong, stern, unremitting portraits of societies, often

Nights). 1960: *Rocco e i suoi fratelli (GB & US: Rocco and His Brothers).* 1962: †*Boccaccio '70.* 1963: *Il gattopardo (GB & US: The Leopard).* 1965: *Vaghe stelle dell'orsa (GB: Of a Thousand Delights. US: Stella).* 1966: †*The Witches.* 1967: *The Stranger.* 1969: *La caduta degli dei/Götterdämmerung (GB & US: The Damned).* 1971: *Death in Venice.* 1973: *Ludwig.* 1975: *Gruppo di famiglia in un interno (GB & US: Conversation Piece).* 1976: *L'innocente (GB: The Innocent. US: The Intruder).*

VON STERNBERG, Josef

(Jonas 'Jo' Sternberg) 1894-1969

Austrian-born director with a sensitive, imperious, autocratic nature who ruled his films with rods of iron, created worlds of light, shade, smoke, mist and intricacies of the camera, upset most of Hollywood's aristocracy, conjured up a dozen memorable films, made a world star out of Marlene Dietrich and, with his extravagant gear, characterized always by riding boots, became the target of scores of impersonators; he was a caricature of the more bizarre kind of Hollywood filmmaker. In America from 1911 (after an earlier, brief visit at the age of seven), Sternberg (the 'von' is supposed to have been added in 1924 by a producer seeking a little extra class) worked in numerous menial positions in the film industry, progressing to assistant director by 1921. Although his first film, *The Salvation Hunters*, in 1925, made on a bottom-drawer budget of $5,000, was a success, Sternberg's own nature ensured that he continued to struggle in Hollywood for a year or two. In 1927, though, *Underworld* made Sternberg a reputation that would sustain him for some years to come. In it, and successive gangster films, such as *The Drag Net, The Docks of New York* and *Thunderbolt,* Sternberg created his own gangster night-world, which had as little to do with reality as his later work, but was full of potent images. All of these films featured big, grouchy George Bancroft, a huge rough diamond of a man. But it was to be a very different figure who starred in all Sternberg's best known films from the 1930s: Marlene Dietrich, whom he met for the first time when he went to Germany in 1930 to make *The Blue Angel.* Dietrich moved to Hollywood and together they made *Morocco, Dishonored, Shanghai Express, Blonde Venus, The Scarlet Empress* and *The Devil is a Woman.* If Dietrich is mainly the same *femme fatale* in these films, whether playing Amy Jolly, Shanghai Lilly ('It took more than one man to change my name to Shanghai Lilly' is one

At the height of his fame: the Austrian director Josef **von Sternberg** at work in Hollywood around 1934. Note the characteristic riding boots he always wore on set.

high, and veneers crumbling under exterior pressures. Most of them are impressive, and beautifully decorated with all the visual elegance of a man who was both set designer and costume designer early in his career. However, after 1960, they have progressively less to offer in terms of entertainment. A trip to a late Visconti film became increasingly an occasion for admiration rather than enjoyment. He was born into one of Italy's highest families. Although interested in the cinema from an early age, Visconti's other 'hobbies' – art and breeding racehorses – took up most of his time before he reached 30, although he did make an amateur film in 1932. Unfortunately, this was lost when his family's palatial home was bombed during World War II. In the middle and late 1930s, Visconti worked with Jean Renoir (qv) who later gave him a copy of the American author James M. Cain's *The Postman Always Rings Twice,* which was to form the basis of Visconti's first film, *Ossessione.* A partisan sympathizer during the war, Visconti was arrested by the Nazis in 1944, fortunately only just before liberating Allied armies marched through Italy, enabling him to escape retribution and continue work. From 1947 until 1960, Visconti made a series of elaborate, sometimes scathing dramas of epic proportions, often employing international stars, that form the core of his best

work. These culminated in his best film, the powerful *Rocco and His Brothers,* in which most of Visconti's themes come together in a highly satisfactory and cinematic mixture in which the 152-minute story of the sons of an immigrant Sicilian family looking for work in Milan is constantly absorbing. One can feel more for these characters than for those in *The Leopard, The Damned* and *Conversation Piece* and other stark later works, much though their visual brilliance still makes one shake one's head in wonder. The most famous of Visconti's later films is *Death in Venice;* perhaps it is not completely successful, despite the overall delicacy of the treatment – the boy who forms the object of the Dirk Bogarde character's homosexual fascination is really too pretty and 'obvious' when he should be innocent and unknowing. After a stroke in 1972, Visconti struggled manfully against very poor health, and just managed to complete his last film, *L'innocente,* before his death.

1942: *Ossessione.* 1945: †*Giorni di gloria (D).* 1948: *La terra trema (US: The Earth Trembles).* 1951: *Bellissima.* **Appunti su un fatto di cronaca (D).* 1953: †*Siamo donne (GB: We the Women. US: Five Women).* 1954: *Senso (GB: The Wanton Countess. US: The Wanton Contessa).* 1957: *Le notte bianche (GB & US: White*

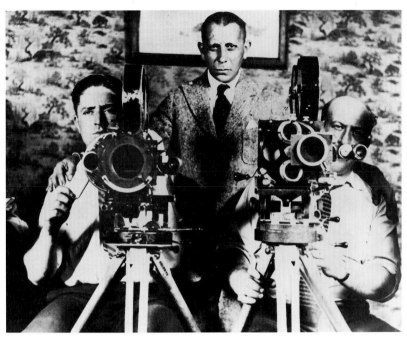

From out of the past looms the forbidding figure of Erich **Von Stroheim**. His own self-indulgence, however, was sometimes undermined by those with even greater power.

of the cinema's great lines) or Catherine the Great, several of these films are still superb combinations of artistry and stage management; they were made with a self-assurance that Sternberg only demonstrated thereafter on parts of *The Shanghai Gesture, Macao* and the little-seen *The Saga of Anatahan*, made in Japan and his last film. He fell out with the establishment, of course, and began the inevitable wanderings, to France, Austria, Britain (for the abortive *I, Claudius*) and Japan. There were a few dull films in which he obviously was not too interested. His best films, though, remain arrogantly, flamboyantly seductive. Sternberg believed in the magic of the movies and, while he was in control of his fortunes, for a while he cast his own spell.

1925: The Salvation Hunters. The Exquisite Sinner (film entirely re-shot by Phil Rosen). †The Masked Bride. 1926: †A Woman of the Sea/The Sea Gull. 1927: †It (uncredited). †Children of Divorce (uncredited). Underworld. 1928: The Last Command. The Docks of New York. The Drag Net. 1929: The Case of Lena Smith. Thunderbolt. 1930: The Blue Angel/Der blaue Engel. Morocco. 1931: Dishonored. An American Tragedy. 1932: Shanghai Express. Blonde Venus. 1934: The Scarlet Empress. 1935: The Devil is a Woman. Crime and Punishment. 1936: The King Steps Out. 1937: I, Claudius (unfinished). 1938: †The Great Waltz (uncredited). 1939: Sergeant Madden.

1940: †I Take This Woman. 1941: The Shanghai Gesture. 1943: *The Town (D). 1950: Jet Pilot (released 1957). 1952: †Macao. 1953: The Saga of Anatahan (US: Ana-Ta-Han).

† unreleased

VON STROHEIM, Erich

(Hans E.S. von Nordenwall, or E. Oswald Stroheim) 1885-1957

Grim-faced Austrian-born actor, director, military expert and general all-round megalomaniac. In today's cinema, it is quite possible that Stroheim could make his 30- or 40-reel films, running some eight or 10 hours, and get away with it, with patrons clamouring for tickets at all-day (or all night?) art house showings. Alas, the backcloth against which Stroheim chose to stage his orgiastic epics of love, lust, hunger, seduction, cruelty and passion was the Hollywood of silent days, and in one man, Irving Thalberg, Stroheim, who boasted a (bogus) military background as an Austro-Hungarian army officer, met his Waterloo. In his later years, he became a familiar character star, once more known, as in World War I times, as 'The Man You Love to Hate'. But he never again regained the power of those heady early years, when he strode like a colossus through the corridors of Universal Studios, had people scurrying to his every command and spent millions of dollars of studio money. Born in Vienna, though his mother was Czech and his

father Silesian (from a town that is now part of Poland), Stroheim soon tired of working as a manager at his father's factory and emigrated to America in 1906. His early years there are (perhaps deliberately) cloaked in mystery, but in 1913 Stroheim emerged in Hollywood, wangling himself jobs as military adviser on war films, and attracting a few acting roles from 1914. He worked extensively for D.W. Griffith, playing roles in such Griffith productions as *The Birth of a Nation* and *Intolerance*, which may have given him a taste for his own extravagance so soon to follow. His first films for Universal, *Blind Husbands* and *The Devil's Pass Key*, are basically sordid little tales involving unlikeable people. But they are full of erotic undercurrents, brilliant details and hypnotic performances from Stroheim himself. By 1922, however, Stroheim was already crossing swords with Thalberg, then the studio's general manager. His third film, *Foolish Wives*, with himself as a fake nobleman conning and blackmailing his way across the Riviera, was hacked from 32 reels to 14 (still well over two hours). Largely through Thalberg's offices, Stroheim was fired half-way through his next film and went to Goldwyn and started work on his masterpiece, *Greed*. It was Stroheim's misfortune that Thalberg had gone to Metro, for the two companies merged to form Metro-Goldwyn-Mayer and consequently *Greed* was pulverized from 42 reels to ten! There are still many powerful and memorable moments in its story of the decline and death of a San Francisco dentist and his wife through greed for gold. Stroheim drove his actors unmercifully, especially in the heat of the Mojave Desert, where he filmed the climax in which the two male protagonists, chained to each other, fight together and die together. Hardly surprisingly, the film in its castrated form was not a commercial success. But Stroheim thumbed his nose at Thalberg by making a tremendous box-office hit out of *The Merry Widow,* although it was hardly the film M-G-M expected, with its hints of sadism and perversion. It was, however, Stroheim's last triumph as a director. There were abortive or half-completed projects to follow, then a long career as an actor, which lasted until his death at 72 from a spinal ailment.

1919: Blind Husbands. 1920: The Devil's Pass Key. 1921: Foolish Wives. 1923: The Merry-Go-Round. 1924: †Greed. 1925: The Merry Widow. 1927: †The Wedding March. 1928: †Mariage du prince. †Queen Kelly. 1933: †Hello Sister/Walking Down Broadway. 1947: †La danse de mort (a few scenes only).

† taken out of the director's hands before issue of release print.

WAGGNER, George (G. Waggoner) 1894-1984
American actor, writer, songwriter, producer and director who came late to directing at 43, but still managed a prolific career, moving from films to television in the early 1950s and directing hundreds of episodes of such popular series as *Cheyenne, Wagon Train, Maverick* and *77 Sunset Strip*. He spent most of his cinema years with Universal, where he made his best-known film, *The Wolf Man*. Despite its brilliant cast – Claude Rains, Warren William, Lon Chaney Jr, Evelyn Ankers, Patric Knowles, Bela Lugosi, Ralph Bellamy – it is not a film that wears well. Waggner himself (the name is sometimes mysteriously spelt with two capital 'G's) seemed unconvinced of his talent as a director, in that he spent as much time being a producer, mostly on Maria Montez fol-de-rols, but also on such goodies as *The Ghost of Frankenstein* and the 1943 version of *The Phantom of the Opera*. Trained as a chemist, Waggner decided on an acting career after military service in World War I and came to Hollywood. His roles were mainly in westerns, and included a portrayal of Buffalo Bill Cody in John Ford's *The Iron Horse*. He worked as a songwriter from 1927 to 1932, and as a screenwriter from 1933 to 1937, at which time he began his career as a director, at first with westerns, although they were hardly in the Ford class. After a little number entitled *Horror Island*, Universal decided to entrust him with *The Wolf Man*, and the resulting film set Lon Chaney Jr. up for a run of several years as the studio's 'master character star'. Waggner left Universal in 1946 and freelanced, mostly with westerns, working in television from 1952. Here he linked up with Warners, directing all their major western series, until the vogue for the genre began to fade in the mid-1960s. Still Waggner was not finished, carrying on his varied career by making numerous episodes of the *Batman* series, and continuing to direct until he was 72. Never throughout his long career did he impose a personal style on a project, but, whatever he was given, efficiency was Waggner's watchword; he kept his films

going well and some of them contain some excellent battle scenes, if no great acting. Indeed, throughout his career, Waggner seemed to be saddled with big, brawny, monolithic actors capable of no great variation. That he made many of them so popular, especially on television, is some tribute to his skill.

1937: *Western Trails*. 1938: *Prairie Justice. Outlaw Express. Guilty Trails. The Black Bandit. Ghost Town Riders*. 1939: *Honor of the West. Mystery Plane. The Phantom Stage. Wolf Call. Stunt Pilot*. 1940: *Drums of the Desert. Horror Island*. 1941: *Sealed Lips. The Wolf Man. Man Made Monster (GB: The Electric Man). South of Tahiti (GB: White Savage)*. 1944: *The Climax*. 1945: *Frisco Sal. Shady Lady*. 1946: *Tangier*. 1947: *Gunfighters (GB: The Assassin)*. 1949: *The Fighting Kentuckian*. 1951: *Operation Pacific*. 1957: *Pawnee (GB: Pale Arrow). Destination 60,000*. 1958: †*Fury River*. 1959: †*Mission of Danger*.

WAJDA, Andrzej 1926-
This Polish director is a man for the moment. Without sadness and anger, his films often count for little, but no-one was more skilled at bringing home the painfulness in the plight of Poland in both World War II and the post-war years – often to the consternation of authorities. Wajda sees the Poles as a people trapped, ultimately with no escape. This sense of entrapment occurs often throughout his films, whether physically (most often) or metaphorically. His characters are trapped in prisons, cellars, sewers, anything that forms the end of the line after a bitter struggle. Or they are trapped by the system, like the elusive central character of *Man of Iron* and *Man of Marble*. Like the heroes of so many of his early films, Wajda himself was a resistance fighter from 1942 onwards, surviving to study fine arts and make a difficult choice between painting and the cinema. After his first feature film, *A Generation*, in 1955, there was no doubt that a new major film-maker had emerged and, by and large, Wajda has sustained a remarkable standard of consistency since that time. *A Generation, Kanal* and *Ashes and Diamonds* not only brought the tragically short-lived Zbigniew Cybulski to the fore as a kind of James Dean of Polish films, but they form a wartime trilogy in which Wajda brings home the full horror of the Poles' war-torn agony to the western world. The images of *Kanal* are particularly haunting, with resistance fighters condemned to wander through the sewers of Warsaw, getting no further towards

freedom than a view of open water through a cluster of iron bars, held as remorselessly underground as was Orson Welles in *The Third Man*. Wajda is especially skilful at assembling the images for greatest impact. He returned to the themes of warfare and oppression from time to time in the ensuing years, particularly in *Landscape After Battle*, set in a 'limbo' camp for displaced Poles still stranded in Germany after World War II. Full of bitterness and hurtful images, it ends on a note of hope, rare in a Wajda film, although Wajda also seems to be trying harder than usual here to make a great movie and it only gradually gains momentum. However, there is no such optimism in the later companion pieces *Man of Marble* and *Man of Iron* which, although other, lesser Wajda films separate them, represent the definitive statement on the Polish situation since the war. Both are brilliantly constructed to give maximum power to the story about a workers' favourite who rises to public prominence through brick-building brilliance in the immediate post-war years, then mysteriously falls from sight. Absorbing from start to finish, the story ends on a note of pessimism seen to be fully justified by subsequent events, which included the suppression of the Solidarity workers' movement, and the (mercifully temporary) internment of Wajda himself. He has since continued his career in France and Poland. Of his later work, only *Danton* – a thought-provoking historical drama – has approached the peaks of his earlier years. Wajda also co-directed a TV mini-series, *As the Years Pass, As the Days Pass*, in 1984.

1950: **Zly Chopiec/The Bad Boy. *Kiedy ty spisz/While You Sleep*. 1951: *Ceramika Ilzecka/Pottery at Ilza (D)*. 1954 *Pokolenie/A Generation*. 1955: **Ide ku Sloncu/Towards the Sun*. 1957: *Kanal*. 1958: *Popiol i Diamenty/Ashes and Diamonds*. 1959: *Lotna*. 1960: *Niewinni Czarodzieje/Innocent Sorcerers*. 1961: *Samson*. 1962: *The Siberian Lady Macbeth (US: Fury is a Woman)*. †*L'amour de vingt ans (GB & US: Love at Twenty)*. 1965: *Popioly/Ashes*. 1967: *Gates to Paradise*. 1968: **Roly-Poly (TV). Wszystko na Sprzedaz/Everything for Sale*. 1969: *Polowanie na Muchy/Hunting Flies*. 1970: *Krajobraz po bitwie/Landscape After Battle*. 1971: *Brzezina/The Birch Wood*. 1972: *Wesele/The Wedding*. 1973: *Pilatus und andere/Pilate and Others*. 1974: *Ziemia Obiecana (GB: Land of Promise. US: Promised Land)*. 1976: *Smuga Cienia/The Shadow Line*. 1977: *Czlowiek z Marmuru/Man of Marble*. 1978: *Bez zwie Czulenia/Rough Treatment. The*

Dead Class (D). 1979: *Panny z Wilko/The Young Girls of Wilko. Noc Listopadowa/November Night.* 1980: *Dyrygent/The Conductor.* 1981: *Czlowiek z Zelaza/Man of Iron.* 1982: *L'affaire Danton/Danton.* 1983: *Eine Liebe in Deutschland.* 1985: *Chronicle of a Love Affair/Chronicles of Love's Casualties (US: A Chronicle of Amorous Accidents).* 1987: *Chatov et les démons.* 1988: *Les possédés/Possessed.* 1990: *Korczak/Dr Korczak.* 1995: *Nastasja.* 1996: *Wielki tydzien/Holy Week.* 1997: *Panna Nikt/Miss Nobody.*

WALKER, Hal
See Webb, Robert D.

WALKER, Stuart 1887-1941
There seem to be two schools of thought on this American director's brief career. One, that he was a hack film-maker whose best 'work' may well have been directed by others; two, that he was an erratic genius, capable of great heights but easily enslaved to the routine. Although he began his career as an actor, Walker had directed and produced plays in Broadway by the time he was called on to Paramount's directorial roster in 1931. His early films were unmemorable, but he used Fredric March and Carole Lombard to great effect in three 1933 films, although the credit of Mitchell Leisen (*qv*) as 'associate director' on two of these films has called Walker's actual contribution into question. Nonetheless, *The Eagle and the Hawk* is an outstandingly frank war film about the effects of combat on pilots in World War I. In several disturbing scenes, the audience is brought face to face with the less appetizing aspects of flying for one's country, and the mental deterioration of Fredric March's character, from the moment he realizes the 'air ace' he has just shot down is a mere boy, is graphically depicted in uncompromising shots that hit an audience right between the eyes. Carole Lombard has a cameo role in this film, merely cast as a 'beautiful lady', but she was the focal point of *White Woman*, a sideshoot from *Red Dust* that proves overheated rather than torrid, but there is some very flattering and atmospheric photography of the star by Harry Fischbeck. Photography also played an interesting part in Walker's second film with Fredric March, *Tonight is Ours*, this time by Theodore Sparkuhl, who greatly aids Walker (and presumably Leisen) to approach the spirit of the Noel Coward original. Also of interest in Walker's small canon are his two Dickens films: *Great Expectations* is

one of the dullest Dickens adaptations on record, but *The Mystery of Edwin Drood* quite vivid, with a memorable performance by Claude Rains as the opium-addicted central character, John Jasper, who secretly covets heroine Rosa Bud. After *The Werewolf of London*, an effective early exercise in the study of lycanthropy with a really pity-arousing performance by Henry Hull, Walker returned to the stage. It seems that he had some talent for misty, moody visuals and attractive central performances but not sufficient to sustain his cinema career.

1931: *The Secret Call. The False Madonna* (GB: *The False Idol*). 1932: *The Misleading Lady. Evenings for Sale.* 1933: *The Eagle and the Hawk. Tonight is Ours. White Woman.* 1934: *Romance in the Rain. Great Expectations.* 1935: *The Mystery of Edwin Drood. Manhattan Moon* (GB: *Sing Me a Love Song*). *Were-Wolf of London.*

WALLACE, Richard 1894-1951
Although hardly ever more than a middle-range American director, Richard Wallace showcased the talents of three decades of Hollywood actresses, including Nancy Carroll, Clara Bow, Janet Gaynor, Tallulah Bankhead, Katharine Hepburn, Maureen O'Hara, Loretta Young, Shirley Temple and Deanna Durbin. His films in the 1920s and 1930s were mostly light dramas for appealing leading ladies; from the late 1930s romantic comedies took over. Wallace's parents originally intended their talented son to be a surgeon, but family funds ran out and a disillusioned Wallace wandered the country with a travelling carnival before gravitating towards Hollywood, where Mack Sennett gave him a job as a cutter in 1918. Wallace stuck with his new profession, rising to editor and director of two-reelers by 1925. The most successful of his early feature films was the first version of *Shopworn Angel* in 1928, with Nancy Carroll and Gary Cooper, by which time Wallace had settled at Paramount, where he was to remain for another ten years. His first film on leaving them in 1938, however, was his most successful. This was the Selznick production *The Young in Heart*, a typically crazy comedy of its time about a family of cardsharps and con-men reformed by one of the kindly old ladies who only exist in Hollywood movies, whom they had originally planned to fleece. Wallace directed very racily, aided by a classy cast that included Roland Young, Billie Burke, Douglas Fairbanks Jr, Janet Gaynor, Paulette Goddard, Richard Carlson and Minnie Dupree as the old

dear. Another Wallace comedy of reputation is *A Night to Remember*, a comedy-thriller about blackmailers and things moving about in the cellar, although this has worn less well, now looking rather stagey. But *The Fallen Sparrow* had John Garfield excitingly dodging Nazis in Manhattan, with lighting, sets and camera-work giving it an edge on most of Wallace's other films of the 1940s, *Because of Him* is a likeable re-teaming of Deanna Durbin and Charles Laughton (they had originally co-starred in *It Started with Eve*), and in *Framed* Wallace gets yet another good female performance, this time from that underrated actress Janis Carter. His last films are very light frivolities with a fading Shirley Temple.

1925: **Jiminy Crickets. *Honeymoon Hotel.* 1926: **So This is Paris. Syncopating Sue.* 1927: *American Beauty* (GB: *The Beautiful Fraud*). *McFadden's Flats. A Texas Steer. The Poor Nut.* 1928: *Lady Be Good. Shopworn Angel. The Butter and Egg Man* (GB: *Actress and Angel*). 1929: *Innocents of Paris. River of Romance.* 1930: *†Seven Days' Leave* (GB: *Medals*). *Anybody's War. The Right to Love.* 1931: *Man of the World. Kick In. The Road to Reno.* 1932: *Thunder Below. Tomorrow and Tomorrow.* 1933: *The Masquerader.* 1934: *The Little Minister. Eight Girls in a Boat.* 1936: *Wedding Present.* 1937: *John Meade's Woman. Blossoms on Broadway.* 1938: *The Young in Heart.* 1939: *The Under-Pup.* 1940: *Captain Caution.* 1941: *A Girl, a Guy and a Gob* (GB: *The Navy Steps Out*). *She Knew All the Answers. Obliging Young Lady.* 1942: *The Wife Takes a Flyer* (GB: *A Yank in Dutch*). *A Night to Remember.* 1943: *Bombardier. The Fallen Sparrow. My Kingdom for a Cook.* 1944: *Bride by Mistake.* 1945: *It's in the Bag!* (GB: *The Fifth Chair*). *Kiss and Tell.* 1946: *Because of Him.* 1947: *Sinbad the Sailor. Framed* (GB: *Paula*). *Tycoon.* 1948: *Let's Live a Little.* 1949: *Adventure in Baltimore* (GB: *Bachelor Bait*). 1950: *A Kiss for Corliss.*

WALSH, Raoul 1887-1981
'Action!', the word that starts the cameras rolling, sums up the career of this American director. Sprawling, brawling, often almost primitive action, teeming across the screen, marks Walsh's stories of comradeship and battles against the odds. He had a talent for making the densest of action sequences seem uncomplicated and uncluttered and his characters, like the scenes they distinguished, often have a raw, unfettered power. Everybody, of course, remembers James Cagney as Cody

Jarrett, with his final maniacal cry of 'Made it Ma! Top of the world!' from the climax of *White Heat*, but there are a dozen like him in Walsh's work, each of them meeting death at the top of their own world, and often being given their epitaphs with the last lines of the film: Humphrey Bogart in *High Sierra*, Errol Flynn in *They Died with Their Boots On* and *Uncertain Glory*, and Cagney again in *The Roaring Twenties*. Walsh's world is one where men are men and women are, by and large, not to be trusted. He had begun with action, assembling, with a co-director, seven reels of newsreel and staged footage purporting to show the life of Pancho Villa. He was one of Griffith's assistants on both *The Birth of a Nation* and *Intolerance*, still pursuing the joint acting and directing careers he had started when joining Griffith in 1912. He continued to produce and often co-write many of his films up to the end of the silent era, achieving his first great box-office success in 1924 with *The Thief of Bagdad*, Douglas Fairbanks' biggest profit-making spectacle. Two years later, he made the famous *What Price Glory?*, a comedy war film about two feuding sergeants; it began a long list of crime films, war films and westerns. One of the first of the latter, *In Old Arizona*, co-directed with Irving Cummings (*qv*) who strangely was nominated for an Oscar with no mention of Walsh, won its leading man, Warner Baxter, an Academy Award, but cost Walsh the sight of an eye in an accident. He directed the young John Wayne in *The Big Trail* and captured the roistering, teeming life of *The Bowery* in a memorable 1933 film with Wallace Beery, George Raft, Fay Wray and child star Jackie Cooper. But Walsh's peak years start from 1939, when he made *The Roaring Twenties*, a marvel of action, editing and economy, covering years and incidents seemingly beyond the compass of its 106 minutes without ever flagging or forsaking its cracking, but even pace. Walsh directed Bogart in *They Drive by Night* and *High Sierra*, did wonderfully well with Cagney in lighter vein in *The Strawberry Blonde*, had Raft again, this time with Edward G. Robinson, in *Manpower*, and took over the Errol Flynn films from Michael Curtiz: *They Died with Their Boots On, Desperate Journey, Gentleman Jim, Northern Pursuit, Uncertain Glory, Objective Burma!* These are all Warners films, a gritty list of great strength that ends its best period with *White Heat* and Bogart again in *The Enforcer*. In the 1950s Walsh was less dominant, but there is still lots of lusty, gutsy adventure. He died in the early hours of New Year's Eve/New Year's Day

of 1980-81.

1914: †*The Life of General Villa. The Double Knot. The Hindu Image/The Mystery of the Hindu Image. The Gunman. Sierra Jim's Reformation. The Final Verdict.* 1915: *The Death Dice. His Return. The Greaser. The Fatal Black Bean. Carmen. The Fencing Master. A Man for all That. Eleven Thirty. The Celestial Code. The Buried Hand. A Bad Man and Others. The Regeneration.* 1916: *Blue Blood and Red. Pillars of Society. The Serpent.* 1917: *The Conqueror. The Honor System. Betrayed. The Innocent Sinner. The Silent Lie. The Pride of New York. This is the Life.* 1918: *On the Jump. The Woman and the Law. The Prussian Cur. Every Mother's Son. I'll Say So.* 1919: *Should a Husband Forgive? Evangeline. The Strongest.* 1920: *From Now On. The Deep Purple.* 1921: *The Oath. Serenade.* 1922: *Kindred of the Dust.* 1923: *Lost and Found on a South Sea Island (GB: Lost and Found).* 1924: *The Thief of Bagdad.* 1925: *East of Suez. The Spaniard (GB: Spanish Love). The Wanderer.* 1926: *The Lucky Lady. What Price Glory? The Lady of the Harem.* 1927: *The Monkey Talks. The Loves of Carmen.* 1928: *Sadie Thompson. Me, Gangster. The Red Dance (GB: The Red Dancer of Moscow).†In Old Arizona.* 1929: *The Cock Eyed World. Hot for Paris.* 1930: *The Big Trail.* 1931: *The Yellow Ticket (GB: The Yellow Passport). The Man Who Came Back. Women of All Nations.* 1932: *Wild Girl (GB: Salomy Jane). Me and My Gal (GB: Pier 13).* 1933: *Sailor's Luck. The Bowery. Going Hollywood.* 1934: *Under Pressure.* 1935: *Every Night at Eight. Baby Face Harrington/Baby Face.* 1936: *Klondike Annie. Big Brown Eyes. Spendthrift. OHMS (US: You're in the Army Now).* 1937: *Jump for Glory (US: When Thief Meets Thief). Hitting a New High. Artists and Models.* 1938: *College Swing (GB: Swing, Teacher, Swing).* 1939: *St Louis Blues. The Roaring Twenties.* 1940: *Dark Command. Manpower. They Drive by Night (GB: The Road to Frisco).* 1941: *High Sierra. The Strawberry Blonde. They Died with Their Boots On.* 1942: *Desperate Journey. Gentleman Jim.* 1943: *Background to Danger. Northern Pursuit.* 1944: *Uncertain Glory.* 1945. *The Horn Blows at Midnight. Objective Burma! †San Antonio (uncredited). Salty O'Rourke.* 1946: *The Man I Love.* 1947: *Pursued. Cheyenne.* 1948: *Fighter Squadron. One Sunday Afternoon. Silver River.* 1949: *White Heat. Colorado Territory.* 1950: †*Montana (uncredited).* †*The Enforcer (GB: Murder Inc. Uncredited).* 1951: *Along the Great Divide. Captain Horatio Hornblower RN (US: Captain*

Horatio Hornblower). Distant Drums. 1952: *The World in His Arms. Blackbeard the Pirate. The Lawless Breed. Glory Alley.* 1953: *Gun Fury. A Lion is in the Streets. Sea Devils.* 1954: *Saskatchewan (GB: O'Rourke of the Royal Mounted).* 1955: *Battle Cry. The Tall Men.* 1956: *The Revolt of Mamie Stover. The King and Four Queens.* 1957: *Band of Angels.* 1958: *The Naked and the Dead. The Sheriff of Fractured Jaw.* 1959: *A Private's Affair.* 1960: *Esther and the King.* 1961: *Marines Let's Go!* 1964: *A Distant Trumpet.*

WALTERS, Charles 1911-1982

It seems amazing that when film fans, even some musical aficionados, have the names of Donen and Minnelli at their fingertips, that of Charles Walters escapes them. While perhaps not as innovative as the others, this American dance director and film-maker turned out beguiling musical entertainments that were almost all successful and often had some very individual touches. Many of his comedies and musicals have great charm, and all are brilliantly photographed in colour and smoothly, imaginatively choreographed, as well as occasionally tugging at the heartstrings. Maybe Walters never made a great film (although *Lili* comes close), but any director whose work includes *Good News, Easter Parade, Lili, Dangerous When Wet, The Tender Trap, High Society, Ask Any Girl, The Unsinkable Molly Brown* and *Walk, Don't Run* has to be accounted in the front flight. Like Stanley Donen and later Bob Fosse (both *qv*), Walters was a dancer who turned to choreography and directed stage musicals. He joined M-G-M in 1942, and created routines for *Du Barry Was a Lady, Girl Crazy, Meet Me in St Louis* (the 'Cake Walk' sequence), *Ziegfeld Follies, The Harvey Girls* and *Summer Holiday*. As a director, Walters worked with Ginger Rogers, Fred Astaire, Judy Garland, Vera-Ellen, Esther Williams and other members of M-G-M's musical stock company, but found a special rapport with Leslie Caron in *Lili*, a charming story of a waif who joins a travelling carnival and becomes involved with a magician and a puppeteer, and the underrated *The Glass Slipper*, beautifully decorated and shot in delicate colours, a version of the Cinderella story which achieves a unique air of whimsical fantasy. *Dangerous When Wet* includes a delightful animated sequence in which Esther Williams swims with Tom and Jerry, while *High Society and The Unsinkable Molly Brown* are vigorous entertainments carried by tuneful scores and personable central performances. *Walk Don't*

Run is a fitting screen farewell from Cary Grant who, with Walters' help, raises a lot of laughs from very little in this remake of the 1943 film *The More the Merrier*. It has an important ingredient noticeable in almost all of Walters' work as choreographer and director: vitality.

1945: *Spreadin' the Jam. 1947: Good News. 1948: Easter Parade. 1949: The Barkleys of Broadway. 1950: Summer Stock (GB: If You Feel Like Singing). 1951: Texas Carnival. Three Guys Named Mike. 1952: The Belle of New York. 1953: Lili. Dangerous When Wet. Easy to Love. Torch Song. 1955: The Glass Slipper. The Tender Trap. 1956: High Society. 1957: Don't Go Near the Water. 1959: Ask Any Girl. 1960: Please Don't Eat the Daisies. 1961: Two Loves (GB: Spinster). 1962: Jumbo/Billy Rose's Jumbo. 1964: The Unsinkable Molly Brown. 1966: Walk, Don't Run.

WANG, Wayne 1949-

Hong Kong-born (named after John Wayne) and American-educated, Wang has enjoyable considerable critical (and some comercial) success with his astute, warmly observed and often gently amusing dissections of Chinese-American life. After obtaining qualifications in film, TV and art, Wang returned to Hong Kong with hopes of joining the industry there. Frustrated at getting a real breakthrough he had returned to San Francisco within two years and started his cinema career there. His first solo film *Chan is Missing*, took some time to set up and was eventually shot in black and white on a tiny budget of $22,000. The cult success of this quirky mystery about two cab drivers trying to track down a vanished friend enabled Wang to make subsequent films on much more lavish budgets. *Dim Sum – A Little Bit of Heart* examined both mother-daughter relationships and the idiosyncracies of Asian cooking, while *Eat a Bowl of Tea* featured Cora Miao (Mrs Wang) and Russell Wong in a charming story of the difficulties of newly weds in New York's post-World War Two Chinatown community. Wang's most ambitious film to date, *The Joy, Luck Club*, saw him extract a series of memorable performances, although the film, a well-presented if sometimes confusing story of Chinese-American life and the chequered histories that lead to the formation of a family network, is less completely successful than the simpler issues of his earlier work. The critics seemed to prefer *Smoke* and *Blue in the Face*, Wang's affectionate portrayals of the small-time denizens of a Brooklyn neighbourhood. Quiet and

"Outrageous" film-maker John **Waters** pictured on the set of one of his less controversial pictures *Cry-Baby*.

sweet-natured, but penetrating in their view of the human character these two films, made back to back, are minor gems.

1974: †Golden Needles (Chinese scenes only). 1975: +A Man, a Woman and a Killer. 1981: Chan is Missing. 1985: Dim Sum – A Little Bit of Heart. 1987: Slam Dance. 1989: Eat a Bowl of Tea. 1990: Life is Cheap ... But Toilet Paper is Expensive. 1993: The Joy Luck Club. 1995: Smoke. Blue in the Face. 1998: Chinese Box. 1999: Anywhere But Here.

WATERS, John 1946 -

From the came cupboard in the cellar that unleashed such directors as Russ Meyer and Edward Wood Jr comes the gleefully offensive Waters who is from Baltimore, Maryland, and is the other side of the coin to Baltimore's rather more traditional directing son, Barry Levinson. Boasting a stock company of extravagant actors whom one critic once unkindly called 'the Waters freak show', Waters has gradually edged closer to a mainstream that must

have trembled at the prospect. In Waters' movies, crime and corpulence are good, traditionalism (unless it be the rock 'n' roll kind) is bad. Disgust in in, good taste is nowhere. The films themselves are violent comic-strip satires. And, in spite of their uneven quality, they have drawn an increasing cult audience over the years. Respectability almost trapped the demonic, trimly moustachioed Waters when he received a director's tribute at the 1997 Deauville Festival. But he shrugged it off again. 'The French invented chic,' he commented, 'so they understand good bad taste. It makes me feel like an ambassador of filth.' Even his autobiography is called *Crackpot*. Fascinated both by violent crime and marginal independent cinema, Waters began shooting his own short films (using himself as cinematographer until the early 1980s). Grabbing his audiences with repellent images and assembling a regular company that included 300-pound transvestite Divine, punk demonette Mink Stole, bizarrely-toothed Edith Massey, grossly overweight Ricki Lake (later to slim down and become a chat show host) and porn queen Traci Lords, Waters attracted both repugnance and fascination with such titles as *Mondo Trasho, Multiple Maniacs* and *Pink Flamingos*. After a long gap in the 1980s, during which he concentrated more on his acting and photography careers, Waters returned, higher-profile if somewhat tamed, with *Hairspray* and *Cry-Baby*, two fairly outrageous and deliberately tacky spoofs of teen movies of the 1950s and 1960s which mixed Waters' own stars with such more accepted icons as Pia Zadora and Johnny Depp. The colour in these films in exactly the right shade of garishness, the direction is as snappy as hell and the supporting cast of grotesques a mine of half-forgotten faces from every decade. Waters was somewhere near his obscene best with *Serial Mom*, in which the dialogue was only faintly less lurid than Kathleen Turner's performance as the housewife who will polish off those around her at the merest hint of offence, including the woman she clubs to death with a leg of lamb for refusing to rewind her videotapes. Sadly, Waters has had less success in raising finance for films in recent times, only adding one film, *Pecker*, in the five years following *Serial Mom*. At the time of writing he is still trying to obtain the funding to make a movie called *Cecil B DeMented*. We're assured it won't be autobiographical.

1964: **Hag in a Black Leather Jacket.*
1966: **Roman Candles.* 1968: **Eat Your Make Up.* 1969: *Mondo Trasho.* 1971: *Multiple Maniacs.* 1972: *Pink Flamingos.* 1975: *Female Trouble.* 1977: *Desperate Living.* 1981: *Polyester.* 1988: *Hairspray.* 1990: *Cry-Baby.* 1994: *Serial Mom.* 1998: *Pecker.*

WATT, Harry 1906-1997

Scottish-born director, writer and documentarist who flew in the front line of the British documentary movement all through its peak years, from 1933 to 1942, before making a few feature films in Australia and Africa, revealing a pleasing sense of locale. After a varied early life, he joined the film unit of the Empire Marketing Board in 1931 as a production assistant. But two years later, he was with the famous GPO film unit under its new chief, the noted documentary producer John Grierson. By this time, Watt had already gained valuable experience working as an assistant to Robert Flaherty *(qv)* on *Man of Aran* (Watt himself would later make a great sea documentary). But for now he found himself making films about Post Office activities, most notable of which was the haunting *Night Mail*, which he co-directed with Basil Wright; here everything on a rail journey from

London to Scotland seems in time with the rhythm of the train. Towards the end of the 1930s, Watt was moving to a more dramatized form of documentary: in *North Sea*, for example, a large part of the footage of the lives of fishermen was taken up with the reconstruction of a storm that had actually recently happened. Watt had a taste of the commercial film world as second-unit director to Alfred Hitchcock *(qv)* on *Jamaica Inn* (1939), before the GPO film unit became the Crown Film Unit and Watt, together with many other prominent documentarists of the period, was soon hard at work chronicling the war and keeping up morale. *London Can Take It* and *The First Days* were stirring notes of defiance, and *Target for Tonight* a thrilling reconstruction of a nighttime bombing raid. Watt was now staging this action with such flair and feel for atmosphere that it was no surprise when he turned to features proper in 1942 with *Nine Men*, a sturdy tale of desert warfare, based on a Russian film, *The 13*. Following the war, Watt went to Australia to make a Fordian Australian western, *The Overlanders* and stayed there for the rather more rugged *Eureka Stockade*. He had considerable success with the popular *Where No Vultures Fly*, about an African game warden, which had only a slight story, but luscious colour camerawork and pictorial values. A sequel, *West of Zanzibar*, was less successful – slow-moving and with a heroine who wore a dozen different dresses in the course of a few days in the African bush. Watt ended his mainstream film career with a return visit to Australia for the tough action film *The Siege of Pinchgut*, which was tense, hard-hitting and quite successful.

1933: **†Six-Thirty Collection (D).* 1934: **†BBC – Droitwich (D).* 1935: **Sorting Office (D).* 1936: **†Night Mail (D).* 1937: **The Saving of Bill Blewitt (D).* **Four Barriers (D).* 1938: **Health in Industry (D).* *North Sea (semi-D).* 1939: **†The First Days (D).* 1940: **†London Can Take It (D).* **Squadron 992 (D).* **Britain at Bay (D).* **Dover – Front Line (D).* 1941: *Target for Tonight (semi-D).* **Christmas Under Fire (D).* 1942: **Dover Revisited (D).* **21 Miles (D).* 1943: *Nine Men.* 1944: *Fiddlers Three.* 1946: *The Overlanders.* 1948: *Eureka Stockade (US: Massacre Hill).* 1951: *Where No Vultures Fly (US: Ivory Hunter).* 1953: *West of Zanzibar.* 1958: **People Like Maria (D).* 1959: *The Siege of Pinchgut (US: Four Desperate Men).* 1962: *Den bride hingst.* 1963: *Messenger of the Mountains.*

WEBB, Robert D. 1903-1990

A rather strange little directing career, this, similar to that of Hal Walker (1896-1972), who had two little bursts of directing at Paramount – although they did include *Road to Utopia* – after serving them for many years. Webb's studio was Twentieth Century-Fox, and he was with them from the early days, although his career had started much earlier, in 1919, when he became a camera assistant. Through the 1930s, he worked as assistant or second-unit director, and it was 1945 before the studio allowed him to make a couple of second-features. Although one of these starred James Dunn, who had just won an Oscar (for *A Tree Grows in Brooklyn*), the film *Caribbean Mystery* did neither Dunn nor Webb much good. Dunn returned to the theatre, and Webb to second-unit direction on such films as *Captain from Castile* and *Prince of Foxes*. His talent for staging period action, however, led to Webb's being reinstated as a director when Fox stepped up their CinemaScope production. *Beneath the 12-Mile Reef, White Feather* and *Seven Cities of Gold* had fine scenic values and stirring action sequences, even if their performers were often vapid and the stories aimed at the younger end of the market. There was nothing vapid, however, about *The Proud Ones*, a gritty, first-rate western, with Robert Ryan turning in his usual honest-to-goodness, hard-hitting job as the physically hampered marshal trying to clean up a lawless town and Jeffrey Hunter matching him. The memorable climax reflected Webb's talent for hammering home action. Webb's reward, if such it was, was to be handed the Elvis Presley debut film, *Love Me Tender*, which made a mint at the box-office, but wasn't actually very good. Webb's work after that has a rather desultory look and, although *Pirates of Tortuga* is a lively swashbuckler with a remarkable cast, by 1963 he was once more back at work on second-unit direction, but had left Fox for Universal. His last film was made in South Africa: ironically, *The Cape Town Affair* was a limp re-working of an earlier Fox hit, *Pick Up on South Street*.

1945: *Caribbean Mystery. The Spider.* 1953: *Beneath the 12-Mile Reef. The Glory Brigade.* 1955: *White Feather. Seven Cities of Gold.* 1956: *On the Threshold of Space. The Proud Ones. Love Me Tender.* 1957: *The Way to the Gold.* 1960: *Guns of the Timberland.* 1961: *Seven Women from Hell. Pirates of Tortuga.* 1967: *The Cape Town Affair.*

WEIR, Peter 1944-

Weir has been called Australia's 'master of mystery and imagination' and most of his films are beautifully bizarre in one way or another. He strayed away from the genre in 1981 with *Gallipoli* but it seemed overly contrived and slightly pretentious. Weir originally studied to become a lawyer, but gradually, at first through working for a theatrical booking agency, gravitated towards the world of entertainment. His first films are faintly disturbing two-reelers, in which one can see some of the qualities his films later projected with more style. Although *Homesdale*, a documentary, was admired, his first big commercial success was *The Cars That Ate Paris*, a monstrous fantasy set in Paris, Australia, where the townsfolk lay traps for unwary night-time motorists. The good people of the town 'treat' the survivors of the crashes and make their living off the pickings from the cars. A marvellous idea, but somewhat uncertainly acted, the film moves too jerkily to maintain interest for long periods. Undoubtedly, though, Weir had caught the eye and his next film, *Picnic at Hanging Rock*, was an unqualified success. A haunting, carefully made period ghost-horror story played out in broad daylight, it concerns a group of Australian schoolgirls and teachers in 1900 who go for a picnic to the towering, primeval Hanging Rock, an excursion from which three of them are never to return. While maintaining a splendid atmosphere of unease, Weir always keeps the explanation of the horrors tantalizingly out of reach. Certainly the best film to come out of Australia in some years, it was followed in the Weir canon by *The Last Wave*, a foolish but stylish chiller about a lawyer who finds himself enmeshed in Aborigine tribal lore when he sets out to defend five black Australians on a charge of murdering a sixth. Weir's confident, if rather slow direction makes the most of some 'jump' moments and creates a film to ponder upon at leisure. In the award-winning *The Year of Living Dangerously,* Weir catches all the turmoil of an impoverished and oppressed country (Indonesia, 1965) as it boils over into revolution. He continued to examine the theme of people alienated from a central society in subsequent films, turning the theme brilliantly to offbeat black comedy in *The Truman Show*.

1967: **Count Vim's Last Exercise.* 1968: **The Life and Times of the Rev. Buck Shotte.* 1970: *†Three to Go.* 1971: *Homesdale (D).* 1972: **Incredible Floridas (D).* 1973: **What Ever Happened to Green Valley? (D).* 1974: *The Cars That Ate Paris.* 1975: *Picnic at Hanging Rock.* 1977: *The Last Wave.* 1978: *The Plumber.* 1981: *Gallipoli.* 1982: *The Year of Living Dangerously.* 1985: *Witness.* 1986: *The Mosquito Coast.* 1989: *Dead Poets Society.* 1990: *Green Card.* 1993: *Fearless.* 1997: *The Truman Show.*

WELLES, Orson (George O. Welles) 1915-1985

Like Von Stroheim and Von Sternberg, although otherwise hardly in similar mould, Wisconsin-born Welles was one of Hollywood's *enfants terribles,* beginning with brilliance but soon falling out with the studio, having his work hacked down and setting off on wanderings round the world, forever in search of another masterpiece and the money to make one. A youthful prodigy, he was in leading roles on stage at 16 and had formed (with producer John Houseman) the famous Mercury Theatre Company at 22. After a noted radio production of *The War of the Worlds* in October, 1938, which seems to have panicked a large percentage of the American populace into believing they were really being invaded by aliens, Welles was called to Hollywood by RKO Radio and given virtual *carte blanche* to make films for them. His first, *Citizen Kane,* still recognized as one of the best pictures ever made, showed a remarkable recognition of the visual possibilities of the cinema, blending newsreel and montage effects with cunningly angled photography to heighten dramatic effect, with a remarkable use of deep focus and an uncommon skill in keeping together the threads of a complicated plot to form an entertaining and constantly fascinating pattern. It was film-making of great power and almost without a flaw but the public did not take to the film despite critical raves. Welles now found his whirl-

Australia's Peter **Weir** (left foreground) briefs Mel Gibson and (on his shoulder) Linda Hunt on the filming of a crowd-packed action sequence for *The Year of Living Dangerously.*

Orson **Welles** and Joseph Cotten at the window of the "New York Enquirer" in a scene from Welles' own classic *Citizen Kane.*

wind career undermining his standing at the studio, as he tried to take on too many things and found that, in his absences, other hands had chopped down his second film, *The Magnificent Ambersons* (still an impressive film, but now with a most peculiar ending) from two-and-a-half hours to 88 minutes, and had also altered the ending of his third film, *Journey into Fear* – although in this case a furious Welles was able to restore the original climax in part on his return. Throughout the 1940s and 1950s, if his dramatic grip was slipping, Welles' visual control remained high, giving great aesthetic pleasure in such sequences as rain pouring from high gutters in the climax to *Journey into Fear,* Welles himself meeting his doom in the clock-tower in *The Stranger,* the climactic hall of mirrors shoot-out in *The Lady from Shanghai,* the Bergmanesque first reel of the otherwise dull *Othello* and the Birnam Wood scenes from *Macbeth.* But projects uncompleted or spanning a period of years had already become the pattern, and, by the late 1940s, the public were clearly more inter-

ested in Welles the actor, with his air of latent menace, undoubted presence and uniquely soft, resonant voice, than in Welles the director. Even an excellent straightforward thriller, *Touch of Evil,* with Welles himself as a fat, wheezing villain, did not succeed at the box-office, although it was the nearest he got to regaining a commercial foothold in Hollywood. He won an Academy Award in 1941 for co-writing the script of *Citizen Kane,* and received a Special Oscar in 1970. His three marriages included one to Rita Hayworth, from 1943 to 1947. He died following a long battle with heart trouble and diabetes.

1934: *†*The Hearts of Age.* 1938: *Too Much Johnson (unreleased).* 1941: *Citizen Kane.* 1942: *The Magnificent Ambersons.* $*Journey into Fear.* †*It's All True.* 1946: *The Stranger.* 1947: *The Lady from Shanghai.* 1948: *Macbeth.* 1951: *Othello.* 1955: *Confidential Report (US: Mr Arkadin).* 1958: *Touch of Evil. The Fountain of Youth.* 1959: †*Don Quixote.* 1962: *The Trial.* 1966: *Chimes at Mid-*

night *(US: Falstaff.* 1968: *The Immortal Story.* 1969: †*The Deep.* 1973: *F for Fake.* 1975: †*The Other Side of the Wind.*

† uncompleted
$ Co-directed

WELLMAN, William A. 1896-1975

This American director was a tough, hard-driving man, and his films always seem happiest when they get out into the open, whether that means the skies of the air films that celebrate his own heroic youth, or the city streets of depressed eras through which wander restless, embittered youths – Wellman clearly felt he might have been one without the intervention of World War I. Reading a number of articles on Wellman, one concludes that his rating has now sunk to an all-time low. It is hard at times to believe one is really reading about the man who made such disparate, but memorable films as *The Public Enemy, So Big, Wild Boys of the Road, A Star is Born, Wings, Nothing Sacred, Beau Geste, Roxie Hart, The Ox-Bow Incident, The Story of G.I. Joe, Yellow Sky, Battleground* and *Track of the Cat.* These are 'men's films' by and large, and if there are sometimes sympathetic portraits of women in them, it is when the women are tough, such as Dorothy Coonan – who in real life became Wellman's fourth wife and stayed married to him until his death from leukaemia – in *Wild Boys of the Road,* Barbara Stanwyck in *So Big* and Ginger Rogers in *Roxie Hart.* Wellman wasn't at his happiest directing the ladies, but he no doubt liked 'Stany', one of the few actresses who, as Fred Astaire said of Eleanor Powell, 'put 'em down like a man'. Wellman's younger days were filled with wanderings and minor brushes with the law before he joined the Foreign Legion in 1914 as an ambulance driver, switching to the Lafayette Flying Corps when the US entered the war. After building up a distinguished record, he was eventually shot down and injured so badly he had to be invalided out of the service. Back in America, he proceeded to make an amazing recovery, but did not join up again, instead earning a living as a stunt pilot in a flying show. He got into films, briefly, as a bit-part player and stuntman, but soon became more interested in the technical side of the business, starting as a props man, but progressing quickly to assistant director, making his first solo feature as director in 1923. Wellman's early films are small-scale westerns, but he soon showed a keen sense of immediacy, which gives an almost-newsreel quality to many of his films, especially, naturally, those that involve wartime action; and his reputation was made when his aviation drama *Wings* (1927, re-released in sound version 1929) won the first best picture Academy Award. Wellman himself never won the best director Oscar, although, with co-writer Robert Carson, he did pick up the screenplay award for *A Star is Born* in 1937. In the latter stages of his career, he drifted into the routine too often for comfort, but his is a generally impressive record.

1923: The Man Who Won. Second Hand Love. Cupid's Fireman. Big Dan. 1924: Not a Drum Was Heard. The Vagabond Trail. The Circus Cowboy. 1925: When Husbands Flirt. 1926: The Boob (GB: The Yokel). The Cat's Pajamas. You Never Know Women. 1927: Wings (and sound version, 1929). 1928: Legion of the Condemned. Ladies of the Mob. Beggars of Life. 1929: Chinatown Nights. The Man I Love. Woman Trap. 1930: Dangerous Paradise. Maybe It's Love. Young Eagles. 1931: Other Men's Women/Steel Highway. The Public Enemy (GB: Enemies of the Public). Night Nurse. Star Witness. Safe in Hell (GB: The Lost Lady). 1932: The Conquerors. The Hatchet Man (GB: The Honourable Mr Wong). So Big. The Purchase Price. Love is a Racket. Frisco Jenny (GB: The Common Ground). 1933: Lilly Turner. Heroes for Sale. Midnight Mary. Wild Boys of the Road (GB: Dangerous Days). College Coach (GB: Football Coach). Central Airport. 1934: Stingaree. Looking for Trouble. 1935: The President Vanishes (GB: Strange Conspiracy). Call of the Wild.

1936: Small Town Girl. Robin Hood of Eldorado. †Tarzan Escapes! (uncredited). 1937: Nothing Sacred. A Star is Born. 1938: Men with Wings. 1939: Beau Geste. The Light That Failed. 1941: Reaching for the Sun. 1942: Thunder Birds. Roxie Hart. The Great Man's Lady. The Ox Bow Incident (GB: Strange Incident). 1943: Lady of Burlesque (GB: Striptease Lady). 1944: Buffalo Bill. 1945: This Man's Navy. The Story of G.I. Joe (later War Correspondent). 1946: Gallant Journey. 1947: Magic Town. 1948: Yellow Sky. The Iron Curtain. 1949: Battleground. 1950: The Happy Years. The Next Voice You Hear. 1951: †It's a Big Country. Across the Wide Missouri. Westward the Women. 1952: My Man and I. 1953: Island in the Sky. 1954: †Ring of Fear (uncredited). The High and the Mighty. Track of the Cat. 1955: Blood Alley. 1956: Goodbye, My Lady. 1957: Darby's Rangers (GB: The Young Invaders). Lafayette Escadrille (GB: Hell Bent for Glory).

WENDERS, Wim 1945 -

Although less prolific than his contemporary Rainer Werner Fassbinder (*qv*), this West German director succeeded in making every one of his new films up to the mid-1980s something of an event. With the strange exception of *The Scarlet Letter*, they all received wide international distribution and are now better known under their English-speaking titles. This is probably caused in some part by the fact that Wenders' style recalls memories of

Hollywood films of 30 years earlier – probably also the reason why Twentieth Century-Fox called him over to Hollywood to make a film for them. His pictures are usually about attempted escapes from inextricable situations, by people who, like Frankenstein and his creature, could go to the ends of the earth and still find fate awaiting them. His cities are unhelpful, unfriendly, black monoliths dotted with harsh lights: the *film noir*, one feels, is in Wenders' soul. After studies at Munich Film School, where he made his first short films, Wenders was quickly into his stride with his first feature at 25. Of the movies that followed, *Summer in the City, The Goalkeeper's Fear of the Penalty, Kings of the Road* and *Alice in the Cities* stay in the mind. But the film that must have attracted Hollywood was *The American Friend*, an adaptation of a novel by American thriller writer Patricia Highsmith. For a start, the film seemed to indicate that Wenders had learned more from the American cinema than modern Hollywood itself. One has only to compare Hollywood attempts to update, for example, Chandler's crime stories in the 1970s with the originals 20 years earlier, then look at Wenders' film in comparison to Hitchcock's *Strangers on a Train* (from another Highsmith novel) to realize that the Hollywood updating has been of the worst kind, broadening, coarsening, losing the brutal innocence of the original. Wenders has plainly seen the folly of these errors of judgment and his film, while approaching the quality of the Hitchcock movie only in spells, is every bit as close to the Highsmith spirit. Up to its first murder, at least, the film is a tightly built, immaculately edited example of what the Hollywood crime film should have led to, after the dark peaks of the 1940s and 1950s. And the location, Hamburg, although retaining something of its own atmosphere, could almost be the Beverly Hills so beloved of the 'Black Mask' school of writers. After this, though, Wenders' career underwent its first hiccups. He helped his dying director friend Nicholas Ray (*qv*) direct one last film, then went to Hollywood. But both *Hammett* (completed in 1980), and his later West German film, *Der Stand der Dinge*, were delayed in release. In 1984, the award-winning *Paris, Texas*, fascinating amusing, dramatic and touching by turns, seemed to have established Wenders' international credentials. His subsequent turning away from American locations (even if he still often used Hollywood stars) has left Wenders with mixed fortunes in the ensuing years. His films, though still quite often festival successes, became less accessible to the general pub-

Hardly looking his 42 years, Wim **Wenders** directs Solveig Dommartin in his 1987 film *Wings of Desire*.

lic, and he seems destined to play out his career with films on the fringes of the mainstream whose target audience outside the continent has appeared much reduced in the 1990s.

1967: *Schauplätze. *Same Player Shoots Again. 1968: *Silver City. *Polizeifilm. 1969: *Alabama – 2000 Light Years. *Drei Amerikanische LPs. 1970: Summer in the City (Dedicated to the Kinks). 1971: Die Angst des Tormanns beim Elfmeter (GB: The Goalkeeper's Fear of the Penalty. US: The Anxiety of the Goalie at the Penalty Kick). 1972: The Scarlet Letter. 1974: Alice in den Städten (GB & US: Alice in the Cities). 1975: Falsche Bewegung (GB: Wrong Movement. US: The Wrong Move). 1976: Im Lauf der Zeit (GB and US: Kings of the Road). 1977: Der amerikanische Freund (GB & US: The American Friend). 1980: †Lightning Over Water. 1981: Hammett. 1982: Der Stand der Dinge (GB & US: The State of Things). Room 666. 1984: Paris, Texas. I Played It for You. 1985: Tokyo – Ga. 1987: Der Himmel über Berlin/Wings of Desire. 1989: A Notebook on Clothes and Cities. 1991: Until the End of the World. 1993: In weiter Ferne so nah/Faraway, So Close. 1995: Arisha, the Bear and the Stone Tiling. 1996: A Trick of the Light. 1997: The End of Violence. 1998: Buena Vista Social Club (D). 1999: Million Dollar Hotel.

WENDKOS, Paul 1922-

This craggy American director did not make it to the top rank despite frequent critical approval. None of his films was especially successful commercially, and he was never handed a really 'big' project to direct. But television seized him eagerly, and gave him far more interesting work, including one of the best-ever TV movies, Haunts of the Very Rich. His best films and TV movies are those which involve us deeply in the fortunes of central characters who are neither good nor bad, but have weaknesses and strengths, doing the best they can in the circumstances. After working in off-Broadway theatre productions, Wendkos started his film career in documentary work for the State Department. His first film proper was a low-budget crime melodrama from an oft-filmed David Goodis novel, The Burglar. Although it was very effective, and contains one of Dan Duryea's most charismatic performances, it was some time before Wendkos really got started in films (1958) and television (1959). Almost immediately, he made one of his best films, Face of a Fugitive, a tremendous western with Fred MacMurray, and had

one of his greatest commercial successes, with the candy-floss concoction Gidget. But they were almost his last cinema triumphs and, of his later work, only the chilling The Mephisto Waltz and the westerns Guns of the Magnificent Seven (better than both other Seven sequels) and Cannon for Cordoba are of note: they move along like express trains with a fluid command of action and personable leading performances. On television, however, Wendkos made a series of films trapping people in their own fates. Haunts of the Very Rich is a disturbing sideshoot of Outward Bound and in Between Two Worlds, as holidaymakers at a lush tropical resort gradually discover that they are all dead .... Fear No Evil is a frightening occult thriller involving a haunted mirror, while The Death of Richie takes us into the real-life horror of a teenage boy hooked on drugs. Robbie Benson's pitiable performance in the leading role is probably his best to date. The mid-1970s proved a particularly rich time for Wendkos in terms of television and The Strangers in 7A, Honor Thy Father (released theatrically outside the United States), The Underground Man, Terror on the Beach and The Legend of Lizzie Borden are also above average of their kind. Despite failing to become a name in the cinema, in fact, Wendkos has plenty to be proud of. Even though sometimes he has descended to rubbish, it has at least been made with relish. And, with the quirky and punchy Scorned and Swindled in 1984, he turned out another of the best TV movies ever made.

1955: *Dark Interlude (D). The Burglar. 1958: The Case Against Brooklyn. Tarawa Beachhead. 1959: Face of a Fugitive. Gidget. Battle of the Coral Sea. 1960: Because They're Young. 1961: Angel Baby. Gidget Goes Hawaiian. 1962: Recoil (TV. GB: cinemas). 1963: Gidget Goes to Rome. 1966: Johnny Tiger. 1967: Attack on the Iron Coast. 1968: Guns of the Magnificent Seven. Hawaii Five-O (TV). 1969: Hell Boats. Fear No Evil (TV). 1970: Cannon for Cordoba. Brotherhood of the Bell (TV). Crisis (TV). 1971: Travis Logan DA (TV). A Tattered Web (TV). A Death of Innocence (TV). A Little Game (TV). The Mephisto Waltz. 1972: The Delphi Bureau (TV). Haunts of the Very Rich (TV). The Family Rico (TV). The Strangers in 7A (TV). Footsteps (TV). Six Characters in Search of an Author (TV). 1973: Honor Thy Father (TV. GB: cinemas). Terror on the Beach (TV). Die, Darling, Die (TV). Blood Feud (TV). Murder in the Slave Trade (TV). 1974: The Underground Man (TV). 1975: The

Legend of Lizzie Borden (TV). Death Among Friends/Mrs R: Death Among Friends (TV). 1976: Special Delivery. 1977: The Death of Richie (TV). Secrets (TV). Good Against Evil (TV). 1978: Betrayal (TV). A Woman Called Moses (TV). 1979: The Ordeal of Patty Hearst (TV). The Victim: An Anatomy of a Mugging (TV). 1980: Hagen (TV). A Cry for Love (TV). The Ordeal of Dr Mudd (TV). 1981: The Five of Me (TV). The Awakening of Candra (TV. Shown 1983). Golden Gate (TV). 1982: Cocaine: One Man's Seduction (TV). Farrell for the People (TV). The Bad Seed (TV). 1983: Intimate Agony (TV). 1984: Scorned and Swindled (TV). 1985: The Execution (TV). Picking Up the Pieces (TV). 1987: Blood Vows: The Story of a Mafia Wife (TV). Right to Die (TV). 1988: The Taking of Flight 847 (TV). The Great Escape II: The Untold Story (TV). 1989: From the Dead of Night (TV). The Flight (TV). Blind Faith (TV). 1990: Deadline Assault/Act of Violence (TV). Presumed Guilty (TV). 1991: White Hot: The Mysterious Murder of Thelma Todd (TV). The Cops Are Robbers (TV). The Chase (TV).

WERKER, Alfred L. 1896-*

There are minor highlights scattered throughout this American director's career, but few of them were in films big enough to make him into a major studio director. There were times though when he elevated quite minor westerns and thrillers to the top of their grade. In Hollywood from the age of 20, Werker at first worked on the production side, but gradually got into direction through his involvement with 'B' westerns at Fox, his studio until 1933. There was an early film about Kit Carson, and two very good others with George O'Brien, The Last of the Duanes and Fair Warning. The latter is particularly good of its kind, packed with rousing action and clever stunts and with a likeable performance from the star. Werker's biggest film was perhaps The House of Rothschild, made in 1934 for Darryl F. Zanuck's new Twentieth Century company, which would soon merge with Fox. This story of the famous banking family, in the late 18th and early 19th century, had some interesting performances, especially from George Arliss and Boris Karloff. The rest of Werker's films in the 1930s were fairly routine, although he was responsible for revamping Erich von Stroheim's Walking Down Broadway into Hello Sister!; he also made the best of Basil Rathbone's Sherlock Holmes films, The Adventures of Sherlock Holmes, with lots of atmosphere and a smooth villain in George Zucco. Of his

One of Hollywood's great sophisticates, James **Whale** was far from his humble origins in the north of England at the time of this publicity shot from the 1930s.

post-war work, *Repeat Performance* is probably his worst film, but it did seem to inspire some good ones, especially *He Walked by Night*, an unrelentingly grim *film noir* about an introverted killer (Richard Basehart), eventually trapped in the sewers of the city; *Lost Boundaries*, one of several goodish racial conscience films made around the late 1940s and early 1950s; and two tough, no-nonsense crime films, *Sealed Cargo* and *Walk East on Beacon!* By this time, Werker was firmly established in second-features, but still had something to offer. Some novel touches kept *Canyon Crossroads* gripping and suspenseful, plus very good acting from Basehart (again) and Phyllis Kirk, while Werker obtained more excellent performances from Fred MacMurray, Dorothy Malone and Walter Brennan in *At Gunpoint*, a suspense western somewhat after *High Noon*, quite superbly directed by Werker, who delivers a climax to satisfy the most avid action fan. *Rebel in Town* is another tough, tense western,

but Werker's last film, *The Young Don't Cry*, was weak and woebegone and he finished off his career in television.

1925: †*Ridin' the Wind.* 1928: †*The Pioneer Scout.* †*The Sunset Legion. Kit Carson.* 1929: †*Chasing Through Europe. Blue Skies.* 1930: †*Double Cross Roads. Last of the Duanes.* 1931: *Fair Warning. Annabelle's Affairs. Heartbreak.* 1932: *The Gay Caballero. Rackety Rax. Bachelor's Affairs.* 1933: *It's Great to be Alive.* †*Hello Sister! Advice to the Lovelorn.* 1934: *The House of Rothschild. You Belong to Me.* 1935: *Stolen Harmony.* 1936: *Love in Exile. Big Town Girl.* 1937: *We Have Our Moments. Wild and Wooly. City Girl.* 1938: *Kidnapped. Gateway. Up the River.* 1939: *The Adventures of Sherlock Holmes (GB: Sherlock Holmes). It Could Happen to You. News Is Made at Night.* 1941: *Moon Over Her Shoulder. The Reluctant Dragon.* 1942: *A-Haunting We Will Go. Whispering Ghosts. The Mad Martindales.* 1944: *My*

Pal Wolf. 1946: *Shock.* 1947: *Repeat Performance. Pirates of Monterey.* 1948: †*He Walked by Night.* 1949: *Lost Boundaries.* 1951: *Sealed Cargo.* 1952: *Walk East on Beacon! (GB: The Crime of the Century).* 1953: *The Last Posse. Devil's Canyon.* 1954: *Three Hours to Kill.* 1955: *Canyon Crossroads. At Gunpoint (GB: Gunpoint).* 1956: *Rebel in Town.* 1957: *The Young Don't Cry.*

* Believed deceased, but date of death uncertain

WHALE, James 1889-1957

If any director can be said to have found beauty in horror, then it was the British-born James Whale. An enigmatic character, Whale was 40 before he came to Hollywood, but he made four classics of the horror genre there. These were *Frankenstein*, *The Old Dark House*, *The Invisible Man* and *Bride of Frankenstein*. Whale was just as effective with dark, unstated horror as with delicate, terrifyingly chilling scenes that had one on the edge of one's seat lest they should fade to black, and scenes of freakish grey horror comedy. Undoubtedly, his understanding of actors gave new dimensions to these films, but the wonder was that such a stage-trained and -bound man should take the measure of the cinema in such a short time. In front of black-and-white backgrounds that could have come from Brueghel or Bosch (or even a demented Rembrandt), Whale moved misguided and misshapen characters so as to arouse a whole host of different emotions in his audience – fear, naturally, but also admiration, pity, foreboding, amusement and aesthetic pleasure. Trained in graphic art, Whale was a newspaper cartoonist until World War I, much of which he spent interned in a prisoner-of-war camp. But he also did some acting, and it was to the theatre he moved from 1919, both as actor and set designer. He turned director in the 1920s, having a tremendous success with the war drama *Journey's End*, and bringing it to New York in 1928. While in America, he became involved in the film industry, at first as dialogue director on a couple of films, then, not unnaturally, as director of the film version of *Journey's End*. That film still touches nerve-ends, although it looks even stagier today than it probably did then. Inheriting the *Frankenstein* project from another director, Whale hired two English actors who were personal friends of his, Colin Clive and Boris Karloff, to play the scientist and the creature, and a legend was on its way. *Frankenstein* is not the greatest of horror films, but it was done with

tremendous style with a number of touches that showed a highly individual imagination at work. *The Old Dark House*
reinforced Whale's liking for English
actors, although the Americans in the cast
of this horror-joke acquit themselves well,
especially Melvyn Douglas and Gloria
Stuart, while Whale's *The Invisible Man*
made a star of another English actor,
Claude Rains, even though he is not seen
until the very end of the film. But *Bride of
Frankenstein* is his greatest achievement, a
celebration of all the possibilities of the
cinema when applied to the fantasy field,
together with some elements, such as the
daringly light musical score, that no-one
had even thought of before. Under
Whale's intelligent direction, Karloff's
portrayal of the monster reaches full
flower; the film is undated and unchanging in its effect. Whale immediately
broadened his horizons to the musical,
and made a memorable version of *Show
Boat*. Whale's work seems less personal
after this; some said that he may have lost
interest in the medium after the unexpected sudden death of his friend Colin Clive
at only 39 from pulmonary tuberculosis.
Others conjectured that his flamboyant
homosexual lifestyle had angered Hollywood moguls. Certainly after the failure
of *The Road Back* in 1937 (mainly thanks
to studio interference), he was quickly
handed lesser assignments. In 1956 Whale
suffered a nervous breakdown and the
following year was found drowned in the
swimming pool of his home. A suicide
note emerged some time later.

1929: $*The Love Doctor*. 1930: $*Hell's
Angels. Journey's End*. 1931: *Waterloo
Bridge. Frankenstein*. 1932: *The Impa-
tient Maiden. The Old Dark House*.
1933: *The Kiss Before the Mirror. The
Invisible Man. By Candlelight*. 1934: *One
More River* (GB: *Over the River*). 1935:
*Remember Last Night? Bride of Franken-
stein*. 1936: *Show Boat*. 1937: *The Road
Back/Return of the Hero. The Great Gar-
rick*. 1938: *Sinners in Paradise. Port of
Seven Seas. Wives Under Suspicion*. 1939:
The Man in the Iron Mask. 1940: *Green
Hell*. 1941: *They Dare Not Love*. 1942:
Personnel Placement in the Navy. 1949:
Hello Out There (unreleased).

$ As dialogue director

WHELAN, Tim 1893-1957

Affable American director whose keen
sense of comedy was little used after the
mid-1930s, when he came to Britain and
worked for various studios, but most
notably for Alexander Korda's London
Films. He returned to America in 1940 to
complete work on Korda's *The Thief of
Bagdad* and stayed there, although he
rarely worked to such good effect as in
England. Whelan began his career as an
actor, mainly in stage comedies. But he
began to be more interested in writing,
and went to Hollywood in 1920. Whelan
worked unspectacularly on screenplays
and writing gags for comedies until a
friendship with Harold Lloyd furthered
his career. He worked on the scripts of
several of Lloyd's funniest of the 1920s,
Safety Last, Girl Shy and *The Freshman*,
and it was Lloyd who encouraged Whelan
to turn his talents to direction. The
opportunity, however, occurred in an
unexpected place – England – and Whelan
liked the working conditions there so
much that after his first film in 1928 he
stayed on and off for another 12 years.
His best American film was a Spencer
Tracy drama, *The Murder Man*, which
gave a first screen role to James Stewart,
but it does not compare with such British
work as *Farewell Again, The Mill on the
Floss, St Martin's Lane* (said to have been
the film that first attracted American producers to Vivien Leigh), *Ten Days in Paris*
and *Q Planes*. These are all lively films,
with genuine senses of atmosphere quite
rare in the British cinema at the time. *St
Martin's Lane*, in particular, really does
seem to have something in common with
the street life of London that other films
struggled unsuccessfully to convey. After
Whelan returned to the States, *International Lady* was a fun spy story, and
Higher and Higher gave Frank Sinatra his
first dramatic role, but otherwise he was
employed on minor musicals and westerns
unworthy of the talent he had shown elsewhere. His best post-war film (although
Rage at Dawn is a vigorous western) was
This Was a Woman, with a powerful performance by Sonia Dresdel; predictably it
was made on a return visit to Britain.

1928: *Adam's Apple*. 1929: *When Knights
Were Bold*. 1933: *It's a Boy. Aunt Sally*
(US: *Along Came Sally*). 1934: *The
Camels Are Coming*. 1935: *The Murder
Man. The Perfect Gentleman*. 1936:
Two's Company. Smash and Grab (US:
Larceny Street). 1937: *The Mill on the
Floss. Farewell Again* (US: *Troopship*).
†*Action for Slander*. 1938: *The Divorce of
Lady X. St Martin's Lane* (US: *Sidewalks
of London*). 1939: *Q Planes* (US: *Clouds
Over Europe*). *Ten Days in Paris* (US:
Missing Ten Days). 1940: †*The Thief of
Bagdad. The Mad Doctor* (GB: *A Date
with Destiny*). 1941: *International Lady*.
1942: *Twin Beds. Nightmare. Seven Days'
Leave*. 1943: *Higher and Higher*. 1944:
Swing Fever. Step Lively. 1946: *Badman's
Territory*. 1948: *This Was a Woman*.

1955: *Rage at Dawn. Texas Lady*.

WIDERBERG, Bo 1930-1997

Swedish director famous for his very
superior TV-commercial style of shooting.
Pastoral shades and pastoral patterns dec-
orate Widerberg's films, whether they are
about doomed lovers or industrial unrest.
They are films to delight lovers of beauty
and antagonize lovers of realism. Arthur
Penn (*qv*) probably combined these sometimes inter-destructive elements better in
Bonnie and Clyde than Widerberg managed to do in any of his films, but the
Swedish director nonetheless enjoyed considerable international success, especially
with *Elvira Madigan* and *Adalen '31*.
Such careful patterns of light and colour
must have surprised those who were regular readers of Widerberg in his role as one
of Sweden's most influential critics of the
early 1960s (earlier he had been a journalist and short-story writer), when he
harangued Swedish cinema for being out
of touch with ordinary people and their
everyday experiences, and published a
searingly critical book called *The Vision
of Swedish Cinema*. The most effective of
his early films is *Raven's End*, immaculately set in 1936, already displaying
Widerberg's care for the right feel and
atmosphere, in the story of a young man
straining to get away from the suffocating
atmosphere of proletarian life in a
Swedish city. The leading man, Thommy
Berggren, was carried forward to Widerberg's most famous film *Elvira Madigan*,
a story of the doomed romance between a
delicately beautiful tightrope walker and
an army officer. Its *amour fou* is deeply
felt, but, although as pleasing to the senses as a visit to an art gallery, it is a shade
too prettified, if given a lift by the music
of Mozart and Vivaldi. It was a one-off
achievement by its leading lady, Pia
Degermark, who, although winning a best
actress award at the Cannes festival that
year (1967) has done little since; other
directors have made her seem merely
vapid, and Widerberg does have a talent
of extracting the maximum of feeling
from even the most placid and inanimate
characters. Widerberg's most enjoyable
film, and deserving of a much wider distribution than the one it had, is *Stubby*,
the story of a seven-year-old footballing
genius. This is very entertaining and full
of delightful little touches, such as the kid
swearing at the referee and being sent off,
or his team-mates having to read him
bed-time stories on away matches. Naturally, there's a fairy-tale ending to such a
fairy-tale, but one told with great panache
and a little gentle satire. In declining
health from 1990, this incurably romantic

filmmaker brought out his first film for seven years in 1995, the well received *All Things Fair*. Two years later he died 'after a long illness'.

1961: *Pojken och Draken/The Boy and the Kite. 1962: Kvarteret Korpen/Raven's End. 1963: Barnvagnen (GB: The Pram. US: The Baby Carriage). 1965: Kärlek 65/Love 65. 1966: Heja Roland!/Thirty Times Your Money. 1967: Elvira Madigan. 1968: †Den Vita Sporten/The White Came. 1969: Adalen '31 (US: The Adalen Riots). 1971: Joe Hill (GB: The Ballad of Joe Hill). 1974: Fimpen/Stubby. 1976: Mannen på Taket/The Man on the Roof. 1979: Victoria. 1984: The Man from Mallorca. 1987: Ormens wäg pa hälleberget/The Serpent's Way. 1988: Up the Naked Rock. 1995: Lust och fagring stor/All Things Fair.

WIENE, Robert 1881-1938

Although few of this German director's films have survived today (nor, according to most writers, do many deserve to), he did create one picture that lives on in our nightmare – *The Cabinet of Dr Caligari*. The beginnings of so many other paths of the horror film can be found in this one story, with its expressionist sets – all crooked and unreal, as if in the vision of a madman – grotesque makeup and story of a sinister doctor whose exhibit at a local fair, a somnambulist, commits brutal murders by night, terrorizing the township. As the framing story comes to its conclusion, it becomes evident that this is indeed the vision of a madman, told by a lunatic in an asylum, where the curator is the sinister doctor himself. No film since has ever illustrated this world of nightmares and lunacy so vividly, installing into its audience a fear of going to bed and dreaming such things themselves. The star of that film (as Cesare, the somnambulist) was Conrad Veidt, who also featured in the only other Wiene film to approach the power of *Caligari*, *The Hands of Orlac*, which has Veidt in demented form as the classical pianist who loses his hands and has the hands of a murderer grafted on. Wiene began his career as an actor, but it was as a writer that he began working in German films at the age of 32. His career was virtually brought to a halt with the Nazis' rise to power, and he fled to France, where he died during production of his last film, *Ultimatum*, which was completed for him by his friend Robert Siodmak (*qv*).

1914: †Arme Eva/Dear Eva. 1915: Die Konservenbraut. Er Rechts, Sie Links. 1916: Der Liebesbrief der Königin/The Empress's Love Letter. Der Mann im Spiegel. Die Räuberbraut. Das wandernde Licht. Der Sekretar der Königin. 1917: Furcht/Fear. 1919: Ein gefahrliches Spiel. Das Kabinett des Dr Caligari/The Cabinet of Dr Caligari. Der Umweg zur Ehe. 1920: Die drei Tänze der Mary Wilford. Genuine. Die Nacht der Königin Isabeau. Die Rache einer Frau. 1921: Hollische Nacht. †Das Spiel mit dem Feuer. 1922: Tragikomedie. Salome. 1923: I.N.R.I/Crown of Thorns. Der Puppenmacher von Kiang-Ning. Crime and Punishment/Raskolnikoff. 1924: Orlacs Hände/The Hands of Orlac. 1925: Pension Groonen. 1926: The Guardsman/Der Gardeoffizier. Die Königin vom Moulin-Rouge. Der Rosenkavalier. 1927: Die Dancer of Barcelona/Die berühmte Frau. Die Geliebte/The Beloved. 1928: Die Frau auf der Folter/A Scandal in Paris. Die grosse Abenteuerin. Leontines Ehemänner. Unfug der Liebe. 1930: Der Andere. 1931: Panic in Chicago. Der Liebesexpress. 1934: Polizeiakte 909. Eine Nacht in Venedig. 1938: †Ultimatum.

WILCOX, Fred McLeod 1905-1964

From this American director's work come several of my fondest recollections of childhood film-going, of Lassie coming home, Margaret O' Brien discovering the secret garden, more Lassie adventures, Robby the Robot on the forbidden planet, and two of my favourite second-features of the 1950s, *Code Two* and *Tennessee Champ*. Why M-G-M gave Wilcox so few films to direct is something of a mystery, since he had a vivid sense of colour, and a keen idea of exactly what would draw the required emotional response from his audience. Most of the films he made could have been very routine, but most of them made a lot of money for the studio. Yet, before he was handed his first Lassie assignment, Wilcox had spent 17 years at the studio, making one short, scores of screen tests and a few films as second-unit director. He was also for many years script clerk to King Vidor (*qv*). The Lassie films are skilfully done, craftily edited and pull pretty well every emotional string. In common with most Wilcox films, they are also attractively, unaffectedly acted. This is certainly true of *The Secret Garden*, a charming, compelling, at times quite chilly fantasy of Victorian childhood, and of *Tennessee Champ*, a very likeable boxing comedy in excellent colour, with Keenan Wynn an amiable rascal. As far as most writers are concerned, however, Wilcox's reputation rests principally with the 1956 *Forbidden Planet*, an outer-space variation of Shakespeare's *The Tempest*. Stupendous sets and exciting action outweigh some rather limp performances in a film which has a great sense of movement.

1938: *Joaquin Murrieta. 1943: Lassie Come Home. 1945: Blue Sierra. 1946: Courage of Lassie. 1948: Hills of Home (GB: Master of Lassie). Three Daring Daughters. 1949: The Secret Garden. 1951: Shadow in the Sky. 1953: Code Two. 1954: Tennessee Champ. 1956: Forbidden Planet. 1960: I Passed for White.

WILCOX, Herbert 1891-1977

This Irish-born director made films that appealed to his audiences' senses of patriotism and nationalism. Despite the lack of a strong personal style, his unerring feel for what would take money at British box-offices kept him in the forefront of his native industry from the mid-1920s until the early 1950s. During this time, his pictures probably made more money on average than those of any other director, Hitchcock included. From 1932, many of his films starred the vivacious blonde actress Anna Neagle, who finally become his wife in 1943. For Wilcox, she would play historical figures, music-hall stars, war heroines and even royalty – all terribly English (with the exception of *Odette*, a war heroine who, after all, was married to a Briton!). A pilot in World War I, Wilcox's first connection with the film industry was as a salesman, but he and his brother soon set up their own distribution company. Wilcox became a producer in 1922, and director the following year. His first film was an assured hit – the record-breaking musical *Chu Chin Chow*. He continued to produce his own films, became a director of British National (which built Elstree Studios in 1926) and later founded the influential British and Dominions company. Hollywood star Dorothy Gish played the first of his many period heroines in *Nell Gwyn* (the same role Miss Neagle would play in a remake eight years later) and Sybil Thorndike was his initial war heroine (Nurse Edith Cavell) in *Dawn*: no prizes for guessing who played the role in Wilcox's 1939 remake. Wilcox also made many very popular light musicals in the 1930s, two enormously successful films about Queen Victoria, some light musicals in Hollywood and some stiff-upper-lip war films which nonetheless make solid entertainment, grafted to an assured formula. Perhaps the most popular of all his films were the post-war high society romances starring Miss Neagle and Michael Wilding. People flocked to get away from austerity and into such escapism as *Piccadilly Incident, The Courtneys of Curzon Street,*

Maytime in Mayfair and *Spring in Park Lane*. By the 1950s Wilcox, so long Britain's premier film showman, no longer had his finger on the pulse of British public taste, and his last few films had a tired look. In 1964, he went into bankruptcy in a case which shocked the nation. But there was still one more comeback, a best-selling autobiography, called *25,000 Sunsets*.

1923: *Chu Chin Chow*. 1924: *Decameron Nights* (and German-language version). *Southern Love*. 1925. *The Only Way*. 1926: *Nell Gwyn*. *London* (US: *Limehouse*). 1927: *Tiptoes*. *Madame Pompadour*. *Mumsie*. 1928: *The Bondman*. *Dawn*. 1929: *The Woman in White*. 1930: *The Loves of Robert Burns*. 1931: †*Chance of a Night Time*. *Carnival* (US: *Venetian Nights*). 1932: *The Blue Danube*. *Goodnight Vienna* (US: *Magic Night*). 1933: *Yes, Mr Brown*. *The King's Cup*. *Bitter Sweet*. *The Little Damozel*. 1934: *The Queen's Affair* (US: *Runaway Queen*). *Nell Gwyn*. 1935: *Peg of Old Drury*. *Limelight* (US: *Backstage*). 1936: *The Three Maxims* (US: *The Show Goes On*). *This'll Make You Whistle*. 1937: *London Melody* (US: *Girls in the Street*). *Our Fighting Navy* (US: *Torpedoed!*). *Victoria the Great*. 1938: *Sixty Glorious*

Years (US: *Queen of Destiny*). 1939: *Nurse Edith Cavell*. 1940: *Irene*. *No, No, Nanette*. 1941: *Sunny*. 1942: *They Flew Alone* (US: *Wings and the Woman*). 1943: †*Forever and a Day*. *The Yellow Canary*. 1945: *I Live in Grosvenor Square* (US: *A Yank in London*). 1946: *Piccadilly Incident*. 1947: *The Courtneys of Curzon Street* (US: *The Courtney Affair*). 1948: *Spring in Park Lane*. *Elizabeth of Ladymead*. 1949: *Maytime in Mayfair*. 1950: *Odette*. 1951: *The Lady with a Lamp*. *Into the Blue* (US: *Man in the Dinghy*). 1952: *Derby Day*. *Trent's Last Case*. 1953: *Laughing Anne*. 1954: *Trouble in the Glen*. *Lilacs in the Spring* (US: *Let's Make Up*). 1955: *King's Rhapsody*. 1956: *My Teenage Daughter* (US: *Teenage Bad Girl*). 1957: *These Dangerous Years* (US: *Dangerous Youth*). 1958: *The Man Who Wouldn't Talk*. *Wonderful Things!* 1959: *The Lady is a Square*. *Heart of a Man*.

WILDE, Cornel (Cornelius Wilde) 1915-1989
Best-known as an actor, idyllically handsome in the days when he played Chopin in *A Song to Remember* and was deluged with critical brickbats and fan-mail from adoring ladies, Wilde proved a sporadic, if interesting director. His films are very

much all of a piece and hearken back to simpler values in life: their disparate locations reflect a restless lifestyle that has seen him forsake advertising for medicine, medicine for fencing, fencing for acting and acting for directing. His best films as a director, however, are well worth having for their primitive vigour and only in his last couple of pictures did his eye drift away from the entertainment factor. The son of Hungarian-Czech parents, Wilde was at his most charismatic in the immediate post war years, but had dropped to co-features by the time he started directing in 1955, by which time he had married his second wife, actress Jean Wallace, who appears in all but two of the films he directed. The films Wilde directed pare their subjects down to basic emotions, and *Storm Fear* is just that, an oppressive study of hatred, replete with tension and thrills (and a few laughs in the wrong places), but an unusual film to come from Hollywood at this uncertain time. *The Devil's Hairpin* and *Maracaibo* were colourful, rattling good adventure stories in the old Hollywood tradition, but with *Lancelot and Guinevere*, the cleanest and freshest version of all of the old legend, Wilde was definitely into his own kind of cinema. *The Naked Prey, Beach Red* and *No Blade of Grass* were further studies of people with all veneer of civilization stripped away. The first of these, an account of a white man hunted

Although the hat and cigar are familiar, Billy **Wilder** was a long way past his prime when he made *Buddy Buddy* in 1981.

barefoot through the bush by a native tribe in 19th century Africa, was easily Wilde's most successful film in commercial terms. His last two films were by far his weakest, exhibiting none of the tension of his earlier work. He died from leukaemia.

1955: Storm Fear. 1957: The Devil's Hairpin. 1958: Maracaibo. 1962: Lancelot and Guinevere (US: Sword of Lancelot). 1964: The Naked Prey. 1967: Beach Red. 1970: No Blade of Grass. 1975: Shark's Treasure. 1983: Flesh and Bullets/Vultures in Paradise.

WILDER, Billy (Samuel Wilder) 1906-

Austrian-born director who came to the fore in the Hollywood of the 1940s after a sparkling writing career, and won two Academy Awards. After 1960, however, the time of the second Oscar, his work became increasingly disappointing and vulgarity eventually got the better of him. In the 1940s and 1950s, however, there were indeed glories to savour. Any retrospective season of Wilder's best work must surely take most, if not all, its films from this period. Having given up law studies in his youth to become a reporter, Wilder fought for some time to break into films as a screenwriter, eventually succeeding in 1929. In 1933, Wilder fled from the Nazis (most of his family were not so lucky and ended their days in concentration camps) and, via France, Britain and Mexico, ended up in Holly wood, where he was employed by Paramount as a writer and, in 1938, began the famous partnership with Charles Brackett, which prospered on such films as *Midnight, Ninotchka, Hold Back the Dawn* and *Ball of Fire*, before they became a writer-producer-director team, with Wilder doing the directing, making their debut as such with the very funny *The Major and the Minor*. Wilder's films kept the studio (Paramount) happy: they consistently made money. The war film *Five Graves to Cairo* was a popular success and the crime drama *Double Indemnity*, although only tolerably well received, has gone down as a classic of its kind – a wife and her lover plan to murder the husband –– and set a new pattern for Barbara Stanwyck's career. Wilder's study of alcoholism, *The Lost Weekend*, was amazingly frank for its time (even with a weak ending) and has some very imaginative and unpalatable sequences that bring home the full force of the hero's addiction: it won four Oscars, including best film, best screenplay, best direction and best actor (Ray Milland). Wilder and Brackett, by now known as The Gold Dust Twins, shared another Oscar for the

screenplay of *Sunset Boulevard*, with Gloria Swanson in her famous role of faded star Norma Desmond; but it was their last film together before they split up. Wilder later collaborated with another writer, I.A.L. Diamond, initially with great success. William Holden, the leading man from *Sunset Boulevard*, moved on to an Oscar for himself in Wilder's gritty and entertaining P-O-W camp thriller *Stalag 17*. The 1950s were vintage years for the team, and produced such classics as *Ace in the Hole*, *Sabrina*, the richly enjoyable courtroom puzzle-game *Witness for the Prosecution*, the underrated *Spirit of St Louis* and two films with Marilyn Monroe, *The Seven-Year Itch* and *Some Like It Hot*. But the highpoint of the decade was the touchingly, mordantly funny *The Apartment*. The film took five Academy Awards – best film, best direction, best screenplay, best art direction and best editing. *Some Like It Hot*, though, had skirted bad taste with some discomfort, and from 1961, with the raucously tedious *One Two Three* and, especially in and after *Kiss Me Stupid*, Wilder and Diamond fell headlong into the pit. Although the warmth of *Avanti!* slowed the decline, by the time of *Buddy Buddy*, the team had nearly disappeared beneath a mass of crass ideas, poor timing and four-letter words.

1934: †Mauvaise graine. 1942: The Major and the Minor. 1943: Five Graves to Cairo. 1944: Double Indemnity. 1945: The Lost Weekend. 1948: The Emperor Waltz. A Foreign Affair. 1950: Sunset Boulevard. 1951: The Big Carnival (GB: Ace in the Hole). 1953: Stalag 17. 1954: Sabrina (GB: Sabrina Fair). 1955: The Seven-Year Itch. 1957: Love in the Afternoon. Spirit of St Louis. 1958: Witness for the Prosecution. 1959: Some Like It Hot. 1960: The Apartment. 1961: One Two Three. 1963: Irma La Douce. 1964: Kiss Me, Stupid. 1966: The Fortune Cookie (GB: Meet Whiplash Willie). 1970: The Private Life of Sherlock Holmes. 1972: Avanti! 1974: The Front Page. 1978: Fedora. 1981: Buddy Buddy.

WILSON, Hugh 1943-

Now seemingly back in the film-making groove after seven years away, Wilson in at ease with all kinds of light entertainment and seems set to continue a middle-range Hollywood career for some time to come. Florida-born Wilson worked in television for many years, beginning as a writer (he has two Humanitas awards for TV writing) but most notably as creator-writer-director on the successful television series *WKRP in Cincinnati*. Other less

successful small-screen work has kept him busy between films, although he won an Emmy in 1988 for best comedy writing on an episode of *Frank's Place*. He began his film career with a co-script credit for *Stroker Ace* (1983) before tackling writing and directing chores on *Police Academy*, the first in an interminable series of cop comedies. Wilson's entry has one big advantage over the rest: it's funny. His knack of getting the most out of characters and situations without ever going over the top makes for some very big laughs. TV kept Wilson away from bigger screens between 1986 and 1993, then he was back with *Guarding Tess*, an amusing account of an infuriating and impossible ex-First Lady who must be guarded night and day. Wilson had his biggest box-office success to date with *The First Wives Club*. This was fun almost all the way, as middle-aged Bette Midler, Diane Keaton and Goldie Hawn deserted by their husbands for younger women, set out to prove there's life in the old bitches yet: revenge begins at 45. Wilson's command of visual comedy ensures some hilarious act pieces.

1984: Police Academy. 1985: Rustlers' Rhapsody. 1987: Burglar. 1994: Guarding Tess. 1996: The First Wives Club. 1998: Blast from the Past.

WINCER, Simon 1943-

The abiding image from this Australian director's work is that of horses on the run. Few if any directors have been able to capture so well the thrilling surge of such a spectacle. No wonder Wincer was chosen to helm Australia's most famous 'horse' film, *Phar Lap*, And yet his major contribution to the moving image will, for many, not be a film at all, but his direction of the classic TV western series *Lonesome Dove* in the late 1980s. After working part-time at a Sydney theatre in his young days, Wincer moved to London, doing time as a stage manager in West End theatre productions there, then moving into British television, where he served as production assistant and assistant director on action and drama series. It wasn't until he returned to Australia that his career in films began to take off. He made his debut as a director with *Harlequin*, an enjoyable sci-fi tall tale about a faith healer and a political plot. Wincer made it tight, tense and intriguing and within four years was helming his first Hollywood film, *D.A.R.Y.L.*, a lively fantasy adventure about a robot boy. Wincer helps make sure that the obvious possibilities of the plot are all made as enjoyable as they should be. There was a good TV movie, *The Girl Who Spelled Freedom*, then Wincer returned to Australia for *The Lighthorsemen*, a film about Australian cavalry fighting in the Palestinian desert of 1917, which has some thrilling charging action sequences. After the overwhelming success of *Lonesome Dove*, Wincer combined his Australian and American outdoor worlds in *Quigley Down Under*, an Aussie 'western' with Hollywood star Tom Selleck as the Yank adventurer far from home. It was not the success its action scenes and the performances of Selleck, Laura San Giacomo and Alan Rickman merited. Wincer is at his best with westerns and outdoor adventures and his biggest success in recent years has been the unexpected hit of *Free Willy*, a film about the release from captivity of a killer whale. Never over-sentimental, the film has more backbone than similar ventures might have done in past years and its story builds to an exhilarating, emotion-tugging climax. Again, Win-

cer could not follow this with another hit, and has recently been working in TV. He also directed two other 'horsey' TV miniseries, *The Last Frontier* (1986) and *Bluegrass* (1988).

1979: Snapshot/The Day Before Halloween. 1980: Harlequin (US: Dark Forces). 1983: Phar Lap. 1985: D.A.R.Y.L. 1986: The Girl Who Spelled Freedom (TV). 1987: The Lighthorsemen. 1990: Quigley Down Under. 1991: Harley Davidson and the Marlboro Man. 1993: Free Willy. 1994: Lightning Jack. 1995: Operation Dumbo Drop. 1996: The Phantom. 1997: Flash (TV). 1998: Escape: Human Cargo (TV).

WINNER, Michael 1935-

Bubbly, voluble, supremely self-confident British director who, like Francis Ford Coppola (*qv*) graduated from nudie movies. Winner was his best in the middle and late 1960s when he came up with some original, intriguing and beguiling entertainments. Since 1970, though, he has been more noteworthy for wasting some big star names in some sticky entertainments that lacked flair, and seemed happy merely to drench the screen in blood and guts. But then Winner has always been one for sensationalism and the main chance. A film gossip writer at 16, his limitless energy propelled him into BBC television at 20 and he had already written screenplays at 22. He continued writing the scripts for his own minor exploitation films before he began to break though to mainline cinema in 1963. He received a certain amount of praise for *The System*, a story of seaside lay-abouts and the sharpie who 'touts' for them, getting them girls. This had a nice sense of location atmosphere and a suitably cynical performance from Oliver Reed, who featured in three of Winner's next four films. These constitute his best work for the cinema, neither are they as overdirected as the later movies. Of especial note are *The Jokers*, a very enjoyable comedy-thriller about two upper-class misfits who decide to steal Britain's Crown Jewels to prove it can be done; and *Hannibal Brooks*, with Reed in the title role as a British prisoner of war who escapes from the Nazis over the Alps with an elephant in tow. Winner films are not generally notable for affecting the emotions, but this one does. The director showed great skill at directing the marathon sequences in *The Games*, in which his actors really look like runners, particularly when near to salt-caked, sweat-soaked exhaustion. That was virtually the last human touch in his work, although he had great commercial success in the mid-1970s with the vigilante movie *Death Wish*, a success he repeated when badly in need of a box-office hit, with *Death Wish II*. But both Winner and his main star, Charles Bronson, looked increasingly passionless and mechanical in the later years of their partnership. The best of his later films, mostly a dismal collection, is *A Chorus of Disapproval*. Armed with a starry cast and decent source material (a play by Alan Ayckbourn), Winner fashioned an affectionate and sometimes funny portrait of the shenanigans within a repertory company in a small Welsh town.

*1958: The Clock Strikes Eight. 1960: Climb Up the Wall. Shoot to Kill. 1961: Old Mac. *Haunted England. Some Like It Cool. Out of the Shadow (US: Murder on the Campus). 1962: *Behave Yourself. Play It Cool. 1963: The Cool Mikado. West 11. 1964: The System (US: The Girl*

Michael **Winner** (right) shows Charles Bronson the way to inflict more death and destruction in *Death Wish 3*.

*Getters). 1965: You Must Be Joking!
1967: The Jokers. I'll Never Forget
What's 'Is Name. 1968: Hannibal Brooks.
1969: The Games. 1970: Lawman. 1971:
The Nightcomers. Chato's Land. 1972:
The Mechanic (later Killer of Killers).
Scorpio. 1973: The Stone Killer. 1974:
Death Wish. 1975: Won Ton Ton, the
Dog Who Saved Hollywood. 1977: The
Sentinel. 1978: The Big Sleep. 1979: Fire-
power. 1981: Death Wish II. 1983: The
Wicked Lady. 1984: Scream for Help.
1985: Death Wish 3. 1986: +Claudia's
Story (uncredited). 1988: Appointment
With Death. A Chorus of Disapproval,
1990: Bullseye! 1992: Dirty Weekend.
1998: Parting Shots.*

WISE, Robert 1914-

American director whose work become
more variable as his career progressed –
generally at his best with small-scale or
sinister subjects. But, strangely, his two
Academy Awards have been for big,
splashy musicals – *West Side Story* and
The Sound of Music – a far cry from the
days when he edited films for Orson
Welles *(qv)*. He had joined RKO at 18, as
an assistant cutter, progressing to editor
by 1939, and working on *Citizen Kane*
and *The Magnificent Andersons*, the second of which Wise helped trim down by
an hour while Welles was away on one of
his peregrinations. His break as a director
came when producer Val Lewton's director for *The Curse of the Cat People* failed
to keep abreast of his tight schedule and
Wise, slated as editor, was brought in. His
best films are tightly clustered in the ten
years that followed, from 1944 to 1953.
He made the best of the Lewton films,
The Body Snatcher, with a screamingly
horrific chase sequence at the end. The
sense of menace lurking just below the
surface was well conveyed in several of
his films, certainly in *Born to Kill*, with
Lawrence Tierney in fearsome mood,
Blood on the Moon and *The House on
Telegraph Hill*. But the best films from
this rewarding period are *The Set-Up*, a
boxing film that really makes the adrenalin flow, thanks to hard-hitting direction
and a typically gritty performance from
Robert Ryan, *The Day the Earth Stood
Still*, a very impressive and sober-minded
science-fiction film that triggered off the
revival of the genre, and *The Captive
City;* a thriller that had something to say,
it was very much the sleeper of its year,
with John Forsythe as the reporter fleeing
desperately one step ahead of the criminals on his heels as he plans to expose the
total corruption in his town. *The Desert
Rats* and *Destination Gobi* are exciting,
flag-waving war films, but after that the

Old-timer Robert **Wise** gets together with the youthful case of his last film, *Rooftops*.

projects got bigger and critical successes
fewer, although *Somebody Up There
Likes Me* was another beautifully made
boxing film and *I Want to Live!* won an
Oscar for Susan Hayward. Two films that
deserved better than they got from critics
and public alike were *Two for the Seesaw*,
virtually a two-hander but poignantly,
brilliantly played by Shirley MacLaine
and Robert Mitchum, and *The Haunting*,
a superb ghost story in which no ghosts
or monsters are ever actually seen, but a
sense of great terror is brilliantly conveyed by use of infra-red photography, a
cacophony of weird noises on the soundtrack, sudden shocks and sheer directorial
skill. Most of his latter films are inflated
and disappointing although the two
Oscar-winners are better than latter-day
critics allow.

*1944: †The Curse of the Cat People.
Mademoiselle Fifi. 1945: The Body
Snatcher. A Game of Death. 1946: Crimi-
nal Court. 1947: Born to Kill (GB: Lady
of Deceit). 1948: Mystery in Mexico.
Blood on the Moon. 1949: The Set-Up.
1950: Two Flags West. Three Secrets.
1951: The House on Telegraph Hill. The
Day the Earth Stood Still. 1952: Some-
thing for the Birds. The Captive City.
1953: The Desert Rats. Destination Gobi.
So Big. 1954: Executive Suite. 1955:
Helen of Troy. 1956: Tribute to a Bad
Man. Somebody Up There Likes Me.
1957: Until They Sail. This Could Be the
Night. 1958: Run Silent, Run Deep. I
Want to Live! 1959: Odds Against
Tomorrow. 1961: †West Side Story. 1962:
Two for the Seesaw. 1963: The Haunting.*

*1965: The Sound of Music. 1966: The
Sand Pebbles. 1968: Star! 1970: The
Andromeda Strain. 1973: Two People.
1975: The Hindenburg. 1977: Audrey
Rose. 1979: Star Trek – the Motion Pic-
ture. 1986: +Wisdom (uncredited). 1989:
Rooftops.*

WITNEY, William 1910-

An enthusiastic director of action through
five decades, Oklahoma-born Witney
spent his entire career making serials and
second-features, a great many of them
westerns. Many of these have a slickness
and crude vigour that, in the eyes of con-
noisseurs of the genre, makes Witney one
of the best of his kind. These serials are
whirlwinds of manic action and sustained
energy and, from 1956, Witney transferred these wild energies to TV westerns
with prolific and often commendable
results. His favourite shot, probably used
for the first time in the 1939 serial
Zorro's Fighting Legion, is a sudden
track-back by the camera, leaving a vast
expanse of ground in a momentarily
empty screen. Then, from the side of the
frame, action comes spilling in, hurtling
away from the camera. The charge that
Witney undoubtedly got from staging
such sequences was vividly transferred to
his audiences. And it seemed he was forever inventing new camera heights and
angles from which to shoot some fresh
piece of mayhem. With dialogue, Witney
was less at ease, although he showed on
occasion that he was capable of making
large-scale adventure films providing the
script allowed him to keep them moving
at his own relentless, exciting gallop. Wit-

ney began his long screen career as a studio messenger in silent days, joining Republic shortly after its inception in 1935. By 1936, he was already script supervisor on serials, and his own directorial career started the following year. His films were mainly serials, before World War II service with the US Marines, after which he was moved on to Roy Rogers westerns, inserting into them a new tough backbone that offended some Rogers purists, who protested that their hero's fights were becoming too violent for his younger fans. This would have cut little ice with Witney, a stickler for rugged realism, who twice nearly burned down sound stages at Republic in his serial days with fires that were all-too-well staged. Witney's no-nonsense approach paid off with some vigorous and ingeniously done action scenes in the Rogers westerns at a time when they were bursting into Trucolor and heading past the 70 minute mark into a higher category of 'B' movie. In 1954 he made his best feature film, *The Outcast*, a fully fledged 90-minute action film with John Derek, fast-moving, tense and exciting throughout its running time. Besides his television work, which includes some quite interesting episodes of

such series as *The High Chaparral, Bonanza, The Virginian* and *Wagon Train*, Witney continued to work for the cinema: *Santa Fé Passage* is another rousing western, involving a wagon train and Indians, crammed with action, *The Bonnie Parker Story*, a hard-edged early life of the famous gun moll and *Master of the World*, a vigorous, if cut-price Jules Verne adventure with Vincent Price and Charles Bronson. He wrote an amusing memoir in 1995 called *In a Door, Out a Door, into a Chase: Moviemaking Remembered by The Guy at the Door.*

1937: *The Trigger Trio.* †*SOS Coast Guard (serial).* †*Zorro Rides Again (serial).* †*The Painted Stallion (serial).* 1938: †*Dick Tracy Returns (serial).* †*The Lone Ranger (serial).* †*Fighting Devil Dogs (serial).* †*Hawk of the Wilderness (serial).* 1939: †*Dick Tracy's G-Men (serial).* †*The Lone Ranger Rides Again (serial).* †*Daredevils of the Red Circle (serial).* †*Zorro's Fighting Legion (serial).* 1940: *Heroes of the Saddle.* †*Hi-Yo Silver! (feature version of The Lone Ranger).* †*Drums of Fu Manchu (serial).* †*The Adventures of Red Ryder (serial).* †*King of the Royal Mounted (serial).* Mysteri-

ous *Dr Satan (serial).* 1941: †*Adventures of Captain Marvel (serial).* †*Jungle Girl (serial).* †*Dick Tracy vs. Crime Inc. (serial).* †*King of the Texas Rangers (serial).* 1942: *Outlaws of Pine Ridge. Spy Smasher (serial). King of the Mounties (serial). Perils of Nyoka (serial).* 1943: *G-Men vs. the Black Dragon (serial).* 1946: *Roll On Texas Moon. Home in Oklahoma. Heldorado.* 1947: *Apache Rose. Bells of San Angelo. Springtime in the Sierras. On the Old Spanish Trail.* 1948: *The Gay Ranchero. Under California Stars. Eyes of Texas. Nighttime in Nevada. Grand Canyon Trail. The Far Frontier.* 1949: *Susanna Pass. Down Dakota Way. The Golden Stallion.* 1950: *Bells of Coronado. Twilight in the Sierras. Trigger, Jr. Sunset in the West. North of the Great Divide. Trail of Robin Hood.* 1951: *Spoilers of the Plains. Heart of the Rockies. In Old Amarillo. South of Caliente. Pals of the Golden West. Night Riders of Montana. Colorado Sundown.* 1952: *The Last Musketeer. Border Saddlemates. Old Oklahoma Plains. South Pacific Trail. The WAC from Walla Walla (GB: Army Capers).* 1953: *Down Laredo Way. Iron Mountain Trail. Shadows of Tombstone. Old Overland Trail.* 1954: *The Outcast (GB: The Fortune Hunter).* 1955: *City of Shadows. Santa Fé Passage. Headline Hunters. The Fighting Chance.*

Hong Kong's top action director, John **Woo**, and the bouncing Belgian, Jean-Claude Van Damme, would appear to be a marriage made in heaven — an off-set shot from Woo's first American film, *Hard Target*.

1956: A Strange Adventure. Stranger at My Door. 1957: Panama Sal. 1958: Juvenile Jungle. The Bonnie Parker Story. Young and Wild. The Cool and the Crazy. 1959: Paratroop Command. 1960: Valley of the Redwoods. The Secret of the Purple Reef. 1961: Master of the World. The Long Rope. 1962: The Cat Burglar. 1964: Apache Rifles. 1965: Girls on the Beach. Arizona Raiders. 1966: †Lost Island of Kioga (feature version of Hawk of the Wilderness). 40 Guns to Apache Pass. 1967: Ride the Wind (TV. GB: cinemas). 1973: I Escaped from Devil's Island. 1975: Darktown Strutters.

WOO, John (Wu Yusen) 1946-

Chinese-born director who made his name with Hong Kong-made films specialising in balletic, almost cartoon-like action bloodbaths. Although not as effective with actors, Woo had little difficulty establishing himself in the Hollywood mainstream after moving to America in 1992. The son of a family who moved to Hong Kong when he was four, Woo made a couple of short films while still at college, then worked as production associate and assistant director with various companies before moving to Golden Harvest in 1973, establishing a cult reputation there with brutal, unsmiling crime thrillers starring such Hong Kong superstars as Jackie Chan and Chow Yun-Fat. One of the films with Chow, *The Killer*, brought him to the attention of influential critics. About an international assassin trying to get out of the game, it represents the highpoint of Woo's ability to choreograph his action to an almost operatic level without ever quite crossing the line to a point where it might make an audience giggle instead of gasp. More lyrical violence pulled in audiences in Woo's subsequent *Once a Thief*, *Hard-Boiled* and *Bullet in the Head* before he re-located to Hollywood. An uncertain start here with *Hard Target*, a Jean-Claude Van Damme vehicle, was followed by progressively more successful films at the box-office. The far-fetched *Face/Off*, full of thundering excitement and bravura performances by stars John Travolta and Nicolas Cage, seems to have established a niche market for Woo that other popular Hong Kong action directors have yet to clamber into.

*1968: *Ouran/Accidentally. *Sijie/Fast Knot. 1973: Tie han rou qing/The Young Dragons (released 1975). 1974: $Guima shuang xing/Games Gamblers Play. Nuzi tai~quan qun yinghui/The Dragon Tamers (GB: Belles of Taekwondo). 1975: Shaolin men/The Hand of Death (GB: Countdown in Kung Fu). 1976: Dinü Hua/Princess Chang Ping. 1977: $Ban*
jinba liang/The Private Eyes. Fa qian han/Money Crazy/Pilferer's Progress. Da shaxing yu xiao motou/Follow the Star. 1978: $Maishen qi/ The Contract. +Haluo yeguiren/Hello, Late Homecomers. 1979: Haoxia/Chivalry's Last Hurrah. 1980: Qian zuoguai/From Riches to Rags. 1981: Modeng tianshi/To Hell with the Devil. Huaji shidai/Laughing Times (credited as Wu Shangfei). 1982: Bacai lin azhen/Plain Jane to the Rescue. 1983: Yingxiong wu lei/ The Sunset Fighter/Heroes Shed No Tears (released 1986). 1984: Xiao jiang/When You Need a Friend. 1985: Liang zhi lao hu/Run, Tiger, Run. 1986: Yingxiong bense/A Better Tomorrow. 1987: Yingxiong bense II/A Better Tomorrow II. 1989: Diexue shuang xiong/The Killer. 1990: Diexue jietou/Bullet in the Head. 1991: Once a Thief. 1992: Hard-Boiled. 1993: Hard Target. 1996: Broken Arrow. John Woo's Once a Thief (TV). 1997: Face/Off. 1998: Blackjack (TV). 1999: King's Ransom. The Devil's Soldier.
$ As Associate Director

WOOD, Edward D. Jr 1922-1978

Generally accepted as the worst film director in sound history – few who have seen his films would dispute the claim – this American film-maker was unique in that he had no idea, in the early years at least, that his films were that bad, and was puzzled by audience disdain. Despite the fact that he rarely lost his enthusiasm and actually got to make some movies that entered the public arena, Wood had little grasp of camera movement or the placing and direction of actors. His writing is stilted and hollow, and the 'exciting', no-budget special effects in his horror films ludicrous to all but the director himself – although, when they are wrestling with rubber monsters, it's one of the few times Wood's actors are not standing or moving stiffly. Although many of Wood's casts were composed of wives, mistresses and friends, he also employed some reputable actors – Bela Lugosi, Lyle Talbot, Gregory Walcott -- most of whom he made look just as bad as the rest, although Lugosi needed little direction of any kind to produce one of his harsh performances of ripe menace. Wood was a cross-dresser with a love of women and horror films, all three elements re-occurring throughout his career. His keenness to make films, plus the fact that the ageing (and ailing) Lugosi had become his friend, enabled him to pull the wool over the eyes of a few producers who didn't realise until their film had been completed that they had been sold a barrel of rotten apples. His 1957 opus *Plan 9 from Outer Space* is often considered the worst film
of all time: it has wondrously wooden dialogue and performance, paper plates standing in for flying saucers and a jackrabbit appearance by Wood's wife's dentist, who stood in when Lugosi died after a few days' filming. Wood's luck ran out in the 1960s and he spent the latter, largely unhappy part of his life writing and (sometimes) appearing in soft-porn films by A.C. Stephen (Stephen C. Apostoloff), a film-maker little better than himself. The most Wood-like of these is the first, *Orgy of the Dead* (1965). Wood may also have directed parts of the self-penned *The Violent Years* and *The Revenge of Dr X*. His last work before his early death was as assistant director on Stephen's *Hot Ice* (1977).

*1952: Hellborn. 1953: *Crossroads Avenger (unsold TV pilot). Glen or Glenda?/I Changed My Sex. 1954: Jail Bait. Bride of the Monster/Bride of the Atom. 1956: +The Violent Years. 1957: Plan 9 from Outer Space. 1959: Night of the Ghouls (GB: Revenge of the Dead). 1961: The Sinister Urge. 1970: +The Revenge of Dr X. Take It Out in Trade. 1971: Necromania.*

WOOD, Sam 1883-1949

A little-appreciated fact about this American director who saw Hollywood right through its vintage years, dying even as his kind of American cinema began to die, was that he could showcase female performances of all kinds, and capture every side of a woman's appeal, whether silly, romantic, courageous, or evil. He would have seemed the ideal director for *Gone with the Wind*, where Scarlett O'Hara is so much the axis of the film, and indeed it was Wood that M-G-M called for when Victor Fleming *(qv)* fell ill and was unable to complete the last few scenes of the film. Almost all the memorable performances in Wood's films were given by ladies, with the exceptions of The Marx Brothers in *A Night at the Opera* and *A Day at the Races* and Robert Donat in *Goodbye Mr Chips!*, cases in which female co-stars, if any, hardly got a look in. But Robert Cummings and Ronald Reagan pale into insignificance beside Betty Field, going mad, and Ann Sheridan in *Kings Row*. It is Ingrid Bergman, wondering where the noses go, we remember in *For Whom the Bell Tolls*, and only Ginger Rogers, winning an Oscar, from *Kitty Foyle*. That virtuoso performance is matched by Joan Fontaine's poisonous *Ivy*, Gladys George's *Madame X* and sparky Jean Arthur in the fresh and funny *The Devil and Miss Jones*, a film that is due for rediscovery. The photography is also usually of a very high standard in Wood's films, and emotions are manipulated within them with a high degree of technical skill. Against this, his work showed an increasing blandness in the 1940s (*Ivy* is a rare latter-day highpoint – how much better Miss Fontaine looked when gone to the bad) and he angered the acting community in his last years by his work for Joseph McCarthy and his House UnAmerican Activities Committee. Wood began his career as an insurance broker, but began to act as an amateur, then took acting up professionally and eventually got into films. By 1915, he had quit acting and become an assistant director with Cecil B. DeMille's (*qv*) unit, and by 1921, was directing Gloria Swanson at Paramount. Swanson and Wood made ten films in a row together, including *Beyond the Rocks* and *Bluebeard's Eighth Wife*. From the late 1920s, however, Wood was with M-G-M, where he remained until his death from a heart attack at 66. He was nominated for an Oscar three times, in 1939, 1940 and 1942.

1919: Double Speed. 1920: The Dancin' Fool. Excuse My Dust. Sick Abed. What's Your Hurry? A City Sparrow. Her Beloved Villain. The Snob. Her First Elopement. 1921: The Great Moment. Peck's Bad Boy. Under the Lash. Don't Tell Everything. 1922: Her Husband's Trademark. Beyond the Rocks. Her Gilded Cage. The Impossible Mrs Bellew. My American Wife. 1923: Bluebeard's Fifth Wife. Prodigal Daughters. His Children's Children. 1924: The Next Corner. Bluff. The Female. The Mine with the Iron Door. 1925: The Re-Creation of Brian Kent. 1926: Fascinating Youth. One Minute to Play. 1927: A Racing Romeo. Rookies. The Fair Co-Ed. 1928: The Latest from Paris. Telling the World. 1929: So This is College. It's a Great Life. 1930: †They Learned About Women. The Girl Said No. Sins of the Children (GB: The Richest Man in the World). Way for a Sailor. Paid (GB: Within the Law). 1931: A Tailor Made Man. The New Adventures of Get-Rich-Quick Wallingford. The Man in Possession. 1932: Huddle (GB: Impossible Lover). Prosperity. 1933: Hold Your Man. The Barbarian (GB: A Night in Cairo). 1934: Stamboul Quest. 1935: A Night at the Opera. Let 'Em Have It (GB: False Faces). 1936: Whipsaw. The Unguarded Hour. 1937: Navy Blue and Gold. A Day at the Races. Madame X. 1938: Lord Jeff (GB: The Boy from Barnardo's). Stablemates. 1939: Goodbye Mr Chips! 1940: Raffles. Our Town. Rangers of Fortune. Kitty Foyle. 1941: The Devil and Miss Jones. 1942: Kings Row. The Pride of the Yankees. 1943:

The Land is Bright (D). For Whom the Bell Tolls. 1944: Casanova Brown. 1945: Guest Wife. Saratoga Trunk. 1946: Heartbeat. 1947: Ivy. 1948: Command Decision. 1949: The Stratton Story. Ambush.

WOODS, Arthur B. 1904-1944

Like the even younger Pen Tennyson (1912-1941), who directed three films in 1939 and 1940 (*There Ain't No Justice, The Proud Valley* and *Convoy*), Arthur Woods was a promising British director killed in action during World War II. He directed light and lively musicals, comedies and thrillers during the 1930s, and was just moving into a bigger class of film when he volunteered for active service. Woods was the son of a shipping millionaire, and his family in turn envisaged careers for him in shipping or medicine. But, as a boy, Woods was fascinated with the cinema and the theatre and, in 1924, abandoned medical studies at Cambridge University to try an acting career. He soon became more interested in the technical side of making films than in treading the boards, and joined the documentary company British Instructional in 1926. From 1929, until 1933, he directed numerous short films in their *Secrets of Nature* series. These one-reel films, rudimentary forefathers of Disney's 'True-Life Adventure' series of the 1950s, were the first such films to use musical backing and voice-over, often humorous commentaries. But they were a very British series, covering native animals, birds, insects and plant life. Woods moved away from the series when he sold his first screenplays, for films later made as *Pride of the Force, I Spy* and *A Southern Maid*. By this time, he had also accumulated some experience in assistant direction in fictional feature films at Elstree Studios. After co-directing *Timbuctoo* with Walter Summers, Woods directed numerous popular entertainment films of the 1930s. In 1940, M-G-M asked him to handle their British production of one of Dorothy L. Sayers' Lord Peter Wimsey novels, *Busman's Honeymoon*, which studio publicity described as a 'love story with detective interruptions'. The film, with delightful performances from Robert Montgomery (as Lord Peter), Constance Cummings and Seymour Hicks, was highly successful, and there was talk of Woods following Victor Saville (coincidentally, both men had co-directed films with the American Tim Whelan, *qv*) to Hollywood. Instead, Woods went into the Royal Air Force and the rest is tragic history.

1929: †Bedtime at the Zoo (D. And others in the 'Secrets of Nature' series). 1930:

Stark Nature. 1933: †Timbuctoo. On Secret Service (US: Spy 77). 1934: Give Her a Ring. Radio Parade of 1935. 1935: †Music Hath Charms. Drake of England. 1936: Rhythm in the Air. One in a Million. Where's Sally? Irish for Luck. 1937: Mayfair Melody. The Windmill. Don't Get Me Wrong. The Compulsory Wife. You Live and Learn. 1938: The Singing Cop. The Dark Stairway. Mr Satan. Glamour Girl. Thistledown. The Return of Carol Deane. Dangerous Medicine. They Drive by Night. 1939: †Q Planes (US: Clouds Over Europe). The Nursemaid Who Disappeared. Confidential Lady. 1940: Busman's Honeymoon (US: Haunted Honeymoon).

WYLER, William (Willy Wyler) 1902-1981

Consistently commendable German-born director who went to Hollywood as a young man and eventually won three Academy Awards there. Emotional impact was the name of Wyler's game, and his most effective acting collaborator was Bette Davis, memorable in the three Wyler films: *Jezebel, The Letter* and *The Little Foxes*. In the years between 1936 and 1946, Wyler was greatly aided in his aims by the deep-focus photography of Gregg Toland, which enabled Wyler to cram his frame with life when it was not adding to the power of a two-shot. After Toland's early death at 44 in 1948, a softer Wyler was evident, but he still managed a number of formidable achievements in disparate genres, culminating in the multi Oscar-winner *Ben Hur* in 1959, after which his career at last began to go downhill. Wyler's films, although in recent times they have undergone critical devaluation, are full of ringing, decisive and memorable emotional moments, and sharply etched acting performances: 14 acting Oscars were won in his films. Most of the public, too, liked what they were seeing: it was crafted for their benefit with such care and attention to detail that the director at one time became known as '90-Take Wyler' for the number of times he would re-shoot his scenes to get exactly the right effect. Born to Swiss parents, Wyler was educated in Switzerland and France (where he studied the violin) before coming to America to work for Universal, whose boss, Carl Laemmle, was a distant relative. After acting in various capacities – including working as a production assistant on the 1925 version of *Ben-Hur* – he began as a director on two-reel (occasionally five-reel) westerns. Despite this roistering apprenticeship, most of Wyler's feature films are pretty serious affairs. He was inconsistent until he made *Dodsworth* in 1936, but then started to make some good and popular films, among them *Dead End* and *Mrs Miniver*, which date less well than the rest, but also *Jezebel*, *Wuthering Heights*, *The Westerner*, *The Little Foxes*, *The Letter*, *The Best Years of Our Lives*, *The Heiress* and *Detective Story*. Wyler did not work in colour until he made *Friendly Persuasion* in 1956, a charmingly natural, beautifully photographed story of a family of Quakers at the time of the American Civil War, with the best comedy scenes in a Wyler film, and some extremely moving moments. It's the sentimental scenes, too, that work best in Wyler's monumental *Ben-Hur*, which won him his third best director Oscar following *Mrs Miniver* and *The Best Years of Our Lives*. This last is an absorbing and at times quite cynical portrait of servicemen returning home after years at war. All three films also won Academy Awards as the best film of their year.

1925. *Crook Buster. 1926: *Don't Shoot. *The Fire Barrier. *The Gunless Bad Man. *The Horse Trader. *Martin of the Mounted. Ridin' for Love. The Stolen Ranch. *The Two Fister. Lazy Lightning. 1927: *Daze of the West. *Galloping Justice. *The Haunted Homestead. *Gun Justice. *The Home Trail. *Kelcy Gets His Man. *The Lone Star. *The Ore Raiders. *The Phantom Outlaw. *The Square Shooter. *Tenderfoot Courage. Straight Shootin' (GB: Range Riders). Blazing Days. *The Silent Partner. Hard Fists. The Border Cavalier. Desert Dust. Thunder Riders. 1928: Anybody Here Seen Kelly? (GB: Has Anybody Here Seen Kelly?). The Shakedown. 1929: The Love Trap. Hell's Heroes. 1930: The Storm. 1931: A House Divided. 1932: Tom Brown of Culver. 1933: Her First Mate. Counsellor at Law. 1934: Glamour. 1935: The Good Fairy. The Gay Deception. 1936: These Three. †Come and Get It. Dodsworth. 1937: Dead End. 1938: Jezebel. 1939: Wuthering Heights. 1940: The Letter. The Westerner. Hell's Heroes (revised and re-edited version of 1929 film). 1941: The Little Foxes. 1942: Mrs Miniver. 1944: The Memphis Belle (D). The Fighting Lady (D). 1946: The Best Years of Our Lives. 1947: †Thunderbolt (D. Completed 1945). 1949: The Heiress. 1951: Detective Story. 1952: Carrie. 1953: Roman Holiday. 1955: The Desperate Hours. 1956: Friendly Persuasion. 1958: The Big Country. 1959: Ben-Hur. 1962: The Children's Hour (GB: The Loudest Whisper). 1965: The Collector. 1966: How to Steal a Million. 1968: Funny Girl. 1969: The Liberation of L.B. Jones.*

YAMAMOTO, Kajiro
See Kurosawa, Akira

YARBROUGH, Jean 1900-1975

This American director slaved for many years in minor capacities in the film industry before getting into the director's chair and, once there, did not enjoy an especially distinguished career; he made some pleasant uninhibited comedies with good quotas of sight gags, a skill probably learned from many years with Hal Roach. Yarbrough had joined Roach in 1922 as a prop man, gradually progressing to gagman and assistant director. It was not until 1936, however, that he began directing two-reelers. For his first few years in features, Yarbrough was associated with such poverty-row companies as PRC and Monogram. But in 1943, he joined Universal and found himself, though still on 'B' movies, with slightly better budgets. One of these, *Weekend Pass,* was a little film of considerable charm, with Noah Beery Jr as a shipyard worker on a weekend's leave, who befriends a runaway girl. Soon afterwards, Yarbrough began a profitable association with Universal's top attractions, the comedy team of Bud Abbott and Lou Costello, whom he steered through five comedy capers, *In Society, The Naughty Nineties, Here Come the Co-Eds, Jack and the Beanstalk* and *Lost in Alaska,* as well as numerous episodes of their television comedy show between 1950 and 1953. His films with them are not quite their best, but far from their worst, *Jack and the Beanstalk* being particularly likeable (and one of their few films in colour). He was involved with lesser comedy series too, including the Joe Palooka, Henry and Bowery Boys romps. Increasingly in television in his later years, Yarbrough's last assignment before his retirement at 70 was a TV film, *The Over-the-Hill Gang,* that reunited him with many of his old friends in the business — Pat O'Brien, Chill Wills, Walter Brennan, Edgar Buchanan and Andy Devine among them.

1936: *Don't Be Like That. *Fight is Right. *Lalapaloosa. *All Business. *And So to Wed. *Bad Medicine. *Dog Blight. *So and Sew. 1937: *A Rented Riot.*

*Horse Play. *Inlawfull. *Rhythm on the Rampage. *Singing in the Air. *Swing Fever. * Trailing Along. *Wife Insurance. 1938: *The Dummy Owner. *A Buckaroo Broadcast. *Berth Quakes. *Hectic Honeymoon. *Music Will Tell. *The Photographer. Rebellious Daughters. *Picketing for Love. *Russian Dressing. 1939: *Crime Rave. *Plumb Crazy. *Start the Music. *Swing Vacation. 1940: *Molly Cures a Cowboy. The Devil Bat. 1941: South of Panama. Caught in the Act. King of the Zombies. The Gang's All Here (GB: In the Night). Father Steps Out. Let's Go Collegiate (GB: Farewell to Fame). Top Sergeant Mulligan. 1942: Law of the Jungle. Freckles Comes Home. Man from Headquarters. So's Your Aunt Emma! Silent Witness (GB: The Attorney for the Defence). She's in the Army. Police Bullets. Criminal Investigator. Lure of the Islands. 1943: So's Your Uncle! Follow the Band. Good Morning, Judge. Get Going. Hi'Ya Sailor. 1944: Weekend Pass. South of Dixie. Moon Over Las Vegas. Twilight on the Prairie. In Society. 1945: Under Western Skies. Here Come the Co-Eds. The Naughty Nineties. On Stage, Everybody. 1946: Inside Job. House of Horrors (GB: Joan Medford is Missing). She-Wolf of London (GB: The Curse of the Allenbys). Cuban Pete (GB: Down Cuba Way). 1947: The Brute Man. 1948: The Creeper. The Challenge. Shed No Tears. Triple Threat. 1949: Henry the Rainmaker. The Mutineers. Angels in Disguise. Leave It to Henry. Master Minds. Holiday in Havana. 1950: Joe Palooka Meets Humphrey. Father Makes Good. Square Dance Katy. Sideshow. Triple Trouble. Joe Palooka in Humphrey Takes a Chance (GB: Humphrey Takes a Chance). Big Timber. 1951: Casa Manana. According to Mrs Hoyle. 1952: Lost in Alaska. Jack and the Beanstalk. 1955: Night Freight. 1956: Crashing Las Vegas. Yaqui Drums. Hot Shots. The Women of Pitcairn Island. 1957: Footsteps in the Night. 1962: Saintly Sinners. 1967: Hillbillys in a Haunted House. 1969: The Over-the-Hill Gang (TV).*

YATES, Peter 1929-

There's a freshness, almost a naiveté, about this British director's best films that makes them most appealing. And, without becoming a 'name' director, he has built up a high percentage of big box-office hits over the years. Although most of his successes have been about action on wheels — the car chase in *Bullitt* is still his most talked-about sequence — he has also made a musical, a romance, a lunatic comedy and a gangster thriller. Yates has been directing (for the theatre to begin with)

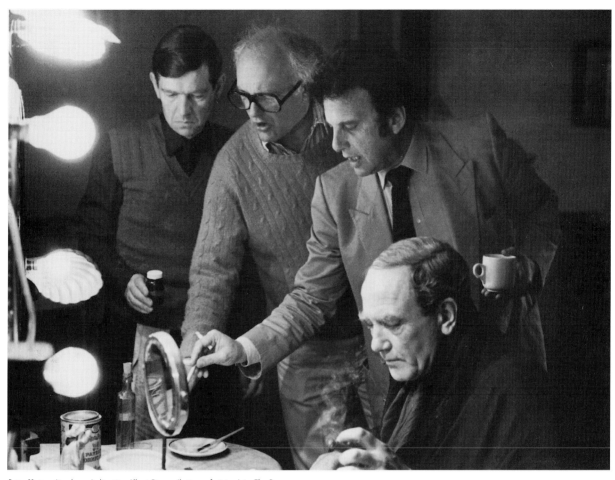

Peter **Yates** (in glasses) directing Albert Finney (bottom of picture) in *The Dresser*.

since he was 19, and got into films as a dubbing assistant at a London sound studio. By 1961, however, he had worked his way up to assistant director and he received his first assignment in 1962, making a pleasantly breezy job of the Cliff Richard musical *Summer Holiday*. This was followed by the inspired idiocy of *One Way Pendulum*, a hang-over from his days with London's Royal Court Theatre, hilarious stuff, but too way-out for mainstream audiences of its time. In 1968, Yates went to America, and hit immediate pay-dirt with *Bullitt*, with its tremendous car chases, Steve McQueen at his most charismatic, a violently fascinating plot, and the emergent Jacqueline Bisset as the female lead. This was followed by the touchingly real, human and everyday *John and Mary*, almost as skilful a manipulation of the emotions as Hoffman's previous film *The Graduate*; *Murphy's War*, an action film (when it got going, which took rather a long time) in attractive locations, which gave Peter O'Toole one of his biggest box-office successes; and the underrated *Mother, Jugs and Speed*, a black comedy-cum-

chase story about three ambulance drivers. *The Deep* was more full of excitement than any follow-up to *Jaws* had any right to be (having Jacqueline Bisset diving about in wet-suit didn't do its box-office prospects any harm) and it was followed by one of Yates' best films, *Breaking Away*. Human values are higher than usual in this offshoot from *American Graffiti*, about four jobless American boys in their first summer since leaving high school. The film gains most from a relationship between bike-mad Dennis Christopher and his mother and father that is both funny and believable. Yates encourages his film to wear its heart on its sleeve, plainly underlining his belief that if script, action and characterization are clearly defined, then the audience reaction will be a positive one. There have been disappointments, too, from Yates, but his films remain events to await with some anticipation. In recent years, they have continued to vary between such polished box-office crime films as *Suspect* and *An Innocent Man*, and warmer, more intimate dramas, such as *Roommates*, in which Yates provided

Peter Falk with the opportunity for an acting *tour-de-force*, as an eccentric old man raising his five-year-old grandson.

1962: *Summer Holiday*. 1964: *One Way Pendulum*. 1967: *Robbery*. 1968: *Bullitt*. 1969: *John and Mary*. 1970: *Murphy's War*. 1972: *The Hot Rock (GB: How to Steal a Diamond in Four Uneasy Lessons)*. 1973: *The Friends of Eddie Coyle*. 1974: *For Pete's Sake*. 1976: *Mother, Jugs and Speed (released 1977)*. 1977: *The Deep*. 1979: *Breaking Away*. 1981: *Eyewitness (GB: The Janitor)*. 1982: *Krull*. 1983. *The Dresser*. 1985: *Eleni*. 1987: *Suspect*. 1988: *The House on Carroll Street*. 1989: *An Innocent Man*. 1992: *Year of the Comet*. 1995: *Roommates*. *The Run of the Country*.

YORKIN, Bud (Alan Yorkin) 1926-
If you wanted a mixture of very good, very bad and pretty indifferent from an American director with just a few films to his credit, you couldn't really do much better than with Yorkin. Basically, he has been much more successful with TV

series, but one or two films have captured the inner workings of the maniac comedy minds of Yorkin and his long-time collaborator Norman Lear. He had joined NBC Television as early as 1949, producing and directing comedy shows with such teams as Martin and Lewis, The Ritz Brothers and Abbott and Costello. His film career, which started in 1963, has been very spasmodic, and by far his funniest film, *Start the Revolution Without Me*, a lunatic relative of The Corsican Brothers with Gene Wilder and Donald Sutherland as two sets of twins, was not a popular success. *Divorce American Style,* in which the rather odd quartet of Dick Van Dyke, Debbie Reynolds, Jason Robards and Jean Simmons worked very well together, was a sparkling satire on the American way of divorce, but its follow-up, *Inspector Clouseau,* the only film in the series without Peter Sellers (Alan Arkin played the title role), was just an embarrassment. Yorkin again had a strong quartet of star players (Ryan O'Neal, Jacqueline Bisset, Warren Oates and Jill Clayburgh) in *The Thief Who Came to Dinner,* a caper comedy-thriller that showed signs of desperation from a director presumably playing it safe for a hit, in that its elements could well have been assembled by computer. It was modestly successful, but after it Yorkin returned to television for a decade, most notably in partnership with Norman Lear again on *All in the Family.* He returned to films in the late 1980s, with a mixture of — you've guessed it — good (*Twice in a Lifetime*), bad (*Love Hurts*) and indifferent (the *Arthur* sequel). More recently he has been both acting and producing. His erstwhile partner Norman Lear (1922-) directed one film, *Cold Turkey* (1970), which unfortunately lived up to its name.

1963: Come Blow Your Horn. 1965: Never Too Late. 1967: Divorce American Style. 1968: Inspector Clouseau. 1969: Start the Revolution Without Me. 1973: The Thief Who Came to Dinner. 1985: Twice in a Lifetime. 1988: Arthur 2 On the Rocks. 1989: Love Hurts.

YOUNG, Harold 1897-1970

Born in America of Irish parents, Young was a brilliant editor who turned director in Britain and made his best film there. In retrospect and with hindsight, he seems to have made a mistake in going back to Hollywood in the mid-1930s, for he was consigned to second-features there and worked on films of decreasing importance for the remainder of his career. After World War I service, Young had gone into the Hollywood film industry as a cutter, quickly climbing the ladder to editor. At one time in the 1920s he was supervising editor of Paramount's European productions, but he was back in Hollywood at the time of his first auspicious meeting with the Hungarian-born director Alexander Korda *(qv),* who was to become such a force in the British film industry. Young first worked for Korda in 1927 on *The Private Life of Helen of Troy,* when Korda was still concentrating on his embryo career as a Hollywood director. The two men got on so well that Korda retained Young's services for most of his subsequent ventures, successively in America, France and (by 1932) England, where Young edited (among others) *The Private Life of Henry VIII* (as supervising editor) and *Wedding Rehearsal,* as well as some films produced but not directed by Korda, such as *The Rise of Catherine the Great* (in America, *Catherine the Great*). After directing a minor quota film, Young's big chance came in 1935, when Korda assigned him to direct *The Scarlet Pimpernel,* after the film's initial director, Rowland Brown, had left under something of a cloud. Today, the film still looks good, with Leslie Howard the quintessential Sir Percy Blakeney and Raymond Massey every inch the evil Chauvelin. The interplay between these two is really the axis around which the film revolves, and how well Young handles it. If the ending seems hurried, the episodes which precede it are much to be relished for their wit and strength. There is little to be said for Young's career on his return to Hollywood, save that it consisted of very minor hoodlum, horror, Nazi and musical offerings and pretty well ended with a small film featuring the Brooklyn Dodgers. Had he remained with Korda in Britain, he would almost certainly have become a director of more than average achievement.

1934: Too Many Millions. 1935: The Scarlet Pimpernel. Without Regret. 1936: My American Wife. Woman Trap. 1937: Let Them Live. 52nd Street. 1938: Little Tough Guy. The Storm. Newsboys' Home. 1939: Code of the Streets. The Forgotten Woman. Hero for a Day. Sabotage (GB: Spies at Work). 1940: Dreaming Out Loud. 1941: Bachelor Daddy. 1942: Juke Box Jenny. The Mummy's Tomb. Rubber Racketeers. There's One Born Every Minute. 1943: Hi 'Ya Chum (GB: Everything Happens to Us). I Escaped from the Gestapo. Hi Buddy. Spy Train. 1944: Machine Gun Mama. The Three Caballeros. 1945: The Frozen Ghost. Jungle Captive. I Remember April. Song of the Sarong. *Phantoms Inc.

1947: Citizen Saint. 1954: Roogie's Bump (GB: The Kid Colossus). 1957: The Amiable Lady.

YOUNG, Terence (Shaun T. Young) 1915-1994

Shanghai-born director in British films whose work as a director has been fairly undistinguished apart from his contributions to the James Bond movies, which include the first and best of them, *Dr No.* He scripted some good war films in the early years of his career, but he has not usually contributed screenplays to films that he directed since embarking in earnest on a directorial career in 1948. In a way, this may have something to do with such a dismal record: Young seems to have had the misfortune to choose (or be assigned) a great many films whose scripts were so poor that few directors could have done much with them. Even though Young's direction does tend towards the stodgy, better directors would have given up on such offerings as *That Lady, Safari, Zarak, Action of the Tiger, Serious Charge, No Time to Die!, The Poppy is Also a Flower, The Rover, Red Sun, The Klansman* and *Bloodline.* The signs are that Young encouraged his players into stridently flamboyant playing in these movies to give them some kind of flavour. This concern with actors led him to gain personable performances from the leading players of the few decent screenplays he has found: Sean Connery in the Bond films, for example, and Audrey Hepburn in *Wait Until Dark.* Young began work as a scriptwriter at Elstree Studios at 21, his first credited solo screenplay being the 1939 film *On the Night of the Fire* (in the United States, *The Fugitive*), with Ralph Richardson. He obtained his first experience of direction during his World War II military service. His career proper as a director picked up with the interesting, if studio-bound *They Were Not Divided* and the mountaineering drama *Valley of the Eagles,* ironically two films that Young wrote himself. *The Red Beret,* with Alan Ladd engendering some resentment at the time as yet another American helping Britain to win the war, is a better action film than contemporary critics allowed, but the years with Warwick Productions were by and large truly wretched ones, although they did prove Young had a talent for directing fierce action, and they introduced him to the team who were later to produce the Bond films. Young directed three of the first four 007 adventures, *Dr No, From Russia With Love* and *Thunderball.* Such box-office blockbusters were understandably hard to follow and, although Young travelled far and wide in search of more hits, he was largely unsuccessful, even if his talent for the staging of colourful action scenes remained undiluted. He died from a heart attack.

1944: †Men of Arnhem (D). 1948: Corridor of Mirrors. Woman Hater. One Night with You. 1950: They Were Not Divided. 1951: Valley of the Eagles. 1952: Tall Headlines (US: The Frightened Bride). 1953: The Red Beret (US: Paratrooper). 1954: That Lady. 1955: †Storm over the Nile. 1956: Safari. Zarak. 1957: Action of the Tiger. No Time to Die! (US: Tank Force). 1959: Serious Charge (US: A Touch of Hell). 1960: Black Tights. Too Hot to Handle. 1961: Orazi e curiazzi/Duel of Champions. 1962: Dr No. 1963: From Russia with Love. 1965: La guerre secrète (GB & US: The Dirty Game). The Amorous Adventures of Moll Flanders. Thunderball. 1966: The Poppy is Also a Flower (GB: Danger Grows Wild). Triple Cross. 1967: Wait Until Dark. L'avventuriero/ The Rover. 1968: Mayerling. 1969: The Christmas Tree. 1970: Cold Sweat. 1971: Red Sun. 1972: The Valachi Papers. 1973: The Amazons. 1974: The Klansman. 1976: Jackpot (unfinished). 1979: Bloodline/Sidney Sheldon's Bloodline. 1980: Inchon! 1983: The Jigsaw Man. 1989: Takeover.

YUZNA, Brian 1945-

The other half of a producer-director team with Stuart Gordon, this American film-maker has, since striking out on his own, been responsible for some of the nastiest, more gruesome, special effects-laden horror films of recent times. He was quiet for a few years in the 1990s, but then returned with more horror, some of it based on his favourite author, H.P. Lovecraft. Born and brought up in North Carolina, Yuzna was a horror and fantasy film fanatic as a teenager but it remained a hobby as an adult: he spent 12 years as an entrepreneur in fine arts, selling real estate and running a restaurant. In 1984, he moved to the Hollywood area and met Gordon, subsequently producing his first three horror films, *Re-Animator, From Beyond* and *Dolls*. His own first film was set in the more familiar territory of Beverly Hills, where the local rich society prove eventually, in a truly eye-popping finale, to be a large group of parasitic alien shape-shifters whose bizarre orgies top anything in the *Alien* films. Yuzna then regressed with *Bride of Re-Animator*, a poor sequel to Gordon's grisly original, but two other continuances of established series are better than their catchpenny titles would suggest, with the inevitable outrageous special effects and broad

graveyard humour that distinguish (if that's quite the right word) all of Yuzna's films. In 1996, he attempted something a little different with a deranged Corbin Bernsen in *The Dentist* (you can imagine the content). By this time Yuzna's films were going straight to video, but *The Dentist* was certainly one of the most successful, and he almost inevitably brought out a sequel (with Bernsen again) three years later.

1989: Society. Bride of Re-Animator (GB: Re-Animator 2). 1990: Silent Night, Deadly Night 4 — Initiation/Initiation: Silent Night, Deadly Night 4. 1991: Bugs (released 1996, revised version of Silent Night, Deadly Night 4). 1992: Return of the Living Dead 3. 1993: †Necronomicon/H P Lovecraft's Neronomicon: Book of the Dead. 1996: The Dentist. 1997: Zen — Intergalactic Ninja. 1998: The Progeny. 1999: Dentist II: Without Novocaine.

ZAMPI, Mario 1903-1963

For an Italian, Mario Zampi had an amazing grasp of the British sense of humour. In the 1950s he made five tremendously enjoyable romps that had something of the Ealing flavour, although there were signs that, just before his early death, he was beginning to lose his golden touch. Zampi was associated with British film-making for over 30 years, although he had started his film career in his native Rome as an actor at 17. He came to Britain in 1923 and, after some minor acting experience on stage and in films, became more interested in the technical side of movie-making. By 1930, he was working for Warner Brothers' British arm at their Teddington studios as a film editor. In 1937, Zampi co-founded Two Cities films with his fellow Italian Filippo Del Giudice; the company subsequently enjoyed a distinguished record, among its films being *In Which We Serve, The Way Ahead, Henry V, The Way to the Stars* (in America: *Johnny in the Clouds*), *Blithe Spirit* and *Hamlet*. Zampi's own directorial career had meantime got under way in 1938, but it was ten years before he made any sort of impact and then it was with

an uncharacteristic film, *The Fatal Night*, only 50 minutes long, but one of the most frightening films ever made, full of horrors not quite or only half-seen, flickering lights and shadows on walls, a triumph, in fact, of the editor's skill. The comedies began in 1951 and the best of them are *Laughter in Paradise* (in which Audrey Hepburn caught the eye as a cigarette girl; it would later be remade, dully, as *Some Will, Some Won't* in 1972), *Top Secret, Happy Ever After, The Naked Truth* and *Too Many Crooks*. Again, Zampi's editing and directing skills complement those of such comedy stars as Alastair Sim, Terry-Thomas, George Cole and Peter Sellers. And these are also films whose sense of fun and enjoyment is infectious. The best bits in them are absolutely hilarious – side-splitting moments of the cinema. This is especially true of *Laughter in Paradise* in which an eccentric will forces the would-be inheritors into various uncharacteristic acts, and *Happy Ever After,* an Irish comedy which drags in practically every known Irish joke and amazingly makes them all seem funny. Like all Zampi's films until the last, which was perhaps his most disappointing, they move at a tremendous pace, and *Too Many Crooks*, about a bunch of bungling burglars, has a riotous car chase which owes something to *The Lavender Hill Mob*, but pre-dates the equally funny one in *The Wrong Arm of the Law*. Zampi surprisingly missed most of the opportunities presented by the school comedy *Bottoms Up!* But if Alastair Sim had played the headmaster, who knows what fresh inspiration Zampi might have found.

1938: Thirteen Men and a Gun. 1940: Spy for a Day. 1947: The Phantom Shot. 1948: The Fatal Night. 1950: Shadow of the Past. Come Dance with Me. 1951: Laughter in Paradise. 1952: Top Secret (US: Mr Potts Goes to Moscow). 1953: Ho scelto l'amore. 1954: Happy Ever After (US: Tonight's the Night/O Leary Night). 1956: Now and Forever. 1957: The Naked Truth (US: Your Past is Showing!). 1959: Too Many Crooks. 1960: Bottoms Up! 1961: Five Golden Hours.

ZEFFIRELLI, Franco 1923-

This Italian director seems to have got himself a formidable reputation without making many good movies. One can rely on Zeffirelli's films to be pretty and this they are, unfailingly. But the attraction remains very much on the surface, with little of substance beneath. Zeffirelli is a master stager of moving images. Thus the little action scenes within the TV-commer-

Franco **Zeffirelli** on location with Olivia Hussey, the star of his 1967 version of *Romeo and Juliet.*

cial style whole are always beautifully staged to give maximum impact: the duel scene, for example, in *Romeo and Juliet,* is in a different class from the rest of the film. But then most of Zeffirelli's background is in the theatre, and design, both in costume and settings, and careful preparation of scenes, are clearly his strengths. Following World War II, he had set out to make a career in acting, but by 1947 had switched to being an assistant director, notably on several films made by Luchino Visconti *(qv).* Since the late 1940s, Zeffirelli has devised, designed and directed many stage plays and operas, gaining a reputation for stylish, tasteful extravagance. He brought this reputation with him into the cinema and confirmed it in his approach to *The Taming of the Shrew,* which is teeming with life, action and colour. He attracted international publicity when searching for two teenagers for his *Romeo and Juliet,* although in the end it proved a matter of swings and roundabouts. The choices, Olivia Hussey and Leonard Whiting, certainly brought a raw freshness to their

roles, but were hardly up to the more subtle nuances of Shakespeare's dialogue. The films, however, made Zeffirelli something of a 'name' in the cinema, although he has only flirted sporadically with the medium since then. *Brother Sun, Sister Moon* was merely weak and watery, and none of the starry cast of *The Champ* could do anything about the pace of a film that bobs and weaves like a punch-drunk punk until it falls asleep on its feet. Zeffirelli continued his fascination with teenage heroines in *Endless Love,* a much watered-down version of a scorching novel. But it was the sheer foolishness of the story rather than any directorial deficiencies that made this one a disappointment. Zeffirelli, though, seems not to have mastered film as a medium, treating many of his films like the grand opera he is so fond of putting on screen. In a string of low-key disasters in the 1980s and 1990s, only his star-studded (but well-cast) 1990 version of *Hamlet* has enhanced his reputation.

1965: Florence – Days of Destruction

(D). 1966: The Taming of the Shrew. 1968: Romeo and Juliet. 1972: Brother Sun, Sister Moon. 1976: Jesus of Nazareth (TV). 1979: The Champ. 1981: Endless Love. 1983: La Traviata. 1986: Otello. 1988: Young Toscanini. 1990: Hamlet. 1993: Sparrow/Storia di una capinera. 1996: Jane Eyre. 1998: Tea With Mussolini.

ZEMECKIS, Robert 1951-

Action fantasy has been the keynote to success for this American director, most of whose latter-day films have been in the blockbuster vein. In 1994, he crowned a spectacular run of success by winning an Academy Award as Best Director for *Forrest Gump.* Things had looked less promising during Zemeckis' formative and early working years. Work as a film cutter with NBC News in Chicago was followed by years of editing commercials. By this time, Zemeckis had met his long-time writing partner Bob Gale, and they wrote several speculative screenplays which, judging by the one Steven Spielberg chose to direct, *1941,* might not have been terribly good. Meanwhile, Zemeckis started his own directorial career with another Zemeckis/Gale script, *I Wanna Hold Your Hand,* about a group of teenage girls trying to see The Beatles on their tour of America. The film lost money, as did the next Zemeckis-Gale project, *Used Cars* (now frequently shown on TV in the wake of Zemeckis' and star Kurt Russell's subsequent successes). Zemeckis withdrew with fingers burned. Four years later, though, he was back to stay when he made an outstanding success out of an unpromising adventure called *Romancing the Stone.* In Zemeckis' hands, it came across as a colourful piece of escapism that's so likeable and fast-moving you forget how silly it all is. Encouraged, Zemeckis put together a winning slice of time-travel fantasy called *Back to the Future* that proved one of America's biggest box-office successes. It was joined in that hallowed hall of fame by Zemeckis' next, *Who Framed Roger Rabbit,* a crafty blend of live-action and animation, two elements that have rarely been as noisily, abrasively or inventively yoked together as in this raucous romp about a down-at-heel gumshoe hired to dig the dirt on the seductive human-toon wife of a cartoon rabbit. Zemeckis seemed to be on auto-pilot with the second film in the *Back to the Future* series; his sure touch of pace for once deserting him. But he and writer Gale made up for it with the third, which moves like a thunderbolt and is full of good fun. Zemeckis and Gale constantly play amusing variations on western traditions after Michael J Fox travels back in time to the Wild West of 1885, and wrap the series up tidily at the end. *Death Becomes Her* was a comparative misfire in the Zemeckis canon, despite prosthetic, state-of-the-effects that almost overcome a limp story about a potion of eternal youth, but it was followed by the legendary *Forrest Gump*, a decidedly different survey of 30 years of American history through the eyes of a simple man (an Oscar-winning role for Tom Hanks), whom special effects place next to numerous celebrities on his miraculously unscathed passage through life. Although the film rarely touches the heart, it struck a chord with filmgoers who made it one of the biggest box-office winners of all time. It was an impossible act to follow and, under the circumstances, it was perhaps hardly surprising that Zemeckis' next, *Contact*, should be pretty much of a flop.

1972: *Field of Honor. 1978: I Wanna Hold Your Hand. 1980: Used Cars. 1984: Romancing the Stone. 1985: Back to the Future. 1988: Who Framed Roger Rabbit. 1989: Back to the Future – Part II. 1990: Back to the Future – Part III. 1992: Death Becomes Her. 1994: Forrest Gump. 1997: Contact.*

ZIEFF, Howard 1929-

American comedy director who came belatedly to a film career after building up a reputation as a maker of way-out TV commercials. Unfortunately his first and best film, *Slither*, was poorly received at the box-office, despite good critical notices, and Zieff has since played fairly safe with big star combinations in tailor-made comedy vehicles. Some laughter has resulted, but by and large this has been a director deprived of his individuality. Like another director of quirky humour and visual inventiveness, Frank Tashlin *(qv)*, Zieff displayed an early skill at drawing and, after enlisting in the US Navy at 17, became a staff artist for *Navy News*, contributing cartoons to the publication. After a period with the navy's school of motion picture photography, Zieff left the service and became a newsreel photographer for a Los Angeles television station. At 25, he had established himself as one of the advertising world's top photographers, and from there moved into making commercials. These usually demonstrated a Goonish sense of humour and were described by one network executive as 'often more entertaining than the programmes'. It seemed inevitable that Zieff would be snapped up by the cinema, but it didn't happen until 1973. 'I'd had motion picture offers before', he admits. 'But nothing really interested me until *Slither* came along.' Zieff's delight in the oddball elements of *Slither* is clear from the results. The freewheeling story contains both zany comedy and sinister chase sequences, with Zieff's handling resulting in a uniquely fresh approach. Zieff s next film, *Hearts of the West*, also had its moments with some well-timed belly-laughs in an otherwise gently funny look at a young stuntman in Hollywood of the early 1930s who by lucky circumstance becomes a western star. Finally it doesn't quite hang together, a fault more clearly visible in *House Calls*, a romantic comedy (with tremendous star value in Glenda Jackson and Walter Matthau) which attempts to be endearing, but succeeds only in spurts. In *The Main Event*, Zieff's observant talent for minor comic details is almost drowned by Barbra Streisand being Barbra Streisand, but *Private Benjamin* is at least half a funny film, if in a thoroughly predictable way, before it goes soft. That accusation could also be aimed at Zieff's big commercial hit *My Girl* and its deplorable sequel *My Girl 2*, but the best film of Zieff's later years is *The Dream Team*. This takes the director's liking for lunacy literally by setting four absentees from the asylum loose in the big city. The film gains momentum with the unwinding of the mainspring of its plot, overcomes our apprehensions at its subject, and proves frequently funny in its later stages.

1973: *Slither. 1975: Hearts of the West (GB: Hollywood Cowboy). 1978: House Calls. 1979: The Main Event. 1980: Private Benjamin. 1984: Unfaithfully Yours. 1988: The Dream Team. 1991: My Girl. 1994: My Girl 2.*

ZINNEMANN, Fred 1907-1997

Austrian-born director who came to Hollywood and won three Oscars, although his work is on the whole not as distiguished as that would suggest. Up to 1960, however, Zinnemann was always capable of coming up with a very good film after one or two misfires. After that his few films proved to be curates' eggs which by and large did not have the courage of their convictions. Some of his commercial successes, on the other hand, such as *The Men, Oklahoma!* and *The Nun's Story* are better films that his severest critics allow, while *High Noon* and *The Sundowners* show a warm understanding of ageing heroes that help to put them at the top of his list of achievements. He was born, like so many directors who started their careers with the beginning of sound, in Vienna, and studied both music and law before dropping each in turn. At 21, he was an assistant cameraman with U.F.A. Studios in Berlin and the following year emigrated to Hollywood, where he endured some hard times before making the contacts that eventually got him a job as an assistant cutter and, by 1931, assistant director. It was M-G-M who gave him his first experience of commercial direction, at first on several of their 'Crime Does Not Pay' two-reelers, one of which, *That Mothers Might Live*, won an Academy Award, then on 'B' features. *Kid Glove Killer* was an honest-to-goodness thriller with some interesting insights into police laboratory work; *Eyes in the Night*

Howard **Zieff** (centre) reunited the stars of *What's Up Doc?*, Barbara Streisand and Ryan O'Neal, for his boxing comedy *The Main Event*. Alas, the film hit the canvas at the box-office.

Getting the needle. Fred **Zinnemann** tutors Audrey Hepburn in the gentle art of nursing for *The Nun's Story*.

– tense, cleverly-worked crime stuff about a blind detective; *The Seventh Cross*, a war film with Spencer Tracy that seemed inspiring at the time; and *Act of Violence*, a suspenseful low-key film about revenge for wartime treachery that contains some of Zinnemann's best direction, with its clever cutting and intelligently found camera angles to increase tension. Zinnemann was gradually becoming a director of importance and confirmed his standing with an Oscar for *From Here to Eternity*, a long but tolerably good adaptation of James Jones' massive novel of World War II. *Oklahoma!* was a great musical with a fiery climax and *The Nun's Story*, with Audrey Hepburn's beautifully wistful performance, a big box-office hit. But Zinnemann bit off more than he could chew, commercially and critically, with *The Member of the Wedding* and *A Hatful of Rain* and, after the inspiration of *The Sundowners, Behold a Pale Horse* was merely soporific and *A Man for all Seasons* a pat and slightly tedious filming of a great play, although it won Zinnemann his third Academy Award. His films continued to be of great length, but Vanessa Redgrave's performance in the otherwise rather tortuous *Julia* was a deserved winner of an acting Oscar.

1934: †*The Wave* (D). 1937: **Friend Indeed.* 1938: **Tracking the Sleeping Death.* **Weather Wizards.* **The Story of Dr Carver.* **That Mothers Might Live.* **They Live Again.* 1939: **While America Sleeps.* **Help Wanted!* **The Ash Can Fleet.* **One Against the World.* **Forgotten Victory.* 1940: **Stuffie.* **A Way in the Wilderness.* **The Old South.* **The Great

Meddler. 1941: **Forbidden Passage. *Your Last Act.* 1942: **The Lady and the Tiger. Kid Glove Killer. Eyes in the Night.* 1944: *The Seventh Cross.* 1946: *My Brother Talks to Horses. Little Mr Jim.* 1948: *The Search.* 1949: *'Act of Violence.* 1950: *The Men.* 1951: *Benjy* (D). *Teresa.* 1952: *High Noon. The Member of the Wedding.* 1953: *From Here to Eternity.* 1955: *Oklahoma!* 1957: *A Hatful of Rain.* 1958: †*The Old Man and the Sea* (uncredited). 1959: *The Nun's Story.* 1960: *The Sundowners.* 1964: *Behold a Pale Horse.* 1966: *A Man for All Seasons.* 1973: *The Day of the Jackal.* 1977: *Julia.* 1982: *Five Days One Summer.*

ZUCKER, David 1947-
and
ZUCKER, Jerry 1950-

Included here to complete the entry on Jim Abrahams, the Zucker brothers co-directed the first three lunatic comedies in the triple filmographies, but have done less solo work. Jerry has had the most notable success, with the major box-office winner *Ghost* which won an Oscar for Whoopi Goldberg, and has generally attempted more serious and ambitious work. David has stuck to comedy, notably with the first two films in the 'Naked Gun' series, of which the second is the more consistently funny. See also Abrahams, Jim.

Together (with Abrahams).
1980: *Airplane!* 1984: *Top Secret!* 1986: *Ruthless People.*

David alone. 1988: *The Naked Gun:*

From the Files of Police Squad. 1991: *The Naked Gun 2½: The Smell of Fear.* 1998: *Basketball.*

Jerry alone. 1990: *Ghost.* 1993: *My Life.* 1995: *First Knight.* 1999: *A Course in Miracles.*

ZWICK, Edward 1952-

A major American director who has yet to enjoy the box-office success he deserves. Zwick initially wrote and directed for the theatre and was awarded a Rockefeller Fellowship to study theatre abroad with some of the more innovative European companies. While on this tour, he worked for Woody Allen on the 1975 film *Love and Death* in Paris, and developed a taste for the cinema. After his short film *Timothy and the Angel* won festival prizes, Zwick came to the attention of the producers of the TV series *Family*. He was invited to write an episode and worked with the series from 1976 to 1980, directing numerous episodes and becoming the show's story editor. He later created another successful small-screen series, *thirtysomething*. Of his TV films, *Special Bulletin* is outstanding, being an edge-of-seat simulation of a 'real event', as nuclear protesters threaten to wipe out half of South Carolina. 'About Last Night...' was a fairly inauspicious start to Zwick's film career, rarely rising above its boy-meets-girl, boy-loses-girl situations. Zwick, however, established himself on the film scene three years later with *Glory*. A stirring war western with some savage and striking battle scenes, this is the story of the first black regiment to fight for the Union during the American Civil War, and a work of major stature. Zwick couldn't find an audience for his captivating female buddy-buddy road movie *Leaving Normal* (he needed stars bigger than Christine Lahti and Meg Tilly), but had better luck (and bigger stars) with the inferior *Legends of the Fall*. Zwick returned to the war theme with *Courage Under Fire*, an underrated *Rashomon*-style film concerning conflicting accounts as to the death of a female helicopter pilot, played by Meg Ryan with more resilience than most critics credited.

1976: *Timothy and the Angel.* 1981: *The Insiders* (TV). 1982: *Having It All* (TV). *Paper Dolls* (TV). 1983: *Special Bulletin* (TV). 1984: *Making Out* (TV). 1986: 'About Last Night...' 1989: *Glory.* 1992: *Leaving Normal.* 1994: *Legends of the Fall.* 1996: *Courage Under Fire.* 1998: *The Siege.*

APPENDIX

ACTORS AS DIRECTORS

In recent times, many actors have taken the reins on their own films, some only once, some several times, often with distinguished, but occasionally disastrous results. Some, such as Clint Eastwood and Sir Richard Attenborough, are dealt with in the main text, as mentioned below. What follows is a reasonably complete list of actors who have directed their own work, and that of others, in the past 50 years.

ALDA, Alan (b 1936).
1980: The Four Seasons. 1985: Sweet Liberty. 1988: A New Life. 1990: Betsy's Wedding.

ALLEN, Woody.
See main text.

ARKIN, Alan (b 1934).
1997: Arigo.

ATTENBOROUGH, Sir Richard (b 1923). *See main text.*

AYKROYD, Dan (b 1951).
1990: Nothing But Trouble.

BACON, Kevin (b 1958).
1996: Losing Chase (TV).

BANDERAS, Antonio (b 1960).
1999: Crazy in Alabama.

BARRY, Don 'Red' (1912-1980).
1954: Jesse James' Women.

BEATTY, Warren
(b 1937). *1978: Heaven Can Wait (co-directed). 1981: Reds (Academy Award). 1990: Dick Tracy.1988: Bulworth.*

BENJAMIN, Richard (b 1938).
1982: My Favorite Year. 1984: Racing With the Moon. City Heat. 1986: The Money Pit. 1987: Little Nikita. My Stepmother is an Alien. 1990: Mermaids. Downtown. 1996: Mrs Winterbourne. 1998: The Pentagon Wars (cable TV).

BENSON, Robby (R Segal)
(b 1956). *1987: Crack in the Mirror. 1989: White Hot. Modern Love.*

BIBERMAN, Abner (1909-1977).
1954: The Golden Mistress (as Joel Judge) 1955: The Looters. Running Wild. 1956: The Price of Fear. Behind the High Wall. 1957: Gun for a Coward. The Night Runner. Flood Tide (GB: Above All Things). 1968: Hawaii Five-0: Once Upon a Time (TV. Co-directed). Too Many Thieves (TV. GB:

cinemas. Co-directed).
BRANAGH, Kenneth.
See main text.

BRANDAUER Klaus Maria
(b 1944). *1989: The Artisan. Seven Minutes/Georg Elser. 1994: Die Wand.*

BRANDO, Marlon (b 1924).
1960: One-Eyed Jacks.

BRAZZI, Rossano (1916-1994).
1966: The Christmas That Almost Wasn't. 1968: Salvara la faccia (US: Psychout for Murder). Sette uomini e un cervello. 1972: Cappucetto rosso, cenerentola...e voi ci credete.

BRIDGES, Beau (Lloyd Bridges III.
B 1941). *1986: The Thanksgiving Promise (TV). 1987: Devil's Odds/The Wild Pair. Seven Hours to Judgment.. 1994: Secret Sins of the Father (TV).*

BROOKS, Albert. *See main text.*

BROOKS, Mel. *See main text.*

BULLOCK, Sandra (b 1964).
1996: Making Sandwiches.

BUSHELL, Anthony (1904-1997).
1949: The Angel With the Trumpet 1951: The Long Dark Hall (co-directed). 1961: The Terror of the Tongs. 1962: A Woman's Privilege.

CAAN, James (b 1938).
1980: Hide in Plain Sight.

CAGNEY, James (1899-1986).
1958: Short Cut to Hell.

CANNON, Dyan (Samille Friesen.
B 1937). *1975: Number One. 1979: For the First Time. 1990: The End of Innocence.*

CARLSON, Richard (1912-1977).
1953: Riders to the Stars. 1954: Four Guns to the Border. 1958: Appointment with a Shadow (GB: The Big Story). The Saga of Hemp

Brown. *1965: Kid Rodelo.*
CARRADINE, David (b 1936).
1974: You and Me. 1981: Americana.

CASSAVETES, John.
See main text.

CHAN, Jackie (Chan Kwong-Sang.
B 1954). *1980: The Young Master. 1982: Dragon Lord. Project A (co-directed). 1985: Police Story. 1988: Police Story Part II. 1989: Mr Canton and Lady Rose. 1990: Armour of God II: Operation Condor. 1992: Police Story III: Supercop. 1998: Who Am I? (co-directed).*

CLARK, Matt (b 1936). *1988: Da.*

CLARKE, Robert (b 1920). *1955: The Hideous Sun Demon (GB: Blood on His Lips).*

CONRAD, William (1920-1994).
1963: The Man from Galveston (TV. GB: cinemas). 1965: My Blood Runs Cold. Brainstorm. Two on a Guillotine. 1971: Side Show (TV).

CONTE, Richard (Nicholas Conte.
1910-1975). *1969: Operation Cross Eagles.*

COOPER, Jackie (b 1921)
1972: Stand up and Be Counted. 1977: Perfect Gentlemen (TV). 1978: Rainbow (TV). 1979: The White Shadow (TV). Sex and the Single Parent (TV). 1980: Marathon. Rodeo Girl (TV). White Mama (TV). 1981: Leave 'Em Laughing (TV). The First Nine Months Are the Hardest (TV). 1982: Rosie: The Rosemary Clooney Story (TV). 1984: The Night They Saved Christmas (TV). 1985: Izzy and Mo (TV).

COSTNER, Kevin (b 1955). *1990: Dances With Wolves (Academy Award). 1997: The Postman.*

CRUISE, Tom (T.C. Mapother. B 1962). *1993: Fallen Angels 2 (TV.*

Co-directed).
CRYSTAL, Billy (b 1947).
1992: Mr Saturday Night. 1995: Forget Paris.

CULP, Robert (b 1930).
1969: Operation Breadbasket. 1970: This Land is Mine. 1972: Hickey and Boggs.

DANTINE, Helmut (1917-1982).
1958: Thundering Jets.

DANTON, Ray (1930-1992).
1972: Crypt of the Living Dead (GB: Vampire Woman). 1973: Deathmaster (GB: The Deathmaster). 1975: Psychic Killer. 1986: The Return of Mike Hammer (TV).

DELON, Alain (b 1935). *1981: Pour la peau d'un flic (US: For A Cop's Hide).*

DEMPSEY, Patrick (b 1966). *1994: Ava's Magical Adventure (TV).*

DE NIRO, Robert (b 1943).
1993: A Bronx Tale.

DENNEHY, Brian (b 1938). *1994: Shadow of a Doubt (TV). 1996: Jack Reed: A Killer Amongst Us (TV). A Father's Betrayal (TV). Jack Reed: Death and Vengeance (TV).*

DEPARDIEU, Gérard
(b 1948). *1984: Le tartuffe.*

DEPP, Johnny (b 1963).
1997: The Brave.

DEREK, John (Derek Harris.
B 1926). *1966: Once Before I Die. 1969: Childish Things. 1972: Confessions of Tom Harris (co-directed). 1975: And Once Upon a Time (US: Fantasies). 1978: Love You. 1981: Tarzan the Ape-Man. 1984: Bolero. 1990: Ghosts Can't Do It.*

DE SICA, Vittorio. *See main text.*

De VITO, Danny (b 1944). *1984: The Ratings Game (TV). 1987: Throw Momma from the Train.*

*1989: The War of the Roses.
1992: Hoffa. 1996: Matilda.*
DOUGLAS, Kirk (Issur
Danielovitch. B 1916). *1973:
Scalawag. 1975: Posse.*

DOUGLAS, Robert (R. D. Fin-
layson. B 1909). *1964: Night
Train to Paris. 1976: Future Cop
(TV). 1978: Columbo: Old Fashioned Murder (TV).*

DRAKE, Tom (1918-1982).
1976: The Keeper.

DUVALL, Robert (b 1931). *1974:
We're Not the Jet Set. 1983: Angelo my Love. 1997: The Apostle.*

EASTWOOD, Clint. *See main text.*

EDWARDS, Anthony (b 1962).
1994: Charlie's Ghost (TV).

ESTEVEZ, Emilio (b 1962). *1986:
Wisdom. 1989: Men at Work.*

FERRER, Jose (1908-1992). *1955:
The Shrike. Cockleshell Heroes.
1956: The Great Man. 1957: I
Accuse! 1958: The High Cost of
Loving. 1961: Return to Peyton
Place. 1962: State Fair.*

FERRER, Mel (Melchior Ferrer.
B 1917). *1945: The Girl of the
Limberlost. 1950: The Secret Fury.
Vendetta (co-directed). 1958:
Green Mansions. 1965: Cabriola
(US: Every Day is a Holiday).*

FIELD, Sally (b 1946). *1996: The
Christmas Tree (TV).*

FINNEY, Albert
(b 1936). *1967: Charlie Bubbles.*

FONDA, Peter (b 1939).
*1971: The Hired Hand. 1973:
Idaho Transfer.*

FORBES, Bryan (John Clarke.
B. 1926) *See main text.*

FOSTER, Jodie (Alicia Foster.
B. 1962). *1991: Little Man Tate.
1995: Home for the Holidays.*

FRAKES, Jonathan (b c1958).
*1996: Star Trek First Contact.
1998: Star Trek Insurrection.*

FREEMAN, Morgan
(b 1937). *1993: Bopha!*

GARCIA, Andy (Andres Garcia-
Menendez. B 1956). *1993:
Cachao. 1996: The Lost City.*

GAZZARA, Ben (Biago Gazzara.
B 1930). *1974: Troubled Waters
(TV). 1975: A Friend in Deed
(TV). 1990: Beyond the Ocean.*

GIANNINI, Giancarlo (b 1942).

*1984: I capitoni (US: Small Fry and
Big Fish). 1986: I numeri del lotto.*
GIBSON, Mel (b 1956). *1993:
The Man Without a Face. 1995:
Braveheart (Academy Award).*

GLASER, Paul Michael (b 1943).
*1986: Band of the Hand. 1987:
The Running Man. 1990: Blue
Lightning. 1992: The Cutting
Edge. 1993: The Air up There.
1996: Kazaam.*

GUILFOYLE, Paul (1902-1961).
*1953: Captain Scarface. 1955: A
Life at Stake. 1960: Tess of the
Storm Country.*

GULAGER, Clu (b 1928).
1969: A Day With the Boys.

HAGMAN, Larry (L Hageman.
B 1931). *1971: Beware! The Blob
(GB: Son of Blob).*

HALL, Jon (Charles Locher. 1913-
1979). *1965: The Beachgirls and
the Monster/ Monster from the Surf.*

HANKS, Tom
(b 1956). *1992: Tales from the
Crypt (TV. Co-directed). 1993:
Fallen Angels (TV.Co-directed).
1996: That Thing You Do!*

HANNAH, Daryl (b 1960).
*1992: *Last Supper.*

HARDIN, Ty (Orson Hungerford.
B 1930). *1964: Boudine. 1988:
The Peace Officer.*

HARRIS, Richard (b 1930).
1969: Bloomfield.

HARVEY, Lawrence (Hirsch
Skikne. 1927-1973). *1963: The
Ceremony. 1968: A Dandy in
Aspic (co-directed). 1969: He and
She. 1973: Welcome to Arrow
Beach (US: Tender Flesh).*

HAWN, Goldie (G Stundlendge-
hawn. B 1945). *1997: Hope (TV).*

HAYDN, Richard (1905-1985).
*1948: Miss Tatlock's Millions.
1949: Dear Wife. 1950: Mr Music.*

HENREID, Paul (P von Hernried.
1908-1992). *1951: For Men
Only/The Tall Lie. 1956: A
Woman's Devotion (GB: War
Shock). 1958: Girls on the Loose.
Live Fast, Die Young. 1964: Dead
Ringer (GB: Dead Image). Ballad
in Blue (US: Blues for Lovers).
1971: Forbidden Knowledge (TV.
Co-directed).*

HESTON, Charlton (John C
Carter. B 1923). *1982: Mother
Lode. 1988: A Man for All Sea-
sons (TV).*

HILL, Terence (Mario Girotti.
B 1939). *1982: Don Camillo.
1991: Lucky Luke. 1994: The
Fight Before Christmas.*

HINES, Gregory (b 1946).
*1994: White Man's Burden. 1996:
Magenta.*

HOGAN, Paul (b 1939). *1989:
The Humpty Dumpty Man.*

HOPKINS, Sir Anthony (b 1937).
1995: August.

HOPPER, Dennis (b 1937).
*1969: Easy Rider. 1971: The Last
Movie. 1987: Colors. 1989: Back-
track (GB: Catchfire). 1990: The
Hot Spot. 1994: Chasers.*

HOSKINS, Bob (b 1942).
*1988: The Raggedy Rawney.
1995: Rainbow.*

HOWARD, Ron. *See main text.*

HOWELL, C Thomas (b 1966).
*1994: Hourglass. 1996: Pure
Danger.*

HUSTON, Anjelica (b 1952).
*1994: Maude Gonne. 1996: Bas-
tard out of Carolina (TV).*

HUTTON, Timothy (b 1960).
1997: Digging to China.

IRELAND, John (1914-1992).
*1953: Hannah Lee (later Outlaw
Territory. Co-directed). 1954: The
Fast and the Furious (co-directed).*

JEFFRIES, Lionel (b 1926). *1970:
The Railway Children. 1972: The
Amazing Mr Blunden. Baxter!/The
Boy. 1977: Wombling Free. 1978:
The Water Babies.*

JONES, L Q (Justice McQueen. B
1927). *1964: The Devil's Bedroom. 1974: A Boy and His Dog.*

KARINA, Anna (Hanne Bayer.
B 1940). *1973: Vivre ensemble.*

KEATON, Diane (D Hall. B 1946).
*1987: Heaven. 1991: Secret Soci-
ety. Wildflower (TV). 1995:
Unstrung Heroes.*

KEITH, David (b 1954).
*1986: The Further Adventures of
Tennessee Buck. 1987: The
Well/The Curse.*

KELLY, Gene (Eugene Kelly. 1912-
1996). *1949: On the Town (co-
directed). 1952: Singin' in the Rain
(co-directed). 1955: Invitation to
the Dance. 1956: The Happy
Road. 1958: The Tunnel of Love.
1962: Gigot. 1967: A Guide for
the Married Man. 1969: Hello,
Dolly! 1970: The Cheyenne Social*

*Club. 1975: Woman of the Year
(TV). 1976: That's Entertainment
Part two (new sequences). 1985:
That's Dancing!*

KINGSLEY, Ben (Krishna Banji.
B 1943). *1993: The Circle of the
White Rose.*

KRABBE, Jeroen (b 1944).
1997: Twee Koffers Vol.1

LADD, Diane (D Ladnier. B 1939).
1995: Mrs Munck.

LAMAS, Fernando (1915-1982).
*1961: The Magic Fountain. 1967:
The Violent Ones.*

LANCASTER, Burt (1913-1994).
*1955: The Kentuckian. 1974: The
Midnight Man (co-directed).*

LANDAU, Martin (b 1928).
*1996: Did You Hear What Hap-
pened to Eddie?*

LARSEN, Keith (b 1926). *1968:
Mission Batangas. 1975: Trap on
Cougar Mountain. 1979: White-
water Sam.*

LAUGHTON, Charles (1899-
1962). *1955: The Night of the
Hunter.*

LAWRENCE, Marc (Max Goldsmith. B 1910). *1963: Nightmare
in the Sun. 1982: Pigs (later
Daddy's Darling. Filmed 1972).*

LEE, Bruce (Li Chen-fan. 1940-
1973). *1973: Way of the Dragon
(US: Return of the Dragon).*

LEMMON, Jack (b 1925).
1971: Kotch.

LEWIS, Jerry. *See main text.*

LOCKE, Sondra (b 1945). *1986:
Ratboy. 1989: Impulse. 1993:
Death in Small Doses (TV). 1997:
Do Me a Favor.*

LORRE, Peter (Laszlo
Lowenstein. 1904-1964). *1951:
Die Verlorene.*

LUPINO, Ida (1914-1995).
*1949: Not Wanted (uncredited
co-director). 1950: Outrage.
Never Fear. 1951: Hard, Fast
and Beautiful. 1953: The
Bigamist. The Hitch Hiker.
1966: The Trouble with Angels.*

MALDEN, Karl (K Mladen
Sekulovich. B 1913).
1957: Time Limit.

MALKOVICH, John (b 1953).
1998: The Dancer Upstairs.

MATTHAU, Walter (W

Matthow. B 1920). *1960: The Gangster Story.*

McCALLUM, John (b 1914). *1956: Three in One. 1971: Nickel Queen.*

McDOWALL, Roddy (b 1928 - 1998). *1971: Tam Lin.*

McGAVIN, Darren (b 1922). *1973: Happy Mother's Day...Love George/Run Stranger Run.*

McGOOHAN, Patrick (b 1928). *1973: Catch My Soul.*

MEREDITH, Burgess (Oliver B Meredith. 1907-1997). *1943: Welcome to Britain. 1944: Salute to France. 1949: The Man on the Eiffel Tower. 1970: The Yin and the Yang of Mr Go.*

MIFUNE, Toshiro (1920-1997). *1963: Goju man-nin no isan.*

MILLAND, Ray (Reginald Truscott-Jones. 1905-1986). *1955: A Man Alone. 1956: Lisbon. 1958: The Safecracker. 1962: Panic in Year Zero. 1968: Hostile Witness.*

MILES, Sir Bernard (1907-1991). *1944: Tawny Pipit (co-directed). 1950: Chance of a Lifetime (co-directed).*

MILLS, Sir John (Lewis Mills. B 1908). *1966: Sky West and Crooked (US: Gypsy Girl).*

MONTGOMERY, George (G Letz. B 1916). *1961: The Steel Claw. 1962: Samar! 1964: From Hell to Borneo. Guerillas in Pink Lace. 1970: Ride the Tiger.*

MONTGOMERY, Robert (Henry Montgomery. 1904-1981). *1946: The Lady in the Lake. 1949: Once More, My Darling. 1950: Your Witness (US: Eye Witness). 1960: The Gallant Hours.*

MOORE, Kieron (K O'Hanrahan. B 1925). *1975: The Progress of Peoples (D). 1979: The Parched Land (D).*

MOREAU, Jeanne (b 1928) *1976: Lumière. 1978: L'adolescente.*

MORROW, Vic (1932-1982). *1962: Last Year at Malibu. 1966: Deathwatch. 1969: Sledge/A Man Called Sledge. 1979: The Evictors.*

MURPHY, Eddie (b 1961). *1989: Harlem Nights.*

MURRAY, Bill (William Doyle-Murray. B 1950). *1990: Quick Change (co-directed).*

NELSON, Gene (G Berg. 1920-1996). *1962: The Hand of Death. 1963: Hootenanny Hoot. 1964: Kissin' Cousins. Your Cheatin' Heart. 1965: Harum Scarum (GB: Harem Holiday). 1967: The Cool Ones. The Perils of Pauline. 1969: Wake Me When the War is Over (TV). 1973: The Letters (co-directed. TV).*

NEWLEY, Anthony (b 1931). *1968: Can Hieronymous Merkin Ever Forget Mercy Humppe and Find True Happiness? 1971: Summertree.*

NEWMAN, Paul (b 1925). *1959: *On the Harmfulness of Tobacco. 1968: Rachel, Rachel. 1971: Sometimes a Great Notion (GB: Never Give an Inch. Co-directed). 1972: The Effect of Gamma Rays on Man-in-the-Moon Marigolds. 1980: The Shadow Box (TV). 1984: Harry and Son. 1987: The Glass Menagerie.*

NICHOLSON, Jack (b 1937). *1971: Drive, He Said. 1978: Goin' South. 1990: The Two Jakes.*

NICOL, Alex (b 1919). *1958: The Screaming Skull. 1960: Then There Were Three (GB: Three Came Back). 1971: Point of Terror. 1985: Striker's Mountain (TV).*

NIMOY, Leonard (b 1931). *1984: Star Trek III: The Search for Spock. 1986: The Voyage Home: Star Trek IV. 1987: 3 Men and a Baby. 1988: The Good Mother/The Price of Passion. 1990: Funny About Love. 1994: Holy Matrimony.*

NOONAN, Tommy (T. Noon. 1921-1968). *1963: Promises! Promise! 1964: Three Nuts in Search of a Bolt.*

O'BRIEN, Edmond (1915-1985). *1954: Shield for Murder (co-directed). 1961: Man-Trap.*

O'KEEFE, Dennis (Edward Flanagan. 1908-1968). *1954: Angela.*

OLDMAN, Gary (b 1958). *1997: Nil by Mouth.*

OLIVIER, Sir Laurence (1907-1989). *1944: Henry V (co-directed). 1948: Hamlet. 1955: Richard III (co-directed). 1956: The Prince and the Showgirl. 1970: Three Sisters.*

PASCAL, Christine (1953-1996). *1977: Félicité. 1983: La garce. 1988: Zanzibar. 1992: Le petit prince a dit. 1996: Adultère mode d'emploi.*

PATE, Michael

(b 1920). *1978: Tim.*

PATRICK, Nigel (N. Wemyss. 1912-1981). *1957: How to Murder a Rich Uncle. 1961: Johnny Nobody.*

PENN, Sean (b 1960). *1991: The Indian Runner. 1995: The Crossing Guard.*

PEPPARD, George (1928-1994). *1978: Five Days from Home.*

PERKINS, Anthony (1932-1992). *1986: Psycho 3.*

PHILLIPS, Lou Diamond (b 1962). *1993: Dangerous Touch. 1994: Sioux City/ Ultimate Revenge.*

PISIER, Marie-France (Claudia Chauchat. B 1944). *1990: Le bal du gouverneur.*

POITIER, Sidney (b 1924). *1971: Buck and the Preacher. 1973: A Warm December. 1974: Uptown Saturday Night. 1975: Let's Do It Again. 1977: A Piece of the Action. 1980: Stir Crazy/Prison Rodeo. 1982: Hanky Panky. 1984: Shootout. 1985: Fast Forward. 1989: Ghost Dad.*

POWELL, Dick (1904-1963). *1953: Split Second. 1956: The Conqueror. You Can't Run Away from It. 1957: The Enemy Below. 1958: The Hunters.*

PRYOR, Richard (b 1940). *1983: Richard Pryor Here and Now. 1985: Jo Jo Dancer.*

QUINN, Anthony (b 1915). *1958: The Buccaneer.*

RATOFF, Gregory. *See main text.*

RAYMOND, Gene (R. Guion). *1948: Million Dollar Week-End.*

REDFORD, Robert. *See main text.*

REEVE, Christopher (b 1962). *1997: In the Gloaming (TV).*

REYNOLDS, Burt. *See main text.*

RICHARDSON, Sir Ralph (1902-1983). *1952: Home at Seven (US: Murder on Monday).*

RICKMAN, Alan (b 1946). *1997: The Winter Guest.*

ROBBINS, Tim (b 1958). *1992: Bob Roberts. 1995: Dead Man Walking, 1998 The Cradle Will Rock.*

ROBERTSON, Cliff (b 1925). *1979: The Pilot.*

ROONEY, Mickey (Joseph Yule. B 1920). *1951: My True Story.*

ROTH, Tim (b 1961). *1998: War Zone.*

SAVALAS, Telly (Aristotle Savalas. 1922-1994). *1976: Mati (released 1985 as Beyond Reason).*

SAXON, John (Carmen Orrico. B 1935). *1988: Death House.*

SCHELL, Maximilian (b 1930). *1969: The Castle. 1970: First Love. 1973: Der Fussgänger/Le piéton. 1976: End of the Game. 1979: Tales from the Vienna Woods. 1980: The Diary of Anne Frank (TV). 1984: Marlene (D). 1990: An American Place.*

SCHWARZENEGGER, Arnold (b 1947). *1990: Tales form the Crypt (TV. Co-directed). 1992: Christmas in Connecticut (TV).*

SCOTT, George C (b 1925). *1972: Rage. 1974: The Savage is Loose.*

SEAGAL, Steven (b 1950). *1993: On Deadly Ground.*

SEBERG, Jean (1938-1979). *1974: Ballad for the Kid.*

SELLERS, Peter (Richard Sellers. 1925-1980). *1961: Mr Topaze (US: I Like Money).*

SHATNER, William (b 1931). *1989: Star Trek V: The Final Frontier. 1994: Tekwar (TV).*

SHEEN, Martin (Ramon Estevez. B 1937). *1990: Cadence (GB: Stockade).*

SHEPARD, Sam (S.S. Rogers. B 1943). *1988: Far North. 1993: Silent Tongue.*

SHIRE, Talia (b 1945). *1994: Before the Night/One Night Stand.*

SILVER, Ron (R. Zimelman. B 1946). *1993: Lifepod (TV).*

SINATRA, Frank (1915 - 1998). *1965: None But the Brave.*

SINISE, Gary (b 1955). *1988: Far from Home. 1992: Of Mice and Men.*

SMITH, Charles Martin (b 1953). *1986: Trick or Treat. 1989: Boris and Natasha in Our Boy Badenov. 1991: 50/50 (released 1993). 1997: Air Bud. +Buffy the Vampire Slayer (TV).*

SORVINO, Paul (b 1939). *1998: The Trouble with Cali.*

STALLONE, Sylvester (Michael S. Stallone. B 1946). *1978: Paradise Alley. 1979: Rocky II. 1982: Rocky III. 1983: Staying Alive. 1987: Rocky IV.*

STARK, Graham (b 1922). *1970: Simon, Simon. 1971: The Magnificent Seven Deadly Sins.*

STERN, Daniel (b 1957). *1993: Rookie of the Year.*

STEVENS, Andrew (b 1955). *1990: The Terror Within 2. 1993: Illicit Dreams. Night Eyes 3. 1994: The Skateboard Kid 2.*

STEVENS, Mark (Richard Stevens. B 1915). *1954: Cry Vengeance. 1955: Timetable. 1957: Gun Fever. 1964: Escape from Hell Island. 1965: Sunscorched.*

STEVENS, Stella (Estelle Eggleston. B 1936). *1980: The American Heroine. 1988: The Ranch.*

STREISAND, Barbra (Barbara Streisand. B 1942). *1983: Yentl. 1991: The Prince of Tides. 1996: The Mirror Has Two Faces.*

SYKES, Eric (b 1923). *1967: The Plank. 1993: The Big Freeze (unreleased).*

TATI, Jacques. *See main text.*
TAYLOR, Don. *See main text.*

THOMAS, Betty (b.1948). *1992: Only You. 1995: The Brady Bunch Movie. 1996: The Late Shift (TV). 1997: Private Parts. 1998: Doctor Dolittle.*

TOBOLOWSKY, Stephen (b 1951). *1988: Two Idiots in Hollywood.*

TODD, Ann (1909-1993). *1965: Thunder in Heaven (D). 1966: Thunder of the Gods (D). 1967: Thunder of the Kings (D).*

TORN, Rip (Elmore Torn. B 1931). *1987: The Telephone.*

TURTURRO, John (b 1957). *1992: Mac. 1998: Illuminata.*

ULLMANN, Liv (b 1939). *1982: Love (co-directed). 1992: Sofia. 1995: Kristin Lavransdatter. 1996: Enskilda samtal/Private Confessions.*

USTINOV, Peter. *See main text.*

VITTI, Monica (Maria Ceciarelli. B 1933). *1989: Scandalo secreto.*

VOIGHT, Jon (b 1938). *1995: The Tin Soldier (TV).*

VON SYDOW, Max (Carl Von Sydow. B 1929). *1988: Katinka.*

WANAMAKER, Sam (Samuel Watenmaker. 1919-1993). *1969: The File of the Golden Goose. 1970: The Executioner. 1971: Catlow. 1977: Sinbad and the Eye of the Tiger. 1979: Charlie Muffin (TV).*

WAYNE, John (Marion Morrison. 1907-1979). *1960: The Alamo. 1968: The Green Berets.*

WEBB, Jack (1920-1982). *1954: Dragnet. 1955: Pete Kelly's Blues. 1957: The DI. 1959: -30- (GB: Deadline Midnight). 1961: The Last Time I Saw Archie. 1969: Dragnet (TV. GB: The Big Dragnet).*

WELLER, Peter (B 1947). *1992: Partners. 1996: Incognito. 1997: Elmore Leonard's Gold Coast (TV).*

WELLES, Orson. *See main text.*

WHITAKER, Forest (b 1961). *1993: Strapped. 1994: The Number Four. 1995: Waiting to Exhale. 1998: Hope Floats.*

WILDE, Cornel. *See main text.*

WILDER, Gene (Jerome Silberman. B 1934). *1975: The Adventure of Sherlock Holmes' Smarter Brother. 1977: The World's Greatest Lover. 1984: The Woman in Red. 1986: Haunted Honeymoon.*

WILLIAMS, Bill (Herman Katt. 1914-1992). *1963: Creatures of Darkness.*

WILLIAMS, Emlyn (George E. Williams. 1905-1987). *1949: The Last Days of Dolwyn. (US: Woman of Dolwyn).*

WILLIAMS, Treat (Richard Williams. B 1952). *1992: *Texan.*

WILLIAMSON, Fred (b 1938). *1976: Mean Johnny Burrows. Adios Amigo. Death Journey. 1977: Joshua. Destinazione Roma (US: Mr Mean). 1983: The Last Fight. The Big Score. 1986: Foxtrap. 1987: The Messenger. 1989: The Kill Reflex. 1992: Steele's Law.*

YOUNG, Karen (b 1958). *1992: *A Blink of Paradise.*

ZETTERLING, Mai (1925-1994) *1963: The War Game. 1964: Loving Couples. 1966: Night Games. 1967: Doktor Glas. 1968: Flickorna/The Girls. 1972: Vincent the Dutchman. 1973: Visions of Eight (co-directed). We har manje nama.*